THE
AMERICAN
DEMOCRACY

THE
AMERICAN
DEMOCRACY

SECOND
EDITION

THOMAS E. PATTERSON

Professor of Political Science
Maxwell School of Citizenship
Syracuse University

McGRAW-HILL, INC.

New York   St. Louis   San Francisco   Auckland   Bogotá
Caracas   Lisbon   London   Madrid   Mexico   Milan   Montreal
New Delhi   Paris   San Juan   Singapore   Sydney   Tokyo   Toronto

2 3 4 5 6 7 8 9 0   DOW   DOW   9 0 9 8 7 6 5 4 3

ISBN 0-07-048835-5

This book was set in Palatino by Black Dot, Inc.
The editors were Peter Labella, Cecilia Gardner, and David A. Damstra;
the designer was Joan E. O'Connor;
the production supervisor was Kathryn Porzio.
The photo editor was Barbara Salz.
R. R. Donnelley & Sons Company was printer and binder.

Cover photo credits:
Lincoln Memorial (Jay Maisel)
Vietnam Memorial (Wally McNamee/Woodfin Camp & Associates)

Part opener credits:
Joe Marquette/Philadelphia Enquirer/Woodfin Camp & Associates
Donna Binder/Impact Visuals
Benn Mitchell/The Image Works
Wally McNamee/Woodfin Camp & Associates
Andrea Pistolesi/The Image Bank
Leonard Harris/Stock, Boston
J. P. Laffont/Sygma
Additional permissions appear on page I-1, and on this page by reference.

Library of Congress Cataloging-in-Publication Data

Patterson, Thomas E.
    The American democracy / Thomas E. Patterson.—2nd ed.
        p.   cm.
    Includes bibliographical references and index.
    ISBN 0-07-048835-5
    1. United States—Politics and government.   I. Title.
  JK274.P358   1993
320.973—dc20   92-17429

ABOUT THE AUTHOR

*T*homas E. Patterson is a professor and past chairman of the department of political science in the Maxwell School of Citizenship at Syracuse University. Raised in a small Minnesota town near the Iowa and South Dakota borders, he was educated at South Dakota State University and the University of Minnesota, where he received his Ph.D. in 1971.

In 1991–92 he was Visiting Professor in the Lombard Chair in the Kennedy School of Government at Harvard University. He has also held teaching positions in Germany and Great Britain.

Patterson is the author or coauthor of several books and dozens of articles, most of them based on his research of political communication. He has held grants from the National Science Foundation, the Ford Foundation, the Mellon Foundation, and the Markle Foundation. His most extensive research project culminated in *The Mass Media Election*, which was named an Outstanding Academic Book, 1980–81, by *Choice*. His current writing projects include a six-country study of political journalists, and a book on the presidential selection process.

He lives with his two grade-school children, Alex and Leigh, who like his story-telling and tolerate his book-writing.

TO ALEX AND LEIGH

CONTENTS

PART TWO

INDIVIDUAL RIGHTS   109

PART THREE

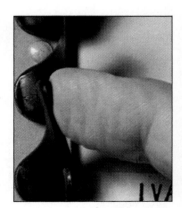

PART FOUR

POLITICAL ORGANIZATION 293

PART FIVE

PART SIX

APPOINTED OFFICIALS   557

PART SEVEN

PREFACE FOR THE INSTRUCTOR

*P*olitical science has been served through the years by some very good introductory American government texts. These texts have been distinguished not so much by the raw material they contain as by their ability to hold the interest of students and help them to integrate the wide array of concepts, facts, and principles that make up the study of American government. I recall to this day the enthusiasm I felt, as an undergraduate, in reading V. O. Key's *Politics, Parties, and Pressure Groups.* Last published in the 1960s, Professor Key's wonderful text was chock-full of ideas, of politics, and of a lucid prose that belied the laborious effort that is required to turn the raw materials of American government into a compelling whole.

This book rests on my belief that it is possible to be comprehensive without being encyclopedic. Although political scientists have developed a deep understanding of American government, this knowledge exists as a set of more or less unrelated observations. When presented in this form in a text, fact is piled upon fact and list upon list, which is almost guaranteed to dull students' interest and thought. I have tried to follow the cardinal rule of always telling students where they are in the text, why they are there, and where they are going.

I also believe that it is possible to be precise without being pedantic. The keys to understanding American government are found, not in abstruse ideas or methods, but in a deep understanding of the broad tendencies that have long characterized the American political experience—namely:

- that American politics since the nation's earliest years has been shaped by a set of governing ideas, which, although subject to dispute in practice, have served the American people as a common bond and source of political action;

- that the American political system is characterized by an extreme fragmentation of authority that has far-reaching implications for the exercise of power and the making of public policy;
- that the United States has an extraordinary range of interests of all kinds—economic, religious, ethnic, regional, and so on—and that this diversity is fundamental to the nature of political conflict and consensus in America;
- that issues which in other countries are fought out through elections and in legislatures are also fought out in America through judicial action and as claims of individual rights; and
- that Americans tend to draw sharp distinctions between what is political, and therefore to be decided in the public arena, and what is economic, and therefore beyond the reach of political majorities under normal conditions.

These ideas are introduced in the first chapter and are discussed frequently in subsequent chapters as tendencies that help to explain a wide range of political actions.

Pedagogical Features

This text has two innovative pedagogical features, each of which represents a deliberate effort to respond to the instructional needs of those who teach and take the basic course:

1. Early in the writing of the first edition of this text, I concluded that it would be enormously helpful if a way could be found to bring into each chapter the judgment of those political scientists who teach the introductory course year in and year out. Any insights for improving the pedagogical value of an introductory text are concentrated among these instructors. This recognition led me to undertake what was, as far as I have been able to determine, the most thorough review process ever undertaken for a new American government text.

We went beyond the normal process of having the draft chapters reviewed by a select number of expert scholars who are recognized experts in the subject matter. After these reviewers had commented on the manuscript, we revised each chapter and sent it out to a dozen or so faculty members at U.S. colleges and universities of all types—public and private, large and small, four-year and two-year. These political scientists, 213 of them in all, had well over a thousand years of combined experience in the teaching of the introductory course. Each of them was asked, in effect, two questions about the chapter they read: "How well does it instruct your students in what they need to know about its subject?" and "How can it be changed so that it better serves your students' needs?"

They had plenty of ideas. For example, after graciously noting that "it is unusual for authors to be interested in the thinking of those of us on the 'frontline' of undergraduate teaching," a professor at a state university suggested three major adjustments in the chapter he had read. I spent the better part of two years rewriting the text in response to these and other reviewers' suggestions.

2. This text has twenty-seven shorter chapters rather than the twenty or so longer ones found in other introductory American government texts. The instructional purpose of this innovation is to give a greater degree of coherence to each chapter. Rather than a single chapter on political parties, for example, I have written one chapter on U.S. party organizations and another on the American party system. When a text's chapters are few in number—one each on parties, Congress, the Constitution, and so on—they tend to lack focus. When more and shorter chapters are used, they can convey a clearer message. My chapter on the American party system, for example, looks squarely at two-partyism: why it exists in America and how fully it channels political competition and choice. These points are stated in the chapter's introduction, developed in the chapter's body, and restated in the conclusion, thus driving home to students their central importance.

This organization of the material permits frequent use of the narrative form of writing, which research has shown to be a superior method of teaching students a "soft" science such as politics. Each chapter contains plenty of facts, but they are always presented in context. If students soon forget many of the details, as they invariably will, they will at least remember the main points.

I believe that most political science professors will find that a text consisting of shorter chapters is a more flexible and effective teaching tool. Each chapter can be read in an hour or less, and thus each lecture's reading assignment can reasonably consist of a full chapter. My experience with teaching the introductory course suggests that many students find it unrewarding to be assigned just part of a chapter at a time because that approach makes it very difficult for them to see the chapter's argument in its entirety. This text makes it easier for students to master each chapter in a single reading.

Innovations in the Second Edition

The response to the first edition of this book was extremely gratifying. The text has been adopted for use at more than 200 American colleges and universities. Moreover, the instructors who adopted the book have stayed with it. A sample survey by the publisher in the book's second year indicated that 95 percent of instructors who had used it the previous year were using it again.

Although the first edition was very favorably received, I have chosen to revise the book substantially for the second edition. I believe that the second-edition changes are the critical one in the life of a text because these revisions can take into account the experiences of those instructors who have actually used the book in the classroom. The thirty-six reviewers of the second edition included a significant proportion of instructors who had adopted *The American Democracy* for use by their students.

Our review process included a full evaluation of the text and resulted in a thorough updating of every chapter. The text was also reorganized slightly at the suggestion of reviewers: the presidency and Congress, which were discussed in three chapters each in the first edition, are discussed in two chapters each in this edition. In addition, a few chapters—those on federalism, representative democracy, civil rights, public opinion, voting, social welfare policy, and foreign and defense policy—were substantially reworked. The chapter on foreign and defense policy, for example, has been completely revised to reflect the great changes that have taken place in world politics since the text's first edition. The new chapter gives as much attention, for example, to the economic dimension of national security as it does to the military dimension. International trade, Japan, multilateralism, the European Community, foreign assistance, and the Middle East are among the subjects that receive substantially more coverage in this edition than in the previous one.

All chapters include two new boxes, one entitled "The Media and the People" and the second entitled "Critical Thinking." These boxes are based on the same philosophy that guided the first edition. All boxed inserts in this text have the purpose of encouraging students to step back and think about what they have been reading. The boxes are not mere fillers or diversions; they are part of a deliberate instructional strategy. The text now presents five kinds of boxed inserts:

- *Dialogues.* At the end of each of the book's seven parts is a pair of brief original essays. These essays, written by some of America's best political scientists, are intended to direct the student's attention back to a recurring issue discussed in the section's chapters. For example, Part Six features one-page essays by Professors Hugh Heclo and Martin Shapiro on the question, "Is Too Much Public Policy Decided by Nonelected Officials in the Bureaucracy and Judiciary?" The authors of the other original essays are Benjamin R. Barber, Morris Fiorina, Louis Fisher, Richard Flathman, Linda L. Fowler, Stephen D. Krasner, Michael Malbin, Jane Mansbridge, Bruce Russett, Robert H. Salisbury, Frank Sorauf, and James Sundquist.
- *How the United States Compares.* Each chapter has a box that compares the United States with other countries on some aspect of politics emphasized in the chapter. American students invariably gain a clearer perspective and a deeper understanding of their own country's politics when they recognize how it resembles and how it differs from politics elsewhere.
- *Analyze the Issue.* Each chapter contains several of these boxes, which ask students to relate current issues or personal experiences to material presented in the chapter—an intellectual exercise that is designed to promote both better scholarship and better citizenship.
- *The Media and the People.* The world of everyday politics is largely beyond our direct observation. We depend on the media to inform us about this world, and these boxes—one in each chapter—are intended to give students a better understanding of the limits of this media-created reality.
- *Critical Thinking.* Each chapter contains a box that asks students to analyze and integrate material presented in the chapter. The purpose is to encourage students to think critically and to make connections between concepts, research findings, and current issues of American politics.

Finally, the second edition contains a new appendix: a chapter-length discussion of state and local politics that is provided for the convenience of those instructors who include a section on state and local politics in their national government course.

Ancillary Package

This text has the standard ancillary materials—an instructor's manual, a study guide, and a test bank. The test bank is available in printed form or on computer disk: IBM (5.25- and 3.5-inch disks), Macintosh, and Apple.

There are also special ancillaries. Unlike the "canned" videotapes that accompany most American government texts, we have developed a set of tapes that are keyed specifically to sections of this text. The videotapes are based on an exclusive agreement with the *MacNeil-Lehrer News Hour;* they focus on current issues of American politics and will be updated as important new issues and controversies emerge. The tapes are designed to stimulate in-class discussion, whether in a lecture or a study-group format.

Students who use this text can also obtain a special subscription price on *The Washington Post National Weekly Edition.* Like many other instructors, I sometimes assign a source of information about current events as required or recommended reading in my undergraduate courses. The weekly edition of the *Post* is an effective option because it is devoted almost exclusively to politics and includes commentary and analysis by some of the country's best journalists, including David Broder, Robert Woodward, George Will, and Meg Greenfield.

Acknowledgments

A great many people contributed to the first and second editions of this book. They include the scholars who gave generously of their professional time and knowledge, the office staff and research assistants who with skill and good humor contributed to every phase of preparation, and the editorial people who offered good judgment and wise counsel in the making of key decisions. I owe a major debt to all who helped.

Bert Lummus, my editor, deserves a very special thanks. He initiated the first edition of this book by asking about my interest in writing it, and he stayed with the project throughout its six years of preparation. He approached the second edition with the same dedication. His keen judgment, steady encouragement, and endless patience have improved every page of this book. No editor could have been more helpful, and I am pleased to say that our years of working together produced a friendship as well as a book. Cecilia Gardner and David Damstra also had a major impact on the book; Cele carefully edited and David meticulously produced every line of every page of both editions. In addition, the following McGraw-Hill people worked on one or both editions and deserve my thanks: Peter Labella, Joan O'Connor, Kathy Porzio, Greg Berge, William Barter, Safra Nimrod, and Barbara Salz.

At Syracuse University, I had word-processing assistance for the first edition from June Dumas, Judith Jablonski, and, for shorter periods, Jacquelyn Meyer and Jennifer Pallone. A large number of graduate assistants and work-study students contributed in one way or another to the first or second edition. I will not try to list them here because they are so many and because their contributions over the years varied so substantially. To each and all of them, I extend my thanks.

I would also like to acknowledge the assistance of the many political scientists who reviewed a portion of the text for the first edition. Their thoughtful and constructive reviews contributed substantially to the favorable response the first edition received. I wish to thank:

John R. Abshire, Tarrant County Junior College
Joseph R. Aicher, Jr., North Carolina Central University
Dennis M. Anderson, Bowling Green State University
Raymond V. Anderson, University of Wisconsin, River Falls
William G. Anderson, Suffolk County Community College
Tom Anton, Brown University
Herrick Arnold, Orange Coast College
David N. Atkinson, University of Missouri, Kansas City
David G. Baker, Hartwick College
Kathleen L. Barber, John Carroll University
Glenn Barkan, Aquinas College
Larry Bartels, University of Rochester
Thomas Barth, University of Wisconsin, Eau Claire
Larry Baum, Ohio State University
Charles S. Bednar, Muhlenberg College
Larry Bennett, DePaul University
Larry Berman, University of California, Davis
Diane Blair, University of Arkansas
Richard Bloss, Chicago State University
John C. Blydenburgh, Clark University
Mary A. Boutilier, Seton Hall University
Gloria J. Braxton, Southern University and A & M College
Jerry Brekke, Northwest Missouri State University
Lynn R. Brink, North Lake College
Roger G. Brown, University of North Carolina, Charlotte
Jere W. Bruner, Oberlin College
Gary Bryner, Brigham Young University
Vincent Buck, California State, Fullerton
Gary J. Buckley, Northern Arizona University
Donald Buzinkai, King's College
Raymond L. Carol, St. John's University
Carol Cassel, University of Alabama
James Cecil, Bemidji State University
Shirley Chapman, East Tennessee University
William L. Chappell, Jr., Columbus College
Ann Charney, Rosary College
Stephen Chen, Lincoln University
Richard Chesteen, University of Tennessee, Martin
Alan Clem, University of South Dakota
Ronald Coan, Canisius College
Robert L. Cord, Northeastern University
Robert J. Courtney, LaSalle University
Jack Crampton, Lewis and Clark College

Mary Paige Cubbison, Miami Dade Community College, South
Everett W. Cunningham, Middle Tennessee State University
David D. Dabelko, Ohio University
Richard J. Dalton, University of Connecticut, Avery Point
Abraham L. Davis, Morehouse College
Paul H. DeForest, Illinois Institute of Technology
Robert DiClerico, West Virginia University
Joel Diemond, Dutchess Community College
John R. Dierst, Eastern Connecticut State University
Robert H. Dixon, Lyndon State College
Lawrence Dodd, University of Colorado
William M. Downer, Thiel College
James W. Dull, University of New Haven
Pat Dunham, Duquesne University
Charles W. Dunn, Clemson University
Gloria S. Durlach, Columbia College
Valerie Earle, Georgetown University
George C. Edwards III, Texas A & M University
Ahmed H. El-Afandi, Winona State University
Larry Elowitz, Georgia College
James Enelow, State University of New York, Stony Brook
Alan S. Engel, Miami University
Joe E. Ericson, Stephen F. Austin State University
Gerald R. Farrington, Fresno City College
Louis Fisher, Congressional Research Service
R. F. Flannery, University of Wisconsin Centers, Sheboygan/Manitowoc
Marvin Folkertsma, Grove City College
Patricia A. Fontaine, Northeast Louisiana University
Richard Foster, Idaho State University
Eugene Fulton, County College of Morris
Anne Freedman, Roosevelt University
Joseph F. Freeman, Lynchburg College
Henry P. French, Jr., State University of New York, Monroe Community College at Rochester
David A. Frolick, North Central College
Arthur L. Galub, Bronx Community College of CUNY
Dan B. German, Appalachian State University
Ernest Giglio, Lycoming College
Terry Gilbreth, Ohio Northern University
Tracey L. Gladstone, University of Wisconsin, River Falls
Henry Glick, Florida State University
Robert Golembiewski, University of Georgia

LeRoy Goodwin, Fort Lewis College
Fred Greenstein, Princeton University
Forest Grieves, University of Montana
Gary Griffith, Temple Junior College
Kathryn Griffith, Wichita State University
Joel Grossman, University of Wisconsin
Martin Gruberg, University of Wisconsin, Oshkosh
Mary E. Guy, University of Alabama, Birmingham
William K. Hall, Bradley University
Beth Halteman, Belmont College
Leroy C. Hardy, California State University, Long Beach
Keith Henderson, State University College, Buffalo
Beth Henschen, Loyola University
John Hibbing, University of Nebraska
Arthur C. Hill, Minneapolis Community College
Thomas R. Hills, Black Hills State College
Herbert Hirsch, Virginia Commonwealth University
Richard D. Hirtzel, Western Illinois University
Douglas I. Hodgkin, Bates College
James B. Hogan, Seattle University
Louisa S. Hulett, Knox College
Margaret A. Hunt, University of North Carolina,
  Greensboro
Jon Hurwitz, University of Pittsburgh
Reverend Emerick J. Hydo, C.M., Niagara University
Willoughby Jarrell, Kennesaw College
Malcom Jewell, University of Kentucky
Loch Johnson, University of Georgia
Evan M. Jones, St. Cloud State University
Hugh E. Jones, Shippensburg University
Robert E. Jones, Belmont Abbey College
Thomas A. Kazee, Davidson College
Robert Keele, University of the South
Richard C. Kelley, University of Washington
Henry Kenski, University of Arizona
Elwyn Kernstock, St. Michael's College
Frank Kessler, Missouri Western State College
Hoyt King, Tennessee State University
Michael P. Kirby, Rhodes College
William Kitchin, Loyola College
Louis Koenig, New York University
Melvin Kulbicki, York College of Pennsylvania
Robert Kvavik, University of Minnesota
Stanley Kyriakides, William Paterson College
  of New Jersey
Walter L. Lackey, Jr., Frostburg State University
Byron G. Lander, Kent State University
Robert Langran, Villanova University
Margaret K. Latimer, Auburn University
James F. Lea, University of Southern Mississippi
Timothy A. Leonard, Siena Heights College
Erwin L. Levine, Skidmore College
Frederick Lewis, University of Lowell
Paul Light, University of Minnesota

James Lindeen, University of Toledo
Connie L. Lobur, State University of New York College
  at Purchase
Duane Lockard, Princeton University
Burdett Loomis, University of Kansas
Joseph Losco, Ball State University
R. Philip Loy, Taylor University
David C. Maas, University of Alaska, Anchorage
L. Sandy Maisel, Colby College
Thomas Mans, Creighton University
Susan H. Marsh, Providence College
John L. Martin, University of Maine
Gerald A. McBeath, University of Alaska, Fairbanks
Charles H. McCall, California State University,
  Bakersfield
James L. McDowell, Indiana State University
Patrick J. McGeever, Indiana University-Purdue
  University, Indianapolis
Donald K. McKee, Upsala College
William McLauchlan, Purdue University
Carl E. Meacham, State University of New York,
  Oneonta
James A. Meader, Augustana College
Daniel R. Minns, American University
Virgil L. Mitchell, Seminole Junior College
James E. Mock, Austin Peay State University
Tommie Sue Montgomery, Agnes Scott College
John E. Monzingo, North Dakota State University
Margaret V. Moody, Auburn University at Montgomery
Richard E. Morgan, Bowdoin College
Thomas J. Morillaro, Nicholls State University
William Morrow, William and Mary College
Kenneth F. Mott, Gettysburg College
Gordon D. Munro, San Bernardino Valley College
Nelda A. Muns, Wharton County Union College
Robert E. Murphy, St. Louis Community College
  at Florissant Valley
Walter Murphy, Princeton University
Marie D. Natoli, Emmanuel College
Arturo Nava, Laredo Junior College
Frederick Neikirk, Westminster College
Patricia M. Nelson, New Mexico State University,
  Carlsbad
David Neubauer, University of New Orleans
Dail Neugaiten, Arizona State University
Stephen L. Newman, York University
G.K. Oddo, University of San Diego
Edwin Allen O'Donnel, Wayne State College
Madelin Olds, Del Mar College
Bruce Oppenheimer, University of Houston
Shirley E. Ostholm-Hinnau, York College
  of the City University
Roger N. Pajari, Georgia Southern College
Wayne Parent, Louisiana State University

John D. Parker, Western Kentucky University
Ronald W. Perry, Arizona State University
Robert K. Peters, Tyler Junior College
Frank Petrusak, College of Charleston
Doris F. Pierce, Purdue University, Calumet
Monte Piliawsky, Dillard University
J. L. Polinard, Pan American University
Freeman W. Pollard, St. Ambrose College
Larry Pool, Mt. View College
Mary Cornelia Porter, Barat College
Bill Postiglione, Quincy College
Herman Pritchett, University of California,
    Santa Barbara
David H. Provost, California State University, Fresno
Brian F. Rader, Northeastern Oklahoma State University
Gene Rainey, University of North Carolina, Asheville
Craig Ramsay, Ohio Wesleyan University
John W. Randall, Jr., University of Alabama, Huntsville
Thomas A. Reilly, Trinity College
Pamela R. Rendeiro, Southern Connecticut State
    University
Bradley R. Rice, Clayton College
Michael Rich, Brown University
Linda K. Richter, Kansas State University
Delbert J. Ringquist, Central Michigan University
George C. Roberts, Indiana University Northwest
David Robinson, University of Houston—Downtown
Ted Robinson, Louisiana State University
Jerel Rosati, University of South Carolina
Gary Rose, Sacred Heart University
Raymond K. Rossiter, Rockland Community College
Annetta St. Clair, Missouri Southern State College
Richard T. Saeger, Valdosta State College
Steven S. Sallie, Boise State University
Frank Schwartz, Beaver College
Lawrence Schwartz, College of Staten Island
Seymour J. Schwartz, Kennedy-King College
    of the City College
Jeffrey A. Segal, State University of New York,
    Stony Brook
Martin Shapiro, Law School, University of California,
    Berkeley
Stewart P. Shapiro, Bentley College
Earl Shaw, Northern Arizona University
John N. Short, University of Arkansas at Monticello
James D. Slack, Cleveland State University
Herbert C. Smith, Western Maryland College
James George Smith, West Chester University
Neil Snortland, University of Arkansas at Little Rock
Robert J. Spitzer, State University of New York,
    Cortland

Terry Spurlock, Henderson County Junior College
Grover Starling, University of Houston
Robert J. Steamer, University of Massachusetts, Boston
Henry Steck, State University of New York, Cortland
Jonathan L. Steepee, California Lutheran College
Jules Steinberg, Denison University
Ronald Stidham, Lamar University
Barbara S. Stone, California State University,
    Fullerton
Emily Stoper, California State University, Hayward
Richard P. Strada, Ocean County College
Sue E. Strickler, Eastern New Mexico University
Theodore Sturm, Robert Morris College
John A. Sullivan, Jacksonville University
George Sulzner, University of Massachusetts
Carl Swidorski, College of Saint Rose
Gary Thompson, Abilene Christian University
H. Christian Thorup, Cuesta College
Charles M. Tidmarch, Union College
Joan Tronto, Hunter College
James Chih-yuan Tsao, Houston Baptist University
John R. Vile, Middle Tennessee State University
Stephen Wainscott, Clemson University
Diane E. Wall, Mississippi State University
Hanes Walton, Jr., Savannah State College
Elizabeth C. Warren, Loyola University of Chicago
James D. Weaver, Marymount College
David G. Wegge, St. Norbert College
Herbert Weisberg, Ohio State University
Warren Weston, Metropolitan State College
R. Eric Weise, University of Cincinnati
Charles Weymann, Los Angeles Valley College
Donald Whistler, University of Central Arkansas
Howard R. Whitcomb, Lehigh University
Bob White, Humboldt State University
Larry D. White, University of Wisconsin Center,
    Fox Valley
John F. Whitney, Jr., Lincoln Land Community
    College
David H. Wicks, Mississippi Valley State University
Henry Wilkins III, University of Arkansas, Pine Bluff
John F. Wilson, University of Hawaii, Manoa
Edward Woodhouse, Rensselaer Polytechnic Institute
Gerald Wright, Indiana University
James P. Young, State University of New York,
    Binghamton
Alton C. Zimmerman, Northwestern Oklahoma State
    University
F. Donald Zucker, Ursinus College
Norman Zucker, University of Rhode Island
Gerald J. Zurat, University of Scranton

The contributions made by the second-edition reviewers were no less helpful. I am deeply grateful for their high standards of professionalism and collegiality. The following list of these reviewers includes the name of one instructor whose comments were unsolicited but invaluable. He sent me a long letter with a list of recommended changes. It was one of the most helpful reviews I have ever received, and led to important adjustments in the second edition. I invite similar comments from any instructor who has ideas on how future editions of this book could be improved.

Danny M. Adkinson, Oklahoma State University
James Chalmers, Wayne State University
Tom Chambers, Golden West College
Kristina K. Cline, Riverside Community College
Stephen Crescenzi, Trenton State College
Paige Cubbison, Miami-Dade Community College
Steve Frank, Saint Cloud State University
Hank Goldman, Rio Hondo College
John Hale, University of Oklahoma
Steve Hatting, College of Saint Thomas
Michael Hawthorne, Pembroke State University
William Hudson, Providence College
Loch Johnson, University of Georgia
George Kaloudis, River College
Robert Kennedy, Georgia Institute of Technology
James D. King, Memphis State University
Marston Leonard, Hillsborough Community College
Carl Lutrin, California Polytechnic State University
Michael Maggiotto, Bowling Green State University

Michael D. Martinez, University of Florida
John McGowan, Villanova University
Bradley J. Miller, Saginaw Valley State University
Michael C. Munger, University of North Carolina, Chapel Hill
Patricia Pauly, University of Kentucky
William Pederson, Louisiana State University, Shreveport
James Perkins, San Antonio College
Russell Renka, Southeast Missouri State University
Michael Rich, Brown University
Donald Roy, Ferris State University
Nadia M. Rubaii-Barrett, New Mexico State University
Lawrence Sullivan, Adelphi University
C. Stephen Tai, University of Arkansas, Pine Bluff
Carol Traut, University of South Dakota
Joseph K. Unekis, Kansas State University
Stephen L. Wasby, State University of New York, Albany
Norman Zucker, Ursinus College

Thomas E. Patterson

PREFACE FOR THE STUDENT:
A GUIDED TOUR OF THE AMERICAN DEMOCRACY

This book describes the American political system, which is one of the most interesting and most intricate in the world. The discussion is comprehensive; a lot of information is packed into each chapter. No student could possibly remember every tiny fact or observation that each chapter contains, but I believe that the main points of discussion are within your grasp if you are willing to reach for them. And once you have acquired these major points, then the smaller points will also be more readily understood.

The text has several features that will help you to understand the major points of discussion. Each chapter has, for example, an opening story that illustrates a central theme of the chapter. This story is followed immediately by a brief summary of the chapter's main ideas.

The "guided tour" below describes further how the organization and the special features of the book can help you in your effort to develop a basic understanding of the American political system.

Thomas E. Patterson

THE TWO-PARTY SYSTEM: DEFINING THE VOTERS' CHOICE

11
CHAPTER

Political parties created democracy and . . . modern democracy is unthinkable save in terms of the parties.

E. E. Schattschneider[1]

OPENING ILLUSTRATION

An illuminating narration of a compelling event introduces the chapter's main ideas.

They were the kind of strange bedfellows that American politics regularly produces. One of them stood for gun control, busing, and an end to the death penalty and proposed that the United States terminate its Star Wars project, MX missile construction, and aid to the Nicaraguan rebels. His running mate held the opposite position on each of these issues. They were the 1988 Democratic ticket: Michael Dukakis of Massachusetts and Lloyd Bentsen of Texas.

The Dukakis-Bentsen partnership was a product of the country's two-party system, which compels candidates and voters with diverse opinions to find common ground. Because the Republican and Democratic parties have dominated U.S. elections for so long and are the only parties with any realistic chance of acquiring political control, Americans nearly take their **two-party system** for granted. However, most democracies have a **multiparty system**, in which three or more parties have the capacity to gain control of government separately or in coalition. Even democracies that have what is essentially a two-party system typically have important smaller parties as well. For example, Great Britain's Labour and Conservative parties have dominated that nation's politics since early in this century, but they have had competition from the Liberal party and, more recently, the Social Democrats.

America's two-party system has important consequences for the nation's

MAJOR CONCEPTS

The first occurrence of a major concept is signaled by **bold type** and accompanied by a concise definition. A complete list of these concepts is found at the end of each chapter, as well as in the Glossary at the back of the book.

[1] E. E. Schattschneider, *Party Government* (New York: Rinehart, 1942), 1.

295

This chapter examines bureaucratic policymaking from the standpoint of the ways in which agencies acquire the power they need in order to maintain themselves and their programs. The chapter shows that career bureaucrats necessarily and naturally take an "agency point of view," seeking to promote their agency's objectives. Moreover, they have substantial resources—expertise, group support, and presidential and congressional backing—that help them to promote their agency's goals. The three constitutional branches of government impose a degree of accountability on the bureaucracy; but the U.S. system of government, with its fragmented authority, frees bureaucrats from tight control. The main points discussed in this chapter are the following:

★ *Because of America's diversity and fragmented system of government, bureaucrats must compete for the power required to administer programs effectively.*

★ *Bureaucrats are committed to the goals of their particular agencies.* Their expert knowledge, support from clientele groups, and backing by Congress and the president help them to promote agency goals.

★ *Agencies are subject to control by the president, Congress, and the judiciary, but these controls place only general limits on the bureaucracy's power.* A major reason agencies are able to achieve power in their own right is that Congress and the president often resist each other's attempts to control the bureaucracy.

★ *The bureaucracy's power is not easily reconciled with the principle of self-government.* Bureaucrats are not directly accountable to the people through elections.

MAIN POINTS

The chapter's three or four main ideas are summarized in the opening pages.

---

political party machines in cities where residents were not personally known to poll watchers. However, the extra effort involved in registering placed an added burden on honest citizens. Turnout in U.S. elections declined steadily after registration was instituted.[7]

Although other democracies also require registration, they place this responsibility on government. In European nations, public officials have the duty to enroll citizens on registration lists. The United States—in keeping with its individualistic culture—is the only democracy in which registration is the individual's responsibility.[8] In addition, registration laws are established by the state governments, and some states make it relatively difficult for citizens to qualify. Registration periods and locations are usually not highly publicized, and many citizens simply do not know when or where to register.[9] Eligibility can also be a problem. In most states, a citizen must establish legal residency by living in the same place for a minimum period, usually thirty days but as long as fifty days, before becoming eligible to register.

States with a tradition of lenient registration laws generally have a higher turnout than other states. Maine, Minnesota, and Oregon allow people to register at their polling place on election day, and these states rank high in voter turnout. Those states that have erected the most barriers are in the South, where

Voter Turnout Incentives
Some countries impose a fine for not voting in elections and have a significantly higher rate of voter turnout than the United States. Would you favor a fine on nonvoters in the United States? Why or why not? Are there other things that some democracies do as a way of increasing voter turnout, such as holding elections on Sundays, that you would support for the United States?

---

[7] Philip E. Converse, "Change in the American Electorate," in Philip E. Converse and Angus Campbell, eds., *The Human Meaning of Social Change* (New York: Russell Sage Foundation, 1972), 281; see also Stanley Kelley, Jr., Richard E. Ayres, and William G. Bowen, "Registration and Voting: Putting First Things First," *American Political Science Review* 61 (June 1967): 359–379. For insights into the impact on electoral behavior of another reform, the Australian ballot, see Jerrold D. Rusk, "The Effect of the Australian Ballot Reform on Split Ticket Voting: 1876–1908," *American Political Science Review* 64 (December 1970): 1220–1238.
[8] Ivor Crewe, "Electoral Participation," in David Butler, Howard R. Penniman, and Austin Ranney, eds., *Democracy at the Polls* (Washington, D.C.: American Enterprise Institute, 1981), 249.
[9] Philip E. Converse with Richard Niemi, "Non-voting among Young Adults in the United States," in William J. Crotty et al., eds., *Political Parties and Political Behavior* (Boston: Allyn & Bacon, 1971), 456.

power that they need if ... cannot be understood ...erican political system,

...her democracies, do not ...arty's platform or the ...ame party do not have a ...s are elected separately, ...ealt with largely after ...ng and power wielding. ...precedence, but so will ...aims on both the presi-...system produces not a ... government in which

...they must seek support ...n from Congress; if not ...en tomorrow. In other ...asis for the lead paragraphs of

"ANALYZE THE ISSUE" BOXES

Boxes in the margins ask searching questions in order to stimulate you to analyze what you are reading.

Near-empty polling stations are a fact of political life in America. Less than 50 percent of voting-age citizens turn out to cast their ballots in nonpresidential election years. (Rob Crandall/Picture Group)

* HOW THE UNITED STATES COMPARES

WOMEN'S EQUALITY

Although conflict between groups is universal, the nature of the conflict is often particularized. Racial conflict in the United States cannot readily be compared with, say, religious conflict in Northern Ireland. The one form of inequality common to all nations is that of gender: nowhere are women equal to men in law or in fact. But there are large differences between countries. The 1988 study by the Population Crisis Committee referred to in Chapter 1 ranked the United States third overall in women's equality, behind only Sweden and Finland. The rankings were based on five areas—jobs, education, social relations, marriage and family, and health—where U.S. women had an 82.5 percent rating compared with men.

The inequality of women is also indicated by their lack of representation in public office. A Royal Commission in Canada compared the national legislatures of industrialized democratic countries in terms of the percentage of women members. The five countries that ranked highest, ranging from 21 percent to 34 percent female lawmakers, were Iceland, Denmark, Sweden, Finland, and Norway. Canada, at 13 percent, was clustered with several western European countries, including Germany and Italy. The United States ranked low—only 6 percent of the members of Congress are women. This percentage is in the same range as that of Spain, Britain, and France. The only country that ranked significantly lower than the United States was Japan, where women constitute only 1 percent of national legislators.

Congressional support for the ERA was an outgrowth of the 1960s civil rights movement and of the changing demands of women.[20] Families were smaller, and more women were entering the labor force.[21] Proponents of the ERA argued that discrimination on the basis of sex could not be [...] distinctions between men and women were maintai[...] was opposed by traditionalists, who argued that the [...] legal protections for women, mainly in the areas of [...] conditions, and family life.[22] A 1982 Gallup survey [...] Americans (including 53 percent of men) favored [...] opposed, and 9 percent had no opinion. Neverthel[...] the support of a majority of state legislators in the th[...] ratification. The proposed amendment was three sta[...] for ratification came and went in 1982. The state le[...] for ratification were concentrated in the South, wher[...] women are stronger.[23]

Equality of rights under the law shall not be denied or abridged by the United States

Women's Legal and Political Gains

Although the ERA did not become part of the C[...] women's rights to the forefront at a time when dev[...] the courts were contributing significantly to the le[...]

[20]Cynthia Harrison, *On Account of Sex: The Politics of Wom[...] University of California Press, 1988).
[21]See Suzanne M. Bianchi and Daphne Spain, *American Women[...] Sage Foundation, 1986).
[22]See Janet K. Boles, *The Politics of the Equal Rights Amendment[...]
[23]See Jane Mansbridge, *Why We Lost the ERA* (Chicago: Univers[...]
[24]See Joyce Gelb and Marian Lief Palley, *Women and Public P[...] University Press, 1982).

---

* CRITICAL THINKING

SHOULD PACS BE ABOLISHED?

American elections have changed greatly in recent years, and one of the most significant and controversial changes has been the increasingly large role played by interest groups through their political action committees (PACs). PACs now provide about a third of all funds contributed to congressional candidates, and their prominence in state and local campaigns is growing.

Most of the criticisms of PACs have been directed at two developments. The first is the tendency of PACs to concentrate their spending on incumbents. The advantages to PACs of an incumbent strategy are obvious. Incumbents usually win, so in backing incumbents PACs are taking less risk than if they back challengers. In addition, a PAC can target incumbents who work in policy areas that are of particular concern to the interest group that the PAC represents. For example, the work of Congress is done primarily in committees, such as the House and Senate banking committees. Banking industry PACs, by focusing on members of these committees, are assured of making contact with the legislators who have the biggest say over policies that affect banking interests.

A second source of concern about PACs is the activities of "independent" PACs. These PACs are not subject to the same contribution limitations as other PACs, provided that they do not directly coordinate their activities with those of a candidate. They have had a prominent role in presidential election campaigns because their expenditures do not count against the expenditure limits imposed on the Republican and Democratic nominees (see Chapter 18). Independent PACs

have spent more than $10 million in each of the recent presidential campaigns, primarily on behalf of the Republican nominees. George Bush benefited from independent PAC support in 1988 in the form of a televised commercial that received widespread attention and apparently hurt his opponent, Massachusetts Governor Michael Dukakis. The commercial portrayed a convicted felon named Willie Horton, who, while on weekend furlough from a Massachusetts prison under a program supported by Dukakis, brutalized a Maryland couple. Some analysts believe that the Willie Horton ad was a turning point in the 1988 race; Dukakis had been ahead in the polls before the commercial was aired.

PACs are favored by those who believe that interest groups should have a large role in campaigns and who prefer a PAC-based system of campaign finance to the previous system. Before the laws were changed in the 1970s to allow PACs to play a larger role in campaign finance, much of the money in elections came from "fat cats"—wealthy contributors who gave thousands, and in some cases millions, of dollars to candidates. No PAC can give more than $5000 to a candidate in a campaign, and PACs get their money from voluntary donations from small contributors. In a sense, PACs allow thousands of like-minded people to pool their contributions in order to influence election campaigns.

Do you think PACs are a problem? If so, should PACs be abolished or simply regulated more closely? If you were to limit the role of PACs, what restrictions would you place on them?

Assessing PACs: The Corporate Advantage

More than 40 percent of all PACs are associated with corporations (see Table 14-1). Examples include the Ford Motor Company Civic Action Fund, the Sun Oil Company Political Action Committee (Sunpac), and the Coca-Cola PAC. The next largest group of PACs consists of those linked to noneconomic groups (that is, public-interest, single-issue, and ideological groups), such as the liberal People for the American Way and the conservative NCPAC (National Conservative Political Action Committee). Ranking third are PACs tied to trade and professional associations, such as AMPAC (American Medical Association) and R-PAC (National Association of Realtors). Labor unions were once the major source of group contributions, but they now rank fourth.

"HOW THE UNITED STATES COMPARES" BOX

Each chapter has a box that compares the United States with other countries in regard to a major political feature.

"CRITICAL THINKING" BOX

Each chapter has a box that asks you to critically analyze and integrate material presented in the chapter.

* THE MEDIA AND THE PEOPLE

CENSORSHIP AND MILITARY OPERATIONS: THE CASE OF THE GULF WAR

The United States' participation in the Persian Gulf war was characterized by substantial restrictions on the press. Military authorities designated a media pool, a small number of journalists allowed to act as stand-ins for the full press corps. They also placed severe restrictions on the journalists' travel and required reporters to have a military escort; allowed journalists to interview only selected soldiers and usually had a superior officer standing nearby as the interviews took place; and subjected all news reports to review by military censors. Journalists critical of the Gulf war were kept out of the media pool and, to further ensure favorable coverage, the U.S. government flew hometown reporters to Saudi Arabia, apparently on the assumption that they would be more likely to write human interest stories about the troops than hard-news stories about the war itself. The press was also kept away from sites that might have produced controversial news reports. For example, at one point U.S. pilots—in what one of them described as "a turkey shoot"—bombed and strafed Iraqi troops who had left their battle positions and were in full retreat from Kuwait; the U.S. military buried the dead in a mass grave before allowing reporters to go to the scene.

The American press protested the military's tight censorship, but in a relatively mild way. A suit by the

Nation and several other liberal publications was not joined by major newspapers or the television networks. The suit charged that the censorship policy had no legitimate national security purpose and that it imposed an unconstitutional prior restraint on freedom of the press. The Justice Department's brief countered that the policy was designed to protect U.S. forces in the Gulf and would be discontinued when conditions in the war zone permitted. The suit was heard after the ground war had ended and after the press restrictions were lifted. Because the restrictions were no longer in effect, a federal judge declared the question moot.

Opinion polls taken during the Gulf war indicated that the large majority of Americans approved of the government's censorship of the press. Most people agreed with the government's position that censorship was necessary in order to protect the troops in the field. According to a March survey by the Times Mirror Center, a 2-to-1 majority said that "military censorship is more important than the media's ability to report important news." The same survey indicated, however,

Summary

In their search for personal liberty, Americans added the Bill of Rights to the Constitution shortly after its ratification. These amendments guarantee certain political, procedural, and property rights against infringement by the national government. Freedom of expression is the most basic of democratic rights. People are not free unless they can freely express their views. Nevertheless, free expression may conflict with the nation's security needs during times of war and insurrection. The courts at times have allowed government to limit expression substantially for purposes of national security. For the past twenty-five years, however, the courts have protected a very wide range of free expression in the areas of speech, press, and religion.

The guarantees embodied in the Bill of Rights originally applied only to the national government. Under the principle of selective incorporation of these guarantees into the Fourteenth Amendment, the courts extended them to state governments, though slowly and unevenly. In the 1920s and 1930s, First Amendment guarantees of freedom of expression were given protection from infringement by the states. The states, however, continued to have wide discretion in criminal proceedings until the

early 1960s, when most of the fair-trial rights in the Fourth through Eighth amendments were given federal protection.

"Due process of law" refers to legal protections that have been established to preserve individual rights. Due process is of two kinds: procedural and substantive. The former consists of procedures or methods (for example, the opportunity of an accused person to have an attorney present during police interrogation) designed to ensure that an individual's rights are respected; the latter consists of legal proceedings that lead to reasonable and fair results (for example, the conditions of imprisonment of an individual convicted of a crime).

Civil liberties are not absolute but must be balanced against other considerations (such as national security or public safety) and against one another when rights come into conflict. The judicial branch of government, particularly the Supreme Court, has taken on much of the responsibility for protecting and interpreting individual rights. The Court's positions have changed with time and conditions, but the Court has generally been more protective of and sensitive to civil liberties than have elected officials or popular majorities.

Major Concepts

Bill of Rights
civil liberties
clear-and-present-danger test
establishment clause
exclusionary rule
freedom of expression

free-exercise clause
preferred position (of First Amendment rights)
prior restraint (of the press)
procedural due process
selective incorporation
substantive due process

Suggested Readings

Abraham, Henry. *Freedom and the Court*, 5th ed. New York: Oxford University Press, 1988. A general survey of judicial interpretations of civil liberties.

Bodenhamer, David J. *Fair Trial: Rights of the Accused in American History.* New York: Oxford University Press, 1991. A comprehensive historical survey of the rights of the accused.

Haiman, Franklyn S. *Speech and Law in a Free Society.* Chicago: University of Chicago Press, 1981. An assessment of the primacy of speech in a free society.

Halpern, Stephen C., ed. *The Future of Our Liberties.* Westport, Conn.: Greenwood Press, 1982. A collection of essays that consider how the freedoms enumerated in the Bill of Rights may be affected by developing conditions in American society.

Lewis, Anthony. *Gideon's Trumpet.* New York: Random House, 1964. A summary of the case of Clarence Gideon and its effects on the right of persons accused of crime to legal counsel.

Mason, Alpheus T. *The Supreme Court: Palladium of*

"THE MEDIA AND THE PEOPLE" BOX

Each chapter has a box that informs you about a major topic pertaining to the media.

SUMMARY

A short discussion, organized around the chapter's main points, summarizes each chapter's content.

KEY TERMS

A list of the chapter's major concepts facilitates review.

SUGGESTED READINGS

Annotated references encourage further pursuit of some of the best works of political science, both classic studies and recent research.

Do Americans Place Too Much Emphasis on Individual Rights?

JANE MANSBRIDGE

I would urge that we voluntarily restrict the frequency with which we invoke "rights" as we talk with one another about the way we ought to live.

Americans do place too much emphasis on individual rights. While reducing that emphasis, I believe we should keep the concept of rights, work to understand which rights are most important, and fight to prevent the most important rights from being diminished.

Philosophically speaking, we could get rid of the concept of rights while still saving a lot of the aspects of it that we like. We could simply agree that some values are more important than others (that, for example, free speech should in most cases be given greater weight than security). At the same time we could, like some non-Western cultures, respect human dignity without having a concept of rights, defined as legitimate claims that individuals always hold against other people and that others have a duty to respect. On balance, however, I would keep the concept of rights, precisely because it adds to the idea of human dignity the notion that others have a duty to respect claims made in its name.

Yet Americans turn too many issues into questions of absolute rights. For example, each side in the abortion debate frames its argument in the language of rights: "a woman's right to control her body" versus "a fetus's right to life." Each side claims the entire moral territory, ruling out discussion of the degree of legitimacy that each moral stance might have at, say, different stages of pregnancy. Similarly, some propo-

nents of the right to free speech cut off debate on substance by asserting that *no* printed matter can be curbed, even those forms of erotica or advertising that all agree cause harm.

In talk about rights, many problems arise from their binary quality—either you have rights or you don't; there is no spectrum of values, no middle ground. In practice, the U.S. Supreme Court introduces balance between one right and another. But the polarizing language of rights discourages balance.

Rights also have the quality of being held "against" other people. This is especially true of the quintessential "right to liberty," which Hobbes defined as "the absence of external impediments." Talk about rights encourages those who engage in it to see others as opponents.

I am not urging that we include in the category of rights only those particularly political claims—to free speech, association, or jury trial—that evolved in the eighteenth century and earlier as important components of democratic life. I would also include the twentieth-century rights—to a job and to the mini-

In paired original essays following each of the text's seven parts, two prominent political scientists discuss a major issue of the American system.

RICHARD E. FLATHMAN

In recent years the favorable attitudes that we have taken toward basic rights against government have quite rapidly extended into other arenas of social life.

The best short answer to this question is twofold: "On the contrary," in that we have not been sufficiently insistent upon and respectful of the rights that we have most properly claimed; "Yes," in that we have a growing tendency to claim too many rights. But how can we know or decide how much emphasis is *too* much?

In many parts of the world, and among a small but often articulate minority in the United States, it is thought that *any* emphasis on individual rights is too much. In this view, concern with individual rights encourages selfishness, breeds competition and conflict, divides and weakens society. Rather than asserting rights against our country and our communities, our fellow citizens, neighbors, and family, we should seek ways to cooperate with and to help them.

As it pertains to government and politics, this attitude toward rights was long ago rejected in the United States. Necessary as they are, all governments are aggregations of power and hence potentially dangerous to their citizens; rewarding as it may be, all politics are struggles for and against power. Division and conflict are engendered not by rights but by government and politics themselves. Convinced of these and related propositions, our founding generations concluded that all citizens should have the protections afforded by a small but basic set of individual rights. Although challenged from time to time, this judgment has remained a prominent feature of the American political culture.

In this view, which I share, the appropriate objection is not to American ideas about rights but to our repeated failure to insist that the rights we regard as basic be extended to all members of our society and be fully respected. For long periods we have denied basic rights to very large groups in our population, and we have regularly committed gross violations of rights that we claim are well established in our law and our morality.

In recent years the favorable attitudes that we have traditionally taken toward basic rights against government have quite rapidly extended into other arenas of social life. The anti-rights view outlined above has clearly become a minority position as regards workplaces and schools, and its proponents may be fighting a losing battle in respect to more private domains such as the church, the club, and even the family. We are now claiming a wide range of rights, we are asserting those rights against one another with remarkable frequency, and we increasingly look to government to enforce respect for those rights.

In many ways this is a welcome development. "Private" institutions such as corporations, unions, and universities have increasingly acquired the characteristics—in particular, great power over their employees, members, and students—that led us to establish rights against governments, while clubs, other private associations, and families perpetrate the very kinds of discrimination from which our basic rights are supposed to protect us. The assumption of a natural cooperativeness and mutuality that usually underlies generalized hostility to individual rights has often proved to be as unwarranted in these private domains as it is in public life.

This expanded emphasis on individual rights nevertheless deserves our watchful concern. Whatever its effects on community and solidarity (and whether or not those are good things), it enhances the authority and power of the single most dangerous institution in any society—namely, government. And by doing that it may insidiously diminish the individuals to whom the new rights are accorded.

Richard E. Flathman is a member of the Department of Political Science at Johns Hopkins University. He is the author of Toward a Liberalism.

THE
AMERICAN
DEMOCRACY

THE AMERICAN HERITAGE: GOVERNING IDEALS

One hears people say that it is inherent in the habits and nature of democracies to change feelings and thoughts at every moment. . . . But I have never seen anything like that happening in the great democracy on the other side of the ocean. What struck me most in the United States was the difficulty experienced in getting an idea, once conceived, out of the head of the majority.

Alexis de Tocqueville[1]

The major-party candidates in the 1992 presidential race had opposing positions on several key issues. The Republican George Bush stood for free trade, restrictions on abortion, and a deep cut in the capital gains tax. He said that changes were needed in the nation's health care system, but he opposed "turning responsibility for medical care over to Washington." The Democrat Bill Clinton's message was that of a progressive southerner. He was pro-choice on the abortion issue and favored economic development policies that "would help business but not at the expense of the workforce." He was opposed to substantial new federal spending programs except in a few areas, including health care and education.

Despite their differences, however, the two candidates had a common vision of the country they each hoped to lead. Threaded into Bush's and Clinton's campaign speeches were references to time-honored American principles: democracy, freedom, equality, national purpose. The same ideals had permeated the speeches of Ronald Reagan and John Kennedy, Franklin Roosevelt and Abraham Lincoln, and Andrew Jackson and Thomas Jefferson. The same ideals have been used to take America to war, to negotiate peace, to inaugurate presidents, to launch major policies, and to celebrate national holidays.[2]

The ideals were also there at the nation's beginning, when they were put into words in the Declaration of Independence and the Constitution. Of course, the practice of these principles has changed greatly during the two centuries that the

[1]Alexis de Tocqueville, *Democracy in America* (1835–1840), ed. J. P. Mayer and A. P. Kerr (Garden City, N.Y.: Doubleday/Anchor), 1969), 640.
[2]See Peter Lawler and Robert Schaefer, *American Political Rhetoric*, 2d ed. (Totowa, N.J.: Rowman and Littlefield, 1990).

United States has been a nation. When the signers of the Declaration of Independence proclaimed in 1776 that "all men are created equal," they did not have in mind racial minorities or women. They were saying that the rigid inequality and absolutism of European governments had been rejected by Americans and would have no place in their future. Today the principle of equality is a more activist concept, including such policies as busing to achieve racial integration in the schools, welfare programs to relieve the suffering of the poor, and affirmative action programs to open colleges and workplaces to women and minorities.

It could be argued that the principle of equality today is so different from that of 200 years ago that it is foolish to see them as sharing the same root. There is in fact no way to show scientifically that American ideals have developed steadily for two centuries. Yet the American political experience has been remarkably enduring.[3] During the same period in which the United States has had one system of government, Germany has been governed as a group of principalities, a monarchy, a parliamentary democracy, a fascist dictatorship, a divided state, and, today, a federal union.

America's continuity has always obscured deep divisions among its people.[4] The claim that America is a melting pot has always been as much fable as fact. When Irish, Italian, and Polish immigrants reached this country's shores, they encountered nativist elements that scorned their ways of life and attacked their religion. The Latinos and Asians who have come here more recently also have been made to feel less than fully welcome. The "English first" movement includes the not-very-subtle message that "true" Americans do not speak Spanish or Vietnamese or Cambodian.

Nevertheless, throughout their history Americans of all colors and creeds have embraced the core principles upon which the nation was founded. They have quarreled over other matters, and over the practice of these principles, but they seem never to have questioned the principles themselves. As Clinton Rossiter concluded, "There has been, in a doctrinal sense, only one America."[5]

This is a book about contemporary American politics, not U.S. history or culture. Yet American politics today cannot be understood apart from the nation's heritage. Government does not begin anew with each generation. It builds on the past. In the case of the United States, the most significant link between past and present has been formed by the nation's founding ideals. This chapter briefly examines the principles that have shaped American politics since the country's earliest years. The chapter also explains basic concepts, such as power and constitutionalism, that are important in the study of government and politics. The main points to be made in this chapter are the following:

★ *The American political culture centers on a set of core ideals—liberty, equality, self-government, individualism, diversity, and unity—that serve as the people's common bond.* These mythic principles have a substantial influence on what Americans will regard as reasonable and acceptable, and on what they will try to achieve.

[3]See, for example, Louis Hartz, *The Liberal Tradition in America* (New York: Harcourt, Brace, 1955).
[4]See Rogers M. Smith, "The American Creed and American Identity: The Limits of Liberal Citizenship in the United States," *Western Political Quarterly* 41 (1988): 225–252; Robert S. Erikson, John P. McIver, and Gerald C. Wright, Jr., "State Political Culture and Public Opinion," *American Political Science Review* 81 (September 1987): 797–813.
[5]Clinton Rossiter, *Conservatism in America* (New York: Vintage Books, 1962), 67.

U.S. politics is remarkable for its historical continuity—although tributes to the connection with the past sometimes take unusual forms. These portraits of past presidents were carried in George Bush's inaugural parade in 1989. (Wally McNamee/Woodfin Camp and Associates)

★ *Politics is the process that determines whose values will prevail in society.* The play of politics in the United States takes place in the context of democratic procedures, constitutionalism, and capitalism.

★ *Politics in the United States is characterized by a number of major patterns, including a highly fragmented governing system, a high degree of pluralism, an extraordinary emphasis on individual rights, and a pronounced separation of the political and economic spheres.*

Political Culture: The Core Principles of American Government

The people of every nation have a few great ideals that affect their political life, but, as James Bryce observed, Americans are a special case.[6] Their ideals are the basis of their national identity. Other people take their identity from the common ancestry that led them gradually to gather under one flag. Thus, long before there was a France or a Japan, there were French and Japanese people, each a kinship group united through blood.[7] Even today, it is kinship that links the French or the Japanese. There is no way to become a Japanese, except to be born a Japanese. Not so for Americans. They are a multitude of peoples linked by a political tradition. The United States is a nation that was founded abruptly in 1776 on a set of ideals that became its people's common bond.[8]

No exact list of these ideals exists. They are not chiseled in stone like the Ten Commandments. Rather, they are habits of mind, a customary way of thinking about the world. They are part of what social scientists call **political culture,** a

---

[6]James Bryce, *The American Commonwealth,* vol. 2 (New York: Macmillan, 1960), 247–254. First published in 1900.

[7]Theodore H. White, "The American Idea," *New York Times Magazine,* July 6, 1986, 12.

[8]Ralph Barton Perry, *Puritanism and Democracy* (New York: Vanguard Press, 1944), 124–125; see also Seymour Martin Lipset, *The First New Nation* (New York: Basic Books, 1963); Hartz, *Liberal Tradition in America.*

term that refers to the characteristic and deep-seated beliefs of a particular people.[9]

The first efforts to analyze the American political culture were impressionistic. The most astute observers were foreign visitors, such as the Frenchman Alexis de Tocqueville and the Englishman James Bryce; their knowledge of another culture heightened their sense of what was distinctive about America's.[10] The modern study of political culture relies on more systematic methods of identifying people's beliefs, such as public opinion polls.[11] Whatever the method or time, however, most analysts have reached similar conclusions about the American political culture. It is said to include the following beliefs in idealized form:

- **Liberty** is the principle that individuals should be free to act and think as they choose, provided they do not infringe unreasonably on the freedom and well-being of others. This ideal includes a distrust of concentrated power, particularly governmental power.

- **Self-government** is the principle that the people are the ultimate source of governing authority and that their general welfare is the only legitimate purpose of government. This ideal includes a faith in free elections and a commitment to majority rule.

- **Equality** holds that all individuals have moral worth and are entitled to fair treatment under the law. This principle also includes the idea that all qualified citizens should have *equal opportunity* for material gain and political influence. The principle does *not* include the idea that people should be *equal in fact* in their material possessions or in their actual political influence.

- **Individualism** is a commitment to personal initiative, self-sufficiency, and material accumulation. This principle upholds the superiority of a private-enterprise economic system and includes the idea that the individual rather than any institution or group is the foundation of society.

- **Diversity** holds that individual differences should be respected and that these differences are a source of strength and a legitimate basis of self-interest. This ideal includes the notion that people of all races, creeds, and nationalities have an equal place in America.

- **Unity** is the principle that Americans are one people and form an indivisible union. This ideal includes the notion that the United States has a special role to play in human history.

These ideals, taken together, are sometimes called "the American Creed." In practice, they mean different things to different people, so it is not particularly

[9]See Gabriel Almond and Sidney Verba, *The Civic Culture* (Boston: Little, Brown, 1963); Donald Devine, *The Political Culture of the United States* (Boston: Little, Brown, 1972); Walter A. Rosenbaum, *Political Culture* (New York: Praeger, 1975); Richard Merelman, *Making Something of Ourselves: On Culture and Politics in the United States* (Berkeley: University of California Press, 1984).

[10]See de Tocqueville, *Democracy in America.*

[11]See, for example, Herbert McClosky and John Zaller, *The American Ethos* (Cambridge, Mass.: Harvard University Press, 1984).

★ HOW THE UNITED STATES COMPARES

AMERICANS AS A POLITICAL PEOPLE

By some standards, Americans are not a very political people. The United States ranks near the bottom, for example, in voter turnout. Barely half of Americans go to the polls in a presidential election, compared with more than 80 percent of eligible voters in most other democratic countries. In Italy, for example, turnout exceeds 90 percent.

In other ways, however, Americans are highly political. In a five-nation study, published as *The Civic Culture*, Gabriel Almond and Sidney Verba asked respondents why they were proud of their country. Of the American respondents, 85 percent identified their political system as the main source of their pride. Respondents in the other four countries—Great Britain, Germany, Italy, and Mexico—were much less likely to mention government. The extreme case was the Italians, only 3 percent of whom mentioned their system of government. Italians instead took pride in their country's physical beauty and its artistic heritage.

The degree of nationalism among Americans is reflected in a 1990–1991 Times-Mirror Center survey that asked respondents in several countries whether they

agreed with the statement, "I am very patriotic." As the accompanying graph shows, Americans ranked at the top; nearly 90 percent claimed to be highly patriotic. The disparity between the United States and Europe was particularly apparent among young adults. In Europe, young adults were substantially less likely to say they were patriotic than were older people. In the United States, the proportion of eighteen- to twenty-four-year-olds who said they were patriotic, 82 percent, was nearly as high as in other age groups.

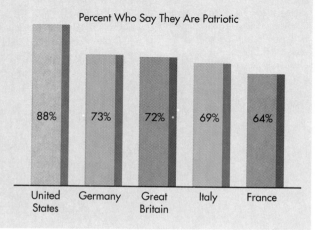

Percent Who Say They Are Patriotic

United States	Germany	Great Britain	Italy	France
88%	73%	72%	69%	64%

SOURCES: Gabriel Almond and Sidney Verba, *The Civic Culture* (Boston: Little, Brown, 1965), 64; Times-Mirror Center for the People and the Press survey, 1990–1991.

useful to give them elaborate definitions at this point in the book. Few observers would argue, however, with the proposition that *a defining characteristic of the American political system is its enduring and powerful set of cultural ideals.* Tocqueville was among the first to see that the main tendencies of American politics cannot be explained without taking into account the country's core beliefs.

Why, for example, does the United States spend less money on government programs for the poor and disadvantaged than do other fully industrialized democracies, including Germany, France, Switzerland, the Netherlands, Spain, Britain, Sweden, Italy, and Japan? Are Americans, even the poorest ones, so much better off than these other people that we have less need for welfare programs? The answer is no. The United States ranks below several of these countries in per capita income and, of all these countries, has in both relative and absolute terms the greatest number of hungry, homeless, and poor people. The reason the United States spends less on social welfare lies chiefly with the emphasis that the American culture places on *individualism*. We have resisted giving government a larger social-welfare role because of our cultural belief that able-bodied individuals should fend for themselves.

The distinctiveness of this cultural belief is evident from a 1991 Times-Mirror

★ ANALYZE THE ISSUE

Self-Criticism as an American Trait
American exceptionalism is the idea that the achievements of Americans are an inspiration to other peoples. The reverse side of American exceptionalism is the tendency of Americans to question whether they are living up to their ideals. The Swedish sociologist Gunnar Myrdal claimed that Americans are more self-critical than any other Western people. What is your opinion? Is it your experience that Americans are a self-critical people? Are you critical of America? What are the advantages and disadvantages of the trait of national self-criticism?

Center survey of opinions in European countries and the United States. When asked whether it is the responsibility of the government "to take care of very poor people who can't take care of themselves," only 23 percent of Americans said they completely agreed. The Germans were the closest to the Americans in their response to this question, but twice as many of them, 50 percent, said they believed that the state should take care of the very poor. More than 60 percent of the British, French, and Italians held this opinion and, among the Spanish, 70 percent claimed that very poor people were the government's responsibility.

Of course, social-welfare policy is not simply an issue of cultural differences. The welfare issue, like all other issues, is part of the rough and tumble of everyday politics everywhere. There are always powerful interests aligned on both sides of important issues. In the United States, the Republican party, business groups, antitax groups, and others have resisted the expansion of the government's social-welfare role, while liberal Democrats, unions, minority groups, and others have from time to time argued for an expansion. Nevertheless, a cultural difference is an unavoidable part of any reasonable explanation of why the United States spends less on social welfare than do European democracies. Americans' belief in individualism, which has no exact parallel in European society, has played a defining role in shaping U.S. welfare policy.

The Power and Limits of Ideals

Early in the settlement of the New World, the idea of "American exceptionalism" emerged. According to this belief, Americans' ideals and accomplishments are an inspiration to other peoples. President Ronald Reagan was a strong advocate of American exceptionalism. In his farewell address, as in several

Even as early Americans were expressing their commitment to the principle of equality, they were allowing slavery to persist. This is the only drawing known to have been made aboard a slave ship as it sailed to America. (National Maritime Museum, London)

The structure of U.S. society helps to promote the American dream of success—for example, by encouraging young people to attend college. (Richard Pasley/Stock, Boston)

other major speeches during his presidency, Reagan quoted John Winthrop's sermon aboard the Puritan ship *Arbella* as it sailed toward America in 1630: "We shall be as a City upon a Hill, the eyes of all people on us."

America's ideals *are* visionary. Their promise is unmistakable. Self-government, liberty, diversity, equality, individualism, and unity are the dream of a society whose aims are noble, one in which power is widely shared and used for the common good.

High ideals do not, however, come with a guarantee that a people will live up to them. The clearest proof of this failing in the American case is the human tragedy that began nearly four centuries ago and continues today. In 1619 the first black slaves were brought in chains to America. Slavery lasted 250 years. Slaves in the field worked from dawn to dark (from "can see, 'til can't"), whether in the heat of summer or the cold of winter. They could be bought and sold, and could be brutally beaten and sexually abused with impunity. The Civil War changed the future of African-Americans but did not assure their equality. Slavery was followed by the Jim Crow era of legal segregation: black people in the South were forbidden by law to use the same schools, hospitals, restaurants, and restrooms as white people. Today African-Americans have equal rights under the law, but in fact they are far from equal. Compared with whites, blacks are three times as likely to live in poverty, twice as likely to be unable to find a job, twice as likely to die in infancy, seven times as likely to be sentenced to death if convicted of an interracial murder.[12] There have always been at least two Americas, one for whites and one for blacks.

The so-called American Dream—the idea that hard work always bring success—also illustrates the gulf between America's ideals and its realities. Compared with Europeans, Americans have a stronger belief that success in life depends on their personal effort rather than on forces outside their control (see

We hold these truths to be self-evident, that all men are created equal; that they are endowed by their Creator with certain unalienable rights; that among these are life, liberty, and the pursuit of happiness.
  Declaration of Independence

[12]U.S. Census Bureau figures, except for the data on sentencing in interracial murders: *New York Times*, April 23, 1987.

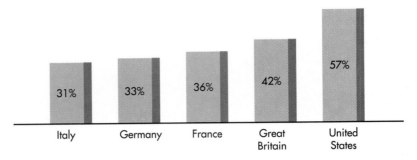

FIGURE 1-1 Opinions about the Source of Personal Success Expressed by Citizens of Major Democracies
Americans are more likely than Europeans to believe that their efforts are the key to personal success. Figures are the percentage of respondents who disagreed with the statement "Success in life is pretty much determined by forces outside our control." *Source: Times-Mirror Center for the People and the Press surveys, 1990–1991.*

Figure 1-1). The United States certainly has been and remains a nation of opportunity for many. Moreover, the society is structured in ways that promote opportunity. No clearer evidence of this exists than the country's elaborate system of higher education, which includes nearly 3,000 two-year and four-year institutions. The democracies of Europe have nothing remotely comparable to this system. College admission in these countries is so restricted that barely a tenth of the young people go to college. Upon entering high school, many European children are steered into a vocational course of study that precludes their subsequent entry into an academic college. The European system is a class-based one; the sons and daughters of the wealthy are almost certain to have the opportunity for a college education, while working-class children are unlikely to get the chance. By comparison, the United States has an open system of college education that is designed to attract nearly all who make the effort to obtain admission. More than a third of young Americans enter college.

This Thomas Nast cartoon from 1882 mocks restrictions on Chinese immigration, reflecting the fact that to some extent our cultural beliefs have always been myths. (Culver Pictures, Inc.)

E PLURIBUS UNUM (EXCEPT THE CHINESE).

Nevertheless, the idea that success is within the reach of all Americans who strive for it is far from accurate. Mexican-Americans in the Southwest, blacks in the inner cities, and poor whites in the depressed industrial belt of the Northeast and Midwest know all too well the limits on their lives. Homelessness, drugs, alcoholism, and family violence have shattered the American Dream for many. In some inner-city schools, the rates of pregnancy and illiteracy are higher than the graduation rate.

A nation's realities will simply never be precisely mirrored in its ideals. The promise of ideals cannot be fully met in practice. To expect otherwise is to misjudge the nature of cultural beliefs and the play of politics. Cultural beliefs have a powerful impact on a nation's politics but not an unlimited one.

CULTURAL BELIEFS AS MYTHS

Cultural beliefs originate in a country's political and social practices, but they are not perfect representations of these practices. They are mythic ideas—symbolic positions taken by a people to justify and give meaning to their way of life.[13] Myths contain elements of truth, but they are far from the full truth. For example, despite the claim that "all men are created equal," equality is not an American birthright. As we will see in Chapter 7, no minority—not blacks, Asians, women, Hispanics, Catholics, or Jews—has advanced toward equality without a struggle. In 1892 Congress suspended Chinese immigration on the assumption that the Chinese were an inferior people. Calvin Coolidge in 1923 asked Congress for a permanent ban on the Chinese, saying that people "who do not want to be partakers of the American spirit ought not to settle in America."[14] Not until 1965 was discrimination against the Chinese and other Asian peoples effectively eliminated from U.S. immigration laws.

The exclusion of the Chinese is not among the stories that we like to tell about ourselves. Such lapses of historical memory can be found among all peoples, but the tendency to recast history is perhaps exaggerated among Americans because our beliefs are so idealistic. How could a people that upholds the ideal of human equality have barred the Chinese, enslaved the blacks, stolen the Indians' lands, subordinated women, and interned the Japanese?

Cultural beliefs can even lull a people into a false sense of what they have accomplished. Some Americans think that by saying they believe in equality, they have achieved it. A 1988 Harris poll showed that two-thirds of white people believe that blacks "get equal pay for equal work." In fact, as U.S. Department of Labor statistics show, blacks in every occupational category are paid less than whites.

One reason America's ideals do not match reality is that they are general principles, not fixed rules of conduct. During the writing of the Declaration of Independence, Thomas Jefferson and John Adams argued over the meaning of liberty. Jefferson contended that its basis was in individual freedom, while Adams centered it on the power of the state to defend itself against other

---

★ ANALYZE THE ISSUE

Cultural Beliefs as Myth and Reality
Cultural beliefs are mythical in that they are combinations of fact and wishful thinking. This mythical dimension can have far-reaching consequences. Consider the 1988 Harris poll in which two-thirds of white Americans said they believed that black Americans "get equal pay for equal work." The reality is otherwise: statistics indicate that, on average, blacks are paid less than whites in every job category. Does the mythical aspect of belief in equality allow white Americans to deceive themselves about how well-off black Americans are? If not, what else might account for the misperception? To what degree do such misconceptions lessen the concern of white Americans with racial equality? Conversely, how does equality as myth promote progress in racial relations?

---

[13]See Claude Lévi-Strauss, *Structural Anthropology* (Chicago: University of Chicago Press, 1983); Clifford Geertz, *Myth, Symbol, and Culture* (New York: Norton, 1974); Albert S. Yee, *Westward to Asia* (in preparation).
[14]Quoted in Ralph Volney Harlow, *The Growth of the United States*, vol. 2 (New York: Henry Holt, 1943), 497.

The American ideal of equality has meant better employment opportunities for women in recent years. (Robert Rathe/ Stock, Boston)

nations. The debate has been restaged countless times in U.S. history. Congressional hearings in 1987 revealed that Lt. Col. Oliver North had broken laws and misused public funds in an effort to assist Nicaragua's anticommunist rebels, the Contras. Representative Lee Hamilton, cochair of the congressional investigative committee, concluded that North's action violated the Constitution and threatened liberty, a judgment that many Americans shared. However, many other Americans, including committee member Senator Orrin Hatch, concluded that North was a hero for his willingness to protect liberty against the external threat of communism.

Conflicts also occur because America's principles cannot be fully reconciled with one another. They derive from somewhat different experiences and philosophical traditions, and there are points at which they conflict. Equality and diversity, for instance, emphasize fairness and a full opportunity for all to partake of society's benefits, whereas liberty and individualism emphasize personal freedom and threats posed to it by political power. Conflict between these beliefs is inevitable. Take the issue of affirmative action. Proponents say that only through aggressive affirmative action programs will women and minorities receive the equal treatment in the job market to which they are entitled. Opponents say that aggressive affirmative action infringes unreasonably on the liberty of the employer and the initiative of the work force. Each side can say that it has America's ideals on its side, and no resort to logic can persuade either side that the opposing viewpoint has merit.

Despite their inexact meanings, conflicting implications, and unfulfilled promise, America's ideals have had a strong impact on its politics. The United States would be a lesser nation today if not for the existence of its core values. All minority groups have gained, for example, from Americans' belief in equality. The idea that every individual has moral worth and is deserving of respect and fair treatment has given weight to demands for equality by those who have not attained it. Consider the situation of women. Since the modern women's rights movement began a quarter century ago, significant changes have taken place in the thinking of Americans of both sexes. The idea that women should have opportunities equal to those of men has changed from the minority opinion to the majority view among men and women alike.[15] There is also a widespread belief that progress toward greater equality for women has been made. A 1991 Gallup poll indicated that about 75 percent of men *and* women believe that women are better off economically, legally, and socially than they were even ten years ago.

The position of women is strengthened by the America cultural belief in the equality of all. The belief alone does not guarantee women equality, but it adds power to their claim. In countries where equality is not a cultural belief, women are at a greater disadvantage. In a 1988 study by the Population Crisis Committee, U.S. women ranked third in the world in their degree of equality with men. The rankings were based on five areas of comparison: employment, education, social relations, marriage and family, and health. American women had an overall score of 82.5 percent, compared with 87 percent for first-ranked Sweden. Women in the United States ranked below men in income and education levels, but they ranked above them in life expectancy, level of nutrition, and health care. In Bangladesh, which ranked last in the study and makes no pretense of sexual equality, women fared much worse than men on all counts, even life expectancy.[16]

In such ways do cultural beliefs lend context to a nation's politics. Ideals serve to define the boundaries of action. They do not determine exactly what people will do, but they have a marked influence on what people will regard as reasonable and desirable. If people believe, as Americans do, that politics exists to promote liberty, equality, self-government, individualism, diversity, and unity, then they will attempt to realize these values through their politics. For example, whenever Americans have faced a crisis of leadership, their belief in self-government has always inclined them to look first to themselves for a solution. They have sought ways to make democracy work better rather than replacing it with a military junta or charismatic leader. This was the case, for instance, when Americans' influence on government was threatened by elitism in the 1820s, by bossism and corruption in the early 1900s, and by a presidency gone haywire in the late 1960s and early 1970s. Each time, as with the introduction of the primary election in the early 1900s, Americans found their answer in electoral reforms designed to make their leaders more responsive to them.

A nation's ideals cannot provide all the answers, but they are the source of many solutions. William James noted that human culture is largely "the resettlements of our ideas."[17] Through trial and error, a society—including American society—finds principles that work for it.

★ ANALYZE THE ISSUE

Affirmative Action and Conflicting Ideals
America's core ideals can conflict, particularly when applied in specific situations. Affirmative action programs, for example, bring into conflict the ideals of liberty and individualism on the one hand and equality and diversity on the other. Which set of ideals do you prize more highly? How far would you go in subordinating one set to the other? Consider your response in the context of affirmative action.

---

[15]Karlyn Keene, "'Feminism' vs. Women's Rights," *The Public Perspective,* November/December 1991, 3–4.
[16]*Los Angeles Times* wire story, June 27, 1988.
[17]William James, *The Principles of Psychology* (New York: Dover Publications, 1950), 638. First published in 1918.

This is a portion of Thomas Jefferson's handwritten draft of the Declaration of Independence, a formal expression of America's governing ideals. (Library of Congress)

THE ORIGINS AND PERSISTENCE OF AMERICA'S GOVERNING IDEALS

In its two centuries as a nation, the United States has changed greatly. The first American settlers lived a rural life near the Atlantic seaboard and were subject to the colonial ambitions of the great European powers. Today's Americans live in an urban society that spans an entire continent and is itself a world power. During its history, the United States has grown from 4 million people to 250 million and from thirteen states to fifty. Yet the political life of the United States has been characterized by remarkable continuity because of the persistence of its founding ideals.

Most observers would agree that this continuity is the most remarkable feature of the country's governing experience. But where did these ideals come from and why do they persist? Although full answers to these questions would fill volumes, even partial answers are instructive.

An Open Country

Our popular history thrives on the illusion that freedom and justice were somehow invented in America in the late eighteenth century. In reality, the outlook of the first white American settlers was shaped by centuries of European life, which, in turn, had been molded by Greco-Roman and Judeo-Christian traditions. The first settlers came to America to live out their ideals, not to think up new ones. As Paul Gagnon has noted, "The first settlers did not sail into view out of a void, their minds as blank as the Atlantic Ocean. . . . Those who sailed west to America came in fact not to build a New World but to bring to life in a new setting what they treasured most from the Old World."[18]

America's special contribution was the enrichment of the freedom and dignity that the first settlers treasured most. The New World's vast wilderness and great distance from the mother country allowed a way of life that was unthinkable in the Old World.[19] Although British kings and Parliament tried to stretch their authority across the Atlantic Ocean, the great distance made it possible for the first white settlers to govern themselves more fully than even they had anticipated. They also found in America more liberty, equality, tolerance, and opportunity than they had imagined. Europe's rigid aristocratic system was unenforceable in frontier America. Ordinary people had no reason to accept servitude when personal freedom was as close as the next area of unsettled wilderness.

Traditional ethnic and religious rivalries, while never far below the surface, were muted by the great task of settling America. Nationalities that warred constantly in Europe had to learn to coexist in America. Diversity became a watchword, and the shared experiences of the New World created a unity and an equality, however uneasy, among groups of people who had never before trusted one another.

It was this heightened sense of freedom and equality amid diversity that Jefferson captured so forcefully in the words of the Declaration of Independence: "We hold these truths to be self-evident, that all men are created equal, that they are endowed by their Creator with certain unalienable rights, that among these are life, liberty, and the pursuit of happiness."

The United States, as the historian Louis Hartz wrote, was "born free."[20] The writing of the Constitution, eleven years after the Declaration, enabled Americans to strengthen their ideals by embodying them in their government. The country's elaborate system of checks and balances is designed to foster liberty by using power to offset power. In most countries final authority is vested in the national government alone, but in the United States it is also vested in state governments. In addition, at both the national and state levels, authority is divided among executive, legislative, and judicial branches. Many other democratic countries have no comparable fragmentation of power. *Extreme fragmentation of governing authority is a major characteristic of the American political system. This fact, as we will see in subsequent chapters, has profound implications for how politics is conducted, who wins out, and what policies result.*

The happiness of society is the end [that is, the purpose] of government.

John Adams

[18]Paul Gagnon, "Why Study History?" *Atlantic Monthly*, November 1988, 47.
[19]White, "American Idea," 12.
[20]Hartz, *Liberal Tradition in America*, 12.

★ THE MEDIA AND THE PEOPLE

LEARNING ABOUT THE AMERICAN WAY

The development of the American political culture was a result of the coincidence of Western values and a New World that offered challenges and possibilities that were not found in the Old. One reason this culture has persisted is the country's natural advantages—in particular, its natural wealth and the protection its ocean barriers provide from potential enemies.

The maintenance of the American political culture also owes, however, to a learning process that social scientists call *political socialization* (which is discussed in detail in Chapter 8). Each generation teaches the next one and thereby contributes to the maintenance of the society's core beliefs. The socialization process starts in the family with exposure to the political views of one's parents and in the schools with the teaching of the country's history and traditions. All told, Americans get a thorough political education, as evidenced by the fact that some of our political catchphrases are so familiar that just about everyone can complete them:

"Government of, by, and for _____."

"The land of the free and the home of _____."

"Life, liberty, and the pursuit of _____."

"All men are created _____."

"One nation, under God, indivisible, with _____."

The mass media have become major agents of political socialization. The news and entertainment media highlight the values of the American political system with consistency and regularity. The messages are seldom delivered in a heavy-handed way, nor do they need to be. They reflect the beliefs of the audience, so that the media pass along and reinforce the culture's values almost automatically. The tendency is most apparent in the case of news about hostile nations. For decades, news about the Soviet Union was accompanied by explicit, and unflattering, comparisons of its values with ours.

Once acquired, cultural beliefs affect a person's view of the world. It is the rare individual who can step back and look at his or her own society in a different light from the one in which the political culture has presented it. Thus, steeped in a political culture that values liberty, equality, self-government, individualism, diversity, and unity, Americans can be expected to see the world along these lines.

A Rich Land

Although a proper constitution can promote a desired form of government, no constitution in and of itself can ensure the existence of such a government. Principles such as liberty and self-government tend to flourish only where wealth is reasonably abundant and widespread. In poor countries physical survival is a far more compelling issue than free speech or open elections.

Extreme poverty leads to a type of politics that restricts personal freedom, initiative, and influence, and contributes to intolerance and divisiveness. When Latin American countries achieved independence in the nineteenth century, they copied the U.S. Constitution but then fell under authoritarian rule. With their history of severe economic inequality based on the clash between the European and native cultures, on dominance by the hierarchical Catholic Church, and on the rigid absolutism of the Spanish governing tradition, the Latin American countries were infertile ground for the implanting of democracy. Even today these nations are struggling to make democracy work against a background of entrenched privilege, abject poverty, and political violence.

The United States has the good fortune to be a rich land. Its vast fertile plains have made it a breadbasket of the world. It ranks among the top three countries worldwide in production of wheat, corn, potatoes, peanuts, cotton, eggs, cattle, and pigs. As for energy resources, the United States is first in uranium production, third in coal reserves, third in natural gas reserves, and sixth in petroleum reserves. In regard to nonfuel minerals, the United States ranks among the top five in copper, lead, sulfur, zinc, gold, iron ore, silver, and magnesium.[21] Americans are a fortunate people; their country's riches have enabled them to pursue a politics of high purpose.

Americans have never fully appreciated the connection between their politics and their country's natural wealth. We have tended to believe that what works for us will also work for others and, indeed, that what works for us would be better for them than what they already have. "Americans who think about the problem of unifying the world," political scientist Harold Lasswell wrote, "tend to follow the precedent set in their own history."[22] Presented after World War I with President Woodrow Wilson's plan for world peace based on American principles, the French premier Georges Clemenceau exclaimed, "This man Wilson with his Fourteen Points! The good Lord had only ten."

Politics: The Struggle for Control

Politics is not simply, or even mostly, about high ideals. It is also about getting one's own way. Most definitions of politics are based on the idea that society's various groups and interests are in competition for power. Even though a society cannot function without a relatively high level of cohesion and cooperation, conflict fills the center stage of politics. Lasswell said that politics is the struggle over "who gets what, when, and how."[23] Defined more formally, **politics** is the process that determines whose values will prevail in society.

The struggle for civil rights is an example of the play of politics. The prominence of civil rights issues in America since the 1950s is a result of the increased awareness of traditionally underprivileged groups, particularly minorities and women, that they have not had equal rights and opportunities. And they have made progress against the political forces arrayed against them by acting politically themselves—through legal action, through lobbying, through elections, through demonstrations. Their efforts have been supported by the cultural ideal of equality, but their political action is what has forced changes in policy.

Political conflict is rooted in two general conditions of society. One is scarcity. Society's resources are finite, but people's appetites are not. There is not enough wealth in even the richest of countries to meet everyone's desires. Conflict over the distribution of resources is the inevitable result. This conflict is perhaps clearest on the issue of how taxes will be spread among various income groups. There is hardly a government program, however, that does not in one way or another redistribute society's resources. When consumers buy milk, for exam-

---

[21]*The New Book of World Rankings* (New York: Facts on File, 1984), 479–480.
[22]Harold D. Lasswell, *World Politics and Personal Insecurity* (New York: Free Press, 1965), 182.
[23]Harold D. Lasswell, *Politics: Who Gets What, When, How* (New York: McGraw-Hill, 1938).

Trying to force the United States to put its ideals into action, these young men were among the pioneers of the modern black civil rights movement. They were arrested for staging a "sit-in" at a whites-only drugstore lunch counter in Jackson, Mississippi, in 1961. (AP/Wide World Photos)

ple, the prices they pay are artificially high because dairy farmers get price supports from government.

Differences in values are the other main source of political conflict. People see things in different ways. The right of abortion is freedom of choice to some and murder of the unborn to others. People bring to politics a wide range of conflicting values—about abortion, about the environment, about national security, about the poor, about crime and punishment, about the economy, about almost everything imaginable.

Opposing values are a persistent source of conflict. School prayer is an example. It was once relatively common for teachers in public schools to lead their students in a prayer or Bible reading at the start of the school day, a practice that some parents opposed. In 1962, in response to a suit brought by a New York parent, the Supreme Court ruled that school prayer violated the constitutional prohibition on the establishment of religion. A year later the Court held that Bible readings were also impermissible. The rulings brought an end to these religious practices in many schools but did not stop the controversy. School prayer still has majority support in opinion polls, and its advocates have repeatedly tried to find a way around the Supreme Court's ruling. In the early 1980s, for example, the Alabama state legislature mandated a minute of silent meditation each school day. The Supreme Court in 1985 held that the minute of silence was unconstitutional, holding that "government must pursue a course of complete neutrality toward religion."[24]

Politics in the United States is not the life and death struggle between opposing groups that typifies some countries, but there are many sources of contention. Perhaps no country has more competing interests than does the United States. Its settlement by people of many lands and religions, its enormous size and geographical diversity, and its economic complexity have

[24]*Engel* v. *Vitale,* 370 U.S. 421 (1962); *Abington School District* v. *Schempp,* 374 U.S. 203 (1963); *Wallace* v. *Jaffree,* 472 U.S. 38 (1985).

made the United States a pluralistic nation. *This feature—competition for power among a great many interests of all kinds—is a major characteristic of American politics that, as later chapters will show, has a substantial impact on how political power is gained and used.*

POWER AND POLICY

Those who prevail in political conflicts are said to have **power,** a term that refers to the ability of persons or institutions to control policy decisions.[25] Power is a basic concept of politics. Power determines which interests will get their way in the making of policy. Those who have sufficient power can impose taxes, permit or prohibit abortions, protect or take private property, provide or refuse welfare benefits, impose or relax trade barriers. With so much at stake, it is perhaps not surprising that power is widely sought and tightly guarded.

When power is exercised through the laws and institutions of government, authority is involved. **Authority** can be defined as the recognized right of an individual, organization, or institution to make binding decisions. By this definition, government is not the only source of authority: parents have authority over their children; professors have authority over their students; firms have authority over their employees. However, government is a special case in that its authority is more encompassing in scope and more final in nature. Government's authority extends to all within its geographical boundaries. It can be used to redefine the authority of the parent, the professor, or the firm. Government's authority is also the most coercive. It includes the power to arrest and imprison, even to punish by death those who violate its rules.

Governments act through policy. In its most general sense, **policy** refers to any broad course of action undertaken by government. U.S. policy toward Japan, for example, consists of a wide range of activities, from trade relations to diplomatic overtures. But *policy* is also used more narrowly to refer to specific programs or initiatives. The Head Start program for improving the educational prospects of poor children, for example, is a policy of government.

Because the allocation of costs and benefits in society is the substance of politics, political scientists have found it useful to categorize policies according to the way in which their costs and benefits are distributed. Some policies provide narrowly concentrated benefits and widely distributed costs. An example is tariffs on imported goods, which benefit domestic producers of those goods at a cost to consumers. Other policies distribute the benefits broadly and concentrate the costs. An example is a steeply progressive income tax that imposes a very high marginal rate on upper-income persons. A third type of policy narrowly distributes both costs and benefits. An example is a license fee on duck hunters that is used to preserve wetlands that serve as breeding grounds for waterfowl. A final type spreads both costs and benefits widely. Social security for retirees, which is funded through payroll taxes on people during their working years, is an example. (Chapters 24–26 examine policy costs and benefits in three policy areas: the economy, social welfare, and foreign affairs.)

[25]Harold D. Lasswell and Abraham Kaplan, *Power and Society* (New Haven, Conn.: Yale University Press, 1950), 75–77.

THE RULES OF THE GAME OF POLITICS

The play of politics takes place according to rules that the participants agree to accept. The rules establish the process by which power is exercised, define the legitimate uses of power, and establish the basis for allocating costs and benefits among the participants. In the American case, the rules of the game of politics include democracy, constitutionalism, and capitalism.

Democracy

Democracy is a set of rules for determining who will exercise the authority of government. Democracy comes from the Greek words *demos,* which means "the people," and *kratis,* meaning "to rule." In simple terms, **democracy** is a form of government in which the people govern, either directly or through elected representatives.

   Democratic government is based on the idea of the consent of the governed, which in practice has come to mean majority rule. The principle of majority rule, in turn, is based on the notion that the view of the many should prevail over the opinion of the few. The many may not be any wiser than the few, but there is no reason to believe that the majority is any more foolish. The one certainty is that the majority includes more people than the minority, and should therefore prevail. Majority rule also reflects a kind of political equality in that the vote of each citizen counts equally, a principle expressed by the phrase "one person, one vote."

★ CRITICAL THINKING

THE PRECONDITIONS OF DEMOCRACY

In 1940 Senator Kenneth Wherry soberly exclaimed, "With God's help, we will lift Shanghai up and up, ever up, until it is just like Kansas City." Like many Americans before and since, Wherry assumed that our form of government could work as well nearly anywhere else. However, democracy has typically flourished in societies where wealth is substantial and widely shared. As the historical experience of Latin American countries indicates, a democratic form of government is not easily maintained where there is widespread poverty and economic inequality.

   Democracy has also worked best in physically secure countries. Living under the threat of conquest by neighboring states is a barrier to a free and open form of government. The Soviet Union is an instructive example. The Soviet state grew out of an impoverished and absolutist feudal society, whose lands were contested by its neighbors. The Soviet Union was itself invaded twice by Germany. The invasion in World War II left 25 million Soviet people dead; by comparison, a half-million American combatants were killed in the same war. It should be no great surprise that the American and Soviet systems—one open and democratic, the other closed and authoritarian—developed in vastly different ways.

   Nevertheless, democracy has begun to spread to what was once the Soviet empire. What do you see as the likelihood of success of this development? What conditions will foster or inhibit the process of democratization in this region?

   Are the countries of Asia, Africa, and the Middle East a different story? They do not share the Western political tradition of the United States and Europe, and differ also in their economic and social systems. Democracy appears to do better when a society's social and economic systems complement its political system (as when all three systems emphasize the importance of the individual). From what you know of the nondemocratic countries of Asia, Africa, and the Middle East, would you predict a democratic future for them? Why or why not?

In practice, democracy in America works primarily through elections. There are other, more direct forms of democracy, such as the town meeting and the initiative, but ours is overwhelmingly a representative system of government in which the people rule indirectly, through the officials they elect.

Democratic procedures, such as free and open elections, are not the same as democratic principles, such as self-government and equality. Rather, democratic procedures serve to promote democratic values. Elections are a *means* by which a people can achieve a greater degree of self-government and equality. Other rules for allocating governing authority, such as a hereditary monarchy, a theocracy, or a dictatorship, are not compatible with democratic principles. Democratic procedures are not, however, a guarantee that democratic values will flourish. The Vietnam war is a case in point. As the military situation worsened, U.S. leaders pressed the South Vietnamese government, America's ally, to adopt a U.S.-style constitution and to conduct a U.S.-style national election. President Lyndon Johnson expected the people of South Vietnam to rally behind their newly acquired democracy. No such thing happened. The Vietnamese people had a feudal legacy, were exhausted by years of internal conflict, were poor and uneducated, and were alienated from their own government because of its distant and corrupt leadership. The right to vote meant little under the circumstances.

Constitutionalism

For many Americans, "democracy" has the same meaning as "liberty"—the freedom to think, talk, and act as one chooses. However, the terms are not synonymous. The concept of democracy implies that the will of the majority should prevail over the wishes of the minority, whereas the concept of liberty implies that the minority has rights and liberties that cannot be taken away by the majority. The democratic model of government has long been accompanied by a fear of tyranny by the majority—the concern that a majority might ruthlessly impose its will on the minority. A more general concern about *all* government is the possibility of abuse of power. James Madison said that the possession of all power in the "same hands, whether of the many or the few, is the path to tyranny."[26]

Constitutionalism is a set of rules that restricts the lawful uses of power. In its original sense, constitutionalism in Western society referred to a government based on laws and constitutional powers.[27] **Constitutionalism** has since come to refer specifically to the idea that there are limits on the rightful power of government over citizens.

In a constitutional system, officials govern according to law, and citizens have basic rights which government cannot take away or deny.[28] An example of constitutionalism in the United States is freedom of speech. Government is prohibited from interfering with the lawful exercise of free speech. No right is absolute, which means that some restrictions are permissible. For example, a

[26]*Federalist* No. 47.
[27]See Charles H. McIlwain, *Constitutionalism: Ancient and Modern* (Ithaca, N.Y.: Cornell University Press, 1983).
[28]Alan S. Rosenbaum, ed., *Constitutionalism: The Philosophical Dimension* (Westport, Conn.: Greenwood Press, 1988), 4.

Free speech is a familiar aspect of American constitutionalism. This protest demonstration took place during the Perisan Gulf crisis of 1990–1991. (Kevin Flach/Impact Visuals)

person could be forcibly removed from the visitors' gallery overlooking the floor of the U.S. Senate for shouting at the lawmakers during debate. Nevertheless, free speech is broadly protected by the courts. During the war in the Persian Gulf, there were hundreds of demonstrations against U.S. policy without a single arrest and conviction for spoken words alone. There were instances where protesters were harassed by officials or other citizens, but those who opposed the war had the opportunity to express their views publicly.

The constitutional tradition in America is at least as strong as the democratic tradition. In fact, *a major characteristic of the American political system is its extraordinary emphasis on individual rights.* Accordingly, the typical American has a keen sense of personal rights. Issues that in other democratic countries would be fought out through elections and in legislatures are, in the United States, worked out through court action as well. Tocqueville said that there is hardly a political issue in America that does not sooner or later become a judicial issue.[29] Abortion rights, nuclear power, busing, toxic waste disposal, and welfare services are among the scores of issues in recent years that have been played out as questions of rights to be settled through judicial action.

This situation reflects the strong influence of cultural beliefs about liberty, equality, and individualism. Through their claims to rights, Americans find protection against majorities and governmental authority. Political debate based on rights, however, tends to be framed in absolute terms, which makes it difficult for the opposing sides to bridge their differences. There is no middle ground in response to the claim, "I know my rights!"

Capitalism

Just as democracy and constitutionalism are systems of rules for allocating society's costs and benefits in American society, so is capitalism. Societies have

---

[29]de Toqueville, *Democracy in America,* chap. 6.

Capitalism, the organizing principle of our economic system, emphasizes marketplace competition and self-initiative. As a result, economic wealth and power are very unequally distributed among Americans. (Jim Richardson/Woodfin Camp & Assoc.)

adopted alternative ways of organizing their economies. One way is socialism, which assigns to government a large role in the ownership of the means of production, in regulating economic decisions, and in providing for the economic security of the individual. Under the form of socialism practiced in democratic countries, such as Sweden, the government does not attempt to manage the overall economy. In communist-style socialism, the government does take responsibility for overall management.

Capitalism is another method for distributing economic costs and benefits. **Capitalism** holds that the government should interfere with the economy as little as possible. Free enterprise and self-reliance are the principles of capitalism. Firms are allowed to operate in a free and open marketplace, and individuals are expected to rely on their own initiative to establish their economic security.

As is the case with the rules of democracy and constitutionalism, the rules of capitalism are not neutral. They enable some interests to gain advantage over others. If democracy responds to numbers and constitutionalism responds to rights, capitalism responds to wealth. Economic power is largely a function of accumulated wealth, whether in the hands of the individual or the firm. "Money talks" in a capitalist system, which means, among other things, that wealthier people will have by far the greater say in the distribution of costs and benefits through the economic system.

The United States does not have a purely capitalist system, in that the government plays a role in regulating the economy and in providing social security (see Chapter 24). The term "mixed economy" is used to define this hybrid form of economic system, with its combination of socialist and capitalist elements. The United States has more elements of the capitalist model and fewer elements of the socialist model than do the countries of Europe. Because of their strong tradition of individualism, Americans tend to restrict the scope of governmental action in the area of the economy. *A major characteristic of the American system is a sharp distinction between what is political, and therefore to be*

★ ANALYZE THE ISSUE

Democracy and Social and Economic Systems
Democracy is more prevalent in countries with a free-market economy than those with a socialist economy. Are a democratic political system and a free-market economic system reinforcing? What do you make of the case of Sweden, which has a stable democracy and yet also has a socialist economy? Does the Swedish example suggest that any explanation of the connection of politics and economics must explore a range of factors, including a country's traditions and natural abundance?

decided in the public arena, and what is economic, and therefore to be settled through private relations. For all practical purposes, this outlook places many kinds of choices, which in other countries are decided collectively, beyond the reach of political majorities in the United States.

An example is health care. Decades ago, the democracies of western Europe established government-paid health systems. All citizens became entitled to full medical care at government expense. Americans' belief in individualism—the idea that able-bodied individuals should provide for themselves—has been an obstacle to the creation of a similar system in the United States. As another example, Americans complain that their taxes are too high, but they actually pay relatively fewer taxes than citizens of European democracies. This situation testifies to the extent to which Americans believe that wealth is more properly allocated through the marketplace than through government.

The past decade has witnessed the triumph throughout most of the world of the capitalist, free-market type of economy. Its chief rival, Soviet-style communism, collapsed from within. In the Soviet system of central planning, the national government controlled all industries and provided the overall management of the economy, deciding what goods would be produced, what their prices would be, and how they would be distributed. Some fifty years ago economist Oskar Lange argued that the computational demands of the Soviet command economy could not be met by *any* organizational structure. He argued, correctly as it turned out, that it was humanly impossible for central planning to handle the computational complexity of price, supply, and demand decisions for a national economy.

As the former Soviet Union and the eastern European countries within its orbit shifted recently toward market-based economic systems, they also moved toward a greater degree of democracy and constitutionalism in their political systems. These different forms of allocating costs and benefits in a society don't necessarily have to go together. However, as the American experience suggests, democracy, constitutionalism, and a free-market economy do reinforce one another in practice. Each is based on the free choices of free individuals.

Studying American Government

The chapters that follow describe and explain the main features of the American governing system. The analysis begins with the constitutional framework of the United States, focusing in Part One (Chapters 1–4) on the governmental structure and in Part Two (Chapters 5–7) on individual rights. The analysis then shifts to the relationship between the American people and their government. Part Three (Chapters 8–10) looks at public opinion, political participation, and voting, while Part Four (Chapters 11–15) examines the intermediaries that enable citizens to act together: political parties, interest groups, and the news media. The functioning of governing institutions and officials is the next general topic. Part Five (Chapters 16–19) examines the nation's elective institutions—Congress and the presidency—and Part Six (Chapters 20–23) looks at the appointive institutions—courts and the government bureaucracy.

Building on all the previous units, Part Seven (Chapters 24–27) examines the major areas of public policy: the economy, social welfare, and foreign affairs. In the final chapter of Part Seven, I venture some judgments about the condition of American democracy.

The chapters are collectively designed to convey a reliable body of knowledge that will enable the reader to begin to think *systematically* about the nature of American government. Systematic thought rests not on the ability to rattle off unconnected facts but on an understanding of general patterns in American politics. Five of these patterns have been highlighted in this chapter. The United States has:

- An enduring set of cultural ideals that are its people's common bond and a source of their political goals
- An extreme fragmentation of governing authority that is based on an elaborate system of checks and balances
- A great many competing interests that are the result of the nation's great size, population diversity, and economic complexity
- A strong emphasis on individual rights that is a consequence of the nation's political traditions
- A sharp separation of the political and economic spheres that has the effect of placing many economic issues outside the reach of political majorities

Each of these patterns will be discussed further in the chapters that follow.

Beneath this book's concern with the broad patterns of American government is a question that must be asked of any democracy: What is the relationship of the people to their government? Thinking about this question is the foundation not only of reasonable judgments about the state of American democracy but also of good citizenship. Responsible citizenship depends finally on an informed perspective, on a recognition of how difficult it is to govern effectively and yet how important it is to try. It cannot be said too often that the issue of governing is the most difficult issue facing any society. Nor can it be said too often that governing is a quest and a search, not a resolved issue. E. E. Schattschneider said it clearly: "In the course of centuries, there has come a great deal of agreement about what democracy is, but nobody has a monopoly of it and the last word has not been spoken."[30]

Summary

The United States is a nation that was formed on a set of ideals that include liberty, equality, self-government, individualism, diversity, and unity. These ideals were rooted in the country's European heritage, and early America's vast open lands and abundant natural resources influenced their growth. They became Americans' common bond and today are the basis of their political culture. Although they are mythic, inexact, and conflicting, these ideals have had a powerful effect on what generation after generation of Americans has tried to achieve politically for themselves and others.

Politics is the process by which it is determined whose

---

[30]E. E. Schattschneider, *Two Hundred Million Americans in Search of a Government* (New York: Holt, Rinehart and Winston, 1969), 42.

values will prevail in society. The basis of politics is conflict over scarce resources and competing values. Those who have power win out in this conflict and are able to control governing authority and policy choices.

The play of politics in the United States takes place through rules of the game that include democracy, constitutionalism, and capitalism. Democracy is rule by the people, which, in practice, refers to a representative system of government in which the people rule through their elected officials. Constitutionalism refers to rules that limit the rightful power of government over citizens. Capitalism is an economic system based on a free-market principle that allows the government only a limited role in determining how economic costs and benefits will be allocated.

Major Concepts

authority	liberty
capitalism	policy
constitutionalism	political culture
democracy	politics
diversity	power
equality	self-government
individualism	unity

Suggested Readings

Geertz, Clifford. *Myth, Symbol, and Culture.* New York: Norton, 1974. An analysis of the mythic and symbolic nature of cultural beliefs.

Graham, George J., Jr., and Scarlett G. Graham, eds. *Founding Principles of American Government.* Chatham, N.J.: Chatham House, 1984. A collection of insightful essays on traditional themes of American government.

Hartz, Louis. *The Liberal Tradition in America.* New York: Harcourt, Brace, 1955. A historical assessment of the liberal tradition that underlies the American political system.

Jennings, M. Kent, and Richard Niemi. *Generations and Politics: A Panel Study of Young Adults and Their Parents.* Princeton, N.J.: Princeton University Press, 1981. A careful study of the relationship over time between the political beliefs of young adults and those of their parents.

Lawler, Peter, and Robert Schaefer, *American Political Rhetoric,* 2nd ed. Totowa, N.J.: Rowman and Littlefield, 1990. A collection of readings that includes speeches by some of America's best political rhetoricians, including Lincoln, Jefferson, and Martin Luther King, Jr.

Lipset, Seymour Martin. *The First New Nation.* New York: Basic Books, 1963. An analysis of America's origins in political ideas.

McIlwain, Charles H. *Constitutionalism: Ancient and Modern.* Ithaca, N.Y.: Cornell University Press, 1983. A study of the historical development of constitutionalism.

Merelman, Richard. *Making Something of Ourselves: On Culture and Politics in the United States.* Berkeley: University of California Press, 1984. An evaluation of culture and politics in the United States.

THE CONSTITUTIONAL FRAMEWORK

The United States has the world's oldest written constitution still in force. France has had fourteen constitutions during the same period in which the United States has had one.

The writing of the U.S. Constitution was a remarkable achievement. When Americans placed themselves under the Constitution in 1789, they achieved what no people before them had accomplished. They had, during a time of grave crisis and without bloodshed, debated a form of government radically different from any that had gone before and then adopted it without resort to arms. The writing and ratification of the Constitution provided the world with a model of peaceful revolution.

The task of the writers of the Constitution was particularly challenging because of the need to design a government that could satisfy three different and somewhat competing objectives at the same time. The most pressing goal, which occasioned the writing of the Constitution in 1787, was to establish a government that could serve as the foundation of an American nation. Only a strong and energetic government could bind the separate American states and their diverse interests. The second aim was to keep the nation's government from being so powerful as to threaten liberty. Liberty had inspired the revolution against England and was Americans' highest political aspiration. Thus the power of the U.S. government would have to be balanced carefully by restraints on that power. Finally, the Constitution would have to embody Americans' desire for self-government. This objective was not wholly compatible with the goal of nationhood, which required a transfer of power to a government that was more distant from the people than were the state governments. Nor was the objective of self-government entirely consistent with the goal of individual liberty, which required that there be limits on the power of the majority.

The chapters of this section focus on the U.S. Constitution and are organized so as to address the document's chief objectives— nationhood (Chapter 2), liberty (Chapter 3), and self-government (Chapter 4). Each chapter explores the circumstances that led the first Americans to value a particular ideal, such as liberty, and then indicates how this ideal was embodied in the Constitution's original provisions, such as the elaborate system of checks and balances. Each chapter then evaluates changes in constitutional thought and action during the country's two centuries and closes with a brief commentary on modern practices. The chapters of the section are intended to demonstrate why the British statesman William Gladstone in 1878 declared the U.S. Constitution to be "the most wonderful work ever struck off at a given time by the brain and purpose of man."   ★   ★   ★

FEDERAL GOVERNMENT: FORGING A NATION

The question of the relation of the states to the federal government is the cardinal question of our Constitutional system. It cannot be settled by the opinion of one generation, because it is a question of growth, and each successive stage of our political and economic development gives it a new aspect, makes it a new question.

Woodrow Wilson[1]

The statistics were grim. Over the next year, 45,000 Americans would die in traffic accidents. Nearly 10,000 of those fatalities would be accounted for by persons under age twenty-five involved in alcohol-related accidents. "Raising the drinking age will reduce fatalities among the younger drivers of this country," claimed an official of the National Highway Traffic Safety Administration. A study conducted for the insurance industry estimated that 1,250 lives a year could be saved if a minimum drinking age of twenty-one were established. In July 1984 Congress passed legislation requiring states either to impose a minimum age of twenty-one for the purchase of alcohol or to lose their share of federal funds for highway construction.[2]

Opponents of the law included restaurant and bar owners and college students on some campuses. A common argument advanced by these groups was that if eighteen-year-olds are considered old enough to vote and to be drafted to fight in war, they should be considered old enough to drink. But the most determined opposition came from some of the states. Issues of public safety and health have traditionally been the constitutional responsibility of state governments rather than the national government. When the drinking-age legislation was passed by Congress, twenty-seven states allowed persons younger than twenty-one to buy alcoholic beverages. These states had two years to raise their legal drinking age or lose their federal highway funds. One

[1]Woodrow Wilson, *Constitutional Government in the United States* (New York: Columbia University Press, 1908), 173.
[2]Details in this paragraph and the paragraphs immediately following are from *U.S. News and World Report*, June 25, 1984, 8; July 9, 1984, 14; and June 9, 1986, 21.

governor described the federal legislation as "blackmail." Another called it "Washington arrogance."

South Dakota was one of several states that challenged the law in court on the grounds that it violated powers reserved to the states by the Tenth Amendment to the U.S. Constitution. These legal challenges failed. In the end, all the states that had permitted persons under twenty-one to drink changed their laws. The financial stakes were too high for the states to stand on principle. New York and Texas, for example, would each have lost $60 million annually in highway funds had they not changed their drinking age, and smaller states such as Connecticut, Iowa, and Hawaii would have lost between $10 million and $15 million annually.

The drinking-age issue is one of thousands of controversies during American history that have hinged on whether national or state authority should prevail. Americans possess what amounts to dual citizenship: they are citizens both of the United States and of the state in which they live. The American political system is a **federal system,** one in which constitutional authority is divided between a national government and state governments: each is assumed to derive its powers directly from the people and therefore to have sovereignty (final authority) over the policy responsibilities assigned to it. The federal system consists of nation *and* states, indivisible and yet separate.[3]

This initial chapter on American constitutionalism focuses on federalism. The nature of the relationship between the nation and the states was the question that dominated all others when the Constitution was written in 1787, and this chapter describes how the issue helped form the Constitution. The chapter's closing sections discuss how federalism has changed during the nation's history and conclude with a brief overview of contemporary federalism. The main points presented in the chapter are the following:

★ *The power of government must be equal to its responsibilities.* The Constitution was needed because the nation's preceding system (under the Articles of Confederation) was too weak to accomplish its expected goals, particularly those of a strong defense and an integrated economy. The Constitution created a stronger national government by granting it significant powers, particularly in the areas of taxation and the regulation of commerce.

★ *Federalism—the Constitution's division of governing authority between two levels, nation and states—was the result of political bargaining.* Federalism was not a theoretical principle, but a compromise made necessary in 1787 by the prior existence of the states.

★ *Federalism is not a fixed principle for allocating power between the national and state governments,* but a principle that has changed in response to changing political needs. Federalism has passed through several distinct stages during the nation's history.

★ *Contemporary American federalism tilts toward national authority.* Expanded national authority reflects the increased interdependence of the various segments of American society as a result of social and economic change.

[3]Richard H. Leach, *American Federalism* (New York: Norton, 1970), 1.

Before the Constitution: The Articles of Confederation

On June 12, 1776, as the thirteen American colonies braced for full-scale revolutionary war against England, the Continental Congress appointed a committee composed of a member from each colony to decide the form of a central government. The task would be difficult. The colonies had always been governed separately, and their residents considered themselves Virginians, New Yorkers, or Pennsylvanians as much as they thought of themselves as Americans. Moreover, the American Revolution was sparked by grievances against the arbitrary policies of King George III of England, and Americans were in no mood to replace him with a powerful central authority of their own making.

These concerns led to the formation of a very weak national government that was subordinate to the states. Under its constitution, known as the Articles of Confederation, each state kept its "sovereignty, freedom, and independence." There was a national Congress, but its members were appointed and paid by their respective state governments. Each of the thirteen states had one vote in Congress, and the agreement of nine states was required to pass legislation. Moreover, any state could block constitutional change: the Articles of Confederation could be amended only by unanimous approval of the states.

The American union held together during the Revolutionary War out of necessity: the states had either to cooperate or to surrender to the British. But once the war ended, the states felt free to go their separate ways. Several states sent representatives abroad to negotiate trade agreements. Others negotiated directly with the Indian tribes. New Hampshire, with its eighteen-mile coastline, even established its own navy. In a melancholy letter to Thomas Jefferson, George Washington wondered whether the United States deserved to be called a nation.

A LACK OF NATIONAL POWER

Under the Articles of Confederation, Congress was denied the powers it needed if it was to achieve national goals. Although Congress had responsibility for defense of the states, it was not granted the power to tax, so it had to rely on the states for the money to maintain an army and navy. During the first six years under the Articles, Congress asked the states for $12 million but received only $3 million—not even enough to pay the interest on Revolutionary War debts. Georgia and North Carolina contributed no money at all to the national treasury between 1781 and 1786. By 1786 the national government was so desperate for funds that it sold the navy's ships and had fewer than 1,000 soldiers in uniform—this at a time when England had an army in Canada and Spain occupied Florida.

Congress was also expected to shape a national economy, yet it was powerless to do so because the Articles forbade interference with the states' commerce policies. States imposed trade barriers among themselves. Connecticut placed a higher tariff on finished goods from Massachusetts than it did on the same goods shipped from England. New Jersey imposed a duty on foreign-made goods shipped from other states. New York responded by taxing goods from New Jersey shipped through New York ports.

County courthouses in Massachusetts in 1786 were the scenes of brawls between angry farmers and those who supported the state's attempts to foreclose on their property because of unpaid debts. The violence of Shays' Rebellion convinced many political leaders that the central government needed to be made more powerful. (The Bettmann Archive)

The Articles of Confederation showed the fallacy of the adage "That government is best which governs least." If England's George III had exposed the dangers of an overly powerful authority, the Articles revealed the consequences of an overly weak authority: public disorder, economic chaos, and inadequate defense.

A NATION IN DISARRAY

By 1784 the nation was unraveling. Congress was so weak that its members often did not bother to attend its sessions. In November of that year the French ambassador reported to his government, "There is in America no general government; [there is] neither Congress, nor president, nor head of any one administrative department."[4]

Finally, in late 1786, a revolt in western Massachusetts prompted leading Americans to conclude that the country's government had to be changed. A ragtag army of 2,000 farmers, armed with staves and pitchforks, marched on county courthouses to prevent foreclosures on their land and cattle. Many of the

[4]Quoted in George Bancroft, *History of the Formation of the Constitution of the United States of America*, 3d ed., vol. 1 (New York: D. Appleton, 1883), 166.

farmers were veterans of the Revolutionary War; their leader, Daniel Shays, had been a captain in the Revolutionary army. They were angered by high taxes on their land and by high interest rates on their mortgages. They had been given assurances during the Revolution that their land, which lay fallow because they were away at war, would not be confiscated for reasons of unpaid debts and taxes. Although many Americans sympathized with the farmers, Shays' Rebellion scared propertied interests, and they called upon Massachusetts' governor to put down the revolt. As he had no state militia to call upon, he asked Congress for help, but it had no army to send. A disgusted George Washington asked why a country that had won a long and difficult war was not able to maintain public order in time of peace.[5] Massachusetts' governor finally raised enough money to hire a militia that put down the rebellion, but the event thoroughly alarmed wealthy interests. They worried that government by mob action would become the rule and would sweep away their privileged position.

Shays' Rebellion dramatized the young country's breakdown and made it clear that a strengthening of national authority was necessary if the United States was to be saved. At the urging of the legislatures of several states, Congress authorized a constitutional convention to be held in late spring of 1787 in Philadelphia. Congress planned a limited convention: the delegates were to meet for "the sole and express purpose of revising the Articles of Confederation."

Negotiating toward a Constitution

The delegates to the Philadelphia constitutional convention ignored the instructions of Congress. Meeting behind closed doors, they drafted a plan for an entirely new form of government. Prominent delegates (among them George Washington, Benjamin Franklin, and James Madison) were determined from the first to establish an American nation built upon a strong central government. Recognizing what appeared likely to happen in Philadelphia, Patrick Henry, a fervent believer in state-level government, said that he "smelt a rat." After the convention had adjourned, he realized that his fears were justified: "Who authorized them," he asked, "to speak the language of 'We, the People,' instead of 'We, the States'?"[6]

That question—"people or states?"—was the central one confronting the Philadelphia convention. If the national government was to be made workable, as Pennsylvania's James Wilson argued, it had to be a government of the people, not of the states. The Confederation was inherently feeble because the central government had no sure way short of war to make a state comply with its laws.

The process of writing the Constitution was not a smooth one. All the delegates were men of substance: they were for the most part lawyers, large landowners, and merchants. They shared a commitment to the interests of the propertied class. But they also had their differences. The Constitution is sometimes portrayed as the work of intellectual geniuses who put politics aside

[5]Catherine Drinker Bowen, *Miracle at Philadelphia* (Boston: Little, Brown, 1986), 10.
[6]William Wirt Henry, *Patrick Henry: Life, Correspondence, and Speeches*, vol. 3 (New York: Scribner's, 1891), 431.

Junius Brutus Stearn's painting, *Washington Addressing the Constitutional Convention.* The Constitution of the United States was written during the summer of 1787 in the East Room of the Old Pennsylvania State House, where the Declaration of Independence had been signed a decade earlier. (The Virginia Museum)

to create a document that they knew would stand for all time. In reality, the Framers of the Constitution fought like any other group of politicians, each promoting the ideas and values in which he believed. What set the Framers apart was their uncommon combination of education and experience and the nature of the times in which they lived. Several of the Framers had a superb education, including tutoring in the classics, and most of them had held high public office. They also had experienced the American Revolution and the problems of nation building. They had thought long about and worked hard at the problems of government, and the Philadelphia convention gave them a unique opportunity to apply the lessons they had learned.

THE GREAT COMPROMISE: A TWO-CHAMBER CONGRESS

Debate at the constitutional convention of 1787 began over a plan put forward by the Virginia delegation, which was dominated by strong nationalists. The Virginia Plan (also called the large-state plan) called for a two-chamber Congress that would have supreme authority in all areas "in which the separate states are incompetent," particularly defense and interstate trade. The Virginia Plan also provided that the states would have numerical representation in Congress in proportion to their populations or tax contributions. Either way, the small states would be greatly outvoted. Small states such as Delaware and Rhode Island would be allowed only one representative in the lower chamber, while large states such as Massachusetts and Virginia would have more than a dozen.

Not surprisingly, the Virginia Plan was roundly condemned by delegates from the smaller states. What was the difference, asked Delaware's John Dickinson, between rule by a foreign power and rule by a few powerful states? The small states rallied around a counterproposal made by New Jersey's William Paterson. The New Jersey Plan (also called the small-state plan) called for a stronger national government with the power to tax and to regulate commerce among the states; in most other respects, however, the Articles would remain in effect. Congress would have a single chamber in which each state, large or small, would have a single vote.

The debate over the New Jersey and Virginia plans dragged on for weeks, and it appeared for a time that the convention was hopelessly deadlocked. Finally a special committee composed of a member from each state reached what is now known as the Great Compromise. The delegates agreed on a bicameral (two-chamber) Congress: the House of Representatives would be apportioned among the states on the basis of population and the Senate on the basis of an equal number of votes (two) for each state.

The small states would never have agreed to join a union in which their vote was always weaker than that of large states, a fact reflected in Article V of the Constitution: "No state, without its consent, shall be deprived of its equal suffrage in the Senate." In retrospect, however, the worries of the small states appear to have been exaggerated. Seldom in U.S. history has a major national issue aligned members of Congress from the large states against those from the small states. Other differences between the states, such as those dividing North and South, have been of far greater significance than differences of size.[7]

THE NORTH-SOUTH COMPROMISE: THE ISSUE OF SLAVERY

The separate interests of the states were also the basis for a second major compromise: a North-South bargain over economic issues. The South had a slave-based agricultural economy, and its delegates feared that the North, which had a stronger manufacturing sector, would gain a numerical majority in Congress and then proceed to enact unfair tax policies. If Congress levied high

[7]Alfred H. Kelley and Winfred A. Harbison, *The American Constitution,* 5th ed. (New York: Norton, 1976), 122.

This illustration shows slaves undergoing inspection by white traders. Southern delegates at the Constitutional Convention sought assurances that Congress would not bar the importation and sale of slaves and that their slave-based agricultural economy would be protected. (Culver Pictures)

TABLE 2-1   U.S. Population and Percentage of African-Americans, by State, 1790

State	Total Population	African-Americans (Percent)
Connecticut	238,000	2.5%
Delaware	59,000	22.0
Georgia	83,000	36.1
Maryland	320,000	21.3
Massachusetts	476,000	1.3
New Hampshire	142,000	0.7
New Jersey	184,000	7.6
New York	340,000	7.6
North Carolina	394,000	26.9
Pennsylvania	434,000	2.3
Rhode Island	69,000	5.8
South Carolina	249,000	43.8
Virginia	748,000	40.9

SOURCE: U.S. Bureau of Census, *Historical Statistics of the United States, Colonial Times to 1970*, Part 1 (Washington D.C.: U.S. Government Printing Office, 1975), 24–36.

import tariffs on finished goods from foreign nations in order to protect domestic manufacturers and placed heavy export tariffs on agricultural goods, the burden of financing the new government would fall mainly on the South. Its delegates also worried that northern representatives in Congress might tax or even bar the importation of slaves.

After extended debate, a compromise was reached. Congress was to be prohibited by the Constitution from taxing exports but could tax imports. In addition, Congress would be prohibited from passing laws to end the slave trade until 1808. The South also gained a constitutional provision requiring each state to return runaway slaves to their state of origin. A final bargain was the infamous "Three-fifths Compromise": for purposes of both taxation and representation in Congress, five slaves were to be considered the equivalent of three white people; in effect, a slave was to be counted as three-fifths of a human being.

Although the Philadelphia convention has been criticized for the compromise over slavery, the issue of slavery was a powerful argument against a union. Northern states had no economic use for forced labor and had few slaves, whereas southern states had based their economies on large slave populations (see Table 2-1). John Rutledge of South Carolina asked during the convention debate whether some of the delegates thought southerners were "fools." He explained that the southern states would form their own union rather than accept one that prohibited slavery.

Federalism: National and State Sovereignty

Viewed historically, the most important constitutional decision of the Philadelphia convention was one that underpinned all the deliberations but was not itself debated at great length. This decision was to institute a federal system, which divided the sovereign power of government between the nation and the states. **Federalism** is the form of government in which **sovereignty,** or ultimate governing authority, is divided between a national government and regional (that is, state) governments. The country had been governed as a **confederacy,** in which sovereignty was vested entirely in the state governments.

Unlike many other features of the U.S. Constitution, the provisions for federalism had no basis in political theory. Indeed, federalism did not exist anywhere in the world before 1787. Other countries had unitary systems of government. A **unitary system** vests sovereignty solely in the national government. Great Britain is an example: its national legislature, the Parliament, has absolute power to decide policy without regard to the authority of the country's other governments. In a political dispute during the 1980s, Parliament, under the leadership of Margaret Thatcher, abolished the Greater London Council, which was part of the city government of London. In contrast, because of federalism, the U.S. national government must act with due regard for the states, which are protected constitutionally from abolishment and from unwarranted interference in their policies.

Within the U.S. federal system, there is a form of unitary government in the relation of the states to their local governments. Local governments derive their sovereignty from the state government; they do not have sovereign (ultimate) authority. That is, although local units often have considerable autonomy, it is granted at the discretion of the state government, which can overturn local policy and in some circumstances can even abolish a local unit.

Federalism was an accommodation of the ideals of unity and diversity. The states already existed and had the loyalty of their people. Virginia's George Mason spoke for nearly all the delegates in Philadelphia in saying that he would never consent to a union that abolished the states. Instead, Americans would be governed as one people through their national government and as

★ HOW THE UNITED STATES COMPARES

FEDERAL VS. UNITARY GOVERNMENTS

Federalism involves the division of sovereignty between a national government and subnational (such as state) governments. It was invented in 1787 in order to maintain the preexisting American states while establishing an effective central government. Since then a number of other countries have established a *federal* government, but most countries have a *unitary* government, in which all sovereignty is vested in a national government. In some cases, countries have developed hybrid versions. Great Britain's government is formally unitary, but Parliament has granted some autonomy to regions. Mexico's system is formally federal, but in actuality nearly all power is concentrated in the national government.

Country	Form of Government
Canada	Federal
France	Unitary
Germany	Federal
Great Britain	Modified unitary
Italy	Modified unitary
Japan	Unitary
Mexico	Modified federal
United States	Federal
Sweden	Unitary

separate peoples through their respective state governments. The federal system gave the states the power to decide local matters on a separate basis, thus providing for a responsiveness to local values and differences. At the same time, federalism gave the national government the power to address issues of broad national scope.[8] Viewed from the perspective of the people, federalism was almost a form of dual citizenship. Americans would be citizens both of a common nation and of individual states.

THE POWERS OF THE NATION AND THE STATES

The Philadelphia convention met to decide the powers of the national government. Accordingly, the U.S. Constitution focuses primarily on the lawful authority of the national government, which is provided through *enumerated* and *implied powers.* Authority that is not in this way granted to the national government is left—or "reserved"—to the states. Thus the states have *reserved powers.*

Enumerated Powers

Article I, section 8, of the Constitution lists, or enumerates, the national government's powers. These seventeen **enumerated powers** are designed primarily to enable the national government to provide for the nation's defense and commerce. Congress is empowered, for instance, to tax, to establish an army and navy, to declare war, to regulate commerce among the states, to create a national currency, and to borrow money. The Constitution also prohibits the states from interfering with the national government's exercise of its lawful powers. Article I, section 10, forbids the states to make treaties with other nations, raise armies, wage war, print money, or make commercial agreements with other states without the approval of Congress.

Furthermore, acts of the national government, when those acts are within its constitutional powers, prevail over conflicting actions by state governments. Article VI of the Constitution grants this dominance in the so-called **supremacy clause,** which states that "the laws of the United States . . . shall be the supreme law of the land."

Implied Powers

The enumeration of powers in the Constitution was intended to limit as well as to grant authority to the national government. By listing the national government's powers one by one, the Framers were placing a restraint on its authority: it could not lawfully assume additional powers. A desire for liberty from oppressive government had inspired Americans to revolt against England eleven years earlier, and it was believed that the preservation of liberty required a government of restricted powers. (This subject is discussed at length in Chapter 3.)

The Framers believed, however, that an overly narrow definition of national

This Constitution, and the laws of the United States which shall be made in pursuance thereof; and all treaties made, or which shall be made, under the authority of the United States, shall be the supreme law of the land; and the judges in every State shall be bound thereby, any thing in the Constitution or laws of any State to the contrary notwithstanding.

U.S. Constitution, Article VI (the supremacy clause)

[8]"The U.S. Constitution Today," report of the Seventy-third American Assembly, Columbia University, April 23–26, 1987.

authority would result in a government incapable of adapting to change. Under the Articles of Confederation, Congress had had authority to exercise only those powers expressly granted it, and partly for that reason it had been unable to respond effectively when the country's changing needs after the Revolutionary War required a more powerful central government. Concerned that the enumerated powers by themselves might be too restrictive of national authority, the Framers added the **"necessary and proper" clause,** or, as it later came to be known, the **elastic clause.** Article I, section 8, gives Congress the power "to make all laws which shall be necessary and proper for carrying into execution the foregoing [enumerated] powers."

Alexander Hamilton (1757–1804) was just thirty-two years old when he served as a delegate to the Constitutional Convention. (Courtesy of the New York Historical Society, NYC)

Reserved Powers

The supremacy clause and the "necessary and proper" clause were of deep concern to some leading Americans of 1787, who worried that the Constitution would lead eventually to national domination of the states. Hamilton tried to quiet their fears by arguing (perhaps less than candidly, for he was an ardent nationalist) that these clauses were merely logical devices. Unless legitimate national laws were declared supreme, Hamilton said, the states could break them at will.[9] And, he said, Congress had to be able to pass the laws necessary to exercise its powers or such powers would be meaningless.[10]

Nevertheless, states'-rights advocates insisted on a constitutional amendment to guard against encroachment by the national government. Ratified in 1791 as the Tenth Amendment to the Constitution, it reads: "The powers not delegated to the United States by the Constitution, nor prohibited by it to the States, are reserved to the States. . . ." The states' powers under the U.S. Constitution are thus called **reserved powers.**

State-to-State Relations

A federal system requires relationships not only between the national and state governments but also among the states themselves. The term **horizontal federalism** has been used to describe the constitutional relationship of the states to one another.

The U.S. Constitution defines several state-to-state obligations. One provision is that states are not permitted to enter into commercial arrangements with other states except as approved by Congress. This provision is intended to prevent two or more states from joining together to gain unfair advantage over another state or states.

The Constitution also requires each state to grant "full faith and credit" to the legal acts and judgments of other states. This means that such legal matters as marriages, wills, court settlements, and contracts rendered in one state are to be upheld by other states. Without the guarantee of full faith and credit, federalism would not work. For example, commerce would grind to a halt if firms incorporated in one state were not allowed to do business in another state or if a party could escape a legal obligation simply by crossing state lines.

[9]*Federalist* No. 28.
[10]*Federalist* No. 33.

Finally, citizens of the various states are afforded "all privileges and immunities of citizens in the several states." This vague clause has come to mean that a state cannot unreasonably discriminate against citizens of other states. A state could not, for example, enact laws that would establish longer prison terms for crimes committed by out-of-state residents. There are exceptions, however, to the concept of equal treatment of in-state and out-of-state residents, particularly in areas of state spending. For example, in-state students receive lower tuition rates at public colleges and universities than do out-of-state students.

THE RATIFICATION DEBATE

The Tenth Amendment symbolized a controversy that had raged since the Philadelphia convention's adjournment. Many Americans feared a powerful national government. Although Anti-Federalists (as opponents of the Constitution were called) recognized a need to strengthen defense and interstate commerce, they did not see why these goals required the creation of a sovereign national government.

To the Anti-Federalists, the sacrifice of states' power to the nation was as unwise as it was unnecessary. They argued that a distant national government could never serve the people's interests as well as the states could. Although Americans had a common language and culture, and thus a reason for union, they also had their differences. The interests of the people of New Hampshire were not identical to those of Georgians or Pennsylvanians, and the Anti-Federalists argued that only state-centered government would protect and preserve this diversity. In support of their contention, Anti-Federalists turned to the French philosopher Montesquieu (1689–1755), who had concluded that the

Recognizing that many issues cross state borders, the Framers of the Constitution established certain state-to-state obligations. Each state must give "full faith and credit" to the legal arrangements of other states and must afford citizens of other states the "privileges and immunities" of its own citizens. (Tony Savino/The Image Works)

leaders of small republics are in closer touch with the people and are more responsive to their concerns.[11]

The Federalists (supporters of the Constitution) responded that the national government would have no interest in submerging the states.[12] The national government would take responsibility for establishing a strong defense and for promoting a sound economy, while the states would retain nearly all other governing functions, including oversight of public morals, education, and safety. The national government, Madison said, would neither want these responsibilities nor have the competence to undertake them.[13]

Madison also took issue with the small-republic theory of Montesquieu. In *Federalist* No. 10, Madison argued that the problem with a small republic is that it is likely to have a dominant faction—whether it be large landholders, financiers, an impoverished majority, or some other group—that is strong enough to take full control of government, using this power to advance its own interests and suppress the interests of others. A large republic is less likely to have such an all-powerful faction. If financiers are strong in one area of a large republic, they are likely to be weak elsewhere, and the same will be true of other interests. "Extend the sphere," wrote Madison in *Federalist* No. 10, "and you take in a greater variety of parties and interests; you make it less probable that a majority of the whole will have a common motive to invade the rights of other citizens." (*Federalist* No. 10 is widely regarded as the greatest political essay ever written by an American. It is reprinted at the back of this book.)

Of course, the debate over ratification was not simply, or even primarily, a dispute over competing theories of government. Sharp political differences were at issue. Commercial interests, for example, were strongly behind the proposed new government, because they saw it as a foundation for a thriving national economy. Agricultural interests were less sure of how they would fare under the new government, so they were more sharply divided for and against the Constitution.

A STRATEGY FOR RATIFICATION

In authorizing the Philadelphia convention, Congress had stated that any proposed change in the U.S. government would have to be "agreed to in Congress" and then "confirmed by [all of] the States." Realizing that this procedure would result in defeat for their proposed constitution, the Framers boldly established their own ratifying process. They instructed Congress to submit the document directly to the states, and it would become law when it had been approved by nine states in special ratifying conventions of popularly elected delegates. This was a masterful strategy: there was no hope that all thirteen state legislatures would approve the Constitution, but nine states through conventions might be persuaded to ratify it.

Despite protests by the Anti-Federalists, ratification proceeded in the manner proposed by the Philadelphia convention. The state conventions began in the late fall of 1787. Delaware became the first state to ratify, and Connecticut,

---

[11]Montesquieu, *The Spirit of the Laws*, vol. 1 (New York: Hafner, 1979), bk. VIII, ch. 16; bk. IX, ch.1.
[12]*Federalist* No.2.
[13]*Federalist* No. 45.

SECRECY AND PUBLICITY
FOR THE NEW CONSTITUTION

The Constitution of the United States was written in secrecy. The delegates to the Philadelphia convention believed that publicity would make their task nearly impossible. Congress had called the convention for the sole purpose of amending the Articles of Confederation. The delegates decided on their own to devise a wholly new constitution. If their plan became widely known, it might fail before a new constitution could be worked out. In addition, the process of writing a constitution would require a great deal of bargaining and compromise. This process would become much more difficult if outside interests pressured the delegates.

The Constitutional Convention was held in the Old Pennsylvania State House, where the Declaration of Independence had been signed eleven years earlier. In order to prevent eavesdropping from the adjoining streets, the windows to the meeting room were boarded up throughout the convention, despite the summer heat. No formal record of the debate was kept, lest it fall into the hands of outsiders. If not for James Madison's extensive notes on the proceedings (which were published years later), there would be a scant historical record of what the delegates said during the convention debates. Finally, the delegates adopted a gag rule, forbidding themselves to discuss the proceedings with outsiders.

After the convention had adjourned, however, the delegates were suddenly eager to publicize their work. The most famous of these efforts took place in New York, where Madison, Alexander Hamilton, and John Jay (who was not a delegate to the Philadelphia convention) wrote a series of essays in an effort to persuade New Yorkers to ratify the proposed constitution. Their eighty-five essays were published in a New York City newspaper under the pen name "Publius" and were entitled "The Federalist." The *Federalist Papers* explain the reasoning behind provisions of the Constitution and are widely acknowledged as a great work of political theory.

Georgia, and New Jersey followed, a sure indication that the Great Compromise had satisfied many of the small states. In the early summer of 1788, New Hampshire became the ninth state to ratify. The Constitution was law. But neither Virginia nor New York had yet ratified, and a stable union without these two states was inconceivable: they were as large in area as some European countries and conceivably could survive as independent nations.

Virginia and New York nearly did choose an independent course. In both states the proposed constitution barely passed, and then only after the Federalists in each state agreed to support a series of amendments (a bill of rights) designed to protect individual freedoms. North Carolina and Rhode Island did not give their support until after the new government had begun its work. Only the fear of isolation finally prompted debtor-controlled Rhode Island to ratify.

Federalism in Historical Perspective

Since ratification of the Constitution two centuries ago, no aspect of it has provoked more frequent or bitter conflict than federalism. By establishing two levels of sovereign authority, the Constitution created competing centers of power and ambition, each of which was sure to claim disputed areas as belonging within its realm of authority.

Conflict between national and state authority was also ensured by the brevity of the Constitution. The Framers deliberately avoided detailed provisions, recognizing that brief phrases would give flexibility to the government they were creating. The document does not define what is meant by the "necessary and proper" clause, does not list any of the states' reserved powers, does not indicate whether the supremacy clause allows the states discretionary authority in areas where state and national responsibilities overlap, and does not indicate how *inter*state commerce (which the national government is empowered to regulate) differs from *intra*state commerce (which presumably is reserved for regulation by the states).

Not surprisingly, federalism has been a contentious and dynamic system, its development determined less by constitutional language than by the strength of contending interests and by the country's changing needs. In rough terms, federalism can be viewed as having progressed through three historical eras, each of which has involved a different relationship between nation and states. Let's look at each of these eras in some detail.

AN INDESTRUCTIBLE UNION (c. 1789–1865)

The issue during the first era, which lasted from the Constitution's beginnings in 1789 through the end of the Civil War in 1865, was the Union's survival. The history of America before the Constitution was of government by colonies-turned-states, and it was only to be expected that the states would dispute national policies that they perceived as inimical to their separate interests.

The Nationalist View: *McCulloch* v. *Maryland*

A first dispute over federalism arose early in George Washington's presidency when his secretary of the treasury, Alexander Hamilton, proposed the creation of a national bank. Thomas Jefferson, Washington's secretary of state, opposed the bank on the grounds that its activities would benefit commercial interests and would harm small farmers, who in Jefferson's view were the backbone of the new nation. Jefferson rejected Hamilton's claim that because the government had constitutional authority to regulate currency, the "necessary and proper" clause gave it the power to establish a national bank.

Hamilton's view prevailed when Congress in 1791 established the First Bank of the United States and granted it a twenty-year charter. When the charter lapsed in 1811, Congress did not renew it, but, in 1816, over the objections of state and local bankers, established the Second Bank of the United States. Responding to their complaints, several states, including Maryland, attempted to drive the Second Bank of the United States out of existence by levying taxes on its operations within their borders. Edwin McCulloch, who was head cashier of the U.S. Bank in Maryland, refused to pay the Maryland tax, and the resulting dispute reached the Supreme Court.

John Marshall, the chief justice of the Supreme Court, was, like Hamilton, a strong nationalist, and in *McCulloch* v. *Maryland* (1819) the Court ruled decisively in favor of national authority. In his opinion for the Court, Marshall asserted that the "necessary and proper" clause was "a grant of power, not a restriction." Although the Constitution made no mention of a national bank, it

Our Constitution is in actual operation; everything appears to promise that it will last; but in this world nothing is certain but death and taxes.
Benjamin Franklin, 1789

We admit, as all must admit, that the powers of the government are limited, and that its limits are not to be transcended. But we think the sound construction of the Constitution must allow to the national legislature that discretion, with respect to the means by which the powers it confers are to be carried into execution, which will enable that body to perform the high duties assigned to it, in the manner most beneficial to the people. Let the end be legitimate, let it be within the scope of the Constitution, and all means which are plainly adapted to that end, which are not prohibited, but consistent with the letter and spirit of the Constitution, are constitutional.
John Marshall,
McCulloch v. *Maryland* (1819)

was reasonable, Marshall concluded, to infer that a government with powers to tax, borrow money, and regulate commerce could establish a bank in order to exercise those powers properly. Marshall's argument was a clear statement of **implied powers**—the idea that, through the "necessary and proper" clause, the national government's powers extend beyond a narrow reading of its enumerated powers.

Marshall also addressed the meaning of the Constitution's supremacy clause. Maryland had argued that it had the sovereign authority to tax the national bank even if it was a legal entity. The Supreme Court rejected Maryland's position, concluding that valid national law prevailed over conflicting state law. Because the national government had the power to create the bank, it could also protect the bank from actions by the states, such as taxation, that might destroy it.[14]

The *McCulloch* decision provided the basis for a broad interpretation of the supremacy clause and the "necessary and proper" clause, thus serving as precedent for future assertions of national authority. The *McCulloch* decision also reaffirmed an earlier Supreme Court decision that rejected a Virginia claim that state courts could decide for themselves the extent of national authority under the U.S. Constitution.[15] This constitutional interpretation was of the utmost significance: as Justice Oliver Wendell Holmes, Jr., noted a century later, the Union could not have survived if each state had been allowed its own interpretation of national law.[16]

The States'-Rights View: The *Dred Scott* Decision

Although John Marshall's rulings helped to strengthen national authority, the issue of slavery posed a growing threat to the Union's survival. A resurgence of cotton farming in the early nineteenth century revived the South's flagging dependence on slaves and heightened southerners' fears that Congress might move to abolish slavery. Southerners consequently did what others have done throughout American history: they devised a constitutional argument to fit their political needs. John C. Calhoun of South Carolina argued that the Constitution had created "a government of states united in a political union, not a government of individuals united by what was usually called a social compact."[17] This line of reasoning led Calhoun to his famed "doctrine of nullification," which declared that each state had the constitutional right to nullify a national law.

In 1832 South Carolina invoked this doctrine, declaring "null and void" a tariff law that favored northern interests. President Andrew Jackson retorted that South Carolina's action was "incompatible with the existence of the Union," a position that was strengthened when Congress authorized Jackson to use military force against South Carolina. The state backed down when Congress agreed to amend the tariff act slightly.

John C. Calhoun (1782–1850), a South Carolinian, was a champion of states' rights. (Library of Congress)

[14]*McCulloch* v. *Maryland*, 4 Wheaton 316 (1819).
[15]*Martin* v. *Hunter's Lessee*, 1 Wheaton 304 (1816).
[16]Oliver Wendell Holmes, Jr., *Collected Legal Papers* (New York: Harcourt, Brace, 1920), 295–296.
[17]John C. Calhoun, *The Works of John C. Calhoun* (New York: Russell & Russell, 1968).

States'-rights advocates gained an ally when Roger B. Taney, who held a state-centered view of federalism, became chief justice of the Supreme Court in 1836.[18] In 1857 the Taney Court issued its infamous *Dred Scott* decision, a constitutional debacle that helped propel the nation toward civil war. Dred Scott, a slave, had lived several years with his master in the free territory of Wisconsin, but was living in the slave state of Missouri when his master died. Scott applied for his freedom, citing a federal law—the Missouri Compromise of 1820—that made slavery illegal in a free state or free territory. Six justices, including Taney, concluded that slaves were "beings of an inferior order," who, within the meaning of the Constitution, were "property" rather than "citizens." As property, a slave could never be made free solely by virtue of place of residence.[19]

Dred Scott (1795?–1858). (Library of Congress)

The *Dred Scott* decision outraged public opinion in the North and contributed to a sectional split in the majority Democratic party that enabled the Republican Abraham Lincoln to win the presidency in 1860 with only 40 percent of the popular vote. Lincoln had campaigned for an end to slavery's expansion and for its gradual, compensated abolition. By the time he assumed office, seven southern states had already seceded from the Union. In justifying his decision to wage civil war on these states, Lincoln said, "The Union is older than the states." In 1865 the superior strength of the Union army settled by force the question of whether national authority would be binding on the states.

DUAL FEDERALISM AND LAISSEZ-FAIRE CAPITALISM (c. 1865–1937)

Although the Civil War preserved the Union, new challenges to federalism were surfacing. Constitutional doctrine held that certain policy areas, such as national commerce and defense, were the clear and exclusive province of national authority, while other policy areas, such as public health and morals, belonged clearly and exclusively to the states. This doctrine, known as *dual federalism,* was based on the idea that a precise separation of national and state authority was both possible and desirable. "The power which one possesses," said the Supreme Court in 1876, "the other does not."[20]

The Union is older than the states.

Abraham Lincoln

Nevertheless, American society was undergoing great changes in racial relations and commerce that raised questions about the suitability of dual federalism as a governing concept. Could former slaves gain the full rights of citizenship if they were subject to the discretion of the South's white-dominated state governments? And could the economic problems spawned by the Industrial Revolution be adequately controlled if they were left to the states?

The fact of the matter was that emerging issues of race and commerce required an expansion of national authority. From the 1860s through the 1930s, however, the Supreme Court stood as a major obstacle to national action. This was an era of federalism characterized by state supremacy in racial policy and by business supremacy in commerce policy.

[18]See *Cooley* v. *Board of Wardens of the Port of Philadelphia,* 53 Howard 299 (1851).
[19]*Dred Scott* v. *Sanford,* 19 Howard 393 (1857).
[20]*U.S.* v. *Cruikshank,* 92 U.S. 452 (1876).

Justice John Marshall Harlan was the lone dissenter from the Supreme Court's ruling in *Plessy* v. *Ferguson* (1896) that "separate but equal" accommodations for blacks and whites were constitutional. Harlan wrote: "Our Constitution is color-blind and neither knows nor tolerates classes among citizens. . . . The thin disguise of 'equal' accommodations for passengers in railroad coaches will not mislead anyone nor atone for the wrong this day done." (Library of Congress)

All persons born or naturalized in the United States, and subject to the jurisdiction thereof, are citizens of the United States and of the State wherein they reside. No State shall make or enforce any law which shall abridge the privileges or immunities of citizens of the United States; nor shall any State deprive any person of life, liberty, or property, without due process of law; nor deny to any person within its jurisdiction the equal protection of the laws.
U.S. Constitution,
Fourteenth Amendment

The Fourteenth Amendment and State Discretion

Ratified after the Civil War, the Fourteenth Amendment was intended to protect citizens (especially black Americans) from discriminatory actions by state governments.[21] A state was prohibited from depriving "any person of life, liberty, or property without due process of law," from denying "any person within its jurisdiction the equal protection of the laws," and from abridging "the privileges or immunities of citizens of the United States."

Supreme Court rulings during subsequent decades, however, helped to undermine the Fourteenth Amendment's promise. The Court held, for example, that the Fourteenth Amendment did not substantially limit the power of the states to regulate rights of person and property,[22] and that the Fourteenth Amendment was not meant to prevent discrimination by private owners of hotels, restaurants, and other accommodations that catered to the general public.[23] Then, in *Plessy* v. *Ferguson* (1896), the Court issued its infamous "separate but equal" ruling. A black man, Adolph Plessy, had been convicted of violating a Louisiana law that required white and black citizens to ride in separate railroad cars. The Supreme Court upheld his conviction, concluding that state governments could require blacks to use separate railroad cars and other accommodations as long as those facilities were "equal" in quality to those reserved for use by whites. "If one race be inferior to the other socially," the Court concluded, "the Constitution of the United States cannot put them on the same plane."[24]

With this decision, the Court undercut the Fourteenth Amendment and allowed southern states to establish a thoroughly racist system of legalized segregation. Black children were forced into separate schools that seldom had libraries and usually had few teachers, most of whom had no formal training. Hospitals for blacks had few doctors and nurses and almost no medical supplies and equipment. Legal challenges to these discriminatory practices were generally unsuccessful. The *Plessy* ruling had become a justification for the separate and *unequal* treatment of black Americans. For the next seven decades, the "states'-rights" doctrine was often invoked by southerners as a guise for the perpetuation of racism.

Judicial Protection of Business

Through its rulings after the Civil War, the Supreme Court also provided a constitutional basis for uncontrolled private economic power. By the late nineteenth century, the Industrial Revolution had given rise to huge business trusts, which used their monopoly power to gouge consumers and oppress labor. Individual consumers and workers were powerless to combat the trusts. Government was the only possible counterforce. Which level of government—state or national—would regulate the trusts?

[21]Edward S. Corwin, *The Constitution and What It Means Today,* 12th ed. (Princeton, N.J.: Princeton University Press, 1958), 248.
[22]*Slaughter-House Cases,* 16 Wallace 36 (1873).
[23]*Civil Rights Cases,* 109 U.S. 3 (1883).
[24]*Plessy* v. *Ferguson,* 163 U.S. 537 (1896).

In large part, the answer was that neither level of government would be permitted to do so. In 1886 the Supreme Court, which was dominated by adherents of the doctrine of *laissez-faire capitalism* (which holds that business should be ''allowed to act'' as it pleases), decided that corporations were ''persons'' within the meaning of the Fourteenth Amendment, and thus their

Between 1865 and 1937, the Supreme Court's rulings severely restricted national power. Narrowly interpreting Congress's constitutional power to regulate commerce, the Court forbade Congress to regulate child labor and other aspects of manufacturing. The Court also ruled that the Fourteenth Amendment did not substantially restrict state governments; this allowed state governments to establish racially segregated public schools. (Library of Congress)

property rights were protected from substantial regulation by the states.[25] The Court also weakened the national government's regulatory power by narrowly interpreting its commerce power. The Constitution's **commerce clause** says that Congress shall have the power "to regulate commerce" among the states but does not spell out which economic activities are included in the term "commerce." When the federal government invoked the Sherman Antitrust Act (1890) in an attempt to break up a monopoly on the manufacture of sugar, the Supreme Court blocked the action, claiming that *interstate* commerce included only the "transportation" of goods, not their "manufacture."[26] Manufacturing was deemed part of *intrastate* commerce and thus subject to state regulation only. The distinction is an example of the Court's dual federalism doctrine.

Although the national government subsequently made some inroads on business regulation, the Supreme Court remained an obstacle. An example is the case of *Hammer* v. *Dagenhart* (1918), which arose from a 1916 federal act that prohibited the interstate shipment of goods produced by child labor. The act was popular because factory owners were exploiting children, working them for long hours at low pay. Citing the Tenth Amendment, the Court invalidated the law, ruling that factory practices could be regulated only by the states.[27] However, in an earlier case, *Lochner* v. *New York* (1905), the Court had prevented a state from regulating labor practices, concluding that such action was a violation of firms' property rights.[28]

In effect, the Supreme Court had denied lawmaking majorities the authority to decide economic issues. Neither Congress nor the state legislatures were permitted to substantially regulate big business. As the constitutional scholars Alfred Kelly and Winifred Harbison have concluded, "No more complete perversion of the principles of effective federal government can be imagined."[29]

NATIONAL AUTHORITY PREVAILS (SINCE 1937)

Judicial supremacy in the economic sphere ended abruptly in 1937. For nearly a decade, the United States had been mired in the Great Depression, which President Franklin D. Roosevelt's New Deal was designed to alleviate. The Supreme Court, however, had ruled much of the New Deal's economic recovery legislation to be unconstitutional. A constitutional crisis of historic proportions seemed inevitable until the Court suddenly reversed its position. In the process, American federalism was fundamentally and forever changed.

A National Economy

The Great Depression revealed that Americans had become a national community with national economic needs. During the nineteenth century most people had lived on farms and in small towns. Americans raised much of their own food, and when they became sick or otherwise needed help, they turned to family and friends.

---

[25]*Santa Clara County* v. *Southern Pacific Railroad Co.,* 118 U.S. 394 (1886).
[26]*U.S.* v. *E. C. Knight Co.,* 156 U.S. 1 (1895).
[27]*Hammer* v. *Dagenhart,* 247 U.S. 251 (1918).
[28]*Lochner* v. *New York,* 198 U.S. 25 (1905).
[29]Kelly and Harbison, *American Constitution,* 529.

During the Great Depression, an employment agency's meager listing of available jobs draws a crowd of unemployed men. States could not cope with such a severe economic crisis, so the federal government stepped in with its New Deal programs, forever changing the shape of federal–state relations. (The Bettmann Archive)

By the time of the Great Depression, Americans were enmeshed in a complex and economically interdependent society. More than half of the population lived in cities (only 20 percent did so in 1860), and more than 10 million workers were employed by industry (only 1 million were so employed in 1860). Urban workers typically depended on landlords for their housing, on farmers and grocers for their food, and on corporations for their jobs. Farmers were more independent, but they, too, were increasingly part of a larger economic network. Their income depended on market prices and shipping and equipment costs.[30]

This economic interdependence enabled the United States to achieve unprecedented prosperity, but it also meant that no area of the economy could be protected if things turned sour. When the depression hit in 1929, its effects could not be contained. A decline in spending was followed by a drop in production, a loss of jobs, unpaid rents and grocery bills, and a shrinking market for foodstuffs, which led to a further decline in spending and a continuation of the downward spiral. At the depths of the Great Depression one-fourth of the nation's work force was unemployed.

[30]James E. Anderson, *The Emergence of the Modern Regulatory State* (Washington, D.C.: Public Affairs Press, 1962), 2–3.

The states by tradition had responsibility for the jobless and others who had welfare needs, but they were nearly penniless because of declining tax revenues and the growing ranks of poor people. The New Deal programs were a way out of the crisis; for example, the National Industrial Recovery Act (NIRA) of 1933 called for a massive public works program to create jobs and for coordinated action by major industries. However, the New Deal was opposed by economic conservatives (who accused Roosevelt of leading the nation down the road to communism) and by justices of the Supreme Court. In *Schechter* v. *United States* (1935) the Court invalidated the Recovery Act, ruling that it usurped powers reserved to the states.[31]

The *Schechter* decision and others like it[32] had disastrous implications. The nationwide depression required national solutions, which the states acting separately could not provide. Moreover, when the states did act, the Court was likely to find their policies in violation of the property rights of business, as it did in a 1936 case.[33]

Frustrated by the Court, Roosevelt in 1937 proposed his famed "Court-packing" plan. Roosevelt recommended that Congress enact legislation that would permit an additional justice to be appointed to the Court whenever a seated member passed the age of seventy. The number of justices would increase, and Roosevelt's appointees would presumably be more sympathetic to his programs. Roosevelt's scheme was resisted by Congress, but the controversy ended with "the switch in time that saved nine," when, for reasons that have never become fully clear, Justice Owen Roberts abandoned his opposition to Roosevelt's policies and thus gave the president a 5–4 majority on the Court.

Within months the Court upheld the 1935 National Labor Relations Act, which gave employees the right to organize and bargain collectively.[34] In passing the act, Congress had argued that labor-management disputes were disruptive of the national economy and therefore could be regulated through the commerce clause. The Supreme Court's decision upholding the act marked the end of the Court's interference in applications of the Constitution's commerce clause. In 1946 the Court openly acknowledged the change when it said that "we have nothing to do" with regulating commerce and asserted that Congress's commerce power is "as broad as the needs of the nation."[35] Thus the constitutional path was opened to a substantial increase in the national government's authority. The extent of national power was evident, for example, in the 1964 Civil Rights Act, which forbids racial discrimination by hotels and restaurants on the grounds that they provide lodging and food to travelers engaged in interstate commerce. When the law was challenged, the Supreme Court upheld it, concluding that "commerce" included public accommodations.[36]

The Supreme Court's decisions in regard to the federal government's taxing

---

[31]*Schechter Poultry Co.* v. *United States*, 295 U.S. 495 (1935).
[32]See, for example, *Carter* v. *Carter Coal Co.*, 298 U.S. 238 (1936), and *United States* v. *Butler*, 297 U.S. 1 (1936).
[33]*Morehead* v. *New York ex rel. Tipaldo*, 298 U.S. 587 (1936).
[34]*NLRB* v. *Jones and Laughlin Steel*, 301 U.S. 1 (1937).
[35]*American Power and Light* v. *Securities and Exchange Commission*, 329 U.S. 90 (1946).
[36]See *Heart of Atlanta Motel* v. *United States*, 379 U.S. 241 (1964).

★ CRITICAL THINKING

HOW POWERFUL SHOULD GOVERNMENT BE?

The American political tradition includes a deep suspicion of governing power. The idea is expressed in the adage "That government is best which governs least." Of recent political leaders, none has made more effective use of this sentiment than Ronald Reagan. During the 1980 presidential campaign, he promised "to get the federal government off the backs of the American people." He used this refrain again in his 1984 campaign, even though by then, as president, he had been the ultimate government "insider," in charge of the executive branch, for four years. Although Republican politicians have been more likely to express the theme of small government, Democratic politicians also use it. In the 1992 race for the Democratic presidential nomination, each of the candidates found a way to attack the size of government.

American history suggests, however, that the real issue is not big government per se but whether the power of government is commensurate with what is expected of it. Government can indeed be too big, but it can also be too small. The Articles of Confederation failed because they were too weak to ensure the public order, national security, and economic prosperity that Americans wanted. The Constitution of the United States was written to strengthen the central government. The economic chaos of the Great Depression of the 1930s is another example of the problem of an overly weak government. The New Deal was developed in order to give the federal government a level of power that would match the nation's governing needs.

Do Americans today, whether Republicans or Democrats, ignore the real issue of government—not whether is is too big or too small, but whether it is adequate to its tasks—when it suits their purposes? Can a national government that is weak in the area of either foreign or domestic policy truly serve all the nation's needs? Consider the question in terms of two contemporary issues of public policy, one foreign and one domestic: the use of military and diplomatic power to secure international markets and the use of taxing and spending power to meet the people's health-care needs. Can either of these goals be met without a strong national government?

---

and spending powers followed a pattern similar to its commerce rulings. The Court placed restrictions on federal authority before lifting them in recognition of national needs.[37]

Toward National Citizenship

As Americans became more interdependent economically, they were also growing together in other ways. Changes in transportation and communication made state boundaries seem less relevant. News and people traveled faster and farther than ever before, which raised the level of controversy that surrounded some state practices, particularly in the area of race relations. Was it right that black children in southern states were forbidden by law from attending the same public schools as white children?

The fact is, such practices were soon stopped. As will be discussed in Chapter 7, federal authority has compelled states and localities to eliminate government-sponsored discrimination and, in some cases, to create compensatory opportunities for minorities and women. A key Supreme Court decision was *Brown* v. *Board of Education* (1954), which held that racial segregation in public schools was unconstitutional on the grounds that it violated the Fourteenth Amendment.[38]

---

[37]Louis Fisher, *American Constitutional Law* (New York: McGraw-Hill, 1990), 384.
[38]*Brown* v. *Board of Education of Topeka*, 347 U.S. 483 (1954).

The idea that all Americans are equal in their rights has also permeated other areas. As Chapter 5 will discuss, federal authority, primarily through judicial rulings, has required states to broaden individual rights of free expression and fair trial. For example, the famous *Miranda* ruling, which requires police to inform crime suspects of their rights at the time of arrest, arose out of an interpretation of the Fourteenth Amendment.[39]

Of course, important differences remain in the rights, privileges, and immunities of the citizens of the separate states, as could be expected in a federal system. The death penalty, for example, is legal in some states but not others, and states differ greatly in terms of the quality of services, such as public education, that they provide their people. Nevertheless, national citizenship— the notion that Americans should be equal in their rights, regardless of the state in which they reside—is a much more encompassing idea today than in the past.[40]

Federalism Today

Dual federalism was never as exact in practice as it was claimed to be in principle. Although it was relatively clear which level of government, national or state, had primary responsibility for a given policy area, such as defense or education, there were areas of overlap. During the 1800s, for example, the federal government provided land and other assistance to the states in an effort to promote the building of transportation and educational systems. The nation's land-grant colleges are a result of this assistance.

Since the 1930s, however, the relation of the nation to the states has changed so fundamentally that dual federalism is no longer even a roughly accurate description of the American situation. The national government has become deeply involved in health care, education, public housing, nutrition, roads, and other areas traditionally dominated by states and localities. These developments have been accompanied, and to some extent promoted, by corresponding changes in constitutional doctrine. An extreme expression of this doctrine was a 1985 Supreme Court decision, *Garcia* v. *San Antonio Transit Authority*, which held that state and local governments must apply *federal* minimum wage and hour standards to their own employees. The Court noted that the judiciary had experienced great difficulty in drawing a line between "traditional" and "nontraditional" state functions; it concluded that if the states wanted protection from national authority, they would have to look to the political process rather than the courts. Reasoning that members of Congress are elected from states and districts within states, the Court said that the states should depend on these officials for protection against national actions that "unduly burden the states."[41]

★ ANALYZE THE ISSUE

The Supreme Court vs. Congress
In the late 1930s the Supreme Court ended its interference with congressional application of the Constitution's commerce clause. In your view, is the Supreme Court or Congress better equipped to safeguard America's federal system? Keep in mind that members of the U.S. Senate are elected from states and members of the House of Representatives are elected from districts within states.

---

[39]*Miranda* v. *Arizona*, 384 U.S. 436 (1966).
[40]For an interesting assessment of change in what has traditionally been America's most distinctive region, see Robert P. Steed, Laurence W. Moreland, and Tod A. Baker, eds., *The Disappearing South?* (Tuscaloosa: University of Alabama Press, 1990).
[41]*Garcia* v. *San Antonio Transit Authority*, 469 U.S. 528 (1985).

In fact, the states have had strong advocates in Washington. Although Republicans and Democrats alike admit that national change has required Washington to play a larger policy role, Republicans in particular have asked whether the federal government has sometimes gone too far in asserting its authority. Republican presidents Richard Nixon, Ronald Reagan, and George Bush all advocated some version of a "new federalism" in which some areas of public policy for which the federal government had assumed responsibility would be returned to states and localities.

The principal motivation behind proposals for increasing or diminishing federal power, however, has been political rather than constitutional. Even Reagan acknowledged that state authority is sometimes a better idea in theory than in practice. For example, Reagan's backing was critical to passage of the 1984 legislation that forced states to raise the legal drinking age to twenty-one or lose federal highway funds. Reagan claimed that the high incidence of fatal alcohol-related traffic accidents involving youthful drivers made the issue "bigger than the states."

INTERDEPENDENCY AND COOPERATIVE FEDERALISM

The major reason national authority has expanded substantially since the 1930s is that the states and their citizens have become increasingly interdependent. Governing decisions that in a slower-paced age could be reserved for the states must now be made for the nation as a whole. The economy, for example, is not principally local and state; it is national and international in scope. Although state and local officials have sometimes claimed that they can handle their residents' problems better than distant officials in Washington can, they have generally welcomed the federal government's help. Many of the federal programs established or retained in recent decades have been a response to requests made by state and local officials, who have become a strong lobbying group in Washington (see Chapter 14).

Today's system has been described as **cooperative federalism,** a situation in which national, state, and local authorities work together to solve the problems facing the American people.[42] The difference between dual federalism and cooperative federalism has been compared to the difference between a layer cake, whose levels are distinct, and a marble cake, whose levels flow together.[43]

Cooperative federalism is evident in public assistance programs such as Medicaid, which provides health care for the poor. Public assistance was traditionally a responsibility of the states, but, during the Great Depression, the national government also got involved. Today cooperative federalism prevails in Medicaid and many other public assistance programs, which are

- Jointly funded by the national and state governments.
- Jointly administered, with the states and localities providing most of the direct service to recipients and a national agency providing general administration.

[42]See Thomas Anton, *American Federalism and Public Policy* (Philadelphia: Temple University Press, 1989).
[43]Morton Grodzins, *The American System: A New View of Government in the United States* (Chicago: Rand McNally, 1966).

Cooperative federalism brings federal and state government officials together to try to solve major problems. In 1989 President Bush met with state governors and federal officials in an "education summit" held at the University of Virginia. (AP/Wide World)

Public education is a state and local responsibility. This well-equipped classroom in Los Angeles reflects California's commitment to education. Some states, however, spend only half as much per pupil as California does. (J. Wilson/Woodfin Camp and Associates)

• Jointly determined, with both the state and national governments having a say in eligibility and benefit levels, and with federal regulations, such as those prohibiting discrimination, giving an element of uniformity to the various state and local efforts.

Cooperative federalism has altered the states' policy agendas. Through its spending and regulatory activities, which are applied broadly across the states, the federal government has encouraged states to pursue many of the same

TABLE 2-2 Direct Funds Provided by Federal, State, and Local Governments in Selected Policy Areas

Policy Area	Federal Funds	State Funds	Local Funds
Education	7%	49%	44%
Public welfare	56	36	8
Health and hospitals	7	47	45

policies. An effect has been to make the states more alike in their policies than they would otherwise be.[44]

This trend should not be misinterpreted to mean that the states are now powerless and indistinguishable. On the contrary, states and localities have substantial discretionary authority in many of the policy areas that touch Americans' lives most directly—among them public education, safety, health, and transportation. Public education, for example, remains largely a state and local function (see Table 2-2). About 90 percent of the funding for primary and secondary schools is provided by states and localities, which also decide most policy issues, from teachers' qualifications to course requirements to the length of the school year. Any broad claim that public education in America is "controlled" by Washington overlooks the fact that states actually have wide leeway in educational policy. In terms of public school expenditures, for example, New Hampshire, North Dakota, Arizona, and Kentucky spend less than half as much on each pupil as do New York, Minnesota, California, and Colorado.[45]

GOVERNMENT REVENUES AND FISCAL FEDERALISM

The interdependence of the sectors of modern American society is one of two major factors that have compelled the federal government to assume a larger domestic policy role. The other is the federal government's superior ability to tax and borrow. States and localities are in an inherently competitive situation with regard to taxation. People and businesses faced with state or local tax increases can move to another state or locality where taxes are lower. The national government is less constrained by tax competition. Few people would consider moving to another country in order to avoid federal taxes. Moreover, the federal government depends almost entirely on forms of taxation, such as personal and corporate income taxes, that automatically increase revenues as the economy expands. State and local governments depend more heavily than Washington on revenue sources, such as license fees and property taxes, that are comparatively inflexible. The overall result is that the federal government raises more tax revenues than do all fifty states and the thousands of local governments combined (see Figure 2-1). Finally, because it controls the

FIGURE 2-1 Federal, State, and Local Shares of Government Revenue, 1989
The federal government raises more revenues than all state and local governments combined. *Source: Advisory Commission on Intergovernmental Relations,* Significant Features of Fiscal Federalism, *1990 ed., vol. 2 (Washington, D.C.: ACIR, 1990), 32, 38.*

[44]John E. Chubb, "The Political Economy of Federalism," *American Political Science Review* 79 (December 1985): 994–1015.
[45]Advisory Commission on Intergovernmental Relations, *Significant Features of Fiscal Federalism, 1985–86 Edition* (Washington, D.C.: ACIR, 1986), 190.

American dollar, the federal government has a nearly unlimited ability to borrow money to cover its deficits. States and localities can go bankrupt and therefore cannot so easily find creditors who will lend them the money to cover their budget deficits.

The federal government's revenue-raising advantage has helped to make money the basis for many of the relations between the national government and the states and localities. **Fiscal federalism** refers to the expenditure of federal funds on programs run in part through state and local government. The federal government provides money in the form of grants-in-aid; the states can reject such a grant, but if they accept it, they must comply with federal restrictions on its use.

The states have the organization to make fiscal federalism a workable arrangement. The national government could not manage the delivery of governmental services without the help of states and localities, which have the agencies and personnel to carry out government programs at the local level. More than 11 million Americans are employees of state and local governments —close to four times as many as the roughly 3 million who work for the federal government. State and local employment grew rapidly in the late 1960s and early 1970s, when the federal government greatly expanded its assistance to these governments.[46]

Viewed in a broad perspective, federal grants-in-aid have been the basis for nothing less than a quiet revolution in the relations among America's governments.[47] Federal restrictions on the policy decisions of state and local governments were relatively few before the 1950s, but they have proliferated in the form of conditions attached to the receipt of federal assistance. The extent of federal aid since 1955 is shown in Figure 2-2. In terms of actual dollars, federal grants-in-aid climbed from $5 billion in 1955 to $124 billion in 1990. In terms of *constant* dollars (dollars adjusted for the rate of inflation), the 1970s were the period of the most rapid growth in federal aid, from $24 billion in 1970 to roughly $100 billion in 1980.

As the federal government encountered fiscal problems in the late 1970s and early 1980s, the days of massive increases in assistance came to end. Although federal grants increased by $30 billion in actual dollars during the 1980s, they decreased slightly for the decade in terms of constant dollars. The decrease was consistent with Reagan's plan for shifting program authority to states and localities, but was less the result of a changing philosophy than of a changing fiscal reality. While states and localities wanted federal assistance to continue at the same high level, Washington simply did not have the money any more.[48] The states have since encountered serious fiscal problems of their own, in part

---

[46]See James C. Garand, "Explaining Government Growth in the U.S. States," *American Political Science Review* 82 (September 1988): 837–852.

[47]David B. Walker, *Toward a Functioning Federalism* (Cambridge, Mass.: Winthrop, 1981), 102. See also Douglas D. Rose, "National and Local Forces in State Politics," *American Political Science Review* 67 (December 1973): 1162–1173; Morton Grodzins, "Centralization and Decentralization in the American Federal System," in Robert A. Goldwin, ed., *A Nation of States* (Chicago: Rand McNally, 1963), 1–4.

[48]Michael A. Pagano and Ann O'M. Bowman, "The State of American Federalism 1988–1989," *Publius* 19 (Summer 1989):1.

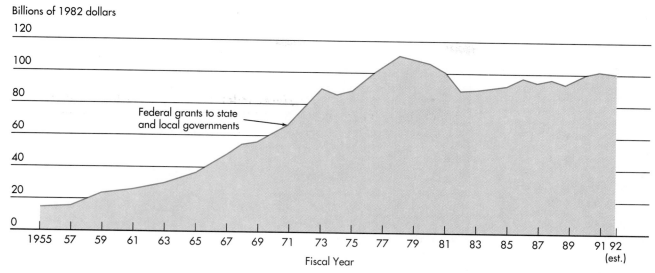

Billions of 1982 dollars

Federal grants to state
and local governments

Fiscal Year

FIGURE 2-2 Federal Grants to State and Local Governments in Constant (1982) Dollars, 1955–1992
Federal aid to states and localities has increased dramatically since the 1950s.
Source: Advisory Commission on Intergovernmental Relations, Significant Features of Fiscal Federalism, *1990 ed., vol. 2 (Washington, D.C.: ACIR, 1990), 42.*

because they have shouldered a larger share of the costs of programs that began through the application of fiscal federalism.

Today, federal funds account for roughly $1 of every $6 spent by state and local governments. State and local governments receive two major types of assistance, categorical grants and block grants, which are differentiated by the extent to which Washington defines the conditions of their use. A third type of grant, "revenue sharing," which gave money directly to states and localities with few restrictions on its use, was terminated a few years ago (see Chapter 25).

Categorical Grants

Most federal aid programs have been in the form of **categorical grants,** so called because the funds can be used only for designated projects. Medicaid funds, for example, can be spent only on health care for the poor, and states that accept Medicaid funds are required to provide health-care coverage to all people on public welfare. Categorical grants are of two types: "project grants," which are awarded on a competitive basis for particular projects (such as the building of a hospital), the cost of which determines the amount of the grant; and "formula grants," which are given for particular programs (for example, Medicaid) and are awarded according to a formula that determines how much the grantee will receive.

Categorical grants serve the power and reelection needs of members of Congress, who are national officeholders but are also representatives of state and local interests. Such grants allow members of Congress to act not only as national legislators but also, in effect, as state governors and local mayors: they have the power to decide some of the policy directions of states and localities.[49]

[49]Charles Schultze, "Federal Spending: Past, Present and Future," in Henry Owen and Charles Schultze, eds., *Setting National Priorities: The Next Ten Years* (Washington, D.C.: Brookings Institution, 1976), 323–369.

Federal funds subsidize road construction in the states, such as this section of Interstate 95 in North Carolina. About $1 out of every $6 spent by state and local governments comes from the federal treasury. (Billy E. Barnes/ Stock, Boston)

Such grants also help members of Congress to build the constituent support necessary to stay in office. They can point to a local hospital wing or school lunch program as something for which they voted to contribute federal funds. Categorical grants are typically drafted so that as many communities as possible can qualify, because members of Congress are not likely to be interested in voting for a grant program that does not include their constitutents. Democrats, whether in Congress or the White House, have been particularly inclined to favor categorical grants,[50] but over the years these grants have come to be accepted by officials of both major parties.

A key issue today is whether the grant money should go to states or to localities. Democratic officials have been stronger advocates of grants that benefit cities, which contain a disproportionate number of poor people, minorities, and other important Democratic constituencies. Republicans have preferred grants to the states, where Republican influence is stronger than it is at the metropolitan level (see Chapter 25).

Block Grants

Although state and local officials welcome categorical grants, they naturally prefer federal money that comes with no strings attached. As a partial response to this sentiment, the Johnson administration in 1966 developed the concept of **block grants.** These grants differ from categorical grants in that they allow states and localities more discretion in the expenditure of funds. The federal government specifies the general area in which the funds must be used, but state and local officials choose the specific projects on which the money will be spent. The first block grant program was established under the Partnership for

[50]See George Break, *Intergovernmental Fiscal Relations in the United States* (Washington, D.C.: Brookings Institution, 1967); Wallace Oates, *Fiscal Federalism* (New York: Harcourt Brace Jovanovich, 1972).

Health Act of 1966. State and local officials were required to use the funds in the health area but could decide for themselves whether to spend the money on medical equipment, say, or on hospital construction. President Reagan made block grants a cornerstone of his New Federalism initiative. Shortly after taking office in 1981, he proposed the consolidation of nearly 100 categorical programs into a small number of block grants. Congress eventually approved merging fifty-seven programs into nine block grants.[51] The move toward block grants meant that fewer conditions were attached to the receipt of federal aid.

President Bush's executive budget for fiscal year 1992 proposed a further decentralization: the federal government would turn over to the states a consolidated grant of $15 billion, taken from grants for housing, community development, and other individual programs. Bush's proposal was not accompanied by the usual rhetoric about block grants versus categorical grants, which was perhaps a sign that a major change is coming in the area of grants-in-aid. In the future, the story may be one of continued cuts in federal assistance and the use of federal regulation (as opposed to federal money) as the primary method of influence on states and localities (see Chapter 25).

Federalism as an Evolving System

Although the influence of Washington over states and localities has leveled off somewhat in the past few years, there is no question that American federalism is substantially more national and interdependent today than a few decades ago. From the perspective of the full sweep of American history, it might be concluded that the Framers' principle of federalism has been negated. But if federalism is regarded as a pragmatic principle, then federalism may have simply changed with the times.[52] In 1787 circumstances required of the national government a small, though critically important, role. Circumstances today often require broad applications of national power. Would the change trouble the Framers? Perhaps; but they were, after all, the nationalists of their time.

Summary

Perhaps the foremost characteristic of the American political system is its division of authority between a national government and the states. The first U.S. government, established by the Articles of Confederation, was essentially a union of the states.

In establishing the basis for a stronger national government, the U.S. Constitution also made provision for safeguarding state interests. The Great Compromise—whereby each state was equally represented in the Senate, as the smaller states demanded, and membership in the House of Representatives was apportioned by population, as the larger states insisted—was the breakthrough that enabled the delegates to the constitutional convention of 1787 to reach agreement. However, this agreement on the structure of Congress has been less historically significant than the Philadelphia convention's pragmatic decision to create a federal system in which sovereignty was vested in both national and state governments. The Constitution

[51]Richard Nathan and Fred Doolittle, *Reagan and the States* (Princeton, N.J.: Princeton University Press, 1987); Timothy J. Conlan, *New Federalism* (Washington: Brookings Institution, 1988).
[52]Valerie A. Earle, "The Federal Structure," in George J. Graham, Jr., and Scarlett G. Graham, eds., *Founding Principles of American Government*, rev. ed. (Chatham, N.J.: Chatham House, 1984), 163.

enumerates the general powers of the national government and grants it implied powers through the "necessary and proper" clause. Other powers are reserved to the states by the Tenth Amendment.

From 1789 to 1865, the nation's survival was at issue. The states found it convenient at times to argue that their sovereignty took precedence over national authority. In the end, it took the Civil War to cement the idea that the United States was a union of people, not of states. From 1865 to 1937, federalism reflected the doctrine that certain policy areas were the exclusive responsibility of the national government, while others belonged exclusively to the states. This constitutional position enabled the South to establish an inferior standard of citizenship for its African-American citizens and promoted the laissez-faire doctrine that big business was largely beyond gov-ernmental control. Federalism as we know it today began to emerge in the late 1930s.

In the areas of commerce, taxation, spending, civil rights, and civil liberties, among others, the federal government now has a very large role, one that is the inevitable consequence of the increasing complexity of American society and the interdependence of its people. National, state, and local officials now work closely together to solve the country's problems, a situation that is described as cooperative federalism. Grants-in-aid from Washington to the states and localities have been the chief instrument of national influence. States and localities have received billions in federal assistance; in accepting that money, they have also accepted both federal restrictions on its use and the national policy priorities that underlie the granting of the money.

Major Concepts

block grants
categorical grants
commerce clause
confederacy
cooperative federalism
enumerated powers
federalism (federal system)
fiscal federalism

horizontal federalism
implied powers
"necessary and proper" clause (elastic clause)
reserved powers
sovereignty
supremacy clause
unitary system

Suggested Readings

Anton, Thomas. *American Federalism and Public Policy: How the System Works.* New York: McGraw-Hill, 1989. An analysis of policy patterns of modern intergovernmental relations, including the role of private interests in federal programs.

Conlan, Timothy J. *New Federalism.* Washington, D.C.: Brookings Institution, 1988. An up-to-date assessment of today's federalism that includes the impact of Reagan's policies and the federal government's budgetary problems.

Federalist Papers. Many editions, including a one-volume paperback version edited by Isaac Kramnick (New York: Penguin, 1987). A series of essays written by Alexander Hamilton, James Madison, and John Jay under the pseudonym "Publius." The essays, published in a New York newspaper in 1787–1788, explained the Constitution and supported its ratification.

Ferrand, Max. *The Records of the Federal Convention of 1787.* New Haven, Conn.: Yale University Press, 1966. A four-volume work that includes all the important records of the Philadelphia convention.

Holcombe, Arthur N. *Our More Perfect Union.* Cambridge, Mass.: Harvard University Press, 1967. Traces federalism's development from eighteenth-century principles to twentieth-century practices.

Lunch, William H. *The Nationalization of American Politics.* Berkeley: University of California Press, 1987. An evaluation of the trend toward nationalization, including the ideological character it has assumed.

Nice, David C. *Federalism.* New York: St. Martin's Press, 1987. An up-to-date survey of the theory and practice of American federalism.

Riker, William. *Federalism: Origins, Operation, Significance.* Boston: Little, Brown, 1964. A critical assessment which concludes that American federalism's virtues are outweighed by its contribution to slavery and state-sponsored racial segregation.

Storing, Herbert. *What the Anti-Federalists Were For.* Chicago: University of Chicago Press, 1981. An analysis of Anti-Federalist thought and its origins.

LIMITED GOVERNMENT: PRESERVING LIBERTY

In framing a government which is to be administered by men over men, the great difficulty lies in this: you must first enable the government to control the governed; and in the next place oblige it to control itself.

James Madison[1]

O n the night of June 17, 1972, a security guard at the Watergate apartment-office complex in Washington, D.C., noticed that the latch on a basement door had been taped open. He called the police, who apprehended five burglars inside the National Democratic Party headquarters. As it turned out, the men had links to Republican President Richard Nixon's Committee to Re-elect the President.

Nixon called the incident "bizarre" and denied that anyone on his staff had had anything to do with the break-in. Nixon was lying, but he realized that telling the truth would bring down his presidency. The Watergate break-in was just one incident in an orchestrated campaign of "dirty tricks" designed to ensure Nixon's reelection. Funded by illegal contributions and conducted through the CIA, IRS, FBI, Secret Service, and Nixon's own operatives (called the White House "plumbers"), the dirty-tricks campaign extended to wiretaps, tax audits, and burglaries of Nixon's political opponents (the "enemies list"), who included journalists and antiwar activists in addition to Democrats. Nixon understood that if his abuse of power became known, his impeachment and removal from office by Congress were distinct possibilities. He told his close aides, "I want you all to stonewall it, let them [the Watergate burglary defendants] plead the Fifth Amendment, cover up, or anything else"[2]

[1] *Federalist* No. 51.
[2] Tape of White House conversation, March 22, 1973.

Although the Nixon White House managed for a time to obstruct justice (in one ploy, the president's assistants asked the CIA to tell the FBI to stop the Watergate investigation on fictitious "national security" grounds), the facts of Nixon's dirty-tricks campaign gradually became known. Initially two persistent *Washington Post* reporters, Bob Woodward and Carl Bernstein, kept the story alive. Additional revelations materialized during special Senate hearings in 1973. Televised to the nation, they portrayed a broad pattern of official corruption that, according to the unconfirmed testimony of former White House counsel John Dean, extended to the president himself.

In early 1974 the House Judiciary Committee began impeachment proceedings, helped along, ironically, by Nixon's own words. During the earlier Senate hearings, a White House assistant had revealed that Nixon had had all his telephone calls and personal conversations in the Oval Office tape-recorded. At first Nixon refused to release transcripts of the tapes, but then made public what he claimed were "all the relevant" ones. The House Judiciary Committee demanded additional tapes, as did the special prosecutor who had been appointed to investigate criminal aspects of the Watergate affair. In late July the Supreme Court of the United States unanimously ordered Nixon to supply sixty-four additional tapes. Two weeks later, on August 9, 1974, Richard Nixon, citing a loss of political support, resigned from office, the first president in U.S. history to do so.

Nixon's downfall was owed in no small measure to the handiwork, two centuries earlier, of the writers of the Constitution. They were well aware that power could never be entrusted to the goodwill of leaders. "If angels were to govern men," James Madison wrote in *Federalist* No. 51, "neither external nor internal controls on government would be necessary." Madison's point, of course, was that leaders are not angels and, as mere mortals, are subject to temptation and vice, including a lust for power—hence the Framers' insistence on constitutional checks on power, as when they gave Congress the authority to impeach a president and remove him from office.

The Framers' goal was **limited government**—government that is subject to strict limits on its lawful uses of power, and hence on its ability to deprive people of their liberty. The essential idea of limited government is captured in the phrase "a government of laws, not of men." Limited government is the essence of constitutionalism. The authority of officeholders is restricted by grants of lawful power; it is illegal for them to rule by whim or dictate.

This chapter examines the foundations of limited government in the United States. The chapter begins with a review of developments that predisposed Americans in 1787 to favor restrictions on political power and then discusses constitutional provisions for limited government and the related issue of judicial review. The chapter concludes with a brief assessment of the Constitution's historical contribution to limited government. The major ideas that are discussed are these:

★ *America during the colonial period developed a tradition of limited government and individual freedom.*

★ *The Constitution provides for a limited national government mainly by defining its lawful powers and by dividing those powers among competing institutions, each of which acts as a check on the others.* The Constitution, with its Bill of Rights, also prohibits government from infringing on individual rights.

★ *The power to decide whether government is acting within its lawful powers rests mainly with the judiciary.*

★ *Historically, the U.S. government has usually (though not always) acted with restraint.* This record is primarily a result of America's diversity and wealth but also stems from the Constitution's provisions for limited government.

The Roots of Limited Government

Early Americans' admiration for limited government was based partly on their English heritage. Other European nations of the eighteenth century implicitly acknowledged the divine right of their kings; England was an exception. British courts had developed a system of precedent known as "common law," which guaranteed trial by jury and due process of law as safeguards of life, liberty, and particularly property. These rights were defended by the courts and ordinarily respected by the king and Parliament.

The English tradition of limited government was enhanced by the Glorious Revolution of 1688–1689. During the preceding century, England had been racked by religious upheaval and political intrigue. Under the Stuart kings James I and Charles I, Protestants were taxed heavily and persecuted for their religious beliefs, while commercial monopolies and other privileges were granted to Catholics. The Stuarts' reign was interrupted by the dictatorship of Oliver Cromwell, a Puritan whose religious intolerance exceeded even that of the Stuarts. When the Stuarts' restoration to the throne in 1660 did not bring domestic peace, the English nobility in 1688 invited William of Orange, a Protestant Dutchman, to become king. He was offered the monarchy on condition that he accept a bill of rights guaranteeing certain liberties to propertied Englishmen. He was also forced to rule through Parliament and was made dependent upon it for an annual subsidy. Parliament further insisted that William accept an Act of Toleration, which gave Protestants of all sects the right to worship freely and publicly.

To the English philosopher John Locke (1632–1704), the arbitrary rule of the Stuarts and of Cromwell conveyed a clear lesson: government must be restrained in its powers if it is to serve the common good. Locke's theory of individual rights and limited government, which had roots that reached back to the Greeks and Romans, became an inspiration to a generation of American leaders. Thomas Jefferson declared that Locke "was one of the three greatest men that ever lived, without exception."[3] In his *Two Treatises of Government* (1690) Locke advanced the liberal principle that people have **inalienable rights** (or **natural rights**), including those of life, liberty, and property. In Locke's view, such rights belonged to people in their natural state before governments were created. When people agreed to come together (or, in Locke's term, entered into a "social contract") in order to have the protection that only

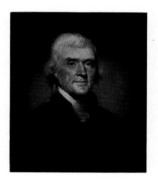

John Locke (*top*) was an English philosopher who contended that every individual has a right to personal liberty. Thomas Jefferson (*bottom*) admired Locke's views and used some of his phrases almost word for word in writing the Declaration of Independence. (*Top:* National Portrait Gallery, London; *bottom:* The White House Historical Association; photograph by the National Geographic Society)

[3] Thomas Jefferson to John Trumball, February 15, 1789, quoted in Dumas Malone, *Jefferson and the Rights of Man* (Boston: Little, Brown, 1951), 211.

organized government could provide, their natural rights were neither taken from them by government nor surrendered by them to government. If the government protected their natural rights, they were obliged to obey it, but if the government failed to protect their rights, they could rightfully rebel against it.[4]

Locke's ideas were part of the Enlightenment, an eighteenth-century European philosophical movement that sought to understand the proper order of nature and society. Locke's ideas dominated Enlightenment theories of government to the same degree that Sir Isaac Newton's ideas dominated Enlightenment theories of science. Locke's revolutionary ideas about rulers and natural rights had special appeal to American colonists because, among all people at this time, they were endowed with the most personal freedom.[5]

COLONIAL AND STATE CONSTITUTIONS

The English tradition of limited government was reflected in the American colonial governments. In each colony there was a right to trial by jury and some freedom of expression.

The first formal constitution among the colonies, the Fundamental Orders of Connecticut, was written in 1639. It gave "freemen" the right to vote and commanded public officials to use their authority for "the public good." The Massachusetts Body of Liberties, drafted two years later, forbade arbitrary sentences by judges and guaranteed a citizen accused of a crime the right to challenge witnesses. Rhode Island's constitution of 1663 was an even bolder step toward limited government: it granted religious freedom for Christians and placed strict limits on the powers of the governor and the town representatives. In other colonies, however, officeholders had fewer restrictions on their authority and citizens had fewer rights. Religious freedom, for example, was not granted by all colonial governments.

When the American colonies declared their independence from England, they adopted state constitutions that defined the limits of government's scope and authority. The new states preferred written constitutions, since they had been governed by formal charters as colonies. In addition, Americans admired the contract theory of government, which was premised on a defined relationship between the people and those who exercised governing authority. By putting the nature of this relationship in writing, Americans believed they were placing limits on the rightful powers of government. No state chose to adopt the British model of an unwritten constitution. (The constitutional structure of Britain's government is defined by custom, common law, and legislative acts.)

THE DECLARATION OF INDEPENDENCE

The Revolutionary War was partly a rebellion against England's failure to respect its own tradition of limited government in the colonies. Many of the colonial charters had conferred upon Americans "the rights of Englishmen,"

[4] John Locke, *The Two Treatises of Government*, ed. Thomas I. Cook (New York: Hafner, 1947), 159–186, 228–247.
[5] Winthrop D. Jordan and Leon F. Litwack, *The United States*, 6th ed. (Englewood Cliffs, N.J.: Prentice-Hall, 1987), 72–74.

but English kings and ministers showed less and less respect for this guarantee as time went on.

The period after the French and Indian War was the turning point. British and colonial soldiers had fought together to drive the French out of Canada and the western territories in 1763, but the British then imposed taxes that created great resentment in the colonies. Britain's seven-year war with France had created a severe financial crisis for the British government, which looked to the prosperous colonies for relief. Americans were forced to garrison English soldiers in their homes, and Parliament in 1765 levied a stamp tax on colonial newspapers and business documents, disrupting commerce and public communication. As the colonists were not represented in the British Parliament that had imposed the tax, the colonial pamphleteer James Otis declared that the Stamp Act violated the fundamental rights of the colonists as "British subjects and men." The colonists convened a special congress, which declared that the only laws binding on the colonies were those enacted by a legislature "chosen therein by themselves."

Although Parliament backed down and repealed the Stamp Act, it then passed the Townshend Act, which imposed taxes on all paper, glass, lead, and tea entering the colonies. In *Letters from a Farmer in Pennsylvania* (1767), John Dickinson claimed that the Townshend duties were punitive and destructive of the goodwill between Britain and its colonies. When other colonists joined the protest, King George III sent additional British troops to America and interfered with colonial legislatures. These actions served only to arouse the colonists further. England then tried to placate the Americans by repealing the Townshend duties except for a nominal tea tax, which Britain retained in order to display its authority. The colonists viewed the tea tax as a petty insult, and in the "Boston Tea Party" of December 1773 a small band of patriots disguised as Indians boarded an English ship in Boston Harbor and dumped its cargo of tea overboard.

Three years later, sporadic acts of defiance had become a full-scale revolution. In a pamphlet called *Common Sense*, which sold 120,000 copies in its first three months, Thomas Paine had claimed that all of Europe—England, too—was rife with political oppression, and that America was humanity's last hope of liberty. "Freedom has been hunted around the globe. . . . Receive the fugitive, and prepare in time an asylum for mankind." The idea was codified in the Declaration of Independence, which Thomas Jefferson prepared and Congress adopted on July 4, 1776. The Declaration honored the British tradition of specific rights by listing their violations by George III and based its argument for inalienable rights on Locke's philosophy. Even two centuries later, the words of the Declaration of Independence are eloquent testimony to the vision of human liberty:

> We hold these truths to be self-evident, that all men are created equal, that they are endowed by their Creator with certain unalienable rights, that among these are life, liberty and the pursuit of happiness.

> That to secure these rights, governments are instituted among men, deriving their just powers from the consent of the governed.

> That whenever any form of government becomes destructive of these ends, it is the right of the people to alter or to abolish it, and to institute new government. . . .

Drafting the Declaration of Independence, a painting by J. L. Ferris. Benjamin Franklin, John Adams, and Thomas Jefferson (standing) drafted the historic document. Jefferson was the principal author; he inserted the inspirational words about liberty, equality, and self-government. (The Bettmann Archive)

Constitutional Restraints on Political Power

The U.S. Constitution was written eleven years after the Declaration of Independence, with a different purpose. The Declaration was a call to revolution rather than a framework for government and therefore could not be used as a blueprint by the men who gathered in Philadelphia in 1787 to write a constitution. Nevertheless, a concern for liberty was no less fundamental to the thinking of the delegates to the constitutional convention than it had been to leaders of the Revolution.

The challenge facing the Framers of the Constitution was how to control the coercive force of government. Fundamentally, government is based on the use of physical force. The German sociologist Max Weber noted that government is defined by its "monopoly of the legitimate use of physical force within a given territory."[6] Government's unique characteristic is that it alone can *legally* arrest, imprison, and even kill the people who break its rules. Force is not the only basis of effective government, but government must have a last-resort option of coercion if its authority is to prevail. Otherwise, persons could break the law with impunity, and society would degenerate to anarchy. Where there is no rule of law, the strong bully the weak.

---

[6] Max Weber, "Politics as a Vocation," in Hans H. Gerth and C. Wright Mills, eds., *From Max Weber: Essays in Sociology* (New York: Oxford University Press, 1958), 78.

The dilemma is that government itself can destroy civilized society by using its monopoly on the legitimate use of force to brutalize and intimidate its opponents. "It is a melancholy reflection," James Madison wrote to Thomas Jefferson shortly after the Constitution's ratification, "that liberty should be equally exposed to danger whether the government has too much or too little power."[7]

The men who wrote the Constitution sought to establish a government strong enough to enforce collective interests, including national commerce and defense, but not so strong as to destroy liberty. In devising a government that was both strong and restrained, the Framers were inclined to err on the side of restraint. Limited government was built into the Constitution through both grants and restrictions of political power.

GRANTS AND DENIALS OF POWER

The Framers chose to limit the national government in part by confining its scope to constitutional **grants of power.** Authority not granted to it was in theory denied to it. In a period when other governments held broad discretionary powers, this was a remarkable restriction.

Unlike the British Parliament, which had largely unrestricted legislative authority, Congress was limited by an enumeration of its powers. As we saw in Chapter 2, Congress's lawmaking is constitutionally confined to seventeen specified powers and to those actions that are "necessary and proper" to the execution of those powers. The U.S. president was similarly restricted by constitutional grants of authority. Unlike the English king, who could invoke broad extraconstitutional authority in a time of crisis, the president was given no extraordinary powers. As for the judiciary, the Framers contained federal judges' authority by forbidding them to make broad rulings on issues of their own choosing. The judiciary can decide only those issues raised by actual cases brought before it by litigants.

The Framers also used **denials of power** as a means of limiting government, prohibiting certain practices that European rulers had routinely used to intimidate their political opponents. The French king, for example, could order a subject jailed indefinitely without charge or trial. (Among the thousands of French victims of this power were the philosophers Diderot and Voltaire.) The U.S. Constitution prohibits such action, granting individuals the right to be brought before a court under a writ of *habeas corpus* for a judgment as to the legality of their imprisonment. Among its other denials of power, the Constitution prohibits religious tests as a qualification for public office, and it forbids Congress and the states from enacting bills of attainder (legislative trials) and from passing *ex post facto* laws, under which citizens could be prosecuted for acts that were legal at the time they were committed.

Finally, the Framers made it difficult for those in power to change the Constitution and thereby increase their lawful authority. An amendment can be proposed only by a two-thirds majority of both houses of Congress or in a national constitutional convention called by the legislatures of two-thirds of the states. Such a proposal must then be ratified by three-fourths of the state

---

[7] Gaillard Hunt, ed., *The Writings of James Madison* (New York: Putnam, 1904), 274.

WHY IS A CONSTITUTION NEEDED?

The Englishman James Bryce ranked America's written constitution as its greatest contribution to the practice of government. He noted that the United States in 1787 gave the world a model of government in which the actions of authorities were subordinate to the words of a written document. The goal was "a government of laws, not of men." The Constitution was to be a higher authority than any act of Congress, any presidential decision, or any Supreme Court ruling.

Bryce did not claim that the Constitution was perfect or free of bias; no human work is. But Bryce suggested that a proper constitution, backed by a people's determination to live under it, can contribute mightily to rule by law. What else but the Constitution and the American tradition of limited government gave Congress the moral authority to pursue, without threat of military coup or popular insurrection, the possibility of impeaching President Nixon? The Watergate scandal and its aftermath were vivid proof that not even the most powerful officer in the U.S. political system stands higher than the Constitution.

The Framers' commitment to limited government grew out of their recognition of the power of government and the corruptibility of human nature. The Framers knew that the power of government is rooted in coercive force. A civil society requires that government have the power to arrest and imprison those who break its rules and prey on other people. Anarchy would result if government could not use force against lawbreakers. Yet their positions do not guarantee that the leaders of government will be scrupulous. Their ambitions, including a lust for power, can lead them to use the coercive power of government to repress the very people they are supposed to serve.

Why do you think these two considerations—the coercive power of government and the corruptibility of human nature—lead almost inevitably to a belief in limited government and to the use of a constitution as a way to control power?

legislatures or by three-fourths of the states in a special national convention before it can become part of the Constitution.

USING POWER TO OFFSET POWER

The Framers believed that political power could not be controlled if it were concentrated in one institution. "The accumulation of all powers, legislative, executive, and judiciary, in the same hands, whether of one, a few, or many, and whether hereditary, self-appointed, or elective," Madison claimed, "may be justly pronounced the very definition of tyranny."[8] Locke, too, had warned against concentrated political power, arguing that those who make the laws should not also be allowed to enforce them. In 1748 the French theorist Montesquieu enlarged this idea into a concept of separated powers, contending that liberty depended on a precise division of executive and legislative authority.

Montesquieu's principle was widely accepted in America, and when the states drafted new constitutions after the start of the Revolutionary War, they built their governments around a separation of powers. Pennsylvania was an exception, and its experience only seemed to prove the necessity of separated powers. Unrestrained by an independent judiciary or executive, Pennsylvania's all-powerful legislature systematically deprived minority groups of their basic rights and freedoms: Quakers were disenfranchised for their religious beliefs, conscientious objectors to the Revolutionary War were prosecuted, and the right of trial by jury was eliminated.

The accumulation of all powers, legislative, executive, and judiciary, in the same hands . . . may be justly pronounced the very definition of tyranny.

James Madison,
Federalist No. 47

[8] *Federalist* No. 47.

In *Federalist* No. 10, Madison asked why popular governments often act according to the interests of overbearing majorities rather than according to principles of justice. He found the cause in "the mischiefs of faction." People, he argued, are divided into opposing religious, geographical, ethnic, economic, and other factions. These divisions are not only natural in society but also desirable, in that free people have a right to their personal opinions and interests. Yet factions can themselves be a source of oppressive government. The threat, Madison noted, arises from "a minority or majority, actuated by interest adverse to the rights of others or to the permanent or aggregate interests of the community." If such a majority or minority faction gains full power, it will use government to advance itself at the expense of all others.

Out of concern for this possibility came the Framers' special contribution to the doctrine of the separation of powers. They did not believe that it would be enough, as Montesquieu had suggested, to divide the government's authority strictly along institutional lines, granting all legislative power to the legislature, all judicial power to the courts, and all executive power to the presidency. This *total* separation would make it too easy for a single faction to exploit a particular kind of political power. A faction that controlled the legislature, for example, could enact laws ruinous to other interests. A better system of divided government is one in which authority is allocated in such a way that no institution can do much on its own. In this situation, political power can be exercised only when institutions cooperate. Since the probability is small that any one faction can gain control over all institutions, factions have to work together, a process that requires each to moderate its demands and thus serves many interests rather than one or a few.[9]

Gilbert Stuart, *Portrait of President James Madison.* Madison is often called "the father of the Constitution" because he was instrumental in its writing and in its ratification (through his contributions to the *Federalist Papers*). (Bowdoin College Museum of Art, Brunswick, Maine)

SEPARATED INSTITUTIONS SHARING POWER: CHECKS AND BALANCES

The Framers' concept of divided powers has been described by political scientist Richard Neustadt as the principle of **separated institutions sharing power.**[10] The separate branches are interlocked in such a way that an elaborate system of **checks and balances** is created (see Figure 3-1, page 70). No institution can act decisively without the support or acquiescence of the other institutions. Madison explained in *Federalist* No. 48 that "unless these departments be so far connected and blended as to give to each a constitutional control over the others, the degree of separation which the maxim requires, as essential to a free government, can never in practice be duly maintained." Thus legislative, executive, and judicial power in the American system came to be divided in such a way that they overlap; each of the three branches of government checks the others' powers and balances those powers with powers of its own.

Shared Legislative Powers

Under the Constitution, Congress has legislative authority, but that power is partly shared with the other branches and thus checked by them. The president

---

[9] See *Federalist* Nos. 47 and 48.
[10] Richard Neustadt, *Presidential Power* (New York: Wiley, 1960), 33.

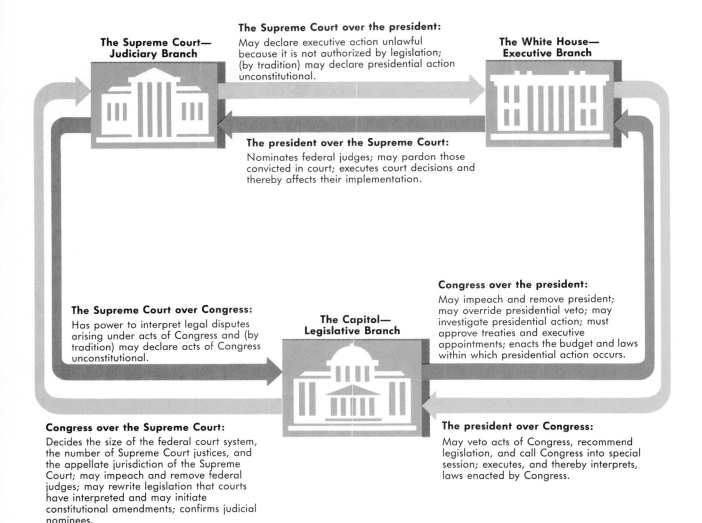

**The Supreme Court—
Judiciary Branch**

The Supreme Court over the president:
May declare executive action unlawful
because it is not authorized by legislation;
(by tradition) may declare presidential action
unconstitutional.

**The White House—
Executive Branch**

The president over the Supreme Court:
Nominates federal judges; may pardon those
convicted in court; executes court decisions and
thereby affects their implementation.

Congress over the president:
May impeach and remove president;
may override presidential veto; may
investigate presidential action; must
approve treaties and executive
appointments; enacts the budget and laws
within which presidential action occurs.

The Supreme Court over Congress:
Has power to interpret legal disputes
arising under acts of Congress and (by
tradition) may declare acts of Congress
unconstitutional.

**The Capitol—
Legislative Branch**

Congress over the Supreme Court:
Decides the size of the federal court system,
the number of Supreme Court justices, and
the appellate jurisdiction of the Supreme
Court; may impeach and remove federal
judges; may rewrite legislation that courts
have interpreted and may initiate
constitutional amendments; confirms judicial
nominees.

The president over Congress:
May veto acts of Congress, recommend
legislation, and call Congress into special
session; executes, and thereby interprets,
laws enacted by Congress.

**FIGURE 3-1 The System
of Checks and Balances**

can veto acts of Congress, recommend legislation, and call special sessions of
Congress. The president also has the power to execute—and thereby to
interpret—the laws made by Congress. The Supreme Court has the power to
interpret acts of Congress that are disputed in legal cases. By tradition, the Court
also has the power of judicial review; it can declare laws of Congress void when
it finds that they are not in accord with the Constitution.

Within Congress, there is a further check on legislative power: for legislation
to be passed, a majority in each house of Congress is required. Thus the Senate
and the House of Representatives have a veto over each other's actions.

Shared Executive Powers

Executive power is vested in the president, but the Framers meant this power to
be constrained by legislative and judicial checks. The president's power to make

treaties, conduct war, and appoint high-ranking officials is subject to congressional approval. Congress can also override the president's vetoes of its legislation with a two-thirds majority in both houses and can impeach a president for wrongdoing and remove him from office. Congress's greatest checks on executive action, however, are its lawmaking and appropriations powers. The executive branch cannot act without laws that authorize its activities or without the money that funds these programs. The judiciary's major check on the presidency is its power to declare an action unlawful because it is not authorized by the legislation that the executive claims to be carrying out.

Shared Judicial Powers

Judicial power rests with the Supreme Court and with lower federal courts, which are subject to checks by the other branches of the federal government. Congress is empowered to establish the size of the federal court system; to restrict the Supreme Court's appellate jurisdiction in some circumstances; and to impeach federal judges and remove them from office. More important, Congress can rewrite legislation that the courts have misinterpreted and can initiate amendments when it disagrees with the courts' rulings on constitutional issues. The president has the power to appoint federal judges with the consent of the Senate and to pardon persons convicted in the courts. The president is also responsible for executing court decisions, a function that provides opportunities to influence the way rulings are implemented.

FEDERALISM AS A FURTHER CHECK ON GOVERNMENT POWER

Theorists such as Locke and Montesquieu had not proposed a division of power between national and local authorities as a further means of protecting liberty.

★ HOW THE UNITED STATES COMPARES

CHECKS AND BALANCES

All democracies place constitutional limits on the power of government. The concept of rule by law, for example, is characteristic of democratic governments but not of authoritarian regimes. Democracies differ, however, in the extent to which political power is restrained through constitutional mechanisms. The United States is an extreme case in that its government rests on an elaborate system of constitutional checks and balances. The system employs a separation of powers among the executive, legislative, and judicial branches. It also includes judicial review, the power of the courts to invalidate actions of the legislature or executive. These constitutional restrictions on power are not part of the governing structure of all democracies.

Country	Separation of Powers?	Judicial Review?
Belgium	No	No
Canada	No	Yes
France	Yes	No
Germany	No	Yes
Great Britain	No	No
Israel	No	Yes
Italy	No	Yes
Japan	No	Yes
Mexico	In theory only	Yes
United States	Yes	Yes

LIMITS ON GOVERNMENT IN THE U.S. CONSTITUTION

Grants of Power: powers granted to the national government by the Constitution. Powers not granted it are denied it unless they are necessary and proper to the carrying out of granted powers.

Denials of power: powers expressly denied to the national and state governments by the Constitution.

Separated institutions sharing power: the division of the national government's power among three branches, each of which is to act as a check on the powers of the other two.

Bill of Rights: the first ten amendments to the Constitution, which specify rights of citizens that the national government must respect.

Federalism: The division of political authority between the national government and the states, enabling the people to appeal to one authority if their rights and interests are not respected by the other authority.

Judicial review: the power of the courts to declare governmental action null and void when it is found to violate the Constitution.

Nevertheless, the Framers came to look upon federalism (discussed in Chapter 2) as part of the system of checks and balances established by the Constitution. Hamilton argued in *Federalist* No. 28 that the American people could shift their loyalties back and forth between the national and state governments in order to keep each under control. "If [the people's] rights are invaded by either," Hamilton wrote, "they can make use of the other as the instrument of redress." Madison wrote in *Federalist* No. 51 that a federal system is a superior form of limited government because power is divided between two distinct governments, as well as among their separate branches. "The different governments will control each other," he said, "at the same time that each will be controlled by itself."

THE BILL OF RIGHTS

Although the delegates to the Philadelphia convention discussed the possibility of placing a list of individual rights (such as freedom of speech and the right to a fair trial) in the Constitution, they ultimately decided that such a list was unnecessary because of the doctrine of expressed powers: government could not lawfully assume powers, such as the abridgment of human rights, that were not authorized by the Constitution. Moreover, the delegates concluded that a bill of rights was undesirable because government might feel free to disregard any right that was inadvertently left off the list or that emerged at some future time.

These considerations did not allay the fears of leading Americans who believed that no possible safeguard against arbitrary government should be omitted. "A bill of rights," Jefferson argued, "is what the people are entitled to against every government on earth, general or particular, and what no just government should refuse or rest on inference." Jefferson had included a bill of rights in the constitution he wrote for Virginia at the outbreak of the Revolutionary War, and all but four states had followed Virginia's example.

Opposition to the absence of a bill of rights in the federal constitution led the Federalists finally to support its addition. Madison himself introduced a series of amendments during the First Congress, which approved twelve of those proposed. Ten of these amendments were subsequently ratified by the states. These amendments, traditionally called the Bill of Rights, took effect in 1791; they include such rights as free expression, property ownership, and due process for persons accused of crimes. (These rights, termed "civil liberties," are the subject of Chapter 5.)

The Bill of Rights is a precise expression of the concept of limited government. Constitutional safeguards of individual rights rest upon a distinction between lawful and unlawful actions of government. In consenting to be governed, the people agree to accept the authority of government in certain areas but not in others, including the area of individual rights. The people's constitutional rights cannot lawfully be denied by governing officials.

The Judiciary as Guardian of Limited Government

The Framers both empowered and limited government through the Constitution. But who was to decide whether the government was operating within its constitutional powers? Who was to be the official guardian of limited government? The Constitution itself makes no direct mention of such authority. Whether by oversight or by design, the Framers did not specifically entrust this power to a particular branch of government, although they did charge the Supreme Court with deciding on "all cases arising under this Constitution."

INTERPRETING THE CONSTITUTION

Most delegates to the Philadelphia convention apparently assumed that the Supreme Court would have the power of **judicial review:** the power of the courts to decide whether a governmental institution has acted within its constitutional powers and, if not, to declare its action null and void. Gouverneur Morris of Pennsylvania said that the judiciary should invalidate laws that were "a direct violation of the Constitution."

The Framers had precedent for judicial review in several states, and a form of it had existed during the colonial period. It is also noteworthy that the power of the courts to declare laws null and void was discussed approvingly at the ratifying conventions of at least eight of the thirteen states.[11]

Nevertheless, because the Constitution did not explicitly provide for judicial review, the question of constitutional interpretation was a political issue waiting to happen. An opening was provided by the Sedition Act of 1798, which had been passed by the Federalist-controlled Congress for the stated purpose of stopping subversive activities by French sympathizers but was actually applied against Jeffersonian Republicans. Thomas Jefferson persuaded the Kentucky legislature to pass the Kentucky Resolutions, which declared that a state could void any national law that it deemed contrary to the Constitution.

[11] Henry J. Abraham, *The Judicial Process*, 5th ed. (New York: Oxford University Press, 1986), 320–322.

★ ANALYZE THE ISSUE

The Bill of Rights and Limited Government
Why did the original Constitution omit the Bill of Rights? Why were the Framers divided over its inclusion? Can you think of any constitutional rights that you might, or might not, have if the Bill of Rights had not been added?

★ ANALYZE THE ISSUE

Limited Government as a Contributor to Judicial Power
Alexis de Tocqueville noted 150 years ago that "scarcely any political question arises in the United States that is not resolved, sooner or later, into a judicial question." Though Tocqueville's observation is an overstatement, it captures an enduring tendency in U.S. politics. Americans turn more readily to the courts to settle disputes than other people do. To what degree do you think this tendency is a result of the concept of limited government that is embedded in the U.S. constitutional structure? Does the tendency give the courts too much power, especially in view of the fact that judges are appointed to office, not elected?

John Marshall forcefully expressed his nationalist views in important Supreme Court decisions during his thirty-four years as chief justice. (Boston Athenaeum Collection)

The Sedition Act would be countered through constitutional review by a state legislature rather than the federal judiciary.

If Jefferson's view had prevailed, chronic abuse of political power could ultimately have resulted. If every governmental institution had the power to rule on the meaning of the Constitution, each would be likely to stretch its self-defined constitutional powers to the limit and beyond.

MARBURY v. *MADISON:* **THE PRINCIPLE OF JUDICIAL REVIEW**

The landmark case of *Marbury* v. *Madison* (1803) became the foundation for judicial review by the federal courts. Judicial review has enabled the U.S. federal judiciary to become one of the most powerful court systems in the world. The judiciaries of many other countries lack this authority. The British high court, for example, cannot invalidate an act of Parliament.

The *Marbury* case grew out of the election of 1800, in which John Adams lost his bid for a second presidential term after a bitter campaign against Jefferson. Between November 1800, when Jefferson was elected, and March 1801, when he was inaugurated, the Federalist-controlled Congress created fifty-nine additional lower-court judgeships, thus giving Adams an opportunity to appoint loyal Federalists to those positions before he left office. However, Adams's term expired before the secretary of state's office could deliver seventeen of the judicial commissions. When Jefferson took office, he ordered his secretary of state, James Madison, to withhold them. William Marbury was one of the seventeen Federalists who were denied a commission, and he asked the Supreme Court to issue a writ of *mandamus* (a court order requiring an official to take a specific action) that would compel Madison to provide it.

Marbury's petition posed a dilemma for the Supreme Court. On the one hand, if it ordered Madison to deliver the commissions, he might refuse to do so; and as the Court could not force him to act, it would be branded as feeble and inconsequential. On the other hand, a decision in Madison's favor might suggest that a president could do anything he wanted, possibly loosening the restraints on government intended by the Constitution.

Chief Justice John Marshall wrote the Court's unanimous opinion. His decision was ingenious, asserting the power of judicial review without forcing the Court into a showdown with the executive branch. The Court ruled that Marbury had a legal right to his commission, thus implicitly criticizing the president for failing in his duty to execute the laws faithfully. However, the Court said it could not issue Marbury a writ because its authority to issue such writs was provided by the Judiciary Act of 1789 rather than by a constitutional amendment. Only through amendment could the Court's original jurisdiction be altered. That being the case, Marshall stated, the provision of the Judiciary Act was unconstitutional.[12]

This decision established the Court's authority without placing it in jeopardy. There was no writ of *mandamus* for Madison to ignore, only a Court opinion critical of his actions. Furthermore, the Court had invalidated an act of Congress, thereby asserting its power to interpret the Constitution. Congress could not retaliate, for it had no way to force the Court to issue a writ if the

---

[12] *Marbury* v. *Madison,* 1 Cranch 137 (1803).

Court refused to do so. John Marshall served as chief justice for more than thirty years after *Marbury*, and his Court did not again invalidate an act of Congress. Nevertheless, *Marbury* had asserted the principle that the lawful powers of government were subject to judicial check. *Marbury* became a precedent for later Court rulings that clearly established the Supreme Court's position as the chief authority on the Constitution's grants of power and thus a critical actor in the preservation of limited government.

Limited Government in Perspective

In the course of their history Americans have not always honored the principle of limited government. The greatest test of the nation's commitment to liberty came shortly after Reconstruction, when the question was whether former slaves would be granted a full measure of freedom. The answer was no. The North turned its back as the South's white majority systematically stripped black people of their constitutional rights, an injustice in which even the Supreme Court of the United States participated by its ruling in *Plessy* v. *Ferguson* (discussed in Chapter 2).

Yet by the standards of a world in which brutal government is all too common, the United States has been relatively successful in restraining political power. Periods of severe repression have been rare in American politics and have seldom lasted very long.[13] When Eldridge Cleaver, a founder of the Black Panther party in the 1960s, returned to the United States from a decade-long voluntary exile brought about by his disillusionment with the country's racial progress, he admonished Americans for not living up to their nation's creed, but added, "With all its faults, the American political system is the freest in the world."[14]

WEALTH, DIVERSITY, AND GEOGRAPHY: CONDITIONS FAVORABLE TO LIMITED GOVERNMENT

The freedom that Americans enjoy cannot be attributed solely, or even primarily, to the Constitution. No document alone can ensure a limited government. During the early nineteenth century, for example, most of the newly independent Latin American countries adopted U.S.-style constitutions, only to fall under authoritarian rule. Even today some Latin American governments rely heavily on intimidation and force to suppress political opposition.

In parts of Latin America, as in some African and Asian countries, politics is an unyielding struggle for survival between the many who are desperately poor and the very few who are rich. In contrast, the politics of the United States has been moderated by the country's great natural wealth. In *Federalist* No. 10 James Madison anticipated that America's economic riches and opportunities would protect it from political extremism. Because property ownership was

---

[13] Robert A. Dahl, *Pluralist Democracy in the United States* (Chicago: Rand McNally, 1967), 370.
[14] Quoted in Thomas J. Maroney, "Supreme Law Checks Powers of Government," *Syracuse Herald American*, May 24, 1987, T5.

Some Latin American governments have at times used military force against their domestic political opponents. Latin America lacks the widespread affluence and economic and social diversity that have moderated political conflict in the United States and permitted limited government to persist. (C. Carrion/Sygma)

widespread, Madison foresaw that conflict would not degenerate into a war between those with property and those without it. Economic divisions would occur instead among differing property interests—landed, industrial, and commercial—each of which would be further divided, as in the case of small and large landholders. The net effect of this economic and social diversity, Madison concluded, would be a moderate level of political conflict that could be settled peacefully within a framework of limited government. The exercise of political power in all cases would depend on a joining of factions, so that each of them would be compelled to respect the rights and interests of the others.

Madison's prediction was reasonably accurate. In 1893 Friedrich Engels, the collaborator of Karl Marx, said that he saw no real chance of a wrenching class struggle in America because of its economic diversity and abundance.[15] And Engels was writing *before* the full fruits of the Industrial Revolution had produced for Americans a standard of living that was the envy of the world.

America's ethnic and religious diversity has also contributed to its tradition of limited government. With the major and tragic exception of racial antagonisms, American political life has not tended toward extreme polarization of one group against another. A nation of immigrants (see Figure 3-2), the United States is home to a population so varied in its national origins and religions that a general struggle between two readily identified and entrenched sides could not easily be sparked. We can perhaps best understand the significance of this diversity by thinking about the dismal situation in countries where two dominant groups are constantly at each other's throats, such as Protestants and Catholics in Northern Ireland, Greeks and Turks in Cyprus, Jews and Palestinians in Israel, and whites and blacks in South Africa.

[15] Daniel Bell, *The End of Ideology* (New York: Collier, 1961), 67.

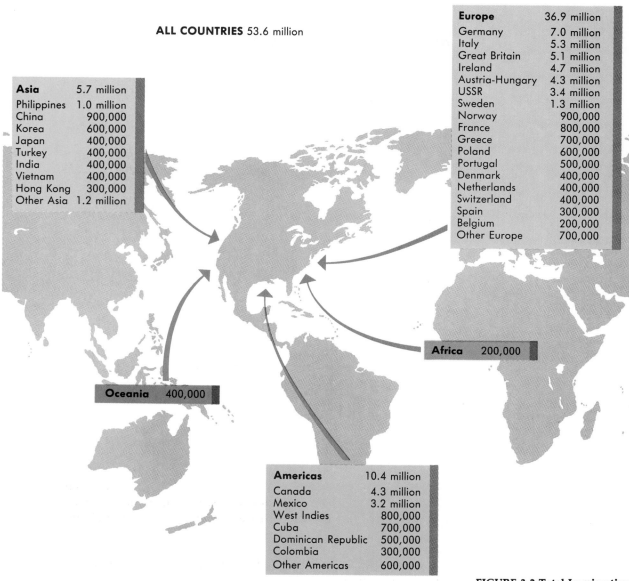

ALL COUNTRIES 53.6 million

Asia	5.7 million
Philippines	1.0 million
China	900,000
Korea	600,000
Japan	400,000
Turkey	400,000
India	400,000
Vietnam	400,000
Hong Kong	300,000
Other Asia	1.2 million

Europe	36.9 million
Germany	7.0 million
Italy	5.3 million
Great Britain	5.1 million
Ireland	4.7 million
Austria-Hungary	4.3 million
USSR	3.4 million
Sweden	1.3 million
Norway	900,000
France	800,000
Greece	700,000
Poland	600,000
Portugal	500,000
Denmark	400,000
Netherlands	400,000
Switzerland	400,000
Spain	300,000
Belgium	200,000
Other Europe	700,000

Africa	200,000

Oceania	400,000

Americas	10.4 million
Canada	4.3 million
Mexico	3.2 million
West Indies	800,000
Cuba	700,000
Dominican Republic	500,000
Colombia	300,000
Other Americas	600,000

FIGURE 3-2 Total Immigration to United States, 1820–1990, by Continent and Country of Origin
Source: U.S. Immigration and Naturalization Service.

Finally, the United States has had the benefit of a favorable geography: the nation's size and the two huge oceans that separate it from Europe and Asia have given it unrivaled protection against possible enemies. The immediate threat of a large-scale invasion by foreign armies has never served as an excuse to entrust power to a repressive regime. As the "Red scares" of the 1920s and 1950s showed, Americans have no special immunity to the political intolerance that can flow from fear of another nation. We can only imagine how much worse these anticommunist witch hunts might have been had the Soviet Union been situated just across the border from the United States rather than in far-off Eurasia.

The Power of Limited Government

The use of power to offset power is traditionally American. Is the approach as viable today as it was 200 years ago? Consider the following: First, Americans today are a relatively well-educated and affluent people with a long tradition of self-government. Could they be expected to uphold limited government even if it were not deeply embedded in their political system? Second, American society today requires a government far more powerful than the one that met its needs in the past. Can modern government be sufficiently powerful when it must operate within the constraints of strong checks and balances? Do these constraints result in a stalemated government rather than an energetic one? Think of examples of policies that support your view.

THE CONSTITUTION'S CONTRIBUTION TO LIMITED GOVERNMENT

Although no constitutional arrangement could have checked political power had the United States lacked these favorable conditions, the American experience indicates that constitutional provisions also contribute to limited government.

Allocation of Power

Of all features of the U.S. constitutional system, none has been more important to the control of power than its allocation among separate branches. Throughout most of the country's history, each branch has jealously guarded its authority from the others, a system that has served to check the power of all three branches. For example, when it became known in late 1986 that officials in the Reagan administration had attempted illegally and covertly to trade weapons for hostages held by the extremist regime in Iran and had then used profits from the weapons sales to sneak arms to Contra rebels fighting against the Sandinista government in Nicaragua, Congress launched an immediate investigation. The inquiry brought the unlawful practices to an abrupt halt, produced administrative changes within the White House designed to prevent such abuses of executive authority, and subjected President Ronald Reagan to sharp criticism.

Those in the Reagan administration who devised and executed the covert Iran-Contra policy defended it by saying it was their duty to take "appropriate" action because Congress had refused to do so. This arrogance on the part of nonelected officials, claiming to know what was best for the country and acting upon it without proper authority, illustrates vividly why the Framers placed so much emphasis on the sharing of power by separate institutions: they recog-

Congress reacted swiftly to protect its powers when news of the Iran-Contra scandal broke. Lt. Col. Oliver North, one of the principal administration officials involved in devising and carrying out the illicit policy, is shown at left testifying at congressional hearings. (Dennis Brack/Black Star)

★ THE MEDIA AND THE PEOPLE

CHECKS ON "THE FOURTH BRANCH OF GOVERNMENT"

The U.S. constitutional system is based on the concept of checks and balances—the notion that all power should be subject to formal limitations. When the Framers wrote the Constitution, this concept was applied to the three branches of government—the executive, the legislature, and the judiciary. The power of each would serve to check and balance the power of the other two.

The press has been called "the fourth branch of government." This term is a relatively new one. At the time the Constitution was written, the press was an adjunct of political authority (see Chapter 15). Not until the late 1800s did the press become an extraordinary political power in its own right. This development occurred when the press became a "mass medium." The spread of mass education and the invention of newsprint in the late 1800s made the newspaper a daily part of Americans' lives. The introduction of radio and television several decades later gave the media an even greater presence in American society.

The power of the press rests with its ability to influence what people think and talk about. The world of politics is beyond firsthand observation, so we depend on the press to bring this world within our reach. In deciding what to cover and what to ignore, the media exert a powerful influence over our images of politics. Some observers claim, in fact, that the media are the preeminent political power in today's society. At his Harvard commencement speech in 1978, the Russian writer Alexander Solzhenitsyn said: "The press has become the most powerful force in Western countries. It has surpassed in power the executive, legislative, and judiciary."

Although most analysts would not go this far, none would deny that the media have considerable political power. Significantly, this power is exercised outside the system of constitutional checks and balances. The press, in fact, is protected from interference by other institutions. The First Amendment says that "Congress shall make no law . . . abridging the freedom of speech, or of the press." The dilemma is that the press is a private institution that is driven as much by its interest in profit as by its sense of public duty. Critics complain that the news media tend to present a relatively trivial and sensational view of politics (see Chapter 15).

Should the press be subject to checks and balances in the same way as the legislative, executive, and judicial branches? What form might these checks and balances take?

nized that political power had to be exercised openly and by multiple institutions if it was to be applied accountably and with restraint.

In the American experience, determined opposition from one branch of government has ordinarily constrained another branch's attempts to overreach its authority. Even during times of grave national crisis, this system of checks and balances has usually held up remarkably well. During the depths of the Great Depression of the 1930s, when the Supreme Court was voiding New Deal programs intended to relieve the nation's suffering, President Franklin D. Roosevelt's plan to undermine the Supreme Court by packing it with additional justices (see Chapter 2) was opposed by Congress even though its majority was solidly behind Roosevelt's New Deal.

Of course, each branch of the national government has significantly broadened its authority since the Constitution was written 200 years ago. Congress's taxing and commerce powers, the president's executive and national security powers, and the judiciary's power over civil rights and social policy are far greater than anything the Framers could have anticipated in 1787. Such developments might be interpreted as contrary to the Framers' plan to limit government by enumerating the powers granted to it. Yet the writers of the Constitution were well aware that government would necessarily evolve in response to social change. The Framers used broad language when they listed the constitutional powers of the national government and added the "necessary and proper" clause so that their concept of a government of elastic powers would not be misunderstood. In the final analysis, however, the Framers recognized that restraints on government rest not with grants and denials of power but with competition for power. "Ambition must be made to counteract ambition," said James Madison. Two centuries later in a Supreme Court case, Justice Antonin Scalia echoed the principle: "In the dictatorships of the world, bills of rights are a dime a dozen. It is the structure of government, the separation of powers and the balancing of powers, that best ensures preservation of rights."[16]

Provision for Judicial Review

Judicial review has been an important element in our system of limited government for two major reasons. First, judicial review was essential if the Court was to be the constitutional equal of the two other branches and thus to have legitimate authority to act against them when necessary. Neither elected branch has much to gain and might have much to lose by being rebuffed by the Supreme Court. Congress and the president have sometimes refrained from initiating policies of questionable constitutionality simply because they knew that the Supreme Court could invalidate their actions, thereby damaging their prestige and calling into question the legitimacy of their actions.[17]

Second, judicial review has proven in the twentieth century to be an important instrument for protecting individual rights, particularly when they are infringed by state and local governments. Since the 1920s the Supreme Court has struck down scores of local and state laws in cases that involved issues of individual rights and liberties, such as state and local infringements of free expression, fair trial, and equal protection under the laws (see Chapters 5 and 7). The authors of the Bill of Rights might be amazed by the range of protections it now encompasses, but they probably would not be surprised that the judiciary has become a prime guardian of individual rights. The Bill of Rights was added to the Constitution to transform what were regarded as inalienable rights into legal rights and thereby, as Justice Robert Jackson noted, "to place them beyond the reach of majorities and officials and to establish them as legal principles to be applied by the courts."[18]

SEPARATION OF POWERS: STILL A GOOD IDEA?

Some contemporary observers are critical of the separation of powers on the grounds that it results in intolerable deadlock and delay.[19] They argue that today's national and international problems require a government that can act quickly and decisively. Recent presidents have voiced a related complaint,

---

[16] *Morrison v. Olson*, 108 S.Ct. 2597 (1988).

[17] Richard M. Johnson, *The Dynamics of Compliance* (Evanston, Ill.: Northwestern University Press, 1967), 10, 11.

[18] Quoted in ibid., 3.

[19] See James Sundquist, *Constitutional Reform and Effective Government* (Washington, D.C.: Brookings Institution, 1986).

A major disadvantage of separation of powers is that sometimes neither the executive nor the legislative branch takes responsibility for action. Shown here is President Bush meeting with congressional leaders in July 1990 to try to work out a budget agreement. But a stalemate over the budget nearly shut the government down in October of that year. (AP/Wide World)

saying that Congress moves too slowly for the nation's good. On March 6, 1991, President George Bush noted that the war in the Persian Gulf had been conducted with speed and efficiency, and he challenged Congress to pass two bills, one dealing with crime and the other with highways, in the next 100 days. The deadline came and went without either bill making it to the president's desk. "I thought 100 days was fairly reasonable—and I wasn't asking the Congress to deliver a hot pizza in 30 minutes," he said to reporters. "I'm disappointed but frankly I'm not surprised."

Critics of congressional inaction have pointed to the parliamentary democracies of Europe, which have limited government without a separation of powers, and thereby have strong executive leadership on issues of public policy. These democracies find it easier to pursue a consistent long-term economic policy and a steadier foreign policy. Moreover, they offer the public a clear line of responsibility: if government policy fails to work, the blame belongs with the prime minister and the governing party. At the same time, these parliamentary democracies provide protection for individual freedoms through tradition, judicial action, and other means.

Few critics have gone so far as to urge that the United States adopt a parliamentary form of government, but numerous modest changes have been suggested to help bring the executive and legislative branches into a closer relationship. These proposals have included constitutional amendments that would allow members of Congress to serve in the president's cabinet and that would provide concurrent terms for the president and members of Congress, thereby enabling presidential and congressional candidates of the same party to run together as a team.

The traditional argument for retaining the separation of powers is that it offers protection against abuses of power and rash policy decisions. Political scientist James Q. Wilson claims that this argument is as valid today as it was at the time the Constitution was written. The separation of powers allows Congress to investigate allegations of executive misconduct, as it did in the case of the Iran-Contra scandal. Parliamentary systems do not have such a safeguard. Wilson concludes, moreover, that the advantages of the separation of powers in avoiding policy mistakes through delayed action are at least as substantial as the advantages of parliamentary government in achieving efficiency through fast action.[20]

The modern debate over the separation of powers reflects the tension that the Framers faced in devising a government that was both strong (see Chapter 2) and limited. In creating such a government, the Framers had to grant it substantial powers and yet restrict the application of those powers. The question of whether the balance the Framers established can serve the nation's needs two centuries later is one that every student of American government should ponder. The essays on pages 106–107 offer opposing views on this question.

Summary

The Constitution was designed to provide for a limited government in which political power would be confined to its proper uses. Liberty was a basic value of America's political tradition and a reason for its revolt against British rule. The Framers wanted to ensure that the government they were creating would not itself be a threat to freedom. To this end, they confined the national government to expressly granted powers. The federal government also was forbidden certain acts (such as *ex post facto* laws) that could be used to intimidate political opponents. Other prohibitions on government were later added to the Constitution in the form of stated guarantees of individual liberties—the Bill of Rights. The most significant constitutional provision for limited government, however, was a separation of powers among the three branches. The powers given to each branch enable it to act as a check on the exercise of power by the others.

The Constitution, however, made no mention of how the powers and limits of government were to be judged in practice. In its historic ruling in *Marbury* v. *Madison,* the Supreme Court assumed the authority to review the constitutionality of legislative and executive actions and to declare them unconstitutional and thus invalid.

The history of the United States, though blemished by episodes of repressive government, has been relatively free of the political oppression that has so often characterized other governments. Limits on government in the United States have apparently been made possible primarily by the nation's abundant wealth, diversity of interests, and geographical situation, which together have had the effect of reducing and moderating applications of political power. But the Constitution has also contributed to limited government, particularly through its provisions for the separation of powers and its stated guarantees of individual rights.

---

[20] James Q. Wilson, "Does the Separation of Powers Still Work?" *The Public Interest* 86 (Winter 1987): 36–52.

Major Concepts

checks and balances
denials of power
grants of power
inalienable (natural) rights

judicial review
limited government
separated institutions sharing power

Suggested Readings

Becker, Carl L. *The Declaration of Independence.* New York: Knopf, 1966. An analysis of the Declaration of Independence and the events that inspired it.

Burns, James MacGregor. *The Vineyard of Liberty.* New York: Knopf, 1982. A well-written historical study of the political, social, and theoretical influences on Americans' conceptions of liberty.

Fisher, Louis. *The Constitution between Friends.* New York: St. Martin's Press, 1978. An analysis of the constitutional relationship of the executive and legislative branches both in the Founders' conception and in subsequent developments.

Locke, John. *The Two Treatises of Government.* New York: Hafner, 1947. Published originally in 1690, Locke's work is a broad statement of the fundamental principles of limited government.

Reid, John Phillip. *The Concept of Liberty in the Age of the American Revolution.* Chicago: University of Chicago Press, 1988. A study of the meaning of liberty to Americans in the late eighteenth century.

Schwartz, Bernard. *The Great Rights of Mankind: A History of the American Bill of Rights.* New York: Oxford University Press, 1977. A historical overview of the Bill of Rights and its importance to limited government in the United States.

White, Morton. *Philosophy, the Federalists, and the Constitution.* New York: Oxford University Press, 1987. An examination of the philosophical arguments underlying the *Federalist Papers*, including the relevance of Locke's ideas.

Wood, Gordon S. *The Creation of the American Republic.* Chapel Hill: University of North Carolina Press, 1969. An examination of American political thought before the Philadelphia convention.

4
CHAPTER

REPRESENTATIVE GOVERNMENT: PROVIDING POPULAR SOVEREIGNTY

The people must be governed by a majority, with whom all power resides. But how is the sense of this majority to be obtained?

Fisher Ames (1788)[1]

The American people were in an angry mood as the 1990 elections drew near. Opinion polls indicated a growing discontent with the performance of government. Taxes were on the rise, the federal budget was in the red, and the economy was stagnant. Yet incumbents seemed above it all, insulated from the consequences of these crises. An unprecedented number of state legislators and members of Congress who had run for reelection in recent elections had won. Congress was the extreme case: 98 percent of House members who had run for another term in the 1988 elections had been reelected.

Advocates of change proposed **term limitation,** or legal restrictions on the number of years that any legislator could remain in office. A Gallup poll indicated that more than 60 percent of Americans favored the idea. Voters in Oklahoma were the first to act. In a September election they decided by a more than 2-to-1 margin to limit state legislators to a maximum of two consecutive six-year terms. California and Colorado voters followed suit in November. The California measure was the more closely contested, but it won out by a margin of 52 to 48 percent. Members of the California senate were restricted to a maximum of two four-year terms, or eight years total. California assembly members would be limited to three two-year terms. A national lobbying group, Americans for Term Limitation, began a campaign to amend the U.S. Constitution to limit service in Congress to twelve years. (Presidents are already limited to two four-year terms by the Twenty-Second Amendment.)

Although term limitation was popular with the voters in 1990, it was opposed by numerous civic leaders, commentators, and political scientists, who argued that effective leaders would be forced out of office along with the poor ones. They also argued that a legislature full of inexperienced representatives would be overwhelmed by the more experienced and more knowledgeable lobbyists and bureaucrats with whom they would have to contend. *The New York Times*, editorializing against term limitation, argued: "If voters think a member of Congress should be shown the gate, let them say so on Election Day."[2]

The issue was also a partisan one. Most of the political groups and leaders who supported term limitation were Republicans, who saw the proposal as a way to break the Democrats' hold on Congress and state legislatures. Republicans had not had control of the U.S. House of Representatives since 1954, and the high reelection rate of incumbents made it unlikely that the Republican party would gain control in the foreseeable future. Not surprisingly, many Democrats were opposed to term limitation. Speaker of the House Tom Foley attacked the idea as inconsistent with the voters' right to elect anyone of their choosing, whether that person be a newcomer or an incumbent with many years of experience in office.

The debate over term limitation during the 1990 elections was a variation on a debate that has been going on since the nation's beginning. What is the proper relationship between the electorate and its representatives? The writers of the Constitution answered that question with an elaborate electoral system that was intended to insulate representatives from the whims of an impassioned majority. The Framers had faith in popular government, but they were also convinced that a democratic government was potentially tyrannical. They feared that a majority might get carried away with the emotions of the moment and support a demagogue who would lead the country to ruin. To guard against the possibility, the Constitution allowed the people to elect directly only the House of Representatives. U.S. senators, federal judges, and the president would be chosen through indirect forms of popular elections.

The Anti-Federalists charged that this arrangement denied to the people the degree of control over their leadership that a democratic government required. The fear was that officeholders would be so far beyond popular control that they would serve themselves rather than the people. And even if they were committed to the public's interests, they would be so far removed from the people as to have no real understanding of their needs. For their critics, these provisions of the Constitution were a blueprint not for a government by the people, but for rule by an entrenched and distant elite.

This chapter traces the debate over representation that has stretched from the ratification of the Constitution in 1787 to the issue of term limitation in the 1990s. The chapter concentrates on the theory and practice of representative

[2]Quoted in Micah L. Sifry, "Let Them Vote for 'None of the Above,'" *The Nation,* September 10, 1990, 240.

★ ANALYZE THE ISSUE

Term Limitation
Term limitation would deal with the problem of entrenched leadership by limiting the number of terms that an elected official could serve. What would be the costs and the benefits if term limitation was widely applied? On balance, do you favor or oppose the idea?

government as originally expressed in the Constitution and as modified by two centuries of governing experience. The major ideas presented in the chapter are these:

★ *The structure of government provided by the Constitution is based on the idea that political power must be separated from immediate popular influences if sound policies are to result.* This idea was central to the Framers' theory of government and still has its advocates today.

★ *The idea of popular government—in which the majority's desires have a relatively direct and immediate impact on public policy—has gained strength since the nation's beginning.* Political parties and primary elections have increased the public's direct influence on the national government. The impulse for these developments has come largely from the American people themselves and from leaders acting on the majority's behalf.

★ *At the root of the debate over the proper form of representative government is an irreconcilable difference of opinion about worst consequences.* Those who fear a concentration of power in the hands of the majority believe that it leads to a government that does not respect the legitimate interests of the minority and produces short-sighted policies. Those who fear a lack of power in the hands of the majority claim that it leads to a government that serves primarily the rights and interests of the upper classes and the governing officials who act as their agents.

▷ *Representation in the Constitution*

To the Framers, a representative government that worked effectively only in good times was undeserving of respect. The true test of a governing system was its ability to withstand the stress of a period of desperation and fear. And in this regard, the record of democracies left much to be desired. In 1786, for example, debtors had gained control of Rhode Island's legislature and made paper money a legal means of paying debts, even though existing contracts called for payment in gold. Creditors were then hunted down and held captive in public places so that debtors could come and pay them in full with worthless paper money. A Boston newspaper wrote that Rhode Island should be renamed *Rogue* Island.

In the Framers' judgment, a great risk of popular government was **tyranny of the majority.** Inflamed by a personality or issue of the moment, the majority could become an irrational mob with no regard for other viewpoints. There would be times, James Madison wrote in *Federalist* No. 10, when "[the] passions . . . , not the reason of the public, would sit in judgment." Moreover, an unreasoning majority would be hard to contain because it would hold to the simpleminded democratic belief that the majority's view is always superior to any view a minority might hold. The fear was not that the government would ignore the majority's will, but that it would comply with the majority's unjust demands. The majority would serve itself at the expense of the minority. Yet, in fact, the minority also had its rights and interests, including property, liberty, and a fair chance to persuade the majority of the merits of its opinions.

The Framers also believed that a government driven by popular demands would be unstable and erratic. To be effective, government requires the stability to weather crises and the purposefulness to see policies through. An unreasoning majority, in the Framers' minds, would not be likely to promote either of these characteristics. The people would change leaders and policies at the first sign that things were not going well, which would serve only to make matters worse.

The Framers were not, as is sometimes alleged, opposed to a government based on popular control. On the contrary, they rejected any form of government that was not rooted in popular sovereignty. Their goal was a popular government that was tempered in ways that would enable it to avoid the worst excesses of democracy. As they read history, "pure" democracy was a dangerous system of government. Said James Madison in *Federalist* No. 10: "It may be concluded . . . that such [uncontrolled] democracies have ever been spectacles of turbulence and contention; have ever been found incompatible with personal security or the rights of property; and have in general been as short in their lives, as they have been violent in their deaths."

The Framers' solution was to combine elements of democracy with elements of republicanism. Today the terms **democracy** and **republic** are used interchangeably to refer to a system of government in which ultimate political power rests with the people through their capacity to choose representatives in free and open elections. In 1787, however, "democracy" and "republic" each had more than one meaning. When the Framers complained about the risks of democracy, they were referring to "pure democracy," in which the people were allowed to decide all issues of policy and leadership directly. The Framers did not reject another meaning of "democracy": government based on the will of the people. The meaning of the term "republic" was more general. It was used in the late 1700s in reference to any government that was not a monarchy. In their use of the term "republic," the Framers had a particular kind of nonmonarchical government in mind: representative government. When elected officials met in representative institutions to decide policy, that was republican government of the type the Framers admired.[3]

Madison summarized the Framers' intent when he said in *Federalist* No. 10 that the Constitution was "a republican remedy" for the excesses historically associated with democratic rule. The objective was a government that would be sensitive to the majority's immediate concerns yet deliberative enough to promote society's more general and enduring interests. No form of self-government could eliminate the threat of majority tyranny or the possibility of political instability, but the Framers believed that these dangers would be greatly diminished by properly structured institutions.[4]

The Framers' concept of **representative democracy** was similar to an idea put forth by the English theorist Edmund Burke (1729–1797). In his *Letter to the Sheriffs of Bristol*, Burke argued that representatives should act as public **trustees:** they are obliged to promote the interest of those who elected them, but the nature of this interest is for them, not the voters, to decide. Burke was concerned about the ease with which society could degenerate into selfishness, and he thought it imperative for representatives not to surrender their judgment to popular whim.

Edmund Burke, English political theorist. (The Bettmann Archive)

---

[3]Martin Diamond, *The Founding of the Democratic Republic* (Itasca, Ill.: F.E. Peacock Publishers, 1981), 62–71.
[4]*Federalist* No. 10.

LIMITED POPULAR RULE

Under the Constitution, all power is exercised through representative institutions. The Constitution has no provision for any form of direct popular participation in the making of public policy. In view of the fact that the United States was much too large to be governed directly by the people in popular assemblies, the Framers felt they had no choice but to establish representative systems. The Framers went beyond necessity, however, and placed officials at a considerable distance from the people they represented (see Table 4-1).

The House of Representatives was the only institution that would be based on direct popular election—its members would be elected for two-year terms of office through vote of the people. Frequent and direct election of House members was intended to make government sensitive to the concerns of popular majorities. The Constitution specified, however, that the House could have no more than one representative for every 30,000 inhabitants; this provision was designed to ensure that each representative would represent a large area and population and thus not be bound too closely to local concerns.[5]

U.S. senators would be appointed by the legislatures of the states they represented. Because state legislators were popularly elected, the people would be choosing their senators indirectly. Every two years, a third of the senators would be appointed to six-year terms. The Senate was expected to check and balance the House, which, by virtue of the more frequent and direct election of its members, would presumably be more responsive to popular opinion.

Presidential selection was an issue of considerable debate at the Philadelphia convention. Hamilton favored a life-term president, but others feared that life tenure would turn the office into a monarchy. Another proposal was to have the president chosen by Congress, but this suggestion was defeated on the argument that it would upset the balance between the legislative and executive branches, since one would be appointing the chief of the other. Direct election of the president was twice proposed and twice rejected because the delegates were uneasy about linking executive power directly to popular majorities.

The Framers finally chose to have the president selected by the votes of electors (the so-called Electoral College). Each state would have as many electors as it had members in Congress and could select them by any method it chose. Each elector would vote for two candidates for president. The candidate who received the largest number of electoral votes, if that number constituted a

[5]Ibid.

TABLE 4-1 Methods of Choosing National Leaders Fearing the concentration of political power, the Framers devised alternative methods of selection and terms of service for national officials.

Office	Method of Selection	Term of Service
President	Electoral College	4 years
U.S. senator	State legislature	6 years (1/3 of senators' terms expire every 2 years)
U.S. representative	Popular election	2 years
Federal judge	Nominated by president, approved by Senate	Indefinite (subject to "good behavior")

Davy Crockett (1786–1836) campaigning for election to the U.S. House of Representatives in Tennessee. Representatives were the only national leaders that the Framers designated to be elected directly by the people. (The Bettmann Archive)

majority (that is, more than 50 percent), would be selected as president; the runner-up would become vice-president. If no candidate won a majority, the election would go to the House of Representatives, which would choose the president from among the top five finishers. The president would serve a four-year term and be eligible for reelection.

With regard to the Supreme Court justices, the Philadelphia convention was in general agreement that they should be appointed rather than elected. At first the delegates decided that the Senate should make the appointments, but they finally chose to have judges nominated by the president and confirmed through approval by the Senate. Once confirmed, the Constitution declared, judges "shall hold their offices during good behavior." Although the selection procedure tied the judiciary to the other branches, the Framers intended to ensure an independent judiciary by allowing judges, in effect, to hold office for life unless they committed a crime. The Supreme Court would be more of a "guardian" institution than a "representative" one.[6]

These differing methods of selecting national officers would not prevent a determined majority from achieving full power if it had sufficient strength and longevity, but control could not be attained easily or quickly. The House of Representatives might surrender to an impassioned majority in a single election, but the Senate, presidency, and judiciary were unlikely to yield so quickly. The delay would reduce the probability that government would degenerate into mob rule. The Framers believed that majority tyranny would be impulsive. Given time, the people would presumably come to their senses.

ANTI-FEDERALIST DISSENT

The Anti-Federalists viewed the Constitution's scheme of representation as at best a severe restriction on majority rule and at worst an elaborate conspiracy by the Federalists to secure power for the wealthy. As the Anti-Federalists saw it,

[6]Leslie F. Goldstein, "Judicial Review and Democratic Theory: Guardian Democracy vs. Representative Democracy," *Western Political Quarterly* 40 (1987): 391–412.

This 1793 cartoon depicts the Anti-Federalists as a "club" gathering to condemn the Federalist government. Jefferson stands with an auctioneer's gavel, wondering "whether 'tis nobler in the mind to knock down [that is, auction off] dry goods with this hammer or with this head to continue some means of knocking down a Government and on its ruins raise myself to Eminence and Fortune." (Historical Picture Service)

the Constitution was not a bulwark against mob rule, but a barrier to rule by the people. The Senate and presidency in particular were seen as elite institutions.

Richard Henry Lee of Virginia criticized even the House of Representatives, which he said had "very little democracy in it" because each of its members would represent a large population and area. Madison had claimed that this arrangement was necessary because otherwise representatives would be "unduly attached" to local interests and "too little fit to comprehend and pursue great and national objects." To Lee and others, such arguments were a mask for elitism—rule by a few who claimed to know the people's interest better than the people knew it themselves.[7]

Modifying the Framers' Work: Toward a More Democratic System

The Framers' conception of self-government was at odds with the one held by many Americans in 1787. The promise that they would govern themselves was one of the reasons that ordinary people had made great sacrifices during the American Revolution. The democratic spirit of the Revolution was reflected in the constitutions of the states. Every state but South Carolina held annual legislative elections, and several states also chose their governors through annual election by the people.[8]

[7]Richard Henry Lee, "Letters from the Federal Farmer," in Forrest McDonald, ed., *Empire and Nation* (Englewood Cliffs, N.J.: Prentice-Hall, 1962), 103–117.
[8]Rosemarie Zagarri, "Two Revolutions," *New Republic*, May 28, 1984, 10.

In this context, the Constitution's provisions for popular rule were rather thin. Of course, the structure of the national government was a more complicated issue than was the structure of the state governments. This consideration, however, did not satisfy the proponents of popular rule, and it was not long after ratification of the Constitution that Americans sought a stronger voice in their own governing. The search has continued throughout the country's history: in no other constitutional area have Americans shown a greater willingness to experiment with new arrangements.

THE ERA OF JEFFERSONIAN DEMOCRACY

Thomas Jefferson, who otherwise admired the Constitution, was among the prominent Americans who questioned its provisions for self-government. To Jefferson, America was the hope of ordinary people everywhere for liberation from rule by the elite few, and he reasoned that the American people might someday rebel against the small governing role assigned them by the Constitution.[9]

Ironically, it was Jefferson who may have spared the nation a bloody revolution over the issue of popular sovereignty. Under John Adams, the nation's second president and a thoroughgoing elitist, the national government increasingly favored the nation's wealthy interests. Adams publicly suggested that the Constitution was designed for a governing elite, while Alexander Hamilton urged him to use force if necessary to suppress popular dissent.[10]

[9]Hannah Arendt, *On Revolution* (New York: Viking, 1963), ch. 6.
[10]Benjamin Ginsberg, *The Consequences of Consent* (New York: Random House, 1982), 22.

The Framers' limitations on popular rule upset many Americans who had sacrificed a great deal in order to win the right to self-government. In this 1775 painting a Minuteman takes a sad leave of his family to go off and fight the British troops. (The Bettmann Archive)

Jefferson asked whether Adams, with the aid of a strong army, planned soon to deprive ordinary Americans of their freedoms altogether. Jefferson challenged Adams in the next presidential election and, upon defeating him, hailed the victory as the "Revolution of 1800."

Although Jefferson was a champion of the common people, he had no clear vision of how a popular government might work in practice. He believed that legislative majorities were the proper expression of the public's interest and accordingly was reluctant to use his presidency for this purpose.[11] Jefferson also had no illusions about a largely illiterate population's readiness for a significant governing role and feared the consequences of inciting the public to pursue their resentment of the moneyed class. An assault on the wealthy, in Jefferson's opinion, would be not only wrong but also destructive of the nation's general prosperity, and therefore ruinous to all. Jeffersonian democracy was thus mainly a revolution of the spirit; Jefferson taught Americans to look upon the national government as belonging to all, not just to the privileged few.[12]

THE ERA OF JACKSONIAN DEMOCRACY

Not until Andrew Jackson became president in 1828 did the country have a powerful leader who was willing and able to involve the public more fully in government. Jackson carried out the constitutional revolution that Jefferson had foreshadowed.

The President as a Popular Leader

Jackson recognized that the president was the only official who could easily claim to represent all the people. Unlike the president, members of Congress were elected from separate states and districts rather than from the whole of the country. Yet the president's claim to popular leadership was diminished by the existence of the Electoral College. If the president and the people were to be brought closer together so that each could draw power from the other, the office would have to rest on popular election. Jackson first tried to persuade Congress to initiate an amendment that would abolish the electoral voting system. Failing in this effort, Jackson persuaded the states to make popular voting the basis for choosing their presidential electors. By 1832, all states except South Carolina had done so.

Jackson's reform is still in effect today and basically places the choice of a president in the voters' hands. The winner of the popular vote in each state is awarded its electoral votes, and the probability is strong that the candidate who wins the popular-vote contest will also receive a majority of electoral votes. Since Jackson's time, only twice has the loser of the popular vote won the presidency (Rutherford B. Hayes in 1876 and Benjamin Harrison in 1888).

The "Spoils System"

Andrew Jackson also sought to put an end to the aristocracy of wealth that had been governing the country through control of public offices. He urged the

---

[11]Robert Dahl, *Pluralist Democracy* (Chicago: Rand McNally, 1967), 92.
[12]This interpretation is taken from Walter Lippmann, *Public Opinion* (New York: Free Press, 1965), 178–179.

CIVIL SERVICE REFORM.

Office-Seeker. "St. Jackson, can't you save us? Can't *you* give us something?"

Andrew Jackson used his presidency to institute rotation in public office, but the result of this civil service "reform" was the spoils system, whereby offices became available every four years for the victorious party to hand out to loyal followers. (New York Public Library)

states to abolish property ownership as a condition for voting, promoted rotation of office as a means of keeping officials in close touch with the people, and appointed common people to high administrative posts. Politically outnumbered, the nation's upper classes could only deride Jackson's policies as a mere "spoils system." Believing that "to the victor belong the spoils," Jackson had appointed his campaign workers to government posts of all kinds (see Chapter 12).

The "Party Constitution"

Jacksonian democracy's greatest contribution to majority government was the grass-roots political party. America's first parties, the Federalists and the Republicans, had developed in the 1790s out of disputes between Hamilton and Jefferson over national policy. These parties were thoroughly dominated by political and community leaders. Ordinary citizens had no large role in them.[13]

Andrew Jackson had a different kind of political party in mind.[14] He wanted a

[13]See Joseph Charles, *The Origins of the American Party System* (New York: Harper & Row, 1961).
[14]See Richard P. McCormick, *The Second American Party System* (Chapel Hill: University of North Carolina Press, 1966).

Jacksonian democracy vastly increased the participation of ordinary citizens in party elections. As this painting (*Verdict of the People*, by George Caleb Bingham) shows, however, "ordinary citizens" at the time did not include women or blacks. (The black man in the foreground is passing by, not participating in the political event.) (Courtesy of the Boatmen's Bank, St. Louis)

party built from the "grass roots"—that is, based on participation at the local level by ordinary citizens. Its strength would be its popular base, not its ties to the elite. By the election of 1832, Jackson's Democratic party had enlisted the participation of thousands of citizens. The election of 1832 also marked the appearance of the party nominating convention in presidential politics.

Jackson's protégé and successor as president, Martin Van Buren, shared Jackson's admiration of political parties. Van Buren was connected with New York City's Tammany Hall, one of the country's first party "machines," and he realized that parties could revolutionize government. In the absence of strong parties, Van Buren concluded, government naturally serves the interests of the rich and powerful. When ordinary citizens are not organized in parties, they lack power; individually they cannot hope to compete against people of wealth and status. Through party organization, however, ordinary citizens can act together as a voting majority that is capable of gaining political control by electing leaders committed to their interests.[15]

This vision of strong national parties was never fully realized in the United States, partly because federalism and the separation of powers have enabled party organizations and leaders in various states and institutions to hold differing views of their party's principles (see Chapter 12). Nevertheless, the development of grass-roots political parties in the 1830s gave the people a powerful means of collective influence. Until then, each voter had a say only in the selection of his single representative. With the advent of grass-roots parties, a majority of individuals throughout the nation, united by affiliation with a political party, could choose a majority of representatives who shared the same

[15]James MacGregor Burns, *The Vineyard of Liberty* (New York: Knopf, 1982), 372.

policy goals. Majority opinion could thereby be more readily translated into public policy. So fundamental was the emergence of the grass-roots party to the influence of the people that the historian James MacGregor Burns has called it America's "second constitution."[16]

When the Frenchman Alexis de Tocqueville visited America in the early 1830s—at the peak of Jacksonian democracy—he felt compelled to say that "in the United States, the majority governs." But Tocqueville's evaluation was not altogether favorable. "I know of no country," he said, "in which there is so little independence of thought and real freedom of discussion as in America." In Tocqueville's judgment, Americans had a tendency to follow blindly the majority's lead. If a majority held an opinion, it seemed to him that others not only failed to question it, but embraced it. Tocqueville was fearful of rule by impulsive majorities.[17]

Alexis de Tocqueville, astute French observer of the young American democracy. (The Bettmann Archive)

I know of no country in which there is so little independence of thought and real freedom of discussion as in America.
Alexis de Tocqueville

THE PROGRESSIVE ERA

After the 1840s, the parties gradually drifted toward localism and favoritism. In the cities especially, they were taken over by powerful party bosses with an appetite for patronage. By the 1880s, some party bosses were in league with the robber barons to block government from regulating business trusts (see Chapter 2).[18]

Progressive reformers looked for ways to weaken the power of corporations and party bosses and to give the public a greater voice in politics. In its Declaration of Principles of 1911, the National Progressive League defined its goal as "the promotion of popular government." The Progressives rejected the Burkean idea (discussed earlier in this chapter) of representatives as trustees; they embraced instead the idea of representatives as **delegates**—officeholders who are obligated to respond directly to the expressed opinions of the people whom they represent.

The Progressive movement was made possible by changes in education and communication during the nation's first century. In 1787 the vast majority of Americans were illiterate, and many of those who could read could not afford the hand-printed newspapers of the time. During the nineteenth century, however, a broad-based public school system was created, and the invention of the high-speed printing press led to the "penny" newspaper. By the time of the Progressive movement, literacy was widespread in America, as was newspaper readership. Ordinary Americans believed themselves to be politically informed and wanted the greater influence that the Progressives promised.

As with other political reform movements, the Progressives were driven as much by political considerations as by a desire for reform. If the movement succeeded, the losers would be big business and Catholic-dominated urban machines. Most Progressives were small businesspeople, small townspeople, and Protestants.

[16]Ibid., 368.
[17]Alexis de Tocqueville, *Democracy in America* (1835–1840), ed. J. P. Mayer (Garden City, N.Y.: Doubleday/Anchor, 1969), bk. I, chs. 15, 16.
[18]See William Allen White, "The Boss System," in Richard Hofstadter, ed., *The Progressive Movement, 1900–1915* (Englewood Cliffs, N.J.: Prentice-Hall, 1963), 104–107.

The public school system, which developed in the nineteenth century, made Americans more literate and thereby better qualified to participate in politics. The Progressive movement's call for increased popular participation in government relied on literate and well-informed citizens. (The Bettmann Archive)

Progressive Reforms

Two of the Progressives' reforms gave voting majorities the direct power to decide policy at the state and local levels. One device was the *initiative,* which allows citizens through petition to place legislative measures on the ballot. A related measure was the *referendum,* which permits legislative bodies to submit proposals to the voters for approval or rejection. The Progressives also sought to give the public recourse against wayward state and local officials through the *recall,* in which citizens petition for the removal of an elected official before the scheduled completion of his or her term of office.

The Progressives also promoted nonpartisan local elections, the extension of the merit system, the conversion of municipal utilities from private to public, the awarding of government contracts through competitive bidding rather than political dealing, and the administration of municipal government through city managers or commissions. These ways of governing were not adopted everywhere. The Progressives were stronger in the newer, less urbanized states of the Midwest and West, and these states were much more likely than those of the East and South to adopt Progressive reforms.

In terms of national politics, a significant Progressive reform was the direct election of U.S. senators, who, before the Seventeenth Amendment was ratified in 1913, had been chosen by state legislatures and were widely perceived as agents of big business (the Senate was nicknamed the "millionaires' club"). Earlier attempts to amend the Senate election procedure were blocked by the senators, who stood to lose their seats if they had to submit to direct vote by the people. Eventually, however, the Senate was persuaded to support an amendment by pressure from the Progressives and by revelations that corporate bribes had influenced the selection of several senators.

Of the many Progressive reforms, the most significant was the *primary election,* which gave rank-and-file voters a voice in the selection of party nominees. Party bosses would no longer have absolute control of nominations, which had been a chief source of their power. No greater blow to political parties can be imagined. When a party does not have the power to select its candidates, it cannot command their loyalty to its organizational and policy goals. Candidates will embrace or reject their party as it suits their needs. In other democracies, which have no primary elections, parties have retained control of the nominating process and therefore have remained strong. (Chapter 12 discusses party organization in detail.)

Political parties in America were further undercut in the early twentieth century by the extension of merit-based civil service, which cost the parties thousands of patronage jobs. By 1916, elections were becoming "advertising-style" campaigns in which candidates appealed to the voters directly rather than through party organizations.[19] The time was coming when no institution of any strength would stand between the voters and their representatives (see Chapters 10 and 12).

Paradoxically, the emergence of candidate-centered campaigns may have ultimately weakened the public's hold on government. The relationship between the individual representative and the voters of his or her election district is the basis of the candidate-centered campaign. The voters have the opportunity to choose a representative, but only in a lesser sense can they be said to have the opportunity to choose a government. Candidates run on individual platforms, so that what happens in one district is not necessarily linked to what happens in another. By comparison, where political parties are strong, as in European democracies, all candidates of the same party run on the same platform. The voters thus have a common choice regardless of the district in which they live. By electing a majority of candidates from one party, the voters are essentially choosing a government based on the platform put forth by that party. A strong party system also makes it easier for a popular majority to

[19]Richard Jensen, "American Election Campaigns," paper delivered at Midwest Political Science Association meetings, Chicago, May 1968.

HOW THE NATIONAL POLITICAL SYSTEM WAS MADE MORE RESPONSIVE TO POPULAR MAJORITIES

EARLIER SITUATION	SUBSEQUENT DEVELOPMENT
Separation of powers, as a means of dividing authority and blunting passionate majorities.	Political parties, as a means of uniting authorities and linking them with popular majorities.
Indirect election of all national officials except House members, as a means of buffering officials from popular influence.	Direct election of U.S. senators, and popular voting for president (linked to electoral votes), as means of increasing popular control of officials
Nomination of candidates for public office through political party organizations.	Primary elections, as means of selecting party nominees.

hold candidates accountable for the actions of government. The in-party is responsible for public policy, and its candidates can be voted out of office if the policy fails. In the case of candidate-centered campaigns, however, the line of responsibility between the candidate and the policies of government is weak or nonexistent. Each candidate can say that he or she does not have the power to enact legislation singlehanded and thus is not personally responsible for policy failure.

The Progressives had the support of two strong presidents, Theodore Roosevelt (1901–1909) and Woodrow Wilson (1913–1921), who shared the Progressives' opposition to business monopolies but also recognized the power inherent in a popular presidency. Roosevelt described the office as a "bully pulpit." Wilson, writing about the president's potential for national leadership, said: "His is the only national voice in public affairs. Let him once win the admiration and confidence of the country, and no other single voice will easily overpower him."[20] Roosevelt and Wilson's conception of the president as national leader, legitimized through election by a majority of voters, helped to change the president's image. In the view of the public, the president was superseding Congress as the chief instrument of democracy (see Chapter 18).

Ironically, as the American system was being opened to greater popular participation early in this century, the power of government was increasing.[21] This parallel development was no coincidence. Although open elections are a means to popular influence, they are also a means by which government accumulates power. Official actions gain legitimacy when they are pursued in the name of a public that has freely chosen a leadership to act on its behalf. Although George Bernard Shaw was overgeneralizing, he was not completely off the mark when he concluded, "The more democratic a government is the more authoritative it is."[22]

Beard's Economic Theory of the Constitution

In the Progressives' view, the Framers had erred in giving the majority too little power. Not surprisingly, the Progressive movement spawned attacks on the Framers. A notable work in this vein is the historian Charles S. Beard's *Economic Interpretation of the Constitution*.[23] Arguing that the Constitution grew out of wealthy Americans' fear of debtor rebellions, Beard claimed that its elaborate systems of power and representation were devices for keeping power in the hands of the rich. As evidence, Beard cited the Constitution's protections of property (see Chapter 6) and referred to James Madison's secret notes on the Philadelphia convention, which showed that property interests were high on the delegates' list of priorities.

Beard further noted that not one of the delegates was a workingman or small farmer. Most of the Framers had large landholdings, controlled substantial

> ★ ANALYZE THE ISSUE
>
> **Reform of Government**
> The Progressive era was a major period of reform. What does it suggest about the ability of self-government to renew itself? Do you see a need for reform today? Is the United States sufficiently democratic? If you believe that it is not, what reforms might reasonably be introduced?

[20]Woodrow Wilson, *Constitutional Government in the United States* (New York: Columbia University Press, 1908), 67.
[21]Ginsberg, *Consequences of Consent*, ch. 1.
[22]George Bernard Shaw to editor of *New Republic*, 1936, reprinted in ibid., August 8 and 15, 1988, 32.
[23]Charles S. Beard, *An Economic Interpretation of the Constitution* (1913; New York: Macmillan, 1941).

interests, or were major bank creditholders. This dominance of the Philadelphia convention by wealthy men reflected the fact that the delegates had been chosen by the state legislatures, which were controlled by the propertied classes. Only Rhode Island's legislature was in nonpropertied hands—and, as Beard noted, only Rhode Island refused to send a delegation to Philadelphia.

Beard's thesis was challenged by other historians, and he later acknowledged that he had not taken the Framers' full array of motives into account. Their concept of separation of powers, for example, was a time-honored governing principle that had previously been incorporated in state constitutions. Nevertheless, the Framers' system of representation was premised on a fear of unrestricted popular majorities and allowed the states to restrict suffrage. The Constitution required only that a state impose no stricter qualifications for voting in elections for the U.S. House of Representatives than were applied to elections for the larger house of the state legislature. The states allowed only propertied white males to vote, and it would seem likely that a majority of the Framers believed that suffrage should be limited to this class. But it would be inaccurate to conclude that the Framers were blatantly antidemocratic by the standards of their time. Property ownership was relatively widespread in America in the late eighteenth century, and in some states half or more of adult white males were eligible to vote.[24]

RECENT DEVELOPMENTS: POLLS, TELEVISION, AND PRESIDENTIAL NOMINATIONS

The Progressive movement declined in the 1920s, after most of its institutional reforms had been achieved. If it had not subsided then, it would surely have done so in the 1930s, when the Western world's trust in majority government was shaken by developments in Europe, particularly in Germany. Germany's Weimar Republic had been founded on popular institutions; it was about as close as any modern nation had come to establishing a pure democracy. When the Weimar Republic degenerated first into chaos and then into Hitler's Third Reich, its demise seemed only to confirm Madison's assertion, quoted earlier in this chapter, that direct democracies are "spectacles of turbulence and contention . . . as short in their lives as they have been violent in their deaths."[25]

Nevertheless, the idea of popular government regained strength in the United States after World War II, when changes in communications, technology, and political organization brought the American people and their representatives into an increasingly close relationship. The new mass medium of television began to enable political leaders to reach the public more easily. And as televised politics became routine, more Americans came to believe that leaders *should* deal with the public directly rather than through political parties.[26]

This perspective was evident during the late 1960s, when reform Democrats

---

[24]Bruce A. Campbell, *The American Electorate* (New York: Holt, Rinehart and Winston, 1979), 12–13.
[25]*Federalist* No. 10.
[26]See Richard L. Rubin, *Press, Party, and Presidency* (New York: Norton, 1981), 191–196.

sought a change in the presidential nominating system. In 1968 the leaders of the Democratic party nominated Hubert H. Humphrey, who, as Lyndon Johnson's vice-president, was associated with the unpopular Vietnam war. Antiwar Democrats challenged the legitimacy of Humphrey's nomination because he had not participated in a single primary election. When Humphrey then lost the general election to Richard Nixon, reform-minded Democrats demanded a change from a nominating system dominated by party leaders to one controlled by the party's rank-and-file voters through primaries and open caucuses. Their position easily prevailed.

Advances in public opinion polling have also drawn the American people and their leaders into a closer relationship.[27] Franklin D. Roosevelt made use of polls to assess public opinion during the Great Depression and World War II, but it was not until the Kennedy administration that polling became a routine part of White House activity. John Kennedy had worked closely with pollster Louis Harris in developing strategy during his 1960 presidential campaign, and he built polling into his White House operations. Since then, every president has used polls to track his popularity and to detect changes in public opinion. Of recent presidents, none has made more use of polls than George Bush. Late in 1991, for example, after polls showed a weakening of the public's support for his presidency and a growing level of concern with rising health costs, Bush directed his staff to begin work on a health-care initiative that would be ready to present to Congress in time for the 1992 presidential election.

Although officeholders do not always do what the polls indicate the American public would like to see done, they are wary of issues on which majority opinion is intense. Vast resources are invested in polling by officials at nearly all levels of government, from city councils to the Congress of the United States. (Public opinion polling is discussed in detail in Chapter 8.)

The Continuing Debate over the Majority's Role

The United States today has a hybrid system of representation, one that combines original countermajoritarian elements with newer majoritarian aspects. The present system of representative government in the United States, as we have seen, has been created piecemeal. New elements have been added to old ones, which in turn have been variously kept, modified, or superseded. In no other area of their constitutional system have Americans been so willing to experiment. Presidential electors and primary elections, for example, are American inventions, which other countries have chosen not to copy.

In certain respects, the U.S. political system is a model of popular control. No other democracy conducts elections for its larger legislative chamber more frequently than does the United States, and no democracy requires more frequent election of its chief executive. In addition, as we just noted, the United States is the only country that relies extensively on primary elections for the selection of party nominees; elsewhere, they are selected by party organiza-

---

[27]See Lawrence R. Jacobs, "The Recoil Effect: Public Opinion and Policy Making in the U.S. and Britain," *Comparative Politics* 24 (January 1992): 199–217.

★ HOW THE UNITED STATES COMPARES

ELECTING AND GOVERNING

All democracies are characterized by free and open elections, but not all democracies have the same electoral systems. The United States has a separation of powers and elects its chief executive separately from its legislators. The result in five of the last six presidential elections has been a divided government, with the presidency held by one party and one or both houses of Congress held by the other. When such a division occurs, the people's influence is diluted. By electing a Republican president and a Democratic-controlled Congress, for example, Americans in a sense deny themselves a majority government.

Parliamentary systems, such as Great Britain's, provide a stronger and more direct opportunity for majority influence through elections. Voters choose the legislators, who then choose one of their members to be the prime minister, who serves as the chief executive. Legislative and executive power are thus combined in one institution, the control of which is determined in each national election. In the United States, control of government is not necessarily at stake in a national election. House elections take place every two years, a presidential election is held every four years, and senators are elected at two-year intervals to six-year terms.

tions. The principle of popular election to office, which the writers of the Constitution regarded as a prerequisite of popular sovereignty but also one to be used sparingly, has been extended further in the United States than anywhere else.

In other respects, however, the U.S. system is less democratic than many others. Popular majorities must work against the barriers to influence—the elaborate system of divided powers, staggered terms of office, and separate constituencies—that were devised by the Framers. In fact, if democracy is defined by the directness with which an electoral majority leads to a governing majority, the American system ranks low in comparison with European systems. In Great Britain, Germany, Sweden, and other European democracies, when the voters go to the polls, one party is almost certain to capture full control of legislative and executive power, leaving no doubt that its policy agenda should prevail. The will of the majority is expressed through the platform of the victorious party. The situation is different in the United States. Since World War II, the voters have elected a president and a majority in one or both houses of Congress from different parties for more years than they have elected a president and a congressional majority of the same party.

The majority's intentions are not at all evident when the White House and Congress are divided between the parties. In 1986, President Reagan's communications director, Patrick Buchanan, accused congressional Democrats of thwarting the will of the American people by opposing Reagan's Central American policy. Buchanan claimed that Reagan's landslide reelection victory in 1984 was a mandate for his policies, including his efforts to influence the outcome of civil wars in El Salvador and Nicaragua. But did Reagan have a clear-cut mandate? The Democrats had won a landslide of their own in 1984, gaining a 253–182-seat advantage in the House of Representatives. The fact is, the U.S. constitutional system gives no precedence to either the president or Congress. The system is based on a separation of powers and different methods of election, which make it difficult for a voting majority to assert its power.

The issue today, as it has always been, is not whether the U.S. political

Democracy requires participation, and the most fundamental way to participate is to vote. Residents of a low-income housing project in Montgomery, Alabama, were targeted in this voter registration drive in 1990. (Steven Rubin/Impact Visuals)

system is democratic but whether it is democratic enough. The history of representative government in America has been a history of periodic reform, and the winds of reform are stirring again. The tradition represented by the Jacksonians and the Progressives is growing in strength.

Modern advocates of popular government point to uncompetitive campaigns, special-interest money, and low voter turnout as signs of a need for political reform. They have proposed a variety of solutions, including term limitation, public financing of campaigns, restrictions on televised political advertising, and automatic voter registration. (Later chapters will examine these topics more fully.)

Other proposals do not stop with election reform. Political scientist Benjamin Barber has recommended, for example, that governing decisions be shifted from the national level to the local level, where the opportunities for direct citizen influence are greater, and from the private sector to the public sector, which would expand the range of policies decided by popular participation. Barber contends that, by not encouraging a greater degree of popular participation, the U.S. system has failed to realize its full democratic potential.[28] His proposal is premised on the view, which stems from the philosophical tradition of Rousseau and John Stuart Mill, that participation in civic life has an enlightening influence on the citizen that can be obtained in no other way. Through participation, the individual gains a sense of civic virtue and commitment that is the foundation for a truly civil society.[29]

---

[28]Benjamin Barber, *Strong Democracy: Participatory Politics for a New Age* (Berkeley: University of California Press, 1984).
[29]Carole Pateman, *Democratic Theory* (New York: Cambridge University Press, 1970), 3.

★ CRITICAL THINKING

"STRONG DEMOCRACY"?

The possibilities for popular government have always been more limited in national politics than local politics. Even at the time of the writing of the Constitution, the United States was too large to be governed except through representative institutions. The New England town meeting could work for a village, but it was unsuited to a large republic. The obstacle of size has led proponents of popular government to look toward local communities as a place where people can participate more directly in government.

A leading proponent of change is Benjamin Barber, who, in *Strong Democracy*, argues that the pessimistic view of human nature that underlies the Constitution contributes to "thin" democracy in America. Barber points out that voting, however important it may be as a symbolic and collective act, can be an insignificant individual act. It is very unlikely that one person's vote will make the difference between victory and defeat in an election campaign. Barber prefers a "strong democracy" in which citizens are provided widespread opportunities for participation, not only as a means of extending their influence, but as a way of developing into full citizens. Barber points out that people spend less time in voting than they do in taking out the garbage and that full citizenship will flower only when people involve themselves deeply and regularly in public affairs. In Barber's view, representative institutions, however important and necessary they may be, are no substitute for a participatory democracy.

Some advocates of popular government would even shift governing decisions from the national level to the local level, and from the private sector to the public sector, for the purpose of expanding the range of policies that could be decided through direct citizen participation. The objective is to achieve "a participatory democracy in all respects," in political theorist Carole Pateman's phrase.

Where do you stand on the issue of popular control? How directly should the people control their leaders? What policies, if any, would you shift from the national level to the local level, or from the private sector to the public sector, in order to increase the direct control of the public over the policies that govern it?

SOURCES: Benjamin Barber, *Strong Democracy: Participatory Politics for a New Age* (Berkeley: University of California Press, 1984); Carole Pateman, *Democratic Theory* (New York: Cambridge University Press, 1970).

Whatever their particular position, advocates of popular government share a central principle: that the people are far and away the most appropriate judges of their own interests. The idea that distant leaders understand the people's interests better than the people themselves has always struck some Americans either as fanciful speculation or as a pretext for self-serving rule by an elite. In this view, the possibility of tyranny by the majority, although a frightening prospect, is far more remote than the likelihood of tyranny by a self-interested elite. Although proponents of popular government recognize a need for effective leadership, they claim that a democratic society must give priority to the expressed wishes of the people, not the presumed wisdom of the leaders.

Although no one would disagree in principle with the idea that the people should govern themselves, there have always been those who believe, as did the Framers, that leaders must be given the opportunity to exercise independent judgment. They reject the notion that government should be run according to public opinion. Robert Nisbet, a conservative writer, has described the idea that public opinion should always prevail as the "great heresy . . . of modern democracies." Former U.S. Senator Thomas Eagleton, a liberal Democrat, has said that polls deprive leaders of the need to lead. "Today, you don't use your brain or your gut, all you use is your pollster," Eagleton said. If a democratic government is to be effective, Nisbet and Eagleton would argue, it cannot be

★ ANALYZE THE ISSUE

Representatives: Trustees or Delegates?
Should representatives act according to their judgment of what is best for the people, or should they act according to the will of their constituents? In other words, do you think representatives should be trustees or delegates?

★ THE MEDIA AND THE PEOPLE

NATIONAL "TOWN MEETINGS"

New communication technologies—including video-conferencing and interactive cable television—may soon bring changes to the practice of popular government. The possibilities are suggested by two pilot projects.

One project enables constituents in five congressional districts to use their home computers to communicate directly with their representative's office in Washington. The number of these messages has been found to peak just before votes are taken during House debates televised on C-SPAN, Congress's cable television network.

The other project, "QUBE," began in the late 1970s in Columbus, Ohio. QUBE used two-way cable to enable viewers to express their opinions on policy issues simply by pressing buttons on a console connected to their TV sets. Some observers predict enthusiastically that national "town meetings" through two-way cable are in America's future. Other observers are not convinced that teledemocracy is such a good idea. They point out that the agenda would be set not by the viewers but by the people who controlled the content of the program, and that the opinions expressed by viewers would not necessarily be representative of the views of the general public.

run by opinion polls, which measure unreflective and often whimsical opinions. It must act through deliberative institutions where established interests and time-honored values, in addition to public sentiments, are taken into account.[30]

The claim that representatives must look inward to their own understanding of the public interest, rather than outward to get the pulse of the people, is as characteristic of modern critics of popular government as it was of Edmund Burke and the Framers. Ironically, the argument finds support in public opinion polls, which show that the policy views of most citizens are seldom backed by an awareness of relevant facts (see Chapter 8). A poll taken in 1991 during the Persian Gulf war, for example, indicated that a majority of Americans believed the United States had clearly warned Iraq that an invasion of Kuwait would be met by military retaliation. In fact, the U.S. government had issued no such warning.

Reasoning from such evidence, proponents of the classical model of representation claim that the public is not equipped to tell its leaders which policies to pursue. In the classical scheme, the principle of majority rule is satisfactorily met when the people have the opportunity through periodic elections to pass judgment on what government has been doing. The fear of defeat at the polls is said to be incentive enough for officials to do their best to represent the people's interests and not their own.[31]

In short, the debate over representative government that began two centuries ago in Philadelphia is still going on. The issue centers on the balance between the influence of popular majorities and the influence of representative institutions. If greater weight is given to popular majorities, can they be trusted to respect the rights and interests of the minority? If the majority is outweighed by representative institutions, can those institutions be trusted to serve the majority's interests, and not those of a powerful minority? These are difficult questions, and we have no final or single answer to them. They will continue to

★ ANALYZE THE ISSUE

Term Limitation Revisited
An "Analyze the Issue" box at the beginning of the chapter asked for your opinion on term limitation. In view of what you have read in the chapter on the issue of representation, has your opinion changed? On balance, do you favor or oppose the idea of term limitation? Why?

[30]Robert Nisbet, "Public Opinion versus Popular Opinion," *Public Interest* 41 (1975): 169.
[31]See, for example, Karl Mannheim, *Freedom, Power, and Democratic Planning* (New York: Oxford University Press, 1950), 156–161.

be debated, and they deserve consideration by any student of American government. Later chapters will explore further the issue of popular influence in America.

Summary

Since 1787 a major issue of American politics has been the public's role in governing. The Framers of the Constitution respected the idea of self-government but distrusted popular majorities. They designed a government that they felt would temper popular opinion and slow its momentum, so that the public's "true interest" (which includes a regard for the rights and interests of the minority) would guide public policy. Different methods were established to select members of the House of Representatives and of the Senate, the president, and federal judges as a means of separating political power from momentary and unreflecting majorities. This philosophy of representative democracy was suggested in the writings of Burke, Locke, and Montesquieu and still has strong advocates to this day.

Since the adoption of the Constitution, however, the public has gradually assumed more direct control of its representatives, particularly through measures affecting the way in which officeholders are chosen. Political parties, presidential voting (linked to the Electoral College), and primary elections are among the devices aimed at strengthening the majority's influence. These developments are rooted in the idea, deeply held by ordinary Americans, that the people must have substantial direct control of their government if it is to serve their real interests. For advocates of majority rule, the alternative is government by privileged interests.

Major Concepts

delegates	term limitation
democracy	trustees
representative democracy	tyranny of the majority
republic	

Suggested Readings

Barber, Benjamin. *Strong Democracy: Participatory Politics for a New Age.* Berkeley: University of California, 1984. Contends that the American political system needs to adopt a participatory model of democracy, as opposed to the prevalent liberal model that harks back to the Framers.

Beard, Charles S. *An Economic Interpretation of the Constitution.* New York: Macmillan, 1941. Argues that the Founders had selfish economic interests uppermost in mind when they wrote the Constitution.

Goldwin, Robert S., and William A. Schambra, eds. *How Democratic Is the Constitution?* Washington, D.C.: American Enterprise Institute, 1980. Essays on various interpretations of the Constitution.

Lippmann, Walter. *The Phantom Public.* New York: Harcourt, Brace, 1925. Argues that the public's capacity to govern directly is extremely limited and that a democracy must take this into account in developing its institutions.

McDonald, Forrest. *We the People: The Economic Origins of the Constitution.* Chicago: University of Chicago Press, 1958. Argues against Beard's thesis that the Framers wrote the Constitution to suit their own economic needs.

Robinson, Donald, ed. *Reforming American Government.* Boulder, Colo.: Westview Press, 1985. A volume of papers by leading thinkers on issues of constitutional reform, including popular government.

Schattschneider, E. E. *The Semisovereign People: A Realist's View of Democracy in America.* New York: Holt, Rinehart and Winston, 1960. Contends that the public's influence depends mainly on fair, open, and partisan competition among elites for power.

Spitz, Elaine. *Majority Rule.* Chatham, N.J.: Chatham House, 1987. An analysis of majority rule which goes beyond the mechanical issue of vote counting.

Tocqueville, Alexis de. *Democracy in America,* vols. 1 and 2, ed. J. P. Mayer. New York: Doubleday/Anchor, 1969. A classic analysis (originally published 1835–1840) of American democracy by an insightful French observer.

Is Our Fragmented System of Government Adequate to Today's Needs?

JAMES L. SUNDQUIST

The risk of governmental impotence is far greater now than in most periods of our history.

The fragmented system of government designed for the United States two centuries ago brings both good news and bad news for us today.

The good news is that the dispersion of powers among the executive, legislative, and judicial branches —and, within the legislature, between the Senate and the House—has accomplished the Framers' purpose: it has forestalled tyranny. No individual or political clique has ever been able to gain enough control over the separated institutions to endanger the country with either of the specters that haunted the delegates to the constitutional convention—an absolute ruler disguised as a democratically elected president, or a rampant congressional majority trampling on the rights of the minority.

But the bad news is that a system that makes it difficult for evil or misguided leaders to assemble the powers of government for wicked or imprudent purposes also, inevitably, hinders the most public-spirited of leaders when they must assemble those powers to achieve proper and even noble ends.

As we enter the third century of our national life, the question is which represents the greater danger: the menace of a government that is too powerful and thus too capable of tyranny, or the threat that a government confronted with enormous challenges at home and abroad will prove too weak to discharge its responsibilities? I am among those who find the latter to be the greater danger. And the risk of governmental impo-

tence is far greater now than in most periods of our history, for two reasons.

First, the advance of technology has enmeshed the United States in an intricately interdependent world economy and an equally intertwined set of global political and security relationships that require the government to act promptly and decisively in concert with other governments to protect and advance the country's interests. When the president, the Senate, and the House pursue independent and contradictory policies, as they often do, the United States cannot cope effectively with the forces and events that weigh in upon it all around the globe.

Second, the difficulty of concerting the powers of government has been greatly increased by a disturbing recent political development: the tendency of the voters to entrust the executive and legislative branches to opposing political parties. In six of the nine presidential elections from 1956 to 1988, the people have chosen a Republican president but have returned Democratic majorities to the House of Representatives and, in four of those elections, to the Senate also. In these circumstances, the conflict between parties that is normal and healthy in a democracy becomes a debilitating struggle within the government itself, between a president and a Congress that simply must get together if they are to accomplish anything constructive.

To deplore a governmental system that fosters disunity where unity is needed, that inhibits the formation and execution of consistent and decisive policies, is of course far easier than to devise acceptable remedies. Perhaps President Bush can find the road to bipartisan harmony that eluded his Republican predecessors Eisenhower, Nixon, Ford, and Reagan, but history and political realism tell us that that is hardly likely. Constitutional reform is not an undertaking for the fainthearted, but it is high time to think seriously about this possible avenue to governmental unity.

James L. Sundquist is Senior Fellow Emeritus at The Brookings Institution. He is the author of Constitutional Reform and Effective Government.

Michael J. Malbin

The country's success has been tied directly to two ideas at the heart of its constitutional system: diversity and the separation of powers.

The single most important point to make about the U.S. Constitution is one that often gets lost in the shuffle. The United States—warts and all—has been a remarkable success. Moreover, the country's success has been tied directly to two ideas at the heart of its constitutional system: diversity (or multiplicity of factions, to use James Madison's terms) and the separation of powers.

Many critics of the Constitution have argued that the separation of powers does such a good job of preventing tyranny that it prevents the government from exercising power. If that argument were true, it would be a severe indictment. If the Framers had wanted a weak government, after all, they could have stayed with the Articles of Confederation.

Has the U.S. government, generally speaking, been paralyzed through most of its recent history? The answer is a pretty clear no—even, as David Mayhew's recent book, *Divided We Govern*, shows, when the presidency and Congress are controlled by different political parties. Much significant legislation was enacted during the administrations of Republican presidents Eisenhower (e.g., education and civil rights), Nixon (environmental and safety regulation), and Reagan (budget, taxes, and defense), when Congress was dominated by Democrats. The process may have been messy, but the results hardly amounted to stalemate.

Even when it comes to that most intractable of recent issues, controlling the budget deficit, the United States is not alone. At least into the late 1980s, the U.S. deficit as a percentage of GNP has generally been about average for industrialized democracies, most of which have parliamentary governments. That does not make the deficit a good thing, but it does raise questions about any separation-of-powers explanation unique to the United States.

What would be the effect of adopting parliamentary-style reforms in the United States? That would depend upon whether the system ended up with multiple parties (or factions) or two disciplined parties. With multiple parties, there is no reason to expect a government that would be any better able to act than is the United States today. One need only think about Italy, Israel, and Belgium to realize how many otherwise healthy, multi-party democracies are unable to come to agreement and act upon some crucial issue or another.

The second broad possibility would be a disciplined two-party system. However, this kind of system is truly rare and cannot be imposed from above. It presupposes a country that is either much less diverse than the United States or polarized around a single, deeply divisive set of issues. In other words, disciplined parties would work at cross-purposes with the most fundamental decision of 1787: the decision to encourage diversity as part of an effort to preserve liberty and make politics less of a life-and-death matter than it is in so many other countries.

None of this means that the United States is perfect. Congressional elections have turned into separate, district-level events, only slightly connected to one another or to the presidency. It is crucial to strengthen organizations that can pull people together and reconnect campaigning to governing. As a small first step, the campaign finance laws could be changed to strengthen parties and to make it easier for congressional challengers to raise seed money. It might also be worth thinking about four-year terms for the House and eight-year terms for the Senate, abolishing the "mid-term" election. Whatever one thinks of these specific ideas, there is obviously a great deal of work to be done. But that work would be done best in a framework that recognizes the virtues of the Constitution's most basic underpinnings.

Michael J. Malbin is Professor of Political Science at the State University of New York/Albany and director of the Center for Legislative Studies at SUNY's Rockefeller Institute of Government.

INDIVIDUAL RIGHTS

2

PART

Constitutional government, as we have just seen in Part One, is partly a matter of the structure of government. However, it is also a matter of individual freedom, of a system in which people have rights and liberties that are constitutionally protected from infringement by government.

The concept of individual rights holds that each person should be free to pursue a life of his or her own choosing, as long as this freedom does not unduly restrict that of other people. This idea came to America from England. The early settlers enjoyed "the rights of Englishmen," which included trial by jury and some freedom of expression. These rights had developed over centuries and gained strength when John Locke declared (in *Two Treatises of Government*, 1690) that the purpose of the state is to protect the natural rights of individuals. The Declaration of Independence (1776) proclaimed that "all men . . . are endowed by their Creator with certain unalienable rights," but when the Constitution was written in 1787, no list of protected rights was included. The Bill of Rights (1791) provided such a list and has been the constitutional focus of individual rights in the United States.

Although individual rights are rooted in principle, they are achieved through politics. The fact that the rights of individuals often conflict with the desires of majorities is the reason for both the constitutional protection of these rights and the reluctance of majorities to grant them. Moreover, rights must be constantly redefined in the light of social, economic, and political change. No matter how "unalienable" Americans' rights have been said to be in theory, they have hardly been so in practice. No group has achieved a greater measure of equality without a struggle, and no significant extension of any right has been won without a fight.

In the nineteenth century, issues of individual rights were almost entirely issues of freedom *from* government. Modern life has made individual rights also an issue of freedom *through* government. Guarantees of rights can be nothing more than empty promises unless government intervenes to correct or compensate for conditions that keep individuals from enjoying genuine freedom. Chapter 5 discusses how civil liberties—specifically, the rights of free expression and fair trial—are protected both from and through government. Chapter 6 extends the analysis into the realm of economic rights. Chapter 7 examines the degree to which Americans' equality of rights and opportunities is affected by considerations of race, sex, color, and creed.   ★ ★ ★

CIVIL LIBERTIES: PROTECTING INDIVIDUAL RIGHTS

A bill of rights is what the people are entitled to against every government on earth, general or particular, and what no just government should refuse, or rest on inference.

Thomas Jefferson[1]

On the night of November 11, 1983, Robert and Sarisse Creighton and their three children were asleep when FBI agents and local police broke into their home. Brandishing guns, they searched the house for a relative of the Creightons who was suspected of bank robbery. When asked to show a search warrant, they said, "You watch too much TV." Failing to find the suspect, they departed, leaving behind three screaming children and two angry parents. The Creightons sued the FBI agent in charge, Russell Anderson, for violating their Fourth Amendment right against unlawful search.

The Creightons won a temporary victory when the Eighth U.S. Court of Appeals, noting that individuals are constitutionally protected against warrantless searches unless officers have good reason ("probable cause") for a search and unless they have good reason ("exigent circumstances") for conducting that search without a warrant, concluded that Anderson had been derelict in his duty. In the judgment of the appellate court, Anderson should have sought a warrant from a judge, who, on the basis of Anderson's information about the suspect's whereabouts, could have decided whether a search of the Creightons' home was justified.

On June 25, 1987, the Supreme Court of the United States overturned the lower court's ruling. The Court's majority opinion said: "We have recognized that it is inevitable that law enforcement officials will in some cases reasonably

---

[1] Julian P. Boyd, ed., *The Papers of Thomas Jefferson*, vol. 12 (Princeton, N.J.: Princeton University Press, 1955), 440.

but mistakenly conclude that probable cause is present, and we have indicated that in such cases those officials . . . should not be held personally liable." Justice John Paul Stevens sharply dissented. He accused the Court's majority of absolving the police of their "constitutional accountability" and of showing "remarkably little fidelity" to the Fourth Amendment.[2] Civil liberties groups endorsed Justice Stevens' view, claiming that the Court's decision gave police an open invitation to invade people's homes on the slightest pretext, thereby diminishing personal liberty. However, the Court's decision was praised by law-enforcement officials and conservatives, who contended that a ruling in the Creightons' favor would have made police hesitant to pursue suspects for fear of a lawsuit if a search failed to produce the person sought.

As this case illustrates, issues of individual rights are complex and political. No right is absolute. For example, the Fourth Amendment protects Americans, not from *all* searches, but from *"unreasonable"* searches." The public would be unsafe if law officials could never search for evidence of a crime or pursue a suspect into a home. Yet the public would also be unsafe if police could frisk people at will or invade their homes with impunity. Such acts are characteristic of a police state, not of a free society. The challenge to a civil society is to establish a level of police authority that balances the demands of public safety with those of individual freedom. The balance point, however, is always subject to dispute. Did FBI agent Anderson have sufficient cause for a warrantless search of the Creightons' home? Or was his evidence so weak that his forcible entry constituted an "unreasonable" search? Law enforcement officials and civil liberties groups had widely different opinions on these questions. Nor did the justices of the Supreme Court have a uniform view. Six of the justices sided with Anderson and three backed the Creightons' position.

This chapter examines issues of **civil liberties:** specific individual rights, such as freedom of speech and protection against self-incrimination, which are constitutionally protected against infringement by government. As we saw in Chapter 3, the Constitution's failure to enumerate individual freedoms led to demands for the **Bill of Rights.** Enacted in 1791, these first ten amendments to the Constitution specify certain rights of life, liberty, and property which the national government is obliged to respect. A later amendment, the Fourteenth, became the basis for extending these protections of individual rights to actions by state and local governments.

Issues of individual rights have become increasingly complex and important. The writers of the Constitution could not possibly have foreseen the United States of the late twentieth century, with its huge national government, enormous corporations, pervasive mass media, urban crowding, nuclear weapons, and the rest. These developments are potential threats to personal freedom, and the judiciary in recent decades has seen fit to expand the rights to which individuals are entitled. However, these rights are constantly being balanced against competing individual rights and society's collective interests. The Bill of Rights operates in an untidy world where people's highest aspirations collide with their worst passions, and it is at this juncture that issues of civil liberties arise. Should an admitted murderer be entitled to recant a confession? Should the press be allowed to print military secrets whose publication might jeopar-

---

[2] *Anderson* v. *Creighton*, 483 U.S. 635 (1987).

dize national security? Should prayer be allowed in the public schools? Should neo-Nazis be allowed to take their anti-Semitic message into predominantly Jewish neighborhoods? Such questions are among the subjects of this chapter, which focuses on the following major points:

★ *Freedom of expression is the most basic of democratic rights, but, like all rights, it is not unlimited.* Free expression recently has been strongly supported by the Supreme Court.

★ *"Due process of law" refers to legal protections (primarily procedural safeguards) that are designed to ensure that individual rights are respected by government.*

★ *During the last half century particularly, the civil liberties of individual Americans have been substantially broadened in law and given greater judicial protection from action by all levels of government.* Of special significance has been the Supreme Court's use of the Fourteenth Amendment to protect these individual rights from action by state and local governments.

★ *Individual rights are constantly being weighed against the demands of majorities and the collective needs of society.* All political institutions are involved in this process, as is public opinion, but the judiciary plays the central role in it and is the institution that is most partial to the protection of civil liberties.

Freedom of Expression

Freedom of political expression is the most basic of democratic rights.[3] Unless citizens can openly express their political opinions, they cannot properly influence their government or act to protect their other rights. They also cannot hear what others have to say, and thus cannot judge the merits of alternative views. And without free expression, elections are a sham, a mere showcase for those who control what is on people's lips and in their minds. As the Supreme Court concluded in 1984, "The freedom to speak one's mind is not only an aspect of individual liberty—and thus a good unto itself—but also is essential to the common quest for truth and the vitality of society as a whole."[4]

It is for such reasons that the First Amendment provides the foundation for **freedom of expression**—the right of individual Americans to hold and communicate views of their choosing. For many reasons, such as a psychological need to conform to social pressure or a fear of harassment, Americans do not always choose to express themselves freely. Nevertheless, the First Amendment provides for freedom of expression by prohibiting laws that would abridge the freedoms of conscience, speech, press, assembly, and petition.

Freedom of expression, like other rights, is not absolute. It does not entitle individuals to say or do whatever they want, to whomever they want, whenever they want. Free expression can be denied, for example, if it endangers national security, wrongly damages the reputations of others, or deprives others of their basic freedoms. An individual's private thoughts are completely free,

Congress shall make no law respecting an establishment of religion, or prohibiting the free exercise thereof; or abridging the freedom of speech, or of the press; or the right of the people peaceably to assemble, and to petition the Government for a redress of grievances.

U.S. Constitution,
First Amendment

---

[3] See Paul L. Murphy, *The Shaping of the First Amendment: 1791 to the Present* (New York: Oxford University Press, 1991.)
[4] *Bose Corp.* v. *Consumers Union of the United States*, 466 U.S. 485 (1984).

Exercising their right of free expression, antiabortion protestors gather outside a Long Island clinic in 1991. Many of them were arrested, however, when their blockade prevented women from entering the clinic and exercising their right to have an abortion. (Meryl Levin/ Impact Visuals)

but words and actions may not be. For example, in 1991 when members of the militant antiabortion group Operation Rescue gathered in protest outside abortion clinics in Wichita, Kansas, they were acting within their constitutional right of free speech. When some of them forcibly restrained pregnant women from entering the clinic, however, they were no longer within their legal rights and were arrested.

In recent decades, free expression has received broad protection from the courts. Today, under most circumstances, Americans can freely verbalize their political views without fear of governmental interference or reprisal. In earlier times, however, Americans were less free to express their political views.

THE EARLY PERIOD: THE UNCERTAIN STATUS OF THE RIGHT OF FREE EXPRESSION

The first legislative attempt by the U.S. government to restrict free expression was the Sedition Act of 1798, which made it a crime to print false or malicious newspaper stories about the president or other national officials. The act was passed by Congress when fear of treason by French sympathizers was high, but its purpose was to muzzle Republican opponents of the Federalist president John Adams. The Sedition Act expired in 1801, but not before lower federal courts, presided over by Federalist judges who did not pretend to be objective, had imposed fines and jail sentences on ten Republican newspaper editors. Thomas Jefferson called the Sedition Act an "alarming infraction" of the Constitution and, upon replacing Adams as president in 1801, pardoned the convicted newspapermen and had their fines returned with interest. As the Supreme Court did not review the sedition cases, however, the judiciary's position on the lengths to which the government could legally go in restricting free expression remained an open question.

The Court also did not rule on free speech during the Civil War era, when the

---

★ HOW THE UNITED STATES COMPARES

CIVIL LIBERTIES

Individual rights are a cornerstone of the American governing system and receive strong protection from the courts. The government's ability to restrict free expression is severely limited, and the individual's right to a fair trial is protected through elaborate due-process guarantees.

According to Raymond Gastil, the United States is one of only twenty countries that deserve a top rating for their protection of civil liberties. Also in this group are Canada, Japan, and all western European democracies except Finland, France, Germany, and Spain, which are in the second rank. Their constitutional protections are

not so well developed as those of the countries in the top group. Most Latin American countries are in either this second category or the third one, at which some censorship and political imprisonments occur. Gastil's rankings bottom out at seven, a level that includes some Communist, African, and Middle East countries. In these nations, the state is oppressive, granting individuals almost no freedom of expression and routinely using brutal methods to suppress political opposition.

SOURCE: Raymond D. Gastil, *Freedom in the World: Political Rights and Civil Liberties* (Westport, Conn.: Greenwood Press, 1985).

---

government severely restricted individual rights. In one instance during Reconstruction, Congress actually prevented the Court from issuing a judgment. The case involved a Mississippi newspaper editor who had sought to arouse citizens against the Union occupation and had been jailed without charge by military authorities. He appealed his imprisonment to the Supreme Court on a writ of *habeas corpus* (discussed in Chapter 3). Fearful that his release would encourage other Confederate diehards to resist Reconstruction policies, Congress passed a law that barred the Supreme Court from hearing appeals involving those policies. In 1869 the Court accepted this congressional "court-stripping" and declined to rule on the editor's appeal.[5]

Not until 1919 did the Court rule on a case that challenged the national government's authority to restrict free expression. Two years earlier, Congress had passed the Espionage Act, which prohibited forms of dissent deemed to be harmful to the nation's effort in World War I. Nearly 2,000 Americans were convicted for such activities as interfering with draft registration and distributing antiwar leaflets. The Supreme Court upheld one of these convictions in *Schenck* v. *United States* (1919), ruling unanimously that the Espionage Act of 1917 was constitutional. In the opinion written by Justice Oliver Wendell Holmes, the Court said that Congress could restrict speech that was "of such a nature as to create a clear and present danger" to the nation's security. This **clear-and-present-danger test** implied the converse: government could not restrict political speech that presented no such danger.[6]

The Supreme Court did not adhere to its own standard, however. Less than a year after *Schenck*, the Court upheld the conviction of six anarchists for writing a pamphlet protesting the U.S. government's attempts to overthrow the newly formed Bolshevik regime in Russia.[7] Holmes dissented, writing that the anarchists' "silly leaflet" posed no substantial threat to the United States. Along

Supreme Court justice Oliver Wendell Holmes, Jr. (1841–1935). (UPI/ Bettmann Newsphotos)

---

[5] *Ex parte McCardle,* 7 Wallace 506 (1869).
[6] *Schenck* v. *United States,* 249 U.S. 47 (1919).
[7] *Abrams* v. *United States,* 250 U.S. 616 (1919).

Personal Freedom vs. National Security
During the writing of the Declaration of Independence, Thomas Jefferson and John Adams disagreed over the meaning of liberty. For Jefferson, it meant personal freedom. For Adams, it had to do with establishing a state powerful enough to protect an American way of life, of which personal freedom was only a part. Since the dawn of the atomic age, the tensions between personal freedom and national security have increased beyond anything Adams and Jefferson could have imagined. How far would you go in allowing government to restrict personal freedom for reasons of national security?

with Justice Louis D. Brandeis, Holmes subsequently argued that government should not be allowed to limit expression unless it posed an "imminent" danger to national security.[8]

THE MODERN PERIOD: PROTECTING FREE EXPRESSION

Until the twentieth century, the tension between national security interests and free expression was not a pressing dilemma for the United States. The country's great size and ocean barriers provided such protection from potential enemies that it had little to fear from internal subversion. World War I, however, intruded upon America's isolation, and World War II brought it to an abrupt end. Since then, Americans' rights of free expression have been defined largely in the context of national security concerns.

The Communist Threat and Limits on Free Expression

During the cold war that followed World War II, many Americans perceived the Soviet Union as bent on destroying the United States through internal subversion and global expansion. Senator Joseph McCarthy's sensational allegations that communists had infiltrated key positions in the U.S. government intensified public anxiety. In this climate of fear, the Supreme Court allowed government to put substantial limits on free expression. In *Dennis* v. *United States* (1951) the Court upheld the convictions of eleven members of the U.S. Communist party who had been prosecuted under the Smith Act of 1940, which made it illegal to advocate the forceful overthrow of the U.S. government.[9]

Fears of communist subversion began to subside in the mid-1950s, and the Court modified its *Dennis* position. In *Yates* v. *United States* (1957), the lower-court convictions of fourteen Communist party members were overturned because evidence indicated that they had not directly advocated lawless action. The Court said that their advocacy was "theoretical" and therefore protected by the First Amendment.[10] In subsequent rulings the Court stated that only active, high-ranking communists with a "specific intent" to destroy the U.S. government are subject to conviction.[11]

The "Preferred Position" Doctrine

Since the late 1950s, court decisions involving *political* expression (other types of expression, such as obscenity, are a different matter, as we shall see) have generally followed a legal doctrine outlined by Justice Harlan Fiske Stone in 1938. Stone argued that although government had broad discretion in certain areas, such as economic policy, the Court should carefully scrutinize legislative attempts to restrict First Amendment rights. These rights, Stone said, should have a "preferred position" in a democratic society. If those in power can limit

---

[8] *Whitney* v. *California*, 274 U.S. 357 (1927).
[9] *Dennis* v. *United States*, 341 U.S. 494 (1951).
[10] *Yates* v. *United States*, 354 U.S. 298 (1957).
[11] *Noto* v. *United States*, 367 U.S. 290 (1961); *Scales* v. *United States*, 367 U.S. 203 (1961).

free expression, they can control what people will come to know and think. For this reason, Stone contended, laws that restrict free expression require "more exacting [judicial] scrutiny . . . than most other types of legislation."[12]

Although the Supreme Court has not explicitly endorsed Stone's position, its decisions since the late 1950s have been consistent with the **preferred position** doctrine regarding First Amendment rights. The judiciary has held that government officials must show that national security is directly and substantially imperiled before they can lawfully prohibit citizens from voicing their political views. This demanding criterion was widely applied during the Vietnam war, when, despite the largest sustained protest movement in the country's history, not a single American was convicted solely because of spoken objections to the government's Vietnam policy. (Some dissenters were found guilty on other grounds, such as inciting to riot and disturbing the peace.)

The Supreme Court distinguished, however, between verbal speech and "symbolic speech." During the Vietnam period the Court upheld the conviction of David O'Brien for burning his draft registration card on the steps of the South Boston Courthouse. The Supreme Court acknowledged that O'Brien's act had a "communicative element"—that in a way it *was* political expression—but ruled against him all the same, saying that the government can prohibit action that threatens a legitimate public interest as long as the main purpose in doing so is not to inhibit free expression. The Court held that the federal law prohibiting the destruction of draft cards was designed primarily to provide for the military's personnel needs.[13]

Yet the Supreme Court in 1989 upheld the burning of the American flag as a form of symbolic expression. The 5-4 ruling came in the case of Gregory Lee Johnson, a member of the Communist Youth Brigade. In 1984 Johnson had set

[12] *United States* v. *Carolene Products Co.,* 304 U.S. 144 (1938).
[13] *United States* v. *O'Brien,* 391 U.S. 367 (1968).

Civil rights attorney William Kunstler (*right*), with defendant Gregory Lee Johnson (*second from right*), addresses reporters outside the Supreme Court building. Kunstler defended Johnson in the celebrated case that ultimately established flag burning as a constitutionally protected form of political expression. (Bob Daugherty/ AP/Wide World Photos)

fire to a U.S. flag outside the hall in Dallas where the Republican National Convention was being held. As he did so, a crowd chanted, "America, the red, white and blue, we spit on you." The Supreme Court rejected the state of Texas's argument that a flag burning is, in every instance, an imminent danger to public safety. Justice Anthony Kennedy wrote that, although he personally despised flag burning, the Constitution protected the act: "If there is a bedrock principle underlying the First Amendment, it is that the Government may not prohibit the expression of an idea simply because society finds the idea itself offensive or disagreeable."[14] A year later the Court struck down a new federal statute, passed by Congress in reaction to the Johnson ruling, that had made it a federal crime to burn or deface the flag.[15]

The Supreme Court's flag-burning decisions were opposed in opinion polls by a large majority of Americans and were broadly attacked by leaders of both parties. Senate Majority Leader George Mitchell (D-Maine) said that the Court's ruling "cheapened the flag." By 97-3, the Senate supported a resolution by Mitchell and Senate Minority Leader Robert Dole (R-Kan.) that expressed "profound disappointment" in the Court's position. President George Bush said that, to him, flag burning was "dead wrong."

Press Freedom and Prior Restraint

Freedom of the press received strong judicial support during the Vietnam period. In *New York Times Co. v. United States* (1971) the Court ruled that the *Times*'s publication of the "Pentagon papers" (secret government documents revealing official deception about the success of the United States' conduct of the war) could not be blocked by the Department of Justice, which claimed that publication would hurt the war effort. The documents had been illegally obtained by antiwar activists, who had turned them over to the *Times* and other news organizations for publication. The Court ruled that "any system of prior restraints" on the press is unconstitutional unless the government can clearly justify the restriction.[16]

The unacceptability of **prior restraint**—government prohibition of speech or publication before the fact—is basic to the current doctrine of free expression. The Supreme Court has said that any attempt by government to prevent expression carries "a 'heavy presumption' against its constitutionality."[17] News organizations and individuals are legally responsible after the fact for what they report or say (for example, they can be sued by an individual whose reputation is wrongly damaged by their words), but generally government cannot stop them in advance from expressing their views.

An exception is coverage of military operations. During the Persian Gulf war, U.S. journalists on station in Saudi Arabia had to work within limits placed on them by military authorities. Journalists were not allowed to travel freely, could talk only with selected soldiers, and had their news reports censored (see box). In another exception to the doctrine of prior restraint, the courts have upheld

★ ANALYZE THE ISSUE

Rights in Conflict
In *Nebraska Press Association v. Stuart* (1976), the Supreme Court overruled a Nebraska judge who had issued a "gag order" forbidding the press to report the lurid details of a crime. The judge reasoned that the accused's right to a fair trial would be jeopardized if the press sensationalized the crime. How would you have ruled in this case? Can you think of other situations in which rights come into conflict? What criteria would you use in resolving such conflicts? Do you believe that any right or rights should take precedence over all others? If so, why?

[14] *Texas* v. *Johnson,* 109 S. Ct. at 2544 (1989).
[15] *United States* v. *Eichman,* No. 89-1433 (1990).
[16] *New York Times Co.* v. *United States,* 403 U.S. 713 (1971).
[17] *Nebraska Press Assn.* v. *Stuart,* 427 U.S. 539 (1976).

★ THE MEDIA AND THE PEOPLE

CENSORSHIP AND MILITARY OPERATIONS: THE CASE OF THE GULF WAR

The United States' participation in the Persian Gulf war was characterized by substantial restrictions on the press. Military authorities designated a media pool, a small number of journalists allowed to act as stand-ins for the full press corps. They also placed severe restrictions on the journalists' travel and required reporters to have a military escort; allowed journalists to interview only selected soldiers and usually had a superior officer standing nearby as the interviews took place; and subjected all news reports to review by military censors. Journalists critical of the Gulf war were kept out of the media pool and, to further ensure favorable coverage, the U.S. government flew hometown reporters to Saudi Arabia, apparently on the assumption that they would be more likely to write human interest stories about the troops than hard-news stories about the war itself. The press was also kept away from sites that might have produced controversial news reports. For example, at one point U.S. pilots—in what one of them described as "a turkey shoot"—bombed and strafed Iraqi troops who had left their battle positions and were in full retreat from Kuwait; the U.S. military buried the dead in a mass grave before allowing reporters to go to the scene.

The American press protested the military's tight censorship, but in a relatively mild way. A suit by the *Nation* and several other liberal publications was not joined by major newspapers or the television networks. The suit charged that the censorship policy had no legitimate national security purpose and that it imposed an unconstitutional prior restraint on freedom of the press. The Justice Department's brief countered that the policy was designed to protect U.S. forces in the Gulf and would be discontinued when conditions in the war zone permitted. The suit was heard after the ground war had ended and after the press restrictions were lifted. Because the restrictions were no longer in effect, a federal judge declared the question moot.

Opinion polls taken during the Gulf war indicated that the large majority of Americans approved of the government's censorship of the press. Most people agreed with the government's position that censorship was necessary in order to protect the troops in the field. According to a March survey by the Times Mirror Center, a 2-to-1 majority said that "military censorship is more important than the media's ability to report important news." The same survey indicated, however, that the public had a high level of confidence in both the military and the media. Fully 45 percent of the respondents said that press coverage of the war was "excellent."

U.S. journalists from the press pool film the allied land offensive during the Persian Gulf war. The military's restrictions on press coverage provoked a debate about whether such censorship is justified on national security grounds or is a violation of the constitutional right of press freedom. (P. Durand/Sygma)

the government's authority to ban uncensored publications by certain past and present government employees, such as CIA agents, who have taken part in classified national security activities.

FREE EXPRESSION AND STATE GOVERNMENTS

In 1790 Congress rejected a proposed amendment to the Constitution which would have applied the Bill of Rights to the states. They had their own bills of rights, and anyway, early Americans were more worried about the power of the national government than about the power of the states. Thus the freedoms guaranteed in the Bill of Rights were initially protected only from action by the national government, a constitutional arrangement that the Supreme Court upheld in 1833.[18] A century later, however, the Court began to protect individual rights from infringement by state governments. The vehicle for this change was the Fourteenth Amendment to the Constitution.

The Fourteenth Amendment and the States

No State shall . . . deprive any person of life, liberty, or property, without due process of law.
U.S. Constitution,
Fourteenth Amendment

Ratified in 1868, the Fourteenth Amendment forbids a state to deprive any person of life, liberty, or property without due process of law. It was not until *Gitlow* v. *New York* (1925), however, that the Supreme Court decided that the Fourteenth Amendment applied to state action in the area of freedom of expression. Although the Court upheld Benjamin Gitlow's conviction for violating a New York law that prohibited advocacy of the violent overthrow of the U.S. system of government, the Court indicated that the states were not completely free to limit expression:

> For present purposes we may and do assume that freedom of speech and of the press—which are protected by the First Amendment from abridgement by Congress —are among the fundamental personal rights and "liberties" protected by the due process clause of the Fourteenth Amendment from impairment by the states.[19]

Having developed this new interpretation of the Fourteenth Amendment, the Supreme Court proceeded during the next decade to overturn state laws that restricted expression in the areas of speech, press, religion, and assembly and petition.[20] The most famous of these judgments came in the case of *Near* v. *Minnesota* (1931). Jay Near was the publisher of a Minneapolis weekly newspaper that regularly made scurrilous attacks on blacks, Jews, Catholics, and labor union leaders. His paper was closed down on authority of a state law that banned "malicious, scandalous, or defamatory" publications. Near appealed the shutdown, and the Supreme Court ruled in his favor, saying that the Minnesota law was "the essence of censorship." Chief Justice Charles Evans Hughes wrote the Court's opinion: "The fact that the liberty of the press may be

---

[18] *Barron* v. *Baltimore*, 7 Peters 243 (1833).
[19] *Gitlow* v. *New York*, 268 U.S. 652 (1925).
[20] *Fiske* v. *Kansas*, 274 U.S. 30 (1927) (speech); *Near* v. *Minnesota*, 283 U.S. 697 (1931) (press); *Cantwell* v. *Connecticut*, 310 U.S. 296 (1940) (religion); and *DeJonge* v. *Oregon*, 299 U.S. 253 (1937) (assembly and petition).

abused by miscreant purveyors of scandal does not make any the less necessary the immunity of the press from previous restraint."[21]

When the Fourteenth Amendment was debated in Congress after the Civil War, there was no indication that its framers meant it to protect First Amendment rights from state action. Seventy years later the Supreme Court justified the change by reference to **selective incorporation**—the absorption of certain provisions of the Bill of Rights, particularly freedom of speech and press, into the Fourteenth Amendment so that these rights would be protected from infringement by the states. The Court asserted that such rights are an indispensable condition of American life because "neither liberty nor justice would exist if they were sacrificed."[22]

Limiting the Authority of States to Restrict Expression

Since the 1930s, the Supreme Court has broadly protected freedom of expression from action by the states and by local governments, which derive their authority from the states. A leading free-speech case was *Brandenburg* v. *Ohio* (1969). The appellant was a Ku Klux Klan member who, in a speech at a Klan rally, had been recorded as saying, "If our president, our Congress, our Supreme Court, continues to suppress the white Caucasian race, it's possible that there might have to be some revenge taken." He was arrested and convicted of advocating force under an Ohio law prohibiting "criminal syndicalism," but the Supreme Court reversed the conviction, saying that

> the constitutional guarantees of free speech and free press do not permit a state to forbid or proscribe advocacy of the use of force or of law violation except where such advocacy is directed to inciting or producing imminent lawless action, and is likely to produce such action.[23]

In a key case involving the right to assemble peaceably, the U.S. Supreme Court in 1977 upheld a lower-court ruling against local ordinances of Skokie, Illinois, which had been invoked to prevent a parade there by the American Nazi party. The Nazis had chosen Skokie for their assembly in order to dramatize their message of hate: the town had a large Jewish population, including many survivors of Nazi Germany's concentration camps. The American Nazis ultimately called off the parade, but not because they were compelled by law to do so. The Supreme Court has held that the right of free expression takes precedence over the mere *possibility* that a riot or some other evil might result from what is said. Before government can lawfully prevent a speech or rally, it must show persuasively that an evil is almost certain to result from the event and must also demonstrate that there is no alternative way (such as assigning police officers to control the crowd) to keep the evil from happening.

The Supreme Court has recognized, however, that freedom of assembly may conflict with the routines of daily life. Accordingly, individuals do not have the right to hold a public rally in the middle of a busy intersection during rush hour,

---

[21] *Near* v. *Minnesota*, 283 U.S. 697 (1931).
[22] *Palko* v. *Connecticut*, 302 U.S. 319 (1937).
[23] *Brandenburg* v. *Ohio*, 395 U.S. 444 (1969).

nor do they have the right to command immediate access to a public auditorium. The Court has held that public officials can regulate the time, place, and conditions of public assembly, provided that these regulations are reasonable and do not discriminate on the basis of what is likely to be said at these gatherings. Officials have an obligation to accommodate public gatherings and to treat all groups—including those that espouse unpopular views—in accordance with reasonable standards.

In sum, the Supreme Court's position on the power of state and local governments to limit free political expression is relatively straightforward: they cannot lawfully impose substantial infringements on what people may say or write. If anything, the Court has been less tolerant of restrictions imposed by states and localities because, unlike the national government, they are not responsible for national security and thus cannot justify limiting free expression on that basis.

LIBEL AND SLANDER

The constitutional right of free expression is not a legal license to avoid responsibility for the consequences of what is said or written. If information that is known to be false and that greatly harms a person's reputation is published (libel) or spoken (slander), the injured party can sue for damages. The ease or difficulty of winning such suits has obvious implications for free expression. Individuals and organizations are less likely to express themselves openly if they stand a good chance of subsequently losing a libel or slander suit.

A leading decision in this area is *New York Times Co.* v. *Sullivan* (1964), in which the Court overruled an Alabama state court that had found the *Times* guilty of libel for printing an advertisement that accused Alabama officials of physically abusing black citizens during civil rights demonstrations. The Court ruled that libel of a public official requires proof of "actual malice," which was defined as a knowing or reckless disregard for the truth with intent to damage the official's reputation.[24] Although later decisions refined the Court's position, this imposing standard of proof remains essentially intact today. It is very difficult to prove that a publication was intentionally malicious in its reporting on a public figure.

A widely publicized lower federal court decision in 1985 revealed how nearly complete is the protection of the news media against libel cases brought by public figures. During Israel's invasion of Lebanon in 1983, *Time* magazine had reported that Israeli defense minister Ariel Sharon had tacitly consented in advance to a massacre of Palestinian refugees by Lebanese Christian forces. Sharon sued *Time* in a U.S. court, charging that the story was false, careless, and deliberately malicious. The jury agreed with Sharon that *Time* had been wrong in its allegation and had been careless about trying to ascertain the facts. But the jury concluded that *Time* had not acted with actual malice; its basic motivation in reporting the story, the jury believed, was not to harm Sharon's reputation. Sharon therefore lost the case.

The Sharon case notwithstanding, the greatest protection against a libel judgment is truthfulness. The Court in a 1990 decision held that expressions of

---

[24] *New York Times Co.* v. *Sullivan*, 376 U.S. 259 (1964).

Museum visitors examine Robert Mapplethorpe's photographs in the Cincinnati exhibit that was the focus of a recent controversy over the definition of obscenity. (Michael Keating–Cincinnati Enquirer/Gamma-Liaison)

opinion deserve "full constitutional protection" against the charge of libel as long as they do not contain "a provably false factual connotation."[25] In 1991 the Supreme Court held 7-2 that even quotations made up by a writer or journalist were not grounds for a libel judgment as long as the words of the fabrication did not materially alter what the person had actually said.[26]

The press has less protection against a libel judgment when its target is a "private" person rather than a "public" figure such as Sharon. The courts have reasoned that information about private individuals is less basic to the democratic process than information about public figures and that the press accordingly must take greater care in ascertaining the validity of claims about a private citizen.

The courts have made it easier to sue successfully for slander (spoken words) than for libel (published material). Because the press acts as a surrogate for the public, the courts have reasoned that plaintiffs seeking judgments against the press for libel must meet a tougher standard of evidence than plaintiffs seeking judgments against ordinary citizens for slander.

OBSCENITY

In 1990 the director of a Cincinnati museum, Dennis Barrie, was arrested on an obscenity charge for holding an exhibit that included homoerotic art by the photographer Robert Mapplethorpe. Although Barrie was acquitted in a jury trial, his arrest provoked a controversy that extended to Congress. Conservative Senator Jesse Helms (R-N.C.) attempted unsuccessfully to withdraw appropriations for the National Endowment for the Arts (NEA), which had partially underwritten the Mapplethorpe exhibit. Helms described Mapplethorpe's work

[25] *Milkovich* v. *Lorain Journal*, No. 89-645 (1990).
[26] *Masson* v. *The New Yorker*, No. 89-1799 (1991).

as "homosexual pornography." Representative Fred Grandy (R-Iowa) defended the NEA, saying, "You can't have art without risk."[27]

Obscenity is a form of expression that is not protected by the First Amendment. However, the Supreme Court has had difficulty in defining which publicly disseminated sexual materials are obscene and which are not. The Court has struggled to develop a standard that gives predictability to the law without endangering First Amendment rights.

Declaring that because "what would offend the people of Maine or Mississippi might be found tolerable in Las Vegas or New York City," Chief Justice Warren Burger wrote in *Miller* v. *California* (1973) that obscenity must be judged by "contemporary community standards."[28] The Court has also reasoned, however, that local standards cannot be the sole criterion of obscenity. In *Jenkins* v. *Georgia* (1974), for example, the Court overturned a local court's conviction of a theater owner who had shown a film (*Carnal Knowledge,* starring Jack Nicholson) that included scenes of a partially nude woman. The scenes were regarded by the Court as neither "patently offensive" nor aimed at people's "prurient interest"—two criteria the Court has used in judging obscenity. In 1987 the Court ruled that sexual material could not be judged obscene simply because the "average" local resident might object to its content. Apparently "community standards" are to be judged in the context of a "reasonable person"—someone who would judge material on the merits of its content. Sexual content is not in itself evidence that a book, magazine, or film is obscene.[29] To be obscene, sexual content must be of a particularly offensive type—still a rather vague criterion.

The justices of the Supreme Court continue to have difficulty in reaching agreement on issues of obscenity, as a 1991 decision showed. The case involved an Indiana public-decency law banning nude entertainment in barrooms and other public establishments. Five of the justices concluded that erotic nude dancing was not a protected form of expression. The other four justices disagreed and voted against the ban.[30]

The Supreme Court has distinguished between obscene materials in public places and in the home. A unanimous ruling in 1969 held that what adults read and watch in the privacy of their homes cannot be made a crime.[31] The Court created an exception to this rule in 1990 by upholding an Ohio law making it a crime to possess pornographic photographs of children.[32]

Freedom of Religion

Free religious expression is the precursor of free political expression, at least within the English tradition of limited government. England's Glorious, or Bloodless, Revolution of 1689 centered on the religious issue and resulted in the Act of Toleration, which gave members of all Protestant sects the right to

---

[27] "Free Speech vs. Obscenity," *Media Monitor* 4 (December 1990): 2–3.
[28] *Miller* v. *California,* 413 U.S. 15 (1973).
[29] *Pope* v. *Illinois,* (1987).
[30] *Barnes* v. *Glen Theatre,* No. 90-26 (1991).
[31] *Stanley* v. *Georgia,* 394 v. 557 (1969).
[32] *Osborne* v. *Ohio,* No. 88-5986 (1990).

worship freely and publicly. The English philosopher John Locke (1632–1704) extended this principle, arguing that legitimate government could not inhibit free expression, religious or otherwise. The First Amendment reflects this tradition, providing for freedom of religion along with freedom of speech, press, assembly, and petition. In regard to religion, the First Amendment reads: "Congress shall make no law respecting an establishment of religion, or prohibiting the free exercise thereof." The prohibition on laws aimed at "establishment of religion" (the establishment clause) and its "free exercise" (the free-exercise clause) applies to states and localities through the Fourteenth Amendment.

THE ESTABLISHMENT CLAUSE

The **establishment clause** has been interpreted by the courts to mean that government may not favor one religion over another or support religion over no religion. (This position contrasts with that of a country such as England, where Anglicanism is the official, or "established," state religion, though no religion is prohibited.) The Supreme Court's interpretation of the establishment clause has been described as maintaining a "wall of separation" between church and state, which includes a prohibition on nondenominational support for religion.[33] The Court has taken a pragmatic approach, however, permitting some establishment activities but disallowing others. The Court has permitted states to provide secular textbooks for use by church-affiliated schools,[34] for instance, but has forbidden states to pay part of the salaries of teachers in church-affiliated schools.[35] Such distinctions follow no strict logic but are based on judgments of whether government action involves *excessive* entanglement with religion."[36] In allowing public funds to be used by religious schools for secular textbooks but not for teachers' salaries, the courts have indicated that, whereas it is relatively easy to ascertain whether the content of a particular textbook promotes religion, it would be much harder to determine whether a particular teacher was promoting religion in the classroom.

The Court has developed a three-point test that a law providing aid to religion must pass to be considered constitutional: first, the main purpose of the aid must be secular and not religious; second, the main effect of the assistance must not be to promote one religion or religion per se; and third, the aid must not excessively involve the government in religion.[37] These restrictions do not, for example, allow substantial government grants to religious schools but do permit lesser contributions under some circumstances, such as the provision of secular textbooks and copies of standardized examinations. Some of the Court's applications of the three-point test have been controversial. The Court in 1983, for instance, upheld a Minnesota law allowing parents a tax deduction for certain school expenses, including tuition, incurred by their children. The Court reasoned that, because the tax deduction was available to parents with children

[33] See Frank J. Sorauf, *Wall of Separation: The Constitutional Politics of Church and State* (Princeton, N.J.: Princeton University Press, 1976).
[34] *Board of Regents* v. *Allen,* 392 U.S. 236 (1968).
[35] *Lemon* v. *Kurtzman,* 403 U.S. 602 (1971).
[36] Ibid.
[37] Ibid.

in either public or private (including nonreligious) schools, the law's purpose was not to support religion.[38] Opponents claimed that the law promoted religion because the parents of public school children, who pay no tuition, were entitled to smaller tax deductions than parents who paid tuition to send their children to private schools, most of which were affiliated with a church.

Since the early 1960s, the Court has held that the establishment clause prohibits the saying of prayers in public schools. In the *Engel* (1962) case, the Court ruled against the Board of Regents of New York State, which had written a nondenominational prayer to be recited in the public schools at the start of each day. Even though no particular religion was favored in the prayer, the Court concluded that the prayer promoted religion over nonreligion.[39] A year later the Court struck down Bible readings in public schools.[40]

Religion is a strong force in American life, and the Supreme Court's position on school prayer has had strong opposition, particularly from Protestant fundamentalists. A recent attempt to circumvent the prayer ruling was an Alabama law permitting the public schools to set aside one minute each day for silent prayer or meditation. In 1985 the Court voted 6-3 to declare Alabama's minute of silence unconstitutional, ruling that "government must pursue a course of complete neutrality toward religion."[41] Whether the Supreme Court would invalidate a silent-meditation law that was less clearly religious in its intent than Alabama's is an open question that is sure to be tested in future cases.

Government must pursue a course of complete neutrality toward religion.

U.S. Supreme Court,
Wallace v. Jaffree (1985)

Advocates of school prayer have pressured Congress to propose a constitutional amendment permitting some form of prayer in the public schools. In 1984 the U.S. Senate rejected by eleven votes a school-prayer amendment that had the support of President Ronald Reagan. A change in the constitutional status of religion might also come about through changes in the Supreme Court's membership.[42] Chief Justice William Rehnquist and three other current justices (Byron R. White, Sandra Day O'Connor, and Antonin Scalia) have indicated a willingness to lower some of the barriers between church and state, although no justice has advocated eliminating the barriers completely.

★ ANALYZE THE ISSUE

Free Exercise of Religion and Criminal Law
The Supreme Court held in a 6-3 decision in 1989 that American Indians who follow a centuries-old custom of using peyote (a narcotic) for religious purposes can be prosecuted under state drug laws. Do you side with the six justices who upheld the state law? Or do you side with the three justices who concluded that the use of peyote was protected by the First Amendment's guarantee of the free exercise of religion? What are the reasons for your opinion?

THE FREE-EXERCISE CLAUSE

The First and Fourteenth amendments also prohibit governmental interference with the "free exercise" of religion. The idea behind the **free-exercise clause** is clear: Americans are free to hold any religious belief they choose.

Although people are free to believe what they want, they are not always free to act on their beliefs. The courts have tolerated government interference with the exercise of religious beliefs when such interference is the secondary result of a compelling and overriding social goal. An example is the legal protection of children with life-threatening illnesses whose parents refuse on religious grounds to permit medical treatment. A court may order that such children be

---

[38] *Mueller* v. *Allen,* 463 U.S. 388 (1983).
[39] *Engel* v. *Vitale,* 370 U.S. 421 (1962).
[40] *Abington School District* v. *Schempp,* 374 U.S. 203 (1963).
[41] *Wallace* v. *Jaffree,* 472 U.S. 38 (1985).
[42] See Leo Pfeffer, *Religion, State and the Burger Court* (Buffalo, N.Y.: Prometheus Books, 1984).

The Amish practice of having children leave school after eighth grade to work full time is in conflict with laws regulating child labor and school attendance. The courts have tended to resolve the conflict by ruling that the custom is protected by the Constitution's guarantee of free exercise of religion. (Amy Sancetta/AP/ Wide World Photos)

given medical assistance because the social good of saving their lives overrides their parents' free-exercise rights. And in 1986 the Supreme Court concluded that military regulations requiring standard headgear took precedence over an Orthodox Jewish serviceman's practice of wearing a yarmulke.[43]

In some circumstances exceptions to certain laws have been permitted on free-exercise grounds. The Supreme Court ruled in 1972 that Wisconsin could not compel Amish parents to send their children to school beyond the eighth grade because this policy violated a centuries-old Amish religious practice of having children leave school and begin work at an early age.[44] The Court has also held that Quakers, unlike adherents of most other religions, cannot be compelled to serve in the military because their religious doctrine encompasses a conscientious objection to war. In upholding free exercise in such cases, the Court may be said to have violated the establishment clause by granting preferred treatment to people who hold a particular religious belief. The Court has recognized the potential conflict between the free-exercise and establishment clauses and, as in other such situations, has tried to strike a reasonable balance between the competing claims.

When the free-exercise and establishment clauses cannot be balanced, the Supreme Court has been forced to make a choice. In 1987 the Court ruled unconstitutional a Louisiana law requiring that creationism (the Bible's account of how the world was created) be taught along with the theory of evolution in public school science courses. Creationism, the Court concluded, is a religious doctrine, not a scientific theory; thus its inclusion in public school curricula violates the establishment clause by promoting a religious belief. Creationists viewed the Court's decision as a violation of their right to the free exercise of religion; they claimed that their children were being forced to study a theory, evolution, that contradicts the Bible's account of the origins of the human race.

---

[43] *Goldman* v. *Weinberger*, 475 U.S. 503 (1986).
[44] *Wisconsin* v. *Yoder*, 406 U.S. 295 (1972).

Rights of Persons Accused of Crimes

Near the end of its 1991 term, the Supreme Court overturned several of its own precedents, all in the area of the rights of people accused of crimes. The Court ruled that police had the freedom to search containers in cars that had been stopped on suspicion of crime; that a "coerced confession" did not invalidate a conviction if other evidence supported the judgment; that a lawyer's mistake could force a state prisoner to forfeit an appeal to the federal courts; and that a victim's character and the grief of the victim's family could be taken into account in death sentence proceedings.

The retiring Justice Thurgood Marshall decried these decisions of the Court's majority as a "far-reaching assault upon the Court's precedents."[45] How could the law be one thing today and another tomorrow? Had the Constitution changed, or was it just that the membership of the Court had changed? Marshall answered the question by noting that recent appointees to the Court had partisan and legal views very different from his own. His retirement would leave only one justice who had been appointed by a Democratic president. The other eight justices were all Republican appointees, who formed a majority with a narrower conception of the rights of the accused than had prevailed a decade or two earlier.

PROCEDURAL DUE PROCESS

The history of liberty has largely been the history of the observance of procedural guarantees.
Justice Felix Frankfurter

Justice Felix Frankfurter once wrote that "the history of liberty has largely been the history of the observance of procedural guarantees."[46] Due process of law is rooted in the idea of ensuring justice for all, with special emphasis on persons accused of crimes. "Due process" refers to legal protections that have been established to preserve the rights of individuals. The most significant form of these protections is **procedural due process;** the term refers primarily to procedures that authorities must follow before a person can legitimately be punished for an offense. (A second form, substantive due process, is discussed in the next section.)

The U.S. Constitution provides for several procedures designed to protect a person from wrongful arrest, conviction, and punishment (see box). A person has, according to Article I, section 9, "the privilege of the writ of habeas corpus." Any person taken into police custody is entitled to seek such a writ, which requires law-enforcement officials to bring him or her into court and state the legal reason for the detention. If the reason is inadequate, the court must order the prisoner's immediate release. The Fifth and Fourteenth amendments provide generally that no person can be deprived of life, liberty, or property without due process of law. And specific procedural protections for the accused are spelled out in the Fourth, Fifth, Sixth, and Eighth amendments:

> *The Fourth Amendment* forbids the police to conduct searches and seizures unless they have probable cause to believe that a crime has been committed.

---

[45] "Good for the Left, Now Good for the Right," *Newsweek,* July 8, 1991, p. 20.
[46] *McNabb* v. *United States,* 318 U.S. 332 (1943).

The Fifth Amendment protects against double jeopardy (being prosecuted twice for the same offense); self-incrimination (being compelled to testify against oneself); indictment for a crime except through grand jury proceedings; and loss of life, liberty, and property without due process of law.

The Sixth Amendment provides the right to have legal counsel, to confront witnesses, to receive a speedy trial, and to have a trial by jury in criminal proceedings.

The Eighth Amendment protects against excessive bail or fines and prohibits the infliction of cruel and unusual punishment on those convicted of crimes.

Defining Procedural Protections

These procedural protections have always been subject to interpretation. The Fourth Amendment, for example, protects people against "unreasonable searches" of their persons, homes, and belongings. In a 1968 decision, the Supreme Court said that a determination of whether a search was "reasonable" could be based only on the concrete facts of the individual case.[47] The admissibility in court of evidence obtained in an unreasonable search has also varied. In *Weeks* v. *United States* (1914), the Court formulated the **exclusionary rule,** which prohibits the use in federal trials of evidence obtained by illegal search and seizure.[48] In subsequent decades, the Supreme Court expanded the application of the exclusionary rule, but, in the 1980s, restricted the rule's application, concluding that in some circumstances illegally obtained evidence can be admitted in trials if the procedural errors are small, inadvertent, or ultimately inconsequential.

Allowing the States to Differ. At first, the exclusionary rule applied only to federal cases. States in their criminal proceedings were not bound by the rule. Nor were states compelled, as was the federal government,[49] to provide attorneys for felony defendants who could not afford to pay for legal counsel. There were limited exceptions, such as a 1932 ruling that a defendant charged in a state court with a crime carrying the death penalty had to be provided with an attorney.[50] The Court's general position, however, was that the states themselves could decide what procedural rights their residents would have.

A noteworthy case was *Palko* v. *Connecticut* (1937). A Connecticut court had convicted Frank Palko of killing two policemen, and he was sentenced to life imprisonment. But Connecticut had a statute that permitted law-enforcement authorities under certain conditions to appeal a sentence on the grounds that legal errors had been made at the trial. The authorities had wanted Palko to receive the death penalty, so they appealed the decision. Palko was tried again on the same charges, and this time was sentenced to death. He appealed to the U.S. Supreme Court, claiming that Connecticut's second trial violated his right not to be tried twice for the same crime. The Fifth Amendment to the U.S. Constitution prohibits double jeopardy, and so do many state constitutions, but

[47] *Sibron* v. *New York*, 392 U.S. 59 (1968).
[48] *Weeks* v. *United States*, 232 U.S. 383 (1914).
[49] *Johnson* v. *Zerbst*, 304 U.S. 458 (1938).
[50] *Powell* v. *Alabama*, 287 U.S. 45 (1932).

PROCEDURAL DUE-PROCESS RIGHTS IN ACTION: A HYPOTHETICAL CASE

Perhaps the best way to illustrate how procedural due-process rights protect the individual is to present a hypothetical case. Let us say that John Q. Student has been selling illegal drugs on campus. In order for the police to arrest Mr. Student legally, they must have "probable cause" to do so—some indication that a crime has been or is about to be committed, such as evidence linking Mr. Student to drug sales. If the police apprehend Mr. Student merely because they wonder how he got the money to pay for the new sports car he is driving and then happen to discover evidence of drug trafficking, he may avoid conviction on the grounds that his Fourth Amendment protection against illegal search and seizure has been violated.

When Mr. Student is arrested, the police may search for evidence, although the extent of this search is subject to Fourth Amendment limitations. In general, the Supreme Court has held that the area that can be searched without a warrant is limited to the suspect's person and the immediate area, and then only to preserve the evidence and to protect the arresting officers from harm. Ordinarily, police should have a search warrant to look for evidence in a suspect's house or place of business; to obtain such a warrant, police must go to a judge and show probable cause.

After Mr. Student has been arrested, police interrogation should not begin until he has been informed of his rights, including the right to remain silent (Fifth Amendment) and the right to have an attorney present (Sixth Amendment). Mr. Student also has the right to be brought before a judge without undue delay and informed of the charge against him. If he is not, Mr. Student can apply for a writ of *habeas corpus* to secure his release. At his hearing, Mr. Student also has the right to seek reasonable bail (Eighth Amendment), an amount normally based on the severity of the alleged crime and the likelihood that the accused person will return for trial if he or she is released on bail.

If Mr. Student is charged with a federal crime, an indictment must be handed down by a grand jury, which hears evidence from the prosecution and determines whether this evidence is strong enough to suggest that Mr. Student has indeed violated the law and should be indicted to stand trial. Most states do not make extensive use of the grand jury; rather, they let prosecutors directly file a bill of information with a court, detailing the charge and the evidence. After an indictment, the bail decision is reviewed by the court. In more serious cases, bail can be revoked if it has not already been denied. In federal cases, the Bail Reform Act of 1966 requires that accused persons be released on their own recognizance if they are unable to make bail, unless the judge has adequate evidence to believe that they will not appear for trial or are dangerous to others.

Under the Sixth Amendment, Mr. Student is entitled to a "speedy trial." But court backlogs and assorted other delays can push a criminal trial back as much as a year after an arrest. Jury trials are required (Sixth Amendment) for serious crimes unless that right is waived by the defendant. Most juries consist of twelve persons. On the federal level and in most states, a unanimous jury verdict is needed for a conviction. At his trial, Mr. Student cannot be forced to give testimony against himself (Fifth Amendment) and has the right to confront witnesses against him (Sixth Amendment). There are also prohibitions on the introduction by the prosecution of illegally obtained evidence (Fourth Amendment), although the Supreme Court has relaxed this ban in certain instances, such as when the evidence would eventually have been discovered anyway.

If Mr. Student is convicted, he may appeal the verdict to a higher court. While the Constitution does not guarantee an appeal after conviction, the federal government and all states permit at least one appeal. The Supreme Court has ruled that the appeal process cannot discriminate against poor defendants. At a minimum, government must provide convicted persons unable to pay the costs of an appeal with free legal counsel and transcripts of the original trial.

The Constitution limits the punishment that Mr. Student can be given for his crime. The Eighth Amendment forbids "cruel and unusual punishment," a provision that the Supreme Court cited in 1972 when it temporarily halted the death penalty because the states were imposing it arbitrarily. A few years later, the Court declared that the death penalty as such was constitutionally permissible.

Our discussion of Mr. Student's case presumes that all his rights were respected by the police and the courts. However, there is often a marked difference between procedural rights and actual practices. For example, police sometimes conduct sweep searches, frisking people on the street without having any reason to believe they have committed a specific crime. A person found to be carrying a concealed weapon, stolen property, or drugs is likely to be arrested, tried, and convicted, for it is very difficult to prove in court that the police had no reasonable basis for the search that led to the arrest.

SOURCE: Much of the material on arrest, search, interrogation, formal charge, trial, appeal, and punishment which informs this example is derived from Walter F. Murphy and Michael N. Danielson, *Robert K. Carr and Marver H. Bernstein's American Democracy* (Hinsdale, Ill.: Dryden Press, 1977), 465–474.

at the time Connecticut's did not. The Supreme Court refused to overturn Palko's second conviction, and he was executed.[51]

Justice Benjamin Cardozo wrote the Court's *Palko* opinion, which stated that the Fourteenth Amendment protects rights "fundamental" to liberty but not other rights provided in the Bill of Rights. Free expression is a "fundamental" right, since it is "the indispensable condition of nearly every other form of freedom." Some procedural due-process rights, such as protection against double jeopardy, are not in the same category, Cardozo claimed.

Selective Incorporation of Procedural Rights. Not until the 1960s did the Court broadly require states to safeguard procedural rights. Changes in public education and communication had made Americans more aware of their rights, and the civil rights movement had dramatized the fact that rights were administered very unequally: the poor and minority-group members had many fewer rights in practice than other Americans. In response, the Supreme Court in the 1960s "incorporated" Bill of Rights protections for the accused in state courts by ruling that these protections are covered by the Fourteenth Amendment's guarantee of due process of law (see Table 5-1). This incorporation process began with *Mapp* v. *Ohio* (1961). Dollree Mapp's home had been entered by Cleveland police, who, though they failed to find the drugs they were looking for, did discover some pornographic material. Mapp's conviction for its possession was overturned by the Supreme Court on the grounds that she

> *Freedom of expression is the matrix, the indispensable condition, of nearly every other form of freedom.*
> Benjamin Cardozo,
> *Palko v. Connecticut (1937)*

---

[51] *Palko* v. *Connecticut,* 302 U.S. 319 (1937).

TABLE 5-1 Selective Incorporation Bill of Rights protections have been extended through the Fourteenth Amendment to include action by the states.

Supreme Court Case	Year	Constitutional Right at Issue
Gitlow v. *New York*	1925	First Amendment's applicability to free speech
Fiske v. *Kansas*	1927	Free speech
Near v. *Minnesota*	1931	Free press
DeJonge v. *Oregon*	1937	Freedom of assembly and of petition
Cantwell v. *Connecticut*	1940	Religious freedom
Mapp v. *Ohio*	1961	Unreasonable search and seizure
Gideon v. *Wainwright*	1963	Right to counsel
Malloy v. *Hogan*	1964	Self-incrimination
Pointer v. *Texas*	1965	Right to confront witnesses
Miranda v. *Arizona*	1966	Self-incrimination
Klopfer v. *North Carolina*	1967	Speedy trial
Duncan v. *Louisiana*	1968	Jury trial in criminal cases
Benton v. *Maryland*	1969	Double jeopardy

Warren Burger *(top)*, chief justice of the Supreme Court from 1969 to 1986, and William Rehnquist *(bottom)*, the current chief justice. *(Top:* Yoichi R. Okamoto/Photo Researchers; *bottom:* UPI/ Bettmann Newsphotos)

had been subjected to unreasonable search and seizure.[52] With this decision, the Court extended the exclusionary rule to state trial proceedings.

Two years later, the Court's decision in *Gideon* v. *Wainwright* (1963) required the states to furnish attorneys for poor defendants in all felony cases. Clarence Gideon, an indigent drifter, had been convicted and sentenced to prison in Florida for breaking into a poolroom. He had no lawyer, nor was he entitled to one under the Florida constitution. He appealed on the grounds that he had been denied due process because he could not afford to pay an attorney. The Supreme Court agreed, thus extending the right to free legal counsel to defendants in state felony trials.[53]

During the 1960s the Court also ruled that defendants in state criminal proceedings cannot be compelled to testify against themselves;[54] have the rights to remain silent and to have legal counsel when they are arrested;[55] have the right to confront witnesses who testify against them;[56] must be granted a speedy trial;[57] have the right to a jury trial;[58] and cannot be subjected to double jeopardy.[59] The most famous of these cases is *Miranda* v. *Arizona* (1966), as a result of which police are required to tell suspects about their rights at the time of arrest. Ernesto Miranda had confessed during police interrogation to kidnapping and raping a young woman. His confession led to his conviction, which he successfully appealed to the Supreme Court on the grounds that he had not been informed of his rights to remain silent and to have legal counsel present during interrogation. Using other evidence of Miranda's crime, the state of Arizona then retried and again convicted him. He was paroled from prison in 1972 and four years later was stabbed to death in a bar fight. Ironically, Miranda's assailant was read his *"Miranda* rights" when police arrested him. By now the wording has become familiar: "You have the right to remain silent. . . . Anything you say can and will be used against you in a court of law. . . . You have the right to an attorney."

By 1969, when Chief Justice Earl Warren retired, nearly all the rights guaranteed by the Fourth through the Eighth amendments had been extended to defendants in state trial proceedings. Evidence indicates that local and state law-enforcement and judicial officials do not always uphold these rights fully,[60] but legal protections have been greatly expanded in the course of the century.

Weakening the Exclusionary Rule

As the Warren Court expanded defendants' rights during the 1960s, many law-enforcement officials, politicians, and private citizens accused the Court of "coddling criminals" to such an extent that law-abiding people were not safe on the streets and in their homes. When Richard Nixon won the presidency after

[52] *Mapp* v. *Ohio,* 367 U.S. 643 (1961).
[53] *Gideon* v. *Wainwright,* 372 U.S. 335 (1963).
[54] *Malloy* v. *Hogan,* 378 U.S. 1 (1964).
[55] *Miranda* v. *Arizona,* 384 U.S. 436 (1966). See also *Escobedo* v. *Illinois,* 378 U.S. 478 (1964).
[56] *Pointer* v. *Texas,* 380 U.S. 400 (1965).
[57] *Klopfer* v. *North Carolina,* 386 U.S. 213 (1967).
[58] *Duncan* v. *Louisiana,* 391 U.S. 145 (1968).
[59] *Benton* v. *Maryland,* 395 U.S. 784 (1969).
[60] See Richard L. Medalic, Leonard Zeitz, and Paul Alexander, "Custodial Police Interrogation in Our Nation's Capital: The Attempt to Implement *Miranda,*" *Michigan Law Review* 66 (1968): 1347.

promising to restore "law and order" in the country, expectations were widespread that government would pursue a tougher line on issues of crime. Although Nixon appointed four new justices to the Supreme Court, its positions on the rights of the accused did not undergo wholesale change during the 1970s or early 1980s.

Since then, however, a shift in the Court's philosophy has clearly been evident. The greatest change has been to the exclusionary rule barring the use of illegally obtained evidence in criminal cases. In 1983 the Court allowed the use of evidence obtained without a properly issued search warrant when the "totality of circumstance" suggests that the police are justified in their action.[61] Then in two key 1984 decisions the Court ruled that evidence discovered under a faulty warrant can be used in a trial if the police acted in "good faith"[62] and that illegally obtained evidence can be used against a defendant if the prosecution can prove that it would have discovered the evidence anyway.[63]

The Supreme Court terms that ended in 1990 and 1991 are widely viewed as marking a turning point. As has always been true of the Supreme Court's positions, this shift came about through political change. The conservative Ronald Reagan had been elected president in 1980, and three Supreme Court seats had become vacant during his two terms of office. Reagan appointed a conservative jurist to fill each vacancy, and the three jurists—Sandra Day O'Connor, Antonin Scalia, and Anthony Kennedy—provided the votes that resulted in two very significant changes in the treatment of persons accused or convicted of crime.

First, police have been granted wider discretion in their pursuit and treatment of criminal suspects. Legal scholar David O'Brien concludes that recent

[61] *Illinois* v. *Gates,* 462 U.S. 213 (1983).
[62] *United States* v. *Leon,* 468 U.S. 897 (1984).
[63] *Nix* v. *Williams,* 467 U.S. 431 (1984).

The conservative majority on the Supreme Court has relaxed the restrictions on search and seizure by police. For example, it is legal for police forces to set up roadblocks to apprehend drunk drivers as long as they proceed systematically—stopping every fourth vehicle, say, rather than examining drivers on the basis of arbitrary criteria such as age or appearance. (Dan Chidester)

Republican appointments to the Supreme Court have made it "more deferential to law enforcement than at any time in over thirty years."[64] The Warren Court had concluded that the Fourth Amendment required police to have "probable cause" to believe a crime had occurred before search or seizure activity was legal and had held police to strict standards in the treatment of suspects. The Court relaxed these requirements considerably in its 1990 and 1991 judgments, as the following rulings illustrate:

> Protection against unreasonable seizure does not prohibit the admission in court of evidence discarded by a fleeing subject, even when the police had no reason to suspect the individual of any wrongdoing. The Court concluded that a fleeing individual has not been "seized" and therefore is not protected by the Fourth Amendment.[65]

> Roadside checkpoints where police systematically stop drivers to examine them for signs of intoxication do not violate the right to protection against unreasonable search.[66]

> Protection against unreasonable search is not violated if police stop a car because they suspect that it contains something illegal and then search a closed container in the car without obtaining a court-approved warrant. The ruling overturned an earlier case in which the Court held that a closed container in the trunk could not be searched without a warrant.[67]

> The requirement of a "prompt" hearing by a judge is not violated if police hold a suspect for as long as forty-eight hours before a judge decides whether the arrest was justified.[68]

> Protection against self-incrimination does not extend to a *coerced* confession if it can be regarded as "harmless error" in that other evidence is adequate to sustain the conviction.[69]

The second area in which the Supreme Court in 1990 and 1991 restricted the rights of the accused involved appeals to federal courts by people who had been convicted of crime in state courts. Chief Justice William Rehnquist had said publicly that the federal courts were bogged down in "frivolous" and multiple appeals. The Supreme Court addressed his concerns in opinions that:

> Restricted the jurisdiction of federal courts in appeals based on petitions for a writ of *habeas corpus* from people convicted in state courts.[70] (*Habeas corpus* gives defendants access to federal courts in order to argue that their rights were violated when they were convicted in state courts.)

> Restricted the ability of a convicted person to bring even an initial *habeas corpus*

---

[64] David M. O'Brien, "The High Court Changes Course," *The Public Perspective* 2 (July/August 1991): 6–7.
[65] *California* v. *Hodari D.,* No. 89-1632 (1991).
[66] *Michigan* v. *Sitz,* No. 88-1897 (1990).
[67] *California* v. *Acevedo,* No. 89-1690 (1991).
[68] *Riverside* v. *McCoughlin,* No. 89-1817 (1991).
[69] *Arizona* v. *Fulminante,* No. 89-839 (1991).
[70] See *Butler* v. *McKellar,* No. 88-6677 (1990).

★ CRITICAL THINKING

WHEN SHOULD PROCEDURAL ERROR RESULT IN A NEW TRIAL?

Roger Coleman, a coal miner, was convicted of rape and murder in a Virginia court and was sentenced to death. He sought to appeal the conviction on several grounds, including evidence that one of the jurors had told friends he wanted to sit on the case in order to make sure Coleman was convicted. The volunteer attorneys who handled the appeal were not fully familiar with Virginia courts and filed the appeal a day after the deadline for doing so. Prosecutors moved to deny the appeal on procedural grounds, and the motion was upheld by Virginia's highest court. Coleman filed a *habeas corpus* petition to have the appeal heard in federal court. In 1991 the Supreme Court held that Coleman had forfeited his right to bring the petition because of the procedural error. The Court's ruling overturned a 1963 precedent which had held that state prisoners were entitled to seek federal *habeas corpus* petitions as long as they had not "deliberately bypassed" state courts.

In its decision, the Supreme Court said that it was fair to penalize Coleman because he had no right to an attorney at this stage of legal proceedings. He had a right to counsel during his trial but, according to a Supreme Court ruling two years earlier, did not have a right to free counsel for purposes of filing a federal *habeas corpus* petition. The Court also held that state procedures should be respected, even if the death penalty has been applied. The Court referred to "the respect that Federal courts owe the states and the states' proceedings and rules."

What reasoning would lead you to conclude that justice was served in the *Coleman* ruling? What reasoning would lead you to conclude otherwise?

Coleman v. Thompson, No. 89-7024 (1991).

petition if his or her attorney's procedural error invalidates the petition. The decision overturned an earlier ruling that state prisoners could seek a federal suit as long as they had not "deliberately bypassed" state courts.[71] (see box).

Restricted prison inmates' ability to raise new issues after the first round of federal court appeals failed. The Court held that federal judges must dismiss second or subsequent petitions as an "abuse of the writ" (of *habeas corpus*) except in unusual circumstances.[72]

Although these and other decisions have weakened the legal position of persons accused and convicted of crime, analysts disagree about the broader implications of the rulings. Proponents say that the Court's recent direction has primarily eliminated loopholes that in the past have allowed guilty persons to go free on minor technicalities. Detractors see a darker consequence, noting that police can always claim to have acted in good faith in violating an individual's person or property, whatever their true motives at the time. One of the Supreme Court's own justices, John Paul Stevens, has even suggested on several occasions that the Bill of Rights is being downgraded into an "honor code" for police.

However, no one claims that recent decisions have returned the standard of

[71] *Coleman v. Thompson*, No. 89-7662 (1991); *Keenay v. Tamaya-Reyes*, No. 90-1859 (1992).
[72] *McCliskey v. Zant*, No. 89-7024 (1991).

justice to the low level that prevailed before the 1960s. Some of the Warren Court's precedents remain in effect, including the most important one of all: the principle that procedural protections guaranteed to the accused by the Bill of Rights must be observed by the states as well as by the federal government. In addition, the current Supreme Court has extended the rights of the accused in a few areas. In 1991, for example, the Court reaffirmed and extended a 1986 ruling that black defendants are denied their rights when prosecuting attorneys use peremptory challenges (that is, rejections without explanation) to exclude black potential jurors, so that the trial is conducted with an all-white jury.[73] The 1991 Court term also included a decision that once a defendant asks for a lawyer, the police must halt their questioning until the lawyer arrives.[74]

SUBSTANTIVE DUE PROCESS

Most issues of criminal justice have centered on procedural due process. However, beyond the question of whether proper legal procedures have been followed is the more general question of **substantive due process**—the requirement that the government and its laws be reasonable in their purposes and consequences. Adherence to proper legal procedures (procedural due process) does not necessarily produce reasonable outcomes (substantive due process). In recent years, for example, courts have addressed the issue of whether properly convicted persons are treated justly when they are confined in overcrowded, filthy, or outmoded jails and prisons. Courts have ordered officials in some cases to relieve inmate overcrowding and to improve prison facilities.

A difficulty with judgments about substantive due process is that they are relatively subjective. At what point between the extremes of dungeons and country clubs do jail conditions become unjust? Recognizing the subjective nature of such judgments, the courts have shied away from such decisions, preferring to leave them in the hands of legislative bodies. The Supreme Court in 1991 made it harder for inmates to sue over prison conditions by ruling that they would have to show "deliberate indifference" to conditions by prison officials.[75]

The legal standard for assessing substantive due process is whether the policy in question appears reasonable and fair by contemporary expectations. At one time in Western society, pickpockets were put to death by hanging. A death sentence for petty theft is regarded today as unjust and would not meet the standard for substantive due process. The standard is vague enough, however, to provoke deep divisions of opinion, even among justices of the Supreme Court. A divided Court in 1991 upheld a Michigan law that mandated life imprisonment without parole for a nonviolent first-offense conviction for possession of as little as 1.5 pounds of cocaine.[76]

★ ANALYZE THE ISSUE

Defining "Cruel and Unusual Punishment"
The Supreme Court in 1991 upheld a state law that mandated life imprisonment without parole for a nonviolent first-offense conviction for possession of as little as 1.5 pounds of cocaine. The conviction had been appealed on grounds that the sentence constituted cruel and unusual punishment. What is your opinion? Is a sentence of life imprisonment without parole justifiable for someone who has no prior criminal record and who commits a nonviolent crime? Would you have the same opinion if some crime other than drug possession was involved?

---

[73] See *Batson* v. *Kentucky*, 476 U.S. 79 (1986); *Edmonson* v. *Leesville Concrete Company*, No. 89-7743 (1991); *Powers* v. *Ohio*, No. 89-5011 (1991).
[74] *Minnick* v. *Mississippi*, No. 89-6332 (1991).
[75] *Wilson* v. *Seiter*, No. 89-7376 (1991).
[76] *Harmelin* v. *Michigan*, No. 89-7272 (1991).

The Right of Privacy

Until the 1960s, Americans' constitutional rights were confined largely to those enumerated in the Bill of Rights. This situation prevailed despite the Ninth Amendment, which reads: "The enumeration in the Constitution, of certain rights, shall not be construed to deny or disparage others retained by the people."

In 1965, however, the Supreme Court added to the list of individual rights, declaring that Americans have "a right of privacy." This judgment arose from the case of *Griswold* v. *Connecticut*, which challenged a state law prohibiting the use of birth-control devices, even by married couples. The Supreme Court invalidated the statute, concluding that a state had no business interfering with a married couple's decision in regard to the use of contraceptives. The Court did not base its decision on the Ninth Amendment, but reasoned instead that an underlying right of privacy gave rise to such individual protections as the freedom from unreasonable search and seizure. "We deal with a right of privacy older than the Bill of Rights," concluded Justice William O. Douglas.[77]

The right of privacy was the basis for the Supreme Court's ruling in *Roe* v. *Wade* (1973), which gave women full freedom to choose abortion during the first three months of pregnancy.[78] (During the second three months of pregnancy, the Court said, a state could regulate abortions, but only to safeguard the health of the woman. In the final three months, a state could ban abortion except when the woman's life was endangered by her pregnancy.) In a 7-2 decision that overturned a Texas law prohibiting abortion except to save the life of the mother, the Supreme Court said that the right of privacy is "broad enough to encompass a woman's decision whether or not to terminate her pregnancy."

After *Roe*, antiabortion activists sought to reverse or weaken the Court's ruling. Attempts to pass a constitutional amendment that would ban abortions were unsuccessful, but abortion foes succeeded in some of their efforts, such as their campaign to establish laws that prohibit the use of government funds to pay for abortions for poor women. Then, in *Webster* v. *Reproductive Health Services* (1989), the Supreme Court upheld a Missouri law that prohibits abortions in public hospitals and by public employees.[79] The ruling was in part a consequence of the efforts of antiabortion groups to influence Supreme Court appointments during the Reagan presidency. The Missouri law was upheld by a 5-4 majority and all three Reagan appointees on the Court (Justices O'Connor, Scalia, and Kennedy) voted with the majority.

The *Webster* decision was followed within two years by restrictions on abortions by state legislatures in Louisiana, Utah, Missouri, and Pennsylvania. In 1991 the Court in a 5–4 ruling held that family-planning clinics that receive federal funds could be barred by regulation from counseling their clients on abortion. The regulation was adopted by the Reagan administration to replace

[77]*Griswold* v. *Connecticut*, 381 U.S. 479 (1965).
[78]*Roe* v. *Wade*, 401 U.S. 113 (1973).
[79]*Webster* v. *Reproductive Health Services*, No. 88-605 (1989).

an earlier regulation, based on the same 1971 statute, that had required health counselors to inform pregnant women of all their rights, including the right to an abortion. Chief Justice Rehnquist said that the federal government was not required to "subsidize" speech about abortion.[80]

The 1989 and 1991 rulings were followed in 1992 by a judgment in the Pennsylvania abortion case *Planned Parenthood* v. *Casey*. Pennsylvania's law placed a 24-hour waiting period on women who sought an abortion, required doctors to counsel women on abortion and alternatives to abortion, required a minor to have a parent's consent or a judge's approval before having an abortion, and required a married woman to notify her husband before obtaining an abortion. The law had the backing of the Bush administration, and anti-abortion advocates saw the law as an opportunity for the Supreme Court to overturn *Roe* v. *Wade*. In a decision that surprised many observers, the Court by a 5–4 margin reaffirmed the "essential holding" of *Roe* v. *Wade*: that a woman, because of the constitutional guarantee of privacy, has a right to abortion during the early months of pregnancy. The Court also ruled, however, that states can regulate abortion as long as they do not impose an "undue burden" on women seeking abortion. The Court concluded that the 24-hour waiting period, physician counseling, and the informed-consent requirement for minors were not undue burdens and were therefore constitutional. The spousal-notification requirement, however, was judged to place a "substantial obstacle" in the path of women seeking abortion and was thereby declared unconstitutional.[81]

This ruling brought denunciation from both proabortion and antiabortion advocates, and abortion will certainly be a leading controversy for years to come. The American public is sharply divided on the issue, and there are a great many deeply committed activists on both sides.[82] The Supreme Court itself is divided. The four justices who voted in the minority in the Pennsylvania case would have overturned *Roe* v. *Wade*. The Supreme Court's oldest member and the author of *Roe* v. *Wade*, Justice Harry Blackmun, underscored the tenuous nature of the Court's abortion position. "I am 83 years old," he said. "I cannot remain on this Court forever, and when I do step down, the confirmation process for my successor may well focus on the issue before us today."

The Courts and a Free Society

A free and democratic nation has a vital stake in maintaining individual freedoms. The United States was founded on the belief that individuals have an innate right to personal liberty—to speak their minds, to worship as they choose, to be free of police intimidation. The greatest threat to individual rights in a democratic society is a popular majority backed by elected leaders determined to carry out its will. Majorities have frequently preferred policies that would diminish the freedom of those who hold minority views, have unconventional lifestyles, or simply "look different" from the majority.

FIGURE 5-1 Opinions on the Abortion Issue
Americans are deeply divided over abortion, with the prochoice position having a numerical edge. *Source: Yankelovich-Clancy-Shulman survey for Time and CNN, April 4–5, 1989, and April 9–10, 1990.*

★ ANALYZE THE ISSUE

Abortion and Parental Consent
In 1990 and again in 1992 the Supreme Court upheld a state law prohibiting teenaged girls from obtaining abortions without first either telling their parents or obtaining permission from a judge. The Court majority agreed that without the judicial-bypass option, the requirement that both parents give their consent was unconstitutional. What is your opinion on the issue? Do you think abortion should be permitted at all? If you believe that abortion should be legal, where do you stand on the issue of parental consent? Should a young woman under eighteen be required to have the permission of one or both parents, or neither parent, in order to obtain an abortion?

---

[80]*Rust* v. *Sullivan*, No. 89-1391 (1991).
[81]*Planned Parenthood* v. *Casey*, No. 91-744 (1992).
[82]Charles H. Franklin and Liane C. Kosaki, "Republican Schoolmaster: The U.S. Supreme Court, Public Opinion, and Abortion," *American Political Science Review* 83 (1989): 751–772.

Americans are highly supportive of rights and freedoms expressed in abstract terms but are much less supportive—and in some cases antagonistic—when confronted with those same rights in practice.[83] Although nearly all Americans say that they favor free expression as a general principle, for example, a significant proportion oppose the expression of certain viewpoints. Surveys conducted by the National Opinion Research Center between 1976 and 1982 found that most Americans would ban from public libraries a book by an atheist, communist, homosexual, militarist, or racist. Only 37 percent of those interviewed said they would ban books by none of the authors, and 22 percent were willing to remove the books of all the authors.[84] The rights of the accused receive even less public support. Most Americans apparently fear crime more than they respect due-process rights that they themselves expect never to need. A 1989 Washington Post-ABC News Poll indicated that most Americans were quite willing to sacrifice individual rights for the battle against drugs. A majority of respondents favored mandatory drug testing of all Americans, approved the idea of police searches of the homes of suspected drug dealers even without a court order, and favored the random search of cars for drugs.

When conditions are favorable, many politicians have been willing to play on the public's fear of crime and insensitivity to civil liberties issues—as when scores of politicians rode the "law and order" issue to election victory during the 1960s. Nor is the Supreme Court entirely insulated from these popular moods. Nevertheless, the judicial branch can normally be expected to grant

---

[83]See Herbert McClosky and Alda Brill, *Dimensions of Tolerance* (New York: Sage Foundation, 1983); David C. Lawrence, "Procedural Norms and Tolerance: A Reassessment," *American Political Science Review* 70 (1976): 80–100; Michael Corbett, *Political Tolerance in America* (New York: Longman, 1982).

[84]See Howard D. White, "Majorities for Censorship," *Library Journal*, July 1986, 33.

★ ANALYZE THE ISSUE

The Necessity of the Bill of Rights
The Bill of Rights was added to the Constitution despite the Framers' objection that it was unnecessary. Whose position—the Framers' or those who advocated the Bill of Rights—do you think history supports? Can you think of additional rights that you might have today if the Framers' position had prevailed? Can you think of rights that you might *not* have today if their view had prevailed?

Abortion rights activists protest the Supreme Court's 1991 ruling in *Rust* v. *Sullivan*. The Court found constitutional a "gag rule" forbidding counselors at federally funded clinics to discuss abortion with patients. (Mike Albans/AP/Wide World Photos)

more consideration to the individual citizen, however unpopular his or her views or actions, than will the elected branches, which are more responsive to majority and established interests.

How far the Supreme Court will go in protecting a person's rights depends on the facts of the case, the existing status of the law, prevailing social needs, and the political leanings of the justices. The political dimension, as we have seen, is a critical one. Republican and Democratic appointees to the Supreme Court tend to see legal issues differently. All the justices, however, regard the protection of individual rights as one of the Court's most significant responsibilities, a perspective that is owed in no small measure to the Bill of Rights. It transformed the inalienable rights of life, liberty, and property into legal rights, thus putting them under judicial protection.[85]

Civil liberties are not blessings that government kindly bestows on the individual. Because of their constitutional nature, these rights are above government. In fact, it can be said that government exists to protect these rights. True, government does not always act lawfully; the temptations of power and the pressures of the majority can at times lead governmental institutions to usurp individual rights. The courts are not immune to these influences and have the additional pressure of the obligation to seek an accommodation between the claims of individuals and the collective interests of society (which, of course, include respect for civil liberties). However, while the courts have not always sided with individuals in their claims to rights, it is at least as noteworthy that they have not always sided with government in its claims against the individual.

The judiciary's importance to the preservation of civil liberties has increased as society has grown in complexity. Large, impersonal bureaucracies—public and private—are a defining characteristic of the modern age, and their power can easily dwarf the individual. Courts of law are an exception. The isolated citizen, who standing alone carries no weight with huge bureaucracies, is the center of attention in legal proceedings. Not surprisingly, then, individuals have increasingly turned to the courts for protection. In its 1990–1991 term, 30 percent of Supreme Court cases involved criminal law issues, a much higher percentage than even a few decades ago.

Courts alone cannot provide adequate protection for individual rights. A civil society rests also on enlightened representatives and a tolerant citizenry. If, for example, politicians and the public encourage police to infringe the rights of vaguely threatening minorities or nonconformists, the judiciary's protection of persons accused of crimes will not ensure justice. It may be said that the test of a truly civil society is not its treatment of popular ideas and of its best citizens but its willingness to tolerate ideas that the majority detests and to treat even its unpopular citizens with respect.

---

[85]Alpheus Thomas Mason, *The Supreme Court: Palladium of Freedom* (Ann Arbor: University of Michigan Press, 1962), 58.

Summary

In their search for personal liberty, Americans added the Bill of Rights to the Constitution shortly after its ratification. These amendments guarantee certain political, procedural, and property rights against infringement by the national government. Freedom of expression is the most basic of democratic rights. People are not free unless they can freely express their views. Nevertheless, free expression may conflict with the nation's security needs during times of war and insurrection. The courts at times have allowed government to limit expression substantially for purposes of national security. For the past twenty-five years, however, the courts have protected a very wide range of free expression in the areas of speech, press, and religion.

The guarantees embodied in the Bill of Rights originally applied only to the national government. Under the principle of selective incorporation of these guarantees into the Fourteenth Amendment, the courts extended them to state governments, though slowly and unevenly. In the 1920s and 1930s, First Amendment guarantees of freedom of expression were given protection from infringement by the states. The states, however, continued to have wide discretion in criminal proceedings until the early 1960s, when most of the fair-trial rights in the Fourth through Eighth amendments were given federal protection.

"Due process of law" refers to legal protections that have been established to preserve individual rights. Due process is of two kinds: procedural and substantive. The former consists of procedures or methods (for example, the opportunity of an accused person to have an attorney present during police interrogation) designed to ensure that an individual's rights are respected; the latter consists of legal proceedings that lead to reasonable and fair results (for example, the conditions of imprisonment of an individual convicted of a crime).

Civil liberties are not absolute but must be balanced against other considerations (such as national security or public safety) and against one another when rights come into conflict. The judicial branch of government, particularly the Supreme Court, has taken on much of the responsibility for protecting and interpreting individual rights. The Court's positions have changed with time and conditions, but the Court has generally been more protective of and sensitive to civil liberties than have elected officials or popular majorities.

Major Concepts

Bill of Rights	free-exercise clause
civil liberties	preferred position (of First Amendment rights)
clear-and-present-danger test	prior restraint (of the press)
establishment clause	procedural due process
exclusionary rule	selective incorporation
freedom of expression	substantive due process

Suggested Readings

Abraham, Henry. *Freedom and the Court*, 5th ed. New York: Oxford University Press, 1988. A general survey of judicial interpretations of civil liberties.

Bodenhamer, David J. *Fair Trial: Rights of the Accused in American History.* New York: Oxford University Press, 1991. A comprehensive historical survey of the rights of the accused.

Haiman, Franklyn S. *Speech and Law in a Free Society.* Chicago: University of Chicago Press, 1981. An assessment of the primacy of speech in a free society.

Halpern, Stephen C., ed. *The Future of Our Liberties.* Westport, Conn.: Greenwood Press, 1982. A collection of essays that consider how the freedoms enumerated in the Bill of Rights may be affected by developing conditions in American society.

Lewis, Anthony. *Gideon's Trumpet.* New York: Random House, 1964. A summary of the case of Clarence Gideon and its effects on the right of persons accused of crime to legal counsel.

Mason, Alpheus T. *The Supreme Court: Palladium of*

Freedom. Ann Arbor: University of Michigan Press, 1962. An assessment of the Supreme Court's role in protecting individual rights.

Murphy, Paul L. *The Shaping of the First Amendment: 1791 to the Present.* New York: Oxford University Press, 1991. A description of the development and application of First Amendment principles in American history.

O'Brien, David M. *The Public's Right to Know.* New York: Praeger, 1981. A penetrating analysis of the Supreme Court and the First Amendment.

Rutland, Robert A. *The Birth of the Bill of Rights, 1776–1791.* New York: Macmillan, 1962. A description of the historical developments leading to the addition of the Bill of Rights to the U.S. Constitution.

Sorauf, Frank J. *Wall of Separation: The Constitutional Politics of Church and State.* Princeton, N.J.: Princeton University Press, 1976. A well-written account of religious freedom as a constitutional issue.

ECONOMIC RIGHTS: EXPRESSING INDIVIDUALISM

6

The true foundation of republican government is the equal right of every citizen, in his person and in his property.

Thomas Jefferson[1]

I n 1974 Allied Structural Steel closed down its operations in Minnesota. The closing triggered the implementation of a Minnesota law requiring companies that go out of business in the state to secure the pension benefits of their laid-off employees. The law was enacted to prevent companies from absconding with pension funds that had been set aside for workers.

Allied Steel sued the state of Minnesota, arguing that it was protected by the **contract clause** (in Article I, section 10) of the U.S. Constitution, which forbids a state to pass laws that impair "the obligation of contracts." Allied's contract with its workers stated that the company had sole discretion to determine the status of pension benefits. Allied contended that it could not be forced to provide pension benefits to its former employees. In *Allied Structural Steel Co.* v. *Spannaus,* the Supreme Court of the United States ruled in Allied Steel's favor. Minnesota's law was judged to impinge severely, not incidentally, on Allied's pension contract with employees and thus was concluded to violate the contract clause of the Constitution.[2]

The *Allied* case is an example of the stakes that can be involved in a dispute over property rights. **Property rights** are rights of ownership, use, and contract. Property rights are defined mainly through common law (judge-made law arising out of legal disputes between private parties). Common law dictates, for example, that individuals have a right to establish a home of their own.

The U.S. Constitution also provides property protections. In addition to the

---

[1] Quoted in Catherine Drinker Bowen, *Miracle at Philadelphia* (Boston: Atlantic-Little, Brown, 1966), 71–72.
[2] *Allied Structural Steel Co. v. Spannaus,* 438 U.S. 234 (1978).

contract clause, the Constitution's Fifth Amendment prohibits the national government from depriving individuals of their property rights except through due process of law and from taking private property for public use without just compensation to the owner. The Fourteenth Amendment extends due-process protection of property to include actions by state governments.

These constitutional provisions are intended to keep government from unreasonably infringing on the rights of individuals who already hold property or are parties to contracts. The Constitution does *not* grant each citizen a right to economic security: the document is silent on the issue of whether a citizen is entitled to a minimum standard of living. However, legal protections of property are not designed simply to allow individuals to do whatever they want with the property they have accumulated.[3] In theory, property rights are granted to promote both individual interests *and* the common good. For example, corporations are protected in their property rights not only because such protection is beneficial to individual stockholders but also because it can benefit workers (through, for example, income security and stable employment) and consumers (through, for example, a dependable supply of goods).

Property rights have a constitutional history rivaling that of personal liberties. The Philadelphia Convention of 1787 was convened because of threats to property, and the contract clause of the Constitution was a direct result. The clause is one of the few explicit protections of individual rights in the body of the Constitution (as opposed to its amendments) and was one of the few protections that applied to the states from the very beginning of the nation. (It will be recalled from Chapter 5 that protections in the Bill of Rights did not apply to state action until the twentieth century.) In addition, commerce and property issues dominated the Supreme Court's agenda until the 1930s. Although property issues since then have taken a back seat to issues of free expression and fair trial, they remain important. In a 1991 decision, Chief Justice William Rehnquist declared that the principle of adherence to precedent is stronger in "cases involving property and contract rights" than in those involving personal liberties.[4]

This chapter discusses individual rights and opportunities in the economic realm, focusing particularly on how these rights and opportunities reflect basic cultural values and affect Americans' everyday lives. Related economic issues are covered in later chapters, notably in Chapters 24 ("Economic Policy") and 25 ("Social-Welfare Policy"). The main points of this chapter are the following:

★ *Property rights are protected through due process from infringement by government.* This protection is consistent with the concept of *negative government,* which holds that personal liberty is enhanced when the power of government is strictly constrained.

★ *Government intervention can promote economic fairness and security.* The concept of *positive government* holds that government intervention to promote liberty is necessary when individuals are subject to social and economic forces beyond their control.

---

[3] Richard A. Posner, "What Am I? A Potted Plant?: The Case against Strict Constructionism," *New Republic,* September 28, 1987, 23.
[4] *Payne* v. *Tennessee,* No. 90-5721 (1991).

For many Americans, home ownership epitomizes the right of property and the personal freedom associated with it. (Gabe Palmer/Stock Market)

★ *A prevailing principle in the United States is equality of opportunity.* Unlike many other democracies, the United States has not established an individual right to economic security.

★ *In its idealistic form, economic individualism fosters human growth and accomplishment; in its perverse form, it culminates in selfishness and elitism.*

Property and Liberty

In a classic study, the political scientist Robert Lane asked workingmen to talk about freedom. They made scant mention of the right to a fair trial or free expression. They spoke instead of the freedom that extends from property. One worker said, "I work where I want to work, I spend my money where I want to spend it. . . . What else—what else could you want?" Another worker stated, "When the day is over, I come home to my family and [then] if we want to go somewhere in the car, we can go. . . . I just like the system we have."[5]

Americans place a very high value on the freedom that property can provide. The sociologist Herbert Gans found that "middle Americans"—that majority of the population who are neither rich nor poor—are oriented primarily toward family and are distrustful of large institutions. Gans discovered that homeownership is particularly valued by middle Americans, who seek in a house the privacy and freedom of action that is otherwise elusive. They place much less emphasis on political expression or collective goods than on their personal well-being, a tendency that Gans labels "middle American individualism."[6]

[5] Quoted in Robert E. Lane, *Political Ideology* (New York: Free Press, 1962), 21, 24.
[6] Herbert J. Gans, *Middle American Individualism: The Future of Liberal Democracy* (New York: Free Press, 1988); Michael Schudson, "Pumping Polyester," *The Nation*, June 4, 1988, 794.

Opinion polls reveal how firmly attached Americans are to private property and to the country's economic system (see Figure 6-1). By 87 percent to 4 percent, for example, Americans agree that "private ownership of property is as important to a good society as freedom."

NEGATIVE GOVERNMENT

Personal property and liberty have always been closely linked in Americans' minds. In the Europe left behind by the first American immigrants, ordinary persons had no significant opportunity to own property. Nearly all land was vested in the church and a small aristocracy. A growing commercial class existed, but its profits were subject to confiscatory taxation. The effect was that most people had no sphere of privacy: even the most intimate aspects of their lives were subject to the prying eyes of the ruling class.

America offered an alternative. Its open land and vast wilderness made it relatively easy for individuals to acquire property and establish an independent life. The situation appealed to the new immigrants, most of whom were Protestants from the British Isles and northern Europe whose religious values made virtues of hard work and thrift. Rather quickly, these early Americans came to believe that their liberty included the freedom to establish themselves economically and that their rights included those of property.[7]

[7] James W. Ely, *The Guardian of Every Other Right: A Constitutional History of Property Rights* (New York: Oxford University Press, 1991); Seymour Martin Lipset, *The First New Nation* (New York: Basic Books, 1963), ch. 3; Joyce Appleby, *Capitalism and a New Social Order: The Republican Vision of the 1790s* (New York: New York University Press, 1984).

FIGURE 6-1 Opinions on Property and Capitalism
Americans strongly believe in the value of property rights and free enterprise. *Source: Adapted from Herbert McClosky and John Zaller,* The American Ethos: Public Attitudes toward Capitalism and Democracy *(Cambridge, Mass.: Harvard University Press, 1984), 133, 140 (Tables 5-1 and 5-3).*

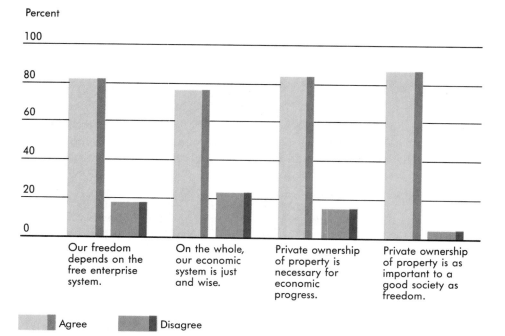

To the writers of the U.S. Constitution, protection of property was primarily an issue of restraints on government. Of course, government had to have economic resources of its own, so it had to have the power to tax property. But, in the Framers' view, government's chief economic duty was *not* to interfere in property relations. The Framers' fear of tyrannical majorities was primarily a fear of legislative majorities that would undermine private rights of property. A concern with property also explains the Framers' admiration for a strong judiciary: during the debtor rebellions, the courts had remained steadfast in their commitment to creditors.

The Framers' philosophy included the idea of **negative government,** which holds that government governs best by staying out of people's lives, thus giving individuals as much freedom as possible to determine their own pursuits. Liberty is enhanced when government refrains from acting. As Thomas Jefferson said in his first inaugural address in 1801,

> [A] wise and frugal government, which shall restrain men from injuring one another, which shall leave them otherwise free to regulate their own pursuits of industry and improvement, and shall not take from the mouth of labor the bread it has earned. This is the sum of good government.

The concept of negative government is embodied in the contract clause and the Fifth and Fourteenth amendments of the Constitution. These provisions are barriers to government usurpation of property. The Constitution protects property chiefly through due process of law, which, as we noted in Chapter 5, can take either substantive or procedural form.

In America's colonial times, work was hard but opportunities were abundant; as a result, people's commitment to self-reliance was heightened. (The Bettmann Archive)

*No State shall . . . make
anything but gold and silver
coin a tender in payment of
debts; [nor] pass any . . . law
impairing the obligation of
contracts.*

U.S. Constitution,
Article I, section 10
(the contract clause)

*No person shall . . . be
deprived of life, liberty, or
property, without due process
of law; nor shall private
property be taken for public
use without just compensation.*

U.S. Constitution,
Fifth Amendment

*No State shall . . . deprive any
person of life, liberty, or
property, without due process
of law.*

U.S. Constitution,
Fourteenth Amendment

SUBSTANTIVE DUE-PROCESS PROTECTION OF PROPERTY

For a lengthy period in American history, substantive due process, which is concerned with the reasonableness of a law (see Chapter 5), was a major protection of propertied interests, particularly big business. Through its substantive due-process rulings, the Supreme Court blocked legislation affecting such areas as workers' wages, hours, and unions. In *Lochner* v. *New York* (1905), for example, the Court invalidated a New York statute that forbade bakery firms to require employees to work more than sixty hours a week. The Court said: "There is no reasonable ground for interfering with the . . . right of free contract. . . . They [bakers] are in no sense wards of the state."[8] The right of contract was presumed to protect business from governmental regulation of employer-employee relations. Sir Henry Maine wrote that the Constitution's contract clause "is the bulwark of American individualism against democratic impatience and socialist fantasy."[9]

The Supreme Court's support of business interests had begun long before *Lochner*. The Court concluded in 1810 that the Constitution's contract clause, which was originally designed to govern the relationship between individual creditors and debtors, also barred states from impairing contracts involving corporate parties.[10] A few years earlier, in a precedent-setting Philadelphia jury trial, union organizers were found guilty of conspiracy, a verdict that effectively gave business an overwhelming advantage in its relations with labor.

By the late nineteenth century, business reigned supreme in the United States

[8] *Lochner* v. *New York*, 198 U.S. 25 (1905).
[9] Quoted in Geoffrey R. Stone, Louis M. Seidman, Cass R. Sunstein, and Mark V. Tushnet, *Constitutional Law* (Boston: Little, Brown, 1986), 1428.
[10] *Fletcher* v. *Peck*, 6 Cranch 87 (1810).

Until the 1930s the Supreme Court tended to protect the property interests of businesses, even at the expense of workers' safety and health. At the turn of the century most factories were dark, dirty, and hazardous. (The Bettman Archive)

(see Chapter 2). As President Calvin Coolidge was later to say, "The business of America is business." The idea of individualism at the personal level had, at the level of the economic system, become the doctrine of *laissez-faire capitalism*. As we saw in Chapter 1, **individualism** stresses the values of hard work and self-reliance and holds that the individual should be left to succeed or fail on his or her own. Individualism and a capitalist economic system complement each other. Capitalism's principles of competition, profit, and private enterprise parallel individualism's emphasis on striving, achievement, and self-reliance.[11]

In the era of laissez-faire capitalism, government left business alone on the assumption that the free market is largely self-regulating and will ultimately produce for society the greatest possible social and economic benefits. As it turned out, though, unbridled capitalism became destructive of individualism. Large trusts dominated nearly every sector of the economy and virtually controlled the lives of their workers, most of whom labored sixty hours a week or more for meager wages under conditions so unsafe that more than a thousand were killed or critically injured every week. James Madison had recognized that private economic power could jeopardize personal liberty, but he had concluded that the threat was small in comparison with the dangers posed by powerful government. A century later, economic change had rendered Madison's analysis obsolete. The iron grip that the business trusts had on workers and consumers was every bit as oppressive as any governmental power Americans had known.

The destructive force of the Great Depression in the 1930s finally awakened Americans to the folly of laissez-faire capitalism. As we saw in Chapter 2, it took the Supreme Court longer than other government institutions to recognize the need for change. In 1937, however, the Supreme Court reversed its opposition to government regulation of the marketplace and largely abandoned its use of substantive due process to protect business interests. In so doing the Court, in effect, accepted a dissenting argument that Justice Oliver Wendell Holmes had made thirty years earlier in *Lochner:* "A constitution is not intended to embody a particular economic theory, whether of paternalism or . . . laissez-faire."[12]

Although today's Supreme Court has indicated that it might resurrect on a limited basis the doctrine of substantive due process as applied to property issues, its basic position is that broad economic policy is largely the responsibility of legislatures, not courts. Although the Supreme Court has never said so directly, this reversal of precedent was based on a belated recognition that individual property rights—although a good unto themselves—must also be judged on their contribution to the common good. They are a means to desirable social and economic goals, and it is largely up to the majority, not to the courts or powerful corporations, to decide the nature of these goals.

MODERN DUE-PROCESS PROTECTION OF PROPERTY

Today due-process protection of property is largely procedural rather than substantive. In general, procedural due process requires that government follow

---

[11] Herbert McClosky and John Zaller, *The American Ethos: Public Attitudes toward Capitalism and Democracy* (Cambridge, Mass.: Harvard University Press, 1984), 113.
[12] *Lochner* v. *New York,* 198 U.S. 25 (1905).

★ ANALYZE THE ISSUE

Property Rights and the Community
Richard A. Epstein of the University of Chicago Law School has said that courts should strike down rent controls, zoning, the minimum wage, and social security on the grounds that these laws and entitlements violate property and contract rights. What is your view of Epstein's position? What would be the effect of his proposal on community life?

proper procedures when it takes action that is potentially harmful to an individual (see Chapter 5). For example, the Fifth and Fourteenth amendments prohibit government from taking private property without giving the owner adequate compensation. Government can legally take private property for public purposes (a power known as *eminent domain*)—to build a road, for example—but it must pay the owner a fair price. If the owner contends that the proposed public purpose is not a valid one or that the offered price is too low, he or she can take the government agency to court to resolve the difference.

Property rights are less straightforward today than they were in the past. As American society has become increasingly complex, it has also become increasingly "public." Actions by individuals are more likely now to affect other individuals—that is, to have a public impact. The judiciary has recognized this fact in upholding, for example, zoning and antipollution laws that place substantial restraints on the uses that people can make of their own property.

Government's power of eminent domain provides another example. Years ago, the courts held that the Fifth Amendment's reference to "public use" meant that property taken by government had to become public property, as in the case of private land that is taken in order to construct a public park. Today the courts hold that "public use" can mean merely a public benefit. In 1954, for example, the Supreme Court upheld the action of a District of Columbia planning commission when it took over a department store in a blighted neighborhood for the purpose of letting a private developer make the area more attractive. The Court ruled that this use of eminent domain was justified "once the public purpose [that is, beautification of the area] had been established."[13]

On the whole, however, Americans are still substantially protected in their property from detrimental government action. A noteworthy recent example is the *Nollan* case. The California Coastal Commission granted the Nollan family a permit to build a beach house on their ocean-front property, subject to the condition that the public be allowed to walk along the beach. Such permit conditions are a means by which state and local governments have forced private developers to take public and environmental considerations into account. The Nollans believed that the California Coastal Commission had exceeded its authority, and they challenged the public-access condition of their permit. In 1987 the Supreme Court ruled in the Nollans' favor, concluding that, although government had the authority to protect the public's view of the ocean, the requirement concerning public access to the beach was a "taking" that could not be imposed on the Nollans without compensation.[14]

The *Nollan* decision reaffirmed a position taken decades earlier by Justice Oliver Wendell Holmes, who argued that a taking occurs when governmental action greatly diminishes the value of private property, even if that property remains in the hands of its private owners.[15] Holmes foresaw that private property would increasingly be subject to public encroachment as population density increased.

---

[13] *Berman* v. *Parker*, 348 U.S. 26 (1954).
[14] *Nollan* v. *California Coastal Commission*, 107 U.S. 314 (1987).
[15] David A. Farber, "'Taking' Liberties," *New Republic*, July 27, 1988, 200.

Property and Equality

Individualism and strong property rights encourage people to become economically unequal. They are urged to achieve, and, if they are successful, their accumulated property is protected by law. In a sense, property rights are the modern equivalent of the feudal order. Instead of status defined by ancestry, as was the case under feudalism, status is defined by property relationships: employer-employee, creditor-debtor, capital-labor, landowner-tenant.

In the early nineteenth century economic inequality was not a critical issue in America, for two major reasons. First, Americans were economically more equal than other peoples. There was no aristocratic class in America. Second, as long as economic opportunities were relatively open and abundant, Americans could claim an equality of opportunity. Alexis de Tocqueville noted both sides of the American character—its egalitarian spirit and its individualistic competitiveness. He said, "America thus exhibits in her social state an extraordinary phenomenon. Men are there seen on a greater equality . . . than in any other country of the world, or in any age." But Tocqueville also noted that "in no other country in the world is the love of property keener or more alert than in America."[16]

By the late nineteenth century, however, liberty and equality in the economic sphere had come into conflict. In the industrial age, the power of capital and labor were vastly unequal, and most factory workers had no real hope of advancement. As Franklin D. Roosevelt was later to say, "Equality of opportunity as we have known it no longer exists."[17]

POSITIVE GOVERNMENT

Constitutional doctrine until the 1930s essentially held that governmental inaction in the economic realm meant neutrality toward the contending parties. Of course, this theory was not at all neutral in practice. The doctrine legitimized the power of capital and property interests over labor and propertyless interests.

The prevailing doctrine was narrow even by the standards of the preindustrial age. When John Locke wrote that "the preservation of their property is the reason why men enter into society," he was not thinking simply in terms of land, buildings, money, and other tangibles. The word "property" in Locke's time had the larger meaning of everything peculiar to oneself, including such intangibles as a person's beliefs and well-being. A person's labor was as much property in this sense as were his or her physical possessions. James Madison's *Essay on Property* (1792) was based on the same conception of property. Madison wrote that conscience is the "most sacred of all property" and that it is therefore a greater crime to infringe on a person's conscience than on a person's home.[18]

★ ANALYZE THE ISSUE

Events That Force Political Change
In their concern with patterns and processes, political scientists sometimes fail to acknowledge that great events have the power to change government. The Great Depression of the 1930s, for example, challenged Americans to harness the power of a modern economy and a mass society without destroying what they treasured from their past. Franklin Roosevelt's New Deal was designed to do exactly that. How did its policies (such as public works programs, social security, and bank depositors' insurance) hark back to old ways and yet reach toward new ones?

In no other country in the world is the love of property keener or more alert than in America.

Alexis de Tocqueville

---

[16] Alexis de Tocqueville, *Democracy in America* (1835–1840) (Garden City, N.Y.: Doubleday/Anchor, 1969), 55.
[17] Quoted in Advisory Commission on Intergovernmental Relations, *Conditions of Contemporary Federalism* (Washington, D.C.: ACIR, 1985), 115.
[18] Louis Fisher, *American Constitutional Law* (New York: McGraw-Hill, 1990), 465.

In the food stamp program, as in all other government entitlement programs, eligibility criteria determine who is "entitled" to receive the benefits. (Kevin Horan/Picture Group)

The Supreme Court's adoption of a narrower view of property stemmed in part from the justices' backgrounds. They were all trained in the field of law, which was dominated by issues of tangible property, and many of them had considerable wealth of their own. In promoting a narrow doctrine of property, they were upholding the type of property with which their work and their social class made them most familiar.

The industrial age exposed the faults in the Supreme Court's doctrine of property. Nonintervention by government during the era of the business trusts left workers at the mercy of private interests much more powerful than they. The reformer Henry George said that the argument for a hands-off policy by the government was like insisting that each individual "should sink or swim for himself in crossing a river, ignoring the fact that some had been artificially supplied with corks and others artificially loaded with lead."[19]

This recognition that gross economic inequality undermines human freedom and dignity became the justification for **positive government**—the idea that government intervention is necessary in order to enhance personal liberty when individuals are buffeted by economic and social forces beyond their control. Whereas the concept of negative government had regarded government as the

[19] Quoted in McClosky and Zaller, *American Ethos*, 87.

enemy of liberty, the concept of positive government holds that government action can give individuals greater control over their lives. This objective can be met when government acts to offset repressive social and economic forces or provides individuals with the means to resist those forces.

The concept of positive government found its first and fullest expression in the United States in Franklin Roosevelt's New Deal, which rested on the twin ideas that government must act to correct inequities in the free market and that it must protect individuals from severe economic hardship. Because the marketplace is driven by an uncompromising commitment to profit, government is obligated to intervene in order to promote human values, including freedom from want and freedom from market exploitation. This "new public philosophy," as Samuel Beer and others have labeled it, found expression in a great many New Deal policies and programs.[20] Among them were child-labor laws, a minimum wage, the right of labor to bargain collectively, business regulation of varying types, public works projects, unemployment compensation, and social security for the elderly, infirm, handicapped, and widowed.

Since the 1930s, the concept of positive government has extended beyond what even the most ardent New Dealer might have imagined. Government now has ongoing responsibilities for regulating, promoting, and monitoring economic relationships and for protecting individuals from the vagaries of the marketplace. Nevertheless, the idea of positive government has not replaced that of negative government. The two ideas coexist, sometimes uneasily, in American public opinion and public policy. As James David Barber notes, Americans want "security *and* opportunity, money *and* liberty, fairness *and* variety."[21] They want freedom from government and yet they want government to protect them from personal deprivation and loss of control.

"NEW" ECONOMIC RIGHTS: ENTITLEMENT PROGRAMS

A **right** is an individual claim that has legal status and is protected through due process of law. In recent years, traditional rights of property, derived from the Constitution, have been augmented by property rights established through ordinary (statutory) law. These rights include "welfare payments, job rights, garnishment procedures, unemployment compensation, and environmental rights."[22] Many of the more important of these newer rights involve government *entitlement programs*. The benefits provided by such programs cannot be denied to individuals who are "entitled" to them by virtue of meeting the criteria for eligibility. Social security benefits are an example. These benefits cannot lawfully be denied an individual who has reached the statutory retirement age and who otherwise meets the conditions of eligibility, including payment of social security taxes for a specified period.

As with constitutional rights, people who believe they have been wrongly denied an entitlement can resort to due-process proceedings. They can bring suit against the government in order to get a court determination as to whether

[20] Samuel Beer, "In Search of a New Public Philosophy," in Anthony King, ed., *The New American Political System* (Washington, D.C.: American Enterprise Institute, 1978), 6–13.
[21] James David Barber, *The Pulse of Politics* (New York: Norton, 1980), 317. (Emphasis added.)
[22] Fisher, *American Constitutional Law*, p. 464.

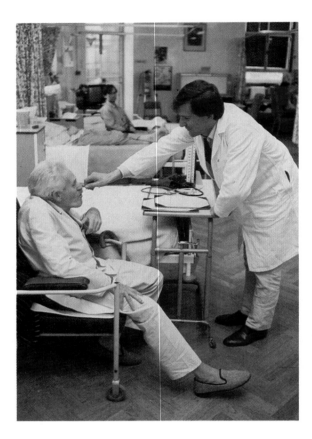

European democracies emphasize economic security more than the United States does. Most of them, including England, offer government-paid health care to all their citizens. Here, a doctor makes the rounds of a London clinic. (S. Steen/ Gamma-Liaison)

they should receive the benefit. Due process has also been a means by which individuals have sometimes forced government to expand entitlement programs. In cases involving public housing and other forms of assistance, courts at times have ordered government to expand eligibility to include categories of citizens who appear to have been arbitrarily excluded by a government agency. For the most part, however, the judiciary has held that questions of welfare services are matters for the elected branches to decide. The "intractable economic, social, and even philosophical problems presented by public welfare assistance programs are not the business of this Court," said the Supreme Court in 1970.[23]

Today the range of entitlement programs that have been established through statute is quite extensive, and these programs have become every bit as significant to many Americans' lives as traditional rights of property and contract. Citizens expect government to protect their economic security through such entitlement programs as

Social security for retirees

Medical benefits for the poor (Medicaid) and for eligible retirees (Medicare)

---

[23] *Dandridge* v. *Williams,* 397 U.S. 471 (1970).

Aid to Families with Dependent Children (AFDC)

Food stamps for low-income individuals and families

School lunch subsidies for poor children

Public housing for low-income families

Equality of Opportunity: The American Way

All democratic societies promote both economic liberty and economic security, but they do so in varying ways and to different degrees. Economic security has a higher priority in European democracies than in the United States. European democracies have instituted such programs as government-paid health care for *all* citizens, compensation for *all* unemployed workers, and retirement benefits for *all* elderly citizens. By comparison, the United States provides these benefits only to *some* citizens in each category. For example, not all elderly Americans receive social security benefits. Eligibility is confined to those persons (including their spouses) who contributed special payroll taxes during their working years. If they paid social security taxes for a long enough period when they were employed, they get the benefits. Otherwise, they do not, even if they are in dire economic need.

Such policy differences between Europe and the United States stem from cultural and historical differences. Democracy developed in Europe in reaction to centuries of aristocratic rule, the inequities of which brought the issue of human equality to the forefront. When strong labor and socialist parties then emerged as a consequence of industrialization, European democracies initiated sweeping social-welfare programs that brought about greater economic equality. In contrast, American democracy emerged out of a tradition of limited government that emphasized personal freedom. Equality was a lesser issue, and class consciousness was weak. No major labor or socialist party emerged in

---

★ HOW THE UNITED STATES COMPARES

GOVERNMENT'S RESPONSIBILITY FOR A PERSON'S WELL-BEING

Central to Americans' long tradition of individualism is self-reliance, the ideas that people should take care of themselves and that anyone who tries hard enough can succeed. This cultural belief has been altered somewhat by events and policies of the past century, but it remains strong. Western Europeans stress individualism, too, but they tend to be more willing than Americans to give government a leading social-welfare role.

Government Should Take Responsibility For	PERCENT WHO AGREE		
	United States	Great Britain	Germany
Providing good medical care	42%	74%	63%
Looking after old people	41	58	51
Guaranteeing jobs	34	55	60
Providing adequate housing	25	60	39
Reducing income inequality	13	25	29

SOURCE: Russell J. Dalton, *Citizen Politics in Western Democracies* (Chatham, N.J.: Chatham House Publishers, 1988), 100.

America during industrialization to represent the working class, and there was no persistent and strong demand for welfare policies that would bring about an economic leveling.

These differing legacies are evident today in the opinions of Americans and Europeans toward liberty and equality. When asked in a Gallup study whether they placed a higher value on freedom or on equality, Americans chose freedom by 72 percent to 20 percent. Among Europeans, the margin was only 49 percent to 35 percent.[24]

Although there has been a modest trend during the twentieth century to restrict traditional property rights in order to promote equality, the United States lags behind Western Europe in this respect. An example is labor rights.[25] Employees in the United States do not have much, if any, say in the running of the firms they work for. In comparison with European workers, they also have fewer collective bargaining and job security rights. In fact, it was not until the enactment of the National Labor Relations Act (also called the Wagner Act) in 1935 that employers were required to negotiate pay and working conditions with employees' unions. This requirement has altered but not equalized the rights of employers and employees. During the past two decades business has made a concerted effort to undermine labor unions. In a 1984 case the Supreme Court ruled in favor of a company that had filed for bankruptcy for the purpose of voiding its labor contracts.[26] After filing, the corporation resumed its operations with new, nonunion workers hired at much lower wage and benefit levels.

The probusiness tradition in America goes back to the time when Lockean notions of property were narrowed to refer only to tangible property, excluding personal labor. Americans have never had a vision of a moral order based on an explicit notion of economic justice. On the basis of his study of political values, Karl Lamb concluded that most Americans "cannot really imagine a society that would provide substantial material equality."[27]

Instead, Americans place their trust in the economic marketplace. They look upon jobs and the personal income that comes from work as the proper basis of economic security. The uncertainties of the economy and the small wages that some jobs produce are slight concerns. Americans tend to look upon equality as an issue of economic opportunity rather than economic sharing. Americans are disinclined to help the poor through welfare payments; they prefer that the poor be given training and education so that they can learn to help themselves (see Table 6-1). This attitude is consistent with Americans' preference for **equality of opportunity,** which is the idea that individuals should have an equal chance to succeed on their own. The concept embodies equality in its emphasis on giving everyone a fair chance to get ahead. Yet equality of opportunity also embodies liberty because it allows people to succeed or fail on their own as a result of what they do with their opportunities. The presumption is that people will end up differently—some rich, some poor. It is sometimes

[24] McClosky and Zaller, *American Ethos,* 18.
[25] See, for example, Robert C. Grady, "Workplace Democracy and Possessive Individualism," *Journal of Politics* 52 (1990): 146–166.
[26] *National Labor Relations Board* v. *Bildisco and Bildisco,* 465 U.S. 513 (1984).
[27] Karl A. Lamb, *As Orange Goes: Twelve California Families and the Future of American Politics* (New York: Norton, 1974), 178.

★ CRITICAL THINKING

DOES "WORKFARE" ENCOURAGE SELF-RELIANCE OR IS IT INVOLUNTARY SERVITUDE?

Individualism exalts self-reliance, and many Americans believe that self-reliance is within the capacity of nearly everyone. When Gallup pollsters asked in 1985 whether a lack of effort or circumstances beyond one's control are more often to blame if a person is poor, only 34 percent of the respondents attributed poverty mainly to uncontrollable circumstances. Such opinions account for the persistence of the idea of "workfare"—the requirement that able-bodied welfare recipients either work in unpaid jobs or receive training for employment. In the early 1980s Congress rejected workfare as national policy but in 1988 enacted a national workfare law. The law directs the states to establish education and work programs designed to put those on welfare to work. As an enticement for those with young children, the law has a child-care support provision. Welfare recipients who meet the eligibility criteria for the workfare program have no choice but to participate if they want to retain their welfare benefits.

Proponents claim that workfare can break the pattern of welfare dependency that can envelop entire families for several generations. When a welfare recipient is trained or employed, in this view, the probability increases that he or she will eventually find gainful, permanent employment. Opponents say that the large majority of people on welfare are there because of circumstance, such as job layoffs at their former place of work, and not because they choose not to work. Opponents also say that because workfare forces welfare recipients to do any job that officials assign, it amounts to involuntary servitude.

What is your position on workfare? Do you believe that significant numbers of welfare recipients will find gainful employment as a result of a workfare program? Or do you believe that workfare is ineffective and a form of involuntary servitude? (For further information on the subject of welfare and work, see Chapter 25.)

said that equality of opportunity offers individuals an equal chance to become unequal.

In practice, equality of opportunity works itself out primarily in the private sector, where Americans compete for jobs, promotions, and other advantages. However, a few public policies have the purpose of enhancing equality of opportunity. The most significant of these policies is public education.

TABLE 6-1 What Americans Believe Should Be Done to Help the Poor
Americans look toward education rather than welfare as the best solution to problems of poverty.

Form of Assistance	Percent Favoring
Give money to the poor	1%
Do nothing and wait for a strong economy to lift up the poor	2
Provide government services for the poor	5
Create government jobs for the poor	20
Give poor people education and training for jobs in the private sector	72
	100%

SOURCE: 1985 *Los Angeles Times* survey.

Workfare—the performance of public services, such as maintaining the grounds of a housing project, in exchange for government-paid financial assistance—is gaining in popularity as an alternative to welfare "handouts." (Kevin Horan/Picture Group)

PUBLIC EDUCATION: LEVELING THROUGH THE SCHOOLS

In the nation's first century of existence, the question of whether government should provide free education to all children divided the landed wealthy from the advocates of broad-based democracy. The wealthy feared that an educated public would challenge their entrenched power. The democrats wanted to provide more people with the foundation for economic advantage.

The democrats won out. Public schools sprang up in nearly every community and were open free of charge to children who could attend. The contrast with Europe was stark. There, schooling was a privilege that was reserved largely for the upper classes. Leon Sampson, a nineteenth-century American socialist, commented on the difference: "The European ruling classes . . . were open in their contempt for the proletariat. But in the United States equality, and even classlessness, the creation of wealth for all and political liberty were extolled in the public schools." Sampson concluded that Americans had a unique conception of equality: everyone was primed to become a capitalist. "It is," he said, "a socialist conception of capitalism."[28]

Of course, public education has never been a uniform experience for American children. Cities in the late nineteenth century neglected the education of many immigrant children, who were thereby placed at a permanent disadvantage. And southern schools for black children in the segregationist era were designed to keep them down, not lift them up.

[28] Quoted in Michael Harrington, *Socialism* (New York: Bantam, 1973), 142.

Today, whether an American child gets a good education depends to a significant extent on the wealth of the community in which he or she resides. In 1973 the Supreme Court ruled that education of high quality is not a right to which all children are entitled. The Supreme Court concluded that education "is not among the rights afforded explicit protection under [the] Constitution. Nor . . . [is it] implicitly so protected." A state is obliged only to provide "an 'adequate' education for all children," not "equal quality of education."[29] The Supreme Court reaffirmed its position in 1988 by declaring that education is not a "fundamental right" and that schools can require even poor families to pay fees in return for services for their children.[30]

Nevertheless, the United States through its public schools has educated a broad segment of the population. Arguably, no country in the world has made an equivalent effort to give children, whatever their parents' backgrounds, an equal opportunity in life through education. The United States ranks first in the world in per capita spending on education and first in the proportion of adults receiving a college education.[31] In the United States, about 40 percent of young people eventually go on to college, compared with less than 15 percent in Britain, for example.

A CRISIS IN EDUCATION?

Although the United States ranks first in the world in education spending, the results are not comparably impressive. Critics have said that a high school

[29] *San Antonio Independent School District* v. *Rodriguez,* 411 U.S. 1 (1973).
[30] *Kadrmas* v. *Dickinson Public Schools,* 487 U.S. 450 (1988).
[31] Sidney Verba and Gary Orren, *Equality in America* (Cambridge, Mass.: Harvard University Press, 1985), ch. 1.

The Supreme Court has held that states are required to give all children, of all socioeconomic strata, an adequate education. The extent, causes, and remedies of the education system's failures in that effort are sources of recurrent controversy. (Michael Weisbrot/Stock, Boston)

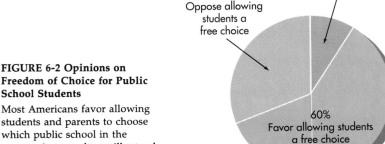

FIGURE 6-2 Opinions on Freedom of Choice for Public School Students

Most Americans favor allowing students and parents to choose which public school in the community a student will attend. *Source: Gallup poll, May 5–June 11, 1989.*

diploma in some school systems now means next to nothing, that many graduates can barely read and write. Indeed, by some estimates a fourth of the country's adult population is illiterate or nearly so. Among minority-group members the incidence is much higher—about half of African-Americans and Hispanics cannot read and write at more than an elementary level.[32] The performance of American students on standardized exams, such as the Scholastic Aptitude Test (SAT), has declined in comparison with earlier periods.

Several reasons for the apparently weak performance of the American educational system have been put forward. One is the extraordinary amount of time that the country's children spend watching television as compared with studying. Another is the sharp increase in the number of minority-group members (such as Hispanics) for whom English is a second language. Still another is the weakening of institutions, such as the family and the church, that have traditionally helped to educate youth.

The decline in the quality of American public education has alarmed parents and educators and has led to proposals for alternative approaches.[33] Some communities now allow parents to choose the public school their children will attend. The schools in effect compete for students, and those that attract the most students are rewarded with the largest budgets. A 1989 Gallup poll indicated that Americans favor such a policy by a 2-to-1 margin (see Figure 6-2). Advocates of the policy contend that it compels school administrators and teachers to do a better job and gives students the option of rejecting a school that is performing poorly. Opponents of the policy say that it creates a few well-funded schools and a lot of poorly funded ones, yielding no net gain in education quality. Critics also claim that the policy discriminates against poor and minority-group children, whose parents are less likely to be knowledgeable enough to steer them toward the better schools.

Oregon adopted a statewide merit system in 1991 that is based more on competition between students than between schools. The system includes a statewide test of tenth-graders which determines whether a student is held back

[32] Jonathan Kozol, *Illiterate America* (Garden City, N.Y.: Anchor Press/Doubleday, 1985).
[33] See John E. Chubb and Terry M. Moe, *Politics, Markets, and America's Schools* (Washington, D.C.: Brookings Institution, 1990).

for remedial work, enters a job-training track, or enters a college preparatory track. This program, with its reliance on test scores to determine who can prepare for college, has been compared with European systems. Business groups and other advocates of the Oregon plan say that it will lead to a better educated and more economically competitive population. Critics maintain that the Oregon policy is undemocratic because it segregates students into two classes—those certified to be worthy of college training and those suited for vocational education only.[34]

The issue of whether to have a classless educational system goes to the heart of the issue of equal opportunity. On the one hand, a system that seeks to enhance the education of top students works to the disadvantage of the poor and others who, for reasons of language or life circumstances, are less prepared to do well when they enter school. An elite-centered school system widens the gap between the country's richer and poorer groups. On the other hand, making students compete with one another for the best education can be justified in terms of the country's individualistic tradition; moreover, it better prepares some students for the skill requirements of an increasingly technological society and global economy.

Although education has traditionally been primarily a state and local issue, it has increasingly become an issue of national politics as well. George Bush said he wanted to be known as "the education president" and in 1991 proposed changes in the country's education system, including national testing to measure school performance. However, the proposals were not backed up by major new funding provisions. Democrats charged that Bush was not really serious about improving education quality. This dispute was one more sign that the debate over what to do about American education will not end soon.

[34] "Putting Value in Diplomas," *Newsweek,* July 15, 1991, 62.

★ THE MEDIA AND THE PEOPLE

REPORTING ON AMERICAN EDUCATION

News coverage about the U.S. education system in recent years has been markedly negative. The media's message is that the system is not performing at a level that matches the nation's needs. For example, *Washington Post* columnist George Will wrote, "Today the principal threat to America is America's public education establishment."

Given that the performance of the education system is presented in a negative way, it is not surprising that the proposals for changing the system receive favorable press coverage. Reports about education reflect the pragmatic "we can fix it" attitude that typifies the reporting about a range of U.S. policy issues. Among the proposals mentioned frequently in the news are national

testing, school choice, magnet schools, and an increase in funding for preschool programs for poor children. The news is dominated by conservative proposals (for example, school choice) rather than liberal ones (for example, bilingual education). The most discouraging message is the prevalent suggestion that the United States does not have enough money to solve its education problems.

Education is the top children's issue in the news. More stories are written about education than about children's health, the plight of poor children, family disintegration, and child abuse.

SOURCE: "Saving the Children," *Media Monitor* 5 (August/ September 1991), 1–4.

> *Thus not only does democracy make every man forget his ancestors, but it hides his descendants and separates his contemporaries from him; it throws him back forever upon himself alone and threatens in the end to confine him entirely within the solitude of his own heart.*
>
> Alexis de Tocqueville,
> *Democracy in America*

Individualism: A Mixed Blessing

Americans' beliefs about economic rights and opportunities have been molded primarily by a commitment to individualism. The point can hardly be overstated. Americans have an unusually strong belief that personal effort is the key to success (see Figure 6-3).

The first observer to reflect on this relationship was Alexis de Tocqueville, who in the 1830s questioned whether individualism was altogether a good thing. He acknowledged that individualism had contributed to America's economic progress but was concerned that individualism led Americans to value their private lives over citizenship and their self-interest over the public interest. Others have since reached the same judgment, concluding that individualism is the source of much that is undesirable—as well as much that is admirable—in American society.

A SELF-CENTERED PUBLIC

Individualism can degenerate into crass materialism, fostering a society in which human needs become marketplace commodities. The issue becomes, says Jennifer Hochschild, "what's mine" rather than "what's fair."[35] The United States is the only advanced industrial democracy that has no comprehensive system of government-paid health care for all citizens. Health care is not a recognized right of each citizen, so the quality of the health care Americans receive depends to a considerable degree on their ability to pay. In some democracies this policy would be thought unconscionable (all western Europeans have a right to government-funded health-care services), but in the United States it is not even particularly controversial. Recently, the rising costs of health services and the increasing numbers of Americans who cannot afford adequate medical care have given new urgency to the question of a government-funded health-care system. But the question has been phrased in pragmatic terms, not moral ones. That is, the issue is not whether all Americans are

[35] Jennifer Hochschild, *What's Fair?* (Cambridge, Mass.: Harvard University Press, 1981).

FIGURE 6-3 Opinions on the Relationship between Hard Work and Success
Americans are much more likely than Europeans to believe that personal effort is the key to success. Figures are the percentage that disagree with the statement "Hard work offers little guarantee of success." *Source: Times-Mirror Center for the People and the Press survey.*

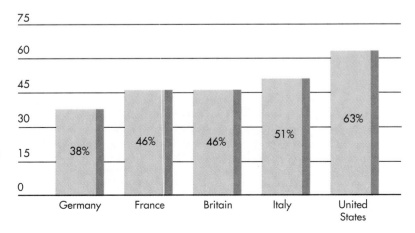

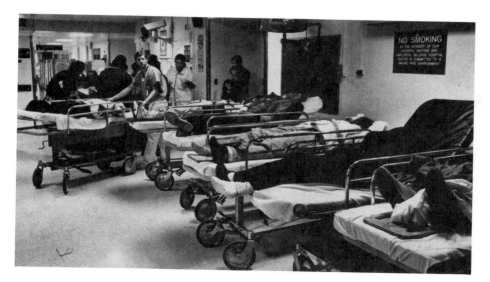

As health-care costs in the United States continue to skyrocket, the relatively few government-funded care providers are becoming overwhelmed by the numbers of patients who have no health insurance and cannot afford private medical care. One result is that hospital emergency rooms now must cope with people who resort to them for routine treatment as well as with patients who need immediate attention. (© 1991 George Cohen/Impact Visuals)

entitled to adequate health care, but whether rising costs are putting health care beyond the means of too many people.

Individualism diminishes Americans' inclination toward collective action. Only about half of America's adult citizens went to the polls to elect a president in 1992. In contrast, turnout levels of 70 to 90 percent are common in other democracies. One reason for the difference is that Americans are more inclined to believe that they can get what they want through the private sector. Americans have an interest in politics, but they are immersed in their economic pursuits.[36] In fact, when they are highly active politically, it is often for the purpose of advancing their economic interests. The United States ranks first in the number of its lobbying groups, most of which have the goal of promoting a special economic interest, not the common interest.

AN ECONOMIC ELITE

A critical perspective on American politics, **elite theory,** holds that the people and their elected representatives have less to say about how the United States is run than does an economic elite composed of wealthy individuals and corporate managers. This elite controls the country's agenda by dominating its financial resources.[37] The richest 1 percent of Americans own 33 percent of the nation's total wealth, and the top 100 corporations (out of a total of 200,000) control half of all industrial assets.

Elite theorists also point to the inordinate degree of influence that the wealthy have over public policy through their connections, direct and indirect, to political leaders. Wealthy individuals occupy a disproportionate number of top positions, particularly in executive agencies and in the Senate. In addition, the economic elite is said to have inside influence over officials because they

★ ANALYZE THE ISSUE

Individualism vs. the Common Good

For many early Americans, the sum of good government was the sum of individual satisfaction, a view that many of today's Americans accept. Alexis de Tocqueville could not accept it, and his view, too, has its modern adherents. Tocqueville argued that individualism leads people to judge everything by its material value and to place their self-interest above the common good. Which of these views reflects your own opinion?

[36] See Gans, *Middle American Individualism.*
[37] See G. William Domhoff, *Who Rules America Now?* (Englewood Cliffs, N.J.: Prentice-Hall, 1983).

Class Consciousness
Wealth is distributed very unequally in the United States. The richest 1 percent of the population control more than 30 percent of the nation's wealth; the poorest 20 percent control less than 5 percent of the wealth. Yet Americans are not highly class conscious. Why is this? Is America's individualistic culture part of the explanation? Do racial divisions among poorer Americans interfere with the development of class awareness?

The Question of a Ruling Elite
Elite-theory and Marxist sociologists claim that ordinary Americans are duped by elites into supporting a society that does not foster their best interests. One supposed strategy is pervasive advertising, which creates a blind demand for products, enriches the elite, and pacifies the masses with material possessions. Can you think of other examples that seem to support elite theory? Are there examples that disprove it? Do you think America is indeed run by a ruling elite?

contribute a large share of the campaign funds that candidates receive and because they underwrite many foundations, "think tanks" (research institutes), and policy groups that provide ideas and forums to officials. Finally, the economic elite is tied to powerful interest groups, particularly the corporations and trade associations that account for more than half of all Washington lobbying groups.[38]

Individualism is a powerful component of elite influence. In comparison with European democracies, the United States has very low effective tax rates, particularly on high incomes and accumulated capital, supposedly because such low rates constitute incentives and rewards for individual efforts. Even more important to moneyed interests is Americans' mistrust of big government, an attitude that stems from individualism and results in a tendency to leave to the private sector many of the decisions that in other democracies are made by government. Banking, natural resources, health care, and air transportation are among the economic sectors that are controlled by private firms in America but by government agencies elsewhere.

Individualism results in a sharp distinction between that which is properly public (political) and that which is properly private (economic). The public component is subject to partisan debate and action. The private component, which includes most economic relationships, is not. Americans, says political scientist Robert Lane, have a preference for market justice rather than political justice.[39] They prefer to see benefits distributed primarily through the economic marketplace rather than through the policies of government. A result is that most of the power and resources of the country's wealthiest interests are effectively beyond the reach of a political majority. Although ordinary people are profoundly affected by the decisions of moneyed interests, they continue to believe that these decisions belong not to themselves but to the holders of property. Thus, although (as we saw in Chapter 2) the Supreme Court decided in 1937 that the Constitution was no longer a powerful protector of business interests, these interests are still protected in significant ways by Americans' persistent belief that politics and economics are largely different realms.

The power of America's economic elite is often exaggerated; it is a mistake to assume that because the nation's politics serves the interests of this elite, it serves *only* those interests. Elite analysis also breaks down when it is ahistorical; some analysts attribute the power of moneyed interests to a grand conspiracy rather than to a cultural bias in favor of economic accumulation and power. But in any case the extraordinary power of wealthy interests in America is both a consequence and a cause of the country's individualistic culture.

HUMAN ENERGY AND PROGRESS

Individualism as a fundamental value cannot be judged by its costs alone. It has the capacity to liberate human energy and imagination, thereby contributing to societal progress and individual growth.

An individualistic society is open and fluid rather than closed and stratified.

[38] Ibid., ch. 1.
[39] Robert E. Lane, "Market Justice, Political Justice," *American Political Science Review* 80 (1986): 383; also see Jennifer Nedelsky, *Private Property and the Limits of American Constitutionalism* (New York: Oxford University Press, 1990).

By law and custom, there are few formal distinctions—no titles, no fixed class lines—that sharply separate Americans from one another. To a considerable degree, each American must create his or her own place in society. Although material striving is one consequence, another and more salutary effect is that Americans are not locked into inferior social positions. There are fewer barriers to social mobility in the United States than in nearly any other society. Race is the dramatic exception: nonwhites confront formidable obstacles to advancement. For whites, at any rate, American society is relatively open, a condition that is owed largely to individualism. As Tocqueville noted more than a century and a half ago, there is a natural social equality in a country in which a person's achievement is admired more than his or her family background.[40]

The bias that individualism produces against governmental power also has its positive side. For one thing, personal privacy is strengthened when people believe strongly in limited government. Governmental invasion of property and, to a lesser degree, of person is naturally resisted. Government is more intrusive and repressive in most other societies than it is in the United States.

In addition, big government by its nature is less flexible government. Countries that have a larger public sector than the United States have special difficulties, including bureaucratic rigidity, economic inflexibility, and welfare dependency. Such societies suffer an incalculable loss of human initiative; this is a large part of the reason that several European democracies, as well as the former Soviet Union and China, have recently placed more emphasis on economic individualism. It has a proven power to unleash human energy and imagination and thereby to stimulate human development.

Summary

Liberty for the first American immigrants included the right to better themselves economically and to be protected through law in their property holdings. The Constitution codified this idea in the contract clause; property rights are also included within the due-process protections of the Fifth and Fourteenth Amendments. The idea behind the granting of individual economic rights is that they are worthwhile in themselves and contribute to the collective good through the social and economic benefits that result from them.

The historic conception of liberty in the United States was freedom from government (negative government). This conception and the nation's open frontier fostered a belief in rugged individualism. Economic self-reliance complemented Americans' commitment to equality; as long as personal liberty and opportunity were provided, Americans could seek individual economic gain without encountering insurmountable barriers and without imposing great costs on others. The Industrial Revolution altered these conditions: concentrated corporate power enabled business monopolists to restrict the freedom and institutionalize the inequality of workers. This pattern was reinforced by the Supreme Court, which, through substantive due process, protected corporations from governmental regulation of employment practices.

In contrast, the premise of the New Deal was that government must act affirmatively to help individuals control their lives and achieve their full human potential (positive government). Acceptance of the New Deal by the American people tempered their commitment to individualism and allowed government to begin to play a significant role in providing economic security. In the United States, however, the balance between economic equality and individualism is still tilted more toward individualism than it is in other advanced industrialized democracies. Entitlement to social security, for example, is not a universal right of elderly Americans but instead depends on whether the individual has contributed special payroll taxes during his or her working years. Unlike some democracies, however, the United States attempts

[40] Tocqueville, *Democracy in America*, 550.

to provide all children with an education that will give them equality of opportunity.

Idealistically, individualism is a commitment to human potential and accomplishment, but it can devolve into selfishness and elitism. Untempered materialism diminishes public life and creates a selfish reluctance to share society's resources with the less privileged. Elite power stems from the concentration of wealth and the tendency to separate political issues from economic ones, thus leaving large areas of American life subject to control by powerful private interests. Although materialism and an economic elite are undeniably elements of American society, the significant question is whether these elements are as pervasive and decisive as critics claim them to be. No simple answer is possible. To ordinary Americans, political and economic life in the United States is not a stark choice between economic security and opportunity or between public power and private power. A blend of values—individual security and opportunity, public choice and private discretion—constitutes Americans' conception of the good society.

Major Concepts

contract clause	negative government
elite theory	positive government
equality of opportunity	property rights
individualism	right

Suggested Readings

Chubb, John E., and Terry M. Moe. *Politics, Markets, and America's Schools.* Washington, D.C.: Brookings Institution, 1990. The authors recommend a new system of public education designed around parent-student choice and school competition.

Domhoff, G. William. *Who Rules America Now?* Englewood Cliffs, N.J.: Prentice-Hall, 1983. An assessment of wealth and power that concludes that the United States is run largely by and for an economic elite.

Ely, James W. *The Guardian of Every Other Right: A Constitutional History of Property Rights.* New York: Oxford University Press, 1991. An analysis of the close relationship between property rights and the Constitution, from colonial times to the present.

Goldwin, Robert A., and William A. Schambra, eds. *How Capitalistic Is the Constitution?* Washington, D.C.: American Enterprise Institute, 1982. A series of essays on the relationship of a liberal democratic society to a capitalist economic system.

Hochschild, Jennifer. *What's Fair?* Cambridge, Mass.: Harvard University Press, 1981. A careful study of Americans' conceptions of fairness, with an emphasis on economic issues.

McClosky, Herbert, and John Zaller. *The American Ethos: Public Attitudes toward Capitalism and Democracy.* Cambridge, Mass.: Harvard University Press, 1984. A survey-based analysis of Americans' attitudes toward economic and political issues.

Mintz, Beth, and Michael Schwartz. *The Power Structure of American Business.* Chicago: University of Chicago Press, 1985. An examination of intercorporate connections, with some references to relationships between corporate and political entities.

Nedelsky, Jennifer. *Private Property and the Limits of American Constitutionalism: The Madisonian Framework and Its Legacy.* Chicago: University of Chicago Press, 1990. Argues that the Framers' focus on property has had a substantial impact on the development and theory of American politics.

O'Brien, David M. *Privacy, Law, and Public Policy.* New York: Praeger, 1979. An assessment of privacy and its status in law and policy.

EQUAL RIGHTS: STRUGGLING TOWARD FAIRNESS

I have a dream that one day this nation will rise up and live out the true meaning of its creed: "We hold these truths to be self-evident: that all men are created equal."
Martin Luther King, Jr.[1]

*I*n 1991 the producers of ABC television's _Prime Time Live_ put hidden cameras on two young men, equally well dressed and groomed, and then sent them on different routes to do the same things—search for an apartment, shop for a car, look at albums in a record store. The cameras recorded the reactions the two men received. One was greeted with smiles and was invited to buy, often at good prices. The other man was treated with suspicious looks, was sometimes made to wait, and was often asked to pay more. Why the difference? The explanation was simple: the young man who was routinely well received was white; the young man who was treated badly was an African-American.

The Urban Institute had conducted a similar experiment a few months earlier. The experiment used pairs of specially trained white and black male college students who were the same in all respects—education, work experience, speech patterns, physical builds—except for their race. The students responded individually to nearly 500 classified job advertisements in Chicago and Washington, D.C.. The black applicants got fewer interviews, had shorter interviews, and were given fewer job offers than the white applicants. An Urban Institute spokesperson said, "The level of reverse discrimination [favoring blacks over whites] that we found was limited, was certainly far lower than many might have been led to fear, and was swamped by the extent of discrimination against black job applicants."[2]

These two experiments suggest why some Americans are still struggling for equal rights. In theory, Americans are equal in their rights, but in reality, they

[1]Speech of Martin Luther King, Jr., in Washington, D.C., August 2, 1963.
[2]_Washington Post_ wire story, May 14, 1991.

are not now equal, nor have they ever been. African-Americans, women, Hispanic-Americans, the disabled, Jews, American Indians, Catholics, Asian-Americans, homosexuals, and members of nearly every other minority group have been victims of discrimination in fact and in law. The nation's creed—"all men are created equal"—has encouraged minorities to believe that they deserve equal justice and has given weight to their claims for fair treatment. But full equality is far from being a universal condition of American life. In fact, inequality is built into almost every aspect of our society. To take but one example: African-Americans with a correctable heart problem are three times less likely to receive the necessary surgery than are whites with the same problem.[3]

This chapter focuses on **equal rights,** or **civil rights**—terms that refer to the right of every person to equal protection under the laws and equal access to society's opportunities and public facilities. We saw in Chapter 5 that "civil liberties" refer to specific *individual* rights, such as freedom of speech, that are protected from infringement by government. "Equal rights" or "civil rights" have to do with whether individual members of differing *groups*—racial, sexual, and the like—are treated equally by government and, in some areas, by private parties. To oversimplify, civil liberties deal with issues of personal freedom, and civil rights deal with issues of equality.

Although the law refers to the rights of individuals first and to those of groups in a secondary and derivative way, this chapter concentrates on groups because the history of civil rights has been largely one of group claims to equality. The chapter emphasizes the following main points:

★ *Disadvantaged groups have had to struggle for equal rights.* African-Americans, women, Native Americans, Hispanic-Americans, and Asian-Americans have all had to fight for their rights in order to come closer to equality with white males.

★ *Americans have attained substantial equality under the law.* They have, in legal terms, equal protection of the laws, equal access to accommodations and housing, and an equal right to vote. Discrimination by law against persons because of race, sex, religion, and ethnicity is now largely a thing of the past.

★ *Legal equality for all Americans has not resulted in* de facto equality. African-Americans, women, Hispanic-Americans, and other traditionally disadvantaged groups have a disproportionately small share of America's opportunities and benefits. Existing inequalities, discriminatory practices, and political pressures are still major barriers to their full equality. Affirmative action and busing are policies designed to help the disadvantaged achieve full equality.

The Struggle for Equality

Equality has always been the least completely developed of America's founding concepts. Not even Thomas Jefferson, who had a deep admiration for the "common man," believed that broad meaning could be given to the claim of the

[3]Reported on *CBS Evening News,* January 16, 1989.

Declaration of Independence that "all men are created equal." Jefferson rejected any suggestion that people should be equalized in their possessions, interests, positions, or opinions. To Jefferson, "equality" had a restricted, though significant, meaning: people are of equal moral worth and as such deserve equal treatment under the law.[4] Even then, Jefferson made a distinction between free men, who were entitled to legal equality, and slaves, who were not.

The history of America shows that disadvantaged groups have rarely achieved an additional degree of legal equality without a struggle. Equality is seldom bestowed by the more powerful upon the less powerful. Resistance to granting disadvantaged groups a greater degree of equality is rooted in prejudice and privilege. Certain groups have always claimed superiority over other groups on the basis of superficial differences such as skin color. Even today, more than a fourth of white Americans claim that the black race is "less able" than their own race.[5] Legal discrimination serves the material interests as well as the status needs of a dominant group. The classic case was the white southern plantation owner, for whom slavery was an issue not of human freedom and dignity but of economics—of a lavish lifestyle built on the sweat and blood of the black race.

Equality is a subject that loses urgency when it is considered apart from its historical context. The compelling need for the 1964 Civil Rights Act and other such laws, and the great triumph their passage represents, cannot be understood without an awareness of the long struggle that led up to them. We can establish this context by looking briefly at the efforts of African-Americans, women, Native Americans, Hispanic-Americans, and Asian-Americans to achieve fuller equality.

AFRICAN-AMERICANS

Of all America's problems, none has been so persistent as the white race's unwillingness to yield a fair share of society's benefits to members of the black race. The ancestors of most African-Americans came to this country as slaves, after having been captured in Africa, shipped in chains across the Atlantic, and sold in open markets in Charleston and other southern seaports. When the Constitution was being written in 1787, the question was not whether black people would become free citizens, but whether they would even be counted as human beings. It was finally decided, and written into Article I of the Constitution, that each slave would be counted as three-fifths of a person for purposes of taxation and representation.

It took a civil war to bring slavery to an end, but the conflict did not stop institutionalized racism. When Reconstruction ended in 1877 with the withdrawal of federal troops from the South, southern whites regained power and gradually reestablished racial segregation by enacting laws that prohibited black citizens from using the same public facilities as whites.[6] The Supreme Court accepted this arrangement in *Plessy* v. *Ferguson* (1896), ruling that

> ★ ANALYZE THE ISSUE
>
> **The Impact of Federalism on Equality**
> Disadvantaged groups have achieved a greater degree of equality primarily through federal laws and federal court rulings, rather than through state and local measures. What do you think are the main reasons for this development? Do James Madison's arguments (in *Federalist* No. 10) about the greater diversity of the nation under a federal system apply to the situation? Do issues of equality affect your opinion about whether a federal system is preferable to a unitary one?

[4]Robert Nisbet, "Public Opinion versus Popular Opinion," *Public Interest* 41 (1975): 171.
[5]Paul M. Sniderman with Michael Gray Hagen, *Race and Inequality* (Chatham, N.J.: Chatham House, 1985), 30.
[6]The classic analysis of this system of legalized segregation is C. Vann Woodward, *The Strange Career of Jim Crow*, 3d rev. ed. (New York: Oxford University Press, 1974).

"separate" facilities for the two races did not violate the equal-protection clause of the Fourteenth Amendment, which had been ratified after the Civil War to protect black people, as long as the facilities were "equal."[7]

The Court at first refused even to uphold its own weak standard, allowing southern states and communities to maintain inferior facilities for their black residents. Public schools for African-Americans nearly always had fewer teachers and books and less classroom space than did those for whites. In some cases, no facilities at all were established for the black community; for example, in the whole of the Deep South, there were no state medical or dental colleges for African-Americans. Black leaders challenged these discriminatory state and local policies through legal action, but not until the late 1930s and 1940s did the Supreme Court begin to modify its *Plessy* position.[8] The Court began modestly by ruling that where no public facilities existed for African-Americans, they must be allowed to use those reserved for whites.[9]

The *Brown* Decision

Substantial relief for African-Americans was finally achieved in 1954 with *Brown* v. *Board of Education of Topeka,* arguably the most significant ruling in Supreme Court history. The case began when Linda Carol Brown, a black child in Topeka, Kansas, was denied admission to an all-white elementary school that she passed every day on her way to her all-black school, which was twelve blocks farther away. The case was initiated on her behalf by the National Association for the Advancement of Colored People (NAACP) and was argued

---

[7]*Plessy* v. *Ferguson,* 163 U.S. 537 (1896).
[8]See Loren Miller, *The Petitioners* (New York: Meridian Books, 1967).
[9]*Missouri ex rel. Gaines* v. *Canada,* 305 U.S. 57 (1938).

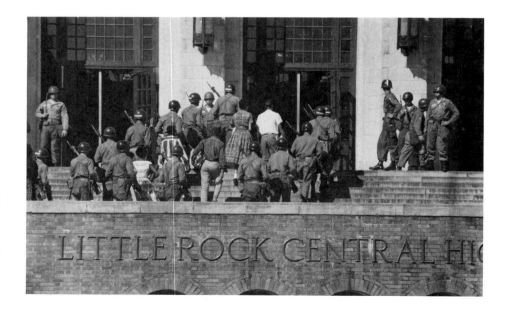

Federal troops protect black students desegregating Little Rock Central High School after the Supreme Court's *Brown* ruling in 1954 that segregated public schools were unconstitutional. The ruling set off a wave of protests throughout the South. (Burt Glinn/Magnum)

Under police orders, Birmingham firefighters turn the full force of their firehoses on black civil rights demonstrators in July 1963. Such images of hatred and violence shook many white Americans out of their complacency regarding race relations. (AP/Wide World Photos)

before the Supreme Court by Thurgood Marshall, who later became the Court's first black justice.[10] In its decision, the Court fully reversed its *Plessy* doctrine by declaring that racial segregation of public schools "generates [among black children] a feeling of inferiority as to their status in the community that may affect their hearts and minds in a way unlikely ever to be undone. . . . Separate educational facilities are inherently unequal."[11]

A 1954 Gallup poll indicated that a sizable majority of southern whites opposed the *Brown* decision, and billboards were quickly erected along southern roadways that called for the impeachment of Chief Justice Earl Warren. In the so-called Southern Manifesto, southern congressmen urged their state governments to "resist forced integration by any lawful means." In 1957 rioting broke out when Governor Orval Faubus called out the Arkansas National Guard to block the entry of black children to the Little Rock public schools. To restore order and carry out the desegregation of the Little Rock schools, President Dwight D. Eisenhower used his power as the nation's commander in chief to place the Arkansas National Guard under federal control. For their part, northern whites were neither strongly for nor strongly against school desegregation. A Gallup poll taken shortly after the *Brown* decision indicated that a slim majority of whites outside the South agreed with it.

Separate educational facilities are inherently unequal.
Brown v. Board of Education of Topeka (1954)

[10]See Richard Kugler, *Simple Justice: The History of* Brown v. Board of Education *and Black America's Struggle for Equality* (New York: Knopf, 1977).
[11]*Brown v. Board of Education of Topeka*, 347 U.S. 483 (1954).

The Black Civil Rights Movement

After *Brown*, the struggle of African-Americans for their rights became a political movement. Perhaps no single event turned national public opinion so dramatically against segregation as a 1963 march led by Dr. Martin Luther King, Jr., in Birmingham, Alabama. An advocate of nonviolent protest, King had been leading peaceful demonstrations and marches for nearly eight years before that fateful day in Birmingham.[12] As the nation watched in disbelief on television, police officers led by Birmingham's sheriff, Eugene ''Bull'' Connor, attacked King and his followers with dogs, cattle prods, and firehoses.

The modern civil rights movement peaked with the triumphant March on Washington for Jobs and Freedom of August 2, 1963. Organized by Dr. King and other civil rights leaders, it attracted 250,000 marchers, one of the largest gatherings in the history of the nation's capital. ''I have a dream,'' the Reverend King told the gathering, ''that my four little children will one day live in a nation where they will not be judged by the color of their skin but by the content of their character.''

A year later, after a months-long fight in Congress that was marked by every parliamentary obstacle that racial conservatives could muster, the Civil Rights Act of 1964 was enacted. As we'll discuss later in this chapter, the legislation provided African-Americans and other minorities with equal access to public facilities and prohibited job discrimination. Even then, southern states resorted to legal maneuvering and other delaying tactics to blunt the new law's impact. The state of Virginia, for example, established a commission to pay the legal expenses of white citizens who were brought to court for violations of the federal act. Nevertheless, momentum was on the side of racial equality. The murder of two civil rights workers during a voter registration drive in Selma, Alabama, helped to sustain the momentum.[13] President Lyndon Johnson, who had been a decisive force in the battle to pass the Civil Rights Act, called for new legislation that would end racial barriers to voting.[14] Congress's answer was the 1965 Voting Rights Act.

The Aftermath of the Civil Rights Movement

After 1965 the civil rights movement went awry. The rising expectations of African-Americans were not met in terms of jobs and other benefits, and rioting occurred in Detroit, Newark, Los Angeles, and other cities between 1966 and 1968. In addition, the attention of Washington policymakers had been distracted from the civil rights movement by the escalating war in Vietnam, which was also siphoning away federal funds that might have been used for education, training, and jobs programs for poor African-Americans (see Chapter 25). When King was murdered in 1968, the most active phase of the modern civil rights movement came to an end.

The most significant progress in history toward the legal equality of all

---

★ ANALYZE THE ISSUE

Why Are Black Americans Losing Ground?
Although the lives of black Americans have improved in absolute terms since the mid-1960s, their lives have not improved much in comparison with those of whites. The job and income gaps have grown; the education gap, which had been closing, is now widening; and the life expectancy of blacks has started to drop while that of whites continues to increase. Why are blacks going backward in these important respects? Is it mainly because no major new policy initiatives have been made in their behalf in recent years and some existing programs have been cut back? Or is it mainly because of the destructive impact of drug abuse, violence, and family disintegration within the black community? If both these reasons apply, are they connected? Can anything but racism, historical and contemporary, be at the bottom of the whole problem?

---

[12]See Francis M. Wilhoit, *The Politics of Massive Resistance* (New York: George Braziller, 1973).
[13]See David J. Garrow, *Protest at Selma: Martin Luther King and the Voting Rights Act of 1965* (New Haven, Conn.: Yale University Press, 1978).
[14]See Steven A. Shull, *The President and Civil Rights Policy: Leadership and Change* (Westport, Conn.: Greenwood Press, 1989).

The Rev. Martin Luther King, Jr., became the nation's conscience as he led the black civil rights movement from the Montgomery, Alabama, bus boycott in 1955 until his murder in 1968. Here he delivers his famous "I have a dream" speech at the Lincoln Memorial in Washington, D.C., to a crowd of 250,000 people in 1963. (UPI/Bettmann Newsphotos)

Americans occurred during the 1960s. Yet Dr. King's dream of a color-blind society has remained elusive.[15] By some indicators, the status of African-Americans has actually deteriorated since King's death. According to U.S. Department of Labor statistics, the unemployment rate for African-Americans in the late 1960s was less than 50 percent higher than the rate for whites; by 1992 it was more than 100 percent higher. During the same period, the gap in the incomes of black and white Americans has widened, not narrowed. The income of the average African-American family is about 60 percent of the average white family's (see Figure 7-1).

[15]See Sar Levitan, William Johnson, and Robert Taggert, *Still a Dream* (Cambridge, Mass.: Harvard University Press, 1975).

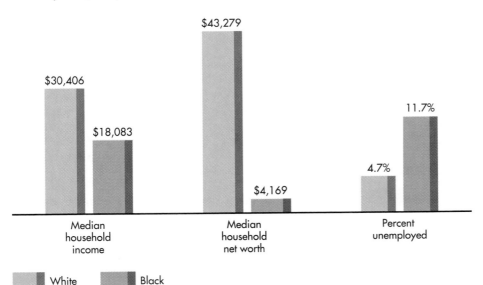

FIGURE 7-1 Indicators of the Economic Status of Whites and Blacks in the United States. White Americans tend to be better off financially than black Americans. The prevalence of poverty among blacks is both a cause and an effect of persistent racial discrimination. *Source: U.S. Bureau of the Census*, Statistical Abstract of the United States, 1990 *(Washington, D.C.: U.S. Government Printing Office, 1990). All data are from 1988.*

Even the legal rights of African-Americans do not, in practice, match the promise of the civil rights movement.[16] A 1988 Harris poll indicated, for example, that only 17 percent of African-Americans agreed with the statement that "blacks and whites are treated equally by the justice system." Well-publicized incidents provide support for the perception. One of the most notorious occurred in March 1991, when an amateur photographer videotaped Los Angeles policemen kicking and clubbing Rodney King, a black man they had stopped along a roadway. Recorded transmissions on police radio made it clear that King's beating was racially motivated.

WOMEN

The United States carried over from English common law a political disregard for women, forbidding them to vote, hold public office, and serve on juries. Upon marriage, a woman essentially lost her identity as an individual and usually surrendered her right to own and dispose of property without her husband's consent. Marriage made husband and wife into "one person," with the man in charge. Even the wife's body was not fully hers. A wife's adultery was ruled by the Supreme Court to be a violation of the husband's property rights![17]

The first women's rights convention in America was held in 1848 in Seneca Falls, New York, after Lucretia Mott and Elizabeth Cady Stanton had been barred from the main floor of an antislavery convention.[18] Thereafter, however, the movement for women's rights became closely aligned with the abolitionist movement, and women had some expectation that black emancipation would also bring them their civil rights. However, the passage of the post–Civil War constitutional amendments proved to be a setback for the women's movement. The Fifteenth Amendment, for example, said that the right to vote could not be abridged on account of race or color, but said nothing about sex.[19] After decades of struggle, the Nineteenth Amendment was finally adopted in 1920, forbidding denial of the right to vote "by the United States or by any state on account of sex."

In view of this entire disfranchisement of one-half the people of this country, . . . and because women do feel themselves aggrieved, oppressed, and fraudulently deprived of their most sacred rights, we insist that they have immediate admission to all the rights and privileges which belong to them as citizens of the United States.

Elizabeth Cady Stanton et al., *Declaration of Seneca Falls Convention*

The Equal Rights Amendment

In 1923 women's leaders proposed another constitutional amendment, one that would guarantee equal rights for women. The amendment failed to gain congressional approval then and on several subsequent attempts. Finally, in 1973, the Equal Rights Amendment (ERA) received congressional approval and went to the state legislatures for ratification. The proposed amendment stated: "Equality of rights under the law shall not be denied or abridged by the United States or by any state on account of sex."

---

[16]See Derrick Bell, *And We Are Not Saved: The Elusive Quest for Racial Justice,* (New York: Basic Books, 1987).

[17]*Tinker* v. *Colwell,* 193 U.S. 473 (1904).

[18]For a history of the women's rights movement, see Eleanor Flexner, *Century of Struggle,* rev. ed. (Cambridge, Mass.: Harvard University Press, 1975).

[19]See Ellen Carol DuBois, *Feminism and Suffrage: The Emergence of an Independent Women's Movement in America, 1848–1869* (Ithaca, N.Y.: Cornell University Press, 1978); Susan Cary Nicholas, *Rights and Wrongs* (Old Westbury, N.Y.: Feminist Press, 1979).

★ HOW THE UNITED STATES COMPARES

WOMEN'S EQUALITY

Although conflict between groups is universal, the nature of the conflict is often particularized. Racial conflict in the United States cannot readily be compared with, say, religious conflict in Northern Ireland. The one form of inequality common to all nations is that of gender: nowhere are women equal to men in law or in fact. But there are large differences between countries. The 1988 study by the Population Crisis Committee referred to in Chapter 1 ranked the United States third overall in women's equality, behind only Sweden and Finland. The rankings were based on five areas—jobs, education, social relations, marriage and family, and health—where U.S. women had an 82.5 percent rating compared with men.

The inequality of women is also indicated by their lack of representation in public office. A Royal Commission in Canada compared the national legislatures of industrialized democratic countries in terms of the percentage of women members. The five countries that ranked highest, ranging from 21 percent to 34 percent female lawmakers, were Iceland, Denmark, Sweden, Finland, and Norway. Canada, at 13 percent, was clustered with several western European countries, including Germany and Italy. The United States ranked low—only 6 percent of the members of Congress are women. This percentage is in the same range as that of Spain, Britain, and France. The only country that ranked significantly lower than the United States was Japan, where women constitute only 1 percent of national legislators.

Congressional support for the ERA was an outgrowth of the 1960s civil rights movement and of the changing demands of women.[20] Families were smaller, and more women were entering the labor force.[21] Proponents of the ERA argued that discrimination on the basis of sex could not be eliminated as long as legal distinctions between men and women were maintained. Ratification of the ERA was opposed by traditionalists, who argued that there is a need to retain special legal protections for women, mainly in the areas of the military draft, working conditions, and family life.[22] A 1982 Gallup survey indicated that 55 percent of Americans (including 53 percent of men) favored the ERA, 36 percent were opposed, and 9 percent had no opinion. Nevertheless, the ERA failed to gain the support of a majority of state legislators in the thirty-eight states needed for ratification. The proposed amendment was three states short when the deadline for ratification came and went in 1982. The state legislatures that did not vote for ratification were concentrated in the South, where traditional attitudes about women are stronger.[23]

Equality of rights under the law shall not be denied or abridged by the United States or by any state on account of sex.

Proposed Equal
Rights Amendment

Women's Legal and Political Gains

Although the ERA did not become part of the Constitution, it helped bring women's rights to the forefront at a time when developments in Congress and the courts were contributing significantly to the legal equality of the sexes.[24]

[20]Cynthia Harrison, *On Account of Sex: The Politics of Women's Issues, 1945–1968* (Berkeley: University of California Press, 1988).
[21]See Suzanne M. Bianchi and Daphne Spain, *American Women in Transition* (New York: Russell Sage Foundation, 1986).
[22]See Janet K. Boles, *The Politics of the Equal Rights Amendment* (New York: Longman, 1977).
[23]See Jane Mansbridge, *Why We Lost the ERA* (Chicago: University of Chicago Press, 1986).
[24]See Joyce Gelb and Marian Lief Palley, *Women and Public Policies* (Princeton, N.J.: Princeton University Press, 1982).

Among the congressional initiatives that have helped women are the Equal Pay Act of 1963, which prohibits sex discrimination in salary and wages by some categories of employers; the Civil Rights Act of 1964, which prohibits sex discrimination in programs that receive federal funding; Title IX of the Education Amendment of 1972, which prohibits sex discrimination in education; and the Equal Credit Act of 1974, as amended in 1976, which prohibits sex discrimination in the granting of financial credit.

The Fourteenth Amendment's equal-protection clause has also become an instrument of women's equality. The *Brown* decision encouraged women's rights activists to believe that the equal-protection clause could be the basis for sex-discrimination rulings. In *Reed* v. *Reed* (1971) the Supreme Court invoked equal protection for the first time in a case involving women's rights, declaring unconstitutional an Idaho statute that gave preference to men in appointments as administrators of the estates of dead children.[25]

The 1984 *Grove City* case, which involved alleged sex discrimination, was a setback for women's rights advocates: the Supreme Court concluded that the antidiscrimination requirements of federal grants to educational institutions applied only to activities funded directly, in whole or in part, with federal money.[26] However, in 1988 Congress over-rode the veto of President Ronald Reagan to alter this policy through legislation that prohibits discriminatory practices in any activity of organizations that receive federal funding.

Women have made clear gains in the area of appointive and elective offices.[27] In 1981 President Reagan appointed the first woman to serve on the Supreme Court, Sandra Day O'Connor. The Democratic party in 1984 chose Geraldine Ferraro as its vice-presidential nominee, the first time a woman has run on the national ticket of a major political party. In Nebraska in 1986, both the Republican nominee and Democratic nominee for governor were women—another political first. Despite such signs of progress, women are still a long way from political equality with men.[28] Women occupy less than 5 percent of the nation's gubernatorial and congressional offices, and women who hold lower public offices are more likely than their male counterparts to perceive significant obstacles to their political advancement.[29]

Job-Related Issues: Comparable Worth and Sexual Harassment

In recent decades, increasing numbers of women have sought employment outside the home. Government statistics indicate that one in eight women worked outside the home in 1950 compared with nearly five in eight in 1990. Women have made gains in many traditionally male-dominated fields. For example, women now make up a third of the new lawyers who enter the job market each year.

The increased number of women in the workplace has brought demands for

[25]*Reed* v. *Reed,* 404 U.S. 71 (1971).
[26]*Grove City College* v. *Bell,* 465 U.S. 555 (1984).
[27]Susan J. Carroll, *Women as Candidates in American Politics* (Bloomington: Indiana University Press, 1985).
[28]Mary Lou Kendrigan, *Political Equality in a Democratic Society: Women in the United States* (Westport, Conn.: Greenwood Press, 1984).
[29]Timothy Bledsoe and Mary Herring, "Victims of Circumstance: Women in Pursuit of Political Office," *American Political Science Review* 84 (1990): 213–224.

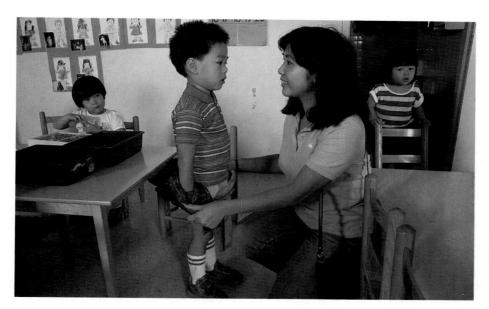

The majority of women with preschool-age children work outside the home, a situation that has created political pressures for affordable day care. (Jacques Chenet/Woodfin Camp & Associates)

increased support for programs such as day-care centers and parental leave. Public support for these programs is relatively high among both men and women. A 1990 Gallup poll indicated, for example, that 72 percent of women and 66 percent of men favored a proposed federal law that would require employers to provide up to twelve weeks of unpaid leave for employees, male or female, who have a new baby or a serious illness in the immediate family.

Nevertheless, women are less than equal to men when it comes to job opportunities and benefits. Women hold a disproportionate number of the poorer-paying jobs. On average, women earn only about three-fourths as much as men. This situation has led to demands by women for equal pay for work that is of similar difficulty and responsibility and that requires similar levels of education and training—a concept called **comparable worth.** A comparable-worth policy would eliminate salary inequities resulting from the fact that some occupations are dominated by women and others by men. This view was the basis for a legal suit against the state of Washington brought by a group of female state employees, who won in a lower court but were reversed by a U.S. court of appeals. Advocates of comparable worth did persuade the Minnesota and Iowa legislatures to enact new salary structures that may eventually provide employees of those states with equal pay, regardless of sex, for jobs requiring comparable training and skills.[30] On the national level, though, the Reagan and Bush administrations opposed the concept of comparable worth, contending that market forces alone should dictate salaries in the private sector.[31]

Discrimination against women in the workplace includes sexual harassment. In 1980 Carolyn Kohlberer, who worked in a St. Paul, Minnesota, printing

★ ANALYZE THE ISSUE

Comparable Worth
Should women receive the same pay as men if their jobs, though different from those held by men, require similar levels of education and experience? Establishment of the doctrine of comparable worth is a major goal of some women's groups. Can it be accomplished on a large scale without disrupting the nation's economy? Can women achieve full equality without achieving income parity with men? Which of these considerations do you think is more important? Which is more likely to win out?

[30]See, however, Sara M. Evans and Barbara Nelson, *Wage Justice* (Chicago: University of Chicago Press, 1989).
[31]See Ellen Frankel Paul, *Equity and Gender* (New Brunswick, N.J.: Transaction Books, 1989).

Employees in certain job categories dominated by women—day-care workers, secretaries, and so on—are paid less than those in male-dominated jobs with similar educational requirements and levels of responsibility. The concept of comparable worth is proposed as a remedy for such inequities. (Richard Kalvar/ Magnum)

plant, complained to management after seeing pinups of nude women in a supply cabinet. Her male supervisor reprimanded her for opening the cabinet. She complained again after a male co-worker made lewd comments to her and another grabbed her breasts. When no action was taken, she sued and received a favorable settlement. Ms. Kohlberer's treatment at work was not unlike that of thousands of other women, which has led to laws that prohibit sexual harassment. The legal standard for what constitutes sexual harassment is known as the "reasonable woman" standard. The question in each case is whether a reasonable woman would be offended by a supervisor's or co-worker's request for sexual favors, a display of sex-related pictures or objects, sexual language, or physical contact.[32] The issue received extraordinary national attention in 1991 in conjunction with the nomination of Clarence Thomas for a seat on the Supreme Court. University of Oklahoma law professor Anita Hill charged that Thomas had sexually harassed her when he was her supervisor a decade earlier at the Equal Employment Opportunity Commission.

NATIVE AMERICANS

When white settlers began arriving in America in large numbers during the seventeenth century, 8 to 10 million Native Americans were living in the territory that would become the United States. By 1900, the Native American population had plummeted to less than 1 million. Diseases brought by white settlers had taken a toll on the various Indian tribes, but so had wars and massacres. "The only good Indian is a dead Indian" is not simply a hackneyed expression from cowboy movies. It was part of the strategy of westward

[32]"Confusion Exists on Issue of Harassment," *Minneapolis Star Tribune,* October 13, 1991, 1A, 4A, 5A.

expansion, as settlers and U.S. troops alike mercilessly drove the eastern Indians from their ancestral lands to the Great Plains, then took those lands too.

Today Native Americans number more than 1 million, of whom about half live on or close to reservations set aside for them by the federal government. Those who retain ties to a reservation are among America's most impoverished, illiterate, and jobless citizens. Native Americans are less than half as likely to attend college as other Americans, their life expectancy is more than ten years less than the national average, and their infant mortality rate is more than three times higher than that of white Americans.

The civil rights movement of the 1960s at first did not include Native Americans. Then, in the early 1970s, militant Native Americans occupied the Bureau of Indian Affairs in Washington, D.C., and later seized control of the village of Wounded Knee on a Sioux reservation in southwestern South Dakota, exchanging gunfire with U.S. marshals. These episodes brought attention to the grievances of Native Americans and may have contributed to the passage in 1974 of legislation that granted Native Americans on reservations a greater measure of control over federal programs that affected them. Native Americans had already benefited from the legislative climate created by the civil rights movement of the 1960s. In 1968 Congress had enacted the Indian Bill of Rights, which gives Native Americans on reservations constitutional guarantees that are similar to those held by other Americans.

In recent years Native Americans have filed suit to reclaim lost ancestral lands and have won a few settlements. But they stand no realistic chance of getting back even those lands that had been granted them by federal treaty but were later sold off or simply taken forcibly by federal authorities. Native Americans were not even official citizens of the United States until an act of Congress in 1924. This status came too late to be of much help; their traditional way of life had already been seriously eroded.

As a result of federal government policy, most Native Americans live on reservations, and many aspects of their traditional way of life have been destroyed. (Rene Burri/Magnum)

HISPANIC-AMERICANS

The fastest-growing minority in the United States is Hispanic-Americans, people with Spanish-speaking backgrounds. The 1990 census counted 22.4 million Hispanics living in the United States, an increase of 53 percent over the 1980 census; and it is projected that Hispanics will replace African-Americans as the nation's largest racial or ethnic minority group by the year 2000. They have emigrated to the United States primarily from Mexico and the Caribbean islands, mainly Cuba and Puerto Rico. About half of all Hispanics in the United States were born in Mexico or trace their ancestry there. Hispanics are concentrated in their states of entry; thus Florida, New York, and New Jersey have large numbers of Caribbean Hispanics, while California, Texas, Arizona, and New Mexico have many immigrants from Mexico. More than half the population of Los Angeles is of Hispanic—mostly Mexican—ancestry.

The term "Hispanic" can be misleading if it is construed to mean a group of people who all think alike. Hispanics cover a wide political spectrum, from the conservative, Republican-leaning Cuban-Americans of southern Florida to the liberal, Democratic-leaning Puerto Ricans of the Northeast. Hispanic-Americans share a common language, Spanish, but they are not monolithic in their thinking.

Migrant Workers

The most publicized civil rights actions involving Hispanic-Americans were the farm workers' strikes of the late 1960s and the 1970s, which aimed at gaining basic labor rights for migrant farm workers. Migrants were working long hours for low pay, traveling from place to place as crops became ready for harvesting. They usually lived near the fields where they worked, in shacks without electricity or plumbing. They were unwelcome in many local schools, and sometimes in local hospitals as well, because few of them had health insurance or the money to pay for their medical care.

Farm owners at first refused to bargain with migrant workers over pay, hours, conditions, or benefits. Only after several years of strikes and a surprisingly effective nationwide boycott of California grapes and lettuce did California in the 1970s pass a law giving migrant workers the right to bargain collectively through their organization, the United Farm Workers. The strikes were led in California by Cesar Chavez, who himself grew up in a Mexican-American migrant family.[33] Chavez's tactics in California were copied in other states, particularly Texas, but the results were less successful.

Illegal Aliens

Hispanic-Americans have benefited from laws and court rulings aimed primarily at protecting other groups. Thus, although the Civil Rights Act of 1965 was largely a response to the condition of black people, its provisions apply broadly. Just as it is unlawful to deny a hotel room to an individual because he or she is black, so it is unlawful to do so because he or she is a Native American, Asian,

---

[33]See Peter Matthiessen, *Sal si Puedes: Cesar Chavez and the New American Revolution* (New York: Random House, 1969).

Hispanic-Americans are growing in political and cultural influence as their numbers increase in California and other states. (Alon Reininger/Woodfin Camp & Associates)

or Hispanic. The fact that Hispanics have made gains as a result of the efforts of other groups, however, does not mean that they feel a common bond with those groups. In some communities, Hispanic-Americans and African-Americans in particular have had a tense relationship, reflecting competition over jobs and status.

Hispanics face some distinctive problems. The fact that many do not speak English is the main reason for a 1968 amendment to the 1964 Civil Rights Act that funds public school programs offering English instruction in the language of children for whom English is a second language. In addition, many Hispanics are illegal aliens; these individuals do not have the full rights of citizens. In *De Canas* v. *Bica* (1976), for example, the Supreme Court upheld a state law barring illegal aliens from employment.[34]

In 1986 Congress passed landmark immigration and naturalization legislation, the Simpson-Mizzoli Act, which primarily affected Hispanics. The legislation provided that illegal aliens who could prove that they had lived continuously in the United States for five years were eligible to become citizens. The act also mandated fines for employers who knowingly hired aliens without work permits; the resulting lack of job openings would eliminate the main reason for aliens to enter the country illegally. The legislation was intended partly to relieve employment and social-service pressures on states bordering Mexico, which is the country of origin of most illegal aliens. Hispanic-American leaders had mixed reactions to the legislation, welcoming the provision granting citizenship to aliens of long-standing residence but worrying that the deportation of nonqualified aliens would result in the breakup of families. The number of illegal aliens who applied to become citizens fell short of government projections. Apparently some aliens were suspicious of the program, believing that they would be arrested and deported when they applied for citizenship at the offices of the Immigration and Naturalization Service. Nevertheless, more

[34]*De Canas* v. *Bica*, 424 U.S. 351 (1976).

than 2 million Hispanics responded to the Immigration Reform and Control Act and will become eligible for citizenship and the vote in the 1990s.

Growing Political Power

Hispanic-Americans are an important political force in some states and communities, and their influence is likely to increase substantially in the next decade or two.[35] In recent years, only about half of Hispanic adults have been registered to vote. If all Hispanic adults were registered, they would make up a voting bloc of more than 10 million people.

More than 4,000 Hispanic-Americans nationwide hold public office. In 1974 Arizona and New Mexico elected governors of Spanish-speaking background. New Mexico elected its second Hispanic governor in 1982.

The growing political and cultural influence of Hispanics, however, has made them a target for criticism in some cities. For example, some non-Hispanic residents of Miami have become increasingly vocal in their opposition to bilingual education, claiming that Spanish-speaking residents (most of whom are of Cuban background) are making little effort to learn English or adjust to their new culture and are thus turning Miami into a Spanish-speaking city.

ASIAN-AMERICANS

Chinese and Japanese laborers were the first Asians to come to the United States in large numbers. They were brought into western states during the late 1800s to work in mines and to build railroads. When the need for this labor declined, Congress in 1892 ordered a temporary halt to Chinese immigration. Over the next three decades informal agreements kept all but a few Asians out of the country. In 1921 the United States ended its traditional policy of unlimited immigration and established immigration quotas based on country of origin. Western European countries were given large quotas and Asian countries tiny ones. About 150 Japanese a year were allowed to immigrate until 1930, when Congress excluded them entirely. Japan had protested a California law that prohibited persons of Japanese descent from buying property in the state. Rather than finessing what was called "the California problem," Congress bluntly told Japan that its people were not wanted in the United States.[36]

This discrimination against Asians did not change substantially until 1965, when Congress enacted legislation that adjusted the immigration quotas to favor those who had previously been disadvantaged. This change in the law was a product of the 1960s civil rights movement, which, as we have indicated, sensitized national leaders to all forms of discrimination. About half a million people now emigrate to the United States each year, and a majority come from Asian and Latin American countries. By the year 2000, Asian-Americans will number about 12 million, or between 4 and 5 percent of the total U.S.

---

[35]See F. Chris Garcia and Rudolph O. de la Garza, *The Chicano Political Experience* (Duxbury, Mass.: Duxbury Press, 1977).
[36]James Truslow Adams, *The March of Democracy*, vol. 4 (New York: Scribner's, 1933), 284–285.

Asian-American children, whose cultures emphasize the importance of education, benefit from government-mandated programs of English instruction in the children's first language. (Elizabeth Crews/Stock, Boston)

population. Most Asian-Americans live on the West Coast, particularly in California.

The rights of Asian-Americans have been expanded primarily by court rulings and legislation, such as the Civil Rights Act of 1964, that were responses to the problems of other minorities. In a few instances, however, the rights of minorities have been defined by actions of Asian-Americans. For example, in *Lau* v. *Nichols* (1974), a case involving Chinese-Americans, the Supreme Court ruled that public schools with a large proportion of children for whom English is a second language must offer English instruction in the children's first language.[37]

Asian-Americans are an upwardly mobile group. The values of most Asian cultures include a commitment to hard work, which, in the American context, has included an emphasis on academic achievement. For example, Asians make up a disproportionate share of the students at California's leading public universities, which base admission primarily on high school grades and standardized test scores. However, Asian-Americans are still underrepresented in certain areas of the workplace. According to U.S. government figures, Asian-Americans account for about 5 percent of professionals and technicians, nearly the same as their percentage of the population. Yet they hold less than 2 percent of managerial jobs; past and present discrimination has kept them from obtaining their fair share of top business positions.

[37]*Lau* v. *Nichols,* 414 U.S. 563 (1974).

★ ANALYZE THE ISSUE

Homosexual Rights
In 1986 the Supreme Court ruled that the Constitution does not give consenting adults the right to have private homosexual relations. Do you approve or disapprove of this ruling? When asked this question in a Gallup poll, 51 percent of the respondents said that they approved and 41 percent said that they disapproved (8 percent had no opinion). With its ruling, the Supreme Court said, in effect, that homosexuals are not a legally protected category, unlike certain other groups, including racial minorities, women, and the elderly. What legal, political, or other considerations might justify society in treating homosexuals differently from these other groups?

EXTENDING THE STRUGGLE FOR EQUAL RIGHTS: THE DISABLED, THE ELDERLY, AND CHILDREN

Women and racial and ethnic minorities are not the only groups whose members suffer from discrimination. Almost any group that is vulnerable or is a minority has experienced discrimination in some form. Three such groups that have been receiving increased attention from government are the disabled, the elderly, and children.

For years the disabled were thought of as a tiny proportion of the American population and therefore more of a special-interest group than a civil rights classification. But, according to the U.S. Census Bureau, more than 37 million Americans are physically impaired and between 13 and 14 million have a disability so severe that they are unable to perform some critical function, such as hearing, seeing, or walking. They constitute about 5 percent of the population—a sizable minority.

A major goal for the disabled is easier access to the mainstream of society. The 1973 Rehabilitation Act has moved them toward this goal. So has the Education for All Handicapped Children Act of 1975, which mandates that all children, however severe their disability, receive a free, appropriate education. Before the legislation, 1 million handicapped children were receiving no education and another 3 million were receiving an inappropriate one (as in the case of a blind child who is not taught Braille or is not provided with instructional materials in Braille). In 1987 Congress enacted the Employment Opportunities for Disabled Americans Act, which allows disabled individuals to earn a moderate income without losing their Medicaid health coverage. A more sweeping bill is the 1990 Americans with Disabilities Act, which extends to the disabled the protections enjoyed by other disadvantaged groups.

The government has also been moving to protect elderly Americans from discrimination. The Age Discrimination Act of 1975 and the Age Discrimination in Employment Act of 1967 outlaw discrimination against older workers in hiring for jobs in which age is not clearly a crucial factor in job performance. More recently, mandatory retirement ages for most jobs have been eliminated by law. Retirement at age seventy can no longer be arbitrarily decided by management; it must be justified by the nature of the particular job or the performance of the particular employee.

America's youngest citizens—its children—have also come under increasing protection from government. Among the children's rights that have recently been propounded are an adequate education, bilingual education for those for whom English is a second language, and safeguards in the event of physical abuse or other forms of mistreatment in the home. Children were once regarded as the "property" of their parents but now are regarded as persons in their own right and thus deserving of equal protection under the laws.

SOURCE: Mary Johnson, "Overcoming the Social Barriers," *The Nation,* April 9, 1988, 489–494.

Equality under the Law

The catchphrase of nearly any group's claim to a fairer standing in American society has been "equality under the law." The importance that people attach to legal equality is understandable. When made into law, claims to equality assume a power that they do not otherwise have. Once secure in their legal rights, people are in a stronger position to seek equality on other fronts, such as the economic one. Also once encoded in law, a claim to equality can force officials to take positive action on behalf of a disadvantaged group. For example, some communities refused to allow the children of illegal aliens to attend public school until a 1982 Supreme Court ruling required them to do so.[38] Americans' claims to legal equality are contained in a great many laws. Among the most noteworthy are the equal-protection clause of the Fourteenth Amendment, the Civil Rights Acts of 1964 and 1968, and the Voting Rights Act of 1965.

[38]*Plyler* v. *Doe,* 457 U.S. 202 (1982).

Through protest demonstrations in 1988, students at Gallaudet College, which was founded to provide higher education for the hearing-impaired, succeeded in obtaining the appointment of the college's first hearing-impaired president. The students argued that the appointment of a president with normal hearing would be a severe setback in the effort of handicapped people to achieve equal rights. (Paul Conklin)

EQUAL PROTECTION: THE FOURTEENTH AMENDMENT

The Fourteenth Amendment, which was ratified in 1868, declares in part that no state shall "deny to any person within its jurisdiction the equal protection of the laws." Through this **equal-protection clause,** the courts have protected such groups as black people and women from discrimination by state and local governments.

As we noted in Chapter 2, the Supreme Court initially interpreted the Fourteenth Amendment so narrowly that the South's white-dominated governments found it easy to relegate black people to second-class status. By law, they were not allowed to attend the same schools, use the same public restrooms, or go to the same hospitals as white people. In 1954, however, the Supreme Court issued its historic decision in *Brown* v. *Board of Education of Topeka*, which declared that racial segregation of public schools violates the equal-protection clause of the Fourteenth Amendment.[39]

No State shall . . . deny to any person within its jurisdiction the equal protection of the laws.

U.S. Constitution,
Fourteenth Amendment
(equal-protection clause)

The Reasonable-Basis Test

The equal-protection clause does not require government to treat all groups or classes of people the same way in all circumstances. In fact, laws routinely treat people unequally. For example, minimum age restrictions have been placed on voting, driving, and drinking. By law in most states, twenty-one-year-olds can drink alcohol but twenty-year-olds cannot. Inequality is also written into the tax

[39]*Brown* v. *Board of Education of Topeka*, 347 U.S. 483 (1954).

code: people who make more money pay taxes at a higher marginal rate than people who make less money.

The judiciary allows such inequalities because they are held to be "reasonably" related to a legitimate government interest. In applying this **reasonable-basis test,** the courts give the benefit of the doubt to government. It need only show that a particular law has a sensible basis. For example, the courts have held that the goal of reducing fatalities from alcohol-related accidents involving young drivers is a valid reason for imposing a twenty-one-year minimum age requirement for the purchase of alcohol.

The Strict-Scrutiny Test

Although the reasonable-basis test applies to most social classifications, it does not apply to racial or ethnic classifications, particularly when these categories serve to discriminate against minority-group members. Any law that attempts a racial or ethnic classification is subject to the **strict-scrutiny test,** under which such a law is unconstitutional in the absence of an overwhelmingly convincing argument that it is necessary. Such an argument is nearly impossible to construct; after all, what could justify a law that treated people less favorably merely because their skin is not white?

The strict-scrutiny test has virtually eliminated race and ethnicity as permissible classifications when the effect is to put members of a minority group at a disadvantage. The Supreme Court's position is that race and national origin are **suspect classifications**—that such classifications have invidious discrimination as their purpose and therefore any law containing such a classification is in all likelihood unconstitutional.

The "Intermediate"-Scrutiny Test

The strict-scrutiny test emerged after the 1954 *Brown* ruling and became a basis for invalidating laws that discriminated against black people. As other groups, especially women, began to organize and press for their rights in the late 1960s and early 1970s, the Supreme Court gave early signs that it might expand the scope of suspect classifications to include gender. In the end, however, the Court announced in *Craig* v. *Boren* (1976) that sex classifications were permissible if they served "important governmental objectives" and were "substantially" related to the achievement of those objectives.[40] The Court thus placed sex distinctions in an "intermediate" (or "almost suspect") category, to be scrutinized more closely than some other classifications (for example, income levels) but, unlike racial classifications, justified in some instances.

The intermediate-scrutiny test is so inexact that some scholars question its validity as a legal principle. Nevertheless, when evaluating claims of sex discrimination, the judiciary applies a stricter level of scrutiny than is required by the reasonable-basis test. Rather than allowing government broad leeway to treat men and women differently, the Supreme Court has recently invalidated most of the laws it has reviewed that contain sex classifications. In 1983, for example, the Court disallowed lower monthly pension payments to women

---

[40]*Craig* v. *Boren,* 429 U.S. 190 (1976).

★ CRITICAL THINKING

DISCRIMINATION BY PRIVATE ORGANIZATIONS

Private organizations are often within their constitutional rights in discriminating against women and members of racial or religious minorities. The Fifth and Fourteenth amendments prohibit only discrimination by government bodies.

Nevertheless, the government has tried to discourage private organizations from discriminating. One tactic is to deny them tax benefits. In 1983, for example, the Supreme Court upheld the IRS's decision to withdraw the tax-exempt status of Bob Jones University, a private religious college that prohibits interracial dating and marriage among its students. The government also prohibits a private organization from receiving federal funds if it engages in discriminatory practices.

What is your opinion in these instances? Should private organizations be denied government privileges, such as tax-exempt status, if they pursue discriminatory practices?

Many country clubs and other private social organizations, such as the Jaycees, the Rotary, and the Elks, have used discriminatory tactics to remain nearly all white, all gentile, and all male, particularly at the leadership level. Membership in such organizations provides opportunities to make important business connections, so excluded groups are put at a disadvantage. Accordingly, a number of successful lawsuits have been filed on the ground of restraint of trade. And in one noteworthy case the Minneapolis and St. Paul chapters of the Jaycees voted to admit women, whereupon the national Jaycees revoked their charters. In *Roberts* v. *United States Jaycees* (1984), the Supreme Court ruled that the Jaycees must admit women in states, including Minnesota, that have statutes barring sex discrimination in any "place of public accommodation"—such as the restaurants and halls in which the Jaycees hold their meetings.

What is your opinion of this ruling? How far would you go in limiting discrimination by private organizations? What constitutional justification exists for your position?

merely because they tend to live longer than men. The Court concluded that women were entitled to monthly payments comparable to those of men.[41] In a 1991 "equal-protection" decision the Court ruled that employers could not exclude pregnant women from jobs on the grounds of possible danger to the fetus. The case involved a battery manufacturer which had barred pregnant women from jobs that would expose them to lead.[42]

Yet the Supreme Court has upheld some sexually discriminatory laws. In *Rostker* v. *Goldberg* (1980), for example, the policy of male-only registration for the military draft was upheld on grounds that the exclusion of women from combat duty serves a legitimate and important purpose.[43] It is safe to say that the Supreme Court would never have upheld a draft system that required registration of black men but not of white men. At the very least, the judiciary applies a less strict level of scrutiny to sexual classifications than to racial classifications.

EQUAL ACCESS: THE CIVIL RIGHTS ACTS OF 1964 AND 1968

The Fourteenth Amendment applies only to action by government. As we saw in Chapter 2, the Supreme Court ruled after the Civil War that the language of

[41]*Arizona* v. *Norris*, 459 U.S. 904 (1983).
[42]*Automobile Workers* v. *Johnson Controls*, No. 89-1215 (1991).
[43]*Rostker* v. *Goldberg*, 453 U.S. 57 (1980).

the Fourteenth Amendment could not be construed as forbidding discrimination by private parties. Owners could legally bar black people from restaurants, hotels, and other accommodations, and employers could freely discriminate in their job practices.

Accommodations and Jobs

Since the 1960s private firms have had much less freedom to discriminate for reasons of race, sex, ethnicity, or religion. The Civil Rights Act of 1964, which is based on the commerce power of Congress under the Constitution, entitles all persons to equal access to restaurants, bars, theaters, hotels, gasoline stations, and similar establishments serving the general public. The legislation also bars discrimination in the hiring, promotion, and wages of employees of medium-sized and large firms. The Civil Rights Act of 1964 does not regulate people's beliefs, friendships, or use of their own homes—no legislation could put an end to prejudice and discrimination in these realms—but the act does prohibit discriminatory conduct in public places, such as restaurants and motels, and in employment situations involving interstate commerce. A few forms of job discrimination are still lawful under the Civil Rights Act of 1964. For example, an owner-operator of a small business can discriminate in hiring his or her co-workers, and a religious school can take the religion of a prospective teacher into account.

The Civil Rights Act of 1964 has nearly eliminated the most overt forms of discrimination in the area of public accommodations. Some restaurants and hotels may provide better service to white customers, but outright refusal to serve African-Americans or other minority-group members is rare. Such a refusal is a violation of the law and could easily be proven in many instances. It is harder to prove discrimination in job decisions; accordingly, the act has been less effective in rooting out employment discrimination—a subject that will be discussed in detail later in the chapter.

Housing

The Civil Rights Act of 1968 prohibits discrimination in housing. A building owner cannot ordinarily refuse to sell or rent housing because of a person's race, religion, ethnicity, or sex. More than three-fourths of all housing transactions—sales and rentals—are covered by the antidiscrimination provisions of the 1968 Civil Rights Act. Exceptions are allowed for owners of small multifamily dwellings who reside on the premises and for owners of three or fewer houses who sell or rent without using an agent and who do not indicate a discriminatory preference when advertising the property.

Despite legal prohibitions on discrimination, housing in America remains highly segregated. Less than a third of African-Americans live in a neighborhood that is mostly white. One reason is the fact that the annual income of most black families is substantially below that of most white families. Low income tends to limit the areas in which black families can afford to live. A second reason is the legacy of discriminatory practices that were common in the past. Until 1948, when the Supreme Court outlawed them,[44] "restrictive covenants" in the deeds to many properties barred their sale to African-Americans, Jews, Catholics, or members of other designated "undesirable" groups. Banks

★ ANALYZE THE ISSUE

White Americans' Acceptance of Racial Integration

Comparisons of opinion polls taken in the 1960s and in the 1990s indicate that white Americans have become more accepting of integration in schools, housing, and other aspects of American life. Yet such comparisons also show that white Americans are less supportive of federal intervention to promote racial integration. Are these opinions contradictory? From the poll results, what conclusions would you draw about what most white Americans *really* think about racial progress?

Persistent and illegal discriminatory practices of real estate interests and mortgage lenders have made it difficult for minority families to buy into the American Dream of home ownership. (Jon Feingersh/Stock, Boston)

contributed to housing segregation by "redlining"—refusing to grant mortgage loans in certain neighborhoods. This practice drove down the selling prices of homes in these neighborhoods, which led to an influx of African-Americans and an exodus of whites. "Blockbusting" was a tactic used by some unscrupulous real estate firms: they frightened white homeowners into selling at low prices by moving a black family into a previously all-white neighborhood. Redlining and blockbusting are prohibited by the 1968 Civil Rights Act, but many of the segregated neighborhoods that they helped to create still exist.

A 1991 study by the Federal Reserve Bank made it clear that racism is still a factor in the lending practices of many banks (see Table 7-1). Although banks are bound by law not to discriminate in mortgage loans, the study indicated that nationwide, many more applications for mortgages from blacks than from whites—34 percent to 14 percent—were rejected. Even when high-income black applicants were compared with high-income white applicants, the difference persisted. Banks rejected more than twice as many well-paid black applicants. The rejection rate of Hispanic-American and Asian-American applicants also exceeded that of white applicants.[45]

EQUAL BALLOTS: THE VOTING RIGHTS ACT OF 1965

Free elections are perhaps the foremost symbol of American democracy, yet the right to vote has only recently become a reality for many Americans, particularly those of the black race.

The Nineteenth Amendment, which in 1920 gave women the right to vote, effectively ended resistance to women's suffrage; paradoxically, resistance to black suffrage was intensified by the Fifteenth Amendment, which in 1870 gave black persons the right to vote. Southern whites invented a series of devices that were designed to keep African-Americans from voting and thus to prevent

[44]*Shelley* v. *Kraemer*, 334 U.S. 1 (1948).
[45]Federal Reserve Bank data, 1991.

TABLE 7-1 Denial Rates for Home Purchase Loans (1990) Minority-group applicants are much more likely to be denied a mortgage loan than are white applicants.

	PERCENTAGE REJECTED				
CITY	Total	Asian	Black	Hispanic	White
Atlanta	13.8%	11.1%	26.5%	13.6%	10.5%
Baltimore	8.6	7.3	15.6	10.1	7.5
Boston	12.9	15.4	34.9	21.2	11.0
Chicago	9.9	10.4	23.6	12.1	7.3
Dallas	12.5	9.3	25.6	19.8	10.7
Detroit	11.7	9.1	23.7	14.2	9.7
Houston	15.5	13.3	33.0	25.7	12.6
Los Angeles	14.7	13.2	19.8	16.3	12.8
Miami	18.0	16.9	22.9	17.8	16.0
Minneapolis	7.1	6.4	19.9	8.0	6.1
New York	18.7	17.3	29.4	25.3	15.0
Oakland	11.4	11.6	16.5	13.3	9.6
Philadelphia	11.3	12.1	25.0	21.0	8.3
Phoenix	16.4	12.8	30.0	25.2	14.4
Pittsburgh	13.3	12.2	31.0	13.9	12.0
St. Louis	14.0	9.0	31.8	13.5	12.1
San Diego	11.4	11.2	17.8	15.1	9.8
Seattle	11.8	11.6	18.3	16.8	10.7
Washington, D.C.	8.2	8.7	14.4	8.9	6.3

SOURCE: Federal Reserve Bank.
Figures refer to 1–4 family homes purchased with conventional, FHA, FMHA, and VA mortgages. Refinancings are not included.

them from having an electoral weapon with which to fight discrimination.[46] Through poll taxes, whites-only primary elections, and rigged literacy tests as a qualification for registration to vote, African-Americans in many areas of the South were effectively disenfranchised. For example, almost no votes were cast by African-Americans during the years 1920—1946 in North Carolina.[47]

Barriers to black participation in elections began to crumble in the mid-1940s, when the Supreme Court declared that whites-only primary elections were unconstitutional.[48] Two decades later, through the Twenty-fourth Amendment, poll taxes were outlawed.

The major step toward equal voting rights for African-Americans was passage of the Voting Rights Act of 1965, which forbids discrimination in voting and registration. This legislation empowers federal agents to register voters and to oversee participation in elections. The threat of federal agents descending on county courthouses was enough to persuade officials in most southern communities to allow African-Americans to register and vote, but agents had to intervene actively in some locations. The Voting Rights Act, as interpreted by the courts, also eliminated literacy tests: local officials can no longer deny

[46]See J. Morgan Kousser, *The Shaping of Southern Politics: Suffrage Restriction and the Establishment of the One-Party South, 1880–1910* (New Haven, Conn.: Yale University Press, 1974).
[47]V. O. Key, Jr., *Southern Politics* (New York: Knopf, 1949), 495.
[48]*Smith* v. *Allwright*, 321 U.S. 649 (1944).

registration and voting for reasons of illiteracy. In fact, officials in communities where a language other than English is widely spoken are now required by law to provide ballot materials in that other language.

From the late 1950s to 1968, black registration and voting rose sharply (see Figure 7-2); the increase was especially pronounced in the South. In Mississippi, black registration rose by 900 percent in just the five years from 1965 to 1970. The influx of black voters into the southern electorate does not mean that race is no longer an issue in the region's politics. David Duke, a former wizard of the Ku Klux Klan, finished second in Louisiana's 1991 governor's election. He received a majority of the white vote and might have been elected if professional and trade associations had not promised to cancel scheduled conventions in New Orleans if he won. Nevertheless, the impact of race in southern elections has been diminished and white candidates who might previously have run blatantly racist campaigns have been forced to moderate their appeals to bigotry.[49]

African-Americans have also had some success in winning election to public office. Although the percentage of black elected officials nationwide is still far below the proportion of African-Americans in the population, it has risen sharply since the early 1960s.[50] As of 1992, there were more than twenty black members of Congress and 200 black mayors—including the mayors of some of the largest cities, such as New York City, Los Angeles, Atlanta, and Detroit. In 1989, Douglas Wilder of Virginia became the first African-American to be elected governor in the South since the Civil War Reconstruction.

Congress renewed the Voting Rights Act in 1970, 1975, and 1982. The 1982

[49]See Richard Scher and James Button, "Voting Rights Act: Implementation and Impact," in Charles S. Bullock III and Charles M. Lamb, eds., *Implementation of Civil Rights Policy* (Monterey, Calif.: Brooks/Cole, 1983), ch. 2; Jack Bass and Walter DeVries, *The Transformation of Southern Politics* (New York: Basic Books, 1976), 47.
[50]See Michael B. Preston, Lenneal J. Henderson, Jr., and Paul Puryear, eds., *The New Black Politics* (New York: Longman, 1982).

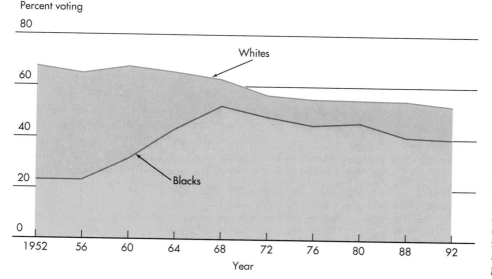

FIGURE 7-2 **Voter Turnout in Presidential Campaigns among Black and White Americans, 1952–1992**
Voter turnout among black Americans rose dramatically during the 1960s as legal obstacles to their voting were removed. *Source: National Election Studies, 1952–1988; trend projections, 1992.*

In 1989 Tom Bradley was elected to a fifth term as mayor of Los Angeles. An increasing number of minority-group members have been elected to public office. (Rick Browne/Stock, Boston)

extension is noteworthy because it renews the act for twenty years and requires states and localities to clear with federal officials any electoral change that has the effect, intended or not, of reducing the voting power of a minority group. This provision has the potential to enable minorities to increase their electoral influence. When congressional-district boundaries were redrawn in the wake of the 1990 census, several states, including North Carolina and Florida, created odd-shaped districts that were designed to give minority-group voters a numerical majority. In two 1991 decisions, the Supreme Court held that the Voting Rights Act's provisions on district boundaries also apply to state and local judicial elections.[51]

Equality of Result

The struggles of America's disadvantaged groups have resulted in significant progress toward equal rights, particularly during the past few decades. Through acts of Congress and rulings of the Supreme Court, most forms of government-sponsored discrimination—from racially segregated public schools to gender-based pension plans—have been banned.

However, civil rights problems involved deeply rooted conditions, habits, and prejudices and affect whole categories of people, not just isolated individuals here and there. For these reasons, a new civil rights policy rarely produces a sudden and dramatic change in society. Despite their greater equality in law, America's traditionally disadvantaged groups are still substantially unequal in their daily lives. Consider the income disparity between white and minority families. The average Asian-American family's income is three-fourths that of the average white family's. For Hispanic-American families, the average is two-thirds that of white family's. The average falls to three-fifths for black families, and still lower for Native Americans.

Such figures reflect ***de facto* discrimination,** which is discrimination that is a consequence of social, economic, and cultural biases and conditions. This type of discrimination is different from ***de jure* discrimination,** which is discrimination based on law, as in the case of segregation in southern public schools during the pre-*Brown* period. No law says that other Americans cannot have incomes as high as those of white males, but higher average incomes for white males are a fact of American life. *De facto* discrimination is difficult to root out because it is embedded not in the law but in the very structure of society. **Equality of result** is the aim of policies intended to reduce or eliminate *de facto* discriminatory effects so that members of traditionally disadvantaged groups may obtain the same benefits as members of traditionally advantaged groups. Such policies are inherently more controversial than those that provide equality under the law. Many Americans believe that government's responsibility extends no further than the removal of legal barriers to equality. This attitude conforms with the country's individualistic tradition and is a major reason for the lack of any large-scale governmental effort to reduce the economic and social gaps between Americans of varying racial and ethnic backgrounds.

[51]*Chisom* v. *Roemer*, No. 97–757 (1991); *Houston Lawyers* v. *Texas Attorney General*, No. 90–757 (1991).

However, a few policies—notably affirmative action and busing—have been designed to achieve equality of result.

WORKPLACE INTEGRATION: AFFIRMATIVE ACTION

The difficulty of converting newly acquired legal rights into everyday realities is evident in the fact that, with passage of the 1964 Civil Rights Act, which prohibited discrimination in employment, it did not suddenly become easier for women and minorities to obtain jobs for which they were qualified. Many employers maintained a deliberate though unwritten preference for white male employees, while other employers adhered to established employment procedures that continued to keep women and minorities at a disadvantage; membership in many union locals, for example, was handed down from father to son. Moreover, the Civil Rights Act did not compel employers to show that their hiring practices were not discriminatory. Instead, the burden of proof was on the woman or minority-group member who had been denied a particular job. It was costly and often difficult to prove in court that one's sex or race was the reason that one had not been hired. In addition, a victory in court affected only the individual in question; such case-by-case settlements were no remedy for a situation in which established hiring practices kept millions of women and minority-group members from competing equally for job opportunities.

A broader remedy was obviously required, and the result was the emergence during the late 1960s of affirmative action programs. **Affirmative action** is a deliberate effort to provide full and equal opportunities in employment, education, and other areas for women, minorities, and individuals belonging to other traditionally disadvantaged groups. Affirmative action requires corporations, universities, and other organizations to establish programs designed to ensure that all applicants are treated fairly. Affirmative action also places the burden of proof on the providers of opportunities; to some extent, they must be able to demonstrate that any disproportionate granting of opportunities to white males is not the result of discriminatory practices.

Differing Views of Affirmative Action

Opportunity in America has never been as equal in practice as it is in theory. When women and members of minority groups seek a job or a promotion, they are more likely than white males to find that an employer wants someone else. Few employers today are likely to say outright that they prefer a white male to a woman or a black person, but the statistics speak for themselves. White males get more jobs, better pay, and more promotions than do members of other groups.

In the abstract, affirmative action is not a controversial idea. Most Americans say that minorities and women deserve a truly equal chance at jobs and other opportunities. Yet affirmative action programs are controversial in practice because in some instances they can end up favoring women and minorities over white males, an outcome that is called "reverse discrimination." Although there is no evidence that reverse discrimination is rampant (and plenty of evidence that white males still have an edge in educational and marketplace opportunities), the idea that minorities and women may receive preferential treatment in particular instances has resulted in attacks on affirmative action.

Most Americans have no real enthusiasm for a policy that is designed in part to make up for past wrongs. For example, 76 percent of the respondents in a national survey said that programs giving preference to minorities in hiring and promotion are "unfair to qualified people who are not members of a minority," whereas only 10 percent said that such preference is "necessary to make up for a long history of discrimination."[52]

The Reagan and Bush administrations objected to "quotas" for women and minorities. President Reagan, for example, fired the chairman and two other members of the Civil Rights Commission who believed that aggressive affirmative action programs were necessary to protect the rights of women and minorities; eased the affirmative action regulations for employers doing business with government; and supported suits brought by white workers who claimed to have been victimized by affirmative action quotas or other preference systems. The justification for these policies was the claim that past discrimination against women and minorities was not a good enough reason for practices that might now discriminate against white males.[53]

Civil rights groups have argued, in contrast, that affirmative action must be broadly and aggressively applied if the effects of past discrimination and lingering prejudice are to be overcome. A Gallup poll found in 1982 that respondents—women as well as men—favored a male boss to a female boss by nearly 4 to 1 (see Table 7-2). In such a climate of opinion, strong government

[52]Herbert McClosky and John Zaller, *American Ethos: Public Attitudes toward Capitalism and Democracy* (Cambridge, Mass.: Harvard University Press, 1985), 93.
[53]See Allan P. Sindler, *Equal Opportunity* (Washington, D.C.: American Enterprise Institute, 1983); Alan Goldman, *Justice and Reverse Discrimination* (Princeton, N.J.: Princeton University Press, 1978).

TABLE 7-2 Attitudes toward Women Bosses Both men and women say they would prefer a male boss, an indication of cultural bias.

IF YOU WERE TAKING A NEW JOB AND HAD YOUR CHOICE OF A NEW BOSS, WOULD YOU PREFER TO WORK FOR A MAN OR A WOMAN?			
Characteristics of Respondents	*Prefer Male Boss*	*Prefer Female Boss*	*No Difference*	*No Opinion*
All respondents	46%	12%	38%	4%
Sex				
Male	40	9	46	5
Female	52	15	30	3
Education				
College	41	13	42	4
High school graduate	47	13	37	3
Less than high school	51	7	35	7
Age group				
18–24	33	21	40	6
25–29	41	16	38	5
30–45	45	12	39	4
50 plus	53	7	37	3

SOURCE: *Gallup Poll Reports*, 1982, 196–197.

action is said to be imperative. If a union, business, university, fire department, or other organization has no or few female or minority employees or members, then it should be ordered by government to give them preferential treatment in hiring or admission. In such cases, some innocent white males may lose out, but this cost is an unavoidable necessity if discrimination against women and minorities is to be curtailed.[54] This perspective on affirmative action was held by the Carter administration. President Carter, for example, initiated "set-aside" contracts on public projects, reserving a portion of all funding for minority-owned businesses; imposed heavy "back pay" penalties on businesses found to have inadequate affirmative action programs; and developed a long-term plan for the federal government to hire members of five "designated" minorities (the same five we discussed earlier: African-Americans, women, Native Americans, Hispanic-Americans, and Asian-Americans) in proportion to their numbers in the U.S. population.

The Supreme Court's Shifting Position on Affirmative Action

Affirmative action was first tested before the Supreme Court in *University of California Regents* v. *Bakke* (1978).[55] Alan Bakke, a white man, had twice been denied admission to the medical school of the University of California at Davis, even though his admission test scores were higher than those of several minority-group students who had been accepted. Bakke sued, claiming that the medical school had admitted less qualified minority students through an affirmative action program that set aside sixteen places for such students. In a 5–4 decision with six separate opinions, the Court ruled in Bakke's favor and ordered the university to admit him. Although the *Bakke* case was a setback for advocates of affirmative action, the Supreme Court did not invalidate the policy. The Court said that race could be one consideration in admission policy, along with such other considerations as test scores and extracurricular activities, as long as no rigid racial quotas were imposed.[56]

Bakke was followed by two rulings in favor of affirmative action programs, one of which—*Fullilove* v. *Klutznick* (1980)—upheld a quota system that required 10 percent of federal public works funds to be set aside for minority-owned firms.[57]

The Reagan administration began in 1981 to press its view that racial preferences were rarely, if ever, justified. It won a legal victory in 1984 when the Supreme Court ruled that the city of Memphis could lay off members of its fire department on a "last hired, first fired" basis and did not have to retain black firefighters who had low seniority. Their jobs, the Court said, could not be saved at the expense of white firefighters who had more seniority.[58] Then, in a 1986 case, the Court invalidated a layoff plan of Jackson, Michigan, which kept

[54]See Robert M. O'Neill, *Discrimination against Discrimination* (Bloomington: Indiana University Press, 1975).
[55]See Allan P. Sindler, *Bakke, DeFunis, and Minority Admissions: The Quest for Equal Opportunity* (New York: Longman, 1978).
[56]*University of California Regents* v. *Bakke*, 438 U.S. 265 (1978).
[57]*Steelworkers* v. *Weber*, 443 U.S. 193 (1979); *Fullilove* v. *Klutznick*, 448 U.S. 448 (1980).
[58]*Firefighters* v. *Stotts*, 459 U.S. 969 (1984).

some black schoolteachers on the job while white teachers with more seniority were released.[59]

The Reagan administration interpreted the Court's ruling in these cases as invalidating *any* affirmative action program that favored minority-group members who had not been individually victimized by discrimination. However, the Memphis and Jackson cases validated this "victim-specific" concept only in regard to job layoffs, leaving open the question of whether it also applied to job hirings and promotions. In two rulings announced at the close of its 1986 session, the Supreme Court rejected the Reagan administration's contention that civil rights remedies should benefit only specific, identifiable victims of discrimination.

In one case, the Court upheld by a 5–4 vote a lower-court order that required New York City's Sheet Metal Workers Local No. 28 to develop a program that would give 29 percent of its memberships to African-Americans and Hispanic-Americans. The formerly all-white union local had disobeyed two earlier lower-court orders to open its ranks to minorities. In such cases of "longstanding or egregious discrimination," Justice William Brennan wrote, "requiring recalcitrant employees in unions to hire and to admit qualified minorities in the work place may be the only effective way to ensure the full enjoyment of the rights protected by Title VII [of the Civil Rights Act of 1964].[60]

The Court had seemed to clarify the legal status of affirmative action. Preferential treatment of women and minorities could be justified in cases where discrimination had been severe, whether or not the minority-group members or women who benefited from this treatment were personally victimized by the past pattern of discrimination. However, preferential treatment could not be applied in a way that infringed on the rights of white employees to keep their jobs.

In a series of recent cases, however, the Supreme Court limited substantially the job protections available to minorities. The addition to the Court of conservative justices who had been appointed by Reagan resulted in decisions that weakened affirmative action policy. The Court concluded that affirmative action programs may be approved only after close scrutiny by a court and that such programs are not free of challenge at a later time by white workers who were not part of the original agreement. The Court thereby opened the door to challenges across the country to existing affirmative action programs.[61] Then in a decision with potentially far-reaching consequences, the Court held that, in some circumstances, minority employees must prove that racial imbalances in employment have no valid business purpose—once again placing the burden of proof on the employee.[62]

In another ruling, the Court excluded *racial harassment* on the job from statutory protection. A credit union employee in North Carolina had claimed that she was required to do menial tasks because she was black. The Supreme Court disallowed her claim, which was based on a Reconstruction-era statute.

---

[59]*Wygant* v. *Jackson*, 476 U.S. 238 (1986).
[60]*Local No. 28, Sheet Metal Workers* v. *Equal Employment Opportunity Commission*, 478 U.S. 421 (1986); see also *Local No. 93, International Association of Firefighters* v. *Cleveland*, 478 U.S. 501 (1986).
[61]*Martin* v. *Wilks*, 490 U.S. 755 (1989).
[62]*Wards Cove Packing* v. *Antonio*, 490 U.S. 642 (1989).

Writing for a 5–4 majority, Justice Anthony Kennedy said the statute prohibited racial discrimination at the time of the employment contract but not on the job.[63] The Court also cast doubt on the legality of *minority set-aside* programs for government contracts, which led more than a score of cities to dismantle their programs.[64]

The Civil Rights Act of 1991

These Supreme Court decisions brought strong condemnations from civil rights and women's rights groups and led in 1990 to the passage in Congress of a civil rights bill that would have reversed several of the decisions. President Bush vetoed the measure, calling it a "quota" bill. Bush then worked against efforts in Congress to achieve a compromise on a new version of the bill. He changed his mind a year later, however, after he was pressured to do so by moderate Republicans in Congress and after polls indicated that he was losing support among women and minority-group members.

With the threat of a veto removed, Congress in late 1991 passed a civil rights bill that provides employment protections for women and minority-group members. The legislation makes it easier for job discrimination victims (including sexual harassment victims) to sue for damages. The legislation also shifted the burden of proof back to employers in cases where they have relatively few women or minority-group members among their employees. The employer must show in some circumstances why a lopsidedly white male work force is the result of business necessity and not the result of systematic discrimination against women or minorities. As part of the compromise that led to passage of the legislation, it contains a provision that bans the adjustment of employment-related test results to boost the scores of minority-group members (a practice called "race norming").

SOCIAL INTEGRATION: BUSING

In 1944 the Swedish sociologist Gunnar Myrdal gained fame for his book *An American Dilemma,* whose title referred to deep-rooted racism in a country that proclaimed itself to be the epitome of an equal society.[65] Since then, legal obstacles to the mixing of the races have been nearly eliminated. Public opinion has also changed significantly in the past half century. In the early 1940s a majority of white Americans believed that black children should not be allowed to go to school with white children; today only 5 percent of white Americans express this belief. There are also visible signs of black progress. In the past two decades, increasing numbers of African-Americans have attended college, received undergraduate and graduate degrees, obtained jobs as professionals and managers, and moved into suburban neighborhoods.

However, the majority of black people still live largely apart from white people. The reality of American life today is racial segregation. More than two-thirds of African-Americans live in neighborhoods that are all or mostly

[63]*Patterson* v. *McLean Credit Union,* 491 U.S. 164 (1989).
[64]*City of Richmond* v. *J. A. Croson,* Co., 488 U.S. 469 (1989).
[65]Gunnar Myrdal, *An American Dilemma: The Negro Problem and Modern Democracy* (New York: Harper, 1944).

The controversy over court-ordered busing that erupted in Boston and other northern cities in the early 1970s revealed that racial antagonism was not only a southern problem. (Peter Southwick/Stock, Boston)

black; more than two-thirds of black children go to schools that are mostly black; two-fifths attend schools that are more than 90 percent black.

The *Swann* Decision

In 1971 the Supreme Court took the controversial step of requiring the busing of children in some circumstances. Affirming a lower-court decision, the Supreme Court held in *Swann* v. *Charlotte–Mecklenburg County Board of Education* that the busing of children from one neighborhood to another was a permissible way for courts to compel the integration of public schools where past years of official segregation had created residential patterns that had the effect of keeping the races in separate schools. Busing, the Court said, was allowed as a tool "in the interim period when remedial adjustments are being made to eliminate the dual school system."[66]

Few policies of recent times provoked so much controversy as the introduction of forced busing.[67] Angry demonstrations lasting weeks took place in Charlotte. When busing was ordered in Detroit and Boston, the protests turned violent. Unlike *Brown*, which affected mainly the South, *Swann* also applied to northern communities in which African-Americans and whites lived apart as a result of economic and cultural differences as well as discriminatory real estate practices. A 1972 University of Michigan survey indicated that more than 80 percent of white Americans disapproved of forced busing, and the proportion has not changed significantly since then.

[66]*Swann* v. *Charlotte–Mecklenburg County Board of Education*, 402 U.S. 1 (1971).
[67]See Jennifer L. Hochschild, *The New American Dilemma* (New Haven, Conn.: Yale University Press, 1985); Michael W. Giles and Thomas G. Walker, "Judicial Policy-Making and Southern School Segregation," *Journal of Politics* 37 (1975): 936.

★ THE MEDIA AND THE PEOPLE

THE NEWS IN BLACK AND WHITE

Because whites and blacks in America live apart to a significant degree, the portrayal of race relations in the news media is for many people the most important source of their understanding of the other race. An analysis of national media coverage of race relations by Robert Lichter and Linda Lichter, editors of *Media Monitor*, provides insights about this portrayal. The Lichters analyzed more than 300 news stories on the television network evening newscasts and in national newsmagazines in 1989.

The leading topic in these stories about race relations was crime, which accounted for about 25 percent of the news coverage. For example, the media gave heavy coverage to events that surrounded an apparently racially motivated murder in the Bensonhurst section of Brooklyn and riots that accompanied the killing of two black men by a Miami policeman. Other major topics included election politics (for example, the election of Douglas Wilder as Virginia's first black governor), civil rights history (for example, the discussion accompanying the film *Mississippi Burning*), education (for example, the issue of racism on campuses), and affirmative action (for example, the Supreme Court decision that struck down minority set-asides).

The TV and magazine stories about race relations were dominated by controversy and "bad news." They painted a picture not so much of a harmonious interracial society as of a country divided between black and white. Most stories were critical of the way in which African-Americans are treated by whites. Many stories were weighted heavily toward those authorities who argue that racism is deeply embedded in American society, as opposed to those who claim that racism is an isolated phenomenon.

The social institution that was most often singled out for criticism was business. Thus, some news stories charged banks with redlining and other discriminatory practices. Education was also cited as a problem area, as in the case of news stories about culturally biased testing procedures. The news media were pessimistic in their assessment of race relations. More than half of the authorities quoted in the news stories said that racism was on the increase and only a fifth said that racism was in decline.

SOURCE: "The News in Black and White," *Media Monitor* 4 (February 1990), 1–6.

The Course and Impact of Busing

Busing has never had the strong support of elected officials. Congress on several occasions came close to forbidding the use of federal funds to assist busing in any way. Richard Nixon was president when the *Swann* decision was announced, and he ordered the Justice Department to act slowly on busing cases; he hoped that opposition to busing would attract racially conservative whites to the Republican coalition. Under President Reagan a decade later, the Justice Department effectively ceased to pursue probusing lawsuits. In fact, the Reagan administration endorsed an antibusing initiative passed by voters in the state of Washington, but the Supreme Court ruled the law unconstitutional because it was based on racial categories and as such failed the strict-scrutiny test.[68] The Court has also ruled that federal judges may order local governments to increase school taxes in order to pay for programs to remedy segregation that stems from constitutional violations.[69]

However, the Supreme Court in 1991 held that formerly segregated school districts may be released from court-ordered busing requirements if they can

[68]*Washington* v. *Seattle School District*, 458 U.S. 457 (1982).
[69]*Missouri* v. *Jenkins*, No. 88–1153 (1990).

show that they have taken all "practicable steps" to eliminate the "vestiges" of the era of state-sponsored segregation. The Court did not spell out what it meant by "practicable" or "vestiges," thereby leaving open to lower courts the question of when busing could lawfully be terminated. The Court acknowledged that a possible reemergence of one-race schools was not necessarily a bar to lifting a busing order.[70]

Despite the controversy surrounding it, busing remains a part of national policy. Thousands of children throughout the nation are bused out of their neighborhoods each school day for purposes of school integration. Busing has provided equality of result for some black children, but its effectiveness has been undercut by public and official resistance. In part because of the adverse reactions to busing, the Supreme Court has limited across-district busing to situations where it can be shown that school district boundaries were purposely drawn so as to segregate the races.[71] Since school districts in most states coincide with community boundaries, the effect of this position has been to insulate most suburban schools from integration plans. As a result, the burden of busing has fallen most heavily on poorer whites and African-Americans in the inner cities.

PERSISTENT DISCRIMINATION: SUPERFICIAL DIFFERENCES, DEEP DIVISIONS

Discrimination has been called America's curse. In a country that is otherwise bountiful and generous, superficial differences—sex, skin color, country of origin—are sources of deep divisions and stark contrasts. To cite but one example: a child born in the United States has more than twice the chance of dying before reaching his or her first birthday if that child is black rather than white. The difference in the infant mortality rates of whites and African-Americans reflects differences in their nutrition, medical care, and education—in other words, differences in their access to the most basic commodities of a modern society.

Racial discrimination, today as in the past, is at the root of these differences. America's professed commitment to equality for all has a decidedly narrow focus—on equality under the law but not on the opportunity to share fully in everything that American society has to offer. No greater challenge faces America as it approaches the twenty-first century than the rooting out of discrimination based on sex, race, and ethnicity.

Summary

During the past few decades, the United States has undergone a revolution in the legal status of its traditionally disadvantaged groups, including African-Americans, women, Native Americans, Hispanic-Americans, and Asian-Americans. Such groups are now provided equal protection under the law in such areas as education, employment, and voting. Discrimination by race, sex, and ethnicity has not been eliminated from American life but is no longer substantially backed by the force of law.

Traditionally disadvantaged Americans have achieved

[70]*Board of Education* (Oklahoma City) v. *Dowell*, No. 89–1080 (1991).
[71]*Milliken* v. *Bradley*, 418 U.S. 717 (1974).

fuller equality primarily as a result of their struggle for greater rights. The Supreme Court has been an important instrument of change for minority groups. Its ruling in *Brown* v. *Board of Education* (1954), which declared racial segregation in public schools to be an unconstitutional violation of the Fourteenth Amendment's equal-protection clause, was a major breakthrough in equal rights. Through its busing, affirmative action, and other rulings, the Court has also mandated the active promotion of integration and equal opportunities.

However, as civil rights policy involves large issues concerned with social values and the distribution of society's resources, questions of civil rights are politically potent. For this reason, legislatures and executives as well as the courts have been deeply involved in such issues, sometimes siding with established groups and sometimes backing the claims of underprivileged groups. Thus Congress, with the backing of President Lyndon Johnson, enacted the landmark Civil Rights Act of 1964; but Congress and recent presidents have been ambivalent about or hostile to busing for the purpose of integrating public schools.

In recent years affirmative action programs, designed to achieve equality of result for African-Americans, women, Hispanic-Americans, and other disadvantaged groups, have been a civil rights battleground. Affirmative action has had the strong support of civil rights groups and has won the qualified endorsement of the Supreme Court but has been opposed by those who claim that it unfairly discriminates against white males. Busing is another issue that has provoked deep divisions within American society.

Major Concepts

affirmative action	equal rights (civil rights)
comparable worth	equality of result
de facto discrimination	reasonable-basis test
de jure discrimination	strict-scrutiny test
equal-protection clause	suspect classifications

Suggested Readings

Barsh, Russel Lawrence, and James Youngblood Henderson. *The Road: Indian Tribes and Political Liberty.* Berkeley: University of California Press, 1979. An analysis of Native Americans' quest for their civil rights.

Bell, Derrick. *And We Are Not Saved: The Elusive Quest for Racial Justice.* New York: Basic Books, 1987. An analysis of the struggle, including the political and legal strategies, for racial justice.

Evans, Sara M., and Barbara Nelson. *Wage Justice.* Chicago: University of Chicago Press, 1989. A study of Minnesota's comparable-worth policy that concludes that policy alone will not provide women with economic justice.

Faludi, Susan. *Backlash: The Undeclared War against American Women.* New York: Crown, 1991. A critical view of American society's treatment of women.

Garcia, F. Chris, and Rudolph O. de la Garza. *The Chicano Political Experience.* Duxbury, Mass.: Duxbury Press, 1977. An analysis of the Mexican-American political movement.

Gelb, Joyce, and Marian Lief Paley. *Women and Public Policies.* Princeton, N.J.: Princeton University Press, 1982. An assessment of women's position and influence in public policy.

Kugler, Richard. *Simple Justice: The History of* Brown v. Board of Education *and Black America's Struggle for Equality.* New York: Random House, 1977. The best evaluation of the *Brown* case and its impact on school desegregation.

Lemann, Nicholas. *The Promised Land: The Great Black Migration and How It Changed America.* New York: Knopf, 1991. A history of the migration to northern cities of southern blacks.

Lukas, J. Anthony. *Common Ground.* New York: Knopf, 1985. A study of three families caught up in the controversy over forced busing to achieve racial integration in the public schools of Charlestown, Mass.

Mansbridge, Jane. *Why We Lost the ERA.* Chicago: University of Chicago Press, 1986. A study of the defeat of the Equal Rights Amendment, focusing on strategy and the indirect benefits of the effort to pass the ERA.

Do Americans Place Too Much Emphasis on Individual Rights?

JANE MANSBRIDGE

I would urge that we voluntarily restrict the frequency with which we invoke "rights" as we talk with one another about the way we ought to live.

Americans do place too much emphasis on individual rights. While reducing that emphasis, I believe we should keep the concept of rights, work to understand which rights are most important, and fight to prevent the most important rights from being diminished.

Philosophically speaking, we could get rid of the concept of rights while still saving a lot of the aspects of it that we like. We could simply agree that some values are more important than others (that, for example, free speech should in most cases be given greater weight than security). At the same time we could, like some non-Western cultures, respect human dignity without having a concept of rights, defined as legitimate claims that individuals always hold against other people and that others have a duty to respect. On balance, however, I would keep the concept of rights, precisely because it adds to the idea of human dignity the notion that others have a duty to respect claims made in its name.

Yet Americans turn too many issues into questions of absolute rights. For example, each side in the abortion debate frames its argument in the language of rights: "a woman's right to control her body" versus "a fetus's right to life." Each side claims the entire moral territory, ruling out discussion of the degree of legitimacy that each moral stance might have at, say, different stages of pregnancy. Similarly, some proponents of the right to free speech cut off debate on substance by asserting that *no* printed matter can be curbed, even those forms of erotica or advertising that all agree cause harm.

In talk about rights, many problems arise from their binary quality—either you have rights or you don't; there is no spectrum of values, no middle ground. In practice, the U.S. Supreme Court introduces balance between one right and another. But the polarizing language of rights discourages balance.

Rights also have the quality of being held "against" other people. This is especially true of the quintessential "right to liberty," which Hobbes defined as "the absence of external impediments." Talk about rights encourages those who engage in it to see others as opponents.

I am not urging that we include in the category of rights only those particularly political claims—to free speech, association, or jury trial—that evolved in the eighteenth century and earlier as important components of democratic life. I would also include the twentieth-century rights—to a job and to the minimum level of goods necessary for belonging to the community. However, I *would* urge that we voluntarily restrict the frequency with which we invoke rights as we talk with one another about the way we ought to live. Several rights, like the right not to be tortured, deserve the position of absolute non-negotiability implicit in the word "right." Often, however, we use the word "right" the way a five-year-old uses "need" ("Mommy, I *need* that candy!")—that is, as an indication that we feel strongly about a subject and as a substitute for persuasive arguments. When we talk about an issue, let's ask, "Is it necessary to frame this as a question of rights? Couldn't I think of it as a question of what would be good, or good for people?"

Jane Mansbridge is Professor of Political Science at Northwestern University. She is the author of Beyond Adversary Democracy.

**RICHARD E.
FLATHMAN**

In recent years the favorable attitudes that we have taken toward basic rights against government have quite rapidly extended into other arenas of social life.

The best short answer to this question is twofold: "On the contrary," in that we have not been sufficiently insistent upon and respectful of the rights that we have most properly claimed; "Yes," in that we have a growing tendency to claim too many rights. But how can we know or decide how much emphasis is *too* much?

In many parts of the world, and among a small but often articulate minority in the United States, it is thought that *any* emphasis on individual rights is too much. In this view, concern with individual rights encourages selfishness, breeds competition and conflict, divides and weakens society. Rather than asserting rights against our country and our communities, our fellow citizens, neighbors, and family, we should seek ways to cooperate with and to help them.

As it pertains to government and politics, this attitude toward rights was long ago rejected in the United States. Necessary as they are, all governments are aggregations of power and hence potentially dangerous to their citizens; rewarding as it may be, all politics are struggles for and against power. Division and conflict are engendered not by rights but by government and politics themselves. Convinced of these and related propositions, our founding generations concluded that all citizens should have the protections afforded by a small but basic set of individual rights. Although challenged from time to time, this judgment has remained a prominent feature of the American political culture.

In this view, which I share, the appropriate objection is not to American ideas about rights but to our repeated failure to insist that the rights we regard as basic be extended to all members of our society and be fully respected. For long periods we have denied basic rights to very large groups in our population, and we have regularly committed gross violations of rights that we claim are well established in our law and our morality.

In recent years the favorable attitudes that we have traditionally taken toward basic rights against government have quite rapidly extended into other arenas of social life. The anti-rights view outlined above has clearly become a minority position as regards workplaces and schools, and its proponents may be fighting a losing battle in respect to more private domains such as the church, the club, and even the family. We are now claiming a wide range of rights, we are asserting those rights against one another with remarkable frequency, and we increasingly look to government to enforce respect for those rights.

In many ways this is a welcome development. "Private" institutions such as corporations, unions, and universities have increasingly acquired the characteristics—in particular, great power over their employees, members, and students—that led us to establish rights against governments, while clubs, other private associations, and families perpetrate the very kinds of discrimination from which our basic rights are supposed to protect us. The assumption of a natural cooperativeness and mutuality that usually underlies generalized hostility to individual rights has often proved to be as unwarranted in these private domains as it is in public life.

This expanded emphasis on individual rights nevertheless deserves our watchful concern. Whatever its effects on community and solidarity (and whether or not those are good things), it enhances the authority and power of the single most dangerous institution in any society—namely, government. And by doing that it may insidiously diminish the individuals to whom the new rights are accorded.

Richard E. Flathman is a member of the Department of Political Science at Johns Hopkins University. He is the author of Toward a Liberalism.

CITIZEN POLITICS

3

PART

*S*elf-government is a grand idea, resting as it does on the notion
that government is obliged to obey the people. An older idea,
still in place in much of the world, is that the people are obliged
to obey government.

"We, the people" are the opening words of the U.S. Constitution.
The American political system asks that its citizenry be a reasoning
and participatory public, not an unruly mob or a quiescent mass. This
requirement is confounded, however, by the practical need to reduce
complex alternatives and diverse opinions to simple choices before the
people can act. It is impossible for 252 million people to rule directly.
They can govern only through systems of representation, in which
their influence does not include control over the day-to-day decisions
of government.

The role of citizen is accordingly a difficult one. The individual
citizen is asked to take time to participate in public affairs and yet
does not have the opportunity to exert great influence over these
affairs. Not surprisingly, individuals differ in their willingness to
exercise their citizenship. Some people cannot be bothered with
public affairs, and others spend considerable time at it. Most
Americans fall between the two extremes, giving some time to politics
but not immersing themselves in it. Nevertheless, the integrity of the

[1]Harold D. Lasswell, *Democracy through Public Opinion* (Menasha, Wis.: Banta, 1941), 15.

American political system depends on popular influence. As Harold Lasswell once wrote, the "open interplay" of the people and their government is "the distinguishing mark of popular rule."[1]

Part Three probes this open interplay along three dimensions: the people's opinions, their participation, and their votes. Chapter 8 examines the way Americans think politically and the effect of their opinions on the policies of government. Chapter 9 explores the nature and implications of citizens' participation in politics. Chapter 10 considers why Americans vote as they do and how their votes affect representative institutions.   ★   ★   ★

PUBLIC OPINION AND POLITICAL SOCIALIZATION: FORMING THE PEOPLE'S VIEWS

To speak with precision of public opinion is a task not unlike coming to grips with the Holy Ghost.

V. O. Key, Jr.[1]

When Iraqi tanks rolled into Kuwait in early August of 1990, most Americans were ill equipped to pass judgment on what was happening. They knew almost nothing about Iraq or Kuwait—what kind of leadership these countries had, what the conflict was all about, or what kind of relationship each country had with the United States at the time of the invasion.

Within days, however, as President George Bush moved from a cautious response to a decision to deploy U.S. troops in the Persian Gulf region, public opinion on the issue began to form. An August 9–12 Gallup poll indicated that 82 percent of Americans approved of Bush's decision to send troops. A 64 percent majority said they would approve of the use of force to remove Iraq from Kuwait, although polls showed that Americans preferred a peaceful settlement of the crisis. A CBS News/New York Times poll in early October found that Americans by a 3-to-2 margin were opposed to *immediate* military action against Iraq.

Bush's words soon became more militant; he said at one point that Saddam Hussein, the Iraqi ruler, was "worse than Hitler." The American public grew increasingly pessimistic about the effectiveness of the economic boycott imposed on Iraq by the United Nations. Between early August and early October, according to ABC News/Washington Post polls, the percentage of Americans who thought the boycott would succeed dropped from 53 to 38. A warlike mood crept over the country. When the United States attacked Iraqi troops by air on January 16, 1991, an ABC News/Washington Post poll indicated that 76 percent

---

[1] V. O. Key, Jr., *Public Opinion and American Democracy* (New York: Knopf, 1961), 8.

As the American public learned more about the events surrounding the Iraqi invasion of Kuwait in August 1990, a strong public opinion emerged that supported President Bush's responses to the crisis. (Pedrick/The Image Works)

of Americans approved of the decision to go to war. Weeks later, a majority of Americans also expressed approval when a cease-fire was declared. Although earlier polls had shown that Americans had come to believe that the United States should not stop fighting until Saddam Hussein had been deposed, the polls now indicated acceptance of Bush's announcement that the military objective had been met when the last Iraqi forces were driven out of Kuwait.

The unfolding of the Gulf crisis is a revealing example of the influence of public opinion on government. Public opinion rarely compels officials to take a particular action. Bush was not forced by public opinion to attack Iraqi forces, but, as he moved away from economic sanctions and toward the military option, public opinion supported the change. And at war's end, public opinion would have allowed Bush to continue the military action if he had chosen to do so.

Public opinion has an important place in democratic societies because of the concept that government springs from the will of the people. The idea that government should attend to the opinions of ordinary citizens is deeply embedded in democratic thought. However, public opinion is a far more elusive phenomenon than conventional commentary suggests. It is widely assumed that there is a clear-cut public opinion on current issues, but in fact, as the Gulf war illustrates, public opinion is seldom exact when it comes to questions of how to accomplish an agreed-upon goal. Americans came to believe that Iraq had to be made to leave Kuwait, but how and when that might be done was left to the discretion of the Bush administration.

This chapter discusses public opinion and its influence on the U.S. political system. A major theme is that public opinion is a powerful and yet inexact force in American politics. The policies of the U.S. government cannot be understood apart from public opinion; at the same time, public opinion is not a precise determinant of public policies. This apparent paradox is explained by the fact that self-government in a large and complex country necessarily entails a division of labor between the public and its representatives; the result is a government that is tied only loosely to its public and a public that can influence only the general direction of its government. The main points made in this chapter are the following:

★ *Public opinion consists of those views held by ordinary citizens which government takes into account in making its decisions.* Public officials have many means of gauging public opinion, such as elections and mass demonstrations, but increasingly have relied on public opinion polls to make this determination.

★ *The process by which individuals acquire their political opinions is called political socialization.* This process begins during childhood, when, through family and school, Americans acquire many of their basic political values and beliefs. Socialization continues into adulthood, during which peers, political institutions and leaders, and the news media are major influences.

★ *Americans' political opinions are shaped by several frames of reference. Five of the most important are ideology, group attachments, partisanship, political culture, and a pragmatic outlook on politics.* These frames of reference form the basis for political consensus and conflict among the general public.

★ *Public opinion has an important influence on government but ordinarily does not directly determine what officials will do.* Public opinion works primarily to impose limits and directions on the choices made by officials.

The Nature of Public Opinion

Public opinion is a relatively new concept in the history of political ideas. Not until democracy began to flourish in the nineteenth century did the need arise to obtain some idea of what the public was thinking on political issues. If democracy is government of and for the people, then the public's political opinions are a central concern. Nevertheless, there has always been considerable disagreement about the impact that public opinion should have on government actions. Of course, there is agreement on basic principles. No democrat, past or present, would reject the idea that a just government rests on popular consent or that the people are in some sense the ultimate source of governing wisdom and strength.[2] Beyond these abstractions, however, the range of viewpoints on the proper role of public opinion is wide.

At one extreme are those who claim that government *by* public opinion is perilous. One such analyst, Robert Nisbet, says the idea that "public opinion must somehow govern, must therefore be incessantly studied, courted, flattered and drawn upon . . . is the great heresy . . . of modern democracies." Nisbet targets opinion polls for special criticism, saying that the opinions expressed through polls are unreflective and largely whimsical public reactions to current events. Nisbet claims that government has an obligation to respond only to the

[2] Robert Nisbet, "Public Opinion versus Popular Opinion," *Public Interest* 41 (1975): 167.

References to "American public opinion" can be misleading, because American society consists of many publics, not just one. Americans may divide into publics on the basis of age, sex, race, occupation, and many other dimensions. (Roy Morsch/Stock Market)

enduring and fundamental beliefs that citizens share as members of an ongoing political community. He labels these beliefs "public opinion" and distinguishes them from "popular opinion," which he defines as the transitory thoughts that citizens have about topical events.[3]

In making this distinction, Nisbet is attempting to locate modern thinking about public opinion within the classical liberal tradition expressed in such writings as the *Federalist Papers*. James Madison had differentiated between the public's momentary passions and its enduring interests, a distinction similar to Nisbet's differentiation between popular opinion and public opinion. For Madison as for Nisbet, governments are obligated to respond only to the public's shared and enduring beliefs.[4]

In contrast, other analysts contend that almost any opinion held by ordinary citizens—whether stable or fleeting, reasoned or emotional—should be taken into account by government. George Gallup, who founded the public opinion polling industry in the United States, promoted this view. He wrote: "We are often told that the function of leadership is to lead. . . . This is an attractive and appealing concept of leadership and one which has intrigued mankind from the earliest days. Unfortunately, it fits perfectly such eminent leaders as Adolf Hitler, Benito Mussolini, and Premier Stalin." Gallup questioned whether remote leaders can ever be trusted to serve the public. He believed that leaders should be in tune with the citizenry. "In a democracy," Gallup said, leaders "should have available an accurate appraisal of public opinion and take some account of it in reaching their decision. . . . The task of the leader is to decide how best to achieve the goals set by the people."[5]

[3] Ibid.
[4] *Federalist* No. 10.
[5] George Gallup, "Polls and the Political Process—Past, Present, and Future," *Public Opinion Quarterly* 40 (Winter 1965): 547–548.

Gallup's argument fits into the Jacksonian and Progressive traditions. We noted in Chapter 4 that the Jacksonians and Progressives had a strong faith in the judgment of the ordinary citizen and a suspicion of leaders who were not directly accountable to the people. Modern-day Jacksonians and Progressives see public opinion polls not as ephemeral and unreliable snapshots of the public's mood, but as a strong foundation of popular government. Whereas leaders at any earlier time could always claim to be in step with the public's wishes, today's leaders can do so only if the polls show that the public agrees with them.

The ideas of Robert Nisbet and George Gallup are only two of many views on the proper role of public opinion in a democratic society. There is no consensus on the subject. The various ideas are normative ones; they stem from different values and hence do not lend themselves to factual analysis. Nisbet represents the view that systems of leadership are at the core of effective democratic government. Gallup represents the view that public sentiment should dominate. Such differences are fundamental and, in America, are at least as old as the dispute between Federalists and Anti-Federalists over the Constitution's provisions for popular influence.

A WORKING DEFINITION OF PUBLIC OPINION

"Public opinion" is an ordinary term, but it refers to a complex reality. Although the term is typically used in reference to the whole society, it is not very meaningful to lump all citizens together as if they constituted a single coherent public.[6] In fact, Americans form *many* publics.[7]

One thing that divides Americans into a variety of publics is the fact that they differ greatly in their level of attention to politics. Some people pay close attention to politics, but most people do not, and some people pay hardly any attention at all. As a result, the level of knowledge that the average citizen has about public affairs is usually quite low. Fewer than half of adult Americans can name the Speaker of the House of Representatives or the U.S. senators from their state. Half of them do not know the length of a term in the U.S. House of Representatives (the answer is two years), and a similar proportion do not know how many U.S. senators each state has (the answer is two). When a 1987 poll asked Americans to identify the chief justice of the Supreme Court, only 8 percent could recall William Rehnquist's name.[8] Other polls have shown that most adult Americans do not know, even in rough terms, when the Civil War took place or when the United States entered the First World War. Their knowledge of geography is no better. On a map of the world, a majority of Americans cannot locate Vietnam, Sweden, or South Africa. A fifth of the citizenry cannot even find the United States.[9]

When it comes to questions of policy choices, such as the military action that might be taken in response to an international crisis, the public's level of awareness is also remarkably low. Here again the Gulf war provides a sobering

★ ANALYZE THE ISSUE

Forming Opinions without Information
The level of the public's knowledge about some policy issues is shockingly low. How does this situation affect the public discussion of policy problems? What circumstances affect whether a citizen is likely to possess much factual information about a policy issue? Can you think of an issue about which a citizen could have a thoughtful opinion without having much information?

---

[6] Harwood L. Childs, *Public Opinion* (Princeton, N.J.: Van Nostrand, 1965), 12.
[7] Jerry L. Yeric and John R. Todd, *Public Opinion* (Itasca, Ill.: F. E. Peacock, 1983), 3.
[8] Market Facts Survey, June 1987.
[9] Warren E. Leary, "Two Superpowers' Citizens Do Badly in Geography," *New York Times*, November 9, 1989, A6.

★ ANALYZE THE ISSUE

The Nature of Public Opinion
What is public opinion? How might public opinion actually differ from what pollsters refer to as public opinion? How might it differ from what the writers of the Constitution thought of as public opinion (see Chapter 4)?

example. Although Americans, through television, paid closer attention to the Gulf war than to any other event in recent memory, they were relatively uninformed about it. In a survey conducted six months after Iraq's invasion of Kuwait and three weeks into the American bombing campaign, a large majority of respondents agreed with the claim that the U.S. government had warned Saddam Hussein that Iraq would face military retaliation if it invaded Kuwait. In fact, the U.S. government had issued no such warning; the decision to attack Iraqi forces came after Iraq's invasion took place. A significant minority of respondents even judged Kuwait to be a democracy (it is a monarchy).[10]

Obviously, in defining "public opinion" we cannot assume that all citizens are equally interested in and informed about all aspects of political life. Accordingly, we shall take **public opinion** to mean those opinions held by ordinary citizens which officials take into account when they choose to act or not to act. So defined, public opinion can be the views of many or a few people. On one question public opinion may be the views held by one set of citizens; on another question, the views of a quite different set. Government does not necessarily have to follow expressed opinion in each case; it can also reject, divert, or try to alter opinion. The central point is that the opinions of private citizens become public opinion when government takes them into account.[11]

ESTIMATING PUBLIC OPINION THROUGH POLLS

Public officials have numerous ways of assessing public opinion. Election returns are a time-honored method. The vote is routinely interpreted by the press and politicians as a sure indicator of the public's mood—whether liberal or conservative, angry or satisfied, quiet or intense. Letters to the editor in newspapers and the size of crowds at mass demonstrations are other means to judge what the public is thinking.

All these indicators of public opinion are important and deserving of attention by those in power. These indicators are not, however, a particularly good way to discover what is on the minds of the people. Elections offer the people only a yes-or-no choice between candidates, and different voters will make the same choice for quite different reasons. The winning candidate may claim that the public has based its choice on a particular issue or inclination, but election returns mask a much more complex reality. As for letter writers and demonstrators, they are not at all representative of the general population. Less than 1 percent of Americans participate each year in a mass demonstration, and fewer than 10 percent write to the president or a member of Congress. Studies have found that the views of letter writers and demonstrators are more intense and more extreme than those of other citizens.[12]

Opinion polls are a more reliable method for determining what ordinary citizens are thinking. It is certainly the case that the poll or survey has become the most relied-upon method of measuring public opinion. More than 100

---

[10] Survey by Sut Jhally, Justin Lewis, and Michael Morgan, February 2–4, 1991, cited in *The Nation*, March 18, 1991.
[11] The original formulator of this common view of public opinion is unknown. Its foremost advocate was V. O. Key, Jr. See Key, *Public Opinion and American Democracy*, 14–15.
[12] Sidney Verba and Norman H. Nie, *Participation in America: Political Democracy and Social Equality* (New York: Harper & Row, 1972), 281–284.

organizations are in the business of conducting public opinion polls. Some, like the Gallup Organization, conduct polls that are then released to the news media by syndication. Most large news organizations also have their own in-house polls; one of the foremost of these is the CBS News/New York Times poll, which conducts about fifteen surveys annually for use in the *Times* and on CBS's newscasts. Finally, there are polling firms that specialize in conducting surveys for candidates and officeholders.

The Theory of Opinion Sampling

In a **public opinion poll,** a relatively small number of individuals—the **sample**—are interviewed for the purpose of estimating the opinions of a whole **population,** such as the students of a college, the residents of a city, or the citizens of a country. How is it possible to measure the thinking of a large population on the basis of a small sample? How can interviews with, say, 1,000 Americans provide a reliable estimate of what 250 million are thinking? The answer is found in mathematical probabilities. The general idea of mathematical probabilities can be illustrated by the hypothetical example of a huge jar filled with a million marbles, half of them red and half blue. If a blindfolded person reaches into the jar, the probability of selecting a marble of a given color is 50-50. And if 1,000 marbles were chosen in this random way, red marbles and blue marbles would be selected roughly 500 times apiece.

The probabilities of opinion polling are similar. If individuals are selected at random and if enough of them are chosen, their views will tend to be representative—that is, roughly the same as the views held by the population as a whole. The accuracy of a poll is usually expressed in terms of **sampling error,** which is a function of sample size. The larger the sample, the smaller the sampling error (see Table 8-1). A properly drawn sample of 1,000 individuals has a sampling error of plus or minus 3 percent, which is to say that the proportions of the various opinions expressed by the people in the sample are

TABLE 8-1 Approximate Sampling Error by Number of Opinion-Poll Respondents The larger a poll's sample, the smaller the error in estimating the opinions of the population from which the sample is taken.

Approximate Number of Respondents	Approximate Sampling Error
200	±7%
275	±6
375	±5
600	±4
1,075	±3
2,400	±2
9,600	±1

Note: Figures are based on a 95 percent confidence level. This means that for a given sample size (e.g., 600), the chances are 19 in 20 (95 percent) that the sample will produce results that are within the sampling error (e.g., ± 4 percent) of the results that would have been obtained if the whole population had been interviewed.

George Gallup (*seated*) and his staff meet on the day after the election of 1948. Gallup's American Institute of Public Opinion had wrongly predicted that Republican Thomas E. Dewey would beat Democrat Harry Truman. The Gallup organization subsequently revised its polling procedures and has correctly predicted the outcome of every election since 1948. (AP/Wide World)

likely to be no more than 3 percent larger or smaller than those of the whole population. For example, if 55 percent of a sample of 1,000 respondents say that they intend to vote for the Republican candidate for president, then the chances are high that 52 to 58 percent (55 percent plus or minus 3 percent) of the whole population plan to vote for the Republican.

The impressive record of the Gallup poll in predicting the outcomes of presidential elections indicates that the theoretical accuracy of polls can be matched in practice. For example, the Gallup poll came within 1 percent of the actual vote in predicting the 1988 Bush-Dukakis race. The Gallup Organization has erred badly only once: it stopped polling several weeks before the 1948 election and missed a late trend that carried Harry Truman to victory over Thomas E. Dewey.

Methods of Sampling

Mathematical estimations of poll accuracy require a **probability sample**—a sample in which each individual in the population has a known probability of being selected at random for inclusion. In practice, pollsters can only approximate this ideal. Because pollsters rarely have a complete list of all individuals in a population from which to draw a random sample, they usually base their sample on telephones or locations. Random-digit telephone sampling is the most commonly used technique. Pollsters use computers to pick random telephone numbers, which are then dialed by interviewers to reach respondents. Because the computer is as likely to pick one telephone number as any

★ THE MEDIA AND THE PEOPLE

THE USE OF POLLS BY THE PRESS

Public opinion polls are widely acknowledged to be the most accurate method of gauging what the public is thinking. Many polls are conducted by government and by candidates for public office. Others, such as the Gallup poll, are produced by independent polling organizations. Recently, however, the news media has become a major source of public opinion polls.

Opinion polls are identified with "precision journalism," which aims to bridge what Walter Lippmann called the gap between "the news" and "the truth." Lippmann argued that the news should not be confused with the truth, claiming that the subjects of news coverage and the pressures of news delivery are obstacles to accurate reporting. It occurred to some, including Phillip Meyer (then a reporter with Knight newspapers and now a journalism professor at the University of North Carolina), that news accuracy could be improved if the media had better in-house research. Meyer's influential book, *Precision Journalism* (1973), offered a blueprint for newsroom research, including the extensive use of polls. The first news organizations to develop a polling capacity were CBS News and *The New York Times,* which teamed up to sponsor their own poll. The New York Times/CBS News poll is now conducted about fifteen times annually. The ABC, CNN, and NBC television networks; *Washington Post* and *USA Today* newspapers; and *Time* and *Newsweek* magazines are among the other news organizations that commission their own polls.

Seldom does a major news event occur without one news organization or another conducting a poll about it. The media's reliance on polls is particularly pronounced during a presidential election campaign. In the early years of polling, from the 1930s through the 1950s, a leading newspaper, such as *The New York Times* or *Washington Post,* might have contained a dozen or so poll-based stories during the entire campaign. Today, a leading newspaper may run as many as a dozen poll-based stories in a week, many of them relying on the newspaper's own polls. Poll stories are also given greater prominence in the daily news than in the past. Social scientist Kevin Keenan's comparison of network television coverage of the 1972 and 1984 campaigns, for example, indicated that half of all poll stories in 1984 were broadcast as either the lead story or the next-to-lead story. In contrast, only 14 percent of poll stories in 1972 were carried in the first or second position on the nightly newscasts.

SOURCES: Walter Lippmann, *Public Opinion* (New York: Free Press, 1965); Phillip Meyer, *Precision Journalism* (Bloomington: Indiana University Press, 1973); Kevin Keenan, "Polls in Network Newscasts in 1984 Presidential Race," *Journalism Quarterly* 63 (1985): 616–618.

other and because 95 percent of U.S. homes have a telephone, a sample selected in this way is usually assumed to be representative of the population.[13]

A major drawback to telephone interviewing is that many people refuse to answer phone questions for more than 10 or 15 minutes. Accordingly, when longer interviews are required, they are often conducted face to face. To achieve randomness in this situation, census data are used to select locations (such as city blocks) at random; interviewers then go to these sites to locate and talk with respondents. Whatever the probability sampling method used, the goal is to obtain a representative sample; only then can the pollster have confidence in the accuracy of the results.

Some polls are not based on probability sampling. For example, news reporters sometimes conduct "man-in-the-street" interviews to obtain individuals' responses to political questions. Although a reporter may imply that the views of those interviewed are representative of the general public's, the fallacy

[13] See William R. Klecka and Alfred J. Tuchfarber, "Random Digit Dialing: A Comparison to Personal Surveys," *Public Opinion Quarterly* 42 (Spring 1978): 105–114.

"Man-in-the-street" interviews are not reliable because where and when the interview is conducted affects the type of sample chosen. A poll like this one, held in a shopping mall, will probably sample a disproportionate number of homemakers, whose views are unlikely to reflect those of the population as a whole. (Spencer Grant/Stock, Boston)

of this reasoning should be readily apparent. The sample will be biased by where and when the reporter chooses to conduct the interviews. For example, interviews conducted on a downtown street at the noon hour will include a disproportionate number of business employees who are taking their lunch breaks. Housewives, teachers, factory workers, not to mention farmers, are among the many groups that would be underrepresented in such a sample.

A somewhat more reliable form of nonprobability sample is the "quota sample." When this method is used, respondents are categorized by type and a quota is set for each type. For example, a survey might call for a quota sample consisting of 45 percent white females, 45 percent white males, 5 percent black

Polls can show the direction of public opinion but not the intensity of it. These protesters took to the streets to demonstrate their intense opposition to the Persian Gulf war. (N. Tully/Sygma)

females, and 5 percent black males. These quotas could have been set on the basis of data indicating that the population being studied is 90 percent white and evenly divided by gender. Once the quotas are set, interviewers then locate respondents who fit the designated descriptions. Quota samples have been known to produce reasonably representative findings, but they do not regularly yield results that are as reliable as those associated with probability samples. Quota samples tend to overrepresent individuals who are highly "visible"— that is, individuals, such as regular shoppers, who are easy for interviewers to approach. Less visible people, such as those who seldom leave their homes or workplaces, are typically underrepresented in quota samples.

Sources of Polling Errors

Even when probability sampling is used, there are many potential sources of error beyond that of the sampling error. For example, failure to follow acceptable sampling procedures can result in an unrepresentative sample; thus, if interviewers are unwilling to go into slum neighborhoods, the resulting poll will underreport the opinions of low-income people.

The placement and wording of survey questions can also affect poll results. In a series of polls between 1973 and 1983, the Roper Organization found a 10 percent fluctuation back and forth in Americans' opinions as to whether their health needs would be better served by a national system of government-paid health insurance or by the existing system of private health care. The Roper Organization determined, finally, that the zigzag pattern was a function, not of a true fluctuation in public opinion, but of whether the question was asked by itself (in which case more people preferred the national system) or at the end of a series of questions about the respondent's own experiences with medical care (in which case more people preferred the present system).[14] The wording of questions can similarly result in inconsistent findings. During Senate confirmation hearings on the appointment of Robert Bork to the Supreme Court in 1987, national polls differed by almost 20 points in the proportion of respondents who opposed Bork's nomination. When the questions mentioned allegations about Bork's weak record on civil rights, the pollsters found a higher level of opposition than was registered by polls whose questions did not remind respondents of these allegations.

Polls can also be misleading if they include questions on subjects to which people have given little or no thought. For example, most Americans have not thought carefully about whether Puerto Rico, currently a U.S. commonwealth, should be granted statehood. If a polltaker were to ask whether Puerto Rico should become the fifty-first state, most respondents would probably offer a yes or no answer, but it seems highly unlikely that they would have a reasoned opinion on the question.

Finally, polls are less than satisfactory in measuring *intensity*, or the strength of feeling that people have about a given issue. Polls are reasonably good at assessing *direction*, which is a measure of whether opinion on a particular question is favorable (positive) or unfavorable (negative); but they are not good

---

[14] Burns W. Roper, "The Subtle Effects of Context," in *The Public Perspective* 1 (January/February 1990): 25.

at indicating intensity. Unlike mass demonstrations or other active expressions of public opinion, polls do not capture the passion that some political issues generate. Polls taken during the Vietnam war, for example, indicated that, until the last stage of the conflict, a majority of the American people favored U.S. involvement. Yet, of the demonstrators who took to the streets to express their opinion, the vast majority were opponents of U.S. policy. They had a level of intensity that the polls could not measure. The Nixon administration used the phrase "silent majority" to refer to those citizens who backed the war but were not heard from publicly.

Political Socialization: How Americans Learn Their Politics

Analysts have long been interested in the process by which public opinion is formed. Almost a century ago James Bryce proposed that opinion formation takes place in stages, beginning with the public's first impression of an issue, continuing through a period of public deliberation on the issue, and concluding with a public action—such as the enactment of legislation—that settles the issue.[15] We now know that the process of opinion formation is far more varied and haphazard than Bryce believed. Citizens arrive at their opinions by any number of routes, most of them quite casual and unreflective and many of them involving elaborate psychological defense mechanisms.

The learning process by which people acquire their opinions, beliefs, and values is called **political socialization.** For most Americans, the process starts in the family with exposure to the political views of the parents. The schools later contribute to the process, as do the mass media, friends, and other influences. Political socialization is thus a lifelong process.

THE PROCESS OF POLITICAL SOCIALIZATION

The process of political socialization in the United States has several major characteristics. First, although socialization continues throughout life, most people's political outlook grows firmer with age. This tendency is less a function of age itself than of an accumulated attachment to particular ideas or values. Of course, the fact that the United States is a diverse and mobile society increases the possibility of a basic change in a person's political views, especially when childhood and adult experiences are at odds. However, individuals have psychological defenses for their ingrained beliefs: when faced with challenging situations, they can readily muster reasons for clinging to their original views. Republicans of long standing, for example, typically have more favorable opinions of *any* action of an incumbent Republican president than do longtime Democrats, and vice versa.

Thus, early political attachments often persist despite major changes later in life. Someone who has believed the same thing for fifty years cannot be expected to change his or her mind just because someone comes along who claims to have a better idea. It is life experience, not abstract logic, upon which

[15] James Bryce, *The American Commonwealth*, vol. 2 (New York: Macmillan, 1900), 247–254.

people base their personal and political philosophy. For this reason, when change in political attitude comes, it usually occurs among younger adults, who are less fixed in their opinions than older people and are therefore more responsive to changing political conditions. During the 1980s, for example, most longtime Democrats remained loyal to their party, whereas many younger voters with Democratic backgrounds switched their support to Ronald Reagan and the Republican party. The economic hard times of the period and the blow that the Iranian hostage crisis dealt to America's international prestige led many young people to identify with the Republican party (see Chapter 10).

A second characteristic of political socialization is that it is fairly uncritical. Most people do not think long and hard about their political preferences; they acquire many of them through subtle influences. Basic ideas about race, gender, and political party, for example, are often formed uncritically in childhood, much in the way that loyalty to a particular religion, typically the religion of one's parents, is acquired.

It is the rare individual who can step back and see the world differently from the way in which he or she has spent years learning to see it. Steeped in a certain way of looking at things, individuals can be expected to continue to think and act according to that way. Dramatic political conversion is uncommon and, when it has occurred on a large scale, it has nearly always been preceded by an extraordinary event that shakes people out of their complacency. Without the Great Depression, for example, Americans almost certainly would not have accepted the philosophy of Roosevelt's New Deal, with its emphasis on government intervention in the economy and on regulation of business.[16] The Vietnam war, the Watergate scandal, and the deep economic recession that faced Americans in the late 1970s and early 1980s are other examples of events that helped to change the direction of American politics by altering the pattern of conventional beliefs.

A third characteristic of political socialization in the United States is that it is relatively casual. It is not the rigid program of indoctrination that some societies impose on their people. Americans are not forced to take formal courses that extol the virtues of the U.S. political system. Nevertheless, Americans receive a thorough political education. Their country's values are impressed upon them by every medium of communication: newspapers, daily conversations, television, movies, books.[17] The result is a level of national pride that few countries, if any, can match (see box.)[18]

THE AGENTS OF POLITICAL SOCIALIZATION

As we have noted, the socialization process takes place through a variety of influences, including family, schools, peers, the mass media, and political leaders and events. It is helpful to consider briefly some ways in which these

[16] See Kristi Andersen, *The Creation of a Democratic Majority, 1928–1936* (Chicago: University of Chicago Press, 1979); Norman H. Nie, Sidney Verba, and John R. Petrocik, *The Changing American Voter*, rev. ed. (Cambridge, Mass.: Harvard University Press, 1979), 60; Stuart Oskamp, *Attitudes and Opinions* (Englewood Cliffs, N.J.: Prentice-Hall, 1977), 131.
[17] See James E. Combs, *Polpop: Politics and Popular Culture in America* (Bowling Green, Ohio: Bowling Green University Press, 1984).
[18] Institute for Social Inquiry, University of Connecticut tracking poll, January 12–24, 1991.

⋆ HOW THE UNITED STATES COMPARES

NATIONAL PRIDE AND POLITICAL SOCIALIZATION

Polls show that Americans take great pride in their country and its political system. The citizens of other leading democracies—France, Britain, and Germany among them—do not express anywhere near the same degree of national pride. The difference reflects the political socialization processes in the various countries. Patriotic messages and practices are more prevalent in the United States than elsewhere. The pledge of allegiance to the U.S. flag has no counterpart in Western European democracies. The national anthem of these countries is also not routinely played at public events, whereas "The Star-Spangled Banner" is used to open high school, college, and professional sporting events. In other ways as well, from entertainment to news, Americans are constantly reminded of their country's greatness.

Degree of National Pride	United State	France	Great Britain	Germany*
Very proud	87%	42%	58%	20%
Quite proud	10	39	30	42
Not proud	2	15	11	32
No opinion	1	4	1	6
	100%	100%	100%	100%

* This 1985 poll was taken in West Germany
SOURCE: New York Times/CBS New polls, 1985.

so-called *agents of socialization* affect the opinions that people have. Although these agents will be discussed separately, it should be kept in mind that, by and large, their influences overlap. Many of the same political values that people acquire at home and in school, for example, are emphasized regularly by the mass media and political leaders.[19]

The Family

The family is a powerful agent of socialization because children begin with no political attitudes of their own and are likely to accept uncritically those of their parents.[20] The reasons are fairly simple. The family has a near-monopoly on the attention of the young child, who also places great trust in what a parent says. By the time the child is a teenager and is not likely to listen to any advice a parent might offer, many of the beliefs and values that will stay with the child throughout life are already in place.

Some of these orientations are overtly political. Many adults are Republicans or Democrats today largely because they accepted their parents' party loyalty.[21] They now can give all sorts of reasons for preferring their party to the other. But the reasons came later in life; the loyalty came first, during childhood. The family also contributes to basic orientations that, while not directly political, have political significance. For example, the American family tends to be more

[19] See Murray Edelman, *Politics as Symbolic Action* (Chicago: Markham, 1971).
[20] See M. Kent Jennings and Richard Niemi, "The Transmission of Political Values from Parent to Child," *American Political Science Review* 62 (March 1968): 169–184.
[21] M. Kent Jennings and Richard G. Niemi, *Generations and Politics* (Princeton, N.J.: Princeton University Press, 1981), 91.

In school, children are taught love of country and flag as they learn about national heroes and historical events. Such political socialization during childhood has a profound influence on the individual's basic political views. (Jerry Berndt/Stock, Boston)

egalitarian than families in other nations, and American children often have a voice in family decisions. Such basic American values as equality, individualism, and personal freedom have their roots in patterns of family interaction.[22]

Opinions on specific issues of public policy are less substantially influenced by childhood experiences.[23] And, of course, a critical event, such as the Great Depression or the Vietnam war, may intervene to disrupt family influences.

Schools

The school, like the family, has its major impact on basic political beliefs and values rather than on specific issues of policy. The school teaches the young allegiance to flag and country, steeping them in the exploits of national heroes and telling them about the superiority of the country's economic and political systems.[24] U.S. schools are perhaps more instrumental in building support for the political system than the schools in most other democratic countries. The pledge of allegiance, which opens the school day throughout the United States, has no parallel in European democracies. The role of U.S. schools in the teaching of patriotic values was evident during the Gulf crisis, when schoolchildren were encouraged by their teachers to write letters to soldiers stationed in the Middle East. Newly returned soldiers were invited by schools to discuss their experiences with the children.

Americans' sense of social equality is also developed in part through the school. Most American children, regardless of family income, attend public

[22] See David Easton and Jack Dennis, *Children in the Political System* (New York: McGraw-Hill, 1969); Gabriel Almond and Sidney Verba, *The Civic Culture* (Boston: Little, Brown, 1965), 276.
[23] Kent Tedin, "The Influence of Parents on the Political Attitudes of Adolescents," *American Political Science Review* 68 (December 1974): 1579–1592; M. Kent Jennings and Richard G. Niemi, *The Political Character of Adolescence* (Princeton, N.J.: Princeton University Press, 1974).
[24] See Robert D. Hess and Judith V. Torney, *The Development of Political Attitudes in Children* (Chicago: Aldine, 1967), 219.

schools; the curriculum is fairly standard nationwide, at least in the lower grades. By contrast, European children of working-class parents are more likely to be segregated from those of wealthier families, either by financial exclusion from upper-class private schools, as in Britain, or by early placement in vocational programs, as in Germany.

The college experience also contributes to political socialization. The sense of a citizen's obligations—to vote, to be active in community affairs, to take an interest in political news—is stronger among college-educated people than among people with less education. Support for individual rights, such as freedom of speech, is also stronger among this group. These tendencies are due in part to the direct effects of a college education; in the classroom and out, college students learn about and experience civic life. College-educated people are also likely to have more of the skills and contacts that promote political involvement, from which can flow consistent opinions. For example, freedom of expression, like other rights, is prized most highly by those citizens who make active use of it.

Peers

Members of peer groups—friends, neighbors, and co-workers—tend to have similar political views. Belonging to a peer group usually reinforces what a person already believes. One reason is that most people trust the views of their friends and associates. Another is that they may be reluctant to deviate too far from what their peers think.

An intriguing hypothesis holds that social pressures can prevent deviant opinions from being freely expressed. In her book *The Spiral of Silence*, Elisabeth Noelle-Neumann contends that most individuals want to conform and are afraid to speak out against a dominant opinion, particularly when the issue has a strong moral component.[25] Thus a highly educated person who believes that environmental protection is being carried too far may be unwilling to express that opinion openly because the belief is regarded as wrongheaded in well-educated circles.

The Mass Media

Experts agree that the mass media are a powerful socializing agent, but there are disagreements on the exact nature of media influence. Some observers claim, for example, that violence on television promotes a lack of respect for life and property, particularly among young people. Other observers reject this linkage, asserting that the media are a minor influence compared with family and peers. Nevertheless, young people devote a great deal of time to the media, particularly to entertainment programs on TV. Television has a general, although diffuse and largely unmeasurable, effect on young people's tastes in clothing and food, and on their social and political values as well.[26]

News programs and newspaper stories are also an important influence on public opinion,[27] particularly in regard to what people see as the major issues

---

[25] See Elisabeth Noelle-Neumann, *The Spiral of Silence* (Chicago: University of Chicago Press, 1984).
[26] See Combs, *Polpop.*
[27] Benjamin I. Page, Robert Y. Shapiro, and Glenn R. Dempsey, "What Moves Public Opinion?" *American Political Science Review* 81 (March 1987): 23–44.

facing the country.[28] In the early fall of 1986, for example, national polls indicated that drug abuse had become the issue that was uppermost in people's minds. This widespread concern developed in the wake of a string of sensational news reports that drug abuse was becoming an epidemic—even though, in fact, the level of drug abuse had not increased significantly during the preceding six years. (Chapter 15 discusses this agenda-setting role of the media in detail.)

Political Leaders and Institutions

People look to political leaders and institutions, particularly the presidency and the political party, as guides to opinion. The level of public approval of a nuclear arms limitation agreement with the USSR rose in 1987 after President Ronald Reagan endorsed the idea. In broader terms, political leaders play a significant role in shaping political debate and opinion through the symbols and slogans they use.[29] Their way of framing issues can become the viewpoint of citizens, as in the case of Woodrow Wilson's claim that the United States was entering World War I in order to "make the world safe for democracy."

The ability of a president to mold opinion has definable limits, however. Consider the case of President Gerald Ford, who quickly gained the public's confidence after he succeeded Richard Nixon in the wake of the Watergate crisis in 1974. A Gallup poll indicated that 71 percent of Americans initially held a high opinion of Ford's leadership. Two months into his presidency, however, Ford pardoned Nixon for any crimes he might have committed while in office. This development caused a rapid 20-point plunge in Ford's public-approval rating. Ford claimed that the pardon was necessary if the nation was to put Watergate behind it and get on to other business, but the American public, which had become convinced of Nixon's guilt, was in no mood to let Nixon—or Ford—off the hook so easily. (Chapters 10, 11, 18, and 19 discuss further the impact of political leaders and institutions on public opinion.)

Frames of Reference:
How Americans Think Politically

What are the frames of reference that guide the political thinking of Americans? The question is important in at least two respects. First, the way in which citizens think politically provides clues about the way in which public opinion is likely to affect government. We have already seen that most people are poorly informed about the details of politics and policy. It would therefore be unrealistic to expect public opinion to determine the details of policy programs. Yet public opinion could be expected to have an influence on the general direction of public policy. But which direction? Do the people want policies that are conservative, liberal, or something in between?

A second reason it is important to understand how the people think politically is that a shared frame of reference can bring citizens together in the pursuit of a common goal. The opinions of millions of Americans would mean

[28] See Donald Shaw and Maxwell McCombs, *The Emergence of Political Issues* (St. Paul, Minn.: West, 1977).
[29] See David Green, *Shaping Political Consciousness: The Language of Politics in America from McKinley to Reagan* (Ithaca, N.Y.: Cornell University Press, 1988).

almost nothing if each of these opinions was different from all the others. If enough people think the same way, however, they may be able to exert political power. And, of course, if there are sizable numbers of people who think in opposing ways, the likelihood of political conflict rises sharply.

The subject of how Americans think politically fills entire books; here we will outline four of the major frames of reference through which Americans evaluate political alternatives. The first tends to unite Americans; the other three give rise to differences of opinion among them.

CULTURAL THINKING: COMMON IDEAS

As we indicated in Chapter 1, Americans are unusual in their commitment to a set of ideals that nearly define the nature of the American political experience. Such principles as individualism, equality, and self-government have always meant somewhat different things to different people but nonetheless are a source of opinion consensus.[30] For example, most Americans reject government programs aimed at redistributing wealth from richer citizens to poorer ones. Such policies are common in Western Europe but have had little appeal for Americans, who have a deep-seated belief in individualism. Consider the widespread support that Americans express for social security because retirees have "earned" these benefits through the payroll taxes they paid during their working years. In the context of individualism, whether a benefit has been earned is a standard for judging whether it is truly deserved.

There are limits, of course, to the degree to which Americans' basic beliefs give direction and uniformity to their policy opinions. For nearly two centuries black Americans were inferior by law to white Americans, despite the American creed that "all men are created equal." Such inconsistencies speak to the all-too-human capacity to voice one idea and live another.

Nevertheless, Americans' political ideals are a powerful influence on public opinion. They affect the way in which disputes are argued and affect what people regard as reasonable and desirable. Americans' ideals serve to define the general boundaries of acceptable political action and opinion.

IDEOLOGICAL THINKING: THE OUTLOOK FOR SOME

Are You a Liberal or a Conservative?
Do you favor government programs that would give each American economic security? Do you favor a broad conception of individual rights? Do you believe that the United States should place less emphasis on military power in the exercise of its foreign policy? If you answered yes, you are probably a liberal. If you answered no, you are probably a conservative.

Commentators on public opinion in the United States often use such ideological words as "liberal" and "conservative" in describing how ordinary citizens think about political issues. In the early 1980s, for example, analysts spoke of "a conservative tide" that was supposedly sweeping the country and displacing the liberal trend that had dominated American politics for most of the preceding fifty years. Liberalism and conservatism are examples of an **ideology,** a consistent pattern of opinion on particular issues that stems from a basic underlying belief or beliefs.[31] As used in contemporary politics, **conservatism**

[30] See Donald Devine, *The Political Culture of the United States* (Boston: Little, Brown, 1972); Richard Merelman, *Making Something of Ourselves* (Berkeley: University of California Press, 1984); John White, *The New Politics of Old Values* (Hanover, N.H.: University Press of New England, 1988).
[31] Alternative conceptualizations that are potentially useful have not been widely explored. See, for example, Pamela Johnston Conover and Stanley Feldman, "Belief System Organization in the American Electorate: An Alternative Approach," in John C. Pierce and John L. Sullivan, eds., *The Electorate Reconsidered* (Beverly Hills, Calif.: Sage, 1980); Shawn Rosenberg, Dana Ward, and Stephen Chilton, *Political Reasoning and Cognition* (Durham, N.C.: Duke University Press, 1988).

Percent who agreed

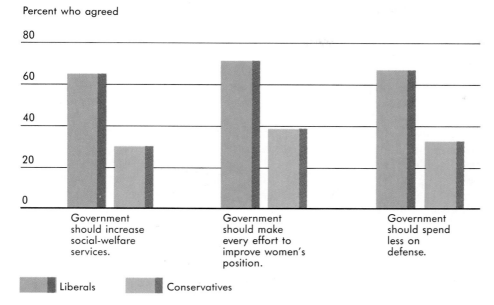

FIGURE 8-1 Correlation between Political Ideology and Opinion on Selected Policy Issues
Liberals are more likely than conservatives to support social-welfare spending and social change and less likely to support defense spending.
Source: National Election Studies data, 1984.

includes beliefs in economic individualism, traditional social values, and a strong defense establishment. **Liberalism** refers to support for social-welfare programs and activitist government, tolerance for social change and diversity, and opposition to "excessive" military spending and interference abroad. Of course, individuals can call themselves liberals or conservatives without subscribing to all or any of the associated beliefs. Yet, as Figure 8-1 illustrates, self-identified liberals and conservatives divide somewhat along the expected dimensions.

Liberalism and conservatism are relatively sophisticated patterns of thought. They require that citizens have general beliefs that they can apply when they respond to an emerging policy alternative. When a new problem or program comes along, a true liberal or conservative judges it by whether or not it calls for activist government or promotes social change.

Given the lack of information that some citizens have about politics, it is perhaps no surprise that about half of adult Americans cannot say what is meant by "liberalism" and "conservatism" and that an additional one-fourth cannot readily apply these ideas to particular policy issues. Most Americans even reject the labels "liberal" and "conservative" and prefer instead to be called "moderate." A 1989 CBS News/New York Times poll indicated that fully 50 percent of Americans saw themselves as moderates, 28 percent as conservatives, and 20 percent as liberals.

After looking in vain for evidence of ideological thinking on the part of the large mass of citizens, Philip Converse concluded, "The common citizen fails to develop global views about politics."[32] Converse's assertion was challenged by later scholarship that indicated ideological thinking was somewhat more

---

[32] Philip Converse, "The Nature of Belief Systems in Mass Publics," in David Apter, ed., *Ideology and Discontent* (New York: Free Press, 1965), 206.

prevalent than he had estimated. Some scholars, however, defended Converse's findings, saying that the differences between his study and later studies was an artifact of differences in the way they measured ideology.[33] All scholars agree, however, that only a minority of citizens—as few as one in ten and no more than one in three—readily understand and apply an ideological frame of reference to political issues.

In fact, Americans tend to be relatively pragmatic, judging policy choices more by their effectiveness than by their ideological "correctness." When Ronald Reagan took office in 1981, for example, most Americans, although they had doubts about many of his conservative ideas, were willing to give them a try. The idea of a new approach was less worrisome to most Americans than the fear of the nation's continuing high rates of inflation and unemployment. This type of pragmatism is what the historian Daniel Boorstin labeled "the genius of American politics."[34] Rather than sticking doggedly to fixed ideologies, Americans have traditionally been willing to try new approaches when the old ones no longer seem to be working. A reason for this pragmatism is that class conflict in the United States has been relatively subdued, which has kept lower-income groups from embracing the socialist idea that wealth should be redistributed from richer to poorer. In European democracies, where class conflict has historically been more substantial, there are major socialist and labor parties that contribute to a more ideological form of partisan politics (see Chapters 9 and 11).

[33] John L. Sullivan, James E. Pierson, and George E. Marcus, "Ideological Constraint in the Mass Public," *American Journal of Political Science* 22 (May 1978): 233–249; Eric R. A. N. Smith, *The Unchanging American Voter* (Berkeley: University of California Press, 1989).
[34] See Daniel Boorstin, *The Genius of American Politics* (Chicago: University of Chicago Press, 1953). A concept that resembles pragmatic thinking is proposed by Shanto Iyengar, "How Citizens Think about National Issues," *American Journal of Political Science* 29 (November 1985): 878–900.

Class conflict lies at the heart of partisan politics in many European countries, giving an ideological twist to public opinion there. Here, French labor union members are protesting a government policy of austerity. (A. Nogues/Sygma)

Income level is one of the group orientations that can affect public opinion. Thus, lower-income Americans are more likely than wealthier people to believe that the government should subsidize the construction of reasonably priced housing. (Rick Reinhard/Impact Visuals)

Although ideology is not an overriding factor in American public opinion, there are at least three reasons for regarding it as an influence of some importance. First, the proportion of citizens who think ideologically, though a minority, is still sizable. Moreover, the proportion increases whenever the available political alternatives are more ideological than normal.[35] For example, when the Democrat Lyndon Johnson, a strong proponent of activist government, campaigned in 1964 against the Republican Barry Goldwater, an equally strong advocate of governmental restraint, the proportion of voters who described their choices in ideological terms doubled from the level in the previous election.[36]

Second, liberalism and conservatism occasionally take on transcendent symbolic meanings. They become associated with much that is good or bad in American politics. In 1964 conservatism was associated in some people's minds with racism and a callous disregard for the poor and the elderly; Johnson was able to exploit this association in his campaign against Goldwater. During the 1988 campaign, the Republican George Bush repeatedly referred to his Democratic opponent, Michael Dukakis, as "a liberal," knowing that some Americans equate liberalism with government waste and social disorder. As the proportion of Americans who perceived Dukakis as a liberal increased during the 1988 campaign, his support decreased.[37]

[35] See John C. Pierce, "Party Identification and the Changing Role of Ideology in American Politics," *Midwest Journal of Political Science* 14 (1970): 25–42; John C. Pierce and Douglas D. Rose, "Non-Attitudes and American Public Opinion," *American Political Science Review* 68 (June 1974): 629–649; Bruce A. Campbell, *The American Electorate* (New York: Holt, Rinehart and Winston, 1979), 148–156.

[36] John Osgood Field and Ronald E. Anderson, "Ideology in the Public's Conceptualization of the 1964 Presidential Election," *Public Opinion Quarterly* 33 (1969): 380–398.

[37] Conclusion based on a comparison of May and September 1988 polls conducted for Times-Mirror Company by the Gallup Organization.

Third, and perhaps most important, ideology is concentrated among those who are most active politically. They understand ideological debate, and many of them are strong liberals or conservatives. Studies indicate, for example, that the political activists who serve as delegates to the national presidential nominating conventions are much more ideological than either the voters within their party or the public as a whole (see Chapter 12). Activists are the most vocal of citizens, which gives added visibility to their ideas. They are also a vital link between leaders and the larger public. In his book *The Paradox of Mass Politics*, W. Russell Neuman explored the low level of information and the relatively unsophisticated level of political thinking on the part of most citizens and asked how democracy could possibly be made to work. He answered his own question by referring to the activist stratum, which he estimated to include no more than about 5 percent of the citizenry. The activists, he argued, serve to bridge the gap between the leaders and the led: although they are members of the mass public, activists are connected through their activities to officeholders, party officials, and other political leaders.[38]

GROUP THINKING: THE OUTLOOK OF MANY

Converse's study indicated that groups are a more important reference for Americans than is ideology; subsequent studies have confirmed his finding.[39] Many Americans see politics through the lens of a group to which they belong or with which they identify. These individuals nearly always pay closer attention to issues that affect the group's interests than to more remote issues. Farmers, for example, are more likely to follow agricultural issues than they are labor-management issues. A group outlook is a source of both consensus and conflict. Farmers generally approve of government price supports for commodities; this opinion unites farmers but pits them against other groups, including consumers.

Because of the country's great size, settlement by various immigrant groups, and economic pluralism, Americans are a very diverse people. Later chapters will examine group tendencies more fully, but it is useful here to mention a few of the major group orientations.

Religion

Religious differences have always been a source of solidarity within a group and conflict with outsiders. Gone, presumably forever, is the virulent anti-Catholicism and anti-Semitism that many Protestants directed at immigrants from southern and eastern Europe upon their arrival in America. Today religious differences are evident mainly in the context of social policy issues, such as school prayer and abortion. For example, fundamentalist Protestants and Roman Catholics oppose legalized abortion more strongly than do other Protestants, Jews, and those who have no religious affiliation.

A different alliance characterizes opinions on social-welfare issues, such as

---

[38] W. Russell Neuman, *The Paradox of Mass Politics* (Cambridge, Mass.: Harvard University Press, 1986).
[39] Converse, "The Nature of Belief Systems."

food programs for the poor. Catholics and Jews are more supportive of such programs than are Protestants, with fundamentalists being more strongly opposed than Protestants as a whole.

Income

Personal income level has less influence on political opinion in the United States than in Europe, but it is nevertheless related to opinions on certain economic policy issues. For example, lower-income Americans are more supportive of social-welfare programs, business regulation, and progressive taxation than are those in higher-income categories.

Occupation

Related to income, but different in its political significance, is occupation. Occupation affects how Americans view issues that narrowly affect their livelihoods. To list just a few examples, physicians have opposed a nationalized health service, which would provide government-paid medical care to all Americans; farmers have been the strongest proponents of agricultural subsidies; and factory workers have supported strong collective bargaining legislation. The interplay of occupation and opinion will be examined more closely in Chapters 13 and 14, where interest groups are discussed.

Region

Region has declined as a basis of political differences, but growing up in a particular section of the country is still associated to a degree with opinions on such issues as civil rights and national defense. For example, southern whites are less favorably disposed toward civil rights and more supportive of defense spending than are whites in other geographical areas.

Race

Race is a significant source of opinion differences. For example, African-Americans are more supportive of social-welfare programs and less trustful of government than are whites. Blacks are also more in favor of affirmative action, busing to achieve racial integration in the schools, and other measures designed to promote racial equality.

Gender

Although male-female differences of opinion are small on most issues, gender does affect opinion on some questions. Perhaps surprisingly, these issues are not primarily those that touch directly on sexual equality. Opinion polls indicate that men and women are about equally supportive of affirmative action and do not hold significantly different opinions on abortion rights or the proposed Equal Rights Amendment to the Constitution. But men and women do divide on issues involving physical coercion by the state. For example, in an ABC News/Washington Post survey on January 16, 1991, the night that the

TABLE 8-2 Differences in Male–Female Opinion on Selected Issues Men are more likely than women to support the use of force by the state.

| | PERCENT WHO AGREE | |
FORCE-RELATED ISSUE	Men	Women
Describe self as a "hawk"—want to step up military effort in Vietnam (1968)	50%	32%
Favor death penalty for those convicted of murder (1988)	83	75
Favor the use of troops if Soviet Union invaded Western Europe (1990)	66	50
Approve of U.S. having gone to war with Iraq (1991)	84	68

SOURCES: Gallup, April 4–9, 1968; Gallup, Sept. 25–Oct. 1, 1988; Gallup, Oct. 23–Nov. 15, 1990; ABC News/Washington Post, Jan. 16, 1991.

United States went to war with Iraq, 84 percent of men but only 68 percent of women said they approved of the action. Table 8-2 provides poll results that indicate the extent of male-female differences on several issues involving the use of physical force.

PARTISAN THINKING: THE LINE THAT DIVIDES

In the everyday play of politics, there is no source of opinion that more clearly divides Americans than their partisanship—their loyalty to one political party or another. Republicans and Democrats disagree on a significant range of policy issues. Social welfare is an example. Democrats are much more supportive of welfare services than are Republicans; a 1989 Gallup poll, for example, indicated that 63 percent of Democrats but only 38 percent of Republicans favored more government spending on food programs for low-income families.

Partisanship is the major frame of reference by which many people make their political judgments. Although party loyalty is a declining influence, it is still the dominant one in the context of mainstream politics. Americans' evaluations of presidential candidates, for example, are substantially affected by current issues, the performance of government, and the personalities of the candidates; but, election after election, partisanship remains the best predictor of the vote. (Partisan differences will be examined in depth at various points later in this book, particularly in Chapters 10, 11, 24, and 25.)

Effective government cannot be conducted by legislators and officials who, when a question is presented, ask themselves first and last not what is the truth and which is the right and necessary course, but "What does the Gallup Poll say?"

Walter Lippmann

The Influence of Public Opinion on Policy

Questions of how people frame and acquire their political opinions are relevant to the issue of the influence those opinions should have on government policy. Obviously, opinions that are framed on the basis of deeply held values and that are acquired as a result of prolonged deliberation or lengthy experience should weigh more heavily in political action than hastily acquired opinions that derive

★ CRITICAL THINKING

SHOULD LEADERS GOVERN ACCORDING TO OPINION POLLS?

These days, public officials and candidates for public office routinely use public opinion polls to keep track of what the people are thinking. During the Vietnam war, President Lyndon Johnson would sometimes carry a copy of the latest poll in his pocket and wave it at reporters to support his claim that his war policies had majority support.

Some observers have argued that polls contribute to effective government by keeping political leaders from getting too far out of line with the public's thinking. Polls can dissuade political leaders from thinking that the view of those who are speaking the loudest is also the common view. When a policy is contrary to the public's desires, people may choose to disregard or undermine it, thus making it counterproductive or inefficient. Further, when government pursues a course of action with which a large proportion of the public disagrees, it risks a loss of public confidence, which can adversely affect its ability to lead. The Reagan administration, flying high from 1981 to 1985, was brought low in 1986 by public reaction to news of its secret sales of weapons to Iran. The administration had not paid sufficient attention to polls that revealed the deep antagonism Americans still felt toward Iran because it had held sixty-three embassy personnel and other Americans hostage in 1979–1981.

Other observers claim that poll results cannot substitute for leadership. "Effective government," Walter Lippmann wrote, "cannot be conducted by legislators and officials who, when a question is presented, ask themselves first and last not what is the truth and which is the right and necessary course, but 'What does the Gallup Poll say?'" Lippmann reinforced his argument by pointing out that the mass public does not have accurate and detailed information from which to select among policy options. He concluded that leaders must take the responsibility for devising workable policies that the public, in the long run, will accept. Opinion polls can be a useful guide in this process but are insignificant in comparison with good leadership and effective policy institutions. During his presidential term, for example, Jimmy Carter proposed five consecutive inflation-fighting programs, changing his plans with each shift in public sentiment without having invested the political capital necessary to get Congress and the country behind any of the efforts. The nation—and Carter—might have been better served by a steadfast commitment to a single course of action.

What is your view on the use of polls in governing? Should leaders rely heavily on public opinion polls in making their governing decisions? Or should leaders follow their own judgment of the public interest when deciding issues of policy?

SOURCES: Bruce E. Altschuler, *LBJ and the Polls* (Gainesville: University of Florida, 1990); James R. Beninger and Robert Giuffra, Jr., "Public Opinion Polling: Command and Control in Presidential Campaigns," in Alexander Heard and Michael Nelson, eds., *Presidential Selection* (Durham, N.C.: Duke University Press, 1987), 214; Larry J. Sabato, *The Rise of Political Consultants* (New York: Basic Books, 1981), 321.

---

from, for example, a government propaganda campaign. In the latter situation, people are voicing opinions that have been placed in their heads by manipulative officials. When these opinions are then used to justify particular policies, officials are merely adding the veneer of public approval to actions they planned to take anyway. The result is not government of and by the people but government of and by those in authority.

As it happens, public opinion is not so easily manipulated in most instances. Studies of persuasion through mass communication have found that people's views are relatively resistant to change.[40] The attitudes that people bring to a situation tend to persist and to affect the formation of new opinions.

Government, in the last analysis, is organized opinion. Where there is little or no public opinion, there is likely to be bad government, which sooner or later becomes autocratic government.

W. L. Mackenzie King, Prime Minister of Canada (1927)

[40] See Dan D. Nimmo and Keith R. Sanders, *Handbook of Political Communication* (Beverly Hills, Calif.: Sage, 1981).

PUBLIC OPINION AND POLICY CHANGE

A fundamental principle of democracy is that the people's view ought to prevail on public issues. The difficulty comes in putting this principle into practice. A democracy is typically said to be "rule by the people" and is different from an authoritarian regime. The distinction implies that what an authoritarian ruler does in one system the people do in the other. But the comparison is faulty. Government by the people in a literal sense would mean that 175 million adult Americans were in charge—which is to say that no one would be in charge.[41] The result would be chaos. Everyone would want things run his or her way, meaning that nothing would be accomplished.

In a society of any appreciable size, it is simply not possible for the people directly to formulate public policies and programs. Thankfully, democracy does not depend on such an arrangement. Democracy can be said to exist when the people's representatives take their constituents' interests and desires into account in significant ways when making policy decisions. By this standard, America's government is democratic, albeit imperfectly so.

In a study covering 1935 to 1979, Benjamin Page and Robert Shapiro found considerable congruence between changes in public opinion and subsequent changes in public policy, particularly on highly visible issues about which opinion change was large and stable. They examined 357 cases of opinion change and then determined what policy change, if any, ensued during the following year.[42] The results of their study are summarized in Table 8-3. Overall, Page and Shapiro found that policy changed in the same direction as

[41] E. E. Schattschneider, *The Semisovereign People* (New York: Holt, Rinehart and Winston, 1980), ch. 8.
[42] Benjamin I. Page and Robert Y. Shapiro, "Effects of Public Opinion on Policy," *American Political Science Review* 77 (March 1983): 175–190.

TABLE 8-3 Congruence between Changes in Public Opinion and Changes in Policy, 1935–1979 Public policy tends to change in the same direction as changes in public opinion.

	All Cases	Only Cases Involving a Policy Change
Public opinion and policy changed in the same direction	43%	66%
Public opinion and policy changed in opposite directions	22	34
No policy change	33	
Unclassified	2	
	100%	100%

Note: Each case is an instance in which public policy preferences changed significantly, according to repeated administration of identical survey items.

SOURCE: Benjamin I. Page and Robert Y. Shapiro, "Effects of Public Opinion on Policy," *American Political Science Review* 77 (March 1983): 178.

Bags containing the bodies of American soldiers killed in the Vietnam war await shipment back to the United States. The large number of American casualties during the war helped to turn public opinion against U.S. involvement in Vietnam. (UPI/Bettmann Newsphotos)

opinion change in 43 percent of the cases and changed in the opposite direction in only 22 percent of the cases. Even in the latter cases, the researchers found that the policy change was nearly always minor in scope. Page and Shapiro concluded, "When Americans' policy preferences shift, it is likely that congruent changes in policy will follow."[43]

PUBLIC OPINION AND THE BOUNDARIES OF ACTION

The influence of public opinion on policy takes several forms. It is relatively rare for public opinion to be so powerful as to force leaders to act. It can happen that existing opinion supports a certain course of action so strongly that officials have little choice but to take that course. An example is the public outrage against Japan following the bombing of Pearl Harbor in 1941. Even if Congress had wanted to react differently, it would have had no choice but to bow to public opinion and declare war on Japan.

Public opinion can also block action by leaders. During his first presidential term, Ronald Reagan proposed a change in the social security system, but he quickly backed down in the face of widespread public opposition, particularly from senior citizens groups. The founder of social security, Franklin D. Roosevelt, understood that public opinion would preserve his program. "No damn politician," he reportedly said, "can ever scrap my social security program."[44] Roosevelt recognized that if social security were funded by payroll

[43] Ibid., 189.
[44] Quoted in Arthur M. Schlesinger, Jr., *The Coming of the New Deal* (Boston: Houghton Mifflin, 1958), 309.

In the modern world the intelligence of public opinion is the one indispensable condition of social progress.
Charles Eliot,
President of Harvard
University (1869)

taxes, future generations of workers would feel that they had rightfully earned their retirement benefits and therefore would fight to maintain them.

Ordinarily, however, public opinion gives policymakers room to maneuver, serving only as a guiding force. It establishes a boundary within which officials can act, but does not force a particular action upon them. When Iraq invaded Kuwait in August 1990, George Bush had a range of options that the American people had indicated they would accept. He chose the war option, but he could also have selected an extended economic boycott or other sanctions against Iraq without incurring the displeasure of the American public.

Finally, public opinion is a sanctioning force. As a policy develops, opinions about its effectiveness emerge and generate support for or opposition to it. Few issues of recent times illustrate this aspect of public opinion's influence more clearly than does the Vietnam war. Two years into a major buildup of U.S. forces in Vietnam, Americans had soured on President Lyndon Johnson's commitment of a half-million U.S. soldiers to a war that was not being won. A November 1965 Gallup poll had indicated that a solid majority of the American public (64–21 percent) supported the escalation, and a majority approved of Johnson's later decision to carry the war to North Vietnam by the aerial bombardment of Hanoi, its capital city, and Haiphong, its major seaport. However, in early spring of 1968, with his public approval rating down to 40 percent from a high of 70 percent two years earlier, and with a majority of Americans now convinced that the escalation had been a mistake, Johnson announced that he would not seek reelection. Public opinion had not forced Johnson to increase the U.S. role in Vietnam; but once he had done so, he had to deal with the public's expectation that the escalation would win the war. In the end, it was the American people, not the generals and politicians, who concluded that Johnson's policy was a failure and a change of leadership was needed.

The recognition by elected leaders that they must satisfy public opinion is a powerful constraint on their actions, as Chapter 10 will discuss more fully. Later chapters will also examine directly the impact of public opinion in particular policy areas: the economy (Chapter 24), social welfare (25), and foreign affairs (26).

Summary

Public opinion can be defined as those opinions held by ordinary citizens which government takes into account in making its decisions. Public officials have many ways of assessing public opinion, such as the outcomes of elections, but have increasingly come to rely on public opinion polls. There are many possible sources of error in polls, and surveys sometimes present a misleading portrayal of the public's views. However, a properly conducted poll can provide an accurate indication of what the public is thinking and can dissuade political leaders from thinking that the views of the most vocal citizens (such as demonstrators and letter writers) are also the views of the broader public.

Individual opinions gain power to the degree that others share a similar view. Public opinion thus has the force of numbers. A major source of common opinions among Americans is their cultural beliefs, such as individualism, which result in a range of acceptable and unacceptable policy alternatives. Agreement can also stem from a shared ideology, although most citizens do not have a strong and consistent attachment to liberal or conservative policies. In addition, individuals share opinions as a result of a shared party loyalty or a shared group circumstance, notably religion, income, occupation, region, race, or gender.

The process by which individuals acquire their political

opinions is called political socialization. During childhood the family and schools are important sources of basic political attitudes, such as beliefs about the parties and the nature of the U.S. political and economic systems. Many of the basic orientations that Americans acquire during childhood remain with them in adulthood; but socialization is a continuing process. Major shifts in opinion during adulthood are usually the consequence of changing political conditions; for example, the Great Depression of the 1930s was the catalyst for wholesale changes in Americans' opinions on the government's economic role. There are also short-term fluctations in opinion that result from new political issues, problems, and events. Individuals' opinions in these cases are affected by prior beliefs, peers, political leaders, and the news media. Events themselves are also a significant short-term influence on opinions.

Public opinion has a significant influence on government but seldom determines exactly what government will do in a particular instance. Public opinion serves to constrain the policy choices of officials. Some policy actions are beyond the range of possibility because the public will not accept change in existing policy or will not seriously consider policy that seems clearly at odds with basic American values. Evidence indicates that officials are reasonably attentive to public opinion on highly visible and controversial issues of public policy.

Major Concepts

conservatism	probability sample
ideology	public opinion
liberalism	public opinion poll
political socialization	sample
population	sampling error

Suggested Readings

Backstrom, Charles H., and Gerald Hursh-Cesar. *Survey Research*, 2d ed. New York: Macmillan, 1981. A how-to-do-it book on public opinion polling.

Hess, Robert D., and Judith V. Torney. *The Development of Political Attitudes in Children*. Chicago: Aldine, 1967. A study of how children learn about politics.

Key, V. O., Jr. *Public Opinion and American Democracy*. New York: Knopf, 1961. A thorough examination of public opinion and its relation to the governing process.

Lippmann, Walter. *Public Opinion*. New York: Free Press, 1965. The classic analysis of public opinion (originally published in 1922).

McCloskey, Herbert, and John Zaller. *The American Ethos: Public Attitudes toward Capitalism and Democracy*. Cambridge, Mass.: Harvard University Press, 1984. A study of how Americans' ideals underpin capitalism and democracy and narrow the range of political choices.

Miller, Warren E., et al. *American National Election Studies Data Sourcebook*. Cambridge, Mass.: Harvard University Press, 1980. A compendium of the results of opinion surveys conducted by the University of Michigan's famed Survey Research Center.

Neuman, W. Russell. *The Paradox of Mass Politics: Knowledge and Opinion in the American Electorate*. Cambridge, Mass.: Harvard University Press, 1986. An assessment of how democracy works, given that most citizens are not particularly interested in or informed about policy and government.

Noelle-Neumann, Elisabeth. *The Spiral of Silence*. Chicago: University of Chicago Press, 1984. An intriguing theory of how public opinion is formed and muted.

Yankelovich, Daniel. *Coming to Public Judgment*. Syracuse, N.Y.: Syracuse University Press, 1991. A prescriptive book on how the public can be brought more fully into the policy process despite the complexity of modern issues.

9

POLITICAL PARTICIPATION: INVOLVING THE PEOPLE

We are concerned in public affairs, but immersed in our private ones.
Walter Lippmann[1]

*T*he American people were angrier at Washington in 1992 than they had been in years. The House of Representatives was muddied by a check-cashing scandal, the Senate was still reeling from earlier accusations of influence peddling in conjunction with the savings and loan scandal, and the presidency seemed adrift in the midst of a weak economy, a defiant Congress, and a budget deficit so huge that there was almost no money for new initiatives. Some pundits predicted that Americans would vent their frustrations with the national government by turning out in record numbers to "vote the rascals out" in the November election.

In the end, however, about half the adult population stayed home on election day. Out of nearly 200 million people of voting age, fewer than 100 million showed up at the polls. Despite the public's expressions of anger at their elected representatives and despite a concerted get-out-the-vote campaign by public-service groups and the news media, the number of people who did not vote was far greater than the number of votes the winning party received in either the presidential or congressional races.

Voting is a form of **political participation**—a sharing in activities designed to influence public policy and leadership. Political participation involves other activities in addition to voting, such as joining political parties and interest

[1] Walter Lippmann, *Public Opinion* (1922; New York: Free Press, 1965), 36.

groups, writing to elected officials, demonstrating for political causes, and giving money to political candidates.

Democratic societies are distinguished by their emphasis on citizen participation. The concept of self-government rests on the idea that ordinary people have a right, even an obligation, to involve themselves in the affairs of state. A political system that claims to operate in the public's interest is not necessarily a truly democratic system; citizens must also be given meaningful opportunities to participate in the process. From this perspective, the extent of political participation—how much and by whom—is a measure of how fully democratic a society is.[2]

The question of participation also extends to the reasons people are politically involved or not involved. If differences in degree of participation are of a purely individual nature, there is less cause for concern than if the differences have a systemic base. It is one thing if political participation is like attendance at a rock concert, which is mostly a matter of individual taste and proximity, and quite another if participation is like attendance at an elite prep school, which is mostly a matter of social privilege. A democratic political system implies that society will not place substantial barriers in the way of those who want to participate. As we will see in this chapter, differences in the extent of political participation among Americans are explained by both individual and systemic factors, although the latter are more influential in the United States than in most other Western democracies. One result is that the participation rate in U.S. elections is less than that of other countries, particularly among citizens of lower income and less education. The major points made in this chapter are the following:

★ *Voter turnout in U.S. elections is low in comparison with that of other democratic nations.* The reasons for this difference include the nature of U.S. election laws, particularly those pertaining to registration requirements and the scheduling of elections, but the fundamental reason seems to be Americans' belief that election outcomes are not very important to their lives. This view is especially prevalent among people with lower incomes and less education.

★ *Most citizens do not participate actively in politics in ways other than voting.* Only a small proportion of Americans can be classified as political activists.

★ *Most Americans make a sharp distinction between their personal lives and national life.* This attitude reduces their incentive to participate and contributes to a pattern of participation dominated by citizens with higher levels of income and education.

Voter Participation

At the nation's founding, **suffrage**—the right to vote—was restricted to property-owning males. Tom Paine ridiculed this policy in *Common Sense*. Observing that a man whose only item of property was a jackass would lose his

[2] Sidney Verba and Norman H. Nie, *Participation in America: Political Democracy and Social Equality* (New York: Harper & Row, 1972), 1.

After a hard-fought, decades-long campaign, American women finally won the right to vote in 1920. (Culver Pictures)

right to vote if the jackass died, Paine asked, "Now tell me, which was the voter, the man or the jackass?" It was not until the 1820s that a majority of states had extended suffrage to propertyless white males, a change made possible by their continued demand for the vote and by the realization on the part of the wealthy that the nation's abundance and openness were natural protections against an assault on property rights by the voting poor.

Women did not secure the vote until 1920, with the ratification of the Nineteenth Amendment. In the 1870s Susan B. Anthony tried to vote in her hometown of Rochester, New York, asserting that she had a right to do so as a U.S. citizen. The men who placed her under arrest charged her with "illegal voting" and insisted that her proper place was in the home. By 1920, men had run out of pretexts for keeping the vote from women. The best argument that the antisuffragists could muster was that women should not vote because they had no voting experience. Senator Wendell Phillips expressed the pro-suffrage view: "One of two things is true: either woman is like man—and if she is, then a ballot based on brains belongs to her as well as to him. Or she is different, and then man does not know how to vote for her as she herself does."[3]

The right of citizens of the United States to vote shall not be denied or abridged by the United States or by any State on account of sex.
    U.S. Constitution,
    Nineteenth Amendment

Black Americans had to wait nearly fifty years longer than women to be granted full suffrage. Blacks seemed to have won the right to vote with passage of the Fifteenth Amendment after the Civil War, but as we saw in Chapter 7, they were effectively disenfranchised in the South by a number of electoral tricks, including poll taxes, literacy tests, and whites-only primary elections. The poll tax was a fee of several dollars that had to be paid before one could register to vote. Since most blacks in the South were too poor to pay it, the poll tax barred them from voting. Not until the ratification of the Twenty-fourth

[3] Quoted in Ralph Volney Harlow, *The Growth of the United States* (New York: Henry Holt, 1943), 312.

Amendment in 1964 was the poll tax outlawed in national elections. Supreme Court decisions and the Voting Rights Act of 1965 swept away other legal barriers to fuller participation by black Americans.

Today virtually any American—rich or poor, man or woman, black or white—who is determined to vote can legally and actually do so. Americans attach great importance to the power of their votes. They claim that voting is their greatest source of influence over political leadership and their strongest protection against an uncaring or corrupt government.[4] In view of this attitude and the historical determination of various groups to gain voting rights, the surprising fact is that Americans are not enthusiastic voters. Millions of them choose not to vote regularly, a habit that sets them apart from citizens of other western democracies.

The right of citizens of the United States to vote shall not be denied or abridged by the United States or by any State on account of race, color, or previous condition of servitude.
U.S. Constitution,
Fifteenth Amendment

FACTORS IN VOTER TURNOUT: THE UNITED STATES IN COMPARATIVE PERSPECTIVE

Voter turnout is the proportion of persons of voting age who actually vote in a given election. Since 1920 the level of turnout in presidential elections has never exceeded 63 percent; thus a third or more of voting-age persons stayed away from the polls at each election (see Figure 9-1). Turnout is even lower in nonpresidential elections: at no time since 1920 has it reached 50 percent. When

[4] See Gerald Pomper with Susan Lederman, *Elections in America*, 2d ed. (New York: Longman, 1980), ch. 1; Jack Dennis, "Support for the Institution of Elections by the Mass Public," *American Political Science Review* 64 (1970): 819–835.

★ HOW THE UNITED STATES COMPARES

VOTER TURNOUT

The United States ranks near the bottom among the world's democracies in the percentage of eligible citizens who vote in national elections. One reason for this low voter turnout is that individual Americans are responsible for registering to vote, whereas in most other democracies, voters are automatically registered by government officials. In addition, unlike some other democracies, the United States does not encourage voting by penalizing citizens who do not participate, as by fining them.

Country	Voter Turnout	Personal Registration?	Penalty for Not Voting?
Italy	94.0%	No	Yes
Austria	89.3	No	No
Belgium	88.7	No	Yes
Sweden	86.8	No	No
Greece	84.9	No	Yes
Netherlands	84.7	No	Yes
Australia	83.1	Yes	Yes
Denmark	82.1	No	No
Norway	81.8	No	No
West Germany	81.1	No	No
New Zealand	78.5	Yes	No
France	78.0	Yes	No
Great Britain	76.0	No	No
Canada	67.4	No	No
United States	52.6	Yes	No

SOURCE: David Glass, Peverill Squire, and Raymond Wolfinger, "Voter Turnout: An International Comparison," *Public Opinion*, December/January 1984, 50.

Percent of voting-age population who voted

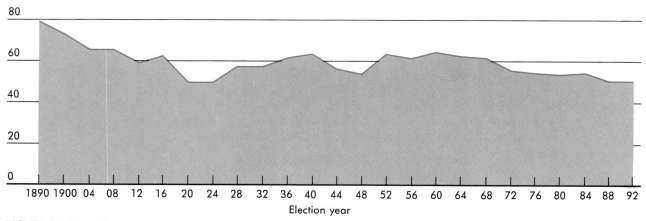

FIGURE 9-1 Voter Turnout
in Presidental Elections,
1896–1992
Voter turnout declined after
registration was instituted at the
turn of the century and has
stayed low for most national
elections ever since. *Source: Data
for 1896–1968 from U.S. Bureau of
Census,* Historical Statistics of the
United States, Colonial Times to
1970, Part 2 *(Washington, D.C.:
U.S. Government Printing Office,
1975),* 1071; *data for 1972–1988,
Federal Election Commission; data
for 1992 estimated.*

a mere 37 percent of adults voted in the high-stakes congressional elections of
1986, the cartoonist Rigby showed a stray cat wandering into a polling place
and an election clerk asking it hopefully, "Are you registered?"[5] The voting rate
in U.S. elections is always low enough so that people who do not vote greatly
outnumber the voters who provide the winning candidate's margin of victory.
In the 1968 presidential election Richard Nixon defeated Hubert Humphrey by
just 510,635 votes, while 62 million adult Americans did not participate.

Nonvoting is far more prevalent in the United States than in nearly all other
democracies. In recent decades, turnout in major national elections has averaged less than 60 percent in the United States, compared with more than 90
percent in Italy, more than 80 percent in Australia and West Germany, and
more than 70 percent in Great Britain and Canada.[6] The disparity in turnout
between the United States and other nations is not so great as these official
voting rates indicate. Some nations calculate turnout solely on the basis of
eligible adults, while the United States bases its figures on all adults, including
noncitizens and other ineligible groups. Nevertheless, even when such statistical disparities are corrected, turnout in U.S. elections remains low in comparison with that of nearly every other western democracy.

The major reasons that Americans vote at such a comparatively low rate
include registration requirements, the frequency of elections, and the lack of
clear-cut differences between the major political parties.

Registration Requirements

Before Americans are allowed to vote, they must be registered—that is, their
names must appear on an official list of eligible voters. **Registration** began
around 1900 as a way of preventing voters from casting more than one ballot
during an election. Such fraudulent activities had become a favorite tactic of

[5] Example from Gus Tyler, "One Cheer for the Democrats," *New Leader*, November 3, 1986, 6.
[6] G. Bingham Powell, "Voting Turnout in Thirty Democracies," in Richard Rose, ed., *Electoral
Participation: A Comparative Analysis* (Beverly Hills, Calif.: Sage, 1980), 6.

political party machines in cities where residents were not personally known to poll watchers. However, the extra effort involved in registering placed an added burden on honest citizens. Turnout in U.S. elections declined steadily after registration was instituted.[7]

Although other democracies also require registration, they place this responsibility on government. In European nations, public officials have the duty to enroll citizens on registration lists. The United States—in keeping with its individualistic culture—is the only democracy in which registration is the individual's responsibility.[8] In addition, registration laws are established by the state governments, and some states make it relatively difficult for citizens to qualify. Registration periods and locations are usually not highly publicized, and many citizens simply do not know when or where to register.[9] Eligibility can also be a problem. In most states, a citizen must establish legal residency by living in the same place for a minimum period, usually thirty days but as long as fifty days, before becoming eligible to register.

States with a tradition of lenient registration laws generally have a higher turnout than other states. Maine, Minnesota, and Oregon allow people to register at their polling place on election day, and these states rank high in voter turnout. Those states that have erected the most barriers are in the South, where

[7] Philip E. Converse, "Change in the American Electorate," in Philip E. Converse and Angus Campbell, eds., *The Human Meaning of Social Change* (New York: Russell Sage Foundation, 1972), 281; see also Stanley Kelley, Jr., Richard E. Ayres, and William G. Bowen, "Registration and Voting: Putting First Things First," *American Political Science Review* 61 (June 1967): 359–379. For insights into the impact on electoral behavior of another reform, the Australian ballot, see Jerrold D. Rusk, "The Effect of the Australian Ballot Reform on Split Ticket Voting: 1876–1908," *American Political Science Review* 64 (December 1970): 1220–1238.

[8] Ivor Crewe, "Electoral Participation," in David Butler, Howard R. Penniman, and Austin Ranney, eds., *Democracy at the Polls* (Washington, D.C.: American Enterprise Institute, 1981), 249.

[9] Philip E. Converse with Richard Niemi, "Non-voting among Young Adults in the United States," in William J. Crotty et al., eds., *Political Parties and Political Behavior* (Boston: Allyn & Bacon, 1971), 456.

Near-empty polling stations are a fact of political life in America. Less than 50 percent of voting-age citizens turn out to cast their ballots in nonpresidential election years. (Rob Crandall/Picture Group)

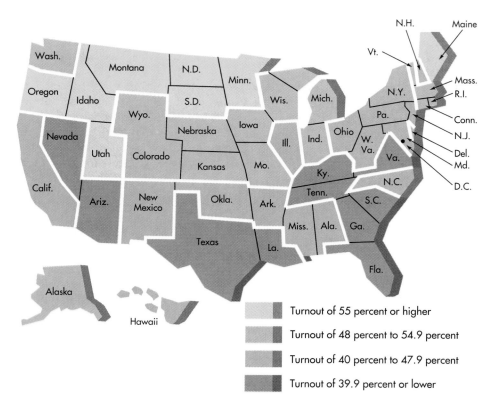

FIGURE 9-2 Mean State-by-State Voter Turnout in All Presidential, Gubernatorial, Senatorial, and House Elections, 1981–1988 Southern states have a tradition of more restrictive registration laws, and even today they tend to have the lowest rates of voter turnout. *Source: Virginia Gray, Herbert Jacob, and Robert Albritton,* Politics in the American States: A Comparative Analysis, *5th ed. (Glenview, Ill.: Scott, Foresman, 1990), table 3.1.*

Turnout of 55 percent or higher

Turnout of 48 percent to 54.9 percent

Turnout of 40 percent to 47.9 percent

Turnout of 39.9 percent or lower

restrictive registration was originally intended to prevent black people from voting. These historical differences continue to be reflected in state voter turnout levels (see Figure 9-2).

It has been estimated that if all states adopted simple registration procedures —for example, lengthening the registration period, allowing weekend and evening registration, and locating registration facilities near workplaces—voter turnout would increase by about 9 percent.[10] In a presidential election, this increase would mean an additional 10 million voters.

Why, then, have not all states simplified their registration procedures? One reason is that many state and local officials, regardless of what they may say publicly, are not very interested in adding lots of new voters to the registration lists. Poor and less-educated citizens are the ones most easily discouraged by restrictive registration laws, and their influx into the electorate could alter the political balance of power in a state, county, or city. The same self-interest prompts officials in many college towns to resist student registration. Until recently, college students in Syracuse, New York, had to complete a lengthy questionnaire to establish their eligibility to register. The procedure discouraged most students from trying to register in Syracuse and allowed local officials to disqualify other students on the basis of "wrong" responses on the questionnaire. Of 900 students who applied to register in Syracuse in 1986, only 150 were permitted to do so.

[10] Raymond E. Wolfinger and Steven J. Rosenstone, *Who Votes?* (New Haven, Conn.: Yale University Press, 1980), 78–79.

Frequency of Elections

Another factor that reduces voter turnout is the frequency with which Americans are asked to vote. No other democracy has elections for the lower chamber of its national legislature (the equivalent of the U.S. House of Representatives) as often as every two years, and none schedules elections for chief executive as often as every four years.[11] In addition, elections of state and local officials in the United States are often scheduled separately from national races. Two-thirds of the states elect their governors in nonpresidential election years,[12] and 60 percent of U.S. cities hold elections of municipal officials in odd-numbered years.[13]

This staggered scheduling reflects in some cases a deliberate effort by state and local officials to insulate their election races from the possible effects of other campaigns. During Franklin D. Roosevelt's four terms as president, for example, Republicans in several states, including New York and Connecticut, backed constitutional amendments that required gubernatorial races to be held in nonpresidential years. The purpose was to prevent other Democratic candidates from riding into office on Roosevelt's coattails.

The frequency of U.S. elections reduces turnout by increasing the effort required to participate in all of them.[14] Most European nations have less frequent elections, and the responsibility of voting is thus less burdensome. Many European nations also schedule their elections on Sundays or declare

[11] Crewe, "Electoral Participation," 230.
[12] Malcolm Jewell and David Olson, *American State Politics and Elections* (Homewood, Ill.: Irwin Press, 1978), 50.
[13] A. Karnig and B. Walter, "Municipal Elections," in *Municipal Yearbook, 1977* (Washington, D.C.: International City Management Assn., 1977).
[14] Richard Boyd, "Decline of U.S. Voter Turnout," *American Politics Quarterly* 9 (April 1981): 142.

In Austin, Texas, a door-to-door drive simplifies voter registration. Many people fail to register to vote in states that impose more complex requirements and restrictions. (Bob Daemmrich/The Image Works)

election day to be a national holiday, thus making it more convenient for working people to vote. In the United States, elections are traditionally held on Tuesdays, and most people must vote before or after work.

The contrast with European practice is especially marked in the case of primary elections. The United States is the only democratic nation in which party nominees are commonly chosen by voters through primary elections rather than by party leaders.[15] Consequently, Americans are asked to vote twice to fill a single office. Many voters skip the primaries, preferring to vote just once, in the general election. In contested statewide and presidential primaries, the average voter turnout is about 30 percent, substantially lower than the turnout in general elections.

Party Differences

An additional explanation for low voter turnout in the United States has to do with voters' perception that there is not much difference between the major political parties. Roughly a third of Americans claim that it is largely irrelevant whether the Republicans or the Democrats gain control of government.[16] This belief is not entirely unfounded. The two major American political parties do not normally differ greatly in their policies. Each party depends on citizens of all economic interests and social backgrounds for support; consequently, neither party can afford to take an extreme position that would alienate any sizable segment of the electorate. For example, both parties share a commitment to the private enterprise system and to a basic social security system (see Chapter 11).

Parties in Europe tend to divide more sharply over economic policies. There the choice between a conservative party and a socialist party may mean a choice between private and government ownership of major industries. Studies indicate that turnout is higher in nations whose political parties represent clear-cut alternatives, particularly when religious or class divisions are involved. Conversely, turnout is lower when, as in the United States, a nation's parties compete for the loyalty of voters of all religions and classes.[17] European parties, particularly those on the left, are also more closely tied to other organizations, such as labor unions, which assist in the mobilization of the electorate.[18]

WHY SOME AMERICANS VOTE AND OTHERS DO NOT

Even though turnout is lower in the United States than in other democracies, some Americans do vote in all or nearly all elections.. But other Americans seldom or never vote. What accounts for such *individual* differences?

The factors that account for differences in public opinion (see Chapter 8) are not in all cases related to turnout differences. The turnout rates of men and women, for example, are similar. Among older women the voting rate is

---

[15] Austin Ranney, "Candidate Selection," in Butler, Penniman, and Ranney, *Democracy at the Polls*, 88.
[16] Angus Campbell, Philip E. Converse, Warren E. Miller, and Donald E. Stokes, *The American Voter* (New York: Wiley, 1960), 104. More recent studies show no significant change in this attitude.
[17] Crewe, "Electoral Participation," 251–253; Powell, "Voting Turnout."
[18] Powell, "Voting Turnout."

Older Americans have more deeply ingrained political views and are more likely to vote than are younger citizens. (James Kamp/Black Star)

somewhat below that of men, but once age and educational differences are accounted for, sex is not related to turnout differences.[19] Race was once a very significant predictor of turnout but has become less important. African-Americans still have a substantially lower turnout rate than whites, but the difference, which is about 10 percent in presidential elections, is far less than the 40 percent that existed even as recently as 1960 (see Chapter 7).

Large differences in voter turnout are associated with citizens' sense of civic involvement, age, education, and socioeconomic class.

Feelings of Civic Duty, Alienation, and Apathy

Regular voters are characterized by a strong sense of **civic duty**—that is, they regard participation in elections as one of the responsibilities of citizenship. On the night of the 1984 presidential election, early returns from the East indicated that Ronald Reagan would win reelection by a landslide, yet regular voters in the West were undeterred. Although they knew that their votes would not affect the outcome, they voted anyway in order to fulfill their duty as citizens.

Your every voter, as surely as your chief magistrate, exercises a public trust.

Grover Cleveland

A sense of civic duty is an attitude that most individuals acquire during their political socialization in childhood and adolescence. When parents vote regularly and take an interest in politics, their children are likely to grow up believing that voting is an obligation of citizenship. Schools reinforce this belief by stressing the value of civic involvement.

A sense of civic duty can be undermined by political disillusionment.[20] Turnout in U.S. presidential elections dropped by 10 percentage points between

[19] Warren E. Miller, Arthur H. Miller, and Edward J. Schneider, *American National Election Studies Sourcebook* (Cambridge, Mass.: Harvard University Press, 1980), table 5.23.
[20] U.S. Bureau of the Census, *Current Population Reports,* ser. P-20, no. 344 (Washington, D.C.: U.S. Government Printing Office, 1979).

1960 and 1980, a time when Americans' trust and confidence in governmental institutions and parties declined under the onslaught of the Vietnam war, the Watergate scandal, economic stagnation, and other national problems. Believing that government was beyond their control, some citizens became alienated from the political process and concluded that participation was pointless.[21] In this context, the term **alienation** describes people's feelings of powerlessness and their sense that government does not care about the views of people like themselves.[22] The level of alienation appeared to drop somewhat during the early 1980s, but some analysts have suggested that it is again on the increase.[23]

Alienation rises and falls with political conditions. A more constant factor in low participation and, in general, a more important one is **apathy,** or a general lack of interest in or concern with politics. Citizens who seldom or never vote typically have a weak sense of civic responsibility and a low level of interest in politics. They simply do not care about politics. Just as some people would not attend the Super Bowl if it were free and being played across the street, some people would not bother to vote if a ballot were delivered to their door.

Age

During the Vietnam war, men aged eighteen and over were eligible to be drafted into military service yet were not eligible to vote in many states if they were under twenty-one. A slogan became familiar: "If someone is old enough to die for his country, he is old enough to vote." Bowing to intense public pressure, Congress in early 1971 enacted the Twenty-sixth Amendment, lowering the voting age to eighteen.

Ironically, most young adults have not bothered to exercise this right. Younger people are less likely to have the political concern that can come with homeownership, permanent employment, and a family.[24] In presidential elections, the voting rate among citizens under the age of thirty is 15 percentage points lower than that among older citizens. Failure to vote among the young helps to explain the 10-percentage-point drop in turnout in presidential elections between 1960 and 1980: the postwar "baby boom" resulted in an abnormally large number of young people eligible to vote in the 1960s and 1970s, and the trend was exaggerated when the Twenty-sixth Amendment (ratified in 1971) gave eighteen-year-olds the right to vote.[25]

[21] Howard L. Reiter, "Why Is Turnout Down?" *Public Opinion Quarterly* 43 (Fall 1979): 297–311; see also Paul R. Abramson, John H. Aldrich, and David W. Rhode, *Change and Continuity in the 1980 Elections* (Washington, D.C.: Congressional Quarterly Press, 1982).
[22] See, for example, Norman H. Nie, G. Bingham Powell, and Kenneth Prewitt, "Social Structure and Political Participation," *American Political Science Review* 63 (September 1969).
[23] Frances Fox Piven and Richard A. Cloward, *Why Americans Don't Vote* (New York: Pantheon, 1988), ch. 4.
[24] Verba and Nie, *Participation in America,* 139; John M. Strate, Charles J. Parrish, Charles D. Elder, and Coit Ford III, "Life Span Civic Development and Voting Participation," *American Political Science Review* 83 (June 1989): 443–465.
[25] Boyd, "Decline of U.S. Voter Turnout," 136. The trend toward increased turnout between 1920 and 1960 supports Boyd's explanation. The period was marked by a decline in the birth rate, particularly during the Depression of the 1930s.

Percent voting

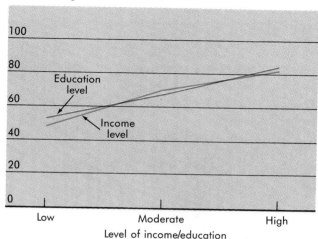

FIGURE 9-3 Voter Turnout and Levels of Income and Education
Americans of lower income and less education are much less likely to vote. *Source: Adapted from Raymond E. Wolfinger and Steven J. Rosenstone,* Who Votes? *(New Haven, Conn.: Yale University Press, 1986), 17, 21.*

Education

Education level is closely related to turnout level among Americans. The more years of education that individuals have, the more likely they are to vote. The differences are striking. Persons with a college education are about 40 percent more likely to vote than persons with a grade school education (see Figure 9–3). Researchers have concluded that education generates a greater interest in politics, a higher level of political information, a greater confidence that one can make a difference politically, and peer pressure to participate—all of which are related to the tendency to vote.[26]

Education, in fact, is the single best predictor of voter turnout. This fact led some analysts in the 1950s to conclude that increasing the overall level of education was the way to increase levels of turnout. Paradoxically, the overall education level of the American people increased throughout the 1960s and 1970s but turnout dropped. Political scientists have concluded that the positive effect of increased education levels has been more than offset by people's declining political loyalties and by their heightened sense of alienation.[27]

Socioeconomic Status

Turnout is also strongly related to socioeconomic status, as measured by income level (see Figure 9–3). Americans at the bottom of the socioeconomic ladder are about one-third less likely to vote in presidential elections than those at the top.[28] The difference is even larger in primaries and in nonpresidential elections.[29]

In European democracies, socioeconomic status does not affect turnout to such a high degree. Europeans of lower income levels are encouraged to

---

[26] M. Margaret Conway, *Political Participation in the United States,* 2d ed. (Washington, D.C.: Congressional Quarterly Press, 1991), 23–25.
[27] Ibid., 122–123.
[28] Wolfinger and Rosenstone, *Who Votes?* 17–21.
[29] Nelson W. Polsby, *Consequences of Party Reform* (New York: Oxford University Press, 1983), 158.

Voters in New York City's Harlem turned out in record numbers during the Great Depression, a time when the Democratic party appealed directly to lower-income voters with its New Deal programs. (UPI/Bettmann Newsphotos)

participate by class-based organizations and traditions—strong socialist parties, politically oriented trade unions, and class-based political ideologies.[30] In Britain, for example, the Labour party emerged with the growth of trade unionism and enrolled many manual laborers. Since 1918 the Labour party's membership card has carried a broad pledge "to secure for the workers by hand or by brain the full fruits of their industry." When the Labour party came to power in 1945, it made good on this promise to the working class by placing key industries under government ownership and adopting new social-welfare programs. A major policy was government-paid medical care for all Britons, which was of particular benefit to lower-income people.

Although social class has declined in importance, European political traditions and institutions continue to encourage lower-class voter participation in ways that the U.S. political system does not.[31] The United States does not have, and never has had, a major socialist or labor party.[32] The Democratic party by and large represents poorer Americans, but their interests tend to be subordinated to the party's concern for the American middle class, which, because of its size and voting regularity, is the key to victory in U.S. elections.

Some analysts point out that, once education level is controlled, income is a small factor in Americans' participation level. However, this observation does not adequately account for the absence of a lower-class political party in the U.S. system. The real test of the impact of income is whether poor people would turn out at a higher level if the party alternatives were different. Voting patterns during the Great Depression of the 1930s indicate that they would. In response to social security, public works projects, and other unprecedented class-based

[30] Verba and Nie, *Participation in America,* 340.
[31] Mark Kesselman and Joel Kreiger, *European Politics in Transition* (Lexington, Mass.: Heath, 1987), 87.
[32] Arthur T. Hadley, *The Empty Polling Booth* (Englewood Cliffs, N.J.: Prentice-Hall, 1978), 40.

New Deal programs, turnout rose sharply among lower-income citizens.[33] Their voting rate stayed high throughout the 1950s because the New Deal agenda remained the focus of domestic policy debate. As class-based appeals declined after 1960, turnout among lower-class citizens dropped sharply. By the early 1980s, turnout among those at the bottom of the socioeconomic ladder had dropped by 25 percent from its 1960 level. Turnout at the top declined by only 4 percent. Today barely two-fifths of unemployed and working-class Americans vote even in a presidential election.[34]

Conventional Forms of Participation Other Than Voting

In one sense, voting is an unrivaled form of citizen participation. Free and open elections are the defining characteristic of democratic government, so voting is regarded as the most basic duty of citizens.[35] Voting is also the only form of citizen participation engaged in by a majority of adults in every democratic country.[36]

In another sense, however, voting is a restricted form of participation. Citizens have the opportunity to vote only at a particular time and place, and only on those predetermined items listed on a ballot. Voting takes up less than an hour a year for most citizens, and there is no guarantee that candidates will be able to keep the promises they made to the voters during the campaign. There are other forms of participation that offer a greater opportunity for personal influence or involvement. These may be divided into campaign activities, community activities, and attentiveness to the news.

CAMPAIGN ACTIVITIES

A citizen may engage in such campaign-related activities as working for a candidate or a party, attending election rallies or meetings, contributing money, and wearing a candidate's campaign button. The more demanding of these activities, such as doing volunteer work for a candidate or a party, require a lot more time and effort than voting. These activities are also less imbued with notions of civic duty than is voting.[37] Not surprisingly, the proportion of citizens who engage in these activities is relatively small. For example, about one in seven adult Americans say they frequently or sometimes work for a party or a candidate. The actual proportion is probably much less, since people have a tendency in polls to overstate their level of political participation.

Campaign participation is higher in the United States than in Europe.[38] A

★ ANALYZE THE ISSUE

Changes in Forms of Political Participation
Elections are the traditional means by which citizens try to exert political influence. Yet as citizens can vote only yes or no on candidates, elections do not give voters much flexibility of choice. Does this fact lessen any concern you may have about low voter turnout? Add another fact: as voting has declined some other forms of political activity that give citizens more control have increased. These alternatives include going to court over policy issues and informing public officials of opinions on a policy controversy. Some analysts suggest that the United States is shifting from a representative democracy to a participatory one. Does this idea seem plausible to you?

[33] Seymour Martin Lipset, *Political Man* (Garden City, N.Y.: Doubleday/Anchor, 1963), 194.
[34] Walter Dean Burnham, "The Class Gap," *New Republic*, May 9, 1988, 30, 32.
[35] Richard Rose and Harve Mossawir, "Voting and Elections: A Functional Analysis," *Political Studies Quarterly* 15 (1967): 173.
[36] Joseph Schumpeter, *Capitalism, Socialism, and Democracy* (New York: Harper Torchbooks, 1950), 269.
[37] W. Russell Neuman, *The Paradox of Mass Politics* (Cambridge, Mass.: Harvard University Press, 1986), 176.
[38] Samuel H. Barnes and Max Kaase, *Political Action: Mass Participation in Five Western Democracies* (Beverly Hills, Calif.: Sage, 1979), 168–169.

five-country comparative study found that Americans ranked ahead of citizens of Germany, Austria, the Netherlands, and Great Britain in such activities as volunteering to work for a party or a candidate during an election campaign (see Table 9–1).

One reason Americans, even though they vote at a lower rate than Europeans, are more likely than Europeans to work in a campaign is that they have more opportunities to do so.[39] Elections take place more often in the United States, and citizens can become involved in an election campaign by volunteering to work for either a party or a candidate (see Chapter 12). In Europe, campaigns are organized through the parties, and participation opportunities for those who are not party members are restricted. Moreover, the United States is a federal system, which results in campaigns for national, state, and local offices. A citizen who wishes to engage in campaign activity is almost certain to find an opportunity at one level of office or another. Most of the governments of Europe are unitary in form (see Chapter 2), which means that there are fewer elective offices and thus fewer campaigns in which to participate.

COMMUNITY ACTIVITIES

Political participation extends beyond campaigns and elections to involvement in the community. Citizens can join community groups, work to accomplish community goals, and let officials know their opinions on community matters. These forms of participation offer the citizen a substantial degree of control over the timing and extent of their participation. The chief obstacle to participation is not opportunities, which are abundant, but the motivation to join in. Most

[39] Russell J. Dalton, *Citizen Politics in Western Democracies* (Chatham, N.J.: Chatham House, 1988), 43.

TABLE 9-1 Conventional Political Participation in Five Countries Americans are more politically active than Europeans in areas other than voter turnout.

ACTIVITY	PERCENT OF CITIZENS WHO PARTICIPATE				
	United States	Austria	Germany	Great Britain	Nether-lands
Campaign activity					
Convince others					
how to vote	19%	17%	22%	9%	10%
Attend meetings	18	18	22	9	6
Work in campaign	14	5	8	5	3
Community activity					
Work with group to					
solve community problems	37	14	14	17	18
Contact officials	27	12	11	11	13
Sign petitions	58	34	31	22	21
Communication activity					
Read political news	74	58	73	66	74
Discuss politics					
with others	64	45	43	46	52

SOURCE: Samuel H. Barnes and Max Kaase, eds., *Political Action* (Beverly HIlls, Calif.: Sage Publications, 1979), 541–542.

It is not difficult for the interested citizen to get involved in a political campaign. With frequent elections on three different levels—national, state, and local—Americans have countless opportunities to participate in the political process by working for a candidate. (Bob Daemmrich/ Stock, Boston)

people choose not to get involved, particularly when it comes to community activities that are relatively time-consuming. About a third of adult Americans claim that they frequently or sometimes work in a group effort to solve a community problem, and about a fourth claim to contact government officials frequently or sometimes; in these areas, Americans are more active than are Europeans (see Table 9–1).

Compared with local communities in Europe, those in the United States have more authority over policy issues, which is an added incentive to participation. In addition, the United States has a tradition of community participation that goes back to colonial days. Americans are accustomed to this form of participation, although many of the community groups to which they belong are only secondarily political in their orientation. (Group participation is discussed in greater detail in Chapters 13 and 14.)

FOLLOWING POLITICS IN THE NEWS

Campaign work and community participation are active forms of political involvement. There is also a passive form of participation: following politics by reading newspapers and newsmagazines and by listening to news reports on television or radio. It can safely be said that no act of political participation takes up more of people's time than does news consumption. The news is important to citizen participation: if people are to participate effectively and intelligently in politics, they must be aware of what is taking place in their communities, in their nation, and in the world.

News about politics is within easy reach of nearly all Americans. More than 95 percent of U.S. homes have a television set, and more than 60 percent

★ THE MEDIA AND THE PEOPLE

WHERE PEOPLE GET THEIR NEWS

Television is the major source of news for most Americans. This statement is based partly on polls, such as those conducted annually by the Roper Organization, which ask Americans where they get most of their news. The 1985 Roper poll, for example, indicated the following pattern: television, 64 percent; newspapers, 40 percent; radio, 14 percent; other, 12 percent. (The total exceeds 100 percent because respondents could name more than one source of news.) These data suggest that television is far and away the nation's most important information source. However, the data are misleading in that they indicate only where people get "most" of their news, not how much news they actually get. People who say they get "most" of their news from television do not necessarily get a lot of television news. For instance, they may watch a television news program every now and then but never read a newspaper. When people's news habits are measured by the frequency with which they read or watch the news, television and the newspaper are of nearly equal importance as information sources. The number who read the newspaper almost daily is about the same as the number who watch television news on a daily basis. Such individuals constitute a minority of citizens: most people do not follow either the newspaper or television news on a daily basis.

In the case of dramatic events, television exposure makes a greater impact than newspaper exposure. The images that Americans developed of the Persian Gulf war, for example, were primarily visual images that they acquired from television. The one image that stayed in people's minds more than any other was television footage of America's Patriot missiles intercepting Iraqi SCUD missiles in midair.

In the case of events that are less dramatic, newspaper exposure may have the greater impact. Research has shown that newspaper readers can more readily recall news stories they have seen and tend to acquire more political information from their news exposure. There are several reasons for this finding. Newspaper readers, first, have more control over content. A newspaper can be read and digested as quickly or as slowly as the reader desires. Television viewers, in contrast, must watch their news stories flow one after another, with the time they can spend on each story determined by the time it takes to broadcast it. Second, viewers obtain less information, for television stories typically contain only as many words as the first two paragraphs of a newspaper story. The average television news story is only about a minute long and provides almost no background information to the story. Finally, television news receives less attention from its audience than a newspaper does. In its early years, as the communication theorist Marshall McLuhan noted, television was a "high-involvement" medium, but it no longer draws the undivided attention of its viewers. Newspaper readers too can be distracted, but the act of reading requires more concentration than does the act of viewing.

SOURCES: Thomas E. Patterson, *The Mass Media Election* (New York: Praeger, 1980), ch. 6; Jarol B. Manheim, "Can Democracy Survive Television?" *Journal of Communication* 26 (Spring 1976): 84–90.

receive a newspaper. However, the regular audience for news is smaller than these figures suggest. If the regular audience for politics is defined as those who read a newspaper's political sections almost daily or watch television newscasts almost daily or both, then slightly more than 40 percent of Americans qualify (see box). About 30 percent of the citizenry follow the news intermittently. About 30 percent of all adult Americans pay no appreciable attention to either television news or newspapers.[40]

For many citizens, news exposure is the only significant form of contact with the world of politics. Yet the role of the news audience is akin to that of spectators at a sporting event, not of the players. Marshall McLuhan character-

[40] Thomas E. Patterson, *The Mass Media Election* (New York: Praeger, 1980), ch. 6.

ized the modern world of mass communication as a "global village," suggesting that the media, particularly television, have effectively linked citizens everywhere.[41] Robert Entman is closer to the truth when he describes news-centered politics as "democracy without citizens."[42]

In a disturbing trend, many young people are ignoring the news. A 1990 survey conducted by the *Times-Mirror* Center for the People and the Press found that Americans under thirty years of age know less and care less about politics than any generation of the last half century and pay less attention to newspapers. They are inclined toward television usage, but, at that, do not pay much attention to television news. In fact, during the 1980s, the percentage of persons over fifty in the network news audience rose from 50 percent to 60 percent. A lot of young people apparently cannot be bothered with news about politics in any form.

Nevertheless, Americans spend more time following the news than Europeans do. They read and discuss politics more frequently than Europeans do (see Table 9-1). They also watch more news on television. Unlike the United States, most European countries do not have around-the-clock television. There are also fewer television networks and less cable television in Europe than in the United States.

CATEGORIES OF CONVENTIONAL PARTICIPATION

Citizens who work in campaigns, are active in the community, or pay close attention to the news have the same general characteristics as those who vote regularly. Compared with the population as a whole, they are older, have higher incomes, are more highly educated, are more likely to have a strong sense of civic duty, and are less likely to feel politically alienated or apathetic.

Sidney Verba and Norman Nie have developed a typology that provides a profile of citizen participation. They identify six categories of citizens according to level and type of participation:[43]

1. *Inactives* (22 percent of population): They take virtually no part in politics; they seldom or never even vote.
2. *Voting specialists* (21 percent): They vote regularly or occasionally but are otherwise politically inactive.
3. *Parochialists* (4 percent): They confine their political activities to occasional contacts with public officials over personal problems.
4. *Communalists* (20 percent): They are active in cooperative community groups (e.g., Lions Club, hospital auxiliary) but dislike the conflict-ridden atmosphere of politics and thus do not participate in politics per se (except for voting).
5. *Campaigners* (15 percent): They participate in political parties or other election-related activities.
6. *Complete activists* (11 percent): They take an active role in both community organizations and political organizations.

[41] Marshall McLuhan, *Understanding Media: The Extensions of Man* (New York: McGraw-Hill, 1964).
[42] Robert Entman, *Democracy without Citizens* (New York: Oxford University Press, 1989).
[43] Verba and Nie, *Participation in America,* 78–81.

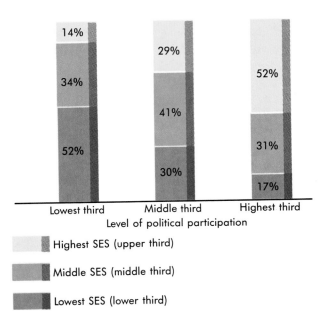

FIGURE 9-4 Socioeconomic Status (SES) of Americans at Three Levels of Political Participation
The highest levels of political participation are found among people at the high socioeconomic level. *Source: Adapted from Sidney Verba and Norman H. Nie,* Participation in America: Political Democracy and Social Equality *(New York: Harper & Row, 1972), 131 (fig. 8-3).*

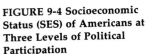

Highest SES (upper third)

Middle SES (middle third)

Lowest SES (lower third)

Citizens in the first four categories are not highly active in politics. Verba and Nie's final two categories, totaling 26 percent of voting-age adults, include the real political activists. However, that 26 percent figure substantially overestimates the number of true activists. The "campaigner" and "complete activist" categories include citizens who once actively participated in politics but no longer do so and citizens whose involvement is marginal—for example, an individual whose sole participatory act is to serve as a poll watcher on election day. When political activism is defined more rigorously to exclude previously or marginally active participants, the proportion of highly involved citizens drops sharply. W. Russell Neuman concludes: "Roughly speaking, only one in twenty Americans can confidently be described as actively involved. . . . Such activities as attending campaign meetings [and] contributing to political organizations . . . are, all things considered, rare phenomena."[44]

Citizens of higher socioeconomic status are by far the most politically active individuals. They are most likely to possess the financial resources and communication skills that encourage participation and make it personally rewarding.[45] Verba and Nie's study provides a rough indication of the extent to which higher-status individuals fill the ranks of the activists. Among citizens who are *most* active in politics, three times as many are at the top socioeconomic level as are at the bottom level[46] (see Figure 9-4).

[44] Neuman, *Paradox of Mass Politics*, 99.
[45] Verba and Nie, *Participation in America*, 80. See also Lipset, *Political Man*, ch. 3; Clifford W. Brown, Jr., Roman B. Hedges, and Lynda W. Powell, "Modes of Elite Political Participation: Contributors to the 1972 Presidential Candidates," *American Journal of Political Science* 24 (May 1980): 261–262.
[46] Verba and Nie, *Participation in America*, 340.

Unconventional Activism: Social Movements and Protest Politics

Before mass elections became prevalent, the public often resorted to riots and disorders as a way of expressing dissatisfaction with government. The advent of elections allowed the masses to communicate their views in an institutionalized and less disruptive way. Elections are double-edged, however. Although they are commonly viewed as a means by which the people control the government, *elections are also a means by which the government controls the people.*[47] Because they have been freely chosen by the people to rule, representatives can claim that their policies reflect the popular will and must therefore be obeyed by all. Elections provide those in power with a powerful argument for the legitimacy of their policies, and most citizens accept the claim.

Voting in elections is also limited to the choices that are offered. In the U.S. two-party system, the meaningfulness of the vote depends to some degree on whether the citizen accepts the alternatives offered by the Republican and Democratic parties. If neither choice is acceptable, voting becomes a hollow act, even a counterproductive one in that it lends legitimacy to the victorious party. An alternative for those who are dissatisfied with the status quo is participation in a social movement. **Social movements,** or political movements, as they are sometimes called, refer to broad efforts to achieve change by citizens who feel that government is not properly responsive to their interests.[48] Their efforts are sometimes channeled through traditional forms of participation, such as political lobbying, but citizens can also take to the streets in protest against government. Through demonstrations, picket lines, and marches, protesters dramatize their opposition to official policies.

Social movements do not always succeed, but they sometimes assist otherwise politically weak persons to force government to respond to their desires. For example, the timing and scope of the landmark 1964 Civil Rights Act and 1965 Voting Rights Act can be explained only as a response by Congress to the pressure created by the civil rights movement. The movement was in great part nonviolent, but it existed outside established channels—civil disobedience was one of its techniques—and it challenged existing power structures. Another effective social movement in the 1960s was the farm workers' movement, whose protests led to landmark legislation and court decisions that improved the working and living conditions of migrant workers.[49]

Protest can pose a serious threat to established authority, and government at times has responded violently to dissent.[50] In May 1970, during demonstrations against the Vietnam war, several unarmed students at Kent State University and Jackson State College were shot to death and others were wounded by national guardsmen who had been sent onto the campuses to restore order. The majority of the general public sides with authorities in such situations. In a *Newsweek*

---

[47] See Benjamin Ginsberg, *The Consequences of Consent* (New York: Random House, 1982), ch. 2.
[48] Conway, *Political Participation,* 76–78.
[49] J. Craig Jenkins, *The Politics of Insurgency: The Farm Workers Movement in the 1960s* (New York: Columbia University Press, 1985).
[50] See Jerome K. Skolnick, *The Politics of Protest* (New York: Ballantine, 1969).

★ ANALYZE THE ISSUE

Riots as Political Behavior
In early 1989 an off-duty police officer in Miami shot and killed a speeding motorcyclist. The motorcyclist was black, and his death sparked a riot in Miami's black community which lasted several days. Riots are spontaneous outbursts of collective violence, and data show that the incidence of riots (that is, the number of riots in relation to total population) is higher in the United States than in Canada, France, Germany, Great Britain, and nearly all other Western democracies. Does this fact surprise you? What do you think accounts for the relatively high rate of rioting in the United States?

TABLE 9-2   Opinions about Peace Demonstrations during the Gulf War, 1991
Most Americans believed that protests against the war were "a bad thing."

	ARE CURRENT DEMONSTRATIONS . . . ?		
	A Bad Thing	*Not a Bad Thing*	*No Opinion*
All respondents	63%	34%	3%
Male	58	40	2
Female	67	28	5
18-29 years	57	40	3
30-49 years	58	39	3
50 years and over	72	23	5
College grads	47	47	6
Some college	59	37	4
High school grads	68	30	2
Not high school grads	76	20	4
Republicans	71	26	3
Democrats	61	35	4
Independents	57	40	3

SOURCE: Gallup poll, January 23–26, 1991.

poll, 58 percent of respondents blamed the Kent State killings on the student demonstrators, while only 11 percent blamed the guardsmen.

Most citizens apparently believe that the proper way to express disagreement over public policy is through voting and not through protesting, despite the First Amendment's guarantee of the right "peaceably to assemble." In a 1972 University of Michigan survey, only 15 percent of those interviewed expressed approval of the Vietnam protests. Only 1 to 2 percent of the American public took to the streets in protest at any time during the 1960s and 1970s. Public opinion about demonstrations against the Gulf war was also negative, although less so than for protests against the Vietnam war, perhaps because U.S. involvement in the Gulf was shorter and more successful. A Gallup poll in early 1991 indicated that by a 2-to-1 margin Americans believed it was "a bad thing for Americans to be demonstrating against the war when U.S. troops are fighting overseas." This view was particularly pronounced among women, older persons, Republicans, and persons with lower education levels (see Table 9-2).

Recent American history would be very different had not the civil rights, women's rights, Vietnam protest, and other major social movements pressed their claims on government. Social movements have been the most effective way for groups outside the political mainstream to make significant claims on society. A successful social movement often evolves into conventional forms of politics. After the 1960s, for example, African-Americans shifted from protest politics to activities such as lobbying and voter registration drives.

Protest politics in America goes back to the Boston Tea Party and earlier, but it has taken on new forms in recent years. Protest was traditionally a desperate act, which began, often spontaneously, when a group had lost hope that it could succeed through more conventional methods. Today, however, protest is usually a calculated act—a means of bringing added attention and impetus to a cause.[51] These tactical protests often involve a great deal of planning, including, in some instances, the busing of thousands of people to Washington for a rally staged for television. Civil rights, environmental, agricultural, and pro- and antiabortion groups are among those that have staged tactical protests in Washington within the past few years.

Citizens who participate in social movements tend to be younger than nonparticipants, which is a reversal of the situation with voting. In fact, age is the best predictor of protest activity.[52] Participants in social movements also tend to emphasize nonmaterial values more than do nonparticipants. Social movements often develop in response to real or perceived injustices and thus attract idealists.[53]

Participation and the Potential for Influence

Although Americans claim that political participation is important, most of them do not practice what they preach. As we have seen, most citizens take little interest in participation except to vote, and a significant minority cannot even be persuaded that voting is worth their while. Americans are obviously not completely apathetic: many millions of them give their time, effort, and money to political causes, and nearly 90 million go to the polls in presidential elections. Yet sustained political activism does not engage a large proportion of the public. Moreover, many of those who do participate are drawn to politics by

[51] Dalton, *Citizen Politics in Western Democracies*, 59–61.
[52] Ibid., 68.
[53] Ronald Inglehart, "Post-Materialism in an Environment of Insecurity," *American Political Science Review* 75 (1981): 880–900; Edward N. Mueller and Mitchell A. Seligson, "Inequality and Insurgency," *American Political Science Review* 81 (1987): 425–451.

Most Americans do not regard political participation as an effective way of dealing with their personal problems. However, many are willing to work with local community organizations to improve their lives. (Bob Daemmrich/The Image Works)

a habitual sense of civic duty rather than by an intense concern with current issues.

INDIVIDUALISM AND COLLECTIVE ACTION

The emphasis that American culture places on individualism tends to discourage a sense of urgency about political participation. "In the United States, the country of individualism *par excellence*," William Watts and Lloyd Free write, "there is a sharp distinction in people's minds between their own personal lives and national life."[54] Although wars and severe recessions can lead the American public to rely on government, most people under most conditions expect to solve their own problems. This is not to say that Americans have a disdain for collective action. In their communities particularly, citizens frequently take part in collective efforts to support a local hospital, improve the neighborhood, and the like. But Americans tend not to see their material well-being as greatly dependent on involvement in politics of the traditional kind.

At times, in fact, Americans appear to be almost oblivious of the swirl of national politics. During the early 1950s, when Senator Joseph McCarthy was claiming that Communists had infiltrated the highest ranks of government and McCarthy's critics were saying that he was trampling on the civil liberties of innocent people, Samuel Stouffer asked a sample of Americans what their major concerns were. Although McCarthy's charges were the subject of front-page headlines and special live television broadcasts seen by millions, only 2 percent of the interviewees mentioned communism or civil liberties as a major concern. The respondents spoke instead of their jobs, the education of their children, their plans to buy a home, and other personal goals.[55]

Of course, Americans' paramount interest in their private lives does not preclude a political commitment. Nevertheless, because Americans are not very class-conscious and because they trust their ability to get ahead on their own, they regard politics as an important activity but hardly a life-or-death proposition. Many people do not even define citizenship in political terms.[56] Their model of the "good citizen" is as likely to be someone who is an economic pillar of the community as someone who is actively involved in politics.

POLITICAL PARTICIPATION AND SOCIOECONOMIC STATUS

During the 1950s and 1960s, many political scientists argued that low turnout largely reflected an apathetic satisfaction with the status quo. They also argued that low turnout did not matter a great deal because survey data showed that voters and nonvoters had similar preferences in regard to policies and candidates; election outcomes would not change if everyone voted. This viewpoint

[54] William Watts and Lloyd A. Free, eds., *The State of the Nation* (New York: University Books, Potomac Associates, 1967), 97.
[55] Samuel Stouffer, *Communism, Conformity, and Civil Liberties* (Garden City, N.Y.: Doubleday, 1955), 61.
[56] Harry Holloway with John George, *Public Opinion*, 2d ed. (New York: St. Martin's Press, 1986), 157.

★ CRITICAL THINKING

WHAT KIND OF CITIZENS WILL YOUNG ADULTS BECOME?

Recent surveys indicate that young Americans differ significantly from older citizens in ways that suggest a decline in democracy. Young adults have always been somewhat less involved in politics than older adults. They are less likely to vote, to participate in community organizations, and to follow the news.

These differences between generations have become sharper. Today's Americans under thirty years of age pay less attention to politics than any generation of young people since polling began in the 1930s. The current generation is so apolitical that it even defines good citizenship in an unusual way. Surveys by Peter D. Hart Research Associates in 1988 and 1989 found that fewer than 15 percent of those between the ages of fifteen and twenty-five believed that voting was an essential part of good citizenship. About half of them defined good citizenship in terms of caring personal relationships. When asked directly what public activities

they would be willing to contribute to, respondents ranked most highly two activities—an anti-drunk-driving campaign and a neighborhood crime watch—that are more personal than civic in nature.

When respondents in the Hart surveys were asked how they would spend additional leisure time, nearly half mentioned recreational activities and one-fourth said they would spend the extra time with family and friends. Not a single respondent mentioned civic or political participation. A significant minority even said that they could not imagine a circumstance in which they would be willing to fight for their country.

What do you make of these findings? Do the attitudes of young people today indicate that American democracy is imperiled? Why are today's young people less committed to public life than their parents and grandparents? What steps might be taken to instill in them a sense of civic duty?

---

continues to have its advocates[57] but is less persuasive today.[58] As the income gap widened in the 1980s, so did the gap between the political opinions of lower- and upper-income Americans. As Walter Dean Burnham notes, "It is no longer possible to assume a quiet consensus, a happy apathy. [There are now] significant differences between the preferences of voters and non-voters."[59]

These differences are most pronounced on class-based issues and reflect the differences in voter turnout between citizens of high and low socioeconomic status. As we have seen, high-status citizens can look after themselves; they have the personal skills and resources to take part in politics on their own. "The rich have the capacity to participate with or without assistance," Benjamin Ginsberg writes. "When assistance is given, it is primarily the poor who benefit."[60] Other democratic countries give the poor such assistance by placing the burden of registering voters on government and by fostering class-based political organizations. By comparison, the poor in the United States must arrange their own registration and have a choice only between major political parties that are attuned primarily to people of higher economic status.

An overall effect, more pronounced in the 1970s and 1980s than at any other time since the 1920s, is to give American politics a decidedly middle-class slant.

[57] Wolfinger and Rosenstone, *Who Votes?*, 110.
[58] See Piven and Cloward, *Why Americans Don't Vote*.
[59] Burnham, "The Class Gap," 30; see also Stephen Earl Bennett and David Resnick, "The Implications of Nonvoting for Democracy in the United States," *American Journal of Political Science* 34 (August 1990): 771–802.
[60] Ginsberg, *Consequences of Consent*, 49.

The relatively high participation rate of the country's middle-class citizens, who constitute the bulk of the population in any case, tends to direct public policies to their benefit. Studies indicate that representatives are more responsive to the demands of participants than to those of nonparticipants,[61] although it must be kept in mind that participants do not always promote only their own interests. It would be a mistake, however, to conclude that large numbers of people regularly support policies that impose great costs on themselves.

In sum, the pattern of *individual* political participation in the United States parallels the distribution of influence that prevails in the private sector. However, the issue of individual participation is only one piece of the larger puzzle of who rules America and for what purposes. Subsequent chapters will provide additional pieces.

Summary

Political participation is a sharing in activities designed to influence public policy and leadership. A main issue of democratic government is the question of who participates in politics and how fully they participate.

Voting is the most widespread form of active political participation among Americans. Yet voter turnout is significantly lower in the United States than in other democratic nations. The requirement that Americans must personally register in order to establish their eligibility to vote is one reason for lower turnout among Americans; other democracies place the burden of registration on governmental officials rather than on the individual citizen. The fact that the U.S. holds frequent elections also discourages some citizens from voting regularly. Finally, the major American political parties, unlike many of those in Europe, do not clearly represent the interests of opposing economic classes; thus the policy stakes in American elections are correspondingly reduced. Some Americans do not vote because they think that policy will not change greatly regardless of which party gains power.

Only a minority of citizens engage in the more demanding forms of political activity, such as work on community affairs or on behalf of a candidate during a political campaign. The proportion of Americans who engage in these more demanding forms of activity exceeds the proportion of Europeans who do so. Nevertheless, only about five in every twenty Americans will take an active part in a political organization at some point in their lives, although perhaps no more than one in twenty is highly active in politics at any given time. Most political activists are individuals of higher income and education; they have the skills and material resources to participate effectively and tend to have a greater interest in politics. More than in any other western democracy, political participation in the United States is related to socioeconomic status.

Social movements are broad efforts to achieve change by citizens who feel that government is not properly responsive to their interests. These efforts sometimes take place outside established channels; demonstrations, picket lines, and marches are common means of protest. Protesters are younger and more idealistic on average than other citizens, but they are a very small proportion of the population. In addition, protest activities do not have much public support, despite the country's tradition of free expression.

Overall, Americans are only moderately involved in politics. They are concerned with political affairs but immersed in their private pursuits, a reflection in part of our culture's emphasis on individualism. The lower level of participation among poorer citizens has particular significance in that it works to reduce their influence on public policy and leadership.

---

[61] See Verba and Nie, *Participation in America*, 332; V. O. Key, Jr., *Southern Politics* (New York: Vintage Books, 1949), 527.

Major Concepts

alienation
apathy
civic duty
political participation

registration
social movements
suffrage
voter turnout

Suggested Readings

Barber, Benjamin. *Strong Democracy: Participatory Politics for a New Age.* Berkeley: University of California Press, 1984. A provocative assessment of citizenship in the modern age.

Conway, M. Margaret. *Political Participation in the United States,* 2d ed. Washington, D.C.: Congressional Quarterly Press, 1991. An up-to-date analysis of political participation patterns.

Edelman, Murray. *Politics as Symbolic Action.* Chicago: Markham, 1971. A sweeping analysis of political "participation" defined broadly.

Entman, Robert. *Democracy without Citizens: Media and the Decay of American Politics.* New York: Oxford University Press, 1989. A critical evaluation of citizen involvement in the context of news about politics and public affairs.

Piven, Frances Fox, and Richard A. Cloward. *Why Americans Don't Vote.* New York: Pantheon, 1988. An analysis of nonvoting which focuses on registration requirements and calls for simplified procedures.

Verba, Sidney, and Norman H. Nie. *Participation in America: Political Democracy and Social Equality.* New York: Harper & Row, 1972. The most comprehensive study to date of American political participation. Stresses the relationship of social class to political involvement.

Wolfinger, Raymond E., and Steven J. Rosenstone. *Who Votes?* New Haven, Conn.: Yale University Press, 1980. A careful statistical analysis of voters and nonvoters based on a large survey conducted by the U. S. Bureau of the Census.

VOTE CHOICE: ELECTING THE NATION'S LEADERS

The electoral process is of greatest interest because of its importance in the wider political system. However much voting may tell about the psychology and sociology of human choice, it is important because of the importance of the [policy] decisions to which it leads.
Angus Campbell et al., The American Voter[1]

The 1964 presidential election was a classic political confrontation. Barry Goldwater, the Republican nominee, was a diehard opponent of federal activism. In his book *The Conscience of a Conservative*, Senator Goldwater had argued for a return to the pre–New Deal free-market economy and for sharp cutbacks in the federal government's social-welfare programs.[2] During his presidential campaign Goldwater gave substance to his philosophy by saying that he would seek to abolish mandatory social security. Goldwater also opposed the use of federal authority to achieve racial desegregation. He was one of the few nonsouthern senators to vote against the 1964 Civil Rights Act.

Lyndon Johnson, the Democratic nominee in 1964, was Goldwater's antithesis in both personality and philosophy. Johnson was committed to an activist federal government. As a young congressman from Texas in the late 1930s, Johnson had nearly worshipped Franklin D. Roosevelt and the New Deal, and upon becoming president in 1963 he had urged the immediate passage of a comprehensive civil rights bill. When he was asked during the 1964 campaign about the extent of his activism, Johnson responded, "We're in favor of a lot of things, and we're against mighty few."[3]

The choice available to voters in 1964 could not have seemed clearer, and the outcome could hardly have been more one-sided. Johnson received 60 percent of the popular vote, a landslide nearly unmatched in the history of presidential elections. As the election returns came in, Johnson's victory was heralded as a sign that he had a mandate from the people to carry out the programs he had advocated during the campaign. The fact is, however, that election results by

[1]Angus Campbell, Phillip Converse, Warren Miller, and Donald Stokes, *The American Voter* (New York: Wiley, 1960), 4.
[2]Barry Goldwater, *The Conscience of a Conservative* (Shepardsville, Ky.: Victor, 1960).
[3]Quoted in David Broder, *The Party's Over* (New York: Harper & Row, 1971), 45.

themselves do not reveal much about the voters' thinking, except their preference for one candidate over another. The reasons people vote as they do are always more complex and less definitive than the election returns suggest. After studying the Goldwater-Johnson vote, Stanley Kelley concluded that Johnson's majority was composed of voters attracted for a lot of different reasons. Some were concerned with social security, others with foreign policy, still others with racial issues. Kelley concluded, "American voters are of many minds, and [their] heterogeneity of opinion can be expected to reduce the likelihood of mandates in most elections and to make even rarer [any] highly specific mandates."[4]

Elections are the primary instrument of self-government in modern democracies. The idea of self-government would be meaningless if the sole function of the vote was to give one leader rather than another a position of official authority. The question of the relationship of voting to public policy is thus a central concern. Although election returns do not shed much light on this question, election surveys do. Since the 1930s, scholars and pollsters have regularly surveyed voters to discover the reasons for their decisions about candidates, including the part that policy issues have played. Using survey evidence, this chapter argues that citizens exercise an important degree of policy influence through their votes, but they do so in a way that is both less direct and less substantial than is commonly assumed. The main ideas discussed in this chapter are the following:

★ *The voters' partisan loyalties are embedded in policy developments, and party-line voting can be a substantial expression of the electorate's policy preferences.* However, the United States is currently in a period of dealignment, in which party loyalties have been weakening and the electorate is increasingly responsive to transitory influences.

★ *Realigning elections occur with the emergence of a powerful issue that cuts across existing political divisions.* By responding strongly to this issue, the electorate "chooses" a significant and enduring change in national policy. Although rare, a realigning election is the most powerful form of popular influence through voting.

★ *In most campaigns, most voters do not choose a candidate on the basis of policy promises (a form of choice known as prospective voting). Indeed, voters are as likely to reward or punish the "in-party" for the success or failure of policies it has already pursued (a form of choice known as retrospective voting) as they are to evaluate candidates on promises of future action.*

★ *Although citizens rarely decide through their votes exactly what government will do, the vote is nonetheless a significant constraint on political leaders.*

Party-Line Voting

The New York Times judged the information important enough to give it front-page coverage on a Sunday. The July 13, 1991, story opened with the line:

---

[4]Stanley Kelley, Jr., *Interpreting Elections* (Princeton, N.J.: Princeton University Press, 1983), 137–140.

"After a decade of party growth, Republicans have drawn almost even with the Democrats nationally, and ahead, though barely, in the allegiance of whites and adults under the age of 40." Sixty years had elapsed since the Republicans had been in the same position. The Great Depression of the 1930s had carried the Democratic party to majority status, which it had held onto for decade after decade. The gap between the parties had widened and narrowed at various times during those sixty years—for example, the Republicans lost ground in the early 1970s because of the Watergate scandal—but the Democrats were always in the lead. Even as late as 1980, Democrats outnumbered Republicans by more than 15 percentage points.

PARTY IDENTIFICATION

The *Times's* story centered on **party identification,** a term that refers to a person's ingrained sense of loyalty to a political party. Party identification is not formal membership in a party, but instead a psychological attachment to a party—the feeling that "I am a Democrat" or "I am a Republican." Scholars and pollsters have typically measured party identification with a question of the following type: "Generally speaking, do you think of yourself as a Republican, a Democrat, an independent, or what?" Since the 1960s, about 70 percent of adult Americans have called themselves Democrats or Republicans; until recently, as noted above, people who identified themselves as Democrats substantially outnumbered those who thought of themselves as Republicans (see Table 10-1).

Early studies of party identification concluded that partisan attitudes were highly stable and seldom changed over the course of adult life.[5] Subsequent studies, however, have shown that party loyalties are more fluid than originally believed; they can be influenced by the issues and candidates of the moment.[6]

[5]See Campbell et al., *American Voter,* chs. 3–4.
[6]Martin P. Wattenberg, *The Decline of American Political Parties,* 1952–1984 (Cambridge, Mass.: Harvard University Press, 1990).

Many people identify with the Republican or Democratic party. A few people identify *very* strongly with their chosen party. (Matthew McVay/Stock, Boston)

TABLE 10-1 Party Identification, 1952–1992 Party loyalties weakened in the late 1960s, and the proportion of independents increased.

Party Identification	YEAR										
	1952	1956	1960	1964	1968	1972	1976	1980	1984	1988	1992
Strong Democrat	22%	21%	21%	26%	20%	15%	15%	18%	17%	17%	16%
Weak Democrat	25	23	25	25	25	25	25	23	20	18	18
Independent, leaning Democrat	10	7	8	9	10	11	12	11	11	12	11
Independent	5	9	8	8	11	13	14	13	8	11	11
Independent, leaning Republican	7	8	7	6	9	10	10	10	14	12	12
Weak Republican	14	14	13	13	14	13	14	14	15	14	16
Strong Republican	13	15	14	11	10	10	9	8	13	14	15
Other	4	4	4	2	1	3	1	3	2	2	2

SOURCES: Survey Research Center, Center for Political Studies, University of Michigan, 1952–1988; multiple surveys, 1992.

Nevertheless, most adults do not switch their partisanship easily, and some adults never waver from an initial commitment to a party. They may cross party lines to vote for a candidate of the opposing party whom they like, but they do not give up their basic loyalty to the party of their choice.

Partisans and Vote Choice

Party loyalty is a significant influence on vote choice. Some states and districts are so heavily Republican or Democratic that the candidate of the majority party nearly always wins. Perhaps a fifth of all Senate seats and a larger proportion of House seats are safely in the hands of one party or the other. Democratic nominees in Louisiana, for example, have won every U.S. Senate election since the Reconstruction era of the 1870s. Republicans thought they could loosen the Democrats' hold on Louisiana when the popular longtime senator Russell Long retired in 1986. President Ronald Reagan even made two personal appearances on behalf of the Republican candidate, W. Henson Moore, in the election's closing days; but Moore still lost to the Democrat, John B. Breaux. Republicans concede that Breaux, who was forty-two years old when he was elected, may well hold the Louisiana seat until his death or retirement.

In general, a nominee for public office can expect the support of most of those who identify themselves with the nominee's party. Since 1960, Democratic identifiers' support for Democratic presidential nominees has ranged from a high of 89 percent to a low of 58 percent. Republican identifiers have been more loyal: their support for Republican nominees has ranged between 94 percent and 76 percent. At the congressional level, about 80 percent of partisans back their party's nominee.[7]

About a third of voters prefer to call themselves "independents" rather than Republicans or Democrats, but most independents lean toward one party or the other. These independents behave in ways similar to voters who have a weak

[7]Albert D. Cover and David R. Mayhew, "Congressional Dynamics and the Decline of Competitive Congressional Elections," in Lawrence C. Dodd and Bruce I. Oppenheimer, eds., *Congress Reconsidered*, 2d ed. (Washington, D.C.: Congressional Quarterly Press, 1981), 74–75.

The Democractic "Solid South" more or less ended in 1964, when Barry Goldwater, the Republican presidential candidate, drew the strong support of voters in South Carolina and other states in the Deep South. (Max Scheler/Black Star)

party commitment; they can be persuaded to back candidates of the other party but usually support candidates of the party that they feel more positive about.[8]

Is Party Loyalty "Blind"?

Some people's party loyalty is merely blind partisanship. There are Republicans and Democrats who know very little about their party's traditions, policies, or group commitments.[9] For many of these individuals, partisanship is an "inherited" identity. They are Republicans or Democrats primarily because their parents had been, but they have never acquired a clear understanding of the policy support implied by a vote for their inherited party.[10] One study found that party perceptions unrelated to issues characterize 17 percent of voters—a point illustrated by the North Carolina Democrat who said, "I've always been a Democrat just like my daddy."[11] Other partisans have simply closed their minds to the possibility of voting for candidates of the opposing party.

[8]John E. Stanga and James F. Sheffield, "The Myth of Zero Partisanship: Attitudes toward American Political Parties, 1964–84," *American Journal of Political Science* 31 (1987): 829–855; William H. Flanigan and Nancy H . Zingale, *Political Behavior of the American Electorate*, 7th ed. (Washington, D.C.: Congressional Quarterly Press, 1991), 52.
[9]Campbell et al., *American Voter*, ch. 3.
[10]See Herbert Hyman, *Political Socialization* (New York: Free Press, 1959); Fred I. Greenstein, *Children and Politics* (New Haven, Conn.: Yale University Press, 1965); M. Kent Jennings and Richard Niemi, *The Political Character of Adolescence* (Princeton, N.J.: Princeton University Press, 1974), 37–62.
[11]Quoted in Campbell et al., *American Voter*, 246.

It would be wrong to assume, however, that party-line voting typically lacks a policy component. Party loyalties are not randomly distributed across the population. They are embedded in social and economic conditions and have been molded by historical forces. They have a basis in policy.[12] As long as no new issues arise to change the fundamental basis of party conflict, most people simply have no good reason to abandon their existing party loyalties. V. O. Key noted that, in terms of their policy preferences, most voters are where they ought to be in their loyalty to one party or the other.[13] The fact that blue-collar workers voted strongly Democratic in the 1950s, for example, might be taken as evidence that they acted on blind partisanship, since the majority of them had a Democratic party identification; yet it was also the case that these 1950s blue-collar Democrats believed that the Democratic party, which had sponsored policies such as minimum wage laws and collective bargaining for organized labor, was more likely than the Republican party, which had opposed these measures, to serve their interests.

The real test of blind partisanship is whether voters stay with their party even when its policies conflict with their interests. The 1960s revealed that most partisans do not behave in this unthinking way. As new issues that arose in the 1960s cut across the partisan divisions created by the New Deal, voters tended to reject their party if they believed it was on the wrong side of an issue that was crucial to them.[14] The issue of black civil rights, for example, helped to turn the "Solid South" into a Republican presidential stronghold after nearly a century of staunch support for the Democratic party.[15] In response to northern Democrats' leadership on civil rights, southern Democrats voted overwhelmingly for the conservative Republican Goldwater in 1964. He won only 40 percent of the national vote but carried the states of Alabama, Georgia, Louisiana, Mississippi, and South Carolina. In Mississippi he received fully 87 percent of the votes cast, whereas in 1956, before civil rights became an important partisan issue, Mississippi had cast 72 percent of its votes for the Democratic presidential candidate, Adlai Stevenson.

In sum, party voting should be regarded not as blind loyalty, but as a generalized commitment that is based on a melding of personal, political, and historical influences. Partisan loyalty has roots in public policies, although not necessarily in current issues, as will be discussed later in the chapter.

Primary Elections: Where Partisanship Matters Very Little

Partisan loyalty is a key factor in general elections, but not in primary elections, in which candidates of the same party compete for nomination. Facing a choice within their party, voters in a primary election cannot use partisanship as their guide, and their preferences can be volatile. In the race for presidential

---

[12]See William G. Jacoby, "The Impact of Party Identification on Issue Attitudes," *American Journal of Political Science* 32 (1988): 643–661.

[13]V. O. Key, Jr., *The Responsible Electorate* (Cambridge, Mass.: Belknap Press of Harvard University Press, 1966), ch. 1.

[14]David E. RePass, "Issue Salience and Party Choice," *American Political Science Review* 60 (June 1971): 398–400.

[15]See Dorothy Davidson Nesbit, "Changing Partisanship among Southern Party Activists," *Journal of Politics* 50 (1988): 322–334.

Paul Tsongas's victory in New Hampshire's 1992 Democratic presidential primary election swung the media spotlight his way. Bill Clinton's victories a few weeks later on Super Tuesday gained him the spotlight. Such early publicity is likely to enhance a candidate's chances of winning the party's nomination. (Jim Heemstra/Picture Group)

nomination, each state holds a separate primary, and a candidate who wins an early contest, such as the New Hampshire primary or the Iowa caucuses, can sometimes parlay that victory into success in subsequent primaries, particularly when there is no strong, well-known opponent. The media attention that comes to a candidate who wins an early primary can move thousands of voters in his direction.[16] After Paul Tsongas won the New Hampshire primary in 1992, his nationwide support among Democratic voters in polls jumped several points. All recent New Hampshire winners have gained public support immediately after this state's early primary.[17]

Primary elections are less important in congressional races than in presidential contests, but they are the main threat to incumbents in constituencies that are lopsidedly Democratic or Republican.[18] However, voters rarely abandon a member of Congress in a primary election unless the incumbent is involved in a scandal or is widely perceived to have lost touch with local interests. Although one-fourth of congressional incumbents face primary challenges in an average election year, few of them lose.[19] (Chapters 16 and 18 provide further information on primary elections.)

[16]See Larry Bartels, *Presidential Primaries and the Dynamics of Public Choice* (Princeton, N.J.: Princeton University Press, 1988), ch. 8.
[17]William C. Adams, "As New Hampshire Goes . . . ," in Gary Orren and Nelson Polsby, *Media and Momentum* (Chatham, N.J.: Chatham House, 1987), ch. 3.
[18]Maisel, Louis Sandy. *From Obscurity to Oblivion: Running in the Congressional Primary* (Knoxville: University of Tennessee Press, 1982).
[19]Harvey L. Schantz, "Contested and Uncontested Primaries for the U.S. House," *Legislative Studies Quarterly* 5 (November 1980): 548; Arthur D. McNitt and Jim Seroka, "Intraparty Challenges of Incumbent Governors and Senators: 1956–1976," *American Politics Quarterly* 9 (July 1981): 321–340.

DEALIGNMENT: THE DECLINE OF PARTISANSHIP

In the 1950s partisanship was far and away the most important single influence on vote choice. About 80 percent of adults claimed to identify with the Republican or Democratic party, and nearly half of them said that their party loyalty was strong. By the early 1970s, however, the proportion of partisans had dropped to nearly 60 percent, most of whom said they had only a weak attachment to the party of their choice. Correspondingly, the proportion of Americans who described themselves as "independents" had nearly doubled—rising above 30 percent.

The trend away from party identification in the late 1960s and early 1970s was coupled with widespread **split-ticket voting.**[20] In 1960 more than 60 percent of the electorate cast "straight" ballots (supporting the entire ticket of candidates of one party for all offices), whereas in 1972 about 65 percent cast "split" ballots (dividing their votes among candidates of both parties for various offices). "Perhaps the most dramatic political change in the American public over the past two decades," Nie, Verba, and Petrocik wrote in 1976, "has been the decline of partisanship."[21]

The decline has been termed a party **dealignment,** a partial but lasting

[20]Norman H. Nie, Sidney Verba, and John Petrocik, *The Changing American Voter,* enlarged ed. (Cambridge, Mass.: Harvard University Press, 1979), 47, 53. See also Walter Devries and V. Lance Terrance, *The Ticket-Splitter* (Grand Rapids, Mich.: Eerdmans, 1972); David B. Hill and Norman R. Luttbeg, *Trends in American Electoral Behavior* (Itasca, Ill.: F. E. Peacock, 1983), 35; John A. Ferejohn, "On the Decline of Competition in Congressional Elections," *American Political Science Review* 71 (March 1977): 166–176.
[21]Nie, Verba, and Petrocik, *Changing American Voter,* 364.

★ HOW THE UNITED STATES COMPARES

INFLUENCES ON VOTING CHOICES

The major influences on the vote are party loyalties, class and group attachments, issues, and candidate characteristics. However, the relative influence of these factors can vary significantly from one election to the next and from one country to the next. One study of postwar elections in western democracies found that the American electorate is somewhat more responsive to issues and somewhat more volatile than are nearly all European electorates. One reason for this difference is that party loyalties, although they have been declining in all western societies, are substantially weaker in the United States than elsewhere. The independent voters that are an important part of American elections are not found in other democratic systems.

Another reason is that voting choices in the United States are not affected so strongly by class and group attachments, a fact that makes Americans more respon-sive to short-term influences, such as current issues. If Americans were more class conscious, for example, they would undoubtedly have stronger commitments to liberal and conservative alternatives within the party system.

Finally, the length of American election campaigns increases the likelihood that disruptive incidents will arise and affect the voters' choices. All recent U.S. presidential campaigns, for example, have included mistakes and gaffes that have badly hurt a candidate and helped his opponent. In Europe, national election campaigns last only a few weeks and have a relatively consistent focus.

SOURCE: Ian Budge and Dennis J. Farlie, *Explaining and Predicting Elections: Issue Effects and Party Strategies in Twenty-Three Democracies* (London: Allen & Unwin, 1983), chs. 3, 5.

The Impact of Ticket Splitting

Many people believe it is better to vote for the person than for the party. But is it? Ticket splitting can produce a divided government, in which one party controls the presidency and the other controls one or both houses of Congress. This has happened in most of the recent presidential elections. Divided government can result in deadlock and makes it easier for officials to disclaim responsibility for problems: each side can say that the problems are the other party's fault. How important are these considerations? What could be an argument in favor of ticket splitting?

movement away from partisan loyalties. A dealignment is characterized by a greater responsiveness among the electorate to short-term influences, such as the candidates and issues of the moment, than to the long-term influence of party identification.

Declining partisanship has meant less stability in vote choices. In the 1940s and 1950s, when voters' party loyalties were stronger than they are today, presidential campaigns changed few people's minds. About 80 percent of the voters made their choice early in the campaign and stayed with it. Even the late deciders were not entirely open to persuasion; the large majority ended up supporting the candidate of their party.[22] Today's voters are more easily influenced by a campaign's issues, events, and candidates. The 1980 Carter-Reagan contest is an extreme example. A third of the voters claimed not to have made their choice until the campaign's final two weeks, and 10 percent said they did not decide until election day itself. Today, if an election is close for other reasons, victory is likely to go to the presidential candidate who campaigns more effectively.[23]

Why Dealignment Persists

The decline of partisanship began in the 1960s, when cross-cutting issues emerged and started to shake existing loyalties. The civil rights issue, for example, was unsettling not only to many southern Democrats but also to some white northern Democrats, particularly blue-collar workers and members of ethnic groups, who felt that black Americans were making rapid gains at their expense.[24] The lengthy conflict in Vietnam also tested Americans' patience with elected leaders of both parties, and the Watergate scandal of the early 1970s seemed to indicate that incompetence and corruption were widespread in government. Americans' trust in their elected representatives dropped sharply, as did their faith in political parties. By 1976, 55 percent of the public claimed, on balance, to dislike *both* the Democratic and Republican parties. Twenty years earlier, only half as many voters had expressed displeasure with both parties.[25]

Since the 1970s the images of the parties, particularly those of the GOP, have improved somewhat (although they are still not very positive), and the erosion of partisan identification has stabilized, but at a substantially lower level than a few decades ago. Partisanship today is a far cry from what it once was, and most analysts see little likelihood of a dramatic reversal. One reason is that the voters of today are better educated and are more inclined to believe that they can get along without a partisan commitment. Many voters are now satisfied to judge the candidates for themselves, on the basis of what they see and hear through the media rather than on the basis of party traditions and performance.

Another, and perhaps the most powerful, factor working against partisanship is the social-welfare programs established in the 1930s and later. Economic downswings no longer produce the extraordinary personal hardships of earlier

[22]See Bernard Berelson, Paul Lazarsfeld, and William McPhee, *Voting* (Chicago: University of Chicago Press, 1954), 18.
[23]See Joe McGinniss, *The Selling of the President, 1968* (New York: Trident Press, 1968).
[24]Frederick G. Dutton, *Changing Sources of Power* (New York: McGraw-Hill, 1971), ch. 6.
[25]Nie, Verba, and Petrocik, *Changing American Voter*, 364.

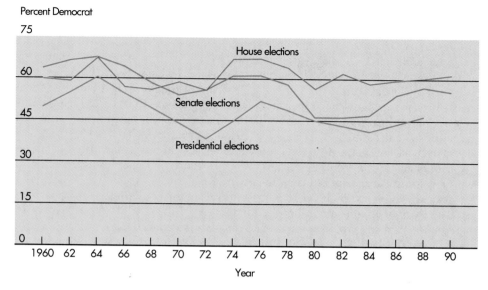

FIGURE 10-1 Democratic Party's Percentage of the Two-Party Presidential Vote and of House and Senate Elections. 1960–1990 In recent years, the Democrats have dominated congressional races but have fared poorly in presidential elections.

periods; social security, unemployment compensation, and other government programs protect most Americans from abject poverty, hunger, and hopelessness. Americans become less desperate in times of recession and thus are less likely to see the relevance of party politics to their lives.

A third possible obstacle to unabashed partisanship is the complexity of modern life and public policy. Americans want better jobs, more leisure, and higher incomes, but they also want cleaner air and water, services for the elderly and disadvantaged, and assistance programs for the impoverished. As Americans become increasingly unwilling to choose between public and private progress or to consider the two spheres separable, they are less likely to be persuaded by either the Republican argument for a less active government or the Democratic argument for a more active government. In today's politics, simple choices are becoming scarcer, so the chances are decreasing that either party will gain the full support of an enduring electoral majority. The electoral system may have reached a new equilibrium in which party still matters, but less than it did in the past.[26]

Dealignment and Divided Government

A consequence of the weakening partisan loyalties has been **divided government**—the situation where control of the presidency and one or both chambers of Congress is divided between the parties. Since 1968 the Republicans have dominated presidential elections, while the Democrats have prevailed in congressional voting. Both patterns have been quite one-sided (see Figure 10-1). The Republicans won the presidency narrowly in 1968, but have since had wide victory margins in most of the races. The GOP also controlled the Senate

[26]Everett Carll Ladd, "On Mandates, Realignments, and the 1984 Presidential Election," *Political Science Quarterly* (Spring 1985): 1–16.

between 1980 and 1986 but otherwise has not been very successful in congressional elections. The Democratic majority in the House has ranged upwards of 55 percent.

Some analysts have suggested that voters prefer this situation—that they want a Republican president to serve as a check on a Democratic Congress and vice versa. Surveys indicate that most Americans believe that divided government has advantages, but there is no strong evidence that voters weigh this consideration heavily when making their own choice among congressional and presidential candidates. The vote for president and the vote for Congress are decided by somewhat different factors. Name recognition, for example, is of no consequence in the general election for president but is a critical factor in congressional races, particularly those for the House. About twice as many voters know a House incumbent's name as know the challenger's name, which works strongly to the incumbent's advantage.[27] In the 1950s, fewer than 10 percent of partisan voters defected to the House candidate of the opposing party. Now about 20 percent do so, and most of them are attracted to incumbents—presumably because they attach more significance to their sense of familiarity with the incumbent than to his or her party affiliation.[28]

In sum, the divided government of today reflects the weakening of partisanship, the link that historically tied presidential and congressional election outcomes together. As straight-ticket voting began to decline in the 1960s, so did the likelihood that the same party would control both the presidency and the Congress.

REALIGNING ELECTIONS: REPUDIATING THE PARTISAN PAST

Dealignment is a development that apparently has no strict precedent historically. Major shifts in partisanship in the past have instead been realignments. A **realignment** is a relatively abrupt change in partisan loyalties, coalitions, and issues.[29] A realignment involves five basic elements:

1. The disruption of the existing political order because of the emergence of one or more unusually powerful and divisive issues
2. The widening of divisions between the parties
3. The occurrence of an election contest in which one party has a strong advantage
4. A major change in policy through the action of the newly dominant party
5. An enduring change in the party coalitions, which works to the lasting advantage of the newly dominant party

Only a few elections in U.S. history have had all five elements, and they have been termed **realigning,** or *critical,* **elections.** The most recent of these elections

---

[27]Kent L. Tedin and Richard W. Murray, "Public Awareness of Congressional Representatives: Recall v. Recognition," *American Politics Quarterly* 7 (October 1979): 509–517; Ferejohn, "On the Decline of Competition," 166–175.

[28]Cover and Mayhew, "Congressional Dynamics," 74–75; Robert S. Erikson, "The Advantage of Incumbency in Congressional Elections," *Polity* 3 (1971): 395–405.

[29]For the classic analysis of realignments, see Walter Dean Burnham, *Critical Elections and the Mainsprings of American Politics* (New York: Norton, 1970).

The new order begins: Franklin D. Roosevelt rides to his inauguration with outgoing president Herbert Hoover after the realigning election of 1932. (UPI/Bettmann Newsphotos)

took place in 1932. (Chapter 11 includes a brief discussion of the earlier realigning elections.)

The Realignment of 1932

The probusiness Republican party had been in firm control of national government since the depression of 1893, holding a majority in one or both houses of Congress except for a six-year period (1913–1918) that overlapped the tenure of the period's only Democratic president, Woodrow Wilson. This Republican era was characterized by laissez-faire capitalism. President Calvin Coolidge summed up his party's philosophy when he said, "The business of America is business."

The Great Depression brought an end to Republican dominance. The Republican Herbert Hoover was president when the stock market crashed in 1929, and many Americans blamed Hoover, his party, and its business allies for the economic catastrophe that followed. To the millions of Americans who lost their jobs, homes, and self-esteem, Hoover offered only platitudes about patience, claiming that the nation's economy would soon rebound without government intervention. In the congressional elections of 1930, the Democrats came within one seat of capturing the U.S. Senate and gained a 220–214 edge in the House of Representatives, which the Republicans had previously controlled by 100 seats. In 1932 the electorate resoundingly rejected Hoover,

The fundamental strength of the nation's economy is unimpaired.
Herbert Hoover (1930)

The country needs and, unless I mistake its temper, the country demands bold, persistent experimentation.
Franklin D. Roosevelt (1932)

choosing the Democratic presidential nominee, Franklin D. Roosevelt, by a margin of 58 to 42 percent, and handing control of the Senate to the Democrats.

As a candidate, Roosevelt had not promised a sweeping "new deal"; but his first months in office were characterized by unprecedented policies in the areas of business regulation, social welfare, and public works programs. Even though these policies marked an abrupt departure from those of the past, they won support from a public mired in hard times. A 1936 Gallup poll indicated that 61 percent of Americans backed Roosevelt's social security program, while only 27 percent opposed it. If Roosevelt had not provided social security, public works programs, and other innovative policies, his campaign for reelection in 1936 would have fallen as flat as Hoover's had four years earlier. Not all of Roosevelt's policy initiatives were equally popular, but his public support undoubtedly stemmed from a widespread belief that he was leading the country in the right direction.[30]

The sweeping policy changes that follow a realigning election are lasting ones. The Roosevelt years, for example, established a new governing philosophy with broad popular appeal which limited what future political leaders could reasonably propose. When Barry Goldwater, the Republican presidential candidate in 1964, argued for a return to the economic and welfare policies of the 1920s, he was widely branded a reactionary and was soundly defeated at the polls.

Realignments and Party Identification

The lasting impact of realignments is due in large part to their effect on party identification. In the 1930s, the Democratic party was widely perceived as the party of the common people and of social security, while the Republican party was seen as the party of business and wealthy interests. The Democratic party's image was more appealing to first-time voters; they came to identify with the Democratic party by a 2-to-1 margin.[31] These new partisans helped establish the Democrats as the nation's majority party. By 1940, according to Gallup polls, Democrats outnumbered Republicans, and their continuing plurality enabled the Democratic party to dominate national politics for decades. Between 1932 and 1968, the Republicans had only one successful presidential candidate, Dwight D. Eisenhower, and held control of Congress only twice, in 1947–1948 and 1953–1954.

As for older voters, the 1930s realignment did not change the party loyalties of most of them. Although Roosevelt won the votes of some long-standing Republicans in 1932 and 1936, he did not convert many of them permanently to his party. Their Republicanism was bolstered by an accumulation of past voting decisions and political beliefs, including a commitment to the economic individualism for which their party still stood. Similarly, older Democrats generally had little reason to rethink their party identification. The strength of the Democratic party in the 1930s and 1940s resided in the nation's working

★ ANALYZE THE ISSUE

Dealignment as the Prelude to Realignment
Some analysts believe that a dealignment, rather than a realignment, is taking place among the American electorate. What has not been widely debated is the question of whether a dealignment increases the likelihood that sometime soon a full realignment will occur. Why might a dealignment set the stage for a far-reaching realignment?

[30]Key, *Responsible Electorate*, 56.
[31]See Kristi Andersen, *The Creation of a Democratic Majority, 1928–1936* (Chicago: University of Chicago Press, 1979).

Economic prosperity is a key factor in determining a president's chances of being returned to office. One reason that Ronald Reagan was reelected by a landslide in 1984 was that many voters perceived themselves as being better off economically than they had been before he came to office. (Dennis Brack/Black Star)

class, which had suffered most deeply from the Depression and benefited most directly from the Democratic administration's New Deal programs.

A party realignment inevitably loses strength, because the issues that gave rise to it cannot remain dominant indefinitely. By the late 1960s, when the Democratic party was divided over Vietnam and civil rights, Kevin Phillips claimed that the New Deal era was over and a realignment favorable to the Republicans was under way.[32] When the anticipated Republican majority failed to materialize, Phillips attributed the outcome to the damage done to the Republican party by the Watergate scandal.

A Different Kind of Realignment? The Reagan Presidency

The possibility of a new realignment favorable to the Republicans was raised again by Ronald Reagan's victories in 1980 and 1984, which had some features in common with previous realignments. Reagan's first election resulted from widespread dissatisfaction with incumbent president Jimmy Carter's handling of the economy. Moreover, like Roosevelt's New Deal, Reagan's policies were a sharp departure from the past. Reagan sought to reverse the growth of national government and in 1981 persuaded Congress to enact the largest cuts in taxes and government spending in the nation's history. Such policies encouraged Americans to believe, as they had done in the 1930s, that large and important differences existed between the parties. The Republican party came to be widely regarded as the party of a smaller, less activist national government and the Democrats as the party of a larger, more intrusive government.[33] And, like

[32]See Kevin Phillips, *The Emerging Republican Majority* (New Rochelle, N.Y.: Arlington House, 1969).
[33]See Wattenberg, *Decline of American Political Parties.*

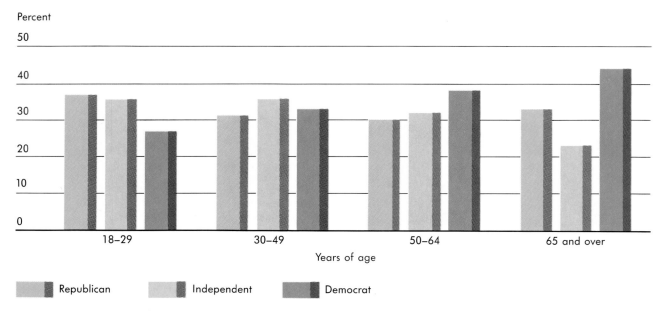

Percent

Republican   Independent   Democrat

FIGURE 10-2 Percentage of American Adults Who Identified Themselves as Republicans, Independents, or Democrats in 1991, by Age Group
Younger voters are the most heavily Republican age group.
Source: Gallup poll. Based on surveys from October 1989–February 1991 combined.

Roosevelt, Reagan won reelection to a second term by a landslide, largely because the electorate responded favorably to his economic recovery policies. Other parallels between the 1930s and 1980s are also evident. First-time voters identified mainly with the president's party (see Figure 10-2), and the numerical dominance of the previous majority party in terms of party identifiers was lost. And, of course, the Republicans retained control of the White House when George Bush, Reagan's vice-president, won the election of 1988.

Some analysts contend, in fact, that the party system underwent a realignment during the Reagan-Bush period, although on a smaller and more gradual scale than the 1930s realignment. They point in particular to the formerly Democratic "Solid South," which has become staunchly Republican in presidential politics.[34] Other analysts have argued against the realignment conclusion, saying that recent developments are notably different from the 1930s in important respects. For one thing, the Republicans did not capture both houses of Congress or sweep state offices in any of those years. For another, the public has not been completely sold on the Reagan-Bush governing philosophy. Although a philosophy of lower taxes and a smaller federal government has had broad appeal, surveys indicate that most Americans prefer to retain many of the federal social programs that Reagan and Bush wanted to cut or eliminate (see Chapters 24 and 25).

Whether labeled a partial realignment or not, the period since Reagan's 1980 election has been marked, as we noted earlier, by significant changes in party

[34]See Harold W. Stanley, "Southern Partisan Changes: Dealignment, Realignment or Both?" *Journal of Politics* 50 (1988): 64–88; Earl Black and Merle Black, *Politics and Society in the South* (Cambridge, Mass.: Harvard University Press, 1987); Robert H. Swansbrough and David M. Brodsky, eds., *The South's New Politics: Realignment and Dealignment* (Columbia: University of South Carolina Press, 1988); Dewey L. Grantham, *The Life and Death of the Solid South* (Lexington: University of Kentucky Press, 1988); Alexander P. Lamis, ed., *The Two-Party South* (New York: Oxford University Press, 1988).

identification. Should the Republican party continue to build its edge among younger voters, it might conceivably come to dominate U.S. elections at all levels. A more likely scenario is a continuation of divided outcomes, where the Republicans prevail in elections for some offices and the Democrats for other offices. In fact, the unprecedented decline in party voting in the past quarter century almost makes talk of a majority party somewhat off the mark. Party identification is still an important influence on how individuals will vote in a given election, but American elections increasingly hinge on other factors, particularly incumbency and government performance.

Public Policies as Influences on Vote Choice

As we noted at the beginning of this chapter, the interpretation of elections as mandates holds that voters consciously choose between candidates on the basis of promises made during the campaign. **Prospective voting** is a term used to describe this forward-looking form of voting. Prospective voting requires that voters know the issue positions of the candidates and choose the candidate whose promises match their own issue preferences.

Issues have a significant influence on the vote, but not to the same degree or in quite the same way as the mandate thesis would suggest. Most voters are not particularly well informed about the candidates' policy positions and usually base their choice on other factors. In addition, the mandate interpretation grossly oversimplifies the nature of the vote by assuming that the electorate can be divided into two groups, a majority that supported the winning candidate on every major issue and a minority that unequivocally opposed the winner. The reality is that candidates build their electoral majorities by persuading voters with different policy preferences to support them.[35]

PROSPECTIVE VOTING:
THE LESS COMMON FORM OF POLICY VOTING

Contrary to the prospective-voting model's assumption that voters are well informed, the fact is that most voters are not very knowledgeable about election issues. In U.S. House campaigns, less than half the voters can recall the two major parties' nominees in their district and even fewer know these candidates' stands on the issues.[36] The voters know more about U.S. Senate candidates, but not a lot more in many cases. In presidential races, most voters know the candidates by name but often cannot identify their policy positions.[37] During the 1976 campaign, for example, the Democratic candidate, Jimmy Carter, proposed a public-sector jobs program as a way of reducing unemployment. His Republican opponent, Gerald Ford, took a stand against the idea. By the campaign's end, roughly half of the voters were unaware of Ford's or Carter's position on the public jobs issue.[38]

[35]V. O. Key, Jr., *Public Opinion and American Democracy* (New York: Knopf, 1961), 460.
[36]Edie N. Goldenberg and Michael W. Traugott, *Campaigning for Congress* (Washington, D.C.: Congressional Quarterly Press, 1984), ch. 9.
[37]Scott Keeter and Cliff Zukin, *The Uninformed Choice* (New York: Praeger, 1983), chs. 4, 5.
[38]Thomas E. Patterson, *The Mass Media Election* (New York: Praeger, 1980), 155.

Obstacles to the Public's Awareness of Issues

Several influences combine to limit the electorate's awareness of issues. One problem is media coverage. Many campaigns for Congress, particularly the campaigns of nonincumbents and metropolitan-area House candidates, get almost no attention from the press.[39] Presidential elections get a lot of attention, but the news media concentrate not on the issues, but on the strategic aspects of the candidates' pursuit of office. The media stress the day-to-day mechanics of campaigning—the candidates' travels, their organizational efforts, their tactics—as well as voting projections and returns, results of opinion polls, and so on. By covering campaigns as if they were horse races, the media deemphasize substantive questions of policy.[40]

Another reason for the public's limited awareness of issues is that candidates do not always make their positions on issues altogether clear. They are sometimes deliberately vague about their intentions, either because they fear that taking a firm stand will lose them votes or because they do not have specific policies in mind. In the 1968 presidential election, Richard Nixon dodged the Vietnam issue by claiming that he had a "secret plan" for ending the war, a plan that he said could not be revealed to the American public because the enemy would also learn of it.

Finally, voters can hardly be aware of issues if they are inattentive to them. If the voters would pay close attention to election campaigns, they could learn about policy issues. But most people do not follow campaigns intently and do not necessarily come to recognize even highly publicized issues.[41] In the 1948 presidential election, for example, the Democratic candidate, Harry S Truman, campaigned vigorously for repeal of the Taft-Hartley Act and for controls on wages and prices to reduce the inflation rate. The Republican nominee, Thomas E. Dewey, strongly opposed these proposals. Yet only 16 percent of the voters could correctly identify the stands of both candidates on both issues.[42] Surveys during more recent elections have produced similar findings.

Issue Voting That Yields No Mandate

Even when the voters are well informed on election issues, a campaign does not necessarily result in a mandate for the winning candidate.[43] The 1972 presidential election is a case in point. The Vietnam war was the leading issue in 1972, and the major parties' nominees held sharply opposing positions on the war. The Democratic challenger, George McGovern, proposed an immediate withdrawal of U.S. forces from Vietnam, while the Republican incumbent, Richard Nixon, promised a continuation of his policy of gradual disengagement. Vietnam had become a national obsession by 1972, and Americans listened to and learned from the candidates. About 80 percent of voters knew of Mc-

[39]Peter Clarke and Susan Evans, *Covering Campaigns* (Stanford, Calif.: Stanford University Press, 1981); Charles M. Tidmarch and Brad S. Karp, "The Missing Beat: Press Coverage of Congressional Elections in Eight Metropolitan Areas," *Congress and the Presidency* 10 (Spring 1983): 47–61.

[40]Patterson, *Mass Media Election*, ch. 3.

[41]Ibid., chs. 7–10.

[42]Berelson, Lazarsfeld, and McPhee, *Voting*, 227.

[43]See Richard W. Boyd, "Popular Control of Public Policy," *American Political Science Review* 66 (June 1972): 429–449; John L. Sullivan and Robert E. O'Connor, "Electoral Choice and Popular Control of Public Policy," *American Political Science Review* 66 (December 1972): 1256–1268.

★ THE MEDIA AND THE PEOPLE

MEDIA CAMPAIGN MESSAGES AND THE VOTE

The Framers of the Constitution feared that the people would be exploited by demagogues. Americans would flock to the polls and deal self-government a death blow by electing a leader who had aroused their worst instincts. What the Framers could not have foreseen was that the people would confront election messages that are more discouraging than persuasive. Yet the story of the modern media campaign is a story of messages that do as much to alienate the voters as to inform and motivate them.

Presidential election news emphasizes the strategic game played by the candidates rather than their policy positions or leadership capabilities. Election news also has a negative bent. Presidential candidates are presented in unflattering terms. Bad news about the candidates takes precedence over good news. Soon after Arkansas Governor Bill Clinton broke to the front of the Democratic pack of presidential contenders in early 1992, he became the subject of news stories about his alleged marital infidelity. Four years earlier, Democratic frontrunner Gary Hart's campaign had been derailed by a similar scandal. Unfavorable gossip about the private lives of candidates, it seems, has more news value than does information about their policy stands or political experience.

Televised political advertising also tends to be negative in tone. Media consultants have perfected what is called the "attack ad"—a blistering, negative assault on the opponent. In the 1988 campaign, the Bush camp, instead of engaging Michael Dukakis on the issues,

decided to attack his patriotism and to blame him personally for the actions of the criminals of his state. A key television ad showed a revolving door that was meant to represent the Massachusetts prison furlough program; the suggestion was that Dukakis, as the state's governor, was personally responsible for crimes committed by furloughed prisoners. The ad was part of what seasoned observers called the meanest and most negative presidential campaign in memory.

Election polls suggest that such negative messages undermine the public's confidence not only in candidates but also in the electoral process itself. The messages that flow from the mass media of communication during a presidential campaign do not give people much reason to believe that they are participating in the noble process of democratic governance. The messages also do not give the public the kind of information that would be most useful in making an educated choice between the contenders. Although there are many other reasons for the relatively low level of voter turnout and voter information in U.S. elections, the type of campaign message that flows through the mass media is surely a contributing factor.

SOURCES: Thomas E. Patterson, *The Mass Media Election* (New York: Praeger, 1980); Thomas E. Patterson and Richard Davis, "The Media Campaign: Struggle for the Agenda," in Michael Nelson, ed., *The Elections of 1984* (Washington, D.C.: Congressional Quarterly Press, 1985), ch. 4; Thomas E. Patterson, "The Press and Its Missed Assignment," in Michael Nelson, ed., *The Elections of 1988* (Washington, D.C.: Congressional Quarterly Press, 1989), 93–109.

Govern's proposal for immediate disengagement and nearly 70 percent linked Nixon to a policy of phased withdrawal.[44]

Nevertheless, Nixon's huge victory over McGovern in 1972 was not a mandate for his Vietnam policy. In a careful analysis of Nixon's win, Stanley Kelley found that Nixon's position on Vietnam won him more support than any other issue did (see Table 10-2); yet the number of voters who cited his stand on Vietnam as the reason they voted for him was far short of a majority. Moreover, Nixon's supporters who did cite Vietnam had opposing opinions: some thought his policy was the best way to achieve peace, while others saw it as designed to win the war.[45]

Kelley's findings support what Norman Nie, Sidney Verba, and John Petrocik

[44]Thomas E. Patterson, Robert D. McClure, and Kenneth J. Meier, "Issue Voting," paper presented at the annual meeting of the American Political Science Association, September 1976, Chicago.
[45]Kelley, *Interpreting Elections*, 139.

TABLE 10-2 Percentage of Voters Who Cited Various Issues as a Reason for Preferring a Candidate in the 1972 Presidential Election The idea of election mandates is not supported by the evidence. Voters have different reasons for choosing the same candidate.

Issues	Percent Favoring Winner (Nixon)	Percent Favoring Loser (McGovern)
Vietnam war, peace	33.6%	18.4%
Foreign policy	20.7	6.1
Détente with USSR	4.1	1.0
Policy toward China	7.4	1.6
New Deal issues	28.6	39.5
Monetary and fiscal policy	6.5	8.6
Welfare	17.3	5.2
Race-related issues	6.0	4.0
Social change issues	15.2	8.1

SOURCE: Adapted from Stanley Kelley, Jr., *Interpreting Elections* (Princeton, N.J.: Princeton University Press, 1983), 138.

discovered when they studied presidential elections from 1952 to 1976 for evidence of the impact of issues.[46] Early in this period, the candidates' policy proposals had relatively little influence on voters' decisions. The public's degree of concern with issues then increased in the 1960s and early 1970s as a result of Vietnam, the civil rights movement, and urban unrest. Yet the voters who responded strongly to issues of any kind, even during this politically intense period, made up, by generous estimate, only about half of the electorate.[47]

Thus the common idea that victorious candidates have a popular mandate for their policy ideas simply does not conform with the facts. After his landslide victory in 1984, Ronald Reagan claimed that the voters had "voiced their support" for his proposed increase in defense spending. The electorate chose Reagan for a variety of reasons, but a desire for higher defense expenditures was not one of them: polls indicated that most voters favored either maintaining military spending at the current level or reducing it. In fact, opinion surveys in 1984 indicated that a majority of voters were closer to Walter Mondale's issue positions than they were to Reagan's. Reagan won anyway, and by a wide margin. The reality is that Reagan's electoral majority, like nearly all such majorities, was a coalition of minorities.

As could be expected, prospective voting is even less common in congressional races. In most cases, voters simply do not have the necessary information about the candidates' issue positions to choose between them on this basis.

RETROSPECTIVE VOTING: THE MORE COMMON FORM OF POLICY VOTING

V. O. Key, Jr., argued that prospective voting is neither the only way nor the best way for the electorate to exercise control over public policy. Key noted that

[46]Nie, Verba, and Petrocik, *Changing American Voter.*
[47]Ibid., 377.

candidates' promises do not always provide a sound basis for voting. A newly elected president, for example, may find that Congress has not the slightest interest in supporting the program that he promised the voters during his campaign. For such reasons, Key suggested that the public is better advised to cast its votes on the basis of government's past performance, which is not only a more tangible basis for decision but also one that is more easily calculated. The voter merely needs to decide whether government has performed well or poorly since the last election.[48]

Key used the term **retrospective voting** to describe the situation in which voters support the incumbent party when they judge its policies to have been successful[49] and oppose it when they conclude that its policies have failed. Retrospective voting is a somewhat weaker form of public control than prospective voting, because it occurs after the fact: government has already acted, and nothing can change what has already taken place. Nevertheless, retrospective voting can be an effective form of popular control over policy because it forces officeholders to *anticipate* the voters' likely response in the next election. "The fear of loss of popular support," Key concluded, "powerfully disciplines the actions of government."[50]

The fear of loss of public support powerfully disciplines the actions of government.
V. O. Key, Jr.

Reward or Punish? Evaluating the In-Party

Key presented evidence from the 1936–1960 presidential elections that indicated that voters' candidate preferences were generally consistent with their evaluation of whether the incumbent administration had done a good or poor job of handling policy problems.[51] This kind of evidence overestimates the extent of retrospective voting. Voters who support the incumbent administration are likely to say that it has been doing a good job even if this judgment is not the reason they are backing the in-party's candidate. Similarly, those who oppose the in-party's candidate, whatever their actual reasons for doing so, are likely to say that the "ins" have been doing a poor job.

Nevertheless, as Key concluded, a substantial number of voters do base their judgments of presidential candidates on a look backward at how government has been performing.[52] The 1980 presidential campaign is a case in point. The electorate in 1980 did not respond enthusiastically to the prospect of Ronald Reagan's election. His conservative economic ideas and belligerent attitude toward the Soviet Union worried many voters, and opinion surveys indicated that Reagan was the least popular presidential winner since polling began in the 1930s.[53] He won because the electorate was even less enthusiastic about the incumbent, Jimmy Carter. High inflation and unemployment in the late 1970s had made the U.S. economy weaker than it had been at any previous time since

[48]Key, *Responsible Electorate*, ch. 1.
[49]Ibid., 61.
[50]Ibid., 10.
[51]Ibid., 7–8.
[52]Gerald Pomper with Susan Lederman, *Elections in America*, 2d ed. (New York: Longman, 1980), 218.
[53]Arthur H. Miller and Martin P. Wattenberg, "Policy and Performance Voting in the 1980 Election," paper presented at the annual meeting of the American Political Science Association, September 1981.

Incumbent president Jimmy Carter (*left*) shakes hands with Republican challenger Ronald Reagan (*right*) before their television debate in 1980, during which Reagan invited voters to make a retrospective judgment of Carter's presidency. (UPI/ Bettmann Newsphotos)

the Great Depression of the 1930s, and the Iranian hostage crisis, which remained unresolved on the eve of the 1980 election, had severely damaged America's international prestige. In the closing statement of his televised debate with Carter in 1980, Reagan asked Americans whether they were "better off" than they had been four years earlier, when Carter had become president. If you are better off, said Reagan, "you should vote for Carter." If not, "you should vote for me." Reagan's appeal asked for a retrospective judgment from voters, and they complied. Carter's performance in office lost him the support in 1980 of more than one-fourth of the voters who had backed him in 1976.[54]

The in-party's congressional candidates, too, can lose out when the voters conclude that government has not performed well.[55] In 1980 Carter's fellow Democrats lost a net total of thirteen Senate seats and thirty-three House seats. National conditions also have an indirect effect on election outcomes: potentially strong opponents are more likely to run against House and Senate incumbents when the electorate is dissatisfied with government's performance.[56]

The influence of national issues on congressional races helps to explain the phenomenon called "presidential coattails."[57] The term commonly refers to the greater electoral success of congressional candidates who belong to the same party as the winning presidential candidate: they are said to ride into office on the president's coattails. Although the pattern is often said to occur because a

[54]Kathleen A. Frankovic, "Public Opinion Trends," in Gerald Pomper, ed., *The Election of 1980* (Chatham, N.J.: Chatham House, 1981), 97.
[55]Morris P. Fiorina, *Retrospective Voting in American National Elections* (New Haven, Conn.: Yale University Press, 1981), 81.
[56]Gary C. Jacobson and Samuel Kernell, *Strategy and Choice in Congressional Elections* (New Haven, Conn.: Yale University Press, 1981), 2–3.
[57]See James E. Campbell, "Explaining Presidential Losses in Midterm Congressional Elections," *Journal of Politics* 47 (November 1985): 1140; James E. Campbell, "Predicting Seat Gains from Presidential Coattails," *American Journal of Political Science* 30 (February 1986): 165.

presidential candidate's popularity rubs off on his party's congressional candidates, this factor actually has only a little to do with it. A larger factor is national conditions. The same conditions that benefit one party's presidential candidate are a boost to its congressional candidates.

Congressional elections, however, are affected to a lesser extent by national conditions than is the presidential race.[58] For one thing, voters distinguish between the incumbent president's contribution to national conditions and the smaller influence of any individual member of Congress.[59] In addition, congressional races, particularly those for the House of Representatives, have become somewhat insulated from policy and political developments. The proportion of incumbents who have been reelected has increased in recent decades, and their margins of victory have widened. The 1992 congressional elections were an exception; the turnover in Congress was higher after 1992 than it had been in years. The public's dissatisfaction with the ethical standards and performance record of Congress resulted in the retirement and defeat of an abnormally large number of its members. But incumbents ordinarily get a huge advantage at election time from the office they hold. The personal staffs of members of Congress tripled between 1960 and 1980, which gave incumbents the basis for publicity efforts, constituency services, and other activities that have enabled them to increase their public support on an ongoing basis. In addition, incumbents usually have more campaign funds and a higher level of name recognition than their challengers, which, in an era of weakened partisanship, are major sources of advantage in an election campaign.

The 1990 congressional elections are a dramatic illustration of the extent to which performance issues have been diminished by the advantages of incumbency. Public anger was high in the fall of 1990 as a result of Congress's

---

[58] See Alberto Alesina and Howard Rosenthal, "Partisan Cycles in Congressional Elections and the Macroeconomy," *American Political Science Review* 83 (1989): 373–398.
[59] Fiorina, *Retrospective Voting.*

The president sometimes tries to help other members of his party with their campaigns. Here, George Bush (*left*) makes an appearance at a fund-raiser for fellow Republican Bob Martinez (*right*), governor of Florida. (Chris O'Meara/AP/Wide World Photos)

inability to work out a deficit reduction plan, its enactment of a pay raise for its members, and the cozy relationship that was discovered to exist between several senators and Charles Keating, a leading figure in the savings and loan scandal. Nevertheless, on election day, only one incumbent senator and less than 5 percent of House incumbents were defeated at the polls. The results of the 1990 elections are in sharp contrast with those of a realigning election nearly a century ago. In 1894, angry at economic hard times, the electorate cleaned out Congress, turning a 218–127 Democratic majority in the House of Representatives into a 244–105 Republican majority.[60] (The advantages of congressional incumbency are discussed further in Chapter 16.)

Economic Performance as a Key to Reelection

George Bush's victory in 1988 further illustrates the importance that voters attach to past governmental performance. The nation's economy in 1988 was in the midst of the longest sustained upturn in a half century, and opinion polls showed that a majority of Americans believed that the Republican party was more likely than the Democrats to keep the country prosperous. This circumstance, more than any promise of future action or any personality traits of Bush, was the key to his victory. He had the support of more than 85 percent of the voters who had backed Reagan four years earlier.

In 1992, however, the U.S. economy was in its longest recession since World War II, and Bush had political trouble. He was under criticism from congressional conservatives of his own party and had to fend off a conservative primary challenge from broadcast commentator Pat Buchanan. His presidential approval ratings in the previous year, when he was the triumphant commander of allied forces in the Persian Gulf war, had been the highest recorded for a president. In 1992, however, three-fourths of the American public expressed concern about his handling of the economy. Bush's reelection chances, which had once seemed all but certain, were suddenly precarious.

In general, economic conditions play a large role in the electorate's response to the in-party. "Voters are disposed," Seymour Martin Lipset concludes, "to credit or blame incumbent administrations for the state of the economy."[61] As voters' confidence in a party's ability to ensure prosperity rises or falls, so does their support for its presidential candidate.[62] The voters' opinions about which party is better for economic prosperity has been closely related to party success (see Figure 10-3). Since 1952, the Democratic share of the two-party presidential vote has stayed above 50 percent when a majority of the public perceived it as the party of prosperity. Conversely, the Democratic vote has stayed below 50 percent when the Republican party was more widely perceived as the party of prosperity.[63] This pattern reflects the essential pragmatism of the American electorate which we noted in Chapter 8. If an incumbent administration

[60]R. Hal Williams, *Years of Decision* (New York: Wiley, 1978), 162; see also Paul W. Glad, *McKinley, Bryan, and the People* (Philadelphia: Lippincott, 1964), 92.
[61]Seymour Martin Lipset, "The Economy, Elections, and Public Opinion," *Tocqueville Review* 5 (Fall 1983): 431.
[62]D. Roderick Kiewiet, *Macro-Economics and Micro-Politics* (Chicago: University of Chicago Press, 1983), 154–158.
[63]*Gallup Reports*, April 1985.

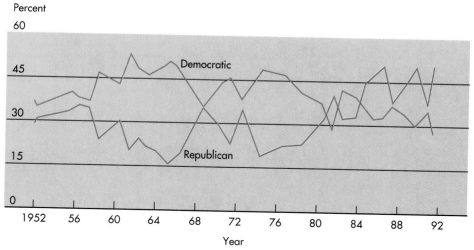

FIGURE 10-3 The Public's Perception of the Relative Ability of the Democratic and Republican Parties to Promote Prosperity, 1952–1991 Voters' support for a party's presidential candidate has typically been related to their opinion of the party's ability to manage the economy. *Source: Gallup poll, March 1, 1991. Respondents were asked whether the Democratic or Republican party would do "a better job of keeping the country prosperous."*

presides over an apparently healthy or improving economy, it can expect a good response at the polls.

Realigning Elections: A Strong Case of Retrospective Voting

Most national elections result in only moderate changes in public policy. Each newly elected president or Congress has innovative policy ideas, some of which will be enacted into law. But wholesale changes in national policy are rare. During periods of peace and prosperity, elected officials tend to believe that existing policies are working and to avoid tampering with them. Officeholders are more likely to seek alternative policies during difficult periods, but even then they confront significant political obstacles to major changes. Powerful interests that benefit from existing programs will resist radically new approaches. Congress's opposition to the president, or vice versa, can also kill new ideas. The American system of checks and balances generally works to protect the status quo. Unless the executive and legislative branches are united in their determination to forge ahead in a new direction, no significant action is likely.

This pattern changes abruptly with a realigning election, which can be regarded as a strong case of retrospective voting. Although the electorate does not actually decide the particulars of new programs through its vote in such elections, it does reject an existing policy direction and express a demand for new policies appropriate to the crisis. Historically, the peak years in the enactment of innovative national legislation have coincided roughly with periods of realignment.[64]

Elections and Citizen Influence: Some Conclusions

Cynical observers claim that elections provide only the illusion of popular control of policy. In their view, the electorate chooses leaders who then go their merry way, usually hand in hand with a wealthy elite. This portrayal of the

[64]Benjamin Ginsberg, "Elections and Public Policy," *American Political Science Review* 70 (1976): 49.

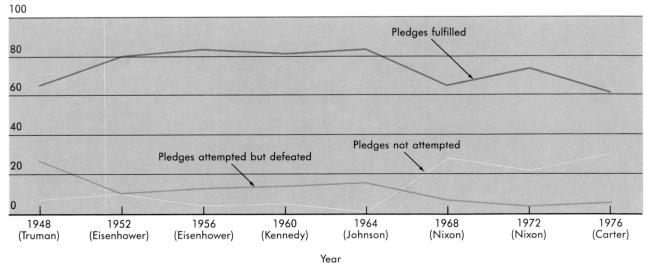

Percentage of campaign pledges

FIGURE 10-4 Percentage of
Platform Pledges Fulfilled,
Defeated, and Not Attempted,
1948–1976
Contrary to widespread belief,
winning presidential candidates
keep most of their campaign
promises. *Source: Gerald M.
Pomper with Susan S. Lederman,
Elections in America, 2d ed. (New
York: Longman, 1980), 162–163.*

influence, or lack thereof, exerted by voters is overdrawn. The threat of a loss of
popular support as a result of failed or unresponsive policies forces officeholders to pay attention to the electorate. The vote is a potentially lethal political
weapon: it can end a politician's career.

Candidates know the risk. More than a year before his 1992 reelection bid,
George Bush proposed major innovations in the field of education policy. The
proposal was apparently a response to charges that Bush was indifferent to
domestic problems, preferring to concentrate on foreign policy issues. Bush and
his advisers concluded that he needed a domestic policy initiative to which he
could point during the upcoming campaign. Education policy was chosen after
polls indicated that a wide spectrum of Americans were concerned about the
quality of their children's schooling. However, candidates' promises are not
mere vote-getting ploys.[65] Although candidates take positions that they believe
will gain them votes, they tend to follow through on their commitments.
Political scientist Gerald Pomper's study of party platforms from 1944 to 1976
(see Figure 10-4) revealed that winning candidates and parties fulfilled well
over half of their campaign pledges.[66] Indeed, the major obstacle to fulfillment
of platform pledges appears to be not bad faith but political roadblocks—as
when a Republican president cannot persuade a Democratic Congress to enact
his programs.

Arguments that voting does not significantly influence policy also tend to
ignore the fact that preferences of the electorate help to define the limits of
public policy. Candidates can advance certain policy proposals only at the risk
of losing their public support. As we saw at the beginning of this chapter, this is
what happened to Barry Goldwater when he proposed that mandatory social

*Political leaders develop a
strong sense of what the
permissible bounds of policy
are.*

Angus Campbell et al.,
The American Voter

[65]Ian Budge and Richard I. Hofferbert, "Mandates and Policy Outputs," *American Political Science
Review* 84 (1990): 111–132.
[66]Pomper, *Elections in America,* ch. 8.

★ CRITICAL THINKING

IS IT BETTER TO VOTE RETROSPECTIVELY THAN PROSPECTIVELY?

The civics-book model of voting that is taught in high schools suggests that a rational voter is a person who evaluates the candidates on the basis of their stands on issues. The voter is encouraged to discover how the candidates intend to handle the major problems of the day, and then to vote for the candidate whose positions are closest to his or her own.

The political scientist V. O. Key, Jr., argued that there were two basic problems with this prospective voting model. He noted, first, that it places extraordinary information demands on the voters. They have to pay close attention to the campaign and interpret accurately the candidates' statements. Second, the voters have to deal with the uncertainty that accompanies candidates' promises. Are the candidates sincere in their commitments? Will their commitments outlast the campaign and the changes that inevitably take place in the country's policy needs?

In Key's view, voters would be better advised to select their candidates retrospectively. He said that they should consider the past performance of the incumbent and, depending on whether they judge the performance to be effective or ineffective, vote for either the incumbent or a challenger. Key noted that the retrospective model places fewer information demands on voters and is based on the actual performance of government rather than on promises of future action.

Do you agree with Key's assessment? What are the drawbacks of retrospective voting? Are there particular times when prospective voting or retrospective voting is the more advisable basis of decision? In the last presidential election was your choice of a candidate based more on the past performance of government or on the promises of the candidates?

SOURCE: V. O. Key, Jr., *The Responsible Electorate* (Cambridge, Mass.: Belknap Press of Harvard University Press, 1966).

security be abolished. Most presidential candidates would have accepted social security as a settled issue that the public did not want reopened. As Angus Campbell and his colleagues noted, "Political leaders develop a strong sense of what the permissible bounds of policy are."[67]

[67]Campbell et al., *American Voter*, 547.

Stung by criticism that he was more interested in foreign affairs than in domestic problems, and aware that that perception among voters could hurt his chances for reelection in 1992, George Bush in 1991 launched a series of school appearances and education-policy statements that were intended to portray him as "the education president." (Dirck Halstead/Gamma-Liaison)

Finally, the importance of voting is underestimated if due attention is not paid to the long-term effects of realigning elections, such as that of 1932, and of other key elections, such as that of 1980. Such elections result in long-term and significant policy changes that are rooted in public dissatisfaction with existing conditions and are shaped in part by public demands stemming from this dissatisfaction. To ignore this type of electoral influence is to ignore perhaps the single most important way in which the voters give direction to national policy.

These observations do not amount to a claim that voting alone drives the American policymaking process. Many important policy issues are not addressed in elections but instead are decided out of the view of the general public. The voters' preferences clearly have more impact on policy at some times than at others, more impact on larger issues than on smaller ones, and more impact on government's general performance than on its specific actions. As Walter Lippman said, "The popular will does not direct continuously but . . . intervenes occasionally."[68] Thus a complete accounting of how policy is made in America and who benefits from it requires the study not only of elections and voting but also of other institutions and behaviors. Subsequent chapters will undertake these investigations.

Summary

Americans view themselves as a self-governing people largely in terms of their right to choose representatives in free elections. Yet voting does not by itself give the public control over policy. A central question, therefore, is the degree to which issues of policy and performance drive vote choices.

A basic influence on vote choice is party identification, which can cause a voter to support candidates from one party only. Such party-line voting, however, is mainly a response to the parties' policy tendencies and traditions. Although party loyalty has declined, over 60 percent of American voters still identify themselves with either the Republican or the Democratic party. For most partisans, particularly during periods when the parties' policies differ clearly and substantially, party-line voting is an important way of expressing a preference for general policy goals. However, the influence of partisanship on election results has declined sharply in the past two decades as we have undergone a dealignment, or decrease in party identification.

A realignment occurs when new and powerful issues emerge and disrupt the normal pattern of party politics. Realigning, or critical, elections offer voters the opportunity to have a large and lasting impact on national policy. In responding to these issues and then by endorsing the action of the party that takes power, the electorate helps to establish a new governing philosophy and its associated policies. A realignment is maintained in part through the development of loyalties among first-time voters to the new governing party and its policies.

Prospective voting is one way the public can exert influence on policy through elections. It is the most demanding approach to voting: voters must develop their own policy preferences and then must educate themselves about the candidates' positions. The voters must also set aside other considerations, such as the candidates' personalities. Yet most voters do not respond to issues in this way. The degree of prospective voting rises and falls with the importance of the issues of the day, but the electorate as a whole is generally not well informed about the candidates' stands and is only partially inclined to vote for candidates on the basis of the policies they advocate.

Retrospective voting demands less from voters: they need only decide whether the government has been performing well or poorly in terms of the goals and values they hold. The evidence suggests that the electorate is, in fact, reasonably sensitive to past governmental performance, particularly in relation to economic prosperity, and that such judgments affect voting to a significant degree, especially in presidential elections.

The vote is an important influence on public policy. This influence takes the form of general limits on policy debate and action, not of mandates for the specific policies advocated by the winning candidate. The power of the vote rests ultimately on its potential to penalize: elected representatives risk being voted out of office if their policy actions fail to satisfy the electorate.

[68]Walter Lippmann, *Phantom Public* (New York: Harcourt, Brace, 1925), 3.

Major Concepts

dealignment
divided government
party identification
prospective voting

realignment (realigning election)
retrospective voting
split-ticket voting

Suggested Readings

Andersen, Kristi. *The Creation of a Democratic Majority.* Chicago: University of Chicago Press, 1979. An analysis of the changes in the electorate between 1928 and 1936 which established the Democrats as the nation's majority party.

Bartels, Larry M. *Presidential Primaries and the Dynamics of Public Choice.* Princeton, N.J.: Princeton University Press, 1988. One of the first book-length, data-based studies of presidential primary voters.

Berelson, Bernard, Paul Lazarsfeld, and William McPhee. *Voting.* Chicago: University of Chicago Press, 1954. One of the pioneering survey research studies of voting behavior, focusing on the 1948 election.

Black, Earl, and Merle Black. *Politics and Society in the South.* Cambridge, Mass.: Harvard University Press, 1987. A careful analysis of the underlying economic and demographic changes that have contributed to the changing politics of the South.

Campbell, Angus, Phillip Converse, Warren Miller, and Donald Stokes. *The American Voter.* New York: Wiley, 1960. The classic study of the influences affecting individual voters, concentrating on the elections of 1952 and 1956.

Fiorina, Morris P. *Retrospective Voting in American National Elections.* New Haven, Conn.: Yale University Press, 1981. A sophisticated study of the nature and prevalence of retrospective voting.

Flanigan, William H., and Nancy H. Zingale. *Political Behavior of the American Electorate,* 7th ed. Washington. D.C.: Congressional Quarterly Press, 1991. A concise, up-to-date summary of the literature on voting behavior.

Key, V. O., Jr. *The Responsible Electorate.* Cambridge, Mass.: Belknap Press of Harvard University Press, 1966. A provocative analysis of voting as a response to government's performance.

Nie, Norman H., Sidney Verba, and John Petrocik. *The Changing American Voter,* enlarged. ed. Cambridge, Mass.: Harvard University Press, 1979. A reassessment of the nature of the American electorate in view of the political changes of the 1960s and early 1970s.

Popkin, Samuel L. *The Reasoning Voter: Communication and Persuasion in Presidential Campaigns.* Chicago: University of Chicago Press, 1991. A careful analysis of how voters respond to campaign communication.

Wattenberg, Martin P. *The Decline of American Political Parties, 1952–1984,* enlarged ed. Cambridge, Mass.: Harvard University Press, 1990. An assessment of changes in party identification since the 1950s and what the changes mean for American elections.

Are Americans Responsible as Citizens?

BENJAMIN R. BARBER

Responsibility means that all people take responsibility for at least some public decisions and acts at least some of the time.

If by "citizens" we mean voters who take themselves to the polls every year or two, about half of the eligible electorate are responsible citizens. (Just 50 percent of Americans voted in the 1988 presidential election.) But if we mean what the ancient Athenians meant—active participants in public office, assembly discussion (every ten days or so), periodic juries and magistracies often chosen by lot from census rolls—then the only people in modern America worthy of the name citizen are professional politicians and public servants. Indeed, although women, slaves, and resident foreigners were excluded from citizenship, about 22 percent of Athenians participated actively in politics, as compared to the 24 percent, on average, of Americans who participate in the far less demanding civic task of voting.

Perhaps the most fundamental question of modern democratic politics, then, is, "What does it mean to be a citizen?" Social scientists often use the language of "elites" and "masses," which suggests not rational individuals engaged in civic activity, but pawns of social forces who simply vote their background or religion or class interests and are stuck in permanent classes defined by their socioeconomic status. And even where the idea of a rational voter is advanced, advocates of representative democracy are satisfied with a minimalist definition of the citizen, associating civic virtue with getting people to the polls. This occasional act by "watchdogs" who otherwise leave governing to the governors is seen as the whole of citizenship.

If, however, by democracy we mean not the selection of accountable representatives to undertake all the real tasks of government, but the burdensome practices of collective self-government, then citizenship becomes a task that, as Oscar Wilde said of socialism, takes up a great many free evenings. To be a competent citizen capable of community self-government requires individuals to deliberate as members of a community—to think "publicly" in a language of civic discourse that does more than merely express sectarian private interests. It also demands that citizens participate—in juries, in referenda, in assembly discussion, and in the rest of the work of democracy. Citizenship in this sense is an acquired art, resting on extended civic education, civic training, and above all civic experience. Responsibility is taught by giving people responsibility—and this includes the right to make mistakes.

Responsibility cannot of course mean that all people take responsibility for all public decisions and acts all of the time; but it can mean that all people take responsibility for at least some public decisions and acts at least some of the time. Responsibility of this kind cannot be ceded to great leaders. As socialist leader Eugene V. Debs once warned his supporters, "Too long have the workers of the world waited for some Moses to lead them out of bondage. He has not come. He will not come. I would not lead you out if I could; for if you could be led out, you could be led back in again."

The language of civic responsibility, like so many other valuable currencies, has been eroded by inflation. We are now urged to believe that voting once every four years constitutes the essence of patriotism. But as Rousseau remarked, "Freedom is a food easy to eat but hard to digest." To digest freedom and transform it into fuel for the sinews of a living democracy is the real challenge of citizenship. Americans have yet to meet it, and until they do, their boast of being responsible citizens of a free country will ring hollow.

Benjamin R. Barber is Walt Whitman Professor and Director of the Walt Whitman Center for the Culture and Politics of Democracy at Rutgers University. He is the author of Strong Democracy, The Conquest of Politics, *and (with Patrick Watson) the book and TV series* The Struggle for Democracy.

MORRIS P. FIORINA

It often seems that academic critics of the American citizen are whining simply because more citizens don't share and act on their concerns.

Are Americans responsible citizens? A generation ago political scientists debated a related question: Were Americans sufficiently well informed to merit the term "rational" voters? An exasperated E. E. Schattschneider finally inquired, "Who . . . are these self-appointed censors who assume that they are in a position to flunk the whole human race? . . . Democracy was made for the people, not the people for Democracy." Schattschneider's observation is as appropriate now as then.

Critics of citizen responsibility employ standards of judgment that incorporate assumptions about political life. A number of the assumptions typically made are problematic:

1. Government has some higher purpose—to lead the populace to a more elevated moral plane, to spread democracy throughout the world, and the like.
2. Participation in government is educational and morally uplifting for the citizen. In particular, it fosters an appreciation of the common good.
3. Contemporary citizenship has deteriorated from some past stage of higher development—that of the ancient Greeks, or at least of nineteenth-century Americans.

Each of these assumptions is questionable. As for the first, most Americans are not crusaders. What they want from government is the safety and stability that will enable them to pursue their happiness as they define it. Rather than a crusading government, they want a government that does its job in the background with a minimum of fuss, like the electric company.

Citizens regard politics more as a necessary evil than as an opportunity for moral development.

The second assumption is faulty on two counts. First, it assumes that communication inevitably produces understanding. On the contrary, getting to know one's neighbors may only reveal that they are more narrowminded and vicious than one had imagined. And, far from producing consensus about the common good, deliberation may only produce the knowledge of particularistic interests necessary to construct a winning logroll that benefits special interests at the expense of the broader community interest. Second, this assumption tends to discount the myriad nongovernmental activities in which citizens engage. All across America, citizens generously volunteer their time for school committees, church groups, youth sports, and a host of community activities. Intellectuals might want citizens to spend their time in meetings discussing the Third World debt problem, but most citizens prefer to stay closer to home.

The third assumption is most likely wrong in fact. High levels of political involvement in the past by no means indicate a more committed, more virtuous citizenry. They may only indicate a lack of alternative forms of entertainment. Crowds of Americans endured four-hour speeches and debates in the nineteenth century primarily because they didn't have TVs. And in an era of seven-day work weeks, election day was a welcome holiday. If an increase in political participation is such a high priority today, we need only resurrect various practices from our glorious past—the spoils system, machine politics, and paying for votes.

Obviously, these comments are overstatements intended to provoke, but the underlying point is serious. On what basis can anyone presume to decide what responsible citizenship is? It often seems that academic critics of the American citizen are whining simply because more citizens don't share and act on *their* concerns. The present era of increasing internationalization of political arrangements poses new challenges. I am fairly optimistic that the American citizenry will meet these challenges. I am less hopeful that the academic critics, yearning for some glorified version of ancient Athens, will do so.

Morris P. Fiorina is Professor of Government at Harvard University. He is the author of Retrospective Voting in American National Elections.

POLITICAL ORGANIZATION

*I*magine that all adult Americans were placed heel to toe in a line: the line would stretch across the country, from New York City to Los Angeles and back, five times over. Imagine further that there is a man in the line who seeks to influence others. He shouts out his opinions as loudly as possible, his voice carrying the length of a football field in either direction. Assume now that everyone within earshot is persuaded by the man's arguments and accepts his views. What proportion of the American public has he influenced? The answer is a tiny share: 0.000001. If the proportion seems trivial, then consider the following fact: few flesh-and-blood citizens have influence over as many other people as does our imaginary man.

This hypothetical situation suggests why Americans, like any other democratic people, depend on political organization. No citizen acting alone is likely to have a measurable influence on national policies. Some Americans find it difficult to accept the fact of their individual powerlessness, but it is a reality of life in a nation of 252 million people. They acquire power only when they join together in common purpose.

This joining comes through political organization, one form of which is the political party, discussed in Chapters 11 and 12. Democratic government is almost inseparable from parties, which formed at the grass roots in the 1800s to provide a means by which citizens could act together as an effective majority. Interest groups, the subject of Chapters 13 and 14, are another vehicle of collective action. The interests that they represent tend to be specialized ones, such as soybean farmers or oil companies. Groups have always been a strong force in American politics, and their influence has become even more pronounced in recent decades. The news media, examined in Chapter 15, are a third linking organization. Newspapers, television, radio, and newsmagazines enable citizens to keep in touch with one another and with their leaders. The present era is often described as the age of communications, testimony to the media's current pervasiveness and power.

All democracies depend on parties, groups, and the media to organize their publics, but the United States does so in almost unique ways. America's political parties are among the weakest in the world, while its interest groups and media are among the strongest. The reasons for this state of affairs are many, and the consequences are significant. Organization enables Americans to make their voices heard, and the precise nature of this organization—weak parties, strong groups, and powerful media—determines whose voices will be the loudest.   ★   ★   ★

THE TWO-PARTY SYSTEM: DEFINING THE VOTERS' CHOICE

11
CHAPTER

Political parties created democracy and . . . modern democracy is unthinkable save in terms of the parties.

E. E. Schattschneider[1]

hey were the kind of strange bedfellows that American politics regularly produces. One of them stood for gun control, busing, and an end to the death penalty and proposed that the United States terminate its Star Wars project, MX missile construction, and aid to the Nicaraguan rebels. His running mate held the opposite position on each of these issues. They were the 1988 Democratic ticket: Michael Dukakis of Massachusetts and Lloyd Bentsen of Texas.

The Dukakis-Bentsen partnership was a product of the country's two-party system, which compels candidates and voters with diverse opinions to find common ground. Because the Republican and Democratic parties have dominated U.S. elections for so long and are the only parties with any realistic chance of acquiring political control, Americans nearly take their **two-party system** for granted. However, most democracies have a **multiparty system,** in which three or more parties have the capacity to gain control of government separately or in coalition. Even democracies that have what is essentially a two-party system typically have important smaller parties as well. For example, Great Britain's Labour and Conservative parties have dominated that nation's politics since early in this century, but they have had competition from the Liberal party and, more recently, the Social Democrats.

America's two-party system has important consequences for the nation's

---

[1] E. E. Schattschneider, *Party Government* (New York: Rinehart, 1942), 1.

politics. Neither major party can win an election by drawing its votes from only a small sector of the population; as a result, the two parties tend to appeal to many of the same interests. The policy traditions and tendencies of the Republican and Democratic parties do not differ sharply and consistently. For example, each party is committed to social security for the elderly and to substantial expenditures for national defense. Parties in European multiparty systems tend to be more programmatic. Each party has its distinctive platform and voting bloc. Of course, once in power, European parties are forced to adjust their programs to the prevailing realities. France's Socialist party, for example, won power in 1981 by attacking the center-right parties for failing to protect working-class and middle-class citizens from downward economic mobility (*déclassement*), but the nation's weak economy forced the Socialists to retain many of the pro-business policies of the previous government.[2] Nevertheless, European multiparty systems offer voters a more clear-cut set of choices than does the American two-party system.

To critics, the American parties' failure to take sharply different policy positions means that they offer the public no genuine alternatives. To their admirers, however, America's major parties provide political stability and yet are different enough to give voters a real choice. This chapter investigates America's two-party system and the type of choice it provides the public. It argues that the Republican and Democratic parties do offer a real and significant choice, but only at particular times and on particular issues. The main points discussed in this chapter are the following:

★ *Throughout most of the nation's history, political competition has centered on two parties.* This two-party tendency is explained by the nature of America's electoral system, political institutions, and political culture. Minor parties exist in the United States but have been unable to compete successfully for governing power.

★ *The Republican and Democratic coalitions are very broad.* Each includes a substantial proportion of nearly every economic, ethnic, religious, and regional grouping in the country.

★ *To win an electoral majority, each of the two major parties must appeal to a diverse set of interests; this necessity normally leads them to advocate moderate and somewhat overlapping policies and to avoid taking detailed positions on controversial issues.* Only during national crises are America's parties likely to present the electorate with starkly different policy alternatives.

The History of the Two-Party System

Although many Americans distrust political parties and question their role, the fact is that democracy would be nearly meaningless without political parties. The party is the only institution that has the purpose of developing *broad* policy and leadership choices and then presenting them to the voting public for acceptance or rejection. Through the alternatives they offer in elections, parties

[2] Paul J. Best, Kul B. Rai, and David F. Walsh, *Politics in Three Worlds* (New York: Wiley, 1986), 324.

Congressional Pugilists.

1. *Jonathan Dayton, Speaker.*   2. *Jonathan W. Condy, Clerk.*

He in a trice struck Lyon thrice
Upon his head, enrag'd sir,

Who seiz'd the tongs to ease his wrongs,
And Griswold thus enjcy'd, sir.

Congress Hall,
in Philad'a, Feb. 15, 1798.
S. E. Cor. 6th & Chestnut St.

FIRST FIGHT IN CONGRESS.

Party conflict developed early in the nation's history. The conflict turned violent one day in 1798 on the floor of the House of Representatives, when Roger Griswold *(at right)*, a Federalist, attacked Matthew Lyon, a Republican. (New York Public Library)

give the public an opportunity to express its preferences about the direction government should take.

Of course, parties are not the only means by which the public can exert influence. Interest groups such as the AFL-CIO and the American Medical Association provide individuals with the opportunity to act collectively. However, most such groups articulate the narrow and specific demands of a *minority* interest in society. In the United States, with its individualistic culture and tradition of freedom of association, group activity is more fragmented than in many other nations. Major political parties function in a different way. The party's goal is to create a *majority* by bringing together individuals with diverse interests. A **political party** is an ongoing coalition of interests joined together to try to get their candidates for public office elected under a common label.[3] Parties serve to pull diverse interests together and in the process offer the public broad policy and leadership alternatives.

Political parties developed spontaneously in the United States. They were not established by the Constitution, and most of America's early leaders were suspicious of parties. George Washington in his Farewell Address warned the nation of the "baneful effects" of parties, and James Madison likened parties to special interests. However, Madison's initial misgivings about parties gradually gave way to a grudging admiration; he recognized that they were a way for like-minded people to work together toward common goals. Gradually parties

Let me now . . . warn you in the most solemn manner against the baneful effects of party.

George Washington
Farewell Address, 1796

[3] Leon D. Epstein, *Political Parties in Western Democracies* (New York: Praeger, 1967), 9.

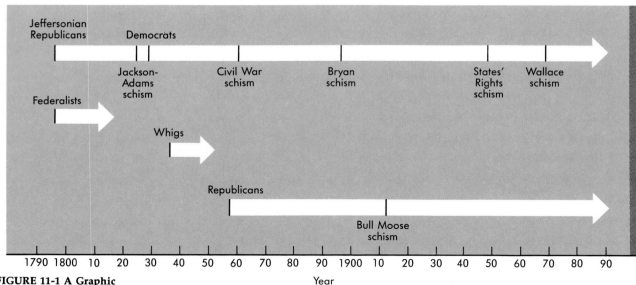

FIGURE 11-1 A Graphic History of America's Major Parties

became the engine of democracy—the instrument by which a mass public could exercise political influence.

THE FIRST PARTIES

Political parties in the United States originated in the rivalry within George Washington's administration between Thomas Jefferson and Alexander Hamilton: as we saw in Chapter 4, Jefferson defended states' rights and small landholders, while Hamilton promoted a strong national government and wealthy interests. After Hamilton's ideas prevailed in Congress, Jefferson and his followers formed a political party, the Republicans (see Figure 11-1). By adopting this label, which was associated with popular government, the Jeffersonians sought to portray themselves as the rightful heirs to the American Revolution's legacy of self-government and political equality.

Hamilton responded by organizing his supporters into a formal party—the Federalists—and in the process created America's first competitive party system. The Federalists took their name from the faction that had supported ratification of the Constitution, thereby implying that they were the Constitution's true defenders. However, the Federalists' preoccupation with commercial and wealthy interests alienated many people. Under President John Adams, for example, the Federalists tried to intimidate new immigrants—most of whom were poor—by the Alien Acts, which gave government the right through presidential order to deport or imprison political dissenters who had not yet obtained citizenship. These repressive acts fueled Jefferson's claim that the Federalists were bent on establishing a government for the rich and wellborn. After Adams's defeat by Jefferson in the election of 1800, the Federalists and their discredited philosophy never again held sway.

During the so-called Era of Good Feeling, when James Monroe ran unopposed in 1820 for a second presidential term, it appeared as if the nation might exist without parties. Monroe told Andrew Jackson that free government could survive without parties. Yet by the end of Monroe's second term, policy disputes had split the Republican party into the National Republicans, led by John Quincy Adams, and the Democratic Republicans (later shortened to Democrats), led by Andrew Jackson. The National Republicans resembled the earlier Federalists in their support of commercial interests and a larger role for the national government, while the Democrats viewed themselves as Jefferson's rightful successors, since they favored small landholders and states' rights.

The idea of a government without party competition is utopian. The alternative is likely to be, not government for the common good, but government for and by a small elite. In Mexico a single party has dominated government for most of this century and, despite its roots in the popular revolution of 1910, has become the instrument of the nation's wealthiest families. For all its faults, competition between parties is the only system that can regularly mobilize collective influence on behalf of the many who are individually powerless against those few who have extraordinary wealth and prestige.[4] Because they are a vast numerical majority, ordinary citizens have the potential for great power in a democratic system, but that potential cannot become reality unless the people are collectively organized.

It was this realization that led Andrew Jackson during the 1820s to reassert the principle of party. By mobilizing the mass citizenry through party action, Jackson sought to break the hold of the Virginia and Massachusetts aristocracy on the presidency, opening the way to a government that was more directly responsive to ordinary citizens. At the peak of Jacksonian democracy in the 1830s, Alexis de Tocqueville wrote: "The People reign in the American political

---

[4] Walter Dean Burnham, "The End of American Party Politics," in Walter Dean Burnham, ed., *Politics/America: The Cutting Edge of Change* (New York: Van Nostrand, 1973), 132.

★ ANALYZE THE ISSUE

The Advantages of Political Parties

The United States has the world's oldest representative government; it also has the world's oldest political parties. Is this just a coincidence? If you believe that it is, then why have political parties emerged in *every* democracy? Can you think of an effective alternative means—such as interest groups or the mass media—by which citizens can acquire collective influence? What are the advantages and disadvantages of parties in comparison with these alternative means of bringing citizens together?

Robert Cruikshank's *All Creation Going to the White House* satirized the inauguration of Andrew Jackson, who—as a democratic gesture—invited the public to join in the celebration. (Historical Picture Services)

world as the Deity does in the universe."[5] Tocqueville exaggerated the people's true power but caught the spirit of popular government that was behind the development of popularly based parties under Andrew Jackson.

GRASS-ROOTS PARTIES

Jackson's idea of a political party differed from Thomas Jefferson's. Whereas Jefferson's party had been well organized only at the leadership level, Jackson sought a "grass-roots" party, one that was built from the bottom up and was designed to encourage wide participation. Jackson's Democratic party consisted of committees and clubs at the national, state, and local levels, with membership open to all eligible voters. During the 1828 campaign the Democrats staged public parades, rallies, and barbecues throughout the nation. These popular entertainments, along with more liberal suffrage laws, contributed to a nearly fourfold rise in voter turnout.[6]

In the 1830s the Democrats faced a new opposition party, the Whigs. The Whigs consisted of a diverse set of interests, including states'-rights advocates from the South who felt that the Democrats had abandoned them, former National Republicans who favored a strong central government, and members of the single-issue Anti-Masonic party. About all that these diverse groups had in common initially was their hostility to the strong-willed Jackson, whom they called "King Andrew I." By 1840, however, the Whigs had transformed themselves into an effective opposition party by imitating the Democrats' tactics—grass-roots organization, mobilization of the electorate, and the nomination in 1840 of a national military hero, William Henry Harrison, as their presidential candidate.[7]

This competitive two-party system was short-lived. In the 1850s both parties were torn apart by the slavery issue. Many southern Whigs gravitated to the more pro-slavery Democratic party. Northern Whigs and some antislavery northern Democrats joined a new sectional organization, the Republican party, which opposed the extension of slavery into the new western territories. In 1860 the Democratic party's northern faction nominated for president Stephen A. Douglas, who held that the question of whether a new territory permitted slavery was for a majority of its voters to decide, while the southern faction nominated John C. Breckinridge, who called for the legalization of slavery in all territories. The Democratic vote in the fall election was split sharply along regional lines between these two candidates—with the result that the Republican nominee, Abraham Lincoln, was able to win the presidency with only 40 percent of the popular vote. The Republicans had eclipsed the Whigs and become America's other major party. However, the U.S. party system essentially collapsed in 1860, for the only time in the nation's history.[8] The issues of slavery and union were too basic and serious to be settled through peaceful elections. The presidential victory of the Republican Abraham Lincoln marked

[5] Alexis de Tocqueville, *Democracy in America* (Garden City, N.Y.: Doubleday/Anchor, 1969), 60.
[6] See Richard P. McCormick, *The Second American Party System: Party Formation in the Jacksonian Era* (Chapel Hill: University of North Carolina Press, 1966).
[7] Glyndon G. Van Deusen, "The Whig Party," in Arthur M. Schlesinger, Jr., ed., *History of the U.S. Political Parties*, vol. 1 (New York: Chelsea House, 1973), 344.
[8] William Crotty, "The Party Symbol and Its Changing Meaning," in William Crotty, ed., *The Party Symbol* (San Francisco: W. H. Freeman, 1980), 6.

not the peaceful resolution of these issues but the beginning of a war between the states.

REPUBLICANS VS. DEMOCRATS: THE ENDURING PARTY SYSTEM

After the Civil War, the nation settled into the pattern of competition between the Republican and Democratic parties that has prevailed ever since. The durability of these two parties is due not to their ideological consistency but to their remarkable capacity for adaptation during periods of crisis. Realigning elections of the kind that occurred during the Great Depression of the 1930s (see Chapter 10) have produced essentially different Democratic and Republican parties—with new bases of support, new policies, and new philosophies.

The Civil War realignment brought about a thorough change in the party system. The Republicans replaced the Democrats as the nation's majority party. The Republicans were the dominant party in the larger and more populous North; the Democratic party was left with a stronghold in what became known as "the Solid South." During the next three decades the Republicans controlled the presidency except for Grover Cleveland's two terms, and they held a majority in one or both houses of Congress for all but four of those years. Cleveland's initial victory in 1884 was made possible only by a split in Republican ranks. The GOP denied nomination to its own incumbent, Chester A. Arthur, and turned instead to James G. Blaine ("the Man from Maine"), who, it appears, had the support neither of progressive Republicans nor of his own running mate, John A. Logan.

The election of 1896 resulted in a further realignment of the Republican-Democratic party system. Three years earlier, an economic panic following a bank collapse had resulted in a severe depression. The Democratic Cleveland was president when the panic occurred, and that circumstance worked to the advantage of the Republicans. They gained strength in the East particularly because of fear of cheap credit, a policy advocated by the Democrats' 1896 presidential nominee, William Jennings Bryan. During the four decades between the 1890s realignment and the next one in the 1930s, the Republicans held the presidency except for Woodrow Wilson's two terms and had a majority in Congress for all but six years. As was the case with Cleveland, Wilson could not have won except for dissension within Republican ranks. In the election of 1912, the Republican vote for incumbent William Howard Taft was split by the Bull Moose party candidacy of Theodore Roosevelt, which enabled Wilson to win with less than 45 percent of the total vote.

As was discussed in Chapter 10, the Great Depression of the 1930s triggered a thoroughgoing realignment of the American party system. The Democrats became the country's majority party, and the political and policy agenda favored a significant social and economic role for the national government. Franklin D. Roosevelt's election in 1932 began a thirty-six-year period of Democratic presidencies that was interrupted only by Dwight D. Eisenhower's two terms in the 1950s. In 1968 the Republicans won the presidency and have since dominated the office. The Democrats, however, have dominated Congress since 1930, losing control of both House and Senate only in 1947–1948 and 1953–1954, and of the Senate in 1980–1986.

Thus, although the United States has had a two-party system for nearly the whole of its history, this system, at most times, has been dominated by one of

Abraham Lincoln said that this portrait of him by Mathew Brady, which he used in his campaign literature, contributed to his election to the presidency as a Republican in 1860. (Library of Congress)

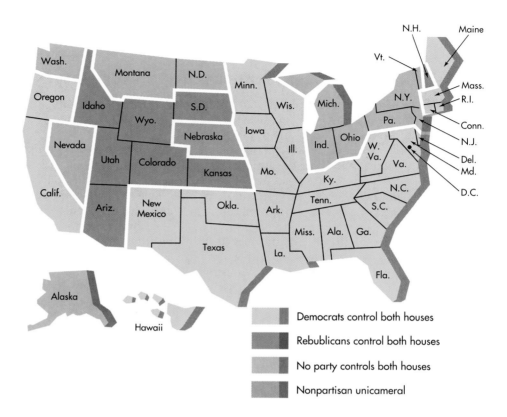

FIGURE 11-2 Party Control of State Legislatures, 1990
Intense party competition is not found in most states.
Source: The World Almanac, 1991 *(New York: Pharos Books, 1991), 92–95.*

Democrats control both houses

Rebublicans control both houses

No party controls both houses

Nonpartisan unicameral

the two parties. Intense two-party competition is not the norm on the state and local levels either. In most states, for example, both houses of the legislature are controlled by the same party (see Figure 11-2). Party dominance tends to follow regional lines. Since the Civil War, Democrats have held sway over southern politics—the South's revenge on the party of Lincoln; only in recent decades has the region begun to see more party competition. The Republican party also has its traditional strongholds, such as New England and the rural Midwest, although Democratic candidates have recently improved their showing in these areas. As political power has shifted toward the government in Washington in the past few decades, states and localities have become less insulated from national influences, and their parties' strengths have become more evenly matched. However, vigorous two-party competition is still the exception rather than the rule in states and localities.

Minor Parties in America

Although American politics has come to center on two major parties, there have always been minor parties—more than a thousand during the nation's history.[9] Most of them have been short-lived, and only a few have had a lasting impact.

---

[9] See Frank Smallwood, *The Other Candidates: Third Parties in Presidential Elections* (Dartmouth, N.H.: University Press of New England, 1983); Steven J. Rosenstone, Roy L. Behr, and Edward H. Lazarus, *Third Parties in America* (Princeton, N.J.: Princeton University Press, 1984).

A minor party, by definition, has no chance of acquiring a significant share of governing power. Minor parties exist largely to advocate positions that their followers believe are not being adequately represented by either of the two major parties. When a minor party gains a large following, which has happened a few times in history, the major parties are inevitably transformed. They are forced to pay attention to the problems that are driving people to look outside the two-party system for leadership.

TYPES OF MINOR PARTIES

Minor parties may be formed in response to the emergence of a single controversial issue, out of a commitment to a certain ideology, or as a result of a rift within one of the major parties.

Single-Issue Parties

Some minor parties form around a single issue of overriding concern to its supporters. The present-day Right-to-Life party, for example, was formed to oppose the legalization of abortion. Of course, right-to-life interest groups have also formed in opposition to legalized abortion. In fact, single-issue parties are similar to interest groups in that each is preoccupied with a narrow and specific policy area. The difference is that a single-issue party places candidates for public office on the ballot, whereas an interest group, although it may otherwise be active in election campaigns, does not. (Interest groups are discussed in detail in Chapters 13 and 14.)

Some single-issue parties have seen their policy goals enacted into law. The Prohibition party contributed to the ratification in 1919 of the Eighteenth Amendment, which prohibited the manufacture, sale, and transportation of alcoholic beverages (but was repealed in 1933). Single-issue parties usually disband when their issue is favorably resolved or fades in importance.[10]

---

[10] Daniel A. Mazmanian, *Third Parties in Presidential Elections* (Washington, D.C.: Brookings Institution, 1984), 143–144.

The National Prohibition party, shown here at its national convention in Indianapolis in 1892, sought to prohibit the sale of all alcoholic beverages. Single-issue parties tend to last only as long as the issue holds any importance in national politics. (The Bettmann Archive)

In 1896 the Populist party—a strong ideological party—nominated William Jennings Bryan as its presidential candidate. Bryan was also the Democratic nominee in that election. (Brown Brothers)

Ideological Parties

Other minor parties are characterized by their ideological commitment, or concern for a broad and radical philosophical position, such as redistribution of economic resources. Modern-day ideological parties include the Citizens party, the Communist party, the Socialist Workers party, and the Libertarian party, each of which operates on the fringe of American politics. Their combined popular vote has been less than 1 percent of the total in recent presidential elections. Ideological parties tend to gain strength during times of social and political upheaval. The Socialist party received 6 percent of the presidential vote in 1912, largely from voters dissatisfied with the monopolistic practices of business trusts.[11]

One of the strongest ideological parties in the nation's history was the Populist party. Its candidate in the 1892 presidential election, James B. Weaver, gained 8.5 percent of the national vote and won twenty-two electoral votes in six western states. The party, which is classified as a "protest party" by some scholars, began as a protest movement in response to the economic depression and business monopolies of the 1890s.[12] It had an agrarian base, a result of the anger of small farmers over low commodity prices, tight credit, and the high rates charged by railroad monopolies to transport farm goods. The Populist platform called for government ownership of the railroads, a graduated income tax, low tariffs on imports, and elimination of the gold standard. The Populist party in 1896 endorsed the Democratic presidential nominee, William Jennings Bryan, and its support probably hurt the Democrats nationally.[13] Large numbers

★ ANALYZE THE ISSUE

The Role of Minor Parties
At the end of the nineteenth century, neither the Republican nor the Democratic party was providing substantial leadership in addressing problems spawned by the Industrial Revolution. How does this fact help to explain the rise of the Populists? What does the story of the Populist party suggest about the role and eventual fate of minor parties?

[11] Ibid., 58–59.
[12] Walter Dean Burnham, *Critical Elections and the Mainsprings of American Politics* (New York: Norton, 1970), 27; see also Lawrence Goodwyn, *The Populist Movement* (New York: Oxford University Press, 1978).
[13] James L. Sundquist, *Dynamics of the Party System* (Washington, D.C.: Brookings Institution, 1973), 140.

of "Gold Democrats" left their party in fear of the inflationary consequences of Bryan's advocacy of the free coinage of silver.

The 1992 campaign of billionaire H. Ross Perot resembled that of an ideological party, even though he ran as an independent candidate rather than as a party nominee. Perot's populist-style campaign was based not on a single issue but on broad public dissatisfaction with the ethical standards and performance record of established policymakers, Republicans and Democrats alike.

Factional Parties

The Republican and Democratic parties are relatively adept at managing internal conflict. Although each party's support is diverse, the differences among its varying interests can normally be reconciled. However, there have been times when factional conflict within the major parties has led to the formation of minor parties.

The most successful of these factional parties at the polls was Theodore Roosevelt's Bull Moose party. In 1908 Roosevelt, after having served eight years as president, declined to seek a third term despite the GOP's overtures. Roosevelt hand-picked William Howard Taft for the Republican nomination, expecting him to continue the Progressive tradition that he, Roosevelt, had established. When Taft as president showed neither Roosevelt's enthusiasm for a strong presidency nor Roosevelt's commitment to business regulation, relations between the two men soured. In 1912 Roosevelt challenged Taft for the Republican presidential nomination. Progressive Republicans backed Roosevelt, but Taft won the nomination with the backing of conservative Republicans and the Republican National Committee. Roosevelt led a Progressive walkout to form the Bull Moose party (a reference to Roosevelt's claim that he was "as strong as a bull moose"). Roosevelt won 27 percent of the presidential

Theodore Roosevelt campaigns in Atlantic City, N.J., in 1912 with a symbol of his Bull Moose party. (UPI/Bettmann Newphotos)

vote to Taft's 25 percent, but the split within Republican ranks enabled the Democratic nominee, Woodrow Wilson, to win the presidency.

The States' Rights party in 1948 and the American Independent party in 1968 are other examples of strong factional parties. Each of these parties was formed by southern Democrats who were angered by northern Democrats' support of racial desegregation. The States' Rights platform asserted that the Truman administration was "totalitarian" in its disregard for states' rights.

Factional parties usually flourish for just one or two elections, and their electoral appeal is typically tied to a powerful issue and a well-known candidate. When Theodore Roosevelt returned to Republican ranks in 1916, the Bull Moose party as such ceased to exist, although Senator Robert La Follette ran a strong campaign as a Progressive in 1924, receiving 16 percent of the national vote. George Wallace was the founder and 1968 presidential nominee of the American Independent party (AIP). Wallace considered making a second presidential run under the AIP's banner in 1972 but decided finally to seek the mainstream Democratic nomination, leaving the AIP without a candidate. In 1976, in what turned out to be its last campaign, the AIP nominated the segregationist Lester Maddox, a former Georgia governor, who received less than 1 percent of the national vote.

Deep divisions within a party give rise to factionalism, and such wounds are not easily healed. Conservative Republicans were never very comfortable with Progressivism, and it eventually came to be represented mainly by the Democratic party, beginning with Wilson and continuing in the New Deal policies of Franklin D. Roosevelt. Similarly, the conflict over civil rights that began within the Democratic party during the Truman years continued for the next quarter century, resulting first in widespread support by many southern whites for Republican presidential candidates and later in their general loyalty to the Republican party. In short, such factional splits usually represent irresolvable conflicts within a major party that eventually help to redefine the divisions between the two major parties.

Some factional candidates have run not under a party label but as independents. The most prominent such candidate in recent years was John Anderson, a congressman from Illinois who, having failed in a bid for the 1980 Republican nomination for president, continued to campaign as an independent. Anderson attracted support among some liberal Republicans who were dissatisfied with their party's nomination of Ronald Reagan, liberal Democrats seeking an alternative to the incumbent president, Jimmy Carter, and independent voters. Anderson's support in opinion polls reached nearly 25 percent during the summer of 1980; it appeared that he had an outside chance of winning the presidency if the electorate otherwise divided closely between Carter and Reagan. When it later became evident that Anderson would lose, his support dwindled rapidly. In the end he received only 7 percent of the presidential vote. Anderson tried to counter the slippage by denying that his candidacy was indirectly contributing to the election of either Carter or Reagan. "A vote for Anderson is a vote for Anderson" was his rallying cry. Nevertheless, of voters who had at one time indicated a preference for Anderson, about half cited his inability to win as a reason for their defection. Anderson's maverick candidacy had no apparent lasting impact on the composition of the two major parties.

THE DILEMMA OF MINOR PARTIES

Only one minor party, the Republican party, has ever achieved majority status. Minor parties in America have a recurrent dilemma. Their followers are motivated by issue positions that are vital to them but unattractive to other voters. To increase its following, a minor party must broaden its platform; in so doing, however, it risks alienating its original supporters. Yet if it remains small, it cannot win elections and may eventually wither away.

Historically, the influence of minor parties has resided mainly in the response of the major parties to the issues they raise. Strong support for a minor party can encourage one or both major parties to try to capture its backers. For example, George Wallace's strong showing in the South in 1968 apparently prompted the Nixon administration to develop its "southern strategy," which included nomination of a southern conservative to the Supreme Court and opposition to court-ordered busing for purposes of school integration.[14] Richard Nixon reportedly believed that if Wallace's followers could be won over, the GOP would replace the Democrats as the nation's dominant party.

Why Only Two Parties?

Minor parties come and go, but the two major parties go on and on. What accounts for their persistence? The long tradition of the Republicans and Democrats is obviously a factor in their current strength. Most voters give serious consideration only to the Republican and Democratic nominees, and the news media devote nearly all their coverage to the major parties.[15] These tendencies, however, do not explain why only two parties took firm root in the United States in the first place.

THE ELECTORAL SYSTEM

One reason for America's two-party system is the fact that the nation chooses its officials through plurality voting in **single-member districts**.[16] Each constituency elects a single candidate to a particular office, such as U.S. senator or representative; only the party that gets the most votes (a plurality) in a district wins the office. This system discourages minor parties. Assume, for example, that a minor party received exactly 20 percent of the vote in each of the nation's 435 congressional races. Even though one in five voters nationwide backed the minor party, it would win *no* seats in Congress because none of its candidates placed first in any of the 435 single-member-district races. The winning candidate in each case would be the major-party candidate who received the larger proportion of the remaining 80 percent of the vote.

---

[14] Mazmanian, *Third Parties*, 85–87.

[15] Michael Robinson and Margaret Sheehan, *Over the Wire and on TV* (New York: Russell Sage Foundation, 1983), 73.

[16] The classic account of the relationship of electoral and party systems is Maurice Duverger, *Political Parties* (New York: Wiley, 1954), bk. II, ch. 1; see also Giovanni Sartori, *Parties and Party Systems* (Cambridge, England: Cambridge University Press, 1976); Douglas Rae, *The Political Consequences of Electoral Laws* (New Haven, Conn.: Yale University Press, 1967).

By comparison, most European democracies use some form of **proportional representation,** in which seats in the legislature are allocated according to a party's share of the popular vote. Germany's electoral system, for instance, combines single-member districts and proportional representation. Each party not only nominates candidates to run in single-member local districts but also prepares a ranked list of national candidates. All single-member-district winners receive seats in the Bundestag, the German legislature. Each party then can select candidates from its list until its legislative seats total roughly its proportion of national votes. Thus in the federal elections of 1983, the Green party won slightly more than 5 percent of the national vote. Although none of its candidates placed first in an election district, the party was able to choose candidates from its list to occupy about 5 percent of the Bundestag's seats. If the Green party had been competing under the rules of the American electoral system, it would not have won any seats.

The adverse effect of electoral laws on U.S. minor parties is evident also in the election of the president. A presidential race is a winner-take-all contest, and only a strong party has any chance of gaining the office. The presidency can be won with less than a majority of the popular vote, as was the case in 1968, when Republican Richard Nixon was elected with only a 43 percent plurality. In that election George Wallace won 13.5 percent of the national vote as the American Independent party candidate, but his relatively strong showing gave him no share of executive power. By comparison, in France there must be a runoff election between the two candidates who receive the most votes if neither receives a majority—50 percent or more—of the vote. Minor parties that fare poorly in the first election can bargain with the final contenders, trading support in the runoff election for policy concessions or cabinet positions in the new government. In this way, the French system—unlike the American one—provides an incentive for smaller parties to compete.

Election laws can discriminate against minor parties. Some states make it difficult for minor parties to get their candidates on the ballot by requiring that a party receive a certain proportion of the vote in one election in order to have its candidates automatically placed on the next election's ballot. A party that does not meet this requirement must collect the signatures of a large number of registered voters before its candidates can appear on the ballot in a future election. In his 1968 presidential bid, Wallace had to collect 2.7 million signatures in order to get his name on the ballot in every state.[17]

Finally, minor-party candidates are disadvantaged in presidential politics by a federal law that requires them to get at least 5 percent of the popular vote in order to qualify for public funds and then permits them to receive only an amount equal to the ratio of their vote total to the average vote total of the two major-party nominees. Independent candidate John Anderson received $4.2 million after he won 7 percent of the 1980 presidential vote. Reagan and Carter had seven times as many votes, on average, and each received $29 million. Moreover, Reagan and Carter were given their money in late summer, after the major-party conventions, whereas Anderson did not become eligible for public funds until he exceeded the 5 percent threshold on election day in November. Anderson conducted his fall campaign on borrowed money.

---

[17] Robert J. Huckshorn, *Political Parties in America,* 2d ed. (Pacific Palisades, Calif.: Brooks/Cole, 1983), 70.

Germany's electoral system allocates legislative seats on the basis both of single-district voting and of the overall proportion of votes a party receives. This system requires that the German voter cast two ballots in legislative races: one to choose among the candidates in the particular district and one to choose among the parties. Shown here is a ballot from a West German election held in 1987 (before East and West Germany were reunified). The left-hand column lists the candidates for the legislative seat in a district, and the right-hand column lists the parties. (Note the relatively large number of parties on the ballot.)

PARTY PRAGMATISM

The pragmatic nature of America's major parties also contributes to their persistence. Because the Republican and Democratic parties have opened their ranks to people of all views, they have been able to accommodate individuals who might otherwise have allied themselves with minor parties. In Congress, for example, members with sharply different political philosophies find it possible to coexist in the same party. Consider Jesse Helms of North Carolina and Robert Packwood of Oregon, both Republican members of the Senate. Helms and Packwood are often on opposite sides of an issue. In fact, Packwood, a liberal Republican, sides more often with some of his Democratic Senate colleagues than he does with Helms.

Europe's legislative parties, in contrast, generally insist on the loyalty of their elected representatives. A member of the French National Assembly who votes with the opposition party on a key legislative measure may be denied renomination. Conflicts within French parties have at times forced dissident leaders to leave and form new parties. The broad base of American parties makes this response unlikely: party mavericks in Congress usually find that they gain more power by staying in the party and acquiring the seniority that leads to positions of committee leadership. Although Senator Packwood is less conservative than most of his Republican colleagues, his seniority has made

WHAT IF THE UNITED STATES HAD PROPORTIONAL REPRESENTATION?

Politics is a game played under certain rules. These rules are often regarded as neutral in their effect: they define how the game is played and won but do not themselves influence the outcome. However, this view is naive. The rules can and do affect who wins and who loses.

A clear example is electoral systems. The United States has a single-member-district system in which the election winners are those candidates who get the most votes in a district. Each district elects a single legislator —the candidate who is its top vote-getter. Most European countries, by comparison, have proportional representation systems, in which seats in the national legislature are distributed according to each party's share of the popular vote. The European system makes it possible for smaller parties to win legislative seats. A party that receives 15 percent of the national vote, for example, will get about 15 percent of the legislative seats. In contrast, the American system discourages smaller parties. A party that receives 15 percent of the national vote might win no seats in Congress. Only if its vote was concentrated in particular geographical areas would it have a chance of finishing ahead of a major party in any district.

Which system—the proportional or the single-member district—do you prefer? Why? Is one system inherently better suited to the Unites States than the other? Why?

If the United States had an electoral system based on proportional representation, it would probably have more than two competitive parties. What might these other parties be? Do you think one of them might be a socialist party? Do you think one might be a regional party and, if so, which region? How about a party representing the fundamentalist Christian right? Black people? Women? Others? Would proportional representation make a great or only a marginal difference in U.S. politics?

Can you think of any other changes in the rules of the game that would alter the distribution of power in the American political system?

him the ranking Republican on the Senate Finance Committee and thus an influential voice in the formulation of Republican positions on tax issues within the Senate.

The fragmentation of power that characterizes the American political system gives the major parties almost no choice but to accept divisions within their ranks. Because members of Congress are highly responsive to the interests of the states and districts they represent, members of the same party can find themselves at odds over national issues. Yet in attending to their constituents' needs and demands, they build an electoral base separate from that of their party nationally. The party is thus not in a position to dictate what its congressional representatives will do once they are in office.[18]

The pragmatism that helps to maintain the two major parties in a dominant position is also dictated by federalism. Because the parties compete for national, state, and local offices, where the issues and divisions can differ significantly, they cannot realistically demand that their candidates adhere to a common philosophy.[19]

Policy Formulation and Coalition Formation in the Two-Party System

The overriding goal of a major American political party is to gain control of government by getting its candidates elected to office. This goal can be stated

[18] Frank Sorauf, *Party Politics in America*, 5th ed. (Boston: Little, Brown, 1984), 42–43.
[19] Duverger, *Political Parties*, bk. II, ch. 1.

Political party members in America do not feel tied to one ideological view, as many of their European counterparts do. For example, the Republican senators pictured here cover the ideological spectrum: Jesse Helms (*center*) represents the conservative wing of the party and Mark Hatfield (*right*) the liberal end, with John Warner (*left*) in between. (Wide World Photos)

more broadly in terms of the party system's major function: the organization of political conflict.[20] The parties transform conflict over society's goals into electoral competition in which the losers accept the winners' right to make policy decisions. In this **party competition,** which is at the core of the democratic process, the parties form coalitions of interests, articulate policy and leadership positions, and compete for electoral dominance. In the process, political parties give individual citizens a choice among various leaders and policies.

The choice that parties offer, however, depends significantly on the type of party system in which they operate. Because there are only two major American parties, their policies and bases of support differ from what could be expected if numerous parties were in competition. To gain control of the government, the Republicans or Democrats must attract a majority of the electorate, and so must appeal to a broad and diverse set of interests. The need to gain wide support usually leads both parties to advocate moderate policies and to avoid taking highly specific positions on controversial issues. American parties, Clinton Rossiter said, are "creatures of compromise."[21]

Rossiter's characterization describes American parties with reasonable accuracy during normal times. In periods of national crisis or political realignment, however, the parties have sometimes pursued policies that have sharply divided Americans and offered them a clear choice. To be complete, a description of the alternatives provided by the major American parties must include their actions in periods both of stability and of change, as the following discussion indicates.

The American people are quite competent to judge a political party that works both sides of a street.

Franklin D. Roosevelt

[20] E. E. Schattschneider, *The Semisovereign People: A Realist's View of Democracy in America* (New York: Holt, Rinehart and Winston, 1961), 86–96.
[21] Clinton Rossiter, *Parties and Politics in America* (Ithaca, N. Y.: Cornell University Press, 1960), 11.

Italy has many political parties, offering clear-cut alternatives to the country's voters. The Italian Communist party is shown here convening in March 1990 to discuss its response to the collapse of communism in Eastern Europe. In the United States, by contrast, the two major parties moderate their views in order to appeal to the broad center of the political spectrum. (F. Origlia/Sygma)

SEEKING THE POLITICAL CENTER

In Europe's multiparty systems, the various parties of the left (liberal), right (conservative), and center (moderate) typically offer voters sharply defined alternatives. A far-left party, for example, may advocate government control of all key industries, while a far-right party may propose the elimination of all but the most essential social-welfare programs. These differences are substantial and reflect the wide spectrum of political opinions in European societies and the need of each party to stake out a clear position along this spectrum.[22]

By comparison, most Americans prefer moderate policies to ideological extremism, so the two major parties tend to stay close to the center of the political spectrum.[23] Any time a party makes a pronounced shift toward either extreme, the middle is left open for the opposing party. Barry Goldwater, the Republican presidential nominee in 1964, proposed the elimination of mandatory social security and said he would consider the tactical use of small nuclear weapons in such wars as the Vietnam conflict—extreme conservative positions that cost him many votes. At the opposite end of the spectrum, liberal George McGovern, nominated by the Democrats in 1972, advocated an immediate and unconditional withdrawal of U.S. combat troops from Vietnam and a guaranteed annual income for every American family; he was resoundingly defeated in the general election.

Republican and Democratic candidates usually try to develop stands that will have broad appeal or at least will not alienate significant blocs of voters. Often this strategy results in campaigns in which the candidates avoid committing themselves to unequivocal stands on controversial issues. This tendency has

[22] Duverger, *Political Parties,* 372–392.
[23] See Anthony Downs, *An Economic Theory of Democracy* (New York: Harper & Row, 1957), chs. 7 and 8.

been thoroughly documented in Benjamin Page's study of presidential campaign rhetoric from 1928 to 1976.[24] The main issue of the 1968 campaign, for example, was the United States' involvement in Vietnam, but neither Richard Nixon nor Hubert Humphrey outlined a detailed plan for dealing with that issue (see box).

At times, however, the parties have strayed from the political center and still prevailed. In 1980 Ronald Reagon campaigned on a platform calling for sharp cuts in domestic spending programs and for a confrontational policy toward the Soviet Union (see Chapter 10). These positions were worrisome to most Americans, but they still preferred Reagan to the Democratic incumbent, Jimmy Carter, who most Americans felt had mishandled the presidency.

The lesson of Reagan's victory and some others, such as Franklin D. Roosevelt's in 1932, is that the center of the American political spectrum can be moved. Candidates risk a crushing defeat by straying too far from established ideas during times of general satisfaction with government, but they may do so with some chance for victory when times are turbulent. Then, if conditions improve, the American public may show their support for the new president's initiatives by reelecting him, thereby contributing to the creation of a new political center.

Changes in the presidential nomination system since 1972 have made it more difficult for presidential candidates to avoid taking stands on issues.[25] To win

---

★ THE MEDIA AND THE PEOPLE

HOW CANDIDATES TALK ABOUT ISSUES

The following excerpt from Richard Nixon's televised acceptance speech at the 1968 Republican convention illustrates the tendency of major-party candidates to talk in generalities, identifying problems that need the government's attention but avoiding taking clear-cut positions on controversial issues. Nixon's vague statements on Vietnam are particularly revealing. The Vietnam war was the issue uppermost in voters' minds in 1968, but it was also an issue over which Americans were sharply divided, so Nixon was careful to speak about it in broad terms and link it to problems that were bothersome to all.

As we look at America, we see cities enveloped in smoke and flame. We hear sirens in the night. We see Americans dying on distant battlefields abroad. We see Americans hating each other; fighting each other; killing each other at home. And as we see and hear these things, millions of Americans cry out in anguish: Did we come all this way for this? Did American boys die in Normandy and Korea and in Valley Forge for this?

When the strongest nation in the world can be tied down for four years in a war in Vietnam with no end in sight . . . then it's time for new leadership for the United States of America. . . . Never has so much military and economic and diplomatic power been used so ineffectively. And if after all of this time and all of this sacrifice and all of this support there is still no end in sight, then I say the time has come for the American people to turn to new leadership—not tied to the mistakes and the policies of the past. That is what we offer to America. And I pledge to you tonight that the first priority foreign policy objective of our next Administration will be to bring an honorable end to the war in Vietnam.

---

[24] Benjamin I. Page, *Choices and Echoes in Presidential Elections* (Chicago: University of Chicago Press, 1978), 132, 153–156.

[25] Denis G. Sullivan, Jeffrey L. Pressman, and F. Christopher Arterton, *Explorations in Convention Decision Making* (San Francisco: W. H. Freeman, 1976).

TABLE 11-1   Ideology of Voters and National Delegates, by Party, 1988

Ideology	Democratic Delegates	Democratic Voters	All Voters	Republican Voters	Republican Delegates
Liberal	39%	25%	20%	12%	1%
Conservative	5	22	30	43	60

SOURCE: *New York Times*, August 14, 1988, 32.

nomination, presidential contenders must appeal directly to primary electorates, which tend to be somewhat ideological. Republican primary voters are more conservative on the whole than other Republicans, and Democratic primary voters tend to be somewhat more liberal than other Democrats.[26] The national convention delegates who choose the presidential nominees are even more ideologically oriented (see Table 11-1). To satisfy these primary voters and convention delegates, candidates must sometimes take strong stands that they might otherwise try to avoid.

PARTY COALITIONS

The groups and interests that support a party are collectively referred to as the **party coalition.** In multiparty systems, each party is supported by a rather narrow range of interests. European parties tend to divide along class lines, with the center and right parties drawing most of their votes from the middle and upper classes and the left parties drawing theirs from the working class. By comparison, America's two-party system requires each party to accommodate a wide range of interests in order to gain the voting plurality necessary to win elections. The art of campaigning is to persuade people who think differently to vote alike. The Republican and Democratic coalitions are therefore very broad. Each includes voters of every racial, ethnic, religious, regional, and economic grouping (see Figure 11-3). Only one sizable group aligns itself overwhelmingly with one party: 90 percent of black Americans have voted Democratic in recent presidential elections.[27]

Although the Republican and Democratic coalitions overlap, they are hardly identical. Each party likes to appear to be all things to all Americans, but in fact each builds its coalition through a process of both unification and division. If a party did not stand for something—if it never took sides—it would lose all support.

Since the 1930s, the major policy differences between the Republicans and the Democrats have involved the national government's role in solving social and economic problems. Each party has supported government action to promote economic security and social equality, but the Democrats have

---

[26] See Jeane Kirkpatrick, *The New Presidential Elite* (New York: Russell Sage Foundation, 1976), ch. 10; Norman H. Nie, Sidney Verba, and John Petrocik, *The Changing American Voter* (Cambridge, Mass.: Harvard University Press, 1976), ch. 12.

[27] For thorough analyses of where the Republican and Democratic parties have found their votes in recent presidential campaigns, see Robert Axelrod, "Where the Votes Come From: An Analysis of Electoral Coalitions," *American Political Science Review* 66 (March 1972): 11–20; "Communications," *American Political Science Review* 68 (June 1974): 717–720; "Communications," *American Political Science Review* 76 (June 1982): 393–396.

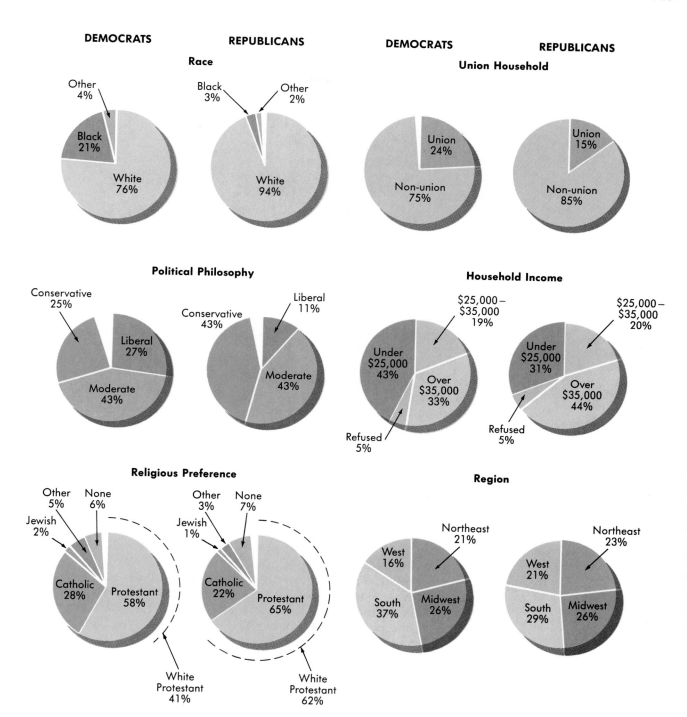

FIGURE 11-3 The Makeup of the Republican and Democratic Party Coalitions
Source: New York Times/CBS News Polls, March 19–22, May 9–12, and July 5–8, 1988, reported in New York Times, July 17, 1988, 16. Data are based on responses of self-identified Democrats (n = 1,177) and self-identified Republicans (n = 994).

The Republican party has started to try to make inroads among black Americans, who have long sided with the Democratic party. Neither major party can afford to ignore the interests of any sizable voting bloc. (Cynthia Johnson/Gamma-Liaison)

consistently favored a greater degree of governmental involvement. Major social-welfare and civil rights programs have been enacted during Democratic administrations, particularly those of Franklin Roosevelt and Lyndon Johnson. To some extent, the national Democratic party's coalition reflects this tradition: it draws support disproportionately from society's "underdogs"—blacks, union members, the poor, city dwellers, Jews, and other "minorities."[28] Of course, many formerly underprivileged groups that are now part of the middle class have remained loyal to the Democratic party, which also includes a significant proportion of the nation's better-educated and higher-income voters.

Throughout the 1970s, the Republican coalition consisted mainly of white, middle-class Protestants. Richard Scammon and Ben Wattenberg described the Republicans as the party of the unpoor and the unblack—in short, the exact opposite of the Democratic party.[29] This characterization ignored the overlapping nature of the parties; if three-fifths of Catholics in 1970 were Democrats, then two-fifths—a hefty proportion—were Republicans. The same was true of working-class Americans. Nevertheless, the Republican coalition was, overall, remarkably homogeneous for an American major party.[30] However, the GOP has recently made inroads among such traditionally Democratic groups as Catholics, Hispanics, and blue-collar workers, and the two major parties are, today, roughly equal in numerical strength among the voters (see Chapter 10).

There is a self-limiting feature to the national party coalitions. The larger

[28] See Richard L. Rubin, *Party Dynamics: The Democratic Coalition and the Politics of Change* (New York: Oxford University Press, 1976).
[29] Richard M. Scammon and Ben J. Wattenberg, *The Real Majority* (New York: Coward, McCann & Geoghegan, 1970), chs. 4–5.
[30] Everett Carll Ladd, *Where Have All the Voters Gone?* (New York: Norton, 1978), xxii.

party can dominate the other only by building a broader coalition, but this broader base can ultimately be its undoing: the party cannot continue indefinitely to satisfy all the groups in its coalition.[31] As a party attracts more interest groups, the likelihood of conflict among them increases. The Democratic party, for example, could not possibly have met the demands of both black Americans and white southerners over the long term. Perhaps the surprising aspect of the Democrats' New Deal coalition was not its eventual decline but its longevity— its survival for almost fifty years. If the Republican party should gain a clear-cut majority status, it too can be expected to have problems in managing its coalition. Indeed, a source of internal division may already exist in the growing role of fundamentalist Christians within the GOP. In the presidential elections of 1980 through 1988, 75 percent of fundamentalists voted Republican, but the fundamentalists' strong views on school prayer, abortion, and other social issues are not shared by many traditional Republicans.

Popular Influence and America's Two-Party System

"It is the competition of political organizations that provides the people with the opportunity to make a choice," E. E. Schattschneider once wrote. "Without this opportunity popular sovereignty amounts to nothing."[32] Thus the competitive nature of America's two major parties is a central issue in any evaluation of the nation's politics. Do the parties in fact give the public a meaningful choice?

Critics who contend that public policy in America is controlled by a wealthy elite argue that the two parties do not offer a real alternative.[33] These critics emphasize the tendency of Republican and Democratic policies to converge and, when it comes to potentially divisive issues, to be less than clear-cut.[34] In truth, the U.S. two-party system does not produce the range of alternatives offered by Europe's multiparty systems. For nearly a century, for example, Europe has had major socialist parties, whereas the U.S. party system has never offered socialism as a serious alternative. Each U.S. major party has embraced private enterprise to a degree not found elsewhere. Of course, the American public has shared this attachment to private initiative, although from time to time polls have indicated public support for social-welfare alternatives. In the two decades following World War II, for example, the American public, by a bare majority and apparently without much intensity, indicated a preference for a comprehensive system of government-paid health care. President Truman did propose legislation for such a health-care system in the late 1940s, but the plan never came close to receiving the necessary congressional approval.

Noting such examples, leftist critics argue that America's major parties are tools of upper-class interests. Ironically, the Republican and Democratic parties

★ ANALYZE THE ISSUE

Two Parties, Limited Choice
The public's only hope for sustained, predictable influence is concerted action. The Democratic and Republican parties provide the opportunity for such action, but at the cost of a substantial narrowing of the options. On what major issues to do you think the parties are furthest apart? Closest together? Which issues are the most significant—those on which the parties' positions are most similar or those on which they most differ?

---

[31] See John R. Petrocik, *Party Coalitions: Realignments and the Decline of the New Deal System* (Chicago: University of Chicago Press, 1981).
[32] Schattschneider, *Semisovereign People,* 140.
[33] See G. William Domhoff, *Who Rules America Now?* (Englewood Cliffs, N.J.: Prentice-Hall, 1983), 117–129.
[34] Donald M. Wittman, "Parties as Utility Maximizers," *American Political Science Review* 67 (June 1973): 498.

★ HOW THE UNITED STATES COMPARES

PARTY SYSTEMS

For nearly 160 years, electoral competition in the United States has centered on the Republican and Democratic parties. By comparison, most democracies have a multi-party system, in which three or more parties receive substantial support from voters. The difference is significant. In a two-party system, the parties tend to have overlapping coalitions and programs, because each party must appeal to the middle-of-the-road voters who provide the margin of victory. In multiparty systems, particularly those with four or more strong parties, the parties tend to separate themselves, as each tries to secure the enduring loyalty of voters who have a particular viewpoint. Whether a country has a two-party or multiparty system depends on several factors, including its traditions, its social composition, and the nature of its electoral system.

NUMBER OF COMPETITIVE PARTIES

Two	Three	Four or More
New Zealand	Canada	Belgium
United States	Germany	Denmark
	Great Britain	France
		Israel
		Italy
		Netherlands
		Norway
		Sweden

★ ANALYZE THE ISSUE

The Similarity of the Two Major Parties
George Wallace attacked the Republican and Democratic parties by saying that "there's not a dime's worth of difference" between them. Do you agree with Wallace's contention? Would it make much difference today if the Republicans rather than the Democrats had majorities in both the House and the Senate?

have not been spared by critics on the right, either. After all, it was George Wallace, a conservative, who made the slogan "Not a dime's worth of difference between them" the basis for a third-party campaign. Wallace contended that the Republican and Democratic parties were both overly solicitous of the opinions of minorities and liberals. Indeed, until Ronald Reagan's election in 1980, most of the attacks on the parties from political circles (as opposed to academic circles) came from the right, not the left.

Nonetheless, the Republican and Democratic parties do offer somewhat different alternatives and, at times, a clear choice. When Roosevelt was elected president in 1932, Johnson in 1964, and Reagan in 1980, the parties were relatively far apart in their priorities and programs. Roosevelt's New Deal was an extreme alternative within the American political tradition and caused a decisive split along party lines. Similarly, voters had a real choice between Johnson's Great Society initiatives and the alternatives proposed by Goldwater. And Reagan's tax, spending, and defense priorities pitted Republicans against Democrats in bitter debate. In each case, the nature of the conflict was predictable, given the two parties' differing policy traditions and electoral coalitions.

America's parties tend to draw apart as public dissatisfaction and demands for new alternatives grow. In such periods of unrest as the 1930s, 1960s, and 1980s, the Democratic and Republican parties have clearly promoted different interests within society. When the parties later began to converge again, that trend was always in part a reflection of a change in the distribution of public attitudes.

The continuous adjustment of America's two parties to the mood of the electorate reflects their competition for power. Each party has a realistic chance of winning a national election and thus has an incentive to respond to changes in public opinion. Viewed differently, a competitive opposition party is the public's best protection against an unresponsive government; the out-party provides the electorate with an alternative. Even in its weakened position after the Roosevelt years, the Republican party was strong enough to provide an alternative when the public's dissatisfaction with the Democrats rose, as in 1952, 1968, and 1980 at the presidential level and in 1946, 1952, and 1980 at the congressional level.

It is the case, moreover, that the public perceives important differences between the parties that are consistent with each party's traditions (see Chapter 10). A 1991 New York Times/CBS News poll, for example, indicated that Americans believed the Republican party was more likely to practice fiscal restraint, promote economic prosperity, nominate good presidential candidates, and build a strong military; they thought the Democratic party was more likely to improve the health-care system, keep the nation out of war, do a better job of handling unemployment, and pay attention to the concerns of people like themselves (see Figure 11-4).

FIGURE 11-4 Perceptions of the Differences between the Republican and Democratic Parties
Source: New York Times/CBS News survey, 1991. Reported in Adam Clymer, "Poll Finds G.O.P. Growth Erodes Dominant Role of the Democrats," New York Times, July 14, 1991, 1.

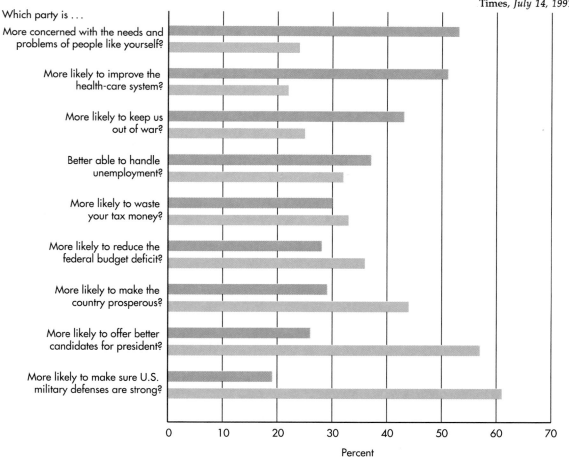

Which party is . . .

More concerned with the needs and problems of people like yourself?

More likely to improve the health-care system?

More likely to keep us out of war?

Better able to handle unemployment?

More likely to waste your tax money?

More likely to reduce the federal budget deficit?

More likely to make the country prosperous?

More likely to offer better candidates for president?

More likely to make sure U.S. military defenses are strong?

Percent

Democratic party   Republican party

In sum, America's parties do offer the public a real choice, even if the alternatives are not so sharply defined as those in some other democratic nations. Without political parties the American public would be in a weak position to influence the broad direction of public policy through elections. However, the capacity of America's party system to propose coherent and consistent alternatives may be undergoing a long-term decline. The candidate-selection process in the United States has become more and more individualistic: within each party, candidates are increasingly free to define for themselves the policies on which they will campaign. The significance of this development to the public and to the parties is discussed in the next chapter.

Summary

Political parties serve to link the public with its elected leaders. In the United States this linkage is provided by a two-party system; only the Republican and Democratic parties have any chance of winning control of government. Most other democracies have a multiparty system. The fact that the United States has only two major parties is explained by several factors: an electoral system—characterized by single-member districts—that makes it difficult for third parties to compete for power; each party's willingness to accept political leaders of differing views; and a political culture that stresses compromise and negotiation rather than ideological rigidity. America's two major parties are also maintained by laws and customs that support their domination of elections.

Because the United States has only two major parties, each of which seeks to gain majority support, they normally tend to avoid controversial or extreme political positions. The parties typically pursue moderate and somewhat overlapping policies. Their appeals are designed to win the support of a diverse electorate with moderate opinions. This form of party competition is reflected in the Republican and Democratic coalitions. Although the two parties' coalitions are not identical, they do overlap significantly: each party includes large numbers of individuals who represent nearly every significant interest in the society. Nonetheless, the Democratic and Republican parties sometimes do offer sharply contrasting policy alternatives, particularly in times of political unrest. It is at such times that the public has its best opportunity to make a decisive difference through its vote.

Major Concepts

multiparty system
party coalition
party competition
political party

proportional representation
single-member districts
two-party system

Suggested Readings

Burnham, Walter Dean. *Critical Elections and the Mainsprings of American Politics.* New York: Norton, 1970. The classic analysis of how long-term stability in the electoral process is punctuated periodically by major change.

Duverger, Maurice. *Political Parties.* New York: Wiley, 1954. A classic analysis of types of party systems, their origins, and their effects.

Eldersveld, Samuel J. *Political Parties in American Society.* New York: Basic Books, 1982. An overview of the organization, role, and activities of America's two major parties.

Jewell, Malcolm, and David Olson. *American State Political Parties and Elections,* 2d ed. Homewood, Ill.: Dorsey Press, 1982. A broad overview of state parties with comparative information on the competitiveness of the two-party system at the state level.

Mazmanian, Daniel A. *Third Parties in Presidential Elec-tions.* Washington, D.C.: Brookings Institution, 1984. An assessment of the influence of America's third-party movements, including George Wallace's 1968 campaign.

Page, Benjamin I. *Choices and Echoes in Presidential Elections.* Chicago: University of Chicago Press, 1978. A study of the campaign appeals of the major parties' presidential nominees from 1932 to 1976.

Rosenstone, Steven J., Roy L. Behr, and Edward H. Lazarus. *Third Parties in America.* Princeton, N.J.: Princeton University Press, 1984. An analysis of America's third parties and their impact on the two-party system.

Sartori, Giovanni. *Parties and Party Systems.* Cambridge, England: Cambridge University Press, 1976. A comparative and theoretical assessment of the world's party systems.

PARTY ORGANIZATIONS: CONTESTING ELECTIONS

By the standards of political parties of most Western democracies, the American party organizations are comparatively weak and insubstantial.

Frank J. Sorauf[1]

*T*he 1968 Democratic convention was a last hurrah for party leaders. Led by Mayor Richard Daley, the boss of Chicago's powerful political machine, they delivered the presidential nomination to Lyndon Johnson's vice-president, Hubert H. Humphrey, who had not entered a single primary. His chief opponent for the nomination was Senator Eugene McCarthy, who had fought his way through a dozen state primaries. Party leaders such as Daley regarded McCarthy as a spoiler whose attacks on the Johnson administration's handling of the Vietnam war had driven a wedge in party unity, jeopardizing the Democratic party's chances in the fall election. Rejecting McCarthy's bid, they turned to Humphrey.

Four years later it was Mayor Daley's turn to be voted down at a Democratic convention. After the 1968 campaign, which ended in Humphrey's narrow defeat by Richard M. Nixon, reform elements within the Democratic party forced a change in the rules for selecting convention delegates. Party leaders in a state would no longer be permitted to hand-pick a slate of delegates. All states would have to choose their delegates openly, either through primary elections or through caucuses in which all party voters were invited to participate. Daley defied the new rules and arrived at the 1972 convention as head of an Illinois delegation of old-line party regulars. The convention was controlled by delegates loyal to George McGovern, and they voted to unseat the Daley delegation. In a classic scene of confrontation between the old order and the new, Daley shook his fist in rage at the podium and stalked out of the

---

[1] Frank J. Sorauf, *Party Politics in America*, 5th ed. (Boston: Little, Brown, 1984), 61.

convention, vowing that his Chicago machine would not participate in the fall campaign.

Daley's fall from national power symbolizes the fate of party leaders and organizations in the twentieth century. As the century began, the parties were in firm control of U.S. elections, but individual candidates gradually took command. By the 1960s, the presidential nominating convention was the last party stronghold in national politics. When party leaders after 1968 were denied control of convention delegates, the transition from **party-centered politics** to **candidate-centered politics** was virtually complete. The reality of today's national elections is that candidates have most of the initiative and influence. Candidates for the presidency and for Congress raise most of their own funds, form their own campaign organizations, and choose for themselves the issues that they will emphasize. Parties still play a very important part in election campaigns, but their role is secondary to that of the candidates.

The public's hostility toward political parties is a main reason for the change. The individualistic and egalitarian elements of the nation's political culture create resentment among the public against any concentration of power, including the power of party bosses.[2] Americans have sought to control party organizations through restrictive laws (such as those requiring primary elections) that no other democracy has imposed on its parties. As a result, U.S. **party organizations** are among the weakest in the world and U.S. candidates are among the most independent. Americans prefer a more nearly direct form of democracy—one in which their relationships with candidates are not mediated by party organizations.

Each U.S. party is really three parties in one. There is, first, the party in the electorate, which consists, as we saw in Chapter 10, of the voters who identify with it. Second, there is the party in office, which consists, as was evident in Chapter 11, of those officials elected under its label. And third, there is the party as organization staffed and led by activists, which is the subject of this chapter. The following points are emphasized in the chapter:

★ *The ability of America's party organizations to control nominations, campaigns, and platforms has declined substantially.* Although the parties continue to play an important role, elections are now controlled largely by the candidates, each of whom is relatively free to go his or her own way. This situation is distinctly American. In other democracies, party organizations continue to dominate elections.

★ *U.S. party organizations are decentralized and fragmented. The national organization is a loose collection of state organizations, which in turn are loose associations of autonomous local organizations.* This feature of U.S. parties can be traced to federalism and the nation's diversity, which have made it difficult for the parties to act as instruments of national power.

★ *Candidates' relative freedom to run on platforms of their own devising diminishes the electorate's capacity to influence national policy in a predictable direction.* The candidate choice made by voters in any one constituency has no necessary relation to the choices of voters in other constituencies.

[2] Judson L. James, *American Political Parties* (New York: Pegasus, 1969), 60.

Sometimes a candidate who is not the party's choice can win the primary, as Democratic Senator Bill Bradley did in his first run for the Senate in 1978. (Owen Franken/Sygma)

Elections and the Decline of Party Control

The main business of America's major parties is the contesting of elections. Unlike some European parties, which contribute to public education by publishing newspapers and conducting issue forums, U.S. parties concentrate almost entirely on election campaigns. Ironically, U.S. parties do not completely control any aspect of these campaigns, not even the selection of candidates to run on their tickets. In 1978 Bill Bradley, former New York Knicks basketball star, entered the U.S. Senate race in New Jersey against a candidate supported by Democratic party leaders and the state's governor. Bradley defeated the party's choice in the primary and then went on to win the general election. This is not an isolated example. Candidates who are not recruited by the party often run and sometimes win. Even candidates who have the party's backing are more concerned with marketing themselves than with promoting their party.[3] As William Crotty has noted:

> It is a politics of every candidate for himself, each with an individual campaign organization loyal only to the candidate and disbanded after the election. It is an antiparty politics of fragmentation and transitory candidate organizations. It is a politics with no core, no sense of collective effort. And, it should be added, it is a politics that has captured the political world.[4]

[3] See Robert Agranoff, "The New Style of Campaigning: The Decline of Party and the Rise of Candidate-Centered Technology," in Robert Agranoff, *The New Style in Election Campaigns*, 2d ed. (Boston: Holbrook Press, 1976), 3–48.
[4] William Crotty, "The Party Symbol and Its Changing Meaning," in William Crotty, ed., *The Party Symbol* (San Francisco: W. H. Freeman, 1980), 13.

In the nineteenth and early twentieth centuries, the situation was different. The party organizations were in control of nominations, elections, and platforms. The story of how and why they lost their commanding position is basic to an understanding of the parties' present role and influence.

CONTROL OF NOMINATIONS

Nomination refers to the selection of the individual who will run as the party's candidate in the general election. The legendary William Marcy ("Boss") Tweed of New York City's Tammany Hall machine once remarked, "I don't care who does the electing just so I can do the nominating."[5] Tweed was merely stating the obvious. His Democratic machine so thoroughly dominated New York City elections in the late nineteenth century that his hand-picked nominees were virtually guaranteed election. Even in constituencies where the parties are competitive, the nominating decision is a critical choice because it narrows a large field of potential candidates down to the final two, one Republican and one Democrat.

Party-Controlled Nominations

Until the early twentieth century, nominations were the responsibility of party organizations. In smaller communities where voters had personal knowledge of potential candidates, the parties often had no practical alternative but to nominate popular individuals who wanted to run. In the cities, however, the party organizations were in a commanding position. Party label was the prime influence on urban voters, so it was essential for candidates to have party backing. To receive nomination, an individual had to be loyal to the party organization, a requirement that included a willingness to share with it the spoils of office—government jobs and contracts.

Political spoils enabled party organizations to acquire campaign workers and funds but were also the foundation of party corruption. Unscrupulous party leaders were in a position to extort money from those seeking political favors. When Richard Croker, a Tammany leader, was asked his opinion of the unrestricted coinage of silver, the major political issue of the 1890s, he replied, "I'm in favor of all kinds of money—the more the better."[6]

Widespread corruption made the party organizations targets of Progressive reformers, who had, in addition to a desire for clean government, a partisan objective. The Progressive movement was led by native-born Protestant Republicans whose values were at odds with those of the big-city machines, which were Democratic organizations founded on the support of working-class Catholic immigrants. The machines operated not on the high principle of the public interest, but on the low principle of exchange.[7] They took contributions

[5] James W. Davis, *National Conventions in an Age of Party Reform* (Westport, Conn.: Greenwood Press, 1983), 4.
[6] William L. Riordon, *Plunkitt of Tammany Hall* (New York: Dutton, 1963), xvi.
[7] Dennis R. Judd, *The Politics of American Cities* (Boston: Little, Brown, 1984), ch. 3; for a discussion of the machines' policy orientations, see John Allswang, *Bosses, Machines, and Urban Voters* (Baltimore: Johns Hopkins University Press, 1986).

from business interests in return for favors from City Hall, and then used those contributions to woo the ethnic voters whose support enabled them to control city government. In their day, the machines were the closest things that the United States had to full-service welfare agencies. Jim Pendergast's Kansas City machine, for example, handed out more than government jobs to the party faithful. When they were penniless in winter, the Pendergast machine delivered fuel to their homes. Hundreds of families had turkey and trimmings at the free dinners that "Big Jim" staged each Christmas.[8]

The Progressives fumed over the power of the machines and sought to destroy them through the principle of "party democracy"—the idea that party organizations should properly be run by ordinary voters and not by entrenched bosses. The idea appealed to Americans' sense of individualism and egalitarianism, and gained strong support in many state legislatures. Laws were passed requiring the parties to choose their organizational leaders by secret ballot, to print public notices of their meetings, and to make all major policy decisions in public session.

Primary Elections

The most serious blow struck by the Progressives against the power of the party bosses was the **primary election** (or direct primary) as a method of choosing party nominees. In place of the older system of party-designated nominees, the primary system placed nominations in the hands of voters. In an 1897 speech, Robert M. La Follette, Sr., the Progressive movement's acknowledged leader, advised, "Go back to the first principles of democracy: go back to the people. Substitute for both the caucus and convention a primary election."[9] The philosophy was not unlike that of the Populist party, which preceded the Progressive movement by a few years. A Populist theme was the intent to turn the machinery of government over to the people.

The first primary election law was enacted in 1903 by Mississippi. Within a decade most states had adopted primaries as the means of choosing party nominees for some public offices. Today all states but Virginia have primary elections for contested nominations for U.S. Senate and House seats, and about thirty states use primaries to select their delegates to the presidential nominating conventions (see Chapter 19). Most states have "closed" primaries, in which participation is limited to voters registered or declared at the polls as members of the party whose primary is being held. Less than a fifth of the states use "open" primaries, a form that allows independents and voters of either party to vote in a party's primary, although voters are prohibited by law from participating in both parties' primaries simultaneously. Alaska and Washington have a third form of primary, known as the "blanket" primary. These states provide a single primary ballot listing both the Republican and Democratic candidates by office. Each voter can cast only one vote per office, but can select a candidate of either party. Louisiana has a variation on this form in which all candidates are listed on the ballot but are not identified by party.

[8] Lyle W. Dorsett, *The Pendergast Machine* (New York: Oxford University Press, 1968), 42.
[9] Robert M. La Follette, Sr., *La Follette's Autobiography* (Madison, Wis.: R. M. La Follette, 1913), 197–198; quoted in Sorauf, *Party Politics in America,* 210.

Senator Robert M. La Follette, Sr., of Wisconsin pushed for Progressive reforms, including the use of primary elections to select the parties' candidates. (State Historical Society of Wisconsin)

The closed primary is preferred by party regulars because it restricts participation to those who are registered with the party. The open and blanket primaries allow "outsiders" to influence party nominations, thus weakening party control more than the closed primary does.

Primaries have not completely eclipsed the party organizations. Successful candidacies are normally built on more than raw ambition.[10] Many politicans begin their careers as party volunteers; in this capacity they gain the attention of party leaders, who help them to win their first elective office. From there they move up the ladder. Nevertheless, primaries were the severest blow imaginable to party organizations. Because of primaries, candidates have the option of seeking office on their own, and, once elected (whether with or without the party's help), they can build an independent electoral base that effectively places them beyond the party's control.[11]

Some states have even passed laws limiting party activities during primary election campaigns in order to help ensure that nominations will not be controlled by organizational leaders. One effect of such laws is to discourage the development of strong parties; they are hamstrung by laws that effectively limit the power they will be permitted to acquire. California and Oregon, for instance, prohibit party organizations from endorsing candidates in primary elections. Utah requires the parties to nominate two candidates for each office unless one candidate receives 70 percent of the vote at the state party convention. Other states, including New York and Colorado, allow parties to

---

[10] James, *American Political Parties*, 68.
[11] Sarah McCally Morehouse, "The Effect of Pre-Primary Endorsements on State Party Strength," paper delivered at the 1980 meeting of the American Political Science Association, August 1980, 17.

endorse candidates for nomination but require them also to list on the primary ballot any candidate who gets the support of a certain proportion of the delegates at the state convention (25 percent in New York). New York's parties are also prohibited by law from giving financial support to primary election candidates. The decline of party influence in New York is reflected in the fact that in a number of recent races for governor and U.S. senator, the party-endorsed candidates have lost the primary elections.

The absence of primaries in Europe is one of the main reasons the parties there have remained strong. They control nominations, and European candidates must operate within the party organizations. A popular leader will be given fairly wide latitude by the party, but it is the parties, not the candidates, who are at the center of elections. The European philosophy of party democracy has been unlike that of the United States. Rather than imposing legal restrictions on party activities, European nations have allowed the parties to regulate their own affairs, counting on the threat of electoral defeat to keep them in line. By all accounts, European parties are no less honest than U.S. parties and are considerably more effective.[12]

CONTROL OF ELECTION CAMPAIGNS

Workers, money, and media have always been the key resources in campaigns, but their relative importance has changed over time, as has their control by parties and candidates.

Party Workers

From their grass-roots inception in the Jacksonian era, U.S. parties have depended on a relatively small number of active members. The parties have never had the large dues-paying memberships that characterize some European socialist and labor parties. Even the party machines in their heyday did not attempt to enroll the party electorate as active members. The machine's lowest organizational echelon was the precinct-level unit. Each precinct had several hundred voters but only two party workers, a precinct captain and his assistant.

Patronage was the traditional source of party workers. To get or keep government employment, individuals had to work for the party during election campaigns. Instituted during Andrew Jackson's presidency, this "spoils system" was a perennial target of reformers, and when antiparty sentiment intensified around 1900, the Progressives saw an opportunity to deprive party leaders of their work force. About 10 percent of federal jobs had been placed under civil service in 1883, and the Progressives demanded that merit-based hiring be expanded. As government jobs in the early twentieth century shifted from the patronage to the merit category, the party organizations lost vigor. Today, because of the expanded size of government, thousands of patronage jobs still exist. These government employees help to staff the parties, but many of them are more loyal to the politician for whom they work than to a party organization. In addition, the courts have placed restrictions on patronage

---

[12] Samuel J. Eldersveld, *Political Parties in American Society* (New York: Basic Books, 1982), 96–97.

The media can do a more thorough job of promoting candidates than party organizations ever could. Ann Richards is shown here taping a radio commercial during her successful campaign for the Texas governorship in 1990. (Bob Daemmrich/Stock, Boston)

systems. In a recent ruling, the Supreme Court held that the Constitution prevents the use of partisan criteria in the hiring, promotion, and retention of most public workers.[13]

The parties today get help from volunteers as well as from patronage workers. However, many volunteers are more interested in debating the issues than in distributing party leaflets, and because they are not patronage employees, they cannot be compelled to perform tedious campaign tasks or to work long hours.[14] Another problem with volunteers is that they often have more interest in a particular candidate than in the party.[15] In 1972 anti–Vietnam war activists took over numerous Democratic party organizations in order to secure national-convention delegates for George McGovern but then abandoned those organizations after he failed to win the presidency.

Money and Media

Campaigns for higher office have changed fundamentally in recent decades. The "old politics," which emphasized party rallies and door-to-door canvassing, was based on a large supply of workers. The "new politics" centers on the media and depends on money—lots of it. U.S. Senate campaigns cost well over $1 million, and House campaigns average close to $500,000 (see Chapter 16).

Candidates for major office spend a larger percentage of their budgets on televised political advertising and other media activities than they do on

[13] *Rutan* v. *Republican Party of Illinois*, 88–1872.
[14] See James Q. Wilson, *The Amateur Democrat* (Chicago: University of Chicago Press, 1962); Robert S. Hirschfield, Bert E. Swanson, and Blanche D. Blank, "A Profile of Political Activists in Manhattan," *Western Political Quarterly* 15 (1962): 489–506.
[15] Joseph Schlesinger, *Ambition and Politics* (Chicago: Rand McNally, 1966), 125–133.

grass-roots organizing (see Figure 12-1). The key operatives in the modern campaign are television consultants, pollsters, and direct-mail fund-raising specialists, all of whom operate outside the formal party organizations. These advisers and their services have loosened the parties' hold on candidates.[16] Televised advertising in particular enables candidates to communicate directly and easily with the electorate, thereby reducing the need for grass-roots party workers.[17]

The news media reflect the increase in candidate-centered campaigns. Election news is devoted almost entirely to what the candidates say and do.[18] In earlier times, news coverage of campaigns during the nominating stage was filled with speculation as to what party kingmakers might do. Now, because the nominees are decided in primaries, party leaders are barely visible in election news. Press coverage simply mirrors the reality of today's campaigns: they are candidate-centered, so the news is too.[19]

Candidates also dominate election fund-raising. At the turn of the century, when party machines were at their peak, most campaign funds passed through the hands of party leaders. Today the parties provide only 10 percent of the money spent on congressional campaigns. Candidates now get most of their funds through direct solicitation of individual contributors and interest groups' political action committees (PACs, discussed in Chapter 14).

In European democracies, parties continue to dominate campaign resources. British parties, for example, hire and assign the campaign manager for each of their parliamentary candidates. These managers are party agents and are expected to see that the party's interests, as well as those of the candidates, are

---

[16] Alan R. Gitelson, M. Margaret Conway, and Frank B. Feigert, *American Political Parties* (Boston: Houghton Mifflin, 1984), 84.
[17] See David S. Broder, *The Party's Over* (New York: Harper & Row, 1972).
[18] See Peter Clarke and Susan Evans, *Covering Campaigns: Journalism in Congressional Elections* (Stanford, Calif.: Stanford University Press, 1983); Thomas E. Patterson, *The Mass Media Election* (New York: Praeger, 1980), chs. 3–5.
[19] See Clarke and Evans, *Covering Campaigns.*

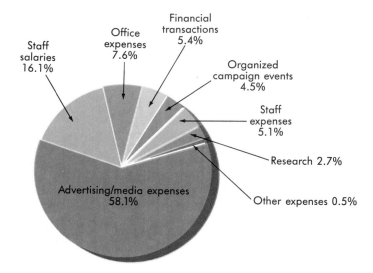

FIGURE 12-1 Allocation of Campaign Expenditures in Races for the U.S. House of Representatives
More congressional campaign funds are spent on the mass-communications media than on grass-roots organization. *Source: Edie N. Goldenberg and Michael W. Traugott,* Campaigning for Congress, *(Washington, D.C.: Congressional Quarterly Press, 1984), 86.*

Staff salaries 16.1%
Office expenses 7.6%
Financial transactions 5.4%
Organized campaign events 4.5%
Staff expenses 5.1%
Research 2.7%
Advertising/media expenses 58.1%
Other expenses 0.5%

★ THE MEDIA AND THE PEOPLE

POLITICAL PARTIES "DON'T GET NO RESPECT"

The comedian Rodney Dangerfield's trademark line is "I don't get no respect." America's political parties could say as much about their coverage by the news media. The press pays a great deal of attention to elected public officials but almost none to organizational party leaders. These leaders are less visible even than interest-group leaders, who tend to get press coverage when an important issue affecting their group surfaces.

The news media's inattention to party organizations reflects trends in both journalism and politics. The news is primarily about people rather than institutions or organizations. National, state, and local party functionaries are less significant as individuals than as organizational operatives. But since organizations are not ordinarily the focus of news, party leaders are not routinely sought out by journalists for news stories. In addition, journalists operate in the reality of a political system that is candidate-centered rather than party-centered. The president, members of Congress, state governors and legislators, mayors and city council members—all these are considered more newsworthy than members of their party organizations because journalists, like everyone else, see elected officials as the central figures of American party politics.

The media's inattention undoubtedly goes a long way toward explaining why party organizations have such a poor public image. There is an old saying that if something is important it will be in the news. Parties are seldom in the news, so, by this reasoning, they must not be very important. In fact, many Americans have a difficult time thinking of reasons that parties *might* be important. The lack of public support for their role makes it more difficult for American political parties to carry out their role effectively.

adequately represented in parliamentary campaigns. Further, European nations allot free television time for campaign messages, which is granted directly to the parties rather than to candidates (see box). Such differences reflect the fact that European elections are party-centered. European candidates do not have the freedom to organize and run on their own, and this constraint has kept them from taking control of campaign media and money.

CONTROL OF PARTY PLATFORMS

Beginning in the 1830s and for more than a century thereafter, U.S. parties had control of the national platforms adopted at the presidential nominating conventions held every four years. Each state party sent a delegation to the national convention, and most of the delegates were high-ranking organizational and elected party officials. The first real business at each convention was the formulation of the policy proposals that made up the platform, and the delegates took the platform seriously as a statement of their common interests and commitments. (Ticket balancing—the practice of choosing a vice-presidential nominee from a different region and wing of the party than the presidential choice—served the same purpose.)

Modern platforms have a somewhat different status than earlier ones because national conventions themselves have changed. Until Franklin D. Roosevelt went to the 1932 Democratic convention to accept his party's nomination in person, prospective nominees by tradition did not attend the convention. William Jennings Bryan was present at the 1896 Democratic convention but was not regarded as a presidential contender until he gave his electrifying

To me, party platforms are contracts with the people.
Harry S Truman

Like many other politicians, State Senator Gonzalo Barrientos of Texas (*at right*) relies more on his own efforts than on his party organization to raise funds and to conduct election campaigns. (Bob Daemmrich/The Image Works)

In 1988 George Bush picked a relatively obscure senator, Dan Quayle of Indiana, to be his running mate. Delegates to the Republican party convention had no say in the selection, but they ratified it by nominating Quayle unanimously. (UPI/Bettmann Newsphotos)

platform speech. The convention was the showcase of the party, not of the nominee.

Today the convention is essentially controlled by the candidate who has accumulated the support of a majority of delegates in the state primaries and caucuses that precede the convention. The loyalty of these delegates, most of whom are *not* high-ranking party organizational and elected leaders, is mainly to the prospective nominee, not to the party (see Chapter 18).

Accordingly, the modern platform is tailored to the views of the potential nominee. For purposes of party unity, recent nominees-to-be have accepted platform compromises with their opponents and have even given their own followers leeway in drafting the platform. But recent nominees have insisted that major "planks" in the platform conform to their own views and that controversial minor planks be omitted. In addition, the vice-presidential nominee can no longer be regarded as the party's choice: the delegates now accept whomever the presidential nominee designates for the second spot on the ticket. In the 1988 Democratic race, for example, Michael Dukakis, who had accumulated a majority of the delegates before the Democratic convention, hand-picked Lloyd Bentsen as his running mate and directed that three platform planks proposed by his chief rival, Jesse Jackson, be rejected by the Democratic national convention. Bentsen was chosen and the Jackson planks were defeated, just as Dukakis instructed.

National platforms have never been officially binding on presidential candidates, much less on candidates for the House and Senate, who have traditionally embraced, ignored, or rejected platform planks as it suited their purposes to

★ HOW THE UNITED STATES COMPARES

POLITICAL PARTIES AND TELEVISION CAMPAIGNING

The Republican and Democratic parties are weak organizationally. They do not have full control over the nomination of candidates and are not the centers of campaign organization. For the most part, candidates in the United States set up their own campaigns, raise their own funds, and determine their own platforms. This pattern is unusual. In most other democracies, party organizations choose the nominees, devise platforms on which candidates must run, and coordinate campaign activities. The United States is atypical for many reasons, among them a cultural bias against political parties and a federal system and demographic diversity that make party unity difficult to achieve.

The candidate-centered nature of U.S. elections is evident even in the use of television. In most democracies, televised campaigning on behalf of candidates takes place through the parties, which receive free air time to make their appeals to voters. U.S. parties do not receive unrestricted free time, but instead may buy advertising time. The candidates, however, have nearly all the money, so it is they who buy and control the advertising time. Some democracies prohibit parties and politicians from buying television time to advertise their appeals.

Country	Paid TV Ads Allowed?	Unrestricted Free TV Time Provided?
Canada	Yes	Yes
France	No	Yes
Germany	No	Yes
Great Britain	No	Yes
Italy	No	Yes
Japan	Yes	Yes
Mexico	Yes	Yes
United States	Yes	No

do so. However, the transition from party-centered to nominee-centered conventions has reduced the applicability of the national platform to congressional campaigns. When the parties' organizational and elected leaders, including members of Congress, had control of the platform, they aimed to persuade the delegates to approve planks on which they could campaign. And by virtue of participation in the deliberations, they had a commitment to the platform. Today most candidates for Congress do not pay much attention to the national platform. They run on a platform of their own choosing.

In European democracies, a party's candidates are expected to campaign on the national platform and, if elected as a governing majority, to support its planks, which are formulated in conjunction with organizational leaders, particularly in the case of labor and socialist parties. In Great Britain's Labour party, for example, the national platform is prepared by an executive committee dominated by organizational leaders but also including elected party representatives.

Party Organizations Today

The influence of U.S. parties has declined relative to that of candidates, but parties are not about to die out. Some scholars suggest that parties in fact are stronger today than in the recent past, even though less strong than at earlier times.[20] Political leaders and activists need an ongoing organization through which they can communicate and work together, and the parties meet that need. Moreover, certain activities, such as voter registration drives, benefit all of a party's candidates and are therefore more efficiently conducted through party organizations. Indeed, efficiency is an important reason that national and state party organizations are staging a comeback of sorts. They have recently

[20] See Cornelius P. Cotter, John F. Bibby, and Robert J. Huckshorn, *Party Organization in American Politics* (New York: Praeger, 1986).

A century ago party bosses so dominated the electoral process that they were regularly accused of stuffing the ballot boxes. This 1871 cartoon by Thomas Nast shows Boss Tweed saying: "You have the liberty of voting for anyone you please; but we have the liberty of counting in any way we please." (The Bettmann Archive)

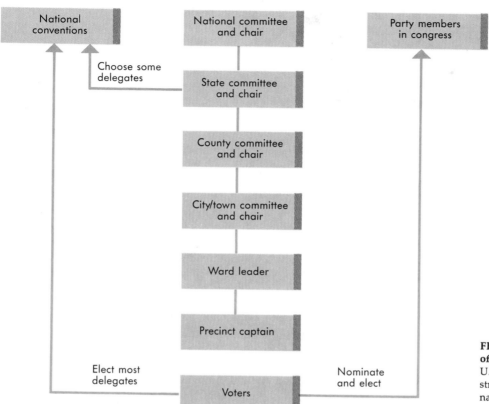

FIGURE 12-2 Organization of the Political Party
U.S. parties today are loosely structured as alliances of national, state, and local organizations.

developed the capacity to assist candidates with polling, research, and media production, which are costly but essential ingredients of a successful modern campaign. Scholars who study local party organizations have also noted signs of party renewal. All agree, however, that the modern age is one of candidate-centered politics.

Structurally, U.S. parties are loose associations of national, state, and local organizations (see Figure 12-2). The national party organizations have almost no say in the decisions of state organizations, and the latter, in turn, cannot tell the local organizations what to do. By comparison, European parties tend to be hierarchical: national parties in Great Britain, for example, have the power to select parliamentary nominees, although they usually follow the recommendations of the local organizations. The major reason that U.S. parties are not hierarchical is the nation's federal system and tradition of local autonomy. Because each governing level in the United States is a competing center of power and ambition, the parties at the national, state, and local levels are able to reject the authority of other levels.

LOCAL PARTY ORGANIZATIONS

U.S. parties are organized from the bottom up, not from the top down. There are about 500,000 elective offices in the United States, of which fewer than 500 are contested statewide and only two—the presidency and vice-presidency—

★ ANALYZE THE ISSUE

**The Effect of
Decentralization on the
Political Parties**
E. E. Schattschneider wrote,
"Decentralization is by all
odds the most important
characteristic of the American
party system." What do you
think is the basis for this
observation? How does
decentralization affect the
parties' ability to serve as
instruments of national
policy?

are contested nationally. All the rest are local offices, so, not surprisingly, at least 95 percent of party activists work within local organizations. In addition, as former Speaker of the House Thomas P. "Tip" O'Neill often said, "All politics is local." Distant events may interest voters, but local conditions are more likely to affect how they vote. Parties are organized at the local level—where the votes are.

It is difficult to generalize about local parties because they vary greatly in their structure and activities. But local parties tend to be strongest in urban areas and in the Northeast and Midwest, where parties traditionally have been more highly organized.[21] In any case, local parties tend to specialize in elections that coincide with local electoral boundaries. Campaigns for mayor, city council, state legislature, county offices, and the like activate local parties to a greater degree than do statewide and national contests. Local parties are less highly involved in campaigns for the U.S. House of Representatives because most congressional districts overlap the boundaries of several local party organizations, and they are not accustomed to working together closely. Nevertheless, parties are active in congressional campaigns and, according to Paul Herrnson, have adapted successfully to the change toward candidate-centered politics.[22]

The Decline of the Big-City Machines

For most Americans, local party organizations are synonymous with the party machines that once flourished in the nation's cities. Well-staffed and tightly disciplined, the machines were welfare agencies for the poor, vehicles of upward mobility for newly arrived immigrant groups, and brokers of public jobs, contracts, and policies for those willing to meet the price. But above all, the machines could win elections, even if victory required stuffing ballot boxes with fraudulent votes.

The party machines deserve their notoriety, but they should not be viewed as representative of party politics in America. Their reign was relatively short: machines emerged during the latter half of the nineteenth century and within a few decades were in retreat in the face of economic and political changes. Moreover, the party machines were located primarily in the big cities of the Northeast and Midwest. Many southern and western cities did not have machinelike parties, and smaller communities rarely had highly organized parties.

Today only a few local parties, including the Democratic organizations in Albany, Philadelphia, and Chicago, bear any resemblance to the old-time machines. Of these organizations the most famous is Chicago's, which is today much less formidable than it was under the first Mayor Daley (his son was elected as Chicago's mayor in 1989) but is still a force to be reckoned with. The Daley machine was built on more than 30,000 patronage jobs in Cook County and Chicago government. Each of Chicago's 3,500 precincts had a precinct captain, and nearly all of them held government jobs. Each captain's responsibility was to get to know the precinct's voters and gain their support. The

[21] Richard J. Tobin and Edward Keynes, "Institutional Differences in the Recruitment Process," *American Journal of Political Science* 19 (November 1975): 674.
[22] Paul S. Herrnson, "Do Parties Make a Difference?: The Role of Party Organizations in Congressional Elections," *Journal of Politics* 48 (1986): 589–615.

Chicago mayor Richard Daley (*at microphones*) was the last of the big-city party machine bosses. He "ruled" Chicago during his 20-year, six-term reign. (UPI/Bettmann Newsphotos)

precinct captains reported to fifty ward leaders, who also held patronage positions and were the link between City Hall and the voters, offering them services in exchange for support at the polls.[23] During his twenty-year reign (1956–1976) as boss of Chicago's Democratic machine, Richard J. Daley gained a national reputation as a political kingmaker. His support was instrumental in the success of John F. Kennedy's drive for the 1960 Democratic presidential nomination. He may even have "stolen" the general election for Kennedy. Daley delayed reporting some of Chicago's returns until the vote totals from downstate Illinois were nearly complete, buying himself time to calculate how many Chicago votes were needed to swing the state in Kennedy's favor. Kennedy narrowly won Illinois, the result, some observers have claimed, of ballot-box stuffing by the Daley machine. It is a fact that without Illinois's votes, Kennedy would have lost the election to Richard Nixon.

Nonmachine Local Organizations

In most urban areas the party organizations are important but bear no resemblance to the old-style machines. These organizations do not have enough workers to staff even a majority of precincts on an ongoing basis. However, they do become active during campaigns, when they open campaign headquarters, conduct voter registration drives, send mailings or deliver leaflets to voters, and help get out the vote (see Table 12-1). The importance of these activities should not be underestimated. Efforts to get out the vote on election day, for example, can make the difference in a close race. In most cities the party organizations also play a role in the nomination of candidates for local office. Many nominees come from party ranks or are solicited by party leaders. Sometimes the organization's backing of a candidate will discourage others from waging a primary fight, and even if a nomination for local office is contested, the party organization is likely to prevail. Most local campaigns are not well funded, and the party's backing of a candidate often spells the difference.

[23] See Milton Rakove, *Don't Make No Waves, Don't Back No Losers* (Bloomington: Indiana University Press, 1975).

TABLE 12-1 Characteristics and Activities of Local Democratic and Republican Parties Most local party organizations are relatively inactive except during election periods.

	Local Democratic Parties	Local Republican Parties
Chairperson devotes at least six hours per week to party business during election periods	77%	78%
Chairperson devotes at least six hours per week to party business during nonelection periods	24	26
Organization has formal annual budget	20	31
Organization has paid, full-time staff	3	4
Organization has a telephone listing	11	16
Organization has a campaign headquarters during election periods	55	60
Organization contributes money to candidates	62	70
Organization prepares press releases during campaigns	55	55
Organization sends mailings to voters	47	59
Organization conducts voter registration drives	56	45

SOURCE: Adapted from James L. Gibson, Cornelius P. Cotter, John F. Bibby, and Robert J. Huckshorn, "Whither the Local Parties?" *American Journal of Political Science* 29 (February 1985): 149–151.

In other localities the party's role is less substantial. In some rural areas, the parties barely exist, if at all. In most suburbs, wards, and smaller communities, the parties exist organizationally but because they have little money and few workers, they are not able to operate effectively as electoral organizations.[24] The individual candidates must carry nearly the full burden. As one candidate in such a locality remarked, "I cannot count on the party to do what it should—like registration, hand out literature, arrange coffees and meetings, and turn out the vote. The party should also at least provide poll watchers, but often [does not]."[25]

Party organizational strength at the local level may have increased slightly in recent years.[26] Today's party activists include many well-educated people who have strong communication and organizational skills, and they have used these skills to good advantage in their party work. Local organizations have recently also received some organizational support from the state and national levels, which they have used to adapt to today's poll- and media-oriented campaigns.

[24] Robert J. Huckshorn, *Party Leadership in the States* (Amherst: University of Massachusetts Press, 1976), 234.
[25] Quoted in Malcolm Jewell and David Olson, *American State Political Parties and Elections*, 2d ed. (Homewood, Ill.: Dorsey Press, 1982), 185.
[26] James L. Gibson, John P. Frendreis, and Laura L. Vertz, "Party Dynamics in the 1980s: Change in County Party Organizational Strength, 1980–84," *American Journal of Political Science* 33 (1989): 67–90.

STATE PARTY ORGANIZATIONS

At the state level, each party is headed by a central committee made up of members of local party organizations and local and state officeholders. These state central committees do not meet regularly, and they provide only general policy guidance for the state organizations. Day-to-day operations and policy are directed by a chairperson, who is a full-time, paid employee of the state party. The central committee appoints the chairperson, but it often accepts the individual recommended by the party's leading politician, usually the governor or a U.S. senator.[27]

In recent decades the state parties have expanded their budgets and staffs considerably, and so have been able to play a more active electoral role. On average, state parties now have an annual budget of about $500,000 and a staff of about ten people.[28] In contrast, thirty years ago about half of the state party organizations had no permanent staff at all. Heightened party competition is one reason that state party staffs have expanded. For example, Georgia's Democratic leaders in the early 1980s felt they had no choice but to enlarge their state organization because the Republicans had bolstered theirs and were making inroads on public offices that Democrats had held since the Reconstruction era, after the Civil War.[29] The increase in state party staffs is due largely to improvements in communication technology, such as computer-assisted direct mail, which have made it easier for political organizations of all kinds, parties included, to raise funds. Having acquired an ability to pay for permanent staffs, state parties have developed them in order to expand their activities, which range from polling to issues research to campaign management. (These activities are discussed in detail later in this chapter.)

State party organizations concentrate on statewide races, including those for governor and U.S. senator,[30] and also emphasize races for the state legislature. They play only a small role in campaigns for national or local offices, and in most states they do not endorse candidates in statewide primary contests. Some states, such as New York and Connecticut, hold party conventions to endorse candidates for nomination to state office. The local party organizations designate the delegates to these conventions.

NATIONAL PARTY ORGANIZATIONS

The national party organizations are structured much like those at the state level: they have a national committee, a national party chairperson, and a support staff (see Figure 12-3). The national headquarters for the Republican and Democratic parties are located in Washington, D.C. Although in theory the

[27] Jewell and Olson, *American State Political Parties,* 67–70.

[28] James L. Gibson, Cornelius P. Cotter, John F. Bibby, and Robert J. Huckshorn, "Assessing Party Organizational Strength," *American Journal of Political Science* 27 (May 1983): 200; John F. Bibby, Cornelius P. Cotter, James L. Gibson, and Robert L. Huckshorn, "Parties in State Politics," in Virginia Gray, Herbert Jacob, and Kenneth N. Vines, eds., *Politics in the American States* (Boston: Little, Brown, 1983), 77.

[29] Robin Toner, "Georgia Democrats Say Lance Move Helps Party," *New York Times,* July 8, 1985, A–13.

[30] See, for example, Sarah McCally Morehouse, "Money versus Party Effort: Nominating for Governor," *American Journal of Political Science* 34 (1990): 706–724.

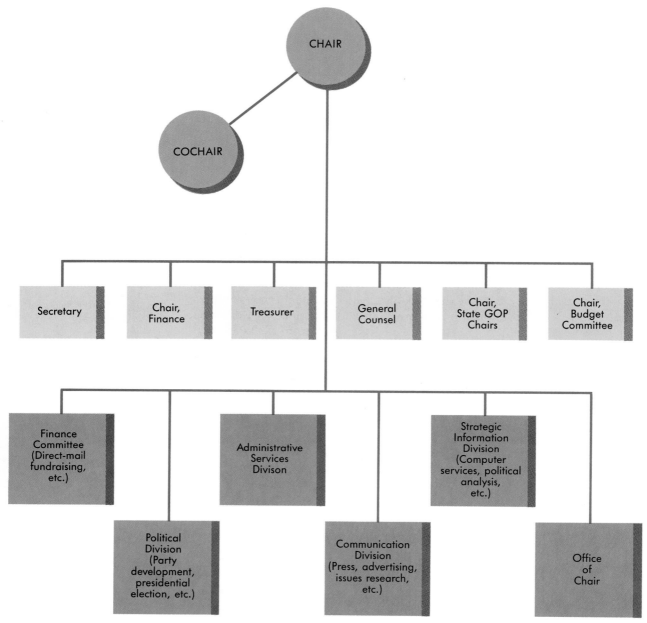

**FIGURE 12-3 Organization
Chart of the Republican
National Committee**
*Source: Graham Paterson,
Republican National Committee
(1989).*

national parties are run by their committees, neither the Democratic National Committee (DNC) nor the Republican National Committee (RNC) has great power. "A national committee," the columnist Thomas Stokes once said, "never nominated anybody, never elected anybody, never established party policy."[31] Although Stokes's claim is a slight exaggeration, it is true that the RNC (with more than 150 members) and the DNC (with more than 300

---

[31] Quoted in Hugh A. Bone, *American Politics and the Party System,* 3d ed. (New York: McGraw-Hill, 1965), 202.

Ron Brown (*center*) was chosen as chairman of the Democratic National Committee in 1989. This position has become more symbolic than influential in recent years. (R. Maiman/ Sygma)

members) are too cumbersome to act as deliberative bodies. Besides, neither party can afford the expense of having its national committee meet for the long periods that would be required to forge party policy. Consequently, the national committees are convened only periodically, to ratify decisions made by a smaller core of party leaders.

The RNC and the DNC include members chosen by each of the state parties and recently have striven for demographic representation as well. "Each national committee," Samuel Eldersveld wrote, "seeks to include blacks, women, persons from labor, business, and farm organizations, as well as representatives from different ethnic, socioeconomic, and age groups."[32] With all these efforts to achieve balance in other areas, the DNC and RNC are still not ideologically representative. Democrats on the DNC are more liberal as a whole than rank-and-file Democrats, and Republicans on the RNC are more conservative than rank-and-file Republicans.[33]

The national party's day-to-day operations are directed by a national chairperson chosen by the national committee. When a party controls the White House, the president's choice for chairperson is accepted by the committee. The position of party chair was once highly coveted because its occupant was expected to run the party's presidential campaign and coordinate patronage appointments. These responsibilities have since been assigned elsewhere, so the position of chair has declined in importance.

The national party administers the quadrennial presidential nominating convention. This is a major responsibility, but it carries no political power. Influence at the national conventions rests with the delegates, who are chosen in the states they represent, although the national party organizations are legally empowered to tell state organizations how to choose and certify their

[32] Eldersveld, *Political Parties in American Society*, 106.
[33] William Crotty, "National Committees as Grass-Roots Vehicles of Representation," in Crotty, *Party Symbol*, 33–49.

In organizing their campaigns, candidates for major office depend more heavily on professional consultants than on party leaders. One of these consultants is Richard Viguerie, who pioneered the use of computerized mailings to raise funds for Republican candidates. (Dennis Brack/Black Star)

national convention delegates.[34] When it comes to electoral activity, the national party organizations concentrate on campaigns for national office—the Senate, House, and presidential races. Both the Republican and Democratic national parties raise campaign funds and distribute them directly to their candidates for Congress.

A NEW PARTY ROLE: SERVICING CANDIDATE-CENTERED CAMPAIGNS

Facing the fact that campaigns have become candidate-centered, the national and state parties have assumed a service role, helping candidates to conduct their personal campaigns. A key figure in this development was William Brock, who became the GOP's national committee chair in 1976. He believed that one way to revive the Republican party, which was in disarray after the Watergate scandal and Nixon's resignation, was to strengthen the national organization. With its close ties to business and upper-middle-class interests, the Republican party has always had a fund-raising advantage over its rival party, and Brock sought to capitalize on this advantage through a nationwide direct-mail fund-raising campaign. By 1982 the Republican party's mailing list included

[34] *Cousins* v. *Wigoda*, 419 U.S. 477 (1975); *Democratic Party of the United States* v. *La Follette*, 450 U.S. 107 (1975).

over one million names and had been used to raise $130 million for the party's election efforts.[35]

Brock also decided that the GOP would take full advantage of new campaign technologies. The national Republican organization developed campaign management "colleges" for candidates and their staffs, compiled massive amounts of electoral data, sent field representatives to assist state and local party leaders, and established a media production division. The media division prepares advertising packages for candidates and assists them in buying commercial time on television and radio. In 1980 the Republican party used its in-house media capacity to produce a national advertising campaign, the first time that a party had done so. Based on the theme "Vote Republican—for a Change," the $9.5 million campaign attacked the Democrats for their handling of national government.[36]

In 1982 the Democratic party followed Brock's lead, mounting a national advertising campaign against Ronald Reagan's economic policies, but its later start and less affluent followers have kept the Democrats behind the GOP in spending (see Figure 12-4).[37] Modern campaigns, as David Adamany notes, are based on a "cash economy," and Democrats are relatively cash-poor.[38]

Fund-raising problems are not the only reason for the Democratic party's inability to match the Republicans' organizing efforts. The Democrats are a more deeply divided party, and the national organization has been preoccupied with the issue of fair representation of the party's various factions, including organized labor, women, racial minorities, and southerners.[39]

Because of their expanded activities, the national parties now play a more important role in election campaigns. The range of services they provide, from candidate schools to polls to media assistance to money, is impressive. The role

[35] Larry Sabato, "New Campaign Techniques and the American Party System," in Vernon Bogdanor, ed., *Parties and Democracy in Britain and America* (New York: Praeger, 1984), 202–206.
[36] Ibid.
[37] See Peter Byrne Edsall, *The New Politics of Inequality* (New York: Norton, 1984).
[38] David Adamany, "Political Parties in the 1980s," in Michael J. Malbin, ed., *Money and Politics in the United States* (Chatham, N.J.: Chatham House, 1984), 114.
[39] See Denis G. Sullivan, Jeffrey L. Pressman, Benjamin I. Page, and John J. Lyons, *The Politics of Representation: The Democratic Convention, 1972* (New York: St. Martin's Press, 1974).

Millions of dollars

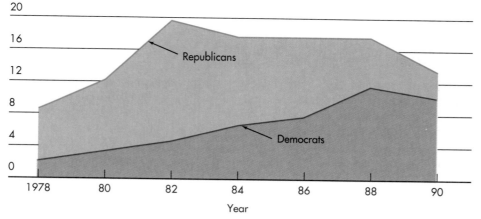

FIGURE 12-4 Democratic and Republican Party Spending, 1978–1990
The Republican party significantly outspends the Democratic party. The figures include spending on behalf of congressional candidates by national, state, and local party committees.
Source: Federal Elections Commission.

of national party organizations in the funding of campaigns is particularly crucial. Even more important than the Democratic and Republican national committees to the funding of congressional races are the Democratic and Republican campaign committees in the House and Senate, each of which raises its own funds to distribute to congressional candidates. By the late 1980s, these campaign committees provided about 90 percent of party contributions in congressional campaigns.[40] Not a lot of money is involved; congressional candidates get the largest share of their campaign funds from nonparty sources. The congressional committees' contributions, however, have extra weight because they are targeted for competitive races and are timed for maximum impact, such as the closing days of a tight race.

The relationship of parties to candidates is primarily one of service, not of power.[41] Rather than lose an office to the opposition, a party will even contribute to the campaign of a party maverick. In 1986 the national Democratic party made the U.S. Senate race in Florida a top priority, even though its candidate, Bob Graham, had some policy views that were closer to those of Senate Republicans than of his fellow Democrats.

Party Organizations and the Public's Influence

Strong political parties give the public its greatest potential for influence. When a party is cohesive and disciplined enough to adopt a national platform on which all its candidates are willing to run, the electorate has its best opportunity to decide the policies by which the nation will be governed. Voters in all constituencies have a common choice and thus can act together in the election.

Because European parties are strong, national organizations, they can offer this type of choice to their electorates. U.S. parties have not provided it, and today's campaigns do not come anywhere near doing so. Each candidate is relatively free to establish a personal platform. Because candidates of the same party in different constituencies stand for different things, the electorate nationally has only a limited opportunity to elect a lawmaking majority pledged to a common set of policies. Of course, U.S. elections produce governing majorities, and it is safe to assume that most elected officials of a particular party share certain ideas. There are common bonds among elected representatives of the same party even when they run and win on their own.[42] But this is a far cry from a system in which voters everywhere have the same choice.

THE ADVANTAGES AND DISADVANTAGES OF CANDIDATE-CENTERED CAMPAIGNS

Candidate-centered campaigns have some advantages. First, they contribute flexibility and new blood to electoral politics. When political conditions and

[40] Frank J. Sorauf, *Money in American Elections* (Glenview, Ill.: Scott, Foresman, 1988), 132.
[41] Gibson et al., ''Assessing Party Organizational Strength,'' 206; Charles H. Longley, ''National Party Renewal,'' in Gerald M. Pomper, ed., *Party Renewal in America* (New York: Praeger, 1980), 69–86.
[42] William J. Keefe, *Congress and the American People* (Englewood Cliffs, N.J.: Prentice-Hall, 1980), 101.

issues change, self-directed candidates quickly adjust, bringing new problems and possible solutions to the forefront. By comparison, strong party organizations sometimes have difficulty adapting to new realities. For example, the British Labour party in recent years was controlled by old-line activists who were unwilling to recognize that weaknesses in the British economy called for changes in the party's employment and welfare policies.

Second, candidate-centered campaigns encourage national officeholders to be responsive to local interests. Where strong national parties exist, overarching national interests take precedence over local concerns. In France, the Basque and Brittany regions are severely underdeveloped, but their calls for a greater share of the country's resources have gone largely unheeded by major-party representatives in the National Assembly. Members of the U.S. Congress, in contrast, are keenly sensitive to subnational interests. In building personal followings among their state and district constituents, members of Congress respond to local needs. Nearly every significant domestic program enacted by Congress is adjusted to accommodate the interests of states and districts that would otherwise be hurt by the policy. The Johnson administration's Model Cities program of the 1960s, for example, was originally formulated as a way to revitalize the nation's depressed urban centers, such as New York, Detroit, and Chicago. However, members of Congress from states and districts with no large cities refused to vote for the program until it was modified to include smaller and thriving cities within their constituencies, such as Cody, Wyoming; Bangor, Maine; and San Jose, California.

In other respects, however, candidate-centered campaigns are decidedly inferior to party-centered ones. Officeholders' accountability to the public is diminished by candidate-centered politics. If national policy goes awry, an individual member of Congress can always blame the problem on "others" in Congress or on the president.[43] For example, no one in Congress took responsibility for the inefficient use of resources entailed in extending the Model Cities program to cities that were not in dire need of federal assistance. Responsibility is less easily evaded when parties are stronger, because governing success or failure is then a party matter and members of the majority party must share in the credit or blame.

The problem of accountability is apparent from surveys that have asked Americans for their evaluations of Congress as a whole and of their own member of Congress in particular (see Figure 12-5). In the 1960s, the public's judgment about the performance of Congress declined sharply, and it has remained low ever since. Yet, for most of this period, a high proportion of the American people have indicated that they believe their own member of Congress is doing a good job in Washington. This attitude has prevailed in so many districts that the net result in most elections has been a Congress whose membership is little changed from the previous one.

Candidate-centered campaigns are also characterized by the prominent influence of special interests. In a party-based system, power can rest on sheer numbers, so heavy emphasis is placed on appeals to the mass public. In a candidate-based system, by contrast, superior campaign funding is prized. In U.S. elections, money increasingly has come from special interests; in the last

It is time we face facts. The Democratic party has changed. Once it was a real grass-roots organization, sustained by an active membership and able to deliver votes to candidates who stuck up for its platform (and withhold votes from those who didn't). Today it is little more than a fund-raising umbrella for a self-perpetuating club of politicians who feel a greater obligation to their campaign contributors and to other incumbents, regardless of party, than they do to the voters who elected them.

Tony Mazzocchi,
Secretary-Treasurer,
Oil, Chemical, and Atomic
Workers Union, 1991

[43] David E. Price, *Bringing Back the Parties* (Washington, D.C.: Congressional Quarterly Press, 1984), 116.

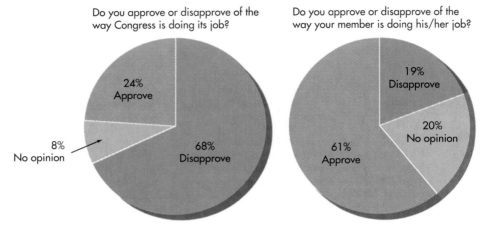

Do you approve or disapprove of the way Congress is doing its job?

24% Approve

8% No opinion

68% Disapprove

Do you approve or disapprove of the way your member is doing his/her job?

19% Disapprove

20% No opinion

61% Approve

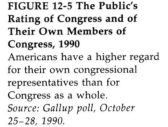

FIGURE 12-5 The Public's Rating of Congress and of Their Own Members of Congress, 1990
Americans have a higher regard for their own congressional representatives than for Congress as a whole.
Source: Gallup poll, October 25–28, 1990.

decade alone, group contributions through PACs have increased threefold in congressional campaigns. When the narrow demands of special interests predominate, candidates are less able to respond to broader national needs. (Chapter 14 discusses the relationship between candidates and interest groups, including PACs, more fully.)

Finally, candidate-centered campaigns can easily degenerate into meaningless showmanship. The 1986 congressional elections are a case in point. They were marked by what Nelson Polsby has called a "policy craze," which is an issue of the moment that is guaranteed to appeal to voters.[44] The policy craze in 1986 was illegal drugs, which was an ideal issue in that no candidate can lose votes for condemning drug dealers. When the news media began to focus on the spread of "crack," a new and inexpensive form of cocaine, congressional candidates quickly jumped on the bandwagon. So did President Ronald Reagan, who was actively campaigning for Republican Senate candidates. Reagan proposed and Congress passed legislation allocating millions of dollars to combat drug trafficking and drug abuse. Incumbent members of Congress held hastily scheduled news conferences to announce that they had voted for the new legislation, and many of them stressed the drug issue in their campaign advertising. After the election, however, the issue died out almost as quickly as it had flared up. When he submitted his budget to Congress the following January, Reagan had deleted all funding for the new drug programs. Only a few members of Congress strenuously objected.

Of course, expediency has always been a characteristic of election politics, whatever the time and whatever the nation. But it peaks when candidates work on their own for election. Unconstrained by a strong party's policy tradition and commitments, candidates are tempted to do whatever it takes to get elected.

THE PRESIDENT AS PARTY SURROGATE

As campaigns in the United States have become increasingly candidate-centered, competition over policy issues has focused on the president. On broad national issues, his initiatives have come to serve as a basis of division, with

[44] Nelson Polsby, *Consequences of Party Reform* (New York: Oxford University Press, 1983), 147.

★ CRITICAL THINKING

CAN U.S. ELECTIONS BE TRULY COMPETITIVE WITHOUT STRONGER PARTIES?

Candidate-centered campaigns are peculiarly American and are often portrayed as the perfect form of electoral competition. The ideal citizen in high school civics textbooks is the one who votes for "the person, not the party." This image is deceptive, however. Candidate-centered elections in fact are deeply anticompetitive. The classic analysis of candidate-centered politics is V. O. Key's study of the one-party "Solid South" in the 1940s. Key observed that candidate-based politics inevitably devolves into conflict between ad hoc coalitions built around personality and special interests. This brand of election campaign is decipherable, if at all, only by those few citizens who are keenly attentive to politics. The ordinary voter, said Key, is continually confronted with "new issues" and "new choices." The contending candidates may be competing over something, but the voter can never be quite sure what it is.

Candidate-centered campaigns are more nearly private than public in the way they are conducted. Campaign money flows not through a public organization, but directly to the self-promoting candidate; the operatives of the modern campaign—the pollster, the strategist, and the media consultant—are employees of the candidate; the platform is whatever the candidate decides it will be; the communication is largely one-way, from the candidate to the voters.

Candidate-centered campaigns also deprive the electorate as a whole of the opportunity to exercise its collective judgment. Competition takes place within constituencies, and not across them as well. What happens in one constituency has no necessary relationship to what happens in other constituencies. Each race is self-contained, a situation that has resulted in the nearly automatic reelection of incumbents. Where is the competition over national policy in elections that cannot look beyond the local scene?

A strengthening of the political party's role in elections would go a long way toward restoring competition to American elections. Few people seem to recognize the simple truth that the party is the only institution that has a vested interest in the election of nonincumbents to office. To be meaningful, competition requires the mounting of strong challenges across the board to incumbents; parties alone can provide such competition. This point is not mere speculation. Comparisons of the United States, which lacks competitive elections, and European democracies, which do not, make it abundantly clear that the difference is attributable mainly to the difference between weak parties and strong parties. Why do you think Americans have failed to recognize the full contribution that parties can make to meaningful competition? Do Thomas Jefferson's words about the American states—"we would have to invent them if they did not already exist"—apply to parties in late twentieth-century America?

U.S. parties will never—for reasons of law, culture, and tradition, among others—be as strong as their European counterparts. Can you think of any steps that could nevertheless be taken, in areas such as campaign finance and media communication, that would strengthen the parties enough to make American elections more competitive?

SOURCE: V. O. Key, Jr., *Southern Politics* (New York: Knopf, 1949).

candidates aligning themselves either with or against the president's policies. This tendency for the president to act as a surrogate for the parties as the center of policy debate has lent a degree of commonality to electoral competition in various parts of the nation. It can also give continuity to policy conflict, as it did in the early 1980s, when Reagan's policies resulted in relatively stable coalitions in Congress and created a policy debate that bridged the elections of 1980, 1982, and 1984.

In at least three respects, however, presidential politics is inferior to party politics. First, whatever the president's policy preferences and personal idiosyncrasies, they overshadow the ideas of all other individuals and define national debate. In contrast, a party agenda is formulated by a broader spectrum of leadership and thus provides a more fully representative set of views. Second,

In May 1986 great fanfare surrounded the Reagan administration's legislation to fight drug abuse. 1986 happened to be a congressional election year, and candidates used their antidrug stand to appeal to the voters. The following year, however, funding to implement the legislation was cut as the "policy craze" faded. (Pam Price/Picture Group)

presidential politics lacks permanence: when a president leaves office after four or eight years, his policy agenda goes with him. In party politics, policy commitments outlast the term of any single administration. Finally, modern presidents have had difficulty maintaining their power throughout their terms of office: all presidents since Franklin D. Roosevelt have suffered prolonged periods of incapacity or loss of the public's confidence. When the president is unable to lead, the country has no other obvious source of guidance. In party politics, party tradition and philosophy are continuing sources of direction.

THE PARADOX OF MODERN U.S. ELECTIONS

Wistful longings for a return to the party politics of yesteryear have a touch of both unreality and amnesia. The parties are never going to regain their former level of influence, and they were far from perfect in the first place. After all, it was abusive practices by party leaders that led to the introduction of primary elections—America's drastic cure for the mischiefs of party.

Yet, and this is the central point, the electorate's opportunity to have a broad and consistent influence on national policy has been weakend by the decline of parties. Election outcomes now depend more heavily than in the past on incumbency, personality, and campaign spending. These factors are not necessarily trivial, but they are inferior in importance to the sustained issues of party politics. Popular rule is not a question of a Congress filled with incumbents or ingratiating personalities but of a Congress filled with members committed to policy directions that the people through their votes have had a reasonable chance to accept or reject. The common belief that it is better to vote "for the person, not the party" conforms with Americans' trust in individualism but makes little sense as a guideline for collective voting. When candidates run personal campaigns, and are judged on them, the effect is to shift the point of decision from the electoral process to the legislative process, where 100 senators and 435 representatives finally bring their separate agendas together. This is the great paradox of modern U.S. elections: they appear to strengthen the public's hold on the policy agenda by making the candidate-voter relationship in any given constituency a more direct one; yet they actually weaken that hold by making it more difficult for voters in different constituencies to act together.

Of course, as we noted in Chapter 11, the two parties differ in their policy tendencies and constituency interests, so party labels still provide the electorate with a guide to candidates' policy leanings. Voters in different constituencies are thus given some opportunity for collective action, and their choice of a Democratic or Republican majority in Congress does affect the direction of national policy. Yet the history of democratic societies indicates that the potential for popular influence cannot be fully realized without effective organization.[45] Grass-roots parties—"the people's constitution," in the historian James MacGregor Burns's phrase—were established in the early nineteenth century to enable the mass public to assert its collective voice more forcefully.[46]

Americans either never learned this history lesson very well or have forgotten it. The public today has no real appreciation of parties and would welcome their further decline. A majority of Americans, for example, say that presidential nominees should be chosen by national primaries rather than in party conventions. Most candidates also have no desire to see a return of strong parties. Although they approve of the parties' new service role, candidates would not welcome any change that placed them in a position subordinate to the parties.

Parties survived the shift to candidate-centered campaigns and will persist, but their heyday has passed. A continuation of candidate-centered politics is the outlook for the future.

Summary

America's political parties are relatively weak organizations. They lack control over nominations, elections, and platforms. Candidates can bypass the party organization and win nomination through primary elections. Individual candidates also control most of the organization and money necessary to win elections and run largely on personal platforms.

Primary elections are the major reason for the organizational weakness of America's parties. Once the parties lost their hold on the nominating process, they became subordinate to candidates. More generally, the political parties have been undermined by election reforms, some of which were intended to weaken the party and others of which have unintentionally done so. Recently the state and national party organizations have expanded their capacity to provide candidates with modern campaign services and are again playing a prominent role in election campaigns. Nevertheless, party organizations at all levels have few ways of controlling the candidates who run under their banner. They assist candidates with campaign technology, workers, and funds but cannot compel candidates' loyalty to organizational goals.

America's parties are decentralized, fragmented organizations. The relationship among local, state, and national party organizations is marked by paths of common interest rather than lines of authority. The national party organization does not control the policies and activities of the state organizations, and they in turn do not control the local organizations. The fragmentation of parties prevents them from acting as cohesive national organizations. Traditionally the local organizations have controlled most of the party's work force because most elections are

---

[45] Benjamin Ginsberg, *The Consequences of Consent* (New York: Random House, 1982), 145.
[46] James MacGregor Burns, *The Vineyard of Liberty* (New York: Knopf, 1982), 351.

contested at the local level. Local parties, however, vary markedly in their vitality.

America's party organizations are flexible enough to allow diverse interests to coexist within them; they can also accommodate new ideas and leadership, since they are neither rigid nor closed. However, because America's parties cannot control their candidates or coordinate their policies at all levels, they are unable to present the voters with a coherent, detailed platform for governing. The national electorate as a whole is thus denied a clear choice among policy alternatives and has difficulty influencing national policy in a predictable and enduring way through elections.

Major Concepts

candidate-centered politics
nomination
party-centered politics

party organizations
primary election (direct primary)

Suggested Readings

Allswang, John. *Bosses, Machines, and Urban Voters*. Baltimore: Johns Hopkins University Press, 1986. A penetrating study of the party machines that once flourished in America's cities.

Crotty, William, ed. *The Party Symbol*. San Francisco: W. H. Freeman, 1980. A series of articles by leading scholars on the activities and influence of contemporary American parties.

Ehrenhalt, Alan. *The United States of Ambition*. New York: Times Books, 1991. A provocative book that claims that self-starting politicians are the reason the U.S. government has a scarcity of sound leadership.

Frantzich, Stephen E. *Political Parties in the Technological Age*. New York: Longman, 1989. An insightful analysis of how parties are adapting to the information age.

Herrnson, Paul S. *Party Campaigning in the 90's*. Cambridge, Mass.: Harvard University Press, 1988. An analysis that indicates political parties continue to have an important organizational role in the United States.

Huckshorn, Robert J. *Party Leadership in the States*. Amherst: University of Massachusetts Press, 1976. A study of parties in the states based on a survey of party leaders.

Kayden, Xander, and Eddie Mahe, Jr. *The Party Goes On*. New York: Basic Books, 1985. An assessment of how the two major parties have adapted to the political changes of recent decades.

Sorauf, Frank J. *Money in American Elections*. Glenview, Ill.: Scott, Foresman, 1988. A careful study of the flow of money in U.S. election campaigns.

THE INTEREST-GROUP SYSTEM: ORGANIZING FOR INFLUENCE

13

The flaw in the pluralist heaven is that the heavenly chorus sings with a strong upper-class bias.

E. E. Schattschneider[1]

*U*ntil Candy Lightner came along in May 1980, they had not thought of themselves as a group, even though they had something tragically important in common—the death of children or other family members in traffic accidents caused by drunk drivers. Lightner taught them to view themselves as a political lobby and gave them a name—Mothers Against Drunk Driving (MADD).

Perhaps no other small group in recent times has pressed its view so forcefully as MADD. Its intense grass-roots campaign resulted in a 1984 law that withholds federal highway funds from states with a legal drinking age under twenty-one. Through appearances on television news shows, letters to key members of Congress, and personal appeals to President Ronald Reagan, MADD won a campaign that at first appeared unlikely to succeed because of opposition by powerful restaurant and liquor lobbies. Since then, MADD has pressured state legislatures and local law-enforcement officials to toughen penalties for people convicted of driving while intoxicated.

MADD is one of thousands of organizations known as interest groups. An **interest group** is a set of individuals who are organized to promote a shared political interest. Also called a "faction" or "pressure group" or "special interest," an interest group is characterized by its formalized organization and

---

[1] E. E. Schattschneider, *The Semisovereign People: A Realist's View of Democracy in America* (New York: Holt, Rinehart and Winston, 1960), 35.

Candy Lightner, founder of Mothers Against Drunk Driving (MADD). (AP/Wide World Photos)

by its pursuit of policy goals that stem from its members' shared interest. Thus college students as a whole do not constitute an interest group, because they are not an organized collectivity. Similarly, a bridge club is not an interest group, because it does not seek to influence the political process. However, the organizations listed below—corporations, industry associations, nonprofit social-service agencies, lobbying organizations—*are* interest groups because, despite their differences, they all meet the definition's two criteria: each is an organized entity and each seeks to further its members' interests through political action.

AFL-CIO	The National Grange
U.S. Chamber of Commerce	AT&T
Sierra Club	Planned Parenthood
Association of Wheat Growers	American Petroleum Institute
American Association of University Professors	Common Cause
Mobil Oil	Americans for Democratic Action

National Organization for Women

American Civil Liberties Union

American Bar Association

General Motors

American Realtors Association

Liberty Foundation

Interest groups promote public policies, encourage the political participation of their members, support candidates for public office, and work to influence policymakers. Interest groups are thus similar to political parties in certain respects, but the two types of organizations differ in important ways. Major political parties address a broad range of issues so as to appeal to diverse blocs of voters. By comparison, interest groups focus on specific issues of immediate concern to their members; farm groups, for example, concentrate on agricultural policy.

The fact that interest groups exist to promote the interests of their members has given them a dubious reputation. However, blanket criticisms of interest groups are misplaced. Such groups are a basic means for people to achieve the ideal of self-government. Although citizens have common concerns, they also have disparate ones, and it is appropriate for them to look to government to protect their special interests. The elderly, for instance, have certain needs, such as financial security, that can be met only through government policies for the aged. The same can be said of farmers, consumers, corporations, minorities— indeed, of nearly every interest in society. Without groups to articulate and pursue the goals of various interests in society, government would be less aware of those interests and less able to promote them. Thus the issue is not whether government should be responsive to groups but whether particular groups have undue political influence.

A leading theory of American politics—**pluralism**—holds that society's interests are substantially represented through the activities of groups. An extreme statement of this view was Arthur F. Bentley's claim in 1908 that society is "nothing other than the complex of groups that compose it."[2] Although modern pluralists make far less sweeping claims, they do contend, on balance, that the group process is open to a great range of interests, nearly all of which benefit from organized activity in one significant way or another.

This chapter examines the degree to which various interests in American society are represented by organized groups. These groups will be considered to constitute a group *system*, much as political parties make up a party system. The major question about the group system is its representativeness. Which interests are highly organized through groups? Which are not? The chapter argues that the pluralist viewpoint exaggerates the representativeness of the group system and that economically powerful interests dominate the group system. The main points made in the chapter are the following:

★ *Although nearly all interests in American society are organized to some degree, those associated with economic activity, particularly business enterprises, are by far the most thoroughly organized.* Their advantage rests partly on the fact that their economic activities provide them with resources (especially money) that can be used for political purposes. Also, economic

---

[2] Quoted in Norman J. Ornstein and Shirley Elder, *Interest Groups, Lobbying, and Policymaking* (Washington, D.C.: Congressional Quarterly Press, 1978), 11.

organizations are relatively easy to maintain because they provide individuals with private goods (such as wages and jobs) that are tangible incentives for membership.

★ *Groups that do not have economic activity as their primary function often have organizational problems.* They pursue public or collective goods (such as a safer environment) that are available even to individuals who are not group members, so individuals may choose not to pay the costs of membership.

★ *The interest-group system overrepresents business interests and higher-income groups,* although their advantage has diminished in recent decades.

Types of Interest Groups

In the 1830s the Frenchman Alexis de Tocqueville wrote that the "principle of association" was nowhere more evident than in America.[3] Tocqueville's observation has been echoed many times since then, for an obvious reason: organized groups have always flourished in the United States. The country's tradition of free association has made it easy for Americans to join together for political purposes, and their diverse interests have given them reason to seek influence through specialized groups. Perhaps no other nation has so many separate economic, ethnic, religious, social, and geographic interests as the United States. Moreover, the nation's fragmented political system provides numerous points of access for interest groups; because of federalism and separation of powers, numerous political institutions at all levels of government are available for groups to lobby. Not surprisingly, manufacturing, labor, agriculture, and other leading interests have not only national organizations but also separate state and local lobbies. Groups spent $29 million in 1990 to lobby New York's state government alone. The top spender was Philip Morris, which spent $566,223 in a successful effort to defeat a proposed statewide ban on the sale of cigarettes in vending machines.

The extraordinary number of groups in the United States does not indicate, however, that the nation's various interests are equally well organized. Organizations develop when people with shared interests have the opportunity and the incentive to join together.[4] Some individuals have the skills, money, contacts, or time to participate effectively in group politics, but others do not. Moreover, some groups are inherently more attractive to potential members than others and thus find it easier to build large or devoted followings. Finally, organizations differ in their access to financial resources and thus differ also in their capacity for political action.

Therefore, a first consideration in regard to group politics in America is the issue of how thoroughly various interests are organized. These differences are of critical importance. Group politics is the politics of organization. Interests that are highly organized stand a good chance of having their views heard by policymakers. Poorly organized interests stand a good chance of being ignored.

★ ANALYZE THE ISSUE

The Differences between Groups and Parties
Political parties and interest groups are the organizations through which people have traditionally obtained representation. How do groups differ from parties? How are groups like parties? Can either substitute for the other?

[3] Alexis de Tocqueville, *Democracy in America* (Garden City, N.Y.: Doubleday/Anchor, 1969), bk. II, ch. 4.
[4] See Peter Clarke and James Q. Wilson, "Incentive Systems: A Theory of Organizations," *Administrative Science Quarterly* (1961): 129–166; William P. Browne, "Benefits and Membership: A Reappraisal of Interest Group Activity," *Western Political Quarterly* 29 (June 1976): 258–273.

TABLE 13-1 Number of Members of Some Large Economic Groups Compared with other groups, those representing economic interests have larger memberships.

Group	Number of Members
AFL-CIO	14,100,000
Council of Better Business Bureaus	240,000*
National Association of Manufacturers	13,500*
United Farm Workers	100,000
American Medical Association	271,000
American Bar Association	360,000
American Farm Bureau Federation	3,300,000

*Member firms.

SOURCE: *Encyclopedia of Organizations, 1990,* 24th ed. (Detroit: Gale Research, 1989).

ECONOMIC GROUPS

No interests are more fully or effectively organized than those that have economic activity as their primary purpose. Corporations, labor unions, farm groups, and professional associations are organized primarily for economic reasons (see Table 13-1). They exist to make profits, provide jobs, improve pay, or protect an occupation. They do not exist for political purposes, but they do lobby government. Their political activity is secondary to their economic activity. For example, although corporations routinely seek favorable policies from government, they function chiefly to produce economic goods and services. For the sake of discussion, such organizations will be called **economic groups,** although it is important to recognize that their political goals can include policies that transcend narrow economic interests. Thus the AFL-CIO concentrates on labor objectives, but it also takes positions on broader issues of foreign and domestic policy.

Business Groups

Writing in 1929, E. Pendleton Herring noted, "Of the many organized groups maintaining offices in [Washington], there are no interests more fully, more comprehensively, and more efficiently represented than those of American industry."[5] Although corporations do not dominate the group system to the same degree as they did in the past, Herring's general conclusion still holds: more than half of all groups formally registered to lobby Congress are business organizations. Nearly all large corporations and many smaller ones are politically active. They concentrate their activities on policies that touch directly on business interests, such as tax, tariff, and regulatory decisions.

Business organizations are also represented through associations. Some of these "organizations of organizations" seek to advance the general interests of business and industry and to articulate a business perspective on broad policy

[5] E. Pendleton Herring, *Group Representation before Congress* (Washington, D.C.: Brookings Institution, 1929), 78.

The AFL-CIO's slogan "Solidarity Works" becomes increasingly ironic as union membership declines from year to year and the political influence of organized labor declines accordingly. (Jim West/Impact Visuals)

issues.[6] One of the oldest associations is the National Association of Manufacturers (NAM), which was formed in 1894. The NAM includes 13,500 manufacturing firms and has worked to restrain labor unions, to reduce federal taxes on corporations, and to block unfavorable regulation of business by government. Another large business association is the U.S. Chamber of Commerce, which represents more than 180,000 medium-sized and small businesses.[7] The Chamber has a Washington headquarters located near the White House with a support staff of more than 400 employees. Because the Chamber of Commerce and the NAM represent firms of various types, they generally lobby for policies beneficial to the business sector as a whole.

Business is also organized through trade associations confined to a single industry. These associations vary enormously in their lobbying budgets; for example, the American Petroleum Institute and the National Association of Home Builders have annual budgets of $10 million each, whereas the Bow Tie Manufacturers Association and the Post Card Manufacturing Association each spend only $10,000 annually. Trade associations carry on the bulk of corporate lobbying. Because each trade association represents a single industry, it can promote the interests of member corporations even when these interests conflict with those of business generally. Thus, while the Chamber of Commerce promotes a free-trade policy, some trade associations seek protective tariffs because their member firms need barriers against foreign competition.[8]

[6] Kay Lehman Schlozman and John T. Tierney, *Organized Interests and American Democracy* (New York: Harper & Row, 1986), 41; see also Graham Wooton, *Interest Groups, Policy, and Politics in America* (Englewood Cliffs, N.J.: Prentice-Hall, 1985), 103.
[7] Schlozman and Tierney, *Organized Interests*, 24, 41.
[8] See Robert H. Salisbury, John P. Heinz, Edward O. Leumann, and Robert L. Nelson, "Who Works with Whom? Interest Group Alliances and Opposition," *American Political Science Review* 81 (December 1987): 1217–1234.

Labor Groups

Since the 1930s, organized labor has been politically active on a large scale. Its goal has been to promote policies that benefit workers in general and union members in particular. In 1988, for example, organized labor worked hard and successfully for passage of legislation requiring companies to give workers sixty days' notice before they closed a plant or laid off employees.

Although some independent unions, such as the United Mine Workers, lobby actively, the dominant labor group is the AFL-CIO, which maintains its national headquarters in Washington, D.C. The AFL-CIO has more than one hundred affiliated unions, including the International Brotherhood of Electrical Workers, the Sheet Metal Workers, the Communication Workers of America, and, as of 1987, the giant International Brotherhood of Teamsters.

The AFL-CIO has more than 14 million members, which represents a considerable decline in recent years. At one time about a third of the U.S. work force was unionized, but only about one-sixth of all workers currently belong to unions. Skilled and unskilled laborers have been the core of organized labor, and their numbers are decreasing while professionals, technicians, and service workers are increasing in number. Professionals have shown little interest in union organization, perhaps because they identify with management or see themselves as economically secure. Service workers and technicians are also more difficult for unions to organize than traditional laborers because they work closely with managers and, often, in small offices.

However, unions have made important inroads in recent decades in their efforts to organize public employees. Teachers, postal workers, police, firefighters, and social workers are among the public-employee groups that have become increasingly unionized. The effectiveness of these unions is limited by federal and state laws forbidding public employees to strike. In 1981 the Professional Air Traffic Controllers Organization (PATCO) called a strike over pay and working conditions; President Reagan responded by firing 11,500 federally employed controllers.

Agricultural Groups

Farm organizations are another large economic lobby. The American Farm Bureau Federation is the largest of the farm groups, with roughly 3 million members. The National Farmers Union, the National Grange, and the National Farmers Organization are smaller farm lobbies. Agricultural groups do not always agree on policy issues. For instance, the Farm Bureau has sided with agribusiness and owners of large farms, while the Farmers Union has promoted the interests of smaller, "family" farms.

There are also numerous specialty farm associations, including the Association of Wheat Growers, the American Soybean Association, and Associated Milk Producers. Each association acts as a separate lobby to try to obtain policies beneficial to its members' narrow agricultural interests.

Professional Groups

Most professions have lobbying associations. Perhaps the most powerful of these groups is the American Medical Association (AMA), which, with its

This 1873 lithograph illustrates the benefits of membership in the National Grange, an agricultural interest group. (Library of Congress)

271,000 members, has about half of the nation's physicians among its members. The AMA has opposed government involvement in medical practices and is widely held responsible for blocking comprehensive government-paid medical care in the United States. Other professional groups are the American Bar Association and the American Association of University Professors, each of which maintains a lobbying office in Washington.

NONECONOMIC GROUPS

Although economic interests are the best organized and most conspicuous groups, they have no monopoly on group activity. There are a great number and variety of other organized interests, which we shall refer to collectively as **noneconomic groups** (see Table 13-2). The members of groups in this category are drawn together not by the promise of direct economic gain but by **purposive incentives**—opportunities to promote a cause in which they believe.[9] Whether a group's goal is to protect the environment, reduce the threat of nuclear war, return prayer to the public schools, feed the poor at home or abroad, outlaw or retain legal abortion, or whatever, there are citizens who are willing to participate simply because they believe the policy goal is a worthy one.[10] Purposive incentives are powerful enough that nearly every conceivable interest within American society has a group that claims to represent it. Most

[9] See Clarke and Wilson, "Incentive Systems," 135.
[10] Jeffrey M. Berry, *The Interest Group Society* (Boston: Little, Brown, 1984), 77.

TABLE 13-2 Number of Members of Some Large Noneconomic Groups A few noneconomic groups have large memberships, but their memberships are smaller and less stable than those of the largest economic groups.

Group	Number of Members
National Organization for Women	250,000
American Civil Liberties Union	275,000
National Association for the Advancement of Colored People	400,000
John Birch Society	50,000
Amnesty International of the United States	300,000
National Urban League	50,000
Ralph Nader's Public Citizen	100,000
Common Cause	265,000

SOURCE: *Encyclopedia of Organizations, 1990,* 24th ed. (Detroit: Gale Research, 1989).

noneconomic groups are of three general types: public-interest groups, single-issue groups, and ideological groups.

Public-Interest Groups

THE LEAGUE OF WOMEN VOTERS

Public-interest groups are those that attempt to act in the broad interests of society as a whole. Despite their label, public-interest groups are not led by people elected by the public at large, and the issues they target are ones of their own choosing, not the public's. Nevertheless, there is a basis for distinguishing such groups from economic groups: the latter seek direct material benefits for their members, while the former seek benefits that are less tangible and more broadly shared. For example, the National Association of Manufacturers, an economic group, seeks policies favorable to large corporations, while the League of Women Voters, a public-interest group, seeks policies—such as simplified voter registration—that can benefit the public in general.

The League of Women Voters has existed for decades, but more than half of the currently active public-interest groups have been formed since 1960. Among the more visible of these newer organizations are Common Cause and Ralph Nader's Public Citizen. Each of these groups gets some of its resources from small contributors. Common Cause has about 265,000 members, whose annual dues help to support a large national staff of lobbyists, attorneys, and public relations experts. Founded in 1970 by John Gardner (formerly Lyndon Johnson's secretary of health, education, and welfare), Common Cause, which describes itself as "a national citizens' lobby," concentrates on political reform in such areas as campaign finance. Common Cause, in its recent "People vs. PACs" campaign, pressed for fundamental campaign reform, including the reduction of PAC influence. Nader first came to national attention in 1965, when his book *Unsafe at Any Speed* exposed the poor safety record of General Motors' Corvair automobile. His Public Citizen group works primarily on consumers' issues, including pollution control, auto safety, and pure food and drugs.

The Proliferation of Interest Groups

Do groups beget groups in a continuous sequence of development? Consider the environmental lobby, which now includes three times as many groups as it did in the 1960s. In response to demands from existing environmental groups, the federal government in the 1960s passed major environmental legislation (such as the Clean Water Act), which spawned protective environmental groups. These specialized groups then pressed for more specialized legislation, which in turn spawned even more specialized groups. Is hyperpluralism—the runaway proliferation of specialized groups—an inevitable consequence of activist government?

Single-Issue Groups

A single-issue group is organized to influence policy in just one area. Notable current examples are the various right-to-life and pro-choice groups that have formed around the issue of abortion. The number of single-issue groups has risen sharply in the past two decades, and they now lobby on almost every conceivable issue, from nuclear arms to day-care centers to drug abuse. Single-issue groups with a national membership are the most prominent, but a vast number of single-issue groups are organized and operate autonomously on the local level. They sometimes form networks or coalitions with similar groups to make their views known on national issues. An example is the "solidarity committees" which support the rights of Palestinians in the Middle East.

Environmental groups are sometimes classified as public-interest groups, but they may also be considered single-issue organizations in that most of them seek to influence public policy in a specific area, such as pollution reduction, wilderness preservation, or wildlife protection. The Sierra Club is one of the oldest of such groups; it was formed in the 1890s to promote the preservation of scenic areas. Also prominent are the National Audubon Society, the Wilderness Society, the Environmental Defense Fund, and the Izaak Walton League. Between 1960 and 1970, membership in environmental groups tripled in response to increased public concern about the quality of the environment.[11] Since then, membership in environmental groups has continued to grow. Greenpeace USA, founded in 1978, has rapidly become one of the largest and best-known environmental groups in the country.

Ideological Groups

Some groups are concerned with a broad range of policies from a general philosophical or moral perspective. Americans for Democratic Action (ADA), for example, supports liberal positions on social, economic, and foreign policy issues. Like many other groups, ADA rates members of Congress according to how closely their votes on various issues match its own positions. The Christian Moral Government Fund is another example of an ideological group; along with a number of other groups with similar goals,[12] it was formed to restore "Christian values" to American life and policy. Ideological groups on both the left and the right have proliferated since the 1960s.[13]

Groups such as the National Organization for Women (NOW) and the National Association for the Advancement of Colored People (NAACP) can also be generally classified as ideological groups. Their aim is to promote the broad interests of a particular demographic segment of society. The NAACP was formed in 1909 to promote the political interests of racial minorities, primarily through initiating lawsuits on their behalf.

[11] Carol S. Greenwald, *Group Power* (New York: Praeger, 1977), 181; Robert Cameron Mitchell, "National Environmental Lobbies and the Apparent Logic of Collective Action," in Clifford S. Russell, ed., *Collective Decision Making* (Baltimore: John Hopkins University Press for Resources for the Future, 1979), 93–98.
[12] See Steve Bruce, *The Rise and Fall of the New Christian Right* (New York: Oxford University Press, 1988); Allen D. Hertzke, *Representing God in Washington* (Knoxville: University of Tennessee Press, 1988); Matthew Moen, *The Christian Right and Congress* (Tuscaloosa: University of Alabama Press, 1989).
[13] See Alan Crawford, *Thunder on the Right* (New York: Pantheon, 1980).

Public Citizen, a public-interest group founded by Ralph Nader (*at right*), promotes consumer interests by working for such measures as laws requiring juice-drink producers to reveal on labels the amount of natural fruit juice in their products. (UPI/Bettmann Newsphotos)

Greenpeace USA, a single-issue environmental group, is well known for its dramatic forms of protest. When New York City hosted Fleet Week in the spring of 1989, some hardy Greenpeace activists sailed out into the harbor to publicize the hazards of nuclear-powered ships. (UPI/Bettmann Newsphotos)

A SPECIAL CATEGORY OF INTEREST GROUP: GOVERNMENTS

While the vast majority of organized interests in the United States represent private concerns, a growing number of interest groups represent governments, both foreign and subnational.

The National Association for the Advancement of Colored People (NAACP) is an ideological group that has long been active in the field of civil rights. (T. L. Litt/ Impact Visuals)

The U.S. federal government makes policies that directly affect the economic development, political stability, and security of nations throughout the world. Arms sales, foreign aid, immigration, and import restrictions and other trade practices have a great impact on foreign nations. For this reason, most foreign nations supplement the political efforts made through their embassies with the services of paid lobbying agents in Washington. Although lobbying by foreign governments is subject to some restrictions, most governments have managed to circumvent these vague regulations. In addition to sending their own agents to Washington, many countries hire American lobbyists to assist their efforts. Roughly 1,000 registered agents represent foreign nations' interests in Washington.[14]

Subnational governments within the United States also have a major stake in many of the policies decided on in Washington. States, cities, and other governmental units go to Washington separately and in groups to lobby Congress. While most major cities across the United States and two-thirds of the states have at least one Washington lobbyist, cooperative lobbying is perhaps more important. The intergovernmental lobby includes such groups as the Council of State Governments, the National Governors Conference, the National Association of Counties, the National League of Cities, and the U.S. Conference of Mayors. These organizations are, in essence, the trade associations of subnational governments. They represent the broad interests of cities and states while still allowing individual member cities and states to lobby for their particular interests. A second component of the intergovernmental lobby consists of organizations representing the concerns of bureaucratic specialists at the subnational level—for example, highway engineers, county welfare directors, and housing and redevelopment officials.

[14] Schlozman and Tierney, *Organized Interests,* 54.

★ THE MEDIA AND THE PEOPLE

HIGH-PROFILE GROUPS

Although journalists like to describe the news as a mirror held up to society, the news is actually a highly selective portrayal of reality. There are no objective standards for choosing a few news stories each day out of the millions of events that have taken place that day. The choices are based on conventions. Journalists look for that which is new, interesting, and important. They also tend to tell the news through familiar figures. News coverage of the United States Senate, for example, is not spread evenly across the institution's 100 senators. Instead a few highly visible senators—such as Robert Dole and Edward Kennedy—dominate news of the institution.

The same tendencies hold for coverage of interest groups. There are tens of thousands of interest groups in the United States, but the news brings to light only a few of them. A group is unlikely to receive news coverage unless it is embroiled in a controversy. Journalists are drawn to conflict because it provides a more dramatic form of news. A result is that group activity appears more conflictual than it actually is. Although groups sometimes fight for narrow advantage, they also work together. Moreover, most of their activity involves service to their members, which rarely is presented in the news.

News about groups is also biased toward a particular type of group—the mainstream group that is readily recognizable to the general public. Journalists have limited space and time within which to work, which inclines them to seek out familiar figures. Senator Kennedy gets more coverage than many senators because the press does not have to explain who he is before starting into a news story. By the same token, a spokesperson for the United States Chamber of Commerce is an easy figure to quote in a news story since no explanation of the Chamber is required. Furthermore, the opinions of a Chamber of Commerce authority can be presented as if they were representative of the business community as a whole, whereas the opinions of a spokesperson for some little-known trade association would not have the same legitimacy. For such reasons, journalists in their news selections tend to avoid less prominent groups.

The National Conference of Mayors represents the interests of cities in cooperative lobbying of the White House and Congress. (Michael Hirsch/Gamma-Liaison)

The interests of subnational governments vary greatly. The problems of frostbelt states differ from those of sunbelt states; cities in the industrial Northeast face problems that are almost unknown in cities of the Southwest. These differences impose limits on the effectiveness of the intergovernmental lobby. Nonetheless, its presence in Washington has demonstrably influenced many major policy decisions that affect state and local governments.[15]

Why Not All Interests Are Equally Well Organized

We have seen that economic interests are the most thoroughly organized. A further indication of their advantage is the fact that their Washington lobbyists outnumber those of noneconomic groups by roughly 4 to 1. There are in Washington:

4,000 lobbyists representing labor unions and trade and professional associations

1,250 lobbyists representing individual corporations

1,250 lobbyists representing noneconomic groups[16]

The predominance of economic interests was predicted in *Federalist* No. 10, in which James Madison declared that property is "the most common and durable source of factions." Stated differently, nothing seems to matter quite so much to people as their pocketbooks and livelihoods. Actually, several factors give economic groups an organizational advantage: their size, the incentives they offer members, and their resources.

THE SIZE FACTOR

The most common and durable source of factions has been the various and unequal distribution of property.
Federalist No. 10

Many economic interests naturally form into small rather than large groups. As the economist Mancur Olson notes, a small group has an inherent advantage in that each of its members stands to benefit sufficiently from a collective effort.[17] The U.S. automobile industry, for example, has its Big Three—General Motors, Ford, and Chrysler. Each firm's contribution to a collective lobbying campaign can make a measurable difference and produce extraordinary benefits. If U.S. automakers can persuade government to limit auto imports from Japan, for example, each stands to make millions in additional profits. Thus the Big Three automakers have a powerful incentive to work together.

The automobile industry is representative of U.S. industry as a whole. The business sector is divided into numerous industries, most of which include only a small number of major firms. Virtually every industry, from oil to steel to cereals, has its own trade association. About 1,000 trade associations are

---

[15] See Donald H. Harder, *Urban Governments Come to Washington* (New York: Free Press, 1974).
[16] *Washington Representatives, 1984*, 8th ed. (Washington, D.C.: Columbia Books, 1984). In addition to the 6,500 lobbyists enumerated above, 2,500 Washington lobbyists (mainly lawyers and consultants) represent multiple clients.
[17] Mancur Olson, *The Logic of Collective Action* (Cambridge, Mass.: Harvard University Press, 1965), 147.

represented in Washington, and they spend well over $100 million annually on lobbying.

The situation confronting most industries is far different from that of, say, consumers, who number in the millions. The huge numbers of individual consumers make any one of them seem insignificant. John Doe in New York and Jane Roe in Montana may recognize that there would be advantages if all consumers could join together in a single group, but they also realize the impossibility of forming such an organization. Getting millions of people to work together is infinitely more difficult than getting a few firms to collaborate.

THE LURE OF INCENTIVES

Many economic groups offer prospective members a powerful incentive to join: **private goods** (or **individual goods**), which are the benefits that a group can grant directly to the individual member. For example, workers in the state of Michigan cannot hold automobile assembly jobs unless they belong to the United Auto Workers (UAW). Union membership is the qualification that enables an individual to obtain an auto worker's job, which is a private good.

Not all economic groups are in such a monopoly position. Agricultural organizations, for example, provide crop insurance, marketing arrangements, farming information, and other private goods to members, but these are benefits that farmers can obtain elsewhere. As a result, most farmers are not dues-paying members of a farm group. In general, however, the incentives provided by economic groups are stronger than those offered by other types of groups. Economic interests are highly organized in part because they serve the individual economic needs of potential members. A secure job or a higher income is, for most individuals, a powerful incentive to join a group.

Most noneconomic groups, in contrast, offer **collective goods** (or **public goods**) as an incentive for membership. These goods are benefits in which everyone can share. An environmental group that seeks tougher air-pollution laws, for example, is seeking a collective good; if government should enact such legislation, the resulting benefit—cleaner air—is provided to all citizens, whether or not they belong to the group. This characteristic of collective goods reduces the incentive of individuals to contribute to a group's efforts because they can get a "free ride," receiving the benefits but paying none of the costs. This situation, accordingly, is called the **free-rider problem.**

The free-rider problem arises because it is not rational, in the economic sense, for people to join a group that pursues a collective good.[18] If such a group succeeds in its goals, individuals will get the benefit even if they have not contributed to the cause. Participation in such groups is not rational in another sense as well: the contribution of any individual is so small that it does not affect the group's success in any significant way. Common Cause is no more or less effective if it gains or loses a single contributor. Why, then, should an individual bother to join such a group?

The free-rider problem becomes less troublesome when an issue is so compelling or a leader so charismatic that many potential members are roused to join a group. Membership in Common Cause rose to 350,000 in 1974, when

---

[18] Ibid., 64.

The Sierra Club is a single-issue group that attracts members by offering them such individual benefits as weekend outings. (John Eastcott/Yva Momatiuk/ The Image Works)

the group conducted a nationwide direct-mail membership drive during the televised coverage of the Senate Watergate hearings. Common Cause subsequently lost more than 100,000 members, however, as public concern over honesty in government abated.

Another way in which noneconomic groups can overcome the free-rider problem is to create individual benefits, akin to those offered by economic groups, to make membership more attractive. The Sierra Club, for example, provides wilderness treks and other social benefits (known as "solidarity incentives") to its members. Many groups provide an organizational newsletter or magazine to their members. Such individual incentives are apparently more important to an organization's capacity to retain existing members than to its ability to attract new ones. The Environmental Defense Fund (EDF) is the only large environmental group that offers no newsletter or other services to individual members. Perhaps as a result, EDF also has the highest membership turnover among major environmental groups.

A group that has surmounted the free-rider problem is the American Association of Retired Persons (AARP). With 20 million members, it is a very powerful lobbying group on issues affecting the elderly (see box). The AARP closely resembles an economic group in that, although it depends on voluntary membership contributions, it offers members certain economic incentives, such as member discounts at hotels and restaurants, and concentrates on issues that directly affect the economic well-being of retirees. AARP members are so responsive to policies affecting them that they generate more mail to Congress than any other group.[19] In 1989, Congress decided to require increased payments for nursing-home care from higher-income social security recipients. AARP members flooded the Capitol with calls and letters, and Congress reversed itself.

[19] Ernest Wittenberg and Elisabeth Wittenberg, *How to Win in Washington* (Cambridge, Mass.: Basil Blackwell, 1989), 81.

ACCESS TO RESOURCES

Finally, economic groups have the advantage of ready access to the resources that facilitate organization. Political activity does not come cheap. If a group is to make its views known, it normally must possess a headquarters, an expert staff, and a communication capacity. Economic groups can siphon the requisite money and expertise from their economic activities. For example, a portion of the dues that unions, farm groups, and professional associations receive from their members can be used for lobbying purposes. Corporations have the greatest natural advantage: they can apply corporate funds to the support of their political activities. In 1990, when the Persian Gulf crisis resulted in skyrocketing gasoline prices, the nation's oil giants spent some of their windfall profits on television and print advertising aimed at dampening public criticism that suggested they were exploiting the situation. The oil companies blamed government for policies that impeded their attempts to discover additional oil fields, which would free the country from its dependence on Middle Eastern oil.

Noneconomic groups have a harder time gathering the resources that are necessary for effective political activity. Changes in communication technology have eased the free-rider problem somewhat and have contributed to the sharp increase in the number of noneconomic groups in recent decades. The power of television to dramatize issues and personalities has given a boost to some noneconomic groups. Without television's coverage, such issues as civil rights and the environment would have attracted less interest, and such figures as Jerry Falwell and Ralph Nader would have had smaller followings.

Even more important than television are computers. In the past, a fledgling organization almost had to locate potential members one by one and persuade them personally to join. Today, however, group organizers can buy mailing lists and flood the mails with computer-typed "personal" letters asking recipients to

★ CRITICAL THINKING

CATASTROPHIC HEALTH CARE AND THE SENIOR CITIZENS' LOBBY

With the backing of President Reagan in the closing period of his presidency, Congress enacted a catastrophic health insurance plan that was designed to protect elderly Americans from losing their life savings in paying for medical care if they had a catastrophic illness. The program was designed to be self-financing, with its potential recipients, rather than taxpayers in general, paying the bill. All eligible senior citizens would pay $4 monthly for medical insurance coverage, and high-income seniors would pay a tax surcharge that ranged as high as $800 annually.

A year after its enactment, the plan was effectively dead. The senior citizens' lobby had fought against it, targeting its financing mechanism as the reason. Retirees wanted catastrophic health-care coverage but did not want to pay for it. Why, they argued, should they be singled out to pay for a social-welfare program when other programs were funded out of general revenues? Congress backed down in the face of the intense pressure, as did President Bush, who had taken office in the interim and who had initially opposed repeal of the law.

What does this episode say about the public's expectations of government? About the nature of political leadership? About the power of a determined lobby? Was the seniors' lobby selfish in its demand for "free" medical coverage? Is there merit to the lobby's argument that other social-welfare recipients are not required to pay directly for the services they receive?

TABLE 13-3   Advantages and Disadvantages Held by Economic and Noneconomic Groups   Compared with economic groups, noneconomic groups have fewer advantages and more disadvantages.

Economic Groups	Noneconomic Groups
Advantages	*Advantages*
Economic activity provides the organization with resources necessary for political action.	Members are likely to support leaders' political efforts because they joined the group in order to influence policy.
Individuals are encouraged to join the group because of economic benefits they individually receive (e.g., wages).	*Disadvantages*
	The group has to raise funds especially for its political activities.
In the case of firms within an industry, their small number encourages organization because the contribution of each firm is significant.	Potential members may choose not to join the group because their individual contribution may be too small to affect the group one way or another.
Disadvantages	Potential members may choose not to join the group because they get collective benefits even if they do not join (the free-rider problem).
Persons within the group may not support leaders' political efforts because they did not join the group for political reasons.	

pay a small annual membership fee. For some citizens, a donation of $25 to $50 represents no great sacrifice and offers the personal satisfaction of involvement in a worthy cause.

From the organization's perspective, a direct mailing does not have to produce an extraordinary response to be successful. The immediate goal is to raise enough money to maintain the organization and its lobbying efforts; the goal can be met if only a small percentage of the people who receive fund-raising letters respond to them. Yet a weak response, which is the typical case, limits an organization's activities and its claim to represent a vital interest. In fact, some noneconomic groups could not survive if they depended on financial support from the general public; these organizations get most of their funds from charitable foundations or wealthy donors.[20]

On the whole, however, the organizational advantage rests with economic groups. In resources as in other respects, they have the edge on noneconomic groups. (see Table 13-3)

The Group System: Indispensable but Flawed

As we noted in the introduction to this chapter, pluralist theory holds that organized groups provide for the representation of society's many and diverse interests. On one level, this claim is beyond dispute. Without groups to carry

---

[20] Jack L. Walker, "The Origins and Maintenance of Interest Groups in America," *American Political Science Review* 77 (June 1983): 398–399.

Many noneconomic interest groups lack the financial resources to publicize their needs, so they must rely on dramatic protests to attract media attention to their cause. These disabled Americans are demonstrating in front of the White House to urge passage of the Americans with Disabilities Act in 1990. (Johnson/Gamma-Liaison)

the message, most of society's interests would have great difficulty in gaining government's attention and support. Yet the issue of representation is also a question of whether all interests in society have a fair chance to succeed, and here the pluralist argument is less compelling.

THE CONTRIBUTION OF GROUPS TO SELF-GOVERNMENT

Group activity is an essential part of self-government. A major obstacle to popular sovereignty is the sheer difficulty that public officials encounter in trying to discover what the people want from government. As we saw in Chapter 8, public opinion cannot be accurately observed directly. To discover it, lawmakers consult public opinion polls, talk with experts, meet with constituents, follow the news, and assess the meaning of recent elections. Organized groups are an additional means of determining popular sentiment. Through their political activities, they provide policymakers with a heightened sense of the policy concerns of various interests in society. Groups communicate with an uncommon clarity and vigor.[21] On any given issue, the policy positions that are likely to be expressed most clearly and directly are those held by organized interests.

Organized groups also give officials an indication of the intensity with which popular opinions are held. Officials may ignore an issue that evokes almost no intensity, while an issue that provokes strong feelings, whether from a large or

---

[21] V. O. Key, Jr., *Public Opinion and American Democracy* (New York: Knopf, 1961), 428.

The Decline of Voting and the Rise of Groups
Between the 1960s and the 1990s, voter turnout in the United States declined as group activity increased. Is it possible to look upon these trends as the institutionalization of middle-class politics? (Consider not only which citizens tend to participate in groups but also which ones have tended to drop out of the voting electorate—see Chapter 9.)

small portion of the public, is likely to require action.[22] Here again, organized groups provide policymakers with relevant cues. When organized interests feel strongly about an issue, they contrive to attract policymakers' attention.

Government does not exist simply to serve majority interests. Smaller interests too have a legitimate claim on public policy. The fact that most people are not retirees or labor union members or farmers or college students or Hispanics does not mean that the special needs and concerns of such "minorities" are undeserving of attention. And what better instrument exists for promoting the interests of such "minorities" than organizations formed around them? Groups are not antithetical to the democratic process: they are basic to it.

THE ECONOMIC BIAS OF THE GROUP SYSTEM

The flaw in the pluralist argument resides in its claim that the group system is representative. Pluralists contend that society's interests compete on a reasonably equal footing through organized groups, that numerous winners emerge from the competition, and that society's general interest is ultimately served by government's responsiveness to a multitude of particular interests. Pluralists recognize that better-organized interests have more influence, but argue that the group process is relatively open and fluid and that few interests are at a serious disadvantage. Each of these claims contains an element of truth, but each is far from the complete truth.

Chiefly, as we have seen, organization is a political resource that is distributed unequally across society. Economic interests, particularly corporations, are the most highly organized, and some analysts argue that group politics works almost entirely to the advantage of business.[23] This generalization was perhaps valid before the 1930s but is less so today. In fact, many of the public-interest groups formed in the 1960s and early 1970s were deliberately created to check and balance the influence of existing groups, particularly corporate lobbies.[24]

Big government has also brought the group political system into closer balance. "Interest group activity," Benjamin Ginsberg writes, "is often more a consequence than an antecedent of the state's programs." In other words, groups form not only to influence policy but also to respond to it. When new programs were created in the 1960s for the benefit of less advantaged interests in society, these interests tended to mobilize to protect their newly acquired benefits. An example is the National Welfare Rights Organization, which was formed during the 1960s *after* new welfare programs were established.[25]

Many of the newer interest groups have had a significant impact in such areas as civil rights, the environment, social-welfare programs for the elderly and the poor, public morality, national security, and business regulation. Moreover, as

[22] Ibid.
[23] See G. William Domhoff, *Who Rules America Now?* (Englewood Cliffs, N.J.: Prentice-Hall, 1983).
[24] See Andrew McFarland, *Public Interest Lobbies* (Washington, D.C.: American Enterprise Institute, 1976); Berry, *Interest Group Society.*
[25] Benjamin Ginsberg, *The Consequences of Consent* (New York: Random House, 1982), 214; see also Frances Fox Piven and Richard A. Cloward, *Poor People's Movements* (New York: Random House, 1979), ch. 5.

★ HOW THE UNITED STATES COMPARES

INTEREST-GROUP SYSTEMS

A century and a half ago, Alexis de Tocqueville noted that the United States was unrivaled in the range and number of its groups. The point remains valid today and is a reflection of the diversity of American society. The United States has more economic, social, religious, ethnic, and other interests than the countries of Europe. The greater diversity of the United States is evident in particular areas of group organization. For example, whereas U.S. farmers are represented through several large general organizations (among them the Farm Bureau, the National Grange, the Farmers Union, and the National Farm Organization), British farmers are represented through only one such organization (the

National Farmers Union). Moreover, the group systems of the United States and western Europe differ in their socioeconomic bias. Because of strong labor unions and other working-class organizations, lower-status Europeans are only marginally underrepresented through groups. By comparison, the group system in the United States has a decided tilt toward persons of higher income and education.

SOURCES: Russell J. Dalton, *Citizen Politics in Western Democracies* (Chatham, N.J.: Chatham House, 1988), ch. 3; Thomas Rochon, "Political Change in Ordered Societies," *Comparative Politics* 15 (1983): 351–353.

Chapter 14 indicates, policy is less often decided today by the actions of one or a few groups. The group system is thus not closed and rigid; it is open to new interests and new patterns of influence.

Nevertheless, it would be inaccurate to conclude that the group system is now fully competitive or fully representative of society's interests. Interests differ significantly in their level of organization and degree of influence through group activity. Well over half of all lobbying groups in Washington are still business-related. The interest-group system has a decided tilt toward America's economically oriented groups, particularly its corporations.

The group system is also slanted toward upper-middle-class interests.[26] Studies indicate that individuals of higher socioeconomic status are disproportionately represented among group members and even more so among group leaders (see Table 13-4). These tendencies are predictable. Educated and affluent Americans have the skills and money that give organizational form to special-interest politics. Less advantaged Americans find it harder to contribute to organized activity even when they sense a need or desire to do so. They lack the money, information, contacts, and communication skills to participate. The nation's traditionally disadvantaged, including the poor, minorities, women, and the young, are greatly underrepresented in the group-politics system. When the Reagan administration in 1981 proposed large reductions in federal spending on programs for the poor and disadvantaged, a weak lobby emerged to fight these cuts. In contrast, a 1985 Reagan proposal to reduce federal loans to college students, most of whom are middle-class, triggered substantial organized opposition.

A lack of organization does not ensure an interest's failure, just as the

---

[26] Sidney Verba and Norman H. Nie, *Participation in America: Political Democracy and Social Equality* (New York: Harper & Row, 1972), 181.

TABLE 13-4 Extent of Participation of Americans in Organizations, by Socioeconomic Status Lower-SES Americans are less likely to participate in organizations than are higher-SES Americans.

	SOCIOECONOMIC STATUS		
	Lowest Third	*Middle Third*	*Highest Third*
Nonmember	56%	34%	20%
Passive member	23	22	21
Active member of only one organization	16	28	24
Active member of more than one organization	6	16	35
	101%	100%	100%

Note: Socioeconomic status is a combined measure based on educational level of respondent and occupation and income of head of household. Membership is based on activity in *any* organization, not just political organizations. The active–passive distinction is based on respondents' own claims to take an active part in the organization or to be merely a passive member.
SOURCE: Sidney Verba and Norman H. Nie, *Participation in America: Political Democracy and Social Equality* (New York: Harper & Row, 1972), 204.

existence of organization does not guarantee success. However, organized interests are obviously in a better position to make their views known. They have at hand the means to get the attention of policymakers. In contrast, underorganized interests must first collect themselves before they can communicate their opinions. Often they are not even able to establish themselves organizationally. Of course, the underorganized are sometimes represented by proxy.[27] For example, the Southern Poverty Law Center, which works solely on behalf of minorities and the poor who run afoul of the justice system, gets most of its funding from upper-middle-class whites. Interest groups of this sort are uncommon, however, and groups organized and funded directly by low-income Americans are even rarer.

The business and class bias of the group system is especially significant because the most highly organized interests are, in a sense, those least in need of political clout. Corporations and affluent citizens are already favored in the distribution of society's material resources. Left alone, market forces operate to increase the concentration of wealth and power; the rich do indeed get richer. The group system does not alter that basic fact.

A MADISONIAN DILEMMA

James Madison recognized the dilemma inherent in group activity. Although he worried that government would fall under the control of a dominant interest, whether of the majority or of the minority, he realized that a free society is obliged to permit the advocacy of self-interest. Unless people can promote the separate opinions that stem from differences in their talents, needs, values, and possessions, they do not have liberty.

[27] See Charles McCarry, *Citizen Nader* (New York: Signet, 1972).

Madison added, however, that "the regulation of these various and interfering interests forms the principal task of modern legislation." Government must attempt to check and balance the demands of groups to ensure that the special interest not rule the general interest. Madison was arguing, in effect, that government, although obliged to foster the conditions that promote self-advocacy, must also operate to keep groups in their proper place. Government is the only institution in society that can greatly alter or offset private power. Among the topics of the next chapter is whether the U.S. government adequately constrains group demands.

> *The diversity in the faculties of men . . . is . . . an insuperable obstacle to a uniformity of interests. The protection of these faculties is the first object of government.*
> Federalist No. 10

Summary

A political interest group is a set of individuals organized to promote a shared political concern. Most interest groups owe their existence to factors other than politics. They form for economic reasons, such as the pursuit of profit, and maintain themselves by making profits (in the case of corporations) or by providing their members with private goods, such as jobs and wages. Their lobbying for political advantage is an outgrowth of their economic activity. Such interest groups include corporations, trade associations, labor unions, farm organizations, and professional associations. Collectively, economic groups are by far the largest set of organized interests, accounting for about three-fourths of registered Washington lobbies.

Other groups do not have the same organizational advantages. They depend on voluntary contributions from potential members who may lack interest and resources, or who recognize that they will get the collective good from a group's activity even if they do not participate (the free-rider problem).

Noneconomic groups include public-interest, single-issue, and ideological groups. Their numbers have increased dramatically since the 1960s despite their organizational problems.

In general, America's group system is relatively open and encompasses nearly all interests in society. However, interests are not equally well organized. Economic interests, particularly corporations, are more fully organized than other interests, and relatively affluent Americans are more fully organized than poorer Americans. As a result, the group system tends to favor interests that are already economically and socially advantaged.

Major Concepts

collective (or public) goods
economic groups
free-rider problem
interest group

noneconomic groups
pluralism
private (or individual) goods
purposive incentives

Suggested Readings

Berry, Jeffrey M. *Lobbying for the People*. Princeton, N.J.: Princeton University Press, 1977. An insightful analysis of public-interest lobbying groups.

Dahl, Robert. *Who Governs?* New Haven, Conn.: Yale University Press, 1961. A classic study of political influence whose major conclusion is that the policy process is open to participation and influence by many interests.

McFarland, Andrew S. *Common Cause: Lobbying in the Public Interest*. Chatham, N.J.: Chatham House, 1984. A case study of a public-interest group, Common Cause.

Moe, Terry M. *The Organization of Interests*. Chicago: University of Chicago Press, 1980. An analysis of economic interest groups as well as their incentive structures.

Olson, Mancur, Jr. *The Logic of Collective Action*, rev. ed. Cambridge, Mass.: Harvard University Press, 1971. An insightful analysis of why some interests are more fully and easily organized than others.

Schattschneider, E. E. *The Semisovereign People: A Realist's View of Democracy in America.* New York: Holt, Rinehart and Winston, 1960. A classic analysis of bias in the interest-group system and a critique of pluralist democracy.

Schlozman, Kay Lehman, and John T. Tierney. *Organized Interests and American Democracy.* New York: Harper & Row, 1986. A recent survey of interest groups and their activities.

Wittenberg, Ernest, and Elisabeth Wittenberg. *How to Win in Washington.* Cambridge, Mass.: Basil Blackwell, 1989. A practical guide to group organization and lobbying.

GROUP ORGANIZATION: LOBBYING FOR SPECIAL BENEFITS

14

The emerging public philosophy, interest group liberalism, has sought to solve the problems of public authority in a large modern state by defining them away . . . and by parceling out to private parties the power to make public policy.

Theodore Lowi[1]

They first met over breakfast in 1978 at Washington's Sheraton-Carlton Hotel and thereafter were known as the "Carlton Group." Each member was a lobbyist for a major U.S. corporation, and collectively they were determined to reestablish business power.

The late 1960s and early 1970s had been unusually difficult times for U.S. corporations. Over their objections, Congress had passed tough new laws that required firms to spend billions to safeguard workers' health and safety and to reduce industrial pollution. U.S. industry was operating at less than 75 percent of capacity as a result of softened consumer demand stemming from high rates of inflation and unemployment. To make matters worse, Japanese and European firms were cutting into the United States' share of world markets. Not since the 1930s had American business been at such a low ebb.

The Carlton Group had a strategy for halting the decline. The lobbyists would push for continued deregulation of U.S. business, which had begun in 1977 with the airline industry. Their major objective, however, was a change in the tax laws. Although corporate tax rates had declined steadily since the 1950s, the Carlton Group sought the virtual elimination of business taxes. Under its plan, corporations would receive an accelerated depreciation allowance on new equipment and other tax breaks that would allow many of them to avoid taxes almost entirely.

The Carlton Group spent three years refining its plan and convincing legislators of its merits. Seminars were held, publications distributed, and private meetings arranged with key officials. In 1981 the Carlton Group achieved its goal. At the urging of the new Reagan administration, Congress enacted the accelerated depreciation allowance for business. General Electric

---

[1] Theodore J. Lowi, *The End of Liberalism*, 2d ed. (New York: Norton, 1979), 43–44.

was one of hundreds of major corporations that benefited from the change. Although GE made a profit of $6.5 billion in 1981–1983, it paid no federal taxes at all during the period; in fact, the company received $283 million in federal tax rebates.

Supporters of the 1981 tax change claimed that it enabled U.S. corporations to replace outmoded plants and equipment with new ones that would help America compete more effectively with Japan and Germany. Critics maintained that business had instead used much of its additional capital to take over existing companies and to build plants in such countries as Mexico and Taiwan, where labor costs are lower than in the United States.

This sequence of events illustrates both the value of interest-group lobbying and the reasons for concern about it. By and large, interest groups have a better understanding of their problems and needs than public officials do. It is therefore important that public policy decisions be informed by the views of the interests likely to be affected by them. Lobbying enables groups to bring their views to policymakers' attention. Yet the logic of democratic politics implies that policies of benefit to special interests should also be broadly beneficial and should promote definable public goals. Lobbying, then, should not merely serve the narrow interests of particular groups.

This chapter examines the lobbying process by which interest groups seek to promote their advantage and then evaluates the impact of this process on national policy. The chapter demonstrates that the group process is indispensable and produces narrowly beneficial policies, but that groups have acquired too much policy influence and have significantly reduced government's capacity to respond effectively to society's broad interests. The main points made in the chapter are the following:

★ *Lobbying and electioneering are the traditional means by which groups communicate with and influence political leaders.* Recent developments, including "grass-roots lobbying" and PACs, have given added visibility to groups' activities.

★ *Groups can exert influence in a wide variety of ways and through many points of access to the legislative, executive, and judicial branches.*

★ *Most public policies are decided through iron triangles and issue networks, which facilitate the influence of interest groups.*

★ *When public policy is decided solely by group demands, the group process does not serve the collective interest, regardless of the number of separate interests that benefit from the process.*

Inside Lobbying: Seeking Influence through Official Contacts

Modern government provides a supportive environment in which interest groups can seek to achieve their policy goals. First, modern government is involved in so many interest areas—business regulation, income maintenance, urban renewal, cancer research, and energy development, to name only a few—that hardly any interest in society could fail to benefit significantly from having influence over federal policies or programs. Moreover, most of what

The action orientation of government enhances the influence of interest groups. When a severe drought struck the United States in 1988, the federal government quickly stepped in with aid to farmers. (George Mars Cassidy/The Picture Cube)

government does is decided without much publicity and with the participation of a relatively small group of officials. These conditions, as E. E. Schattschneider noted, are conducive to group influence.[2]

Second, modern government is oriented toward action. Officials are inclined to look for policy solutions to problems rather than to let problems linger. For example, when a severe drought caused a decline in farm production and income in many parts of the country in 1988, Washington did not leave farmers to sink or swim but quickly mobilized to help them out through government programs. As a result of this action orientation, groups can expect officials to be predisposed to act on their claims.

A group's ability to take advantage of its opportunities for influence depends on any number of factors, including its size, its financial strength, and the nature of its policy demands.[3] Although groups cannot control all these factors, they can choose their persuasive strategies. According to Norman Ornstein and Shirley Elder, the two main strategies may be thought of as "inside lobbying" and "outside lobbying."[4] Each strategy involves communication between public officials and group lobbyists, but the strategies differ in what is communicated, who does the communicating, and who receives the communication. Let's begin by discussing **inside lobbying,** which is based on group efforts to develop and maintain close ("inside") contacts with policymakers. (Outside lobbying will be described in the next section.)

ACQUIRING ACCESS TO OFFICIALS

Inside lobbying is designed to give a group direct access to officials in order to influence their decisions. Access is a critical first step. Unless a group can get the attention of officials, it has no chance of persuading them to support its position.

[2] E. E. Schattschneider, *The Semisovereign People: A Realist's View of Democracy in America* (New York: Holt, Rinehart and Winston, 1960), 20–46.
[3] Jeffrey Berry, *Lobbying for the People* (Princeton, N.J.: Princeton University Press, 1977), 62
[4] Norman Ornstein and Shirley Elder, *Interest Groups, Lobbying, and Policymaking* (Washington, D.C.: Congressional Quarterly Press, 1978), 82–86.

In the early nineteenth century, agents for interest groups would wait in the lobbies of legislative buildings to talk with officials. These agents came to be known as lobbyists, and that label is still applied to group representatives. Groups themselves are sometimes referred to as lobbies. The process in which groups and their representatives engage is called **lobbying.** The term refers broadly to efforts by special interests to influence public policy through contacts with public officials.

Lobbying once depended significantly on tangible inducements, sometimes including indirect or even outright bribes. This old form of lobbying survives today. Through personal and family contributions, Charles H. Keating, Jr., owner of Lincoln Savings and Loan, contributed hundreds of thousands of dollars to the campaigns of five U.S. senators, each of whom interceded on his behalf with the Federal Home Loan Bank Board, which was investigating Lincoln's finances. When asked whether his contributions helped him, Keating said, "I certainly hope so." The investigation of Lincoln Savings lagged for two years, costing taxpayers an estimated $1.3 billion.

But modern lobbying generally involves more subtle and sophisticated methods than providing money or personal favors to officials. It focuses on supplying officials with information and indications of group strength which will persuade them to adopt the group's perspective.[5] As one lobbyist explained:

[5] Robert H. Salisbury and Paul Johnson, "Who You Know versus What You Know," *American Journal of Political Science* 33 (February 1989): 175–195.

Access to public officials and the capacity to provide them with useful information are crucial to effective inside lobbying. (Dennis Brack/Black Star)

In the late 1980s five U.S. senators got into trouble for accepting large campaign contributions from Charles Keating and then acting on behalf of Keating's beleaguered savings and loan. The "Keating Five" and their lawyers are shown at hearings of the Senate Ethics Committee, defending themselves against charges of influence peddling. (Brad Markel/Gamma Liaison)

"To a large extent, the three B's—booze, bribes, and broads—have disappeared. . . . Today, a good lobbyist must have the ability to draw up factual information—a lot of it—in a short period of time for people on [Capitol] Hill who want it. . . . Nowadays, taking someone to a football game or a goose hunt just doesn't quite make it."[6] Few policymakers today are going to support a group's claim simply because it asks them to. For a group to gain its objectives, it must win out against competing interests and alternative objectives.

A group's chances of success are enhanced if it has effective lobbyists working on its behalf. Some of the best lobbyists are longtime Washington lawyers from prestigious firms who have built effective working relationships with top officials.[7] Former presidential assistants are also in demand as lobbyists, particularly if the president they served is still in the White House. Lyn Nofziger was charged in 1986 with illegal influence peddling because, after leaving his position as a top aide to President Ronald Reagan, he had not waited one year, as the law required, before attempting to influence policy on behalf of group clients. Former members of Congress do not have to wait before they can lobby legally, and they, too, are in great demand as lobbyists. They have the unique right to go directly onto the floor of the House or Senate to speak with current members. Former members usually represent groups with which they had close ties while they were in office. In the 1980s, Representatives Richard Ichord (D-Mo.) and Bob Wilson (R-Calif.) stepped from senior posts on the House Armed Services Committee to jobs with a lobbying firm that represented seven of the nation's major defense contractors.[8]

[6] Quoted in Kay Lehman Schlozman and John T. Tierney, *Organized Interests and American Democracy* (New York: Harper & Row, 1986), 24.
[7] See Joseph Goulden, *The Superlawyers* (New York: Dell, 1973).
[8] Bill Keller, "Former House Members Ichord, Wilson Sign Up with Top Defense Contractors," *Congressional Quarterly*, June 13, 1984, 1052.

Lyn Nofziger, a former political director for the Reagan administration, was charged with violating federal conflict of interest laws by lobbying for clients within a year of leaving his White House position. His conviction was subsequently overturned by a federal appeals court. (Randy Taylor/Sygma)

Money is the essential ingredient of inside lobbying efforts. The American Petroleum Institute, for example, with its abundant financial resources, can afford a downtown Washington office staffed by lobbyists, petroleum experts, and public relations specialists who help the oil companies to maintain access to and influence with legislative and executive leaders.[9] Many groups spend $1 million or more annually on lobbying. Other groups survive with much less, but it is hard to run a first-rate lobbying campaign on less than $100,000 a year. That figure is roughly what Guam paid a firm in 1988 to lobby for legislation that would change Guam's status from that of U.S. territory to U.S. commonwealth in order to give it more control of the policies governing it.[10] Given the costs of maintaining a Washington lobby, the domination by corporations and trade associations is understandable. They have the money to retain high-priced lobbyists, while many other interests do not. The best that some groups can manage is to buy a small share of a lobbyist's time.

PERSUASION THROUGH CONTACT AND INFORMATION

The medium of exchange for most inside lobbying activity is information. Lobbyists focus on supplying officials with information that will persuade them to adopt the interest group's perspective. The lobbyist's job is to build a persuasive case for the group's viewpoint, and this goal can rarely be achieved without convincing information. An argument that is not solidly based on facts is not likely to get very far, so the foundation of effective lobbying is necessarily

[9] Ornstein and Elder, *Interest Groups, Lobbying, and Policymaking,* 70.
[10] Steven Waldman, "The 'Designer Lobbyists,'" *Newsweek,* April 4, 1988, 22.

the presentation of a strong supporting argument for the group's objective. This argument could conceivably be targeted at legislative, executive, or judicial officials.

Lobbying Congress

Members of Congress are frequent targets of inside lobbying efforts. Lobbyists are required by the Federal Regulation of Lobbying Act of 1946 to register with Congress before they can lawfully engage in persuasive activities. The 1946 act is filled with loopholes, however, and the number of lobbyists who actually lobby Congress is substantially greater than the roughly 5,000 who are formally registered to do so. Although lobbyists must reveal whom they represent, what their legislative agenda is, and how much they and their employers spend on lobbying activities, these disclosure requirements provide relatively limited information and are only weakly enforced.

The benefits of a close relationship with members of Congress are substantial. Through its supporters in Congress, a group can obtain the legislative help it needs to achieve its policy goals. By the same token, members of Congress can gain from working closely with lobbyists. The volume of legislation facing Congress is enormous, and members rely on lobbyists they trust to identify bills that deserve their attention and support. Some members of Congress even involve lobbyists directly in their legislative work. One congressional aide explained:

> My boss demands a speech and a statement for the *Congressional Record* for every bill we introduce or co-sponsor—and we have a lot of bills. I just can't do it all myself. The better lobbyists, when they have a proposal they are pushing, bring it to me along with a couple of speeches, a *Record* insert, and a fact sheet.[11]

As would be expected, lobbyists work primarily with members of Congress who share their views.[12] Union lobbyists work most closely with pro-labor legislators, just as business lobbyists work mainly with pro-business legislators. In recent years, in order to improve communication with their congressional allies, some groups have organized informal caucuses.[13] These caucuses meet periodically to discuss pending issues and coordinate legislative strategy. There are about eighty such caucuses in the House and Senate, including, for example, the Oil Caucus, which consists of pro-industry members of Congress from such oil-producing states as Texas, California, Louisiana, and Oklahoma.

Lobbyists' effectiveness with members of Congress depends in part on their reputation for fair play. An effective lobbyist knows when and how to compromise. No group can expect to get everything it seeks and risks complete failure by insisting that all its demands be met. The goal, as one lobbyist put it, is "solution searching": finding a position that is beneficial to the group without

★ ANALYZE THE ISSUE

Regulation of Lobbying
Lobbying presents the risk that special interests will get undue favors through shady influence peddling. As a result, lobbying reform is often discussed, although the idea of regulating lobbying raises First Amendment issues of free speech and petition. To what extent should lobbying be regulated? What forms might regulation take?

[11] Quoted in Schlozman and Tierney, *Organized Interests and American Democracy,* 85.
[12] For the classic study of this process, see Raymond A. Bauer, Ithiel de Sola Pool, and Lewis Anthony Dexter, *American Business and Public Policy* (New York: Atherton, 1963); see also Lester Milbrath, *The Washington Lobbyists* (Chicago: Rand McNally, 1963), 212.
[13] Susan Webb Hammond, Arthur G. Stevens, Jr., and Daniel P. Mulhollan, "Congressional Caucuses: Legislators as Lobbyists," in Allan J. Cigler and Burdett A. Loomis, eds., *Interest Group Politics* (Washington, D.C.: Congressional Quarterly Press, 1983), 275–297.

conceding more than is necessary.[14] Lobbyists are also expected to play it straight with members of Congress. Said one congressman: "If any [lobbyist] gives me false or misleading information, that's it—I'll never see him again."[15]

Of course, lobbying is more than a process of information sharing and solution searching. Through lobbyists, members of Congress have been known to receive favorable stock options, free trips on corporate jets, jobs for friends, low-interest loans, and nearly every other imaginable benefit. The mistake is to assume that such giveaways are the ordinary means by which lobbyists win support. Such practices can violate the law and subject both lobbyist and legislator to adverse publicity and loss of position. It is also a mistake to think of lobbying as arm-twisting. A group that regularly throws its weight around creates resentment and loses access to members of Congress. The safe lobbying strategy is the aboveboard strategy: provide information, rely on longtime friends among members of Congress, and push steadily but not too aggressively for legislative goals.

Lobbying Executive Agencies

As the scope of the federal government has expanded, lobbying of the executive branch has increased in importance. Bureaucrats make key administrative decisions and develop policy initiatives that the legislative branch later makes into law. By working closely with government agencies, groups can influence policy decisions at the implementation and initiation stages. In return, groups assist government agencies by providing them with information and lending support to their funding and programs.[16]

Nowhere is the link between groups and the bureaucracy more evident than in the regulatory agencies that oversee the nation's business sectors. For example, the Interstate Commerce Commission (ICC), which regulates the nation's railroads and truckers, uses information provided by these interests to decide many of the policies governing their activities. The ICC was created in 1887 to protect the public from price fixing and other corrupt practices then prevalent among the railroads. Yet at times—as when it has permitted trucking companies to set high shipping rates—the ICC has acted more as an agent of industry than as a watchdog for the public. The ICC is often cited as an example of agency "capture." The capture theory suggests that regulatory agencies pass through a series of phases that constitute a "life cycle." Early in an agency's existence, it regulates an industry on the public's behalf, but as the agency matures, its vigor declines until at best it protects the status quo and at worst it falls captive to the very industry it is supposed to regulate.[17]

Research on executive agencies has shown that the capture theory describes only some agencies and then only some of the time.[18] "Bureaucratic agencies,"

★ ANALYZE THE ISSUE

The Mutual Dependency of Lobbyists and the Bureaucracy
As government has expanded, lobbying has increasingly been directed at the bureaucracy. Groups and bureaucrats have come to depend on each other for information and support. Is this development inherently more troubling than the traditional pattern of lobbying, which focuses on legislators? Does frequent contact between unelected bureaucrats and interest-group lobbyists have public benefits as well as costs?

---

[14] Jeffrey M. Berry, *The Interest Group Society* (Boston: Little, Brown, 1984), 121–122.

[15] Quoted in Ornstein and Elder, *Interest Groups, Lobbying, and Policymaking*, 77.

[16] See Elizabeth Drew, "Charlie," in Cigler and Loomis, *Interest Group Politics*, 217–250.

[17] See Marver Bernstein, *Regulating Business by Independent Commission* (Princeton, N.J.: Princeton University Press, 1955).

[18] Paul J. Quirk, *Industry Influence in Federal Regulatory Agencies* (Princeton, N.J.: Princeton University Press, 1981); James Q. Wilson, ed., *The Politics of Regulation* (New York: Basic Books, 1980).

The trucking industry is regulated by the Interstate Commerce Commission, which is widely viewed as a "captive" agency. (Johnson/Gamma-Liaison)

John Chubb writes, "need not be pawns of the interest organizations that confront them." In analyzing energy policy, Chubb found that agencies selectively cooperate with or oppose interest groups, depending on which strategy better suits agency purposes.[19] The first concern of any agency is its own well-being, and agency officials are aware that they can lose political support in Congress, which controls agency funding and program authorization, if they show too much favoritism to a special interest. In 1988 it became known that some Pentagon officials had lost sight of this cardinal rule when they gave inside information on weapons-contract bidding to defense corporations, thus allowing these firms to rig their bids and reap millions in illicit profits. Congress responded to the ensuing scandal by demanding new restrictions on defense contracts, thereby reducing the Pentagon's discretionary authority in securing new weaponry.

Lobbying the Courts

Recent broad rulings by the courts in such areas as education and civil rights have made interest groups recognize that the judiciary, too, can help them reach their goals.[20] Interest groups have several judicial lobbying options, including efforts to influence the selection of federal judges. "Right-to-life" groups pressured the Reagan administration to make opposition to abortion a prerequisite for nomination to the federal bench. Although the administration announced no such policy, it did require that nominees be political conservatives —most of whom had antiabortion views.

[19] John E. Chubb, *Interest Groups and the Bureaucracy: The Politics of Energy* (Stanford, Calif.: Stanford University Press, 1983), 200–201.
[20] Joseph Stewart, Jr., and James F. Sheffield, Jr., "Does Interest Group Litigation Matter? The Case of Black Political Mobilization in Mississippi," *Journal of Politics* 49 (August 1987): 780–798; Joseph F. Kobylka, "A Court-Related Context for Group Litigation," *Journal of Politics* 49 (November 1987): 1061–1078.

Amicus curiae ("friend of the court") briefs are another method of judicial lobbying. An *amicus* brief is a written document in which a group states its position on a particular case and thus makes the court aware of a view in addition to those of the plaintiff and defendant. For example, in the landmark affirmative action case *Regents of the University of California* v. *Bakke* (1978), fifty-eight *amicus* briefs representing the positions of more than one hundred organizations were filed with the Supreme Court at its invitation. *Amicus* briefs can also influence the Court's decision to select a particular case for a hearing by showing that interest in the case extends beyond the parties directly involved.[21]

Finally, and most significant, groups can influence public policy through the courts by filing lawsuits. For some organizations, such as the National Association for the Advancement of Colored People (NAACP) and the American Civil Liberties Union (ACLU), legal action is the primary means of lobbying government. The ACLU devotes itself to defending the constitutional rights of individuals, whatever their beliefs. When the predominantly Jewish town of Skokie, Illinois, sought to bar the American Nazi party from marching through its streets in 1977, as we saw in Chapter 5, the ACLU defended the Nazis' First Amendment right to do so.

As interest groups increasingly resort to legal action, they often find themselves pitted against one another in court. Such environmental litigation groups as the Sierra Club Legal Defense Fund, the Environmental Defense Fund, and the Natural Resources Defense Council have frequently sued large oil, timber, and mining corporations.

Although court action is expensive, it can be less costly and more rewarding than legislative lobbying. The NAACP, for example, has emphasized legal action since its founding in 1909 because it recognizes that minorities often lack influence with elected officials. As we saw in Chapter 7, the NAACP financed the 1954 *Brown* case, in which the Supreme Court declared that racial segregation of public schools is unconstitutional. Had the NAACP tried to achieve the same result by lobbying state legislators in the South, it almost certainly would have failed.

WEBS OF INFLUENCE: GROUPS IN THE POLICY PROCESS

Lobbying efforts provide an incomplete picture of how groups obtain influence. To get a fuller picture, it is necessary to consider also two policy processes, iron triangles and issue networks, in which many groups are enmeshed.

Iron Triangles

An **iron triangle** consists of a small and informal but relatively stable set of bureaucrats, legislators, and lobbyists who are preoccupied with the development of policies beneficial to a particular interest.[22] The three "corners" of one such triangle are the Department of Veterans Affairs (bureaucrats), the veterans'

[21] Gregory A. Caldeira and John R. Wright, "Organized Interests and Agenda Setting in the U.S. Supreme Court," *American Political Science Review* 82 (December 1988): 1109–1128.
[22] See J. Leiper Freeman, *The Political Process* (New York: Random House, 1965); Keith E. Hamm, "Patterns of Influence among Committees, Agencies, and Interest Groups," *Legislative Studies Quarterly* 8 (August 1983): 378–426.

★ HOW THE UNITED STATES COMPARES

THE PREVALENCE OF LOBBYING

With its federal system and separate branches of government, the United States is a lobbyist's dream. If unsuccessful with legislators, the lobbyist can turn to executives or the courts. If thwarted at the state level, the lobbyist can turn to the national level of government. By comparison, the governments of most other democratic nations are not organized in ways that facilitate group access and influence. Great Britain's unitary government and parliamentary system, for example, result in a concentration of power in the majority party. Britain's prime minister and cabinet ministers are, at one and the same time, the majority-party leaders, the legislative leaders, and the executive heads. Their support is a great asset for a group but is correspondingly hard to achieve. A group may find it difficult even to get their attention. Not surprisingly, interests in Britain tend to organize nationally and to work through the political parties. Groups in the United States are more likely to function independently of parties and to organize at both the national and state levels.

U.S. lobbying groups are unparalleled in their number, in their spending, and in their impact (through PACs) on election campaigns. In fact, lobbyists of the traditional American type are found in only a few countries. Interest groups are important in all democracies, but the United States, Canada, and Britain are among the few countries in which groups hire lobbyists to intercede with officials on their behalf.

In all Western democracies, interest groups seem to be gaining strength while political parties grow weaker. An explanation is that people's interests have become more focused and less ideological. Some traditional interest groups, such as labor, are on the wane in all democracies, while environmental groups and single-issue groups are on the increase.

SOURCE: Clive S. Thomas, "Interest Groups in Post-Industrial Democracies," *Newsletter of Political Organizations and Parties*, 9, no. 1, 1991, p. 8.

affairs committees of Congress (legislators), and veterans' groups such as the American Legion and the Veterans of Foreign Wars (lobbyists), which together determine most of the policies affecting veterans. Of course, others, including the president and the majority in Congress, are needed to enact new programs to benefit veterans. However, they tend to defer to the policy preferences voiced by the veterans' triangle, because the triangle's members best understand the programs, problems, and policy needs of veterans.

When a group is part of an iron triangle, it has an inside track to those legislators and bureaucrats who are in the best position to promote its cause. And because it has something of value to offer each of them in return, the relationship tends to be ironclad. The group provides lobbying support for the bureaucrats when their agency's funding and programs are at issue, and it has campaign contributions to give its congressional allies. The American Dairy Association, for example, contributes more than $1 million each election year to members of Congress (nearly all of them from farm states) who serve on the House and Senate Agriculture committees. Figure 14-1 summarizes the benefits that flow to each member of an iron triangle.

Issue Networks

An iron triangle represents the pattern of influence only in certain policy areas, such as aspects of agriculture and public works. Iron triangles were once more dominant than they are today. The most common pattern of influence now is

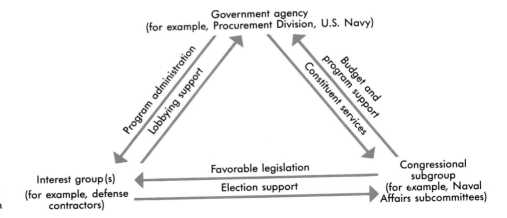

FIGURE 14-1 How an Iron Triangle Benefits Its Participants
An iron triangle works to the advantage of each of its participants—an interest group, a congressional subgroup, and a government agency.

the issue network. An **issue network** is an informal grouping of officials, lobbyists, and policy specialists (the "network") who are brought together by their shared interest and expertise in a particular policy area (the "issue").

Issue networks are a result of the increasing complexity and interconnectedness of policy problems. The complexity of modern issues often makes it essential that a participant have specialized knowledge of the issue at hand in order to join in the debate. Someone who lacks this knowledge may try to influence the debate but is not likely to be taken seriously by those who are in the know. Thus, unlike iron triangles, where one's position is everything, an issue network is built around policy expertise. On any given issue, the participants might come from a variety of executive agencies, congressional committees, interest groups, and institutions, such as universities or "think tanks." And, unlike iron triangles, issue networks are less stable and less clearly defined. As the issue develops, new participants may join the debate and old ones drop out. Once the issue is resolved, the network disbands.[23]

An example of an issue network is the set of participants who would come together if Congress proposed a major change in the requirements for constructing nuclear power plants. In earlier times this issue might have been settled by an iron triangle consisting of the Nuclear Regulatory Commission, the nuclear power industry, and the energy committees in Congress. Today, however, the issue network that would form would also include energy policy specialists and representatives of environmental groups, consumer advocacy groups, oil companies, and labor unions, to name just a few.

Interest groups are at home within issue networks. In fact, because groups focus narrowly and constantly on the particular policy area of concern to them, their expertise is a valued part of an issue network's debate. Of course, unlike an iron triangle, which is dominated by like-minded groups, an issue network can involve opposing groups.

★ **ANALYZE THE ISSUE**

The Relative Influence of Iron Triangles and Issue Networks
Some observers claim that issue networks are signs that government has become overly subject to stalemate and specialization. The argument has some validity, but is it too one-sided? Consider agricultural policy. When iron triangles were at their peak, agricultural policy was decided chiefly by agricultural groups and officials. Today, in the era of issue networks, consumer- and environment-oriented groups and officials also play major parts in setting agricultural policy. Are issue networks therefore an improvement on iron triangles?

[23] Hugh Heclo, "Issue Networks and the Executive Establishment," in Anthony King, ed., *The New American Political System* (Washington, D.C.: American Enterprise Institute, 1978), 87–124; Thomas L. Gais, Mark A. Peterson, and Jack L. Webb, "Interest Groups, Iron Triangles, and Representative Institutions in American National Government," *British Journal of Political Science* 14 (1984): 161–185.

Regulating the construction of nuclear power plants requires policy expertise, which issue networks are uniquely qualified to provide. (Tannenbaum/ Sygma)

Outside Lobbying: Seeking Influence through Public Pressure

Although interest groups may rely on their Washington lobbying alone, this approach is not likely to be successful unless it is backed up by evidence of a connection to the public. Elected officials particularly, but also bureaucrats, are always more receptive to a lobbying group if it can demonstrate convincingly that its concerns reflect those of a vital constituency. Accordingly, groups make use of constituency connections when it seems advantageous to do so. They engage in **outside lobbying,** which involves bringing public ("outside") pressure to bear on policymakers.[24] The "outside" approach typically takes the form of either *constituency advocacy* or *electoral action*.

CONSTITUENCY ADVOCACY: GRASS-ROOTS LOBBYING

Some groups depend heavily on **grass-roots lobbying**—that is, pressure designed to convince government officials that a group's policy position has broad public support.[25] To mobilize constituents, groups can mount advertising and public relations campaigns through the media. They can also encourage their members to write or call their elected representatives, or even see their representatives personally. In 1988, for example, more than 700 insurance agents visited congressional offices in a successful effort to protect the insurance business from encroachment by banks. Senator William Proxmire (D-Wis.),

[24] Ornstein and Elder, *Interest Groups, Lobbying, and Policymaking,* 88–93; Berry, *Interest Group Society,* 151.
[25] Kay Lehman Schlozman and John T. Tierney, "More of the Same: Washington Pressure Group Activity in a Decade of Change," *Journal of Politics* 45 (May 1983): 363–364.

★ THE MEDIA AND THE PEOPLE

LOBBYING AND NEW MEDIA TECHNOLOGIES

Interest groups are discovering that new technologies can help their lobbying efforts. Television satellites, computers, and high-speed printers are changing the way interest groups operate.

In the area of telecommunications, the U.S. Chamber of Commerce broke new ground with Biznet, its closed-circuit satellite TV network. The network links together the Chamber's member organizations throughout the country. "Think of the increase in influence on the public policy-making process when we have real-time access to our members and they have real-time access to Washington," noted Richard Lesher, the Chamber's president. With the network, the Chamber can alert its members rapidly to events on Capitol Hill. Grass-roots campaigns can be developed in a matter of days rather than weeks. The Chamber's network also enables companies to set up two-way televised meetings with members of Congress to discuss bills. Biznet has inspired at least one imitator, the AFL-CIO's Solidarity Satellite Network. The network is used for closed-circuit meetings at which labor leaders in various cities confer on labor policy.

Computers have greatly simplified the job of compiling mailing lists and targeting people for direct-mail campaigns. Sophisticated computer systems allow organizations to identify their members by congressional district and even by precinct, as well as by occupation, age, party registration, and any other variable that is of interest to them. The Chamber of Commerce uses its computers and detailed information on member firms—such as number of employees, revenues, and plant locations—to refine its mail campaigns to include only those firms directly affected by pending legislation.

Changes in printing technology, such as high-speed laser printers, make it possible to increase the number of letters sent while making each one look personalized. In one direct-mail campaign, a high-speed printer produced personalized form letters with slightly varying messages, each printed with the individual constituent's name and address, for the constituents to sign and send on to their representatives in Congress. Proxy mailings are sometimes sent without the constituent's direct knowledge. The National Education Association (NEA) got the permission of 100,000 teachers to sign their names to NEA-generated letters on a variety of issues. The NEA signs and sends out the letters and telegrams as they are needed. This method has its drawbacks, however. When Senator William Cohen of Maine responded to proxy letters generated by an organization, he discovered that some of the constituents who had supposedly just written to him were dead.

These expensive innovations cannot guarantee an increase in the political clout of an interest group. As one printer candidly admitted, "The best technology in the world cannot make a dead issue look like it's alive, or a badly written letter look like it's well written."

SOURCES: Jeffrey M. Berry, *The Interest Group Society* (Boston: Little, Brown, 1984), 154–155; Burdett A. Loomis, "A New Era: Groups and the Grass Roots," in Allan J. Cigler and Burdett A. Loomis, eds., *Interest Group Politics* (Washington, D.C.: Congressional Quarterly Press, 1983), 169–190; *New York Times*, October 12, 1983, B-9; Bill Keller, "Computers and Laser Printers Have Recast the Injunction: 'Write Your Congressman,'" *Congressional Quarterly Weekly Report*, September 11, 1982, 2245–2247; William J. Lanouette, "Chamber's Ponderous Decision Making Leaves It Sitting on the Sidelines," *National Journal*, July 24, 1982, 1298–1301; Mark Green and Andrew Buchsbaum, "How the Chamber's Computers Con the Congress," *Washington Monthly*, May 1980, 48–50.

then chair of the Banking Committee, was impressed: "There are more insurance agents in New Jersey alone than there are banks in the entire country."[26]

A more dramatic grass-roots lobbying tactic consists of public protest or demonstration—as when in 1978 a group of 2,000 farmers attracted national attention to agricultural problems by driving their tractors around the White House and the Capitol building in Washington.

As with other forms of influence, the impact of grass-roots lobbying is

[26] Quoted in Ernest Wittenberg and Elisabeth Wittenberg, *How to Win in Washington* (Cambridge, Mass.: Basil Blackwell, 1989), 51.

Grass-roots lobbying brought 2000 farmers to Washington in 1978. The trucks and tractors circling the White House and the Capitol were visible reminders to federal officials that agricultural workers were experiencing hard times. (Arthur Grace/Sygma)

difficult to assess.[27] Some members of Congress downplay the influence it has on them, but nearly every congressional office monitors letters and phone calls from constituents as a way of tracking public opinion. In 1988 Senator William Cohen (R-Maine) received 9,000 letters on the issue of military assistance for the Contra rebels in Nicaragua. Most of the letters were prompted by Neighbor to Neighbor, a grass-roots group that opposed U.S. aid to the Contras.[28] Cohen voted against the appropriation.

Grass-roots lobbying has occasionally been known to backfire. In 1983 insurance companies initiated a grass-roots campaign of 500,000 form letters to selected members of Congress. The letters demanded a stop to pending legislation that would require insurance companies to alter their property and casualty coverage. Angered by the tone and volume of the letters, some members of Congress threatened to close tax loopholes that benefited insurance companies.[29] The campaign stopped abruptly.

Grass-roots lobbying works better for groups whose members are well educated and thus more likely to write or phone their representatives. In the early 1980s the Sierra Club and other environmental groups, which have an educated membership, employed a successful letter-writing campaign that helped alter the Reagan administration's policies regarding the commercial use of federal lands.

[27] Richard E. Cohen, "Controlling the Lobbyists," *National Journal*, December 31, 1983, 2591; Burdett A. Loomis, "A New Era: Groups and the Grass Roots," in Cigler and Loomis, *Interest Group Politics*, 184; Linda L. Fowler and Ronald G. Shaiko, "The Grass Roots Connection," *American Journal of Political Science* 31 (August 1987): 484.
[28] Nancy Cooper, "Nowhere to Run, Nowhere to Hide," *Newsweek*, February 1, 1988, 31.
[29] Steven Pressman, "Critics Attack Industry Drive against Unisex Insurance Bills," *Congressional Quarterly*, July 9, 1983, 1401–1403.

Former White House Press Secretary James Brady, who was shot and partially paralyzed during the 1981 assassination attempt on President Reagan, celebrates a hard-fought victory against the National Rifle Association, a powerful gun lobby. Over the NRA's objection, the Senate had just passed a bill requiring a 5-day waiting period for handgun purchases. (Wide World Photos)

TRYING TO DELIVER THE GROUP VOTE

"Reward your friends and punish your enemies" is a political adage that describes roughly how interest groups view election campaigns. As part of an "outside" strategy, organized groups work to elect their supporters and defeat their opponents. Although they are less influential than they are commonly assumed to be, they can have some real impact on an election. The mere possibility of electoral opposition from a powerful group can keep an officeholder from openly obstructing its interests.

Groups with a large membership try to exert influence by urging their members to vote for or against particular candidates. Many candidates are not willing to test whether a group's vote will hurt their chances of victory. Opposition from the National Rifle Association (NRA) is a major reason the United States has lagged behind other Western societies in its handgun-control laws, although polls show that most Americans favor such laws. The NRA's power has weakened as gun-related crime has increased, but the NRA has staunch supporters in every congressional district and works to defeat candidates who favor gun control in almost any form. The NRA even has a "test" that it offers candidates. Allen O'Donnell, a Nebraska college professor, received an A-minus on his NRA test, while his primary election opponent got an A and received the NRA's support. O'Donnell lost the primary.[30]

THE RISE OF PACs: CONTRIBUTING MONEY

Another way in which interest groups try to gain influence is by contributing money to candidates' campaigns. As one lobbyist said, "Talking to politicians is

[30] Allen O'Donnell, personal communication.

fine, but with a little money they hear you better."[31] By this standard, groups are coming through loud and clear: they contribute millions of dollars to political campaigns. Although PAC money does not literally "buy" votes in Congress, it does buy access. Members of Congress listen to the groups that underwrite their campaigns.

Because the potential for abuse is high, the role of interest groups in campaign finance has long been a matter of controversy. In the late nineteenth century corporations poured millions into legislative election campaigns in order to block attempts at business regulation. In 1907 Congress passed legislation that prohibited corporate contributions to candidates for federal office. However, under-the-table corporate payments became common, and there was no law prohibiting a wealthy businessperson from giving a large personal donation to a candidate. The Watergate affair helped to change these practices. President Richard Nixon's reelection campaign was heavily underwritten by wealthy donors and corporate money that had illegally been channeled ("laundered") through Mexican banks. In response, Congress strengthened laws requiring candidates to account for the sources of their funds and placed a ceiling on the contributions they could receive from a single source.

However, these reforms opened the door to a larger overall funding role for interest groups through provisions that relaxed legal restrictions on **political action committees (PACs)**.[32] Through its PAC, a group can raise money for election campaigns by soliciting *voluntary* contributions from members or employees. A group cannot give organizational funds (such as corporate profits or union dues) to candidates, but it can give funds that it raises by soliciting voluntary contributions.

PACs are admired by those who believe that a campaign finance system

[31] Quoted in Mark Green, "Political PAC-Man," *New Republic*, December 13, 1982, 20.
[32] See Frank Sorauf, *Money in American Elections* (Boston: Scott, Foresman, 1988).

As this 1889 cartoon by Joseph Koppler shows, at the end of the last century big business attempted to run the show in Congress through its enormous (and unregulated) campaign contributions. (The New York Historical Society, New York City)

based on pooled contributions by individuals is superior to one in which candidates rely heavily on a few wealthy donors.[33] However, critics claim that PACs give interest groups altogether too much influence over public officials.[34] Whichever view is accepted, there is no doubt that the emergence of PACs as a leading source of campaign funds is one of the most significant developments of recent elections.[35]

PAC Spending as a Factor in Election Campaigns

Before the reforms of the early 1970s, PACs were a modest component of campaign financing. As late as 1974 there were only about 600 PACs, and their contribution to congressional candidates was $11.6 million—about 15 percent of all funds received by those candidates. The number of PACs increased sharply in the late 1970s, however (see Figure 14-2), and so did their contributions. There are now roughly 5,000 PACs and, during the 1989–1990 election cycle, PAC contributions to congressional campaigns reached $150 million, about 30 percent of total contributions to these campaigns.

As PAC money can be raised earlier and more quickly than money from individual contributors, PACs have become a critical factor in getting congressional campaigns off the ground. Their role is less significant in presidential

[33] See Michael J. Malbin, "Of Mountains and Molehills," in Michael J. Malbin, *Parties, Interest Groups, and Campaign Finance Laws* (Washington, D.C.: American Enterprise Institute, 1981), 157–177.
[34] See Fred Wertheimer, "Common Cause Declares War on Political Action Committees," *Common Cause*, March/April 1983; Elizabeth Drew, *Politics and Money: The New Road to Corruption* (New York: Macmillan, 1983); Philip M. Stern, *The Best Congress Money Can Buy* (New York: Pantheon, 1988).
[35] See Drew, *Politics and Money;* Larry Sabato, *PAC Power: Inside the World of Political Action Committees* (New York: Norton, 1984); Ronald J. Hrebenar and Clive S. Thomas. eds., *Interest Group Politics in the American West* (Salt Lake City: University of Utah Press, 1987).

FIGURE 14-2 Growth in the Number of PACs, 1974–1990 The number of PACs began to increase sharply after campaign finance reforms were enacted in the early 1970s. *Source: Federal Elections Commission.*

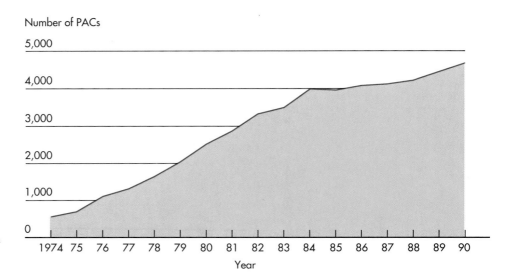

Number of PACs

5,000

4,000

3,000

2,000

1,000

0

1974 75 76 77 78 79 80 81 82 83 84 85 86 87 88 89 90

Year

campaigns, which are larger in scale and publicly funded in part and therefore depend on a wider range of funding sources than do congressional campaigns.

A PAC is legally limited in the amount it can contribute to the campaign of a candidate for federal office. The ceiling is $10,000 per candidate—$5,000 in the primary campaign and $5,000 in the general election campaign. However, there is no legal limit on how many candidates a PAC can support.

PACs have conducted increasing numbers of "independent" campaigns on behalf of certain candidates. In such cases, provided that the PAC's campaign is not coordinated with the candidate's own effort, the PAC is not bound by the $10,000 spending limit. The National Conservative Political Action Committee (NCPAC) has led the way in independent campaigns by developing its own television advertising and grass-roots efforts to elect conservatives and defeat liberals. NCPAC has spent several million dollars in each congressional election year since 1980, and it ran a $12 million independent campaign in 1984 to reelect President Reagan.

PAC Support for Incumbents

Members of Congress who seek reelection have a high success rate—over 70 percent for senators and over 90 percent for representatives. In 1990 the reelection rate for House incumbents exceeded 95 percent, while only one Senate incumbent was defeated. PACs are well aware of the fact that incumbents are likely to win and thus to remain in a position to make policy. For this reason, the great bulk of PAC contributions are given to incumbents seeking reelection. "We have a friendly incumbent policy," said one PAC director, expressing a common view. "We always stick with the incumbent when we agree with them both."[36] In 1990 House and Senate incumbents received $120 million from PACs, eight times the $15 million their challengers received.

That these PACs feel compelled to contribute to lawmakers who have no opponent shows that what is being sought is access and influence.
Joan Claybrook,
President of Public Citizen

The tendency of PACs to back incumbents has blurred long-standing partisan divisions in campaign funding. Business interests traditionally have been pro-Republican, but corporate PACs have been reluctant to anger Democratic incumbents. The result is that Democratic candidates for Congress, particularly in the House, have received nearly as much support from business-related PACs as have Republicans.[37]

Other PACs, especially those organized to promote a particular public policy or ideology, are less pragmatic than corporate PACs. The Christian Moral Government Fund, for example, backs only candidates who take conservative stands on such issues as school prayer, abortion, and pornography. A few PACs even demand that candidates commit themselves in writing to the group's policies. In 1982 PeacePAC required recipients of its contributions to sign a pledge to support a nuclear freeze and to oppose funding of the B-1 bomber and the MX missile.[38]

---

[36] Quoted in Larry Sabato, *PAC Power*, 72.
[37] Michael Barone and Grant Ujifusa, *The Almanac of American Politics, 1986* (Washington, D.C.: National Journal, 1985), 2147–2152.
[38] Larry Sabato, "Parties, PACs, and Independent Groups," in Thomas E. Mann and Norman Ornstein, eds., *The American Elections of 1982* (Washington, D.C.: American Enterprise Institute, 1983), 92.

★ CRITICAL THINKING

SHOULD PACS BE ABOLISHED?

American elections have changed greatly in recent years, and one of the most significant and controversial changes has been the increasingly large role played by interest groups through their political action committees (PACs). PACs now provide about a third of all funds contributed to congressional candidates, and their prominence in state and local campaigns is growing.

Most of the criticisms of PACs have been directed at two developments. The first is the tendency of PACs to concentrate their spending on incumbents. The advantages to PACs of an incumbent strategy are obvious. Incumbents usually win, so in backing incumbents PACs are taking less risk than if they back challengers. In addition, a PAC can target incumbents who work in policy areas that are of particular concern to the interest group that the PAC represents. For example, the work of Congress is done primarily in committees, such as the House and Senate banking committees. Banking industry PACs, by focusing on members of these committees, are assured of making contact with the legislators who have the biggest say over policies that affect banking interests.

A second source of concern about PACs is the activities of "independent" PACs. These PACs are not subject to the same contribution limitations as other PACs, provided that they do not directly coordinate their activities with those of a candidate. They have had a prominent role in presidential election campaigns because their expenditures do not count against the expenditure limits imposed on the Republican and Democratic nominees (see Chapter 18). Independent PACs

have spent more than $10 million in each of the recent presidential campaigns, primarily on behalf of the Republican nominees. George Bush benefited from independent PAC support in 1988 in the form of a televised commercial that received widespread attention and apparently hurt his opponent, Massachusetts Governor Michael Dukakis. The commercial portrayed a convicted felon named Willie Horton, who, while on weekend furlough from a Massachusetts prison under a program supported by Dukakis, brutalized a Maryland couple. Some analysts believe that the Willie Horton ad was a turning point in the 1988 race; Dukakis had been ahead in the polls before the commercial was aired.

PACs are favored by those who believe that interest groups should have a large role in campaigns and who prefer a PAC-based system of campaign finance to the previous system. Before the laws were changed in the 1970s to allow PACs to play a larger role in campaign finance, much of the money in elections came from "fat cats"—wealthy contributors who gave thousands, and in some cases millions, of dollars to candidates. No PAC can give more than $5000 to a candidate in a campaign, and PACs get their money from voluntary donations from small contributors. In a sense, PACs allow thousands of like-minded people to pool their contributions in order to influence election campaigns.

Do you think PACs are a problem? If so, should PACs be abolished or simply regulated more closely? If you were to limit the role of PACs, what restrictions would you place on them?

Assessing PACs: The Corporate Advantage

More than 40 percent of all PACs are associated with corporations (see Table 14-1). Examples include the Ford Motor Company Civic Action Fund, the Sun Oil Company Political Action Committee (Sunpac), and the Coca-Cola PAC. The next largest group of PACs consists of those linked to noneconomic groups (that is, public-interest, single-issue, and ideological groups), such as the liberal People for the American Way and the conservative NCPAC (National Conservative Political Action Committee). Ranking third are PACs tied to trade and professional associations, such as AMPAC (American Medical Association) and R-PAC (National Association of Realtors). Labor unions were once the major source of group contributions, but they now rank fourth.

TABLE 14-1 Number and Percentage of Political Action Committees (PACs) in Five Categories Most PACs represent business: corporations and trade associations make up 62% of the total.

Category	Number	Percentage
Corporate	2,116	45%
Noneconomic	1,337	29
Trade/membership association	796	17
Labor	372	8
Agriculture	60	1
All categories	4,681	100%

SOURCE: Federal Election Commission figures, 1990.

SINGLE-ISSUE POLITICS AND THE DECLINE OF POLITICAL PARTIES

As the growth of PACs illustrates, group activity has expanded rapidly in recent decades. Through inside and outside lobbying, group politics now intrudes heavily on the policymaking and electoral processes (see Table 14-2). Some analysts describe the situation as the triumph of **single-issue politics:** separate groups organized around nearly every conceivable policy issue, with each group pressing its demands and influence to the utmost.

For example, in 1979 the National Association of Home Builders (NAHB) was barely visible on Capitol Hill. The NAHB's weakness showed as the federal government used high interest rates to curb inflation while the housing industry fell into a depression-like slump. Three years later, however, the NAHB's lobbyists were being listened to more carefully. What had happened? First, the builders had beefed up their Washington lobby from one staff person and a half-time secretary to seven full-time staffers and a budget of $500,000. Next, the NAHB had worked to politicize its members by establishing government-affairs "schools" in which more than 2,000 home builders learned how Congress and political campaigns work. Finally, the NAHB had expanded its

TABLE 14-2 Tactics Used in Inside and Outside Lobbying Strategies Inside and outside lobbying are based on different tactics.

Inside Lobbying	Outside Lobbying
Developing contacts with legislators and executives	Encouraging group members to write or phone their representatives in Congress
Providing information and policy proposals to key officials	Seeking favorable coverage by news media
Forming coalitions with other groups	Encouraging members to support particular candidates in elections
	Targeting group resources on key election races
	Making PAC contributions to candidates

largely ineffective political action committee, BUILD-PAC. In 1978 BUILD-PAC had only $38,000 to contribute to political candidates, but by 1982 it had raised more than $1 million to become one of the wealthiest political action committees.[39]

Why have groups become so much more visible and powerful than ever before? As we discussed earlier, modern communication technology has made it easier for groups to organize for influence, and modern government offers numerous benefits that groups have a stake in maintaining. Of equal significance, however, is the fact that political parties have declined in importance. Whereas candidates in U.S. elections once turned to the parties for help, they now increasingly turn to groups. The candidate-centered campaigns of today run on money and media appeals, not on volunteer labor and party loyalty. Groups have an abundance of the resource—money—that is the foundation of the modern campaign for public office. Until recent decades, interest groups in Washington confined their efforts largely to inside lobbying. The outside lobbying of today—grass-roots pressure and PAC contributions—is a relatively new development and coincides with the decline of parties.

Group politics differs from party politics. As we noted in Chapter 12, parties seek to forge a majority, and this effort draws them naturally toward an emphasis on broad issues and interests. Parties do not ignore narrow interests, but they must subordinate any particular interest to a wider interest so that they can offer platforms that will appeal to the public in general. Thus democratic countries that have stronger political parties tend to have weaker interest groups. Power in these societies flows through the parties; to get a share of power, a group is forced to tone down its demands. U.S. parties have never been strong enough to control groups fully, but they have less control over them now than at nearly any time in the past. Parties are even losing the competition for citizens' loyalties; today most adult Americans believe they are better represented by interest groups than by parties.

Underlying the decline of parties and the upsurge of groups are the individualism and diversity that characterize American society. Groups represent the differences among citizens, not their similarities. Groups might be termed the organizational form of individualism: they are a means by which people in a pluralistic society find it possible to advance their particular political concerns.[40]

Groups and the Collective Interest

In *Federalist* No. 10 James Madison considered the conditions under which the pursuit of self-interest could also serve the collective interest of society. We noted at the end of Chapter 13 that although Madison lamented the tendency of a given group to further its own interests at the expense of other interests in society, he did not believe that groups could ever be persuaded as a matter of

[39] Timothy D. Schellhardt, "Builders Try to Wield Political Cash to Get Housing Aid from Congress," *Wall Street Journal*, March 25, 1982; *Builder*, January 1983, 174, and January 1985, 255.
[40] See William P. Browne, "Organized Interests and Their Issue Niches," *Journal of Politics* 52 (May 1990): 477–509.

routine to subordinate their cause to the good of the whole society. And the thought that the power of government might be used to repress group interests were abhorrent to Madison.

Madison concluded that the only feasible solution to the problem of self-interested factions was a governing system that prevented groups from judging the worth of their own cause. Liberty required that any group be allowed to act as "advocate," but good sense required that it not be allowed also to act as "judge." As we saw in Chapter 3, Madison's constitutional solution was a separation of powers which would make it nearly impossible for a single group to gain full control of government and thus be in a position to judge the merits of its own cause. Each group would have to work with others, and they would decide the merits of a given group's particular claim in the course of deciding issues of policy.

Madison's concerns are as relevant today as they were two centuries ago. Groups are a means by which society's various interests obtain representation. Yet the role of groups must also be assessed by their contribution to society's collective interest. Do the policies that result from group politics serve the common good? Pluralism and interest-group liberalism offer opposing opinions on this question.

A FAVORABLE VIEW OF GROUP INFLUENCE: PLURALISM

As we noted in Chapter 13, pluralism holds that society is roughly the sum of the separate interests that constitute it. Pluralists even question whether such terms as "the common good" and "the collective interest" are very useful. If people disagree on the goals of society, as they always do, how can it be said that people have a "common" or "collective" concern? As an alternative, pluralists would substitute the sum of people's separate interests as a rough approximation of society's collective interest.

The relevant question then becomes not whether a single interest gets its way in a particular instance, but whether many and varied (that is, plural) interests win out at one time or another. The logic of this proposition is that, because society has so many interests, the common good is ultimately served by a process that enables a great many interests to gain favorable policies. Thus if manufacturing interests prevail on one issue, environmentalists on another, farmers on a third, minorities on a fourth, and so on until a wide range of particular interests are served, the collective interest of society has been promoted.[41]

As pluralist theory maintains, it is a mistake to assume that the only meritorious policies are those, such as national defense and public education, that broadly affect nearly everyone in society. In fact, few policies apply to the public generally; most bestow a particular benefit on a specific interest. Examples include government loans to students, price supports for farmers, national parks for vacationers, protective tariffs for steelmakers, and school lunch programs for the children of poor families. Representation in a complex

---

[41] See Robert Dahl, *Who Governs?* (New Haven, Conn.: Yale University Press, 1961); Robert Dahl, *Dilemmas of Pluralist Democracy* (New Haven, Conn.: Yale University Press, 1982); William Kelso, *American Democratic Theory: Pluralism and Its Critics* (Westport, Conn.: Greenwood Press, 1978).

society requires attention to special needs, and the policies that address these needs can also advance broader objectives. For example, when government intervened in the mid-1980s to protect thousands of farms threatened by bankruptcy, the action also brought greater stability to the general economy and protected the production of food grains and other commodities on which the country as a whole depends.

Pluralists also point out that groups do not always get their way, particularly on those issues that touch society broadly. For example, the Tax Reform Act of 1986, which some regard as the most significant overhaul of the U.S. tax code in history, was passed despite intense opposition from powerful interests, each of which wanted its tax loopholes preserved.[42]

AN UNFAVORABLE VIEW OF GROUP INFLUENCE: INTEREST-GROUP LIBERALISM

Although pluralist theory offers some compelling arguments, it also has questionable aspects. In a direct attack on pluralism, Theodore Lowi argues that there is no concept of society's collective interest in a system that allows special interests to determine for themselves which policy benefits they receive, regardless of how many interests are served.[43] The fact that a great number and variety of interests receive a slice of the pie is beside the point if each group decides for itself what its slice is going to be. When each group makes its own choice, the basis of decision in each case is not majority (collective) rule but minority (special-interest) rule.

In making his argument, Lowi accepts Madison's point that no interest should be allowed to be both advocate and judge. But whereas Madison's major concern was about a single interest that might capture full political control, Lowi's observation is based on the ability of various groups to come close to monopolizing power in their special areas. The policies that result favor the interests not of a majority but of a series of minorities. The iron triangle is the clearest example, with a particular group working in tandem with legislators and bureaucrats who have a stake in promoting the group's interest. Of course, the policy proposals that emerge from an iron triangle must still gain the acceptance of other officials, and this necessity serves as a restraint. But the sheer volume of modern legislation prevents most such policies from being studied closely and thus from acquiring the support of a true deliberative majority.

It is seldom safe to assume that what a popular majority favors is what a special-interest group wants. Consider the case of the federal law that required auto dealers to list the known defects of used cars on window stickers. The law was repealed after an extensive lobbying campaign financed by contributions of more than $1 million by the National Association of Automobile Dealers to the reelection campaigns of nearly 200 members of the U.S. House of Representatives.[44] Although an overwhelming majority of the general public would surely

---

[42] Jeffrey H. Birnbaum and Alan S. Murray, *Showdown at Gucci Gulch* (New York: Random House, 1987).

[43] Lowi, *End of Liberalism*.

[44] Berry, *Interest Group Society*, 172.

Sometimes the interests of a group clearly diverge from the majority opinion, as when the National Association of Auto Dealers lobbied successfully against legislation that would have required auto dealers to inform customers about any defects in used cars. (Sam Pierson/Photo Researchers)

have favored retention of the law, the car dealers' view prevailed. As Mancur Olson said of such situations, "Small groups . . . can often defeat the large groups . . . which are normally supposed to prevail in a democracy."[45]

Lowi uses the term **interest-group liberalism** to describe the tendency of officials to support the policy demands of the interest group or groups that have a special stake in a policy. Interest-group liberalism constitutes a partial abdication by government of its authority over policy. In practical terms, it is the group, not the government, that is deciding policy. The adverse effects include a weakening of majoritarian institutions and an inefficient use of society's resources: groups get what they want, whether or not their priorities are those of society as a whole. Lowi also points out that interest-group liberalism dulls the public spirit: a concern for justice (doing the "right thing") gives way to a concern for jurisdiction (deciding which groups have the "right" to prevail in a particular policy area).[46]

HOW MADISON'S SOLUTION IS NOW PART OF THE PROBLEM

Ironically, Madison's constitutional solution to the problem of factions has become part of the problem. The American system of checks and balances, with a separation of powers at its core, was designed primarily to block control by a *majority* faction. Madison did not believe that a minority posed a significant threat, because "if a faction consists of less than a majority, relief is supplied by the republican principle, which enables the majority to defeat its [that is, the minority faction's] sinister views by regular vote." Yet by the same token a

[45] Mancur Olson, Jr., *The Logic of Collective Action: Public Goods and the Theory of Groups*, rev. ed. (Cambridge, Mass.: Harvard University Press, 1971), 127–128.
[46] Lowi, *End of Liberalism*, 295–298; see also Ornstein and Elder, *Interest Groups, Lobbying, and Policymaking*.

★ ANALYZE THE ISSUE

Special and General Interests
Is the sum of special interests nearly the same as the general interest? An answer to this question requires a judgment about the degree to which people's interests are more separate than general. An answer also requires a judgment about the degree to which government's response to special interests limits its ability to respond to general needs.

majority faction, by definition, has enough votes to get its way and thus to be in a position to sacrifice "both the public good and the rights of other citizens" to its selfish ends.[47]

Madison's solution to this problem has more or less worked as planned. Throughout U.S. history majorities have been frustrated in their efforts to gain full power by America's elaborate system of divided government. This same system, however, has made it relatively easy for minority factions—or, as they are called today, special-interest groups—to get their way. Madison did not anticipate that divided government would lead to the delegation of authority in particular policy areas to small sets of officials. Nevertheless, this development occurred, and it provides an almost perfect context for group influence. A group with a special interest in a particular policy area does not have to win majority backing; it has only to persuade the small set of officials in charge. And because these officials are likely also to benefit from actions beneficial to the group, they are inclined to serve its purposes. Only by great effort—more effort than any official can muster for each and every policy decision—can society's broad interest be imposed on decisions made in these small policy realms. Chapters 16 and 20 will discuss this problem further.

Summary

Organized interests seek influence largely by lobbying public officials and contributing to election campaigns. Lobbying serves primarily to provide policymakers with information and to alert them to group members' views. Using an "inside strategy," lobbyists develop direct contacts with legislators, government bureaucrats, and members of the judiciary in order to persuade them to accept their group's perspective on policy. Through iron triangles and issue networks particularly, groups develop the access to and influence with policymakers which result in policies favorable to them.

Groups also use an "outside strategy," seeking to mobilize public support for their goals. This strategy relies in part on grass-roots lobbying—encouraging group members and the public to communicate their policy views to officials. "Outside" lobbying also includes efforts to elect officeholders who will support group aims. Groups endorse candidates and urge their members to vote for them and, most important, contribute money to candidates' election campaigns. Through political action committees (PACs), organized groups now provide nearly a third of all contributions received by congressional candidates.

Public policy has increasingly been decided through the activities of organized groups. As society has become more complex and its sectors more interdependent, public policy has become more technical and increasingly targeted at particular problems. This situation works to the advantage of organized interests because they concentrate their attention on specific policy areas and have the expertise necessary to participate in the making of complex policy decisions. Interest groups have also gained strength because of the decline of political parties. Elected officials have turned to groups for campaign assistance, and this development has enhanced the influence of groups on policy.

The policies that emerge from the group system bring benefits to many of society's interests, and in some instances these benefits also serve the general interest. But when groups can essentially dictate policies, the common good is not served. A major challenge of democratic politics is to keep special interests in their proper place. They must be allowed to advocate their point of view, but they cannot also be permitted to judge the merits of their claims. Increasingly, interest groups have become both advocate and judge, and this is a development that cannot serve the common good.

---

[47] *Federalist* No. 10.

Major Concepts

grass-roots lobbying   lobbying
inside lobbying   outside lobbying
interest-group liberalism   political action committees (PACs)
iron triangle   single-issue politics
issue network

Suggested Readings

Birnbaum, Jeffrey H., and Alan S. Murray. *Showdown at Gucci Gulch.* New York: Random House, 1987. A well-written case study of the Tax Reform Act of 1986, during which Congress substantially ignored the opposition of powerful special interests.

Chubb, John E. *Interest Groups and the Bureaucracy: The Politics of Energy.* Stanford, Calif.: Stanford University Press, 1983. An assessment of interest groups' influence which refutes the common idea that the bureaucracy is captive to groups.

Cigler, Allan J., and Burdett A. Loomis, eds. *Interest Group Politics.* Washington, D.C.: Congressional Quarterly Press, 1983. A useful set of readings on the activities and influence of America's interest groups.

Eismeier, Theodore J., and Philip H. Pollock III. *Business, Money, and the Rise of Corporate PACs in American Elections.* Westport, Conn.: Quorum Books, 1988. An analysis of the role and influence of corporate PACs in U.S. campaigns.

Lowi, Theodore J. *The End of Liberalism,* 2d ed. New York: Norton, 1979. A thorough critique of interest groups' influence on American politics.

McFarland, Andrew A. *Public Interest Lobbies: Decision-Making on Energy.* Washington, D.C.: American Enterprise Institute, 1976. A study of public-interest groups' lobbying on energy policy.

Malbin, Michael J., ed. *Parties, Interest Groups, and Campaign Finance Laws.* Washington, D.C.: American Enterprise Institute, 1980. A collection of readings on the role of interest groups and political parties in campaign finance.

Milbrath, Lester W. *The Washington Lobbyists.* Chicago: Rand McNally, 1963. A study of Washington lobbyists, based on interviews with them.

Ornstein, Norman, and Shirley Elder. *Interest Groups, Lobbying, and Policymaking.* Washington, D.C.: Congressional Quarterly Press, 1978. A review of interest-group activities which discusses the strategies of groups' attempts to exert influence.

Sabato, Larry. *PAC Power: Inside the World of Political Action Committees.* New York: Norton, 1984. An assessment of the factors that have led to an increase in the numbers and influence of PACs.

15
CHAPTER

THE NEWS MEDIA: LINKING THE PEOPLE AND THEIR LEADERS

The press in America . . . determines what people will think and talk about—an authority that in other nations is reserved for tyrants, priests, parties and mandarins.
—Theodore H. White[1]

*I*n November 1979, Islamic fundamentalists stormed the U.S. embassy in Iran, seized fifty-two of its occupants, and held them hostage for more than a year. Each day of the hostage crisis, every newspaper and television news program in the United States gave the story prominent play. One television news program, ABC's *Nightline*, was born of the crisis; the newscast's initial purpose was to provide Americans with a daily update on the situation, and its anchorman, Ted Koppel, began each night's report by noting the number of days that had elapsed since the hostages had been taken. By the time Koppel presented "America Held Hostage: Day 365," his news program was firmly established, and the American people were thoroughly disillusioned by their government's handling of the crisis. They blamed President Jimmy Carter, and he lost his bid for a second presidential term. (The hostages were finally released after 444 days, minutes after Ronald Reagan was inaugurated as president.)

Not all significant developments receive such intense media coverage. After World War II, black Americans in the rural South began to head for the urban North in search of better jobs. Each day, hundreds of blacks left such states as Mississippi, Georgia, and North Carolina for cities such as Detroit, New York, and Chicago. As they moved in, large numbers of whites moved out, in response both to the lure of the suburbs and to racial fears. By the end of the 1950s the political, economic, and social composition of urban America had been fundamentally changed. Few developments in this century have had so

[1] Theodore H. White, *The Making of the President, 1972* (New York: Bantam Books, 1973), 327.

The mass movement of American blacks from the rural South to the cities of the North during the 1940s and 1950s is portrayed in this painting, one of a series collectively entitled *The Migration of the Negro* by the black artist Jacob Lawrence. Although the black migration had a decisive impact on American politics, it was not front-page news. (The Phillips Collection, Washington)

large or lasting an impact on the nation as the postwar black migration. Yet this major population shift was seldom even mentioned in the news, let alone emblazoned in the headlines.

Although the news has been compared to a mirror held up to society,[2] it is actually a highly selective portrayal of reality. The news is mainly an account of overt, obtruding events, particularly those that can be immediately seen as significant and dramatic.[3] Thus the situation in Iran became headline news at the instant the U.S. embassy was seized, and it remained newsworthy until the hostages were released. The black migration to the North was not considered news, because it was a slow and steady process, dramatic only in its long-term implications. The columnist George Will once suggested that the postwar migration of black Americans could have become news only if a ribbon had been stretched across the Mason-Dixon line as the one-millionth black person crossed it on the way north.[4] Reporters would then have had an event to cover.

News organizations and journalists, of either the print media (newspapers and magazines) or the broadcast media (radio and television), are referred to collectively as the *press* or the *news media*. The press has become an increasingly visible and powerful institution in American politics. Its heightened influence is attributable both to developments within the media themselves, particularly the emergence of television in the 1960s as a politically important medium, and to developments within politics, notably the trend toward individualistic leadership. As political leaders have begun to operate independently of political parties (see Chapter 12), they have turned to the media to help them build public support.

[2] See Sig Mickelson, *The Electronic Mirror* (New York: Dodd, Mead, 1972).
[3] Walter Lippmann, *Public Opinion* (New York: Free Press, 1965), 215, 221, 226.
[4] Comment at the annual meeting of the American Association of Political Consultants, Washington, D.C., 1977.

Like political parties and interest groups, the press has thus become a key link between the public and its leaders. This chapter will show, however, that the news media are a very different kind of intermediary than either parties or groups and that problems arise when the press is expected to perform the same functions as a party or an interest group. The chapter begins with a review of the news media's historical development and current tendencies in reporting. Examination of these topics helps to explain the nature of the press and to distinguish its foundations from those of other linking mechanisms, such as political parties. The final section indicates what roles the news media can and cannot be expected to perform adequately in the American political system. The main ideas presented in this chapter are the following:

★ *The American press was initially tied to the nation's political party system (the partisan press) but gradually developed an independent position (the objective press).* In the process, the news shifted from a political orientation, which emphasized political values and ideas, to a journalistic orientation, which stresses newsworthy information and evaluations.

★ *Although the United States has thousands of separate news organizations, they present a common version of the news which reflects journalists' shared view of what the news is.* Freedom of the press in the United States does not result in a robust marketplace of ideas.

★ *In fulfilling its responsibility to provide public information, the news media effectively perform three significant roles—those of signaler (the press brings relevant events and problems into public view), common carrier (the press serves as a channel through which political leaders can address the public), and watchdog (the press scrutinizes official behavior for evidence of deceitful, careless, or corrupt acts).* These roles are within the news media's capacity because they fit with the values, incentives, and accountability of the press.

★ *The press cannot do the job of political institutions, even though it sometimes tries to do so.* The nature of journalism as it has evolved is incompatible with the characteristics required for the role of public representative.

The Development of the News Media: From Partisanship to Objective Journalism

Democracy requires a free flow of information. Communication enables a free people to keep in touch with one another, with their leaders, and with important events. Recognizing the vital role of the press in the building of a democratic society, Thomas Jefferson wrote in 1787, "Were it left to me to decide whether we should have a government without newspapers, or newspapers without a government, I should not hesitate a moment to prefer the latter."[5]

America's early leaders were quick to see the advantages of promoting the establishment of newspapers. At Alexander Hamilton's urging, the *Gazette of the United States* was founded by John Fenno to promote the policies of George Washington's administration. Hamilton was secretary of the treasury and

---

[5] Thomas Jefferson to Colonel Edward Carrington, January 16, 1787.

★ THE MEDIA AND THE PEOPLE

AMERICA'S NEWSPAPERS: LOCALISM AND CONCENTRATION

America's great size influenced the development of its first newspapers. In England during the late eighteenth century, a few newspapers had already developed national circulations. However, national newspapers were not feasible in a nation the size of the United States at a time when it took more than a week to travel from New York to South Carolina. Thus separately owned dailies were established in all cities and in many small towns. Today systems of high-speed transportation and communication make national newspapers possible in the United States, as evidenced by the *Wall Street Journal* and *USA Today*. However, Americans retain a preference for local newspapers. There are about 1,700 local-circulation dailies in the United States, and they account for more than 95 percent of newspaper readership—a reflection of the public's interest in news of the community as well as of the nation.

Despite its local-circulation base, however, the ownership of newspapers has become increasingly concentrated. In 1935 only one in six newspapers was part of a publishing chain; now about two of every three dailies are owned by a chain. Of the nation's 155 publishing groups, a few—such as Knight-Ridder and Newhouse—own more than fifteen dailies. The largest chain is Gannett News, which publishes the national newspaper *USA Today* as well as eighty-two dailies in thirty-two states, Guam, and the Virgin Islands. Chain newspapers account for nearly 75 percent of daily newspaper circulation in the United States. Local editors in these groups depend for some of their news on the chain's Washington news bureau and are occasionally instructed by the national chain on editorial policy. Endorsements of presidential candidates by local papers, for example, are sometimes decided by their chain's ownership.

The newspaper industry has also become concentrated in a second way. For most of the nation's history, larger communities had competing newspapers. In 1920, 700 U.S. cities had two or more newspapers. New Yorkers at that time could choose from more than a dozen dailies. Now they have less than a handful. Even at that, New Yorkers have more options than readers elsewhere. In the past decade, major newspapers in Chicago, Philadelphia, and Washington have folded. Newspaper competition still exists in a dozen cities, and a third of the nation's population continues to have a choice among local newspapers; but the high costs of newspaper publishing have gradually narrowed Americans' newspaper options.

SOURCES: Edwin Emery and Michael Emery, *The Press in America* (Englewood Cliffs, N.J.: Prentice-Hall, 1984), 680; Daniel B. Wackman, Donald M. Gillmor, Cecilie Gaziano, and Everette E. Dennis, "Chain Newspaper Autonomy as Reflected in Presidential Campaign Endorsements," *Journalism Quarterly* 52 (Fall 1975): 411–420.

supported Fenno's paper by granting it the Treasury Department's printing contracts. Jefferson, who was secretary of state and Hamilton's adversary, complained that the newspaper's content was "pure Toryism." Jefferson persuaded Philip Freneau to start the *National Gazette* as the opposition Republican party's publication and supported it by granting Freneau authority to print State Department documents.[6] Leaders of the U.S. Senate and House later came to have their own newspapers of record, to which they granted printing contracts and from which they received editorial support.[7]

Early newspapers were printed on hand presses, a process that limited production and kept the cost of each copy beyond the reach of ordinary citizens—most of whom could not read anyway. Leading papers such as the *Gazette of the United States* had fewer than 1,500 subscribers and could not have survived without party support. Not surprisingly, the "news" they printed was

Were it left to me to decide whether we should have a government without newspapers, or newspapers without a government, I should not hesitate a moment to prefer the latter.

Thomas Jefferson

---

[6] Culver Smith, *The Press, Politics, and Patronage* (Athens: University of Georgia Press, 1977), 2, 15, 39–55.
[7] Robert O. Blanchard, *Congress and the News Media* (New York: Hastings House, 1974), 8.

a form of party propaganda.[8] In this era of the **partisan press,** publishers openly took sides on partisan issues. Their employees were expected to follow the party line. President James K. Polk once persuaded a leading publisher to fire an editor who was critical of Polk's policies.[9]

THE DECLINE OF THE PARTISAN PRESS

Technological changes helped bring about the gradual decline of America's partisan press. After the invention of the telegraph in 1837, when editors could receive timely information on developments in Washington and the state capital, they had less reason to fill their pages with partisan harangues.[10] Another major innovation was the high-speed rotary press (invented in 1845), a breakthrough that enabled commercially minded publishers to print their newspapers rapidly and cheaply and thus to increase their profit potential.[11] The *New York Sun* was the first paper to pass on the benefit of high-speed printing to subscribers by reducing the price of a daily copy from six cents to a penny. The *Sun's* circulation rose to 5,000 in four months and to 10,000 in less than a year.[12] Increased circulation and revenues gave newspapers independence from government and parties, a change that some political leaders welcomed. "The freedom and independence of the press," a congressional committee concluded in 1873, "is best maintained by the people, and their subscriptions are a more legitimate means of support than the patronage of the federal government."[13]

By the late nineteenth century, several American newspapers were printing 100,000 or more copies a day, and their large circulation enabled them to charge high prices to advertisers. This development increased the profitability of newspapers but put pressure on editors and publishers to voice the political opinions of major advertisers, just as they had earlier reflected the views of party leaders. "One set of masters," political scientist V. O. Key, Jr., wrote, "had been replaced by another."[14]

The years around 1900 marked the height of newspapers' power and the depths of their sense of public responsibility.[15] A new style of reporting— "yellow journalism"—had emerged as a way of boosting circulation.[16] The "yellow" press—so called because some of these newspapers were printed on cheap yellow paper—emphasized "a shrieking, gaudy, sensation-loving, devil-may-care kind of journalism which lured the reader by any possible means."[17]

---

[8] Frank Luther Mott, *American Journalism, a History: 1690–1960* (New York: Macmillan, 1962), 114–115.
[9] Smith, *Press, Politics, and Patronage,* 163–168.
[10] Doris A. Graber, *Mass Media and American Politics* (Washington, D.C.: Congressional Quarterly Press, 1980), 36.
[11] See Michael Schudson, *Discovering the News* (New York: Basic Books, 1978).
[12] Mott, *American Journalism,* 122–123, 220–227.
[13] Quoted in Smith, *Press, Politics, and Patronage,* 241.
[14] V. O. Key, Jr., *Public Opinion and American Democracy* (New York: Knopf, 1961), 388.
[15] Commission on Freedom of the Press, *A Free and Responsible Press* (Chicago: University of Chicago Press, 1974), 62–63.
[16] Mott, *American Journalism,* 220–227, 241, 243.
[17] Edwin Emery, *The Press and America: An Interpretive History of the Mass Media* (Englewood Cliffs, N.J.: Prentice-Hall, 1977), 350.

$50,000 REWARD.—WHO DESTROYED THE MAINE?—$50,000 REWARD.

EDITION FOR GREATER NEW YORK

NEW YORK JOURNAL

AND ADVERTISER.

DESTRUCTION OF THE WAR SHIP MAINE WAS THE WORK OF AN ENEMY.

$50,000!		**$50,000!**
$50,000 REWARD! For the Detection of the Perpetrator of the Maine Outrage!	Assistant Secretary Roosevelt Convinced the Explosion of the War Ship Was Not an Accident.	$50,000 REWARD! For the Detection of the Perpetrator of the Maine Outrage!
	The Journal Offers $50,000 Reward for the Conviction of the Criminals Who Sent 258 American Sailors to Their Death. Naval Officers Unanimous That the Ship Was Destroyed on Purpose.	

NAVAL OFFICERS THINK THE MAINE WAS DESTROYED BY A SPANISH MINE.

Yellow journalism was characterized by its sensationalism. William Randolph Hearst's *New York Journal* whipped up public support for a war in Cuba with Spain through inflammatory reporting on the sinking of the battleship *Maine* in Havana Harbor in 1898. (Historical Pictures Service)

A circulation battle between William Randolph Hearst's *New York Journal* and Joseph Pulitzer's *New York World* is believed to have contributed to the outbreak of the Spanish-American War through sensational (and largely inaccurate) reports on the cruelty of Spanish rule in Cuba. A young Frederic Remington (who later became a noted painter and sculptor), working as a news artist for Hearst, planned to return home because Cuba appeared calm and safe; but Hearst cabled back, "Please remain. You furnish the pictures and I'll furnish the war."[18]

THE RISE OF OBJECTIVE JOURNALISM

The excesses of yellow journalism led some publishers to consider how the news could be reported more responsibly. Their goal was to establish the newspaper as an unbiased medium of timely public communication. One step they took was to separate the newspaper's advertising department from its news department, thus reducing the influence of advertisers on news content. A second development was a new model of reporting called **objective journalism,** which was based on the reporting of "facts" rather than opinions and was "fair" in that it presented all sides of partisan debate.[19]

A chief advocate of this new form of journalism was Adolph Ochs of *The New York Times*. Ochs bought the *Times* in 1896, when its circulation was 9,000; four years later, its readership had grown to 82,000. Ochs told his reporters that he "wanted as little partisanship as possible . . . as few judgments as possible."[20] The *Times*'s approach to reporting appealed to educated readers particularly,

[18] Quoted in Mott, *American Journalism*, 529.
[19] See Theodore Peterson, "The Social Responsibility Theory of the Press," in Fred Siebert, Theodore Peterson, and Wilbur Schramm, eds., *Four Theories of the Press* (Urbana: University of Illinois Press, 1956).
[20] Quoted in David Halberstam, *The Powers That Be* (New York: Knopf, 1979), 208–209.

and by the early twentieth century it had acquired a reputation as the country's best newspaper.

Objective reporting was also promoted through newly formed journalism schools. Among the first of these professional schools were those at Columbia University and the University of Missouri. The Columbia School of Journalism opened in 1912 with a $2 million grant from Pulitzer.

Today most newspaper publishers emphasize objective reporting. Although publishers invariably slant the news slightly in favor of their own political position, they report both Republican and Democratic views and stress factual descriptions of news events. Many publishers even try to achieve some balance in their opinion columns. In the early 1970s, for example, *The New York Times* hired the conservative columnist William Safire as a counterweight to such liberal columnists as Tom Wicker and Anthony Lewis. Newspapers' partisan bias has traditionally been most evident in their endorsements of candidates during election campaigns, but even this form of advocacy has diminished. One-fourth of America's daily newspapers no longer endorse candidates, while most of the others do so without regard for the candidates' party affiliations.[21]

A few American newspapers continue to cover politics in much the manner of the nineteenth-century press. The *Manchester* (N.H.) *Union Leader* is noted for its partisan reporting of New Hampshire's pivotal presidential primary. In one notorious incident, the *Union Leader* helped to bring down the campaign of Senator Edmund Muskie of Maine, the early favorite for the 1972 Democratic presidential nomination. In a front-page editorial titled "Sen. Muskie Insults Franco-Americans," the paper made reference to a letter (later discovered to be a forgery) that claimed Muskie had laughed upon hearing an ethnic slur referring to French-Canadian Americans, who are a significant portion of New Hampshire's population, as "Canucks." The next day the paper alleged that Muskie's wife had a foul mouth and drank heavily. Muskie went to the front steps of the newspaper's building and made a speech defending his wife, appearing to weep as he spoke. The national press claimed Muskie's reaction was a sign that he did not have the emotional stability required of a president, and his campaign collapsed shortly thereafter.[22]

THE DEVELOPMENT OF THE BROADCAST MEDIA

Radio and Television: The Truly National Media

Until the early twentieth century, the print media were the only form of mass communication. Within a few decades, however, there were hundreds of radio stations throughout the nation, many of which were linked in national networks, such as the Red and Blue networks of the National Broadcasting Corporation (NBC). Franklin D. Roosevelt used radio for his famous "fireside chats" with the American people. Business-minded newspaper editors had been critical of his New Deal programs, and Roosevelt found that radio was a

---

[21] Roger Gafke and David Leathold, "A Caveat on E & P Poll on Newspaper Endorsements," *Journalism Quarterly* 56 (Summer 1979): 384; Joseph E. Pillegge, Jr., "Two-Party Endorsements in a One-Party State," *Journalism Quarterly* 58 (Autumn 1981): 449–453.

[22] David H. Everson, *Public Opinion and Interest Groups in American Politics* (New York: Franklin Watts, 1982), 101–102.

Franklin D. Roosevelt was the first president to make effective use of the radio to communicate directly with the American people. He broadcast a series of "fireside chats" that reached millions of listeners across the country. (Brown Brothers)

way of getting his messages directly to the people, without having to filter them through editors and reporters. Broadcasting was also revolutionary in a second way: it was the first truly *national* mass medium. Newspapers had local circulation bases, whereas radio could reach millions of Americans across the country simultaneously.

Television followed radio, and by the late 1950s more than 90 percent of American homes had a television set. The political potential of television was evident as early as 1952, when 17 million homes tuned in to the national Republican and Democratic party conventions.[23] However, television newscasts of the 1950s were brief, lasting no more than fifteen minutes, and relied on news gathered by other organizations, particularly the Associated Press and other wire services. In 1963 CBS expanded its evening newscast to thirty minutes in an effort to overtake NBC's lead in audience ratings.[24] The popularity of President John F. Kennedy's televised press conferences helped to persuade CBS executives that the American people were eager for more television news. NBC and ABC followed suit by expanding their evening newscasts to thirty minutes, and the audience ratings of all three networks rose.

At the same time, the television networks greatly increased their news-division staffs, and television quickly became the principal news medium of national politics. In the 1960s there was no twenty-four-hour Cable News Network (CNN) or other cable newscasts, and there were no regularly scheduled late-night network news programs such as ABC's *Nightline*. Americans in most parts of the country now have access to television news around the

[23] Leo Bogart, *The Age of Television* (New York: Frederick Unger, 1956), 213.
[24] Theodore H. White, *America in Search of Itself: The Making of the President, 1956–1980* (New York: Harper & Row, 1982), 172–173.

clock if they want it. Although the quantity of television news is higher, the quality may be lower. The networks have reduced their news staffs to try to compensate for declining revenues caused by a loss of audience to cable. Television news also has become more entertainment-oriented, from the weekly shouting matches on CNN's *McLaughlin Group* to the gossipy and breezy content of "infotainment" news shows (see box).

Government Licensing and Regulation of Broadcasters

At first the government did not carefully regulate broadcasting. The result was a communication mess. Nearby stations often used the same or adjacent radio frequencies, interfering with each other's transmissions. Finally, in 1934, Congress passed the Communications Act, which requires that broadcasters be licensed and meet certain performance standards. The Federal Communications Commission (FCC) was established to administer the act and to develop regulations pertaining to such matters as signal strength, advertising rates and access, and political coverage.

The principle of scarcity justifies the licensing and regulation of broadcast media. Because the number of available broadcasting frequencies is limited, those few individuals who are granted a broadcasting license are expected to serve the public interest in addition to their own. In principle, licensing is a means of controlling broadcasting. If a station fails to comply with federal broadcast regulations, the FCC can withdraw its license.

The government's licensing power, however, has not significantly undermined broadcasters' independence. During the early 1970s, for example, the

---

★ CRITICAL THINKING

AN UNINFORMED PUBLIC—WHOSE FAULT?

Survey after survey has demonstrated that the general public is not well informed about politics and public affairs. On most policy issues, a majority of citizens are unable to describe what the issue is all about or who is involved (see Chapter 9).

Some analysts place the blame mainly on the press, which, they say, is more concerned with entertaining its audience than informing it. The news is presented in simplified and colorful ways. The news is weak on detailed information and the context of events. It tells what has happened without providing the background information that would enable the audience to make sense of what has happened. The news is also negative in tone: bad news takes precedence over good news. The longest running political stories tend to be those about trouble—scandals, blunders, and the like. Critics conclude that these news tendencies lead the public to devalue news of politics.

Other observers place the blame for the public's low level of information squarely on the public itself. They say that the news is filled with information and that it contains many more facts than any citizen could possibly absorb. They point out that there is almost no vital piece of information about a policy issue that is not reported by the media at one time or another. These observers say that the problem is the public's failure to take notice of the news.

In your opinion, is the press or the public primarily to blame for the citizenry's low level of political awareness? What changes in news coverage might improve the public's understanding of politics? How might the public be encouraged to pay closer attention to the news?

Nixon administration allegedly pressured the FCC to refuse to renew the licenses of broadcast stations owned by the *Washington Post*, which was leading the investigation of the Watergate scandal. The FCC took no action. The FCC seldom even threatens to revoke a license, for fear of being accused of restricting freedom of the press. A broadcast station can apply for renewal of its license by postcard and is virtually guaranteed FCC approval, which covers seven years for radio and five for television.

Because broadcast frequencies are a scarce resource, licensees are required by law to be somewhat evenhanded during election campaigns. Section 315 of the Communications Act imposes on broadcasters an "equal time" restriction, which means that they cannot sell or give air time to a political candidate without granting equal opportunities to other candidates running for the same office. (Election debates are an exception; broadcasters can sponsor them and limit participation to nominees of the Republican and Democratic parties only.) During campaigns broadcasters are also required to make air time available for purchase by candidates at the lowest rate charged to commercial advertisers.

Until recently broadcasters were also bound by the "fairness doctrine," an FCC regulation that compelled broadcasters to provide "reasonable" opportunities for the airing of opposing opinions on major public issues. In 1987 broadcasters, on the grounds that the fairness doctrine infringed on press freedom, persuaded the FCC to rescind it.

Freedom and Conformity in the U.S. News Media

Some democracies impose significant legal restraints on the press. The news media in Britain are barred from reporting on anything that the government has labeled an "official secret," and the nation's tough libel laws inhibit the press from publishing any allegation about an individual unless it can provide supporting evidence. In France the leading public television channel is under the directorship of the government and seldom criticizes the party in power. When Valéry Giscard d'Estaing was France's president (1974–1981), he reportedly had a telephone "hot line" from his office to the network's editorial room which he could use to influence news coverage.

In the United States, as we saw in Chapter 5, the First Amendment gives the press substantial protection. The courts have consistently upheld the right of U.S. newspapers to report on politics as they choose. The government cannot block publication of a news story unless it can convincingly demonstrate in court that the information would jeopardize national security. U.S. libel laws also strongly favor the press. A public figure who is attacked in a news story cannot collect libel damages unless he or she can demonstrate convincingly that the news organization was false in its accusations, careless in its search for the truth, and malicious in its intent.

Moreover, the U.S. government provides the news media with indirect economic support. Newspapers and magazines have a special postal rate that helps them to keep their circulation costs low, and broadcasters pay only a few dollars annually in license fees. Such policies have contributed to the development of a truly enormous news industry in the United States: 1,700 daily newspapers, 7,500 weeklies, 9,000 radio stations, five national television news

★ ANALYZE THE ISSUE

Broadcasting without the Fairness Doctrine
In 1987 the FCC rescinded the fairness doctrine, which had required broadcasters to air opposing opinions on major issues. The FCC concluded that broadcasters should be free to cover issues as they wish, even if this means that some opinions do not get aired. Do you agree with the FCC's position? Consider whether the scarcity of broadcast frequencies compels different interpretations of freedom of the press for broadcasters and for print journalists.

TABLE 15-1   Audience Size of Selected U.S. Media

Media	Audience Size
Daily Newspapers, City	
Los Angeles Times	1,114,929
New York Times	1,058,636
Chicago Tribune	756,728
Washington Post	747,610
San Francisco Chronicle/Examiner	702,506
Detroit Free Press	629,182
Atlanta Journal Constitution	466,227
Seattle Times/Post-Intelligencer	442,407
Phoenix Republic/Gazette	441,985
Miami Herald/News	424,563
Daily Newspapers, National	
Wall Street Journal	1,857,131
USA Today	1,347,450
Weekly Newsmagazines	
Time	4,094,935
Newsweek	3,211,958
U.S. News & World Report	2,311,534
Network Evening News, Daily	
CBS Television	
NBC Television	23,000,000*
ABC Television	

*Data are based on number of households viewing the news. However, estimated television viewing dwindles in the summer, network audiences vary, and in many homes the television is left on continuously even though no one may be watching a particular program.

SOURCES: *SRDS* (Standard Rate and Data Service), June 12, 1991, vol. 73, no. 6., p. a6 (city newspapers) and pp. 178–180 (national newspapers); *SRDS,* May 27, 1991, vol. 27, no. 5, pp. 498–510 (weekly newsmagazines); *Electronic Media,* June 17, 1991, vol. 10, no. 25; p. 44 (evening newscasts).

networks, 1,000 local television stations, and 6,000 cable television systems.[25] The audience reach of leading news organizations is truly substantial (see Table 15-1).

In view of the great number and the freedom of news organizations in the United States, it might be expected that there would be great variation in the national news that Americans receive. And certainly the argument for a free press hinges on the expectation that a robust "marketplace of ideas" will result. Press freedom is intended to produce full and open debate, in which all significant opinions on leading issues are widely disseminated and thoroughly voiced so that the public can weigh the competing arguments and choose among them on their merits. To encourage the airing of diverse points of view, U.S. laws prohibit any owner from monopolizing print and broadcast media

[25] Ernest C. Hynds, *American Newspapers in the 1980s* (New York: Hastings House, 1980); Annual Report, Federal Communications Commission, fiscal year 1985.

★ HOW THE UNITED STATES COMPARES

THE MEDIA

The United States ranks first in the world in several media categories, including the number of radio receivers (2.10) and television sets (0.62) per capita. The United States ranks lower than nearly twenty other countries in daily newspaper circulation (0.28 per capita). Japan has the highest rate of newspaper circulation (0.57 per capita), and all the remaining countries in the top ten are European.

All democracies have vigorous news systems, but their characteristics vary somewhat. Whereas most western European countries have strong public broadcasting networks, the United States depends almost entirely on private broadcast organizations, such as ABC, CBS, NBC, and CNN. Party-based newspapers are strong in many countries, including Norway, which subsidizes them from public funds. By comparison, the partisan press in the United States is nearly dead.

Many governments censor their news media, exercising daily control over news content and closing down news organizations that criticize official policy. News media in democratic societies, including the United States, have much greater freedom.

As for public attitudes about the media, a 1988 study indicated that 69 percent of Americans have confidence in their media whereas less than 50 percent of German, British, French, and Spanish citizens have confidence in their media. In addition, a plurality of Americans, Spaniards, and Britons said that their media have too much power, while pluralities in France and Germany held that the media have "just about the right amount" of power.

SOURCES: *The New Book of World Rankings* (New York: Facts on File, 1984), 395, 398, 408; Laurence Parisot, "Attitudes about the Media: A Five-Country Comparison," *Public Opinion*, January/February 1988, 19.

within a community or from holding more than a few broadcast licenses nationwide.

Nevertheless, most Americans receive a relatively uniform version of the news. Each day, newspapers and broadcast stations from coast to coast are likely to highlight the same national news stories and to interpret them in identical ways. Any number of terms—pack journalism, group think, media concentration, the decline of the critical press—have been used to describe the fact that news reporting today is fairly homogeneous and straightforward, a far cry from a robust and contentious marketplace of ideas. The basic reason the news is pretty much the same everywhere is that objective journalism, with its emphasis on facts and salient events, provides journalists with a basis for agreement. They do sometimes disagree about which facts, events, and issues are more important than others, but this polite selectivity is a far cry from the disputes and diversity that characterized the nineteenth-century partisan press.

Of course, today's news organizations do differ in *how* they tell a given story. Broadcast news tends to be, in effect, headline news with pictures. A thirty-minute network news broadcast typically presents a dozen or so stories in the twenty-two minutes allotted to news content (the other eight minutes being devoted to commercials); each story is less than two minutes long, on average. Newspapers have the space to present news developments in greater depth; some, like *The New York Times* (which proclaims itself to be "the newspaper of record"), provide substantial detail. The reporting styles of newspapers also vary. Although most of them present the news in an understated way, others tend toward sensationalism. For example, when New York City's government faced bankruptcy in the mid-1970s and President Gerald Ford rejected a request

DAILY ⊙ NEWS

NEW YORK'S PICTURE NEWSPAPER ®

FORD TO CITY: DROP DEAD

Vows He'll Veto Any Bail-Out

Abe, Carey Rip Stand

Stocks Skid, Dow Down 12

President Gerald Ford's rejection in 1975 of New York City's request for federal loan guarantees was reported very differently by the city's two major newspapers, the more sensational *Daily News* and the more staid *Times. (Top:* courtesy of the *Daily News;* bottom: courtesy of *The New York Times)*

The New York Times

FORD, CASTIGATING CITY, ASSERTS HE'D VETO FUND GUARANTEE; OFFERS BANKRUPTCY BILL

Sadat Urges U.N. to Help In Resuming Geneva Talk

N.S.A. CHIEF TELLS OF BROAD SCOPE OF SURVEILLANCE

'BAILOUT' BARRED

President's Plan Has Provision for Safety in Event of Default

for a federal bailout, the *New York Daily News* gave its whole front page to the now-famous headline: "Ford to City: Drop Dead." *The New York Times*, in contrast, gave the story a standard-size front-page headline. Such differences in approach, however, do not disguise the fact that most news organizations tell their audiences the same stories each day.

The stories may also be increasingly superficial, presenting more imagery and less substance. Studying changes in television election news coverage, sociologist Kiku Addato found that the average "sound bite," or block of uninterrupted speech by a presidential candidate, dropped from 42.3 seconds in 1968 to 9.8 seconds in 1988. In fact, no candidate at any time during the 1988 campaign was shown speaking, without interruption, for a minute or more on network evening newscasts. By comparison, during the 1968 campaign, a fifth of all candidate sound bites were a minute or more in length. Furthermore, the voiceless candidate was the norm in 1988 newscasts; only 37 percent of the time that the candidates' images were on the screen were their voices also heard. In contrast, the candidates in 1968 were pictured speaking 84 percent of the time their images were on the screen.[26]

DOMINATION OF NEWS PRODUCTION

Another reason for the lack of diversity in national news reporting is that a small number of news organizations generate most of it. The quintessential case of concentrated news production is radio, with its "canned" network-provided news; almost no local radio station in the country produces its own national news reports.

The Associated Press (AP) is the major producer of news stories. It has 300 full-time reporters stationed throughout the country and the world to gather news stories, which are relayed by satellite to subscribing newspapers and broadcast stations. More than 95 percent of the nation's dailies are serviced by AP, and some also subscribe to other wire services, such as Reuters and the New York Times.[27] Smaller dailies lack the resources to gather news outside their own localities and thus depend almost completely on wire-service reports for their national and international coverage.[28] They may give these reports a local or partisan slant, but most of what they say is reprinted word for word from the wire-service dispatches. Even major news organizations, such as *The New York Times*, depend heavily on AP for reports about developments in the more remote areas of the country and the world.[29]

Television news production is similarly dominated by just a few organizations. The five major networks—ABC, CBS, NBC, PBS, and CNN—generate most of the news coverage of national and international politics. For news of the nation and the world, local stations depend on videotransmissions fed to them by the networks. The Persian Gulf war provided a dramatic example. When the allied bombing of Baghdad began on January 16, 1991, CNN had a correspon-

[26] Kiku Addato, *Sound Bite Democracy* (Cambridge, Mass.: Harvard University Kennedy School of Government, 1990), 2.
[27] Graber, *Mass Media and American Politics*, 36.
[28] Maxwell E. McCombs and Donald L. Shaw, "Structuring the 'Unseen Environment,'" *Journal of Communication*, Spring 1976, 18–22.
[29] Lawrence W. Lichty, "The News Media: Video versus Print," *Wilson Quarterly* 6 (1982): 53.

dent in the Iraqi capital who singlehandedly provided much of the world with its only news about what the war looked like from inside Iraq. It was reported that even senior Iraqi military staff were watching CNN for information about what the allies were doing.

NEWS VALUES AND IMPERATIVES

Competitive pressures also lead the producers of news to report the same stories. No major news organization wants to miss an important story that others are reporting. It is also easier to report what others are saying. In some foreign capitals, it is common for American journalists to hang around the U.S. embassy, sharing sources and story possibilities with one another. The pressures *not* to be different are overwhelming. "Even at the best newspapers," Timothy Crouse notes, "the editor always gauges his own reporters' stories against the expectations that the stories [of other news organizations] have aroused."[30] Television news, too, displays a follow-the-leader tendency.[31]

The networks, wire services, and a few elite dailies, including *The New York Times, Washington Post, Wall Street Journal, Los Angeles Times,* and *Chicago Tribune,* establish a national standard of story selection. Whenever one of them uncovers an important story, the others jump on the bandwagon. The chief trendsetter among news-gathering organizations is the New York Times, which has been described as "the bulletin board" for other major newspapers, newsmagazines, and television networks.[32] Herbert Gans notes, "When editors and producers are uncertain about a selection decision, they will check whether, where, and how the *Times* has covered the story; and story selectors see to it that many of the *Times*' front-page stories find their way into television programs and magazines."[33]

The imperatives of the fast pace of daily journalism also tend to make the news homogeneous.[34] Journalists have the task each day of filling a newspaper or broadcast with stories. Their job is to produce an edition every twenty-four hours. Thus editors assign reporters to such beats as the White House and Congress, which can be relied on for a steady supply of news. On these beats the reporters of various news organizations see and hear the same things, exchange views on what is important, and, not surprisingly, produce similar news stories.

Finally, a common set of professional values guides journalists in their search for news.[35] Reporters are on the lookout for aspects of situations that lend themselves to interesting news stories—novel, colorful, and compelling developments.[36] Long practice at storytelling leads journalists to find significance in

[30] Timothy Crouse, *The Boys on the Bus* (New York: Ballantine, 1973), 20.
[31] Edward J. Epstein, *News from Nowhere: Television and the News* (New York: Random House, 1973), 37.
[32] White, *Making of the President, 1972,* 346–348.
[33] Quoted in Kathleen Hall Jamieson and Karlyn Kohrs Campbell, *The Interplay of Influence* (Belmont, Calif.: Wadsworth, 1983), 9–10.
[34] See David Manning White, "The Gatekeeper," *Journalism Quarterly* 27 (Fall 1950): 383–388; Joseph S. Fowler and Stuart W. Showalter, "Evening Network News Selection," *Journalism Quarterly* 51 (Winter 1974): 712–715; John Chancellor and Walter R. Mears, *The News Business* (New York: Harper & Row, 1983).
[35] David L. Paletz and Robert M. Entman, *Media Power Politics* (New York: Free Press, 1981), 16.
[36] James David Barber, "Characters in the Campaign: The Literary Problem," in James David Barber, ed., *Race for the Presidency* (Englewood Cliffs, N.J.: Prentice-Hall, 1978), 114–115.

CNN is one of five major networks that dominate news coverage of national and international events. During the Persian Gulf war the whole world relied on the reports of CNN correspondent Peter Arnett, the only American reporter sending news out of the capital of Iraq at the time of the allied bombing. (Sygma)

the same things. Experienced journalists claim that they "know news when they see it," which is to say that they have a common understanding of what the news is.[37] After the White House press corps has listened to a presidential speech, for example, nearly all of the journalists in attendance are in agreement on what was most newsworthy about the speech, often only a single statement within it.

The News Media as Link: Roles the Press Can and Cannot Perform

When the objective model of reporting came to dominate American news coverage, the relationship between the press and the public was fundamentally altered. The nineteenth-century partisan press gave its readers blatant cues as to how to evaluate political issues and leaders. In the presidential election campaign of 1896, the *San Francisco Call* devoted 1,075 column-inches of photographs to the Republican ticket of McKinley-Hobart and only 11 inches to the Democrats, Bryan and Sewell.[38] Many European newspapers still function in this way, guiding their readers by applying partisan or ideological values to current events. The *Daily Telegraph,* for example, is an unofficial but fiercely loyal voice of Britain's Conservative party.

In contrast, the U.S. news media act primarily as transmitters of information. Objective journalism asks the American reporter to play the role of neutral observer, and the media are thus very different from the political parties and interest groups, the other major links between the public and its leaders. The

[37] Bernard Rushko, *Newsmaking* (Chicago: University of Chicago Press, 1975), 105.
[38] Lippmann, *Public Opinion,* 214.

force that drives the media is the search for interesting and revealing stories; parties and interest groups exist to articulate particular political opinions and values.

This distinction provides a basis for determining what roles the media can and cannot be expected to perform. The press is capable of fulfilling only those public responsibilities that are compatible with journalistic values: the signaler role, the common-carrier role, and the watchdog role. The media are less successful in their attempts to perform a fourth, politically oriented role: that of public representative.

THE SIGNALER ROLE

As journalists see it, one of their responsibilities is to play the **signaler role,** alerting the public to important developments as soon as possible after they happen: a state visit to Washington by a foreign leader, a bill that has just been passed by Congress, a change in the nation's unemployment level, a demand by dairy farmers for higher milk prices, a terrorist bombing in a foreign capital.

The signaler role is one that the American media perform extremely well. U.S. news organizations compete to be the first to discover and communicate news developments, and they have the resources to do the job effectively. The press is poised to converge on any fast-breaking major news event anywhere in the nation and nearly anywhere in the world. For instance, soon after Iraq invaded Kuwait in August 1990, there were several hundred U.S. reporters and technicians on assignment in the Middle East, mainly in Saudi Arabia. Although they had to work within the constraints of U.S.-imposed censorship on news about the Gulf crisis, they were producing enough stories to fill the round-the-clock American news process.

The media are particularly well suited to signal developments from Washington. More than half of all reported national news emanates from the nation's capital, most of it from the White House and Congress. Altogether, about 10,000 people in Washington work in the news business. The key figures are the leading correspondents of the television networks and major newspapers, the heads of the Washington news bureaus, and a few top editors.[39]

Agenda Setting

You [journalists] deal in the raw material of opinion, and, if my convictions have any validity, opinion ultimately governs the world.
Woodrow Wilson

The press, in its capacity as signaler, has the power to focus the public's attention. The term "agenda setting" has been used to describe the media's ability to influence what is on people's minds. By covering the same events, problems, issues, and leaders—simply by giving them space or time in the news—the media place them on the public agenda. The press, as Bernard Cohen notes, "may not be successful much of the time in telling people what to think but it is stunningly successful in telling them what to think about."[40]

---

[39] See Allen Barton, "Consensus and Conflict among American Leaders," *Public Opinion Quarterly* 38 (Winter 1974–1975): 507–530; Stephen Hess, "A Washington Perspective," paper presented at the Donald S. McNaughton Symposium, sponsored by Syracuse University, New York City, April 1985.

[40] See Bernard C. Cohen, *The Press and Foreign Policy* (Princeton, N.J.: Princeton University Press, 1963), 13.

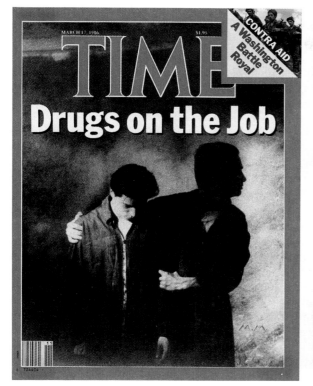

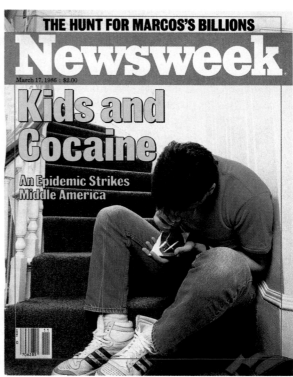

In their signaler role, the news media serve the public interest by identifying major problems, such as drug abuse. (*Left:* courtesy of Time Inc.; *right:* courtesy of *Newsweek* magazine)

This influence is most obvious in such situations as the Gulf war, an event that quickly aroused widespread public attention. When the allies started their air raid on Baghdad, the ABC, CBS, and NBC networks began an unprecedented forty-two continuous hours of coverage. News of the war was almost inescapable. The press's agenda-setting capacity is evident in less dramatic circumstances, too. In March 1986, for example, both *Time* and *Newsweek* ran cover stories on drug abuse and then ran two more cover stories on drugs within six months. Newspapers around the country picked up the drug theme, as did radio and television stations. *U.S. News & World Report* devoted its July 28 cover story to drug abuse, calling it "the nation's no. 1 menace." On September 2 CBS ran a news documentary on drugs titled *48 Hours on Crack Street*. This mounting coverage of drugs had a clear impact on the public agenda. Gallup polls taken early in 1986 indicated that drug abuse was of small concern to most citizens, but by September 1986 a Gallup poll indicated that drug abuse had become the national problem of greatest concern to Americans. The only explanation for the change was the media's attention to the issue: statistics showed that the actual level of drug abuse in 1986 was no higher than it had been during the previous five years.[41]

Studies indicate that the media's agenda-setting influence is substantial, affecting even the relationship between leaders and policymakers and the

[41] The example is from Adam Paul Weisman, "48 Hours on Crack Street: I Was a Drug-Hype Junkie," *New Republic,* October 6, 1986, 15.

public.[42] When the student-led prodemocracy demonstration in Beijing's Tiananmen Square broke out in April 1989, Americans saw it live on television. The Chinese government had invited the U.S. networks to cover a visit to Beijing by Soviet President Mikhail Gorbachev, but the journalists were more interested in reporting on the demonstration. The American public also saw the protesters erect their version of the Statue of Liberty and watched in horror when the students were brutally attacked by army tanks on June 4. Television coverage made it impossible for U.S. policymakers to treat the protest simply as an internal dispute among the Chinese people. Although some voices within the Bush administration soon began to hint that it was interested in lifting the trade sanctions imposed on China immediately after the Tiananmen Square massacre, public outrage did not fade enough to permit the policy change until 1991.

Forecasting

In another extension of the signaler role, the press attempts to alert the public to what lies ahead. In this area, the press's performance is only as good as the sources on which journalists rely for information. Their forecasts are often off the mark or ignore alternative scenarios. The 1968 Tet offensive during the Vietnam war is a classic example. Vietnamese communists used the Tet holiday lull to catch American forces off guard and launch attacks on major South Vietnamese cities. In Saigon, they penetrated the U.S. embassy's inner perimeter before being driven back. The embassy attack was widely interpreted by the media as a symbol of the futility of America's presence in Vietnam and led

[42] See, for example, F. Cook, T. Tyler, E. Goetz, M. Gordon, D. Protess, D. Leff, and H. Molotch, "Media and Agenda Setting: Effects on the Public, Interest Group Leaders, Policy Makers, and Policy," *Public Opinion Quarterly* 47 (1983): 16–35.

Media coverage of the events at Beijing's Tiananmen Square in June 1989 put a worldwide spotlight on the brutality of the Chinese government's attack on the prodemocracy movement. Public outrage prompted by reports of the massacre forced the United States to stiffen its China policy for a time. (Jacques Langevin/Sygma)

The president's views are always sought after by journalists. Here, President Bush's vacation in Maine is interrupted for questions about the attempted coup against Soviet leader Mikhail Gorbachev in August 1991. (Dirck Halstead/Gamma-Liaison)

many prominent journalists to conclude that the war was unwinnable.[43] However, the real story of Tet, Peter Braestrup has concluded, was that the Vietnamese communists suffered such heavy troop losses that they were unable to mount another major offensive for four years. Braestrup concludes that if the press had emphasized enemy casualties during Tet, the United States might have been encouraged to pursue the Vietnam conflict to victory.[44]

Whether in this particular case the press was right or wrong is of secondary significance. The main point is that the press has no crystal ball. Journalists work too rapidly and with too few facts to do well what even experts (such as military intelligence analysts) have difficulty doing. Journalists may be denied access to information, especially on issues of national security, without which reasonable predictions cannot be made. It is not surprising, then, that the media's forecasts are often inaccurate. For example, at some point during each of the seven presidential elections from 1968 to 1992, the consensus in the press as to who would become the Republican or Democratic nominee turned out to be wrong.[45] After the Iowa caucuses, which began the formal campaign in 1988, the press seemed to be convinced that George Bush, who had finished third behind Robert Dole and Pat Robertson, was in deep trouble. "Bush is dead," said NBC's Ken Bode. A week later Bush easily won New Hampshire's primary, and he breezed to his party's nomination.

THE COMMON-CARRIER ROLE

Journalists base many of their news stories on the words of political leaders. The press thus plays what is labeled a **common-carrier role,** serving as an open

[43] See George Bailey, "Television War: Trends in Network Coverage of Vietnam, 1965–70," *Journal of Broadcasting* 20 (1976): 147–158; James Reston, "The End of the Tunnel," *New York Times*, April 30, 1975, 41.
[44] See Peter Braestrup, *The Big Story*, 2 vols. (Boulder, Colo.: Westview Press, 1977).
[45] See Gary Orren, "The Nomination Process: Vicissitudes of Candidate Selection," in Michael Nelson, ed., *The Elections of 1984* (Washington, D.C.: Congressional Quarterly Press, 1985), 27–82.

channel through which political leaders and the public can communicate. "It is my job," a reporter explained, "to report the position of the politician whether I believe it or not."[46]

The value of the media's common-carrier role to the public is obvious. Citizens cannot very well support or oppose what their leaders are planning and doing if they do not know what those plans and actions are. The importance of the press's function as a common carrier is also obvious from the viewpoint of political leaders. If leaders are to gain the public's attention, they must have news exposure. Not surprisingly, leaders go out of their way to build relationships with reporters: they brief them on important plans, grant them access to confidential matters, and provide them working space in Congress, the White House, and other government offices.[47]

The press reciprocates the interest of political leaders in developing a close relationship.[48] Journalists are always on the lookout for fresh stories, and political leaders are their prime source. Franklin D. Roosevelt, an early master of the art of media manipulation, held twice-weekly press conferences in the Oval Office to release information about his upcoming programs. Reporters called these sessions "the best show in town" and eagerly sought to participate, even though Roosevelt's ground rules were strict. When he gave reporters confidential information, he expected it not to appear in the next day's headlines.[49]

Media critics complain that the press neglects its responsibilities as a common carrier by failing to allocate its coverage fairly.[50] The press virtually ignores all political parties except the Democrats and Republicans and devotes disproportionate amounts of coverage to established interest groups, such as the AFL-CIO; and it devotes substantially more attention to the president than to all the members of Congress combined. As the one political figure known to nearly all Americans, the president is presumed to be newsworthy whether he is at work in the White House or at play on vacation. Helen Douglas, the UPI's White House correspondent, has described her job as the "body watch"—keeping track of where the president is and what he is doing.[51] Congress fares poorly by comparison. Congress is an institution that is not personified by a single individual, and the press is less interested in reporting on institutions than on people. Reflecting on the press's tendency to downplay the newsworthiness of Congress, Thomas P. "Tip" O'Neill said, "If I could accomplish one thing as Speaker of the House of Representatives, it would be to teach the

---

[46] Quoted in Richard Davis, "News Media Coverage of National Political Institutions," Ph.D. dissertation, Syracuse University, 1986.

[47] William Rivers, *The Other Government: Power and the Washington Media* (New York: Universe Books, 1982), ch. 1; Michael Baruch Grossman and Martha Joynt Kumar, *Portraying the President* (Baltimore: Johns Hopkins University Press, 1981), 83.

[48] See Leon V. Sigel, *Reporters and Officials* (Lexington, Mass.: D. C. Heath, 1973); Hugh Heclo, "Introduction: The Presidential Illusion," in Hugh Heclo and Lester M. Salamon, *The Illusion of Presidential Government* (Boulder, Colo.: Westview Press, 1981), 8; Ben H. Bagdikian, "Congress and the Media: Partners in Propaganda," *Columbia Journalism Review* 12 (January/February 1974): 3–10.

[49] B. H. Winfield, "Franklin D. Roosevelt's Efforts to Influence the News during His First-Term Press Conferences," *Presidential Studies Quarterly* 9 (Spring 1981): 189–199. See also George Juergens, *News from the White House* (Chicago: University of Chicago Press, 1981), 65.

[50] See Herbert I. Schiller, *Mass Communications and American Empire* (Boston: Beacon Press, 1971); Epstein, *News from Nowhere*.

[51] Grossman and Kumar, *Portraying the President*, 420.

American public that the Congress is a coequal branch of the federal government."[52]

THE WATCHDOG ROLE

Traditionally the American press has accepted responsibility for protecting the public from deceitful, careless, incompetent, and corrupt officials.[53] In this **watchdog role** the press stands ready to expose any official who violates accepted legal, ethical, and performance standards.

The most notable exercise of the watchdog role in recent decades took place during the Watergate scandal. Bob Woodward and Carl Bernstein of the *Washington Post* spent months uncovering evidence that high-ranking officials in the Nixon White House were lying about their role in the burglary of the Democratic National Committee's headquarters and in the subsequent cover-up. Virtually all of the nation's media picked up on the *Post's* revelations. In the end, even the most diehard Republicans found it all but impossible to deny that President Nixon had acted unlawfully. Nixon was forced to resign, as was his attorney general, John Mitchell. The Watergate episode is a dramatic reminder that a vigilant press is one of society's best safeguards against abuses of political power.

Some critics say that the news media occasionally go overboard in performing their watchdog role. In 1991, for example, the press for several weeks made headlines out of the travels of White House chief of staff John Sununu. He had flown on government planes and driven in his government-paid limousine when not on official business. The White House tightened the rules for Sununu's travel, which might have ended the controversy if the press had not extended the story. There were news reports saying that Sununu's finances were a mess and that many White House staffers disliked Sununu and would not mind seeing him fired. A leading weekly news magazine predicted that Sununu would soon be fired. He resigned in December 1991.

A more common criticism is the opposite: that the media are not diligent enough in their watchdog role. There is an inherent tension between the watchdog and common-carrier roles. The watchdog role demands that the journalist maintain a skeptical posture toward political leaders and keep them at a distance. The common-carrier role requires the journalist to maintain close ties with political leaders. When the two roles conflict, the watchdog role is usually the one that is sacrificed. Except in a few cases, such as Watergate, Washington reporters have not been particularly zealous in uncovering official wrongdoing. A study revealed that American journalists are substantially more dependent on, and friendlier with, top officials than are western European journalists.[54] A symbol of this closeness is the White House press room. The White House is the most prestigious "beat" in Washington, and many of the nation's top journalists have worked it. Those who cover the White House from the inside, however, get most of their news from official sources and are expected to treat the

<aside>
★ ANALYZE THE ISSUE

Journalistic Advocacy
During the race for the Republican nomination in 1988, George Bush refused to admit that he had played any role in the Iran-Contra affair. In a controversial on-the-air shouting match with Bush, CBS news anchor Dan Rather tried to force Bush to acknowledge an involvement. Who was Rather representing in this instance—Bush's Republican rivals, the Democratic party, the American people, CBS, himself? What does this incident suggest to you about the proper limits of journalistic advocacy?
</aside>

---

[52] Thomas P. O'Neill, Jr., "Congress: The First 200 Years," *National Forum* 64 (Fall 1984): 20–21.
[53] See Rivers, *The Other Government*; Douglass Cater, *The Fourth Branch of Government* (Boston: Houghton Mifflin, 1955).
[54] Thomas E. Patterson, "Irony of the Free Press," paper presented at the International Communication Association meeting, Chicago, May 1991.

News pictures like this famous one, of children burned by napalm bombs dropped by U.S. planes, brought the reality of the Vietnam war home to the American people. (Huynh Cong/Associated Press)

president favorably. Reporters who violate this understanding often are denied access to top officials and are excluded from special White House activities, such as dinners for visiting heads of state.

The media's watchdog role is also compromised to some degree by the fact that politicians have become increasingly adept at recognizing the material that the media seek in news stories and creating situations that provide it.[55] It is always easier for the press to respond to what officials give it than to look for stories on its own. There is no guarantee that an investigation, which may take weeks or months, will result in a story. On the other hand, there is always a story to be written when the president gives a speech or Congress holds a hearing.

Despite all these difficulties, the watchdog role is a crucial one and one that the American press takes pride in performing. The media see themselves as standing guard over the guardians, thereby playing an indispensable part in a properly functioning democratic system.

THE PUBLIC REPRESENTATIVE ROLE

The mass media are an increasingly important and powerful institution in American society. They have become more influential as some other institutions, most notably the political parties, have lost strength. Traditionally the **public representative role**—that of spokesperson for and advocate of the public—belonged to political leaders, political institutions, and political organizations. Today, however, many reporters seem to believe that *they* represent the public. "[Our] chief duty," newscaster Roger Mudd claims, "is to put before the nation its unfinished business."[56]

[55] See Martin Linsky, *Impact: How the Press Affects Federal Policymaking* (New York: Norton, 1986).
[56] Quoted in Max Kampelman, "The Power of the Press," *Policy Review* 6 (1978): 19.

Although the press has to some degree always acted as a stand-in for the people, the tendency for journalists to play the role of public advocate has increased significantly since the 1960s.[57] Vietnam and Watergate convinced many journalists that their judgments were superior to those of political leaders. "The press," declared Ben Bradlee, executive editor of the *Washington Post*, "won on Watergate."[58] *The New York Times*'s James Reston said much the same thing about Vietnam: "Maybe historians will agree that the reporters and the cameras were decisive in the end. They brought the issue of the war to the people, before the Congress and the courts, and forced the withdrawal of American power from Vietnam."[59]

Are reporters really in a position to know what is best for the American people? There are at least two basic reasons for concluding that the media are not well suited to the role of public representative: they do not promote a consistent point of view, and they are not adequately accountable to the public.

"News from Nowhere"

First, representation requires a point of view. Politics is essentially the mobilization of bias—that is, it involves the representation of particular values and interests. Political parties and interest groups, as we saw in Chapters 11 through 14, exist to represent particular interests in society. But what political interests do the media represent? CBS News executive Richard Salant once said that his reporters covered stories "from nobody's point of view."[60] What he was saying in effect was that journalists do not consistently represent the political concerns of any group in particular. They respond to news opportunities, not to political interests.

Presidential elections provide an example. News coverage of presidential campaigns does not focus on the policy and leadership choices facing the American people but instead emphasizes the "horse race" between the candidates—who is winning and who is losing (see Figure 15-1). Moreover, the candidates' blunders and gaffes tend to make more news headlines than their stands on domestic and foreign policy.[61] In the 1984 campaign, for example, a major controversy was the refusal of the Democratic vice-presidential candidate, Geraldine Ferraro, to make public her family's income-tax returns. In 1992 the Democratic candidate Bob Kerrey told an off-color joke in New Hampshire the same day that his primary opponent Bill Clinton unveiled his economic program. Clinton's speech was virtually ignored by the press, while Kerrey's joke made headlines. Such stories meet the media's standards for newsworthiness, but they hardly contribute to the fulfillment of the role of public representative.

The press is better geared to the role of critic. Studies indicate that journalists tend to be more liberal and Democratic in their preferences than are other elite

Without criticism and reliable and intelligent reporting, the government cannot govern.
Walter Lippmann

[57] Ibid.; Leonard Downie, Jr., *The New Muckrakers* (New York: New American Library, 1976); James Boylan, "Newspeople," *Wilson Quarterly* 6 (1982).
[58] Quoted in Kampelman, "Power of the Press," 18.
[59] Reston, "End of the Tunnel," 41.
[60] Quoted in Epstein, *News from Nowhere*, ix.
[61] See Thomas E. Patterson, *Mass Media Election* (New York: Praeger, 1980), chs. 3–5.

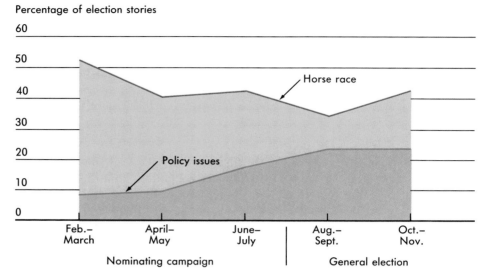

FIGURE 15-1 Network News Coverage of Policy Issues and of the "Horse Race" during the 1988 Presidential Campaign The media emphasize the "horse race" rather than the issues when they report on election campaigns. During the 1988 presidential campaign, the news media never came close to giving the same amount of coverage to the policy issues as they did to the "horse race" aspects—that is, which candidates were pulling ahead and which were falling behind. *Source: Figures based on author's content analysis of 1988 election news coverage.*

groups, such as corporate executives and lawyers,[62] but there is no clear evidence that the news itself reflects journalists' personal biases. For example, the Democratic president Jimmy Carter took more of a bashing from the press than did the Republican president Ronald Reagan. The media do not consistently build up liberal and Democratic positions and tear down conservative and Republican ones, or vice versa. Journalists tend to criticize *all* sides—liberals as well as conservatives, Democrats as well as Republicans.[63]

Such criticism has value: a public that is aware of the policy failures and personal shortcomings of its political leaders is better equipped to hold them accountable for their actions. Yet political criticism is not the same as public representation, which involves advocacy of certain interests and values.

Lack of Accountability

Second, the news media do not have the level of public accountability required of a public representative. Political institutions are made responsible to the public by formal mechanisms of accountability, particularly by regular elections. If representatives fail to serve as effective advocates, their constituents can vote them out of office. The vote thus provides officeholders with an incentive to discover what the people want and gives the public an opportunity to indicate whether it agrees with what officials are doing in its name. The public has no comparable hold over the press. Irate citizens can stop reading or viewing when they disagree with what journalists are advocating, but no daily newspaper or television station has ever gone out of business as a result.

[62] Robert Lichter and Stanley Rothman, "Media and Business Elites," *Public Opinion,* October/ November 1981, 42.
[63] See C. Richard Hofstetter, *Bias in the News* (Columbus: Ohio State University Press, 1976); Michael J. Robinson and Margaret A. Sheehan, *Over the Wire and on TV* (New York: Russell Sage Foundation, 1983); Michael J. Robinson and Austin Ranney, eds., *The Mass Media in Campaign '84* (Washington, D.C.: American Enterprise Institute, 1985).

The First Amendment virtually negates the press's claim to represent the public. Freedom of the press places the media beyond the control of popular majorities, and the people's representatives cannot properly be a self-appointed group, whether journalists or anyone else.

Organizing the Public in the Media Age

The mass media increasingly mold Americans' ideas about politics. The United States is in a "media age," in which communication is instantaneous, the news is omnipresent, and some journalists become national celebrities. The press seems at times to be all-knowing and all-powerful, an illusion that leads its critics and defenders alike to expect the press to give coherence to the nation's politics. This expectation is unrealistic. The problem is that the news media are not truly a political institution and have no stake in organizing public opinion and policy choices. The press is a private institution that is in the public news business. Walter Lippmann once noted:

> The press is no substitute for [political] institutions. It is like the beam of a searchlight that moves restlessly about, bringing one episode and then another out of darkness into vision. Men cannot do the work of the world by this light alone. They cannot govern society by episodes, incidents, and interruptions.[64]

Lippmann's point was not that news organizations are somehow inferior to political organizations but that each has a different role and responsibility in society. Democracy cannot operate effectively without a free press that is acting effectively in its signaler, common-carrier, and watchdog roles. To keep in touch with one another and with government, citizens must have access to timely and uncensored news about public affairs. In other words, the media must do their job well if democratic government is to succeed. However, the media cannot also be asked to do the job of political institutions. For reasons already noted, the task is beyond the media's capacity.

As previous chapters have emphasized, the problem of citizen influence is the problem of organizing the public so that people can act together effectively. The news media merely appear to solve this problem. The fact that millions of people each day receive the same news about their government does not mold them into an organized community. The news creates a pseudocommunity: citizens feel they are part of a functioning whole until they try to act upon their news awareness. The futility of media-centered democracy was dramatized in the movie *Network* when its central character, a television anchorman, became enraged at the nation's political leadership and urged his viewers to go to their windows and yell, "I'm mad as hell and I'm not going to take it anymore!" Citizens heeded his instructions, but the main effect was to raise the network's ratings. It was not clear what officials in Washington were expected to do about several million people leaning out their windows and shouting a vague slogan at the top of their lungs. The film vividly illustrated the fact that the news can raise public consciousness as a prelude to organization, but the news itself

★ ANALYZE THE ISSUE

The News Media's Rights and Responsibilities
The news media have a favored position in law. They are the only private institution that enjoys special constitutional protection. Does the First Amendment's guarantee of freedom of the press place a special obligation on the media to behave responsibly? The media have become an increasingly powerful force in American politics. Is there a corresponding need for new checks and balances on the power of the media?

[64] Lippmann, *Public Opinion,* 221.

cannot organize the public in any meaningful way. When public opinion is already formed, the media can serve as a channel for the expression of that opinion. But when public opinion is lacking, the media cannot establish it.

Summary

In the nation's first century, the press was allied closely with the political parties and helped the parties to mobilize public opinion. Gradually the press freed itself from this relationship and developed a form of reporting, known as objective journalism, that emphasizes the fair and accurate reporting of newsworthy developments. The foundation of modern American news rests on the presentation and evaluation of significant events, not on the advocacy of partisan ideas. The nation's news organizations do not differ greatly in their reporting; broadcast stations and newspapers throughout the country emphasize many of the same events, issues, and personalities, following the lead of the major broadcast networks, a few elite newspapers, and the wire services.

The press performs four basic roles in a free society. In their signaler role, journalists communicate information to the public about events and problems that they consider important, relevant, and therefore newsworthy. The press also serves as a common carrier, in that it provides political leaders with a channel for addressing the public. Third, the press acts as a public protector or watchdog by exposing deceitful, careless, or corrupt officials. The American media can and, to a significant degree, do perform these roles adequately.

The press is less well suited, however, to the other role it plays, that of public representative. This role requires a consistent political viewpoint and public accountability, neither of which the press possesses. The media cannot be a substitute for effective political institutions. The press's strength lies ultimately in its capacity to inform the public, not in its claims to represent the people.

Major Concepts

common-carrier role
objective journalism
partisan press

public representative role
signaler role
watchdog role

Suggested Readings

Altheide, David L., and Robert P. Snow. *Media Worlds in the Postjournalism Era*. New York: Aldine-De Gruyter, 1991. An analysis of the mass media and culture, including the conditions that lead journalists to present a version of reality that serves the media's own ends.

Bagdikian, Ben H. *The Media Monopoly*, 3d ed. Boston: Beacon Press, 1990. An examination of the growing power of the press, including tendencies toward monopolies of ownership and news production.

Epstein, Edward J. *News from Nowhere: Television and the News*. New York: Random House, 1973. A behind-the-scenes look at the organizational influences affecting the production of network television news.

Gans, Herbert J. *Deciding What's News*. New York: Vintage Books, 1980. A study of journalists' news values, focusing on major organizations, including CBS News and *Time* magazine.

Graber, Doris A. *Processing the News*, 2d ed. New York: Longman, 1988. A careful assessment of how people make use of news.

Grossman, Michael Baruch, and Martha Joynt Kumar. *Portraying the President*. Baltimore: Johns Hopkins University Press, 1981. A study of relations between the White House and the press.

Iyengar, Shanto, and Donald R. Kinder. *News That Matters*. Chicago: University of Chicago Press, 1987. An assessment of the impact of television news on the public's perceptions of politics.

Patterson, Thomas E., and Robert D. McClure. *The Unseeing Eye*. New York: Putnam, 1976. An analysis of television coverage of a presidential election campaign.

Robinson, Michael J., and Margaret A. Sheehan. *Over the Wire and on TV*. New York: Russell Sage Foundation, 1983. Analysis of television and wire-service news coverage of the 1980 presidential election.

Sabato, Larry J. *Feeding Frenzy: How Attack Journalism Has Transformed American Politics*. New York: The Free Press, 1991. An argument that recent tendencies in journalism are warping the democratic process.

Has the Rise of Interest Groups Offset the Decline of Political Parties?

ROBERT H. SALISBURY

The growth in the number and variety of interest groups in Washington has run parallel with a decline in their net impact on policy.

Does the explosion of private-interest presence in the nation's capital signal a comparable increase in the influence of these groups? Do they now dominate the policymaking process to the exclusion of other considerations? Have they replaced political parties as the main mechanisms driving the political system? I think the answer to each of these questions is no; indeed, I think that the growth in the number and variety of interest groups in Washington has run parallel with a decline in their net impact on policy.

Part of this decline in influence has resulted from the great expansion in the number and effectiveness of various types of citizens' groups. Citizens' groups draw heavily upon well-educated middle-class Americans for support, and as this segment of society has grown, so have the organizing possibilities for such groups. These groups often disrupt the older established linkages between government officials and private groups. The links among congressional committees, executive agencies, and interest groups have been destabilized and often undermined by the vocal participation of groups that point out adverse third-party or externality effects of policy—harm to the environment from pesticide runoff, for example, or the high costs consumers must pay for zealous enforcement of workplace safety rules. The increasing number of groups has often meant that particular policy issues get bogged down in intergroup conflict, and the organized interests that used to dominate policy outcomes now find themselves confronted by vigorous opposition that sometimes results in policy stalemate.

As interest groups have grown, the structures of government with which they must deal have changed. In Congress, power has been broadly decentralized. Committee chairs have had to share their authority with subcommittee chairs, and every member has come to possess significant staff resources. Moreover, most incumbents have managed to insulate themselves against electoral defeat. From the perspective of the interest groups, there are now many more members who must be persuaded before any policy can be enacted. From the members' perspective, most of them are less dependent for reelection on the support of particular interest groups. Meanwhile, in the executive branch there has been a steady shift of power toward the Executive Office of the President and, indeed, the White House Office itself. These are much more difficult for lobbyists to penetrate than the operating units of cabinet departments or the independent agencies and commissions.

Finally, federal policy itself has immensely greater import for nearly every person or institution than it did a few decades ago. This fact helps to explain why, despite decreased clout, the number of interest groups in Washington has continued to grow. All sorts of groups—universities, business corporations, local governments, churches—need to know the potential impact of policy, not just in order to influence policy decisions but to adapt their own actions more effectively. Accordingly, they must send people to Washington to monitor the policymaking process. A great deal of what today's interest groups seek from their representatives is information, not influence. Shaping the future has become more and more difficult for them to do; if they can obtain the information needed to predict it and then adjust to it, their investment in Washington representation will be amply repaid.

Robert H. Salisbury is Chair and Souers Professor of American Government at Washington University. Articles on the role of interest groups in American politics, the focus of his recent work, have appeared in the American Political Science Review, *the* National Journal of Political Science, *the* American Journal of Political Science, *and other journals.*

FRANK J. SORAUF

The rise of groups and the decline of parties have meant a new mix in the influence of these intermediaries between citizens and their government.

When two changes, both of enormous political importance, occur more or less simultaneously, one cannot avoid looking for connections. The decline of American political parties and the proliferation of interest groups both became evident in the 1960s and 1970s, so we naturally ask: Has one replaced the other? Has one trend offset the other? Has one *caused* the other?

Rather than being cause and effect, the rise of groups and the decline of parties seem to reflect the same changes in American society. Parties flourished when we were a less educated, less politically sophisticated society. Parties gave a simple and easily grasped structure to the complexities of American politics. Truth or wisdom was in one party or the other; for the individual partisan, the party defined the good guys and the bad guys. Today, however, many Americans would rather pick and choose among candidates and issues than accept the whole "package" of party candidates and issues. They find in groups a more specific and focused kind of choice, for groups seem better able to reflect the politics of a complex and heterogeneous society.

Americans, then, are exchanging one kind of politics, one kind of representation, for another. The change has enormous consequences. It means a more specialized, precise, and targeted representation of the political goals of individual Americans; it is, indeed, now much easier for the individual with a single interest to find representation for it. It also means a system in which relatively small but intense and committed groups can outweigh much larger groups; the successes of the National Rifle Association in forestalling gun control testify to that. And it means a kind of representation in which the interests of middle-class Americans are better represented, if only because they have the time and resources that permit them to join and work for groups. That is why we have seen the rise of a middle-class agenda—issues of the environment, lifestyle, equality, and morality, for instance —along with the rise of group politics.

However, the increase in group activity has not really "offset" the decline of political parties. Rather, the changes in the fortunes of the two have altered the nature of representation in American politics. Because both serve as mobilizers of individual Americans, the rise of groups and the decline of parties have meant a new mix in the influence of these intermediaries between citizens and their government.

Inevitably, the new mix affects the operation of the American democracy. The greater specialization and effectiveness of interest groups necessarily result in a fragmentation of the American electorate, a fragmentation that many observers think leads to deadlock in American legislatures. Whatever may be the shortcomings of the two major parties in trying to encompass a majority of Americans in a single coalition, they were in their heyday unsurpassed vehicles for mobilizing majorities. Their decline shifts the burdens of majority building from political intermediaries to increasingly burdened institutions of government.

Frank J. Sorauf is a member of the Department of Political Science at the University of Minnesota. He is the author of Money in American Elections.

ELECTED REPRESENTATIVES

A merican democracy, it is sometimes said, is government by the people. So it is, but in a figurative sense. Direct democracy is a practical impossibility in a nation of the size and complexity of the United States. Americans are governed through representatives. There is no alternative.

As we indicated in Chapters 4 and 8, a debate has long raged over the proper relationship between a people and its representatives. One view holds that the representative must follow the expressed opinion of the constituency. Another view, first elaborated two centuries ago by the English theorist Edmund Burke, holds that the representative is obligated to exercise personal judgment in making policy decisions. The debate is essentially an issue of which interests will be the objects of public policy. The notion that representatives should take instructions from their constituents is based on the assumption that if they do not, they will promote the interests of themselves and their social class over the true interests of the people. In contrast, Burke's idea that representatives should follow their consciences is based on the assumption that if they listen too closely to those who elected them, they will serve local or narrow interests rather than the national or general interest.

The governing system of the United States, partly by design and partly by accident, embodies elements of both these concepts of representation. The presidency is a truly national office that inclines its incumbent to take a national view of issues, while Congress is both a national institution and a body that is subject to powerful constituency influence. U.S. senators and representatives are elected from states and from districts within states, so that they are subject to strong local pressures. Chapters 16 and 17 show how the election, organization, and policymaking of Congress reflect both national and local influences. In contrast, Chapters 18 and 19 reveal how the president's election, role, and power are affected by the office's national political base. Collectively, these four chapters indicate how local and national factors come together in relations between the executive and legislative branches and between these two branches and their constituents, the American people. ★ ★ ★

CONGRESSIONAL ELECTION AND ORGANIZATION: SHARING THE POWER

16

A decentralized system [of power serves] the immediate needs of members of a professionalized Congress.

Lawrence Dodd and Richard Schott[1]

I n 1987 Congress began work on legislation that would address the growing U.S. trade imbalance; the trade deficit had hit a yearly high of $171 billion. At one time the United States had had the greatest trade surplus in the world, but by the early 1980s it had become a debtor country, with a huge trade deficit. Congress was determined to reverse this trend. The proposed legislation was based on the principle of free trade and provided for economic penalties to be imposed on countries that exported goods to the United States but erected barriers to the importation of American goods. In its original form the bill was relatively straightforward and just 200 pages long. By the time it reached the floors of the House and Senate in 1988, however, the bill had been loaded down with so many amendments that it ran to more than 1,000 pages.

The trade bill had ballooned because many members of Congress had succeeded in creating local exceptions to the free-trade principle that underlay the legislation. Senator Max Baucus of the lamb-producing state of Montana proposed a provision that called for federal payments to sheep producers who were financially harmed by imports. Representative Don Bonker of the lumber-rich state of Washington developed a measure that would protect certain U.S. wood products, including plywood paneling, from foreign imports. Representative Beryl Anthony, whose state of Arkansas has a Timex assembly plant, inserted a provision that would protect foreign watch companies that had production facilities in the United States.[2]

---

[1]Lawrence C. Dodd and Richard L. Schott, *Congress and the Administrative State* (New York: Wiley, 1979), 326.
[2]"The Making of a Mishmash," *Time*, March 28, 1988, 49.

The story of the trade bill illustrates the dual nature of Congress: it is both a lawmaking institution for the country and a representative assembly for states and districts. Members of Congress must bargain and compromise in the process of producing legislation because they have both an individual duty to serve the interests of their separate constituencies and a collective duty to protect the interests of the country as a whole. Often, their duty to constituency takes precedence over their duty to country. Attention to constituency interests is the common denominator of an institution in which each member must please the voters back home in order to win reelection. Congressional elections have been described as "local events with national consequences."[3]

This chapter explains the nature of congressional election and organization. In the next chapter we will examine congressional policymaking. The following points are emphasized in this first of two chapters on Congress:

★ *Congressional elections tend to have a strong local orientation and to favor incumbents.* Congressional office provides incumbents with substantial resources (free publicity, staff, and legislative influence) that give them (particularly House members) a major advantage in election campaigns.

★ *Congress is organized in part along political party lines; its collective leadership is provided by party leaders of the House of Representatives and the Senate.* However, these party leaders do not have great formal powers. Their authority rests mainly on the fact that they have been entrusted with leadership responsibility by other senators or representatives of their party.

★ *The work of Congress is done mainly through its committees and subcommittees, each of which has its leader (a chairperson) and its policy jurisdiction.* The committee system of Congress allows a broad sharing of power and leadership, which serves the power and reelection needs of Congress's members but fragments the institution.

Congress as a Career: Election to Congress

In the nation's first century, service in the Congress was not a career for most of its members. Before 1900 at least a third and sometimes as many as half of the seats in Congress changed hands at each election. Most members left voluntarily. Because travel was slow and arduous, serving in the nation's capital required them to spend months away from their families. And because the national government was not the center of power and politics that it is today, many politicians preferred to serve in state capitals.

The modern Congress is very different.[4] Service in Congress is a career for most of its members. They are professional politicians, and a seat in the U.S. Senate or House is as far as most of them can expect to go in politics. The pay (about $125,000 a year) is reasonably good, and the prestige of their office is

---

[3]Randall B. Ripley, *Congress: Process and Policy,* 3d ed. (New York: Norton, 1983), 76.
[4]See John R. Hibbing, "Voluntary Retirements from the House in the Twentieth Century," *Journal of Politics* 44 (November 1982): 1020–1034.

CONSTITUTIONAL QUALIFICATIONS FOR SERVING IN CONGRESS

Representatives: "No person shall be a Representative who shall not have attained to the age of twenty-five years, and been seven years a citizen of the United States, and who shall not, when elected, be an inhabitant of that State in which he shall be chosen" (Article I, section 2).

Senators: "No person shall be a Senator who shall not have attained to the age of thirty years, and been nine years a citizen of the United States, and who shall not, when elected, be an inhabitant of the State for which he shall be chosen" (Article I, section 3).

substantial, particularly if they serve in the Senate. A lengthy career in Congress is what most of its members aspire to attain.

Today the biggest obstacle to having a congressional career is winning a seat in the first place. As we noted in Chapter 10, incumbents, particularly members of the House, have a good chance of being returned to office again and again (see Table 16-1).[5] In recent House elections, about 90 percent of incumbents, on average, have decided to seek reelection, and fewer than 10 percent of them have lost. Senate seats are less secure.[6] Since 1970 the success rate of incumbent

[5]Robert S. Erikson, "Is There Such a Thing as a Safe Seat?" *Polity* 8 (Summer 1976): 627–628; James L. Payne, "The Personal Electoral Advantage of House Incumbents, 1936–1976," *American Politics Quarterly* 8 (October 1980): 465–482; see also Stephen E. Frantzich, "Opting Out: Retirement from the House of Representatives," *American Politics Quarterly* 6 (July 1978): 251–273.
[6]Joseph Cooper and William West, "The Congressional Career in the 1970s," in Lawrence C. Dodd and Bruce I. Oppenheimer, eds., *Congress Reconsidered*, 2d ed. (Washington, D.C.: Congressional Quarterly Press, 1981), 99.

Like all other members of Congress, Senator Ted Stevens of Alaska tries to win reelection by serving the interests of his constituents while in office. Here Stevens testifies about the damage to Alaskan fishing grounds caused by the *Exxon Valdez* oil spill of 1989. (John Duricka/AP/Wide World)

TABLE 16-1   House and Senate Incumbents Reelected and Not Seeking Reelection, 1954–1990   Congressional incumbents who seek reelection have a very high rate of success.

	HOUSE INCUMBENTS		SENATE INCUMBENTS	
	Percent Not Seeking Reelection	*Percent Reelected of Those Seeking Reelection*	*Percent Not Seeking Reelection*	*Percent Reelected of Those Seeking Reelection*
1954	6%	93%	18%	75%
1956	5	95	18	86
1958	8	90	18	64
1960	6	93	15	97
1962	6	92	12	83
1964	8	87	6	85
1966	5	88	9	88
1968	5	97	18	71
1970	7	95	12	77
1972	9	94	18	74
1974	10	88	21	85
1976	11	96	24	64
1978	11	94	30	60
1980	8	91	15	55
1982	9	90	9	93
1984	6	96	12	90
1986	10	98	18	75
1988	6	98	21	85
1990	6	96	17	97

SOURCE: *Congressional Quarterly Weekly Report,* various dates.

senators has averaged about 75 percent, ranging from a low of 55 percent (1980) to a high of 97 percent (1990).

Most congressional incumbents win by a safe victory margin (see Table 16-2). In nearly half of recent Senate contests, the winner has received more than 60 percent of the vote. The proportion of one-sided contests is even higher in House races. Whereas in the 1950s nearly half of all House races were won with less than 60 percent of the vote, only about a fourth of House races have been that close in recent elections.[7] A backlash in the 1990 and 1992 elections against Congress's performance on budget issues, and allegations of widespread ethics violations by its members, lowered substantially the victory margin of contested House races from what it had been in 1988. Nevertheless, the winner in most House races won by a comfortable margin.

[7]David R. Mayhew, "Congressional Elections: The Case of the Vanishing Marginals," *Polity* 6 (1974): 295–317; see also Cooper and West, "The Congressional Career in the 1970s," 99; Melissa P. Collie, "Incumbency, Electoral Safety, and Turnover in the House of Representatives, 1952–1976," *American Political Science Review* 75 (March 1981): 119–131.

USING INCUMBENCY TO STAY IN CONGRESS

Getting reelected is a high priority for members of Congress.[8] They may be more interested in issues of public policy than in reelection activities, but they must stay in Congress if they are to realize their policy goals. In Lawrence Dodd's phrase, members of Congress strive for **electoral mastery**—a strong base of popular support that will free them from constant worry over reelection and allow them to pursue other goals.[9]

Most incumbents succeed in building a level of popular support that will guarantee their reelection time and again. In the 1986–1990 period fewer congressional seats changed hands than at any other time in American history. This development took place despite substantial public discontent with the

[8]David R. Mayhew, *Congress: The Electoral Connection* (New Haven, Conn.: Yale University Press, 1974), 16.
[9]Lawrence C. Dodd, "A Theory of Congressional Cycles," in Gerald Wright, Leroy Rieselbach, and Lawrence C. Dodd, *Congress and Policy Change* (New York: Agathon, 1986).

TABLE 16-2 Percentage of House and Senate Incumbents Who Won Reelection by 60 Percent or More of the Vote, 1956–1990

	House Incumbents	Senate Incumbents
1956	59%	
1958	63	43%
1960	59	
1962	64	
1964	59	44
1966	68	
1968	72	
1970	77	45
1972	78	
1974	66	
1976	72	41
1978	78	
1980	73	
1982	69	39
1984	77	
1986	86	
1988	87	53
1990	79	

SOURCES: Data for 1956–1982 from Norman Ornstein et al., *Vital Statistics on Congress, 1984–1985* (Washington, D.C.: American Enterprise Institute, 1984), 53–54; for 1984, *Congressional Quarterly Almanac*, vol. 40 (Washington, D.C.: Congressional Quarterly, 1984), 7B–31B; for 1986, *Congressional Quarterly Weekly Report* 44 (November 8, 1986): 2864–2870; for 1988 and 1990, Federal Election Commission.

performance of Congress as a whole. Safe incumbency reflects a serious decline in partisan competition, a condition attributable in large part to the important advantages that incumbents, both Democrats and Republicans, have over their election opponents.

Claiming Credit

Members of Congress sometimes seek **pork-barrel legislation,** a term that refers to laws whose tangible benefits are targeted solely at a legislator's **constituency**—the body of citizens eligible to vote for him or her. ("Pork" was the term for political graft or corruption in the late nineteenth century; when legislators adopted the practice of placing numerous items of pork into a single bill, people began to say, "Now the pork is all in one barrel.") The $600 billion annual appropriations bill for 1988, for example, included $2.6 million that Senator Ted Stevens secured for Alaska fishermen so that they could "develop fishery products"; $60,000 that the University of Massachusetts obtained for its Belgian Endive Research Center, thanks to the efforts of Congressman Silvio Conte, the ranking minority member on the House Appropriations Committee; and a $6.4 million federal grant for development of an Idaho ski resort, the result of Senator James McClure's efforts.

Pork-barrel politics is often ridiculed by the public, but the voters themselves are the main reason it continues. Constituents may disagree on issues of national policy, but they do not object when federal pork-barrel projects pour into their area. And in general, voters demand that their representatives think of local interests as their highest priority. The Republican House whip, Newt Gingrich of Georgia, escaped defeat in 1990 by fewer than 1,000 votes, in part because he had not paid close attention to the demands of striking Eastern Airlines workers in his suburban Atlanta district.

Members who look after the needs of their constituents are in a position to deny responsibility for Congress's governing failures. In fact, incumbents often campaign against Congress itself, criticizing its policy failures while denying any personal responsibility for them.[10]

Performing Services

The availability of staff resources is another advantage of incumbents. Each House member receives an office allowance of about $500,000 a year, which enables him or her to hire a personal staff of about twenty full-time staff members. Senators have larger budgets that vary in size with the population size of the states they represent. Senators' personal staffs average about forty employees.[11] Congressional staffs doubled in size during the 1960s, when members of Congress decided they needed more help to keep pace with their growing legislative load (see Table 16-3). However, most members of Congress use their personal staffs primarily to perform services in order to build support among constituents, a practice that is known as **service strategy.** Congressional staffers spend the bulk of their time not on legislative matters but on

TABLE 16-3 Approximate Number of Personal Staff Members Employed by Members of Congress, 1960–1990, by Chamber
The size of Congress members' personal staffs increased greatly after the 1960s.

Year	Senate	House
1960	1,275	2,875
1970	2,250	4,950
1980	3,925	7,200
1990	4,400	7,950

SOURCE: Staff, Office of Disbursing (Senate) and Office of Clerk of the House.

[10]Richard F. Fenno, Jr., *Home Style: House Members in Their Districts* (Boston: Little, Brown, 1978), 167.
[11]Norman Ornstein et al., *Vital Statistics on Congress, 1984–1985* (Washington, D.C.: American Enterprise Institute, 1984), 1221.

THE INCUMBENCY ADVANTAGE

Incumbent members of Congress, particularly those in the House, have an extraordinary reelection rate. Their domination of the communication process is a major contributing factor in their reelection success. One reason is that members of Congress can use their office staffs to communicate directly with constituents through personal letters and franked mail.

Members of Congress also communicate with the public by means of the free publicity they get from the news media. All U.S. senators and most House members receive fairly close coverage from local media. Except for House members from large cities such as New York, Chicago, and Los Angeles, which have numerous congressional districts within their boundaries, members of Congress are locally prominent individuals and are thus considered newsworthy. Moreover, local reporters tend to give favorable coverage to members of Congress.

Another media advantage for incumbents comes through their ability to raise campaign funds. These funds are used primarily to produce and air televised political advertising. Many challengers, in contrast, do not have the funds for a major advertising campaign.

The chief disadvantage that incumbents have is that news about members of Congress generated by the national media is often negative, particularly when alleged ethics violations are involved. Sexual misconduct and financial misdeeds are the usual topics of such news stories, which can contribute to an incumbent's downfall. The comedian Jay Leno recently joked: "There are three stages to being a congressman. When they're first elected and unknown, you see them on the local news. Then when they get popular you see them on the network news. Then when they get really big—*America's Most Wanted.*"

SOURCES: Charles M. Tidmarch and Brad S. Karp, "The Missing Beat," *Congress and the Presidency* 10 (Spring 1983): 47–61; Peter Clarke and Susan Evans, *Covering Campaigns* (Stanford, Calif.: Stanford University Press, 1981); "Keeping an Eye on Congress," *Media Monitor* 4 (January 1990):6.

---

constituency relations, including responding to the thousands of letters that each member of Congress receives annually from individual constituents.[12] When citizens encounter delays or other obstacles in applying for social security, government loans, and other federal benefits, their representative or senator can often assist by persuading the bureaucracy to act quickly or favorably.[13] Congressional observers disagree on exactly how many votes can be won through these small favors,[14] but there is no doubt that constituency service helps—particularly in House races, in which the incumbent's attentiveness to local people and problems is often a major campaign issue.

Generating Publicity

Members of Congress also boost their chances of reelection by keeping their names before the voters. At public expense, each House member is allowed twenty-six visits to his or her district each year and each senator can take about forty trips home. In addition, each member of Congress is permitted several free mailings annually to constituent households; not surprisingly, the use of this privilege, known as the *frank*, peaks during election years.[15] Congressional staffs

---

[12]See John S. Saloma III, *Congress and the New Politics* (Boston: Little, Brown, 1969), 185; Harrison W. Fox and Susan Webb Hammond, "The Growth of Congressional Staffs," in Harvey C. Mansfield, ed., *Congress against President*, vol. 32, no. 1, of *Proceedings of the Academy of Political Science* (1975), 119.

[13]Fenno, *Home Style*, 101.

[14]For the opposing views, see Morris P. Fiorina, *Congress: Keystone of the Washington Establishment*, 2d ed. (New Haven, Conn.: Yale University Press, 1989), ch. 7, and John R. Johannes, *To Serve the People* (Lincoln: University of Nebraska Press, 1984), ch.8.

[15]Congressional Quarterly, *How Congress Works* (Washington, D.C.: Congressional Quarterly Press, 1983), 142–143.

When Massachusetts was redistricted in 1812, Governor Elbridge Gerry had the lines of one district redrawn in order to ensure that a candidate of his party would be elected. The cartoonist Elkanah Tinsdale, noting that the strangely shaped district resembled a salamander, called it a "Gerry-mander." (The Bettmann Archive)

also churn out newsletters and press releases designed to publicize the member for whom they work.[16] Some congressional offices are quite shameless in their use of the frank to get free publicity. Certain House members, for example, routinely send congratulatory letters to all graduating high school seniors in their districts, an effort that is designed to impress these newly eligible voters and their parents. The letters are individually signed—by a machine that duplicates the member's signature.

Gerrymandering: An Advantage for House Incumbents

Every ten years, after each population census, the 435 seats in the House of Representatives are reapportioned among the states in proportion to their population. States that have gained population since the last census may acquire additional seats, while those that have lost population may lose seats. After the 1990 census, California, Texas, and Florida were among the states that gained seats in the House. New York, Illinois, and Michigan were among those that lost seats.

The responsibility for redrawing House election district boundaries after a reapportionment—a process called **redistricting**—rests with the state governments. States are required by law to make their House districts as nearly equal in population as possible.[17] In establishing this principle in the early 1960s, the Supreme Court reasoned that districts of varying size give voters in smaller districts a larger voice in government, thus violating the "one person, one vote" principle of democratic government. Before this ruling, states commonly attempted to influence House elections through **malapportionment,** a situation in which election districts have greatly unequal populations.

Redistricting is a threat to House incumbents. Turnover in House elections is typically higher after a new census than in previous elections. The newly redrawn districts include voters who are unfamiliar with the incumbent, thereby diminishing a major advantage that incumbents have over their challengers. Moreover, in the case of a state that loses congressional seats there will be more incumbents then there are districts; thus incumbents may have to

[16]See Diana Evans Yiannakis, "House Members' Communication Styles," *Journal of Politics* 44 (November 1982): 1049–1073.
[17]*Wesberry* v. *Sanders,* 376 U.S. 1 (1964).

compete against each other in either a primary or general election. This situation occurred in New York after the 1990 census.

The effect of redistricting on House turnover would be greater if not for **gerrymandering**—the deliberate redrawing of an election district's boundaries to give a particular party or candidate an advantage. The Supreme Court has ruled that legislative redistricting for partisan political advantage is unconstitutional but has left open the question of what exactly constitutes redistricting of this type.[18] Because of the Court's position, majorities in state legislatures, whether Republican or Democratic, were cautious when redistricting after the 1990 census, but they tended naturally to draw district boundaries in a way that would not hurt candidates of their party.

The state legislatures also tended to protect House incumbents of both parties by creating heavily Republican districts around Republican incumbents and heavily Democratic districts around Democratic incumbents. Incumbents of both parties get protected for both practical and political reasons. Incumbents complain loudly and may initiate court action if they feel they have been unfavorably singled out in a partisan redistricting plan. A more important reason is that an incumbent member of Congress is always a formidable opponent. It is risky for a party to jeopardize the reelection chances of its potential winners by forcing them into a race with an incumbent of the opposite party. A safer strategy is to concede the race by stacking the district with voters of the incumbent's party, which means that other districts will have fewer of these partisan voters.

Of course, gerrymandering is not a tool that can be applied to U.S. Senate races. The electoral district for such races is defined not by population but by geography: it consists of the entire state, and each state—large or small—elects two senators.

THE PITFALLS OF INCUMBENCY

Incumbency is not without its pitfalls. The potential problems are several: troublesome issues, personal misconduct, and strong challengers.[19]

Troublesome Issues

Disruptive issues are a potential threat to incumbents. As we discussed in Chapter 10, incumbents become less secure when the nation's economy is doing poorly. The 1980 elections, for example, were waged against the backdrop of a severe recession overseen by a Democratic administration. The Democrats had a net loss of thirty-three House seats and thirteen Senate seats; the loss of the thirteen seats enabled Republicans to take control of the Senate.

Personal Misconduct

Members of Congress know they must stay away from scandal, but a few cannot seem to avoid it. Life in Washington can be fast-paced, glamorous, and expensive, and some members of Congress get caught up in influence peddling,

[18]*Davis v. Bandemer*, 478 U.S. 109 (1986). See Bernard Grofman, ed., *Political Gerrymandering and the Courts* (New York: Agathon Press, 1991).
[19]See Thomas E. Mann, *Unsafe at Any Margin: Interpreting Congressional Elections* (Washington, D.C.: American Enterprise Institute, 1978).

sex scandals, and questionable ways of inflating their salaries. Even the top leaders are not immune, as evidenced by the experience of former Speaker of the House Jim Wright. In addition to being accused in 1988 of a conflict of interest between his private business dealings and some of his legislative efforts, Wright was criticized for receiving $55,000 in "royalties" from a book written in his name by an aide and published by a friend. Almost all the copies sold went to interest groups such as the Teamsters union, which bought 2,000 copies.[20]

Improper behavior by members of Congress can sometimes be traced to the political demands placed upon them. They are expected to serve interests within their constituencies, and, in turn, they look to these interests for campaign support. The "Keating Five" are a case in point. Five senators—Alan Cranston (D-Calif.), Dennis DeConcini (D-Ariz.), John Glenn (D-Ohio), John McCain (R-Ariz.), and Donald Riegle, Jr. (D-Mich.)—intervened in 1987 with federal thrift regulators investigating Lincoln Savings and Loan Association, a failing thrift institution owned by Charles Keating. Keating had contributed almost a third of a million dollars to the senators' campaigns and had given another $1 million to political organizations at their request. In 1991 the Senate Select Committee faulted four of the senators for poor judgment and cited the fifth, Senator Cranston, for a more serious breach of ethics. Cranston, a four-term senator who was in poor health, resigned his position as majority whip and announced that he would not seek reelection in 1992.

The House check-writing scandal of 1992 was even more damaging to congressional incumbents. After the public reacted angrily to the news of the scandal, numerous incumbents announced their intention to retire. A first casualty was New York's Robert Mrazek. He had previously announced that he would run for the U.S. Senate, but he quit his campaign within weeks of the revelation that he had written more bad checks than any other House member.

Strong Challengers: A Special Problem for Senators

Finally, incumbents are vulnerable to strong challengers. Senators are particularly likely to face formidable opponents: after the presidency, the Senate is the top rung of the political ladder, and membership is highly coveted. Governors and House members are frequent challengers for Senate seats, and they have the electoral base, reputation, and experience to compete effectively.[21] Moreover, the U.S. Senate lures wealthy challengers. John D. (Jay) Rockefeller IV spent $12 million, most of it his own money, in winning election to the U.S. Senate from West Virginia in 1984. The willingness of strong challengers to take on Senate incumbents is a major reason that Senate campaigns have remained somewhat competitive in recent decades.

House incumbents have less reason to fear strong challengers.[22] A House seat is often not appealing enough to induce prominent local politicians, such as mayors or state legislators, to risk their political careers in a challenge to an incumbent. Political scientists Linda Fowler and Robert McClure speak of "the

---

[20]Ibid.
[21]See Alan I. Abramowitz, "A Comparison of Voting for U.S. Senator and Representative in 1978," *American Political Science Review* 74 (September 1980): 633.
[22]Linda L. Fowler, "Candidate Perceptions of Electoral Coalitions," *American Politics Quarterly* (October 1980): 484.

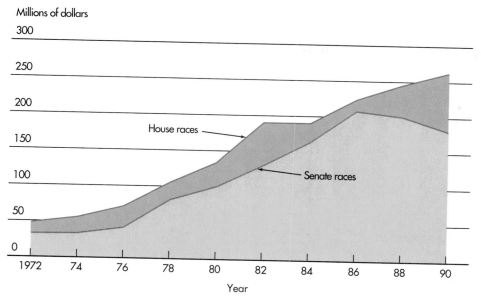

FIGURE 16-1 Congressional Campaign Expenditures, 1972–1990
The cost of running for congressional office has risen sharply as campaign techniques—television advertising, opinion polling, and so on—have become more elaborate and sophisticated. *Source: Federal Election Commission.*

unseen candidates"—potentially strong House challengers who end up deciding that the costs of a campaign outweigh the benefits.[23] This situation frequently leaves the field open to weak opponents with little or no governmental or political experience.[24] In a district where one party has a lopsided advantage, the incumbent may even run unopposed. In the 1990 elections, a fifth of House seats were uncontested by the weaker party.

CAMPAIGN SPENDING

Incumbents have a decided advantage when it comes to raising funds. The costs of recent congressional campaigns have risen to a total of roughly $450 million, a sixfold increase over the campaigns of the early 1970s (see Figure 16-1). These rising expenditures reflect the impact of inflation (the value of the dollar declined by more than half during the period) and the high cost of modern campaign techniques, such as polling, television advertising, and voter targeting.

About half of all campaign contributions come from individuals, most of whom donate $100 or less to a candidate. These individual donations are raised largely through computer-based direct-mail solicitations. Political action committees (PACs, discussed in detail in Chapter 14) are the second major source of contributions. PACs put up about 30 percent of congressional campaign funds, twice as much as two decades ago. Political party organizations provide about 10 percent of campaign money, although the proportion is higher for Republicans than for Democrats. Parties also affect the flow of election funds by identifying key races, on which PACs may then focus their financial support.

Politics has got so expensive that it takes lots of money to even get beat with.

Will Rogers

[23]Linda L. Fowler and Robert D. McClure, *Political Ambition* (New Haven, Conn.: Yale University Press, 1989); see also Jonathan S. Krasno and Donald Philip Green, "Preempting Quality Challengers in House Elections," *Journal of Politics* 50 (November 1988), 878.
[24]Thomas Kazee, "Recruiting Challengers in U.S. House Elections," *Legislative Studies Quarterly* (August 1983): 469–480.

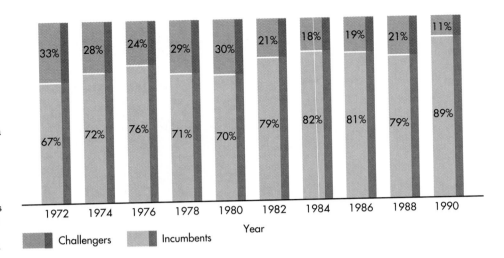

FIGURE 16-2 Allocation of PAC Contributions between Incumbents and Challengers in Congressional Races That Included an Incumbent, 1972–1990
In allocating campaign contributions, PACs favor incumbent members of Congress over their challengers by a wide margin. *Source: Estimated from Federal Election Commission data.*

★ ANALYZE THE ISSUE

The Influence of PACs
Many people believe that PACs exercise too much influence over politics and government. However, attempts by some members of Congress to curb the power of PACs have not attracted majority support. Is it likely that such congressional support will ever materialize? Why, or why not? Does the fact that members of Congress set the ground rules for congressional campaigns, including levels of PAC support, represent a threat to democracy?

Finally, candidates' personal funds account for about 10 percent of campaign spending.[25]

The amount of money that is required to run a successful campaign varies widely, depending on the nature of the constituency and of the competition.[26] Major-party Senate candidates spent, on average, about $2 million in 1990, double the average $1 million spent in 1980. The 1990 contest between Jesse Helms and Harvey Gantt in North Carolina was one of the most expensive Senate races in history, with Helms outspending Gantt by $13.4 million to $7.8 million, for a combined total of $21.2 million. House campaigns are much less expensive than Senate campaigns, but a House campaign costing $500,000 is no longer unusual, and million-dollar contests may become commonplace in the 1990s.

Though money has been called "the mother's milk of politics," money does not always decide an election; in most elections it is not even the main factor. Political scientist Gary Jacobson has demonstrated that money is no higher than third in importance, ranking behind partisanship and incumbency.[27] Nevertheless, the flow of money in congressional campaigns is significant both in itself and as an indicator of the other crucial factors, particularly the advantages of incumbency and the extent of electoral competitiveness.

A study by *Congressional Quarterly* found that only 10 percent of incumbents said they had had trouble raising enough money to conduct an effective campaign, compared with 70 percent of challengers.[28] Over half of House incumbents in recent elections have outspent their opponents by a ratio of 5-1 or more. PACs overwhelmingly favor incumbents (see Figure 16–2). In the

[25]Thomas E. Mann, "Election and Changes in Congress," in Thomas E. Mann and Norman J. Ornstein, eds., *The New Congress* (Washington, D.C.: Brookings Institution, 1981), 46.
[26]Barbara Hinckley, *Congressional Elections* (Washington, D.C.: Congressional Quarterly Press, 1981), 22–23; Barbara Hinckley, "House Re-elections and Senate Defeats: The Role of the Challenger," *British Journal of Political Science* (October 1980): 459–460.
[27]See Gary C. Jacobson, *Money in Congressional Elections* (New Haven, Conn.: Yale University Press, 1980).
[28]*Congressional Quarterly Guide to Congress*, 3d ed. (Washington, D.C.: Congressional Quarterly Press, 1982), 666; see also David A. Leuthold, *Electioneering in a Democracy* (New York: Wiley, 1968).

1990 elections, incumbents received eight times as much money in PAC contributions as their opponents did. About half the U.S. senators seeking reelection in 1990 each received $1 million or more from PACs, and fifteen House members each received half a million dollars or more.

Many challengers are able to raise only enough money for a token campaign. In 1988 about half of House challengers had less than $100,000 with which to try to unseat an incumbent. "Spending is particularly important for non-incumbents," political scientist Barbara Hinckley notes. "It significantly increases recognition and affects the vote."[29] Challengers who spend heavily have at least a chance of victory; those who spend little are almost certain to lose. In contrast, incumbents normally spend heavily only when they face a serious challenger.[30]

Senate races tend to attract well-funded challengers, but incumbents still derive a financial advantage from a variety of funding sources, including individual contributors, PACs, and political party sources. In recent years Senate incumbents have filled large campaign "war chests" well in advance of their reelection campaigns, partly in order to discourage potentially strong challengers from running against them. A year before the 1990 Senate races, Bill Bradley (D-N.J.) and Phil Gramm (R-Texas) had raised more than $6 million each for their reelection campaigns. Gramm ended his 1990 campaign with a surplus of $4 million, which he can use to ward off potential challengers if he runs again in 1996.

A race without an incumbent—called an **open-seat election**—nearly always brings out a strong candidate from each party and involves heavy spending, especially when party competition in the state or district is strong. In 1990, for example, there were twenty-eight open-seat races for the House; on the

[29]Hinckley, *Congressional Elections*, 29.
[30]Edie N. Goldenberg and Michael W. Traugott, *Campaigning for Congress* (Washington, D.C.: Congressional Quarterly Press, 1984), 81.

Senator Phil Gramm of Texas greets a supporter on the way to a fund-raising event that added to Gramm's $6 million reelection campaign war chest. (Najlah Feanny/SABA)

The Public's Influence on Representatives
Members of Congress now win election largely through their own efforts rather than through political parties. In this situation, does the influence that constituents have on their particular representative in Congress have any necessary relation to the larger question of whether the public as a whole has influence over Congress as a whole? In answering, bear in mind that each member of Congress is but one of 435 House members or 100 senators.

Any government is free to the people under it where the laws rule and the people are a party to the laws.

William Penn

average, each pair of major-party candidates spent roughly $750,000 for the House races.

CONGRESS AS A WHITE, MALE, LAWYER-DOMINATED INSTITUTION

Members of the House and the Senate are elected to represent their constituents, but the fact is that the average representative is very different from the average American in virtually every respect.[31] Although their membership is increasing, women and minorities are substantially underrepresented in Congress. In the thirty years from 1953 to 1982, an average of only about twenty women and twenty members of minority groups were among the 535 House and Senate members. The House is slightly more representative of the population than the Senate, mainly because House members have smaller, more homogeneous constituencies. In the 102d (1991–1992) Congress, the House had thirty-one women, twenty-six African-Americans, and twelve Hispanic-Americans, while the Senate had two women, one Asian-American, and no African-Americans or Hispanic-Americans.

Safe incumbency is a major obstacle to the election to Congress of more women and minorities. They have been no more successful than other challengers in dislodging congressional incumbents. In elections to state and local office, where incumbency is less important, women and minority candidates have made greater progress (see Chapter 7).

Members of Congress are drawn heavily from the legal profession. Although only one in every 350 Americans is a lawyer, nearly one in every two members of Congress is a lawyer. Attorneys are attracted to politics in part by Congress's role in lawmaking and by the public visibility that a campaign for office helps build, which can make a private law practice more successful. Along with lawyers, professionals such as businesspeople, educators, bankers, and journalists account for more than 90 percent of congressional membership.[32] Blue-collar workers, clerical employees, and homemakers are seldom elected to Congress. Farmers and ranchers are not as rare; a fair number of House members from rural districts have agricultural backgrounds.

Congressional Leadership

The way in which Congress works is closely related to the way in which its members win election. That is, the resources of Congress are designed in significant part to help members build electoral support. As a result, the emphasis in Congress is as much on the individual members as it is on the institution as a whole. The Speaker of the House and the other top leaders of Congress are important to its operation, but, unlike their counterparts in European legislatures, they have only limited authority over the members they lead.

[31]See David Vogler, *The Politics of Congress*, 3d ed. (Boston: Allyn & Bacon, 1984), 59–60, 64; *Congressional Quarterly Weekly*, January 7, 1989, 113.
[32]Compiled from "Characteristics of Congress," *Congressional Quarterly Weekly Report*, vol. 49, January 12, 1991, 118–127.

Speaker of the House Thomas Foley (*podium at left*) swears in the mostly male, mostly white members of the 102d Congress in 1991. (Greg Gibson/AP/Wide World)

PARTY LEADERSHIP IN CONGRESS

The House and Senate are organized along party lines. When members of Congress are sworn in at the start of a new two-year session, they automatically join either the Democratic or Republican caucus in their chamber. These caucuses select **party leaders** to represent the party's interests in the full chamber and to give some central direction to the body's deliberations.

The U.S. Capitol in Washington, D.C., with the Senate wing in the foreground. The House of Representatives meets in the wing at the left of the central rotunda (under the dome). The offices of the House and Senate party leaders—Speaker, vice-president, majority and minority leaders and whips—are located in the Capitol; other members of Congress have offices in buildings nearby. (Ellis Herwig/Stock, Boston)

The House Leadership

The main party leaders in the House are the Speaker, majority leader, majority whip, minority leader, and minority whip. The Constitution provides only for the post of Speaker, who is to be chosen by a vote of the entire House. In practice, this means that the Speaker is selected by the majority party's members, since only they have enough votes to choose one of their own. (Table 16-4 shows the party composition of Congress during the past two decades.)

The Speaker is often said to be the second most powerful official in Washington, after the president. The Speaker has the right to speak first on legislation during House debate and has the power to recognize members—that is, give them permission to speak from the floor. Since the House places a time limit on floor debate, not everyone has a chance to speak on a bill, and the Speaker can sometimes influence legislation simply by exercising the power to decide who will speak and when.[33] The Speaker also chooses the chairperson and majority-party members of the powerful House Rules Committee, which controls the scheduling of bills for debate.[34] Legislation the Speaker wants passed is likely to reach the floor under conditions favorable to its enactment; for example, the Speaker may ask the Rules Committee to delay sending a bill to the floor until he has lined up enough votes for its passage. The Speaker has other ways of directing the work of the House. He assigns bills to committees, can place time limits on the reporting of bills out of committees, and assigns members to conference committees. (The importance of these powers over committee action will become apparent later in this chapter and in the next.)

The Speaker is active in developing the party's position on issues and in persuading party members in the House to follow his lead.[35] The Speaker chairs the House Steering and Policy Committee, which has ongoing responsibility for developing and promoting the majority party's legislative program. Although the Speaker cannot compel party members to support this program, they look to him for leadership. The Speaker can draw upon shared partisan views and has a

[33]Barbara Sinclair, *Majority Leadership in the U.S. House* (Baltimore: Johns Hopkins University Press, 1983), 34–41.
[34]See Bruce Oppenheimer, "The Rules Committee: New Arm of Leadership in a Decentralized House," in Lawrence C. Dodd and Bruce I. Oppenheimer, eds., *Congress Reconsidered* (New York: Praeger, 1977), 96–116; Spark M. Matsunga and Ping Chen, *Rulemakers of the House* (Urbana: University of Illinois Press, 1976).
[35]Barbara Hinckley, *Stability and Change in Congress*, 2d ed. (New York: Harper & Row, 1978), 113–114; Sidney Waldman, "Majority Leadership in the House of Representatives," *Political Science Quarterly*, Fall 1980, 377.

TABLE 16-4 Number of Democrats and Republicans in House of Representatives and Senate, 1971–1992

	1971–72	1973–74	1975–76	1977–78	1979–80	1981–82	1983–84	1985–86	1987–88	1989–90	1991–92
House											
Democrats	255*	243*	290*	293	276	243*	269*	253*	258*	262*	268*
Republicans	180	192	145	142	159	192	166	182	177	173	167
Senate											
Democrats	54*	57*	61*	61	59	47	45	47	54*	55*	56*
Republicans	44	43	39	39	41	53	55	53	46	45	44

*Chamber not controlled by the president's party. 1991–92 House Democrat total includes an independent member who caucuses with the Democratic members.

The leadership of the 102d Congress (*from left to right*): House majority leader Richard Gephardt; House minority leader Robert Michel; Senate majority leader George Mitchell; Speaker of the House Thomas Foley; and Senate minority leader Robert Dole. (Lisa Berg/New York Times)

few rewards at his disposal for cooperative party members; he can, for instance, help them obtain public spending projects for their districts and favorable committee assignments for themselves.

The Speaker is assisted by the House majority leader, who is elected by the majority party's members. The majority leader acts as the party's floor leader, organizing the debate on bills and working to line up legislative support. Typically, the majority leader is an experienced and skilled legislator.[36]

The majority-party whip has the important job of soliciting votes from party members and of informing them when critical votes are scheduled. Whips have been known to track down members who are out of town and persuade them to rush back to Washington for an important vote. As voting is getting under way on the House floor, the whip will sometimes position himself where he can easily be seen by party members and let them know how the leadership wants them to vote by giving a thumbs-up or thumbs-down signal.

The minority party has its own leaders in the House. The House minority leader heads the party's caucus and policy committee and plays the leading role in developing the party's legislative positions. If the president is also of the minority party, the minority leader will work closely with him on legislative issues. The minority leader is assisted by a minority whip, who is responsible for lining up party members' support on legislation and informing them when votes are scheduled.

To a significant degree, the power of all party leaders in the House rests on the trust placed in them by the members of their party. They do not have strong formal powers, but they are expected to lead. If they are adept at promoting ideas and building coalitions, they will be able to exercise considerable power within their chamber.

The Senate Leadership

In the Senate, the most important party leadership position is that of the majority leader, who heads the majority-party caucus. The majority leader's role is much like that of the Speaker of the House, in that he formulates the majority's legislative policies and strategies and seeks to develop influential

[36]Roger H. Davidson and Walter J. Oleszek, *Congress and Its Members* (Washington, D.C.: Congressional Quarterly Press, 1981), 171.

★ HOW THE UNITED STATES COMPARES

LEGISLATIVE LEADERSHIP AND AUTHORITY

The U.S. House and Senate are separate and co-equal chambers, each with its own leadership and rules. This type of legislative structure is not found in most democracies. Although many of them have a bicameral legislature like the U.S. Congress, nearly all power is vested in just one of the two chambers. In the British Parliament, for example, the House of Commons is far more powerful than the House of Lords; the latter can delay legislation but cannot kill it. In such a situation legislative power is more concentrated and easier to exercise. Thus in Great Britain the party that controls the House of Commons decides legislative policy. In the United States a party must control both the House of Representatives and the Senate if it is to exercise such power.

Country	Form of Legislature
Canada	One house dominant
France	One house dominant
Germany	One house dominant (except on regional issues)
Great Britain	One house dominant
Israel	One house only
Italy	Two equal houses
Japan	One house dominant
Mexico	Two equal houses
United States	Two equal houses

relationships with his colleagues. Like the Speaker, the Senate majority leader chairs the party's policy committee and acts as the party's voice in the chamber.[37] The majority leader works closely with the president in developing legislative programs if they are of the same party. When Howard Baker was the Senate majority leader, he said that part of his job was to act as President Reagan's "point man" in the Senate.[38] For example, when the Reagan administration in 1981 sought congressional approval for the sale of AWACS surveillance planes to Saudi Arabia, Baker advised the White House not to press for a vote in order to give undecided senators enough time to study the effect of the sale on the security of Israel. Reagan agreed to hold off, and the sale was eventually approved.[39]

Unlike the Speaker of the House, the Senate majority leader is not the presiding officer of his chamber. The Constitution assigns this responsibility to the vice-president of the United States. However, since the vice-president is allowed to vote in the Senate only to break a tie, he seldom presides over Senate debates. The Senate has a president *pro tempore*, who, in the absence of the vice-president, has the right to preside over the Senate. President *pro tempore* is largely an honorary position that by tradition is usually held by the majority party's senior member. The presiding official has limited power, since each senator has the right to speak at any length on bills under consideration.

The Senate's tradition of unlimited debate stems mainly from its relatively small size (only 100 members, compared with the House's 435 members). Moreover, senators like to view themselves as the equals of all others in their chamber and are thus reluctant to take orders from their leadership.[40] For such

[37]Robert L. Peabody, *Leadership in the Congress: Stability, Succession, and Change* (Boston: Little, Brown, 1976), 35.
[38]CBS News, February 27, 1987.
[39]Davidson and Oleszek, *Congress and Its Members*, 185.
[40]See Randall B. Ripley, *Power in the Senate* (New York: St. Martin's Press, 1969), 104–106.

reasons, the Senate majority leader's position is weaker than that of the Speaker of the House. One former Senate majority leader, Robert Byrd, jokingly called himself a "slave," saying that he served his fellow Democrats' needs without commanding their votes.[41] The Senate majority leader's actual power depends significantly on his leadership skills.[42] Lacking strong formal powers, he must convince party members that their interests coincide with his.

Like the House, the Senate has a majority whip; however, this position is less important in the Senate because that body's members are less subject to persuasive tactics. Nevertheless, the Senate majority whip sees to it that members know when important votes are scheduled and ensures that the party's strongest advocates on a legislative measure are present for the debate. "The leadership must have the right members at the right place at the right time," said Senator Byrd.[43]

Finally, the Senate has a minority leader and minority whip, whose roles are comparable to those performed by their counterparts in the House. As befits "a chamber of equals," the majority leadership in the Senate usually consults the minority leadership on the scheduling of legislation.

COMMITTEE CHAIRPERSONS: THE SENIORITY PRINCIPLE

Party leaders are not the only important leaders in Congress. Most of the work of Congress takes place in the meetings of its thirty-eight standing (permanent) committees and their numerous subcommittees, each of which is headed by a chairperson. A committee chair schedules committee meetings, determines the order in which committee bills are considered, presides over committee discussions, directs the committee's majority staff, and can choose to lead the debate when a committee bill reaches the floor of the chamber for a vote by the full membership. (The process by which a bill becomes a law is discussed in Chapter 17.)

Committee chairs are always members of the majority party, and they almost always have the most **seniority**—the most consecutive years of service on a particular committee. The seniority principle for selecting committee chairs began in the Senate in the mid-nineteenth century but was not formally applied in the House until the early twentieth century.[44] Before that time, the Speaker picked all committee chairs, who were then expected to back his policies. Abuses of authority by Speaker Joseph Cannon led the House to end this practice in 1911.

The seniority principle remained virtually absolute until the House Democratic majority decided in the early 1970s that committee chairs would henceforth be chosen by secret ballot. Abuses by some committee chairs led to the change. Virginia's Howard Smith, who chaired the House Rules Committee

Dan Rostenkowski (D-Ill.), chairman of the House Ways and Means Committee. (Dennis Brack/Black Star)

[41]Frank H. Mackamar, *Understanding Congressional Leadership: The State of the Art* (Pekin, Ill.: Dickson Center, 1981), 9.
[42]Randall B. Ripley, *Party Leaders in the House of Representatives* (Washington, D.C.: Brookings Institution, 1967), 12–14.
[43]Quoted in ibid., 185.
[44]See Nelson W. Polsby, Miriam Gallagher, and Barry S. Rundquist, "The Growth of the Seniority System in the U.S. House of Representatives," *American Political Science Review* 63 (September 1969): 787–807.

in the 1950s and 1960s, would sometimes leave Washington for his Virginia farm when civil rights legislation reached his committee. Because the Rules Committee could not meet unless he called it into session, Smith's absence was sometimes enough to persuade the full committee to "table" a bill, or set it aside. A committee chair now has less discretionary power; for example, a majority of the committee members can vote to convene meetings in the chair's absence.

Although the seniority principle is no longer absolute, the House majority has seldom deviated from it. Two of the exceptions took place in 1991, when Glen Anderson of Public Works and Frank Annunzio of House Administration were voted out of their chairmanships. Both men were in their seventies and were regarded as relatively ineffective leaders.

The seniority system persists because it has several important advantages: it reduces the number of bitter power struggles that would occur if the chair were decided by open competition, provides experienced and knowledgeable committee leadership, and enables members to look forward to the reward of a position as chair after years of committee service.[45] Seniority gives ambitious members of Congress a reason to work on the business of their committees. If committee leadership were subject to control by party leaders or the president, members would have an incentive to curry favor with this leadership rather than devoting their efforts to mastery of a committee's work. As it is, however, an ambitious member of Congress will pay attention to the committee's business because, through the seniority system, he or she might someday put this expertise to use as chairperson or ranking minority member of the committee.[46]

The enduring tendency for seniority to serve as the basis for allocation of committee chairs places these leaders largely outside the power of the House or Senate's elected leaders.[47] The Speaker of the House and the Senate majority leader often have little choice but to defer to senior committee members on policy issues within their jurisdictions.[48] Seniority in committee also reduces the power of party leaders in another way: the principle ensures that the persons who chair the committees will normally keep their posts indefinitely. Faced with an antagonistic chairperson, party leaders will sometimes wait until proposed legislation goes from the committee to the full chamber before trying to influence its content.[49]

SUBCOMMITTEE CHAIRPERSONS

Congressional organization and leadership extend into subcommittees, which are smaller units within each committee formed to conduct specific aspects of

[45]See Barbara Hinckley, *The Seniority System in Congress* (Bloomington: Indiana University Press, 1971), 111.
[46]Kenneth Shepsle, "Representation and Governance: The Great Legislative Tradeoff," paper presented at the Constitutional Bicentennial Conference, Nelson A. Rockefeller Center, Dartmouth College, Hanover, N.H., May 5, 1987, 19–20.
[47]Hinckley, *The Seniority System in Congress*, 111, 112.
[48]Lawrence C. Dodd and Bruce I. Oppenheimer, "The House in Transition: Change and Consolidation," in Dodd and Oppenheimer, *Congress Reconsidered*, 2d ed., 46–55.
[49]Ripley, *Congress*, 242–243.

the committee's business. The House has nearly 150 subcommittees and the Senate about 100, each with a chairperson who decides its order of business, presides over its meetings, and directs its staff.

Before reforms were enacted in the 1970s, subcommittees were controlled largely by committee chairs. Some committee chairs appointed themselves to head each of their subcommittees. A few committees, such as House Ways and Means (taxation), did not even have subcommittees: all power was vested in the full committee and thus was concentrated in its chairperson.

In 1973, in a move intended partly to limit the power of Ways and Means chairman Wilbur Mills of Arkansas, whose alcoholism had made him erratic, House Democrats adopted the so-called Subcommittee Bill of Rights, which requires each House committee of more than twenty members to maintain at least four subcommittees. The House also determined that no representative can chair more than one committee and one subcommittee at a time, and it placed selection of subcommittee chairs in the hands of majority-party members of each committee.[50] These measures give House subcommittees a substantial degree of independence from their committee and its chair.

In 1977 the Senate altered its subcommittee structure, limiting to three the number of committee and subcommittee chairs that a senator can hold at the same time. In both the House and the Senate, seniority on the full committee is a primary criterion, but not always the decisive one, in the selection of a subcommittee's chair.[51]

Reform leaders contended that these subcommittee changes would make Congress "more democratic."[52] Indeed, an effect of the subcommittee reforms has been to create a broader congressional leadership corps. At present about half of the majority party's House members chair a committee or subcommittee. In the smaller Senate, all members of the majority party, even those newly elected, normally head at least one committee or subcommittee. However, members of Congress had more than democracy on their minds in enacting the reforms of the 1970s. By creating more leadership positions, they were serving their personal reelection and power needs.[53] Less senior members would no longer have to wait many years before rising to a position of institutional authority.

The increased importance of subcommittees has multiplied the problems of the elected congressional leadership, but there have been compensating reforms to strengthen the position of the party leaders, particularly the Speaker of the House. Since the 1970s, for example, the Speaker has had more control over the routing and scheduling of bills. Nevertheless, the distinguishing feature of congressional leadership is its dispersion across the membership, not its concentration in a few top positions.

> ★ ANALYZE THE ISSUE
>
> **Institutional Power vs. Individual Power**
> The history of congressional organization, at least in the twentieth century, is the history of conflict between institutional power and individual power. Can this conflict ever be resolved? Is it possible for Congress as a whole and its individual members to be strong at the same time? Which position—a strong Congress or individually powerful members—appears to win out generally? Why? What are the consequences for the American governing system?

[50]See Steven H. Haeberle, "The Institutionalization of the Subcommittee in the United States House of Representatives," *Journal of Politics* 40 (November 1978): 1054–1065.
[51]Thomas R. Wolanin, "Committee Seniority and the Choice of House Sub-Committee Chairmen, 80th–91st Congresses," *Journal of Politics* 36 (1974): 687–702.
[52]David Rhode, "Committee Reform in the House of Representatives and Subcommittee Bill of Rights," *Annals of the American Academy of Political and Social Sciences* 411 (1974): 39–47; Leroy N. Rieselbach, "Assessing Congressional Change, or What Hath Reform Wrought or Wreaked?" in Dennis Hale, ed., *The United States Congress* (Boston: Boston College Press, 1982), 179–181.
[53]David E. Price, "Congressional Committees in the Policy Process," in Dodd and Oppenheimer, *Congress Reconsidered*, 2d ed., 162.

The Committee System

When Congress first met in 1789, it had no committees. However, committees formed within a few years in the House, and the first Senate committees were established in 1816. At present there are twenty-two standing committees in the House and sixteen in the Senate (see Table 16-5). A **standing committee** is a permanent committee with responsibility for a particular area of public policy. Both the House and the Senate, for example, have a standing committee that specializes in handling foreign policy issues. Other important standing committees are those that deal with agriculture, commerce, the national budget, the interior (natural resources and public lands), defense, government spending, labor, the judiciary, and taxation. House committees, which average about thirty-five members each, are larger than the Senate committees, with about eighteen members. Each standing committee has legislative authority in that it can draft and rewrite proposed legislation and can recommend to the full chamber the passage or defeat of the legislation it considers.

In addition to its standing committees, Congress has a number of **select committees,** which are created to perform specific tasks and are disbanded after they have done so. They generally do not have legislative authority but can conduct hearings and investigations. At present the Senate has select commit-

TABLE 16-5   The Standing Committees of Congress

House of Representatives	Senate
Agriculture	Agriculture, Nutrition, and Forestry
Appropriations	Appropriations
Armed Services	Armed Services
Banking, Finance, and Urban Affairs	Banking, Housing, and Urban Affairs
Budget	Budget
District of Columbia	Commerce, Science, and Transportation
Education and Labor	Energy and Natural Resources
Energy and Commerce	Environment and Public Works
Foreign Affairs	Finance
Government Operations	Foreign Relations
House Administration	Governmental Affairs
Interior and Insular Affairs	Judiciary
Judiciary	Labor and Human Resources
Merchant Marine and Fisheries	Rules and Administration
Post Office and Civil Service	Small Business
Public Works and Transportation	Veterans' Affairs
Rules	
Science, Space, and Technology	
Small Business	
Standards of Official Conduct	
Veterans' Affairs	
Ways and Means	

The Senate Select Committee on Indian Affairs reviews legislation that affects Native Americans living on reservations, including the Taos Pueblo in New Mexico. (Paul Conklin)

tees on aging, ethics, Indian affairs, and intelligence. The House has select committees on aging; children, youth, and families; hunger; intelligence; and narcotics abuse and control.

Congress also has joint committees, composed of members of both houses. These committees—the joint Economic, Library, Printing, and Taxation committees—perform advisory or coordinating functions for the House and the Senate.

Finally, Congress has **conference committees,** which are joint committees formed temporarily to work out differences in House and Senate versions of a particular bill. The role of conference committees is discussed more fully in the next chapter.

Congress could not possibly handle its work load without the help of its committee system. About 10,000 bills are introduced during each two-year session of Congress; the sheer volume of this legislation would paralyze the institution if it did not have a division of labor. Yet the very existence of committees and subcommittees helps to fragment Congress: each of these units is relatively secure in its power, jurisdiction, and membership.[54]

COMMITTEE POWER

At times, particularly when bills dealing with major issues are introduced, the full membership of Congress takes decisive action. On most bills, however, the full chamber merely votes to confirm or modify decisions made previously by committees and subcommittees. When a committee recommends passage of a bill, the measure has about a 90 percent chance of being approved by the full House or Senate, although about a third of these bills are amended on the floor.[55] Moreover, committees are the burial ground of most legislation intro-

[54]See George Goodwin, Jr., *The Little Legislatures* (Amherst: University of Massachusetts Press, 1970).
[55]Ripley, *Congress*, 199–201.

duced in Congress. Only about 10 percent of the bills that committees consider reach the floor for a vote; the others are "killed" when committees decide that they do not warrant further consideration and table them. The full House or Senate can overrule these committee rejections but seldom does so.

In the House particularly, subcommittees now rival full committees in their power. Most legislative work—hearings, debates, and the basic reworking of bills—is done by the subcommittees rather than by the full committees.[56] Unless a subcommittee's members are seriously divided or have highly unrepresentative views, their decision on a bill usually prevails when it is considered by the full committee.[57] Senate subcommittees, in contrast, serve more as advisory bodies to the full committees than as separate decisionmaking bodies within the committees.[58]

Although the power of committees and subcommittees should not be underestimated, statistics on their influence can be misleading. The fact that committee recommendations are followed about 90 percent of the time does not mean that committees hold 90 percent of the power in Congress. In making their decisions, committees are mindful that their positions can be reversed by the full chamber, just as subcommittees recognize that the full committee can overrule their actions. Consequently, committee and subcommittee decisions are made in anticipation of the probable responses of other members of Congress. Always committee and subcommittee members must ask whether their colleagues are likely to accept their recommendations.

It is the case, moreover, that the increased delegation of power to the subcommittees has made floor action more important than in the past. The membership of subcommittees is smaller, less senior, and less stable than that of the committees; so subcommittees are less expert and less politically representative than the committee of which they are a part. Accordingly, their work is more likely to be questioned and altered when it reaches the Senate or House floor.

COMMITTEE JURISDICTION

★ ANALYZE THE ISSUE

Do Committees Serve Their Constituencies or the Country?
The membership of congressional committees is not representative of Congress as a whole. The agriculture committees, for example, are filled with farm-state senators and representatives. This kind of arrangement obviously serves the interests of members of Congress and their specific constituencies. But does it also serve the interests of the country as a whole? Why, or why not?

The 1946 Legislative Reorganization Act requires each bill introduced in Congress to be referred to the proper committee. An agricultural bill introduced in the Senate must be assigned to the Senate Agriculture Committee, a bill dealing with foreign affairs must be sent to the Senate Foreign Relations Committee, and so on. This requirement is a major source of each committee's power. Even if its members are known to oppose certain types of legislation, bills clearly within its **jurisdiction**—the policy area in which it is authorized to act—must be sent to it for deliberation.

However, House and Senate leaders do have some direction when they assign certain bills to committee. Although the House Education and Labor Committee has primary jurisdiction over education policy, for example, more

---

[56]Richard Hall and C. Lawrence Evans, "The Power of Subcommittees," *Journal of Politics* 52 (1990): 335–355.
[57]Dodd and Oppenheimer, "The House in Transition," in Dodd and Oppenheimer, *Congress Reconsidered*, 2d ed., 41.
[58]See Steven S. Smith and Christopher J. Deering, *Committees in Congress* (Washington, D.C.: Congressional Quarterly Press, 1984), 125–165.

Former First American Bankshares chairman Clark Clifford (*left*) and former First American president Robert Altman (*right*) testify before the House Banking Committee, which in 1991 held hearings to investigate whether the Bank of Credit and Commerce International (BCCI) had illegally acquired First American in 1982. (Rick Reinhard/Impact Visuals)

than a dozen other House committees have some responsibility for education policy, so that the Speaker has a choice when some education bills are to be assigned. In other cases, a bill may be broad enough to be reasonably assigned to any of several committees. In 1963 Senate majority leader Mike Mansfield sent a comprehensive civil rights bill to the Senate Commerce Committee, most of whose members were liberal northerners. He purposely avoided the Senate Judiciary Committee, which normally handles civil rights measures, because it was dominated by southerners who were likely to oppose the bill. Mansfield's justification for referring the bill to the Commerce Committee was that the proposed legislation would prohibit the disruptive effects that racial discrimination in public restaurants, hotels, and transportation facilities has on interstate commerce.

In 1973 House subcommittees were given secure jurisdictions like those of the committees: bills must be referred to the appropriate subcommittees within two weeks of their arrival in committee. The Senate has adopted a similar practice. Thus responsibility in Congress is thoroughly divided, with each subcommittee having formal authority over a small area of public policy.[59] The House Foreign Affairs Committee, for instance, has eight subcommittees: Africa, Asia and the Pacific, Europe and the Middle East, Human Rights and International Organizations, Inter-American Affairs, International Economic Policy and Trade, International Operations, and Internal Security and Scientific Affairs. Each of these subcommittees has nine members, and these few individuals largely determine the content and the fate of most bills in their policy domain.

COMMITTEE MEMBERSHIP

Each committee includes Republicans and Democrats, but the majority party holds the majority of seats on each committee and subcommittee. Democrats

---

[59]See Norman Ornstein, ed., *Changing Congress: The Committee System, Annals of the American Academy of Political and Social Sciences* 411 (1974): 1–176; Leroy N. Rieselbach, *Congressional Reform in the Seventies* (Morristown, N.J.: General Learning Press, 1977).

currently have a majority in both the House and the Senate, so they outnumber Republicans on every congressional committee.

The ratio of Democrats to Republicans on each committee is approximately the same as the ratio in the full House or Senate, but there is no fixed rule on this matter, and the majority party sets the proportions as it chooses (mindful that at the next election it could become the chamber's minority). In the early 1980s, House Democrats granted themselves oversized majorities on a few key committees. The Senate and the presidency were under Republican control, and House Democrats wanted to ensure themselves an offsetting influence. The Democrats had precedent for their action. When Republicans gained control of the House in 1946–1948 and 1952–1953, they granted themselves extraordinary majorities on some committees in order to enhance their policy position.

Number of Committee Memberships

The number of committee seats that an individual member of Congress may hold is limited. A senator can sit on only two major committees, such as Foreign Relations and Finance, and can hold appointments on just one or two additional committees. House members who serve on the Ways and Means, Appropriations, or Rules Committee may normally hold only that one appointment, because of the power and prestige attached to those committees. Other House members are limited to membership on two committees, and these assignments are usually to one major committee, such as the Armed Services Committee, and one of lesser importance, such as the District of Columbia Committee. Subcommittees also have limits on membership. Each member of a House committee is prohibited from holding a seat on more than two of its subcommittees.

Obtaining a Committee Assignment

Each standing committee has a fixed number of members, and a committee must have a vacancy before a new member can be appointed. These vacancies usually occur at the start of a new congressional session, when the committee positions of members who have retired or been defeated for reelection are reallocated. On nearly all committees, members retain their seats unless they decide to relinquish them or are forced to do so by changes in party ratios or committee size. There are a few exceptions; for example, members of the House Rules Committee from the majority party are subject to appointment by the Speaker, who can also remove them at will.

Each party has a special committee in the House and Senate which has responsibility for deciding who will fill vacancies on standing committees. Several factors influence these decisions, including the preferences of the legislators themselves. About 80 percent of newly elected members of Congress receive a committee assignment that they have requested.[60] New members usually ask for assignment to a committee on which they can serve their

[60]David W. Rhode and Kenneth A. Shepsle, "Democratic Committee Assignments in the House of Representatives," *American Political Science Review*, September 1973, 889–905; see also Kenneth A. Shepsle, *The Giant Jigsaw Puzzle: Democratic Committee Assignments in the Modern House* (Chicago: University of Chicago Press, 1978).

★ CRITICAL THINKING

NATIONAL OFFICE, LOCAL ORIENTATION: GOOD OR BAD?

Whereas legislators in most other democracies are pre-occupied with national affairs, members of the U.S. Congress divide their attention between national and local concerns. Membership in Congress provides U.S. senators and representatives with the large personal budgets and staffs they need to retain the support of constituents in the home state or district—support that they must have if they are to be reelected. Incumbency also makes it relatively easy for members of Congress to raise money for their reelection campaigns—typically half a million dollars or more for representatives and several million dollars for senators. Many members focus so intently on constituent services and public relations that, in effect, their reelection campaigns last as long as their term of office.

In contrast, members of the Canadian House of Commons concentrate on national issues because their chances of reelection depend heavily on their party's nationwide popularity. Members of the House of Commons have only a small amount of staff help, and most of them spend only small amounts of money on their reelection campaigns. Moreover, lengthy tenure is not a hallmark of service in Canada's Parliament. Turnover in the House of Commons was 51 percent in the country's 1984 elections and 41 percent in its 1988 elections.

What are the relative advantages and disadvantages of the American system? In serving their constituencies, do members of Congress also serve the interests of the country as a whole better than they would if they were preoccupied with national-level problems? Does the existence of a president in the U.S. system (Canada has no separate executive branch) lessen your concern about the local orientation of most members of Congress?

constituents' interests and at the same time increase their reelection prospects.[61] In 1984, for example, when Phil Gramm was elected to the Senate from Texas, a state that depends heavily on the defense industry, he requested a position on the Armed Services Committee.

Members of Congress also prefer membership on one of the most important committees, such as Foreign Relations or Finance in the Senate and Ways and Means or Appropriations in the House. Such factors as members' intelligence, experience, party loyalty, ideology, region, length of congressional service, and work habits weigh heavily in the determination of appointments to these prestigious committees. In both the House and the Senate, however, the choice rests with the special party committees established for the purpose of deciding standing-committee assignments.[62]

Obtaining a Subcommittee Assignment

Subcommittee assignments are handled differently. The members of each party on a committee decide who among them will serve on each of its subcommittees. The members' preferences, seniority, and personal backgrounds and the interests of their constituencies are key influences on subcommittee assignments. Of the members of the Tobacco and Peanuts Subcommittee of the House

---

[61]See Richard F. Fenno, Jr., *Congressmen in Committees* (Boston: Little, Brown, 1973); see also Charles S. Bullock III, "Motivations for U.S. Congressional Committee Preferences," *Legislative Studies Quarterly* 1 (1976): 201–212.
[62]Irwin N. Gertzog, "The Routinization of Committee Assignments in the U.S. House of Representatives," *American Journal of Political Science* 20 (1976): 693–712.

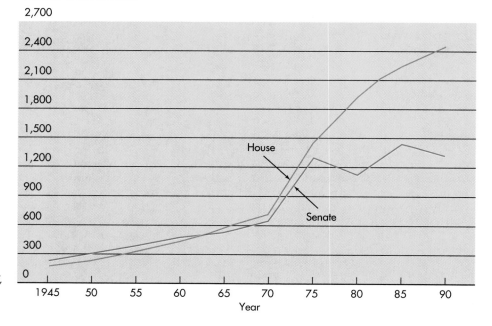

Number of staff members

FIGURE 16-3 Number of Staff Members Employed by Congressional Committees, 1947–1990
The number of committee staff members has increased sharply since the mid-1960s. *Sources: 1947–1980, Roger H. Davidson and Walter J. Oleszek,* Congress and Its Members *(Washington, D.C.: Congressional Quarterly Press, 1981), 238; 1985, 1990, Staff, Clerk of House Office and Senate Disbursing Office.*

Agriculture Committee, for example, nearly all are from the South—the region where most of the nation's tobacco and peanut crops are grown.

Institutional Support for the Work of Congress

The range and complexity of the policy issues that Congress must confront have greatly increased in this century. As an initial response to policy complexity, Congress gave the president additional staff and authority (see Chapter 18). This approach gradually placed Congress at a substantial disadvantage to the president. The withholding of crucial information about the progress of the Vietnam war by Presidents Johnson and Nixon persuaded many members of Congress that they could not maintain their institution as a coequal branch unless it had a larger and more expert staff. Accordingly, Congress increased its committee staffs and created and expanded its legislative bureaucracy, which consists of four agencies: the General Accounting Office, the Congressional Research Service, the Congressional Budget Office, and the Office of Technology Assessment.

COMMITTEE STAFFS

About 4,000 people are employed by the House and Senate committees and subcommittees (see Figure 16-3). Unlike the members' personal staffs, which concentrate on constituency relations, the committee staffs perform an almost entirely legislative function. They help to draft legislation, prepare reports, and participate in altering bills within committee. Committee staffs are also responsible for organizing legislative hearings—inviting witnesses, preparing questions, informing committee members of proposed legislation, and sometimes participating in hearings when members are absent.[63]

Although its institutional staff enhances Congress's legislative capacity, it also contributes to the fragmentation of congressional power. By specializing in their committees' or subcommittees' policy areas, staff members increase Congress's emphasis on a narrow range of issues. They are often more familiar with the technical details of legislation than are the members themselves.[64]

A committee's or subcommittee's employees are hired and fired by its chair or its ranking minority member. As a result, they usually adapt to his or her way of doing things.[65] Nevertheless, staff members' knowledge of a committee's or subcommittee's work enables them to influence its decisions. Some staff members, on their own initiative, even prepare drafts of legislation; by thus acting as "unelected representatives," they blur Congress's lines of authority even further.[66] Upon leaving the Senate in 1986, Barry Goldwater of Arizona complained that some staff members "don't have anything to do, so they sit down and write amendments and bills. My god, the number of bills on the calendar every year is unbelievable."[67]

However, congressional staffers work within an institution where loyalty and

[63]Michael J. Malbin, "Delegation, Deliberation, and the New Role of Congressional Staff," in Mann and Ornstein, *New Congress*, 156–160; see also Harrison W. Fox and Susan Webb Hammond, *Congressional Staffs* (New York: Free Press, 1977).
[64]Robert H. Salisbury and Kenneth A. Shepsle, "Congressional Staff Turnover and the Ties-That-Bind," *American Political Science Review* 75 (June 1981): 381–396.
[65]Thomas P. Murphy, *The Politics of Congressional Committees* (Woodbury, N.Y.: Barron's, 1978), 38.
[66]Michael J. Malbin, *Unelected Representatives: Congressional Staff and the Future of Representation* (New York: Basic Books, 1980), 28.
[67]Quoted in *Time*, November 10, 1986, 25.

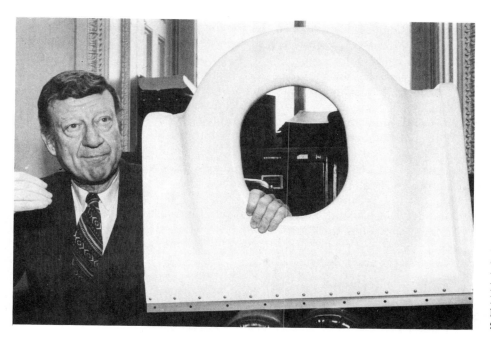

Findings by the General Accounting Office in the mid-1980s triggered a congressional investigation of wasteful defense spending. Here Senator William Roth (R-Del.) displays a plastic toilet-seat cover for a P-3 airplane, for which the Lockheed Corporation had tried to charge the U.S. Navy $640 apiece; Lockheed later agreed to drop the price to $100. (AP/Wide World)

deference to elected representatives are the norm. Staff members have room to initiate and advocate policy, but they can find themselves out of a job if they try too hard to force their ideas on the elected members of Congress.[68]

CONGRESSIONAL AGENCIES

We noted above that Congress has four agencies to provide it with information and technical advice. The 6,800 employees of these agencies help to lessen Congress's dependence on the executive branch for information relevant to legislative decisions.

The General Accounting Office (GAO), with about 5,400 employees, is the largest congressional agency. Formed in 1921, it has the primary responsibility of overseeing executive agencies' spending of money that has been appropriated by Congress.[69] Recently the GAO was much in the news for bringing abuses by defense contractors to Congress's attention. (In one notorious instance, the GAO reported that the government was paying more than $1,000 apiece for wrenches available in hardware stores for less than $10.) In the past decade Congress has broadened the GAO's responsibilities to include program evaluations, such as a major study on the need to reform government-paid health programs.

Created in 1914, the Congressional Research Service (CRS) is the oldest congressional agency and is part of the Library of Congress. (The CRS was originally the LRS—Legislative Reference Service.) The CRS is a nonpartisan reference agency. If a member of Congress wants historical or statistical information for a speech or bill, the CRS will provide it. It also prepares reports on pending legislative issues, although it makes no recommendations as to what action Congress should take. Finally, the CRS provides members with status reports and summaries of all bills currently under consideration in Congress. The 1,000-member staff of the CRS sometimes complains that it is too much Congress's errand boy (responding, for example, to a member's request for information with which to reply to a constituent's letter) and not enough of a research institute.

The Congressional Budget Office (CBO) is the newest agency, created by the Congressional Budget and Impoundment Control Act of 1974. The main role of the CBO's 200 employees is to provide Congress with projections of the nation's economic situation and of government expenditures and revenues.[70] The Office of Management and Budget (OMB) furnishes similar projections to the president, who incorporates them into the annual budget he submits to Congress. The CBO's figures enable Congress to scrutinize the president's budget proposals more thoroughly.

The Office of Technology Assessment (OTA), established in 1972, assesses technology policies and evaluates policy proposals in such areas as oil exploration and communications. Most of the work of the OTA's 200 employees could be done by other agencies, and some members of Congress have proposed that it be abolished.

---

[68]Samuel C. Patterson, "The Professional Staffs of Congressional Committees," *Administrative Science Quarterly* 15 (1970): 22–37.
[69]See Frederick C. Mosher, *The GAO* (Boulder, Colo.: Westview Press, 1979).
[70]See Joel Havemann, *Congress and the Budget* (Bloomington: Indiana University Press, 1978), ch. 6.

In some ways, congressional agencies have strengthened Congress's ability to act as a collective body. Before the CBO was formed, for example, Congress lacked the authoritative information that is needed to challenge the president's budget proposals. Congress is still at a disadvantage, but the CBO's budget estimates give the House and Senate Budget committees (also formed in 1974) a basis for an institutional response (see Chapters 17 and 24).

In other ways, however, congressional agencies contribute to the fragmentation of Congress. These agencies are set up to serve all members of Congress, not just the top leadership. The party leaders obtain information from the congressional agencies that they can use in developing major proposals and in contesting the judgments of the executive branch. But these agencies are designed mainly to provide information directly to individual members, committees, and subcommittees. They use this information to advance their own goals, which in many cases do not coincide with those of the party leadership.

The next chapter examines further how conflicts between the institutional needs of Congress and the individual needs of representatives and senators affect the role that Congress plays in national policy.

Summary

Members of Congress, once elected, are likely to be reelected. Members of Congress have large staffs and can pursue a "service strategy" of responding to the needs of individual constituents. They also can secure pork-barrel projects for their state or district and thus demonstrate their concern for constituents. House members gain a greater advantage from these activities than do senators, whose larger constituencies make it harder for them to build close personal relations with voters and whose office is more likely to attract a strong challenger. Incumbency does have some disadvantages. Members of Congress must take positions on controversial issues, may blunder into a political scandal or indiscretion, or face strong challengers; any of these conditions can reduce their reelection chances. By and large, however, the advantages of incumbency far outweigh the disadvantages, particularly for House members. Incumbents' advantages extend into their reelection campaigns. Their influential positions in Congress make it easier for them to raise campaign funds.

Congress is a fragmented institution. It has no single leader; the House and Senate have separate leaders, neither of whom can presume to speak for the other chamber. The principal party leaders of Congress are the Speaker of the House and the Senate majority leader. These party leaders derive their influence less from their formal authority than from having been entrusted by other members of their party with the tasks of formulating policy positions and coordinating party strategy. Individual party members can choose to follow or ignore their leader's requests.

The committee system is a network of about 40 committees and 250 subcommittees, each with its separate chairperson. Each chair has influence on the policy decisions of the committee or subcommittee through the scheduling of bills and control of staff. Although the seniority principle is not absolute, the chair of a committee or subcommittee is usually the member from the majority party who has the longest continuous service. Party loyalty is not normally a criterion in the selection of chairs. As a result, committee and subcommittee leaders may or may not have the same national policy objectives as the party leaders.

It is in the committees that most of the work of Congress is conducted. Each standing committee of the House and Senate has jurisdiction over congressional policy in a particular area (such as agriculture or foreign relations), as does each of its subcommittees. In most cases, the full House and Senate accept committee recommendations about passage of bills, although amendments to bills are quite common and committees are careful to take other members of Congress into account when making legislative decisions. Congress is a legislative system in which influence is widely dispersed, an arrangement that suits the power and reelection needs of its individual members.

In recent decades, the individualistic nature of Congress has been intensified by staffing changes. Larger committee and subcommittee staffs now make it easier for members of Congress to pursue their separate power and reelection goals. Congressional agencies strengthen the ability of Congress to act as a collective body by lessening the institution's dependence on the executive branch for information relevant to legislative issues, but they also make it easier for members of Congress to function independently.

Major Concepts

conference committee	party leaders
constituency	pork-barrel legislation
electoral mastery	redistricting
gerrymandering	select committee
jurisdiction	seniority
malapportionment	service strategy
open-seat election	standing committee

Suggested Readings

Cain, Bruce, John Ferejohn, and Morris P. Fiorina. *The Personal Vote.* Cambridge, Mass.: Harvard University Press, 1987. A careful analysis of the relationship between constituency service and electoral independence.

Davidson, Roger H., and Walter J. Oleszek. *Congress against Itself.* Bloomington: Indiana University Press, 1977. An assessment of the congressional reform movement of the early 1970s.

Fenno, Richard F., Jr. *Home Style: House Members in Their Districts.* Boston: Little, Brown, 1978. A penetrating analysis of the varying relationships between House members and their constituents.

Fiorina, Morris P. *Congress: Keystone of the Washington Establishment,* 2d ed. New Haven, Conn.: Yale University Press, 1989. An analysis of how incumbent members of Congress use their office to win reelection.

Fowler, Linda L., and Robert D. McClure. *Political Ambition: Who Decides to Run for Congress.* New Haven, Conn.: Yale University Press, 1989. A study of why potentially strong challengers often choose *not* to run against a House incumbent, thereby reducing the voters' alternatives.

Gertzog, Irwin N. *Congressional Women: Their Recruitment, Treatment, and Behavior.* New York: Praeger, 1984. A study of women in Congress as candidates and representatives.

Jacobson, Gary C. *The Electoral Origins of Divided Government.* Boulder, Colo.: Westview Press, 1990. A study that challenges some aspects of the thesis that House elections are largely insulated from electoral change.

Malbin, Michael J. *Unelected Representatives: Congressional Staff and the Future of Representation.* New York: Basic Books, 1980. A careful assessment of the impact of congressional staffs on the legislative process.

Smith, Steven S., and Christopher J. Deering. *Committees in Congress.* Washington, D.C.: Congressional Quarterly Press, 1984. A comprehensive look at the House and Senate committee systems.

CONGRESSIONAL POLICYMAKING: BALANCING NATIONAL GOALS AND LOCAL INTERESTS

17
CHAPTER

There are really two Congresses, not just one. Often these two Congresses are widely separated; the tightly knit, complex world of Capitol Hill is a long way from the world of [the member's district or state]—not only in miles, but in perspective and outlook as well.

Roger Davidson and Walter Oleszek[1]

The process of approving a budget for fiscal year 1991 was beset with difficulties from the very beginning. Congress expressed its unhappiness with President Bush's budget proposal as soon as it arrived on Capitol Hill. After it had languished without congressional action for three months, Bush requested a "bipartisan budget summit" with Congress's top leaders. On September 30, after negotiations that threatened several times to end in deadlock, Bush and the congressional leadership announced that they had reached an agreement. Both sides had made substantial compromises. Bush and Republican congressional leaders had backed down on their opposition to new taxes, and Democratic congressional leaders had held back on domestic programs they favored. All that remained was for the Republican and Democratic leaders of Congress to persuade the members to back the compromise proposal. How could it fail; after all, it had the backing of the president and the House and Senate leadership of both parties.

Five days later, the compromise was dead. It had been voted down in the House of Representatives. The federal government had no budget and was forced to shut down all nonessential operations for several days. "We are the laughingstock of the nation," said Representative Silvio Conte (R-Mass.).[2]

The budget compromise had come apart because of the diverse and conflicting interests of the legislators. The House and Senate leadership had known that the budget package did not match any senator's or representative's desires perfectly, but argued that the provisions required sacrifices from all sides. Senate Majority Leader George Mitchell (D-Maine) urged senators to take a pragmatic view of the proposal. He asked, "Do we want to make a law or do we want to make a statement?" As it happened, most members preferred to make a

---

[1] Roger H. Davidson and Walter J. Oleszek, *Congress and Its Members,* 2d ed. (Washington, D.C.: Congressional Quarterly Press, 1985), 7.
[2] *Congressional Quarterly Weekly Report* 1990, 3471–3473.

statement. Representative David Obey (D-Wis.) expressed a widely held view when he said, "We've had this phony bipartisanship that said, 'Let's not fight because we don't have the votes.' If you don't have the votes, at least let people know what you stand for." Obey had led an unsuccessful assault on the Reagan administration's tax and budget policies in the early 1980s, and he claimed that the compromise proposal was unfair to poorer Americans. Representative Newt Gingrich (R-Ga.), who is as conservative as Obey is liberal, also opposed the bill. As Senate Republican whip, he had been part of the compromise negotiations, but he came out against the proposal, saying that its provision for a tax increase on wealthier Americans was a step in the wrong direction.[3]

The role of Congress in national policymaking is examined in this chapter. Because Congress is a large and complex organization whose members vary widely in their concerns and positions, the observations made in this chapter are necessarily broad. Nevertheless, there are discernible patterns to the policy actions of Congress and its members. Arguably, the most significant of these patterns is the one that emerged in deliberations over the budget for fiscal year 1991—the adjustment of broad national goals to more specific local and partisan ones.

This chapter describes the patterns of congressional policymaking in the context of Congress's three major functions: lawmaking, representation, and oversight. The main points made in the chapter are the following:

★ *Congress is limited by the lack of direction and organization usually necessary for the development of comprehensive national policies.* Congress looks to the president to initiate most broad policy programs but has a substantial influence on the timing and content of those programs.

★ *Congress is well organized to handle policies of relatively narrow scope.* Such policies are usually worked out by small sets of legislators, bureaucrats, and interest groups.

★ *Individual members of Congress are extraordinarily responsive to local interests and concerns,* although they also respond to national interests. These responses often take place within the context of party tendencies.

★ *Congress oversees the bureaucracy's administration of its laws,* but this oversight function is of less concern to members of Congress than is lawmaking or representation.

★ *Congress is admired by those who favor negotiation, deliberation, and the rewarding of many interests, particularly those with a local constituency base. Critics of Congress say that it hinders majority rule, fosters policy delay, and caters to special interests.*

The Lawmaking Function of Congress

The Framers of the Constitution expected Congress to be the leading branch of the national government. It was to the legislature—the embodiment of representative government—that the people were expected to look for policy

---

[3] Ibid.

leadership. Moreover, Congress was granted the **lawmaking function**—the authority to make the laws necessary to carry out the powers granted to the national government. The capacity to make the laws is, beyond doubt, the greatest power of a civil government. During most of the nineteenth century, Congress, not the president, was clearly the dominant national institution.[4] Aside from a few strong leaders such as Jackson and Lincoln, presidents did not play a major legislative role. In fact, Congress frequently made it clear that presidential advice was not wanted. Then, as national and international forces combined to place greater leadership and policy demands on the federal government, the president became a vital part of the national legislative process.

Today Congress and the president substantially share the lawmaking function. However, their roles differ greatly. The president's major contribution is made on the small number of broad legislative measures that arise each year, although Congress also plays a large part in the disposition of such bills. In addition, Congress has the lead—and in most cases nearly the full say—on the narrower legislation that constitutes the great majority of the roughly 10,000 bills introduced during a two-year congressional session.

An understanding of Congress's lawmaking role requires an awareness of how laws are made. The lawmaking process is an elaborate one that reflects the organizational complexity of Congress and the diffusion of power within it.

HOW A BILL BECOMES LAW

The basic steps in enacting a law are summarized in Figure 17-1. The first step in the legislative process is the creation of a bill. A **bill** is a proposed legislative act. Many bills are prepared by executive agencies, interest groups, or other outside parties, but members of Congress also draft bills and only they can formally submit a bill for consideration by their chamber. If a bill is passed by both the House and Senate and signed by the president, it becomes a **law** and thereby takes effect.

From Committee Hearings to Floor Debate

Once a bill is introduced by a member of the House or Senate, it is given a number and a title. Ordinarily, the bill is then sent to the appropriate committee, which assigns it to one of its subcommittees. Most bills that reach a subcommittee are set aside on the grounds that they are not worthwhile. If a bill seems to have merit, the subcommittee will schedule hearings on it. This is a critical stage in a bill's development. The subcommittee invites testimony on the proposed legislation by lobbyists, administrators, and experts, who inform members about the policy in question, provide an indication of the support the bill has, and may disclose weaknesses in the proposal. After the hearings, if the subcommittee still feels that the legislation is warranted, members recommend the bill to the full committee, which can hold additional hearings. The full committee may decide to kill the bill by taking no action on it but usually accepts the subcommittee's recommendation for passage. In the House, both

[4] See Ernest Griffith and Francis Valeo, *Congress: Its Contemporary Role*, 5th ed. (New York: New York University Press, 1975), ch. 1.

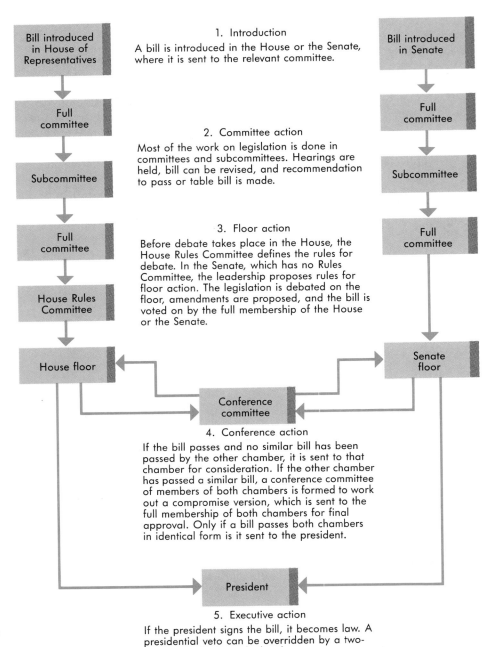

1. Introduction
A bill is introduced in the House or the Senate, where it is sent to the relevant committee.

Bill introduced in House of Representatives

Bill introduced in Senate

Full committee

Full committee

2. Committee action
Most of the work on legislation is done in committees and subcommittees. Hearings are held, bill can be revised, and recommendation to pass or table bill is made.

Subcommittee

Subcommittee

Full committee

Full committee

3. Floor action
Before debate takes place in the House, the House Rules Committee defines the rules for debate. In the Senate, which has no Rules Committee, the leadership proposes rules for floor action. The legislation is debated on the floor, amendments are proposed, and the bill is voted on by the full membership of the House or the Senate.

House Rules Committee

House floor

Senate floor

Conference committee

4. Conference action
If the bill passes and no similar bill has been passed by the other chamber, it is sent to that chamber for consideration. If the other chamber has passed a similar bill, a conference committee of members of both chambers is formed to work out a compromise version, which is sent to the full membership of both chambers for final approval. Only if a bill passes both chambers in identical form is it sent to the president.

President

5. Executive action
If the president signs the bill, it becomes law. A presidential veto can be overridden by a two-thirds majority in each chamber.

FIGURE 17-1 How a Bill Becomes a Law
Although the legislative process can be short-circuited in many ways, this diagram describes the most typical way in which a bill becomes law.

the full committee and a subcommittee can "mark up," or revise, a bill; in the Senate, markup is usually reserved for the full committee.

Once a bill is reported out of committee, it needs to be scheduled for floor debate by the full chamber. In the House, the Rules Committee has the power to determine when the bill will be voted on, how long the debate on the bill will last, and whether the bill will receive a "closed rule" (no amendments will be permitted), an "open rule" (members can propose amendments relevant to any of the bill's sections), or something in between (for example, only certain sections of the bill will be subject to amendment). The Rules Committee has this scheduling power because the House is too large to operate effectively without strict rules for the handling of legislation by the full chamber.

Most House bills of importance are scheduled for floor action under the Union Calendar, which sets the order of debate for finance and economic bills, and the House Calendar, which covers nonfinancial and noneconomic bills. There are also separate calendars for noncontroversial bills and private bills. On certain days, noncontroversial and private bills can be called up for a floor vote without action by the Rules Committee. (Private bills grant privileges or payments to individuals; for example, a private bill might allow a particular person to immigrate to the United States even though he or she does not meet the immigration requirements. In contrast, public bills deal with programs and broad categories of people and are what is normally meant by "legislation.")

The House and Senate require that a quorum (a majority of members) be present to conduct business on the floor. In order to expedite business, the House often adjourns to the Committee of the Whole. This committee consists of all House members and meets on the floor of the House but requires a quorum of only 100 members and has relatively informal procedures. Once agreement is reached in the Committee of the Whole, the House will reconvene and proceed to vote on the legislation at hand.

The Senate has no Rules Committee, relying instead on the majority leader to schedule its bills. All Senate bills are subject to unlimited debate unless a three-fifths majority of the full Senate votes for **cloture,** which limits debate to 100 hours. Cloture is a way of thwarting a Senate **filibuster,** a procedural tactic whereby a minority of senators prevent a bill from coming to a vote by holding the floor and talking until other senators give in and the bill is withdrawn from consideration. Filibustering is an honored tradition in the Senate, and in the past the chamber rarely voted to invoke cloture. Although the filibuster remains an important weapon of the Senate minority, successful cloture votes are now more common; in a recent eight-year period, cloture was voted on eighty-seven times and was invoked on thirty-one of those occasions.[5]

The Senate also differs from the House in that its members can propose *any* amendment to *any* bill. Unlike House amendments, those in the Senate do not have to be germane to a bill's content. For example, a senator may propose an antiabortion amendment to a bill dealing with defense expenditures. Such amendments are called *riders* and are frequently introduced.

Strom Thurmond of South Carolina leaves the Senate cloakroom after setting the record for the longest filibuster by a single senator. Thurmond spoke against the Civil Rights Act of 1957 for an uninterrupted twenty-four hours and nineteen minutes. (AP/Wide World)

From Floor Debate to Enactment into Law

To become law, a bill must be passed in identical form by both the House and the Senate. About 10 percent of all proposals that are approved by both chambers—the proportion is larger for major bills—differ in important respects in their House and Senate versions and are referred to a conference committee to resolve their differences. Slight differences in House and Senate versions of a bill are normally worked out informally, without a conference.

[5] Randall B. Ripley, *Congress,* 3d ed. (New York: Norton, 1983), 148–149.

★ ANALYZE THE ISSUE

The Slowness of Congress
Congress has been called the "slow" branch of the national government. How do its fragmentation and the complexity of the process by which it enacts a bill into law help account for Congress's reputation? What are the advantages and disadvantages of this slow institutional pace?

Each conference committee is formed temporarily to handle a particular bill; its members are usually appointed from the House and Senate standing committees that worked on the bill originally. The conference committee's job is to bargain over the differences in the House and Senate versions and to develop a compromise version. It then goes to the House and Senate floors, where it can be passed, defeated, or returned to conference, but not amended. Nongermane amendments, however, can be voted on separately, so that each chamber has an opportunity to reject part of a conference committee's proposed version of a bill while accepting another part.

After identical versions of a bill have passed both houses, the bill goes to the president for signature or veto. If the president signs the bill, it immediately becomes law. If the president exercises the *veto*, a refusal to sign a bill, it is sent back to its originating chamber with the president's reasons for the veto. Congress can *override* a veto by vote of a two-thirds majority of each chamber; the bill then becomes law. If the president fails to sign a bill within ten days (Sundays excepted) and Congress has remained in session, the bill automatically becomes law anyway. If the president fails to sign a bill within ten days and Congress has adjourned for the term, the bill does not become law. This last situation is called a *pocket veto* and forces Congress in its next session to start from the beginning: the bill must again pass both chambers and is again subject to presidential veto.

The MX missile program survived repeated congressional challenges in 1985 at both the authorization and appropriation stages. An unfavorable vote at either stage could have meant the end of the MX program. (Gamma Liaison)

Sam Nunn, chairman of the Senate Armed Services Committee. Nunn's knowledge of and opinions on defense-related issues are respected by other senators of both parties. (Gamma Liaison)

A program or project enacted into law may require an appropriation of funds. For instance, if Congress authorizes the U.S. Navy to build a new aircraft carrier, the carrier cannot be built unless Congress also appropriates the necessary funds. *This funding legislation must go through the same steps as the earlier authorizing legislation:* passage of identical appropriations bills in both houses, subject to presidential veto. Should the appropriations bill be defeated, as such bills occasionally are, the authorizing law is effectively negated.

CONGRESS IN RESPONSE: BROAD POLICY ISSUES

The formal process by which a bill becomes law suggests that Congress and the president play legislative roles that are largely independent of each other. This impression is misleading. In practice, the lawmaking roles of Congress and the president are intertwined. Moreover, whether Congress or the president takes the lead depends on the type of policy at issue.

Some of the policy questions addressed by the national government transcend local or group boundaries. A sluggish economy, for example, affects Americans of all regions and of most occupational groups. Such issues normally call for a broad and well-coordinated policy response. Congress is not well suited to the development of such policies. Its strengths are deliberation and compromise. When a policy question requires comprehensive planning, the leadership usually comes from the president, with Congress playing a responsive role.

Fragmentation as a Policymaking Limitation

Congress's fragmentation makes it difficult for it to take the lead in developing policies that address broad national problems. "Congress remains organized," James Sundquist notes, "to deal with narrow problems but not with broad

Congress remains organized to deal with narrow problems but not with broad ones.

James Sundquist

★ ANALYZE THE ISSUE

Party Unity and Fragmentation in Congress
The best predictor of the way individual members of Congress will respond to legislation is their party affiliation, Republican or Democratic. In view of this fact, do you think it makes sense for voters in congressional elections to "vote for the person, not the party"? Why, or why not? Then consider this question: Can anything but party unity overcome the fragmentation that besets Congress?

ones."[6] Congress is not one house but two, and each chamber has its separate leadership. Moreover, neither the Speaker of the House nor the Senate majority leader has the authority to bind the chamber's majority to a legislative program. Not surprisingly, the party leaders in Congress do not routinely initiate major legislative programs. Their personal staffs do not even include the broad range of experts who could enable them to undertake such a policy role consistently.

The committee system of Congress is likewise not designed to handle broad national issues. Such issues transcend committee jurisdictions, and neither the House nor the Senate has any institutionalized way for its committees to work together to originate major bills. The House has experimented with ad hoc committees formed for this purpose, with mixed results.[7] In 1977 House Speaker Thomas P. ("Tip") O'Neill appointed a temporary committee to develop an energy bill, which eventually was passed by Congress.[8] However, the bill had begun as President Jimmy Carter's energy program. It had been split among five standing committees upon reaching the House, and the temporary committee's job was mainly to put the five pieces together once the standing committees had done their work.[9]

The reelection needs of members of Congress are a further obstacle to its initiation of national solutions to national problems. It is difficult for senators or representatives to look beyond the special needs of their own districts or states. The energy crisis of the 1970s, for example, required decisions on the pricing of oil and natural gas, on taking the windfall profits that oil producers had made from higher oil prices, and on funding research on synthetic fuels. The view of the nation's energy policy needs held by members of Congress from oil-producing states such as Texas and Louisiana differed sharply from that of members from other states, whose ideas also varied in accordance with their states' energy resources and requirements.[10]

To be sure, Congress sometimes does take the lead on large issues.[11] Except during Roosevelt's New Deal, Congress has been a chief source of major labor legislation, including the Taft-Hartley Act of 1947 (which legalized state right-to-work laws), the Landrum-Griffin Act of 1959 (which holds union officials to sound administrative and democratic practices), and plant-closing legislation in 1988 (which requires companies to notify workers sixty days before a plant closing or mass layoff). Congress also developed the Water Pollution Control Act of 1964, the Clean Air Act of 1963, and other environmental legislation.[12] Congress took the lead in the 1980s on tax simplification. Several proposals, including the Kemp-Roth and Bradley-Gephardt bills, became the foundation for the Tax Reform Act of 1986, a comprehensive

[6] James L. Sundquist, "Congress and the President: Enemies or Partners?" in Lawrence C. Dodd and Bruce I. Oppenheimer, eds., *Congress Reconsidered* (New York: Praeger, 1977), 240.
[7] James L. Sundquist, "Congress, the President, and the Crisis of Competence in Government," in Lawrence C. Dodd and Bruce I. Oppenheimer, eds., *Congress Reconsidered*, 2d ed. (Washington, D.C.: Congressional Quarterly Press, 1981), 362–364.
[8] See Bruce I. Oppenheimer, "Congress and the New Obstructionism: Developing an Energy Program," in ibid., 275–295.
[9] For a broader perspective on committee and policy initiatives, see Gerald Wright, Leroy Rieselbach, and Lawrence C. Dodd, *Congress and Policy Change* (New York: Agathon, 1986).
[10] Oppenheimer, "Congress and the New Obstructionism," 282–285.
[11] Ronald C. Moe and Steven C. Teel, "Congress as Policy-Maker," *Political Science Quarterly* 85 (1970): 467–468.
[12] See Charles O. Jones, *Clean Air: The Policies and Politics of Pollution Control* (Pittsburgh: University of Pittsburgh Press, 1975).

★ THE MEDIA AND THE PEOPLE

CONGRESS IN THE NEWS

Speaker of the House Thomas P. "Tip" O'Neill once wrote that if there was one thing he could do before his retirement, it would be to persuade the news media and the American people that Congress was a coequal branch of the government. O'Neill retired without achieving his goal. Americans tend to see the president as more active and more important than Congress. This perception arises in part from the way the news media cover the two branches. A study by political scientist Richard Davis of television and newspaper coverage of national politics found that the presidency receives more than half again as much coverage as Congress does. The tendency toward "presidentialization" of the news is more pronounced on television than in newspapers but is characteristic of both media.

Furthermore, when Congress does get coverage from the media, it is often presented in the context of executive-legislative relations rather than as a powerful institution in its own right. In fact, two-thirds of all news about Congress is also about the president, whereas only a third of presidential news makes any reference to Congress. Even the president's leisure activities are considered newsworthy by reporters—a situation that grates on members of Congress, who believe that their institution cannot exercise its proper constitutional role as long as the media fail to report it coequally.

Davis's study included the following findings, based on news coverage during the 1969–1984 period:

Three National Political Institutions as Primary or Secondary Focus of News Stories, 1969–1984 (percent)

News Stories	Presidency	Congress	Supreme Court
Primary focus	57%	35%	8%
Secondary focus of story about:			
Presidency	—	34	1
Congress	67	—	1
Supreme Court	18	5	—

SOURCE: Richard Davis, "News Coverage of National Political Institutions," Ph.D. dissertation, Syracuse University, 1986. Based on 617 news stories sampled from *CBS Evening News*, *Los Angeles Times*, and *Syracuse Post-Standard*.

overhaul of the personal and corporate tax codes. Federal aid to education, nuclear energy, and urban development are other areas in which Congress has played an initiating role.[13] Nevertheless, Congress does not ordinarily develop broad policy programs and carry them through to passage. "Congress," Arthur Maass notes, "is limited by the lack of resources and organization typically needed for these tasks.[14]

Presidential Leadership, Congressional Response

In general, Congress depends on the president to initiate broad policy proposals, and for good reason: the president is strong in ways that Congress cannot match.

First, whereas Congress's authority is fragmented, the president is a singular authority.[15] The president seeks the advice of others within the executive branch, but ultimately the decision is his to make. His decision may not be easy: some national problems are difficult to understand fully, let alone to manage effectively.[16] Runaway inflation admittedly bewildered President Carter, who

---

[13] See Gary Orfield, *Congressional Power: Congress and Social Change* (New York: Harcourt Brace Jovanovich, 1975).

[14] Arthur Maass, *Congress and the Common Good* (New York: Basic Books, 1983), 14.

[15] See Paul C. Light, *The President's Agenda* (Baltimore: Johns Hopkins University Press, 1982).

[16] Hugh Heclo, "Introduction: The Presidential Illusion," in Hugh Heclo and Lester M. Salamon, *The Illusion of Presidential Government* (Boulder, Colo.: Westview Press, 1981), 1–2.

proposed program after program—five in all—in a frantic effort to control it. Nevertheless, the president does not have to have a majority consensus within the executive branch in order to act. As sole chief executive, he can choose a course of action on his own and direct his assistants to prepare a legislative proposal for implementing it. Accordingly, the presidency is capable of a degree of policy planning and coordination that is far beyond the normal capacity of Congress. "It is the difference," one congressman said, "between an organization headed by one powerful man and a many-headed organization."[17]

Another advantage that the president enjoys is his national political base, which focuses public attention on his actions and lends a national perspective to his choices. The president must take regional and state concerns into account, but they do not affect his decisions as much as they influence those of members of Congress. In a way, the president's situation is the reverse of that of a member of Congress: the president cannot ignore state and local interests, but he must concentrate on national ones if he hopes to retain power.

Presidential leadership means that Congress will pay attention to the White House, not that it will accept whatever the president proposes. But Congress welcomes presidential initiatives as a starting point for its own deliberations. Frequently Congress will delay action on a problem until the president submits his plan. In the 1980s, for example, several attempts in Congress to strengthen air-pollution standards were defeated by the opposition of industry and President Reagan. New legislation was finally enacted in 1990 after President Bush had proposed clean-air measures that strengthened the hand of proenvironmental forces. Congress went further than the administration desired, but Bush's plan provided the impetus that was needed to move the legislation along.

Organizational changes have improved Congress's ability to evaluate and modify presidential proposals. For example, as we mentioned in Chapter 16, the Congressional Budget Office (CBO) was created as part of the Budget and Impoundment Control Act of 1974, which also established the House and Senate budget committees. These committees initially had the task of proposing spending ceilings that, when approved by the full Congress, determined the size of the federal budget, both overall and within major categories, such as defense and interior.[18] However, the federal government's fiscal problems have since prompted changes in the federal budgetary process that lessen the role of the budget committees. Under a new budgetary process enacted in 1990, the budget committees help to set priorities (but not the overall level of expenditures) within the domestic, international, and military spending categories. Spending in each category is capped according to a set of rules that are designed to trim the nation's chronic budget deficit and that limit Congress's budget options. (The federal budget process that was enacted in 1990 is described in Table 17-1. It can be assumed that the process will be revised again after the budget deficit is brought under control, which is projected to happen in fiscal year 1995 at the earliest.)

Congress's budgetary role is necessarily a reactive one. Congress cannot play the initiating role because it lacks the unified leadership that would enable it to

---

[17] Quoted in Ripley, 326.
[18] See Allen Schick, *Congress and Money* (Washington, D.C.: Urban Institute, 1980); Lance T. LeLoup, *The Fiscal Congress* (Westport, Conn.: Greenwood Press, 1980).

TABLE 17-1 Annual Congressional Budget Schedule (Simplified) The federal budget process was changed in 1990 to reflect the budgetary problems that have resulted from the large federal deficit.

Date	Action
First Monday in January	President gives Congress his budget proposal and economic forecast.
April 15	Congress completes work on budget resolution.
June 30	Congress completes work on appropriations bills.
October 1	Start of fiscal year.
15 days after Congress adjourns	Automatic spending cuts are determined if appropriations exceed legal limits.

set priorities among hundreds of agencies and programs. In 1986 President Reagan submitted to Congress a budget that he knew was unacceptable to its Democratic leaders and challenged them to write a budget of their own. After six months they threw in the towel, acknowledging that differences of opinion within Democratic ranks made the task impossible. They settled on the same program allocations that the previous year's budget had contained.

Of course, the same factors that make it difficult for Congress to initiate broad policy also make it difficult for the president to persuade Congress to accept his initiatives. There is no permanent congressional majority waiting eagerly to line up behind the president's programs. As we will discuss in Chapter 19, Congress has rejected outright roughly half of all major presidential proposals in recent decades and has modified others substantially. Congressional majorities must constantly be created because each member has his or her own reelection base and does not have to take orders from any congressional leader. Much talk and bargaining precede the passage of comprehensive legislation, which also normally requires the stimulus of an urgent, major problem.[19] When a president tries to act ahead of events and public opinion, Congress is likely to drag its feet. Gerald Ford attempted to awaken congressional concern over the looming problems of inflation and energy during the mid-1970s but could not get Congress to move. Said Ford, "There are just roadblocks up there [on Capitol Hill] that are apparently unbreakable until we get a real crisis. . . . That is the way [the system works], right or wrong."[20]

Determined opposition from a sizable minority will often defeat a presidential initiative because so many tactics for blocking legislation are available in Congress.[21] A bill must pass through two legislative chambers that differ from each other in size, constituency, and term of office and even, at times, in majority party.[22] Inaction or rejection by either chamber is sufficient to kill a bill. If a bill can be stopped at any one of several points—House or Senate

★ ANALYZE THE ISSUE

The Line-Item Veto
Several modern presidents, including Reagan and Bush, have wanted Congress to give them the line-item veto on budgetary legislation. As things stand, the president can either veto a whole bill or let it become law in its entirety. A line-item veto would enable the president to veto particular budget items while affirming others. What is your view on the line-item veto? Would it greatly undermine Congress and thereby upset the balance of power between the executive and the legislative branches?

[19] Light, *President's Agenda*, 90–91.
[20] Interview in *Newsweek*, December 9, 1974, 33–34.
[21] Lewis A. Froman, Jr., *The Congressional Process* (Boston: Little, Brown, 1967), 18.
[22] Benjamin Page, "Cooling the Legislative Tea," in Walter Dean Burnham and Martha Wagner Weinberg, *American Politics and Public Policy* (Cambridge, Mass.: MIT Press, 1978), 171–187.

Congress is particularly adept at handling issues that are narrow in scope and that coincide with the jurisdiction of a particular committee. Price supports for agricultural products are an example. (Dennis Stock/Magnum Photos)

committee, House or Senate floor, authorization step or appropriations step—it usually *is* stopped, unless its backers reach a compromise with its opponents. Senator Robert Dole (R-Kan.) compared Congress to a wet noodle: "If it doesn't want to move, it's not going to move."[23]

CONGRESS IN THE LEAD: NARROW POLICY ISSUES

Only a small proportion of the bills addressed by Congress deal with broad national issues of widespread interest. The rest cover smaller problems of less general interest. The leading role in the disposition of these bills falls not on the president but on Congress and, in most cases, on a relatively small number of its members.

Congress's standing committees and their subcommittees decide most legislative issues.[24] Interest groups and bureaucratic agencies with a stake in a particular policy issue tend to concentrate their persuasive efforts on the committee that is responsible for formulating legislation in that policy area. Hearings on proposed legislation are held by a committee or subcommittee, not by the full membership of Congress. The testimony introduced at the hearings is published, but transcripts of congressional hearings run to over a million pages annually, far more than any member of Congress could read. Members of Congress consequently have little choice but to trust the judgment of committees and subcommittees.

Of course, committees and subcommittees do not operate in a vacuum.[25]

[23] Quoted in Martin Tolchin, "How Senators View the Senate," *New York Times*, November 25, 1984, 40.
[24] See George Goodwin, *The Little Legislatures* (Amherst: University of Massachusetts Press, 1970); Joseph K. Unekis and Leroy N. Rieselbach, *Congressional Committee Politics* (New York: Praeger, 1984); Richard F. Fenno, Jr., *Congressmen in Committees* (Boston: Little, Brown, 1973).
[25] See Donald R. Matthews and James A. Stimson, *Yeas and Nays: Normal Decision-Making in the U.S. House of Representatives* (New York: Wiley, 1975).

Other members of Congress look for signs of trouble, as when a committee's vote divides sharply along party or ideological lines. In such a case the committee's recommendation on a bill is more likely to be debated, amended, or defeated on the floor. Committees also develop reputations for fair play. A committee that regularly seeks excessive benefits for a special interest can expect all its bills to start receiving close scrutiny on the floor. Some committees, such as the House Ways and Means Committee, pride themselves on drafting legislation that the full chamber will find acceptable. A question in each case is whether the committee has done its job in weighing the needs of a special interest against the general interest. For example, most members of Congress are not opposed in principle to special tax incentives for individuals and firms engaged in risky ventures, but they do not always feel that these entrepreneurs should be given tax breaks at the expense of other taxpayers.

Big government and social complexity have increased the pressure on committees to weigh the effects of their decisions on other policy areas and to respond to the views of people outside the committee. As we saw in Chapter 14, **iron triangles** (small, stable sets of bureaucrats, lobbyists, and legislators with a shared policy commitment) have given way in large part to **issue networks** (relatively open and fluid networks of bureaucrats, lobbyists, legislators, and policy specialists who are linked by a shared policy expertise, not by a common policy goal). Unlike iron triangles, issue networks cut across committee boundaries, with the result that members of a committee now operate less independently than they once did. Major environmental issues, for example, will draw the close attention of representatives and senators from most states and several committees.

Another congressional subgroup of importance is the **caucus,** which is an informal group of legislators with a shared interest who meet to exchange information and coordinate a legislative strategy designed to foster that interest. As we noted in Chapter 16, the traditional caucuses are composed of the party

The congressional black caucus is an informal group whose aim is to represent the concerns of African-Americans to Congress as a whole. Here, Representatives John Conyers of Michigan (*left*) and Louis Stokes of Ohio (*right*) appear as witnesses before the Senate Judiciary Committee during its confirmation hearings for Supreme Court nominee Clarence Thomas. (John Duricka/AP/Wide World)

members in each chamber—the House and Senate Republican and Democratic caucuses. For our purposes in this chapter, the relevant caucuses are the newer ones that have been formed around constituent interests.[26] Some of these caucuses are regional; for example, there is a Northeast-Midwest Caucus as well as a Sunbelt Caucus. The black, Hispanic, and women's caucuses consist of members of Congress who belong to these demographic groups. Many caucuses have formed around constituency interests of members of Congress; the textile, steel, automotive, and agricultural caucuses are examples.

Whether the major influence on a particular bill comes from a subcommittee, committee, iron triangle, issue network, or caucus, the crucial point in each case is that a subset of Congress's members is essentially making national policy on behalf of the whole institution. Woodrow Wilson described Congress as a system of "little legislatures," referring to its dependence on subsets of members to do its work. Many of the bills that these "little legislatures" formulate will pass the full House or Senate with little or no alteration by other members. Because the legislative issues with which subsets of legislators deal are often narrow and technical, other members of Congress may neither know enough nor care enough to examine bills closely as long as they believe that the specialists are doing an acceptable job.

A related point is that Congress is organized to operate with a division of labor. The same fragmentation that makes it difficult for Congress to take the lead on a broad issue makes it easy for Congress to tackle scores of narrow issues simultaneously. Most of the legislation passed by Congress is "distributive"—that is, it distributes benefits to a particular group while spreading the costs among the general public. Agricultural price supports, veterans' benefits, and business tax incentives are only a few examples of such policies. They are the type of policy that Congress is organizationally best suited to handle.

Congress's ability to lead on narrow issues, but not broad ones, might seem to make it a less than "coequal" branch of the national government. Any such conclusion, however, should be made in the context of institutional developments in other democratic countries. Elsewhere, the complexity of modern policymaking has led to a clear-cut subordination of the legislature to the executive. The legislature serves as an arena of debate and acts as a check on executive power; but, realistically speaking, it is not an independent lawmaking body. The U.S. Congress, by comparison, has retained a significant lawmaking role, in part because of its constitutional separation from the executive, but also in part because its committee system gives it an independent source of policy leadership and expertise. The fragmented structure of Congress has, paradoxically, protected it from capture by the president while at the same time making it dependent on the president for leadership on broad issues.[27]

[26] See Burdett A. Loomis, "Congressional Caucuses and the Politics of Representation," in Dodd and Oppenheimer, *Congress Reconsidered*, 2d ed., 204–220; Susan Webb Hammond, Arthur G. Stevens, and Daniel P. Mulhollan, "Congressional Caucuses," in Allen J. Cigler and Burdett A. Loomis, eds., *Interest Group Politics* (Washington, D.C.: Congressional Quarterly Press, 1983), ch. 12.

[27] See Kenneth Shepsle, "Representation and Governance: The Great Legislative Tradeoff," paper presented at the Constitutional Bicentennial Conference, Nelson A. Rockefeller Center, Dartmouth College, Hanover, N.H., May 5, 1987.

The Representation Function of Congress

In the process of making laws, the members of Congress represent various interests within American society, giving them voice and attention in the national legislature. Congress, with its individually elected, constituent-based membership and its decentralized system of power and work, has been characterized as a representative body *par excellence*. It expresses the concerns of countless interests, from those that would protect a local landmark from the wrecking ball to those that would devise a new banking system in the wake of the savings and loan scandal. The various members of Congress spread their time and energy across a wide range of interests. Congress may not be particularly effective in balancing interests in the process of making national law, but it is superb as a forum of expression for diverse interests.[28]

The proper approach to the **representation function** has been debated since the nation's founding.[29] The writers of the Constitution tied members of Congress to their home states and districts, so that the interests of these entities would be represented in national politics. The diversity of America was to be reflected in its Congress, which would also respond to broad national concerns. A recurrent issue has been whether the primary concern of a representative should be the interests of the nation as a whole or those of his or her own constituency.[30] These interests always overlap to some degree but rarely coincide exactly. Policies that are of maximum benefit to the full society are not always equally advantageous to particular localities, and can even cause harm to some constituencies. To the writers of the Constitution, the higher duty was to the nation. James Madison said in *Federalist* No. 10 that members of Congress should be those persons "least likely to sacrifice" the national interest to "local prejudice."

The local-national distinction was discussed in Chapter 4 in terms of the trustee and delegate models of representation. The trustee model holds that elected representatives are obligated to act in accordance with their own judgment as to what policies are in the best interests of society. The delegate model claims that elected representatives are obligated to carry out the expressed wishes of those who elected them to office. The choice is not a simple one, even for a legislator who is inclined toward either the delegate or trustee orientation. To be fully effective, a member of Congress must be reelected time and again, a necessity that compels him or her to pay attention to local demands. Yet, as part of the nation's legislative body, no member can easily put aside his or her judgment as to the nation's needs. In making the choice, most members of Congress, it appears, tend toward a local orientation, albeit one that is modified by both overarching and partisan concerns, as the following discussion explains.

Representation of National and Local Interests
Members of Congress are representatives both of the nation and of particular states and districts. These representative roles often complement each other but sometimes conflict. When should a representative place the needs of the nation ahead of the needs of his or her particular state or district? When should local needs dominate? Try to place your answers in the context of a specific issue, such as energy, trade, or defense-spending policy.

[28] Morris P. Fiorina, "The Decline of Collective Responsibility in American Politics," *Daedalus* 109 (1980): 40.
[29] See Herbert Storing, *What the Anti-Federalists Were For* (Chicago: University of Chicago Press, 1981).
[30] See David J. Vogler and Sidney R. Waldman, *Congress and Democracy* (Washington, D.C.: Congressional Quarterly Press, 1985); David C. Kozak, *Contexts of Congressional Decision Behavior* (Lanham, Md.: University Press of America, 1984).

The effects of acid rain on forests and lakes are mainly a concern of people who live in northeastern states and, accordingly, to members of Congress from those states. (Peter Miller/Photo Researchers)

REPRESENTATION OF STATES AND DISTRICTS

Most members of Congress say that they are in Washington primarily to serve the interests of the state or district that elected them.[31] As natural as this claim may appear, it is noteworthy that members of the British House of Commons or the French National Assembly would not be likely to say the same thing: they consider their chief responsibility to be service to the nation, not to their localities. The unitary governments and strong parties of Britain and France give their politics a national orientation. The federal system and weak parties of the United States force members of Congress to take responsibility for their own reelection campaigns and to be wary of antagonizing local interests.[32] They are particularly reluctant to oppose local sentiment on issues of intense concern, even when larger national objectives are at stake.[33] For example, the Civil Rights Act of 1964, which forbids racial discrimination in public accommodations such as hotels and restaurants, was supported by only twelve House members from the South.

The committee system of Congress promotes representation of local rather

[31] See Richard F. Fenno, Jr., *Home Style: House Members in Their Districts* (Boston: Little, Brown, 1978).
[32] See Thomas A. Flinn and Harold L. Wolman, "Constituency and Roll Call Voting," *Midwest Journal of Political Science*, May 1966, 193–199; Fenno, *Home Style*, ch. 1; John W. Kingdon, *Congressmen's Voting Decisions* (New York: Harper & Row, 1981), 19; Randall B. Ripley, *Party Leaders in the House of Representatives* (Washington, D.C.: Brookings Institution, 1967), 140–141.
[33] Thomas E. Cavanaugh, "The Calculus of Representation," *Western Political Quarterly*, March 1982, 120–129.

than national interests.[34] Although recent studies of committees indicate that the views of committee members are not radically different from the views of the full House or Senate membership,[35] committee membership is hardly random. Many senators and representatives sit on committees and subcommittees with policy jurisdictions that coincide with state or district interests (see Figure 17-2). For example, farm-state legislators dominate the membership of the House and Senate Agriculture committees; westerners dominate the Interior committees (which deal with federal lands and natural resources, most of which are concentrated in the West); and legislators from states and districts with important military installations dominate the Armed Services committees.

Constituency interests are also advanced by **logrolling,** the common practice of trading one's vote with another member so that each gets what he or she most wants. The term dates to the early nineteenth century, when a settler would ask neighbors for help in rolling logs off land being cleared for farming, with the understanding that the settler would reciprocate when the neighbors were cutting trees. In Congress, logrolling often occurs in committees where constituency interests vary from member to member. Senator Sam Ervin of North Carolina expressed the general attitude of many committee members when he said to Senator Milton Young of North Dakota, his colleague on the Agriculture Committee, "Milt, I would just like you to tell me how to vote about

[34] Roger H. Davidson, "Representation and Congressional Committees," *Annals of the American Academy of Political and Social Science,* January 1974, 48–62.

[35] Keith Krehbiel, "Are Congressional Committees Composed of Preference Outliers?" *American Political Science Review* 84 (1990): 149–164; Richard L. Hall and Bernard Grofman, "The Committee Assignment Process and the Conditional Nature of Committee Bias," *American Political Science Review* 84 (1990): 1149–1166.

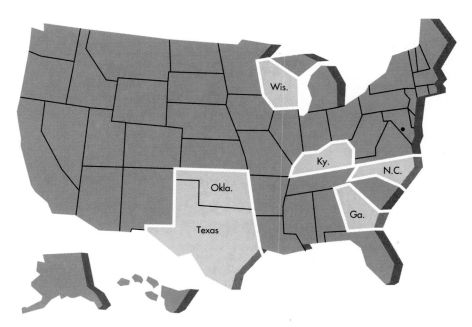

FIGURE 17-2 States Represented by Membership on the House Tobacco and Peanut Subcommittee, 1991–1992
Members of Congress try to get assigned to committees and subcommittees whose jurisdictions allow them to help their constituents. Nearly all the members of the Tobacco and Peanut Subcommittee of the House Agriculture Committee are from the states (singled out on map) in which most of the nation's peanuts and tobacco are grown. *Source: Staff, House Agriculture Committee.*

wheat and sugar beets and things like that, if you just help me out on tobacco and things like that.''[36]

Nevertheless, representation of constituency interests has its limits. A representative's constituents have little interest in most issues that come before Congress and even less information about them.[37] Whether the government should appropriate a few million dollars in foreign aid for the Central African Republic or should alter patent requirements for copying machines is not the sort of issue that local people are likely to know or care about. Moreover, members of Congress often have no choice but to go against the wishes of a significant portion of their constituency. The interests of small and large farmers in an agricultural state, for example, can differ considerably. Congress sometimes delays action on controversial issues, forcing the president to take the heat from the opposing sides. Congress cannot always duck such issues, however, and when its members are forced to vote, they know that by agreeing with one portion of their constituency they will antagonize another.

REPRESENTATION OF INTERESTS THROUGH GROUPS

Congress is almost ideally designed to represent interest groups. Its committees and subcommittees have legislative responsibility for policies that touch directly on particular groups, and members of Congress are receptive to lobbying efforts.

At one time, the representation of groups was nearly synonymous with the representation of constituents. The relationship of a farm-state senator to agricultural interests is an example. Such relationships are still important, but, as society has become increasingly complex and interdependent, interests have cut across constituency boundaries. The representation of groups has accordingly taken on new dimensions. One indicator is the emergence in recent decades of "outside lobbying"—pressure from the grass roots (see Chapter 14). Some of this pressure comes from the member's constituents, but much of it comes from networks of like-minded people who have a shared goal, not by virtue of living in the same state or district, but by virtue of shared values. Environmental issues, for example, typically transcend election districts.

Recent studies indicate that lobbying and PAC money result in "representation" for groups.[38] Indeed, research by Richard Hall and Frank Wayman suggests that, in some policy areas, committee members are more responsive to organized interests than to the views of unorganized voters within their districts.[39]

REPRESENTATION THROUGH PARTIES

"The two biggest lies," Senator Thomas Eagleton once remarked, are "one, to say a senator never takes into account the political ramifications of a vote and

---

[36] Quoted in Charles O. Jones, "Representation in Congress: The Case of the House Agriculture Committee," *American Political Science Review* 55 (1961): 358–367.
[37] See Aage R. Clausen, *How Congressmen Decide* (New York: St. Martin's Press, 1973).
[38] See John R. Wright, "Contributions, Lobbying, and Committee Voting in the U.S. House of Representatives," *American Political Science Review* 84 (1990): 417–438.
[39] Richard L. Hall and Frank W. Wayman, "Buying Time: Moneyed Interests and the Mobilization of Bias in Congressional Committees," *American Political Science Review* 84 (1990): 797–820.

secondly, almost an equal lie, is to say the only thing a senator considers is politics."[40] Arthur Maass agrees that Congress's concern for the common good is vastly underestimated by most observers. He notes, for example, that committees routinely weigh the impact of special-interest legislation on other interests and on the nation as a whole.

It is seldom the case, however, that the interests of the nation are clear-cut and unanimous. There are some broad goals, to be sure, that unite Americans. Nearly all would agree, for example, on the need for an adequate national defense and a strong economy. When it comes to specific policies, however, there are usually competing views of the national interest. Seldom can a member of Congress choose an action that is universally embraced. Thus the whole nation is not a very useful reference point for representation. The legislator must take sides. In other words, the member of Congress must decide which interests within the nation he or she will represent. By and large, the basis of this representation is partisanship.

Although members of Congress, unlike their counterparts in many European legislatures, are not bound to a legislative program of their party, they share partisan traditions and viewpoints, which affect their policy choices (see Figure 17-3). Roll-call votes in Congress often align a majority of the Democratic members against a majority of the Republicans.[41] The typical member of Congress votes with his or her party's majority about 70 percent of the time.[42] Divisions along party lines are common in committee voting as well.[43]

Party influence is also evident in the president's relationship with Congress. He serves as a legislative leader not so much for the whole Congress as for members of his party.[44] More than half of the time, opposition and support for presidential initiatives divide along party lines. A president can expect prob-

The happiness of society is the end [that is, the purpose] of government.

John Adams

FIGURE 17-3 Percentage of Roll-Call Votes in House and Senate in Which a Majority of Democrats Voted against a Majority of Republicans, 1970–1990
As a result of partisan traditions, Democrats and Republicans in Congress are often on opposite sides of issues. *Sources: 1970–1988,* Congressional Quarterly Weekly, *November 19, 1988, 3334–3335; 1989–1990,* Congressional Quarterly Weekly, *December 22, 1990, 4188.*

[40] Quoted in Davidson and Oleszek, *Congress and Its Members,* 398.
[41] Richard E. Cohen, "Rating Congress—A Guide to Separating the Liberals from the Conservatives," *National Journal,* May 8, 1982, 800–810.
[42] See Keith T. Poole and R. Steven Daniels, "Ideology, Party, and Voting in the U.S. Congress 1959–1983," *American Political Science Review,* 79 (June 1985): 373–399; *Congressional Quarterly Weekly Report,* January 15, 1983, 107; David E. Price, *Bringing Back the Parties* (Washington, D.C.: Congressional Quarterly Press, 1984), 54.
[43] Glenn R. Parker and Suzanne L. Parker, "Factions in Committee: The U.S. House of Representatives," *American Political Science Review,* March 1979, 52–63.
[44] See Steven A. Shull, *Domestic Policy Formation: Presidential-Congressional Partnership?* (Westport, Conn.: Greenwood Press, 1983); Matthews and Stimson, *Yeas and Nays.*

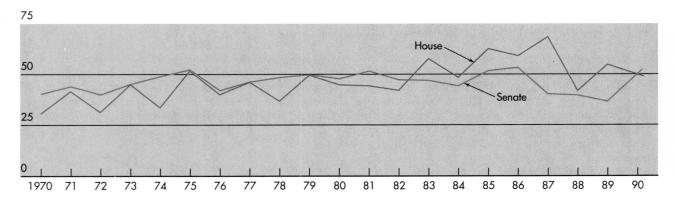

TABLE 17-2 Liberal/Conservative Voting Pattern of Senate and House Democrats and Republicans
Democrats and Republicans in Congress are on opposite sides of the fence ideologically.

VOTING PATTERN	ECONOMIC LEGISLATION				NONECONOMIC LEGISLATION			
	Senate Democrats	Senate Republicans	House Democrats	House Republicans	Senate Democrats	Senate Republicans	House Democrats	House Republicans
Liberal	83%	9%	82%	3%	74%	22%	80%	9%
Conservative	17	91	18	97	26	78	20	91
	100%	100%	100%	100%	100%	100%	100%	100%

SOURCE: Adapted from "Ideological Portrait of Congress," *National Journal,* January 28, 1989, 206.

lems with Congress when it is controlled by the opposing party or when divisions within his own party prevent him from fully mobilizing its support (see Chapter 19).

The influence of partisanship is also evident in the liberal or conservative pattern of the individual member's voting record (see Table 17-2).[45] For example, on major economic legislative issues during the 1987–1988 congressional sessions, 83 percent of Senate Democrats and 82 percent of House Democrats had an overall liberal voting record, compared to only 9 percent of Senate Republicans and 3 percent of House Republicans. The differences between Republicans and Democrats were less pronounced on noneconomic issues but were still very substantial.[46]

[45] See Helmut Norpoth, "Exploring Party Cohesion in Congress," *American Political Science Review,* December 1976, 1171; Kingdon, *Congressmen's Voting Decisions,* 19.
[46] "Ideological Portrait of Congress," *National Journal,* January 28, 1989, 206.

★ HOW THE UNITED STATES COMPARES

PARTY UNITY IN THE LEGISLATURE

All democratic legislatures are organized by party, but they differ greatly in the degree of control exercised by parties. At one extreme are those countries in which a single legislative chamber dominates, one party has a majority in that chamber, and the members of the majority party display a high level of unity. In such countries, which currently include Great Britain and Germany, the majority party in the legislature essentially dictates national policy. At the other extreme are multiparty systems in which no party has a legislative majority and national policy is worked out in bargaining among a coalition of parties. If the parties find themselves unable to agree on national policy, however, the government may collapse. Belgium's coalition government was disbanded in 1987 for this reason.

With its fixed terms for legislators, the U.S. system precludes a collapse of government, but party control of Congress is always somewhat uncertain. For one thing, the Republicans may control one chamber while the Democrats control the other, as was the case in 1981–1986. For another, Congress is not characterized by a high level of party unity. It is common for one-fourth or more of Democratic or Republican members to vote against their party's position on important legislative issues. The effect of this lack of a reliable party majority is to weaken Congress's ability to provide national leadership.

★ CRITICAL THINKING

HOW MUCH AUTHORITY SHOULD PARTY LEADERS IN CONGRESS HAVE?

In 1981, soon after taking office, Republican President Ronald Reagan pressed Congress for drastic cuts in domestic spending. His budget proposals included stricter eligibility requirements for social security recipients, cuts in public-service jobs and child nutrition programs, the disqualification of a million food-stamp recipients, the reduction of the maximum term of unemployment benefits from thirty-nine weeks to twenty-six, and cuts in federal loan programs for college students. Reagan argued that only deep budget cuts would restore the nation's faltering economy, and the U.S. Senate had a Republican majority that was prepared to follow his leadership. The House of Representatives was a different matter. It had a 243–192 Democratic majority, and the Speaker of the House was Thomas P. "Tip" O'Neill, a feisty liberal Democrat.

O'Neill had served in Congress during the period when Democratic presidents and congressional majorities had initiated many of the programs that Reagan proposed to chop, and O'Neill had supported all of them. He believed firmly that government was obligated to help society's underdogs and was determined to fight Reagan's proposals with all the authority of the Speaker's office. Appealing to the Democratic majority that had placed him in the House's top position, O'Neill called for the defeat of Reagan's plan. O'Neill himself describes the outcome:

I screeched and I hollered and I fought his [Reagan's] program every way I could, but there are times that you just can't buck a trend. I got clobbered so badly that I felt like the guy in the old joke who gets hit by a steamroller. Somebody runs to tell his wife about the accident.

"I'm taking a bath right now," she says. "Could you just slip him under the door?"

That's what happened to me during the President's first year, except that they didn't bother to slip me under the door. They just left me lying out on the street.

Speaker O'Neill's clobbering, as Congress enacted into law one Reagan proposal after another, illustrates the key fact that congressional power is diffused. In most democratic countries, power in the national legislature is centralized: there is a dominant chamber and the top leaders are powerful, the committees weak, and the parties unified. The U.S. Congress is unusual in being such a fragmented institution: it has two equal chambers, elected leaders with limited powers, a vast network of relatively independent and powerful committees and subcommittees, and members who are free to follow or ignore other members of their party.

Which form of legislature do you prefer—one in which power is centralized or one in which it is decentralized? What are the advantages and disadvantages of each? Is either form better suited to political conditions in America? Why?

SOURCES: Thomas P. (Tip) O'Neill with William Novak, *Man of the House: The Life and Political Memoirs of Speaker Tip O'Neill* (New York: Random House, 1987); John E. Schwarz and L. Earl Shaw, *The United States Congress in Comparative Perspective* (Hinsdale, Ill.: Dryden Press, 1976).

LAWMAKING VS. REPRESENTATION

There is a conflict between the lawmaking and representation functions. A high level of responsiveness to local opinion diminishes the capacity of Congress to legislate for the nation as a whole. The needs of the nation are rarely the sum of local needs. It is important in the long run that all states receive fair treatment in national lawmaking, but taking all states into account in every act of Congress is not conducive to effective lawmaking. The same quality—a strong local orientation—that makes Congress a superb representative institution also makes it a less than ideal national legislative body.

The fear that the national interest is at the mercy of narrow, parochial concerns can be exaggerated. Representation is a complex process, and local and national interests complement each other more often than they conflict with each other. Moreover, changes in campaign technology and congressional staffing have enabled members of Congress to pursue local interests aggressively while also representing national interests. Members of Congress have no good reason to ignore the vote-getting potential of pork-barreling and constituent service; the legwork these efforts require can usually be delegated to staff and interested groups, while the member gets the credit for their accomplishments. The goodwill that a member accumulates through such activities can give him or her greater confidence about reelection and thus more freedom to address national problems.

The Oversight Function of Congress

Although Congress enacts the laws governing the nation and appropriates the money to implement them, the administration of these laws is entrusted to the executive branch. Congress has the responsibility to see that the executive carries out the laws faithfully and spends the money properly, a supervisory activity that is referred to as the **oversight function** of Congress.

THE PROCESS OF LEGISLATIVE OVERSIGHT

Oversight is carried out largely through the committee system of Congress and is facilitated by the parallel structure of the committees and the executive bureaucracy: the Foreign Affairs committees of Congress oversee the work of the State Department, the Agriculture committees look after the Department of Agriculture, and so on. The Legislative Reorganization Act of 1970 spells out each committee's responsibility for overseeing its parallel agency:

> Each standing committee shall review and study, on a continuing basis, the application, administration, and execution of those laws, or parts of laws, the subject matter of which is within the jurisdiction of that committee.

★ ANALYZE THE ISSUE

Congressional Oversight of Executive Lawmaking
Oversight has traditionally ranked behind lawmaking and representation in Congress's priorities, but most legislation now originates in the executive branch, which has the expertise and working knowledge of government programs that are the foundation of modern public policy. Is Congress's chief role, like it or not, coming to be that of overseer of the executive's legislative ideas and administrative actions?

However, oversight is easier to mandate than to carry out. If congressional committees were to try to monitor all the federal bureaucracy's activities, they would have no time or energy to do anything else. Most members of Congress are more interested in working out new laws and looking after constituents than in laboriously keeping track of the bureaucracy. Although Congress is required by law to maintain "continuous watchfulness" over programs, committees have little incentive to take a hard look at programs that they have enacted or upon which their constituent groups depend. Oversight normally is not pursued aggressively unless members of Congress are annoyed with an agency, have discovered that a legislative authorization is being grossly abused, or are reviewing a program for possible major changes.[47]

If a committee believes that an agency has mishandled a program, it can

[47] See Morris S. Ogul, *Congress Oversees the Bureaucracy* (Pittsburgh: University of Pittsburgh Press, 1976); Morris S. Ogul, "Congressional Oversight Structures and Incentives," in Dodd and Oppenheimer, *Congress Reconsidered*, 2d ed., 317–331.

Exercising its oversight functions, the House Committee on Science, Space, and Technology held hearings into the explosion of the *Challenger* space shuttle. Here NASA administrator James Fletcher (*left*) and Ron Truly, NASA's associate administrator for space (*right*), testify before the committee. (John Duricka/AP/Wide World)

investigate the matter.[48] Congress's investigative power is not listed in the Constitution, but the judiciary has not challenged the power, and Congress has used it extensively. The Watergate and Iran-Contra affairs prompted congressional investigations, which have also been used to focus attention on national problems such as crime, poverty, and health care.

When serious abuses by an agency are suspected, a committee is likely to hold hearings. Except in cases involving "executive privilege" (the right to withhold confidential information affecting national security), executive-branch officials are compelled to testify at these hearings. If they refuse, they can be cited for contempt of Congress, which is a criminal offense. In 1990, in response to allegations that former Secretary of Housing and Urban Development (HUD) Samuel R. Pierce, Jr., and other HUD officials had granted illegal loans and otherwise conspired to defraud the government, a House subcommittee concluded that Pierce had channeled government funds to friends and lied to Congress about his actions. The subcommittee recommended that the special prosecutor investigating the HUD scandal explore the charge of perjury and bring Pierce to account if the allegation was substantiated. The investigative work of Congress and the special prosecutor helped bring about administrative and personnel changes within HUD.

Most federal programs must have their funding renewed every year, a requirement that gives Congress crucial leverage in its ongoing oversight function. If an agency has acted improperly, Congress may reduce the agency's appropriation or tighten the restrictions on the way its funds can be spent. A major difficulty is that the House and Senate Appropriations committees must review nearly the entire federal budget, a task that limits the amount of attention they can give any particular program.[49] Some programs are also

[48] See James Hamilton, *The Power to Probe: A Study of Congressional Investigations* (New York: Vintage Books, 1976).
[49] See Allen Schick, "The Battle of the Budget," in Harvey C. Mansfield, Sr., *Congress against the President* (New York: Praeger, 1975).

reviewed for renewal each year by the House and Senate committees that authorized them. These committees, however, are busy with new legislation and are not greatly interested in conducting annual reviews of existing programs. They prefer to wait until administrative problems surface and then respond with investigations.[50]

LEGISLATIVE DEVICES FOR RESTRAINING THE BUREAUCRACY

Oversight conducted after the bureaucracy has acted has an obvious drawback: if a program has been administered improperly, some damage has already been done. For this reason, Congress in recent years has developed ways of limiting the bureaucracy's discretion in advance. One method is to include detailed instructions in appropriations bills. Department of Defense appropriations, for example, now often specify cost-accounting procedures that bureaucrats must use. Such instructions serve to limit bureaucrats' flexibility when they spend funds on programs and provide a firmer basis for holding them accountable if they disregard the intent of Congress.

Another oversight device is the "sunset law," which fixes a date on which a program will end (or "fade into the sunset") unless it is renewed by Congress.[51] Such laws are a response to the fact that any program, once established, tends to be perpetuated by the bureaucrats who run it and by the interests that gain from it. Sunset provisions help to prevent a program from outliving its usefulness because, once its expiration date is reached, Congress can reestablish it only by passing a new law.

The "legislative veto" is a more intrusive and controversial oversight tool.[52] It requires that an executive agency have the approval of Congress before it can take a specified action. The Department of Defense, for example, cannot close a military facility unless Congress permits it to do so. Legislative vetoes are under challenge as an unconstitutional infringement on executive authority, and their future is unclear. (Congress's oversight tools are discussed more fully in Chapter 21.)

As indicated in Chapter 16, Congress has come to rely heavily on the General Accounting Office (GAO) to oversee executive agencies' spending and, more recently, their program performance. Some of the more blatant misuses of federal funds, particularly in the Department of Defense, have been uncovered by the GAO and then referred to the appropriate committees of Congress.

OBSTACLES TO OVERSIGHT

Members of Congress acknowledge the importance of their oversight function but find the task a largely unrewarding and troublesome one. Because they depend on the bureaucracy to do its own work effectively, members of

---

[50] Fred R. Harris and Paul L. Hain, *America's Legislative Process* (Glenview, Ill.: Scott, Foresman, 1983), 436–437.

[51] See Joel D. Aberbach, "Changes in Congressional Oversight," *American Behavorial Scientist* 22 (May–June 1979): 495–502.

[52] See James L. Sundquist, *The Decline and Resurgence of Congress* (Washington, D.C.: Brookings Institution, 1981), ch. 12; John R. Bolton, *The Legislative Veto* (Washington, D.C.: American Enterprise Institute, 1979).

Depositors line up outside the Bank of New England in Lynn, Massachusetts, in 1990, waiting to withdraw their money because they fear the bank is about to become insolvent. The recent nationwide rash of bank failures coupled with the savings and loan scandal demonstrated the inadequacy of congressional oversight over the huge, complex banking industry. (Lisa Bul/AP/Wide World)

Congress generally seek close and friendly relations with administrators. Oversight works against such relationships; it involves surveillance and the prospect of conflict between bureaucrats and members of Congress.

The biggest obstacle to effective oversight is the sheer magnitude of the task. With its 3 million employees and $1 trillion budget, the bureaucracy is beyond comprehensive scrutiny. Even some of Congress's most publicized oversight activities are relatively trivial when viewed against the sheer scope of the bureaucracy. For example, congressional investigations into the Defense Department's purchase of small hardware items, such as wrenches and hammers, at many times their market value do not begin to address the issue of whether the country is overspending on the military. Whatever their symbolic significance as evidence of bureaucratic waste, overpriced hand tools represent pocket change in a defense budget of billions of dollars. The real oversight question is whether the defense budget as a whole provides cost-effective national security. It is a question that Congress has neither the capacity nor the determination to investigate fully.

The inadequacy of the oversight process was perhaps never more apparent than in the savings and loan scandal. Although there were early signs that several of the nation's major thrifts were engaged in risky ventures and were not complying with federal regulations governing their activities, Congress did not act decisively to compel the agencies that regulated thrift activity to enforce their regulations more strictly. The delay in clamping down on runaway thrifts, which was in truth as much the fault of executive agencies as of the Congress, cost the American taxpayers untold billions of dollars.

Members of Congress have stronger personal incentives to function as lawmakers and representatives than to act as overseers. They tend to be keenly interested in oversight only when it promises substantial political rewards. From time to time a member of Congress can gain wide publicity through oversight activity. In the early days of television, Senator Estes Kefauver of

Institutional Reform of Congress
In the opinion of some observers, Congress can no longer make satisfactory policy decisions. Today's problems are supposedly too big and too technical to be handled by an institution that has no strong central authority. Is this argument persuasive? Have the Congressional Budget Office and other modernizing efforts helped Congress respond more promptly and effectively to urgent issues? Can you think of other changes that would help?

Tennessee became a national figure and almost won the 1952 Democratic presidential nomination because of publicity gained from hearings he chaired. The Iran-Contra hearings in 1987 brought national attention to several members of Congress, including Senator George Mitchell of Maine and Representative Lee Hamilton of Indiana.[53]

Oversight is also a useful political tool for a party when it has a congressional majority but does not control the presidency. Through oversight, Congress can pressure the administration to alter its policies. In 1982, in response to allegations that the Environmental Protection Agency (EPA) was permitting some corporations to circumvent laws regulating the disposal of toxic wastes, Congress scheduled hearings on the question. When the EPA's top administrators claimed they had President Reagan's backing and refused to provide requested information, Congress issued subpoenas. When it was rebuffed again, Congress forced the resignation of the EPA administrator, Anne Burford, and pursued the prosecution of another agency official, Rita Lavelle, who was convicted and sentenced to a six-month prison term. As a result of the investigation, the EPA brought its activities more closely into line with existing laws.

Appointment hearings have also become a time when Congress can put pressure on the president. In 1991 the nomination of Robert Gates to head the Central Intelligence Agency was held up for several months in the Democrat-controlled Senate so that the allegation that Gates had played a role in the Iran-Contra affair, which was a potential embarrassment for President Bush, could be probed.

Congress: The Truly "American" Institution?

Of all U.S. political institutions, Congress most closely reflects the central principles of American culture. Thus the individualism that pervades American society is evident in the independence of members of Congress. They are self-reliant politicians who are both part of and apart from the institution they serve. This characteristic is especially evident when candidates for Congress attack the institution for its failings and then, once in office, use all the institution's resources to keep themselves there.

The diversity of American society is also reflected in Congress. This is not to say that Congress is a microcosm of the U.S. population. Far from it. As we saw in Chapter 16, Congress is like other major institutions of American society in the overrepresentation among its members of wealthy white males. But Congress is diverse in the sense that it is a vast network of small legislatures, with each committee having its separate leaders and members, and each having jurisdiction over some aspect of American life. Agriculture, labor, education, commerce, and other economic sectors have their own special committees in Congress. It is hard to conceive of a national legislature structured to parallel the economic sectors of society more closely than the Congress of the United States. There is also the fact that individual representatives and senators are at

---

[53] See William S. Cohen and George J. Mitchell, *Men of Zeal: A Candid Inside Story of the Iran-Contra Hearings* (New York: Viking, 1988).

The hearings to confirm Robert Gates as director of the Central Intelligence Agency gave Senate Democrats a chance to look into Gate's alleged role in the Iran-Contra scandal. (Rick Reinhard/Impact Visuals)

least as closely tied to the interests of their separate districts and states as they are to the common national interest.

Congress is not an institution where simple majorities rule. Separate majorities in the two chambers and within relevant committees are normally required for enactment of significant legislation. For this reason Congress is sometimes portrayed as a weak institution. However, the power to prevent change is as significant as the power to accomplish change. Congress is actually extraordinarily strong: its fragmentation makes it a bulwark of the status quo. This was the intention of the Framers of the Constitution: they designed Congress in such a way that the majority could rule, but only if that majority was exceptionally strong. A narrow majority is usually insufficient in Congress, given its two chambers and their separate constituencies and different methods of selection.

What the writers of the Constitution failed to anticipate was the degree to which members of Congress would, because of their local base, cater to the demands of special interests. The Framers were intent on designing an institution that would forestall majority tyranny; in doing so, they created an institution that facilitates access and influence by minority interests. The fragmentation of the legislative structure and the local pressures on representatives contribute to a high degree of responsiveness to interest groups. Supporters of Congress say that this tendency gives strength to the nation's special interests while satisfying many of their legitimate demands on government. Critics see a congressional process biased toward established interests (see Chapter 14).

Conflicting opinions on Congress are inevitable. The strengths of Congress are its representativeness, its concern with local interests, and its function as an arena for achieving balance and compromise. The major weakness of Congress lies in the fact that small and nationally unrepresentative sets of interests control what should be national policy and use that control to benefit themselves disproportionately. Thus, in a sense, the strengths of Congress are also its weaknesses. Congress could not at once be both a nationally and a locally oriented institution. In a large and diverse nation, there is merit in an institution that stays in touch with grass-roots sentiment. The question is whether Congress leans too far in that direction.

Summary

The major function of Congress is to enact legislation. Congress is not well suited to the development of broad and carefully coordinated policy programs. Its divided chambers, weak leadership, and committee structure, as well as the concern of its members with state and district interests, make it difficult for Congress to initiate solutions to broad national problems. Congress looks to the president for such proposals but has strong influence on the timing and content of major national programs. Presidential initiatives are passed by Congress only if they meet its members' expectations and usually only after a lengthy process of compromise and negotiation.

Congress is more adept at handling legislation dealing with problems of narrow interest. Legislation of this sort is decided mainly in congressional committees, where interested legislators, bureaucrats, and groups concentrate their efforts on issues of mutual concern. Narrowly focused bills emerging from committees usually win the support of the full House or Senate. Committee recommendations are always subject to checks on the floor, and larger policy groups—issue networks and caucuses—have increasingly intruded on the committee process. Nevertheless, most narrow policy issues are settled primarily by subgroups of self-interested legislators rather than by the full Congress, although the success of these subgroups in the long run can depend on their responsiveness to broader interests.

A second function of Congress is the representation of various interests. Members of Congress are highly sensitive to the state or district on which they depend for reelection. As a result, interest groups that are important to a member's state or district are strongly represented in Congress. Members of Congress do respond to overriding national interests, but for most of them, local concerns generally come first. National and local representation often work through party representation, particularly on issues that have traditionally divided the Democratic and Republican parties and their constituencies.

Congress's third function is oversight, the supervision and investigation of the way the bureaucracy is implementing legislatively mandated programs. Oversight is usually less rewarding than lawmaking or representation and receives correspondingly less attention from members of Congress.

Congress is a slow and deliberative institution. It is also a powerful one; the process by which a bill becomes law is such that legislative proposals can be defeated or stymied rather easily. Congress is admired by those who believe that broad national legislation should reflect a wide range of interests, including local ones; that policies developed through a lengthy process of compromise and negotiation are likely to be sound; and that minorities should be able to obtain selective benefits and should have ways of blunting the impulses of the majority. Critics of the congressional process argue that it serves special interests, particularly entrenched economic groups; makes it hard, and sometimes impossible, for majorities to get their way; and prevents timely responses to pressing national needs.

Major Concepts

bill
caucus
cloture
filibuster
iron triangles
issue networks

law
lawmaking function
logrolling
oversight function
representation function

Suggested Readings

Arnold, R. Douglas. *Congress and the Bureaucracy.* New Haven, Conn.: Yale University Press, 1979. A study of Congress's relationships with the bureaucracy.

Fenno, Richard F., Jr. *Home Style: House Members in Their Districts.* Boston: Little, Brown, 1978. A penetrating analysis of the varying relationships between House members and their constituents.

Johnson, Loch K. *A Season of Inquiry.* Chicago: Dorsey Press, 1988. An insightful study of congressional oversight of intelligence activities.

Kingdon, John W. *Congressmen's Voting Decisions.* New York: Harper & Row, 1981. A study of congressional voting based in part on surveys of members of Congress.

Ogul, Morris S. *Congress Oversees the Bureaucracy.* Pittsburgh: University of Pittsburgh Press, 1976. An assessment of Congress's oversight function, with instructive case studies.

Orfield, Gary. *Congressional Power: Congress and Social Change.* New York: Harcourt Brace Jovanovich, 1975. An analysis of important shifts in congressional influence following reforms and events of the early 1970s.

Reid, T. R. *Congressional Odyssey.* San Francisco: Freeman, 1980. A lively and insightful study of the passage of a Senate bill.

Vogler, David J., and Sidney R. Waldman. *Congress and Democracy.* Washington, D.C.: Congressional Quarterly Press, 1985. Addresses the question of whether members of Congress should serve their constituents' interests or a common national interest.

18
CHAPTER

PRESIDENTIAL OFFICE AND ELECTION: LEADING THE NATION

[The president's] is the only voice in national affairs. Let him once win the admiration and confidence of the people, and no other single voice will easily overpower him.

Woodrow Wilson[1]

*I*n 1972 Richard Nixon demonstrated why the presidency has been described as "both the most dynamic and most dangerous of our political institutions."[2] At the same time that Nixon was reopening U.S. relations with China, suspended since the communist takeover in 1949, he was ordering the saturation bombing of large areas of Cambodia. The two policies began in secrecy, but they led in opposing directions and had vastly different consequences. The opening to China was a brilliant diplomatic move that heightened tensions between China and the Soviet Union, drew China toward the West, and contributed to developments that led the Soviet Union, more than a decade later under Mikhail Gorbachev, also to reach out to the West. The bombing of Cambodia, in contrast, violated international law, rained death and destruction on the people of that tiny nation, and, when it became publicly known, undermined relations between the United States and its allies and created tension between the executive and legislative branches of the national government.

The characterization of the presidency as "both the most dynamic and most dangerous" of U.S. political institutions refers to the leeway inherent in the office's constitutional authority.[3] The writers of the Constitution sought to establish an energetic presidency but also wanted to constrain the powers of the office. The Framers knew what they wanted from a president—national

---

[1]Woodrow Wilson, *Constitutional Government in the United States* (New York: Columbia University Press, 1908), 67.
[2]Robert Hirschfield, ed., *The Power of the Presidency*, 3d ed. (New York: Aldine, 1982), 3.
[3]James W. Davis, *The American Presidency* (New York: Harper & Row, 1987), 13.

President Richard Nixon and his wife, Pat, visit the Great Wall of China in 1972. Nixon resumed U.S. diplomatic relations with China, even as he was secretly intensifying U.S. involvement in the war in Southeast Asia—a demonstration of why the presidency is characterized as the most dynamic and yet most dangerous of U.S. institutions. (AP/Wide World)

leadership, statesmanship in foreign affairs, command in time of war or insurgency, enforcement of the laws—but could devise only general phrases to describe the president's constitutional authority. Compared with Article I, which enumerates Congress's specific powers, Article II of the Constitution contains relatively vague statements on the president's powers.

The Constitution vests executive authority in a single chief executive. The Framers debated briefly the possibility of a three-person executive (one president each from the northern, middle, and southern states) but rejected the idea on the grounds that a joint office would be sapped of its energy by constant infighting. The Framers worried that a single executive might become too powerful but believed that adequate protection against such a threat was provided by the separation of powers and the president's selection by electors. Although the president would represent the people, he would not be chosen directly by them. This arrangement would protect him against excessive public demands and at the same time deny him the reserve of power that direct public election could confer.

The Framers did not anticipate that the president would someday be chosen through popular election. The Framers also did not foresee all the leadership implications of the president's national office. Senators and representatives are chosen by voters within a single state or district, a limitation that diminishes the claim of any one of them to national leadership. Moreover, since the House and the Senate are separate bodies, no member of Congress can speak for the whole institution. The president, in contrast, is a nationally elected official and the sole chief executive. These features of the office enabled presidents, as the executive demands on government increased during the twentieth century, to assume powers and leadership that helped to transform the presidency into a permanently more powerful office.

This chapter explains why the presidency has become a stronger office than the Framers envisioned. The chapter also examines the presidential selection process and the staffing of the modern presidency, both of which contribute to the president's prominence in the American political system. The main ideas of the chapter are these:

★ *Public expectations, national crises, and changing national and world conditions have required the presidency to become a strong office. Underlying this development is the public support that the president acquires from being the only nationally elected official.*

★ *The modern presidential election campaign is a marathon affair in which self-selected candidates must plan for a strong start in the nominating contests and center their general election strategies on media, issues, and a baseline of support.* The lengthy campaign process serves to heighten the public's sense that the presidency is at the center of the U.S. political system.

★ *The modern presidency could not operate without a large staff of assistants, experts, and high-level managers, but the sheer size of this staff makes it impossible for the president to exercise complete control over it.*

Foundations of the Modern Presidency

Over the course of American history, each of the president's constitutional powers has been extended in practice beyond the Framers' intention. For example, the Constitution grants the president command of the nation's military, but only Congress can declare war. In *Federalist* No. 69 Alexander Hamilton wrote that a surprise attack on the United States was the only justification for war by presidential action. President Thomas Jefferson disputed even this exception, claiming that he could respond to invasion with only defensive action unless Congress declared war. Since Jefferson, however, the nation's presidents have sent troops into military action abroad more than 200 times. Of the twelve wars included in that figure, only five were declared by Congress.[4] Each of America's most recent wars—the Korean, Vietnam, and Persian Gulf wars—was undeclared.

The Constitution also empowers the president to act as diplomatic leader. He is granted the authority to receive ambassadors, and thus has the power to decide which nations will have the formal diplomatic recognition of the United States. The president is further empowered to appoint U.S. ambassadors and to negotiate treaties with other countries, subject to approval by the Senate. The Framers anticipated that Congress would have responsibility for developing foreign policy, while the president would oversee its implementation.[5] However, the president has become the principal architect of U.S. foreign policy and has even acquired the power to make treaty-like arrangements with other nations, in the form of executive agreements. In 1937 the Supreme Court ruled that such agreements, signed and approved only by the president, have the same legal status as treaties, which require approval by a two-thirds vote of the

---

[4]See Barry M. Blechman and Stephen S. Kaplan, *Force without War* (Washington, D.C.: Brookings Institution, 1978).
[5]Edward S. Corwin, *The President: Office and Powers, 1787–1957* (New York: New York University Press, 1959), 180–181.

THE PRESIDENT'S CONSTITUTIONAL AUTHORITY

Commander in chief. Article II, section 2: "The President shall be commander in chief of the Army and Navy of the United States, and of the militia of the several states."

Chief executive. Article II, section 2: "He may require the opinion, in writing, of the principal officer in each of the executive departments, upon any subject relating to the duties of their respective offices, and he shall have power to grant reprieves and pardons for offences against the United States, except in cases of impeachment."

Article II, section 2: "He shall have power, by and with the advice and consent of the Senate, to make treaties, provided two thirds of the senators present concur; and he shall nominate, and by and with the advice and consent of the Senate, shall appoint ambassadors, other public ministers and consuls, judges of the Supreme Court, and all other officers of the United States, whose appointments are not herein otherwise provided for, and which shall be established by law."

Article II, section 2: "The President shall have power to fill up all vacancies that may happen during the recess of the Senate, by granting commissions which shall expire at the end of their next session."

Article II, section 3: "He shall take care that the laws be faithfully executed, and shall commission all the officers of the United States."

Chief diplomat. Article II, section 2: "He shall have power, and with the advice and consent of the Senate, to make treaties, provided two thirds of the senators present concur."

Article II, section 3: "He shall receive ambassadors and other public ministers."

Legislative promoter. Article II, section 3: "He shall from time to time give to the Congress information of the state of the Union, and recommend to their consideration such measures as he shall judge necessary and expedient; he may, on extraordinary occasions, convene both houses, or either of them, and in case of disagreement between them, with respect to the time of adjournment, he may adjourn them to such time as he shall think proper."

Senate.[6] Since World War II, presidents have negotiated more than 9,000 executive agreements, as compared with roughly 500 treaties ratified by the Senate.[7]

In addition, the Constitution vests "executive power" in the president, giving him the responsibility to execute the laws faithfully and to appoint major administrators, such as heads of the various departments of the executive branch. In *Federalist* No. 76 Hamilton indicated that the president's real authority as chief executive was to be found in this appointive capacity. Presidents have indeed exercised substantial power through their appointments, but they have found their administrative authority—the power to execute the laws—to be of even greater value, because it enables them to determine how laws will be interpreted and applied. President Ronald Reagan, for example, used his executive power to halt the use of federal funds by family-planning clinics that offered abortion counseling.

Finally, the Constitution provides the president with legislative authority, including use of the veto and the opportunity to recommend proposals to Congress. The Framers expected this authority to be used in a limited and largely negative way. George Washington acted as the Framers anticipated: he proposed only three legislative measures and vetoed only two acts of Congress. Modern presidents have a different, more activist view of their legislative role. They routinely submit legislative proposals to Congress and often veto legisla-

[6]*United States v. Belmont*, 57 U.S. 758 (1937).
[7]Raymond Tatalovich and Byron W. Daynes, *Presidential Power in the United States* (Monterey, Calif.: Brooks/Cole, 1984), 263.

Perceiving himself as the people's steward, President Teddy Roosevelt took on the business trusts that were using their domination of markets to gouge consumers. (Culver Pictures)

tion they find disagreeable. The champion of the veto is Franklin D. Roosevelt, who during his twelve years in office rejected 635 acts of Congress.

The presidency is a more powerful office than the Framers envisioned for many reasons, but two features of the office in particular—national election and singular authority—have enabled presidents to make use of changing demands on government to claim the position of national leader.

AN EMERGING TRADITION OF STRONG PRESIDENTS

The first president to assert forcefully a claim to popular leadership was Andrew Jackson, who had been swept into office in 1828 on a tide of public support that broke the hold that the upper classes had had on the presidency until then. Jackson used his popular backing to challenge Congress's claim to national policy leadership, contending that he was "the people's tribune."

Jackson's view of the presidency, however, was not shared by most of his successors during the nineteenth century, because national conditions did not routinely call for strong presidential leadership. The prevailing conception of the presidency was the **Whig theory.** In this view, the presidency was a limited or constrained office whose occupant was confined to the exercise of expressly granted constitutional authority. The president had no implicit powers for dealing with national problems, but was primarily an administrator, charged with carrying out the expressed will of Congress. "My duty," said President James Buchanan, a Whig adherent, "is to execute the laws . . . and not my individual opinions."[8]

[8]Quoted in Wilfred E. Binkley, *President and Congress*, 3d ed. (New York: Vintage, 1962), 142.

Theodore Roosevelt rejected the Whig tradition when he took office in 1901. He embraced the **stewardship theory,** which called for a strong, assertive presidential role. As "steward of the people," Roosevelt said, he was obliged "to do anything that the needs of the Nation demanded unless such action was *forbidden* by the Constitution or by the laws."[9] Thus, in Roosevelt's view, presidential authority was not limited by any restrictions inherent in expressed grants of power; it stopped only at points specifically prohibited by law. Moreover, the stewardship view holds that the presidency includes the role of legislative initiator, a leader who formulates policy proposals and prods Congress to act on them. Accordingly, Roosevelt, among other initiatives, attacked the business trusts, promoted conservation, and persuaded Congress to enact standards for the safety of foods, drugs, and transportation.[10]

Roosevelt's image of a strong presidency was shared by Woodrow Wilson, but his other immediate successors reverted to the Whig notion of the limited presidency.[11] Herbert Hoover's restrained conception of the presidency prevented him from taking decisive action even during the economic devastation that followed the Wall Street crash of 1929. Hoover argued that he lacked the constitutional authority to establish public relief programs for jobless and penniless Americans.

Hoover's successor, Franklin D. Roosevelt, shared the stewardship theory of his distant cousin Theodore Roosevelt, and FDR's New Deal signaled the end of the limited presidency. Today the presidency is an inherently strong office.[12] The modern presidency becomes a more substantial office in the hands of a persuasive leader such as Lyndon Johnson or Ronald Reagan, but even a less forceful person such as Gerald Ford or Jimmy Carter is now expected to act assertively. This expectation not only is the legacy of former strong presidents but also stems from the need for presidential leadership in periods of national crisis and from changes that have occurred in the federal government's national and international policy responsibilities.

The president can exercise no power which cannot be fairly and reasonably traced to some specific grant of power or justly implied.

William Howard Taft

THE NEED FOR PRESIDENTIAL LEADERSHIP IN NATIONAL CRISES

National crises have enabled presidents to assume powers beyond those provided in the Constitution. Emergencies usually demand speed of action and singleness of purpose. Congress—a large, divided, and often unwieldly institution—is poorly suited to such a response. In contrast, the president, as sole head of the executive branch, can act quickly and decisively. Abraham Lincoln's response to the outbreak of the Civil War is a notable example. Acting on his own authority, Lincoln called up the militia, blockaded southern ports, increased the size of the army and navy, ordered conscription, suspended the writ of *habeas corpus,* and placed part of the nation under martial law. When Congress convened in 1861, after Lincoln's war orders had already taken effect,

[9]Theodore Roosevelt, *An Autobiography* (New York: Scribner's, 1931), 383.
[10]George C. Edwards and Stephen J. Wayne, *Presidential Leadership* (New York: St. Martin's Press, 1985), 6–7.
[11]See Richard M. Pious, *The American Presidency* (New York: Basic Books, 1979), 83.
[12]Robert Hirschfield, "The Power of the Contemporary President," in Aaron Wildavsky, ed., *The Presidency* (Boston: Little, Brown, 1969), 137.

Japanese-Americans assemble for evacuation from San Francisco to inland detention camps in April 1942. President Franklin Roosevelt ordered this drastic program in the crisis atmosphere that followed the Japanese attack on Pearl Harbor. His order was upheld by the Supreme Court as a lawful exercise of the president's authority as commander in chief. (Library of Congress)

it acknowledged the validity of his actions by passing a law stating that his directives had the same authority "as if they had been issued and done under the previous express authority and direction of the Congress of the United States."[13]

Similarly, Congress formally endorsed Franklin Roosevelt's directive, issued in the wake of the Japanese attack on Pearl Harbor in 1941, that ordered the evacuation of 135,000 Japanese-Americans living on the West Coast. Fearing subversive activities among these Japanese-Americans, Roosevelt instructed federal authorities to seize their property and relocate them in detention camps farther inland until the war's end. Japanese-Americans challenged the legality of Roosevelt's order, but the Supreme Court upheld their forced evacuation from coastal areas (although it voided their involuntary detention).[14]

In such instances the other branches of government have had little choice but to accept presidential claims to extraordinary powers. Constitutionality has given way to perceived necessity in times of crisis. Lincoln's critics called him a dictator, but a congressional majority affirmed that his extraconstitutional actions had been necessary to save the Union.

National crises have had a lasting impact on the conduct of the executive office. Modern presidents are expected to be powerful in part because some of their predecessors assumed extraordinary powers in critical times. Lincoln, Roosevelt, and other strong presidents left a legacy for later presidents. Every strong president has seen his power as flowing from a special relationship with the American people. As Harry S Truman noted in his memoirs, "I believe that

The Increase in Presidential Power
It has been said that constitutionality bends to necessity. How does this axiom help to explain the increased power and responsibility that the president has acquired during the twentieth century? Is the axiom strictly accurate, given that the provisions for presidential authority in Article II of the Constitution are relatively vague in any case?

[13]Tatalovich and Daynes, *Presidential Power*, 322–323.
[14]*Korematsu* v. *United States*, 323 U.S. 214 (1944); *Ex parte* Endo, 323 U.S. 283 (1944).

the power of the President should be used in the interest of the people and in order to do that the President must use whatever power the Constitution does not expressly deny him."[15]

THE NEED FOR PRESIDENTIAL LEADERSHIP OF AN ACTIVIST GOVERNMENT

During most of the nineteenth century the United States did not need a strong president. The federal government's policymaking role was small, as was its bureaucracy. Moreover, the nation's major issues were of a sectional nature (especially the North-South split over slavery) and thus suited to action by Congress, which represented state and local interests. The U.S. government's role in world affairs was also small.

Today the situation has greatly changed. The federal government has such broad national and international responsibilities that strong leadership from presidents is essential.

Foreign Policy Leadership

The president has always been the foreign policy leader of the United States, but during the nation's first century that role was a rather undemanding one. The United States avoided getting entangled in the turbulent politics of Europe, and though it was involved in foreign trade, its major preoccupation was its internal development. By the end of the nineteenth century, however, the nation was seeking to expand the world market for its goods, and the size and growing industrial power of the United States was attracting more attention from other nations. President Theodore Roosevelt advocated an American economic empire, looking south toward Latin America and west toward Hawaii, the Philippines, and China (the "Open Door" policy) for new markets. However, the United States' tradition of isolationism remained a powerful influence on national policy. The United States fought in World War I but immediately thereafter demobilized its armed forces. Over President Woodrow Wilson's objections, Congress then voted against the entry of the United States into the League of Nations.

World War II fundamentally changed the nation's international role and the president's role in foreign policy. In 1945 the United States emerged as a global superpower, a giant in world trade, and the recognized leader of the noncommunist world. The United States today has formal diplomatic relations with three times as many nations as it did in the 1930s; a military presence in nearly every part of the globe; and an unprecedented interest in trade balances, energy supplies, and other international issues affecting the nation's economy.[16]

The effects of these developments on America's political institutions have been largely one-sided. Because of the president's constitutional authority as chief diplomat and military commander and the special demands of foreign policy leadership, the president, not Congress, has taken the lead in addressing the United States' increased responsibilities in the world. (The special demands

[15]Harry S Truman, *1946–1952: Years of Trial and Hope* (New York: Signet, 1956), 535.
[16]Davis, *American Presidency*, 25–26.

A hallmark of Franklin Delano Roosevelt's presidency was his strong leadership in formulating domestic policies to combat the Great Depression. He is shown here signing the legislation that created the social security system in 1935, surrounded by congressional and administration leaders who had helped draft the bill. (UPI/Bettmann Newsphotos)

of foreign policy and how they work to the president's advantage are discussed more fully in Chapter 19.)

Domestic Policy Leadership

The change in the president's domestic leadership has also been substantial. Throughout most of the nineteenth century Congress jealously guarded its constitutional powers, making it clear that domestic policy was its business. James Bryce wrote in the 1880s that Congress paid no more attention to the president's views on legislation than it did to the editorial positions of prominent newspaper publishers.[17]

By the early twentieth century, however, the national government was taking on regulatory and policy responsibilities imposed by the nation's transition from an agrarian to an industrial society, and stronger presidential leadership was becoming necessary. In 1921 Congress conceded that it lacked the centralized authority to coordinate the growing national budget and enacted the Budget and Accounting Act, which provided for an executive budget.[18] Federal departments and agencies would no longer submit their annual budget requests directly to Congress. The president would oversee the initiation of the budget, compiling the various agencies' requests into an overall budget, which he would submit to Congress for its approval.

During the Great Depression of the 1930s, Franklin D. Roosevelt's New Deal responded to the public's demand for economic relief with a broad program that involved a level of policy planning and coordination that was beyond the capacity of Congress. In addition to initiating public works projects and

---

[17]James Bryce, *The American Commonwealth* (New York: Commonwealth Edition, 1908), 230.
[18]Davis, *American Presidency*, 20.

social-welfare programs aimed at providing immediate relief, the New Deal made the government a partner in nearly every aspect of the nation's economy. If economic regulation was to work, unified and continuous policy leadership was needed, and only the president could provide it. Later Congress institutionalized the president's economic role with the Full Employment Act of 1946, which assigns to the president an ongoing responsibility for economic growth. This act entrusts the president with the authority "to use all practicable means . . . to promote maximum employment, production, and purchasing power."

Roosevelt's power, like that of the strong presidents before him, rested on the support of the American people.[19] In the early 1930s the nation was in such desperate condition that Americans would have supported almost anything Roosevelt did. "If he burned down the Capitol," said the humorist Will Rogers, "we would cheer and say 'Well, we at least got a fire started.'"[20]

Presidential authority has continued to grow since Roosevelt's time. In response to pressures from the public, the national government's role in such areas as education, health, welfare, safety, and protection of the environment has expanded greatly, which in turn has created additional demands for presidential leadership.[21] Big government, with its emphasis on comprehensive planning and program coordination, favors executive authority at the expense of legislative authority. *All* democracies have seen a shift in power from their legislature to their executive. In Britain, for example, the prime minister has taken on responsibilities that once belonged to the cabinet or the parliament.

The president's preeminence as domestic policy leader does not mean that Congress no longer plays a significant role.[22] As we saw in Chapter 17, some major policy initiatives of recent decades—including labor relations, public housing, atomic energy, and environmental protection—have emanated from Congress, which has also modified or rejected many presidential proposals during this period.[23] Moreover, Congress tends to seek the president's leadership only on particular types of legislative measures—principally those that address truly national issues from a national perspective.[24] (The president's domestic policy role is discussed further in Chapter 19.)

Choosing the President

As the president's policy and leadership responsibilities changed during the nation's history, so too did the process of electing presidents. The changes do not parallel each other exactly, but they are related politically and philosophically. As the presidency drew ever closer to the people, their role in selecting the president grew ever more important.

[19]Ibid., 25.
[20]Quoted in Arthur M. Schlesinger, Jr., *The Coming of the New Deal* (Boston: Houghton Mifflin, 1958), 13.
[21]Hugh Heclo, "Introduction: The Presidential Illusion," in Hugh Heclo and Lester M. Salamon, eds., *The Illusion of Presidential Government* (Boulder, Colo.: Westview Press, 1981), 6.
[22]James Sundquist, *The Decline and Resurgence of Congress* (Washington, D.C.: Brookings Institution, 1981), 150.
[23]Richard M. Pious, "Sources of Domestic Policy Initiatives," in Harvey C. Mansfield, ed., *Congress against the President* (New York: Praeger, 1975), 108–109.
[24]John Kingdon, *Congressmen's Voting Decisions* (New York: Harper & Row, 1973), 170–171.

TABLE 18-1   The Four Systems of Presidential Selection

Selection System	Period	Features
1. Original	1788–1828	Party nominees are chosen in congressional caucuses. Electoral College members act somewhat independently in their presidential voting.
2. Party convention	1832–1900	Party nominees are chosen in national party conventions by delegates selected by state and local party organizations. Electoral College members cast their ballots for the popular-vote winner in their respective states.
3. Party convention, primary	1904–1968	As in system 2, except that a *minority* of national convention delegates are chosen through primary elections (the majority still being chosen by party organizations).
4. Party primary, open caucus	1972– present	As in system 2, except that a *majority* of national convention delegates are chosen through primary elections.

THE DEVELOPMENT OF THE PRESIDENTIAL SELECTION SYSTEM

The process by which the United States selects its chief executive has evolved through four cumulative systems (summarized in Table 18-1 and described below), each of which resulted from popular reforms that were aimed chiefly at granting the American people a larger say in choosing the president.[25] The major justification for each of the reforms was **legitimacy,** the idea that the selection of the president should reflect the will of the people.[26]

The First and Second Systems: Electors and Party Conventions

The delegates to the Constitutional Convention of 1787 were steadfastly opposed to popular election of the president. They feared that popular election would make the office too centralized and too powerful, which would undermine the principles of federalism and separation of powers. The Framers devised a novel system, which came to be called the Electoral College. Under the Constitution, the president is chosen by a vote of electors who are appointed by the states. Each state is entitled to as many electors as it has members of Congress, and each state determines its own method for selecting its electors. The candidate who receives the majority of electoral votes is elected president.

In the first two presidential elections, the electors unanimously selected George Washington, the only presidential candidate in history to receive the votes of all electors. Nevertheless, the Framers anticipated that in some

[25]Thomas R. Marshall, *Presidential Nominations in a Reform Age* (New York: Praeger, 1981); James W. Ceaser, *Reforming the Reforms: A Critical Analysis of the Presidential Selection Process* (Cambridge, Mass.: Ballinger, 1982), 81; James W. Ceaser, *Presidential Selection: Theory and Development* (Princeton, N.J.: Princeton University Press, 1979).
[26]Ceaser, *Presidential Selection*, 19.

elections no candidate would gain the electoral majority required by the Constitution, in which case the House of Representatives (with each state having one vote) would select the president from among the top five votegetters (later changed to the top three by the Twelfth Amendment). The House soon did decide an election, choosing Thomas Jefferson in 1800.

Jefferson's election by the House resulted from a development that the Framers had not foreseen. In its original form, the Constitution provided that each elector would cast two ballots. The candidate who placed first, provided that he received the votes of a majority of electors, became president, and the second-place candidate became vice-president. The Framers had not anticipated the emergence of political parties and the formation of party tickets. In 1800 Jefferson teamed with vice-presidential candidate Aaron Burr on the Republican party's ticket, and each elector who voted for Jefferson also voted for Burr, which led to a tie and nearly a constitutional crisis when Burr tried to persuade the Federalists in Congress to elect him as president. Jefferson finally prevailed on the thirty-fifth House ballot. After he took office, the Twelfth Amendment was enacted to prevent ties in the Electoral College; the amendment provides that each elector shall cast one ballot for a presidential candidate and one ballot for a vice-presidential candidate.

In the 1790s, party members in Congress assumed the power to name a presidential nominee. Their choice was not binding on the electors, who could vote as they pleased; but the need for party unity and the prestige of the Congress led most electors to follow the recommendation of their party's congressional caucus, earning it the title of "King Caucus."[27]

In 1824, however, Republican caucus leaders bypassed the war hero Andrew Jackson and Secretary of State John Quincy Adams, who had emerged as leaders of the party's rival factions. Instead they nominated Secretary of the Treasury William Crawford of Georgia, who they believed would be easy to control once he was in the White House. A number of states had established popular voting for president, and Jackson and Adams took their campaigns to the people. Jackson polled 152,933 popular votes to Adams's 115,696, while Crawford received fewer than 50,000 votes. Jackson also placed first in the electoral voting (which was separate from the popular voting) but had less than a majority; so the final decision passed to the House of Representatives, which chose John Quincy Adams on the first ballot.[28]

Jackson was outraged by Adams's election, believing that an elite conspiracy had denied him the presidency. After he ran again and won in 1828, Jackson set about altering the presidential election system so that it would give the people a stronger voice. He could not persuade Congress to support a constitutional amendment which would have eliminated the Electoral College, but did obtain the next-best alternative: he persuaded the states to tie their electoral vote to the popular vote. Under Jackson's reform, which is still in effect today, each party in a state has a separate slate of electors who gain the right to cast a state's electoral votes if their party's candidate places first in the state's popular voting. Thus the

[27]See Noble E. Cunningham, Jr., "Presidential Leadership, Political Parties, and the Congressional Caucus, 1800–1824," in Patricia Bonami, James MacGregor Burns, and Austin Ranney, eds., The American Constitutional System under Strong and Weak Parties (New York: Praeger, 1981), 1–20.
[28]Neal R. Pierce and Lawrence Longley, The People's President (New Haven, Conn.: Yale University Press, 1981), 49–52.

John F. Kennedy was the first president whose nomination clearly derived from victories in the primaries. As a Catholic and a junior senator, Kennedy had no chance of winning the Democratic presidential nomination in 1960 unless his primary campaign was successful. Kennedy is shown campaigning in West Virginia, a heavily Protestant state whose primary he won. (AP/Wide World)

popular vote directly affects the electoral vote, and one candidate is likely to win both forms of the presidential vote. Since Jackson's time, only Rutherford B. Hayes (in 1876) and Benjamin Harrison (in 1888) have won the presidency after having lost the popular vote.

Jackson also eliminated King Caucus. In 1832 he convened a national party convention to nominate the Democratic presidential candidate. The parties had their strength at the grass roots, among the people, whereas Congress was dominated by the wealthy interests against which Jackson was fighting. Since Jackson's time, presidential nominees have been formally chosen at national party conventions.

The Third and Fourth Systems: Primaries and Open Races

The system of presidential selection that Jackson had created remained intact until the early twentieth century, when the Progressives initiated primary elections as a way of wresting control over presidential nominations from party bosses. In 1904 Florida became the first state to choose its national convention delegates through a presidential primary. Some other states followed suit, but most either stayed with the older system of party selection or adopted nonbinding primaries. As a result, party leaders continued to control a majority of the convention delegates who selected the presidential nominees.

Through 1968, a strong showing in the primaries enabled a candidate to demonstrate popular support but did not guarantee nomination. In 1952, for example, Senator Estes Kefauver beat President Harry Truman in New Hampshire's opening primary and went on to win twelve of the thirteen primaries he entered; however, Kefauver was denied nomination by party leaders, who believed that his views were inconsistent with the party's traditions.

In 1968, the Democratic nomination went to Vice-President Hubert Humphrey, who had not entered a single primary and was closely identified with the Johnson administration's Vietnam war policy. After Humphrey narrowly lost the 1968 general election to Richard Nixon, reform-minded Democrats forced changes in the nominating process. The new rules gave rank-and-file party voters more control by requiring that states choose their delegates through either primary elections or **open party caucuses** (meetings open to any registered party voter who wants to attend). Although the Democrats initiated the change, the Republicans were also affected by it. Most states that adopted a presidential primary in order to comply with the Democrats' new rules also required Republicans to select their convention delegates through a primary. Today it is the voters in state primaries and open caucuses who play the decisive role in the selection of the Democratic and Republican presidential nominees.

The modern presidential selection process is a long and grinding process that bears almost no resemblance to the way in which other democratic countries select their chief executives. When Helmut Kohl gained a third term as Germany's chancellor in 1990, the campaign lasted just a few weeks. The typical campaign for prime minster of Great Britain lasts about three weeks. By comparison, a U.S. presidential campaign officially spans nine months and actually starts much earlier. The main reason the U.S. campaign lasts so long is that the voters choose the nominees as well as the final winner. No European democracy uses primary elections as a means of choosing its nominees for public office.

THE CAMPAIGN FOR NOMINATION

The recent changes in the nominating process have made the race for the presidency more wide open than ever before.[29] Nevertheless, a presidential campaign is lengthy and demanding, which discourages some potential candidates from making the run.[30] Recent nominating campaigns, except those in which an incumbent president is seeking reelection, have typically attracted about a half-dozen or more contenders. Most of them are not well known to the nation's voters before the campaign, and few have a significant record of national accomplishment. Among the active Democratic candidates when the 1992 primaries began, for example, not one had a national reputation.

Media and Momentum

A key to success in the nominating campaign is what candidates and journalists call **momentum**—a strong showing in the early contests which leads to a buildup of public support in subsequent ones. If candidates start off poorly, reporters will lose interest in covering them, contributors will deny them funding, political leaders will not endorse them, and voters will not give further thought to supporting them.

[29]John H. Aldrich, *Before the Convention* (Chicago: University of Chicago Press, 1980), ch. 2; Thomas E. Cronin, *State of the Presidency* (Boston: Little, Brown, 1980), 28.
[30]See Robert E. DiClerico and Eric M. Uslaner, *Few Are Chosen* (New York: McGraw-Hill, 1984).

★ ANALYZE THE ISSUE

The New Elite in the Nomination Process
The process of choosing presidential nominees has greatly changed in the past few decades. Among other things, the old elite of party leaders—governors, mayors, members of Congress, and party chairs—has given way to a new elite of journalists and the candidates' hired consultants—pollsters, media specialists, and the like. What are the implications of this shift? In regard to this change alone, is the new system an improvement over the old?

For these reasons, presidential contenders now give extraordinary attention to the early contests, particularly the first primary in New Hampshire.[31] The media also gives New Hampshire close scrutiny (see Figure 18-1). Even though New Hampshire's primary selects less than 1 percent of the national convention delegates, it receives more news coverage than any other presidential primary.[32] The candidates fight for the media's attention, but the spotlight is not always advantageous. Bill Clinton was the leading Democrat in New Hampshire polls in 1992 until he was accused in the press of adultery and dodging the Vietnam draft. Clinton lost the New Hampshire primary to Paul Tsongas but was able to regain the momentum with victories on Super Tuesday, when most of the southern states held their primaries.

Although the dynamics of momentum help to explain why the early leader often wins nomination, it does not account for initial success or enduring appeal. Why does one candidate start strongly or maintain strength while another does not? There is no single answer, but a candidate must have strength of one kind or another to prevail. Issues can be important: the main reason George McGovern won the Democratic nomination in 1972 was that his anti-Vietnam stance attracted a stable and committed voting bloc. Critical events can also matter: the international crisis that resulted when Iranian militants took control of the U.S. embassy in Teheran in late 1979 gave President Carter's popularity a temporary boost that enabled him to turn back Senator Edward Kennedy's challenge for the 1980 Democratic nomination. Public familiarity is another factor: George Bush's successful drive to the 1988 Republican nomination owed mainly to support built up during his vice-presidency. In short, political influences of varying kinds have a strong impact on nominating races. Presidential nominations are not decided strictly by momentum and superior strategy. Since 1968 the preprimary poll leader in contested nominations has won about half the time.

[31]See Hugh Winebrenner, *The Iowa Precinct Caucuses* (Ames: Iowa State University Press, 1987); Gary R. Orren and Nelson W. Polsby, eds., *Media and Momentum: The New Hampshire Primary and Nomination Politics* (Chatham, N.J.: Chatham House, 1987).
[32]Michael J. Robinson and Margaret A. Sheehan, *Over the Wire and on TV* (New York: Russell Sage Foundation, 1983), 174.

FIGURE 18-1 States Sized in Proportion to News Coverage Given Their Presidential Nomination Contests, 1984
The Iowa caucuses and the New Hampshire primary dominate news coverage of state nominating contests. *Source: William C. Adams, "As New Hampshire Goes . . . ," in Gary R. Orren and Nelson W. Polsby, eds.,* Media and Momentum: The New Hampshire Primary and Nomination Politics *(Chatham, N.J.: Chatham House, 1987), ch.3.*

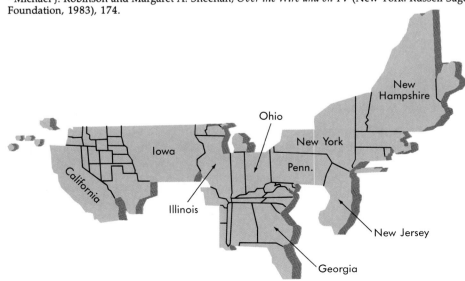

Bill Clinton is surrounded by supporters after he announces his bid for the 1992 Democratic presidential nomination. (Haviv/SABA)

★ THE MEDIA AND THE PEOPLE

MOMENTUM AND THE NEW HAMPSHIRE PRIMARY

Every candidate for the presidential nomination seeks to build up momentum by making a strong early showing that can be parlayed into an ever-increasing level of support. The state contest that traditionally has had the greatest impact on momentum is New Hampshire's primary. A win in New Hampshire provides a media bonanza for the winner. After narrowly winning New Hampshire's 1976 Democratic primary, for example, Jimmy Carter appeared on the covers of *Time* and *Newsweek* and received 2,600 lines of coverage within those issues, compared with 300 lines for all five of his Democratic challengers combined. Within a week of his New Hampshire triumph, Carter's name recognition nationwide jumped from 20 percent to 80 percent, and his support among Democratic voters tripled. In the same week, all of Carter's opponents either stood still or dropped in the polls.

Voting in primaries is not affected by partisan loyalties, since all candidates are of the same party. Without partisanship as an anchor, vote swings in response to momentum can be substantial. After Michael Dukakis

won the New Hampshire primary in 1988, his nationwide support among Democratic voters in polls doubled. Most New Hampshire winners in recent elections have, like Dukakis, gained significant public support immediately after this primary.

A candidate's early triumph can often be extended into continued success. When the voters are poorly informed about the contenders, which is often the case in nominating races, the news coverage that comes to a candidate because of an early win can persuade a high percentage of undecided voters. Their attention is directed toward one contender, so, not surprisingly, those without an existing strong preference may be inclined to support him. In 1976 Carter apparently gained half or more of his votes in subsequent early primaries from the momentum achieved by his victory in New Hampshire's primary.

SOURCES: Thomas E. Patterson, *The Mass Media Election* (New York: Praeger, 1980), chs. 5, 11; Larry Bartels, *Presidential Primaries and the Dynamics of Public Choice* (Princeton, N.J.: Princeton University Press, 1988), ch.8.

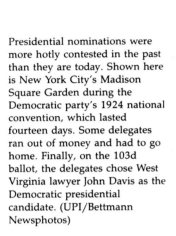

Presidential nominations were more hotly contested in the past than they are today. Shown here is New York City's Madison Square Garden during the Democratic party's 1924 national convention, which lasted fourteen days. Some delegates ran out of money and had to go home. Finally, on the 103d ballot, the delegates chose West Virginia lawyer John Davis as the Democratic presidential candidate. (UPI/Bettmann Newsphotos)

Candidates in primary elections are assisted by the Federal Election Campaign Act of 1974 (as amended in 1979). This act provides for federal "matching funds" to be given to any candidate who raises at least $5,000 in individual contributions of up to $250 in each of twenty states. In general, this federal support mainly helps lesser-known contenders—the sort who in the past had trouble raising enough money to compete effectively. Now any candidate who raises funds in the legally prescribed way is given an equal amount by the U.S. Treasury. Candidates who accept matching funds must agree to limit their expenditures to a set amount, which is adjusted each election year to account for inflation. In 1992 the spending limit for each candidate for the nominating phase of the campaign was roughly $25 million.

The National Party Conventions

National party conventions were once tumultuous affairs during which lengthy, heated bargaining took place before a presidential nominee was chosen. An extreme case was the Democratic convention of 1924, at which delegates took 103 ballots and ended up nominating an unknown "dark horse," John W. Davis. Today's conventions are relatively tame; not since 1952 has a nomination gone past the first ballot. The leading candidate has usually acquired enough delegates in the primaries and caucuses to lock up the nomination before the convention even begins. Nevertheless, the party convention is a major event. It brings together the delegates elected in state caucuses and primaries, who then vote to approve a party platform and to nominate the party's presidential and vice-presidential candidates.

Some recent conventions have been the scenes of major disputes. The strategies and issues of nominating campaigns can so alienate the losers that they cannot accept defeat gracefully. In 1968, when the Vietnam war was at issue, Democratic contender Eugene McCarthy at first refused to support the party's nominee, Hubert Humphrey, even though they were both from Minnesota and had been personal friends. However, national conventions are ordinarily occasions for cementing party unity and building bridges to party voters. As many as 150 million Americans watch part of the proceedings on national television, and for many of them it is a time of decision. About a fourth of voters solidify their presidential choice during the conventions, and most of them decide to back the nominee of their preferred party.[33]

The party conventions choose the vice-presidential nominees as well as those for president. Nomination to run for the vice-presidency was once scorned by leading politicians, including Daniel Webster and Henry Clay. Said Webster, "I do not propose to be buried until I'm really dead."[34] No politician today shares this view of the vice-presidency. Although it is a relatively powerless office, it has become the inside track to the presidency: five of the nine presidents between 1948 and 1992 were former vice-presidents (Truman, Johnson, Nixon, Ford, and Bush).

By tradition, the choice of the vice-presidential nominee rests with the presidential nominee. Critics have argued that the vice-presidential nomination should be decided in open competition, since the vice-president stands a good chance of becoming president someday. The chief argument for keeping the existing system is that the president needs a vice-president in whom he has complete confidence. Although presidential nominees always seek a running mate who will not be a liability, it does not always work out that way. In 1988, Bush's running mate, Senator Dan Quayle of Indiana, was discovered to have pulled strings to avoid the draft during the Vietnam war. Bush kept Quayle in the background during the fall campaign.

★ ANALYZE THE ISSUE

The Relative Importance of Primary and General Elections
Voter turnout is roughly 20 percentage points lower in presidential primaries than in the general election. This pattern suggests that the public regards the general election as the more important of the two—but is it? Consider the fact that the nominating races eliminate all the presidential alternatives except two, one of whom is certain to win.

THE CAMPAIGN FOR ELECTION

The winner in the November general election is almost certain to be either the Republican or the Democratic nominee. A minor-party or independent candidate, such as George Wallace in 1968, John Anderson in 1980, or Ross Perot in 1992, can draw votes away from the major-party nominees but stands almost no chance of defeating them.

A major-party nominee has the critical advantage of support from the party faithful. Earlier in the twentieth century, this support was so unwavering that the victory of the stronger party's candidate was almost a certainty. Warren G. Harding accepted the 1920 Republican nomination at his Ohio home, stayed there throughout most of the campaign, and won a landslide victory simply because most of the voters of his time were Republicans. Party loyalty has declined in recent decades, but more than two-thirds of the nation's voters still identify themselves as Democrats or Republicans, and most of them support their party's presidential candidate.[35] Even Democrat George McGovern, who

---

[33]William Flanigan and Nancy Zingale, *Political Behavior of the American Electorate*, 4th ed. (Boston: Allyn & Bacon, 1979), 172–173.
[34]Quoted in Stephen J. Wayne, *Road to the White House*, 2d ed. (New York: St. Martin's Press, 1984), 131.
[35]See Norman H. Nie, Sidney Verba, and John Petrocik, *The Changing American Voter* (Cambridge, Mass.: Harvard University Press, 1979), 48–59.

George Bush, Ross Perot, and Bill Clinton (*left to right*) take questions from citizens during the second debate of the 1992 presidential campaign, at the University of Richmond. (Reuters/Bettmann)

had the lowest level of party support among recent nominees, was backed in 1972 by nearly 60 percent of his party's voters.

Republican nominees have usually found it easier to keep their party's loyalists in line.[36] The GOP has been the more homogeneous party, and campaign appeals to traditional social values, partriotism, restrained government spending, lower taxes, and a strong defense have usually maintained the Republican vote. In 1992, however, a weak economy hurt the Republican effort. George Bush received the votes of 73 percent of Republicans, while Perot got 17 percent and Bill Clinton 10 percent. The Republican coalition has been increasingly divided over social issues. Evangelical Christians and other newer Republican groups have values that conflict with those of traditional Republican groups. Their conflict was evident at the 1992 Republican National Convention, when a platform that called for a total ban on abortions provoked debate between conservatives and moderates.

Election Strategy

Presidential candidates act strategically. In deciding whether to pursue a course of action, they try to estimate its likely impact on the voters. For incumbents and challengers alike, some of these issues will be questions of past performance. During the 1992 campaign, a sign on the wall of Clinton's headquarters in Little Rock read, "The Economy, Stupid." The slogan was the idea of James Carville, Clinton's chief strategist, and was meant as a reminder to the candidate and the staff to keep the campaign focused on the nation's sluggish economy, which ultimately was the issue that defeated Bush. As in 1980, when incumbent Jimmy Carter lost to Ronald Reagan during tough economic times, the voters were motivated largely by a desire for change.

[36]See John Kenneth White, *The New Politics of Old Values*, 2d ed. (Hanover, N.H.: University Press of New England, 1991).

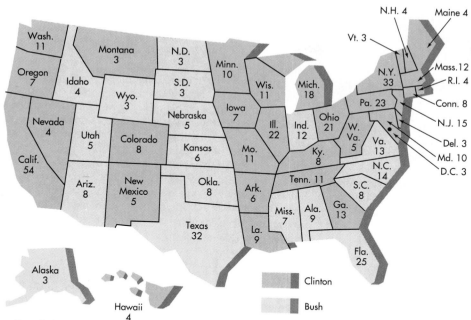

FIGURE 18-2 Electoral Votes in the Fifty States and States Carried by the Presidential Candidates in the 1992 Election The larger a state's population is, the more electoral votes it has—and the more important it is to presidential candidates. Each state's electoral votes are shown here, along with the states carried by candidates Bill Clinton and George Bush in the 1992 election. To win the presidency, a candidate must receive 270 of the national total of 538 electoral votes. Clinton won 32 states and the District of Columbia for 370 electoral votes, while Bush took 18 states and 168 electoral votes. Ross Perot did not finish first in any state and thus received no electoral votes.

Candidates try to project a strong leadership image. Whether voters accept this image, however, depends more on external factors than on a candidate's personal characteristics. In 1991, after the Persian Gulf war, Bush's approval rating reached 91 percent, the highest level recorded since polling began in the 1930s. A year later, with the Gulf war a receding memory and the nation's economy in trouble, Bush's approval rating dropped below 40 percent. Bush tried to stir images of his strong leadership of the war, but voters remained preoccupied with the economy.

The candidates' strategies are shaped by many considerations, including the constitutional provision that each state shall have electoral votes equal in number to its representation in Congress. Each state thus gets two electoral votes for its Senate representation and a varying number of electoral votes depending on its House representation. Altogether, there are 538 electoral votes (including three for the District of Columbia, even though it has no voting representatives in Congress). To win the presidency, a candidate must receive at least 270 votes, an electoral majority.

Candidates are particularly concerned with winning the most populous states, such as California (with 54 electoral votes), New York (33), Texas (32), Florida (25), Pennsylvania (23), Illinois (22), and Ohio (21). Victory in the eleven largest states alone would provide an electoral majority, and presidential candidates therefore spend most of their time campaigning in those states.[37] Because the winner of the popular vote in a state receives all of that state's electoral votes (except for Maine and Nebraska), a relatively small popular-vote margin can produce a lopsided electoral-vote margin. Clinton received only 43 percent of the popular vote in 1992, compared with Bush's 38 percent and Perot's 19 percent; but Clinton won in states that gave him an overwhelming 370 electoral votes, compared with 168 for Bush and none for Perot (see Figure 18-2).

[37]Raymond Tatalovich, "Electoral Votes and Presidential Campaign Trails, 1932–1976," *American Politics Quarterly*, October 1979, 489–498.

★ CRITICAL THINKING

WHY DID CLINTON WIN THE PRESIDENCY?

During the 1992 campaign, Bill Clinton was widening his lead in New Hampshire when Gennifer Flowers claimed in an interview with the weekly supermarket tabloid, *The Star*, that she had had a 12-year affair with the Arkansas governor. Soon thereafter *The Wall Street Journal* reported that in the 1960s Clinton had manipulated an ROTC commitment in order to avoid service in Vietnam. The candidate's own poll in New Hampshire showed a drop of 17 points in his support. At the urging of some Democratic insiders, Clinton's camp planned to quit if he finished third in New Hampshire; he placed second by a few points.

Clinton was able to remain in the race, despite these looming scandals, in part because the field of Democratic candidates was weak. Many of the strongest Democratic leaders, including Mario Cuomo of New York and Richard Gephardt of Missouri, had chosen not to run in 1992. The general view among Democrats in 1991, when potential candidates were making their decisions to run, was that George Bush was nearly unbeatable; his leadership of the Gulf war had pushed his approval rating to the highest level ever recorded for a president.

His primary-election victories on Super Tuesday enabled Clinton to reclaim the lead for the Democratic nomination. However, his pending nomination did not appear to be worth very much. He was mired in third place in the polls, trailing not only President Bush but also independent candidate Ross Perot.

Clinton got an unexpected boost on the second day of the Democratic National Convention in July: Perot announced that he was quitting the race. Within a few days, Clinton had a 25-point lead over Bush, the greatest swing in the presidential vote ever recorded by pollsters. Perot's supporters had turned overwhelmingly to Clinton. Bush's approval rating had dropped into the 40 percent range in early 1992, reflecting the public's dissatisfaction with his handling of the economy.

In the remaining months of the campaign, Perot reentered the race and Bush fought back, but Clinton never lost his lead. He won by a 5 percent margin.

Why did Clinton win in 1992? Was he just plain lucky? Would he have won his party's nomination even if Cuomo, Gephardt, and others had been in the race? Did he win the general election, or is it more accurate to say that Bush lost it?

Media and Money

The modern presidential campaign is a media campaign. Whereas candidates once relied heavily on party organization and rallies to carry their messages to the voters, they now rely on the media, particularly television. Candidates strive to produce effective "sound bites" for TV news, preparing their speeches with an eye toward including a pithy 10-second statement that the television networks will find compelling enough to highlight on the evening newscasts. In 1992, they also discovered the power of the "new media," making frequent appearances on such programs as *Larry King Live* and *The Phil Donahue Show*.

Television is the forum for the major confrontation of the fall campaign—the presidential debates. The first televised debate took place in 1960 between Kennedy and Nixon, and an estimated 100 million people saw at least one of their four debates.[38] Televised debates resumed in 1976 and have become an apparently permanent fixture of presidential campaigns. Studies indicate that presidential debates influence the votes of only a small percentage of the electorate. However, presidential elections are sometimes decided by a few percentage points, and the lesser-known candidate usually benefits more than his opponent from televised debates. In 1976 President Ford became rattled during a television debate and said that Eastern Europe was "not under the

[38]Sidney Kraus, ed., *The Great Debates* (Bloomington: Indiana University Press, 1962), 190.

domination of the Soviet Union,'' a claim that hurt his image as a master of foreign affairs and contributed to his defeat by Jimmy Carter.

In 1992 the candidate who benefited most from the exposure provided by the three televised debates was Ross Perot. He had dropped out of the race in July, but reentered in late September. His decision to quit the race was a costly one; he had stood at nearly 30 percent in the polls when he left but was at less than 10 percent when he reentered. In the debates he was disarmingly direct, folksy, and iconoclastic. He won 19 percent of the national vote, and slightly more than half of those who supported him said that his debate performance had been very important in their decision.[39]

The television campaign includes political advertising. Televised commercials are by far the most expensive part of presidential campaign politics. Since 1976, political commercials on television have accounted for about half of the candidates' expenditures in the general election campaign. Kathleen Hall Jamieson describes the role of advertising in the modern campaign as "packaging the presidency."[40] In 1922 Bush and Clinton each spent more than $30 million on advertising in the general election, and Perot spent even more. Perot relied heavily on "infomercials"—30-minute and hourlong commercials that emphasized substance over slogans.

The Republican and Democratic nominees are each eligible for a federal grant for their general election campaigns. The grant was set at $20 million in 1975 and is adjusted for inflation during each campaign. Clinton and Bush each received a grant of about $55.2 million in 1992 for their general election campaigns. The only string attached to this funding is that candidates who accept it can spend no additional funds on their campaigns (though their party can spend additional money on their behalf). Presidential candidates can choose not to accept public funding, in which case the amount they spend is limited only by their ability to raise money privately. However, all major-party nominees since 1976 have accepted public funding. Other candidates for the presidency qualify for federal funding if they receive at least 5 percent of the vote and do not spend more than $50,000 of their own money on the campaign. Perot spent over $60 million of his own money on his 1992 campaign, so he was ineligible for federal funding.

Because of the recent decline in partisanship, the uses that candidates make of money and media have more influence than they would have had in the past. As was explained in Chapter 10, most votes are not won or lost by what happens during the campaign (party loyalty and government performance are the determining factors), but the voters are more volatile than in the past. In 1992 Clinton trailed Bush in June, but he got a record bounce of 25 percent at the time of the Democratic National Convention and never fell behind again.

The Winners

The winners of all recent presidential elections, as it has been throughout the nation's history, have been white males. The great majority of presidents have been well-to-do Anglo-Saxon Protestants. Except for four army generals, no man has won the presidency who has not first held high public office (see Table

---

[39]"Perot: Eccentric Perhaps, but No Joke," *The New York Times*, November 5, 1992, p. B4.
[40]Kathleen Hall Jamieson, *Packaging the Presidency* (New York: Oxford, 1984).

★ ANALYZE THE ISSUE

The Perot Factor
Ross Perot's 19 percent of the presidential vote in 1992 was the highest total for an independent or third-party candidate since Theodore Roosevelt's 27 percent in 1912. Election-day polls indicated that Perot voters would have split evenly between Clinton and Bush if Perot had not been in the race. Some analysts believe, however, that Perot helped Clinton by focusing criticism on the Bush presidency. In addition, a significant rise in turnout, from 50 percent in 1988 to 54 percent in 1992, has been attributed in part to Perot's candidacy. In election-day polls, 14 percent of Perot voters said they would have stayed home if Perot had not been on the ballot. What influence did the Perot candidacy have on your thinking about the 1992 campaign? Do you see the possibility of a Perot candidacy in 1996?

★ ANALYZE THE ISSUE

Voter Turnout: Reversing the Trend
In 1992 voter turnout was 54 percent, which represented the first significant increase in turnout since 1960. Analysts attributed the increase to people's anger over economic conditions and the independent candidacy of Ross Perot, who appealed to people who had not voted in recent elections. From your recall of the 1992 campaign, do you accept these explanations of the increase in voter turnout? Can you think of any other reasons for the increase?

18-2). Nearly a third of the nation's presidents had previously been vice-presidents, and most of the rest were former U.S. senators, state governors, or top federal executives.

Staffing the Presidency

When Americans go to the polls on election day, they have in mind the choice between two individuals, the Democratic presidential nominee and the Republican nominee. In effect, however, they are choosing a lot more than a single executive leader. They are also picking a secretary of state, the director of the FBI, the chair of the Federal Reserve Board, and a host of other executives, all of whom are presidential appointees.

The duties of the modern presidency far exceed the capacity of one person. The president must rely on a great many other people to carry out the responsibilities of office, a situation that Thomas Cronin calls the "swelling" of the presidency.[41]

A newly elected president gains important advantages from his authority to appoint more than 2,000 assistants, experts, and administrators. First, his

TABLE 18-2   The Path to the White House for Twentieth-Century Presidents

President	Years in Office	Highest Previous Office	Second-Highest Office
William McKinley	1897–1901	Governor	U.S. representative
Theodore Roosevelt	1901–1908	Vice-president*	Governor
William Howard Taft	1909–1912	Secretary of war	Federal judge
Woodrow Wilson	1913–1920	Governor	None
Warren G. Harding	1921–1924	U.S. senator	Lieutenant governor
Calvin Coolidge	1925–1928	Vice-president*	Governor
Herbert Hoover	1929–1932	Secretary of commerce	War relief administrator
Franklin D. Roosevelt	1933–1945	Governor	Assistant secretary of navy
Harry S. Truman	1945–1952	Vice-president*	U.S. senator
Dwight D. Eisenhower	1953–1960	None (Army general)	None
John F. Kennedy	1961–1963	U.S. senator	U.S. representative
Lyndon Johnson	1963–1968	Vice-president*	U.S. senator
Richard Nixon	1969–1974	Vice-president	U.S. senator
Gerald Ford	1974–1976	Vice-president*	U.S. representative
Jimmy Carter	1977–1980	Governor	State senator
Ronald Reagan	1981–1988	Governor	None
George Bush	1989–1992	Vice-president	Director, CIA
Bill Clinton	1993–	Governor	State Attorney General

*Became president on death or resignation of incumbent.

[41]Thomas E. Cronin, *The State of the Presidency*, 2d ed. (Boston: Little, Brown, 1980), 243.

The White House contains, on the first floor, the president's Oval Office, other offices, and ceremonial rooms. The First Family's living quarters are on the second floor. (Jake McGuire)

appointees are a source of policy information. Modern policymaking depends on detailed information, and control of information is a source of considerable power. Second, the president's appointees extend his reach into the huge federal bureaucracy, helping him exert some influence on the day-to-day workings of government. Quite simply, the president puts "his people" in top positions of the executive branch. Not surprisingly, presidents have tended to appoint individuals who share their partisan views. However, the degree to which presidents have stressed partisanship has varied considerably. In his initial appointments, President Bush sought to balance the partisanship issue with his desire to put together a team of skilled managers.[42] Among recent presidents, Reagan was the most adamant about partisan loyalty as a criterion for appointment; he perceived career bureaucrats as hostile to many of his ideas and believed that he needed Republicans as conservative as himself in top positions.[43] Of Reagan's first-term appointees, 82 percent were Republicans, 15 percent were unaffiliated, and 3 percent were Democrats. By comparison, of Carter's appointees, 58 percent were fellow Democrats, 35 percent were unaffiliated, and 7 percent were Republicans.[44]

PRESIDENTIAL APPOINTEES AND THE PROBLEM OF CONTROL

Although the president's appointees are a valuable asset, they also pose a problem: because they are so numerous, they represent a challenge to his

[42]Joel D. Aberbach, "The President and the Executive Branch," in Colin Campbell and Bert A. Rockman, eds., *The Bush Presidency: First Appraisals* (Chatham, N.J.: Chatham House, 1991), 238–240.

[43]See James P. Pfiffner, *The Strategic Presidency: Hitting the Ground Running* (Chicago: Dorsey Press, 1988).

[44]Davis, *American Presidency*, 296.

Like all newly inaugurated presidents, George Bush made politically compatible appointments to positions in the executive branch. However, Bush also made an effort not to be too partisan, looking for appointees who had relevant managerial as well as political credentials. (Susan Steinkamp/SABA)

control of the presidential office. Most appointees are not under the president's direct supervision and have considerable freedom to act on their own initiative —not necessarily in accord with the president's wishes. Truman had a wall chart in the Oval Office listing more than 100 officials who reported directly to him, and often told visitors, "I cannot even see all of these men, let alone actually study what they are doing."[45] Since Truman's time the number of bureaucratic agencies has more than doubled, compounding the problem of presidential control over subordinates.

To assist him in administering the executive branch of the federal government, the president appoints the members of the organizations that make up the Executive Office of the President and the heads of the various cabinet departments. These and other presidential appointees differ in their backgrounds, proximity to the Oval Office, duties, and policy views. All these factors affect the president's ability to control their activities, as can be seen from a closer examination of who his appointees are and what they do.

The Executive Office of the President

In 1939 Congress created the Executive Office of the President (EOP) on the recommendation of a committee formed in 1936 by President Roosevelt and headed by management expert Louis Brownlow.[46] The Brownlow committee had concluded that effective functioning by the executive branch required a level of coordination that only a well-staffed presidency could provide.[47]

Since 1939 the EOP has become the command center of the executive branch[48] and is itself a small bureaucracy. It currently consists of ten organiza-

---

[45]Quoted in James MacGregor Burns, "Our Super-Government—Can We Control It?" *New York Times*, April 24, 1949, 32.
[46]Edwards and Wayne, *Presidential Leadership*, 187.
[47]Adapted from Richard P. Nathan, *The Administrative Presidency* (New York: Wiley, 1983), 36. Based on *Report of the President's Committee on Administrative Management* (Washington, D.C., January 1973).
[48]Davis, *American Presidency*, 240.

FORMAL AND INFORMAL REQUIREMENTS FOR BECOMING PRESIDENT

Formal Requirements. Article II of the U.S. Constitution requires a president to be:
• at least thirty-five years old
• a natural-born U.S. citizen
• a resident in the United States for at least fourteen years
Informal Requirements. In the nation's history, presidents have been:
• male, without exception
• white, without exception

• Protestant, with the exception of John F. Kennedy
• married, with the exceptions of James Buchanan and Grover Cleveland (who married in the White House)
• career public servants—four were army generals, thirteen were vice-presidents (seven succeeded upon a president's death, one upon a president's resignation), eight were federal administrators, and the remainder were U.S. senators, U.S. representatives (only one), or state governors.

tions (see Figure 18-3). The leading ones are the White House Office (WHO), which consists of the president's closest personal advisers; the Office of Management and Budget (OMB), which consists of experts who formulate and then administer the federal budget; the National Security Council (NSC), which assists the president on foreign and military affairs; and the Council of Economic Advisers (CEA), which advises the president on the national economy.[49] The Office of the Vice-President is also part of the EOP.

The Vice-President.   Although the vice-president works in the White House, he is not necessarily a member of the president's inner circle of advisers. The Constitution assigns the vice-president no policy authority. Accordingly, whether the vice-president plays a large or small role is the president's choice. Jimmy Carter gave Walter Mondale more responsibility than any previous

[49]Hugh Heclo, ''The Changing Presidential Office,'' in Arnold J. Meltsner, ed., *Politics and the Oval Office* (San Francisco: Institute for Contemporary Studies, 1981), 163.

FIGURE 18-3 Executive Office of the President
The Executive Office of the President acts as the president's personal bureaucracy, helping him to manage the rest of the executive branch.

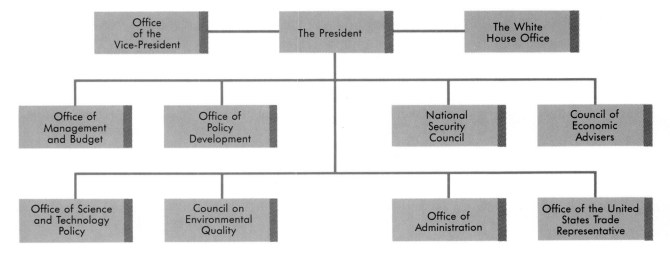

White House chief of staff John Sununu performed valuable services for President Bush, but he was forced to resign after months of reports about his high-handedness with colleagues and his use of government vehicles for personal travel. (AP/Wide World)

vice-president had received, and Mondale served as one of Carter's confidants. George Bush was given fewer duties than Mondale, but he played a substantial role in the Reagan administration as a liaison with Congress and as chair of the crisis-management team within the National Security Council. When he became president, Bush gave Dan Quayle many of the duties he had performed during his vice-presidency. Quayle became head of the National Space Council, which makes recommendations on the space program, and chair of the President's Council on Competitiveness, which reviews federal regulations that affect business.

Earlier vice-presidents played smaller roles. Many of them were selected for their ability to attract votes rather than because of their close association with the president. Lyndon Johnson was Senate majority leader before becoming John Kennedy's vice-president and was selected because Kennedy believed that he would not win the presidency unless he carried Texas, Johnson's home state. As vice-president, Johnson was given few tasks and responsibilities, playing second fiddle to Kennedy's personal advisers, such as Ted Sorensen and McGeorge Bundy.

Presidential Assistants.   Of the EOP's ten organizations, the White House Office serves the president most directly and personally. The WHO consists of the president's personal assistants, including his close personal advisers, press agents, legislative and group liaison aides, and special assistants for domestic and international policy. They work in the White House, and the president can hire and fire them at will. Total loyalty to the president is expected of these staff members.

The president's personal assistants do much of his legwork for him and serve as his main source of advice. Because of their closeness and loyalty to the president, they are among the most powerful individuals in Washington. They are not expert advisers in the sense of having studied or worked for years in a specialized policy field, but they typically have political experience. When George Bush took office, he appointed John Sununu as his top White House assistant. Sununu had been governor of New Hampshire for six years. Before becoming Bush's chief of staff, he had headed Bush's victorious New Hampshire primary campaign, which was widely seen as the turning point in Bush's drive toward the 1988 Republican nomination.

Although no modern president could function effectively without his close assistants, they can also cause problems. In trying to conserve the president's time or their own influence with him, they may withhold views or information that he could use. At times advisers have also presumed to undertake important initiatives without first obtaining the president's approval, leading others to question whether he is actually in charge of his office.[50] Finally, some advisers are arrogant in the use of their power. Sununu was forced to resign in 1991 because his high-handed methods had alienated dozens of White House staffers and members of Congress.

Policy Experts. The president is also served by the policy experts in the EOP's other organizations, who include economists, legal analysts, national security specialists, and others. Modern policymaking cannot be conducted in the absence of such expert advice and knowledge. For example, the president has broad responsibilities for guiding the nation's economy. Advising him in this effort is the Council of Economic Advisers, headed by three economists who are assisted by an expert staff. The CEA gathers information to develop indicators of the economy's strength and applies economic theories to various policy alternatives. In the early 1960s the CEA chairman, Walter Heller, advised President Kennedy to propose a cut in business taxes as a means of bringing the nation's economy out of a recession. Kennedy accepted Heller's advice, persuaded Congress to enact the legislation, and gained public support when the economy rebounded.

The advantages of having expert advice are sometimes offset by the fact that many policy specialists have a narrow view of the nation's priorities. They may think that problems in their policy area are of utmost urgency, and they tend to believe that their preferred solutions are the only satisfactory ones. This outlook does not always serve the president's needs. Proposing "the best policy solution" means little if Congress finds it politically unacceptable.

These experts constitute another group that makes demands on the president's attention. Cecil Crabb and Kevin Mulcahy's study of the National Security Council, for example, concluded that the NSC complicates foreign policy decision making "by generating confusion about who is really in charge of American foreign policy."[51] Is the State Department or the NSC at the center of foreign policy? The infighting between State and NSC has worked against the team effort that presidents seek from their appointees.

The President's Cabinet

The heads of the fourteen executive departments, such as the Department of Defense and the Department of Agriculture, constitute the president's **cabinet.** They are appointed by the president, subject to confirmation by Congress.

---

[50]Stephen Hess, *Organizing the Presidency* (Washington, D.C.: Brookings Institution, 1976), 162–163.
[51]Cecil V. Crabb, Jr., and Kevin V. Mulcahy, *Presidents and Foreign Policy Making* (Baton Rouge: University of Louisiana Press, 1986), 81.

The cabinet is a tradition but has no formal authority, because the Constitution says nothing about it. When Abraham Lincoln was once unanimously opposed by his cabinet, he said, "Seven nays and one aye—the ayes have it." Although the cabinet once served as the president's main advisory group, it has not played this role since Herbert Hoover's administration. Dwight D. Eisenhower tried in the 1950s to restore the cabinet to its former prominence, but he eventually gave up. As national issues have become increasingly complex, the cabinet has become outmoded as a policymaking forum: department heads are likely to understand issues only in their respective policy areas.[52] Cabinet meetings have been largely reduced to gatherings at which only the most general matters are discussed.

Although the cabinet as a collective decisionmaking body is a thing of the past, the cabinet members, as individuals who head major departments, are important figures in any administration. They understand that their first responsibility is to carry out the president's instructions. Nevertheless, the president chooses most of them for their prominence in politics, business, government, or the professions. They may also bring to their office a high level of policy expertise and a group commitment.[53] For example, the secretary of commerce is normally a prominent business leader committed to the business community's goals. The loyalty of cabinet secretaries can be split between their commitment to the president and their concern for interests represented by their departments.[54] Their stature and ideas can sometimes lead them to act too independently. President Carter believed that he had no choice in 1978 but to fire Joseph Califano, his secretary of health, education, and welfare, for disloyalty after Califano had repeatedly expressed disagreement with Carter's policies in statements to reporters and members of Congress.

Other Presidential Appointees

In addition to cabinet secretaries, the president appoints the directors and top deputies of federal agencies, members of federal commissions, and heads of regulatory agencies. Although they work for the president, these appointees do not always serve the president's interests as fully as might be expected. Even top appointees sometimes come to adopt the perspective of the bureaucratic organizations in which they work. They may be "captured" by their organization because they spend nearly all their time on its activities and depend heavily on the expertise of career bureaucrats. About 70 percent of presidential appointees have two years or less of federal government experience, and most are less familiar with agency activities than are the careerists who work under them.[55]

If presidential appointees are to influence career bureaucrats, they must gain their confidence. However, career bureaucrats are likely to be more committed

---

[52]R. Gordon Hoxie, "The Cabinet in the American Presidency, 1789–1984," *Presidential Studies Quarterly*, Spring 1984, 226–228.
[53]See Jeffrey E. Cohen, *The Politics of the United States Cabinet* (Pittsburgh: University of Pittsburgh Press, 1988).
[54]Richard F. Fenno, Jr., *The President's Cabinet* (Cambridge, Mass.: Harvard University Press, 1959), 218.
[55]Hugh Heclo, *A Government of Strangers: Executive Politics in Washington* (Washington, D.C.: Brookings Institution, 1977), 161.

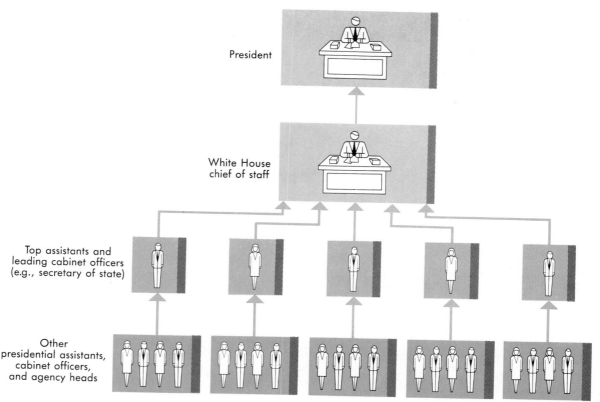

President

White House chief of staff

Top assistants and leading cabinet officers (e.g., secretary of state)

Other presidential assistants, cabinet officers, and agency heads

to their agencies' goals than to the president's.[56] The civil service system protects careerists, so they cannot easily be removed from their positions even if they work against the president's objectives. To gain their cooperation, presidential appointees must achieve a working compromise between the president's goals and those of the bureaucratic organizations. Such delicate maneuvering requires managerial skills that many inexperienced appointees lack. Chapters 20 and 21 examine more closely the relationship between presidential appointees and career bureaucrats.

ORGANIZING THE EXTENDED PRESIDENCY

Effective use of appointees by the president requires two-way communication. The president cannot possibly meet regularly with all his appointees or personally oversee their activities. Yet if he is to be in control, he must receive essential advice from his subordinates and have means of communicating his views to them.

Presidents have relied on a variety of techniques to regulate the flow of information to and from the Oval Office. One arrangement, used by Eisenhower, Nixon, Reagan, and Bush, resembles the way the military and most corporations are organized. It places the president at the top of an organizational pyramid and his personal assistants, each of whom is assigned specific responsibilities, at the next levels (see Figure 18-4). All information and

FIGURE 18-4 Managing the Presidency: The Pyramid (Hierarchical) Form of Organization
In the pyramid form that some presidents have used to organize their staffs, information and recommendations that lower-level advisers wish to communicate to the president must be transmitted through—and thus "filtered" by—first top-level aides and then the White House chief of staff.

[56]Joel D. Aberbach and Bert A. Rockman, "Clashing Beliefs within the Executive Branch," *American Political Science Review* 70 (June 1976): 461.

★ HOW THE UNITED STATES COMPARES

HEADS OF STATE AND HEADS OF GOVERNMENT

Most democracies divide the executive office between a head of state, who is the ceremonial leader, and a head of government, who is the policy leader. In Great Britain these positions are filled by the queen and the prime minister, respectively. In democracies without a hereditary monarchy, the position of head of state is usually held by an individual chosen by the legislature. Germany's head of state, for example, is a president, who is elected by the Federal Assembly; the head of government is a chancellor, who is chosen by the majority party in the lower house (Bundestag) of the Federal Assembly. The United States is one of a few countries in which the roles of head of state and head of government are combined in a single office, the presidency. The major disadvantage of this arrangement is that the president must devote considerable time to ceremonial functions, such as hosting dinners for visiting heads of state. The major advantages are that the president alone is the center of national attention and that his power as head of government is enhanced by his prestige as the personification of the American state.

Country	Head of State	Head of Government
Canada	Governor general (representative of the British monarch)	Prime minister
France	President	Premier
Germany	President	Chancellor
Great Britain	Queen	Prime minister
Italy	President	Prime minister
Japan	Emperor	Prime minister
Mexico	President	President
Sweden	King	Prime minister
United States	President	President

recommendations from lower levels must be submitted to these top aides, who decide whether the reports should be forwarded to the president. This hierarchical arrangement, with its multiple levels of supervision, permits more effective control of subordinates. The pyramid form of organization also has the advantage of freeing the president from the need to deal with the many minor issues that reach the White House.

A major disadvantage of the pyramid form is the danger that presidential advisers will make decisions themselves that should be passed along for the president to make. Another disadvantage is that the pyramid form can result in misdirected or blocked information.[57] The president may be denied access to opinions that his close advisers decide are wrong or unimportant. The risk is that he will not be able to take important views and facts into account as he makes his policy decisions, so that they are more likely to prove ineffective.[58]

A second approach to staff organization was developed by Franklin D. Roosevelt and adapted by Presidents Kennedy, Johnson, Ford, and Carter. Each placed himself at the center of the organization, accessible to a fairly large number of advisers (see Figure 18-5). This "hub-of-the-wheel" (or circular) form allows more information to reach the president and provides him with a greater range of options and opinions. Roosevelt and Kennedy were particularly adept at operating within this organizational framework; each surrounded himself with talented advisers and knew how to make them work together as a team even while they generated competing ideas.

[57]Richard T. Johnson, *Managing the White House* (New York: Harper & Row, 1974), 238.
[58]See Irving Janis, *Victims of Groupthink* (Boston: Houghton Mifflin, 1972).

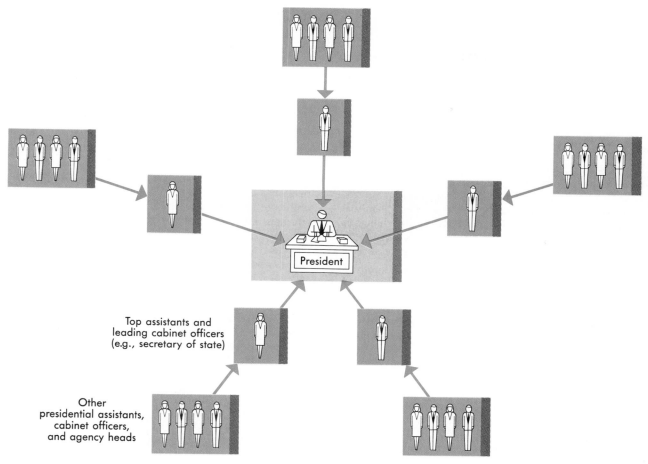

Top assistants and
leading cabinet officers
(e.g., secretary of state)

Other
presidential assistants,
cabinet officers,
and agency heads

FIGURE 18-5 Managing the Presidency: The Hub-of-the-Wheel (Circular) Form of Organization
In the hub-of-the-wheel form of organization, the president is at the center of a circle composed of a fairly large number of top-level aides, each of whom has direct access to the president. Lower-level advisers have correspondingly closer access to the president than they do in the pyramidal form.

Unfortunately, this system encourages personal rivalries. As assistants vie for the president's attention and for control of policy areas, their competition can undermine the team effort the president is looking for. Moreover, the president may become so overloaded with staff opinions that he loses sight of larger issues. This criticism was often leveled at President Carter; it was said that Carter knew the details of every policy issue but had difficulty establishing priorities and placing policies in the broader context that leads to effective action. Carter himself came to recognize that his hub-of-the-wheel organization was overloading him with detail, and he changed to a more hierarchically organized staff; the results, however, were not notably different.

Ultimately, the problem of presidential control is beyond an organizational solution.[59] The president's responsibilities are so broad that he cannot do the job without hundreds of assistants whom it is impossible for him to supervise directly no matter how he organizes them. The modern presidency is thus a double-edged sword. Today's president has greater responsibilities than his

[59]See Peri E. Arnold, *Making the Managerial Presidency: Comprehensive Reorganization Planning* (Princeton, N.J.: Princeton University Press, 1986).

predecessors, and the increase in his responsibilities expands his opportunities to exert power. At the same time, the range of these responsibilities is so broad that he must rely on staffers who may or may not act in his best interests. The modern president's recurring problem is to find some way of making sure that his aides serve his interests above all others. The subject of presidential control of the executive branch will be discussed further in Chapters 20 and 21.

Summary

The presidency has become a much stronger office than the Framers envisioned. The Constitution grants the president substantial military, diplomatic, legislative, and executive powers, and in each case the president's authority has increased measurably. Underlying this change is the president's position as the one leader chosen by the whole nation. The public's support and expectations underlie presidential claims of broad authority.

National crises have contributed to the growth of presidential power. The public looks to the president during national emergencies, in part because Congress is poorly suited to the decisive and continuous action that emergencies require. Changing world and national conditions have also enhanced the presidency. These changes have placed new and greater demands on the federal government, demands that the president is in some ways better able than Congress to meet.

The nation has had four systems of presidential selection. The first centered on Congress and the Electoral College, the second on party conventions, the third on a convention system with some state primaries, and the current one on state primaries and open caucuses as the dominant method of choosing presidential nominees. Each succeeding system has been more "democratic" in that it was designed to give the public greater influence in the choice of the president and thus to make the selection more legitimate.

To gain nomination, a strong showing in the early primaries is necessary because news coverage and other resources flow toward winning candidates. This momentum is a critical factor in nominating races but normally benefits a candidate who by virtue of past record, stands on issues, ideology, or other factors already is in the strongest position to win nomination. Once nominated, the major-party candidates receive federal funds for the general election campaign; much of this money is spent on televised political advertising. The candidates themselves spend their time traveling around the nation, concentrating on the states with large numbers of electoral votes and trying to get favorable coverage from the journalists who follow their every move. The Democratic nominee should have the advantage in the general election because the Democrats are the nation's majority party, but the Republicans have benefited from the fact that the Democratic coalition has often come unraveled in presidential elections during the past two decades.

Although the campaign tends to personalize the presidency, the responsibilities of the modern presidency far exceed any president's personal capacities. To meet their obligations, presidents have surrounded themselves with large staffs of advisers, policy experts, and managers. These staff members enable the president to extend control over the executive branch while providing him with the information necessary for policymaking. All recent presidents have discovered, however, that their control of staff resources is incomplete and that some things that others do on their behalf actually work against what they are trying to accomplish.

Major Concepts

cabinet
legitimacy (of election)
momentum

open party caucuses
stewardship theory (of the presidency)
Whig theory (of the presidency)

Suggested Readings

Arnold, Peri E. *Making the Managerial Presidency: Comprehensive Reorganization Planning.* Princeton, N.J.: Princeton University Press, 1986. Suggests that the very notion of a managerial presidency creates expectations of the office that cannot be met.

Campbell, Colin, and Bert A. Rockman, eds. *The Bush Presidency.* Chatham, N.J.: Chatham House, 1991. An early appraisal of the Bush administration.

Ceaser, James W. *Presidential Selection: Theory and Development.* Princeton, N.J.: Princeton University Press, 1979. A historical review of the philosophy and practice of presidential selection.

Crabb, Cecil V., Jr., and Kevin V. Mulcahy. *Presidents and Foreign Policy Making.* Baton Rouge: Louisiana State University Press, 1986. An analysis of the impact of bureaucratic growth on policymaking, focusing on the foreign policy area during the years from Roosevelt to Reagan.

Davis, James W. *The American Presidency.* New York: Harper & Row, 1987. A highly readable and comprehensive overview of the modern presidency.

Natoli, Marie D. *American Prince, American Pauper: The Contemporary Vice Presidency in Perspective.* Westport, Conn.: Greenwood Press, 1985. A look at the modern vice-presidency.

Orren, Gary R., and Nelson W. Polsby, eds. *Media and Momentum: The New Hampshire Primary and Nomination Politics.* Chatham, N.J.: Chatham House, 1987. An evaluation of the New Hampshire primary and its impact on presidential nominations.

Patterson, Thomas E. *The Mass Media Election.* New York: Praeger, 1980. A study of the news media's coverage of a presidential campaign and the voters' response to this coverage.

Pfiffner, James P. *The Strategic Presidency: Hitting the Ground Running.* Chicago: Dorsey Press, 1988. An analysis of how a newly elected president can convert electoral support into power in office.

PRESIDENTIAL POLICYMAKING: ELICITING SUPPORT

The president's job in the constitutional system is not to lead a followership; it is to elicit leadership from the other institutions of self-government and help make that leadership effective.

Hugh Heclo[1]

President Ronald Reagan was riding high after being reelected by a landslide in 1984. He was being likened in power and popularity to Franklin D. Roosevelt, another president who had come into office during hard economic times and had gained broad support on the strength of his policy initiatives, personal confidence, and communication skills. During his first year and a half as president, Reagan's popularity plummeted, but, as the U.S. economy began to recover in late 1982, his public support steadily rose. In 1984 he was reelected by a landslide. By the end of 1986, however, the Reagan presidency was in trouble. Reagan had put his reputation on the line in the fall's congressional election by campaigning hard on behalf of Republican Senate candidates, only to see a ten-seat shift toward the Democrats that gave them a majority in the Senate. A few weeks later the White House was engulfed in the Iran-Contra scandal. And then there was the gloomy economic picture: a record national debt, a record trade deficit, and an unemployment rate stalled at 7 percent. The opinion of many Washington insiders was that Reagan had become a lame-duck president who would serve his remaining two years without notable accomplishments or distinction. The next year was a troubled one for Reagan, but he then successfully negotiated a strategic arms limitation agreement with the Soviet Union and, during his last year in office, his popularity was again very high.

The Reagan story is but one in the saga of the ups and downs of the modern presidency. Lyndon Johnson's and Richard Nixon's dogged pursuit of the Vietnam war led to talk of "the imperial presidency," an office so powerful that constitutional checks and balances were no longer an effective constraint on it.[2] Within a few years, because of the undermining effects of Watergate and of changing international conditions during the Ford and Carter presidencies, the

---

[1] Hugh Heclo, "Introduction: The Presidential Illusion," in Hugh Heclo and Lester M. Salamon, eds., *The Illusion of Presidential Government* (Boulder, Colo.: Westview Press, 1981), 2.
[2] Arthur M. Schlesinger, Jr., *The Imperial Presidency* (Boston: Houghton Mifflin, 1973).

watchword was "the imperiled presidency," an office too weak to meet the nation's demands for executive leadership.[3] Reagan's policy successes before 1986 renewed talk heard in the Roosevelt and Kennedy years of "a heroic presidency," an office that is the inspirational center of American politics.[4] George Bush's handling of the Gulf crisis—leading the nation into a major war and emerging from it with the highest public approval rating ever recorded for a president—bolstered the heroic conception of the office.

No other political institution has been subject to such varying characterizations as the modern presidency. One reason is that the formal powers of the office are somewhat limited, and thus presidential power changes with national conditions, political circumstances, and the office's occupant. The American presidency is always a *central* office in that the president is constantly a focus of national attention. Yet the presidency is not an inherently powerful office in the sense that presidents always get what they want. Presidential power is conditional. It depends on the president's personal capacity but even more on the circumstances—on whether the situation demands strong leadership and whether the political support for that leadership exists. When conditions are favorable, the president will appear to be almost invincible. When conditions are adverse, the president will seem vulnerable. This chapter examines the correlates of presidential success and failure in policymaking, focusing on the following main points:

★ *Presidential influence on national policy is highly variable.* Whether a president succeeds or fails in getting his policies enacted depends heavily on the force of circumstance, the stage of his presidency, his partisan support in Congress, and the foreign or domestic nature of the policy issue.

★ *The president's election by national vote and his position as sole chief executive ensure that others will listen to his ideas; but, to lead effectively, he must have the help of other officials and, to get their help, must respond to their interests as they respond to his.*

★ *The president often finds it difficult to maintain the high level of public support that gives force to his leadership.* The American people have unreasonably high expectations of the president and tend to blame him for national problems.

Factors in Presidential Leadership

At times presidents can make critical decisions on their own authority.[5] In December 1989 George Bush met secretly with his top advisers to plan a military action that would topple the Panamanian dictator Manuel Noriega. Bush decided on an invasion by U.S. army and marine units, supported by

[3]See Thomas Franck, ed., *The Tethered Presidency* (New York: New York University Press, 1981); Richard M. Pious, *The American Presidency* (New York: Basic Books, 1979); Harold M. Barger, *The Impossible Presidency* (Glenview, Ill.: Scott, Foresman, 1984); George Reedy, *The Twilight of the Presidency* (New York: New American Library, 1970).
[4]See Grant McConnell, *The Modern Presidency* (New York: St. Martin's Press, 1967); Clinton Rossiter, *The American Presidency* (New York: Harcourt, Brace & World, 1960).
[5]George C. Edwards III and Stephen J. Wayne, *Presidential Leadership: Politics and Policy Making* (New York: St. Martin's Press, 1985), 291.

American troops move through Panama City in 1989 on the orders of President George Bush, acting as commander in chief of the armed forces. Undertaking such short-term military actions without the formal consent of Congress is legal under the War Powers Act. (A. Tannenbaum/ Sygma)

helicopter gunships and armored vehicles. After he gave the final orders for the invasion, he headed off to a Christmas party. Not until the party was over, and the troops had started to deploy, did Bush inform congressional leaders that the United States would invade Panama within hours.

Such dramatic initiatives as Bush's invasion of Panama suggest that presidents regularly have the power of command. In fact, however, such unilateral policymaking is uncommon. The president operates within a system of separate institutions that share power. Thus significant presidential action normally depends on the approval of Congress, the cooperation of the bureaucracy, and sometimes the acceptance of the judiciary. Since other officials have their own priorities, the president does not always get his way. His responsibility to initiate and coordinate policy places him at the center of attention, but other institutions have the authority that can make his leadership effective. Congress in particular —more than the courts or the bureaucracy—holds the key to presidential success. Without congressional authorization and funding, most presidential proposals are nothing but ideas, empty of substance. Theodore Roosevelt expressed a wish that he could "be the president and Congress, too," if only for a day, so that he would have the power to enact as well as propose policies.

Given that the president must elicit support from others if he is to succeed, what is the record of presidential success? One way to judge is to measure the extent to which Congress backs legislation on which the president has taken a stand. By this indicator, presidents are reasonably successful (see Figure 19-1). Congress has agreed with the president in more than 50 percent of its votes in most years of recent decades. The low year was 1987, when only 45 percent of the proposals backed by Reagan won congressional approval. Another low point was 1990, when Congress agreed with George Bush on only 47 percent of legislative issues.[6] The high point of presidential-congressional agreement was

[6]George Hager, "Bush's Success Rate Sinks to Near-Record Low," *Congressional Quarterly Weekly Report,* vol. 48, no. 51, December 22, 1990, 1484.

Percentage of bills on which Congress
supported president's position

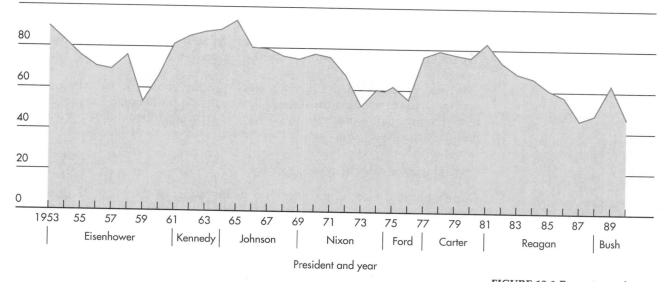

President and year

1965, when Lyndon Johnson's positions coincided with Congress's votes in 93 percent of cases.[7]

A tougher test of presidential success is the proportion of White House initiatives that are enacted by Congress. It is one thing for a president to take a

[7]*Congressional Quarterly Almanac, 1983* (Washington, D.C.: Congressional Quarterly Press, 1984), 19C.

FIGURE 19-1 Percentage of Bills Passed by Congress on Which the President Announced a Position, 1953–1990

In most years the president has been supported by Congress on a majority of policy issues on which he has taken a stand. *Source:* Congressional Quarterly Weekly, *December 22, 1990, 4185.*

President Lyndon Johnson addresses a joint session of Congress in 1965. Johnson had an extraordinary record of success with Congress, which adopted the great majority of his legislative proposals. (René Burri/Magnum)

stand on a bill that is already before Congress, but quite another thing for the president to develop a legislative proposal and then see Congress enact it into law. No president has come close to getting enactment of all the programs that he placed before Congress. The average success rate is just below 50 percent, but there has been wide variation.[8] Johnson saw 69 percent of his 1965 initiatives enacted, whereas Nixon attained only 20 percent in 1973. Moreover, presidents have had markedly less success on their more ambitious proposals than on lesser ones.[9]

Whether a president's initiatives are likely to succeed or fail depends on several factors, including the force of circumstance, the stage of the president's term, the president's partisan support in Congress, and the foreign or domestic nature of the policy proposal. Let us examine each of these factors.

THE FORCE OF CIRCUMSTANCE

During his first months in office and in the midst of the Great Depression, Franklin D. Roosevelt accomplished the most sweeping changes in domestic policy in the nation's history. Congress moved quickly to pass nearly every New Deal initiative he proposed. In 1964 and 1965 Lyndon Johnson pushed landmark civil rights and social-welfare legislation through Congress on the strength of the civil rights movement, the legacy of the assassinated President Kennedy, and large Democratic majorities in the House and Senate. When Reagan assumed the presidency in 1981, high unemployment and inflation had greatly weakened the national economy and created a mood for significant change, which enabled Reagan to persuade Congress to enact some of the most drastic taxing and spending laws in history.

From presidencies such as these has come the popular impression that presidents singlehandedly decide national policy. However, each of these periods of presidential dominance was marked by a special set of circumstances: a decisive election victory that gave added force to the president's leadership, a compelling national problem that convinced Congress and the public that bold presidential action was needed, and a president who was mindful of what was expected and who vigorously advocated policies consistent with those expectations.

When conditions are favorable, the power of the presidency appears awesome. The problem for most presidents is that conditions are not normally conducive to strong leadership. The political scientist Erwin Hargrove suggests that presidential influence depends largely on circumstance.[10] Some presidents serve in periods when important problems are surfacing in American society but have not yet become critical. Such a situation, Hargrove contends, produces a "president of preparation," who opens the way for major policy changes but is no longer in office by the time the change is made. Kennedy was one such president; he recognized that federal intervention would be necessary to bring social justice to black Americans, but because conditions were unfavorable, he

[8]George C. Edwards III, *Presidential Influence in Congress* (San Francisco: W. H. Freeman, 1980), 14.
[9]Robert J. Spitzer, "The Presidency and Public Policy," *Political Science Quarterly,* Fall 1979, 441–457.
[10]Erwin Hargrove, *The Power of the Modern Presidency* (New York: Knopf, 1974).

★ CRITICAL THINKING

IS A PRESIDENT'S "CHARACTER" AN ESSENTIAL COMPONENT OF HIS SUCCESS?

Because the presidential office is vested in a single individual, a president's personal traits are often claimed to have a profound effect on his performance. In a widely discussed book, *The Presidential Character*, the political scientist James David Barber suggests that a president's orientation toward power ("active" or "passive," in Barber's terms) and politics ("positive" or "negative") affects his capacity to lead.

In Barber's view, "active" presidents are more effective than "passive" presidents. Active presidents have a drive to lead and succeed. They devote great energy to the presidency, apply its power fully, and have clear objectives in mind. Passive presidents feel less need to take command. They do not work so hard, are more willing to accept the direction of others, and do not make full use of the office's resources. Barber also regards "positive" presidents as more effective than "negative" presidents. Positive presidents thrive on the give-and-take, the limelight, and the thrill of victory that politics can offer. In contrast, negative presidents are driven by an inner compulsion or sense of duty rather than by enjoyment of politics.

If a president is to succeed fully in the open-ended struggle for power in Washington, Barber claims, he must be aggressive in his pursuit of goals and must relish political maneuvering—that is, he must be active-positive. In fact, the presidents that Barber classifies as active-positive have tended to be more successful than any others. Franklin D. Roosevelt is Barber's archetypical active-positive president. He relished politics and was tireless in his pursuit of his policy agenda. Harry Truman and John Kennedy are other presidents whom Barber has classified as active-positives. Each was dogged in his pursuit of policy goals, tireless in his attempts to master the presidential office, and energized by the political maneuvering required to get others to accept his leadership.

As for Barber's other categories, he regards active-negative presidents as potentially the most dangerous. Although they are active in their drive to succeed, their negative traits of compulsiveness and distaste for the routines of politics can result in confrontation, stalemate, or deviousness. Barber places Woodrow Wilson and Richard Nixon in this category. In Wilson's case, unyielding self-righteousness led to a fight with the Senate over joining the League of Nations that destroyed his physical and emotional health and ended in bitter defeat. As for Nixon, his personal insecurity and unwillingness to accept the legitimacy of opposing views led him to develop an "enemies list" and poisoned the atmosphere in the White House, fostering wrongdoing by subordinates and culminating in the Watergate scandal.

Passive presidents, whether of the positive or negative type, are less likely to get into political trouble but are also less likely to achieve. Calvin Coolidge (passive-negative) decided not to seek a second term. He was relieved to be free of the office, which he had taken upon President Warren Harding's death out of a sense of duty rather than a love of politics or a desire to achieve policy goals.

What is your view of the active-passive and positive-negative dimensions of presidential character? Do you accept Barber's conclusion that active-positive presidents are the most likely to succeed? What problems are such presidents likely to encounter? Do you agree with Barber's classification of the individual presidents who were mentioned? Which ones might you classify differently, and why?

SOURCE: James David Barber, *The Presidential Character: Predicting Performance in the White House*, 3d ed. (Englewood Cliffs, N.J.: Prentice-Hall, 1985).

could not get Congress to act. The legislation was passed after his death, when Lyndon Johnson was president. Johnson is an example of what Hargrove calls a "president of achievement." Such a president is likely to have an activist view of his office, but a more crucial factor is that he serves at a time when other leaders and the public are generally agreed on a compelling issue, such as the need for civil rights legislation. This climate of opinion enables the president, if he seizes the moment, to achieve great success. Finally, there is the "president of

Presidential Greatness
A perennial question is
whether the president shapes
events or is shaped by them.
What does history suggest to
you about the general
question of presidential
greatness?

consolidation," who by personal inclination and circumstance solidifies past achievements. One such president was Dwight D. Eisenhower, who proposed few innovative policies of his own but did consolidate the policy changes accomplished two decades earlier under Franklin Roosevelt, a president of achievement.

Of course, presidents have some control over their fate. Through effective leadership they can sometimes rally the public and Congress behind goals that they believe are important. In general, however, presidential achievement is heavily dependent on circumstance. Had Franklin Roosevelt been elected in 1960 rather than 1932, his place in American history would be very different and probably much less conspicuous. Roosevelt's genius lay in the devising of extraordinary policies, not in the creation of conditions that led to their acceptance.

THE STAGE OF THE PRESIDENT'S TERM

If conditions conducive to great accomplishments occur infrequently, it is nonetheless the case that nearly every president has favorable moments. Such moments tend to come during the first months in office. A newly elected president enjoys a "honeymoon" period during which Congress, the press, and the public expect him to propose programs and are predisposed to support them.[11] During George Bush's first 100 days as president, for example, his news coverage on network television was 61 percent positive, after which the positive evaluations dropped below 50 percent.[12]

Not surprisingly, presidents have put forth more new programs in their first year in office than in any subsequent year.[13] James Pfiffner uses the term "strategic presidency" to refer to a president's need to move quickly to take advantage of the policy momentum that is gained from the election.[14] Later in their terms, presidents tend to do less well in presenting initiatives and getting them enacted.[15] They may run out of good ideas or, more likely, deplete their political resources—the momentum of their election is gone and sources of opposition have emerged. Furthermore, if the president blunders or conditions turn sour—and it is hard for a president to serve for any length of time without a serious setback of one kind or another—he will lose some of his credibility and public support. Even highly successful presidents tend to have weak records in their final years. Franklin Roosevelt began his presidency with a remarkable period of achievement—the celebrated "Hundred Days"—but during his last six years in office, few of his major domestic proposals were enacted.

An irony of the presidency, then, is that presidents are most powerful when

[11]See Charles McCall, "Political Parties and Popular Government," in George J. Graham, Jr., and Scarlett G. Graham, *Founding Principles of American Government* (Chatham, N.J.: Chatham House, 1984), 299; Stephen J. Wayne, *The Road to the White House*, 2d ed. (New York: St. Martin's Press, 1984), 264.
[12]"The Honeymoon Is Over," *Media Monitor*, vol. III, no. 10 (December 1989): 3.
[13]Paul C. Light, *The President's Agenda* (Baltimore: Johns Hopkins University Press, 1982), 41–45.
[14]James P. Pfiffner, *The Strategic Presidency: Hitting the Ground Running* (Chicago: Dorsey Press, 1988).
[15]See Darrell M. West, *Congress and Economic Policymaking* (Pittsburgh: University of Pittsburgh Press, 1987).

they are least knowledgeable—during their first months in office. These months can, as a result, be times of risk as well as times of opportunity. An example is the Bay of Pigs fiasco during the first year of John Kennedy's presidency, in which a U.S.-backed invasion force of anticommunist Cubans was easily defeated by Fidel Castro's army.

THE PRESIDENT'S PARTISAN SUPPORT IN CONGRESS

The fact that they represent separate state or district constituencies can place individual members of Congress at odds with one another as well as with the president, whose constituency is a national one. Representatives of urban and rural areas, wealthier and poorer communities, and different regions of the country have conflicting views on some policy issues. To succeed, the president must convince enough members of Congress that their disparate interests can be reconciled with his singular purpose.

No source of division is more important to presidential success than partisanship. The fact that the president does or does not belong to the same party as the House and the Senate majorities and the absolute sizes of those majorities are crucial factors. Between 1952 and 1992, each Republican president—Eisenhower, Nixon, Ford, Reagan, and Bush—had to contend with a Democratic majority in one or both houses of Congress. Congress passed a smaller percentage of the initiatives proposed by each of these presidents than by any Democratic president of the period—Kennedy, Johnson, or Carter.[16]

Democratic presidents have not always had an easy time with Congress, either. The chief obstacle has been southern Democrats, who tend to be more conservative than congressional Democrats from other regions and thus more likely to break party ranks and vote with their Republican colleagues. Even Jimmy Carter, who was from the South himself, had appreciably less support from his fellow southern Democrats. In 1978, for example, his legislative positions were supported by an average of only 50 percent of southern congressional Democrats, compared with nearly 70 percent of congressional Democrats from other regions.[17] On such issues as social welfare and individual rights, southern Democrats have frequently combined with Republicans (in the "conservative coalition") to block many of the legislative initiatives of Democratic presidents. Over the past two decades, a majority of Republicans and a majority of southern Democrats have voted together on about a fifth of all congressional votes. When they have done so, they have prevailed most of the time.[18]

Nevertheless, Democratic majorities in Congress have given Democratic presidents an advantage. Of post–World War II presidents, Lyndon Johnson had the highest success rate with Congress. When his advisers cautioned him about proposing what was to become the Voting Rights Act of 1965, Johnson told them he would push legislation as fast and hard as he could before his "window of opportunity" with Congress closed. Party loyalty and the urgency of poverty and civil rights issues carried the day for Johnson.

[16]*Congressional Quarterly Almanac, 1983*, 20C.
[17]*Congressional Quarterly Almanac, 1978* (Washington, D.C.: Congressional Quarterly Press, 1979), 24C–25C.
[18]See Mark C. Shelley, *The Permanent Majority: The Conservative Coalition in the United States Congress* (University: University of Alabama Press, 1983).

★ HOW THE UNITED STATES COMPARES

SYSTEMS OF EXECUTIVE POLICY LEADERSHIP

The United States instituted a presidential system in 1789 as part of its constitutional checks and balances. This form of executive leadership was copied in Latin America but not in Europe. European democracies adopted parliamentary systems, in which executive leadership is provided by a prime minister, who is a member of the legislature. In recent years some European prime ministers have campaigned and governed as if they were a singular authority rather than the head of a collective institution. France in the 1960s created a separate chief executive office, but retained its parliamentary form of legislature.

The policy leadership of a president can differ substantially from that of a prime minister. As a singular head of an independent branch of government, a president does not have to share executive authority but nevertheless depends on the willingness of the legislative branch to support his leadership. By comparison, a prime minister shares executive leadership with a cabinet, but once agreement within the cabinet is reached, he or she is almost assured of the legislative support necessary to carry out policy initiatives.

Presidential System	Presidential/Parliamentary System	Parliamentary System
Mexico	Finland	Australia
United States	France	Belgium
Venezuela		Canada
		Germany
		Great Britain
		Israel
		Italy
		Japan
		Netherlands
		Sweden

THE FOREIGN OR DOMESTIC NATURE OF THE POLICY PROPOSAL

In the 1960s the political scientist Aaron Wildavsky wrote that, while the nation has only one president, it has two presidencies: one domestic and one foreign.[19] Wildavsky was referring to Congress's differential responses to presidential initiatives in the areas of foreign and domestic policy. He found that since World War II, only 40 percent of presidential proposals in the domestic policy area had been enacted by Congress, compared with 70 percent of foreign policy initiatives. It must be noted that Wildavsky was looking back on a period when there was general agreement on U.S. foreign policy objectives. After World War II, Republican and Democratic leaders alike were agreed on the desirability of containing Soviet communism and establishing U.S. diplomatic, military, and economic influence around the world (see Chapters 26 and 27). Accordingly, presidents had strong backing for their foreign policy leadership. In 1964, for example, Lyndon Johnson urged Congress to ratify the Gulf of Tonkin resolution, which he then used as a mandate to escalate the Vietnam war. The resolution was passed unanimously in the House and with only two dissenting votes in the Senate.

By the late 1960s, however, the Vietnam war had gone sour, and the bipartisan consensus on foreign policy was disrupted. Those deep divisions have endured. The January 1991 authorization of the use of military force in the Gulf war was the first time Congress had voted directly for offensive military action since the Gulf of Tonkin resolution. Bush had asked for the vote in order

[19]Aaron Wildavsky, "The Two Presidencies," *Trans-action*, December 1966, 7.

to strengthen his threat to use military force if Iraq did not withdraw from Kuwait. This time Congress was divided in its response to the president's request. The approval of military action in the Gulf was passed by margins of 52-47 in the Senate and 250-183 in the House.

Wildavsky's two-presidencies thesis is now regarded as an oversimplified conception of presidential influence. Many of the same factors, such as the party composition of Congress, that affect a president's success on foreign policy also affect his success on domestic policy.[20] Nevertheless, presidents are somewhat more likely to get what they want when the issue is foreign policy.[21] Republican presidents in particular have had more success with Congress on foreign policy issues than on domestic issues. Democratic members of Congress have been somewhat more willing to cross party lines in support of a Republican president on issues of foreign affairs.[22] In 1990, when Bush had an overall success rate of 47 percent with Congress, his success rate on foreign policy issues was 60 percent, including important votes on China policy, NATO, and the B-2 stealth bomber.[23]

The idea that partisanship ends "at the ocean's edge" has been most evident in the Senate's response to treaty proposals.[24] During the nation's history the

[20]Lance T. LeLoup and Steven A. Shull, "Congress versus the Executive: The Two Presidencies 'Reconsidered,'" *Social Science Quarterly*, March 1979, 707 (for 1965–1975); Harvey G. Zeidenstein, "The Two Presidencies Thesis Is Alive and Well and Has Been Living in the U.S. Senate Since 1973," *Presidential Studies Quarterly* 2 (1981): 511–525; see also Michael Mumper, "The President and Domestic Policy-Making," *Congress and the Presidency*, Spring 1985, 75–80.
[21]Aage Clausen, *How Congressmen Decide* (New York: St. Martin's Press, 1973), ch. 8; see also Lee Sigelman, "A Reassessment of the Two Presidencies Thesis," *Journal of Politics* 41 (1979): 120.
[22]See Richard Fleisher and Jon R. Bond, "Are There Two Presidencies? Yes; But Only for Republicans," *Journal of Politics* 50 (1988): 747–775; George C. Edwards III, *At the Margins: Presidential Leadership of Congress* (New Haven, Conn.: Yale University Press, 1989).
[23]Hager, "Bush's Success Rate Sinks to Near-Record Low," p. 1485.
[24]See Raymond Tatalovich and Byron W. Daynes, *Presidential Power in the United States* (Monterey, Calif.: Brooks/Cole, 1984), 262.

Presidents rely heavily on their top-ranking cabinet officers and personal assistants in making major policy decisions. During the Cuban missile crisis in 1962, this group of advisers to President John F. Kennedy met repeatedly to help him arrive at his decision to use a naval blockade as a means of forcing the Soviet Union to withdraw its missiles from Cuba. (UPI Photo)

Senate has voted to reject only 1 percent of the treaties proposed by presidents; it has ratified another 15 percent after modifying them; and some treaties have been withdrawn because of Senate opposition. The Senate supports the president on the great majority of treaties in part as a signal to other nations that they can negotiate with the United States through its president. The defeat of a treaty is a rebuke not only to the president but also to the other country or countries that are parties to the treaty.

The Supreme Court has recognized the special requirements of foreign policy, conceding to the president the power to take actions not expressly forbidden by law. As a result, presidents are able to make some major policy decisions—including those on trade agreements, deployments of military forces, and the granting of diplomatic recognition—on their own authority. Thus, for example, Nixon's 1972 agreement with China's premier, Chou En-lai, to renew diplomatic relations between their countries was worked out in secret and presented to Congress after the fact. A more dramatic example of unilateral presidential action is Kennedy's 1962 decision to respond to the Soviet Union's deployment of nuclear missiles in Cuba by imposing an air and sea blockade and ordering U.S. navy ships into position around Cuba. Congressional leaders were told of the plan only minutes before Kennedy announced it on television to the American people. On his own, Kennedy had committed the country to a course of action that could have led to a war between the superpowers.

The president owes his advantage in foreign and defense policy in part to his commanding position with the defense, diplomatic, and intelligence agencies. These are sometimes labeled "presidential agencies." As chief executive, the president is in charge of all federal agencies, but in practice his influence is strongest in those agencies that connect with his constitutional authority as chief diplomat and commander in chief, such as the Departments of State and Defense and the CIA. These agencies have a tradition of deference to presidential authority that is not found in agencies that deal primarily with domestic policy. The Department of Agriculture, for example, responds to presidential direction but is also responsive (perhaps even more responsive) to farm-state senators and representatives. As Chapter 21 describes, bureaucratic support is important to a president's success with Congress, and that support is more likely to be forthcoming when the agency in question is part of the defense, diplomatic, or intelligence bureaucracy.

Staying Strong: How Presidents Help and Hurt Themselves

Although presidents are not nearly so powerful as the news media sometimes make them appear, their capacity to influence the agenda of national debate is unrivaled, reflecting their unique claim to represent the whole country. Whenever presidents direct their attention to a particular issue or program, the attention of others usually follows. But will those others pay attention for long? And will they follow the president's lead? As we have noted, a president's support varies with conditions, some of which are clearly beyond his control. Yet presidents are not entirely at the mercy of history. As sole chief executive, a president is an active participant in his fate and can increase his chances of success by working to create effective relationships with Congress and by developing a strong rapport with the American people.

SEEKING COOPERATION FROM CONGRESS

Presidents cannot assume that support for their policies will automatically materialize. They have to build a following by taking into consideration the interests of other policymakers, who have their own jobs to do and their own interests to satisfy. Bill Clinton had this point in mind when, shortly after his election in 1992, he invited the top Democratic leaders in Congress—Senate majority leader George Mitchell, Speaker of the House Tom Foley, and House majority leader Richard Gephardt—to meet with him. He sought their agreement on a policy agenda that would break the gridlock between the executive and legislative branches. "We've got a big job to do and we've got to do it together," said Clinton.

As obvious as this type of thinking might seem, presidents sometimes think otherwise. As the center of national attention, a president can easily start to believe that his ideas ought to prevail because they are somehow innately better. This line of reasoning invariably gets the president into trouble. Jimmy Carter had not held national office before he was elected in 1976, so he had no clear understanding of how Washington operates. In his memoirs, House Speaker Thomas P. "Tip" O'Neill, a fellow Democrat, said of Carter:

> Jimmy Carter was the smartest public officer I've ever known. . . . His mind was exceptionally well developed, and it was open, too. He was always willing to listen and to learn. *With one exception.* When it came to the politics of Washington, D.C., *he never really understood how the system worked.*[25]

Soon after taking office, for example, Carter vetoed nineteen public works projects that he believed were a waste of taxpayers' money, ignoring the importance that members of Congress attach to obtaining federally funded projects for their constituents. Carter's action set the tone for a conflict-ridden relationship with Congress.

The Veto

One instrument by which presidents can try to force their views on Congress is the veto. Congress can seldom muster the two-thirds majority in each chamber required to override a presidential veto (see Table 19-1), so the threat of a veto can force Congress to accept a presidential demand. When a major civil rights bill was being debated in Congress in 1991, George Bush said flatly that he would veto any bill that imposed hiring "quotas" on employers; his ultimatum forced Congress to alter provisions of the bill. Congress will often accept some compromise with the president in return for his support of a legislative proposal.[26] By and large, however, the veto is more effective as a presidential restraint on Congress than as a device by which a president can force Congress to take positive action on his proposals.[27]

---

[25]Thomas P. (Tip) O'Neill, with William Novak, *Man of the House: The Life and Political Memoirs of Speaker Tip O'Neill* (New York: Random House, 1987), 297 (emphasis added).
[26]Robert J. Spitzer, *The Presidential Veto: Touchstone of the America Presidency* (Albany: State University of New York Press, 1988).
[27]Roderick D. Kiewiet and Matthew D. McCubbins, "Presidential Influence on Congressional Appropriations Decisions," *American Journal of Political Science* 32 (1988): 713–736.

TABLE 19-1   Number and Override of Presidential Vetoes, 1933–1992

President	Years in Office	Number of Vetoes	Number of Vetoes Overriden by Congress
Franklin Roosevelt	1933–1945	635	9
Harry Truman	1945–1952	250	12
Dwight Eisenhower	1953–1960	181	2
John Kennedy	1961–1963	21	0
Lyndon Johnson	1963–1968	30	0
Richard Nixon	1969–1974	43	7
Gerald Ford	1974–1976	66	12
Jimmy Carter	1977–1980	31	2
Ronald Reagan	1981–1988	78	9
George Bush	1989–1992	45	1

SOURCES: *Congressional Quarterly Weekly Report*, January 7, 1989. Bush figures were provided by the White House Office of Legislative Affairs and include vetoes, pocket vetoes, and bills returned unsigned to Congress.

Political scientist Richard Neustadt argues that the veto is actually a sign of presidential weakness, not strength, because it usually comes into play when Congress has refused to go along with the president's ideas.[28] The frequency with which Gerald Ford resorted to the veto kept the Democratic-controlled Congress from getting its way, but it was a strong indication that Ford was failing to get Congress to accept his leadership.

Use of the veto can raise congressional resistance to a president's policy efforts. That resistance can last beyond the issue at hand. After Bush in 1990 vetoed a family and medical leave bill that Democratic leaders in Congress had worked hard to enact, they said pointedly that Bush should not expect much help from them in the future.

The War Powers Act

The Vietnam war is the clearest illustration of the dangers to the nation and to the presidency when a president tries to force his policies on others. The war taught Congress a bitter lesson about presidential usurpation of its constitutional authority to declare war. Presidents Johnson and Nixon repeatedly told Congress that victory was near, providing military estimates of enemy casualties as evidence. Congressional support changed abruptly in 1971 with the publication of *The Pentagon Papers*. These secret government documents revealed that Johnson and Nixon had systematically distorted facts to put the Vietnam situation in a more favorable light. To prevent future presidential wars, Congress in 1973 passed the War Powers Act. Nixon vetoed the measure, but Congress overrode his veto. The act stipulates that:

• Within 48 hours of committing combat troops, the president must inform Congress in writing of his reasons for doing so.

[28]Richard E. Neustadt, *Presidential Power: The Politics of Leadership from FDR to Carter* (New York: Wiley, 1980), 67.

- Unless Congress acts to extend the period, hostilities involving American troops must end in sixty days, although the troops can remain for an additional thirty days if the president declares that extra time is needed for their safe withdrawal.
- Within the extra thirty days, Congress can demand the immediate withdrawal of the troops by passing a concurrent resolution, which is not subject to presidential veto.
- In every possible instance, the president must consult with Congress before dispatching troops into hostile situations or into areas where such situations are likely to arise.

The War Powers Act is perhaps Congress's most significant effort to curb presidential authority in the nation's history. Not surprisingly, every president from Nixon to Reagan has claimed that the act infringes on his constitutional power as commander in chief, and each has refused to comply fully with its provisions. For example, Congress was not formally consulted before Bush's intervention in Panama in 1989, Reagan's invasion of Grenada in 1983, Carter's military mission to rescue hostages in Iran in 1979, or Ford's action to free the crew of the *Mayaguez*, seized by Cambodia, in 1975. In each case the president obeyed the requirement to report the military commitment to Congress within forty-eight hours, but at the same time refused to acknowledge limits on his authority.

Nevertheless, the lessons of Vietnam have been a significant curb on presidential warmaking. Congress has shown no willingness to give the president anything approaching a free hand in the use of military force. This posture was plainly evident when, in response to news of covert arms dealings in the Iran-Contra affair, Congress began a full-scale investigation that threw the Reagan administration into disarray. Thus the effect of executive efforts to circumvent congressional authority in the warmaking area is heightened congressional opposition. Even if the president gains in the short run, he undermines his capacity to lead in the long run by failing to keep in mind that Congress is a coequal branch of the American governing system.

★ ANALYZE THE ISSUE

Foreign Policy: The President vs. Congress
In his first State of the Union address, President Bush said that Congress should stop trying to "micro-manage" foreign policy. Presidents Reagan, Carter, and Ford had the same complaint, holding that the president should have broad discretion in carrying out foreign policy. Should Congress take an active role in setting precise limits on foreign policy, or should the president have this responsibility? What are the advantages and disadvantages of each arrangement?

During its investigation into the Iran-Contra scandal, Congress made clear its displeasure with any exercise of presidential authority that was designed to circumvent the law. (Christopher Morris/Black Star)

President Bush was at least somewhat mindful of congressional relations when he urged Congress in January 1991 to authorize the use of military force against Iraq. Even though opinion polls indicated that most Americans believed that the UN Security Council's resolution against Iraq was a sufficient authorization for an attack on Iraqi forces, Bush felt it was important also to have congressional approval. At the same time, however, Bush made clear that he considered the War Powers Act to be an unconstitutional usurpation of his authority.

Congress as a Presidential Constituency

The powers of the presidential office are insufficient by themselves to keep the president in a position of power. He must have the help of other officials, particularly members of Congress, and in order to get their help, he must respond to their interests as they respond to his. Congress is a constituency that the president must serve if he expects its backing.[29]

A President needs political understanding to run *the government, [although] he may* be *elected without it.*

Harry S Truman

A classic illustration of what presidents can do to help themselves with Congress is the Marshall Plan, a program to aid European countries devastated by World War II. The plan was enacted by Congress in 1948 at the request of Harry S Truman. Truman had become president upon the death of Franklin Roosevelt and was widely regarded in Washington as just a caretaker president who would be replaced by a Republican. (The Republicans had made substantial gains in the 1946 congressional elections.) Truman knew he could not simply demand that Congress make a commitment to the postwar rebuilding of Europe, in view of the cost of such a program (roughly $100 billion in today's dollars) and of its novelty (historically, the United States had stayed free of permanent European entanglements). Truman succeeded in getting congressional approval by subordinating his position to that of others.

First, rather than announce the program himself, Truman gave the task to General George C. Marshall, who had been chief of staff of the armed forces during World War II and was one of America's most widely admired leaders. Second, Truman made a special effort to gain the support of Arthur Vandenberg, a leading Republican senator and chairman of the Senate Foreign Relations Committee. Truman accepted Vandenberg's request that "politics" not be allowed to bog down the plan; he followed Vandenberg's advice on changes in financial and administrative aspects of the plan; and he allowed Vandenberg to choose a Republican, Paul Hoffman, to head the U.S. agency responsible for administering the plan. Through Vandenberg's backing, Truman gained the Republican congressional support that made the Marshall Plan possible.

From cases such as the Marshall Plan, Richard Neustadt concluded that presidential power, at base, is "the power to persuade."[30] More recently, the presidential scholar Fred Greenstein offered the same general conclusion: "Whatever else his qualities, the president needs to be a working politician who can work with or otherwise win over the Washington community."[31]

[29]On the leadership role of the president, see Harold Laski, *The American Presidency* (New York: Harper, 1940), and Nicholas D. Berry, "The Foundation of Presidential Leadership: Teaching," *Presidential Studies Quarterly* 11 (Winter 1981): 99–105.

[30]Neustadt, *Presidential Power*, 33.

[31]Fred I. Greenstein, ed., *Leadership in the Modern Presidency* (Cambridge, Mass.: Harvard University Press, 1988), ch. 10.

Congress's Ultimate Sanction: Impeachment and Removal from Office

In the event of extreme presidential irresponsibility, Congress has an ultimate sanction: its power to impeach and remove the president from office. The procedure is spelled out in Article I of the Constitution. The House of Representatives decides whether the president should be placed on trial by the Senate for what the Constitution calls "high crimes and misdemeanors." If the House impeaches the president, the Senate becomes a tribunal presided over by the chief justice of the Supreme Court and can remove the president from office by a two-thirds vote.

Congress has undertaken action to impeach and remove two presidents. In 1868 Andrew Johnson was impeached and came within one Senate vote of being removed from office for his opposition to Congress's harsh Reconstruction policies in the wake of the Civil War. In 1974 Richard Nixon's involvement in the Watergate cover-up led to a recommendation of impeachment by the House Judiciary Committee. Before the full House could vote on his impeachment, Nixon resigned the presidency. It is generally assumed that if Nixon had not resigned, he would have been impeached and subsequently removed from office.

NURTURING PUBLIC SUPPORT

Public support can have a powerful effect on the president's ability to achieve his policy goals. Much of his power rests on his claim to national leadership, and the legitimacy of that claim is roughly proportional to public support of his performance. As long as the public is behind him, the president's leadership cannot easily be dismissed by other Washington officials. If his public support sinks, they are less inclined to accept his leadership.[32]

Every recent president has had the public's confidence during the "honeymoon" period referred to earlier. When asked in polls whether they "approve or disapprove of how the president is doing his job," 60 to 75 percent of the public has expressed approval of the performance of recent presidents during their first months in office (see Table 19-2). All presidents have slipped from this high point, however, and only Eisenhower, Kennedy, and Reagan left office with an approval rating higher than 50 percent.

Pocketbook issues are most closely related to the president's public support. Research indicates that economic downswings sharply reduce the public's confidence in the president.[33] For example, Bush experienced a precipitous decline in popularity in late 1991, which coincided with a rising unemployment rate and a continuation of the low economic productivity of the previous year. Apparently the best thing that a president can do to ensure his political success is to preside over a healthy economy.

The Gulf war indicated that a foreign policy initiative can also have an extraordinary effect on a president's popularity. Bush's approval rating stood at 60 percent in the last Gallup poll before Iraq's invasion of Kuwait in August

[32]Harvey G. Zeidenstein, "Presidents' Popularity and Their Wins and Losses on Major Issues: Does One Have a Greater Influence over the Other?" *Presidential Studies Quarterly,* Spring 1985, 287–300.

[33]John E. Mueller, "Presidential Popularity from Truman to Johnson," *American Political Science Review* 64 (March 1970): 18–34.

TABLE 19-2 Percentage of Public Expressing Approval of President's Performance, 1945–1992 Presidential approval ratings are typically higher at the beginning of the term than at the end.

President	Years in Office	Average during Presidency	First-Year Average	Final-Year Average
Harry Truman	1945–1952	41%	63%	35%
Dwight Eisenhower	1953–1960	64	74	62
John Kennedy	1961–1963	70	76	62
Lyndon Johnson	1963–1968	55	78	40
Richard Nixon	1969–1974	49	63	24
Gerald Ford	1974–1976	46	75	48
Jimmy Carter	1977–1980	47	68	46
Ronald Reagan	1981–1989	53	58	57
George Bush	1989–	—	65	—

SOURCE: Averages compiled from Gallup polls, 1946–1992.

1990. Two weeks after the invasion, Bush's rating had jumped to 75 percent and it peaked in March 1991 at 91 percent, the highest presidential-approval rating ever recorded in a Gallup poll.

The Media Presidency

A major advantage that presidents enjoy in their efforts to nurture public support is their guaranteed access to the media, particularly television.[34] The

[34]See Michael Baruch Grossman and Martha Joynt Kumar, *Portraying the President* (Baltimore: Johns Hopkins University Press, 1981); Anne Rawley Saldich, *Electronic Democracy* (New York: Praeger, 1979); David L. Paletz and Robert M. Entman, *Media Power Politics* (New York: Free Press, 1981); William C. Spragens, *The Presidency and the Mass Media in the Age of Television* (Washington, D.C.: University Press of America, 1978); Robert E. Denton, Jr., and Dan F. Hahn, *Presidential Communication* (New York: Praeger, 1986).

Americans gather outside the White House to congratulate President Bush after the announcement of victory over Iraq in the Persian Gulf war. As the placard at right indicates, the president's approval rating had soared to a record high of 91 percent. (Markel/Gamma Liaison)

THE PRESIDENT IN THE NEWS

The president's news coverage is a critical factor in his leadership role. The public looks to the president for leadership in part because the news media portray him as the driving force in the American constitutional system. The presidency receives an extraordinary amount of news attention compared with the Congress. The president and his top appointees receive more than half again as much coverage as all members of Congress combined (see Chapter 17). The president is the only top U.S. official who is guaranteed news coverage whenever he claims to have an important statement to make. The president's newsworthiness is such that he is trailed by a large entourage of reporters even when he goes on vacation.

Television in particular is a presidential medium. Television reports its news with pictures and through the actions of persons, which gives the president an advantage over Congress. When the national networks have been criticized for their preoccupation with the president, they have replied that members of Congress get more attention from local media.

Although the president is assured of heavy news coverage by the national media, he cannot be sure that the coverage will be favorable. Presidents have become very adept at managing the news, but the press has a somewhat critical view of all politicians and no president can expect to serve out his term without running into policy problems of one kind or another. Robert Lichter and Linda Lichter are the editors of *Media Monitor*, a publication based on their ongoing content analysis of television news coverage. They have found that critical evaluations of the president often outpace positive ones. For example, George Bush had a press "honeymoon" during his first 100 days in office, but press criticism then began to exceed praise for his handling of the presidency. Interestingly, Bush's news coverage was substantially more favorable on foreign policy issues. Television news stories about Bush's handling of domestic issues often included footage of criticism from congressional Democrats and disaffected groups. In contrast, the president and his advisers were often the only U.S. political figures included in foreign policy news stories.

SOURCE: "The Honeymoon Is Over," *Media Monitor* 3, No. 10 (December 1989): 2–4.

television medium exalts personality, and the president is the most compelling and familiar figure in the American political system. Only he can expect the television networks to give him free air time on demand, and he towers over all members of Congress combined in the amount of news coverage he receives (see box).

The political scientist Samuel Kernell calls it "going public" when the president promotes "himself and his policies by appealing to the American public for support."[35] Such appeals are at least as old as Theodore Roosevelt's use of the presidency as a "bully pulpit" but have increased substantially in recent years.[36] As the president has moved from an administrative leader to a policy advocate and agenda setter, public support has become increasingly important to presidential success.[37] Television has made it easier for presidents to go public with their programs. Ronald Reagan was called the "Great Communicator" in part because of his ability to use television to generate public support for his initiatives. Reagan's strength was the delivery of prepared speeches. Because he lacked a command of policy details, he did not perform

[35]Samuel Kernell, *Going Public: New Strategies of Presidential Leadership* (Washington, D.C.: Congressional Quarterly Press, 1986),1.
[36]Jeffrey Tulis, *The Rhetorical Presidency* (Princeton, N.J.: Princeton University Press, 1987).
[37]Mary E. Stuckey, *The President as Interpreter-in-Chief* (Chatham, N.J.: Chatham House Publishers, 1991).

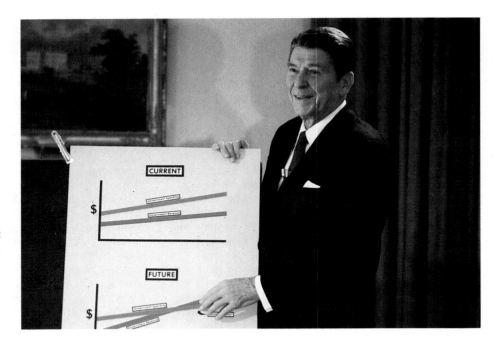

Ronald Reagan became known as the "Great Communicator" because of his skillful televised appeals to the public for support of his policies. However, he was sometimes accused of oversimplifying issues or distorting the facts in the charts and anecdotes he liked to use in presenting his arguments. (Dennis Brack/Black Star)

well in informal settings, particularly when he had to respond to questioning. In one form or another, however, the modern president must find a way to communicate effectively with the public.[38]

Some critics charge that presidents have become more concerned with speaking out about problems than with working to solve them.[39] During the

[38]Lyn Ragsdale, "Presidential Speechmaking and the Public Audience," *Journal of Politics* 49 (August 1987): 704–736.
[39]See Roderick Hart, *The Sound of Leadership* (Chicago: University of Chicago Press, 1987).

A number of times during his presidency, George Bush staged public relations drives to deflect criticism that he was more interested in foreign policy than in domestic problems. Here he addresses reporters on the rim of the Grand Canyon, using the media to try to reassure the public about his concern for the environment. (Larry Downing)

second half of his presidency, for example, Reagan sent budgets to Congress that he knew had no chance of approval and then "went public" to make his point that the national government had become too large and expensive. Reagan's budgets were a statement about big government rather than a blueprint for spending in the next fiscal year.

A good public relations effort on television—and the short memory of the public and the press—can sometimes deflect criticism of the president.[40] Presidents have become adept at putting their preferred "spin" on the news. When it was reported that the performance of U.S. students on standardized achievement exams had declined yet again in 1991, the Bush administration came under attack for its failure to undertake major new initiatives in the education area despite the president's claim to be "the education president." Bush responded immediately with a public appearance at a school in Maine. Pictures of Bush "teaching" a group of students flashed across the news wires and on television news.

A public relations effort can carry a president only so far, however. National conditions ultimately determine the level of public confidence in the president. Lyndon Johnson's popularity soared on the strength of a thriving economy, his legislative triumphs, and his landslide election victory, but then plummeted as the Vietnam war soured, the economy weakened, and riots broke out in inner-city neighborhoods. Johnson's attempts to portray his administration favorably were crushed by the weight of the nation's problems.

Indeed, it could be argued that presidents run a risk by trying to build up their images through public relations. Through their frequent television appearances and claims of success, presidents contribute to the public's expectation that they can control events. During difficult periods, the inevitable disillusionment can be disastrous. If the president is as powerful as he appears to be, why is the nation in such poor shape? When the public asks this question, the answer seems obvious: the president must be failing to govern effectively.

The Public's Response to Crises

International crises nearly always have the effect of increasing the president's public standing, at least initially. Threats from abroad tend to produce a patriotic "rally 'round the flag" reaction that creates widespread support for the president. Every foreign policy crisis in the past four decades has fitted this pattern. Even foreign policy disasters increase public support for the president. Reagan's popularity rose by several percentage points in 1983 after a terrorist bomb killed 241 U.S. Marines whom he had ordered into Lebanon in the midst of its civil war.

Yet ongoing crises can eventually erode a president's support. Within a month after Iranian extremists invaded the U.S. embassy in Teheran in November 1979 and took fifty-nine Americans hostage, Carter's public-approval rating jumped from 32 to 51 percent.[41] The change revived Carter's

---

[40]Bruce Miroff, "Monopolizing the Public Space," in Thomas E. Cronin, ed., *Rethinking the Presidency* (Boston: Little, Brown, 1982), 218–232; see also Lyn Ragsdale, "The Politics of Presidential Speechmaking, 1949–1980," *American Political Science Review* 78 (December 1984): 971–984.

[41]Gallup polls, November 2–5, 1979, and November 30–December 3, 1979.

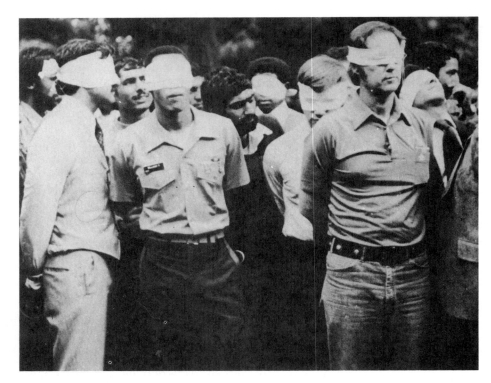

The sight of blindfolded American hostages being put on humiliating display by their Iranian captors in 1979 ultimately had a devastating effect on Jimmy Carter's presidency. The public's expectation that the president can solve the nation's problems placed Carter in the position of either freeing the hostages or being perceived as a failure. (UPI/Bettmann Newsphotos)

prospects for reelection. Before the crisis began, he had trailed Senator Edward Kennedy as the choice of rank-and-file Democrats for the party's 1980 nomination. Kennedy held a 54–31 percent edge in a Gallup poll taken only days before the crisis began; within a few weeks, Carter led, 63–24 percent. As months passed without a resolution of the hostage situation, however, Carter's popularity began to sink and his hold on the presidency again looked shaky. In April, Carter ordered a secret mission into Iran to rescue the American hostages. The mission had to be aborted when two of the U.S. rescue helicopters collided. Nonetheless, Carter's public-approval rating rose by several points: Americans gave him credit for trying. Had Carter's rescue plan succeeded, it is possible that he would have won reelection. As it was, he nearly did pull off a victory when the Iranians seemed to be close to accepting a negotiated settlement on the eve of the November balloting.

Carter's problem stemmed from the public's high expectations of the president—the widespread belief that the president is the one who gets things done. Most Americans see the president as being in charge of the national government, a perception that the political scientist Hugh Heclo calls "the illusion of presidential government."[42] As Godfrey Hodgson puts it, the president is expected to "conduct the diplomacy of a superpower . . . , manage the economy, command the armed forces, serve as a spiritual example . . . , [and] respond to every emergency."[43] Because the public expects so much from

[42]Heclo, "Introduction: The Presidential Illusion," 2.
[43]Godfrey Hodgson, *All Things to All Men* (New York: Simon & Schuster, 1980), 239.

the president, he gets too much credit when things go well and too much blame when things go badly. In a complex world things can easily go wrong for reasons largely beyond the president's control.

Presidents make matters worse for themselves by getting involved in nearly every important national issue and many international ones. A few words spoken by the president are likely to thrust him into the middle of a controversy. It is doubtful that Carter could have done much more than he did about the hostage crisis. In addition to the aborted rescue mission, Carter tried economic sanctions, UN resolutions, third-party negotiations, and nearly every other diplomatic approach imaginable. Nevertheless, the public eventually blamed Carter for failing to secure the release of the hostages, mainly for the simple reason that he was the president.

THE PRESIDENCY: IMPERIAL OR IMPOSSIBLE?[44]

Harry Truman kept a sign on his desk that read, "The buck stops here"—a reference not only to the president's ultimate responsibility for the decisions of his administration but also to the public's view that the president is responsible for national success or failure. Therein lies the paradox of the presidential office. More than from any constitutional grant, more than from any statute, and more than from any crisis, presidential power derives from the president's position as the sole official who can claim to represent the whole American public.

What type of presidency, then, does America have? Is it a powerful office or a weak one? An imperial presidency or an impossible one? The answer is both. When presidents have had strong public support, they have wielded considerable power, giving rise to assertions about an "imperial" presidency. Yet because presidential power rests on a popular base, it erodes when public support declines, which has led to assertions about an "impossible" presidency. An irony is that the presidential office grows weaker as problems mount: just when the country could most use effective leadership, that leadership is often hardest to achieve. The burden on the presidency is substantial. The formal powers of the office are no match for the public's high expectations of their president.[45]

Summary

No president has come close to winning approval of all the programs he has placed before Congress, but the presidents' records of success have varied considerably. The factors in a president's success include the presence or absence of national conditions that require strong leadership from the White House; the stage of the president's term (success usually comes early); the strength of the president's party in Congress; and the focus on the policy issue (presidents do somewhat better in the area of foreign policy than in domestic policy).

As sole chief executive and the nation's top elected leader, the president can always expect that his policy and leadership efforts will receive attention. However, other institutions, particularly Congress, have the authority to make his leadership effective. If the president is to succeed over the long run, he must have a proper

★ ANALYZE THE ISSUE

The President's Personality and the Burdens of Office
The presidency has been described as the world's most demanding job, involving too many great responsibilities and allowing too little time to devote to these duties. Yet the Reagan presidency suggested that the burdens of the job may sometimes be exaggerated. Reagan took frequent vacations and daily naps, delegated responsibility widely, but still managed to leave his imprint on the office and on national policy. What does it take to be a good president, or is no personality type or approach necessarily better than another?

[44]See Harold M. Barger, *Impossible Presidency*, ch.1.
[45]Theodore J. Lowi, *The "Personal" Presidency: Power Invested, Promise Unfulfilled* (Ithaca, N.Y.: Cornell University Press, 1985).

conception of the presidency. Even more important, he must have the help of other officials, and to get their cooperation he must respond to their concerns. The president operates within a system of divided powers, and if he tries to go it alone, he is almost sure to fail.

To retain an effective leadership position, the president also depends on the strong backing of the American people. Recent presidents have made extensive use of the media to build public support for their programs. Yet they have had difficulty maintaining that support throughout their terms of office. A major reason is that the public expects far more from the president than he can deliver.

Suggested Readings

Barber, James David. *The Presidential Character: Predicting Performance in the White House*, 3d ed. Englewood Cliffs, N.J.: Prentice-Hall, 1985. An analysis of presidential performance based on the incumbent's personal traits.

Cronin, Thomas E. *The State of the Presidency*, 2d ed. Boston: Little, Brown, 1980. A detailed analysis of the powers and, especially, the limitations of the American presidency.

Edwards, George C., III. *At the Margins: Presidential Leadership of Congress*. New Haven, Conn.: Yale University Press, 1989. An assessment of the president's influence on Congress, which concludes that the president has a limited ability to lead Congress in directions that it would not otherwise go.

Greenstein, Fred I., ed. *Leadership in the Modern Presidency*. Cambridge, Mass.: Harvard University Press, 1988. A collection of articles on the modern presidency by leading scholars in the field.

Kernell, Samuel. *Going Public: New Strategies of Presidential Leadership*. Washington, D.C.: Congressional Quarterly Press, 1986. A careful analysis of how presidents use the media to build public support for their goals.

Neustadt, Richard E. *Presidential Power: The Politics of Leadership from FDR to Carter*. New York: Wiley, 1980. The classic analysis of the limitations on presidential power.

Spitzer, Robert J. *The Presidential Veto: Touchstone of the American Presidency*. Albany: State University of New York Press, 1988. An insightful analysis of the veto as a modern policy tool.

Tulis, Jeffrey K. *The Rhetorical Presidency*. Princeton, N.J.: Princeton University Press, 1987. Argues that the modern presidency is split between its institutional and rhetorical aspects and that this division limits the president's effectiveness.

Does the President Have Too Much Power in Relation to Congress?

LOUIS FISHER

The central goal of the War Powers Act—to bring about government by 'collective judgment' of the president and Congress—remains an essential objective.

Deciding how to restrain presidential power, especially in foreign affairs, remains one of the thorniest issues of the twentieth century. Even though numerous statutes designed to curb and regulate executive power have been enacted, recent decades have featured a succession of presidential initiatives in Korea and Southeast Asia, the Watergate and Iran-Contra scandals, and several other events that have been costly to the nation and to the prestige of the presidency.

In times of crisis, presidential power naturally expands to meet the emergency. So it was with Abraham Lincoln during the Civil War and with Woodrow Wilson during World War I. However, after each of those conflicts Congress resumed its status as a coequal branch of government. In contrast, the powers transferred to Franklin D. Roosevelt during the Great Depression and World War II did not revert to Congress. What Congress had earlier accepted as a temporary disequilibrium now became a permanent feature of executive–legislative relations.

Particularly disturbing to Congress was the continuation of presidential war powers after World War II ended in 1945. Harry Truman retained various emergency authorities on the grounds that a "state of war" or a "state of emergency" still existed. Not until 1952 did Truman sign a statement terminating the state of war with Japan, and by that time he had already involved U.S. troops in Korea without congressional authority. In 1951 he also announced his intention to send ground forces to Europe, again without seeking congressional approval.

For three months in 1951, the Senate engaged in a "Great Debate" over the president's authority to engage the nation in war. The senators concluded that the policies of the federal government require the approval of Congress and the people after full and free discussion. Secret executive agreements and initiatives, they argued, threaten the liberties of the people. Both chambers of Congress were also stimulated to rethink their own role in foreign affairs.

Dwight Eisenhower tried to forge a common front with Congress. He pointed out that a military commitment by the United States has much greater impact on allies and enemies alike if it represents the collective judgment of the president and Congress.

Under John Kennedy and Lyndon Johnson, however, the relationship between the two branches became progressively more strained and combative. After Richard Nixon had taken several steps to widen the war in Southeast Asia, Congress passed the War Powers Act of 1973 over Nixon's veto.

More than fifteen years of experience with the War Powers Act have proved that its success depends on the willingness of executive officials and members of Congress to cooperate. Some have complained that the act has "failed" because the required presidential reports to Congress are inadequate, because presidents have not consulted sufficiently with Congress, and because the "legislative veto" conferred by the act is unconstitutional. However, the central goal of the act—to bring about government by "collective judgment" on the part of Congress and the president—remains an essential objective. Moreover, the act seems to have succeeded in confining presidential initiatives to short-term military actions, as in Grenada and Libya.

The main lesson of the post–World War II period is that the president needs to secure the understanding and support of Congress and the American people before engaging U.S. forces in hostilities. Such cooperation is in the interest not only of the country and the world but also of the presidency itself.

Louis Fisher is affiliated with the Congressional Research Service. He is the author of **American Constitutional Law.**

LINDA L. FOWLER

The old rationale for the subordination of Congress is no longer valid.

If the debate over the relative power of Congress and the President were decided in purely constitutional terms, it would be easily resolved in favor of Congress. The prerogatives in Article I and the deference of early presidents reflect Madison's view stated in *Federalist* No. 51, that "In republican government, the legislative authority necessarily predominates." In recent years, however, liberals and conservatives have recast the question of institutional power in their struggle for ideological supremacy. On the side of Congress are those who favor Democratic views that emphasize individual welfare and domestic priorities; on the side of the presidency are those who support Republican beliefs about the importance of economic efficiency and activist foreign policies.

Throughout the twentieth century, Congress concentrated authority in the hands of the commander-in-chief. Dissension over the Vietnam war and the Watergate scandal shattered the legitimacy of presidential power, and when divided party control became a permanent feature of the federal government in the 1980s, conflict between the two branches intensified. With the Democrats controlling Capitol Hill and the Republicans controlling the White House, the battle over institutional supremacy surfaced in every facet of government, from Supreme Court nominations, to former House Speaker Jim Wright's negotiations with Nicaragua's Sandinista regime, to strategic weapons systems and domestic spending priorities. Underlying this struggle was profound disagreement over how governmental decisions should be made. When members of Congress had previously deferred to the president, it was because they believed his capacity to act swiftly and secretly was vital to the nation's security against Soviet attack. But with the collapse of the communist bloc and of the cold war consensus, the need became greater for public deliberations over foreign policy options. The House and Senate debates in 1991 on the use of military force against Iraq were potent signals of this new reality.

At the same time, repeated failures by presidents of both political parties to manage the White House staff and the federal bureaucracy have challenged presidential claims to superior institutional competence. Tales of $7,000 toilet seats in the military, evidence of conspiracy during the Iran-Contra affair, and presidential reluctance to chart a responsible fiscal course challenge Congress to oversee the executive more aggressively.

Finally, the erosion of the president's electoral mandate undermined his claim to represent a national constituency. Two decades of declining turnout have created a situation in which presidential landslides are common, but winning candidates capture little more than a quarter of the eligible vote. Presidents have not only lost their coattails, but they often share victory in a state or district with the opposition's congressional nominees. These patterns, along with surveys indicating voters' propensities to select presidential candidates without agreeing with their policies, suggest that presidential elections are less reliable indicators of popular preference than in the past.

Congress cannot do a better job than the president in responding to the demands of the "new world order"; it cannot singlehandedly settle complex economic problems at home; and it cannot offer its uncompetitive election results as barometers of public opinion nationwide. Nevertheless, the old rationale for the subordination of Congress is no longer valid, and there are encouraging signs that Congress has strengthened its internal organization to promote policy coordination and leadership. In such a political climate, presidents and their supporters would do better to seek common ground with Congress than to assert an outdated theory of institutional supremacy.

Linda L. Fowler is professor of political science at Syracuse University. The co-author of Political Ambition: Who Decides to Run for Congress *and the author of the forthcoming book* Candidates, Congress and the American Democracy, *Fowler has published numerous articles on Congress.*

APPOINTED
OFFICIALS

*E*arly in the twentieth century the Supreme Court of the United States was restricted by laws that effectively determined the issues it would address. The great majority of cases reached the Court as mandatory appeals. The Court had no choice but to hear and rule upon these cases, even if they had legal significance only to the parties involved. During this period, the policymaking discretion of bureaucratic agencies was also under substantial limits. These agencies administered laws passed by Congress and assessed situations arising under the laws, but were effectively blocked from issuing regulations that would give new definition to public policy.

Times have changed. Today bureaucratic agencies routinely develop and implement broad regulations. In fact, the number and volume of regulations issued by bureaucratic agencies far exceed the legislative output of Congress. In addition, some of these regulations are as far-reaching as the statutes from which they derive. Affirmative action programs, for example, began when federal agencies required recipients of federal funds to ensure that members of minority groups would share in the opportunities provided by this funding.

The Supreme Court is also a more substantial policymaker today than it was in the past. The Court is more or less free to decide which cases it will hear—and thus which legal issues it will address. Busing to achieve racial integration in the public schools is but one significant public policy that was established through action by the Supreme Court.

Chapters 20 and 21 examine the federal bureaucracy, which is undoubtedly the least appreciated and the most widely misunderstood of the nation's institutions. Chapters 22 and 23 consider the judiciary, which is also misunderstood but is more widely respected than the bureaucracy. The discussion of both the bureaucracy and the judiciary concentrates on the nature of these institutions, their historical development, their roles in modern politics, the recruitment of their officials, their impact on public policy, and their accountability to the public they serve.

The accountability of judges and bureaucrats is a particularly critical issue. These officials are not elected to their positions, yet they affect Americans' daily lives in direct and substantial ways. No observer of American politics would argue that the judiciary and the bureaucracy are more powerful than Congress or the president, but at the same time no observer would say that their power is a secondary concern.   ★ ★ ★

BUREAUCRACY AND BUREAUCRATS: ADMINISTERING THE GOVERNMENT

20

[No] industrial society could manage the daily operations of its public affairs without bureaucratic organizations in which officials play a major policymaking role.

Norman Thomas[1]

When Neil Armstrong set foot on the moon in 1969, most Americans were watching the historic event on television. Armstrong instantly became a national hero, just as Americans had earlier made heroes of Alan Shepard, the first U.S. astronaut to fly into space, and John Glenn, the first American to orbit the earth. Through the power of the press, the space program would continue to make celebrities, if not heroes, of the men and women who risked their lives to fly into space. Then on January 28, 1986, the television cameras made America a witness to tragedy. Seventy-one seconds after liftoff, the space shuttle *Challenger* exploded, killing all seven crew members, including a schoolteacher, Christa McAuliffe.

The *Challenger* disaster led the press, for the first time, to peer deep inside the bureaucracy of the National Aeronautics and Space Administration (NASA). The picture that emerged was one of careless administration, flawed safety procedures, competition over jurisdiction, and denial of responsibility. The presidential commission that was appointed to investigate the tragedy reached the same conclusions. But the news media's portrayal of NASA was incomplete. However courageous America's astronauts might have been, they were not the main force behind the space program. It was the NASA bureaucracy—the aeronautical engineers, the rocket scientists, the top managers, and thousands of other people—that had developed the delivery and control systems that made space missions possible. Yet not until the *Challenger* explosion was NASA's organization brought squarely into public view, and then in a wholly critical way.

---

[1]Norman Thomas, *Rule 9: Politics, Administration, and Civil Rights* (New York: Random House, 1966), 6.

The space shuttle *Challenger* explodes—a human tragedy and an example of bureaucratic blundering. (AP/Wide World Photos)

The U.S. space program illustrates two points about the federal government's bureaucracy. The lesser point is that it rarely gets publicity unless it makes a mistake. The news media infrequently cover the bureaucracy's successes but often report its failures. The bureaucracy also takes a regular beating from politicians. The president and members of Congress have the highly visible role of enacting policy, and they are quick to claim credit when things go well but are often just as quick to shift the blame to the bureaucracy when things go badly. For the most part, their charges are unfair. The federal bureaucracy is far from perfect, but it does not deserve many of the criticisms directed at it.

The more important point that can be drawn from the example of the space program is that the U.S. government could not accomplish its goals without the bureaucracy's contributions. The writers of the Constitution made no mention of a bureaucracy. Modern government, however, would be unthinkable without one. It is America's organizational capacity that makes it possible for us to have such ambitious programs as space exploration, social security, and interstate highways.

This chapter describes the nature of the federal bureaucracy and the personnel who staff it. The discussion aims to clarify the bureaucracy's responsibilities, organizational structure, and personnel management practices. But the chapter also shows that the bureaucracy is very much involved in the play of politics. A recognition of the bureaucracy's political nature is essential to an understanding not only of the bureaucracy's development, which is a focus of this chapter, but also of the bureaucracy's influence, which is the subject of the next chapter. The main points in this first of two chapters on the bureaucracy are the following:

★ *Bureaucracy is an inevitable consequence of complexity and scale.* Modern government could not function without a large bureaucracy. Through hierarchy, specialization, and rules, bureaucracy provides an efficient means for managing thousands of workers and activities.

★ *Government agencies have developed in response to changing national conditions and political demands.* The result is a bureaucracy with hundreds of agencies that are involved inevitably and deeply in the play of politics.

★ *The federal bureaucracy's primary responsibilities are the initiation and development of policy, delivery of services, evaluation of programs, regulation, and adjudication.* Bureaucrats necessarily exercise discretion in carrying out these responsibilities. The bureaucracy does not simply administer policy, it also *makes* policy.

★ *The bureaucracy is expected simultaneously to respond to the direction of partisan officials and to administer programs fairly and competently.* These conflicting demands are addressed through a combination of personnel management systems: the patronage, merit, and executive leadership systems.

★ ANALYZE THE ISSUE

The Bureaucracy's Negative Image
According to opinion polls, most Americans believe that the federal bureaucracy is a relatively ineffective institution. Yet the polls also show that most Americans have had no personal experience that would justify their opinion. What is your view of the federal bureaucracy? Does it do a good, fair, or poor job of carrying out its responsibilities? What is the basis of your opinion?

The Federal Bureaucracy: Form, Personnel, and Activities

Bureaucracy is essentially a method of organizing people and work. As a form of organization, bureaucracy is the most efficient means of getting people to work together on tasks of great magnitude and complexity.

Bureaucracy is a system of organization and control that is based on three principles: hierarchical authority, job specialization, and formalized rules. **Hierarchical authority** refers to a chain of command, whereby the officials and units at the top of a bureaucracy have control over those in the middle, who in turn control those at the bottom. In **job specialization,** the responsibilities of each job position are explicitly defined, and there is a precise division of labor within the organization. **Formalized rules** are the standardized procedures and established regulations by which a bureaucracy conducts its operations.

The mobilization of U.S. and allied troops for the Persian Gulf war was a dramatic example of bureaucracy's ability to get things done. (J. Langevin/ Sygma)

★ ANALYZE THE ISSUE

The Bureaucracy's Fairness
Governor Mario Cuomo of
New York once said,
"Democracy is not meant to
be efficient, it is meant to be
fair." How might a concern
for fairness affect the
operations of the federal
bureaucracy? Is the demand
for fairness a likely reason
why public bureaucracies are
somewhat less efficient than
private ones?

These features are the reason that bureaucracy, as a form of organization, is unrivaled in the efficiency and control it provides. Hierarchy speeds action by reducing conflict over the power to make decisions: the higher an individual's position in the organization, the more decisionmaking power he or she has. Hierarchy is also the basis by which superiors control subordinates and maintain a commitment to organizational goals. Specialization yields efficiency because each individual is required to concentrate on a particular job: specialization enables workers to develop advanced skills and expert knowledge. Formalized rules enable workers to act quickly and precisely because decisions are made on the basis of predetermined guidelines. Formalized rules also enhance control: workers make decisions according to established organizational standards rather than their personal inclinations.[2]

The Persian Gulf war demonstrated the power of bureaucracy as a means of accomplishing tasks. Within five months of Iraq's invasion of Kuwait on August 2, 1990, 540,000 U.S. combat troops and their equipment had been moved into the Gulf region. The orders were sent from the top by President Bush and channeled to each unit and its commander. All personnel had deployment assignments and, once in the Gulf area, an exact mission to perform. This operation could not have been carried out with the same speed and efficiency by any form of organization other than the bureaucratic one.

The characteristics of bureaucratic organizations were first described by the noted German sociologist Max Weber (1864–1920), who concluded that bureaucratic efficiency is achieved at a high price. Bureaucracy transforms people from social beings to rational actors: they perform not as whole persons but as parts of an organizational entity. Their behavior is dictated by position, specialty, and rule. A bureaucracy grinds on, heedless of the personal feelings of its members. In the process, they lose a sense of the place of their narrow role and specialty within the larger context and become bound to rules without regard for the insensitivity of those rules to human circumstance.[3] "Specialists without spirit" was Weber's unflattering description of bureaucrats.[4]

Yet Weber also saw that all large-scale, task-oriented organizations have no realistic alternative to the bureaucratic form.[5] It alone facilitates the coordination of a massive work force. The superiority of the bureaucratic form of organization as a means of accomplishing tasks is apparent from its prevalence. Although Americans tend to associate the word "bureaucracy" with government, bureaucracy is found wherever there is a need to manage large numbers of people and tasks. All major U.S. corporations are bureaucratic organizations. So are most foundations, churches, lobbying groups, and colleges.

THE BUREAUCRACY IN AMERICANS' DAILY LIVES

The U.S. federal bureaucracy has roughly 3 million employees, who have responsibility for thousands of programs. Without hierarchy, job specialization,

[2]H. H. Gerth and C. Wright Mills, eds., *From Max Weber: Essays in Sociology* (New York: Oxford University Press, 1946).
[3]Ralph Hummel, *The Bureaucratic Experience*, 3d ed. (New York: St. Martin's Press, 1987), 2–4.
[4]Max Weber, *The Protestant Ethic and the Spirit of Capitalism* (London: George Allen & Unwin, 1930), 182.
[5]Max Weber, *Economy and Society*, trans. Guenther Roth and Claus Wittich (New York: Bedminster Press, 1968), 23.

and formalized rules, the work of the federal government simply would not get done. The president and Congress may get far more attention in the news than does the bureaucracy, but it is the bureaucracy that has the more immediate impact on the daily lives of Americans. Among its many activities, the federal bureaucracy

Delivers the daily mail

Maintains the national forests and parks

Administers farm programs

Issues social security checks

Conducts diplomatic relations with other nations

Builds dams and generates hydroelectric power

Enforces environmental protection laws

Develops the country's defense systems

Makes loans to small businesses

Provides foodstuffs for school lunch programs

Regulates broadcasting and cable systems

Issues trademarks, patents, and copyrights

Regulates the stock markets

TYPES OF ORGANIZATIONS WITHIN THE FEDERAL BUREAUCRACY

The federal bureaucracy is enormous in its size and complexity. Few organizations in the world can match the number of its employees and administrative units. Even experts do not agree on the exact number of separate and partially independent agencies within the U.S. bureaucracy, although 400 is a reasonable estimate.[6]

The outstanding organizational feature of the federal bureaucracy is its division into areas of specialization. One agency handles veterans' affairs, another specializes in education, a third is responsible for agriculture, and so on. Because each major unit of the bureaucracy exists for a designated purpose, no two are exactly alike. Nevertheless, most of them take one of five general forms: *cabinet department, independent agency, regulatory agency, government corporation,* or *presidential commission.*

Cabinet Departments

The major units within the bureaucracy are the fourteen **cabinet** (or **executive**) **departments** (see Chapter 18 and Table 20-1). Each is headed by a secretary, who serves as a member of the president's cabinet and has responsibility for establishing the department's general policy and overseeing its operations. The

---

[6]On the difficulty of establishing a precise count of government organizations, see David Nachmias and David H. Rosenbloom, *Bureaucratic Government: U.S.A.* (New York: St. Martin's Press, 1980).

TABLE 20-1 Budgets and Number of Employees of Cabinet Departments The executive departments vary greatly in size and budget.

Department	Year Created	Budget (Billions of Dollars)	Number of Employees
State	1789	$3.9	25,633
Treasury	1789	255.2	155,931
Defense[a]	1789	314.6[b]	1,049,422[c]
Interior	1849	5.8	71,233
Justice[d]	1870	6.5	79,082
Agriculture	1889	46.0	110,755
Commerce[e]	1903	3.7	37,756
Labor	1913	25.3	18,050
Health and Human Services[f]	1953	438.7[g]	117,817
Housing and Urban Development	1965	20.2	13,264
Transportation	1966	28.6	64,863
Energy	1977	12.0	16,815
Education	1979	23.1	4,596
Veterans Affairs	1988	29.0	214,040
All departments		$1212.6	1,979,257

[a]Originally the Department of War. In 1947 the departments of the Army, Navy, and Air Force were combined into the Department of Defense.
[b]Military and civilian.
[c]Civilian only.
[d]The attorney general was earlier a member of the president's cabinet, but the Department of Justice was not created until 1870.
[e]Originally the Department of Commerce and Labor. A separate Department of Labor was created in 1913.
[f]Originally the Department of Health, Education, and Welfare. A separate Department of Education was formed in 1979.
[g]Including social security.

SOURCE: *Budget of the United States Government,* 1992 (Washington, D.C.: U.S. Government Printing Office, 1991).

secretary does not ordinarily direct the day-to-day operations of the department; this duty is handled by the department's undersecretary and by deputy or assistant secretaries.

Cabinet departments vary greatly in their visibility, size, and importance. The Department of State is one of the oldest and most prestigious departments, but it is also one of the smallest, with approximately 25,000 employees. The Department of Defense is the largest, with more than 1 million civilian employees (as distinct from the roughly 2 million uniformed members of the armed services). The Department of Health and Human Services has the largest budget; its activities account for nearly a third of all federal spending, much of it for social security benefits. The Department of Energy is one of the newest departments, having been formed in 1977. It has only about 17,000 employees and has yet to attain substantial visibility or reputation.

Each cabinet department has responsibility for a general policy area, such as defense, commerce, transportation, or justice. But executive departments are not monoliths: each department has a number of semi-autonomous operating units that typically carry the label of "bureau," "agency," "division," or

Energy Department seal

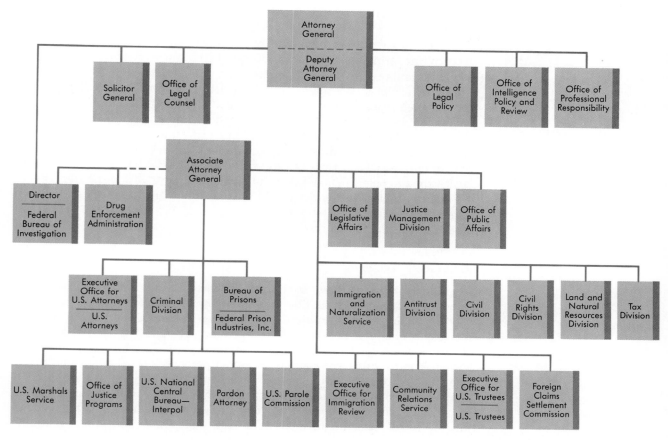

FIGURE 20-1 The U.S. Department of Justice
The major divisions of the U.S. Department of Justice are shown in this organization chart. *Source: The U.S. Government Manual, 1989/1990 (Washington, D.C.: U.S. Government Printing Office, 1990), 372.*

"service." The Department of Justice, for example, has thirteen such operating units: Federal Bureau of Investigation (FBI), Bureau of Prisons, U.S. Marshals Service, U.S. National Central Bureau of the International Criminal Police Organization (Interpol), Immigration and Naturalization Service, Drug Enforcement Administration, Justice Management Division, Antitrust Division, Civil Division, Civil Rights Division, Criminal Division, Environment and Natural Resources Division, and Tax Division.

Although each major operating unit within a cabinet department has a fairly precise mission, these units are usually further divided into smaller working units. The Department of Justice's Criminal Division, for instance, has twelve sections, including Organized Crime and Racketeering, Narcotics and Dangerous Drugs, and Internal Security. Altogether, the Department of Justice's nearly 80,000 employees (who include attorneys, investigators, and clerks) are divided among nearly 100 administrative units. In short, the Department of Justice is itself a large, complex bureaucracy, as Figure 20-1 indicates.

Independent Agencies

Independent agencies resemble the cabinet departments, but most of them have a narrower area of responsibility. They include such organizations as the

SEC seal

EPA seal

Central Intelligence Agency (CIA) and the National Aeronautics and Space Administration (NASA). The heads of these agencies are appointed by the president and report to him but are not members of his cabinet. Like the executive departments, each of the independent agencies is divided into smaller operating units.

Generally, the independent agencies exist apart from cabinet departments because their placement within a department would pose symbolic or practical policy problems. NASA, for example, could conceivably be located in the Department of Defense, but this placement would suggest that the space program is intended almost solely for military purposes rather than also for civilian purposes, such as space exploration and satellite communication. And if NASA tried to balance its defense and civilian missions within the Department of Defense, the balancing act would not last long. Agencies located within a cabinet department inevitably place that department's goals ahead of those of other units of the bureaucracy.

Regulatory Agencies

Regulatory agencies have been created when Congress has recognized the importance of close and continuous regulation of an economic activity. Because such regulation requires more time and expertise than Congress can provide, the responsibility is delegated to a regulatory agency. The oldest regulatory agency is the Interstate Commerce Commission (ICC), which was created in 1887 to control price fixing and other unfair practices of the nation's railroads. The ICC today regulates all surface transportation affecting interstate commerce. Other regulatory agencies include the Securities and Exchange Commission (SEC), which oversees the stock and bond markets, and the Federal Reserve Board, which regulates federal banks and the nation's money supply. Table 20-2 lists some of the regulatory agencies and other noncabinet units of the federal bureaucracy.

Unlike these and other older agencies, which are charged with overseeing a certain industry, the regulatory agencies created since the 1960s are concerned with the business sector in general. Among them are the Occupational Safety and Health Administration (OSHA), which promotes job safety, and the Environmental Protection Agency (EPA), which works to prevent industrial pollution.

Beyond their executive functions, regulatory agencies have certain legislative and judicial functions. They issue regulations, implement them, and then judge whether individuals or organizations have followed them. Some regulatory agencies, particularly the older ones, are "independent" by virtue of their relative freedom from ongoing political control. They are headed by a commission of several members who are appointed by the president and confirmed by Congress but are not subject to removal by the president. Commissioners serve a fixed term, a legal stipulation intended to free their agencies from political interference. The newer regulatory agencies lack such autonomy. They are headed by a single administrator who can be removed from office by the president and is therefore more responsive to the president's goals. (Regulatory agencies are discussed more fully in Chapter 24.)

TABLE 20-2 Selected U.S. Regulatory Agencies, Independent Agencies, Government Corporations, and Presidential Commissions

ACTION	Federal Communications Commission	National Aeronautics and Space Administration	Peace Corps
Administrative Conference of the U.S.	Federal Deposit Insurance Corporation	National Archives and Records Administration	Pennsylvania Avenue Development Corporation
African Development Foundation	Federal Election Commission	National Capital Planning Commission	Pension Benefit Guaranty Corporation
American Battle Monuments Commission	Federal Emergency Management Agency	National Credit Union Administration	Postal Rate Commission
Appalachian Regional Commission	Federal Home Loan Bank Board	National Foundation on the Arts and the Humanities	Railroad Retirement Board
Board for International Broadcasting	Federal Labor Relations Authority	National Labor Relations Board	Securities and Exchange Commission
Central Intelligence Agency	Federal Maritime Commission	National Mediation Board	Selective Service System
Commission on the Bicentennial of the United States Constitution	Federal Mediation and Conciliation Service	National Railroad Passenger Corporation (Amtrak)	Small Business Administration
Commission on Civil Rights	Federal Reserve System, Board of Governors of the	National Science Foundation	Tennessee Valley Authority
Commission on Fine Arts	Federal Trade Commission	National Transportation Safety Board	U.S. Arms Control and Disarmament Agency
Commodity Futures Trading Commission	General Services Administration	Nuclear Regulatory Commission	U.S. Information Agency
Consumer Product Safety Commission	Inter-American Foundation	Occupational Safety and Health Review Commission	U.S. International Development Cooperation Agency
Environmental Protection Agency	Interstate Commerce Commission	Office of Personnel Management	U.S. International Trade Commission
Equal Employment Opportunity Commission	Merit Systems Protection Board	Panama Canal Commission	U.S. Postal Service
Export-Import Bank of the U.S			
Farm Credit Administration			

SOURCE: *The U.S. Government Manual*

Government Corporations

Government corporations are similar to private corporations in that they charge clients for their services and are governed by a board of directors. However, government corporations receive federal funding to help defray operating expenses, and their directors are appointed by the president with Senate approval. The largest government corporation is the U.S. Postal Service, with roughly 800,000 employees. Other government corporations include the Federal Deposit Insurance Corporation (FDIC), which insures savings accounts against bank failures, and the National Railroad Passenger Corporation (Amtrak), which provides passenger rail service.

U.S. Postal Service seal

Presidential Commissions

Some **presidential commissions** are permanently established and provide ongoing recommendations to the president in particular areas of responsibility.

The Environmental Protection Agency uses this tank in New Jersey to test procedures and equipment for cleaning up oil spills. (Martin Rogers/Stock, Boston)

Two such commissions are the Commission on Civil Rights and the Commission on Fine Arts. Other presidential commissions are temporary and disband after making recommendations on specific issues. Temporary commissions during the 1980s included the President's Commission on Central America (charged with recommending a broad Central American policy) and the President's Private Sector Survey on Cost Control, commonly known as the Grace Commission (asked to suggest ways of reducing waste in the administration of federal programs).

FEDERAL EMPLOYMENT

The 3 million civilian employees of the federal government include professionals who bring their expertise to the problems of governing a large and complex society, service workers who perform such tasks as the typing of correspondence and the delivery of mail, and middle and top managers who supervise the work of the various federal agencies.

More than 90 percent of federal employees are hired by merit criteria, which include educational attainment, employment experience, and performance on competitive tests (such as the civil service and foreign service examinations). Merit hiring protects government workers from being fired for partisan reasons. The Supreme Court has ruled that "non-policymaking" public employees cannot be dismissed "on the sole ground of political belief."[7] Their job security is further enhanced by a limited right to a hearing in dismissal actions.[8]

Although federal employees were once underpaid in comparison with their counterparts in the private sector, they now receive reasonably competitive salaries, except at the top levels. The large majority of federal employees have a

---

[7]*Elrod* v. *Burns,* 727 U.S. 347 (1976).
[8]*Board of Regents* v. *Roth,* 408 U.S. 564 (1972).

The U.S. Postal Service, the largest government corporation, moves more mail, and does so more cheaply and reliably, than do the postal bureaucracies of most other industrialized nations. (Mark Antman/The Image Works)

GS (Graded Service) job ranking. The rankings, ranging from GS-1 to GS-18, are determined by job position and the employee's qualifications, such as level of education. Generally, a bachelor's degree is required for a GS-5 appointment, a master's degree for GS-9, and a doctorate for GS-11. A GS-5 starting salary is approximately $17,000, a GS-9 salary about $26,000, a GS-11 about $31,000. An employee's salary increases with length of service. Public employees receive substantial fringe benefits, including full health insurance, liberal retirement plans, and generous vacation time and sick leave.

Public service has its drawbacks. Unlike civil servants in, say, Great Britain or Germany, U.S. bureaucrats are not held in high esteem. Americans tend to look upon government employees as somehow less talented and industrious than people who hold comparable positions in the private sector. The evidence does not justify this perception, but it persists nonetheless and diminishes the satisfaction that federal bureaucrats derive from a career in public service.

Moreover, career bureaucrats are denied some opportunities that are available to workers in the private sector. The Hatch Act of 1939, as amended, prohibits federal employees from holding key positions (such as campaign manager or publicity director) in election campaigns.

In addition, federal employees have few rights of collective action.[9] They can join labor unions, but their unions by law have limited authority: the government maintains full control of job assignments, compensation, and promotion. Moreover, the Taft-Hartley Act of 1947 prohibits strikes by federal employees and permits the firing of workers who do go on strike.[10] In 1981 the 13,000-member Professional Air Traffic Controllers Organization (PATCO)

[9]Sar A. Levitan and Alexandra B. Noden, *Working for the Sovereign* (Baltimore: Johns Hopkins University Press, 1983), 28–29, 39.
[10]See Wilson R. Hart, *Collective Bargaining in the Federal Civil Service* (New York: Harper & Row, 1961), ch. 3.

As the members of the Professional Air Traffic Controllers Organization discovered in 1981, federal employees do not have the same labor rights as do union members in the private sector. President Reagan summarily fired all 11,500 striking PATCO members. (Charles Steiner/Sygma)

decided to ignore the ban and went on strike over pay and working conditions, particularly the strain of monitoring air traffic for long hours without relief. President Reagan immediately invoked the Taft-Hartley Act, officially ordering the 11,500 striking controllers back to work. When they refused, Reagan fired all of them and replaced them with supervisors, military and retired controllers, and nonstriking PATCO members. By 1982, as a rush training program began to provide additional controllers, the union was effectively broken. PATCO eventually filed for bankruptcy, and the striking controllers permanently lost their jobs.[11]

THE FEDERAL BUREAUCRACY'S POLICY RESPONSIBILITIES

We have noted that although the federal bureaucracy is a key policymaking institution, the Constitution does not mention it.[12] Its policymaking authority derives from grants of power to the constitutional branches: Congress, which has legislative power; the president, who has executive power; and the courts, which have judicial power.

Nevertheless, the bureaucracy is far more than an administrative extension of the three branches. It never merely follows orders. The primary function of the bureaucracy is **policy implementation,** which is to say that the bureaucracy carries out the authoritative decisions of Congress, the president, and the courts. Although implementation is sometimes described as "mere administration," it is a highly significant and creative function. The Communications Act of 1934, for example, specifies "public interest, convenience, and necessity" as the guiding principles for regulation of the broadcasting industry, but does not

[11]Levitan and Noden, *Working for the Sovereign,* 101–103.
[12]See John A. Rohr, *To Run a Constitution: The Legitimacy of the Administrative State* (Lawrence: University of Kansas Press, 1986).

go into detail as to what these principles might mean in practice. The responsibility for defining the law falls on the Federal Communications Commission (FCC), a bureaucratic agency created by Congress. Among the FCC's regulations was the "fairness doctrine," which (as we saw in Chapter 15) required broadcasters to present opposing views on controversial and important issues of public policy. In 1987 the FCC removed the restriction, despite objections by many members of Congress. The FCC's decision would have been overridden by Congress in late 1987, but President Reagan's threat of a veto caused the legislation to be set aside.

The fact that policy implementation is never merely "administrative" is made clearer by a brief look at the bureaucracy's major policy activities: *initiation of policy, development of policy, delivery of services, evaluation of programs, regulation,* and *adjudication.* In practice, these activities overlap, but they will be discussed as separate functions of the bureaucracy.

Initiation of Policy

Many ideas for legislative programs are initiated by the bureaucracy. In the course of their work, bureaucrats come up with policy ideas that are then brought to the attention of the president or members of Congress. The origin of the Occupational Safety and Health Act of 1970 is a case in point. A bureaucrat in the Department of Health, Education, and Welfare believed that worker safety was not receiving enough attention and encouraged his brother, a speechwriter for President Lyndon Johnson, to include references to worker safety in some of Johnson's speeches. The references attracted the attention of Department of Labor officials, who then persuaded the White House to include worker safety in the president's legislative program. The AFL-CIO picked up on the issue, as did some members of Congress. When the legislation was being

★ HOW THE UNITED STATES COMPARES

BUREAUCRATIC PERFORMANCE

According to a Harris poll, only one in four respondents have confidence in the performance of the U.S. federal bureaucracy. A comparison with other national bureaucracies, however, suggests that the U.S. federal bureaucracy is relatively effective. In fact, Charles Goodsell, a public administration expert, concludes that America's bureaucracy is among the best in the world. "Some national bureaucracies," he writes, "may be roughly the same [as the U.S. bureaucracy] in quality of overall performance, but they are few in number." In some countries, the bureaucracy is thoroughly inefficient and corrupt. Tasks are completed slowly and sometimes not at all unless a bribe has been paid. In other countries, the bureaucracy is overly rigid, centralized, and remote. The

rules are more important than the policy goals these rules are designed to achieve. Neither of these extreme tendencies is characteristic of the U.S. federal bureaucracy. Comparisons of national postal services, for example, confirm that the U.S. postal bureaucracy is among the world's best. The U.S. mail usually arrives on time, at the right destination, and with the right postage. In many countries, the mail is chronically late, often misrouted, frequently lost, and sometimes posted at the wrong rate.

SOURCE: Charles T. Goodsell, *The Case for Bureaucracy,* 2d ed. (Chatham, N.J.: Chatham House, 1985), 55–60.

As one of the thousands of services provided by the federal bureaucracy, the Department of Agriculture sets standards for the quality of meat and poultry sold to the public and conducts periodic inspections to ensure compliance with those standards. (Cary Wolinsky/Stock, Boston)

considered by congressional committees, bureaucrats who favored an occupational safety and health program were among the expert witnesses.[13]

Development of Policy

Bureaucratic agencies develop public policy. The decisions of Congress, the president, and the courts typically require fleshing out by the bureaucracy.[14] Most legislation, for example, specifies general goals, which bureaucrats then develop into specific programs. Consider the Drug-Free Workplace Act of 1988, which directs all organizations that receive grants from a federal agency to take steps to keep drugs out of the workplace or to face the possible loss of federal funding. The legislation provides that grantees will not lose their funds if drugs enter the workplace, provided that they have made "good-faith efforts" to keep drugs out. But what constitutes a "good-faith effort"? In large part, Congress left it to the bureaucrats to devise the criteria for judging enforcement efforts, which in effect meant that they created the rules by which the Drug-Free Workplace Act would be applied.

Delivery of Services

Agencies are charged with the delivery of services—carrying the mail, processing welfare applications, approving government loans, and the like. Such activities are governed by rules, and in most instances the rules decide what gets done. But some services allow agency employees enough discretion that

[13]Steven Kelman, "Occupational Safety and Health Administration," in James Q. Wilson, ed., *The Politics of Regulation* (New York: Basic Books, 1980), 239–240.
[14]For a different perspective, see Ira Sharkansky, *The Routines of Politics* (New York: Van Nostrand, 1970).

laws end up being applied arbitrarily, a situation that Michael Lipsky describes as "street-level bureaucracy."[15] A classic example is law enforcement. Although in theory law officers are impartial in their work, they routinely discriminate among types of enforcement activity. For example, FBI agents traditionally have concentrated more heavily on combating organized crime and political subversion than white-collar crime.

Evaluation of Programs

Agencies are charged with evaluating the programs they administer. Evaluation is extraordinarily important: it can reveal whether a program is having its intended impact and, if not, how it might be modified to be made more effective. But program evaluation is usually highly subjective. Whether a program is judged effective depends on which standards and evidence are used. For example, the Environmental Protection Agency (EPA) is responsible for implementing laws concerning water, air, and toxic wastes. With such a broad mandate, any number of methods (such as pollution statistics or citations) could be used to assess the effectiveness of EPA programs. In other words, EPA administrators are in a strong position to evaluate their agency's performance in a way that suits their goals. Threatened with budget cuts, for example, the EPA could undoubtedly produce "evidence" that the cuts would have disastrous consequences for the environment.

Regulation

The bureaucracy's policy role is perhaps clearest in its regulatory activities.[16] Lacking the necessary expertise and time, Congress has delegated regulatory responsibilities to specialized agencies. The EPA, for example, can fine a company that is not complying with antipollution standards and can refer serious cases to the Justice Department for further action. Agencies possess considerable discretion in their regulatory function. Consider the difference in the performance of the EPA under presidents Jimmy Carter and Ronald Reagan. The number of cases of industrial pollution referred by the EPA to the Justice Department for prosecution declined from 252 in 1980, Carter's last year in office, to 78 in 1981, Reagan's first year.[17]

Regulation is not confined to specialized agencies. All executive agencies issue binding regulations of one kind or another. The Department of Health and Human Services (HHS), for example, requires health institutions that receive federal assistance to comply with its affirmative action guidelines for the hiring and promotion of women and minorities.

Adjudication

Through reviews and hearings, bureaucrats exercise their responsibility to adjudicate disputes in the manner of the judicial branch. Hearings are held

---

[15]Michael Lipsky, *Street-Level Bureaucracy* (New York: Russell Sage Foundation, 1980).
[16]See Gary C. Bryner, *Bureaucratic Discretion: Law and Policy in Federal Regulatory Agencies* (Elmsford, N.Y.: Pergamon, 1987).
[17]Kenneth J. Meier, *Regulation* (New York: St. Martin's Press, 1985), 164.

TABLE 20-3 Justifications for Major Systems for Managing the Bureaucracy

System	Justification
Patronage	Makes the bureaucracy more responsive to election outcomes by allowing the president to appoint the top officials of executive agencies.
Merit	Provides for *competent* administration in that employees are hired on the basis of ability and allowed to remain on the job and thereby become proficient at their work, and provides for *neutral* administration in the sense that civil servants are not partisan appointees and thus are expected to do their work in an evenhanded way.
Executive leadership	Provides for presidential leadership of the bureaucracy in order to make it more responsive and to give it greater coordination and direction (left alone, the bureaucracy tends toward fragmentation).

before an administrative law officer, who, after hearing the arguments of the opposing sides, rules on the case. The ruling has a comparable status in law to a judicial decision. It can, in the manner of a court decision, be appealed to an appellate court but, barring a successful appeal, the ruling has the full force of law behind it. Adjudication, like lawsuits, is handled on a case-by-case basis. For example, public assistance recipients can request a hearing to contest a ruling that their benefits be terminated. The purpose of such hearings is to provide recipients with an opportunity to present their argument as to why they are still eligible for benefits.

The Development of the Federal Bureaucracy: Politics and Administration

The federal bureaucracy has been two centuries in the making, although most of its development has occurred since the 1930s. A more significant fact is that the organization and staffing of the bureaucracy have been administrative *and* political issues throughout the country's history. Agencies are responsible for carrying out programs that serve the society, and yet each agency was created and is maintained in response to partisan interests. Each agency thus confronts two simultaneous but incompatible demands: that it administer programs fairly and competently and that it respond to partisan claims.

Historically, this conflict has worked itself out in ways that have made the organization of the modern bureaucracy a blend of the political and the administrative. This dual line of development is clearly reflected in the mix of management systems that characterizes the bureaucracy today—the *patronage, merit,* and *executive leadership* systems (see Table 20-3).

SMALL GOVERNMENT AND THE PATRONAGE SYSTEM

The federal bureaucracy was originally small. Under the U.S. Constitution, the states retained responsibility for nearly all domestic policy areas. The federal government's role was confined mainly to defense and foreign affairs, currency and interstate commerce, and the postal system. Accordingly, the First Congress established departments of State, Treasury, and War. Shortly thereafter, a few other agencies were created, including the Department of the Navy and the offices of postmaster general and attorney general. By 1800 the federal government had only 3,000 civilian employees, more than a third of whom were involved in delivering the mail (see Figure 20-2).[18] By 1828 federal employment had risen to a mere 11,000.

In this early period, a large bureaucracy was not required because many of the major federal programs were discrete rather than continuous. Most of the early federal assistance to the states, for example, took the form of land grants. Once the land was deeded to the states, the federal government's role ended. One of the few ongoing activities of the federal government was the delivery of mail, which accounts for the fact that a large proportion of U.S. employees in this period were in the postal service. Until the Civil War, in fact, presidents personally made many of the decisions that today are handled by bureaucrats. President Martin Van Buren, for example, once had to choose the contractor who would build a fire engine that had been authorized by Congress.[19]

The nation's first six presidents, from George Washington through John Quincy Adams, believed that only distinguished men should be entrusted with the administration of the national government. Nearly all top presidential appointees were men of considerable talent, education, and political experience, and many of them were members of socially prominent families. They often remained in their jobs year after year.

The nation's seventh president, Andrew Jackson, did not share his predecessors' faith in the abilities of the wellborn.[20] In Jackson's view, government

The duties of all public office are so plain and simple that men of intelligence can readily qualify themselves for their performance.

Andrew Jackson

[18]Paul Van Riper, *History of the United States Civil Service* (Evanston, Ill.: Row, Peterson, 1958), 19.
[19]Benjamin Ginsberg, *The Consequences of Consent* (New York: Random House, 1982), 208.
[20]Fredrick C. Mosher, *Democracy and the Public Service,* 2d ed. (New York: Oxford University Press, 1982), 64–66.

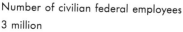

Number of civilian federal employees

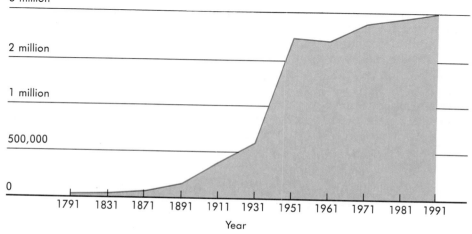

FIGURE 20-2 Number of Persons Employed by the Federal Government, 1791–1991 The federal bureaucracy grew slowly until the 1930s, when an explosive growth began in the number of programs that required ongoing administration by the federal government. *Source:* Historical Statistics of the United States *and* Statistical Abstract of the United States, 1986, 322; 1991 *figure from* Workforce Analysis and Statistics Division, U.S. Office of Personnel Management.

The Bureaucracy's Growth
Although it is sometimes said that bureaucracy begets more bureaucracy, the leading cause of growth in the federal bureaucracy has actually been policy demands emanating from the American people. In effect, the federal bureaucracy was built up from the outside, not the inside. Does knowledge of this fact alter your view of the bureaucracy? Does it alter your opinion of the possibility of a reduction in the size of the bureaucracy?

would be more responsive to the people if it were administered by common men of good sense. "The duties of all public office," Jackson claimed, "are so plain and simple that men of intelligence can readily qualify themselves for their performance."[21] Jackson also believed that top administrators should remain in office for short periods, so that there would be a steady influx of fresh ideas. Jackson's version of the **patronage system** was popular with the public, but critics labeled it a **spoils system**—a device for placing political cronies in high office as a reward for partisan service. In truth, Jackson's desire to reward partisan supporters was tempered by his concern for democratic government. Later presidents, however, were more interested in distributing the spoils of victory. Although Jackson left most lower officials in office, his successors extended patronage to these lesser positions.[22] Party bosses thus had plenty of federal jobs to give to their friends and loyalists, many of whom were incompetent or corrupt.[23] On balance, the patronage system may have actually decreased the bureaucracy's responsiveness to the public.

GROWTH IN GOVERNMENT AND THE MERIT SYSTEM

The patronage system was compatible with the small federal government of the early nineteenth century. Because the government's activities were relatively few and of limited scope, they could be managed by employees who had little or no administrative training or experience. As the century advanced, however, the nature of the bureaucracy changed rapidly, as did the bureaucracy's personnel needs.

An impetus for change was the Industrial Revolution, which was creating a truly national economy and prompting economic groups to pressure Congress to protect and promote their interests. Farmers were initially one of the most demanding groups, looking to the federal government for market and price assistance; in response, Congress created the Department of Agriculture in 1889. Business and labor interests also pressed their claims, and in 1903 Congress established the Department of Commerce and Labor to "promote the mutual interest" of the nation's firms and workers. (The separate interests of business and labor proved stronger than their shared concerns, so in 1913 Labor became a separate department.)[24]

While various economic sectors were advancing their interests, other Americans were demanding protection from economic exploitation. Popular discontent with unfair practices by the railroad monopolies led Congress in 1887 to establish the Interstate Commerce Commission (ICC). The Food and Drug Administration (FDA) was created in 1907 to protect consumers against unsafe products. The Federal Trade Commission (FTC) was formed in 1914 to prevent businesses from limiting competition. Whereas previous agencies had been formed primarily to carry out specific programs enacted by Congress, the ICC, FDA, and FTC were assigned ongoing legislative and judicial functions in

---

[21]Quoted in Van Riper, *History of the U.S. Civil Service*, 36.
[22]Jay M. Shafritz, *Personnel Management in Government* (New York: Marcel Dekker, 1981), 9–13.
[23]Herbert Kaufman, "Emerging Conflicts in the Doctrine of Public Administration," *American Political Science Review* 50 (December 1956): 1060.
[24]James Q. Wilson, "The Rise of the Bureaucratic State," *Public Interest* 41 (Fall 1975): 77–103.

The assassination of President James A. Garfield in 1881 by Charles Guiteau, a disappointed office seeker, did much to end the spoils system of distributing government jobs. (The Bettmann Archive)

addition to administrative ones. That is, they were instructed to develop regulations governing business activity and to investigate alleged violations of federal laws and regulations.

Because of the increased need for continuous administration of government, an ever-larger bureaucracy was required. By 1931 federal employment had reached 600,000, a sixfold increase over the level of the 1880s.[25] With President Franklin Roosevelt's New Deal, the federal work force increased enormously, to 1.2 million by 1940. Roosevelt's programs were generated in response to public demands for relief from the economic hardship and uncertainty of the Great Depression. Administration of these programs necessitated the formation of economic and social-welfare agencies such as the Securities and Exchange Commission (SEC) and the Social Security Board. The effect was to give the federal government an ongoing responsibility for Americans' economic well-being.

A large and active government requires skilled and experienced personnel. This fact was evident long before the 1930s. During the Civil War (1861–1865), President Lincoln complained that the then-dominant patronage system was inadequate to the country's emerging administrative needs. Yet the spoils system survived the Civil War and would have lasted much longer had not President James Garfield been assassinated in 1881 by a disgruntled party worker who had been promised a federal job but had not received it. Garfield's death strengthened the reform movement that was pushing for a **merit system,** or **civil service system,** of government employment. In 1883 Congress passed the Pendleton Act, which established a merit system whereby certain federal employees were hired through competitive examinations or by virtue of having special qualifications, such as an advanced degree in a particular field. The

[25]Nachmias and Rosenbloom, *Bureaucratic Government: U.S.A.*, 39; U.S. Bureau of the Census, *Historical Statistics of the United States: Colonial Times to 1970*, pt. 2 (Washington, D.C.: U.S. Government Printing Office, 1975), 1102.

Pendleton Act was the first national legislation in the field of public personnel administration and was therefore historic. However, the transition to a career civil service was gradual. Only about 10 percent of federal positions in 1885 were filled on the basis of merit; more than 70 percent were merit-based in 1919; and since 1947 the proportion of merit employees has not dipped below 80 percent.[26]

The Pendleton Act created a Civil Service Commission to establish job classifications, administer competitive examinations, and oversee merit employees. The commission was abolished in 1978 and replaced by two independent agencies. The Office of Personnel Management now supervises the hiring and classification of federal employees, and the Merit Service Protection Board handles appeals of personnel actions, such as demotions and dismissals, involving civil service employees.

The merit system is designed to separate the administration of government from partisan politics. The administrative objective is **neutral competence.**[27] A merit-based bureaucracy is "competent" in the sense that employees are hired on the basis of ability and are allowed to remain on the job indefinitely and thereby to become proficient in their work, and it is "neutral" in the sense that employees are not partisan appointees and thus are expected to do their work on behalf of the general public, not just the segment of the public that is loyal to the incumbent administration.

Although the merit system has wide acceptance, it does not guarantee impartial administration. In the process of administering the laws, bureaucrats necessarily make policy choices. Programs are not self-executing; they must be developed and applied by bureaucrats—a fact that both enables and requires them to play a policy role. The issue of the merit system is not, as some of its early advocates claimed, how to eliminate politics from administration but whether bureaucratic politics will be played by partisan appointees or by career civil servants. There is another broad sense in which a merit-based bureaucracy is political: career civil servants stay in their jobs regardless of which party wins elections, and they develop close ties with the interests that benefit from the programs they run. These factors tend to make civil servants powerful advocates of their agencies. Each agency naturally gives higher priority to its concerns than to those of other agencies and to those of Congress or the president. The results include a more fragmented government and a loss of political accountability because bureaucrats are not subject to election.[28] (The next chapter discusses these consequences of bureaucratic government in detail.)

BIG GOVERNMENT AND THE EXECUTIVE LEADERSHIP SYSTEM

As problems with the merit system surfaced after the early years of this century, reformers looked to a strengthened presidency—an **executive leadership system**—as a means of making the bureaucracy more responsive and better integrated.[29] The president was to provide the general leadership that would

---

[26]David H. Rosenbloom, *Federal Service and the Constitution* (Ithaca, N.Y.: Cornell University Press, 1971), 83.
[27]Kaufman, "Emerging Conflicts," 1060.
[28]Ibid., 1063.
[29]Ibid., 1062.

★ THE MEDIA AND THE PEOPLE

COMMUNICATIONS CHANGE AND GROWTH IN THE FEDERAL BUREAUCRACY

The growth in the federal bureaucracy that began in the late 1800s was a result of the increased complexity of American society. As the economy became more diverse and interdependent, problems emerged that demanded governmental solutions. State and local officials were not in a strong position to address these problems, which were largely national in scope. Accordingly, the national government gradually took on additional policy responsibilities.

The communications media contributed to the change. Until the late 1800s, there was, in effect, no mass media of communication in the United States. There were plenty of newspapers, but they did not have large circulations. Then, in the 1880s, newsprint was invented, which, along with the earlier invention of the rotary press, made mass circulation newspapers possible. By the 1890s, newspapers with a daily circulation of a half-million to a million readers were in place in the nation's largest cities. The reading audience was also a product of the times. The Industrial Revolution brought about a migration of Americans from the farms to the cities, which contributed to an increase in public school enrollment and a sharp rise in the nation's literacy rate. An urban middle class, which was the main audience for the mass newspaper, had developed.

The newspapers had a local base, but they also carried news of national politics. For the first time, tens of millions of Americans were kept up-to-date about the daily activities of the government in Washington. The newspapers, in a sense, were helping to build a stronger national community. Citizens began to look more and more toward Washington for solutions to their problems.

This history was repeated again in the 1950s and 1960s with a new set of issues, including education and racial discrimination, and a new mass medium, television. Television is a truly mass medium and, with its national audience, places even more emphasis on national politics than does the newspaper. Television made it easier for politicians like President Lyndon Johnson to build the national support that was necessary to pursue national policy solutions to political problems. A result was further growth in the federal bureaucracy.

overcome agency fragmentation and give the bureaucracy a common direction. As we saw in Chapter 18, Congress in 1939 provided the president with some of the tools needed for fuller control of the bureaucracy. The Office of Management and Budget (OMB) was created to allow the president to examine and adjust the annual budget proposal of each executive agency. The president was also empowered to reorganize the bureaucracy, subject to congressional approval, in order to reduce duplication of activities and strengthen the chain of command from the president to the agencies. Finally, the president was authorized to develop the Executive Office of the President, which oversees the agencies' activities on the president's behalf and assists him in the development of policy programs.

The Senior Executive Service (SES) is a more recently created presidential management tool. Established by Congress in 1978 at the urging of President Carter, the SES represents a compromise between two traditions: a president-led bureaucracy and an expert one.[30] The SES consists of roughly 8,000 top-level career civil servants who receive higher salaries than their peers but who can be assigned, dismissed, or transferred by order of the president. Unlike regular presidential appointees, however, SES bureaucrats cannot be fired; if

[30]See Mark W. Huddleston, "The Carter Civil Service Reforms," *Political Science Quarterly*, Winter 1981–82, 607–622.

the president relieves them of their jobs, they have "fallback" rights to their former rank in the regular civil service. The SES gives the president greater access to and control over individuals who are already expert in the bureaucracy's work. However, the SES is not a panacea: after years of work in the bureaucracy, many top-level bureaucrats have difficulty transferring their loyalty from an agency to the president.

Like the merit and patronage systems, the executive leadership system has brought problems as well as improvements to the administration of government. The chief drawback of placing additional power in the hands of the president has been the possibility that he may abuse it. Richard Nixon did so by using the OMB to impound (that is, fail to spend) more than $40 billion in program funds appropriated by Congress. Nixon claimed that his purpose was to prevent the funds from being spent wastefully or in ways inconsistent with other spending. In reality, however, Nixon disliked the programs in question and withheld the funds in order to prevent their implementation. The impoundment ended only after the courts ruled that Nixon's action was an unlawful infringement on Congress's constitutional authority over spending. To prevent a recurrence of the problem, Congress in 1974 passed legislation that gives the president the authority to withhold funds for only 45 days unless Congress passes legislation to rescind the appropriation.

Other presidents have at times put their administrative management tools to dubious use, but Nixon's impoundment policy most clearly illustrates the weakness of the executive leadership concept. If carried too far, it can threaten the balance of executive power and legislative power on which the U.S. constitutional system is based, and it can make partisanship, not fairness, the criterion by which provision of services is determined.

Despite its potential for abuse, the executive leadership system is a necessary component of any effective strategy for managing the modern federal bureauc-

President George Bush meets in January 1989 with Edwin Derwinski (*second from left*), his appointee as head of the new Department of Veterans Affairs. (Scott Applewhite/AP/Wide World)

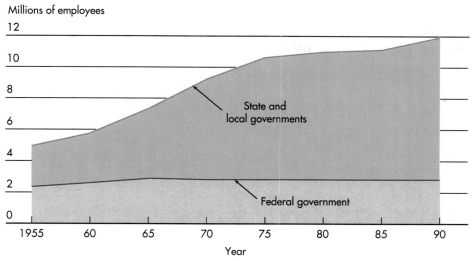

Millions of employees

FIGURE 20-3 Full-Time Civilian Employees of State and Local Governments and of the Federal Government, 1955–1990
Levels of employment in state and local governments have more than doubled in the past thirty years, while the number of federal government employees has remained fairly constant—evidence that the national government does not completely dominate America's system of federalism. *Source: U.S. Advisory Commission on Intergovernmental Relations. Based on statistics compiled by U.S. Bureau of the Census.*

racy.[31] Its size and range make the bureaucracy a management nightmare. Since the 1950s, the number of federal employees has been 2.5 million or more, and that figure actually understates the scope of national programs. In recent decades the federal government has developed and funded many programs that are administered through state and local governments (see Chapters 2 and 25). Their employment level has increased substantially during this period (see Figure 20-3). In addition, the federal government has hired increasing numbers of private consultants and firms to do tasks that would once have been assigned to federal employees.[32] Finally, nearly a third of the bureaucracy's roughly 400 separate and semi-autonomous agencies have been established since the 1950s.[33]

Government agencies have proliferated largely in response to political demands that have arisen from the economic, technological, and social complexity of American society. Examples include the Department of Health and Human Services (which began as the Department of Health, Education, and Welfare in 1953), the Civil Rights Commission (1957), the National Aeronautics and Space Administration (1958), the Department of Housing and Urban Development (1965), the Department of Transportation (1966), the Environmental Protection Agency (1970), the Department of Energy (1977), and the Department of Education (1979).

In the 1980s an economic downturn contributed to a slowing of the bureaucracy's growth, but efforts to streamline the bureaucracy were affected by political demands. Although President Reagan had stated his determination to cut the size of the bureaucracy, he quietly shelved his plan as he learned the timeless lesson that agencies represent powerful constituencies. Reagan further

[31]See Richard W. Waterman, *Presidential Influence and the Administrative State* (Knoxville: University of Tennessee Press, 1989).
[32]See James T. Bennett, "How Big Is the Federal Government?" *Economic Review*, December 1981, 43–49.
[33]Herbert Kaufman, *Are Governmental Organizations Immortal?* (Washington, D.C.: Brookings Institution, 1976), 48–49.

★ CRITICAL THINKING

WHAT IS THE PROPER BALANCE BETWEEN THE MERIT AND EXECUTIVE LEADERSHIP SYSTEMS?

The justification for the merit system is neutral competence, which refers to administration by experienced bureaucrats who apply the law without regard to either their own partisan goals or those of their clients. The merit system is designed to produce this effect by allowing bureaucrats, who are selected on the basis of ability, to stay on the job indefinitely. The merit system is contrasted with the executive leadership system, which, among other things, results in the selection of top bureaucrats who are chosen by the president to carry out his program and whose job tenure may last no longer than the next election.

Some observers claim that the merit system does not achieve its stated goal of neutral competence. They argue that career bureaucrats almost inevitably develop close ties with the interests that benefit from the programs they run. They become political advocates rather than neutral administrators. An argument for the executive leadership model is that there is a democratic justification—the will of the people as expressed in a presidential election—for the bias it introduces into the administration of government. No advocate of the executive leadership model would hold that administration in all respects should be overtly partisan (imagine sending monthly social security checks to Republicans or Democrats only). However, proponents of executive leadership do argue that the driving force in bureaucratic politics (which includes, for example, the struggle over budgetary priorities) should be partisanship as expressed through elections and not partisanship as expressed through an entrenched civil service.

In contrast, supporters of the merit system say that neutral competence—impartial and expert administration—should be the primary goal of a governmental bureaucracy, and that the merit system is the only realistic way of approaching the goal. They argue that career civil servants have a commendable record of impartial public service, which has served the country well. They would not deny the importance of executive leadership to a properly functioning bureaucracy, but would contend that presidential politics should not be allowed to seep into all aspects of administration. The fear is that the public would lose confidence in government because the laws are not being administered impartially.

What balance would you strike between the merit and executive leadership systems? How would you achieve this balance in practice? Would you have the same opinion about the balance if control of the White House were to shift to the other major party?

acknowledged political realities when he proposed in 1987 that the Veterans Administration (VA), an independent agency, be elevated to cabinet status. The VA became the Department of Veterans Affairs by act of Congress in late 1988. Its annual budget of $30 billion includes funds for a medical care system, pensions, and loan benefits for veterans of military service, who, through national organizations such as the American Legion and Veterans of Foreign Wars, are a vocal and powerful lobby.

THE MODERN BUREAUCRACY: A MIX OF MANAGEMENT SYSTEMS

The executive leadership system of public administration has not replaced the merit system, just as the merit system did not eliminate the patronage system. The federal bureaucracy today retains aspects of all three systems, a situation that reflects the tensions inherent in governmental administration. The bureaucracy is expected to carry out programs fairly and impartially, but it is also expected to respond to political forces. The first of these requirements is addressed primarily through the merit system and the second through the executive leadership and patronage systems (see box).

This blending of partisan and nonpartisan elements hardly settles the issues that surround the bureaucracy's influence. The bureaucracy is essentially America's permanent government. Its ongoing programs outlast any president or Congress, and its power, which derives from its size and specialization, is not easily brought under control. The next chapter examines the bureaucracy's power and the problems it poses for democratic government.

Summary

Bureaucracy is a method of organizing people and work; it is based on the principles of hierarchical authority, job specialization, and formalized rules. As a form of organization, bureaucracy is the most efficient means of getting people to work together on tasks of great magnitude and complexity.

The United States could not be governed without a large federal bureaucracy. The day-to-day work of the federal government, from mail delivery to provision of social security to international diplomacy, is done by the bureaucracy. The federal bureaucracy's 3 million employees work in roughly 400 major agencies, including cabinet departments, independent agencies, regulatory agencies, government corporations, and presidential commissions.

Yet the bureaucracy is more than simply an administrative giant. Bureaucrats exercise considerable discretion in their policy decisions. In the process of implementing policy—which includes initiation and development of policy, evaluation of programs, delivery of services, regulation, and adjudication—bureaucrats make important policy and political choices.

Each agency of the federal government was created in response to political demands on national officials. During the country's earliest decades, the bureaucracy was small, a reflection of the federal government's relatively few responsibilities outside the areas of national security and commerce. As the economy became increasingly industrialized and its sectors increasingly interconnected in the late nineteenth century, the bureaucracy expanded in response to the demands of economic interests and the requirement for regulation of certain business activities. During the Great Depression, social-welfare programs and further business regulatory activities were added to the bureaucracy's responsibilities. After World War II, the heightened role of the United States in world affairs and public demands for additional social services fueled the bureaucracy's growth. Government agencies continued to multiply in the 1970s in response to broad consumer and environmental issues as well as to technological change. The bureaucracy's growth slowed in the 1980s because of federal budget deficits and the philosophy of the Reagan administration.

Because of its origins in political demands, the bureaucracy is necessarily political. An inherent conflict results from two simultaneous but incompatible demands on the bureaucracy: that it respond to the demands of partisan officials but also that it administer programs fairly and competently. These tensions are evident in the three concurrent personnel management systems under which the bureaucracy operates: patronage, merit, and executive leadership.

Major Concepts

bureaucracy	merit (civil service) system
cabinet (executive) departments	neutral competence
executive leadership system	patronage system
formalized rules	policy implementation
government corporations	presidential commissions
hierarchical authority	regulatory agencies
independent agencies	spoils system
job specialization	

Suggested Readings

Berry, William D., and David Lowery. *Understanding U.S. Government Growth.* New York: Praeger, 1987. An analysis of government growth in the post–World War II era as a function of economic growth.

Bryner, Gary C. *Bureaucratic Discretion: Law and Policy in Federal Regulatory Agencies.* Elmsford, N.Y.: Pergamon Press, 1987. An exploration of bureaucratic decision making, with an emphasis on regulatory policy.

Gerth, H. H., and C. Wright Mills, eds. *From Max Weber: Essays in Sociology.* New York: Oxford University Press, 1946. Weber's writings on bureaucracy are the classic analysis of this form of organization.

Goodsell, Charles T. *The Case for Bureaucracy.* Chatham, N.J.: Chatham House, 1983. A defense of the bureaucracy against many of the common complaints (e.g., red tape, wastefulness) about it.

Kaufman, Herbert. *Red Tape: Its Origins, Uses, and Abuses.* Washington, D.C.: Brookings Institution, 1977. An analysis of why bureaucratic rules and regulations are seemingly excessive, and why red tape frustrates some interests and benefits others.

Pressman, Jeffrey, and Aaron Wildavsky. *Implementation,* 3d ed. Berkeley: University of California Press, 1984. A case study of a federal job-creation program which assesses the problems of policy implementation.

Rosenbloom, David H. *Public Administration and Law.* New York: Marcel Dekker, 1983. A valuable review by a leading scholar of administrative law.

Stillman, Richard Joseph. *The American Bureaucracy.* Chicago: Nelson-Hall, 1987. A careful overview of U.S. agencies.

Wilson, James Q. *Bureaucracy.* New York: Basic Books, 1989. An insightful analysis of what government agencies do and why they do it.

BUREAUCRATIC POLICYMAKING: COMPETING FOR POWER

The lifeblood of administration is power.
Norton E. Long[1]

Congress enacted the Occupational Safety and Health Act of 1970 "to assure as far as possible every working man and woman in the nation safe and healthy work conditions." The legislation shifted the primary responsibility for occupational safety and health to the federal government from the states, which had addressed the issue largely through compensation payments to workers injured on the job or to the survivors of workers killed on the job. The federal program, in contrast, would focus on the prevention of job-related injuries, illnesses, and deaths. Firms would be subject to stringent health and safety standards and would have to submit to on-site inspectors.[2]

The Occupational Safety and Health Administration (OSHA) was created to administer the program. OSHA was granted broad regulatory power and was authorized to hire specialists, such as safety engineers and industrial hygienists, who could be expected to look out for workers' interests. In its first year OSHA issued more than 4,000 health and safety standards. Most of the standards were based on accepted practices, such as the requirement that fire extinguishers be placed in work areas, but some standards were excessively elaborate or laughably out of date. For example, there were 140 standards for industrial ladders, covering everything from construction materials to the distance between rungs. There was also a regulation that prohibited employers from placing ice in employees' drinking water, a legacy from the days when ice was cut from polluted lakes.

---

[1]Norton E. Long, "Power and Administration," *Public Administration Review* 10 (Autumn 1949): 257.
[2]Kenneth J. Meier, *Regulation* (New York: St. Martin's Press, 1985). The lead paragraphs in this chapter are based on Meier's ch. 8.

While government officials debated the proper role of the Occupational Safety and Health Administration, thousands of people continued to die each year as a result of work-related accidents and illnesses. (Robert Fox/Impact Visuals)

Some of this regulatory overkill was attributable to the growing pains that afflict any new organization. But OSHA's approach also reflected the values of its professional staff. The agency's safety engineers and industrial hygienists believed in the importance of reducing occupational hazards and were intent on vigorously pursuing that goal. A survey indicated that 80 percent of OSHA inspectors believed that business firms would try to evade safety and health requirements unless they were held to high standards of accountability.[3]

Congress was generally supportive of OSHA during its first years but held several hearings at which its overzealousness was criticized. President Jimmy Carter also backed OSHA but demanded that it give more consideration to whether the benefits of specific regulations justified the costs they imposed on businesses. When Ronald Reagan became president, OSHA came under sharp attack. Business had opposed OSHA's formation and welcomed Reagan's cutbacks in its personnel and regulations. Organized labor lashed out at Reagan, claiming that any curtailment of OSHA's activities was a blow to workers' safety and health. Congress held hearings at which witnesses criticized the Reagan administration's handling of OSHA. Meanwhile, the agency's health and safety specialists fought to maintain the effectiveness of their programs.

The battle over OSHA illustrates the nature of bureaucratic politics. The bureaucracy is caught between competing demands and conflicting power centers. The American political system, with its plural interests and fragmented governing authority, requires bureaucrats to play politics. If administrators are to carry out the programs assigned to them, they must have the power to make decisions and put them into effect. Because different interests and officials will have widely varying opinions on the merits of an agency's programs, the agency must fight for power or it will be submerged by those who are working toward other goals and *are* willing to compete for power.

[3]Steven Kelman, "Occupational Safety and Health Administration," in James Q. Wilson, ed., *The Politics of Regulation* (New York: Basic Books, 1980), 255.

This chapter examines bureaucratic policymaking from the standpoint of the ways in which agencies acquire the power they need in order to maintain themselves and their programs. The chapter shows that career bureaucrats necessarily and naturally take an "agency point of view," seeking to promote their agency's objectives. Moreover, they have substantial resources—expertise, group support, and presidential and congressional backing—that help them to promote their agency's goals. The three constitutional branches of government impose a degree of accountability on the bureaucracy; but the U.S. system of government, with its fragmented authority, frees bureaucrats from tight control. The main points discussed in this chapter are the following:

★ *Because of America's diversity and fragmented system of government, bureaucrats must compete for the power required to administer programs effectively.*

★ *Bureaucrats are committed to the goals of their particular agencies.* Their expert knowledge, support from clientele groups, and backing by Congress and the president help them to promote agency goals.

★ *Agencies are subject to control by the president, Congress, and the judiciary, but these controls place only general limits on the bureaucracy's power.* A major reason agencies are able to achieve power in their own right is that Congress and the president often resist each other's attempts to control the bureaucracy.

★ *The bureaucracy's power is not easily reconciled with the principle of self-government.* Bureaucrats are not directly accountable to the people through elections.

The Bureaucracy's Power Imperative

Agencies of the federal bureaucracy must fight for the power that they need if they are to conduct their programs effectively.[4] This fact cannot be understood without consideration of broader tendencies in the American political system, particularly diversity and the separation of powers.

Elections in the United States, unlike those in many other democracies, do not provide a clear mandate for either the winning party's platform or the president's leadership.[5] Because even candidates of the same party do not have a shared agenda and because the president and Congress are elected separately, the task of establishing programs and priorities is dealt with largely after elections and through a process of continuous bargaining and power wielding. The president will insist that his ideas should take precedence, but so will Congress. Moreover, conflicting interests will make claims on both the president and Congress. In short, the American political system produces not a government of clear and accepted objectives, but a government in which objectives are always open to dispute.

If agencies are to operate successfully in this system, they must seek support where they can find it—if not from the president, then from Congress; if not from one interest, then from another; if not today, then tomorrow. In other

---

[4]Long, "Power and Administration." Long's argument provides the basis for the lead paragraphs of this section.
[5]Ibid., 259.

words, agencies must play politics. They must devote themselves to building enough support to permit the effective administration of their programs. If they do not, their goals will suffer because other agencies that *are* willing to play politics will grab the available funding, attention, and support. The importance of this principle has increased because of the federal government's persistent fiscal problems and because of rapid changes in the world, most notably the demise of U.S.-Soviet conflict. These developments require a substantial reallocation of resources across policy areas, and thus across federal agencies. Any agency that is content to sit idly by while new priorities for money and policy are determined is virtually certain to lose out.

THE AGENCY POINT OF VIEW

Bureaucrats have little choice but to look out for their agency's interests, a perspective that is called the **agency point of view.**[6] This perspective comes naturally to most high-ranking civil servants. Their careers within the bureaucracy have taught them to do the job they are assigned, which in all cases is to do their part in making the organization effective. Many bureaucrats are also personally committed to their agency's objectives as a result of having spent years at work on its programs. More than 80 percent of all top careerists reach their high-level positions by rising through the ranks of the same agency.[7] As one top bureaucrat said in testifying before the House Appropriations Committee, "Mr. Chairman, you would not think it proper for me to be in charge of this work and not be enthusiastic about it . . . , would you? I have been in it for thirty years, and I believe in it."[8]

Professionalism also cements agency loyalties.[9] As public policymaking has become more complex, high-level positions in the bureaucracy have increasingly been filled by scientists, engineers, lawyers, educators, physicians, and other professionals. Most of them take jobs in an agency that has programs consistent with their professional values. Consider the case of John Nestor, a physician who tested drugs for the Food and Drug Administration (FDA). Dr. Nestor saw it as his medical and administrative duty to protect the public from unsafe drugs and became angry when a drug that had not been fully tested was approved for sale by the FDA's director, who was a presidential appointee and a supporter of the pharmaceutical industry. "I believe," said Nestor in testimony before a Senate committee, "that hundreds of people . . . suffer daily, and many die because [presidential appointees within the FDA have] failed utterly in . . . enforcing those sections of the law dealing with the safety and mishandling of drugs."[10]

[6]See Robert Harasch, *The Institutional Imperative* (New York: Charterhouse Books, 1973); William A. Niskanen, Jr., *Bureaucracy and Representation* (Chicago: Aldine-Atherton, 1971), 38; Morton H. Halperin, *Bureaucratic Politics and Foreign Policy* (Washington, D.C.: Brookings Institution, 1974), 39–40; Anthony Downs, *Inside Bureaucracy* (Boston: Little, Brown, 1967), 212–218; Herbert Kaufman, *The Administrative Behavior of Federal Bureaucrats* (Washington, D.C.: Brookings Institution, 1981), 4.
[7]Hugh Heclo, *A Government of Strangers* (Washington, D.C.: Brookings Institution, 1977), 117–118.
[8]Quoted in Aaron Wildavsky, *The Politics of the Budgetary Process* (Boston: Little, Brown, 1964), 19.
[9]Frederick C. Mosher, *Democracy and the Public Service*, 2d ed. (New York: Oxford University Press, 1982), ch.2.
[10]Quoted in Kenneth Lassim, *Private Lives of Public Servants* (Bloomington: Indiana University Press, 1978), 96–97.

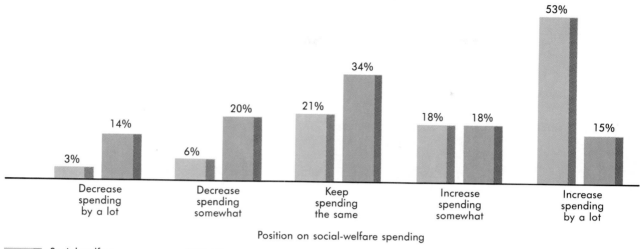

Position on social-welfare spending

Social-welfare bureaucrats

Other bureaucrats

Studies confirm that bureaucrats believe in the importance of their agency's work.[11] One study found that social-welfare administrators are three times as likely as other civil servants to believe that social-welfare programs should have a high budget priority (see Figure 21-1). Another survey found that 80 percent of administrators believe that their agency's budget deserved to be increased substantially.[12]

SOURCES OF BUREAUCRATIC POWER

In promoting their agency's interests, bureaucrats rely on their specialized knowledge, the support of interests that benefit from the programs they run, and the backing of the president and Congress.

The Power of Expertise

Many of the policy problems that the federal government confronts do not lend themselves to simple solutions. Whether the issue is space travel, hunger in America, or trade relations with Japan, expert knowledge is essential to the development of effective public policy. Much of this expertise is held by bureaucrats. Bureaucrats specialize in narrow policy areas, and many have had scientific, technical, or other specialized training that helps them to understand complex issues.[13]

By comparison, elected officials are generalists. To some degree members of

FIGURE 21-1 Attitudes toward Social-Welfare Spending Held by Bureaucrats in Social-Welfare Agencies and in Other Agencies
Bureaucrats who work in social-welfare agencies are much more likely than other bureaucrats to believe that spending on social-welfare programs should be increased. These survey results illustrate the "agency point of view." *Source: Adapted from Joel D. Aberbach and Bert A. Rockman, "Clashing Beliefs within the Executive Branch: The Nixon Administration Bureaucracy,"* American Political Science Review 70 *(June 1976): 461.*

An expert is one who knows more and more about less and less.

Nicholas Murray Butler

[11]See Kenneth J. Meier and Lloyd Nigro, "Representative Bureaucracy and Policy Preferences," *Public Administrative Review* 36 (July/August 1976): 446; Joel D. Aberbach and Bert A. Rockman, "Clashing Beliefs within the Executive Branch," *American Political Science Review* 70 (June 1976): 461.

[12]Advisory Commission on Intergovernmental Relations, *The Intergovernmental Grant System as Seen by Local, State, and Federal Officials,* A-54 (Washington, D.C.: U.S. Government Printing Office, 1977), 184.

[13]Joel D. Aberbach, Robert Putnam, and Bert A. Rockman, *Bureaucrats and Politicians in Western Democracies* (Cambridge, Mass.: Harvard University Press, 1981), 52.

The Career Bureaucracy's Authority

It is sometimes said that bureaucrats should not have policy authority because they are not elected by the people. Is this perspective useful? Does it make any sense to pretend that all authority should rest with elected institutions when government depends also on the continuity, expertise, and impartiality that only a career bureaucracy can provide?

Congress do specialize through their committee work, but they rarely have the time or inclination to acquire a commanding knowledge of a particular issue. The president's understanding of policy issues is even more general. Not surprisingly, bureaucrats are a major source of policy ideas. They are more likely than either the president or members of Congress to be aware of particular problems and to have policy solutions in mind. According to Richard Rose, the president's influence on policy is felt primarily through his decisions about which bureaucratic initiatives to embrace and which to ignore.[14] Congress is in somewhat the same situation; as mentioned in Chapter 20, many bills proposed by members of Congress are conceived by careerists in the bureaucracy.

Not all agencies acquire a great amount of leverage from their staffs' expert knowledge. Those that do have an edge have highly specialized, professional staffs. For example, the expert judgments of the health scientists and physicians in the National Institutes of Health (NIH) are rarely challenged by elected officials. They may question the political assessments of these health professionals but are unlikely to question their scientific evaluations, which are sometimes decisive. For example, as much as some elected officials may have wanted to avoid the issues surrounding the AIDS epidemic during the 1980s, they were eventually forced into action by the warnings of health scientists about the dire consequences of a do-nothing policy.

The power of expertise is conditioned by the extent to which an agency's employees share the same goals. In many agencies, such as the NIH, careerists with different professional backgrounds have similar values. In other agencies professional infighting breaks down this cohesiveness and gives outsiders an opportunity to support the faction whose aims agree with their own. An example is the Federal Trade Commission (FTC), which is divided between its lawyers, who tend to emphasize issues that can be quickly and successfully litigated, and its economists, who tend to stress larger and more complicated issues that have broad implications for national commerce.[15]

Nevertheless, *all* agencies acquire some power through their careerists' expertise.[16] No matter how simple a policy issue may appear at first, it invariably involves more than meets the eye. This situation gives mission-oriented bureaucrats the opportunity to apply their expertise to the agency's advantage.[17] A recognition that the United States has a trade deficit with Japan, for example, is a foundation for policy change, but this recognition does not begin to address such basic questions as the form that the new policy might take, its probable cost and effectiveness, and its connection to other trade issues. Answers to these questions are fundamental to a change in policy, and the officials most likely to have the answers are the trade experts in agencies such as the Commerce Department and the Federal Trade Commission.

The Power of Clientele Groups

Most agencies have **clientele groups,** which are special interests that benefit directly from an agency's programs. Typically, whenever an agency or program

[14]Richard Rose, *Managing Presidential Objectives* (New York: Free Press, 1976), 149.
[15]Meier, *Regulation,* 16.
[16]Jonathan Bendor, Serge Taylor, and Roland Van Gaalen, "Stacking the Deck: Bureaucratic Missions and Policy Design," *American Political Science Review* 81 (September 1987): 873–896.
[17]Samuel Beer, "Political Overload and Federalism," *Polity* 10 (Fall 1977): 11.

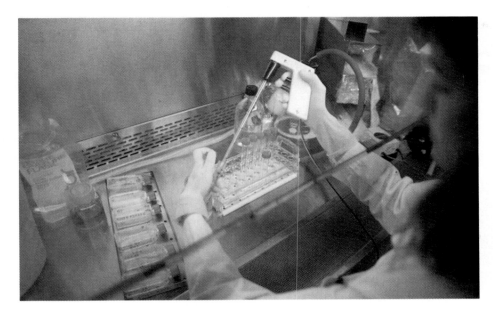

Research on AIDS conducted at the National Institutes of Health provided the expert knowledge that helped the agency to convince elected officials that AIDS-related policy measures were needed. (Shepard Sherbell/Picture Group)

is created, a clientele lobby springs up to protect it.[18] For example, the welfare programs that were part of Johnson's Great Society in the 1960s were quickly

[18]Matthew Holden, Jr., "'Imperialism' in Bureaucracy," *American Political Science Review* 60 (December 1966): 944.

The huge corporate "agribusinesses" make up a large part of the nation's farm sector, form a clientele group, and are a powerful ally of the bureaucrats who administer agricultural programs. (Peter Menzel/Stock, Boston)

taken under the wing of such interest groups as the National Welfare Rights Organization and the American Association of Retired Persons. Clientele groups place pressure on Congress and the president to retain the programs on which they depend.[19] A result is that agency programs, once started, are difficult to terminate. "Government activities," as public administration expert Herbert Kaufman says, "tend to go on indefinitely."[20]

In general, agencies lead and are led by the clientele groups that depend on the programs they administer.[21] Many agencies were created for the purpose of promoting particular interests in society and, because of their permanence, outlook, and resources, are the major channel of representation for these interests. For example, the Department of Agriculture's career bureaucrats are dependable allies of farm interests year after year. The same cannot be said of the president, Congress as a whole, or either political party; these other channels, while not antagonistic to the agricultural sector, must balance its demands against those of other interests. Department of Agriculture careerists have no such conflict: promoting agriculture is their only concern.

An agency can get too cozy with its clientele groups. An example is the role of the Federal Home Loan Bank Board (HLBB) in the savings and loan scandal of the 1980s. The HLBB's examiners did not fully report to the board the problems facing some thrift institutions, and their reports on others were ignored by the board. The HLBB is accused of delaying corrective action until an estimated $500 billion had been lost. In 1989 Congress abolished the HLBB.

The Power of Friends in High Places

Although members of Congress and the president sometimes appear to be at war with the bureaucracy, they need it as much as it needs them. An agency's resources—its programs, expertise, and group support—can assist elected officials in their efforts to achieve their goals. When George Bush came to the White House, he made the problem of drug-related crime a top priority, and he needed the help of Justice Department careerists to make his efforts successful. They were more than eager to help. At a time when other agencies were feeling the pinch of a tight federal budget, Justice was expanding. The department's personnel increased by 20 percent between 1989 and 1992.

Bureaucrats seek favorable relations with members of Congress, too. From the perspective of the bureaucracy, congressional support is vital because agencies' funding and programs are provided through legislation. Agencies that offer benefits to major constituency interests are particularly likely to have close ties to Congress. In some policy areas, more or less permanent alliances—"iron triangles"—form among agencies, clientele groups, and congressional subcommittees.[22] In other policy areas, temporary "issue networks" form among bureaucrats, lobbyists, and members of Congress.[23] As we saw in Chapters 14

[19]See Peter Woll, *American Bureaucracy,* 2d ed. (New York: Norton, 1977), ch.1.
[20]Herbert Kaufman, *Are Government Organizations Immortal?* (Washington, D.C.: Brookings Institution, 1976), 76.
[21]Long, "Power and Administration," 269.
[22]See Harold Seidman, *Politics, Position, and Power: The Dynamics of Federal Organization,* 2d ed. (New York: Oxford University Press, 1975), 150.
[23]Hugh Heclo, "Issue Networks and the Executive Establishment," in Anthony King, ed., *The New American Political System* (Washington, D.C.: American Enterprise Institute, 1978), 102.

TABLE 21-1 Responses of Members of Congress to the Question: "Do You Think It Is Desirable for a Government Agency to Have Close Relations with Its Clientele?"

Response	Percentage Responding "Yes"
Close relations desirable	34%
Close relations, with reservations	39
Depends on situation	3
Distant relations, with reservations	10
Distant relations desirable	13
	99%

SOURCE: Joel D. Aberbach and Bert A. Rockman, "Bureaucrats and Clientele Groups: A View from Capitol Hill," *American Journal of Political Science* 22 (November 1978): 821.

and 17, these alliances enable agencies and interest groups to work toward programs they want and provide members of Congress with electoral support.[24] Not surprisingly, most members of Congress believe that government agencies should maintain close relationships with their clientele groups (see Table 21-1).

A common misperception is that, because the president is the chief executive, he alone has a claim on the bureaucracy's loyalty. In fact, each of the elected institutions has reason to claim proprietorship: the president because of his position as chief executive and Congress because it authorizes and funds the bureaucracy's programs. Neither elected branch is inclined to concede domination over agencies to the other branch,[25] and neither is required by the Constitution to do so. The courts have held that the president can insist that the bureaucracy carry out the laws faithfully while Congress can define through law what an agency must do.[26] Faced with a threat from either Congress or the president, agencies often find that the other becomes an ally. One presidential appointee was bluntly informed of Congress's ability to protect the bureaucracy from intrusions by the executive. The appointee asked a congressional committee whether it had any problem with a planned reduction in his agency's authority. The committee chairman replied, "No, you have the problem, because if you touch that bureau I'll cut your job out of the budget."[27]

The president and Congress are often at odds over the bureaucracy partly as a matter of institutional rivalry. The American system of separate institutions sharing power results in a natural tendency for each institution to guard its turf. In addition, the president and members of Congress differ in their constituencies and thus in the interests to which they are most responsive. For example, although the agricultural sector is just one of many concerns of the president, it is a preoccupation of senators and representatives from farm states; they will fight a president's efforts to cut back agricultural programs. Finally, because the president and Congress are elected separately, the White House and one or

[24]Joel D. Aberbach and Bert A. Rockman, "Bureaucrats and Client Groups: A View from Capitol Hill," *American Journal of Political Science* 22 (November 1978): 821.
[25]Dean Alger, "The Presidency, the Bureaucracy, and the People," paper presented at the annual meeting of the American Political Science Association, New Orleans, 1985.
[26]Louis Fisher, *American Constitutional Law* (New York: McGraw-Hill, 1990), 222, 225.
[27]Quoted in Heclo, *Government of Strangers*, 225.

Anne Burford Gorsuch was forced to resign as head of the Environmental Protection Agency in 1983 after some career employees of the agency leaked information to Congress and the press about her failure to enforce antipollution laws. (AP/Wide World)

both houses of Congress may be in the hands of opposing parties. Of late, this source of executive-legislative conflict has been more often the rule than the exception. Since 1968 there have been only four years in which the same party controlled the presidency and both houses of Congress.

When congressional and presidential ambitions collide, agencies often win out by having either Congress or the White House on their side. Consider the case of the Environmental Protection Agency (EPA) in the early 1980s. The EPA's career staff is dominated by employees who prize environmental protection: pollution-control engineers, health specialists, environmental scientists, and public-interest lawyers.[28] Their values conflicted with those of Reagan's EPA appointees, who were determined to relax the agency's enforcement of antipollution laws in order to benefit business. Through information leaked by EPA careerists, the news media disclosed that the EPA's partisan appointees had privately arranged lenient settlements for firms that had committed serious violations of toxic-waste disposal regulations. The ensuing congressional investigation resulted in the resignation, dismissal, or conviction in court of more than a dozen top EPA officials. Under pressure from Congress and the public, Reagan appointed a new EPA head, William Ruckelshaus, who put the EPA back on the track of vigorous enforcement of environmental protection standards, as its careerists wanted.

Bureaucratic Accountability

Your public servants serve you right.

Adlai Stevenson

Bureaucratic politics raises the specter of a huge, permanent, and uncontrollable organization run by entrenched unelected officials. Adapting the requirements of bureaucracy to those of democracy has been a persistent challenge for public

[28]Meier, *Regulation*, 146.

administration.[29] The issue is **accountability:** the capacity of the public to hold officials responsible for their actions. In the case of the bureaucracy, accountability works primarily through other institutions: the presidency, Congress, and the courts.

ACCOUNTABILITY THROUGH THE PRESIDENCY

All presidents have found the bureaucracy an obstacle to some of their goals. As chief executive, the president may believe that the bureaucracy should be subject to his command; but he is actually able to impose only his general guidance, not direct control, on the bureaucracy.[30] "We can outlast any president" is a common view among bureaucrats. Each agency has its clientele and its congressional supporters, as well as statutory authority for its existence and activities. No president can unilaterally eliminate an agency or its funding and programs. Nor can the president be indifferent to the opinions of career civil servants, because he needs their support and expertise to develop and implement his own policy objectives.

To encourage the bureaucracy to follow his lead, the president has important management tools that have developed out of the "executive leadership" concept discussed in Chapter 20. These tools include reorganization, presidential appointees, and the executive budget.

Reorganization

The bureaucracy's extreme fragmentation—its hundreds of separate agencies —makes presidential coordination of its activities difficult. Agencies pursue independent, even contradictory paths, resulting in an undetermined amount of waste and duplication of effort. For example, some twenty-five units have responsibility for various aspects of national trade policy.[31] More than 100 units have pieces of education policy.

All recent presidents have tried to reorganize the bureaucracy to streamline it and make it more accountable.[32] The most ambitious reorganization plan was Nixon's proposal to combine fifty domestic agencies into four large departments, which would have given him tighter control over domestic policy by placing it under the direction of a few cabinet secretaries. Existing agencies fought Nixon's plan because it threatened their independence. Their clientele groups joined the opposition because they feared the loss of programs. Members of Congress rejected Nixon's plan because of the objections of various interests and also because they recognized that centralization would reduce their influence with the bureaucracy.

Presidents have frequently been able to make less sweeping changes in the

> ★ ANALYZE THE ISSUE
>
> **Overcoming Bureaucratic Resistance**
> A president's policy goals often conflict with those of the careerists in a bureaucratic agency. Can you think of realistic ways in which a president might try to elicit cooperation from bureaucrats who do not share his policy goals?

---

[29]See Bernard Rosen, *Holding Government Bureaucrats Accountable* (New York: Praeger, 1982).
[30]Phillip B. Heymann, *The Politics of Public Management* (New Haven, Conn.: Yale University Press, 1988); James G. Benze, Jr., *Presidential Power and Management Techniques* (New York: Greenwood Press, 1987).
[31]John Helmer, "The Presidential Office," in Hugh Heclo and Lester M. Salamon, eds., *The Illusion of Presidential Government* (Boulder, Colo.: Westview Press, 1981), 55.
[32]See Woll, *American Bureaucracy*, 207–229; Peter Szanton, *Federal Reorganization* (Chatham, N.J.: Chatham House, 1981).

bureaucracy's organization, such as reducing· the autonomy or number of employees of particular agencies.[33] However, minor changes tend merely to upgrade or downgrade programs or to shift activities from one agency to another. A reshuffling of agency responsibilities is usually no cure: the same problems of presidential control typically reemerge in a new place.[34]

Presidents have been more successful in creating new organizations than in eliminating old ones. Lyndon Johnson decided in 1965 that the nation's cities needed massive federal support because of their deteriorating physical condition and declining tax base. The situation helped to persuade Congress to accept Johnson's proposal for a cabinet-level Department of Housing and Urban Development to carry out his urban policies. Bureaucratic growth has been even more pronounced at the agency level. About a third of all federal agencies in existence today have been established since 1960.[35] Ironically, by forming new agencies to meet new problems, presidents have contributed to the bureaucracy's fragmentation and thus to the problem of controlling and coordinating its activities.

Presidential Appointments

Although there is almost no direct confrontation with a bureaucrat that a president cannot win, he does not have time to deal personally with every troublesome careerist. Nor does he have time to make sure that the bureaucracy has complied with his every order. The president relies on his political appointees in the agencies to see that his policies are followed. Although presidential appointees hold the highest positions in each agency, many of them are inexperienced in the bureaucracy's ways and uninformed about the agencies they lead. Such appointees are unlikely to command the respect of career bureaucrats, have no real power to fire them because of civil service regulations, and depend on them for information.[36]

Presidents have increasingly come to recognize that appointments based strictly on patronage are not likely to help them govern. Patronage appointees typically are tied to the president through service in his election campaign, but they rarely have the expertise to administer programs effectively. As a result, presidents have increasingly sought appointees who share their views and are highly knowledgeable.[37] George Bush chose as head of OSHA Gerald F. Scannell, a man who had held several key positions in that agency during the 1970s and who shared Bush's concern with efficient management. Scannell was picked, not to keep OSHA politicized, as it had been during the Reagan administration, but to improve its performance.[38]

[33]Harvey C. Mansfield, "Federal Executive Reorganization: Thirty Years of Experience," *Public Administration Review*, July-August 1969, 339; Stephen J. Wayne, *The Legislative Presidency* (New York: Harper & Row, 1978), 197.
[34]James G. March and Johan P. Olson, "Organizing Political Life: What Administrative Reorganization Tells Us about Government," *American Political Science Review* 77 (June 1983): 281–296.
[35]Kaufman, *Are Government Organizations Immortal?* 48–49.
[36]Thomas Cronin, *The State of the Presidency* (Boston: Little, Brown, 1975), 168.
[37]Kathleen A. Kemp, "The Regulators: Partisanship and Public Policy," *Policy Studies Journal* 11 (March 1983): 386–397.
[38]Joel D. Aberbach, "The President and the Executive Branch," in Colin Campbell and Bert A. Rockman, *The Bush Presidency: First Appraisals* (Chatham, N.J.: Chatham House Publishers, 1991), 240–241.

Regulatory agencies are the clearest illustration of the power of presidential appointments. Because these agencies have broad discretion over regulatory policy, a change in their leadership can have substantial effects. Newly appointed members of regulatory commissions are usually eager to implement the president's regulatory philosophy.[39] For example, President Reagan's appointee to head the Federal Trade Commission, James Miller III, was a strong-willed economist who shared Reagan's belief that consumer protection policy had gone too far and was adversely affecting business interests. In Miller's first year as head of the FTC, the commission dropped one-fourth of its pending cases against business firms.[40]

However, there are limits to what a president can accomplish through his appointments.[41] High-level presidential appointees number in the hundreds, and their turnover rate is high: the average appointee remains in the administration for less than two years before moving on to other employment.[42] No president can keep track of all his appointees, much less instruct them in detail on his intended policies. In addition, some presidential appointees will have a vested interest in the agencies they head. In choosing political appointees, the president is lobbied by groups that depend on agency programs. Rather than antagonize these groups, the president will accept their recommendations in some cases.

A determined president can use political appointees to alter the pattern of relationships between the bureaucracy and its other constituencies, including Congress and clientele groups. The Reagan administration relied on top bureaucrats to carry out programs but tried to keep them out of overall policy decisions and strategy, which were handled, as far as possible, by political appointees. The result, as the political scientist Joel Aberbach's research indicates, was a significant change in the groups with whom top civil servants had contact. Compared with a group of bureaucrats surveyed in 1970, the bureaucrats questioned in 1986–1987 reported more contacts with White House officials and fewer contacts with members of Congress, interest-group representatives, and the general public (see Table 21-2). The 1986–1987 respondents' perception of their political influence was also substantially lower than that of the 1970 group.[43]

The Executive Budget

Faced with the difficulty of controlling the bureaucracy, presidents have come to rely heavily on their personal bureaucracy, the Executive Office of the President (EOP). As we noted in Chapter 18, many decisions once made in agencies are now made by presidential appointees in the EOP.

In terms of presidential management, the key unit within the EOP is the Office of Management and Budget (OMB). Funding, programs, and regulations are the mainstays of every agency, and the OMB has substantial influence on

[39]See David Welborn, *Governance of Federal Regulatory Agencies* (Knoxville: University of Tennessee Press, 1977).
[40]Meier, *Regulation*, 110–111.
[41]See Richard P. Nathan, *The Plot That Failed: Nixon and the Administrative Presidency* (New York: Wiley, 1975).
[42]See Heclo, *Government of Strangers*.
[43]Aberbach, "The President and the Executive Branch," 232–235.

TABLE 21-2   Contacts Reported by Top Federal Executives, 1970 and 1986–1987. Bureaucrats in 1986–1987 reported having more contacts with White House officials than reported in 1970.

Contacts with . . .	POLITICAL APPOINTEES		CIVIL SERVANTS	
	1970	1986–1987	1970	1986–1987
White House	25%	41%	5%	20%
Own department head (cabinet member)	61	48	31	22
Other department head	19	6	18	2
Officials at your level in other departments	57	43	42	30
Members of Congress	42	48	43	20
Political party leaders	8	6	0	0
Interest-group representatives	69	67	69	46
General public	55	67	55	41

SOURCE: Joel D. Aberbach, "The President and the Executive Branch," in Colin Campbell and Bert A. Rockman, *The Bush Presidency: First Appraisals* (Chatham, N.J.: Chatham House Publishers, 1991), 234.

each of them. No agency can issue a major regulation without the OMB's verification that the regulation's benefits outweigh its costs, and no agency can propose legislation to Congress without the OMB's approval. However, the OMB's greatest influence over agencies derives from its budgetary role. At the start of the annual budget cycle the OMB assigns each agency a budget limit in accord with the president's directives. Before the agency's tentative allocation requests are sent back to the OMB, they must be approved by the agency head, who of course is a presidential appointee. The OMB then conducts a final review of all agencies' requests before sending the full budget to Congress in the president's name.

Agencies have certain advantages in budgetary matters which can offset the OMB's influence. Fewer than five OMB analysts monitor the budgets of the typical agency, and they generally know less about its activities than does the agency's larger staff of budgetary experts. Within the overall limits that the OMB places on an agency's budget, the agency has considerable leeway in allocating funds among its various programs. If the person appointed to head the agency is knowledgeable enough, he or she can slant the budget toward the president's goals, but the sheer scope of these agency budgets—involving scores of programs and billions of dollars in some instances—restricts this indirect source of presidential control. Moreover, the work of the president's appointees can be undone by Congress: if the OMB denies an agency's request for a new program, Congress can grant it anyway.

In most cases, an agency's overall budget does not change much from year to year.[44] This fact indicates that a significant portion of the bureaucracy's activities persist regardless of who sits in the White House or Congress.[45] At the program level within an agency, however, major year-to-year changes sometimes occur. A significant increase or decrease in the amount allocated to a program from one year to the next nearly always indicates a shift in the president's priorities.[46]

[44]See Wildavsky, *Politics of the Budgetary Process.*
[45]Benjamin Ginsberg, *The Consequence of Consent* (New York: Random House, 1982), 207.
[46]Harvey J. Tucker, "Incremental Budgeting: Myth or Model?" *Western Political Quarterly* 35 (September 1982): 327–338.

The president also has some authority, after the budget is approved by Congress, to reallocate funds within agencies and to place conditions on their use.

ACCOUNTABILITY THROUGH CONGRESS

Congress has powerful means of influencing the bureaucracy. All agencies depend on Congress for their existence, authority, programs, and funding. The most extreme action that Congress can take is to eliminate an agency's budget or programs. Congress can also pass legislation that reduces an agency's discretion or voids administrative action. However, Congress has no choice but to allow bureaucrats considerable latitude. Congress lacks the institutional capacity to work out complex policies down to the last detail.[47] The bureaucracy would grind to a halt if it had to get congressional approval for all of its policy decisions. Having neither the time nor the capacity to review every regulation of every agency, Congress has no option but to give the bureaucracy a general heading and then let it proceed along that course. In its efforts to resolve the savings and loan crisis, for example, Congress in 1989 created the Resolution Trust Corporation (RTC), which, according to its authorizing statute, is required to oversee the recovery of assets from troubled thrifts in a manner that:

[47]Samuel H. Beer, "Modernization of American Federalism," *Publius* 3 (Fall 1973): 75.

Treasury Secretary Nicholas Brady became chairman of the Oversight Board of the Resolution Trust Corporation, an agency created by Congress in 1989 and given great leeway in coping with the savings and loan crisis. (Marcy Nighswander/ AP/Wide World)

maximizes the net present value sale or other disposition of institutions;

minimizes the impact of such transactions on local real estate and financial markets;

makes efficient use of funds obtained from the Funding Corporation or the Treasury;

minimizes the amount of any loss realized in the resolution of cases; and

maximizes the preservation of the availability and affordability of residential real property for low- and moderate-income individuals.

Obviously, the language of the law gives the RTC broad discretion in deciding how to carry out its lawful responsibilities.

Correcting Bureaucratic Error: Legislative Oversight

Congress has statutory responsibility to oversee the bureaucracy's work, reviewing it to ensure compliance with legislative intentions.[48] As we noted in Chapter 17, however, most members of Congress place less emphasis on oversight than on other major duties. Keeping an eye on bureaucrats does not ordinarily help members of Congress to win reelection[49] and is less rewarding than working on new legislation. Oversight can also interfere with the benefits, such as favorable action on constituents' requests, that members of Congress derive from cooperating with the bureaucracy.[50] For the most part, congressional oversight occurs after the fact. Only when an agency has clearly gotten out of line is Congress likely to take decisive corrective action, holding hearings to ask tough questions and to warn of legislative punishment. Often the mere threat of a congressional investigation is enough to persuade an agency to mend its ways.

Congress has sometimes legislated its own authority to void bureaucratic decisions—a device called the *legislative veto*. When Congress authorized the Alaska oil pipeline, for example, it retained the authority to veto bureaucratic decisions about the pipeline's route. In 1983, however, the Supreme Court voided the use of a legislative veto as interference with the president's constitutional authority to execute the laws, but limited its ruling to the law in question. During the same year, the Court affirmed two lower-court rulings that the legislative veto was unconstitutional. Whether the Supreme Court in some situations will rule differently remains to be tested by future cases, but Congress has from time to time continued to include the legislative veto in bills that presidents have signed into law.[51]

Because oversight is so difficult and unrewarding, Congress has shifted much of its oversight responsibility to the Government Accounting Office (GAO). The GAO's primary function once was to keep track of the funds spent within the bureaucracy; now it also monitors the implementation of policies. The Congressional Budget Office (CBO) also does oversight studies. When the GAO or CBO

---

[48]See Morris Ogul, *Congress Oversees the Bureaucracy* (Pittsburgh: University of Pittsburgh Press, 1976); Randall Ripley and Grace Franklin, *Congress, the Bureaucracy, and Public Policy* (Homewood, Ill.: Dorsey Press, 1976), 225.

[49]Morris Fiorina, *Congress: Keystone of the Washington Establishment* (New Haven, Conn.: Yale University Press, 1977), 91.

[50]Ripley and Franklin, *Congress, Bureaucracy, and Public Policy*, 173–178.

[51]Fisher, *American Constitutional Law*, 280–281.

★ CRITICAL THINKING

HOW ACCOUNTABLE IS THE BUREAUCRACY?

The American political system, with its system of divided authority, gives both the president and Congress a claim on the bureaucracy's allegiance. It also gives both of them tools for holding the bureaucracy accountable.

As chief executive, the president can appoint and fire agency heads and some other top bureaucrats; reorganize the bureaucracy (subject to congressional approval); adjust annual budget proposals of agencies; resist legislative initiatives originating within the bureaucracy; issue executive orders for the bureaucracy to follow; and propose new policies or changes in existing ones which will, if enacted by Congress, affect the bureaucracy's activities.

For its part, Congress can reduce agencies' annual budgets; pass new or revised legislation that affects the bureaucracy's activities; abolish existing programs; investigate the bureaucracy's activities and force bureaucrats to testify about their activities; influence the ap-

pointments of agency heads and some other top bureaucrats; and write legislation with restrictions (for example, "sunset" provisions) on the bureaucracy's discretion.

Which institution, the presidency or Congress, do you think has the better tools for holding the bureaucracy accountable for its actions? Which institution in fact makes the more substantial contribution to the bureaucracy's accountability? Why?

Bear in mind that the bureaucracy is not without tools of its own. Through their expertise and ties with clientele groups, bureaucrats are in a position to develop the agency point of view. In your judgment, is the bureaucracy adequately accountable or does it have too much freedom to pursue its own agenda? How does the constitutional separation of executive and legislative power contribute to the bureaucracy's power and thus to the problem of accountability?

In authorizing construction of the Alaska pipeline, Congress retained authority to veto the bureaucracy's decisions about the pipeline's route. The Supreme Court has since ruled that such legislative vetoes are unconstitutional in some forms and situations. (Michael G. Edrington/The Image Works)

uncovers a major problem with an agency's handling of a program, it notifies Congress, which can then take remedial action.

Restricting the Bureaucracy in Advance

We noted above that congressional oversight takes place *after* the bureaucracy has acted. Of course, an awareness by bureaucrats that misbehavior can trigger a response from Congress helps to keep them in line. Nevertheless, oversight cannot change mistakes or abuses that have already occurred. Recognizing this limit on oversight, Congress has devised ways to constrain the bureaucracy *before* it acts. The simplest method is to draft laws that contain very specific instructions as to how programs are to be administered. Such provisions limit bureaucrats' options when they implement policy.

Another restrictive device is the "sunset law," which, as we saw in Chapter 17, establishes a specific date when a law will expire unless it is reenacted by Congress. Advocates of sunset laws see them as a solution to the problem of the bureaucracy's reluctance to give up programs that have outlived their usefulness.[52] As members of Congress usually want their policies to last far into the future, however, only a few sunset laws have been enacted.

ACCOUNTABILITY THROUGH THE COURTS

The judiciary's influence on agencies is less direct than that of the elected branches, but the courts, too, can and do act to ensure the bureaucracy's compliance with Congress's requirements. Legally, the bureaucracy derives its authority from acts of Congress, and an injured party can bring suit against an agency on the grounds that it has failed to carry out the law properly. Judges can order an agency to change its interpretation of a law. Moreover, the courts have held that agencies must observe the legal standards of due process in making administrative decisions that affect a particular person or group.[53] A welfare recipient, for example, cannot be deprived of benefits without being given an opportunity to contest the decision. Finally, the courts have ruled that the individual bureaucrat is required to respect citizens' constitutional rights.[54] A bureaucrat can be sued for monetary damages by a person whose rights have been violated.[55]

However, the courts have tended to support the bureaucracy if its actions seem at all reasonable. "Courts typically provide agencies wide discretion," David Nachmias and David Rosenbloom conclude. "They greatly defer to the judgment and expertise of administrators."[56] The reason is simple enough: the administration of government would founder if the courts repeatedly reversed

---

[52]See Theodore Lowi, *The End of Liberalism* (New York: Norton, 1979), 309–310.

[53]David H. Rosenbloom, *Public Administration and Law* (New York: Marcel Dekker, 1983); Rosen, *Holding Bureaucrats Accountable*, ch.6.

[54]*Goldberg* v. *Kelly*, 397 U.S. 254 (1970).

[55]*Wood* v. *Strickland*, 420 U.S. 308 (1975). In a few instances involving state and local governments, the Supreme Court has also indicated a willingness to make administrative policy itself. In *Wyatt* v. *Stickney*, the Court established conditions (for example, no more than six patients to a room) that a mental hospital had to meet in order to remain open.

[56]David Nachmias and David H. Rosenbloom, *Bureaucratic Government: U.S.A.* (New York: St. Martin's Press, 1980), 56.

★ THE MEDIA AND THE PEOPLE

THE BUREAUCRACY, THE PUBLIC, AND ACCOUNTABILITY

The career bureaucracy is an institution, pure and simple. The presidency is personified by the president; the Congress by its elected members; and the Supreme Court by its justices. The bureaucracy, in contrast, is faceless. It can be represented by the titles and the symbols of its agencies, but it cannot be represented in any meaningful way through the person of a career bureaucrat or set of career bureaucrats.

As a result, the bureaucracy is the most difficult of all governing institutions for the news media to cover. The media have a tendency to personify the news. Stories of government are typically told through the actions of a leader. The more compelling the leader's role, the more frequent the coverage, which is why the president—the nation's most visible and individually powerful official —receives so much attention from the press. But there is no bureaucratic leadership to whom reporters can turn on a regular basis. Consequently, the bureaucracy is largely ignored by the media except when its activities intersect with those of the president or Congress. Of the four great national institutions of the American political system, the bureaucracy is the least publicized and probably the most misunderstood by the American people.

The bureaucracy's accountability is diminished as a consequence. Public opinion is an important component in the process of holding the president (see Chapter 19), Congress (see Chapter 17), and even the Supreme Court (see Chapter 23) to account for their actions. The public has less influence over the actions of the bureaucracy. Without a proper awareness of the bureaucracy's work —an awareness that the media could help to provide— the public is in a weak position to influence its actions directly. The public's impact can only be indirect, registered through the workings of the three constitutional branches of the government.

agency decisions. The judiciary promotes bureaucratic accountability primarily by encouraging bureaucrats to act responsibly in their dealings with the public and by protecting individuals and groups from the bureaucracy's worst abuses.

ACCOUNTABILITY WITHIN THE BUREAUCRACY ITSELF

A recognition of the difficulty of achieving adequate accountability of the bureaucracy through the presidency, Congress, and the courts has led to the development of mechanisms of accountability within the bureaucracy itself. Two measures, whistle-blowing and demographic representativeness, are particularly noteworthy.

Whistle-Blowing

The bureaucratic corruption that is rampant in some countries is relatively uncommon in the United States. However, in view of the fact that the federal bureaucracy has 3 million employees and thousands of programs, a certain amount of waste, fraud, and abuse is inevitable. **Whistle-blowing,** the act of reporting instances of corruption or mismanagement by one's fellow bureaucrats, is a potentially effective internal check.[57] Whistle-blowing has not been highly successful, however, because superiors are seldom pleased to have their

[57]Roberta Ann Johnson and Michael E. Kraft, "Bureaucratic Whistleblowing and Policy Change," *Western Political Quarterly* 43 (December 1990): 849–874.

Karen Pitts (*left*) and Jaqueline Brever have sued the Rocky Flats plutonium plant near Denver, claiming that they were threatened and forced out of their jobs because managers feared that the two technicians would "blow the whistle" to the FBI about improper handling of toxic and nuclear materials at the facility. (Matthew Wald/New York Times)

lapses made public. In 1988, when Felix Smith, a biologist in the Department of the Interior, reported that the waters of California's San Joaquin Valley were being contaminated by poisonous selenium, his superiors, rather than acting to enforce water-purity standards, tried to transfer him out of the region. A survey conducted by a Senate subcommittee indicated that two-thirds of federal employees will not report instances of mismanagement because they fear reprisals.[58]

To encourage federal employees to come forward when they see instances of mismanagement, Congress has recently toughened laws that protect whistle-blowers from retaliation. Federal law also provides whistle-blowers with financial rewards in some circumstances.

Demographic Representativeness

Although the bureaucracy is not a representative institution in the sense that its officials are elected by the people, it could be representative in the demographic sense. If bureaucrats were a demographic microcosm of the general public, they presumably would treat the various groups and interests in society more fairly. "A public service . . . which is broadly representative of all categories of the population," public administration scholar Frederick Mosher concludes, "may be thought of as satisfying Lincoln's prescription of government 'by the people' in the limited sense."[59]

At present the bureaucracy is not demographically representative at its top levels (see Table 21-3). About 75 percent of managerial and professional positions are held by white males.[60] Women and minorities hold proportionally

[58]Bob Cohn, "New Help for Whistle Blowers," *Newsweek*, June 27, 1988, 43.
[59]Mosher, *Democracy and Public Service*, 13; see also Kathleen Staudt, *Women, Foreign Assistance, and Advocacy Administration* (New York: Praeger, 1985).
[60]Sar A. Levitan and Alexandra B. Noden, *Working for the Sovereign* (Baltimore: Johns Hopkins University Press, 1983), 116.

★ HOW THE UNITED STATES COMPARES

EDUCATIONAL BACKGROUNDS OF BUREAUCRATS

To staff its bureaucracy, the U.S. government tends to hire persons with specialized educations to hold specialized jobs; this approach heightens the tendency of bureaucrats to take the agency point of view. By comparison, Great Britain tends to recruit its bureaucrats from the arts and humanities, on the assumption that general ability and intelligence are the best qualifications for detached professionalism. The continental European democracies also emphasize detached profes-

sionalism, but in the context of the supposedly impartial application of rules. As a consequence, high-ranking civil servants in Europe tend to have legal educations. The college majors of senior civil servants in the United States and other democracies reflect these tendencies.

SOURCE: B. Guy Peters, *The Politics of Bureaucracy*, 3d ed. (New York: Longman, 1989), ch.3. Table adapted from table 3.7, 102–103.

College Major of Senior Civil Servants	Denmark	Germany	Great Britain	Italy	Netherlands	United States
Natural science/ engineering	16%	11%	11%	27%	25%	43%
Social science/ humanities	20	8	87	24	28	27
Law	60	65	—	49	45	24
Other	4	16	2	—	2	6
	100%	100%	100%	100%	100%	100%

few high-ranking posts. However, the employment status of women and minorities has improved somewhat in recent years, and top officials in the bureaucracy include a greater proportion of women and minorities than are found in Congress, the judiciary, the diplomatic corps, or among high-ranking military officers.[61] Moreover, if *all* levels of the federal bureaucracy are considered, it comes reasonably close to being a microcosm of the nation's population.[62]

Although demographic representativeness is symbolically and practically important, it is only a partial answer to the problem of bureaucratic accountability. A fully representative civil service would still be required to play agency politics. The careerists in, say, defense agencies and welfare agencies are not very different in their demographic backgrounds, but they differ markedly in their opinions about policy. Each group believes that the mission of *its* agency should take priority. Such parochial outlooks are inescapable. Bureaucrats naturally come to identify with and promote the interests of the agencies in which they work. The inevitability of agency politics is the most significant of all political facts about the U.S. federal bureaucracy.[63]

[61]Meier and Nigro, "Representative Bureaucracy," 538.
[62]Ibid., 532; see also Steven Thomas Seitz, *Bureaucracy, Policy, and the Public* (St. Louis: Mosby, 1978), 113.
[63]For a broad discussion of the issue of representativeness, see Samuel Krislov and David H. Rosenbloom, *Representative Bureaucracy and the American Political System* (New York: Praeger, 1981).

TABLE 21-3   Federal Job Rankings (GS) of Various Demographic Groups
Women and minority-group members are underrepresented in the top jobs of the federal bureaucracy.

Grade Level*	WOMEN'S SHARE		BLACKS' SHARE		HISPANICS' SHARE	
	1976	1990	1982	1990	1982	1990
GS 1–4 (lowest ranks)	78%	75%	23%	29%	5%	7%
GS 5–8	60	70	19	23	4	6
GS 9–12	20	39	10	12	4	5
GS 13–15 (highest ranks)	5	19	5	6	2	3

*In general, the higher-numbered grades are managerial and professional positions, and the lower-numbered grades are clerical and manual-labor positions.

SOURCE: Office of Personnel Management, 1992.

Bureaucratic Power and American Ideals: An Ongoing Conflict

On the basis of his study of agency policies, B. Dan Wood concluded that "the influence of elected institutions is limited when an agency has substantial bureaucratic resources and a zeal for their use."[64] The power of the bureaucracy is both undeniable and difficult to reconcile with the concept of a self-governing society.[65] Although the incompatibility of the bureaucratic and democratic forms of governing can be overstated,[66] it is true that the two bear little resemblance to each other. Bureaucracy entails hierarchy, command, permanence of office, appointment to office, and fixed rules, whereas democracy involves equality, consent, rotation of office, election to office, and open decision making. At base, the conflict between bureaucracy and democracy centers on the degree of power exercised by unelected officials. The president and members of Congress are accountable to the people through elections. Bureaucrats are not elected, yet they exercise a significant degree of independent power.

The problem cannot be solved by doing away with the bureaucracy. American society would collapse without the defense establishment, education and welfare programs, promotion and regulation of business, transportation systems, financial structures, and the hundreds of other components of the federal bureaucracy. Moreover, the need for public policy to be administered competently makes wholesale administration by partisan appointees unthinkable as a solution to bureaucratic power.

Given the fragmentation of the U.S. governmental structure and the nature of modern life, bureaucratic power will be a persistent feature of American politics and an ongoing challenge to the country's fundamental ideals, particularly the

[64]B. Dan Wood, "Principals, Bureaucrats, and Responsiveness to Clean Air Enforcements," *American Political Science Review* 82 (March 1988): 213.
[65]See Douglas Yates, *Bureaucratic Democracy* (Cambridge, Mass.: Harvard University Press, 1982).
[66]See Larry M. Preston, "Freedom and Bureaucracy," *American Journal of Political Science* 31 (November 1987): 773–795.

principle of self-government. Experts disagree on whether the bureaucracy is adequately accountable (it can never be made perfectly accountable) for its actions,[67] but one thing is certain: the issue of bureaucratic accountability will not disappear. American society in the twenty-first century will grow ever more complex and ever more dependent on technology—and will consequently become ever more reliant on the federal bureaucracy. The gap in competence between the citizen and the politician on the one hand and the bureaucrat on the other will increase, a development that will raise new challenges and problems for a people that seeks to govern itself.

Summary

The federal bureaucracy is actively engaged in politics and policymaking. The fragmentation of power and the pluralism of the American political system result in a policy process that is continually subject to conflict and contention. There is no clear policy or leadership mandate in the American system, so government agencies must compete for the power necessary to administer their programs effectively. Accordingly, civil servants tend to have an agency point of view: they seek to advance their agency's programs and to repel attempts by others to weaken their position. An agency perspective comes naturally to top-level bureaucrats. Their roles, long careers within a single agency, and professional values lead them to believe in the importance of their agency's work. In promoting their agency, civil servants rely on their policy expertise, the backing of their clientele groups, and support from the president and Congress. When they are faced with a threat from either the president or Congress, agencies can often count on the other for support. Institutional rivalry, constituency differences, and party differences are the chief reasons for conflict between the president and Congress over control of the bureaucracy.

Because bureaucrats are not elected by the people they serve yet wield substantial independent power, the bureaucracy's accountability is a major issue. The major checks on the bureaucracy are provided by the president, Congress, and the courts. The president has some power to reorganize the bureaucracy, appoints the political head of each agency, and has management tools (such as the executive budget) that can be used to limit bureaucrats' discretion. Congress has influence on bureaucratic agencies through its authorization and funding powers and through various devices (including sunset laws and investigative hearings) for holding bureaucrats accountable for their actions. The judiciary's role in the bureaucracy's accountability is smaller than that of the elected branches, but the courts do have the authority to force agencies to act in accordance with legislative intent, established procedures, and constitutionally guaranteed rights.

Nevertheless, the bureaucracy is not fully accountable. Bureaucrats exercise substantial independent power, a situation that is not easily reconciled with democratic values, particularly the principle of self-government. Efforts to reconcile the requirements of bureaucracy and democracy must take into account society's interest in having both competent administration and responsive administration.

Major Concepts

accountability
agency point of view

clientele groups
whistle-blowing

---

[67]See Laurence Lynn, *Managing the Public's Business* (New York: Basic Books, 1981).

Suggested Readings

Aberbach, Joel D. *Keeping a Watchful Eye.* Washington, D.C.: Brookings Institution, 1990. A careful assessment of congressional oversight of the bureaucracy.

Burke, John P. *Bureaucratic Responsibility.* Baltimore: Johns Hopkins University Press, 1986. An analysis of bureaucratic responsibility.

Gormley, William T. *Taming the Bureaucracy.* Princeton, N.J.: Princeton University Press, 1989. An analysis of methods of controlling the bureaucracy.

Heclo, Hugh. *A Government of Strangers.* Washington, D.C.: Brookings Institution, 1977. An analysis of political appointees in their relationships with bureaucrats and the president.

Kaufman, Herbert. *Are Government Organizations Immortal?* Washington, D.C.: Brookings Institution, 1976. A look at the factors that allow governmental agencies to persist.

Meier, Kenneth J. *Politics and the Bureaucracy.* North Scituate, Mass.: Duxbury Press, 1979. An assessment of the bureaucracy's political role.

Rohr, John A. *Ethics for Bureaucracy*, 2d ed. New York: Marcel Dekker, 1989. A study of how bureaucrats can use their discretionary power in ways consistent with democratic values.

Yates, Douglas. *Bureaucratic Democracy.* Cambridge, Mass.: Harvard University Press, 1982. An analysis of the conflicting demands of democracy and bureaucracy.

THE FEDERAL JUDICIAL SYSTEM: APPLYING THE LAW

It is emphatically the province and duty of the judicial department to say what the law is. Those who apply the rule to particular cases, must of necessity expound and interpret that rule. If two laws conflict with each other, the courts must decide on the operation of each.

John Marshall[1]

For two weeks in the fall of 1991, the focus of the national news was not the president or a member of Congress, but a federal judge—Clarence Thomas. Thomas had been head of the Equal Employment Opportunity Commission (EEOC) during the Reagan administration and was serving on the U.S. Court of Appeals for the District of Columbia when President Bush nominated him to the nation's highest court. Thomas, an African-American, was chosen to fill the vacancy created by the retirement of Justice Thurgood Marshall, who was the first black person ever to serve on the Supreme Court.

The appointment of Thomas to the Supreme Court was opposed by several major civil rights groups, including the NAACP. The AFL-CIO also formally opposed his confirmation. Thomas had worked against most affirmative action plans while head of the EEOC, and civil rights leaders accused him of turning his back on the needs of minority-group members less fortunate than himself. They also pointed out the irony of Thomas's appointment: he and Bush were both avowed opponents of "quotas," yet Thomas seemed to have been picked to fill the "African-American seat" on the Supreme Court. He was a relatively inexperienced jurist who had not developed a reputation as a leading theorist of the law. When the Thomas hearings were turned topsy-turvy by Anita Hill's allegations that Judge Thomas had sexually harassed her when he headed the EEOC, which was established to protect women and minority-group members from discrimination, the irony was compounded.

The fight over Thomas's nomination reflected a deep division over the direction of the Supreme Court. In his final opinion before resigning from the Court, Justice Marshall accused its conservative majority of a "far-reaching assault" on the Bill of Rights. In recent decisions the Court had restricted the rights of the criminally accused and had ruled that physicians have no

---

[1]*Marbury v. Madison,* 1 Cranch 137 (1803).

The nomination of Clarence Thomas, a conservative, to the Supreme Court was controversial from the outset because it was widely believed that he would tilt the Court further toward the right. Anita Hill's allegation that Thomas had sexually harassed her caused a nationwide uproar but did not prevent Thomas's confirmation. (*Top:* Markel/ Gamma Liaison; *bottom:* David Longstreath/AP/Wide World)

free-speech right to counsel patients on abortion. The Court also appeared ready to reconsider several important precedents, including minority participation in government contracts and the abortion right itself. At stake in the Thomas appointment was the ideological position of the Court. How far to the right would it go?

The Senate hearings gave Americans an opportunity to learn about the workings of the government's judicial branch, which is by far the least publicized and least understood of the three branches of the U.S. government. Yet, as the fight over the Thomas nomination suggested, the judicial branch, from the Supreme Court on down, is a consequential part of the American political system. Although law and politics are sometimes portrayed as separate activities, they are inseparable parts of the governing process. Once a law is established, it is expected to be administered in an evenhanded way; but the law itself is a product of contending political forces, is developed through a political process, and has political content.

This chapter describes the federal judiciary and the work of its judges and justices. The chapter also provides background for the next chapter's analysis of the judiciary's policymaking role. The main points made in this first of two chapters on the judiciary are the following:

★ *Courts are not, as is often assumed, arenas in which neutral judges apply fixed principles of law to the cases brought before them. The judiciary is actively engaged in the making of law and is thus a political as well as a legal institution.*

★ *The federal judiciary includes the Supreme Court of the United States, which functions mainly as an appellate court; courts of appeals, which hear appeals; and district courts, which hold trials.* The courts below the Supreme Court have substantial discretion in their judgments and have the final decision in the great majority of federal cases.

★ *Each state has a court system of its own, which for the most part is independent of supervision by the federal courts.* State courts, not federal courts, handle by far the larger proportion of legal cases that arise each year in the United States, and most of these state cases are not subject to appeal in federal courts.

★ *Political considerations are vitally important in the selection of federal judges and justices.* Because of concern about future judicial performance, presidents have tended to choose persons of their own party and philosophy for nomination to the federal bench.

The Supreme Court of the United States

The writers of the Constitution were determined that the judiciary would be a separate and powerful branch of the federal government but, for practical reasons, did not spell out the full structure of the federal court system. The Constitution simply establishes the Supreme Court of the United States and grants Congress the authority to establish lower federal courts of its choosing.

Congress also has the constitutional authority to determine the number of justices on the Supreme Court and since 1869 has held the number at nine

The Supreme Court building is located across from the Capitol in Washington, D.C. The courtroom, the justices' offices, and the conference room are on the first floor. Administrative staff offices and the Court's records and reference materials occupy the other floors. (Dennis Brack/Black Star)

justices. The chief justice of the United States presides over the Supreme Court and, like the eight associate justices, is appointed by the president with the approval of the U.S. Senate. The Constitution states that the justices "shall hold their offices during good behavior." However, the Constitution contains no precise definition of "good behavior," and no Supreme Court justice has ever been removed from office through impeachment and conviction by Congress. In practice, Supreme Court justices serve until they retire or die.

The Constitution places no age qualifications on federal judicial office; nor does it require that a judge have legal training. Tradition alone dictates that federal judges have an educational or professional background in the law.

THE SUPREME COURT'S JURISDICTION

The Constitution grants the Supreme Court both original and appellate jurisdiction. A court's **jurisdiction** is its authority to hear cases of a particular type. A court of *general* jurisdiction can hear cases of almost any kind, whereas a court of *limited* jurisdiction can hear only cases of a particular kind. The Supreme Court of the United States is an example of a court of general jurisdiction. The U.S. Bankruptcy Court, which hears only bankruptcy cases, is an example of a court of limited jurisdiction. Jurisdiction is also defined by the stage of a legal dispute. **Original jurisdiction** is the authority to be the first court to hear a case. **Appellate jurisdiction** is the authority to review cases that have already been heard in lower courts and are appealed to it by the losing party; such courts are called appeals courts or appellate courts.

The Supreme Court's original jurisdiction embraces legal disputes involving foreign diplomats or two or more states. The Court in its entire history has convened as a court of original jurisdiction only a few hundred times and has rarely done so in recent years.

The Court does its most significant work through its appellate jurisdiction, which extends to cases arising under the Constitution, federal law and regulations, and treaties. The Court also hears appeals involving admiralty or maritime issues and legal controversies that cross state or national boundaries, as when the parties are different states or citizens of different states or when one party is the U.S. government or a foreign government. Appellate courts, including the Supreme Court, do not retry cases; rather, they determine whether a trial court acted in accord with applicable law.

Congress has constitutional authority over the Court's appellate jurisdiction. An early act of Congress in 1789, for example, gave the Supreme Court the authority to hear appeals of lower-court decisions upholding a state law that allegedly violates the Constitution. Various acts of Congress have empowered the Supreme Court to review almost any case originating in a lower federal court or in a state court when a federal question is involved.

The Constitution bars the Court from issuing decisions except on actual cases before it. This restriction prevents the Court from developing legal positions outside the context of the judicial process. A judge must have a case before him or her in order to issue a ruling. As federal judge David Bazelon noted, a judge "can't wake up one morning and simply decide to give a helpful little push to a school system, a mental hospital, or the local housing agency."[2]

THE SUPREME COURT'S PROCEDURES

The primary function of the judiciary is to interpret the law in such a way that rules made in the past (for example, the Constitution or legislation) can be applied reasonably in the present. This function gives the courts—all courts—a role in policymaking. Antitrust legislation, for example, is designed to prevent uncompetitive business practices, but like all such legislation, it is not self-enforcing. If government or another corporation should bring suit against a corporation for an alleged violation of antitrust laws, it is up to the courts to decide whether and how these laws apply to the case at hand.

As the nation's highest court, the Supreme Court is particularly important in determining the meaning and application of laws. Its rulings establish legal precedents that guide lower courts. A **precedent** is a judicial decision that serves as a rule for settling subsequent cases of a similar nature (see Chapter 23). Lower courts are expected to follow precedent—that is, to resolve cases of a like nature in ways consistent with upper-court rulings. For reasons that will be explained later, however, they do not always do so.

Selecting Cases

The Supreme Court's ability to set legal precedent is strengthened by its authority to choose which cases it will hear. Before 1925 the Court did not have much control over its case load; most cases reached it by mandatory appeal—

[2]Quoted in Louis Fisher, *American Constitutional Law* (New York: McGraw-Hill, 1990), 5.

★ THE MEDIA AND THE PEOPLE

PUBLIC CONFIDENCE IN THE SUPREME COURT

When asked in opinion polls, Americans express more confidence in the Supreme Court than they do in the presidency, Congress, or the federal bureaucracy. Federal judges and justices also rank ahead of members of Congress and bureaucrats in public esteem. In fact, members of the federal bench typically rank higher in opinion polls than nearly any other job category. Moreover, public opinion is more consistently favorable toward the judiciary than toward other institutions. In the 1950s and 1960s, the public expressed a great deal of confidence in all federal institutions; but this confidence was undermined in the late 1960s and early 1970s by the Vietnam war, racial riots in the cities, and Watergate. Only about a fifth of the American people expressed confidence in Congress and the presidency by the end of this period. Confidence in all institutions, public and private, including the Supreme Court, also declined during the period, but, in relative terms, the Court's reputation remained strong.

The reasons for the public's confidence in the Supreme Court are many. A deep-seated belief in rule by law—and trust in the leading instrument of this justice—is certainly one reason. Another is the way in which the Supreme Court is handled by the press. Unlike its coverage of Congress and the presidency, the press's coverage of the Court does not go behind the scenes to the bargaining process by which decisions are made. Although compromise and negotiation are a part of Supreme Court decision making, news reports seem almost to imply that justices make choices based only on legal interpretations. The justices are shown to differ in their legal views, but they are not portrayed as political actors in the same way that elected officials are routinely portrayed. Moreover, the press does not probe deeply into the personal and professional lives of the justices. For instance, any difficulties an elderly justice may have in keeping up with the workload or with the intellectual demands of the position are seldom publicized.

The public's confidence in the Supreme Court is an important part of compliance with its decisions. The Court depends on other institutions to carry out its decisions and, in some cases, such as school prayer, depends on voluntary compliance by the public. The likelihood of compliance increases to the degree that officials and citizens regard the Court's rulings as legitimate, particularly when they do not agree with the substance of a ruling.

that is, the Court was required by law to hear them. This situation restricted the Court's capacity to choose cases on the basis of their legal significance. The Judiciary Act of 1925 freed the Court from the burden of mandatory appeals by limiting the types of cases that it was required to hear on appeal.

Today the Supreme Court has broad discretion in choosing the cases it will hear. The large majority of cases reach the Court through a **writ of *certiorari,*** which the justices grant at their discretion. In applying for a writ of *certiorari,* the losing party in a lower-court case explains in writing why its case should be ruled upon by the Supreme Court. Four of the Court's nine justices must agree to accept a particular case before it is granted a writ. Each year roughly 5,000 parties apply for *certiorari,* but the Court accepts only about 150 cases for a full hearing and ruling. The Court issues another 100 to 200 *per curiam* (unsigned) decisions, which are made without a hearing and simply state the facts of the case and the Court's decision. The Court is more likely to grant *certiorari* when the U.S. government is a party to the case. Nearly half of all requests for *certiorari* by the government are accepted by the Court, compared with less than 10 percent of cases requested by other parties.[3]

[3]Joseph Tanenhaus, Marvin Schick, Matthew Muraskin, and Daniel Rosen, "The Supreme Court's Certiorari Jurisdiction," in Glendon A. Schubert, ed., *Judicial Decision-Making* (New York: Free Press, 1963).

Case selection is a vital part of the Supreme Court's work. Through its review of applications for *certiorari*, the Court keeps abreast of legal controversies. Justice William Brennan noted that the *certiorari* process enables the Court to acquire a general idea of the compelling legal issues arising in lower courts and to address those that are most in need of immediate attention.[4] When the Court does accept a case, chances are that most of the justices disagree with the lower court's ruling. In recent years about three-fourths of the Supreme Court's decisions have reversed the judgments of lower courts.[5]

The Court seldom accepts a routine case, even if the justices believe that a lower court has erred. The Supreme Court's job is not to correct every mistake of other courts, but to resolve broad legal questions. As a result, the justices usually choose cases that involve substantial legal issues.[6] This criterion is vague but essentially means that a case must center on an issue of significance not merely to the parties involved but to the nation. As a result, most of the cases heard by the Court raise major constitutional issues, or affect the lives of many Americans, or address issues that are being decided inconsistently by the lower courts or are in conflict with a previous Supreme Court ruling.[7] The last of these situations is particularly likely to propel a case to the Supreme Court, which naturally takes a keen interest in lower-court judgments that depart from its rulings.

Despite its control over its cases, the Supreme Court has a substantial work load. The time required to sift through some 5,000 cases and then to consider fully about 150 of them each year is considerable. Law clerks assist the justices in these tasks. Each justice is entitled to four clerks, who are usually top-ranking recent graduates of the nation's most prestigious law schools. The clerks prepare memos that summarize each case referred to the Court and recommend whether or not the case should be granted *certiorari*. The chief justice's staff then compiles a list of cases that seem to involve sufficiently substantial issues. This list is circulated among the other justices, who can add cases to it. Cases not on this "Discuss List" are automatically dropped from further consideration.

Deciding Cases

Once the Supreme Court accepts a case, it sets a date on which the attorneys for the two sides will present their oral arguments. Strict time limits, usually thirty minutes per side, are placed on these arguments, because each side has already submitted written arguments to the justices.

This open hearing is much less important than the **judicial conference** that follows, which is attended only by the nine justices. Conferences normally take

[4]D. Marie Provine, *Case Selection in the United States Supreme Court* (Chicago: University of Chicago Press, 1980), 62–63.
[5]Henry Glick, *Courts, Politics, and Justice* (New York: McGraw-Hill, 1983), 214.
[6]See Saul Brenner, "The New Certiorari Game," *Journal of Politics* 41 (1979): 649–655; Donald R. Songer, "Concern for Policy Outputs as a Cue for Supreme Court Decisions on Certiorari," *Journal of Politics* 41 (1979): 1185–1194; S. Sidney Ulmer, "Selecting Cases for Supreme Court Review: An Underdog Model," *American Political Science Review* 72 (1979): 902–910.
[7]S. Sidney Ulmer, "The Supreme Court's Certiorari Decisions: Conflict as a Predictive Variable," *American Political Science Review* 78 (1984): 901–911.

place on Wednesday afternoons and Fridays in the Court's private conference room, and the justices are not supposed to discuss the conference's proceedings with outsiders. This secrecy allows the justices to speak freely and tentatively about a case without having to worry that their thoughts will become public.

The chief justice presides over the conference and ordinarily speaks first about a particular case.[8] The other justices then speak in order of their seniority (length of service on the Court); this arrangement enhances the senior members' ability to influence the discussion. After the discussion, the justices usually vote in reverse order of seniority: the least senior justice votes first in most cases and the chief justice votes last.

The chief justice presides over sessions of the Court and acts as its principal spokesman outside the Court. By tradition, however, justices do not speak publicly about cases currently before the Court, so the chief justice's main responsibility is to manage the Court's work load. The chief justice is expected to provide leadership for his colleagues. This leadership is largely inspirational, because the powers of the office of chief justice are nearly the same as those of the other positions on the Court. Consequently, the chief justice's intellectual capacities, knowledge of the law, political awareness, and persuasiveness are significant aspects of his leadership. Charles Evans Hughes is reputed to have been the most effective leader in the Court's history, although John Marshall is generally regarded as the greatest chief justice. The current chief justice, William Rehnquist, is widely viewed as a personally aloof but intellectually assertive leader.

Issuing Decisions and Opinions

After a case has been discussed and decided upon in conference, the Court prepares and issues its decision and one or more opinions. The **decision** indicates which party the Court sides with and by how large a margin. For example, in *Brown* v. *Board of Education of Topeka* (1954), the Supreme Court ruled 9–0 in favor of Linda Brown, a schoolchild who claimed that she had been denied equal protection of the laws when she was refused admission to an all-white public school because she was black.[9] This landmark decision meant that Topeka had to admit Linda Brown to a public school previously reserved for white children, thus setting a precedent for nationwide school desegregation. The unanimous vote indicated that the Court was not likely to reverse its decision.

A Supreme Court decision is accompanied by an **opinion,** which is an explanation of the reasons behind the decision. The reasons may be broad or narrow, but they are ultimately the most important part of a Supreme Court ruling because they inform others of the justices' interpretations of laws. When a majority of the justices agree on the legal basis of a decision, the result is a **majority opinion.** In the *Brown* case, for example, all the justices agreed that government-sponsored school segregation was unconstitutional because it violated the Fourteenth Amendment's guarantee that all Americans are entitled

[8]Lawrence Baum, *The Supreme Court*, 3d ed. (Washington, D.C.: Congressional Quarterly Press, 1989), 117.
[9]*Brown* v. *Board of Education of Topeka*, 347 U.S. 483 (1954).

TYPES OF SUPREME COURT OPINIONS

Majority opinion: a written opinion of the majority of the Court's justices stating the reasoning underlying their decision on a case.

Plurality opinion: a written opinion that in the absence of a majority opinion presents the reasoning of most of the justices who side with the winning party.

Concurring opinion: a written opinion of one or more justices who support the majority position but disagree with the majority's reasoning on a case. This opinion expresses the reasoning of the concurring justices.

Dissenting opinion: a written opinion of one or more justices who disagree with the majority's decision and opinion. This opinion provides the reasoning underlying the dissent.

---

to equal protection of the laws. Enforced segregation of the public schools was therefore constitutionally impermissible. This opinion became the legal basis by which communities throughout the southern states were ordered by lower courts to end their policy of segregating students in their public schools by race.

When he is part of the majority, the chief justice decides which of the justices will write the majority opinion. Otherwise, the senior justice in the majority determines the author. Chief justices have often given themselves the influential task of writing the majority opinion in important cases. John Marshall did so often: *Marbury* v. *Madison* (1802) and *McCulloch* v. *Maryland* (1819) were among the opinions he wrote.

The justice who writes the Court's majority opinion has an important and difficult job, since the other justices who voted with the majority must agree with the written opinion. Because the vote on a case is not considered final until the decision is made public, plenty of compromising and old-fashioned horse trading can take place during the writing stage. The majority opinion often goes through a series of drafts and is circulated among all nine justices. In *Brown* v. *Board of Education,* Justice Felix Frankfurter, the lone initial holdout, was persuaded to make the decision unanimous by the continued urgings of his colleagues and by their willingness to incorporate some of his concerns into the majority opinion.

In some cases there is no majority opinion because a majority of the justices agree on the decision but cannot agree on the legal basis for it. The result is a **plurality opinion,** which presents the view held by most of the justices who side with the winning party. In the *Bakke* case (discussed in Chapter 7), the Court ruled 5–4 that Alan Bakke, a white male, had been wrongly denied admission to medical school because of a quota system that reserved a certain number of admissions for minority students. However, the five justices who ruled in Bakke's favor were divided in their legal reasoning. Four of the justices concluded that Bakke's denial of admission was a violation of the 1964 Civil Rights Act; their view became the plurality opinion. Lewis Powell, the fifth justice who sided with Bakke, believed that Bakke's denial of admission violated a constitutional right. Powell set forth his reasoning in a **concurring opinion,** which is a separate opinion written by a justice who votes with the majority but disagrees with their reasoning.

A justice or justices on the losing side can write a **dissenting opinion** to explain their reasons for disagreeing with the majority position. Sometimes these dissents become a later Court's majority position. In a 1942 dissenting opinion, Justice Hugo Black wrote that defendants in state felony trials should have legal counsel, even if they could not afford to pay for it. Two decades later, in *Gideon* v. *Wainwright* (1963), the Court adopted this position.[10]

The American Judicial System

During the Senate Judiciary Committee's hearings in 1987 on Robert Bork's nomination to the Supreme Court, one of his supporters, Senator Gordon Humphrey (R-N.H.), became exasperated by the line of questioning being pursued by senators who opposed Bork. Noting that the Judiciary Committee had scrutinized Bork five years earlier when he was nominated for a lower-court appointment, Humphrey asked why certain objections to Bork had not been raised back then. Humphrey was particularly incensed by criticisms of legal positions that Bork had taken in lectures and articles written long before he had entered the federal judiciary. If Bork's earlier views were so questionable, Humphrey asked, why had they not been probed in the earlier hearings? Bork's opponents on the Senate Judiciary Committee ignored Humphrey's complaint, probably because they believed that the answer was obvious: a nominee to the Supreme Court should receive closer scrutiny than a lower-court nominee. After all, there are more than 100 federal courts but there is only one Supreme Court, and its position at the top of the country's judicial system gives Supreme Court appointments unparalleled importance.

It is a mistake, however, to conclude that the Supreme Court is the only court

[10]*Gideon* v. *Wainwright*, 372 U.S. 335 (1963).

The Supreme Court is not the only federal court that "matters" in the American judicial system. Most federal cases originate in district courts, and most appealed cases are settled in courts of appeals, never reaching the Supreme Court. (Eli Reed/Magnum)

FIGURE 22-1 The Federal Judicial System
This simplified diagram shows the relationships among the various levels of federal courts and between state and federal courts. The losing party in a case can appeal a lower-court decision to the court at the next-highest level, as the arrows indicate. Decisions can be removed from state courts to federal courts only if they raise a constitutional question.

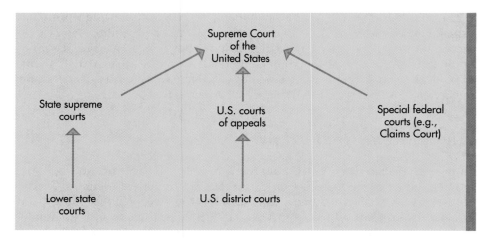

of consequence. Justice Jerome Frank once wrote of the "upper-court myth" that appellate courts and in particular the Supreme Court are the only truly significant judicial arena and that lower courts just dutifully follow the rulings handed down by the appellate level.[11] The reality is very different, as the following discussion will explain.

FEDERAL DISTRICT COURTS

The lowest federal courts are the district courts (see Figure 22-1). There are more than ninety federal district courts altogether—at least one in every state and as many as four in some states. District-court judges, who number about 500 in all, are appointed by the president with the consent of the Senate.

Federal cases usually originate in district courts, which are trial courts, where the parties present their evidence and argue their sides and a decision is rendered in favor of one party or the other. District courts are the only courts in the federal system in which juries hear testimony in some cases, and most cases at this level are presented before a single judge. Some district-court cases involve issues of "private law" (relationships between individuals and between businesses), such as divorce and contract disputes. Other cases involve issues of "public law" (relationships of individuals to government and the rights and obligations of each), such as crimes, political rights, and the government's obligations under the Constitution and under statutes and administrative regulations.

In theory, federal district courts are bound by legal precedents established by the Supreme Court. This requirement was reiterated in a 1982 case, *Hutto* v. *Davis:* "Unless we wish anarchy to prevail within the federal judicial system, a precedent of this Court must be followed by the lower federal courts no matter how misguided the judges of those courts may think it to be."[12]

[11]From a letter to the author by Frank Schwartz of Beaver College, 1986. This section reflects substantially Professor Schwartz's recommendations to the author, as does the later section that addresses the "federal-court myth."
[12]*Hutto* v. *Davis,* U.S. 370 (1982).

There is no question that lower federal courts rely on and follow Supreme Court decisions in their own rulings. However, the idea that lower courts are guided strictly by Supreme Court rulings is part of the "upper-court myth." District-court judges may misapply or misunderstand the Supreme Court's position and deviate from it for that reason. In addition, the facts of a case before a district court are seldom precisely the same as those of a similar case decided by the Supreme Court. In this situation, the lower-court judge must decide whether the facts of the current case are sufficiently different that a different legal principle must be invoked. In some cases, district-court judges have willfully disregarded Supreme Court precedent, finding a basis for decision that allows them to reach a judgment they prefer. For example, after the Supreme Court declared in *Brown* v. *Board of Education* that racial segregation of public schools violated the Fourteenth Amendment's guarantee of equal protection under the law, several southern district-court judges concluded that the issue in question in subsequent school desegregation cases was not equal protection but the maintenance of public order, and that school desegregation could not be allowed because it would disrupt public order. Finally, it is not unusual for the Supreme Court to take a very broad legal position that contains enough generalities and ambiguities to allow lower courts to decide its exact meaning in practice. Trial-court judges then have a creative role in judicial decision making which rivals that of appellate-court judges.

Most federal cases end with the district court's decision; the losing party does not appeal the decision to a higher court. This is another indication of the highly significant role of district-court judges.

FEDERAL COURTS OF APPEALS

When cases are appealed from district courts, they go to a federal court of appeals. These appellate courts make up the second level of the federal court system. Courts of appeals do not use juries. No new evidence is submitted in an appealed case; appellate courts base their decisions on a review of lower-court records. Appellate judges act as supervisors in the legal system, reviewing trial-court decisions and correcting what they consider to be mistakes.

The United States has twelve general appeals courts, each of which serves an area consisting of between three and nine states, except the one that serves the District of Columbia only. There is also the U.S. Court of Appeals for the Federal Circuit, which specializes in appeals of decisions in cases involving patents and international trade. Between four and twenty-six judges sit on each court of appeals, but each case is usually heard by a panel of three judges. On rare occasions, all the judges of a court of appeals sit as a body (*en banc*) in order to resolve difficult controversies, typically ones that have resulted in conflicting decisions within the same circuit. The usual purpose of an *en banc* hearing is to ensure that the judges will decide similar cases in a consistent way.

Courts of appeals offer the only real hope of reversal for many appellants, since the Supreme Court hears so few cases. Fewer than 1 percent of the cases heard by federal appeals courts are later reviewed by the Supreme Court. "Because the Supreme Court only handles several hundred cases a year," Sheldon Goldman points out, "the influence of lower courts is considerable. For most intents and purposes, the courts of appeals function as regional Supreme

Courts for the nation. As a result, we're talking about some major policy makers."[13]

SPECIAL FEDERAL COURTS

In addition to the Supreme Court, the courts of appeals, and the district courts, the federal judiciary includes a few specialty courts. Among them are the U.S. Claims Court, which hears cases in which the U.S. government is sued for damages; the U.S. Court of International Trade, which handles cases involving appeals of U.S. Customs office rulings; and the U.S. Court of Military Appeals, which hears appeals of military courts-martial. Some federal agencies and commissions also have adjudicative powers, and their decisions can be appealed to a federal court.

STATE COURTS

As a consequence of the United States' federal system of government, each state has a court system that exists apart from the federal courts. Like the federal courts, state court systems have trial courts at the bottom level and appellate courts at the top. Some states have two appellate levels, and others have only a single appellate court. States vary in the way they organize and label their courts, but tend to give some lower courts specialized titles and limited jurisdictions. Family courts, for example, settle such issues as divorce and child-custory disputes, and probate courts handle the disposition of the estates of deceased persons. Below such specialized trial courts are less formal trial courts, such as magistrate courts and justice of the peace courts. They handle a variety of minor cases, such as traffic infractions, and usually do not use a jury.

States vary also in their methods of selecting judges. In about a fourth of the states, judges are appointed by the governor, but in most states, judgeships are elective offices. Several states use the "Missouri Plan" (so called because Missouri was the first state to use it), under which a judicial selection commission provides a short list of acceptable candidates from which the governor selects one; after a year on the bench, the judge selected must be approved by the voters in order to serve a longer term. Some other states use nonpartisan or partisan elections to choose their judges. Federalism allows each state to decide for itself the structure of its courts and the method of judicial appointment. Thus, although all federal judges are appointed to office, states are not required to use this method.

Besides the upper-court myth, there exists a "federal-court myth," which holds that the federal judiciary is the most significant part of the judicial system and that state courts play a subordinate role. This view, too, is inaccurate. Upwards of 95 percent of the nation's legal cases are decided in state courts (or local courts, which are agents of the states). Most crimes (from shoplifting to murder) and most civil controversies (such as divorces and corporate disputes) are defined by state or local law. These cases are hardly insignificant, as the federal-court myth implies they are. Moreover, nearly all cases that originate in state courts also end there; the federal courts never come into the picture.

[13]Quoted in Howard Brownstein, "With or without Supreme Court Changes, Reagan Will Reshape the Federal Court," *National Journal*, December 8, 1984, 2238.

In state criminal cases, after a conviction has occurred and after all avenues of appeal in the state court system have been exhausted, the defendant can seek a writ of *habeas corpus* from a federal district court. When a federal court does become involved in a state case, it often confines itself to the federal aspects of the matter, such as whether the defendant in a criminal case received the protections guaranteed by the U.S. Constitution. If a federal court decides, for instance, that state authorities violated a person's constitutional right to a fair trial, the person is not necessarily acquitted; the federal court's decision may require only that the state retry the accused. In addition, the federal court must accept the facts determined by the state court unless such findings are clearly in error. In short, legal and factual determinations of state courts can bind the federal courts—a clear contradiction of the federal-court myth.

However, cases traditionally within the jurisdiction of the states can become federal cases through rulings of federal courts. In *Roe v. Wade* (1973), for example, the Supreme Court concluded that women had a right to abortion under the U.S. Constitution, thus making abortion rights, which had been a state issue, also a federal one.[14]

When court jurisdictions overlap, the governing principle is **comity**—the idea that the laws of a governing authority (such as a state) will be respected even though the dispute is being settled by a court of a different authority (such as another state or the national government). Adherence to this principle is essential if federalism is to work effectively and harmoniously. Consider a state civil suit involving residents of different states. In such situations, the plaintiff (the person who initiates a court suit) can choose to bring the suit either in his or her state court or in federal court; however, if the plaintiff brings the suit in state court, the defendant (the person against whom a suit is brought) can have the case removed to federal court if the suit involves a claim of $50,000 or more. (The idea that the federal judiciary should be able to hear such cases arose in 1787 because of fears that a state court would be biased toward the interests of its own citizens.)

In cases of multiple jurisdiction, confusion would result if no principle existed for deciding which laws apply—those of the plaintiff's state or the defendant's state. Accordingly, the principle of comity dictates that if such cases are removed to the federal judiciary, they are decided under the laws of the plaintiff's state and that the defendant's state must honor the decision. (Of course, federal judges are not controlled by state courts and can interpret the law as they see fit. A federal judge might not interpret a state law in quite the same way as a state judge would, and there is nothing the state judge can do to change the federal ruling.)

Federal Court Appointees

By the time President Ronald Reagan left office in January 1989, he had appointed almost half of all federal judges, filling vacancies that had resulted from resignations, retirements, and deaths. Reagan selected his appointees with care; the new judges were expected to alter liberal principles that had been laid down by federal courts in the previous three decades. Among the areas in

[14]*Roe v. Wade*, 410 U.S. 113 (1973).

Knowing that Clarence Thomas, once he was confirmed, would influence the ideological direction of the Supreme Court for decades, a delegation of Democratic congresswomen marched from the House to the Senate to voice their concern about his nomination. (Marcy Nighswander/AP/Wide World)

which Reagan hoped for significant change were abortion, school prayer, affirmative action, and the rights of the accused. Assistant Attorney General Stephen Markman, who coordinated Reagan's judicial appointments, said that the goal was to appoint judges who were "less likely to be engaged in broad social engineering policies" than their more liberal predecessors.[15]

Appointments of federal judges do represent a significant opportunity for a president to influence national policy because judges have considerable discretion. Although courts make their decisions on the basis of law, "the law" is not always clear-cut in its application to particular cases. In the course of deciding cases that arise under various laws, courts actively create policy. This subject is the focus of the next chapter; here it will suffice to note that no modern president has been willing to leave to chance the question of who will sit on the federal bench. Judges may appear impartial, but they are selected through a highly political process. Each president has sought appointees whose political beliefs reflected his own. The litmus test for Reagan appointees was their commitment to conservative principles.[16]

As most judges retain their positions for many years, a president can influence judicial policy through his appointments long after he himself has left office. Reagan's appointees will be a force on the federal bench well into the twenty-first century. The careers of some Supreme Court justices also provide dramatic testimony to the enduring effects of judicial appointments. Franklin D. Roosevelt appointed William O. Douglas to the Supreme Court in 1939, and for thirty years after Roosevelt's death in 1945 Douglas remained a strong liberal influence on the Court. John Marshall was appointed chief justice in 1801 by the second president, John Adams, and served until 1835, when the seventh president, Andrew Jackson, was in his second term.

[15]Quoted in Kathryn Kahler, "Will Numerous Reagan Appointees Mold a New Judiciary?" *Syracuse Herald-American*, January 24, 1988, E1, E4.
[16]Sheldon Goldman, "Reagan's Second-Term Judicial Appointments: The Battle at Midway," *Judicature* 70 (1987): 327–339.

SELECTING SUPREME COURT JUSTICES AND FEDERAL JUDGES

The formal mechanism for appointments to the Supreme Court and the lower federal courts is the same: the president nominates and the Senate confirms or rejects. Beyond that basic similarity, however, significant differences emerge.

Supreme Court Nominees

Presidents have used a variety of approaches to the task of selecting a nominee to fill a vacancy on the Supreme Court. A president may choose to depend chiefly on his own counsel, ask the Justice Department for advice, or seek the views of interested parties who share his general philosophy.

Interest groups invariably become actively involved in the selection process after the president has announced his choice. When Reagan nominated Sandra Day O'Connor in 1981, her selection was endorsed by several groups that wanted a woman on the Supreme Court. Most nominees are confirmed by wide margins by the Senate, but interest groups occasionally play a significant role in the Senate's rejection of a nominee. In 1969 Clement F. Haynsworth, Jr., a Nixon nominee, was rejected 55-45 by the Senate after strong opposition by organized labor and minority groups (and amid allegations of conflict of interest in his financial dealings).

Perhaps no nominee in Supreme Court history received more attention from a wide array of interest groups than Robert Bork, who was nominated in 1987. In his writings Bork had argued that the 1964 Civil Rights Act's prohibition on discrimination in public accommodations had no constitutional justification, that the Supreme Court's "privacy" decisions (including its *Roe* v. *Wade* ruling on abortion rights) were constitutionally unsound, and that antitrust laws should not be vigorously applied to prevent corporate mergers. These positions caused numerous minority, consumer, and women's groups to oppose Bork's confirmation. Even the American Civil Liberties Union (ACLU), which had a long-standing policy of not taking a position on Supreme Court nominees, came out against Bork. A group of 2,000 law professors, about half the total faculty of accredited law schools in the United States, signed a petition urging that Bork be denied confirmation because of his unbending and extreme legal philosophy. A counterpetition on Bork's behalf was signed by 100 law professors.

One group that always takes a stand on Supreme Court nominees is the American Bar Association (ABA). Its Committee on the Federal Judiciary investigates each nominee and assesses his or her qualifications for appointment to the Supreme Court. This evaluation is less meaningful than it might be, however, because the ABA committee has never judged a nominee to be not qualified—not even G. Harrold Carswell, an undistinguished and perhaps racially biased federal judge whom the Senate refused, 51-45, to confirm in 1970. Carswell's qualifications were so weak that one of his Senate supporters inadvertently contributed to his defeat by offering the now-infamous "mediocrity defense": "There are a lot of mediocre judges and people in Congress," Nebraska's Senator Roman Hruska said, "and they are entitled to a little representation [on the Supreme Court], aren't they?"[17]

---

[17]Quoted in Baum, *Supreme Court,* 37.

Sandra Day O'Connor is sworn in as the first and only female Supreme Court justice. (Sygma)

Within the Senate, a key body is the Judiciary Committee, whose members have responsibility for conducting hearings on judicial nominees and recommending their confirmation or rejection by the full Senate. Nearly 20 percent of presidential nominees have been rejected by the Senate on grounds of judicial qualification, political views, personal ethics, or partisanship. Most of the rejections of nominees in the country's history occurred before 1900, and partisan politics was the main reason. Today a nominee with strong professional and ethical credentials is less likely to be blocked for partisan reasons alone. An exception was Robert Bork, whose nomination was rejected primarily

★ HOW THE UNITED STATES COMPARES

JUDICIAL APPOINTMENT

U.S. courts are highly political by comparison with the courts of most other democracies. First, U.S. courts operate within a common-law tradition, which makes judge-made law (through precedent) a part of the legal code. Many democracies have a civil-law tradition, in which nearly all law is defined by legislative statutes. Second, because U.S. courts operate in a constitutional system of divided power, they are required to rule on conflicts between state and nation or between the executive and legislative branches, which thrusts the judiciary into the middle of political conflicts. U.S. courts have no choice but to act politically. It should not be surprising, then, that federal judges and justices are appointed through an overtly political process in which partisan views and activities are major considerations. Many

federal judges, particularly at the district level, have no significant prior judicial experience and no claim to special legal talent or training. In fact, the United States is one of the few countries that does not mandate formal training for judges.

The pattern is different in most European democracies. Judgeships there tend to be career positions. Individuals are appointed to the judiciary at an early age and then work their way up the judicial ladder largely on the basis of seniority. Partisan politics does not play a large role in appointment and promotion, partly because the courts themselves are less political than their U.S. counterparts. By tradition, European judges see their job as the strict interpretation of statutes, not the creative application of them.

because of strong opposition from Senate Democrats who disagreed with his judicial philosophy.

Bork would probably have been confirmed had his extreme views not been clearly stated in his writings and public speeches. Justice Antonin Scalia is probably as conservative as Bork in his views, but his nomination hearings went smoothly, in part because his views were not "on the record" to the same degree as Bork's. Middle-of-the-road, noncontroversial nominees almost always are approved by the Senate. In practice, the burden of proof rests with the Senate rather than the nominee. To avoid the charge of unprincipled partisanship, the Senate has unofficially accepted the principle that it must build a strong case against confirmation before denying a nominee a seat on the nation's highest court.

Lower-Court Nominees

The president normally gives the deputy attorney general the task of screening potential nominees for lower-court judgeships.[18] **Senatorial courtesy** is also a consideration in these appointments: this tradition, which dates to the 1840s, holds that a senator from the state in which a vacancy has arisen should be given a say in the nomination if the senator is of the same party as the president.[19] If not consulted, the senator involved can request that confirmation be denied, and other senators will normally grant the request as a "courtesy" to a fellow senator.[20] Not surprisingly, presidents have preferred to give senators a voice in judicial appointments. Powerful senators from time to time have even insisted, successfully, on the selection of a candidate of their choosing.

Although the president does not become as personally involved in selecting lower-court nominees as in naming potential Supreme Court justices, lower-court appointments are collectively a significant factor in the impact of a president's administration. Reagan was able to fill more than 300 vacancies in district and appellate courts (compared with three Supreme Court openings), which, as we noted earlier, constituted about half of all judgeships at those levels. Ninety-three percent of Reagan's appointees to the district courts were Republicans, as were 98 percent of his appellate-court nominees.[21]

The Senate is more likely to confirm a president's lower-court nominees than his Supreme Court nominees. Of Reagan's lower-court nominees, only a handful, including Daniel Manion, the son of the founder of the ultraconservative John Birch Society, encountered substantial opposition in the Senate. Manion's critics said he had extreme legal views and lacked judicial experience.

The ABA's Committee on the Federal Judiciary evaluates lower-court appointments. When members of the ABA's committee express reservations about a nominee, as was the case with Manion, the Senate Judiciary Committee tends to investigate the president's choice more thoroughly.

---

[18]For a study of lower-court appointments, see Goldman, "Reagan's Second-Term Judicial Appointments."
[19]Stephen L. Wasby, *The Supreme Court in the Federal Judicial System,* 2d ed. (New York: Holt, Rinehart and Winston, 1984), 75.
[20]Henry J. Abraham, *The Judicial Process,* 5th ed. (New York: Oxford University Press, 1986), 24–26.
[21]Goldman, "Reagan's Second-Term Judicial Appointments," 328, 331.

★ ANALYZE THE ISSUE

A Supreme Court Nominee's Judicial Record
During hearings to confirm his appointment to the Supreme Court in 1990, David Souter was described by some journalists as the "stealth nominee." Just as the stealth bomber cannot be detected by enemy radar, Souter's lack of written opinions (he had spent little time on the federal bench before his nomination) left the senators on the Judiciary Committee somewhat puzzled about his views and abilities. Some senators speculated that President Bush, remembering Robert Bork's rejection by the Senate, had nominated Souter precisely because very little information existed for opponents to use to block his confirmation. Should a judge have a substantial record on the bench before nomination to the Supreme Court?

★ ANALYZE THE ISSUE

Ideology on the Supreme Court
Supreme Court justices normally take ideological positions that are roughly in line with what the presidents who appointed them expected. Of recent justices who have *not* conformed to expectations—including Justices Warren, Blackmun, and Stevens—most have tended to be more liberal than expected, particularly on issues of civil liberties. Do you think this is just a coincidence, or does it suggest something basic about the Court's role in protecting the rights of the individual?

JUSTICES AND JUDGES AS POLITICAL OFFICIALS

In comparing the Supreme Court with the U.S. Senate, where he had served before his appointment to the Court, Justice Harold Burton said that it was the difference between a "monastery" and a "circus."[22] The quiet setting of the Court, the dignity of its proceedings, and the lack of fanfare with which it announces its decisions give the impression that the Court is about as far removed from the world of politics as a governmental institution can possibly be. The reality is different, however. Supreme Court justices are political officials who exercise the authority of a separate and powerful branch of government. And what is true of the justices is true also of lower-court federal judges. All federal jurists are appointed through a political process, bring their political views with them to the courtroom, and have regular opportunities to promote their political beliefs through the cases they decide. In a parting shot at the Supreme Court's conservative majority, retiring Justice Thurgood Marshall asked rhetorically whether the shift in the Court's direction on key issues that had occurred during the 1980s was really based on the law. After all, he said, nothing had changed except "the personnel of this Court."[23]

The Role of Partisanship

Not surprisingly, partisanship is a critical test of potential jurists: presidents nearly always nominate someone from their own party in order to increase the chances of appointing a justice with political views similar to their own. Before nominating Oliver Wendell Holmes, Jr., to the Court, Theodore Roosevelt wrote to Henry Cabot Lodge for his opinion, saying, "I should hold myself as guilty of an irreparable wrong to the nation if I should put in his place any man who was not absolutely sane and sound on the great national policies for which we stand in public life."[24]

Presidents generally manage to appoint individuals who share their political philosophy. Although justices are free to go their own way on the Court, their legal philosophies can be inferred from their prior activities. A study by the judicial scholar Robert Scigliano found that about three of every four appointees have behaved on the Supreme Court approximately as presidents could have expected.[25] Of course, a president has no guarantee that a nominee will fulfill his hopes. Justices Earl Warren and William Brennan proved more liberal than President Dwight D. Eisenhower would have liked. When he was asked whether he had made any mistakes as president, Eisenhower replied, "Yes, two, and they are both sitting on the Supreme Court."[26]

Presidents also tend to choose members of their own party as nominees to lower-court judgeships. All recent presidents except Gerald Ford have selected

---

[22]Quoted in Mary Frances Berry, *Stability, Security, and Continuity: Mr. Justice Burton and Decision-Making in the Supreme Court* (Westport, Conn.: Greenwood Press, 1978), 27.

[23]"Good for the Left, Now Good for the Right," *Newsweek*, July 8, 1991, 20.

[24]Quoted in Walter Murphy and C. Herman Pritchett, eds., *Courts, Judges, and Politics*, 3d ed. (New York: Random House, 1979), 137.

[25]Robert Scigliano, *The Supreme Court and the Presidency* (New York: Free Press, 1971), 146.

[26]Quoted in Baum, *Supreme Court*, 37.

Dwight D. Eisenhower (*right*) discovered to his dismay that Chief Justice Earl Warren (*left*) was more liberal than the president had thought when he nominated Warren to the Supreme Court in 1953. (UPI/Bettman Newsphotos)

more than 90 percent of their district- and appeals-court nominees from among members of their own party.[27]

The fact that judges and justices are chosen through a partisan political process should not be interpreted to mean that they engage in blatant partisanship while on the bench. Judges and justices are officers of a separate branch and prize their judicial independence. All Republican appointees do not vote the same way on cases, nor do all Democrats. Moreover, it is rare for federal judges to support in all cases the position of the president who appointed them. The most dramatic example is·*United States* v. *Nixon* (1974), when the Supreme Court, which included four Nixon appointees, unanimously ruled that President Nixon had to turn over tapes of his private conversations to the special prosecutor investigating the Watergate affair.

Nevertheless, the partisan backgrounds of judges are a significant influence on their decisions. A study of the voting records of appellate-court judges, for example, found that Republican appointees are more conservative than Democratic appointees. Reagan appointees and Nixon/Ford appointees supported civil rights and civil liberties claims in 32 percent and 34 percent of such cases, respectively, compared with 46 percent and 53 percent, respectively, for Johnson and Carter appointees.[28]

Prior Experience and Other Characteristics of Judicial Appointees

In recent years, increasing numbers of federal justices and judges have had prior judicial experience; the assumption is that such individuals are best qualified for

[27]C. Herman Pritchett, *The American Constitutional System* (New York: McGraw-Hill, 1967), 76; Herbert Jacob, *Justice in America: Courts, Lawyers, and the Judicial Process,* 4th ed. (Glenview, Ill.: Scott, Foresman, 1984), 122.
[28]John Gottschall, "Reagan's Appointments to the U.S. Courts of Appeals," 70 *Judicature* 48 (1986): 54.

★ CRITICAL THINKING

SHOULD MERIT PLAY A LARGER ROLE IN JUDICIAL SELECTION?

Over the years the partisanship evident in court appointments has occasionally come under attack. In the early twentieth century, Progressive reformers persuaded some states to exclude their judgeships from party patronage positions. The Missouri Plan (described in the "State Courts" section of this chapter) is a more recent reflection of the belief that partisan loyalty should not play a deciding role in the filling of judicial offices. No such thoroughgoing reform has taken place at the federal level, although Jimmy Carter used selection panels to compile lists of five candidates to fill appellate-court vacancies on the basis of merit. Carter selected from among these candidates, although he nearly always picked a Democrat. Carter's merit system was opposed by some senators, who believed that it reduced their influence on the selection process. Reagan returned the judicial selection process to the earlier system after he took office, and Bush retained that method.

The issue of merit in the case of judges and justices is a complicated one because there is no consensus even on the issue of whether prior judicial experience is desirable for appointees. Justice Felix Frankfurter claimed that "the correlation between prior judicial experience and fitness for the Supreme Court is zero," and felt that the greatest jurists—Oliver Wendell Holmes, Jr., and Benjamin Cardozo among them—were essentially "legal philosophers." Frankfurter's observation is backed by history, in that some of the Court's most influential members—including John Marshall, Charles Evans Hughes, Louis Brandeis, Harlan Stone, Felix Frankfurt-

er, Earl Warren, and Hugo Black—had no significant judicial experience before being appointed to the Court.

C. Herman Pritchett, a leading judicial scholar, suggested that the Court might be best served when the justices collectively have experience in both the legal and political realms. Noting that the Warren Court (1953–1969) had a penchant for tackling issues that in some cases might have been better left to legislative bodies, while the Burger Court (1969–1986) often was preoccupied with narrow points of law, Pritchett observed, "Perhaps there were too many politicians on the Warren Court, but perhaps there [were] too many judges on the Burger Court." The Supreme Court is even more judge-laden today. Recent appointees have been drawn largely from U.S. Courts of Appeals.

What is your view? Should merit be a larger consideration in appointments to the Court, or is it more important that justices be chosen on the basis of their policy views? What are the relative advantages of appointing "politicians" and "judges" to the Supreme Court?

SOURCES: Henry J. Abraham, "The Judicial Function under the Constitution," *News for Teachers of Political Science* 41 (Spring 1984): 12; Felix Frankfurter, "The Supreme Court in the Mirror of Justices," *University of Pennsylvania Law Review* 106 (1957): 781; John Schmidhauser, *Judges and Justices* (Boston: Little, Brown, 1979), 95; C. Herman Pritchett, "High Court Selection," *New York Times*, January 12, 1976, reprinted in Walter Murphy and C. Herman Pritchett, eds., *Courts, Judges, and Politics*, 3d ed. (New York: Random House, 1979), 137.

appointment to the federal bench. Most recent appellate-court appointees have been district or state judges or have worked in the office of the attorney general.[29] Elective office (particularly a seat in the U.S. Senate) was once the typical route to the Supreme Court,[30] but now most justices have held an appellate-court judgeship or high administrative office in the Justice Department before their appointment (see Table 22-1).

The judiciary is not at all demographically representative of the public it serves.[31] White male Protestants are greatly overrepresented on the federal

[29]John Schmidhauser, *Judges and Justices: The Federal Appellate Judiciary* (Boston: Little, Brown, 1979), 84–85.
[30]Joseph B. Harris, *The Advice and Consent of the Senate* (Berkeley: University of California Press, 1953), 313.
[31]Schmidhauser, *Judges and Justices*, ch.3.

TABLE 22-1 Justices of the Supreme Court, 1992 Most recent appointees held an appellate-court position before being nominated to the Supreme Court.

Justice	Year of Appointment	Nominating President	Position before Appointment
Byron White	1962	Kennedy	Deputy attorney general
Harry Blackmun	1970	Nixon	Judge, U.S. Courts of Appeals
William Rehnquist*	1971	Nixon	Assistant attorney general
John Paul Stevens	1975	Ford	Judge, U.S. Courts of Appeals
Sandra Day O'Connor	1981	Reagan	Judge, Arizona Courts of Appeals
Antonin Scalia	1986	Reagan	Judge, U.S. Courts of Appeals
Anthony Kennedy	1988	Reagan	Judge, U.S. Courts of Appeals
David Souter	1990	Bush	Judge, U.S. Courts of Appeals
Clarence Thomas	1991	Bush	Judge, U.S. Courts of Appeals

*Appointed chief justice in 1986.

TABLE 22-2 Background Characteristics of Appointees to U.S. District Courts and U.S. Courts of Appeals, 1963–1988 The judicial appointees of Republican and Democratic presidents have differed in important respects.

CHARACTERISTIC	PRESIDENCY				
	Johnson	Nixon	Ford	Carter	Reagan
Occupation (district judges only)					
Politics/government	21%	11%	21%	4%	13%
Judicial	31	28	35	45	38
Private law	44	58	44	48	47
Professor of law	4	3	0	3	2
Occupation (appellate judges only)					
Politics/government	10	5	8	5	5
Judicial	58	57	75	47	52
Private law	30	36	17	33	27
Professor of law	2	2	0	15	16
Gender					
Male	98	99	98	85	92
Female	2	1	2	15	8
Ethnicity/race					
White	94	96	90	79	94
Black	4	3	5	14	2
Hispanic	2	1	3	6	4
Asian	0	0	3	1	0
Political party					
Democratic	95	7	18	90	4
Republican	5	93	82	5	95
Independent	0	0	0	5	1
Religious background					
Protestant	59	74	70	60	60
Catholic	30	18	20	27	31
Jewish	11	8	10	13	9

SOURCE: Adapted from tables 1 and 3, Sheldon Goldman, "Reagan's Second-Term Judicial Appointments: The Battle at Midway," *Judicature* 70 (April-May 1987): 328, 331.

The justices of the U.S. Supreme Court assemble for their official portrait. From the left, they are: Clarence Thomas, David Souter, Antonin Scalia, Sandra Day O'Connor, Chief Justice William Rehnquist, John Paul Stevens, Harry Blackmun, Byron White, and Anthony Kennedy. (Ken Heinen/AP/Wide World Photos)

Antonin Scalia is the first Italian-American Supreme Court justice. (Arthur Grace/Sygma)

courts, just as they dominate in Congress and at the top levels of the executive branch (see Table 22-2). When Jimmy Carter became president in 1977, he was determined to appoint more women and African-Americans to the courts; numerically, he appointed twice as many women and blacks to the federal bench as all previous presidents combined. Women totaled 20 percent of his appointees and African-Americans 16 percent. Ronald Reagan was more concerned with nominees' ideology than with their race or sex, and women and blacks accounted for only 10 percent of his appointees. Reagan did seek younger people for the federal courts, knowing that such individuals are more likely to remain on the bench for many years, thus prolonging their influence on the law. Reagan's judicial appointees averaged about forty-five years of age, compared with the previous average of more than fifty years. As for religious affiliation, Protestants account for about two-thirds of judicial appointees since 1960.

The Supreme Court itself is also demographically unrepresentative. Until 1916, when Louis D. Brandeis was appointed to the Court, no Jewish justice had ever served. At least one Catholic, but at most times only one, has been on the Court almost continuously for nearly a century. Thurgood Marshall in 1967 became the first black justice, and Sandra Day O'Connor in 1981 became the first woman. Antonin Scalia in 1986 became the Court's first justice of Italian descent. No person of Hispanic or Asian descent has ever been a member of the Court.

The judicial scholar Henry J. Abraham has dismissed concerns about the Supreme Court's demographic makeup, saying that the Court was never meant to be a representative body. Another scholar, Sheldon Goldman, disagrees, saying that "the *best* bench may be composed of persons of all races and both sexes with diverse backgrounds and experiences." Goldman argues that the judiciary's sensitivity to society's diverse interests depends to a degree on the social backgrounds that the justices bring with them to the Court.[32]

Judicial appointments, then, are a critical issue because, as we have emphasized, the judiciary is a political institution as well as a legal one—a point that will be developed further in the next chapter.

Summary

At the lowest level of the federal judicial system are the district courts, where most federal cases begin. Above them are the federal courts of appeals, which review cases appealed from the lower courts. The U.S. Supreme Court is the nation's highest court. Each state has its own court system, consisting of trial courts at the bottom and one or two appellate levels at the top. Cases originating in state courts ordinarily cannot be appealed to the federal courts unless a federal issue is involved, and then the federal courts can choose to rule only on the federal aspects of the case.

The Supreme Court is unquestionably the most important court in the country. The legal principles it establishes are binding on lower courts, and its capacity to define the law is enhanced by the control it exercises over the cases it hears. The most important part of the Court's majority opinion in a case is the legal reasoning underlying the decision: this reasoning guides lower courts in their handling of similar cases. However, it is inaccurate

to assume that lower courts are inconsequential (the upper-court myth). Lower courts have considerable discretion in their evaluation of the facts and applicable laws of the cases before them, and the great majority of their decisions are not reviewed by a higher court. It is also inaccurate to assume that federal courts are far more significant than state courts (the federal-court myth). The vast majority of legal cases that arise each year in the United States are decided in state courts.

Federal judges at all levels are appointed by the president and confirmed by the Senate. Once on the federal bench, they serve until they die, retire, or are removed by impeachment and conviction.

Partisan politics plays a significant role in judicial appointments. Presidents are particularly alert to political philosophy in their selection of Supreme Court justices. Because the nation's top court makes broad policy decisions, presidents have tried to ensure that appointees share their partisan goals.

Major Concepts

appellate jurisdiction	majority opinion
comity	opinion (of the Supreme Court)
concurring opinion	original jurisdiction
decision	plurality opinion
dissenting opinion	precedent
judicial conference	senatorial courtesy
jurisdiction	writ of *certiorari*

[32]Henry J. Abraham, "The Judicial Function under the Constitution," *News for Teachers of Political Science* 41 (Spring 1984): 14; Sheldon Goldman, "Should There Be Affirmative Action for the Judiciary?" *Judicature* 62 (May 1979): 494.

Suggested Readings

Abraham, Henry J. *The Judicial Process,* 5th ed. New York: Oxford University Press, 1986. An explanation of how state and federal courts form the judicial system of the United States.

Ball, Howard. *Courts and Politics: The Federal Judicial System,* 2d ed. Englewood Cliffs, N.J.: Prentice-Hall, 1987. A text that describes the function, organization, and purpose of the federal judicial system.

Baum, Lawrence. *The Supreme Court,* 3d ed. Washington, D.C.: Congressional Quarterly Press, 1989. A survey of the personnel, procedures, and cases of the Supreme Court that assesses its policymaking function.

Carp, Robert A., and Ronald Stidham. *The Federal Courts,* 2d ed. Washington, D.C.: Congressional Quarterly Press, 1990. An analysis of the lower federal court system.

Howard, J. Woodford, Jr. *Courts of Appeals in the Federal Judicial System.* Princeton, N.J.: Princeton University Press, 1981. A recent assessment of the role of federal courts of appeals.

Provine, D. Marie. *Case Selection in the United States Supreme Court.* Chicago: University of Chicago Press, 1980. An analysis of the process by which the Supreme Court chooses the cases it reviews.

Schmidhauser, John. *Judges and Justices: The Federal Appellate Judiciary.* Boston: Little, Brown, 1979. An examination of the backgrounds of Supreme Court justices and federal appeals-court judges.

Scigliano, Robert. *The Supreme Court and the Presidency.* New York: Free Press, 1971. A look at the relationship between the Supreme Court and the presidency, including the subject of presidential nominations of justices.

Woodward, Bob, and Scott Armstrong. *The Brethren.* New York: Simon & Schuster, 1979. Two Washington journalists take a critical look at the Supreme Court from 1969 to 1976.

JUDICIAL POLICYMAKING: DECIDING THE LAW

Judges make choices, but they are not the "free" choices of congressmen.
C. Herman Pritchett[1]

I n its historic ruling in *Brown* v. *Board of Education* (1954), the Supreme Court declared that public school segregation was unconstitutional.[2] However, the Court did not require local officials to take positive steps to promote school integration; it merely forbade them to prevent black children from attending previously all-white schools. Because children of each race lived in segregated neighborhoods, most black children fifteen years after the *Brown* ruling were still not attending school with white children.

To remedy this situation, the Supreme Court held in *Swann* v. *Charlotte-Mecklenburg County Board of Education* (1971) that busing was an acceptable, though not required, means of bringing black and white children together in the public schools.[3] The Court reasoned that, where school segregation is a consequence of past public policies, busing is an appropriate remedy for the injustice. Shortly thereafter, lower courts in many parts of the nation, North and South, were ordering communities to use busing to correct the racial imbalance in their schools. Many whites in the affected communities reacted angrily and sometimes violently.

Was the Supreme Court on solid legal ground when it sanctioned court-ordered busing? Some legalists believe that the Court's decision was justified. They argue that the judiciary should act when legislative majorities are afraid or unwilling to undertake policies that protect the basic rights of minorities.

---

[1]C. Herman Pritchett, "The Development of Judicial Research," in Joel B. Grossman and Joseph Tanenhaus, eds., *Frontiers of Judicial Research* (New York: Wiley, 1969), 42.
[2]*Brown* v. *Board of Education of Topeka,* 347 U.S. 483 (1954).
[3]*Swann* v. *Charlotte-Mecklenburg County Board of Education,* 412 U.S. 92 (1971).

After the Supreme Court's *Swann* decision in 1971, which mandated busing to achieve public school integration, police had to be called out at South Boston High School to maintain order. Some legalists claim that this ruling exceeded the Court's authority. (Ira Wyman/Sygma)

According to this view, the U.S. Constitution has strong moral language—for example, "equal protection of the laws"—that justifies decisions such as the busing ruling.[4] Without busing, many black children would be consigned to a life of permanent inequality.

Other legalists claim that the Court overstepped its authority in approving busing. From their perspective, the problem with the *Swann* decision was that it primarily addressed segregation resulting not from law but from the racial, economic, and social differences that lead blacks and whites to live in separate neighborhoods. This situation is supposedly a political problem, not a legal one, and therefore should have been settled by elected officials, not judges.[5]

The busing example illustrates two key points about court decisions. First, the judiciary is an extremely important policymaking body; some of its rulings, including its busing decisions, are as consequential as nearly any law passed by Congress or any executive action taken by the president. Second, federal courts have considerable discretion in their rulings. The *Swann* decision was not based on any literal reading of the law: the justices invoked *their* interpretation of the Fourteenth Amendment's equal-protection clause.

The judiciary's policymaking significance and discretion have been sources of controversy throughout the country's history, but the controversies have perhaps never been livelier than during recent decades. The judiciary has become more extensively involved in policymaking for many of the same reasons that Congress and the president have been thrust into new policy areas and more deeply into old ones. Social and economic changes have required government to play a larger role in society, and this development has generated a seemingly endless series of new legal controversies. The greater interconnect-

---

[4]See Michael J. Perry, *The Constitution, the Courts, and Human Rights: An Inquiry into the Legitimacy of Constitutional Policymaking by the Judiciary* (New Haven, Conn.: Yale University Press, 1982).
[5]Raoul Berger, *Government by Judiciary: The Transformation of the Fourteenth Amendment* (Cambridge, Mass.: Harvard University Press, 1977).

edness of society and policy has also meant that judicial action will have a more far-reaching impact than it had in early periods, when American life was slower and more compartmentalized.

This chapter examines judicial policymaking, describing how legal and political factors come together to influence court decisions. The chapter also discusses the controversy surrounding the judiciary's policy role. The principle of self-government asserts that lawmaking majorities have the power to decide society's policies. Yet the principles of liberty and equality are checks on the power of lawmaking majorities and justify a significant policy role for the courts. A critical question is how far judges, who are not elected, ought to go in substituting their policy judgments for those of officials who are elected by the people. The main points made in this chapter are the following:

★ *Although the courts have discretion in their decisions, their alternatives are constrained by existing law.* In deciding cases, judges are compelled to consider applicable constitutional law, statutory law, and precedent.

★ *Political factors have a major influence on judicial decisions.* The judiciary is somewhat responsive to political officials and to the public, and court decisions reflect judges' political beliefs.

★ *The judiciary has become an increasingly powerful policymaking body in recent decades, although it still plays less of a policymaking role than Congress or the president.* Many of the leading judicial decisions have been controversial and have raised the question of whether the courts have usurped the powers of elected institutions. Advocates of judicial restraint claim that the judiciary has overstepped its authority, whereas judicial activists say that the judiciary's enlarged policy role is constitutionally appropriate.

Legal Influences on Judicial Decisions

Federal judges and justices are political officials: they constitute one of three coequal branches of the national government. Yet they are not political officers in the same sense as members of Congress or the president. Judges serve in a legal institution and make their decisions in a legal context. As a consequence, their discretionary power is less than that of elected officials. A president or Congress can make almost any decision that is politically acceptable. A court, in contrast, must also explain why the decision is consistent with the law. Thus, existing laws constrain the courts by preventing them from making choices that cannot be justified in legal terms.[6]

In deciding an issue, judges rely not simply on personal preference but also on the legal principles that they see as applicable to the case they are considering. When asked by a friend to "do justice," Oliver Wendell Holmes, Jr., replied, "That is not my job. My job is to play the game according to the rules."[7] In playing according to the rules, judges engage in a creative legal process that requires them to identify the facts of the case, determine and

---

[6]Lawrence Baum, *The Supreme Court* (Washington, D.C.: Congressional Quarterly Press, 1981), 117.
[7]Quoted in Charles P. Curtis, *Law and Large as Life* (New York: Simon & Schuster, 1959), 156–157.

★ ANALYZE THE ISSUE

The Political Becomes the Judicial

The Supreme Court has distinguished between political questions (within the authority of elected officials) and judicial questions (within the authority of the judiciary). However, the Court sometimes decides that a political question has become a judicial question, as in its rulings on abortion (1973), apportionment of state legislatures (1963), and school desegregation (1954). Is the political-judicial distinction therefore a phony one—merely a line drawn where the Supreme Court chooses to draw it at any given moment? Why, or why not?

SOURCES OF LAW THAT CONSTRAIN THE SUPREME COURT'S DECISIONS

U.S. Constitution: The Supreme Court is bound by the provisions of the U.S. Constitution. The sparseness of its wording, however, requires the Constitution to be applied in the light of present circumstances. Thus the justices are accorded a substantial degree of discretion in their constitutional judgments.

Statutory law: The Supreme Court is constrained by statutes and by administrative regulations derived from the provisions of statutes. Most laws, however, are some-what vague in their provisions and often have unanticipated applications. As a result, the justices have some freedom in deciding cases based on statutes.

Precedent: The Supreme Court is bound by precedent (or *stare decisis*), which is a legal principle developed in earlier court decisions. Because not all cases have a clear precedent, however, the justices have some discretion in their evaluation of the way earlier cases apply to a current case.

sometimes formulate the relevant legal principles or rules, and then apply them to the case at hand.

THE CONSTRAINTS OF THE FACTS

The Constitution prohibits the courts from ruling except on actual cases brought before it. Thus the judiciary, unlike Congress or the president, is not free to make judgments at any time and on any issue it chooses.

A basic distinction in any legal case is between "the facts" and "the laws." The **facts** of a case, as determined by trial courts, are the relevant circumstances of a legal dispute or offense. In the case of a person accused of murder, for example, key facts would include evidence about the murder and whether the rights of the accused were respected by police in the course of their investigation. The facts of a case are crucial because they determine which law or laws are applicable to the case.

The courts must respond to the facts of a dispute. Thus a case that centers on whether a defendant's right to a fair trial has been abridged cannot be used as an occasion to pronounce judgment on a corporate merger. This restriction is a very substantial one. Consider the period in the 1960s when the Supreme Court broadened most of the due-process protections in the Fourth through Eighth amendments to include states' criminal proceedings. The first of these rulings came in *Mapp* v. *Ohio* (1961), discussed in Chapter 5.[8] The case arose when the defendant claimed that police had violated her Fourth Amendment protection against unreasonable search and seizure. In deciding that the Fourteenth Amendment's due-process clause embraced this protection, the Court did not also rule that all other due-process guarantees were similarly protected. The facts of the *Mapp* case limited the Court's judgment to the search-and-seizure issue. Only through subsequent cases did the Supreme Court decide, one by

[8]*Mapp* v. *Ohio,* 367 U.S. 643 (1961).

one, that certain other rights were also protected by the Fourteenth Amendment's due-process clause.

THE CONSTRAINTS OF THE LAW

In deciding cases, the judiciary is constrained by existing laws. As distinct from the facts of a case, the **laws** of a case are the constitutional provisions, legislative statues, or judicial precedents that apply to the situation. To use an obvious comparison, the laws governing a case of alleged murder differ from the laws that apply to an antitrust suit. When addressing a case, a court must determine which laws are relevant.

Interpretation of the Constitution

The Constitution is a sparsely worded document, and for that reason its language is open to interpretation. For example, the Constitution grants Congress the power to regulate interstate commerce, but the meaning of "commerce" is not spelled out, and the courts have defined it in various ways during the nation's history. Until the early twentieth century the judiciary held that factory practices were not "commerce" but "production" and were thus beyond Congress's legislative authority. Now, however, the courts hold that the commerce clause embraces nearly every business activity. The judiciary's varying interpretations of the commerce clause have reflected the nation's changing economic needs. A function of the judiciary is to apply rules made in the past in ways that are meaningful in the present. The U.S. industrial economy of today bears no resemblance to the agrarian economy of the late eighteenth century, and only an updated interpretation of the commerce clause could meet today's needs.

We are under a Constitution, but the Constitution is what the judges say it is, and the judiciary is the safeguard of our liberty and of our property under the Constitution.
Charles Evans Hughes

Nevertheless, the courts respect the purpose and intent of the Constitution: judges strive for reasonable interpretations of its provisions. The question for a judge is not how the writers of the Constitution would settle today's disputes by yesterday's standards but what the Framers had in mind by a particular provision. For example, in deciding whether wiretapping and other electronic means of surveillance are covered by the Fourth Amendment's prohibition against unreasonable searches and seizures, the issue is what the amendment was designed to protect. Obviously, the Framers could not have meant to protect people against wiretapping per se; electronic surveillance was not invented until 150 years after the Fourth Amendment was ratified. But the Fourth Amendment was intended to protect individuals against snooping by government into their private lives; for this reason, the courts have held that government cannot indiscriminately tap a person's telephone.

Constitutional interpretation is an important part of the work of the federal judiciary, particularly the Supreme Court and U.S. Courts of Appeals. The power of the courts to decide whether a governmental institution has acted within its constitutional powers is called **judicial review** (see Chapter 3). Without this power, the judiciary's claim to be a coequal branch of government would be a weak one. The judiciary would be unable to restrain a Congress that had gone out of control. Yet the process of judicial review pits a court's

★ ANALYZE THE ISSUE

Busing as a Constitutional Issue
Using your knowledge of the Constitution and the Supreme Court's role in the U.S. political system, defend the Court's reasoning in cases involving busing to achieve racial integration in the schools. Now, using that same knowledge, criticize the Court's reasoning in busing cases. Which constitutional argument seems more compelling to you?

★ HOW THE UNITED STATES COMPARES

JUDICIAL REVIEW

The power of U.S. courts is nowhere more evident than in the exercise of judicial review—the voiding of a legislative or executive action on the grounds that it violates the Constitution. Judicial review had its origins in European experiences and thought, but it was first formally applied in the United States when, in *Marbury v. Madison* (1803), the Supreme Court declared an act of Congress unconstitutional. Judicial review was not immediately incorporated into legal doctrine elsewhere but has since become relatively common. Some democracies, including Great Britain, still do not allow broad-scale judicial review, but most democracies now provide for it.

In the so-called American system of judicial review, all judges can evaluate the applicability of constitutional law to particular cases and can declare ordinary law invalid when it conflicts with constitutional law. By comparison, the so-called Austrian system restricts judicial review to a special constitutional court. Judges in other courts cannot declare a law void on the grounds that it is unconstitutional: they must apply ordinary law

as it is written. In the Austrian system, moreover, constitutional decisions are made mainly in response to requests for judicial review by political officials (such as the chief executive).

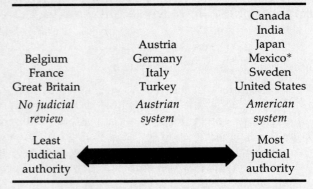

*Mexico is included under the American system even though its judiciary has elements of the Austrian system.

SOURCE: Mauro Cappelletti and William Cohen, *Comparative Constitutional Law* (Indianapolis: Bobbs-Merrill, 1979), ch.4.

judgment against that of another institution and invokes the nation's highest law—the Constitution. The imposing nature of judicial review has led the judiciary, when possible, to prefer statutory rulings to constitutional ones.

Interpretation of Statutes

Statutory law includes legislation that has been enacted by Congress and administrative regulations that have been developed by the bureaucracy from statutory provisions. When a statute is challenged in a case, the judiciary will initially see whether its meaning can be determined by common sense (the "plain-meaning rule").

Congress occasionally structures its debate to ensure that courts will later be readily able to understand its intent. For example, the Civil Rights Act of 1964 was designed in part to prohibit racial discrimination in public accommodations, such as restaurants, hotels, and movie theaters. The act was based principally on the commerce clause, which the Supreme Court had already interpreted broadly. In the congressional debate, the legislation's supporters stressed the adverse effects of racial discrimination on the free flow of commerce. As its supporters in Congress had anticipated, the Civil Rights Act's ban on racial discrimination in public accommodations was later challenged in court. The Supreme Court upheld the law, noting that "the legislative history of the Act is replete with evidence of the burdens that discrimination by race or color places upon interstate commerce."[9]

Not all judges believe that the courts should look beyond the law to determine congressional intent. They argue that words spoken during congressional debate are not necessarily representative of what the majority intended when it passed the legislation at issue. Regardless, the judiciary has no choice at times but to apply its own judgment. Congress can seldom anticipate all the specific applications of a legislative act and therefore uses general language to state the act's purpose. Legislation is often a product of political compromise, which can also result in ambiguous provisions. Such vagueness can give rise to disputes over the implementation of laws, and an individual who is adversely affected by a law-enforcement or administrative official's judgment as to the meaning of a law can seek to have this assessment reversed in the courts.[10]

Interpretation of Precedent

We saw in Chapter 22 that the English common-law tradition that a court's decision on a case should be consistent with previous rulings is called **precedent.** The philosophy underlying the tradition of adherence to precedent is known as *stare decisis* (Latin for "to stand by things that have been settled")—the doctrine that principles of law, once established, should be accepted as authoritative in all subsequent similar cases.

Cases do not always have a clear precedent. This is particularly true of Supreme Court cases. When precedent is more or less obvious, lower courts usually apply it, and the Supreme Court is unlikely to review such cases. The cases that the Supreme Court selects for a full hearing and decision may interest it precisely because their facts differ significantly from those of previous cases. The justices may argue that they are following precedent, while actually they are modifying it substantially. In 1984, for instance, the Court said that the exclusionary rule (discussed in Chapter 5) did not apply to evidence obtained by an illegal search warrant if police obtained it "in good faith."[11] This ruling weakened and substantially modified precedent regarding the exclusion of evidence. At times the Supreme Court disavows precedent entirely. In recent decades the Court has overturned an average of four precedents each year.[12]

A rigid adherence to precedent would not serve a society's needs. The law proceeds in part by trial and error. It must be reinterpreted to meet what Justice Oliver Wendell Holmes, Jr., described as "the felt necessities of the time." The Industrial Revolution of the nineteenth century, for example, brought about *unprecedented* social and economic changes that demanded *unprecedented* court rulings.

Nevertheless, precedent is an important constraint on the courts, including the Supreme Court. To persist in ignoring precedent would be to direct the law onto an unpredictable course, creating confusion and uncertainty among those

> **★ ANALYZE THE ISSUE**
>
> **Precedent as Assurance of Predictability**
> Supreme Court Justice Oliver Wendell Holmes, Jr., claimed that law is founded on the precept of reasonable expectations: people make choices on the assumption that the law will not change overnight. In your judgment, is precedent as important as Holmes claimed it is? Why, or why not?

[9]*Heart of Atlanta Motel* v. *United States*, 371 U.S. 241 (1964).
[10]Samuel Krislov, *The Supreme Court in the Political Process* (New York: Macmillan, 1965), 76–77
[11]*United States* v. *Leon*, 463 U.S. 1206 (1984).
[12]Congressional Research Service, *The Constitution of the United States of America: Analysis and Interpretation* (Washington, D.C.: U.S. Government Printing Office, 1979).

The life of the law has not been logic: it has been experience. In order to know what is [the law], we must know what it has been.

    Oliver Wendell Holmes, Jr.

who must make choices on the basis of their understanding of the law. Judges realize that they have a responsibility to help maintain legal consistency. "The life of the law has not been logic: it has been experience," Justice Holmes wrote. "In order to know what is [the law], we must know what it has been."[13]

Political Influences on Judicial Decisions

Any Supreme Court opinion of reasonable length and importance contains references to previous rulings or to the language of the Constitution or statute law. These opinions reflect the importance of precedent and predictability in the law. It would be inaccurate to conclude, however, that the judiciary is merely following the path laid down by existing legal principles. The law is always somewhat ambiguous, and judges always have some degree of discretion.[14] Judicial discretion is evident, for example, in the frequency of disagreement among Supreme Court justices over how a case should be settled. On most cases of major significance, the justices are divided in their opinions.

The principal reason for divisions among the justices is that judicial opinions reflect not only legal influences but also political ones, which come from both outside and inside the judicial system.

"OUTSIDE" INFLUENCES ON COURT DECISIONS

The courts can make unpopular choices, but, in the long run, their decisions must be seen as fair if they are to be obeyed. In other words, the judiciary cannot ignore the expectations of the general public, interest groups, and elected officials, particularly the president and members of Congress. The precise impact of these outside pressures cannot be measured, but judicial experts agree that the courts are affected by them.

The Force of Public Opinion

Judges are responsive to public opinion, although much less so than are elected officials. In rare instances, public opinion becomes part of the formal basis for a decision. In its ruling in *Gregg* v. *Georgia* (1976), for example, the Supreme Court cited the results of public opinion polling in upholding the constitutionality of the death penalty.[15] In other cases the Court has tailored its rulings in an effort to gain public support or dampen public resistance. In the *Brown* case, for example, the justices, recognizing that school desegregation would be an explosive issue in the South, attempted to defuse the reaction by requiring only that desegregation take place "with all deliberate speed" rather than immediately or on a fixed timetable. The Supreme Court's apparent strategy has been to stay close enough to popular opinion to avoid seriously eroding public support for its decisions.[16]

[13]Oliver Wendell Holmes, Jr., *The Common Law* (Boston: Little, Brown, 1881),1.
[14]Martin Shapiro, *The Supreme Court and Administrative Agencies* (New York: Free Press, 1968), 71.
[15]*Gregg* v. *Georgia*, 428 U.S. 153 (1976).
[16]Stephen L. Wasby, *The Supreme Court in the Federal Judicial System* (New York: Holt, Rinehart and Winston, 1978), 53.

To some extent, judges take public opinion into account in weighing their decisions on such controversial issues as the death penalty. Recently the Supreme Court, perhaps partly in response to the public's frustration, has made it harder for state prisoners in death penalty cases to appeal to the federal judiciary. There are more than 2,500 inmates on death row; there have been 167 executions in the past 16 years; and the appeals process has been lasting an average of eight years. (Shepard Sherbell/SABA)

Some judicial decisions depend almost entirely on voluntary compliance by the public. For example, the day still begins with a prayer in some public schools, but the practice stopped abruptly in most schools in 1962, when the Supreme Court ruled that school prayers violated the First Amendment provision that church and state must remain separate.[17] Most Americans have enough respect for the rule of law to abide by judicial decisions, even those with which they disagree.

The judiciary does not have to follow public opinion slavishly in order to keep its authoritative position. Only a few judicial decisions affect a large portion of the public directly, and most Americans do not want to endure the legal difficulties that might attend violation of the law. Moreover, the fact that public opinion on controversial issues is always divided means that the courts will not stand alone no matter which side of such an issue their rulings favor. As an example, opinion polls indicate that Americans are sharply divided on the issue of a woman's right to obtain an abortion in the early months of pregnancy.

Lobbying the Courts

Interest groups use the courts to advance their policy goals. Although litigation is expensive (the cost of carrying a case all the way to the Supreme Court can run as high as $500,000), it often costs less than lobbying Congress or the executive on a major issue. And obviously some interests, particularly those represented by persons who are in an unpopular or underprivileged minority, may have a better chance of success in a legal suit than with an elected institution.

Some groups that have made extensive use of the judicial alternative are the

[17]*Engel* v. *Vitale,* 370 U.S. 421 (1962).

Twenty years after the Supreme Court's decision in *Roe* v. *Wade* made abortion legal, groups on both sides of the issue are still pressuring the courts. (A. Tannenbaum/Sygma)

American Civil Liberties Union, the Environmental Defense Fund, Jehovah's Witnesses, the American Legion, and the National Association for the Advancement of Colored People. The interest groups that have been most successful in working through the courts are the ones that have been able to perceive the direction in which the courts were already heading. The NAACP, for example, noting that the Supreme Court was nibbling away at the "separate but equal"

Thurgood Marshall (*center*) was the special counsel for the NAACP lawyers who argued the *Brown* school desegregation case before the Supreme Court in 1954. Other members of the team were George E. C. Hayes (*left*) and James Nabret, Jr. (*right*). In 1967 Marshall was appointed to the Supreme Court (and retired in 1991). (UPI/Bettmann Newsphotos)

precedent of *Plessy* v. *Ferguson*, searched out cases that would test the precedent in the area of public school segregation. One of the cases undertaken by the NAACP was that of a Topeka, Kansas, schoolchild, Linda Brown. Brown's case, of course, became the vehicle by which the Supreme Court established a new precedent—namely, that state-sponsored racial segregation of public schools violates the equal-protection clause of the Fourteenth Amendment.

Through *amicus curiae* ("friend of the court") briefs the judiciary can obtain more precise expressions of a group's opinion. When invited by a court to submit such a brief, an interest group gets an opportunity to explain directly its position on a pending case.[18] Conservative groups have had a strong interest in *amicus curiae* participation because they usually support the status quo and have not been as active as liberal groups in promoting their views by initiating suit against established interests.

The Leverage of Public Officials

The influence of groups and the general public on the judiciary is usually registered indirectly, through the elected branches of government. In response to public and group pressure, elected officials try to persuade the judiciary to hand down rulings favored by their constituents. Both Congress and the president have powerful means of influencing the federal judiciary.

Congress is constitutionally empowered to establish the Supreme Court's size and appellate jurisdiction, and Congress can rewrite legislation that it feels the Court has misinterpreted. Although Congress has seldom confronted the Court directly, it has often demonstrated displeasure with Supreme Court rulings, in the hope that the justices would respond favorably. When the Court handed down its *Swann* decision endorsing busing, for example, members of Congress threatened to pass legislation that would prevent the Court from hearing appeals of busing cases. Busing was never used to its full potential in part because of its unpopularity with many members of Congress.

The executive branch is responsible for implementing court decisions and also affects the judiciary by pursuing or overlooking possible legal controversies, thereby influencing the cases that come before the courts. Under President Ronald Reagan, for instance, the Justice Department vigorously backed several suits challenging affirmative action programs and made no great attempt to push cases that would have expanded the rights of racial minorities and women. By these actions, the Reagan administration pressured the judiciary on issues of civil rights.

Acting together, Congress and the president can substantially affect the federal judiciary by expanding its size and selecting judges to fill the new positions. When Democrat Jimmy Carter was president in the 1970s, Congress, which had Democratic majorities in both the House and Senate, created enough new judgeships to nearly double the size of the federal judiciary. These positions were necessary to meet the judiciary's growing case load, but also had the purpose of allowing the appointment of Democratic judges to offset the influence of the Republican judges appointed during the previous eight years by Presidents Richard Nixon and Gerald Ford.

[18]See Lee Epstein, *Conservatives in Court* (Knoxville: University of Tennessee Press, 1985), 80–88.

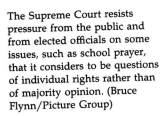

The Supreme Court resists pressure from the public and from elected officials on some issues, such as school prayer, that it considers to be questions of individual rights rather than of majority opinion. (Bruce Flynn/Picture Group)

Although subject to the influence of elected institutions, the judiciary views certain positions as basic to individual rights rather than as matters of majority opinion. In such instances the judiciary seldom lets the public or elected officials dictate its course of action. Despite continuing criticism of its 1962 decision on school prayer, for instance, the Supreme Court has not backed down from its position, refusing even to uphold a 1985 Alabama statute that provided for a minute of silent meditation each day in its public schools. The Court prizes its independence and its position as a coequal branch of government. The fact that judges are not popularly elected and that they hold their appointments indefinitely makes it possible for them to resist pressures from Congress and the president.

"INSIDE" INFLUENCES: THE JUSTICES' OWN POLITICAL BELIEFS

Judges' personal beliefs have a significant influence on their legal opinions.[19] This influence is most evident in the case of the Supreme Court. The justices are frequently divided in their opinions, and the nature of this division can often be predicted on the basis of the justices' political backgrounds. On fair-trial cases in the 1970s, for example, justices William Brennan and Thurgood Marshall, both Democrats when they were appointed to the Court, were "liberals," meaning that they were highly protective of the rights of persons accused of crimes. They were opposed most often on criminal rights cases by justices Warren Burger and William Rehnquist, both of whom were Republicans when they were appointed to the Court and were "conservative" in the sense that they usually sided with the police when police practices conflicted with the rights of the accused. In one four-year period Burger and Rehnquist agreed with each other on 80 percent of the Court's decisions and voted with Brennan and Marshall on less than 50 percent of the cases. Brennan and Marshall, for their part, agreed with each other on more than 90 percent of the cases.[20]

[19]For a general discussion of this research, see Henry R. Glick, *Courts, Politics, and Justice* (New York: McGraw-Hill, 1983), ch. 9.
[20]David Rhode and Harold Spaeth, *Supreme Court Decision Making* (San Francisco: W. H. Freeman, 1976), 138.

The relationship between justices' political beliefs and their decisions is not a simple one. Liberalism and conservatism are not the same among justices as among elected officials. Because justices are constrained by legal principles, their political differences, though not small or inconsequential, are seldom total. For example, today's conservative-leaning Rehnquist Court has modified substantially the criminal justice rulings of the more liberal Warren Court of the 1960s but has not repudiated what is arguably the Warren Court's most important legacy in this area: the broad principle that the Fourteenth Amendment provides substantial protections for the accused in state trial proceedings. Moreover, the position of some justices depends on the type of issue in question.[21] For example, Justice Byron White, who was appointed by the Democratic president John F. Kennedy, proved to be fairly conservative on civil liberties issues, particularly the rights of the accused, but moderate on questions of governmental regulation of the economy.

Most Supreme Court justices hold relatively stable political views during their tenure. Some justices, including Oliver Wendell Holmes, Jr., Earl Warren, and, more recently, Harry Blackmun, have taken a few years on the Court to establish their positions. When he first joined the Court, Blackmun had a voting record that was so close to Chief Justice Warren Burger's that he and Burger, who were from the same home state, were called "the Minnesota Twins." But Blackmun gradually moved toward the views of the Court's more liberal members, particularly on issues of civil liberties. In general, however, most justices stick with their legal positions throughout their time on the nation's highest bench.

As a result, major shifts in the Supreme Court's position usually occur in conjunction with changes in its membership. When the Court in the 1980s moved away from the criminal justice rulings of the 1960s, it was not because the senior justices had changed their views, but because new justices had been appointed who believed that government should have more leeway in its efforts to curb criminal activity. Whereas the Warren Court of the 1950s and 1960s decided in the favor of the accused in two-thirds of criminal cases, the Rehnquist Court of the late 1980s and early 1990s decided in the favor of the accused in one-thirds of such cases.[22]

Shifts in the Court's direction are related to political trends. Although justices are more or less free to follow their own beliefs, they are political appointees who are nominated in part because their legal positions seem to be compatible with those of the president. Pointing out that a new justice has been appointed on average every two years in the Court's history, the political scientist Robert Dahl infers that the policy views of the Court will never be substantially at odds for very long with those of elected officials.[23]

Nevertheless, the Court's membership has its unpredictable aspects. The turnover of justices depends on retirement and death, which occur irregularly. Whether a president will be able to appoint several, one, or no justices is never

Supreme Court justice Harry Blackmun, who wrote the majority opinion in *Roe* v. *Wade* (1973). (Dennis Brack/Black Star)

---

[21]See Glendon Schubert, *The Judicial Mind* (Evanston, Ill.: Northwestern University Press, 1965); Glendon Schubert, *The Judicial Mind Revisited* (New York: Oxford University Press, 1974).
[22]David M. O'Brien, "The High Court Changes Course," *The Public Perspective* 2 (July/August 1991): 6.
[23]Robert A. Dahl, "The Supreme Court and Majority Control," in S. Sidney Ulmer, ed., *Courts, Law, and Judicial Processes* (New York: Free Press, 1981), 214; see also Richard Funston, "The Supreme Court and Critical Elections," *American Political Science Review* 69 (September 1975): 795–811.

★ THE MEDIA AND THE PEOPLE

THE SUPREME COURT: LIBERAL AND CONSERVATIVE

The Supreme Court has become more conservative in recent years. Its decisions, for example, have substantially weakened the exclusionary rule in criminal trials and have given states more authority to regulate abortions. These conservative Court decisions brought expressions of opposition and, in some case, cries of outrage from liberal groups and Democratic officeholders. The opposite situation had prevailed during the 1960s, when the Court had moved to the left in a series of decisions that, for example, broadened the rights of minorities and extended the fair-trial protections of the accused to include action by state governments. At that time, conservative groups and some Republican leaders were vocal opponents of the rulings.

During each of these eras, the Supreme Court received extraordinary attention from the media. It is relatively rare, for example, for the Supreme Court to be the basis for the cover story of a weekly newsmagazine. Yet in the 1960s and again in the early 1990s the Court was the subject of several cover stories in *Time*, *Newsweek*, and

U.S. News & World Report. The media's coverage and the Court's actions had an effect on public opinion. When asked in a 1991 Gallup poll whether the Court was too conservative or too liberal, the larger proportion of respondents said it was too conservative. Comparable polls in the 1960s indicated that a plurality then thought it was too liberal.

The Supreme Court is not ordinarily an issue in political campaigns, but the 1960s and early 1990s were exceptions. Law and order, for example, was a strong issue for Republicans in the presidential election of 1968. Richard Nixon relied on the issue, which he linked to the Supreme Court's decisions on the rights of the accused, to appeal to working-class voters in urban areas. By comparison, the abortion issue appeared to benefit the Democrats in the 1990 elections. Douglas Wilder was helped in the governor's race in Virginia, for example, by his prochoice position on abortion, which appealed most strongly to middle-class voters in the Virginia suburbs of Washington, D.C.

certain. The Republican president Richard Nixon made four Supreme Court appointments during his six years in office, whereas the Democratic president Jimmy Carter made none during his four-year term. Moreover, the influence of new appointees depends on the size of the Court's majority. Important issues have often been decided by a 5-4 vote, and the addition of a single new justice has altered the majority. At other times, however, the existing majority has been more substantial, so two or more new members have been needed to shift the balance.

Judicial Power and Democratic Government

The judiciary symbolizes John Adams's characterization of the U.S. political system as "a government of laws, and not of men." The characterization has value as myth—the vision of impartial justice is undeniably compelling—but the ideal has never fully described the reality. The judicial scholar John Schmidhauser has noted that "laws are made, enforced, and interpreted by men."[24] As an inevitable result, the decisions of the courts bear the indelible imprint of judges' political beliefs.

The issue of judicial power is heightened by the fact that the courts are not a

[24]John Schmidhauser, *The Supreme Court* (New York: Holt, Rinehart and Winston, 1964), 6.

The courts are necessarily creative in formulating judicial policy in response to social and technological change. For example, despite objections from some the courts have held that adding color to black-and-white movies is not a violation of copyright laws. Shown here are black-and-white and color-added versions of the same scene from the movie *Saint Joan*. (Colorization, Inc.)

majoritarian institution. The judges are not elected and cannot easily be held accountable by the public for their decisions—a contradiction of the principle of majority rule. Because the United States has a constitutional system that places checks on the will of the majority, there is obviously an important role in the system for a countermajoritarian institution such as the judiciary. Yet court decisions invariably reflect the political philosophy of the judges, who constitute a tiny political elite that wields significant power.[25]

This power is most dramatically evident when a court declares unconstitutional a law enacted by Congress. Such acts of judicial review place the judgment of unelected judges over the decision of the people's elected representatives. Moreover, a constitutional judgment rendered by the Supreme Court tends to be final. The difficult process of amending the Constitution (needing two-thirds majorities in the House and Senate and approval by three-fourths of the states) makes such amendments an impracticable means of reversing the Supreme Court. In the nation's history only four constitutional amendments (for example, the Sixteenth, which permits a federal income tax) have reversed Supreme Court decisions.

Recognizing the near finality of judicial review, the Supreme Court has applied it with restraint, particularly in regard to presidential or congressional action. In its history, the Court has invalidated on constitutional grounds roughly 125 federal laws and 1,000 state laws and local ordinances—relatively small numbers in the context of two centuries of legislative output. The Court prefers to decide cases on statutory grounds because this approach is less confrontational and gives elected officials the option of changing the law if they disagree with the Court's interpretation of it.

A CREATIVE POLICY ROLE

The judiciary is an important and creative policymaking branch of the government. Of course, there are limits on the judiciary's power. As we have

[25]David M. O'Brien, *Storm Center,* 2d ed., (New York: Norton, 1986), 14–15.

★ ANALYZE THE ISSUE

The Judiciary's Power
Alexander Hamilton called the judiciary the weakest branch of government. How do the Supreme Court's responses in cases involving racial equality illustrate Hamilton's view? Does the Court's behavior also suggest that Hamilton, though correct in his comparison of the relative power of the judiciary as against that of the executive and legislative branches, may have underestimated the power inherent in judicial action?

seen, the courts are constrained by procedures, legal principles, and the limits of what public officials and the American people will accept. Their range of discretion and effective action is narrower than that of either Congress or the president.

However, courts do more than apply the law: they establish law. The English tradition of common law, which was adopted by the United States and which defines most relationships between private parties, is judge-made policy. In addition, when a legislative body enacts a law, it necessarily does so without knowing all the circumstances in which the law may apply in the future. When unforeseen situations arise, judges must make creative decisions. For example, judges have recently had to decide whether copyright laws, enacted before the technological advances that made possible the "colorization" of black-and-white films, permit such coloring.[26]

The structure of the U.S. political system forces a creative role on the judiciary. When the U.S. Constitution established the judiciary as a coequal branch of government, it broke from the English tradition whereby courts had an active role in defining private relationships (*private law*) but were not allowed to define governmental relationships or the relationship of individuals to government (*public law*). Under the U.S. constitutional system, the judiciary in general and the Supreme Court in particular were granted a major role in the sphere of public-law policymaking. The Supreme Court has the responsibility of interpreting the Constitution, overseeing federalism and the separation of powers, and defining individual rights.

The Court bows to the lessons of experience and the force of better reasoning, recognizing that the process of trial and error, so fruitful in the physical sciences, is appropraite also in the judicial function.

Louis D. Brandeis

THE DEBATE OVER THE PROPER ROLE OF THE JUDICIARY

As we noted in this chapter's introduction, the judiciary's policy role has broadened substantially in recent decades in response to social change and new government programs. As a result, the judiciary's authority has been extended into areas that were once regarded as virtually the exclusive domain of elected officials.[27] The Supreme Court has declared, for example, that a state government cannot require a long period of residency in the state as a condition of eligibility for welfare payments. Some recent judicial rulings have not merely forbidden lawmaking majorities to take certain actions but have prescribed actions they must take, such as providing better facilities and programs for inmates of prisons and mental hospitals.

The reactions of liberal and conservative groups to the Supreme Court's recent decisions have depended largely on the degree to which those rulings accord with their own views. In the 1960s, conservatives were outraged at rulings that extended the rights of the criminally accused. More recently, liberals were outraged when the Supreme Court reversed those decisions. However, the question of judicial power goes beyond partisan politics to the basic issue of **legitimacy**—the proper authority of the judiciary in a political system based on the principle of majority rule. In recent decades the judiciary at times has acted almost legislatively by ordering broad social policies, such as

---

[26]Richard Posner, "What Am I? A Potted Plant?" *New Republic*, September 28, 1987, 24.
[27]Donald Horowitz, *The Courts and Social Policy* (Washington, D.C.: Brookings Institution, 1977), 5–9.

Judicial policymaking has extended into areas, such as eligibility requirements for welfare, that had traditionally been handled by elected state officials. (George Cohen/Impact Visuals)

busing and prison reform. In doing so the judiciary has restricted the policy-making authority of the states, has narrowed legislative discretion, and has made judicial action an effective alternative to election victory for certain interests.[28]

Judicial action has have raised important questions. Has the judiciary exceeded its intended authority under the U.S. constitutional system? Has it robbed lawmaking majorities of decisions that are rightfully theirs to make? There are two general schools of thought on these issues: those of judicial restraint and judicial activism. Although these terms are somewhat imprecise and often misused, they are helpful in efforts to clarify opposing philosophical positions on the Court's proper role.[29]

The Doctrine of Judicial Restraint

The doctrine of **judicial restraint** holds that the judiciary should respect precedent and defer to the judgment of legislatures. The restraint doctrine places a high value on the consistency of law and on rule through elected institutions. Although the restraint doctrine does not insist that the judiciary should always uphold precedent or always defer to lawmaking majorities, it does hold that broad issues of the public good should be decided in nearly all cases by the majority through legislation enacted by elected officials. The job of judges is to work within the confines of legislation and precedent, seeking to discover their application to specific cases, rather than searching for new principles that essentially change the meaning of the law.

Advocates of judicial restraint support their position with two major argu-

[28]See Stuart Sheingold, *The Politics of Rights* (New Haven, Conn.: Yale University Press, 1974).
[29]The references cited in the following sections are taken substantially from Henry J. Abraham, "The Judicial Function under the Constitution," *News for Teachers of Political Science* 41 (Spring 1984): 12–14; see also Stephen C. Halpern and Charles M. Lamb, eds., *Supreme Court Activism and Restraint* (Lexington, Mass.: Lexington Books, 1982).

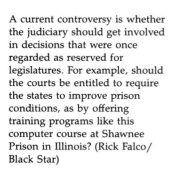

A current controversy is whether the judiciary should get involved in decisions that were once regarded as reserved for legislatures. For example, should the courts be entitled to require the states to improve prison conditions, as by offering training programs like this computer course at Shawnee Prison in Illinois? (Rick Falco/Black Star)

ments. First, they contend that when the Supreme Court assumes policy functions that traditionally belong to elected institutions, it undermines the fundamental premise of self-government: the right of the majority to choose society's policies.[30] Second, judicial self-restraint is admired because it preserves the public support that is essential to the long-term authority of the courts. The judiciary must be concerned with **compliance**—with whether its decisions will be respected and obeyed. The judiciary has no enforcement mechanism of its own and depends for its effectiveness on the support of the public, law-enforcement officials, and elected representatives. If the judiciary thwarts the majority's desires, public confidence in its legitimacy is endangered, and other officials may act to undermine judicial decisions.[31]

The courts must appear to be fair and impartial in their judgments. Those who favor judicial restraint believe that this image is enhanced when court rulings can be clearly justified in the context of established principles. Law professor Gerald Gunther criticized courts for what he claimed were their often high-handed judgments. "One of the saddest lessons of recent decades," Gunther said, "is that judges have given up their explaining function because they just don't believe in it. It's only the result that matters."[32]

Advocates of judicial restraint acknowledge that established law is never so precise as to provide exact answers to every question raised by every case or controversy, so the courts should be empowered to provide remedies in some instances. And in rare circumstances, decisive judicial action may be both appropriate and necessary, as in the historic *Brown* v. *Board of Education* decision (1954). Although the Constitution provides no explicit basis for school desegregation, government-supported racial discrimination violates the princi-

[30]Abraham, "Judicial Function," 14.
[31]Alexander M. Bickel, *The Supreme Court and the Idea of Progress* (New Haven, Conn.: Yale University Press, 1978), 173–181.
[32]Quoted in "Good for the Left, Now Good for the Right," *Newsweek*, July 8, 1991, p. 22.

ple of equal justice under the law. Louis Lusky is among the advocates of judicial restraint who argue that the broad moral language of the Fourteenth Amendment, which says that no state shall deny any person the equal protection of its laws, was adequate justification for the Supreme Court to require state governments to end their policy of segregated public schools.[33]

Yet many advocates of judicial restraint see no constitutional justification for the Supreme Court's busing and abortion decisions. In *Roe* v. *Wade* (1973), for example, the Court struck down state laws prohibiting abortion. The Court justified its ruling not only by citing common law and medical advances but also by claiming that the Fourteenth Amendment implicitly protects a "right of privacy." The Constitution enumerates many specific individual rights, but privacy is not among them. Although most advocates of judicial restraint agree that some right of privacy is implied by the Constitution's guarantee of personal liberty, they do not believe the right is as broad as the Court's majority in *Roe* v. *Wade* claimed it to be.

To advocates of judicial restraint, *Roe* v. *Wade* is an example of judicial interference in the exercise of powers that belong rightfully to the majority through its elected representatives. The question of whether the majority's policies are enlightened or stupid is beside the point. The issue is simply the majority's right to decide for itself the policies, whatever their merits or defects, by which society will be governed. As Justice John Harlan argued in a 1964 opinion: "The Constitution is not a panacea for every blot upon the public welfare; nor should this Court, ordained as a legal body, be thought of as a general haven for reform movements."[34]

The Doctrine of Judicial Activism

In contrast to the judicial-restraint position is the idea that the courts should take a generous view of judicial power and involve themselves extensively in interpreting and enlarging upon the law. Although advocates of this doctrine, which is known as **judicial activism,** acknowledge the principles of precedent and majority rule, they claim that the courts should not be overly deferential to existing legal principles or to the judgments of elected officials. Robert Bork, a former federal judge and a defeated Supreme Court nominee (see Chapter 22), said: "Talk about judicial restraint is troublesome. What's important is that you get it right."[35]

Until recently, the doctrine of judicial activism was associated almost entirely with legalists who believe that the judiciary is obligated to promote social justice by enlarging upon the rights of individuals. These liberal activists are in the centuries-old tradition of **equity,** which holds that courts should resort to general principles of fairness when existing law is insufficient. Liberal judicial activists argue, for example, that fairness for black children requires that in some circumstances some children should be bused to achieve school integration. This reasoning does not extend to all issues of social justice. For example, liberal judicial activists do not regard fundamental decisions about the distribu-

---

[33]Louis Lusky, *By What Right? A Commentary on the Supreme Court's Power to Revise the Constitution* (Charlottesville, Va.: Michie, 1975), 214–216.
[34]*Reynolds* v. *Sims*, 377 U.S. 533 (1964).
[35]"Good for the Left, Now Good for the Right," p. 22.

JUDICIAL ACTIVISM AND THEORIES OF LAW

There are three major theories of law, two of which provide some justification for judicial activism.

The exception is *analytical jurisprudence,* which holds that the law should be applied not according to judges' subjective standards of good or bad, but according to logical applications of legislation. Chief Justice John Marshall expressed this principle when he said that judicial power is exercised "for the purpose of giving effect to the will of the Legislature."

A second theory, *natural law,* gives judges greater leeway. The natural-law theory reflects the belief that there are universal standards of right and wrong that can be discovered through reason. In this view, judicial power can be justified as upholding such standards.

The third theory of law, *sociological jurisprudence,* holds that human law consists of fallible rules made by society to resolve conflicts among competing values. This theory assumes that judges can take into account information about society provided by a broad range of sources, and need not base their decisions exclusively on narrow legal considerations.

tion of wealth as falling within the realm of the judiciary. But in areas where social justice depends substantially on protection of the rights of the individual, the judiciary is said to have a responsibility to act positively and decisively.[36]

Activists who emphasize the Court's obligation to protect civil rights and liberties find justification for their position in the U.S. Constitution's strong moral language and several of its provisions.[37] They view the Constitution as designed chiefly to protect people from unreasonable governmental interference in their lives—a goal that can be accomplished only by a judiciary that is willing to stand up to the lawmaking majority whenever the latter tries to restrict individual choice. They see the Constitution as a charter for liberties, not as a set of narrow rules. An activist interprets the Sixth Amendment's right to counsel, for example, not just as a negative right of a defendant to hire counsel but as a positive right to have a competent lawyer even if the defendant cannot afford one. When the Sixth Amendment was enacted in the late eighteenth century, criminal trials were short and straightforward, and it was at least possible for poor people to defend themselves competently. But criminal law and procedures today are so complex that a defendant without legal counsel would be at a serious disadvantage. Moreover, society today can afford to provide poor defendants with legal assistance. By such reasoning, the judicial-activist school would argue that the Supreme Court was acting properly when it ruled in *Gideon* v. *Wainwright* (1963) that state governments had to provide indigent defendants with counsel at public expense.[38]

Judicial activism is not, however, confined to liberals. In the 1930s conservative activists on the Supreme Court struck down many of the early New Deal programs (see Chapter 2). Judicial activism from the right became an issue again in 1991 when the Supreme Court overturned several precedents. In *Payne* v. *Tennessee,* for example, the Supreme Court reversed two decisions that had

[36]Abraham, "Judicial Function," 13.
[37]Ibid.
[38]*Gideon* v. *Wainwright,* 372 U.S. 335 (1963). Example and argument are from Posner, "What Am I? A Potted Plant?" 25.

Criminal defendants await their day in court in a holding cell in Philadelphia. Judicial activists have ensured that any defendant who cannot afford a lawyer will be provided with legal counsel at public expense. (Chris Gardner/ AP/Wide World)

held that prosecutors could not introduce information on the effect of a capital crime on the victim's family at a sentencing hearing. In his opinion in *Payne*, Chief Justice William Rehnquist wrote that precedent is not "an inexorable command." The judicial activism of the Rehnquist Court has included a deference to majority institutions, but not in all cases. In 1990 the chief justice, in a rare action, asked Congress to restrict the right of people convicted in state courts to file *habeas corpus* appeals in federal courts. Congress rejected the proposal, and in 1991 the Rehnquist Court took action on its own to achieve the goal. In one ruling, the Court held that an inmate could not obtain a federal appeal simply because his or her lawyer had made a procedural mistake during the trial in a state court.[39]

These examples illustrate the difficulty of applying the terms "judicial activism" and "judicial restraint" in consistent ways. In fact, some observers argue that all judges—conservatives, moderates, and liberals—are activists in the sense that their judgments are necessarily creative ones.

Some proponents of judicial activism argue that it is more appropriate on procedural issues, such as protection of individuals' voting rights, than on substantive issues, such as busing and abortion.[40] Other advocates of judicial activism reject the distinction. For example, Arthur Selwyn Miller claims that abortion is an issue of individual rights and is therefore within the policymaking domain of the judiciary. Miller supports the idea that the Constitution implies a broad right of privacy that the courts are obligated to protect.[41]

[39]"Good for the Left, Now Good for the Right," p. 22.
[40]John Hart Ely, *Democracy and Distrust: A Theory of Judicial Review* (Cambridge, Mass.: Harvard University Press, 1980), 74.
[41]Arthur Selwyn Miller, *Toward Increased Judicial Activism: The Political Role of the Supreme Court* (Westport, Conn.: Greenwood Press, 1982), 111.

★ ANALYZE THE ISSUE

Judicial Activism and the Abortion Issue

Roe v. *Wade*, the 1973 Supreme Court decision that legalized abortion on the basis of a woman's right to privacy, is sometimes cited as an example of judicial activism. However, also cited at times as an example of judicial activism is a 1990 decision that upheld a federal regulation decreeing that family planning clinics cannot provide abortion counseling if they receive federal funding. Is judicial activism an accurate description of both, either, or neither of these decisions? Why?

★ CRITICAL THINKING

IS THE SUPREME COURT SUITED TO THE MAKING OF BROAD SOCIAL POLICY?

As the Supreme Court has extended its reach into areas that were once dominated by Congress and the president, some analysts have questioned whether the Court has the capacity (as distinct from the right) to devise workable policies in all these areas. The structure and procedures of the judiciary obviously differ greatly from those of elected institutions. The way in which the Supreme Court gathers information and formulates decisions bears little resemblance to the way in which Congress or the White House carries out its tasks. These differences, Donald Horowitz argues in *The Courts and Social Policy*, prevent the Supreme Court from being a fully effective policymaking body when it comes to such issues as school integration.

Horowitz notes that, unlike members of Congress or executive officials, who usually start their policy deliberations from a general perspective, justices of the Supreme Court start with a particular case, which often involves unusual or extreme circumstances. The Court's initial busing decision in the 1971 *Swann* case, for example, involved Mecklenburg County, North Carolina, which had a long history of government-sponsored racial segregation. Yet the *Swann* decision became binding on a great number of communities, many of which had nothing approaching the level of institutionalized racism in Mecklenburg County.

Horowitz also notes that the Court acts on the basis of less complete information than Congress, which often holds hearings, conducts research, and by other means considers a wide range of facts before deciding on policy. The basic function of courts is to resolve specific disputes, and admissible evidence is generally limited to material directly relevant to the case at hand. Research studies on social conditions, for example, cannot ordi-narily be introduced in a court of law, because pieces of paper cannot be cross-examined on the witness stand. To be sure, the Supreme Court is more likely than lower courts to look for information beyond an immediate case. The justices can, for example, invite interested groups to submit *amicus curiae* ("friend of the court") briefs in the hope that the advice thus obtained will broaden their understanding of a case's implications. The Court has a heavy schedule, however, and time and procedural tradition usually permit only a cursory assessment of information beyond what is contained in the trial record of a lower court.

How important do you judge these limits on the Court's policymaking capacity to be? Why? It is important in your answer to keep in mind the general limits on policymaking. If the criterion for deciding whether an institution should establish broad policies were the likelihood of complete success, no institution would qualify. Every problem associated with judicial policymaking is also a problem confronted by legislative and executive institutions. Congress and the president also must act on the basis of imperfect information. In view of their resources, organization, and incentives, the elected institutions are better at fact finding and are more representative than the Court, but they are not without flaws of their own. Is the difference, however, simply one of degree? Or is there something different about the very nature of the Supreme Court, something that makes its policymaking efforts particularly prone to error?

SOURCE: Donald L. Horowitz, *The Courts and Social Policy* (Washington, D.C.: Brookings Institution, 1977).

THE JUDICIARY'S PROPER ROLE: A QUESTION OF COMPETING VALUES

The dispute between advocates of judicial activism and advocates of judicial restraint cannot be settled by factual analysis. The argument is a philosophical one that involves opposing values. Nevertheless, the debate is important because it addresses the normative question of what role the judiciary *ought* to play in American democracy. Should unelected judges involve themselves deeply in policy by adopting a broad conception of their power, or should they give wide discretion to elective institutions? Should judges defer to precedent, or should they be willing to change course, even at the risk of sending the law down uncharted paths? These questions cannot be answered simply on the basis of whether one personally agrees or disagrees with a particular judicial decision. The answer necessarily depends on a value judgment about the role of the judiciary in a governing system based on the often-conflicting concepts of majority rule and individual rights.

The United States has a constitutional democracy that recognizes both the power of the majority to rule and the claim of the minority to protection of its rights. The judiciary was not established as the nation's moral conscience and does not have a monopoly on the issue of minority interests and rights. Yet the judiciary was established as a coequal branch of government and was charged with the responsibility for protecting individual rights and minority interests. In short, the constitutional question of how far the courts should be allowed to go in substituting their judgment for that of elected institutions and established law is open to interpretation. The trade-off is significant on all issues: minority rights vs. majority rule, states' rights vs. federal power, legislative authority vs. judicial authority. The question of whether judicial restraint or judicial activism is more desirable is one that every student of American government should ponder.

Summary

The courts have less discretionary authority than elected institutions. The judiciary's positions are constrained by the facts of a case and by what is stated in the Constitution, statutes and government regulations, and legal precedent. Yet existing legal guidelines are seldom so precise that judges have no choice in their decisions. The state of the law narrows a judge's options in a particular case, but within these confines there is room for considerable discretion.

As a result, political influences have a strong impact on the judiciary. It responds to national conditions, public opinion, interest groups, and elected officials, particularly the president and members of Congress. Another political influence on the judiciary is the political beliefs of judges, who have personal preferences that are evident in the way they decide on issues that come before the courts.

Federal judges are important policymaking officials because of gaps in the law that require interpretation and because of their role in constitutional interpretation. Is-

sues of federalism, separation of powers, majority power, and individual rights are often resolved through the courts, particularly the Supreme Court. In recent decades the Court has issued broad rulings on individual rights, some of which have required governments to take positive action on behalf of minority interests. As the Court has crossed into areas traditionally left to lawmaking majorities, the legitimacy of its policies has been questioned. Advocates of judicial restraint claim that the justices' personal values are inadequate justification for exceeding the proper judicial role. They argue that the Constitution entrusts broad issues of the public good to elective institutions and that judicial activism ultimately undermines public respect for the judiciary. Judicial activists counter that the courts were established as an independent branch and should not hesitate to promote new principles when they see a need, even if this action puts them into conflict with elected officials.

Major Concepts

compliance
equity
facts (of a case)
judicial activism
judicial restraint

judicial review
laws (of a case)
legitimacy
precedent

Suggested Readings

Berger, Raoul. *Government by Judiciary: The Transformation of the Fourteenth Amendment.* Cambridge, Mass.: Harvard University Press, 1977. A historical study of alleged misinterpretations of the Fourteenth Amendment by a controversial advocate of judicial restraint.

Bickel, Alexander M. *The Supreme Court and the Idea of Progress.* New Haven, Conn.: Yale University Press, 1978. A critical assessment of the policy rulings of the Warren Court from the perspective of an advocate of judicial restraint.

Ely, John Hart. *Democracy and Distrust: A Theory of Judicial Review.* Cambridge, Mass.: Harvard University Press, 1980. A theory of judicial review that advocates activism in some areas but not in others.

Gates, John B., and Charles A. Johnson. *The American Courts.* Washington, D.C.: Congressional Quarterly Press, 1991. A critical assessment of the U.S. court system.

Horowitz, Donald L. *The Courts and Social Policy.* Washington, D.C.: Brookings Institution, 1977. An analysis of the capacity of courts to make broad public policies.

O'Brien, David M. *Storm Center,* 2d ed. New York: Norton, 1990. An analysis of the Supreme Court in the context of the controversy surrounding the role of the judiciary in the U.S. political system.

Perry, Michael J. *Morality, Politics, and Law.* New York: Oxford University Press, 1988. An argument for judicial activism in the determination of individual rights.

Rhode, David, and Harold Spaeth. *Supreme Court Decision Making.* San Francisco: W. H. Freeman, 1976. An analysis of the Court's legal interpretations and decisionmaking patterns.

Is Too Much Public Policy Determined by Nonelected Officials in the Bureaucracy and the Judiciary?

HUGH HECLO

As the power of direct democracy grows, the power of nonelected officials must keep pace if we are to keep our political system in balance.

History taught our forebears three important reasons for designing a national political system with centers of semi-independent, nonelective power over the making of public policy. These reasons still apply today. First, we hope for conduct of the public's business—in the administration of both government programs and justice—that is impartial, or above partisan politics. Second, we desire stability and continuity to shield both public policy and minorities from capricious swings in majority public opinion. Third, expert knowledge—including expertise in impartial weighing of evidence—is needed to inform more partisan judgments about policy issues.

Obviously, impartiality is an elusive ideal; continuity can degenerate into stagnation; expertise can become exclusionary and self-serving in bureaucracies and courts. But the lapses that inevitably occur in practice do not mean that these goals should be abandoned or that these "nonpartisan" expectations should not be imposed on at least some participants in our multifaceted policymaking process.

Today the power of direct democracy—government by mass public opinion—is greater than anything ever imagined by the Founders when they designed our original constitutional structure. We live in a world of nonstop public opinion polling, popular elections to the Senate, an ever-lengthening cycle of presidential campaigns appealing directly to the people, and instantaneous media coverage of political affairs. All these developments would have astonished those early Americans, but their underlying idea of a balanced constitutional structure is far from outmoded. As the power of direct democracy grows, the power of nonelected officials must keep pace if we are to keep our political system in balance with the aid of those "old-fashioned" norms of impartiality, continuity, and expertise.

Today no American judge or bureaucrat, nor any combination of nonelected officials, can sustain a truly unpopular decision against the power of a determined majority. Both bureaucrats and judges depend largely on what is brought to them through legislation and cases; their power of initiating policy is meager. Both ultimately depend on popular consent to carry out their decisions; there is no enforcement power within the United States sufficient to carry out any arbitrary dictates of American bureaucrats or judges.

All of us can find reasons to complain about the decisions of nonelected officials, whether these apply to abortion and school prayer or environmental cleanup and taxes. However, if we try to be objective (or as impartial as a judge or a senior bureaucrat is supposed to try to be but probably never can be), we will see that our complaints are really about particular policy decisions that we dislike and not about some general usurpation of institutional power by nonelected officials.

How would we know if nonelected officials in the United States were determining too much public policy? There is one good test. If that were true, our political institutions would be experiencing a massive hemorrhage of legitimacy—not simply disputes about policy issues (a healthy thing in a cantankerous democracy), but an underlying alienation from elective *and* nonelective components of our constitutional structure. Despite all our complaints, that loss of legitimacy (a feature of regimes such as China's) condition is not characteristic of late twentieth-century America. The important but limited power of nonelected officials is helping to keep representative democracy stable and healthy in the United States.

Hugh Heclo is Clarence J. Robinson Professor of Public Affairs at George Mason University. He is the author of A Government of Strangers: Executive Politics in Washington.

MARTIN SHAPIRO

In a democracy, law ought to be made by the people through their elected representatives.

It is a mistake to believe that because we settle disputes between two individuals by sending them to an impartial third party such as a judge, we should settle public policy disputes that way. Third parties settle individual disputes by applying existing law. Thus, in an auto accident case, the traffic code helps the judge decide which driver was at fault. Policy disputes, in contrast, are about the making of new law. In a democracy, law ought to be made by the people through their elected representatives. We don't want the "impartial" law that someone else thinks is good for us, but law that we devise for ourselves.

We guarantee impartiality in private disputes by finding a third party who knew nothing about the dispute or disputants before the case was brought to him or her. Who would want a dispute about nuclear power or abortion rights to be resolved by someone so out of touch that they had not thought about these important matters before the dispute reached them? Public issues ought to be resolved by people who know a lot about them, but if you know a lot, you will already have decided who is right and who is wrong. Thus, on public questions we need, not impartiality, but popular control; we need decisions to be made by people who know a lot but are subject to election. That means legislators, not judges or bureaucrats.

Judges and bureaucrats themselves say that they resolve issues of public policy by balancing interests. For instance, the Supreme Court says that even the First Amendment right to free speech is not absolute. It is constitutional to arrest a speaker for inciting a riot, because the society's interest in preventing riots outweighs the individual's right to speak. If policy is arrived at by such balancing, it is illogical to try to achieve it in "impartial" judiciaries and bureaucracies rather than in legislatures that are set up specifically to represent various interests and to arrive at compromises, or balances, among those interests.

Bureaucratic and judicial impartiality is mostly a fake, anyway. When the Supreme Court decides that there either is or is not a constitutional right to abortion, it is not being any more impartial about the issue than the rest of us are. Each of the justices is a human being with ideas about right and wrong. How else could the justices decide a question like abortion except by consulting their own values? Granted, in choosing between good and bad, they should choose the good; but what appears to each of them to be the good is going to depend a lot on their own ideas rather than on some impartial weighing of pros and cons.

Very few people who are in the business of making political decisions go through life keeping an open mind about everything. Instead, they arrive at fairly firm judgments about who and what would be best for the country. Once they do so, they are not impartial, but partial to what they think is right. That is as it should be, but it means that the law ought to reflect the public's sense of right and wrong as determined by elected representatives, not by the judiciary and the bureaucracy.

Martin Shapiro is on the faculty of the School of Law at the University of California, Berkeley. He is the author of Who Guards the Guardians: Judicial Control of Administration.

PUBLIC POLICY

T he term *public policy* refers to action (or inaction) by
government which is directed toward a particular goal or
purpose. Busing to achieve racial integration in the public
schools is an example of public policy—a goal-oriented governmental
action.

In a sense, all the preceding sections of this book have led up to
this one. Public policy is the major consequence of political activity.
National policy is decided directly by public officials (discussed in
Parts Five and Six), but these officials operate within a constitutionally
established framework of governmental institutions (Part One) and
individual rights (Part Two), and they make decisions in the context of
public opinion (Part Three) and political organizations (Part Four).
Any realistic assessment of public policy requires that all these factors
be taken into account; this fact is evident in this section's four
chapters, on economic policy (Chapter 24), social-welfare policy
(Chapter 25), national security policy (Chapter 26), and the policy
challenges facing Americans in the years ahead (Chapter 27).

These chapters are designed mainly to provide insights into the
specific policy areas that they discuss. However, some common
patterns emerge. First, U.S. policy is never settled once and for all. As
changes occur in society or in the balance of power between interests,
public policy changes, sometimes substantially. In the past decade, for

example, U.S. policy toward eastern Europe shifted from hostility to cooperation.

Second, U.S. policy tends to be piecemeal and reactive. The nation's fragmented governing structure, diverse interests, and cultural bias against intrusive government make it difficult for policymakers to deal with an issue except in small parts and until it has become a problem. As the unit makes clear, this tendency has advantages as well as disadvantages.

Third, U.S. policy is generated through a process of conflict and consensus. Americans differ in many of their interests, and accordingly they disagree over policy. Some of their differences—over abortion policy, for example—are so fundamental as to be irreconcilable. On most issues of policy, however, competing interests can find common ground if they are willing to search for it. The typical impulse in such situations is to seek compromise, a tendency that itself speaks volumes about the democratic governing process. Public policy is the instrument by which people try to work out solutions to the complex problems of collective life.   ★   ★   ★

ECONOMIC POLICY: CONTRIBUTING TO PROSPERITY

We the people of the United States, in order to . . . insure domestic tranquility . . .
—Preamble, U.S. Constitution

The public's confidence in the economy was thoroughly shaken as 1992 began. The University of Michigan's Index of Consumer Sentiment had fallen to 50 percent, matching the lowest level in the forty years that the index had been compiled. General Motors announced that over the next three years it would close several plants and permanently eliminate 70,000 jobs. IBM planned to cut 20,000 employees. Zales, the jewelry retailer, said it would close 400 stores. An estimated 25 million Americans, a fifth of the work force, had been out of a job at some time in 1991, and the future looked worse. A loss of 100,000 jobs in the banking industry alone was projected for 1992. The country's economic woes awakened memories of another severe downturn sixty years earlier—the Great Depression. Would history repeat itself? Was the United States on the verge of another economic collapse in which millions of Americans would find themselves without work and without hope?

There was one major difference between the 1930s and the early 1990s. When the Great Depression struck, no substantial government programs were in place to stabilize and stimulate the U.S. economy. Moreover, the response to the 1930s crash guaranteed that the economic disaster would worsen. Businesses cut back on production, depositors withdrew their savings, and consumers slowed their spending; all these actions accelerated the downward spiral. In contrast, in the early 1990s government was there to assure depositors that their savings were insured, to encourage consumers to keep spending, and to inform business that government would not allow interest rates to soar.

This chapter examines the economic role of the government, focusing on its promotion and regulation of economic interests and its fiscal and monetary policies, which affect economic growth. Directly or indirectly, the federal government is a party to almost every economic transaction in which Americans engage. Although the private decisions of firms and individuals are the main force in the American economic system, these decisions are made in the context of government policy. Washington seeks to maintain high productivity, employment, and purchasing power; regulates business practices that would otherwise result in economic inefficiencies and inequities; and promotes economic interests. To an important extent, the condition of the U.S. economy depends on how well the government in Washington performs these roles. And certainly no issue is more politically significant than the state of the economy. Americans have high expectations about their financial well-being and, to a large degree, judge their national leaders by whether the economy is doing well or poorly. The main ideas presented in the chapter are the following:

★ *Through regulation, the U.S. government imposes restraints on business activity that are designed to promote economic efficiency and equity.* This regulation is often the cause of political conflict, which is both ideological and group-centered.

★ *Through promotion, the U.S. government helps private interests to achieve their economic goals.* Business in particular benefits from the government's promotional efforts, which take place largely in the context of group politics.

★ *Through fiscal and monetary policy, the U.S. government seeks to maintain a stable and prosperous general economy.* The overall condition of the U.S. economy is generally the leading issue in American electoral politics and has a major influence on each party's success.

Regulating the Economy

An **economy** is a system of production and consumption of goods and services, which are allocated through exchange. When a shopper chooses groceries at a store and pays money in order to take them out the door, that transaction is one of the millions of economic exchanges that make up the economy. Underlying economic exchange is a vast system for the production and distribution of goods. In *The Wealth of Nations* (1776), Adam Smith presented the case for the **laissez-faire doctrine,** which holds that private individuals and firms should be left alone to make their own production and distribution decisions. Smith reasoned that when there is a demand for a good (that is, when people desire it), private entrepreneurs will respond by producing the good and distributing it to points where the demand exists. By the same token, when demand for a good declines, producers will cut back on its production and distribution.

In a capitalist economic system, the incentive that drives this process is profit. Smith argued that the desire for profit is the "invisible hand" that guides the system toward the greatest welfare for all. Left to itself, Smith said, a capitalist economy will produce "a universal opulence extending to the lowest reaches of society." Smith acknowledged that the doctrine of laissez-faire capitalism had a

Adam Smith. (National Portrait Gallery, London)

few limits. Certain areas of the economy, such as roadways and postal services, were natural monopolies and were better run by government than by private firms. In addition, by regulating banking, currency, and contracts, government could give stability to private transactions. Otherwise, Smith argued, the economy was best left in private hands.

In contrast, Karl Marx proposed a worker-controlled economy. In *Das Kapital* (*Capital*, 1867) Marx argued that a free-market system is exploitive because producers, through their control of production and markets, can compel workers to labor at a wage below the value they add to production and can force consumers to pay higher prices for goods than are justified by the cost of production. The effect of capitalism, Marx argued, is to create two social classes—overprivileged capitalists (the bourgeoisie) and underprivileged workers (the proletariat). To end the exploitation of labor, Marx proposed a collective economy. When the workers owned the means of production, the economy would operate in the interest of all people equally.

Marx and Smith represent the extremes of economic theory. No country in the world has an economy that conforms fully to either the laissez-faire or the collectivist model. All national economies today are of "mixed" form in that they contain elements of both private and public control. However, the world's economies vary greatly in their mix. The United States tends toward the private side, whereas China tends toward the collective side. In between, but closer to the American type of economy, are certain European countries whose governments, on behalf of their people, own and operate a number of key industries, including steel, airlines, banking, and oil.

Although the U.S. government itself owns only a few businesses (such as Amtrak and the Tennessee Valley Authority), it plays a substantial economic role through **regulation** of privately owned businesses. U.S. firms are not free to act as they please, but must operate within production and distribution bounds set by federal regulations. Regulatory policy is generally intended to promote either economic *efficiency* or *equity* (see Table 24-1).

Karl Marx. (German Information Center)

Political institutions are a superstructure resting on an economic foundation.
Vladimir Ilich Lenin

TABLE 24-1 The Main Objectives of Regulatory Policy The government intervenes in the economy to promote efficiency and equity.

Objective	Definition	Representative Actions by Government
Efficiency	Fulfillment of as many of society's needs as possible at the cost of as few of its resources as possible	Preventing restraint of trade; requiring producers to pay the costs of damage to the environment; reducing restrictions on business that cannot be justified on a cost-benefit basis
Equity	A system of free and fair economic transactions in which each party gains equally	Requiring firms to bargain in good faith with labor; protecting consumers in their purchases; protecting workers' safety and health

EFFICIENCY THROUGH GOVERNMENT INTERVENTION[1]

Economic **efficiency** requires firms to fulfill as many of society's needs as possible while using as few of its resources as possible. Adam Smith and other classical economists believed that the free market was the optimal means of achieving efficiency. Competition among producers would compel them to use as few resources as possible in producing goods and to charge consumers the lowest possible prices. Inefficient entrepreneurs would be driven out of business by their more efficient competitors, and those who tried to overcharge would be unable to sell their goods and would thus be forced to lower the price to prevailing market levels.

Preventing Restraint of Trade

The assumption that the market always determines price is flawed; the same incentive—the profit motive—that drives producers to respond to demand can drive them to corner the market on a good. If a producer gains a monopoly on a good or conspires with other producers to fix its price, consumers are forced to pay an artificially high price. This form of inefficiency surfaced in the late nineteenth century, when large trusts came to dominate many areas of the U.S. economy, including the oil, steel, railroad, and sugar markets. The trusts were not true monopolies, but they controlled enough of their markets to be able to manipulate production and price levels. Railroad companies, for example, had no competition on short routes, and gouged their customers.[2] Farmers were especially hard hit because they depended on the railroads to get their crops and livestock to market.

> We accept and welcome . . . the concentration of business, industrial and commercial, in the hands of a few, and the law of competition between these, as being not only beneficial, but essential for the future progress of the human race.
>
> Andrew Carnegie,
> U.S. steel manufacturer

In 1887, as the Progressive era dawned, Congress took a first step toward regulating the trusts by enacting the Interstate Commerce Act. The legislation created the Interstate Commerce Commission (ICC), which was charged with regulating railroad practices and fares. Three years later, the Sherman Antitrust Act declared that any business combination or practice in restraint of trade was illegal. A probusiness Supreme Court made these legislative acts less effective than anticipated, so the Mann-Elkins Act (1911) and the Clayton Act (1914) were passed to broaden the government's regulatory authority. The Federal Trade Commission (FTC) was established in 1914 to regulate trade practices.

Today the FTC is one of several federal agencies charged with regulating business competition. In a few cases, the government has prohibited mergers or required divestments in order to increase competition. The largest antitrust suit in the country's history was settled in 1984 when AT&T was forced to sell its regional Bell Telephone companies, which had enabled it to monopolize access to long-distance telephone service. AT&T must now compete for long-distance customers with MCI, Sprint, and other carriers.

In general, however, the government tolerates business concentration. Corporate takeovers and mergers are common, although most of them involve the joining of corporations that are not direct competitors. An example is the

[1]This section relies substantially on Alan Stone, *Regulation and Its Alternatives* (Washington, D.C.: Congressional Quarterly Press, 1982).
[2]James E. Anderson, *The Emergence of the Modern Regulatory State* (Washington, D.C.: Public Affairs Press, 1962), 408.

The government has shifted some of the cost of cleaning up toxic waste dumps and other kinds of pollution from the general public to the firms that discharge the pollutants. (Fred Ward/Black Star)

acquisition of Carrier, a manufacturer of air conditioners, and Otis, an elevator manufacturer, by United Technologies Corporation (UTC). UTC is a conglomerate—a business organization that consists of a number of noncompeting corporations. The government has concluded that conglomerates do not substantially threaten competitive trade practices. But the government has also permitted some mergers of competing firms, such as Chrysler's acquisition of AMC and Pennzoil's takeover of Getty Oil. Although such mergers reduce competition, the government tolerates concentrated ownership in the oil, automobile, and other industries in which high capital costs make it difficult for smaller firms to compete successfully. The government's policy toward corporate giants that act in restraint of trade in these fields has been to penalize them financially. In 1986, for example, Exxon was ordered to rebate $2 billion to gasoline customers because of illegal price fixing. Government acceptance of corporate giants also reflects a realization that market competition no longer involves just domestic firms. For example, the "Big Three" U.S. automakers (General Motors, Ford, and Chrysler) face stiff competition from imports, particularly those from Japan and Germany.

Making Business Pay for Indirect Costs

Economic inefficiencies can result not only from restraint of trade but from the failure of businesses or consumers to pay the full costs of resources used in production. Classical economics assumed that market prices reflect all the costs of production, but this assumption is rarely warranted. Consider the case of persons who become disabled on the job. A large part of the cost of maintaining these now less productive persons is borne, not by their former employers, but by society through public welfare and health-care programs. Or consider companies that dump their industrial wastes in the nearest river. They are polluting a resource that belongs to society rather than to them. The price of these companies' products does not reflect the water pollution, so customers are not paying all the costs that society has incurred in the making of the products. Economists label such unpaid costs **externalities.**

Until the 1960s, the federal government made no great effort to force firms to pay such costs. The impetus to begin doing so came not only from lawmakers but also from the scientific community and public-interest groups. The Clean Air Act of 1963 and the Water Pollution Control Act of 1964 required industry to install antipollution devices to keep air and water pollutants within specified limits. In 1970 Congress created the Environmental Protection Agency (EPA) to monitor compliance with federal regulations governing air and water quality and the disposal of toxic wastes.

EFFICIENCY THROUGH THE MARKETPLACE

Although government intervention is intended to increase economic efficiency, the effect can be the opposite. If government places too many regulatory burdens on firms, they may waste resources in the effort to comply.

Overregulation

In his 1992 State of the Union address, President Bush declared a ninety-day moratorium on new federal regulations, claiming that U.S. business was being hampered by an overzealous bureaucracy. Federal regulations, Bush said, were making U.S. firms less competitive abroad and less profitable at home. Critics accused Bush of using regulation as a scapegoat for economic problems that had more fundamental causes. No one would deny, however, that government regulation raises the cost of doing business.[3] Firms have to hire additional employees simply to monitor and implement federal regulations,[4] which in some instances (for example, pollution control) also require companies to buy and install expensive equipment.

The real issue of regulation is not its cost *per se* but whether the cost is outweighed by the benefits. This concern was the focus of efforts by the Reagan administration in the early 1980s to reduce the regulatory burden on the business sector. The pace of business regulation had more than doubled in the previous decade (see Figure 24-1), and Republicans and Democrats alike agreed

---

[3]William Cilley III and James Miller III, "The New Social Regulation," in Ellen F. Paul and Philip A. Russo, Jr., *Public Policy* (Chatham, N. J.: Chatham House, 1982), 214; David Vogel, "The 'New' Social Regulation in Historical and Comparative Perspective," in Thomas McGraw, ed., *Regulation in Perspective* (Cambridge, Mass.: Harvard University Press, 1981), 214.
[4]Murray Weidenbaum, "An Overview of Government Regulation," *Journal of Commercial Lending*, January 1981, 29.

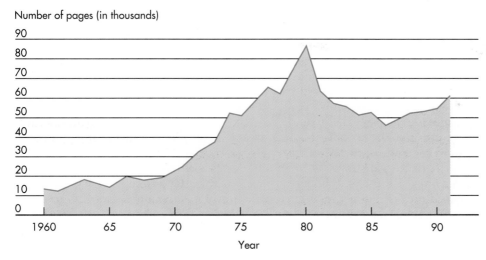

Number of pages (in thousands)

FIGURE 24-1 Number of Pages in *The Federal Register*, 1960–1991
The number of federal regulations, as indicated by the number of pages they occupy in *The Federal Register*, more than doubled during the early 1970s, imposing new costs on U.S. business. *Source: Staff, Office of Federal Register.*

that regulatory activity had gotten out of hand. Regulations that were particularly costly to business without providing offsetting benefits were eliminated.

Later, the issue became highly partisan. The actual costs and benefits of a particular federal regulation are not always easy to calculate, and the Reagan administration used creative arithmetic to get its way. In 1984, for example, the Office of Management and Budget (OMB) blocked a proposed regulation to phase out the use of asbestos, a mineral known to cause cancer. In order to do so, the OMB had to show that the cost of an asbestos ban would exceed the benefit of lives saved by the ban. Although other agencies had placed the value of a human life as high as $2.5 million, the OMB assigned a value of only $208,000, reasoning that deaths from asbestos-caused cancer had to be "discounted" because they occurred years after exposure to asbestos. With the $208,000 figure, the cost to business of the proposed regulation exceeded the benefit to society of lives saved, so the OMB could kill the regulation.[5]

Deregulation

In the early 1930s the airline industry was struggling to get started. Airlines were competing for service between major cities, the routes that were potentially the most profitable. However, the competition for these routes was so intense that airline companies were not profitable enough to accumulate the capital to build large fleets of up-to-date aircraft. In 1938 Congress established the Civil Aeronautics Board (CAB) to regulate airline routes and fares. Major routes were divided among existing carriers, and new flights on these routes were rarely authorized. The CAB also determined fares, setting them high in order to ensure the airlines' profitability. In exchange, airline carriers were required to provide service to smaller cities. The net result was the emergence of a few well-capitalized airline companies, including TWA, Pan Am, American, and United.

In the 1970s the idea of deregulating the airlines came under discussion in Congress. The airlines did not conform to any economist's model of a

[5]"Putting a Price Tag on Life," *Newsweek*, January 11, 1988, 40.

monopoly, so the argument in favor of regulating them for purposes of efficiency was always a weak one. Senator Edward Kennedy (D-Mass.) introduced an airline deregulation bill in 1977. The legislation was opposed by established airlines, which realized that it was a threat to their profits and exclusive routes. They argued that unrestricted competition would make the industry unprofitable. Nevertheless, the idea of **deregulation**—the rescinding of the regulations then in force—had wide support in Congress. Conservatives favored any measure that would allow business to act more freely, and liberals were persuaded that deregulation would result in lower fares, which would benefit consumers. In 1978 Congress passed the Airline Deregulation Act and, soon thereafter, air travelers had more flights to choose from and were paying lower fares. Despite subsequent mergers within the airline industry that have reduced the level of competition, airline travel has remained more competitive and generally less expensive than it was before deregulation.

Striking the Proper Regulatory Balance: The Case of the S&Ls

Congress followed airline deregulation with partial deregulation of the trucking, banking, energy, and communications industries, among others. However, like all other approaches to efficiency, deregulation has not been an unqualified success.[6]

The savings and loan industry is the prime example.[7] When deregulation lifted restrictions on how S&Ls could invest depositors' savings, many of them began to engage in highly speculative ventures, such as commercial real estate. The S&L industry had been hit hard by the high inflation of the 1970s, and S&Ls were hoping that high-yield investments would restore their financial base. Deregulation provided S&Ls the opportunity to make the types of risky investments that had previously been denied to them.

Ironically, the ability of S&Ls to speculate was enhanced by a remaining regulatory device—the Federal Savings and Loan Insurance Corporation (FSLIC). Like the Federal Deposit Insurance Corporation (FDIC), which insures the savings deposits of bank customers, the FSLIC insured S&L savings accounts for a maximum of $100,000 each. The insurance meant that savers were not risking their money when they placed it in S&Ls that were offering extraordinary interest rates in order to attract the funds they needed to pursue their speculative ventures. Financially sound S&Ls were forced to match these high rates in order to keep their customers, and many of them were soon weakened.

By 1989 the S&L industry was in crisis. Bad management, poor investments, and outright fraud had resulted in an industrywide loss of billions of dollars. In order to save what was left of the industry, President Bush and Congress developed a bailout plan that could eventually cost the taxpayers as much as $500 billion. The 1989 legislation also created the Resolution Trust Corporation

---

[6]See Larry N. Gerston, Cynthia Fraleigh, and Robert Schwab, *The Deregulated Society* (Pacific Grove, Calif.: Brooks/Cole, 1988); Susan Tolchin and Martin Tolchin, *Dismantling America* (New York: Oxford University Press, 1985); Roger E. Meiners and Bruce Yandle, *Regulation and the Reagan Era* (New York: Holmes and Meier, 1989).

[7]See Donald F. Kettl, "The Savings and Loan Bailout: The Mismatch between the Headlines and the Issues," *PS: Political Science and Politics* 23 (September 1991): 441–447.

(RTC) to oversee the restructuring of the industry. In the year ending in June 1990, the RTC took control of nearly 500 S&Ls with assets totaling $250 billion. Finally, the FDIC was placed in charge of the S&Ls, thus bringing the nation's banks and S&Ls under a common insurance agency.

The savings and loan crisis shows that the issue of business regulation is not a simple question of whether or not to regulate. On the one hand, too much regulation can burden firms with bureaucratic red tape, costly implementation procedures, and limited options. Federal regulation had made it difficult for S&Ls to respond properly to the inflationary conditions of the 1970s. On the other hand, too little regulation can give firms the leeway to exploit the public unfairly or recklessly. Once free of regulatory constraints, S&Ls engaged in speculative ventures that were virtually certain to carry many of them into bankruptcy. As the S&L crisis illustrates, either too little or too much regulation can result in economic inefficiency. The challenge is to achieve the proper balance between regulatory measures and free-market mechanisms.

EQUITY THROUGH GOVERNMENT INTERVENTION

As we noted earlier, the government intervenes in the economy to bring equity as well as efficiency to the marketplace. **Equity** occurs when an economic transaction is fair to each party. A transaction can be considered fair if each party enters into it freely and is not unknowingly at a disadvantage (for example, if the seller knows a product is defective, equity requires that the buyer also know of the defect).

An early equity measure was the creation of the Food and Drug Administration (FDA) in 1907. Because consumers are often unable to tell whether foods and drugs are safe to use, the FDA works to keep adulterated foods and dangerous or ineffective drugs off the market. In the 1930s, financial reforms were among the equity measures enacted under the New Deal. The Securities and Exchange Act of 1934 and the Banking Act of 1934 were designed in part to protect investors and savers from dishonest or imprudent brokers and bankers. The New Deal also provided greater equity for organized labor, which previously had been in a weak position in its dealings with management. Under the terms of the 1935 National Labor Relations Act (also called the Wagner Act), employers could no longer refuse to negotiate pay and working conditions with employees' unions. The Fair Labor Standards Act of 1938 established minimum wages, maximum working hours, and constraints on the use of child labor.[8]

The 1960s and 1970s produced the greatest number of equity reforms. From 1965 to 1977, ten federal agencies were established to protect consumers, workers, and the public from harmful effects of business activity. Protection of consumers from defective or health-threatening products was a major thrust of this reform period. Among the products declared to be unsafe in the 1960s and 1970s were the insecticide DDT, cigarettes, the Chevrolet Corvair, phosphates, Firestone radial tires, and leaded gasoline.[9]

How Far Should Product Liability Extend?
In early 1992 the Food and Drug Administration called a halt to breast surgery that involved silicone implants, contending that the safety of the implants was at issue. It was revealed that the implant manufacturer, Dow-Corning, had delayed safety research for ten years. The company protested the halt, saying there was no proof that breast implants were unsafe. Consumer advocates said that the company should be held liable in the case of women whose health problems were associated with silicone implants. What is your opinion on this controversy? Should manufacturers for reasons of equity be required to inform the public about all potentially harmful effects of their products?

Health warnings on cigarette packages are an example of government regulation aimed at achieving equity by providing consumers with relevant product information. (George W. Gardner/Stock, Boston)

[8]Henry C. Dethluff, *Americans and Free Enterprise* (Englewood Cliffs, N.J.: Prentice-Hall, 1971), 257.
[9]Vogel, "'New' Social Regulation," 162.

THE POLITICS OF REGULATORY POLICY

Economic regulation has come in waves, as changes in national conditions have produced intermittent bursts of social consciousness.

The Reforms of the Progressive and New Deal Eras

The first wave of regulation came during the Progressive era, when reformers sought to break the power of the trusts by placing constraints on unfair business practices. The second wave came in the New Deal era, when reformers sought to stimulate economic recovery by regulatory policies that they designed as much to save business as to reform it. For example, 1930s banking regulations were meant not only to protect depositors but also to save the banking system, which was threatened by bank closings arising from financial institutions' unsound investments and from mass withdrawals of funds by panicked depositors.

We have always known that heedless self-interest was bad morals; we know now that it is bad economics.

Franklin Delano Roosevelt

Although business fought Progressive and New Deal reforms, long-term opposition was lessened by the fact that most of the resulting regulation applied to a particular industry rather than to firms of all types. This pattern made it possible for an affected industry to gain influence with those officials who were responsible for regulating its activities. By cultivating close ties to ICC commissioners, for example, railroads eventually managed to gain the ICC's approval of uncompetitive shipping rates that gave them high and sustained profits. Although most industries have not coopted their regulators as fully as the shipping industry, it is generally true that business has not been greatly hampered by older forms of regulation and in fact has substantially benefited from it in some cases.

Most of the regulatory functions that were established during the Progressive and New Deal periods are organized in ways that facilitate group access and influence. Some regulatory functions are located within departments, such as the Department of Commerce, that are oriented toward the promotion of particular economic interests. Other functions are carried out by regulatory commissions (including, as we saw in Chapter 20, the ICC, FTC, FCC, SEC, and CAB), whose sole responsibility is the regulation of a given activity or industry. The members of these commissions are appointed by the president with Senate approval but serve fixed terms and are not subject to removal by the president. In other words, regulatory commissioners are relatively independent officials who have broad authority in their policy areas. A regulated interest that acquires influence with commissioners is positioned to obtain favorable policies.

The Era of New Social Regulation

The third wave of regulatory reform, in the 1960s and 1970s, differed from the Progressive and New Deal waves in both its policies and its politics. The third wave has been called the era of "new social regulation" by some economists because of the social goals it addressed in its three major policy areas: environmental protection, consumer protection, and worker safety.[10]

Most of the regulatory agencies established during the third wave have much

[10]Cilley and Miller, "New Social Regulation," 216.

broader policy mandates than those created earlier. They have responsibility not for a single industry but for firms of all types, and their policy scope covers a wide range of activities. The Environmental Protection Agency (EPA), for example, is charged with regulating environmental pollution of almost any kind by almost any firm. Unlike the older agencies that are run by a commission whose members serve for fixed terms, some of the newer agencies, including the EPA, are headed by a single director, who is appointed by the president with Senate approval.

Because newer agencies such as the EPA have a far-ranging clientele, no one firm or industry can easily maneuver itself into a position to influence agency policy to a great extent. There is also strong group competition in some of the newer regulatory spheres; for example, business lobbies must compete with environmental groups such as the Sierra Club and Greenpeace for influence with the EPA.[11] The firms regulated by the older agencies, in contrast, face no powerful competition in their lobbying activities; broadcasters, for example, are largely unopposed in their efforts to influence the Federal Communications Commission, which was established during the New Deal era.

The newer agencies are more responsive to partisan politics. With their stronger commitment to business interests, Republican leaders have been less supportive of environmental, consumer, and worker interests than have Democratic leaders and have thus been less supportive of agencies such as the EPA. When Republican President Ronald Reagan took office, for example, he ordered the EPA to be less vigorous in its enforcement activities than it had been under Democratic President Jimmy Carter (see Chapter 21).

How the Government Promotes Various Economic Interests

The U.S. government has always made important contributions to the nation's economy. The Constitution was written in part to provide for a national government strong enough to promote a sound economy. The Constitution stipulated that the government was to regulate commerce, create a strong currency, develop uniform commercial standards, and provide a stable credit system. The fledgling government also immediately demonstrated its concern for economic interests. Congress in 1789 gave a boost to the nation's shipping industry by placing a tariff on imported goods carried by foreign ships. Since that first favor, the U.S. government has provided thousands of direct benefits to economic interests.

In Chapters 14, 17, and 21 we described how congressional and bureaucratic politics results in the promotion of group interests. Here we will briefly examine a few illustrations of the scope of government's contribution to the interests of business, labor, and agriculture.

PROMOTING BUSINESS

American business is not opposed to government regulation as such. It objects only to regulatory policies that are adverse to its interests. We have noted that,

[11] Vogel, "'New' Social Regulation," 173.

at various times and in differing ways, many federal regulatory agencies have served primarily the interests of the industries they are intended to regulate.

Tax breaks are another way that government promotes business. Firms receive tax credits for capital investments and get tax deductions for capital depreciation. At times, these tax breaks have literally been giveaways. Provisions of the 1981 tax legislation that the Reagan administration engineered through Congress were so generous to business that many corporations got money back from government. Tax loopholes enabled 128 corporations to cut their tax bills to less than zero in at least one of the years between 1981 and 1983. General Electric had profits of $6.5 billion in the 1981–1983 period, but instead of paying taxes, it received $283 million in tax rebates from the federal government.[12]

Over the past forty years the burden of federal taxation has shifted dramatically, from corporations to individuals. A few decades ago, the revenues raised from taxes on corporate income were roughly the same as the revenues raised from taxes on individual income. Today, individual taxpayers carry the heavier burden by a more than 5- to-1 ratio. Some analysts do not regard the change as overly significant, arguing that higher corporate taxes would be passed along to the public anyway in the form of higher prices for goods and services.

Government also promotes business through loans and loan guarantees. In 1979 the Chrysler Corporation was about to go bankrupt. The doctrine of laissez-faire economics would have dictated that any unprofitable and poorly managed company be allowed to fail. Instead, Washington guaranteed $1.5 billion in loans for Chrysler: the federal government would repay the lenders if Chrysler defaulted. Although this loan guarantee came under criticism, it was remarkable only in the amount of money involved. The federal government has guaranteed thousands of business loans and also makes direct loans to businesses. Many firms have received grants and loans from federal, state, or local government for construction and equipment costs. Often, public funding is the price that a community pays to keep or lure a firm. A few years ago, for example, Detroit gave General Motors a $200 million aid package in order to persuade it to build a new assembly plant in the city rather than elsewhere.[13]

The most significant contribution that government makes to business is the traditional services it provides, such as education, transportation, and defense. Colleges and universities, which are funded primarily by governments, furnish business with most of its professional and technical work force and with much of the basic research that goes into product development. The nation's roadways, waterways, and airports are other public-sector contributions without which business could not survive. There is an entire industry—defense contracting—that exists almost entirely on government money. The nation's military power, which is designed for national defense, also protects American business interests abroad. In short, America's business has no better booster than government.

The U.S. government does not, however, have a substantial history of partnerships with business. The Japanese and some European governments

---

[12]"Tax Reform Means End of the Line for Many Corporations' Free Ride," *Syracuse Post-Standard*, April 29, 1988, A–7.
[13]Bryan D. Jones and Lynn W. Bachelor with Carter Wilson, *The Sustaining Hand* (Lawrence: University of Kansas Press, 1986).

The U.S. government has no tradition of direct involvement in private business ventures. In contrast, the Japanese government actively works with Sony and other corporations on technological developments like high-definition television. (Gordon/Rea/SABA)

contribute directly to the development of critical industries or products. An example is the Aerobus, a passenger airliner that was designed and built by a consortium of European governments and corporations. Another example is high-definition television, which Japanese and European companies began to develop with help from their governments in the 1970s. The U.S. effort in the high-definition television field did not get seriously underway until 1989, when Zenith and AT&T formed a partnership using their own funds. Some analysts have suggested that the U.S. government should become more directly involved in business ventures, but the country's free-market tradition has inhibited this development.

American companies have developed a reputation for pursuing short-term profits and corporate takeovers at the expense of long-term market strategies. U.S. government policy does little to discourage this tendency. In the 1980s, instead of borrowing money to build new plants, to buy new equipment, and to develop new products, U.S. corporations borrowed money to buy out other corporations. In some cases, they bought other businesses and sold off the assets to get tax breaks, thereby eliminating jobs. By comparison, Japanese and European firms, supported by government subsidies and tax incentives, have followed long-term investment strategies, which have substantially improved their competitive position in international markets (see Chapter 26).

PROMOTING LABOR

Laissez-faire thinking dominated government's approach to labor well into the twentieth century. The governing principle, developed by the courts in the early nineteenth century, was that workers had limited rights of collective action.

Jesse Jackson marches with striking municipal-hospital workers, members of New York City's Local 1199. Government employees now represent one of the few areas in which union strength is not declining. (Les Stone/Impact Visuals)

Union activity was regarded as interference with the natural supply of labor and the free setting of wages. The extent of hostility toward labor can be seen in the use of federal troops to break up strikes. (Early labor-government relations are discussed in Chapter 6.)

The 1930s brought significant changes. The key legislation was the National Labor Relations Act of 1935, which guaranteed workers the right to bargain collectively and prohibited business from discriminating against union employees and from unreasonably interfering with union activities. The Taft-Hartley Act of 1947 took away some of labor's gains, including compulsory union membership for workers whose workplace is unionized. Under the provisions of Taft-Hartley, each state can decide for itself whether all workers in work units that are unionized must become union members (union shop) or whether a worker can choose not to join the union (open shop). Despite these modifications, the National Labor Relations Act has remained a cornerstone of labor's power. The legislation not only required that business bargain with organized labor but also established the National Labor Relations Board (NLRB), an independent regulatory commission that is empowered to enforce compliance with labor law by both business and labor. Government has also aided labor by legislating minimum wages and maximum hours, unemployment benefits, safer and more healthful working conditions, and nondiscriminatory hiring practices.

Although government support for labor extends beyond these examples, it is not nearly so extensive as its assistance to business. America's individualistic culture has worked against efforts to organize labor and establish labor rights as strong as those in western European democracies.

In the 1980s, backed by the Reagan administration, business launched a broad attack on organized labor which included efforts to undermine employee unions. In one such case, 5,000 striking TWA flight attendants were fired and replaced by new employees who were paid at roughly half the wage rate of the former employees. In labor-management disputes of the 1980s, the NLRB, which was dominated by probusiness Reagan appointees, generally upheld company actions. Some union leaders began to refer to the NLRB as the National Labor Repression Board. In one case labor had the NLRB on its side but lost out before the Supreme Court, which ruled in favor of a company that had filed for bankruptcy for the purpose of voiding its labor contracts.[14] After filing, the corporation resumed its operations with new workers hired at much lower wage and benefit levels. Labor unions were also weakened by a 1992 Supreme Court ruling that declared they almost never have a right to go onto a company's property to distribute union recruitment materials.[15]

At their peak, unions represented a third of the nation's work force. They now represent less than a sixth. Their decline has been paralleled by a decline in the purchasing power of working Americans. Job growth has been concentrated in the nonunion retail trade and service sectors, which, according to Department of Commerce data, pay an average wage of $200 weekly. Unionized manufacturing workers, who earn an average of $450 a week, have been declining in number. Some analysts claim that cheap labor, while advantageous to U.S. business in the short run, is disadvantageous in the long run because lower-income persons do not have the money to buy the new cars, homes, and durable goods that are the backbone of our consumer economy.

[14]*National Labor Relations Board* v. *Bildisco and Bildisco,* 465 U.S. 513 (1984).
[15]*Lechmere* v. *National Labor Relations Board,* 112 S. Ct. 841 (1992).

★ ANALYZE THE ISSUE

Governmental Involvement in Economic Equity
During a strike by its flight attendants, TWA airlines was able to stay in operation with the help of 1,200 unionized attendants who crossed the picket lines. After the strike, TWA kept all these employees and, on the basis of seniority, hired back about a third of the attendants who had stayed out on strike. The union took TWA to court, arguing that seniority alone should have determined which members of the union got their jobs back after the strike. In 1989, by a 6–3 vote, the Supreme Court upheld TWA's action. To what degree does the Court's decision undermine the effectiveness of strikes? Do you agree with the Court's decision? Why, or why not?

In America's first century or so, the government promoted agriculture by offering 160 acres of public land free to homesteaders like this family, photographed in Nebraska in 1877. (Solomon D. Butcher Collection, Nebraska State Historical Society)

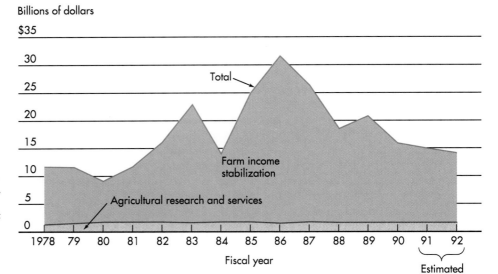

FIGURE 24-2 Federal Expenditures for Agriculture, 1978–1992
Federal assistance to farmers is substantial and is aimed chiefly at stabilizing their yearly income. *Source: Office of Management and Budget,* The United States Budget in Brief, Fiscal Year 1991 *(Washington, D.C.: U.S. Government Printing Office, 1990),* 60.

PROMOTING AGRICULTURE

Until well into the twentieth century, most Americans still lived on farms and in small rural communities. Agriculture was America's dominant business and was assisted by government's land policies. The Homestead Act of 1862, for example, opened government-owned lands to settlement, creating spectacular "land rushes" by offering 160 free acres of government land to each family that staked a claim, built a house, and farmed the land for five years.

Government promotion of agriculture has been complicated by two natural factors. First, farmers' income can fluctuate sharply from one year to the next, depending on market and growing conditions. Second, U.S. farmland is so fertile that it produces more of many crops than can be sold in the marketplace. U.S. agricultural policy has been designed to promote stable farm incomes and control agricultural production, an approach that is both complex and costly.

A brief look at recent government efforts to reduce farm surpluses provides some insight into the tangled web of agricultural tariffs, parity, price supports, and subsidies. Surpluses are a double problem: they keep market prices low because supply exceeds demand, and they require storage at an annual cost of hundreds of millions of dollars. Washington has developed numerous programs designed to reduce farm surpluses. In one such program, the government offered payments to dairy farmers who voluntarily destroyed their dairy herds. Another program gave surplus wheat and other commodities free to farmers who normally grew these commodities but who agreed to take land out of production. In addition, farmers received direct cash payments from government when market prices fell below a specified threshold; the condition for participating in this program, which gave stability to farmers' income, was the removal of some acreage from production. Farm programs provide assistance to both small farmers and to large commercial enterprises (agribusinesses) and cost the federal government billions of dollars annually (see Figure 24-2). (U.S. agricultural policy is discussed further in Chapter 26.)

Maintaining a Stable Economy

Until the 1930s, the federal government adhered to the prevailing free-market theory and made no attempt to maintain the stability of the economy as a whole. The economy was regarded as largely self-regulating. If sellers and buyers looked after their personal interests—with sellers seeking high profits and buyers seeking favorable prices—the result would be abundant goods, jobs, and income. The U.S. economy was indeed fairly prosperous, but periodically—in the late 1830s, early 1870s, and early 1890s—the nation experienced severe economic slumps that resulted in thousands of business failures and high unemployment. During the last of these nineteenth-century depressions, President Grover Cleveland, a Democrat, was urged to create a government jobs program to put the nation's unemployed back to work. He refused, saying that America was founded on self-reliance and that the government had no legitimate basis for interfering with the free market.

The greatest economic catastrophe in the nation's history—the Great Depression of the 1930s—finally brought an end to traditional economics. Franklin D. Roosevelt's emergency spending and job programs, designed to stimulate the economy and put Americans back to work, heralded the change. Roosevelt's efforts to stimulate the economy were controversial, but today government is

★ HOW THE UNITED STATES COMPARES

ECONOMIC POLICY AND PERFORMANCE

All western democracies have market economies. However, democratic countries vary significantly in the degree to which key industries are run by the government. In most democracies, the government owns and operates a number of leading industries, such as the airlines, steel, oil, or banking. But the U.S. government owns and operates very little in the way of industry. The United States also spends less on social welfare than do most other democracies, and consequently has lower tax rates. The U.S. economy differs most obviously from those of other democracies in its sheer size. As measured by gross domestic product (total output of domestic goods and services), the U.S. economy is far and away the world's largest. It is also a strong economy, although most experts rate it as less healthy than the economies of Japan and Germany. A major reason is that the United States has an unfavorable balance of trade. Americans import more goods than they export. By comparison, Japan and Germany are strong exporting nations. SOURCE: *OECD in Figures,* 1991.

Country	Gross Domestic Product (GDP) (Billions of Dollars, 1990)	Total Tax Receipts (Percent of GDP, 1988)	Trade Balance: Exports Minus Imports (Billions of Dollars, 1989)
Canada	$ 579	34.0	$+0.2
France	1192	44.4	+2.7
Germany	1490	37.4	+62.6
Great Britain	978	37.3	−30.7
Italy	1089	37.1	−0.7
Japan	2891	31.3	+43.3
Sweden	230	55.3	+1.1
United States	5330	29.8	−90.5

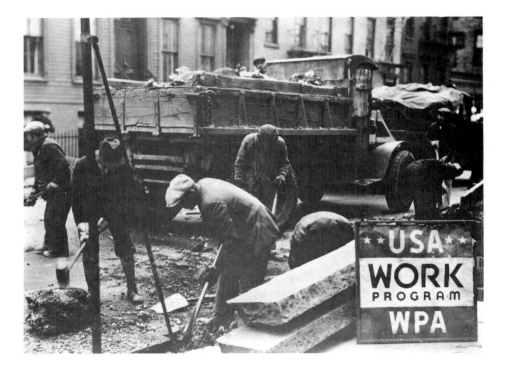

During the Great Depression of the 1930s, the federal government intervened on a massive scale to stabilize the economy. In one New Deal program, the Works Progress Administration, unemployed men were given jobs on public improvement projects, such as the building of roads and parks. (Bettmann Archive)

expected to have ongoing policies for maintaining high economic production, employment, and growth and for controlling prices and interest rates.

Fiscal policy and *monetary policy* are the economic mechanisms on which the government relies most heavily. Each mechanism is complex and is based on several schools of thought. Accordingly, the following discussion attempts merely to outline some of the basic components of fiscal policy and monetary policy.

FISCAL POLICY

The government's efforts to maintain a stable economy are made mainly through its taxing and spending decisions, which together are referred to as its **fiscal policy** (see Table 24-2).

The annual federal budget is the foundation of fiscal policy. George Washington wrote his budget on a single sheet of paper, but the federal budget today is

TABLE 24-2 Fiscal Policy: A Summary   Taxing and spending levels can be adjusted in order to affect economic conditions.

Problem	Fiscal Policy Actions
Low productivity and high unemployment	Increase spending Cut taxes
Excess production and high inflation	Decrease spending Increase taxes

thousands of pages long and takes eighteen months to prepare and enact. The budget is a massive policy statement that allocates federal expenditures among thousands of government programs and provides for the revenues—taxes, social insurance receipts, and borrowed funds—to pay for these expenditures (see Figure 24-3). From one perspective, the budget is the national government's allocation of costs and benefits. Every federal program benefits some interest, whether it be farmers who get price supports, defense firms that obtain military contracts, or retirees who receive monthly social security checks. Not surprisingly, the process of enacting the annual federal budget is a highly political one. Agencies and groups have an obvious stake in promoting their interests.

From another standpoint, that of fiscal policy, the budget is a device for stimulating or dampening economic growth. Changes in overall levels of spending and taxing are means of keeping the economy's normal ups and downs from becoming extreme.

Fiscal policy has its origins in the economic theories of John Maynard Keynes. In *The General Theory of Employment, Interest, and Money* (1936), Keynes noted that employers become overly cautious during a depression and will not expand production, even as wages drop. Challenging the traditional idea that government should draw back during depressions, Keynes claimed that severe economic downturns can be shortened only by increased government spending. By placing additional money in the hands of consumers and investors, government can stimulate production, employment, and spending and thus promote recovery.[16]

Stimulating the Economy

Keynes's theory focused on government's efforts to stimulate consumer spending. This **demand-side economics** emphasizes the consumer "demand" component of the supply/demand equation. When the economy is sluggish, the

[16]See Robert Lekachman, *The Age of Keynes* (New York: Random House, 1966).

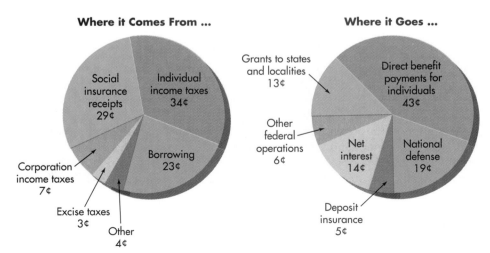

Where it Comes From ...

Social insurance receipts 29¢

Individual income taxes 34¢

Corporation income taxes 7¢

Borrowing 23¢

Excise taxes 3¢

Other 4¢

Where it Goes ...

Grants to states and localities 13¢

Direct benefit payments for individuals 43¢

Other federal operations 6¢

Net interest 14¢

National defense 19¢

Deposit insurance 5¢

FIGURE 24-3 The Federal Budget Dollar, Fiscal Year 1993
Source: Office of Management and Budget, Press Office, 1992.

government can increase its spending, thus placing more money in consumers' hands. With more money to spend, consumers buy more goods and services. This increased demand, in turn, fosters rising production and employment.

The 1980s illustrate the impact that government spending can have on economic growth. Government spending rose sharply during that decade, largely as a result of the greatest peacetime defense buildup in the nation's history. Whereas about $400 billion was spent on defense during Jimmy Carter's presidential term, roughly $1 trillion was expended during each of Ronald Reagan's terms of office. When combined with tax cuts in 1981 and 1986 and spending on domestic programs, the economy received a strong boost from government. All told, the federal government in the 1980s spent $1.5 trillion dollars more than it received in taxes. Consumers had a lot of extra money to spend, which fueled the economy. When Reagan left office in early 1989, the United States was in the sixth year of an uninterrupted economic upswing, the longest such period in the nation's history.

An alternative approach to fiscal policy relies on **supply-side economics,** which emphasizes the business (supply) component of the supply/demand equation.[17] Supply-side economics was a cornerstone of Reagan's policy. He believed that economic growth would flow as easily from stimulation of the business sector as from stimulation of consumer demand. "Reaganomics" included substantial tax breaks for business and upper-income individuals.

Reagan contended that increased prosperity for wealthy Americans would "trickle down" to those at the bottom as production increased and more jobs were created. However, the actual effect was otherwise. The real income of the poorest 20 percent of Americans dropped by more than 10 percent during the 1980s, while the real income of the richest 20 percent rose by roughly 30 percent. Meanwhile, taxes for the poorest 20 percent increased by 3 percent, while taxes for the highest 20 percent decreased by 5 percent.[18] An effect was to discredit the "trickle-down" theory, and the supply-side economics with which it is associated.

Controlling Inflation

High unemployment and low production are only two of the economic problems that government is called upon to solve. Another is inflation, which is an increase in the average level of prices of goods and services. Before the late 1960s, inflation was a minor irritant: prices rose by less than 4 percent annually. But inflation rose sharply during the last years of the Vietnam war and remained high throughout the 1970s, reaching a postwar record rate of 13 percent in 1979. Since then, inflation has moderated (see Figure 24-4) and concern about it has lessened.

To fight inflation, government can apply remedies opposite to those used to fight unemployment and low productivity. Inflation normally occurs when jobs are plentiful and people have extra money to spend. Demand is high in such periods, and prices are pulled up in what is known as "demand-pull" inflation.

---

[17]See Bruce Bartlett, *Reaganomics: Supply-Side Economics* (Westport, Conn.: Arlington House, 1981); Kenneth Hoover and Raymond Plant, *Conservative Capitalism in Britain and the United States* (New York: Routledge, 1989).
[18]House Ways and Means Committee data, 1991.

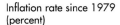

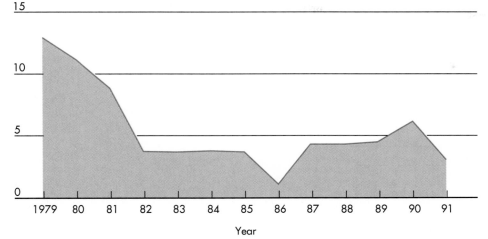

FIGURE 24-4 The Annual Rate of Inflation Price increases have declined in the last decade in comparison with the late 1970s. *Source: U.S. Department of Labor.*

By reducing its spending or by raising personal income taxes, government takes money from consumers, thus reducing demand and dampening prices. In response to rising inflation in the late 1960s, for instance, the federal government cut expenditures by $6 billion and imposed a 10 percent surcharge on personal income taxes.

A Mounting Problem: The National Debt

An ominous aspect of government fiscal policy of the 1980s was the unprecedented size of the national debt; by 1990 it exceeded $3 trillion (up from less than $1 trillion in 1980). Reagan's tax policies in the early 1980s were based partly on the economist Arthur Laffer's prediction that a sizable federal tax cut would actually result in higher tax revenues. Laffer reasoned that lower tax rates would create such a vigorous economy that millions of unemployed people would find jobs and would thus be paying taxes rather than collecting unemployment and welfare payments. As it turned out, the additional tax revenues from new jobs did not, at least in the short run, make up for the tax revenues lost from a 23 percent cut in the tax rates, and the federal government went more deeply into debt. As a direct consequence, enormous amounts of money are required each year to pay the interest on the national debt (see Figure 24-5). The interest payments were more than $200 billion in 1991, a sum larger than the entire federal budget as recently as 1969.

Today interest payments are the third largest item in the federal budget; the only costlier programs are defense and social security. The interest payments each year are roughly equal to all federal domestic spending—for roads, education, prison, food stamps, and the rest—except for social security. The payments exceed by two times the federal taxes paid by corporations and are about the total of federal income taxes paid by Americans who live west of the Mississippi River.

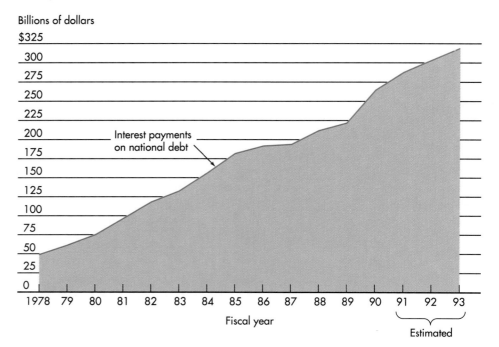

Billions of dollars

FIGURE 24-5 Interest Payments on the National Debt, 1978–1993
Interest on the national debt consumes a huge proportion of each year's federal budget.
Source: Office of Management and Budget, The Budget for Fiscal Year 1992 *(Washington, D.C.: U.S. Government Printing Office, 1991),* 150.

This growing drain on the government's resources has made it very difficult for policymakers to increase the level of spending in order to boost the economy. In early 1992, for example, the U.S. economy was in its longest downturn since World War II, but the government's fiscal condition ruled out any significant new spending programs.

The Fiscal Policy Structure

The president and Congress determine fiscal policy. The Constitution grants Congress the power to tax and spend, but the president normally initiates major policies in these areas and sits atop most of the fiscal policy structure.

The Employment Act of 1946 created the Council of Economic Advisers (CEA) and placed it within the Executive Office of the President (see Chapter 18). Appointed by the president with the approval of the Senate, the three members of the CEA advise the president on economic policy and assist him in preparing his annual economic report to Congress. This statement contains an assessment of the nation's economy and may include legislative proposals. The president also has the services of economic and revenue experts in the Treasury, Labor, and Commerce departments. The Office of Management and Budget (OMB), another presidential staff agency, is the chief instrument of fiscal policy; it prepares the annual budget that the president submits to Congress. The budget contains the president's recommendations on overall government spending and on the allocation of these expenditures among various programs. The combination of taxes and government borrowing necessary to finance this spending is also part of the president's annual budget message.

Congress's ability to affect fiscal policy was improved by the Employment Act of 1946, which established a joint House-Senate committee on the economy. Of much greater importance, however, was the Budget and Impoundment Control Act of 1974 (see Chapter 16). This law requires the president to provide Congress with detailed information on the spending and taxing proposals that underlie his budget. The act also moved the starting date of the government's fiscal year from July 1 to October 1, giving Congress an additional three months to study the president's budget, which reaches the legislature in late January. The act also established the Congressional Budget Office (CBO) to provide the House and Senate with budget analyses, which can be compared with those of the OMB. In addition, the act created the House and Senate Budget committees, which are responsible for proposing spending ceilings for various budget categories. Before 1974, areas of the budget were divided among congressional committees and subcommittees, whose actions were not coordinated so as to stay within specific budgetary limits. Finally, the act restricts the president's ability to impound, or freeze, funds that Congress has appropriated. Congress must approve any impoundments that last more than a short period.

★ CRITICAL THINKING

IS A $4 TRILLION DEBT A NATIONAL DISASTER?

In 1980, Jimmy Carter's last year in office, the national debt was less than $1 trillion. By the start of 1993, the debt had reached the $4 trillion range. In slightly more than a decade, three times as many dollars were added to the federal debt as had been accumulated in the nation's first two centuries. If the national debt were to be paid off tomorrow, each adult American would have to contribute more than $30,000. As it is, the average taxpayer in 1992 paid more than $2,000 in interest on the national debt.

The size of the debt poses several problems for the nation. One is that the rising interest payments on the federal debt have inhibited spending on existing and new programs. Nearly everyone agrees that the U.S. government should spend billions more on education and other pressing national problems. Most policymakers have concluded, however, that the United States simply cannot afford the additional spending. Another problem is that when the government is forced to borrow large sums of money to pay the interest on its debt and to cover its annual deficit, interest rates go up. Faced with these higher rates, other sectors borrow less, which means that there is less business investment and less consumer spending. The economy is weakened accordingly. A third problem with the huge national debt is its unfairness to future generations. We are enjoying the benefits of excess government spending, but our children and grandchildren will be saddled with the need to pay off the debt we have accumulated.

Some economists, however, argue that the negative effects of the national debt are exaggerated. They point out that it often makes sense to borrow. Consumers do it with their credit cards. Families borrow in order to buy a home or car. Businesses borrow in order to grow. Government's position is similar. Government should borrow when the economy requires the stimulus of federal spending or when special circumstances, such as a war, compel it. Most economists would caution against too much government debt, but some have concluded that the United States has only recently approached that point and that, so far, the advantages have outweighed the disadvantages. For one thing, the borrowed dollars are worth more than the inflated dollars with which the debt will someday be repaid. In addition, many of the dollars that the government has borrowed have come from foreign lenders. The Japanese, the Germans, and others have provided revenues that Americans have used for their own purposes.

Which of these positions is the more compelling? Can you think of other arguments for and against the claim that the size of the federal debt is a serious threat to America's future? If you were a policymaker, how would you try to deal with the national debt issue?

As was discussed in Chapter 17, the federal government's recent fiscal problems have forced a reform in the budgetary process. Spending in each of three major categories—domestic, international, and military—is capped according to a set of rules that are designed to keep the overall budget deficit at a prescribed level. The budgetary reform also requires all spending initiatives and tax cuts to be "revenue neutral"; that is, spending increases or tax cuts of one kind must be offset by spending cuts or tax increases of another kind. These changes restrict the use of the federal budget as a fiscal policy tool.

The Politics of Fiscal Policy

Politics plays a significant part in the making of fiscal policy because Democrats and Republicans often disagree over the direction it should take.[19] The Democratic coalition has traditionally included the majority of lower-income and working-class Americans. Accordingly, the party's leaders are sensitive to rising unemployment because blue-collar workers are usually the first and most deeply affected. Chronic unemployment is also characteristic of some largely Democratic groups, such as black Americans, whose rate of joblessness is roughly twice the overall rate. Democrats in Washington have usually responded to a sluggish economy with increased government spending, which offers direct help to the unemployed and stimulates demand. Virtually every increase in federal unemployment benefits during the past fifty years, for example, has been initiated by Democratic officeholders.

Republican leaders are more likely than Democrats to be concerned about inflation. It attacks the purchasing power of all Americans, including higher-income individuals who are less likely than lower-income persons to be affected by rising unemployment rates. Inflation also raises the cost of doing business, because firms must pay higher interest rates for the money they borrow. With its electoral base in business and the middle class, the Republican party usually wants to hold government spending to a level where its inflationary effects are small. Thus, in response to the unusual combination of high inflation and high unemployment in the mid-1970s, Republican President Gerald Ford placed more emphasis on fighting inflation, while his Democratic successor, Jimmy Carter, concentrated initially on reducing unemployment. Each president would have preferred to hold down both unemployment and inflation if he could, but each attacked the problem that was of greater concern to his party's constituents.

Tax policy also has partisan dimensions, even more so perhaps than employment or inflation policy. Republican constituencies—the business community and higher-income Americans—fare better under Republican tax policy than Democratic policy. In 1992, for example, President Bush proposed that the capital gains tax (the tax on profits from the sale of stock, real estate, and other assets) be cut from 28 percent to 15.4 percent for assets held at least three years. About 70 percent of the tax savings would have gone to the richest 1 percent of Americans.

---

[19]See Douglas Hibbs, "Political Parties and Macroeconomic Policy," *American Political Science Review* 77 (December 1977): 1467–1487; David Lowery, "The Keynesian and Political Determinants of Unbalanced Budgets: U.S. Fiscal Policy from Eisenhower to Reagan," *American Journal of Political Science* 29 (1985): 426.

Democratic policymakers have typically sought tax cuts that are more beneficial to working-class and lower-middle-class Americans.[20] Democrats have opposed cuts in the capital gains tax and favored a progressive tax on personal incomes, in which the tax rate goes up as income rises. Although Republicans have also supported this concept, they have preferred to keep the upper-income tax rate at a relatively low level, contending that this policy encourages the savings and investment that are necessary to foster economic growth.

The American tax system does impose higher rates on higher income levels but also contains loopholes (such as tax deductions for interest paid on home mortgages) that benefit mostly higher-income taxpayers. The net effect is that Americans of modest and high incomes have traditionally paid taxes at about the same rate. In comparison with high-income taxpayers in other democracies, wealthy Americans pay relatively little in taxes. The highest tax rate on personal income is 31 percent, compared with 50 percent or more in some European countries.

The powerful hold that the ideal of individualism has on Americans' thinking leads them to want low taxes and to accept relatively modest taxes on the wealthy, but opinion polls show that a growing number of Americans regard the tax system as unfair to middle- and lower-income groups. In one form or another, tax policy is certain to be a major issue of the 1990s.

The Electoral Connection

We noted in Chapter 18 that the issues that affect Americans' pocketbooks have the most influence on their presidential voting decisions. As Seymour Martin Lipset writes, "Voters are disposed to credit or blame incumbent administrations for the state of the economy."[21]

An economic slowdown is a main concern of officials at election time. Rising unemployment and slowing demand can be fatal to a politician; of all economic indicators, the joblessness rate has most consistently been related to swings in election outcomes.[22] Like other presidents before him, George Bush faced the political consequences. The unemployment level rose steadily during 1991 and passed 7 percent at the beginning of 1992. The rise was accompanied by a steady decline in Bush's public support.

Taxes and inflation can also be major election issues. The "taxpayers' revolt" of the late 1970s apparently contributed to the defeat of some incumbent officeholders.[23] In 1980, high inflation contributed to Jimmy Carter's failure to win reelection and to the loss of the Democrats' control of the U.S. Senate.

Officeholders get less credit when the economy is healthy than blame when it

---

★ ANALYZE THE ISSUE

Taxation to Redistribute Income

It is often stated that a goal of taxes is to achieve a partial redistribution of income from wealthier people to poorer ones. According to U.S. Census Bureau figures, the richest one-fifth of Americans receive nearly half of household income, including government benefits, before taxes and still have nearly half after taxes. Meanwhile, the poorest fifth have less than 5 percent of household income, including government benefits, before taxes and less than 5 percent after taxes. Does it surprise you that taxation does so little to redistribute income? Why do you think the effect is so slight?

---

[20]See Richard E. Cohen, "Rating Congress—A Guide to Separating the Liberals from the Conservatives," *National Journal*, May 8, 1982, 800–810.

[21]Seymour Martin Lipset, "The Economy, Elections, and Public Opinions," *Tocqueville Review* 5 (Fall 1983): 431.

[22]D. Roderick Kiewiet, *Macro-Economics and Micro-Politics* (Chicago: University of Chicago Press, 1983), 154–158; Donald R. Kinder and D. Roderick Kiewiet, "Economic Discontent and Political Behavior," *American Journal of Political Science* 23 (1979): 495–527.

[23]Abraham Sharna, "Thomas Hobbes, Meet Howard Jarvis," *Public Opinion*, November/December 1978, 56–59.

Alan Greenspan wields great power as chairman of the Federal Reserve Board, which controls the U.S. money supply. (John Ficara/Woodfin Camp & Associates)

goes bad.[24] A stagnant economy can result in a drop of several percentage points in the vote obtained by the party holding the presidency.[25] The problem for incumbents is the difficulty of getting the economy to respond to their efforts. If government could easily control it, the economy would always be strong. In reality, however, the economy has natural ups and downs that so far have defied mastery by economists and politicians.

MONETARY POLICY

And having looked to Government for bread, on the very first scarcity they will turn and bite the hand that fed them.

Edmund Burke,
British statesman

We noted earlier that fiscal policy is not the only instrument of economic management available to government; another is **monetary policy,** which is based on manipulation of the amount of money in circulation (see Table 24-3). Monetarists such as the economist Milton Friedman hold that control of the money supply is the key to sustaining a healthy economy. Too much money in circulation contributes to inflation because too many dollars are chasing too few goods, so that prices are driven up. Too little money in circulation results in a slowing of the economy and rising unemployment, because consumers lack the ready cash and easy credit that push spending levels up. Monetarists believe in tightening or loosening the money supply as a way of slowing or invigorating the economy.

[24]Howard S. Bloom and H. Douglas Price, "Voter Response to Short-Run Economic Conditions: The Asymmetric Effect of Prosperity and Recession," *American Political Science Review* 69 (1976): 1240–1254.
[25]Edward R. Tufte, *Political Control of the Economy* (Princeton, N.J.: Princeton University Press, 1978), ch. 5; Francisco Arcelus and Allen H. Meltzer, "The Effect of Aggregate Economic Variables on Congressional Elections," *American Political Science Review* 69 (1975): 1232–1239.

★ THE MEDIA AND THE PEOPLE

THE ECONOMY AND AGENDA SETTING BY THE PRESS

Studies of the media's effects have concluded that the press helps to set the country's political agenda by influencing what is uppermost in the minds of policymakers and the American people. The media may not have a powerful influence on people's attitudes, but they do have a major influence on people's attention. The press, as Bernard Cohen once said, "may not be successful much of the time in telling people what to think but it is stunningly successful in telling them what to think about." The economy is a prime example. Persons who have lost their jobs do not have to be told that unemployment is a problem. But jobs are lost every day, year in and year out. There are also new job openings every day. How then do people find out about broader economic tendencies? The news media are a prime source of information about whether the national economy is headed upward or downward.

Economic conditions are always an important news item, and the economy becomes truly big news when a recession hits. During 1991, when the nation was undergoing the longest economic downturn since World War II, the American economy generated more news stories than any other domestic topic. The media also helped convince the American people that their country was in a recession and not simply in a mild economic slump. During the six months from October 1990 through March 1991, according to *Media Monitor*, more than 90 percent of the descriptive terms used by reporters in connection with the economy were negative. On network television, the word "recession" accounted for three-fifths of the descriptive terms. The Bush administration, trying to evade the political repercussions, had been reluctant to say that the economy was in a recession. It is probably fair to say that the news media forced the administration to start using the word. On January 2, 1991, the president's chief economic adviser, Michael Boskin, grudgingly admitted, "The country has probably entered a recession."

Although the agenda-setting power of the news media does not affect people's attitudes directly, it has an important indirect influence. When people are paying attention to one issue rather than another, different attitudes come into play. Early in 1991, when the Persian Gulf conflict was uppermost in people's minds, George Bush's approval rating, 91 percent, was the highest ever recorded by the Gallup poll. Late in 1991, when the economy had moved to the forefront in people's thinking, Bush's approval rating dropped below 50 percent.

SOURCES: Bernard C. Cohen, *The Press and Foreign Policy* (Princeton, N.J.: Princeton University Press, 1963), 13; "Reporting on Recession," *Media Monitor* 5 (May 1991): 1–6; "1991—The Year in Review," *Media Monitor* 6 (January 1992):2.

TABLE 24-3 Monetary Policy: A Summary The money supply can be adjusted in order to affect economic conditions.

Problem	Monetary Policy Action by Federal Reserve
Low productivity and high unemployment (require an increase in the money supply)	Buys securities Lowers interest rate on loans to member banks Lowers cash reserve that member banks must deposit in Federal Reserve System
Excess productivity and high inflation (require a decrease in the money supply)	Sells securities Raises interest rate on loans to member banks Raises cash reserve that member banks must deposit in Federal Reserve System

The Federal Reserve System

Control over the money supply rests not with the president or Congress but with the Federal Reserve System (known as "the Fed"), which was created by the Federal Reserve Act of 1913. The Fed is directed by a board of governors whose seven members serve for fourteen years, except for the chair and vice-chair, who serve for four years. All members are appointed by the president with the approval of the Senate. The Fed regulates the activities of all national banks and those state banks that choose to become members of the Federal Reserve System—about 6,000 banks in all. The key policy decisions made by the Fed's board are carried out through twelve regional Federal Reserve banks, each of which has responsibility for the member banks in its region.

The Fed controls the money supply primarily through three activities. First, it buys and sells securities on the open market. When it buys securities from the public, the Fed puts money into private hands to be spent or invested, thus stimulating the economy. When it sells securities to the public, the Fed takes money out of circulation, thereby slowing spending and investment.

Second, the Fed affects the money supply by lowering or raising the interest charged when member banks borrow money from their regional Federal Reserve bank. When the Fed raises the interest rate for banks, they are discouraged from borrowing from the Federal Reserve, and so they have less money available to lend. Conversely, by lowering the interest rate, the Fed encourages its member banks to borrow, thus increasing their loan funds. When more credit is available, consumers and investors can obtain loans at lower rates and are thereby encouraged to borrow and spend.

Third, the Fed can raise or lower the cash reserve that member banks are required to deposit with the regional Federal Reserve banks. This reserve is a proportion of each member bank's total deposits. By increasing the reserve rate, the Fed takes money from member banks and thus takes it out of circulation; when the Fed lowers the reserve rate, banks keep more of their money and can make more loans to consumers and investors. Essentially, the Fed decides how much money to add to or subtract from the economy, estimating the amount that will permit the most economic growth without leading to an unacceptable level of inflation.

Economists debate the relative effectiveness of monetary policy and fiscal policy, but monetary (money supply) policy has one obvious advantage: it can be implemented more quickly. The Fed can adjust interest and reserve rates on short notice, thus providing a psychological boost to go along with the financial effect. In contrast, changes in fiscal (taxing and spending) policy normally take time to implement because Congress is a slow-acting institution. In late 1991, for example, the Fed dropped the discount rate (the interest rate that the Fed charges its member banks for short-term loans) to its lowest level in twenty-seven years; this action spurred a rally in the financial markets. In the same period, President Bush proposed a tax cut of $300 for each taxpayer, an idea that, though it would have provided the economy with an equally strong stimulus, was widely dismissed as inadequate.

The Politics of Monetary Policy

The Fed's role in managing the national economy has been controversial at times, because its officials are neither elected nor directly responsible to elected representatives. The Fed was established to give stability to the banking system. Only later, with the development of monetarism as a theory of economic management, did the Fed become an instrument for manipulating the national economy.

The Fed's policies are not always popular with elected officials. In 1979, for example, with inflation running at a 13 percent annual rate, the Fed sharply reduced the money supply. By 1981 inflation had come down, but the prime interest rate (the rate that commercial banks charge their major, most creditworthy corporate customers for short-term loans) had soared to a record high of 20 percent. Neither consumers nor investors could afford to take out many loans, and housing construction, business expansion, and consumer spending slowed dramatically. About the only satisfied group was the bankers; high inflation had been eroding the value of their outstanding bank loans. The Reagan administration and Congress pleaded with the Fed to increase the money supply, but the Fed resisted until mid-1982. Once the Fed finally did increase the money supply, the nation's economy began to grow while inflation remained low. In the judgment of some economists, the Fed's decision to loosen credit was a larger factor in the economic recovery that began in late 1982 than were the economic recovery policies of the Reagan administration. If this is true, the obvious question is why the needs of the bankers were initially placed ahead of the needs of the nation.

The issue of the Fed's accountability to elected officials remains unsettled. In 1989 the Fed hiked interest rates in response to rising consumer prices. The Bush administration criticized the Fed's anti-inflationary action, fearing that it would contribute to an economic slowdown, reduce government revenues, and worsen the budget deficit. The Fed reversed course in 1991 in response to indicators of an economic downturn. Washington policymakers acknowledged the importance of the change but complained that the Fed's initial action had been a factor in prolonging the recession. Congress at some future point may decide that an independent Fed can no longer be tolerated and may bring monetary policy under the direct control of elected officials. (The economic role of the government in issues of social welfare and national security is discussed in the next two chapters.)

Summary

Although private enterprise is the main force in the American economic system, the federal government plays a significant role through the policies it selects to regulate, promote, and stimulate the economy.

Regulatory policy is designed to achieve efficiency and equity, which require government to intervene, for example, to maintain competitive trade practices (an efficiency goal) and to protect vulnerable parties in economic transactions (an equity goal). Many of the regulatory decisions of the federal government, particularly those of older agencies, are made largely in the context of group politics; business lobbies have an especially strong influence on the regulatory policies that affect them. In general, newer regulatory agencies have policy responsibilities that are broader in scope and apply to a larger number of firms than those of the older agencies. As a result, the policy decisions of newer agencies are more often made in the context of party politics; Republican administrations are less vigorous in their regulation of business than are Democratic administrations.

Business is the major beneficiary of the federal government's efforts to promote economic interests. Any number of programs, including those to provide loans and research grants, are designed to assist businesses, which are also protected from failure through such measures as tariffs and favorable tax laws. Labor, for its part, gets government assistance through laws concerning such matters as worker safety, the minimum wage, and collective bargaining; yet America's individualistic culture tends to put labor at a disadvantage, keeping it less powerful than business in dealing with the government. Agriculture is another economic sector that depends substantially on government's help, particularly in the form of income stabilization programs, such as those that provide subsidies and price supports.

Through its fiscal and monetary policies, the federal government attempts to maintain a strong and stable economy—one that is characterized by high productivity, high employment, and low inflation. Fiscal policy is based on government decisions in regard to spending and taxing, which are aimed at either stimulating a weak economy or dampening an overheated (inflationary) economy. Fiscal policy is worked out through Congress and the president and is consequently responsive to political pressures. However, because of the difficulty of either raising taxes or cutting programs, there are limits to the government's ability to apply fiscal policy as an economic remedy. Monetary policy is based on the money supply and works through the Federal Reserve System, which is headed by a board whose members hold office for fixed terms. The Fed is a relatively independent body, a fact that has given rise to questions as to whether it should have such a large role in national economic policy.

Major Concepts

demand-side economics
deregulation
economy
efficiency
equity
externalities

fiscal policy
laissez-faire doctrine
monetary policy
regulation
supply-side economics

Suggested Readings

Friedman, Milton, and Walter Heller. *Monetary vs. Fiscal Policy.* New York: Norton, 1969. Opposing arguments by a leading monetarist and a leading Keynesian.

Gerston, Larry N., Cynthia Fraleigh, and Robert Schwab. *The Deregulated Society.* Pacific Grove, Calif.: Brooks/Cole, 1988. An assessment of deregulation and its effects.

Gilder, George. *Wealth and Poverty.* New York: Basic Books, 1984. A defense of the free-market system as economically and morally superior to the welfare state.

Kettl, Donald F. *Deficit Politics: Public Budgeting in Its Institutional and Historical Context.* New York: Macmillan, 1992. Analysis of budgetary politics that aims to explain why the United States suffers repeated annual deficits.

Kiewiet, D. Roderick. *Macro-Economics and Micro-Politics.* Chicago: University of Chicago Press, 1983. An analysis of the relationship between general economic conditions and election outcomes.

Lindbloom, Charles. *Politics and Markets.* New York: Basic Books, 1977. An analysis of the challenges of a mixed economy.

Stone, Alan. *Regulation and Its Alternatives.* Washington, D.C.: Congressional Quarterly Press, 1982. A useful overview of regulatory policy and its purposes.

Wildavsky, Aaron. *The New Politics of the Budgetary Process,* 2d ed. New York: HarperCollins, 1992. An overview of the federal budgetary process, including new developments related to the deficit.

SOCIAL-WELFARE POLICY: PROVIDING FOR PERSONAL SECURITY AND NEED

25
CHAPTER

We the people of the United States, in order to . . . promote the general welfare . . .
Preamble, U.S. Constitution

*J*ohn Jones is a fictitious retired businessman who has a company pension that pays him $1,500 a month. He also receives more than $1,000 a month in interest and dividends on his savings, bonds, and stocks. John's financial obligations are few. He is a widower, and the youngest of his three children graduated from college years ago.

Jane Smith is a fictitious recent divorcée with two children, aged eight and three. Jane was married the summer after she graduated from high school. She had never worked outside the home before her husband left her; without special job skills and with a small child at home, the only work that she could take is a part-time job paying $5 an hour. Jane's net financial assets total less than $500.

John and Jane seem very different, but they do have one thing in common: each gets a monthly social-welfare check from government. Who, John or Mary, receives the larger government check? Who has fewer strings attached to continuing receipt of the check? Who incurs no stigma by taking government handouts? The answer to all of these questions is the same: John.

John is a social security recipient and gets about $750 each month from the government. He applied for social security upon retiring at age sixty-five, and the monthly checks have come regularly ever since. John does not have to worry that the checks will stop coming; he has a lifelong entitlement to them. If John moves to another state, or even to another country, his monthly check will follow. Jane, who lives in New Jersey, gets about $375 a month from the government through the Aid to Families with Dependent Children (AFDC) program. To get this money Jane had to provide proof of her divorce, low income, and lack of assets (she is allowed no more than $1,000 in assets), and she is required to report regularly on whether her economic status has changed.

If her income should rise above the poverty level, she would lose her monthly AFDC support. If Jane should move, say, to Florida, she would have to reapply for AFDC and there would be a waiting period during which she would get no support. Moreover, by moving, she would take a cut in her monthly benefit, to about $250—$125 less than she gets in New Jersey. Finally, Jane carries the mark of a "welfare case" supported by the taxpaying public. John bears no such stigma. He "earned" his monthly check by paying social security taxes during his years of employment.

The U.S. welfare system reflects the country's individualistic culture, tinged with an element of egalitarian compassion. Most Americans are expected to provide for their own economic needs. Economic security is not a right of citizenship. In western European nations a different welfare philosophy prevails. Of course, citizens of these countries are encouraged to work and benefit economically from doing so; but they are considered to be more or less entitled to a minimum standard of living, at government expense if necessary. For example, all citizens of these countries are eligible for government-funded health care. In contrast, Americans believe that it is somehow unfair for people to receive government support unless they have worked for it or are demonstrably unable to work. Moreover, Americans tend to feel that giving public support to able-bodied individuals discourages personal effort and produces welfare dependency. As a consequence, welfare programs based on need, such as AFDC, have less public support than programs based on personal tax contributions, such as social security.

Another powerful influence on U.S. welfare policy is the country's federal system of government. Welfare was traditionally a responsibility of state and local governments; only since the 1930s has the federal government played a major role. A few programs, such as social security, are run solely by the federal government, whereas most programs, such as AFDC, are joint federal-state programs. Because the continuing eligibility of AFDC recipients must be verified at regular intervals, the program is administered by state governments, which have the local offices and employees required for such a task. Each state provides some of the funding for the AFDC program and sets its own level of AFDC benefits. Because the states vary considerably in their ability and willingness to support the program, the amount that AFDC recipients receive depends on where they live. In contrast, as a national program, social security provides uniform benefits regardless of where a recipient resides.

America's traditional values and federal system of government have made welfare policy in the United States a web of complex, untidy, and sometimes logic-defying programs that many liberals and conservatives alike have described as a mess. This chapter accepts that judgment but concludes that the welfare system could hardly be otherwise, given the fact that social welfare is the arena in which nearly all the contending forces of American politics collide. The main points discussed in the chapter are the following:

★ *Poverty is a large and persistent problem in America, affecting deeply about one in seven Americans, including many of the country's most vulnerable individuals—children, female-headed families, and minority-group members.* Social-welfare programs have been a major factor in reducing the extent of poverty in the United States.

> *Few, save the poor, feel for the poor.*
> Letitia Landon

One of the ironies of American domestic policy is that tax deductions on home mortgages for the middle and upper classes are government subsidies, just as are rent vouchers for the poor, but only the latter are stigmatized as "welfare handouts." (*Top*, Sally Weigand/The Picture Cube; *bottom*, Charles Vergara/Photo Researchers)

★ *Welfare policy has been a partisan issue, with Democrats taking the lead on government programs to alleviate economic insecurity.* Changes in social welfare have usually occurred through presidential leadership in the context of majority support for the change.

★ *Social-welfare programs are designed to reward and foster self-reliance or, when this is not possible, to provide benefits only to those individuals who are truly in need.* U.S. welfare policy is *not* based on the assumption that every citizen has a right to material security.

★ *Americans favor social insurance programs (such as social security) over public assistance programs (such as AFDC).* As a result, most social-welfare expenditures are not targeted toward the nation's neediest citizens.

Poverty in America: The Nature of the Problem

In the broadest sense, social-welfare policy encompasses all efforts by government to improve the social conditions of any and all citizens. In a narrower sense, which is the way the term will be used in most of this chapter, social-welfare policy refers to those efforts by government to help individuals avoid becoming burdens to society or, when that is not possible, to help individuals who cannot fully help themselves to meet their basic human needs, including food, clothing, and shelter.

THE POOR: WHO AND HOW MANY?

America's social-welfare needs are substantial. Although Americans are far better off economically than most of the world's peoples, poverty is a large and persistent problem in the United States. The government defines the **poverty line** as the annual cost of a thrifty food budget for an urban family of four, multiplied by three to include the cost of housing, clothing, and other expenses. Families whose incomes fall below that line are officially considered poor. In 1992 the poverty line was set at an annual income of roughly $13,000. About one in seven Americans live at or below the poverty line. In terms of numbers, between 30 million and 35 million American men, women, and children live in poverty. If they could join hands, they would form a line that stretched from New York to Tokyo and back again.

Observers disagree on whether the official poverty line is a valid indicator of the true extent of poverty in the United States. Some benefit programs, such as social security for retirees, provide cash payments to recipients. Other programs provide **in-kind benefits,** which are cash equivalents such as food stamps or rent vouchers. The purpose of in-kind benefits is to ensure that recipients use the support as government intends—on groceries or rent rather than on luxuries. In-kind government benefits are not included in the calculation of family income, which has led some observers to say that the official poverty line overestimates the number of poor people. If in-kind benefits were included, the proportion of the population living below the poverty line would drop about two percentage points.[1]

Other analysts say that the income level set by the government, regardless of how it is calculated, is set too low, that a family of four cannot live adequately on $13,000 a year. They would place the poverty line higher, perhaps in the $15,000–$20,000 range. Arguments about the poverty line are not mere verbal battles. The U.S. government's official poverty line is used to determine eligibility for a number of welfare programs, including food stamps, AFDC, subsidized housing, and government-paid health care.

[1]Sar Levitan, *Programs in Aid of the Poor,* 6th ed. (Baltimore: Johns Hopkins University Press, 1990), 36–37.

★ HOW THE UNITED STATES COMPARES

PERSONS LIVING IN POVERTY

Poverty is more prevalent in the United States than in many other industrialized countries, including Canada, Germany, and Sweden. Although the overall standard of living in the United States is relatively high, poor American families earn less than the poor families in comparable countries for which poverty-level data are available. The reasons are several. Income in the United States is less evenly distributed than in these other countries, and the U.S. government does not spend as much on social-welfare assistance to the poor. If government spending on health care is included (the figures below do not include health-care spending), the difference in welfare spending between the United States and other countries is even more substantial. Many low-income families in the United States receive no help from government; in the other countries, virtually all low-income families receive public assistance in one form or another. Poverty in the United States is also made worse by the relatively large number of single-parent families, although Sweden, which has a similarly large number, has the lowest percentage of persons living in poverty.

Country	Percent below U.S. Poverty Line	Government Expenditures on Social Security and Welfare (Percent of Gross Domestic Product)
Australia	13%	0.7%
Canada	7	not available
Germany	8	2.1
Great Britain	12	1.4
Sweden	6	4.7
United States	13	0.6

SOURCES: Poverty data from Timothy Smeeding and Barbara Boyle Torrey, "Poor Children in Rich Countries," *Science*, November 11, 1988, 873–877; welfare expenditure data from OECD, 1991.

Sheer hard work does not guarantee that a family will rise above the poverty line. A family of four with one employed adult who works forty hours a week at the minimum wage level (about $5 an hour) has an annual income of $10,000, which is well below the poverty line. There are many Americans—mostly household workers, service workers, unskilled laborers, and farm workers—in this position. The U.S. Bureau of the Census estimates that about 40 percent of those in poverty are employed for all or part of the year.

America's poor include individuals of all ages, races, religions, and regions, but poverty is more prevalent among some groups than others. As can be seen from Table 25-1, children are one of the largest groups of poor Americans. Persons under fifteen years of age constitute a third of those who are living below the government's official poverty line. In earlier times, poverty was a problem of the elderly; but, today, because of social security, persons 65 years of age and older make up only 10 percent of the nation's poor.

Most poor children live in single-parent families, usually with the father absent. In fact, 50 percent of *all* Americans living below the poverty line live in families headed by divorced, separated, or unmarried women. These families are at a disadvantage because most women earn less than men for comparable work, especially in nonprofessional fields. Often they cannot find jobs that pay

Of the 32 million Americans who live below the poverty line, 14 million are female heads of households and their children. (Bettye Lane/Photo Researchers)

enough to justify the child-care expenses they incur when they work. In recent years about one in three single-parent, female-headed families have been below the poverty line, compared with one in ten single-parent, male-headed families and one in twenty two-income families. Poverty in America has increasingly become a women's problem, a situation referred to as "the feminization of poverty."

Poverty is also very high among minority-group members. About 10 percent of whites live below the official poverty line, compared with about 30 percent of African-Americans and about 25 percent of Hispanics. About half of poor black families are headed by single women.

Poverty is geographically concentrated. Although it is often portrayed as an urban problem, it is actually more prevalent in rural areas. In 1989, 16 percent of rural residents—as compared with 12 percent of urban residents—lived in families with incomes below the poverty line. The urban figure is misleading, however, in that the poverty rate is very high in inner-city areas, where minority-group members are concentrated. William Julius Wilson has described the inner-city poor as the nation's "underclass."[2]

Suburbs are the safe haven from poverty. Because suburbanites are removed from it, many of them have no sense of the reality of what Michael Harrington called "the other America."[3] Edwin Meese, when he was serving as President Reagan's domestic policy adviser, claimed there were no homeless people in the United States except for the bums who lived on the streets because they

The other America, the America of poverty, is hidden today in a way that it never was before. Its millions are socially invisible to the rest of us. . . . They are not simply neglected . . . they are not seen.

Michael Harrington

[2]William Julius Wilson, *The Truly Disadvantaged: The Inner City, the Underclass, and Public Policy* (Chicago: University of Chicago Press, 1987).
[3]Michael Harrington, *The Other America: Poverty in the United States* (New York: Macmillan, 1962).

preferred to. There are, in fact, hundreds of thousands of homeless people in America, some of whom are women and children. One estimate is that, of every 1,000 homeless people, 120 are adults with children, 100 are single women, and 100 are children without an accompanying adult.[4]

As would be expected, education level is closely related to poverty. More than 20 percent of adults with less than a high school education live in poverty, whereas only 3 percent of college graduates have an income below the poverty line.

A PROBLEM THAT GOT BETTER, ONLY TO GROW WORSE

While campaigning for the presidency in 1960, John F. Kennedy, a millionaire's son, was shocked by the poverty and illiteracy he saw in the Appalachian region of West Virginia. Three years later, as president, Kennedy proposed a set of programs to assist the nation's poor and educationally disadvantaged people, saying that the time had come for "a basic attack on the problems of poverty

If a free society cannot help the many who are poor, it cannot save the few who are rich.

John F. Kennedy

[4]James D. Wright, *Address Unknown: The Homeless in America* (New York: Aldine De Gruyter, 1989).

TABLE 25-1 Percent of Persons in Poverty, by Selected Characteristics (1989) Poverty is more prevalent among some groups than others.

Characteristic	Percent Who Are Poor
AGE:	
Under 15	22%
65 years and over	11
MARITAL STATUS:	
Married-couple families	7
Married-couple families, with children	9
Female householder	36
Female householder, with children	45
PLACE OF RESIDENCE	
Metropolitan residents, outside central city	8
Metropolitan residents, inside central city	18
Nonmetropolitan residents	16
RACE:	
White persons	10
African-Americans	31
Hispanics	26
EDUCATION:	
Less than high school	22
High school graduate	8
Some college	5
College graduate	3

SOURCE: U.S. Bureau of the Census, 1991.

★ THE MEDIA AND THE PEOPLE

THE VISIBILITY OF POVERTY

America is often described as a society in which economic class is not important. Most people are not particularly class conscious; the vast majority label themselves "middle class" and let it go at that. Thus, in a 1992 Roper poll, 92 percent of the respondents described themselves as "middle class" (of which 14 percent and 21 percent called themselves "upper middle class" and "lower middle class," respectively). Only 1 percent said that they were "upper class," and 5 percent described themselves as "lower class."

This lack of class consciousness might be taken as evidence that Americans from all walks of life interact freely and regularly. However, particularly in cities, there is not a great deal of contact between people at the top and bottom of the income ladder. The lifestyle of middle- and upper-income Americans is more suburban than urban, and the automobile rather than public transportation is their major form of conveyance. As a result, they typically have little direct contact with poor people, who rely heavily on public transportation and tend to live within the city proper.

Nor is there much contact through the media. The news is about the powerful, not the poor. Over half of all news stories about politics and public affairs originate from official sources in government. Perhaps it is not surprising, then, that the problems of poverty and homelessness are not very high on Americans' list of priorities. Polltakers have routinely asked Americans what they regard as "the most important problem facing the country today." In the 1981–1991 period, when poverty and homelessness were on the increase, there was only one year (1991) in which poverty was mentioned as the top problem by as many as 10 percent of respondents.

Unfortunately many Americans live on the outskirts of hope—some because of their poverty, some because of their color, and all too many because of both. Our task is to help replace their despair with opportunity.

Lyndon Johnson

and waste of human resources."[5] U.S. Census Bureau data indicated that 22 percent of Americans had incomes below the poverty line in 1960.

After Kennedy's assassination, his successor as president, Lyndon Johnson, pushed hard for the Kennedy initiatives, adding to them many of his own. Johnson did not require much encouragement.[6] He was an activist president who believed that the national government should be deeply involved in social policy. His program, which was labeled the Great Society, included federal initiatives in health care, education, public housing, nutrition, and other areas traditionally dominated by states and localities.[7] In addition to providing direct benefits, these programs had the indirect goal of fostering racial equality. If states and localities wanted a share of federal program funds, they had to use the money in ways that were not racially discriminatory. Thus Johnson's vision of public welfare was broader than that of an earlier Democratic president, Franklin D. Roosevelt, whose New Deal programs had been aimed at economic recovery. In Johnson's view, Americans formed a national community and it no longer made sense for the quality of Americans' public education, health care, or welfare services to depend on the color of their skin or on whether they resided in Mississippi or California or Iowa.[8]

Although Johnson's leadership made the Great Society effort possible, public opinion was a driving force behind a larger federal role in domestic policy.

[5]Quoted in Daniel Patrick Moynihan, *Maximum Feasible Misunderstanding* (New York: Free Press, 1969), xiii.
[6]See Robert D. Plotnick and Felicity Skidmore, *Progress against Poverty* (New York: Academic Press, 1975), 3.
[7]David B. Walker, *Toward a Functioning Federalism* (Cambridge, Mass.: Winthrop, 1981), 102.
[8]See Michael Reagan, *The New Federalism* (New York: Oxford University Press, 1972).

Americans wanted more and better services from government, and when they recognized that federal officials were willing to venture into policy areas traditionally managed by the states (see Chapter 2), they pressured them to act.[9] Antipoverty and civil rights programs were perhaps the least popular of Johnson's initiatives, but they were included in the expansion of the federal government's domestic policy role.

By 1969, the proportion of Americans living below the poverty line had dropped below 15 percent, and the proportion continued to drop, bottoming at 11 percent in 1978. (The U.S. Census Bureau figures on the proportion of Americans living below the poverty line from 1960 to 1992 are shown in Figure 25-1.) In his book *America's Hidden Success*, John Schwarz gave credit for the remarkable change to the War on Poverty. Between 1960 and 1980, welfare spending rose substantially, and there was a sharp reduction in malnutrition among low-income Americans, a decline in infant mortality rates among the poor and minorities, a 50 percent decrease in the number of Americans living in overcrowded and substandard housing, an increase in employment and job skills among poor Americans, and a steep drop in the proportion of Americans living in poverty.[10]

Of course, welfare programs were not the sole influence on this trend, but financial assistance, food stamps, and rent subsidies, among other programs, do help to improve poor people's standard of living. According to the U.S. Census Bureau, the number of Americans living in poverty would increase by about half if there were no welfare programs.

The number of Americans living in poverty began to rise after 1978 as a result of the converging tendencies of a weak economy and a changing federal government. When the U.S. economy in the late 1970s began a long tailspin,

[9]Lloyd A. Free and Hadley Cantril, *The Political Beliefs of Americans* (New York: Simon & Schuster, 1968), 21; see also Eva Mueller, "Public Attitudes toward Fiscal Programs," *Quarterly Journal of Economics* 77 (May 1963): 210–235.
[10]John E. Schwarz, *America's Hidden Success*, rev. ed. (New York, Norton, 1988), 68; and John E. Schwarz, "The War We Won," *New Republic*, June 18, 1984, 19.

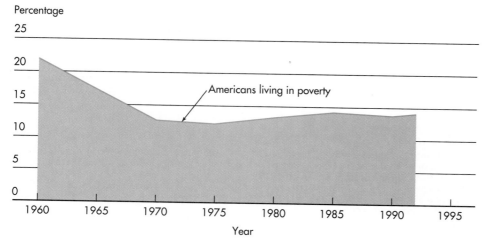

Percentage

FIGURE 25-1 Percentage of Americans Living in Poverty, 1960–1992
The War on Poverty during the 1960s helped to bring about a significant reduction in the percentage of Americans living in poverty, but the figure leveled off as funding for antipoverty programs was cut back beginning in the 1970s. *Source: U.S. Bureau of the Census.*

the effect was devastating to many families. Between 1978 and 1982—a time of two recessions—9.9 million Americans dropped below the poverty line.[11]

The increase during the 1980s in the number of Americans living below the poverty line was also due to cutbacks in federal programs. As the federal welfare commitment had increased substantially in the 1960s and 1970s, polls indicated that a majority of white Americans had become concerned about the level of spending. When he became president in 1981, Ronald Reagan urged sharp cuts in domestic welfare spending and a shifting of policy responsibilities from Washington to the states. Although Congress did not accept most of Reagan's proposals, spending (in terms of actual dollars) and eligibility were trimmed for a number of programs. For example, through a tightening of eligibility rules, more than a million recipients were cut from the AFDC program, and, of those who remained, many had their benefits reduced. Compared with the decade between the late 1960s and late 1970s, when welfare spending per poor person nearly tripled, the 1980s saw a 20 percent decline in actual dollars in welfare spending. All together, several million additional Americans dropped into the ranks of the officially poor as a result of program cutbacks.

The policy change was paralleled by a change in the opinions of white Americans. Opinion surveys conducted by the National Opinion Research Center (NORC) in the early 1970s had indicated that white people were evenly divided when asked to choose between two alternatives: "People should take care of themselves" and "Government should improve living standards of the poor." By 1990, white Americans were overwhelmingly of the opinion that "People should take care of themselves." This opinion is not purely selfish. Many Americans hold to the idea that welfare support creates a vicious cycle of dependency. In his book *Losing Ground*, Charles Murray argued that welfare programs are the foundation for a permanent underclass of unproductive Americans, who live on welfare and who have children who receive no educational encouragement at home and grow up in environments where crime, delinquency, drug abuse, and illegitimacy are commonplace. When the children of these homes reach their teens, said Murray, they behave like the adults around them, so the destructive pattern is perpetuated.[12]

Some Americans are caught in the cycle that Murray describes, but detailed studies of poverty in America indicate that most people are poor by circumstance rather than by intent.[13] A careful ten-year study of American families found that the poor are usually temporarily poor, staying on the welfare rolls for three years or less, and that they are poor for reasons that are hard to control—loss of a job, birth of a child, desertion by the father, and so on.[14]

---

[11]U.S. House of Representatives, Ways and Means Committee, Subcommittee on Oversight and Subcommittee on Public Assistance, *Background Material on Poverty, October 17, 1983* (Washington, D.C.: U.S. Government Printing Office, 1983), ix, 47.
[12]Charles Murray, *Losing Ground: American Social Policy, 1950–1980* (New York: Basic Books, 1984).
[13]See David T. Ellwood and Lawrence H. Summers, "Is Welfare Really the Problem?" *Public Interest* 83 (Spring 1986): 57–78.
[14]*Five Thousand American Families* (Ann Arbor: University of Michigan Institute for Social Research, 1977).

Republicans, Democrats, and Social Welfare

The Bush administration brought no major changes from the Reagan policies. As the contrast between the Reagan-Bush approach and the Kennedy-Johnson approach to welfare would suggest, Republican and Democratic leaders have handled social-welfare policy in very different ways. The differences are also evident in the opinions of the citizens who identify with the two parties. A 1989 Gallup poll indicated that 63 percent of Democrats but only 38 percent of Republicans wanted government to spend more on "food programs for low-income families."

Welfare policy has generally been debated along partisan lines, a reflection of differences in the coalitions and philosophies of the Republican and Democratic parties. With its ties to labor, the poor, and minorities, the Democratic party has nearly always led the way on major federal welfare initiatives, while the GOP has been in opposition. The key House of Representatives vote on the Social Security Act of 1935, for example, found 85 percent of Democrats supporting it and 99 percent of Republicans against it.[15] Republicans gradually came to accept the idea that the federal government has a role in social welfare but have argued that the role should be kept as small as practicable. Thus, in the 1960s, Republican opposition to Johnson's Great Society was substantial. More than 70 percent of congressional Republicans voted against the 1965 Medicare and Medicaid programs, which provide government-paid medical assistance for the elderly and the poor. In the 1980s, against the opposition of congressional Democrats, social-welfare spending was the prime target of Republican President Reagan's efforts to cut the domestic budget.

Although the Republican and Democratic parties have divided over the issue of social welfare, they have also had reason to work together. Social welfare is an ongoing issue because it is a real problem that requires action; there are millions of Americans who need help from government if they are to meet their basic subsistence needs. Thus, Republican Presidents Nixon and Ford did not try to dismantle most of what Johnson had done. It was left to Reagan, who took office in a time of economic trouble, to move welfare policy in a somewhat newer direction. But even Reagan had some help from Democrats, because leaders of both parties have agreed in general that social-welfare spending should serve as a safety net for the poor rather than a device for making Americans economically more equal.

The government's social-welfare effort has included programs to provide jobs and job training, education programs, income measures, and transfer payments. A brief look at each of these government activities will provide further insights into the politics and policies of social welfare.

PROGRAMS TO PROVIDE JOBS AND JOB TRAINING

Employment policy and welfare policy have been loosely linked since the Great Depression, when Franklin Roosevelt combined public jobs programs with

★ ANALYZE THE ISSUE

Welfare Dependency
Charles Murray in *Losing Ground* presents statistics indicating that welfare programs often lead to the chronic dependency of their recipients. John Schwarz in *America's Hidden Success* presents data showing that welfare programs meet people's needs without creating dependency. Which view do you agree with? Is your view based on personal experience, study of the issue, or "educated guessing"?

[15]Everett Carll Ladd, *American Political Parties* (New York: Norton, 1970), 205.

Young Civilian Conservation Corps workers arrive at a work camp in Luray, Virginia, in 1933. The CCC and other Depression-era programs were the first to connect welfare policy with employment policy at the federal level. (UPI/Bettmann)

social security legislation. At one point during the Depression, a fifth of the nation's entire work force was employed on public jobs through the Civilian Conservation Corps and the Works Progress Administration.

There are no contemporary forms of those emergency job programs, and the federal government provides only a moderate amount of funding for employment and job-training programs. Nevertheless, there have been a few notable efforts in the past few decades. Johnson's War on Poverty included several programs designed to train the poor and disadvantaged for the workplace. Among those programs were occupational training for young people (the Job Corps), local initiative opportunities (Community Action programs), and on-the-job training for welfare recipients (the Work Experience Program).

In 1973, an ambitious jobs program, the Comprehensive Employment and Training Act (CETA), began under the Republican administration of Richard Nixon. The CETA program was part of Nixon's "new federalism," in which power, funds, and programs would be shifted from Washington to the states and communities.[16] Local officials were given responsibility for administering CETA's programs. By 1979 CETA was providing jobs for almost 4 million people on a budget of $9.4 billion. Local officials favored the program, but federal officials complained that local governments were using CETA funds for routine administrative expenses and were using CETA workers in place of regular public employees rather than training them for jobs in the private sector. Only about 20 percent of the funds were being spent to train unemployed and underemployed people for future jobs. Also, most local officials did not sufficiently encourage private businesses to hire CETA trainees.[17] Performance

[16]Samuel Beer, "In Search of a New Public Philosophy," in Anthony King, ed., *The New American Political System* (Washington, D.C.: American Enterprise Institute, 1978), 39; Paul R. Dommel, *The Politics of Revenue Sharing* (Bloomington: Indiana University Press, 1976); Henry M. Levin, "A Decade of Policy Developments," in Robert Haveman, ed., *A Decade of Federal Antipoverty Programs* (New York: Academic Press, 1977), 44.
[17]Robert A. Milne, "Welfare Policy in Texas," mimeo, 1980.

improved after national officials developed more stringent regulations to force local officials to administer the program properly, but CETA was terminated in 1983 because of federal budgetary pressures and continuing complaints about its effectiveness.

The program that replaced it, the 1982 Job Training and Partnership Act (JTPA), was more to the liking of the incumbent Republican administration of Ronald Reagan. The program emphasizes training and jobs in the private sector, which is an objective that was consistent with Reagan's philosophy of individualism and smaller government. JTPA program funds are channeled directly to business firms, rather than through local governments. JTPA is today the major federal jobs training program and had a $636 million budget in 1992.

In late 1988 Congress enacted legislation that its sponsors hailed as the most significant reform of the U.S. welfare system since the New Deal. Like CETA and JTPA, the legislation emphasized education, training, and work as the solutions to welfare problems. The legislation was different, however, in its mandatory basis: people on welfare who refused to accept education, training, or work would lose their welfare eligibility.

The 1988 law directs the states to establish education, training, and work programs that are designed to help welfare recipients obtain gainful employment. The legislation also contains a requirement that welfare mothers be provided the child support necessary to enable them to participate in these programs. The federal government provides money (nearly $3 billion in the first year) to fund the programs and the child-care requirement. Individuals who are receiving welfare and meet the eligibility requirements have no choice but to participate in the programs if they want to continue to receive welfare benefits.

The legislation was passed by overwhelming majorities in the Senate and House. Republican members of Congress were persuaded by the legislation's emphasis on training and work in place of income maintenance. Democratic members were attracted by provisions of the legislation, such as the child-support requirement, that are intended to encourage and assist those who would otherwise be penalized by a requirement that they either get job training or lose their welfare payments. Most observers believe that the impact of this recent welfare-reform legislation will not be clear until well into the 1990s.

EDUCATION PROGRAMS

America's individualistic culture includes a recognition of the importance of equality of opportunity (see Chapter 6). If individuals are expected to provide for themselves, logic demands that they be given a reasonable chance to do so. In terms of public policy, this concept is best reflected in the U.S. system of education. Unlike European educational systems, which have a distinct class bias, U.S. primary and secondary schools are relatively egalitarian, and U.S. colleges and universities are open to nearly any high school graduate who wants to attend.

Yet many American children have no hope of obtaining a high-quality education. Many children receive almost no encouragement at home and attend public schools that provide poor instruction, no discipline, and inadequate facilities. These children start out at a disadvantage and cannot reasonably be expected to achieve academic success and a decent life on their own.

Head Start can help disadvantaged preschoolers develop their learning skills, but the program's level of funding permits only a moderate percentage of the eligible children to participate. (Alan Carey/The Image Works)

The United States has one special education program that has survived the political and fiscal battles of recent decades—Head Start. The program provides preschool education for poor children. The program originated with Johnson's War on Poverty but, by the mid-1980s, funding for it had dropped to a level where only 10 percent of the children eligible for Head Start were able to participate. As arguments mounted of poverty's devastating impact on children's development, President Bush and the Democratic Congress concluded that Head Start was the kind of social investment that the country could hardly afford not to make, and it became one of the few domestic programs to receive a substantial funding increase in the early 1990s. Head Start gives the preschool children of poor, often uneducated, parents a better chance to succeed when they get to school and thus a better chance to become productive adults.

INCOME MEASURES

The income of the average American family exceeds $30,000, which, although below the average of several other countries, is substantial enough to provide a reasonable standard of living. Of course, the average income is just that—an average. It hides other averages—for example, the average white family had an income in 1988 that was more than $14,000 higher than the average black family's income—and it hides wide disparities in the income of those individuals at the top and the bottom of the income ladder. The top fifth of Americans in terms of income get 45 percent of the total, while the bottom fifth get slightly less than 5 percent. This ratio of nearly 10:1 is greater than that of European democracies.

Although income-tax policy is mainly an instrument for paying the costs of government, it can also be used to affect the distribution of income across the population. The income that people earn is distributed across a wide range, from very high to very low. Taxation can be used to narrow the range. A **progressive tax** is one in which, as income rises, so does the tax rate on the additional income. By taxing those with higher incomes at a higher rate and those with lower incomes at a lower rate, government can, in effect, redistribute income downward to lower-income groups.

Federal income taxes have a progressive element. A married couple with gross income up to about $10,000 pays no taxes. The rate is 15 percent on the next $30,000 or so, and beyond that level the rate shifts to 31 percent. Other major forms of individual taxation—sales and social security taxes—are not progressive; the tax rate is constant.

Income taxes in the United States have not been the instrument of redistribution that they are in European democracies. An upper tax rate of 50 percent is common in Europe, and there are fewer loopholes, such as the deduction of home mortgage interest, that provide tax breaks for the more well-to-do. In fact, in terms of the actual rate of taxes paid, moderately low income and higher-income Americans are in about the same situation. The higher marginal tax rate on upper-income people is offset by their additional deductions and the existence of nonprogressive taxes such as the social security tax.

Recent changes in the tax code have worked to the benefit of wealthier Americans. Tax reforms in 1981 and 1986, enacted during the Reagan administration, substantially lowered the top tax rate on personal incomes. The Reagan years saw the incomes of the wealthiest one-fifth of Americans increase by almost 10 percent in actual dollars while the incomes of the poorest one-fifth dropped by almost 10 percent. The income gap in America has been felt also by

A high proportion of newly created jobs are in fast-food restaurants and other service businesses, many of which do not pay well enough to provide individuals with long-term economic security. (Hazel Hankin)

those in the lower middle class, who have increasingly found that their dream of home ownership is slipping away. The rise in their incomes has not kept pace with home prices, and a smaller and smaller percentage of them can qualify for a home mortgage. Surveys indicate that a growing percentage of Americans have a sense that they are being left behind, which, if the trend continues, could be politically explosive. The believability of the American Dream—the idea that one could get ahead by working hard enough—has been a reason, historically, why class conflict has not been a large political issue in the United States.

Although well-to-do Americans pay relatively low taxes, the fact that they make a lot of money means, in absolute terms, that they contribute a sizable share of tax revenues. The top 10 percent of taxpayers in terms of income pay about half of the personal income taxes received by the federal government. Some of this tax revenue is redistributed downward to lower-income groups through social-welfare programs.

TRANSFER PAYMENTS

All spending to promote the general welfare is designed to help individuals, but much of it—such as federal funds for public school construction and hospital equipment—is not in the form of direct payments to individuals. Many federal programs, however, do provide benefits directly to individuals, such as social security payments to retired people. These individual-benefit programs are what most people have in mind when they speak of "social welfare." These programs involve what are called **transfer payments,** or government benefits that are given directly to individuals.

Individual-benefit programs are designed to alleviate the personal hardships associated with such conditions as joblessness, poverty, and old age. These programs require the payment of benefits to any individual who is *entitled* to payment by virtue of meeting the established criteria of eligibility. For this reason, each of these programs is termed an **entitlement program.** In this sense, they have the same force in law as taxes. Just as individuals are required by law to pay taxes to government on the income they earn, individuals are entitled by law to receive benefits from government for which they qualify.

The United States has a complex system of social-welfare programs addressing specific needs. No individual-benefit program is universal; each program applies only to those individuals who meet the eligibility criteria. For example, unemployment benefits are not available to all individuals who are out of work. A young person seeking a first job but unable to find one is not eligible for unemployment benefits. Eligible individuals are those who have been laid off from jobs covered by unemployment insurance, and they receive benefits only for a limited period. Such rules are common in the American welfare system and are designed to reward individualism and promote self-reliance or at least to ensure that laziness is not rewarded or encouraged—that is, to limit benefits to the "truly needy."

All told, individual-benefit programs are the major thrust of U.S. social-welfare policy. The federal budget for such programs exceeds $500 billion, which is more money than is spent on any other government activity, including national defense. The various federal programs, from social security to AFDC, differ substantially in their purpose and target population, which the next section will describe in detail.

Individual-Benefit Programs

Until the Great Depression of the 1930s, state and local governments had almost complete responsibility for public welfare. Welfare policy was deemed to fall within the powers reserved to the states by the Tenth Amendment and to be adequately addressed by them because the provision of welfare services was constrained by the country's individualistic culture. Americans were expected to fend for themselves, and when they were unable to do so, they became the responsibility of relatives and friends. In large part, government services were reserved for society's "losers."

Democratic President Franklin Roosevelt's New Deal was important not only for the immediate economic relief it provided but also for its impact on Americans' attitudes.[18] The public jobs projects and welfare programs of the New Deal encouraged Americans to look favorably upon Washington's help. For example, a 1936 Gallup poll indicated that 61 percent of Americans supported Roosevelt's old-age pension plan, while only 27 percent opposed it. "The Social Security Act," Andrew Dobelstein notes, "reflected [the new attitude] that the federal government had responsibility to *promote* the general welfare through specific public welfare programs funded with federal tax dollars."[19]

Since the 1930s the federal government's welfare role has increased immeasurably, and individuals now expect the federal government to ease the loss of income caused by loss of a job, retirement, disability, recession, and the like.

Not all individual-benefit programs are alike, however, in their philosophy or level of public support. Individual-benefit programs fall into two general categories: social insurance and public assistance. Programs in the first category enjoy widespread public support and have a higher degree of funding; programs in the second category encounter substantial public opposition and have a lower degree of funding.

SOCIAL INSURANCE PROGRAMS

More than 40 million Americans receive benefits from social insurance programs—including social security, Medicare, unemployment insurance, and workers' compensation. The two major programs, social security and Medicare, cost the federal government roughly $400 billion per year. Recipients attain eligibility for benefits by virtue of having paid special payroll taxes when they were employed. This is why such programs are labeled **social insurance:** recipients get an insurance benefit under a program that they have helped to fund. This self-financing feature of social insurance programs accounts for their strong public support.

[18]V. O. Key, Jr., *The Responsible Electorate* (Cambridge, Mass.: Belknap Press of Harvard University, 1966), 43.
[19]Andrew W. Dobelstein, *Politics, Economics, and Public Welfare* (Englewood Cliffs, N.J.: Prentice-Hall, 1980), 5.

★ ANALYZE THE ISSUE

Cultural Differences in Welfare Policy
The United States has a greater number of welfare programs and more welfare restrictions than the European democracies. What are the advantages and disadvantages of the American approach to welfare? Of the European approach?

For many elderly Americans, social security benefits make it possible to maintain a dignified, independent life. (Mike Maple/Woodfin Camp & Associates)

Social Security

The premier social insurance program is social security for retirees.[20] The program began with passage of the Social Security Act of 1935 and is funded through payroll taxes on employees and employers. Franklin D. Roosevelt emphasized that retiring workers would be getting an insurance benefit that they had earned through their payroll taxes, not a handout from the government. The result was a program that has gained respectability and permanence, that meets some of the financial needs of Americans upon retirement, and that gives promise of future financial security to those still working. Today social security has Americans' full support. Public opinion polls indicate that upwards of 90 percent of Americans favor current or higher levels of social security benefits for the elderly.

Social security is one of the few entirely federal welfare programs. Washington collects the payroll taxes that fund the program and sends monthly checks directly to recipients, who, on average, get roughly $650 a month. The more than 35 million social security recipients get a total of about $300 billion per year.

Although many people believe that an individual's social security benefits are financed by his or her past contributions, they are actually funded largely through payroll taxes on the current work force. The typical social security recipient gets far more money from the government than he or she has paid into the fund; thus it is necessary to use contributions from the current work force to

[20]See Martha Derthick, *Policy Making for Social Security* (Washington, D.C.: Brookings Institution, 1979).

finance the program. The average recipient takes less than eight years to recover his or her lifetime contributions plus interest and receives "free" benefits from that time forward. In the 1970s expenditures for social security began to exceed contributions as the number of retirees and the size of benefit payments increased. The program would have gone bankrupt in the late 1970s had the social security tax rate not been raised.

In 1981 a bipartisan commission was appointed to study ways of keeping the social security system solvent. The commission recommended that all new federal employees and all employees of nonprofit organizations should be required to contribute to the program, that annual cost-of-living increases in benefits should be delayed by six months, that the payroll-tax increases scheduled throughout the 1980s should go into effect sooner, and that a percentage of the benefits going to retirees with annual incomes over $20,000 should be taxed. The commission's recommendations were enacted in 1983.[21]

The reform of the social security system itself became an issue in 1990, when Senator Daniel Patrick Moynihan (D-N.Y.) attacked the level and use of social security taxes. All employees pay the same social security tax rate up to a certain income level, at which point the tax obligation ends. A person who has an income of $600,000 pays the same tax as one who makes $60,000. Under the 1983 reform, the tax rate and income level were set high enough to guarantee a substantial surplus in the social security trust fund. As a result, many taxpayers pay more social security taxes than they do federal income taxes. Moreover, although the social security tax revenues are technically in "trust," and therefore not to be used for other purposes, the federal government has been using the trust funds to cover its huge budget deficits. Moynihan sought to stop the practice, arguing that one of two undesirable situations had to be true: either the government, through use of the funds, was jeopardizing the future of the social security system, or, through a high social security tax and income ceiling, it was using a devious and regressive tax system to hold down the budget deficit.

Social security is likely to remain a lively political issue for years to come. Because of medical and other advances, Americans live longer than they once did, and our longevity could create a social security crisis during the next century. Roughly 20 percent of the U.S. population—55 million people—will be over age sixty-five in the year 2030, and there may not be enough workers by then to fund the payout to retirees.

Unemployment Insurance

The 1935 Social Security Act provides for unemployment benefits for workers who have lost their jobs involuntarily. Unemployment insurance is a joint federal-state program. The federal government collects the payroll taxes that fund unemployment benefits, but states have the option of deciding whether the taxes will be paid by employers only or by both employees and employers (most states use the first option). Individual states also set the tax rate, conditions of eligibility, and benefit level, subject to minimum standards established by the federal government. Although unemployment benefits vary

[21]See Paul Light, *Artful Work: The Politics of Social Security Reform* (New York: Random House, 1985), ch. 9.

widely among states, they average about a third ($150 a week) of what an average worker makes while employed, and in most cases the benefits are terminated after twenty-six weeks.

The unemployment program does not have the same high level of public support that social security has. The situation reflects in part a common belief that the loss of a job, or the failure to find a new one right away, is somehow a personal failing. Jobless statistics suggest otherwise, however. U.S. Bureau of Labor statistics indicate that, of those who lost their jobs in 1990, for example, only 23 percent had quit working on their own. The others had joined the unemployment ranks because of either a temporary layoff (22 percent) or the permanent elimination of a job position (55 percent).

Medicare

When Franklin Roosevelt was preparing the 1935 Social Security Act, he rejected the idea of providing medical assistance to people who could not afford to pay for it. He feared that the idea was too great a departure from America's individualistic tradition and might jeopardize passage of the retirement program. After World War II, however, most European democracies instituted systems of government-paid health care, and President Harry Truman proposed a similar program for Americans. The American Medical Association (AMA) called Truman's plan "socialized medicine" and "un-American," lobbied hard against it, and threatened to mobilize local physicians to campaign against members of Congress who supported it. Truman's proposal never came

The unemployment-benefits program is based on the insurance principle: workers pay into the fund while they are employed and receive payments from it if they lose their jobs. (David S. Strickler/The Picture Cube)

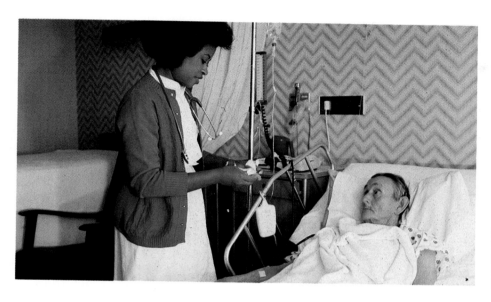

Medicare pays part of the hospitalization and other medical expenses of millions of Americans over age sixty-five. (David Kennedy/TexaStock)

to a vote in Congress. In 1961 President John F. Kennedy proposed a health-care program restricted to social security recipients, but the AMA, the insurance industry, and conservative members of Congress succeeded in blocking the plan.[22]

However, the 1964 elections swept a tide of liberal Democrats into Congress, and the result was Medicare. Enacted in 1965, the program provides medical assistance to retirees and is funded primarily through payroll taxes. Spending on Medicare patients reached $113 billion in 1992. Medicare, too, is based on the insurance principle, so it has gained nearly the same high level of public support as social security. Opinion polls indicate that about 90 percent of Americans prefer that Medicare spending be kept at current levels or increased.

Medicare does not pay all health-care costs for the elderly. It provides for care in a hospital or nursing home, but the recipient must pay part of the initial cost and after 100 days must pay most of the rest. Medicare does not cover all physicians' fees, but enrollees in the program have the option of paying an insurance premium for fuller coverage of these fees. Enrollees who cannot afford the additional premium can apply to have the government pay it.

PUBLIC ASSISTANCE PROGRAMS

Unlike social insurance programs, **public assistance** programs are funded through general tax revenues and are available only to the financially needy. Eligibility for such entitlement programs is established by a **means test,** a demonstration that the applicant is poor enough to qualify for the benefit. In short, applicants for public assistance must prove that they are poor. Public assistance programs are commonly referred to as "welfare" and the recipients as "welfare cases." Opinion polls show that public assistance programs have

[22]For a general overview of disputes over social-welfare policy in the 1950s and 1960s, see James Sundquist, *Politics and Policy* (Washington, D.C.: Brookings Institution, 1968).

less public support than do social insurance programs. For example, fewer than 70 percent of respondents in a 1985 *Los Angeles Times* poll favored current or higher levels of spending on welfare programs for the poor (compared with the 90 percent who favor current or higher levels of spending on social security).

About 30 million Americans receive public assistance, typically through programs established by the federal government, administered mainly by the states, and funded jointly by the state and federal governments. Some Americans have the mistaken impression that public assistance programs account for the lion's share of federal welfare spending. In fact, the federal government spends roughly $125 billion on its major public assistance programs (described below), as against approximately $400 billion on its two major social insurance programs, social security and Medicare.

Supplemental Security Income (SSI)

A major public assistance program is Supplemental Security Income (SSI), which originated as federal assistance to the blind and elderly poor as part of the Social Security Act of 1935. By the 1930s most states had begun or were considering such programs. Although the federal legislation was designed to replace their efforts, the states have retained a measure of control over benefits and eligibility and are required to provide some of the funding. In 1974 programs for poor people who are elderly, blind, or disabled were combined in the SSI program. Because SSI recipients have obvious reasons for their inability to provide for themselves, this public assistance program is not widely criticized. About 5.5 million Americans receive SSI at an annual cost of $18 billion.

Aid to Families with Dependent Children (AFDC)

A more controversial public assistance program is Aid to Families with Dependent Children (AFDC). Partly funded by the federal government but administered by the states, the AFDC program was created in the 1930s as survivors' insurance to assist children whose fathers had died. Almost no one objected to AFDC until it became more and more a program of assistance to families whose male head was absent from the home because of divorce or abandonment. By 1970 about 75 percent of AFDC cases fell into this category, and AFDC had become an object of criticism. Some of the attacks were rooted in social prejudice because many AFDC recipients were unwed minority mothers. The program's skyrocketing costs were also an issue. During the 1960s alone the number of AFDC recipients more than tripled and the costs rose fivefold, to $5 billion. In 1992 the nationwide cost of AFDC was $15 billion, which was used to assist more than 5 million families.

The amounts of monthly AFDC payments are set by each state's government. As a result, AFDC benefits vary widely throughout the nation, depending on the wealth, welfare attitudes, and other characteristics of a state's population (see Figure 25-2). Payments are usually much smaller in areas where voters tend to be antagonistic to government "handouts" than in areas where the public is more tolerant of public welfare. In 1988 Alabama gave the least to AFDC families, an average of $114 a month; Alaska was the most generous

Supplemental Security Income (SSI) is a combined federal–state program that provides public assistance to blind and disabled people. (Spencer Grant/Gamma Liaison)

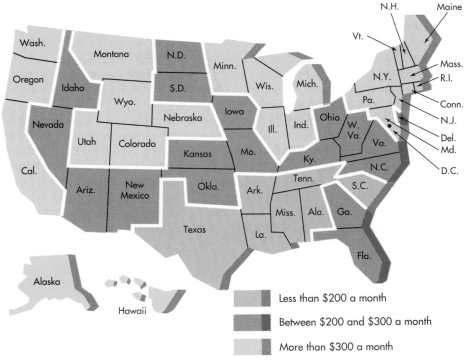

FIGURE 25-2 Average AFDC Payment per Family in the Fifty States, 1988
America's federal system allows the fifty states to establish their own social-welfare policies. A state's policies reflect in part its political traditions, population, and level of economic development. The states vary greatly in their average monthly payments to families under the Aid to Families with Dependent Children (AFDC) program. *Source: Adapted from data compiled by the Social Security Administration.*

state, providing an average of $599 a month per family. By federal law, eligibility for AFDC is restricted to families with net assets below $1,000, and states are permitted to include subsidies for food and housing in calculating whether a family's income is too high to qualify it for AFDC benefits.

Food Stamps

The food-stamp program, which took its present form in 1961, is fully funded by the federal government. Food stamps are available only to people who qualify on the basis of low income. The program is intended to improve the nutrition of poor families by enabling them to purchase qualified items, mainly foodstuffs, with food stamps. Some critics say that food stamps stigmatize their users by making it obvious to onlookers in the checkout line that they are "welfare cases." More prevalent criticisms are that the program is too costly and that too many undeserving people receive food stamps. In the 1980s, by tightening eligibility rules (for example, excluding striking workers and self-supporting students), the Reagan administration cut more than a million recipients from the food-stamp program. In 1992 slightly more than 20 million Americans received food stamps, at a cost of $19.6 billion.

Subsidized Housing

Low-income persons are also eligible for subsidized housing. The federal government spent roughly $20 billion on subsidized housing in 1992, most of which went for housing vouchers rather than the construction of low-income housing units. Under the voucher system, the individual receives a monthly rent-payment voucher, which is given in lieu of cash to the landlord, who then hands the voucher over to the government in exchange for cash. The welfare recipient is given a voucher rather than cash in order to ensure that the funds are actually used to obtain housing. The voucher system is generally preferred to the construction of low-income housing projects because it offers tenants more freedom of choice about where to live. Roughly 6.5 million households received a federal housing subsidy in 1992.

It should be noted that the U.S. government spends much less on public housing than on tax breaks for homeowners, most of whom are middle- and upper-income Americans. Homeowners are allowed a tax deduction for their mortgage interest payments, which in fiscal year 1991 resulted in a $47 billion tax break. Deferred and excluded capital gains on the sale of homes provided an additional tax break of $16 billion. Homeowners are allowed to deduct local property tax payments, which resulted in a $12 billion tax break in 1991. The $75 billion total of these tax concessions was nearly four times as much as was spent by the federal government on housing for low-income families.

Medicaid

When it enacted Medicare in 1965, Congress also established Medicaid, which provides health care for poor people who are already on welfare. It is considered a public assistance program, rather than a social insurance program like Medicare, because it is based on need and funded by general tax revenues.

Half of Medicaid funding is provided by the federal government and half by the states. Nearly 25 million Americans received Medicaid assistance in 1992, at a cost to the federal government of $60 billion.

Before Medicaid, 20 percent of all Americans with incomes below the poverty level had *never* been to a physician. Within a decade of Medicaid's passage, that figure had dropped to 8 percent.[23] Medicaid is attacked because of its cost. As health-care costs have spiraled rapidly upward, far ahead of the inflation rate,

[23]Schwarz, *America's Hidden Success,* 38.

★ CRITICAL THINKING

WHAT TYPE OF HEALTH-CARE SYSTEM SHOULD AMERICA HAVE?

The 1990s brought a new political issue to the forefront, health care. Polls showed that the American people were increasingly worried about their ability to afford medical care. This concern was shared by the business community, which had seen sharp increases in the costs of employee group health programs. Republicans and Democrats alike talked about the need for a change in the country's health-care system.

There are essentially two broad approaches to medical care. One, which exists throughout Europe and in Canada, is a national health system. The government controls such a system, and everyone is entitled to equal access to medical care. Where national health care exists, there is typically a small private program for wealthy individuals who, for one reason or another, choose not to use the government-based system. The alternative approach, which exists in the United States, is based on the private sector but also includes public aspects such as government-paid medical care for the poor (Medicaid) and the elderly (Medicare).

The advantages of a national health-care system are its costs and its coverage. Health care is one area in which government can do the job for less than the private sector. The United States has the most expensive health-care system in the world; it absorbs 13 percent of the gross national product (GNP). By comparison, the national health-care systems of western Europe and Japan account for less than 10 percent of GNP. A national health-care system also provides broader coverage; everyone has access to health care. In the United States, in contrast, access depends to some degree on the ability to pay. In 1992, more than 35 million Americans were too poor to buy their own health insurance and were not covered by private health insurance (for example, group health through an employer) but were not poor enough to qualify for public insurance (Medicaid). The United States performs worse than western Europe and Japan on most indicators (for example, infant mortality rates) of health-system performance.

The advantages of a private-centered health system are its responsiveness to eligible persons and its level of services. In a national health-care system, there is often a long wait to obtain certain services, such as elective surgery, and some services are denied to particular categories of patients (for example, kidney dialysis is not available to all elderly patients who might benefit from it). The private-centered system in the United States has been, moreover, the source of a disproportionate percentage of important medical breakthroughs. Open-heart surgery and organ transplants, for example, were pioneered here. U.S. medicine is widely regarded as the most advanced in the world.

A change can be expected in the U.S. health-care system during the 1990s. One alternative is a national health-care system similar to those of western Europe but having a stronger private component. For example, it is likely that the U.S. government would not assume ownership of the hospitals or force physicians to become public employees. But the system would give all Americans a right of access to health care and would involve a government-prescribed fee structure for medical services. Another alternative is a modified version of the existing private system. A main feature would be the provision of access to health care for nearly all people. For example, employers might be required by law to provide health insurance to their employees.

Which proposal do you favor—a national health-care system or a modified version of the existing private system? Why? Which alternative do you think is more likely to be enacted into law? Why?

so have the costs of Medicaid. It absorbs nearly half of all public assistance dollars spent by the U.S. government.

As is true of other public assistance programs, Medicaid has been criticized for supposedly serving too many people who could take care of themselves if they tried harder. The idea is contradicted, ironically, by the situation faced by many working Americans. There are about 38 million Americans who make too much money to qualify for Medicaid, but who do not make enough money, or do not work at a firm that provides health insurance, to meet their medical care needs.

Culture, Politics, and Social Welfare

Surveys have repeatedly indicated that a majority of Americans are convinced that most people on welfare could get along without it if they tried. Such opinions do not conform with the facts of being poor or jobless in America.[24] Most unemployed Americans have been laid off from jobs because of economic slowdowns; are disadvantaged in finding work because of mental, physical, or educational deficiencies; are too old or ill to work at a regular job; do not qualify for particular jobs because of inexperience (a major problem for young workers); or cannot work profitably because of other factors, such as being a single parent of young children. An economic slowdown alone puts massive numbers of Americans in need of assistance. At the depths of the 1990–1992 recession, more than 10 million people were unemployed

The facts about poverty, however, are sometimes less important to the fate of public assistance programs than the widespread belief that many if not most of the people on welfare do not really deserve help. Because public assistance programs have limited public support, there are constant political pressures to reduce welfare expenditures and to weed out undeserving recipients. Joseph Califano, who was secretary of health, education, and welfare in the Carter administration, complained that he faced constant pressures to reduce welfare expenditures and to devise new ways of weeding out undeserving recipients.[25]

The unwritten principle of social welfare in America, reflecting the country's individualistic culture, is that the individual must somehow earn any social-welfare benefit or, barring that, demonstrate a convincing need for the benefit. The result is a welfare system that is both *inefficient*, in that much of the money spent on welfare never reaches the recipients, and *inequitable*, in that most of the money spent on social welfare never gets to the people who are most in need of help.

INEFFICIENCY: THE WELFARE WEB

The United States has by far the most intricate system of social welfare in the world. Scores of separate programs have been established to address different, often overlapping needs. A single individual in need of public assistance may qualify for many, none, or one of these programs, and the eligibility criteria are

---

★ ANALYZE THE ISSUE

Big Government's Impact on the American Dream
According to a Roper poll, 80 percent of Americans believe that cuts in federal social-welfare programs would threaten the American Dream. Yet 86 percent believe that this same dream is threatened by big government. Do these contradictory opinions represent public support for the status quo, or do they mean something else? Explain your interpretation.

---

[24]See Harrell R. Rogers, Jr., *Crisis in Democracy* (Reading, Mass.: Addison-Wesley, 1978), 164–173.
[25]Joseph A. Califano, Jr., *Governing America* (New York: Simon & Schuster, 1981), 327–328.

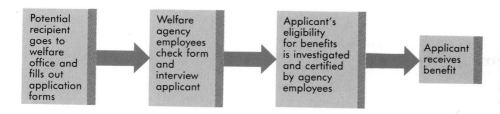

FIGURE 25-3 The Cumbersome Administrative Process by Which Welfare Recipients Get Their Benefits

often perplexing. Consider the case of Gary Myers of Springfield, Missouri, who declared bankruptcy in 1988 because he could not afford to pay $1,400 in hospital bills that his family had incurred. Had Myers made exactly $4 less than his $509 monthly wage as a security guard, he would have qualified for government payment of his medical expenses. Because of the extra $4, however, Myers received nothing.[26]

Beyond the question of the equity of such rules is the question of their efficiency. The unwritten principle that the individual must somehow earn or deserve a particular benefit makes the U.S. welfare system highly labor-intensive. Consider, for example, the AFDC program, which limits eligibility to families with incomes below a certain level and, in most states, to families with a single parent living in the home. Because of these requirements, the eligibility of each AFDC applicant must be periodically checked by a caseworker (see Figure 25-3). Such procedures make programs like AFDC doubly expensive: in addition to payments to the recipients, there are the costs of paying caseworkers, supervisors, and support staffs and of processing the extensive paperwork involved.

Leaders as diverse as George McGovern, Jimmy Carter, Richard Nixon, and the conservative economist Milton Friedman have argued the need to reduce the enormous administrative costs of social welfare. Their ideas have all been variations on the idea of a guaranteed annual income for every American family. Families with little or no income would get regular government payments up to a maximum level. These payments would be sent directly to recipients, just as social security checks are mailed monthly to beneficiaries. Recipients would establish their eligibility by filing an annual tax return documenting their low income. The enormous size and complexity of the welfare bureaucracy could thus be reduced considerably.

Of the various proposals, Nixon's Family Assistance Plan came the closest to becoming law. Recognizing that the concept of a guaranteed income was contrary to the American ideal of individualism, Nixon stressed that the payments of his Family Assistance Plan would "be scaled in such a way that it would always pay to work."[27] Nixon described welfare as "a failure that grows worse every day," and his bill made it through the House of Representatives before being defeated in the Senate by an unlikely coalition of conservatives, who attacked the plan as too costly and likely to produce welfare dependency, and liberals, who feared the program would provide insufficient support for the truly needy.[28]

[26]Matt Clark, "Forgotten Patients," *Newsweek*, August 22, 1988, 52.
[27]Cited in Gilbert Steiner, *The State of Welfare* (Washington, D.C.: Brookings Institution, 1971), 10.
[28]Daniel Patrick Moynihan, *The Politics of a Guaranteed Income* (New York: Random House, 1973), 446.

INEQUITY: THE MIDDLE-CLASS ADVANTAGE

Most Americans hold to the traditional belief in individualism and self-reliance, which they generalize to other people. Although they recognize a need for programs for the poor and disadvantaged, they tend to minimize both the number of such individuals and the extent of their need. The situation means that less-advantaged Americans cannot count on a great deal of political support from other sectors of society.

America's poor and disadvantaged are also in a weak position to help themselves politically. Their numbers are large—one in seven Americans lives below the poverty line—but they have a low rate of voting and do not vote as a bloc. The situation reflects the historical lack of class consciousness among poorer Americans and the absence of strong political organizations (such as a major socialist party) to mobilize them. They are also hampered by traditional American attitudes toward welfare, which diminish the legitimacy of their claim to help and even lead many of them to feel ashamed to ask for it. In view of all the obstacles to political action by the poor and disadvantaged, it is perhaps no surprise that the United States ranks *last* among the leading industrialized democracies in relative level of spending for public assistance. Even the much-heralded War on Poverty of the 1960s was less a war than a skirmish. Weak middle-class support for the effort, reports that the programs were poorly administered and were not reaching the target audience, and the fiscal pressures of the Vietnam conflict combined to undermine the poverty effort. Congressional appropriations for the War on Poverty programs never totaled as much as $2 billion in a given year.

Social security and Medicare are another story entirely. These two social insurance programs have broad public support even though together they cost the federal government roughly $400 billion annually, nearly four times what is spent on the major public assistance programs (see Table 25-2). One major reason for the difference in public funding and approval for social security is that it benefits the majority. Most Americans are either actual or potential social security recipients. It is good politics for elected officials to appeal to the 40 million retired Americans who get a monthly social security check.[29] In 1972 the Republican President Nixon and a Democratic-controlled Congress conducted a virtual auction on social security until they agreed to a 20 percent increase in benefits, which took effect a month before the November election.

Social security recipients do not hesitate to assert their right to benefits; they feel entitled to them by virtue of their payroll-tax contributions. In fact, however, social security is *not* a pure insurance program. As we indicated earlier, recipients receive far greater benefits than they have "earned" through their payroll taxes. So they are, in a sense, getting public assistance: federal dollars beyond what they themselves contributed during their working years.

It is important to note, however, that the existence of social security substantially lessens the demand for other forms of public assistance. Monthly social security checks keep millions of Americans, mostly widows, out of poverty. About a fourth of social security recipients have no other significant source of income. Without social security, they would be completely dependent

[29]See William Mitchell, *The Popularity of Social Security: A Political Paradox* (Washington, D.C.: American Enterprise Institute, 1977).

It's no disgrace t' be poor, but it might as well be.
                Abe Martin

★ ANALYZE THE ISSUE

Social Security's Impact on Poverty
According to U.S. Census Bureau statistics, social security payments have the effect of keeping the proportion of Americans living below the poverty line from increasing to 20 percent from its actual level of 14 percent. Should social security therefore be properly regarded as an antipoverty program? Why, or why not?

TABLE 25-2 Federal Spending for Major Social Insurance and Public Assistance Programs, 1992 Social insurance spending far exceeds public assistance spending.

Program	Number of Recipients (in Millions)		Expenditures (in Billions)
Social insurance			
Social security	40.0		$289
Medicare	32.0		113
		Total	$402
Public assistance			
SSI	5.5		$18
AFDC	5.0*		15
Food stamps	20.0		20
Housing subsidies	6.5*		20
Medicaid	25.0		60
		Total	$133

*Families.

SOURCE: Data are based on estimates provided in *The United States Budget, Fiscal Year 1992* (Washington, D.C.: Office of Management and Budget, 1992), part 4, 4–14.

on public assistance programs. Increases in social security benefits over the past forty years have outpaced inflation and have substantially improved the situation of elderly Americans. Whereas 50 percent of elderly people in the 1950s lived at or below the poverty level, only 15 percent do so today.

Nevertheless, many social security recipients, while legally entitled to the benefits they receive, have no actual financial need for them. Only a third of social security recipients are in the lowest fifth of the population in income. Many recipients are high-income Americans for whom social security is simply additional retirement income. In 1990 families in the top fifth of the income population received more than $50 billion in federal social insurance benefits, which is more money than was spent on AFDC, food stamps, and housing subsidies combined.

The contradictions and difficulties of social welfare in America come together in the contrasting cases of social insurance and public assistance. Although the latter is targeted toward the truly needy, it is less acceptable politically and culturally and receives much less funding. The situation testifies to the strength of traditional American values of individualism and self-reliance and to the power of money and votes.

Social welfare, as we have seen, is the arena in which many of the conflicts of the American political system come together: individualism vs. equality, Congress vs. the president, national authority vs. local authority, public sector vs. private sector, Republicans vs. Democrats, poorer vs. richer. At best, the politics of social welfare is the politics of hope—the expectation that a touch of compassion blended with the provision of opportunity will result in economic security for all. But, of course, not everyone can attain economic security in a system that makes no guarantee that everyone's basic needs will be provided for. Instead, a politics of hope is a trade-off of contradictory values, which ensures that social-welfare policy will be untidy and controversial and, in the end, will not fully satisfy anyone.

Summary

The United States has a complex social-welfare system of multiple programs addressing specific welfare needs. Each program applies only to those individuals who qualify for benefits by meeting the specific eligibility criteria. In general, these criteria are designed to reward and promote self-reliance or, when help is necessary, to ensure that laziness is not rewarded or fostered—in short, to limit benefits to those individuals who truly cannot help themselves. This approach to social welfare reflects Americans' traditional belief in individualism.

Poverty is a large and persistent problem in America. About one in seven people fall below the government-defined poverty line, and they include a disproportionate number of children, female-headed families, minority-group members, and rural and inner-city dwellers. The ranks of the poor are increased by economic recessions and reduced through government welfare programs.

Welfare policy has been a partisan issue, with Democrats taking the lead on government programs to alleviate economic insecurity. Changes in social welfare have usually occurred through presidential leadership in the context of majority support for the change. Welfare policy has been worked out through programs to provide jobs and job training, education programs, income measures, and, especially, transfer payments through individual-benefit programs.

Individual-benefit programs fall into two broad categories: social insurance and public assistance. The former includes such programs as social security for retired workers and Medicare for the elderly. Social insurance programs are funded by payroll taxes on potential recipients, who thus, in a sense, earn the benefits they later receive. Because of this arrangement, social insurance programs have broad public support. Public assistance programs, in contrast, are funded by general tax revenues and are targeted toward needy individuals and families. These programs are not controversial in principle: most Americans believe that government should assist the truly needy. However, because of a widespread belief that most welfare recipients could get along without assistance if they tried, these programs do not have universal public support, are only modestly funded, and are politically vulnerable.

The social-welfare system in the United States is criticized in all quarters, but reform efforts have been largely unsuccessful. A major reason is that opposing sides disagree fundamentally on the nature of the problem. In one view, social welfare is too costly and assists too many people who could help themselves; another view holds that social welfare is not broad enough and that too many disadvantaged Americans live in poverty. In light of these irreconcilable differences, in combination with federalism and the widely shared view that welfare programs should target specific problems, the existing system of multiple programs, despite its administrative complexity and inefficiency, has been the only politically feasible alternative. Yet it results in social spending that is not fully targeted toward the people most in need of help.

Major Concepts

entitlement program	progressive tax
in-kind benefits	public assistance
means test	social insurance
poverty line	transfer payments

Suggested Readings

Blumberg, Paul. *Inequality in an Age of Decline.* New York: Oxford University Press, 1980. An analysis of the perplexing issue of national equality in a period of nonexpanding governmental resources.

Derthick, Martha. *Policy Making for Social Security.* Washington, D.C.: Brookings Institution, 1979. An overview of the development of social security.

Levitan, Sar. *Programs in Aid of the Poor,* 6th ed. Baltimore: Johns Hopkins University Press, 1990. A thorough overview of poverty and poverty programs in America.

Light, Paul. *Artful Work: The Politics of Social Security Reform.* New York: Random House, 1985. An analysis of the issues and politics of the recent reforms of the social security system.

Murray, Charles. *Losing Ground: American Social Policy, 1950–1980.* New York: Basic Books, 1984. An unfavorable assessment of the U.S. welfare system.

Quadagno, Jill. *The Transformation of Old Age Security.* Chicago: University of Chicago Press, 1988. Traces the development of old-age security and the rise of the American welfare state.

Schwarz, John E. *America's Hidden Success,* rev. ed. New York: Norton, 1988. A favorable assessment of the U.S. welfare system.

Wilson, William Julius. *The Truly Disadvantaged: The Inner City, the Underclass, and Public Policy.* Chicago: University of Chicago Press, 1987. An important analysis of poverty in the inner city.

26

FOREIGN AND DEFENSE POLICY: PROTECTING THE AMERICAN WAY

We the people of the United States, in order to . . . provide for the common defense . . .
—Preamble, U.S. Constitution

*I*n early 1992 President George Bush of the United States and President Boris Yeltsin of Russia formally proclaimed an end to the cold war that had divided their countries since the end of World War II forty-five years earlier. "Russia and the United States do not regard each other as potential adversaries," the proclamation stated. "From now on, the relationship will be characterized by friendship and partnership founded on mutual trust and respect and a common commitment to democracy and freedom."

A few weeks before his meeting with Yeltsin, Bush had traveled to Japan with his top Far Eastern advisers and a group of eighteen American corporate leaders, including the heads of the three biggest U.S. automakers, Ford, Chrysler, and General Motors. Bush's trip, which was intended to focus attention on the U.S. trade deficit with Japan, became a nightmare for the president. He became ill at a state dinner, received only vague promises about trade reform from the Japanese, and was widely ridiculed for participating in a much-ballyhooed ribbon-cutting ceremony for a Toys-R-Us store, which had waged a three-year legal battle to break into the Japanese market. Japan had a $41 billion annual trade surplus with the United States, while our president was traveling halfway around the world to help a retail toy store. The columnist George Will described Bush's journey as "the worst foreign trip in the history of presidential travel."[1]

These two sharply contrasting events dramatized the United States' position in a changing world. Its bitter enemy, the Soviet Union, was no longer its main adversary. Its longtime trading partner, Japan, was now a major competitor. The economic future looked gloomy. In 1982, the United States had been the world's biggest creditor nation, holding a net positive international investment in excess of $300 billion. By 1992, the United States was the world's largest

---

[1] George F. Will, "From MEOW to Meow," *Newsweek*, February 10, 1992, 82.

debtor nation, owing more than $500 billion to foreign investors. During the same period, the U.S. balance of trade (that is, of imports against exports) had declined sharply. Americans were buying far more goods from abroad than they were selling overseas, at the cost of millions of jobs. *New York Times* foreign-affairs correspondent Leslie Gelb warned that the country was ''falling apart,'' with great risk to its national security.[2]

As Gelb was aware, national security is an issue of economic strength as well as of military preparedness. The primary goal of U.S. foreign and defense policy is preservation of the American state. This objective requires military readiness in order to protect the territorial integrity of the United States. But the American state is more than a physical entity; it also represents a society of more than 250 million people, whose standard of living depends upon a prosperous economy.

The national security policies of the United States embrace an extraordinary array of activities—so many, in fact, that they could not possibly be addressed adequately in an entire book, much less a single chapter. There are some 160 countries in the world, and the United States has relations of one kind or another—military, diplomatic, economic—with all of them. This chapter narrows the subject of national security policy by focusing on a few main ideas:

★ *The focus of U.S. foreign policy in the past half century was containment of Soviet expansion.* Trillions of dollars were spent and thousands of American lives were lost in the cold war with the Soviet Union.

★ *Since World War II, the United States has acted in the role of world leader,* which has substantially affected its military, diplomatic, and economic policies.

★ *The policy machinery for foreign and defense affairs is dominated by the president and includes military, intelligence, diplomatic, and economic agencies and organizations.*

★ *The United States maintains a high degree of defense preparedness.* This readiness mandates a substantial level of defense spending and a worldwide deployment of U.S. conventional and strategic forces. A consequence of these requirements is a military-industrial complex that benefits from and is a cause of high levels of military spending.

★ *Changes in the international marketplace have led to increased economic interdependence among nations, which has had a marked influence on the United States' economy and on its security planning.* National security today is as much a matter of economic strength as of military power.

The Roots of U.S. Foreign and Defense Policy

For nearly half a century, U.S. defense policy was defined mostly by the country's cold war with the Soviet Union. Most Americans believed that the Soviets aimed to impose communism on the entire world, and that only a

[2] Quoted in Richard J. Barnet, ''Reflections: The Disorders of Peace,'' *The New Yorker,* January 20, 1992, 62.

Great Britain's Winston Churchill, America's Franklin D. Roosevelt, and the Soviet Union's Josef Stalin meet at Yalta in 1945 to discuss the order of the postwar world. (Courtesy of the US Army)

determined United States could prevent that from happening. From the Berlin airlift in 1948–1949 to the Vietnam escalation in 1965 to the Star Wars initiative in 1983, the United States seemed willing to pay any price to halt the spread of communism. Then, suddenly and dramatically in the late 1980s, the Soviet empire began to fall apart. One Soviet republic after another declared its independence until finally, in December 1991, the Soviet Union itself ceased to exist. Today the United States is more secure militarily than at any time since the end of World War II. There were for decades two superpowers, the Soviet Union and the United States. Now there is only one.

With the cold war ended, the United States is positioned to redefine its foreign and defense policies. The country is still at the center of world politics, but its challenges have changed: they are less military and more economic. The conflict with the Soviets consumed energy and resources that were needed at home. As a panel of foreign policy experts concluded recently, "The most urgent challenge for America is to get its own house in order."[3] A strong domestic base, more than a mighty military arsenal, has become the key to global success.

Although the cold war is over, the changes in foreign and defense policy that lie ahead will take place within a context shaped by that conflict. Policy does not begin anew whenever changes occur, even when those changes are as historic as the collapse of the Soviet Union. Decisions made in the past carry into the future, both informing and channeling new ones.

THE UNITED STATES AS GLOBAL SUPERPOWER

U.S. national security policy after World War II was built upon a concern with the power and intentions of the Soviet Union.[4] At the Yalta Conference in 1945,

[3] American Assembly Report (cosponsored by the Council on Foreign Relations), *Rethinking America's Security*, 1991, Harriman, New York, p. 8.
[4] For an overview of Soviet policy, see Alvin Z. Rubenstein, *Soviet Foreign Policy since World War II*, 4th ed. (New York: HarperCollins, 1992).

U.S. President Franklin Roosevelt and Soviet leader Josef Stalin had agreed that eastern European nations were entitled to self-determination within a Soviet zone of influence, which Stalin took to mean governments aligned closely with the Soviet Union. After the war, Soviet occupation forces assisted the communist parties of eastern European nations to capture state power, usually by coercive means. Poland, East Germany, Hungary, Bulgaria, Albania, the Baltic states, and Yugoslavia came under communist control. In 1948 the Union of Soviet Socialist Republics (USSR) completed its domination of eastern Europe by engineering a coup in Czechoslovakia that ousted its democratically elected leadership. In the words of Britain's wartime prime minister, Winston Churchill, an "iron curtain" had fallen across Europe.

The Soviet Union had been attacked twice by Germany in the space of three decades. Between 20 million and 30 million of its citizens (compared with 500,000 Americans) had died in World War II. The United States expected the USSR to create an eastern European buffer zone between itself and Germany, but did not expect the Soviets to use repressive means to do so. The Soviet Union's aggressive action led U.S. policymakers to reassess Soviet aims.[5] Particularly noteworthy was the evaluation made by George Kennan, a U.S. diplomat and expert on Soviet affairs. Kennan concluded that invasions from the west in World Wars I and II had made the Soviet Union almost paranoid in its concern for regional security. Although Kennan believed that the USSR would someday mature into a responsible world power, he contended that it was an immediate threat to neighboring countries and that the United States, although not directly endangered, would have to take the lead in discouraging Soviet aggression. He counseled a policy of "long-term, patient but firm, and vigilant containment."[6]

Kennan's analysis contributed to the formulation of the postwar U.S. security doctrine: containment. The doctrine of **containment** was based on the idea that the Soviet Union was an aggressor nation that had to be stopped from achieving its territorial ambitions.

From Stettin in the Baltic to Trieste in the Adriatic an iron curtain has descended across the Continent.
Winston Churchill, address at Westminster College, Fulton, Missouri, 1946

The Cold War

Although Kennan's assessment of the Soviet Union was influential, it was not accepted in its entirety by Harry S Truman, who had become president after Roosevelt's death in 1945. Truman rejected Kennan's view that the USSR was motivated by a concern for regional security. Truman saw the Soviet Union as an aggressive ideological foe that was bent on *global* domination and that could be stopped only by the forceful use of U.S. power. Truman's view was based on a lesson learned from territorial concessions that Britain and France had made at a conference in Munich in 1938 to Germany's Adolf Hitler; rather than appeasing Hitler, these concessions convinced him that Germany could bully its way to further gains. Thus efforts at appeasement propelled Europe toward World War II. The idea that appeasement only encourages further aggression was the *lesson of Munich,* and it became the dominant view of U.S. policymakers in the postwar period.

Developments in the late 1940s embroiled the United States in a **cold war** with the Soviet Union. The term refers to the fact that the two countries were

★ ANALYZE THE ISSUE

The Effectiveness of the Containment Doctrine
The dominant view among western leaders after World War II was that aggression should never be rewarded because it only encourages the aggressor nation to seek further gains. As a result of this view, western nations concluded that containment was the best strategy to adopt toward the Soviet Union. Do you think this view was the correct one? Can you think of postwar developments that support your position? Do you think this view is still applicable today? Are there recent examples to support your position?

[5] See John Lewis Gaddis, *Strategies of Containment* (New York: Oxford University Press, 1982).
[6] Mr. X. (George Kennan), "The Sources of Soviet Conduct," *Foreign Affairs* 25 (July 1947): 566–582.

STOP Communism!

IT'S EVERYBODY'S JOB

Cold War propaganda, like this poster warning Americans of the danger of Soviet-backed communist encroachment in the Philippines in the late 1940s, contributed to an atmosphere of distrust and fear in the United States. (Library of Congress)

not directly engaged in actual combat (a "hot war"), but were locked into a deep-seated hostility, which lasted forty-five years. From the United States' perspective, the cold war was an extension of containment policy and included support for governments threatened by communist takeovers. In China the Nationalist government had the support of the United States, but it was defeated in 1949 by the Soviet-supplied communist forces of Mao Zedong. In June 1950 the Soviet-backed North Koreans invaded South Korea, and President Truman immediately committed U.S. troops to the conflict, which ended in stalemate with a loss of 35,000 American lives.

In order to contain the Soviet Union itself, the United States encircled it with a ring of military bases and built up its nuclear arsenal. During the 1950s the Eisenhower administration declared its willingness to block Soviet expansionism by all possible means, including the use of nuclear weapons (a policy known as "brinkmanship").

In 1962 President John F. Kennedy took the country close to a war with the Soviet Union. U.S. intelligence sources had discovered that the Soviet Union was constructing nuclear missile sites in Cuba, which lies only 90 miles from Key West, Florida. Kennedy responded with a naval blockade of Cuba and informed the Soviet Union that the United States would attack any Soviet ship that tried to pass through the blockade. At the last moment, Soviet ships heading for Cuba turned around, and Premier Nikita Khrushchev ordered the dismantling of the missile sites. Kennedy himself estimated the odds that the Soviet Union would choose war rather than capitulation at about "1 out of 3."[7]

You have to take chances for peace, just as you must take chances in war. . . . The ability to get to the verge without getting into the war is the necessary art. If you try to run away from it, if you are scared to go to the brink, you are lost.
John Foster Dulles

[7] Quoted in Graham Allison, "Conceptual Models and the Cuban Missile Crisis," *American Political Science Review* 63 (September 1969): 689.

The Cuban missile crisis was a personal triumph for Kennedy, but it provoked an arms race. The Soviets backed down over Cuba in part because they had an inconsequential navy and an inferior nuclear force. Pledging not to be humiliated again, the Soviets began a twenty-year buildup of their naval and nuclear forces.

The Limits of American Power: The Vietnam War

A major turning point of late-twentieth-century U.S. foreign policy was the Vietnam war. It was the most costly application of the containment doctrine: 58,000 American soldiers lost their lives. America's defeat in Vietnam forced U.S. policymakers to reconsider the country's international role.

Vietnam was part of France's colonial empire until the French army was defeated in 1954 by guerrilla forces, which were led by Ho Chi Minh, a nationalist with communist sympathies. The Geneva conference that ended the war resulted in a partitioning of Vietnam: the northern region was placed under Ho Chi Minh's leadership and the southern region under anticommunist leaders. The United States provided economic assistance to South Vietnam, anticipating that its government would quickly develop the public support that would enable it to prevail in a Vietnam unification election that was scheduled for 1956. When it became apparent that Ho Chi Minh would easily win the election, the United States helped to get it canceled and began to increase its military assistance to the South Vietnamese army. By the time of President Kennedy's assassination in 1963, the United States had about 17,000 military advisers in South Vietnam. Lyndon Johnson sharply escalated the war in 1965 by committing U.S. combat units to the conflict. By the late 1960s, 550,000 Americans were fighting in South Vietnam.

U.S. forces were technically superior in combat to the communist guerrillas, but they were at a fatal disadvantage: they were fighting an enemy they could

In the jungle warfare of Vietnam, American soldiers had difficulty finding the enemy and adapting to guerrilla tactics. (UPI/ Bettmann Newsphotos)

not easily identify in a society they did not fully understand.[8] Vietnam was a guerrilla war, with no front lines and few set battles. The United States controlled the air, the sea, and the cities, but the war was to be won in the countryside by an enemy that had popular support and an almost inexhaustible patience developed from decades of war with the French and Americans.

As the war dragged on, American public opinion, most visibly among the young, turned against continued U.S. involvement. The war's unpopularity was the main reason President Johnson decided not to run for reelection in 1968. Richard Nixon, who became president in 1969, continued the war effort, but public opinion forced him to aim not for victory, but for a gradual withdrawal that he called "peace with honor."

The Vietnam war changed the world view of many Americans, citizen and policymaker alike. The *lesson of Vietnam* was that there were limits to their country's ability to get its own way in the world. The United States could not go to war every time the threat of communism surfaced somewhere in the world. Nixon concluded, for instance, that the United States could no longer act as the police—or, as he said, the "Lone Ranger"—for the free world and sought to reduce tensions with communist countries.[9] This new philosophy was highlighted by the Helsinki Accords of 1971, in which the United States accepted the territorial boundaries of eastern Europe—a tacit recognition of Soviet domination of the region. Then Nixon took a historic journey to the People's Republic of China in 1972, the first official contact with that country since the communists took power in 1949.

These diplomatic efforts were accompanied by the Strategic Arms Limitation Talks (SALT), which began in 1969. The SALT talks presumed that the United States and the Soviet Union each had an interest in retaining enough nuclear weapons to deter the other from an attack but that neither side had an interest in mutual destruction. Under the doctrine known as "nuclear parity," the two sides would work to stabilize their arms race (discussed later in this chapter) by agreeing to maintain nuclear arsenals of approximately equal destructive power. Along with the recognition of China and the lowering of East-West trade barriers, the nuclear arms agreements marked the start of a new era of communication and cooperation, or **détente** (a French word meaning "a relaxing"), between the United States and the Soviet Union.[10]

Disintegration of the "Evil Empire"

Although the period of détente during the 1970s marked a major shift in U.S.-Soviet relations, it was not a lasting one.[11] The Soviet invasion of Afghanistan in 1979 convinced U.S. leaders that the USSR was still bent on expansion and threatened western interests in the oil-rich Middle East. Ronald

[8] See David Halberstam, *The Making of a Quagmire: America and Vietnam during the Kennedy Era*, 2d ed. (New York: Random House, 1988); Stanley Karnow, *Vietnam: A History* (New York: Penguin, 1983); Guenter Lewy, *America in Vietnam* (New York: Oxford University Press, 1980).
[9] Charles Kegley and Eugene Wittkopf, *American Foreign Policy* (New York: St. Martin's Press, 1979), 48.
[10] See Paul Y. Hammond, *Cold War and Détente* (New York: Harcourt Brace Jovanovich, 1975).
[11] Robert G. Kaiser, "U.S.-Soviet Relations: Goodbye to Détente," *Foreign Affairs* 59 (Winter 1979/1980): 500–521.

Boris Yeltsin (*holding papers*) speaks from atop a tank in front of the Russian Republic's parliament building in August 1991. Yeltsin was urging the Russian people to resist the attempted coup against Soviet President Mikhail Gorbachev. The coup resisters' extraordinary insistence on democracy contributed to the breakup of the Soviet Union that followed and ushered in a new era in U.S. foreign policy. Instead of a monolithic "evil empire," the United States suddenly had fifteen separate republics to deal with. (AP/Wide World)

Reagan, elected president in 1980, called for a renewed emphasis on U.S. military power as a way of dealing with the Soviet Union, which he described as an "evil empire."[12]

Reagan's proposal for a doubling of defense expenditures during the next five years marked the beginning of the largest peacetime military buildup in the nation's history. Reagan pushed for deployment of new nuclear weapons systems, including MX missiles, cruise missiles, and Pershing missiles. During his presidency 4,500 tanks and 300 attack helicopters were added to the army, the navy got 80 new ships, and the air force acquired 1,300 additional fighter jets. The Soviet Union, for its part, had been building up its conventional and nuclear forces since the Cuban missile crisis of 1962.[13]

U.S. policymakers did not yet realize it, but the Soviet Union was collapsing under its heavy defense expenditures, isolation from western technology and markets, and inefficient centralized command economy. In March 1985 Mikhail Gorbachev became the Soviet leader and proclaimed a need to restructure the Soviet economy and society, an initiative known as *perestroika*. He also ordered the withdrawal of Soviet troops from Afghanistan (which had become his country's Vietnam) and sought to reduce tensions with the United States. In 1987 Gorbachev and Reagan signed a treaty to limit intermediate-range nuclear forces (INF), which was the first time that the two superpowers had agreed to a reduction (as opposed to a ceiling) on nuclear weapons.

Gorbachev's efforts came too late to save the Soviet Union. In 1989 Gorbachev began a withdrawal of Soviet troops from eastern Europe, which accelerated a prodemocracy movement that was already underway in the

[12] See Russell J. Ling, "Reagan and the Russians," *American Political Science Review* 78 (June 1984): 338–355; Seweryn Bialer and Joan Afferica, "Reagan and Russia," *Foreign Affairs* 61 (Winter 1982/1983): 249–271.

[13] See William Zimmerman and Glenn Palmer, "Words and Deeds in Soviet Foreign Policy: The Case of Soviet Military Expenditures," *American Political Science Review* 77 (June 1983): 358–367.

region. Poland initiated major reforms. Hungary dismantled the "iron curtain" that had blocked free travel to Austria. Then, in November, the Berlin Wall and the other barriers between East and West Germany—the most visible symbols of the separation of East and West—came down. Two years later, after an attempted coup by Soviet communists failed to stop the changes, the Soviet Union itself broke apart. On December 8, 1991, the leaders of the Russian, Byelorussian, and Ukrainian republics declared that the Soviet Union no longer existed. A loose and perhaps temporary confederation, the Commonwealth of Independent States, was established in its place.

THE UNITED STATES AS WORLD LEADER

Before World War II, the United States was an **isolationist** country, deliberately avoiding a large role in world affairs. The country had only a small army, although, as an industrial giant that was involved in maritime trade, it had one of the world's largest navies. Its fleet, and the two oceans that separated it from Europe and Asia, protected the United States and kept it at a distance from developments elsewhere in the world.

A different America existed at the end of World War II. It had more land, sea, and air power than any other country in the world, a huge military-industrial base, and several hundred overseas military bases. It negotiated more than fifty treaties, most of which involved a pledge of mutual defense. The United States had become an **internationalist** country, deeply involved in the affairs of other nations.

A World Shaped to America's Liking

As the world's strongest nation, militarily and economically, the United States sought a world suited to its interests. The clearest example is the European Recovery Plan, better known as the Marshall Plan. Proposed in 1947 and named after one of its chief architects, the widely respected General George Marshall, who had become President Truman's secretary of state after the war, the plan was perhaps the most successful U.S. foreign policy initiative of the twentieth century. It called for $3 billion in immediate aid for the postwar rebuilding of Europe, with an additional $10 billion or so to follow. The Marshall Plan was unprecedented both in its scope (today, the equivalent cost would be roughly $100 billion) and in its implications—for the first time, the United States was committed to an ongoing major role in European affairs. The program worked as expected: U.S. assistance through the Marshall Plan enabled the countries of western Europe to regain economic and political stability in a relatively short time.

Our policy [the Marshall Plan] is directed not against any country or doctrine but against hunger, poverty, desperation and chaos. Its purpose should be the revival of a working economy in the world so as to permit the emergence of political and social conditions in which free institutions can exist.

George Marshall

The Marshall Plan was designed, however, for more than the strengthening of the countries of western Europe so that they could better confront the perceived Soviet military and political threat. The plan also conformed to the economic needs of the United States. Wartime production had lifted the country out of the Great Depression, but the end of the war in 1945 brought a recession and renewed fears of hard times. A rejuvenated western Europe would furnish a market for U.S. goods. In effect, western Europe would become a junior partner within a system of international trade dominated by the United States.

America's military power buttressed this international economic system. The worldwide umbrella of U.S. naval and nuclear forces assured the United States and its friends of open markets. The Soviet Union was more or less frozen out of trade with the free world.

U.S. military power was also used to support governments that could be expected to promote America's security and economic goals. In the Middle East, for example, the new state of Israel provided the United States with an opportunity to form a secure friendship in a region that was sometimes hostile to western interests. By helping Israel both militarily and economically, the United States acquired an ally that could be counted on to counter threats from either Arab nationalism or Soviet intervention in the Middle East. Today Israel gets more U.S. aid (about $3 billion annually) than any other country.

A Distorted Vision of America's Ideals

The combination of lofty ideals and tough-minded pragmatism that marked America's actions as world leader was marred by some less admirable tendencies. The fact that the world can be a dangerous place became the justification for policies that were out of step with America's governing principles.

The United States used a simple test—opposition to the Soviet Union and communism—to determine whether any other nation was a friend or foe. In 1973 the CIA participated in a coup that overthrew Salvador Allende, the popularly elected Marxist president of Chile, and brought to power General Augusto Pinochet, a brutal dictator. Two decades earlier the United States had participated in a coup that changed the government of Iran, which borders on the Soviet Union. Iran had nationalized its oil production in 1951, thus taking control away from foreign oil companies. The United States sent CIA agents to undermine the authority of Premier Mohammed Mossadegh and provided arms that enabled the shah of Iran to seize power in 1953. The shah reciprocated by giving U.S. interests more control of oil production and by building Iran into a prowestern regional military power. However, in order to maintain his control within Iran, the shah resorted to increasingly repressive measures, including the torture and murder of his Islamic fundamentalist opponents. (In 1979 they overthrew the shah, seized the oil fields, and established an anti-American government.)

Meanwhile, at home, freedom of speech suffered. In the 1950s the domestic political scene in the United States was dominated by anticommunist hysteria and fear.[14] A leading figure was Senator Joseph McCarthy (R-Wis.), who used innuendo, intimidation, and outright lies to whip up an anticommunist frenzy and to suppress protests against his sweeping allegations of subversion. In the House of Representatives, the Committee on Un-American Activities conducted investigations aimed at uncovering subversive elements that had allegedly infiltrated various areas of American life. The State Department was accused of having "lost" China to the communists and of being a haven for communist sympathizers; many prominent diplomats lost their jobs because of their supposed communist leanings: Trade unionists with any hint of a communist past were eliminated from union bureaucracies. Actors and playwrights be-

★ ANALYZE THE ISSUE

Short-Term Analysis of Policy Costs
When the Marshall Plan was proposed, opponents labeled it a giveaway. Why, they asked, should America give billions to help devastated European nations get back on their feet? Why was this view shortsighted? Can you think of problems today, foreign or domestic, in which an obsessive concern for short-term costs has led policymakers to oppose programs that would provide significant long-term benefits? What are some plausible reasons for officials to fail to take the long view?

[14] See Fred J. Cook, *The Nightmare Decade* (New York: Random House, 1971).

★ CRITICAL THINKING

IS DEMOCRACY COMPATIBLE WITH NATIONAL SECURITY NEEDS?

Alexis de Tocqueville believed that democracies lacked those qualities necessary for the successful conduct of foreign affairs:

> Foreign policy does not require the use of any of the good qualities peculiar to democracy but does demand the cultivation of almost all those which it lacks. . . . A democracy finds it difficult to coordinate the details of a great undertaking and to fix on some plan and carry it through with determination in spite of obstacles. It has little capacity for combining measures in secret and waiting patiently for the result.

A perennial question is whether the rules governing a democracy's national security policy should differ from those that guide its domestic policy. In fact, of course, different rules *are* applied. Certain types of national security information are officially "classified"—the information cannot lawfully be made public. In addition, as we saw in Chapter 19, the president has considerable freedom to act without congressional approval in the national security realm. For instance, the War Powers Act of 1973 allows the president to send U.S. troops into combat abroad for short periods without the approval of Congress. Some people advocate more radical departures from democratic practices in the conduct of national security policy, such as granting the president and the various intelligence agencies broad freedom to operate on their own authority.

An opposing view holds that the national security interests of a democracy are best served when democratic practices are upheld to the fullest extent possible. This view is based on the idea that the true strength of a democracy resides in the will and support of the people. The danger arises when national security concerns override the importance of obtaining popular consent for policy. When the people are kept in the dark about their government's actions and when the policy then goes awry (as it did in Vietnam), the people's faith in government is shaken and their willingness to support the policy effort is diminished.

What is your view on the relationship between democratic practices and national security policy? Is a democratic system a hindrance or an advantage to ensuring national security? Does the answer depend on which issue is involved? Consider the question also from the perspective of an authoritarian regime. What advantages and disadvantages does an authoritarian regime bring to the conduct of foreign policy?

SOURCE: Alexis de Tocqueville, *Democracy in America* (1835–1840), ed. J. P. Mayer (Garden City, N.Y.: Doubleday/Anchor, 1969), 228–229.

---

lieved to have communist loyalties were blacklisted—no major movie studio or theater company would hire them. In some American universities, professors suspected of having communist sympathies were fired.

The worst forms of political repression ended in the mid-1950s, but the cold war continued to have a chilling effect on political debate. For most Americans, the evil of Soviet communism and the need to fight it with force around the globe were gospel. The few skeptics in Congress, like Senator Wayne Morse of Oregon, were portrayed as oddballs. Even policies that made sense domestically required a national security justification. Construction of the interstate highway system, for example, was started in 1958 for the expressed purpose of enabling the rapid transport of military personnel and equipment in case of war.[15]

Even in recent years, criticism of foreign and defense policy has often been cut short by attacks on the critic's patriotism. When the United States invaded

When public excitement runs high as to alien ideologies, is the time when we must be particularly alert not to impair the ancient landmarks set up in the Bill of Rights.

Luther W. Youngdahl,
United States v.
Lattimore, 1953

[15] Barnet, "The Disorders of Peace," 68.

the tiny Caribbean island of Grenada in 1983 to overthrow its communist government, for example, a prominent U.S. senator questioned the legality of the invasion under international law, but said nothing more after his loyalty was questioned by the White House and some of his Senate colleagues.

A NEW WORLD ORDER

The end of the cold war prompted George Bush to call for a "new world order." Although the president did not define it fully, his formulation included at least three components. First, it abandons the assumption that world affairs is a zero-sum game, in which for one nation to gain something, another nation has to lose. Rather, nations can move forward together. Second, the new world order calls for greater attention to problems that are global in scope, such as the environment. Third, the concept emphasizes **multilateralism**—the idea that major nations should act together in response to problems and crises.[16]

Multilateralism characterized the U.S. response to Iraq's invasion of Kuwait in August 1990. Rather than sending U.S. troops to confront Iraqi leader Saddam Hussein's forces singlehandedly, President Bush worked through the United Nations. UN resolutions were adopted that condemned the Iraqi invasion, demanded the unconditional withdrawal of Iraqi forces, and ordered a trade embargo on Iraqi oil. The military force arrayed against Iraq was also nominally a UN force, although it was led by a U.S. commander and consisted mostly of U.S. troops. Several countries that did not contribute troops, such as Germany and Japan, supported the effort with money. The Soviet Union cooperated by promising not to obstruct the allied effort, by sharing intelligence information, and by putting diplomatic pressure on the Iraqi government, with which it had worked closely in the past.

Multilateralism has also characterized the U.S. response to the economic recovery of eastern Europe and the former Soviet Union. The United States has granted some foreign aid to the region, though nothing on the scale of the Marshall Plan. The United States has pressed Japan and western Europe for help in financing the recovery and has encouraged the use of multinational institutions like the International Monetary Fund and the World Bank in the effort.

The Process of Foreign and Military Policymaking

National security is unlike other areas of government policy because it rests on relations with powers outside rather than within a country. Nations have sovereignty within their recognized territory; each nation is the ultimate governing authority over this territory and the people within it. Nations sometimes work together for common goals or against a common opponent, but they do not surrender their sovereignty in the process. In reality, of course, the world is not composed of equal sovereign states. Some are more powerful than

---

[16] For a general view of America's new world role, see Kenneth A. Oye, Robert J. Lieber, and Donald Rothchild, *Eagle in a New World: American Grand Strategy in the Post–Cold War Era* (New York: HarperCollins, 1992)

★ ANALYZE THE ISSUE

Accountability in Foreign Policy
During the summer of 1987, congressional hearings revealed that some staffers on the National Security Council had been involved in illegal arms deals with Iran and covert operations to supply the Nicaraguan Contras. These activities constituted a systematic attempt to avoid the political accountability that is at the core of American democracy. Two of the principal operatives, Lt. Col. Oliver North and National Security Council head John Poindexter, said that their actions were justified by national security concerns—specifically, by the threat of communism in Central America. Do you believe that in this case the end justified the means? In general, how far should the U.S. government be allowed to go in keeping its foreign policy secret from the American people? Explain your position in terms of both democratic accountability and the likely effectiveness of extreme secrecy in foreign policy.

In a revival of multilateralism, the UN Security Council votes to use force against Iraq if that country fails to withdraw from Kuwait by January 15, 1991. Instead of going it alone, the United States worked with the UN throughout the Persian Gulf crisis. (Mark Cardwell/Reuter/ Bettmann Newsphotos)

★ THE MEDIA AND THE PEOPLE

THE GLOBAL VILLAGE

In his classic book, *Understanding Media*, Marshall McLuhan described the modern world as "a global village" because communication technology had brought people everywhere into close and instantaneous contact. However, it took the American press a long time to start bringing the rest of the world to its audience. News reporting in the United States has traditionally been dominated by domestic issues. Only a few newspapers, such as *The New York Times*, made a substantial effort at in-depth international coverage. This pattern began to change after World War II, when the United States took on the role of world leader. As the world became more important to America, the press brought more news of the world to the American people.

The introduction of television accelerated the process: the networks have a national audience and concentrate their coverage on national and international affairs. They devote proportionally more of their news-gathering efforts to international affairs than do newspapers. The most recently established major network, CNN, even has a world edition of its news that is transmitted daily in countries around the globe.

In recent years, the top news story in the U.S. media has often been an international story rather than a domestic one. Between 1989 and 1991, for example, the news story that received the most attention during each of these years was an international one. The breakup of the Soviet bloc was the leading story in 1989 and the Persian Gulf crisis received the most attention in 1990 and 1991. In 1992 a domestic story, the presidential election and the country's economic problems, took center stage.

Opinion polls reflect this pattern. In the past half century, there has been a gradual increase in the proportion of Americans who claim that international affairs is the level of politics that is of greatest interest to them. The size of this proportion is affected, however, by the issues of the moment. Opinion polls in 1992 showed that Americans' attention had shifted from events in Europe and the Middle East to the domestic economy. Nevertheless, in a way that would have been unimaginable earlier in the century, Americans have truly become part of McLuhan's global village.

SOURCES: Marshall McLuhan, *Understanding Media: The Extensions of Man* (New York: McGraw-Hill, 1964); *Media Monitor*, various issues, 1989–1992.

others, and the strong will sometimes force the weak into positions they would not accept voluntarily. Nevertheless, there is no international body that is recognized by all nations as the final (sovereign) authority on disputes between them.

As a result, the chief instruments of national security policy—diplomacy, military force, economic exchange, and intelligence gathering—differ from those of domestic policy.

THE POLICYMAKING INSTRUMENTS

Diplomacy is the process of negotiation between countries. In most cases, nations prefer to settle their differences by talking rather than by fighting. Through negotiation, countries can usually reach agreement on issues they share. By definition, acts of diplomacy involve two (bilateral) or more (multilateral) nations.

Military power is a second instrument of world politics, and it can be used unilaterally—that is, by a single nation acting alone. For most countries, military power is a defensive instrument; they maintain forces, or enter into military alliances with other countries, in order to protect themselves from potential aggressors. Throughout the history of nations, however, there have always been a few countries that used military force more actively. The United States is such a nation. In the nineteenth century, it used force to take territory from the Indian tribes, Mexico, and Spain. Since then, the United States has not pursued territorial goals but has otherwise made frequent use of its military power. Recent examples include the unilateral invasions of Grenada in 1983 and Panama in 1989 and the multilateral war against Iraq in 1991.

Economic exchange is a third instrument of world politics. This form of international relations usually takes one of two forms—trade or assistance. Trade among nations is the more important form. Nearly all countries aspire to a strong trading position so that they will have markets for their products and will have access to outside products. Some countries, however, are so weak economically that they require assistance from more prosperous countries. This assistance, as we saw in the case of the Marshall Plan, is typically designed to help both the weaker and stronger partners.

A fourth instrument of world politics is intelligence gathering, which is the process of discovering what other countries are doing. For many reasons, but primarily because any country can safely assume that every other nation, even its allies, will pursue its own self-interest, nations keep a watchful eye on one another.

THE POLICYMAKING MACHINERY

In the case of the United States, the lead actor in the application of these four instruments of foreign policy is the president. As we indicated in Chapter 19 and will discuss later in this chapter, the president shares power and responsibility for foreign and military·policy with Congress, but he has the stronger claim to leadership because of his constitutional roles as commander in chief, chief diplomat, and chief executive. For example, although President Bush sought and gained congressional approval for the Persian Gulf war, he said that if Congress refused its support, he would order the half million American troops into battle anyway.

The president has an executive agency, the National Security Council (NSC), to advise him on foreign and military issues. The NSC is chaired by the president, and includes the vice president and the secretaries of state and defense as full members, and the CIA director and the chairman of the Joint Chiefs of Staff as advisory members. State, Defense, and the CIA often have conflicting and self-centered ideas about the conduct of security policy, and the NSC acts to keep the president in charge by providing a broader perspective. The NSC's staff of experts is directed by the president's national security adviser, who, with an office in the White House and access to defense, diplomatic, and intelligence sources, has become influential in the setting of U.S. policy. In the Nixon administration, the national security adviser, Henry Kissinger, had a larger voice in foreign policymaking than either the secretary of state or defense. (Kissinger was later appointed secretary of state.)

The complexity of international politics makes it impossible for any individual or government agency to direct U.S. policy singlehandedly. Moreover, as a world power, the United States relies upon outside institutions, such as the United Nations, to pursue some of its policy objectives. The key organizational units in the foreign policy area can be categorized according to their primary functions—defense, intelligence, diplomacy, and trade.

Defense Organizations

The Department of Defense (DOD), which has roughly 2 million uniformed personnel and 1 million civilian employees, is in charge of the military security of the United States. DOD was created in 1947 when the three military services—the army, navy, and air force—were placed under the secretary of defense. Each service has its own secretary, but they report to the defense secretary, who represents all the services in relations with Congress and the president. Each service naturally regards its mission and budget as more important than those of the other services. The secretary helps to reduce the adverse effects of these interservice rivalries.

The secretary of defense is always an important policymaker, but the influence of recent secretaries has varied widely, depending on the secretary's personality and the president's inclinations. Bush's defense secretary, Dick Cheney, played a major and highly visible role, for example, in the planning of the Persian Gulf conflict.

The president also receives military advice from the Joint Chiefs of Staff (JCS). The JCS includes a chairman, a vice chairman, and a member from each of the uniformed services—the army, navy, air force, and marine corps. The JCS helps to shape military strategy and evaluates the military's personnel and weapons needs. Whenever the members of the JCS disagree, the chairman's view prevails. During the Persian Gulf war, General Colin Powell, the first African-American to serve as JCS chair, was deeply involved in strategic decision making, including a controversial recommendation that President Bush halt the fighting before all major Iraqi combat units were destroyed.

Of the country's military alliances, the North Atlantic Treaty Organization (NATO) is the most important. NATO was created as a "forward defense"

General Colin Powell, chairman of the Joint Chiefs of Staff, briefs reporters at the Pentagon during the Persian Gulf war. (Martin Simon/SABA)

against the possibility of a Soviet invasion of western Europe. NATO countries conduct joint military exercises and engage in joint strategic and tactical military planning. The NATO forces, which include troops of the United States, Canada, and most western European countries, are under an integrated command except for France, which since the mid-1960s has maintained full command of its own forces. NATO's communist counterpart until the disintegration of the Soviet bloc was the Warsaw Pact, which consisted of troops of the Soviet Union and its eastern European satellites.

NATO's charter prohibits it from acting "out of area," so it had no authority to act in the Persian Gulf war. Moreover, the demise of the Warsaw Pact threatened NATO's survival. In 1991 NATO was restructured as a smaller, more flexible force that might deal with new risks, such as international terrorism and ethnic rivalries.

Intelligence Organizations

Foreign and military policy requires a high state of knowledge about what is happening in the world and what other countries are planning to do. A large part of the responsibility for the gathering of such information falls on specialized federal agencies, including the Central Intelligence Agency (CIA); the National Security Agency, which specializes in electronic communications analysis; and separate intelligence agencies within the departments of State and Defense. Although the exact amount that the federal government spends annually on intelligence activities is not easily determined, one source has estimated the figure at $30 billion.[17]

Of the various intelligence agencies, the CIA is the most prominent.[18] The

[17] "The CIA's Next Generation," *Newsweek*, February 17, 1992, 27.
[18] See Rhodri Jeffreys-Jones, *The CIA and American Democracy* (New Haven, Conn.: Yale University Press, 1989.)

agency gathers and assesses information on foreign affairs. Much of this effort consists of the routine monitoring of international developments. With the decline of the Soviet threat, which had occupied the agency's attention since its formation in 1947, the CIA is giving more attention to drug trafficking, industrial espionage, and terrorism.

The CIA is prohibited by law from conducting surveillance on individuals and groups within U.S. borders, but it has not always respected this limitation on its activities and has in other ways often abused the trust and secret powers invested in it.[19] Congress in the mid-1970s established House and Senate committees to oversee CIA activities and force it to play by the rules, but this effort was only somewhat successful. William Casey, the director of the CIA under President Reagan, lied to Congress about illegal covert activities in Central America that, in 1986, became known as the Iran-Contra affair.

Diplomatic Organizations

The U.S. Department of State conducts most of the country's day-to-day business with foreign countries through its embassies, headed by U.S. ambassadors. State's traditional duties include negotiating political agreements with other nations, protecting U.S. citizens and interests abroad, promoting U.S. economic interests, gathering foreign intelligence, and representing the United States abroad. For all of its activities and prominence, the State Department is a relatively small organization. Only about 25,000 people—foreign service officers, policy analysts, administrators, and others—work in State. Some observers regard the State Department as tradition-bound and less central to foreign policy decision making than its reputation seems to suggest.[20]

The secretary of state is often described as second in importance only to the president within the executive branch in the determination of national security policy. Whether the secretary, in fact, has this level of influence depends on the president's willingness to rely heavily on the secretary. Dean Rusk, secretary of state under Presidents Kennedy and Johnson, had less influence than top presidential assistants or Secretary of Defense Robert McNamara. In contrast, George Bush chose James Baker as his secretary of state precisely because he wanted Baker to take the lead role in foreign policy.

America's diplomatic efforts also take place through international organizations, such as the Organization of the American States (OAS) and the United Nations. The UN was established after the Second World War by the victorious allies.[21] Its security council, which included the United States, France, Britain, the Soviet Union, and the Republic of China, was to be an instrument of multilateral policymaking; the world's strongest powers would work together to promote global harmony and prosperity. When the United States and Soviet Union entered into the cold war, all hope of such cooperation vanished.

The breakdown of the Soviet bloc in 1989 renewed the possibility that the

---

[19] See Loch K. Johnson, *America's Secret Power: The CIA in a Democratic Society* (New York: Oxford University Press, 1989).

[20] See Barry Rubin, *Secrets of State: The State Department and the Struggle over U.S. Foreign Policy* (New York: Oxford University Press, 1985).

[21] Adam Roberts and Benedict Kingsbury, *United Nations, Divided World* (New York: Oxford University Press, 1988).

The headquarters of the European Community is in Brussels, Belgium. The U.S. government has not yet decided whether the EC represents an economic opportunity, a threat, or both. (Van Parys/Sygma)

world's great powers could work together to achieve common goals. The first major opportunity came in the Persian Gulf conflict of 1990–1991, when the United States led a UN force that first blocked Iraqi forces and then attacked them. Some analysts believe that the UN may finally be able to play the large role in international affairs that was envisioned for it when it was chartered. International terrorism and drug trafficking are among the problems that the UN has recently addressed.

Economic Organizations

The shift in emphasis in global affairs from military forces to economic markets has brought a new set of government agencies, those representing economic sectors, to prominence in foreign affairs. When George Bush made his widely publicized trip to Japan in 1992, he was accompanied, not by the secretary of state or defense, but by the secretary of commerce. The Agriculture, Labor, and Treasury departments are other cabinet agencies that are playing increasingly large roles in foreign affairs. In addition, some specialty agencies are involved in international economics, among them the Federal Trade Commission and the Export-Import Bank of the United States.

The United States also works through international economic agencies, such as the International Monetary Fund (IMF), the World Bank, and the General Agreement on Tariffs and Trade (GATT). These agencies have tended to promote goals, such as economic development and free trade, that are consistent with U.S. policy goals. The IMF and the World Bank were established through the efforts of the United States for the purpose of assisting developing countries. The IMF provides short-term loans so that countries experiencing temporary trade deficits are not forced into drastic action, such as the imposition of high tariffs, that would hurt them and the world economy in the long run. The World Bank makes long-term loans to poorer countries for capital investment projects, such as the construction of factories. The GATT is the formal organization through which nations hold multilateral talks to establish the general rules governing international trade. The GATT operates primarily as a mechanism for reducing tariffs and other barriers to free trade among nations.

There is one major new economic organization of which the United States is not a part. The organization is the European Community (EC), an economic confederation of leading western European countries, including Germany, Italy, France, and Britain. Trade and travel between these countries became unrestricted in 1992, just as trade and travel between U.S. states is unrestricted. The EC forms the world's largest single market; its economy exceeds that of the United States by 30 percent or more. The EC could provide U.S. firms a huge market for their products, but it remains to be seen whether the EC will benefit countries other than its members. In part as a response to the economic clout of the EC, the United States has recently negotiated trade agreements with Canada and Mexico that will bring the economies of the three countries closer together.

The Military Dimension of National Security Policy

The dissolution of the Soviet Union has brought about the first significant scaling back of U.S. defense spending since the end of the Vietnam war (see Figure 26-1). The first round of cuts, in 1991, were in troop strength. The second

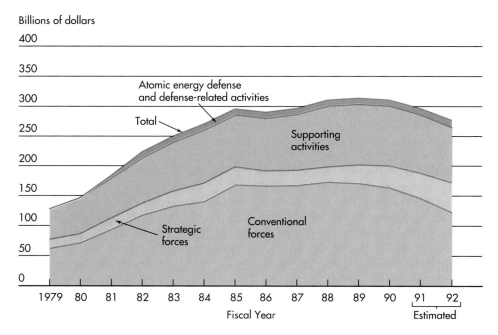

FIGURE 26-1 Defense Spending Spending on national defense, which more than doubled during the 1980s, has begun to decline because of the end of the cold war. *Source: Office of Management and Budget, 1992. The 1991 figure excludes Operation Desert Storm, which was subsidized by other countries.*

★ HOW THE UNITED STATES COMPARES

THE BURDEN OF MILITARY SPENDING

The United States bears a disproportionate share of the defense costs of the NATO alliance. The U.S. military establishment is huge and is deployed all over the world, and the taxpayers spend more than $250 billion per year to maintain it. These expenditures directly account for roughly 5 percent of the U.S. gross national product (GNP). By comparison, defense spending by Germany, Italy, and Canada accounts for 3 percent or less of their GNPs. The percentages for Britain and France are higher but not as high as for the United States. Japan, which is not part of NATO, spends only 1 percent of its GNP on defense. Japan's small military force is confined by World War II peace agreements to the country's islands and the adjoining waters.

The United States has pressured its allies to carry a larger share of the defense burden, but these countries have resisted, contending that the cost would be too high and that their security would not be substantially improved. A partial exception to this situation was the Persian Gulf war. U.S. troops and equipment accounted for the bulk of the military strength arrayed against Iraq, but the financial cost of the war effort was borne by other countries. Germany, Japan, Saudi Arabia, and Kuwait were among the countries that helped to fund the war. In fact, other countries gave the United States $20 billion more than it spent on the war.

The chart below indicates the approximate per capita level of defense spending in the United States and countries with which it is closely aligned.

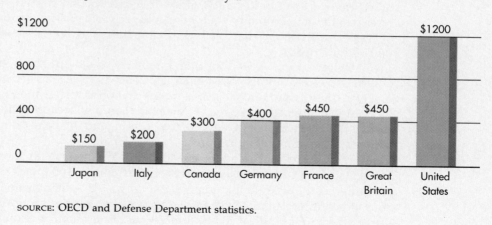

SOURCE: OECD and Defense Department statistics.

round, in 1992, targeted weapons systems. Even so, the so-called peace dividend brought about by the ending of the arms race is relatively modest. Republican leaders have called for a roughly $50 billion reduction in defense spending over five years. Some Democratic leaders have said that the United States could safely make a $100 billion reduction in this period.

Critics have questioned whether U.S. policymakers are truly serious about scaling back the military, but defense cuts are politically difficult to achieve. Military spending buys more than national security; it brings jobs and business to communities. There is also uncertainty about national security: How many ships, planes, tanks, nuclear missiles, and troops are necessary to protect the United States and its worldwide interests? No one knows exactly how much the United States must spend each year to maintain its security. U.S. policymakers have erred on the side of caution. Between 1980 and 1985, for example, military spending doubled even though the country was not at war. Some analysts say that that expenditure was worthwhile because it helped to persuade the Soviet Union, which could not keep pace, that it should abandon its arms race with the United States. Other analysts say that the money would have been better spent at home, since the Soviet Union was already beginning to show signs that it was undergoing political change.

DEFENSE CAPABILITY

Roughly 3 million people are either in the U.S. military or work for it. Another million owe their jobs directly to defense contracts. The United States spends far more on defense, in both relative and absolute terms, than its allies. On a per capita basis, U.S. military spending is more than twice that of other members of the NATO alliance.

Conventional Forces

The United States owes its status as the world's only superpower in part to the strength of its conventional forces. In the Persian Gulf conflict, the U.S. military battled the world's fourth largest army, Iraq's. It was no contest. The United States had far better military equipment and technology. The war lasted about six weeks, with fewer than 200 U.S. casualties and an estimated 50,000–100,000 Iraqi dead.

The United States has troops and military bases in about twenty-five countries. Western Europe has the largest concentration. At the height of the cold war, there were 350,000 U.S. troops stationed there, most of them in Germany. The number has been cut by more than half because of the easing of tensions between East and West. Large contingents of U.S. troops are also stationed in Japan and South Korea.

The Gulf war demonstrated the effectiveness of America's air and sea power. The United States has a dozen aircraft carriers, nearly 100 attack submarines, and hundreds of other fighting and supply ships. U.S. aircraft number in the thousands and are unmatched in performance. American ground troops are supported by thousands of tanks, artillery pieces, armored personnel carriers, and attack helicopters. The U.S. defense budget is second to none in the world, but so is the military power it buys.

Nuclear Forces

The main threat to the physical security of the United States during the cold war was not invasion but nuclear attack. The United States followed a policy of **deterrence,** the idea that the Soviet Union could be deterred from launching a nuclear attack by the knowledge that the United States would retaliate in kind. The cornerstone of deterrence was a theory called "mutually assured destruction" (MAD).[22] Each side develops, builds, and deploys nuclear weapons in the

---

[22] See Jerome H. Kahan, *Security in the Nuclear Age* (Washington, D.C.: Brookings Institution, 1975); Robert Jervis, "Why Nuclear Superiority Doesn't Matter," *Political Science Quarterly* 94 (Winter 1979/1980); Glenn Snyder, *Deterrence and Defense* (Princeton, N.J.: Princeton University Press, 1961); Spurgeon M. Keeny, Jr., and Wolfgang K. H. Panofsky, "MAD vs. NUTS: The Mutual Hostage Relationship of the Superpowers," *Foreign Affairs* 60 (Winter 1981/1982): 287–304.

knowledge that the other side is doing the same. Each side has enough warheads to destroy the other several times over and is inhibited from initiating a nuclear war by the knowledge that it too would be sure to be destroyed.

As of 1990, the United States had more than 10,000 long-range nuclear warheads, of which about 2,000 were on land-based missiles, 5,500 were submarine-based, and 3,500 were bomber-based. America's nuclear weapons are deployed in what is called the "nuclear triad," which refers to the three ways in which nuclear weapons can be launched: by air (bombers), land (missile launchers), and sea (submarines). Each part of the triad by itself is theoretically capable of destroying any country in the world, and together they provide a "second-strike capability"—the ability to absorb a nuclear attack (first strike) and survive with enough nuclear weaponry for massive retaliation (second strike).

Although MAD was the governing principle, not all U.S. leaders fully accepted the thinking behind it. A major shortcoming was that MAD would probably be a credible deterrent only in an extreme situation—if, for example, the United States were about to be conquered. Thus the United States during the Kennedy and Johnson administrations formulated a "flexible-response" strategy, which holds that the United States should use only the level of force, including nuclear force if necessary, that is appropriate to the level of the military threat against it.[23]

The flexible-response strategy requires that the United States also have tactical (battlefield) nuclear weapons in its arsenal. These are short-range, low-yield nuclear weapons that can be used against battlefield targets, such as enemy troop concentrations or artillery batteries. The United States has thousands of these weapons, as do the republics of the former Soviet Union. A major concern with the breakup of the Soviet Union has been control of its nuclear weapons, strategic and tactical. A related concern has to do with the scientists who worked on Soviet nuclear weapons and missile systems. The fear is that these scientists might be hired by hostile countries to help them build nuclear weapons. The United States has worked with Russia and other Soviet republics to prevent the proliferation of nuclear weapons and technology. For example, the United States gave funds for the creation of a Russian institute that is studying peaceful uses of nuclear technology; the institute provides jobs for Soviet nuclear scientists.

THE USES OF MILITARY POWER

U.S. military forces have been trained for or called upon for six types of military action:

Unlimited nuclear warfare, for which MAD is a strategy

Limited nuclear warfare, for which flexible response is a strategy

Unlimited conventional warfare, of which World War II is an example

Limited conventional warfare, of which Korea is an example

Counterinsurgency, of which Vietnam is an example

[23] See Ian Clark, *Limited Nuclear War* (Princeton, N.J.: Princeton University Press, 1982).

Police-type action, of which the detention and repatriation of illegal aliens is an example

Let us take a brief look at each of these military options.

Unlimited Nuclear Warfare

The idea of an all-out nuclear war was always too horrible to imagine, but the fear of nuclear holocaust has diminished greatly since the cold war ended. Following the lead of the United States, the president of the Russian republic, Boris Yeltsin, initiated deep, unilateral cuts in his country's nuclear arsenal. In the past, nuclear arms limitation had required protracted bilateral negotiations; neither the United States nor the Soviet Union would restrict its arsenal without corresponding concessions on the other side.

Limited Nuclear Warfare

Some experts believe that, while the risk of an all-out nuclear attack on the United States has diminished, the possibility that a single nuclear weapon might be used against the United States may have increased slightly. The fear is of an attack not from a republic of the former Soviet Union but from a terrorist group or an "outlaw" regime, such as Iraq, because the technology and materials that are required to build nuclear weapons are more widely accessible than ever before.

Traditional notions of nuclear deterrence make little sense against terrorism. If a terrorist group were to detonate a nuclear warhead in a major U.S. city, it would hardly be rational to destroy a foreign city in response. Accordingly, the United States, Russia, and other nuclear powers are cooperating to reduce the spread of nuclear weapons. One goal of the Persian Gulf conflict was the destruction of Iraq's nuclear weapon development program.

Unlimited Conventional Warfare

The end of the cold war has also reduced the prospect of an unlimited conventional war. A great part of U.S. military preparedness and strategy in the past half century was based on the scenario of an invasion of western Europe by Soviet and eastern bloc forces. When the Soviet Union withdrew its forces from eastern European countries and slashed its defense budget drastically, this possibility became remote. Even if the cold war should begin anew, Russia or any other element of the former Soviet Union would require years to build its military capacity to the point where it was a credible threat to the West.

Limited Conventional Warfare

The Persian Gulf war dispelled the notion, left over from Vietnam, that the United States lacked the will and the might to win a limited conventional war against a well-organized and well-armed foe. The number of Iraq's armor and artillery units, and the combat readiness of its forces as a result of that country's protracted war with Iran, made it a potentially formidable foe. But the war turned out to be no contest, prompting George Bush to say the United States had "kicked the Vietnam syndrome once and for all."

The American people share Bush's view. Polls show the American people are willing to accept the use of military force to stop any country that is "threatening to use chemical or nuclear weapons" or "invading another" country. The strength of this support, however, is contingent on the degree to which America's concerns are shared by other countries. In a 1991 survey the respondents overwhelmingly (85 to 11 percent) said that the United Nations rather than the United States should take the lead in confronting aggressor nations.[24]

A problem of limited conventional wars is that they do not always produce satisfactory results. The military action is likely to be quick and decisive, but the political aspect tends to be troublesome. Many Americans wondered why the Bush administration stopped the Gulf war short of a march on Baghdad and the elimination of Saddam Hussein. The administration's decision was a calculated one. Said one analyst: "The President was not prepared to pay the political price that increased American casualties would have involved or to take responsibility for putting Iraq back together after an unconditional surrender or to figure out how to contain the power of Iran and Syria once the Iraqi regime was destroyed."[25]

Even the smaller conventional wars that the United States has pursued in recent years have not turned out exactly as planned. The U.S. victory in Panama in 1989 ousted the dictator Manuel Noriega, but the drug trafficking that he sponsored did not diminish and the Panamanian economy was badly disrupted.[26]

Counterinsurgency

The Vietnam conflict was an **insurgency,** an uprising by irregular forces against an established government. Insurgencies are an old form of conflict, but they have taken on new importance in the twentieth century as they have become more widespread and more lethal. Insurgencies do not easily yield to military force. As Vietnam made clear, it is difficult to defeat an irregular army, even one that is outmanned and outgunned. Conventional combat units are not very effective against an enemy that can simply run and hide. Even with troops trained in counterinsurgency, a capacity that the U.S. military acquired during the Vietnam war, victory is not assured.

In most Third World countries, insurgencies originate in the grievances of people who are at the bottom of the economic heap. Insurgent forces emerge from the mass of ordinary citizens who are struggling against the monopoly of economic and political power by a tiny elite. Typically this elite controls the military and has the backing of international corporations. In the past, the insurgents often received support in the form of military equipment from the Soviet Union. Most insurgencies were accordingly seen by the United States as a threat to its political and economic interests. When in 1987 the governments

★ ANALYZE THE ISSUE

Insurgencies as Threats to U.S. Interests
Most revolutions in Third World countries have been opposed by the U.S. government. Do most such insurgencies really represent a substantial threat to the interests of the United States? What criteria could be used in judging which Third World revolutions are likely to jeopardize U.S. interests and which are not?

[24] ATI Survey #15, March 1991.
[25] Barnet, "The Disorders of Peace," 62.
[26] Ibid., 64.

A democratic impulse known as "people power," coupled with the belated backing of the United States, helped Corazón Aquino unseat Philippine dictator Ferdinand Marcos in 1986. (Greg Smith/Picture Group)

of Central America developed a general peace plan for the region, the Reagan administration reacted with ambivalence because the plan would have left in place the Sandinista government of Nicaragua, which had declared itself to be outside the sphere of American influence.

U.S. attempts to quell Third World insurgencies have declined somewhat since the Vietnam war, which reduced public support for U.S. military involvement in the internal affairs of other countries. Throughout the 1980s, polls showed that a large majority of Americans were steadfastly opposed to sending American troops into Central America to quell insurgencies there. During most of this period, there was even public opposition to providing military assistance on a small scale. A 1984 Gallup poll, for example, indicated that only 39 percent of the respondents favored giving military advice and equipment to friendly governments in Central America.

U.S. policymakers have become increasingly aware that military power is not likely to stop insurgencies. Abject poverty is a deep-seated condition in Third World countries, and there are always desperate people willing to fill the ranks of the insurgents. Rather than automatically siding with the ruling elite, the United States has increasingly pressured friendly governments to improve the economic and political situation of the underclass as a condition for continued U.S. support. In the Philippines in 1986, for example, the United States withdrew its longtime support from President Ferdinand Marcos and backed reform-minded Corazón Aquino, urging her to carry through on her promises of economic reform, including redistribution of land. The changed outlook of the leaders within the former Soviet Union has also improved the prospects of political solutions to rebellions. Insurgent forces now find it more difficult to obtain the military equipment and supplies to carry on their fight. U.S.-Soviet cooperation in the late 1980s helped bring about negotiated settlements to civil wars in Central America and Africa.

Police-Type Action

With the end of the cold war, U.S. policymakers have begun to pay closer attention to other global problems, including drug trafficking, terrorism, and population movement. The U.S. military has become increasingly involved with these problems. For example, U.S. Special Forces ("Green Berets") have been assigned to South America to help its governments with drug enforcement activities. As another example, U.S. military facilities and personnel were used in 1992 to detain and return hundreds of "boat people" who had fled Haiti in the hope of receiving asylum in the United States.

The use of military troops in some police-type roles can be expected to continue, but military officers have been opposed to the suggestion that U.S. army units be stationed along the border with Mexico to stop the flow of illegal aliens from that country, just as they have opposed suggestions that U.S. troops be used to help keep the peace in drug-ridden inner-city neighborhoods. Given the high cost of keeping a large defense force, and the absence of a highly visible and dangerous enemy like the former Soviet Union, it is likely that new proposals and new pressures to use the troops in unconventional ways will develop.

THE POLITICS OF NATIONAL DEFENSE

All Americans would agree that the physical security of the United States is a paramount concern. The concensus breaks down, however, on specific issues. The Vietnam conflict created deep and lasting divisions of opinion about the proper uses of America's destructive capacity. In contrast, U.S. policy in the Persian Gulf crisis had majority support from start to end.

Elites and the Public

Although public opinion turned against the Vietnam war and ultimately forced U.S. policymakers to withdraw American troops from Vietnam, the public usually plays a reactive rather than a forcing role (see Chapters 8 and 19). It is difficult for the public to assess the options in foreign policy except when a policy clearly produces a disastrous result. In the case of the Persian Gulf crisis, opinion polls indicated that a majority of Americans trusted President Bush's judgment about the best option—economic sanctions or military force. When he chose the military option, and it worked, the American people judged it to have been the right choice.

The major conflicts over defense policy ordinarily take place between political elites. Liberal Democratic elites have been more reluctant than conservative Republicans to support increases in military spending and to use military force as a means of settling international disputes. Institutional perspective has also mattered: presidents have been stronger advocates of military spending and power than has Congress. The president's outlook is perhaps predictable in view of his position as commander in chief of the military. Congressional opposition has been institutional as well as partisan. Members of Congress have sometimes resisted the president's recommendation because they believed that the president was withholding relevant information from them. (See Chapters 17 and 19 for a more detailed discussion of congressional-presidential interaction on policy issues.)

The Military-Industrial Complex

The conjunction of an immense military establishment and a large arms industry is new in the American experience. . . . In the councils of government, we must guard against the acquisition of unwarranted influence, whether sought or unsought, by the military-industrial complex. The potential for the disastrous rise of misplaced power exists and will persist.

Dwight D. Eisenhower

★ ANALYZE THE ISSUE

The Revolving Door
In March 1989 the U.S. Senate narrowly rejected John Tower's nomination to become secretary of defense. One objection raised by Tower's opponents was that after having served as a U.S. senator and a U.S. arms-control negotiator, he had stepped almost immediately through the "revolving door" into well-paid work as a consultant to defense contractors. Do you agree that by doing so, Tower created a serious conflict of interest? Should former members of Congress be required to wait several years before being permitted to work for special interests?

Political disputes over defense policy do not simply involve honest differences of opinion among people who have different views of the world and America's role in it. They also involve billions of dollars in jobs and contracts. Since World War II, the costs of maintaining global nuclear and conventional forces have kept U.S. defense spending at high levels.[27] In fiscal year 1991, the U.S. defense budget was nearly $300 billion, or roughly 6 percent of the gross national product. These enormous expenditures have been justified by reference to the nation's security needs. However, an alternative explanation for high defense spending has been offered: the insatiable demands of the U.S. armed services and defense firms. In his 1961 farewell address, President Dwight D. Eisenhower warned against the "unwarranted influence" and "misplaced power" of what he called a military-industrial complex.[28]

The **military-industrial complex** has three components: the military establishment, the industries that manufacture weapons, and the members of Congress from states and districts that depend heavily on the arms industry. The military-industrial complex is not, as is sometimes suggested, a well-coordinated, unified network of interests engaged in a conspiracy to keep the United States on a wartime footing. Rather, it is an aggregation of interests that benefit from a high level of defense spending, regardless of whether these expenditures can be justified from the standpoint of national security.

Many corporations could not survive without military contracts. Among U.S. aircraft manufacturers, for example, only Boeing and McDonnell-Douglas make passenger planes. Others, such as Northrop and Rockwell, make only military aircraft. Defense firms obviously do not act purely out of nationalistic motives; they are profit-making businesses.[29] Many weapons designs are aggressively sold by industry to the Department of Defense.[30]

The U.S. military does not need much persuading. New weapons systems are naturally attractive to the military establishment; it wants the latest-model tanks, planes, guns, and ships.[31] The cost of modern weaponry is staggering: the army's M-1 tanks cost more than $2 million each; the air force's B-1 bombers, more than $300 million apiece; the navy's Trident II submarines, more than $1 billion each.

Many members of Congress are eager to approve arms contracts (or at least reluctant to oppose them) because of the economic impact such contracts have on constituents. The B-1 bomber, for example, was built with the help of 5,200

[27] Murray L. Weidenbaum, *The Economics of Peacetime Defense* (New York: Praeger, 1974), 25.
[28] See Steve Rosen, *Testing Theories of the Military-Industrial Complex* (Lexington, Mass.: Lexington Books, 1973), 1.
[29] John Perry Miller, "Procurement Policies and Renegotiation," in J. Fred Weston, ed., *Procurement and Profit Renegotiation* (San Francisco: Wadsworth, 1966), 95.
[30] David Sims, "Spoon Feeding the Military: How New Weapons Systems Come to Be," in L. S. Rodberg and Dereck Seyr, eds., *The Pentagon Watchers* (Garden City, N.Y.: Doubleday/Anchor, 1970), 249–250.
[31] See James Fallows, *National Defense* (New York: Random House, 1981).

The Stealth bomber is unveiled in California—one of the newest and most expensive weapons in America's arsenal. (AP/Wide World)

subcontractors located in forty-eight states and in all but a handful of congressional districts. "This geographic spread gives all sections of the country an important stake in the airplane," one assessment of the B-1 concluded.[32] Each $1 billion spent on defense is estimated to create more than 30,000 jobs. A sharp reduction in defense spending would cause havoc in many local economies; about one in ten American jobs is directly or indirectly related to military spending.

Without doubt, some proportion of defense spending reflects the workings of the military-industrial complex rather than the requirements of national security.[33] The problem is that no one knows exactly what this proportion is, and the estimates vary widely.

The Economic Dimension of National Security Policy

Economic considerations are a vital component of national security policy. In the simplest sense, economic strength is a prerequisite of military strength: a powerful defense establishment can be maintained only by a country that is economically well-off.

There is, however, a broader and more important sense in which economic well-being is a core component of national security: economic prosperity enables a people to "secure" their way of life. As President Eisenhower said, it is folly to weaken at home what one is trying to strengthen abroad. The cold war often hid the essential truth of that observation. Global power came to be an end in itself. The Soviet Union paid the highest price. In the end, its status as a military superpower was achieved at the expense of economic growth and

[32] "The B-1: A Flight through Adversity," *Los Angeles Times*, reprinted in *Syracuse Post-Standard*, July 29, 1983, A7.
[33] Seymour Melman, *Pentagon Capitalism* (New York: McGraw-Hill, 1970), 175.

development. The contrast with western prosperity, more so than western military superiority, was ultimately the factor that pressured Soviet leaders to dissolve their country.[34] The United States also paid a high price for its superpower status. In his widely read book, *The Rise and Fall of the Great Powers*, Paul Kennedy concluded that the United States had engaged in "imperial overstretch," straining its resources with its global commitments and, in the process, weakening substantially its domestic economic base.[35]

In economic terms, the world can best be described as tripolar—meaning that economic power is concentrated in three centers. One is the United States, which produces nearly 20 percent of the world's goods and services. A second is Japan, which has 10 to 15 percent of the world's economy. The third and largest economy, at 25 to 30 percent of the world's gross product, is the European Community, which includes the countries of Belgium, Denmark, France, Germany, Great Britain, Greece, Ireland, Italy, Luxembourg, the Netherlands, Portugal, and Spain. These three centers, although they have less than 15 percent of the world's people, account for roughly 60 percent of the world's economic output.

In some respects, the United States is the strongest of these economic superpowers. For one thing, it has the largest market of any single country in the world. For another, the U.S. economy is more well-rounded than that of either the EC or Japan. The United States is strong industrially, agriculturally, and in its natural resources. The EC and Japan are deficient in natural resources; Japan is also weak in its agricultural production. Finally, the United States is unparalleled in its ability to back up its economic requirements with military force, although, as will be explained later, this advantage is less important today than in times past.

In other respects, however, the United States is the weakest of the three economic centers. As was mentioned previously, the United States has the world's largest national debt, its worst trade imbalance, and its greatest credit imbalance. Compared with its competitors, the United States is also weaker in its economic infrastructure; its systems of education and transportation lag behind those of Japan and the EC, which have also developed a more modern industrial base and have made a greater investment in product research. In a widely noted article, Peter G. Peterson, who was secretary of commerce in the Nixon administration, warned that America's imbalances could cripple its future: "The [worst] scenario, of course, is a huge plunge in the dollar, unaffordable imports, a long recession, garrison protectionism and a marked decline in American living standards."[36]

AMERICAN GOALS IN THE GLOBAL ECONOMY

The United States depends on other countries for raw materials, finished goods, and capital to meet Americans' production and consumption demands. Meeting this objective requires the United States to have influence on world markets. The broad goals of the United States in the world economy include:

[34] See Elie Abel, *The Shattered Bloc: Beyond the Upheaval in Eastern Europe* (Boston: Houghton Mifflin, 1990).

[35] Paul Kennedy, *The Rise and Decline of the Great Powers* (New York: Random House, 1988); for an alternative view, see Joseph Nye, *Bound to Lead: The Changing Nature of American Power* (New York: Basic Books, 1990).

[36] Peter G. Peterson, "The Morning After," *Atlantic Monthly*, October 1987, 46.

Sustaining an open system of trade that will promote prosperity at home

Maintaining access to energy and other resources that are vital to the regular functioning of the U.S. economy

Keeping the widening gap between the rich and poor countries from destabilizing the world's economy[37]

Access to Markets and Natural Resources

These three goals were most in reach for the United States in the period after World War II. Industrialized Europe was devastated, but U.S. factories and farmlands had been untouched by the war and were producing more than a third of the world's goods. While European nations were rebuilding, U.S. businesses were in an ideal position to expand. Investment opportunities were open throughout the world, and U.S. business interests had the necessary capital. Middle East oil is an illustration of how American companies exploited their opportunities. Before World War II began, U.S. oil companies controlled one-tenth of Middle Eastern oil reserves; just twenty years later, they controlled six-tenths.[38]

The big oil companies, such as Shell and Mobil, are examples of **multinational corporations**—firms that have major operations in more than one country.[39] These corporate giants have spread their operations, and their financial and political power, across the globe since the end of World War II. By some estimates, multinationals now account for more than a fourth of the total world economy. Many multinationals are headquartered in the United States: more than 500 U.S. firms have an ownership interest of 50 percent or more in foreign affiliates. Some U.S.-based multinationals have pursued policies that are contrary to U.S. security policy. For example, while the U.S. government was providing assistance to insurgents in Angola during the 1980s, U.S. oil firms were managing the oil fields that were the major source of revenue for Angola's Marxist government.

By and large, however, foreign investment by U.S.-based multinationals works to America's advantage in several ways. First, it sends a flow of overseas profits back to the United States, which strengthens the country's financial structure. Second, it assures the United States of the raw materials it needs. American corporations have direct control of certain resources, as in the case of a portion of Middle Eastern oil. Third, it makes other nations dependent on the prosperity of the United States; their economies are linked to the condition of U.S. business.

America's position in the world marketplace, however, has weakened substantially in the past two decades.[40] Whereas the United States at one time could almost define international economic conditions, it is now also defined by them.[41]

★ ANALYZE THE ISSUE

The United States in a Global Economy
All countries are now closely linked in a global economy. How does this situation limit America's foreign policy options? Why might this situation make it even more important for the United States to get its budget deficit under control in order to reduce the amount of money it borrows from other countries?

[37] *Rethinking America's Security*, p. 9.
[38] Harry Magdoff, *The Age of Imperialism: The Economics of U.S. Foreign Policy* (New York: Monthly Review Press, 1969), 43.
[39] See Raymond Vernon, *Storm over the Multinationals* (Cambridge, Mass.: Harvard University Press, 1977); Richard J. Barnet and Ronald E. Muller, *Global Reach: The Power of the Multinational Corporations* (New York: Simon & Schuster, 1975).
[40] William Diebold, Jr., "The United States in the World Economy: A Fifty-Year Perspective," *Foreign Affairs* 62 (Fall 1983): 81–104; see also Walter Russell Mead, *Mortal Splendor: The American Empire in Transition* (Boston: Houghton Mifflin, 1987).
[41] See Robert W. Tucker, "America in Decline: The Foreign Policy Maturity," *Foreign Affairs* 58 (Winter 1979/1980): 449–484.

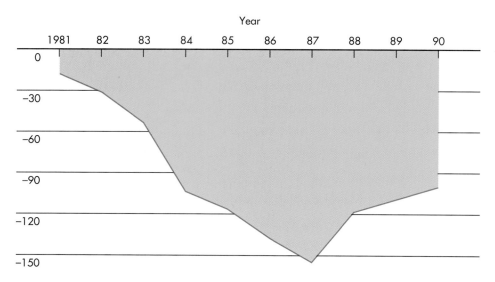

FIGURE 26-2 The Trade Deficit
Since the early 1980s there has
been a severe imbalance of
exports and imports. *Source:
Department of Commerce, 1990*

Germany and Japan, which were once America's junior trading partners, have become powerful economic rivals of the United States. Today Japan, not the United States, is the world's leading exporting nation, and trade between the two countries results in a huge surplus for Japan. For more than a decade, the United States has imported substantially more goods than it has exported (see Figure 26-2). Japan's yen and Germany's deutschemark have become stronger currencies than the American dollar, which once was the monetary standard against which all other currencies were compared. In early 1988 the United States was humbled when Japan and West Germany had to intervene to halt the dollar's drop in value on world financial markets.

In addition, western Europe as a whole has become a less receptive market for U.S. goods; European countries are now one another's best customers, trading among themselves through the EC. Through the GATT talks, the United States is seeking freer access to EC markets. Other new opportunities for U.S. firms reside in an economic partnership with Canada and Mexico and in the emergence of market economies in the countries that formerly constituted the Soviet Union. Some analysts believe that eastern Europe and Russia will provide a boost to international trade unlike anything since the reconstruction era in western Europe after World War II.

Relations with the Developing World

For the United States, economic difficulty has obviously not brought economic deprivation. America remains one of the world's strongest nations economically, and its people continue to have an enviable standard of living. The contrast with the underdeveloped countries is stark. The people of Bangladesh, for example, are desperately poor (the annual per capita income is less than $500), unskilled (the illiteracy rate exceeds 90 percent), and at great risk of dying young (the life expectancy is barely 40 years).

Less economically developed countries are a potential threat to the more developed ones. Political instability in the less developed countries is disruptive of world markets. The Middle East has been a prime example in recent years. The region's vast oil reserves are the fuel that drives the economies of many industrialized countries. The threat that Iraq's invasion of Kuwait posed to the flow of oil to western Europe was a major factor in the decision of the United States and its western allies to go to war with Iraq in 1991.

Less developed countries also offer marketplace opportunities. In order to make progress, they need to acquire the goods and services that more industrialized countries can provide. To foster this demand, the United States and the other industrialized countries provide developmental assistance to poorer countries. These contributions include direct foreign aid and also indirect assistance through international organizations such as the IMF and the World Bank. Since World War II, the United States has been far and away the leading source of aid to the developing countries of the world. The United States is still near the top in terms of its total annual contributions, but is now far down the list in terms of its per capita annual contributions (see Table 26-1).

The budgetary problems of the U.S. government have weakened its ability to influence world affairs through foreign aid. Some U.S. officials have urged that the United States take the lead in implementing a "Marshall Plan" for the fledgling democracies of eastern Europe. They suggest that an economic reconstruction program for the region would greatly reduce the likelihood of a communist resurgence and would ultimately create a strong market for American products. Opponents have said that such a plan, whatever its merits, is too costly for the United States to undertake at the present time.

Military Force as an Instrument of International Economics

The use of force against Iraq illustrated the role that military power can play in the global economy. In general, however, military power has become a less and less effective means of preserving economic leverage.[42] The economies of most

[42] See Robert O. Keohane and Joseph S. Nye, *Power and Interdependence: World Politics in Transition* (Boston: Little, Brown, 1977).

TABLE 26-1 U.S. Assistance to Developing Countries The United States ranks high in terms of total amount spent on development assistance but ranks lowest in terms of per capita expenditure.

	DEVELOPMENT ASSISTANCE	
	Total (Billion)	Per Capita
Canada	$2.4	$ 89
France	7.2	127
Germany	4.8	78
Great Britain	2.6	46
Italy	3.4	59
Japan	9.0	73
Sweden	1.7	196
United States	8.9	36

SOURCE: *OECD in Figures* (Paris: OECD, 1991).

of the world's countries are now so interconnected that military intervention would usually be counterproductive. For example, when Iranian fundamentalists, with the support of their government, took over the U.S. embassy in Teheran in 1979, the United States refrained from retaliating with an attack on Iran's oil fields not only for fear of the hostages' lives but also because the action would have substantially reduced the Middle East's oil-producing capacity.

The United States does not, however, have to use military force in order to get some advantage from its superpower status. Many countries prefer a militarily strong United States to the alternatives. China, for example, does not fear that the United States will use military power against it, but is unsure whether a remilitarized Japan would hesitate to do so. Germany and Russia are two other countries that trust the United States more than they trust each other. Such situations provide the United States with special opportunities for diplomatic and economic influence.

THE FALTERING DOMESTIC BASE OF U.S. PRODUCTIVITY

A strong position in the world economy requires that a country have products or natural resources that other countries want. The United States is the world's leading agricultural producer, which is a major source of its strength in global markets. It could not, however, maintain its standard of living on agricultural exports alone. It must also produce high-quality services and manufactured goods at competitive prices based on the latest technologies. In this respect, the United States has not done particularly well in recent years.

The reasons for some of America's problems in the international marketplace can be seen in a comparison with Japan, which is widely recognized as the world's most successful trading nation.[43] In Chapter 24, we noted that the large share of U.S. investments in the 1980s were spent on mergers and takeovers rather than on capital construction and improvements. During the same period, Japanese investments went primarily into new plants and equipment.

Research and development (R&D) spending is another case of contrasts. The U.S. government in recent years has spent less than half of its R&D money on civilian projects, concentrating instead on the defense area. By comparison, the Japanese government has spent more than 90 percent of its R&D money on civilian projects. Japan's leadership in the new technology of high-definition television, for example, is the result of a nearly twenty-year research collaboration between its government and its leading electronic firms.

In the area of education, the U.S. public school system is basically the same in design as it was a century ago. Japan has restructured its education system to meet what it regards as the demands of a scientific-technological world.

As for other public services, Japan recently began a $3 trillion, ten-year investment in its infrastructure, including its transportation, communication, and waste-disposal systems. The United States is widely recognized to have similar infrastructure needs but has no plans for a comparable investment.

The Japanese private sector has also pursued longer-range market strategies

---

[43] For a general comparison of the United States and Japan, see Samuel Kernell, ed., *Parallel Politics: Economic Policymaking in Japan and the United States* (Washington, D.C.: Brookings Institution, 1991).

than have American firms. The Japanese instrusion in the U.S. auto market, for example, took place over many years and went through several stages. Japanese automakers initially targeted the lower end of the market, gradually establishing a reputation for offering reliable, inexpensive transportation. They then moved into the middle range, producing cars that were more trouble-free than the equivalent American cars. In recent years, they have taken aim at the top end of the auto market with new lines such as Accura, Lexus, and Infiniti. They have priced these luxury cars at a level comparable to American luxury automobiles, but with performance and quality standards comparable to higher-priced European cars. This long-term cultivation of the U.S. auto market has been another Japanese success story. By comparison, U.S. automakers have made no serious effort to penetrate the Japanese market. No U.S. automaker even exports to Japan a car with the steering wheel on the right. (Like the British, the Japanese drive on the left side of the road.)

Most analysts have concluded that the United States must get its own house in order if it is to improve its position in the world economy. The following adjustments have been suggested:

Strengthening the nation's educational system

Changing the laws and attitudes that affect productive investment

Rebuilding the country's transportation and communication infrastructures[44]

Whether the United States will, in fact, take any of these steps anytime soon remains to be seen.

THE POLITICS OF WORLD ECONOMIC POLICY

In 1992, shortly after President Bush returned from the disastrous economic summit meeting in Tokyo described at the beginning of this chapter, a war of words broke out between Japan and the United States. The speaker of the lower house of the Japanese parliament, Yoshio Sakurachi, said he doubted that the Japanese would buy many American goods because U.S. firms "turn out so many defective products." He called American workers "lazy and illiterate" and described the United States as "Japan's subcontractor." His remarks provoked angry replies and retaliation. The Los Angeles County Transportation Commission canceled a $122 million contract with the Sumitomo Corporation of Japan to build rail cars for its new transit system. U.S. Senator Donald Riegle (D.-Mich.) said: "Mr. Sakurachi's attitude in slandering American workers was the same view the Japanese held the day its warplanes struck Pearl Harbor. Their arrogance was gone by 1945, when they learned the full meaning of America's capabilities."[45]

The dispute also revealed deep divisions among U.S. policymakers. No one defended Sakurachi's remarks, but many said that starting a trade war with Japan would hurt the United States far more than it would help. President Bush

[44] *Rethinking America's Security*, p. 10; see also Kendall W. Stiles and Tsuneo Akaha, *International Political Economy* (New York: HarperCollins, 1991).
[45] Material for this paragraph and the next two was obtained from an AP wire story, January 24, 1992.

President George Bush cuts the ribbon to open the new Toys-R-Us store in Kashihara City, Japan. (At left is Kozo Watanabe, Japan's minister of trade and industry; at right is Charles Lazarus, president of Toys-R-Us.) The celebration had been three years in the making, as the U.S. toy retailer struggled with Japan's stringent regulations protecting its domestic businesses. Improving trade relations with Japan is one of the major challenges for U.S. economic policymakers in the 1990s. (Win McNamee/Reuters/ Bettmann Newsphotos)

reiterated his commitment to a free trade policy, which many experts also endorsed. Edward Lincoln, a Brookings Institution scholar, said that the national interest of both the United States and Japan "lies in maintaining a close and relatively friendly economic relationship."

Trade issues have always been a mixture of economics and politics. Protective tariffs, for example, are a political response to economic competition. By placing a tariff on a product from abroad, government can protect domestic producers of that product. All countries subsidize some of their producers in one way or another. On his way to Japan, President Bush stopped in Australia for "friendly" trade talks, but was greeted by farmers who were protesting U.S. trade and price-support laws that protected American sugar, rice, and dairy producers from serious competition.

To oversimplify a bit, the opposing sides on trade issues reflect the **protectionism** and the **free-trade** positions. The protectionist view would place the immediate interests of domestic producers first in nearly all instances by imposing, as necessary, protective tariffs and other measures designed to give them an advantage in the domestic market over foreign competitors. The protectionist view was reflected, for example, in the "America First" campaign of Republican presidential challenger Patrick Buchanan in 1992. The center of protectionist sentiment in the United States, however, is Congress, whose members are responsive to local interests. They try to protect local firms which are being adversely affected by foreign competitors. It is not surprising, for example, that the protectionist campaign against Japanese automakers has been led by members of Congress from the state of Michigan, where the Big Three American automakers have their headquarters.

The free-trade view assumes that the long-term economic interests of all countries are advanced when tariffs and other trade barriers are kept to a minimum. The leadership on free trade has usually come from the White

House, although it is fair to say that most members of Congress, except on vital interests affecting their constituencies, accept the principle that global free trade is preferable to global protectionism. A wall of protective trade measures is widely regarded as a major reason for the severity of the Great Depression of the 1930s. By imposing tariffs to protect their troubled industries, the major industrialized nations kept one another out of markets in which active trade could have helped all of them to recover.

American public opinion in recent decades has generally supported the free-trade position, but adverse economic conditions tend to bring out protectionist sentiments. Polls in the early 1990s indicated that, as the domestic economy worsened, Americans were increasingly supportive of trade restrictions on Japanese products. A 1992 poll found that many Americans regarded Japan's economic power as a greater threat to U.S. national security than Russian military power. Such views were tempered, however, by a widespread belief that America's economic problems were largely of its own making. A 1991 CBS News/New York Times poll indicated that many Americans thought their country was blaming Japan for its own economic shortcomings.

Public opinion in recent years has consistently supported the idea that the United States should turn its attention toward its economy and away from its military. A Gallup survey taken immediately after the Persian Gulf war in 1991 indicated that only 10 percent of Americans thought the United States was spending too little on defense. An ATI survey taken at about the same time indicated that more than three-fourths of Americans believed that the United States "can't afford to defend so many nations."

This last belief seems to reflect the lesson that American elites and officials have drawn from its foreign and military policy experiences during the last half century, particularly during the past decade or so. The consensus is broad enough to suggest that American politics in the 1990s will focus on problems at home.

Summary

From 1945 to 1990, U.S. foreign and defense policies were dominated by a concern with the Soviet Union. During most of this period the United States pursued a policy of containment based on the premise that the Soviet Union was an aggressor nation bent on global conquest. Containment policy led the United States into wars in Korea and Vietnam and into maintaining a large defense establishment. U.S. military forces are deployed around the globe, and the nation has a large nuclear arsenal. The end of the cold war, however, has made some of this weaponry and much of the traditional military strategy obsolete. Cutbacks in military spending and a redefinition of the military's role are underway.

With the end of the cold war, the United States has taken a new approach to foreign affairs, which President George Bush labeled a "new world order." It proposes that nations work together toward common goals and includes efforts to address global problems, such as drug trafficking and environmental pollution. The Persian Gulf War is the most notable example of the multilateralism that is a characteristic of the new world order.

Increasingly, national security is being defined in economic terms. After World War II, the United States helped to establish a global trading system of which it was the leading partner. The nation's international economic position, however, has gradually weakened, owing to domestic problems and to the emergence of strong competitors, particularly Japan and Germany. Many analysts believe that a revitalized economic sector rather than military power holds the key to America's future position in international affairs.

Major Concepts

cold war	internationalism
containment	isolationism
détente	military-industrial complex
deterrence	multilateralism
free trade	multinational corporations
insurgency	protectionism

Suggested Readings

Dallek, Robert. *The American Style of Foreign Policy: Cultural Politics and Foreign Affairs.* New York: Oxford University Press, 1990. A critical assessment of the forces that have shaped American foreign policy in the twentieth century.

Jervis, Robert. *The Illogic of American Nuclear Strategy.* Ithaca, N.Y.: Cornell University Press, 1984. A critical view of U.S. nuclear policy.

Karnow, Stanley. *Vietnam: A History.* New York: Penguin, 1983. A thorough history of American involvement in Vietnam.

Keohane, Robert O., and Joseph S. Nye. *Power and Interdependence: World Politics in Transition.* Boston: Little, Brown, 1977. A penetrating analysis of the effects of global interdependence on U.S. power.

Koistinen, Paul A. *The Military-Industrial Complex.* New York: Praeger, 1980. An analysis of the military-industrial complex and its effect on defense spending and policy.

Oye, Kenneth A., Robert J. Lieber, and Donald Rothchild. *Eagle in a New World: American Grand Strategy in the Post–Cold War Era.* New York: HarperCollins, 1992. A collection of essays on the choices the United States faces now that the cold war has ended.

Quester, George H. *The Future of Nuclear Deterrence.* Lexington, Mass.: Lexington Books, 1986. A forward look at nuclear strategy.

Vernon, Raymond. *Storm over the Multinationals.* Cambridge, Mass.: Harvard University Press, 1977. An analysis of the international political influence of global corporations.

Yergin, Daniel. *Shattered Peace: The Origins of the Cold War and the National Security State.* Boston: Houghton Mifflin, 1977. A study of the origins, policies, and effects of the cold war between the United States and the USSR.

Is the United States Past Its Peak as an Economic and Military Power?

STEPHEN D. KRASNER

The United States has not yet adjusted to its new, more vulnerable international position.

At the end of World War II the United States was the most powerful country in the world. In fact, it was the most powerful state that had ever existed in the 300-year history of the modern international system. It was the only country that possessed nuclear weapons. Its gross national product was three times that of the Soviet Union and six times that of the United Kingdom, the next most economically productive nation in the noncommunist world. American industries held the commanding heights in high-technology industries. The United States was a net exporter of petroleum.

These extraordinary resources made it possible for American leaders to adopt very ambitious foreign policies. The United States created a system of alliances designed to contain the Soviet Union's expansionism. America fought bloody wars in Korea and Vietnam, countries that had few economic resources and were of little strategic importance. Large numbers of American troops were more or less permanently garrisoned in Western Europe and Japan. Defeats, especially the communist victory in China, were attributed to internal betrayal, not to any limitations of American power.

In the past two decades, however, American power has declined, in some areas dramatically. The gross national product of the United States is now only about 40 percent larger than that of Japan, which has half our population and few natural resources. Germany and Japan export more manufactured products than does the United States. The Soviet Union has achieved parity in nuclear weapons. Japan has challenged America's supremacy in high-technology industries. The United States has been a net importer of petroleum since 1970. Even though the United States remains very powerful, it can no longer consider itself able either to control the international environment or to extricate itself from it.

The United States has not yet adjusted to its new, more vulnerable international position. Even crushing setbacks, most notably the loss of the Vietnam war and the quadrupling of oil prices in the 1970s (which could have been prevented if the United States had had surplus productive capacity), have not prompted a fundamental reassessment of American policies. Commitments that were made forty years ago have not been radically changed. A share of the American army is still dedicated to the defense of western Europe, even though western Europe's gross national product is now higher than that of the United States. American leaders continue to treat trade and financial relations with Japan as purely an economic issue, rather than a matter of national power, except in some rare instances where American defense capabilities are directly affected by Japanese control of specific technologies. The stability of the American economy is now hostage to the public and private foreign-investment decisions made in Japan, because neither the American people nor American leaders have been willing to adopt fiscal policies that would close the budget and trade deficits. Hard choices are ahead for Americans, but our attitudes, our history, and our institutions are not particularly well suited to make them.

Stephen D. Krasner is Chair of the Department of Political Science at Stanford University. He is the author of Structural Conflicts: The Third World Against Global Liberalism.

BRUCE RUSSETT

The consolidation of democracy and economic prosperity in the industrialized countries represents a triumph of American hopes and efforts.

The group of economically advanced democracies, which the United States led and nurtured as an alliance throughout the cold war, is still rising in power and influence. As a result, the basic interests of the United States and the values that Americans cherish are more secure than ever. The cold war is over—the West has won.

Immediately after World War II the United States was the world's dominant military and economic power. Europe and Japan were devastated and economically exhausted; the Soviet Union was victorious and had vast new territories under its control, but it too was devastated by the war and remained technologically backward. Against this low point, subsequent American power would necessarily look diminished as the war-torn economies recovered. Just as important, the United States *chose* to help many of its wartime allies and enemies rebuild, thereby hastening its own relative decline from its temporary solitary splendor.

In so choosing, American leaders acted in the true long-term interests of the country. The United States needed strong allies to help contain the perceived threat from Soviet communism. It also needed a prosperous world economy that could serve as both a market for American goods and a source of competitors to supply American markets and keep American producers on their toes. American policy sought these ends, and achieved them. The consolidation of democracy and economic prosperity in the industrialized countries represents a triumph of American hopes and

efforts. So too does the peaceful reunification of Germany.

Communism, by contrast, has been a total political and economic failure—in eastern Europe and the former Soviet Union, in the Third World, and even in China. China's economy prospered only after it became more open to the West and began to abandon socialist ownership and central planning. Other communist economies have stagnated and utterly collapsed. Eastern European states have adopted free markets, and the former Soviet Union (in whatever political form may emerge) is rapidly following. Some of these states have also turned to democracy. Even noncommunist Third World countries have moved away from state control of the economy and from authoritarian political rule. After decades of military dictatorship, many Asian and Latin American countries have returned to democratic government.

Democracy and free-market capitalism are central American values; they are what the cold war was all about. As these values have become entrenched around the world, American security has increased. During the cold war American military power seemed roughly in balance with that of the Soviet Union. The nuclear weaponry of the republics of the former Soviet Union remains in rough balance, but otherwise their military power is vastly diminished. Their former allies in eastern Europe have broken away. As the UN-approved action against Iraq showed, only the United States now has the military power to be effective around the globe.

It is important that the United States not abuse its power as the dominant country in the international system. Cooperation with other powers, and with the UN, is essential to maintain international support and to avoid overreach. Moreover, the United States must improve its technological competitiveness, raise its savings and investment, and shift its economy away from military activities to the global developmental and environmental needs of peacetime. It now can do so in a world that is basically the one that the leaders of postwar America hoped would come into being.

Bruce M. Russett is Dean Acheson Professor of International Relations and Political Science at Yale University. He is the author of Controlling the Sword: The Democratic Governance of National Security.

CONCLUSION: RENEWING AMERICA'S IDEALS

Out of the experiences and ideas of many people in many places in the course of centuries, there has come a great deal of agreement about what democracy is, but nobody has a monopoly of it and the last word has not been spoken.

E. E. Schattschneider[1]

For nearly sixty years, the Gallup poll has regularly asked Americans about their country and its government. For the first few decades, Americans had an optimistic outlook. They were worried about the global threat of totalitarianism, but they felt good about their own country, its future, and the strength of its political institutions. By the late 1960s, however, the Gallup poll was indicating that Americans were growing somewhat disillusioned with their government. During the 1970s, this dissatisfaction with government intensified. Americans' outlook brightened for a few years in the mid-1980s, but then headed downward again. By 1992, less than a third of the Gallup respondents said that they were satisfied with the direction their country was taking.

This decline of confidence has roots in many aspects of American life, but government is the chief culprit in many people's minds. Government is expected to provide peace abroad, a healthy economy, strong systems of health and education, security for the elderly, a clean environment, racial progress, safe streets. In the late 1960s, people began to question whether government was fulfilling its responsibilities adequately. The scope of government kept increasing, but the performance of government was not keeping pace. More was becoming less.

1. E. E. Schattschneider, *Two Hundred Million Americans in Search of a Government* (New York: Holt, Rinehart and Winston, 1969), 42.

The roots of this situation are found in the nature of modern government. One feature of government today is its complexity. Social, economic, and technological change have increased and complicated the relationships between people, organizations, and the natural world in which they operate. The complexity of government has risen proportionally. Public policy issues today can have so many dimensions and so many consequences, some of which are not recognized until years after the fact, that they almost defy resolution. Policymakers often have to struggle just to understand the nature of a problem, let alone develop a sensible policy response. Scores of communities have spent a decade or more trying to find environmentally and financially acceptable ways to dispose of their garbage but have not yet been able to do so. And waste management is probably one of the simpler problems of modern life. Consider poverty in the inner city or competitiveness in the global marketplace. Who has the final answers to problems such as these?

A second characteristic of modern government is its bigness. The scope of public policy is almost beyond imagination. To one degree or another, government has its hand in nearly every aspect of Americans' lives. There are thousands of public policies, nearly all of which contribute positively to society. The sad fact, however, is that no nation, no matter how rich or efficient, has enough resources to do all that is required of it. Hard choices are everywhere. For example, although everyone would like to stop acid rain and the greenhouse effect, which are creating environmental havoc, no one wants to shut down the industries and scrap the automobiles that are the main causes of the problem.

Complexity and bigness have made the work of government exceedingly difficult. Complexity increases both the cost of the search for policy solutions and the probability that policy actions will not turn out as expected. For its part, bigness dilutes the resources of society, forcing trade-offs among goals that all agree are worthwhile. A result is that government does not perform to the level of the public's expectations. Americans often complain that their leaders are not trying hard enough or are not competent enough when, in fact, their leaders are confronted by bewildering and costly choices. Nearly everyone agrees, for example, that the nation's schools must be revitalized if the United States is to compete effectively in the global economy of today; but there is no agreement on what changes must be made, how long the reforms will take, or whether the United States can afford to remake its schools.

In a word, a problem of modern government is "overload." As more and more is expected of government, it becomes less and less capable of performing as expected. This situation poses extraordinary challenges for America's leaders, its people, and its political ideals.

The Challenge of Leadership

Modern leaders need help, lots of it, if they are to govern effectively. Help is available, particularly from the bureaucrats who staff executive agencies and the groups that lobby government. They are storehouses of the information and expertise that are essential components of effective policymaking in the modern age. Government simply could not do its work properly without the specialized contributions of groups and bureaucratic agencies. Yet their help comes at a stiff price: their overriding goal is to further their own narrow interests, not the broad public interest (see Chapters 13–14 and 20–21).

Of course, special interests and the general interest have always been somewhat at odds. The U.S. Constitution's elaborate system of checks and balances was designed to prevent a factional interest from gaining all power and using it to the detriment of other interests and the community as a whole. In *Federalist* No. 51, James Madison explained the necessity of constitutional safeguards against the selfish and potentially tyrannical tendencies of special interests: "In framing a government to be administered by men over men, the great difficulty lies in this: you must first enable the government to control the governed; and in the next place oblige it to control itself." The Framers' system has served its purpose well (see Chapters 2, 3, 5, and 7). In fact, for a long period in U.S. history, constitutional checks and balances were nearly an unqualified benefit. They kept government at bay during the nation's early years, thereby simultaneously preserving individual liberty and promoting social and economic progress and stability (see Chapter 6).

The nation's system of checks and balances is more problematic today. Madison's solution to the problem of factions has itself become a problem. There is a severe tension between the extreme pluralism of contemporary society and a constitutional framework designed primarily to protect against majority tyranny. The growing complexity of society is reflected in the growing number of interest groups, which, as they have multiplied, have also narrowed. Most groups concentrate their demands on a small area of public policy. The same system of checks and balances that was designed to frustrate a majority faction has made it relatively easy for these narrow interests to achieve their specialized goals. The support of a relatively few well-placed policymakers is often all the help that they need (see Chapters 10, 14, 17, and 21). The political consultant Eddie Mahe has described the situation as "the tribalization of politics," saying that it represents the triumph of "the special interest over the general interest."[2]

The nation's system of checks and balances is also a cause of divided government and the lack of accountability that is a major characteristic of divided government. Since the late 1960s the Republicans have dominated the White House and the Democrats have dominated Congress, and each side has blamed the other when policy has gone haywire. The prime example in recent years has been the national debt, which has quadrupled since 1980 to more than $4 trillion. At no time have the president and Congress made an uncompromising effort to reverse the flow of red ink. Neither the executive nor the legislative branch has been willing to scale down its spending demands significantly, and neither side has been willing to accept responsibility for a tax increase. The best that policymakers have so far been able to do was the Gramm-Rudman-Hollings Act of 1985, which commits the federal government to achieve a balanced annual budget by the mid-1990s. The commitment appears to be a hollow one. The budget for fiscal year 1993 reflected a deficit of $400 billion, the largest in the country's history.

---

2. Quoted in "Problems of Governance," A Report to the Ford Foundation, The Maxwell School of Citizenship, Syracuse University, Syracuse, New York, December, 1991, 25.

The Power of Personalized Leadership

In late spring of 1989, millions of students and workers in China began to demand democratic reforms. Beginning with the Tiananmen Square massacre, the country's hard-line leaders used the army and the courts in a brutal suppression of the democracy movement. The goal of the student protesters was summarized in one of their sayings, that it was better to be ruled by ten devils who had to operate within a system of democratic checks and balances than to be ruled by one mandarin, however enlightened he might be in a particular instance. Does the Chinese episode have a lesson to teach Americans? In particular, are there inherent dangers posed by the recent shift in the United States from an institutionalized system of leadership to a more personalized form of leadership?

In the United States, leadership tends to be reactive. Rarely are problems addressed in their early stages. The separation of power within the system makes it difficult in most instances for any leader or set of leaders to muster widespread support for a major policy until a general sense of urgency exists. Separate interests and institutions are not inclined to give up their individual agendas until they are nearly forced by circumstances to do so. Even then, there is no guarantee that decisive leadership will emerge. Policy deadlock and delay are commonplace. A case in point is welfare reform. Although policymakers had come to realize by the late 1960s that the welfare system was in need of a thorough revamping, two decades went by without any basic change because of conflict among various groups and among governing institutions. In one instance, welfare reform had the firm backing of a Republican president and a Democratic-controlled House of Representatives but was blocked by an irresolvable dispute between Senate liberals and conservatives. When a comprehensive welfare bill was attempted again nineteen years later, in 1988, the legislation almost met a similar fate. At one point in the legislative process the proposed law appeared to be dead; several weeks of intense negotiation and compromise were necessary in order to save it.

The shape of America's future will depend substantially on the ability of its leaders to confront the difficult policy issues facing the country. Of all the marks of genuine leadership, none is more crucial than the courage to build public support for burdensome policies—those that require people to sacrifice their short-term and special interests to the long-term and general interest. Such leadership is usually in short supply, and recent years have been no exception. No national emergency, such as a catastrophic war or great depression, forced America's leaders to overspend federal revenues by thousands of billions of dollars in recent years. They did so willfully, bending to immediate pressures and passing on to future generations the burden of the debt.

Such actions are fostered by an ascendant form of candidate-centered politics that serves the personal power and reelection needs of public officials at the expense of their collective accountability and the effectiveness of the institutions within which they operate (see Chapters 12, 16, and 18). The writers of the Constitution warned that leadership wrenched from an institutional context cannot serve the public's true interest, and the axiom is as valid today as it was 200 years ago. A truer measure of the quality of American leadership than the fact that more than 90 percent of officeholders win reelection time after time is the condition of the institutions that, over the long run, give reason and force to public policy.

With their individualistic tradition, Americans have difficulty thinking of institutions rather than a single person exercising leadership. This perspective is the reason that Americans assign the president too much credit when things go well and too much blame when things go badly. This view may be understandable, but it cannot be allowed to determine institutional arrangements. The problem of modern government is not of electing a president big enough for the job but of forging effective instruments of collective leadership and purpose. Historically, political parties have been this instrument. Parties remain strong elsewhere, but not here. It remains to be seen for how long and at what price the United States, alone among western democracies, will persist in the illusion that a leadership system based on political entrepreneurs is preferable to one based on political parties (see Chapters 4, 10–12, 16–19).

The Challenge of Democracy

The scope and complexity of modern government are as much a challenge to the public as they are to leaders. Since the time of Aristotle, the principal objection to democracy has been that the people are prone to rash judgments, that self-government devolves inexorably into majority tyranny. The more appropriate objection today may be that the people are not capable of any public judgment at all—that democracy devolves into formlessness. The complex nature of contemporary issues and their great number combine with the sheer size of the public and the relative insignificance of any one of its members to discourage civic involvement. The problem is not that Americans are indifferent to how they are governed. The problem is that they are too diverse in their ways of life and too pressed for time to recognize easily their common interests and act upon them (see Chapters 8 and 9).

They also live in a world that is not easily scaled down to the level of their daily lives. Proposals for the decentralization of government have come from both the right and the left, but decentralization is neither easily nor fully attainable. Not all problems can be solved by city councils or neighborhood groups. As the political scientist Benjamin Barber recently observed, "There's no question that at the local level democracy works naturally and works well, but it is also the case that we live in a world of institutions and problems that are not only national but also international and interdependent."[3]

A great deal of misplaced romanticism surrounds the concept of democracy. It is not realistic to think that democracy requires individuals to take an active role in all decisions that affect them. Any society of substantial size requires the delegation of broad power and responsibility to a small set of leaders. Yet true democracy requires that individuals be something more than subjects of government and followers of leaders. True democracy requires that citizens have the opportunity to involve themselves in significant ways in public affairs.

Political participation is at a relatively low ebb today. Barely half of all adults bother to vote in a presidential election, and even fewer turn out for other elections; furthermore, those who vote do so as much for reasons of personal habit as out of concern for public policy (see Chapter 9). As for public debate that engages a significant proportion of the citizenry in an active and ongoing way, there is almost none. The closest that most people come to taking part in debate over public policy is watching or reading the news in the privacy of their homes.

True citizenship is "public" rather than "private" in nature. The community, not the individual, is the realm of citizenry. Although individualism can heighten self-esteem and personal security, and in this way strengthen the basis of community, individualism can also, as Tocqueville recognized as early as the 1830s, undermine people's sense of community by degenerating into outright selfishness (see Chapter 6). In addition to its ability to drive people ever deeper into their private affairs, individualism can foster a form of politics in which the chief goal is narrow gain, the public is seen merely in terms of the special interests within it, and the relative strength of the contending interests is regarded as a just basis for public policy (see Chapters 9 and 14).

Thus the sharp rise in interest-group activity since the 1960s is not necessarily

3. Ibid., 27.

an indication of deepening democracy. Although many lobbying groups seek policies that can serve the general interest and actively engage their members in the pursuit of these goals, many others do not. Group membership today is often of the mail-order variety: participation consists of sending money in response to a letter prepared by computer. Moreover, most groups are self-seeking: they aim to promote the narrow interests of their member individuals or firms. Participation in lobbying groups is an essential part of the representational process, but it is not the same thing as active citizenship. There is no genuine sense of "the public" in political participation that is dedicated to the furthering of special interests (see Chapter 14).

Lobbying groups also highlight the gap in the participation rates of rich and poor. Interest-group activity has traditionally been dominated by persons of higher economic status. In recent years there has been a relative decline in the number of groups, such as labor unions, that enroll significant numbers of working-class people, and a relative as well as an absolute increase in the number of groups with a middle-class membership (see Chapter 13). Increasingly, the vote is also dominated by persons with higher levels of income and education; the decline in turnout in recent decades is attributable largely to a sharp drop in participation by those Americans who are in the lowest categories of income and education (see Chapter 9).

Participation differences are part of a widening gap between the poor and the rest of America (see Chapters 24–26). Although critics of American society with a Marxist or elitist perspective have usually concentrated their attention on the richest 1 or 2 percent of the U.S. population, Karl Marx's collaborator, Friedrich Engels, chose to focus on those at the low end. A century ago, Engels claimed that the most remarkable feature of American society was the optimism and progress of its lower-middle and working classes; unlike their counterparts in other industrialized societies, they were not mired in poverty or trapped in their position. As a result, he concluded, they had no reason for a high degree of class antagonism.

However, in recent years, the position of less affluent Americans has deteriorated in relation to the position of those who are better off. The 1980s saw a widening of the gap between the richest and the poorest Americans. The rate of inflation in the 1980s exceeded the average wage increase among Americans in the bottom fifth income bracket and was only slightly less than the average wage increase among middle-income persons. The Americans who made real progress were those who were already at the top of the income ladder; moreover, the richer they were, the more their income increased during the 1980s.[4]

These disparities are attributable in part to public policy. Changes in the tax laws in the 1980s encouraged American business to engage in a leveraged buyout spree that resulted in the flow of capital into mergers and takeovers rather than new plants and equipment. One aspect of this trend was a decrease in the number of manufacturing jobs and an increase in service jobs, which generally pay much less. The pattern was a historical first; always in the past, newer jobs had paid more than older ones. To make matters worse, the tax

---

4. Internal Revenue Service figures, cited in Donald L. Barlett and James B. Steele, "Rules of the Game Rigged to Favor Rich and Influential," *Syracuse Herald American*, January 5, 1992, E4.

codes were changed to shift the tax burden downward. In both absolute and relative terms, more affluent individuals paid lower taxes than the less affluent. The writer Studs Terkel remarked that the politics of the 1980s taught Americans that "it is good to have sharp elbows."[5]

Public policy is not the only, or even the most important, reason for the declining fortunes of many Americans. Technological and scientific changes threaten to make a permanent underclass of those who cannot meet society's new educational, social, and economic demands (see Chapters 24 and 26). There can be no effective citizenship for individuals who have lost the ability to direct their own lives.

Richard Harwood's study for the Kettering Foundation found that Americans feel politically powerless rather than apathetic. They believe that public policy is important, but they feel that the issues have become so intricate that they cannot understand them and so dominated by special interests that they cannot influence them. They are at a loss to know how to exert influence on the political process, which seems to them to take little notice of their concerns.[6]

The challenge of democracy today, as always, is a matter not of a spontaneous outpouring of civic energy by the masses, but of conditions conducive to civic interest and involvement (see Chapters 4, 5, and 7–15). When politics takes on the appearance of a game played among entrepreneurial leaders and the policy process seems designed for the benefit of special interests, democracy will not flourish at any level of society. Indeed, democracy will take on a false character: it will appear to be an issue of what is good for the individual rather than the larger community. A strengthening of democracy can come through attention to those things that, 200 years ago, Thomas Jefferson identified as the proper foundation of public life: sound education, a general prosperity, meaningful work, personal liberty, exemplary leadership, a free and vigorous press, strong face-to-face institutions, a broad sharing of political power, and social tolerance. These are demanding requirements, but democracy is not a trivial pursuit. As the ancient Greeks first recognized, democracy is nothing less than a way of life.

The Challenge of Ideals

For more than 200 years, Americans have been guided by the same set of ideals: liberty, equality, self-government, individualism, diversity, and unity (see Chapter 1). These ideals have challenged each generation, but today, as a result of the complexity and scale of modern government, the challenge has new dimensions.

A crucial difference is that it is no longer so obvious what can be done to achieve a fuller realization of America's traditional ideals. In the past, the question in many cases was not so much what could be done as when and at what cost it would be accomplished. Thus, the ink was barely dry on the Constitution before advocates of popular government began their efforts to extend suffrage and to broaden the range of offices filled by popular election

> ★ ANALYZE THE ISSUE
>
> **The Expansion of Citizenship Responsibility**
> Benjamin Barber argues in *Strong Democracy* that Americans will never truly control their government as long as most of them confine their political participation to voting. Barber argues that citizens must be given added responsibility, including the right to make mistakes. Do you agree with Barber? At the national level, what responsibilities, other than voting, should citizens be given? Can they exercise these responsibilities effectively? Are they likely to exercise them at all, if given the opportunity?

5. Quoted in "Problems of Governance," 16.
6. Ibid., 26.

(see Chapters 4, 9, and 18). This campaign took 175 years; not until 1965, with the passage of the Voting Rights Act, was it truthful to say that the vote belonged to all Americans (see Chapter 7). Like other developments, such as judicial protection of civil liberties from infringement by the state governments (see Chapter 5), the struggle to extend suffrage met strong resistance but could always claim moral superiority: How could it truly be proclaimed that Americans were a self-governing people when whole groups of them were not allowed to participate in the election of their leaders?

Today it is less clear what might be done to advance America's principles. Consider, for example, the question of self-government. At present the United States holds more public elections than any other country, is the only country in which the voters regularly choose party nominees through primary elections, and has laws and procedures that safeguard the right to vote of those who want to exercise it. In view of all this, the question of self-government in America might be thought to be more or less settled. The reality, however, is that self-government is an increasingly difficult challenge, because modern America is more than a representative democracy: it is also a bureaucratic society, a corporate society, a mass-communication society, a scientific-technological society, and more.[7]

Each of these dimensions of contemporary America poses special problems for the practice of self-government. More elections and more voters are not the answer, for example, to the problem of popular control of bureaucratic agencies. The individuals who are elected by the people to represent them in Washington have little real power to redirect federal agencies and programs. What, then, is the answer? The fact is, no one is quite sure. There is agreement on the need to make the bureaucracy more accountable to the people it serves, but there is no agreement on the best way to accomplish this.

The complexity and large scale of modern government have also challenged America's ideals by intensifying the conflicts between them. America's principles have never been fully reconcilable with one another. There are, for example, inherent tensions between the ideal of self-government, which implies that the view of the many should prevail over the opinion of the few, and the ideal of liberty, which implies that individuals have rights and interests that must be preserved. Such tensions were formerly eased by the simplicity of society and government. Thus, during the whole of the nineteenth century there was no reason to abridge personal liberty because of threats from foreign powers (see Chapter 5). However, as society has become increasingly interdependent and government increasingly intrusive, conflicts among America's ideals have grown exponentially. For example, each of the many extensions of individual rights in recent years has narrowed the realm of self-government. It is impossible today to set aside an area of individual discretion—that is, to grant or extend a right—without taking power away from the majority. This fact does not necessarily diminish a claim to a particular right, but it does put the claim in perspective: no right is granted without cost to other values. The axiom applies generally to each and all of America's traditional values.

Of course, politics is not simply a matter of values and ideals. As we noted in Chapter 1, the stakes in political conflict are so high that no ideal has progressed

7. David Mathews, "We, the People . . . ," *National Forum* 50 (Fall 1983): 65.

without a struggle. Women and minority groups, for example, have made significant gains in recent decades, but not because more powerful groups handed them benefits. They had to fight for everything they have received. The debate over affirmative action programs persists despite clear evidence that women and minority-group members are far more likely to encounter employment discrimination than are white men—a reminder that the historical tendency to cling to power and privilege is still in place.

The current challenges to the fuller realization of America's ideals will have to be met under conditions that, in historical perspective, are unfavorable. The advancement of principles such as liberty, equality, and self-government requires that people look beyond their selfish and immediate concerns to the universal and enduring benefits of a society in which power and opportunity are shared by all, not hoarded by those who already possess most of it (see Chapters 1, 4, 6, and 7). This outlook is fostered when people believe that their progress will not be greatly retarded by the progress of others.

In the past, Americans had special advantages that made it easier for them to believe that collective progress was possible. The first of these advantages was the country's open frontier—what the nineteenth-century historian Frederick Jackson Turner called the "Great West."[8] As long as there was abundant cheap land and a shortage of labor in America, there was unbridled opportunity. The second advantage was a result of the timing of America's Industrial Revolution. The industrial age began in the late 1700s in England and spread to western Europe before its major impact was felt in the United States. The delay did not substantially affect prosperity in the United States, because the country was still in the process of westward expansion. However, because of its later start and abundant natural resources, the United States, once industrialization did take firm hold, soon had the most modern and productive industrial sector in the world. The final advantage was provided by the Second World War, which left the industrial capacity of Europe and Japan in ruins. In 1946 the United States, which had emerged from the war with its industrial base intact, was producing more than a third of all goods and services in the world. The result was a level of affluence that no previous society in history had enjoyed.

Since the 1970s, the United States has had to compete on a more nearly equal basis with other highly developed countries. It no longer enjoys an extraordinary advantage, and Americans have struggled economically as they have attempted to adjust to the change (see Chapters 24 and 26). The median family income rose by 89 percent in the twenty years between 1950 and 1970 but by only 13 percent in the twenty-year period from 1970 to 1990.[9]

Widening prosperity lets society avoid making agonizing choices. With the end of the era of fast economic growth in America, however, the future looks less promising than it used to. People now seem more ready to blame others for their problems. Sexual, racial, ethnic, generational, and income conflicts are getting stronger.

This situation is a severe challenge to America's ideals, but also a time when ideals are most needed. It has always been a formidable job to frame society's

★ ANALYZE THE ISSUE

A New Economic Challenge
Walter Lippman observed that the nineteenth century was a "spell of exceptionally fine weather." His observation was certainly true of the United States, which was able to pursue westward expansion and industrialization without much interference by foreign powers and with the benefit of greater natural wealth than any other nation. In the twentieth century, with Europe and Japan devastated by World War II, the United States accounted for more than a third of the global economy. Japan and western Europe have since recovered, however, and are now able to compete head-to-head with the United States. Some analysts say that America is failing to meet the challenge. Others say that the country is merely in a temporary slump. What is your view? What is the basis for your opinion?

---

8. Cited in Ralph Volney Harlow, *The Growth of the United States,* vol. 2 (New York: Holt, 1943), 134.
9. U.S. Bureau of the Census data, 1992.

problems in ways that people can understand and for which they will sacrifice. But societies need ideals. Theodore White said it as well as anyone: "Nations need dreams, goals they seek in common, within which the smaller dreams of individuals can guide their personal lives."[10] Without a governing vision people will lapse, as they have in recent years, into a narrow selfishness. Confronting a similar challenge 200 years ago, the writers of the Constitution plumbed America's ideals in search of a lasting and prosperous union. Today's Americans can do nothing less.

10. Quoted in "Problems of Governance," 15.

STATE AND LOCAL POLITICS

*B*efore there was an American union, there were the American states. When the Framers of the Constitution gathered in Philadelphia in the summer of 1787, they invented a new form of government—federalism—because the states would not consent to a union that required their elimination (see Chapter 2).

Of course, the establishment of the Union meant that the states would have to give up some of their independence. The states did not always do so willingly, as the Civil War and countless lesser disputes over federalism indicate. The cumulative effect of two centuries of federalism, however, has been a gradual diminution of state-to-state differences. In the twentieth century particularly, a "nationalization" of American politics has taken place. Extensions of national power have narrowed the limits within which states can operate:

- Federal regulation has been extended to cover nearly all aspects of business activity, including labor practices, environmental protection, and consumer affairs (see Chapters 2 and 24).
- The national government has established a vast system of social-welfare programs that, although administered primarily through states and localities, are funded and defined largely by Washington (see Chapters 6 and 25).
- Federal grants-in-aid are being used to encourage states and localities to adopt Washington-preferred programs, standards, and priorities in areas such as urban renewal, public education, and law enforcement (see Chapters 2 and 25).
- Federal authority has been used to order states and localities to eliminate government-sponsored discrimination and, in some areas, to create special opportunities for racial minorities and women (see Chapters 6 and 7).
- Federal authority has been exercised to require states to broaden individual rights of free expression and fair trial (see Chapters 5 and 23).

Despite these changes, the state political systems differ in many significant ways. Although Americans, as was indicated in Chapter 1, share a common political heritage that is built around principles such as liberty, equality, and self-government, distinctive regional subcultures persist. These subcultures reflect differences in ethnic settlement patterns, historical episodes, economic conditions, partisan competition, and other influences.

The states in the northern tier of the nation have what the political scientist Daniel Elazar describes as a **moralistic subculture**.[1] This subculture is characterized by an emphasis on "good government" (the public interest), "clean government" (honesty), and "civic government" (public participation). The states that share this subculture were populated primarily by northern Europeans, including the English, Germans, and Scandinavians. Minnesota is an example of a moralistic state; Minnesota has one of the highest rates of voter turnout in the country, one of the lowest rates of political corruption, and a high level of public services, including some of the nation's best public schools.

The middle part of the United States, from Massachusetts to Maryland and then westward through Illinois and Missouri to southwestern states such as Arizona, has an **individualistic subculture.** This subculture is oriented toward private life and economic gain, and politics is largely an extension of this perspective. Political conflict is rough and tumble, and corruption is tolerated if not condoned. Political parties and public office are as much instruments of personal power and gain as instruments of the public interest. Illinois is an example of an individualistic state. The Chicago Democratic party organization was the last of the great political machines in America, and at times it had as much interest in securing patronage as it did in promoting sound government.

A **traditionalistic subculture,** in Elazar's terms, typifies the states of the old Confederacy and a few states bordering on it, such as West Virginia. This subculture reflects the stratified, plantation society out of which it grew: it is conservative in its focus and elitist in its leadership. The politics of a traditionalistic state is likely to be dominated by a small number of prominent leaders, many of whom have gained power through family ties. Government is likely to be a topic of considerable interest in a traditionalistic state, but not because government is activist. In fact, traditionalists prefer a government that reinforces the existing power structure. Until the last decade, when the influence of suburban Washington brought political change to Virginia, it epitomized the traditionalistic subculture. For years, Virginia politics was controlled by elite families, such as the Byrds, who aimed to preserve the racial, social, and economic inequality that had defined Virginia society since the colonial period.

The purpose of this appendix is to describe more fully the American states and the localities that constitute them. The great number of state and local governments, and the variety they exhibit, make difficult an easy summary of what they are all about. Yet there are some general patterns; it is these patterns on which this appendix concentrates. It concludes with a comparison of the states, which will indicate major factors behind differences in their politics and policies. The main points of discussion in this appendix are the following:

★ *All states apply the constitutional principle of separation of powers, but the states otherwise differ from one another, and from the federal government, in the way in which they structure their governments.* The use of elections as a means of choosing officials of all types, including judges and lesser executives (for example, state treasurer), is particularly widespread.

★ *Local governments are not sovereign; they are chartered by their state government, which sets the limits of their power.* Of the units of local government (county, municipality, school district, and special district), the basic unit is the municipality. A municipality may be governed in one of four ways—the strong mayor–council, weak mayor–council, commission, or city manager system.

★ *States and localities have primary responsibility for most of the policies, such as public education, that directly touch Americans' daily lives.* The nature of these policies is affected by the wealth of the state and locality, and also by their political culture, party system, and group system.

States and Localities in the Constitutional System

The Constitution of the United States contains provisions that forbid the states from interfering with the lawful exercise of national authority, and the states are required by the Constitution to provide their citizens with a "republican" form of government. The Constitution also guarantees that each state will have equal representation in the U.S. Senate. Nevertheless, the Constitution was intended primarily to define national power and national institutions and does not say very much about the states or their powers.

In fact, the Framers of the Constitution did not believe it was necessary to define the powers of the states. They held that the Constitution implied that the states held all legitimate governing powers that had not been granted to the national government. This situation was unsettling to states'-rights advocates, who insisted upon a constitutional amendment—the Tenth—which reserves for the states those powers not delegated to the national government (see Chapter 2).

The states have their own constitutions, which vary greatly in length. On average, they are roughly four times the length of the U.S. Constitution. Vermont is the only state whose constitution is shorter than the nation's. Until it was replaced in 1974, Louisiana's constitution was by far the longest and most detailed. At 250,000 words, it was nearly 30 times the length of the U.S. Constitution. The longest state constitution still in effect today is Alabama's, which has approximately 175,000 words and more than 500 amendments.

State constitutions contain many provisions that more properly belong in statutes than in a constitution. Enterprising state legislators have often preferred to embed their favorite policies in constitutional amendments, which are more likely to endure than ordinary laws. For example, many of the state constitutions include benefits for special-interest groups, such as veterans, farmers, and businesses. Minnesota's constitution was amended in the early 1970s to permit the state to give each Vietnam veteran from the state a $600 bonus. California's constitution is filled with all sorts of tax provisions, which, among other things, limit the types and amount of taxation.

Most constitutional scholars would agree that the length of state constitutions is a drawback. As we indicated in Chapter 2, the U.S. Constitution is a sparsely worded document, which has enabled succeeding generations to adapt it to their changing needs. Not so with many of the state constitutions. They are so loaded down with narrow and detailed provisions that they deny policymakers the flexibility to respond effectively to change. The constitutional provisions that bestow benefits on interest groups, for example, do more than convey a special status on a particular group; they also bind the subsequent decisions of policymakers.[2]

Each state's constitution is its supreme law, except where valid national law applies. By the same token, local laws (called ordinances) cannot legitimately conflict with a state's constitution. Local governments are not sovereign. Their authority derives from the state's. The century-old general principle that describes the relationship between state power and localities is called **Dillon's rule**.[3] It holds that local governments are creatures of their state, which in theory even has the power to abolish them. The forced consolidation of school districts and the forced merger of a smaller town with a larger adjoining one are dramatic examples of a state's power over its local units. The most important aspect of Dillon's rule is that local governments must act within constraints placed on them by the state. The state's reach extends even to the issue of whether a local unit of government will provide a particular service. The state of Wisconsin, for example, requires each of its cities to have a solid-waste disposal facility.

States differ markedly in the degree of freedom they grant their local units. The states that grant the highest degree of autonomy to local units, and those that grant the least, are found in all regions of the country. For example, Oregon, North Carolina, and Connecticut rank high on local autonomy, while Idaho, Mississippi, and Massachusetts rank low.

The chief instrument by which a state governs its local units is the **charter.** No local government can exist without a charter, which is issued by the state and defines the limits within which a local unit must operate. By tradition, local charters are restrictive; they spell out in considerable detail what a local government can and cannot do. A typical charter, for example, specifies the types and limits of taxation that a local government may impose on its residents.

There are limits, however, to a state's ability to control its local units. A state government does not have the time, the money, or the staff to make all the decisions concerning its many local units. Nor can a state expect the same restrictions to work equally well for all local units. A charter that is suited to a city of a million inhabitants would probably not be suited to a village of several hundred people. Accordingly, all states give their local units some discretionary authority and make allowance for differences among them. In most cases, the charters for cities are different from those for towns, which in turn differ from those for villages.

Home rule is a device that is designed to give local governments more leeway in their policies. Home rule was first tried in 1875 in Missouri, and it allows a local government to design its own charter, subject to the laws and constitution of the state and also subject to veto by the state. The long-term trend in the states has been toward home rule and other means of granting localities a larger measure of independence.

State Political Structures

All states make use of the principle of checks and balances that underpins the national government (see Chapter 3). There is nothing in the Constitution of the United States that would prohibit a state from adopting a parliamentary form of government, but no state has tried it. The executive, legislature, and judiciary in each state are separate branches that share power. Each branch thus serves as a check on the power of the others.

THE EXECUTIVE BRANCH

Most states wrote their first constitutions during periods when mistrust of executive authority was high; consequently, they provided for relatively weak governors. The model still applies in some states, especially in the South and in New England. In these states, governors are limited in their powers or in the length of their term. North Carolina's governor, for example, does not have the power to veto legislation. The governor of Vermont is elected for a term of only two years. Kentucky's 1891 constitution limits its governor to a single four-year term.

The organization of the executive branch in many states reflects the influence of the Progressives and other popularly based movements. In a number of states, the voters choose one or more of the following executive officials: education commissioner, agriculture commissioner, and public utilities commissioner. Moreover, more than half the states hold separate elections for the offices of secretary of state, attorney general, and treasurer. In other words, the executive office in most states, unlike the presidency, is not unified. The governor is the chief executive but shares executive power with other officials, who have separate electoral bases and who, in some cases, are of the opposite party. In only two states, Maine and New Jersey, is the governor, like the president at the national level, the sole chief executive.

Although the governorship is not a very powerful office in most states, governors have gained power in recent decades.[4] Just as the complexity of modern government has led to an increase in presidential authority (see Chapter 18), it has contributed to an increase in the authority of governors. The initiation of the state budget now resides with the legislature or an independent board rather than the governor in only a handful of states. In 43 states, the governor even has a line-item veto, which allows the option of rejecting a part of an appropriations bill without voiding the whole act. The president of the United States does not have this power.

Of the executive officials other than governor, the most powerful is the attorney general, who is elected to the post in 43 states. The attorney general is the state's chief legal officer and sets priorities for legal action. An attorney general might decide, for example, to concentrate the state's legal resources on environmental protection or investigations of alleged political corruption. The office of attorney general has often been a stepping stone to a governorship or a seat in the U.S. Senate.

THE LEGISLATIVE BRANCH

Like the U.S. Congress, state legislatures are bicameral except in the case of Nebraska's, which is unicameral. In the large majority of states, the two chambers are called the house and the senate.

Like Congress, state legislatures have within their authority the most impressive array of constitutional powers that a democracy can bestow. The legislatures make the laws, appropriate the money, define the structure of the executive and the judiciary, oversee the operations of the other branches, and represent the people. These powers are typically carried out within an organizational structure similar to that of Congress (see Chapter 16). The top leadership in state legislatures are the party leaders, but most of the work is carried out in committees.

For a long period, state legislatures were synonymous with malapportionment. Cities were grossly underrepresented because rural legislators, who had controlled the state legislatures since the days when the United States was a farming nation, refused to reapportion them. Vermont was the extreme case. From 1793 to the 1960s, its legislative distribution did not change. In the state's lower house, each village, town, or city had one representative, regardless of population. Thus, the city of Burlington had exactly the same voting power as the smallest village in the state. Not surprisingly, the policy needs of America's cities were neglected by state legislatures, while the interests of farmers and rural communities were quite well served.

The situation changed abruptly in the early 1960s when the Supreme Court of the United States declared that state legislatures must represent people rather than communities or areas.[5] The "one person, one vote" method of apportioning state legislatures immediately gave a larger share of legislative seats to populated urban areas—although, ironically, the cities never got their full due. By the time the Supreme Court outlawed malapportionment in the 1960s, so many people had moved out of the central cities that the suburbs gained the most advantage from reapportionment. The suburbs, like the rural areas, are more conservative and more Republican than the cities; thus, there has never been a time when the concerns of cities have dominated the actions of state legislatures.

Until recently, most of the state legislatures were relatively unimposing institutions. They were in session only for short periods each year, were deficient in staff and information resources, and were vulnerable to powerful lobbying groups. Beginning in the 1960s, however, they began to meet for longer periods and to expand their staffs. Legislators' pay also increased significantly at this time. The increase was substantial enough in a few states, such as New York and California, to create professional legislators—individuals whose chief occupation is an elective position within a state legislature. New York provides the highest level of compensation; its legislators are paid nearly $60,000 a year in salary. Many of them also hold party or committee leadership positions, for which they receive supplementary allowances (nicknamed "lulus" because they are fixed amounts paid "in lieu of" reimbursement for actual expenses).

Most analysts have welcomed the change toward more professional state legislatures. The Advisory Commission on Intergovernmental Relations, an agency established by Congress, noted in one of its reports: "Today's state legislatures are more functional, accountable, independent, and representative, and are equipped with greater information handling capacity than their predecessors."[6]

Some states, however, have resisted the tendency toward longer sessions, larger staffs, and higher salaries. New Hampshire, Rhode Island, Alabama, Nebraska, and West Virginia are among the states that pay their legislators $10,000 a year or less. The term-limitation movement that is currently underway (see Chapter 4) could restore the "citizen legislature." California, Oklahoma, and Colorado led the move when their voters decided in 1990 to restrict the number of terms that state legislators could serve. Additional states adopted the policy in 1992. Supporters of term limitation argue that "amateur" legislators are more responsive to the public they serve than are long-term incumbents.

THE JUDICIAL BRANCH

As a consequence of America's federal system, as we indicated in Chapter 22, each state has its separate court system. Like the federal system, the state systems have trial courts at the bottom level and appellate courts at the top. About two-thirds of the states have two appellate levels, and the other third have only a single appellate court. Most of the less populated states have determined that they do not need a second appellate level.

The states vary in the way they organize and label their courts. Most of the states have district courts and a supreme court, but the states tend also to give some lower courts specialized titles and jurisdictions. Family courts, for example, settle such issues as divorce and child-custody disputes, and probate courts handle the disposition of the estates of people who have died. Below such specialized trial courts are less formal trial courts, such as magistrate courts and justice of the peace courts. They handle a variety of minor cases, such as traffic infractions, and usually do not use a jury. Jury trial is not a constitutional requirement of the states, nor do they have to follow the federal tradition of a 12-member jury or require a unanimous verdict when a jury is used.

States also vary in their methods of selecting judges. In about a fourth of the states, judges are appointed by the governor, but in most states, judgeships are elective offices. Several states use the Missouri Plan (so called because Missouri was the first state to use it), under which a judicial selection commission provides a short list of acceptable candidates from which the governor selects one; after a trial period of a year or more, the judge selected must be approved by the electorate in a yes-no vote in order to serve a longer term.

State courts are undeniably important. As we indicated in Chapter 22, there is a "federal court myth" that holds that the federal courts are the more significant component of the American judicial system. In fact, the state judiciary is the locus of most court action. Upwards of 95 percent of the nation's legal cases are decided in state courts (or local courts, which are agents of the states.) Moreover, nearly all cases that originate in state courts also end there; the federal courts never enter the picture. Of course, one federal court—the Supreme Court—is a silent partner of the state and local courts, requiring them to act within minimum standards of justice (for example, the prohibition of forced confessions).

Most states have made efforts in recent decades to raise the performance level of their court systems. Administrative and legal procedures have been changed, for example, to expedite the handling of cases. In the past, the pursuit of justice in many state courts was slow and procedurally arbitrary. There are still delays and procedural injustices, but they are less prevalent today as a result of federally imposed standards and state-initiated reforms, such as those that require law-enforcement officials to dismiss a case unless it is presented to a judge or grand jury within a specified period of time.

THE STATE ELECTORAL PROCESS

When the Framers wrote the U.S. Constitution, they allowed for only minimal popular participation. The House of Representatives was the only popularly elected institution and the only one with a short term of office, two years. The democratic spirit of the Revolution of 1776 was more apparent at the state level. Every state but South Carolina held an annual legislative election, and several states chose their governors through annual election by the people.

Today, the states hold elections less frequently, but they have stayed ahead of the federal government in their emphasis on elections as a means of popular influence and control. As was noted previously, most states elect their treasurer, attorney general, and secretary of state by popular ballot. Many states also choose their judges by direct election. No federal judges are chosen by this means.

Citizens as Legislators

State voters also get the opportunity to vote directly on issues of policy. In all states except Delaware, amendments to the state constitution require the approval of the electorate. In addition, more than a third of the states give popular majorities the power of the **initiative,** which allows citizens through signature petitions to place legislative measures on the ballot. If such a measure receives a majority vote, it becomes law, just as if it had been enacted by the state's legislature. A related measure is the **referendum,** which permits the legislature to submit proposals to the voters for approval or rejection. The initiative and referendum were introduced around 1900 as Progressive reforms. The Progressives also sought to protect the public from wayward state and local officials through the **recall,** in which citizens can petition for the removal from office of an elected official before the scheduled completion of his or her term. The state of Arizona would probably have recalled its governor, Evan Mecham, in 1987 had he not been impeached by the state legislature before the recall process could be completed.

Voter Registration and Turnout

Although the states have been electoral innovators, their history also includes attempts to restrict access to the ballot. The clearest example is that of southern states after the Civil War. The Fifteenth Amendment was ratified in 1870, prohibiting states from using race as the basis for denial of suffrage. Southern states responded with a number of devices that were designed to keep African-Americans from voting. Through poll taxes, the grandfather clause, whites-only primary elections, and rigged literacy tests as a qualification for registration to vote, blacks in many areas of the South were effectively disenfranchised.[7]

Action by the national government was necessary to bring a halt to state efforts to disenfranchise large groups of voters (see Chapter 7). Major steps included a Supreme Court decision outlawing whites-only primaries, a constitutional amendment barring poll taxes, and the Voting Rights Act of 1965, which forbids discrimination in voting and registration. However, the legacy of a century of state-supported efforts to keep blacks and poor whites from voting in the South is still evident. The region has the lowest voter turnout rate in the country. By comparison, states such as Minnesota, Wisconsin, and Idaho, which have pioneered methods designed to encourage voting, such as election-day registration, are among the leaders in voter turnout.

The decline in voter turnout in recent federal elections (see Chapter 9) has also been characteristic of state elections. The average turnout in gubernatorial elections that do not coincide with a presidential election, for example, is less than 40 percent—a drop of several percentage points since the early 1960s.[8]

Local Political Structures

If the significance of a level of government was determined strictly on the basis of numbers, the local level would win handily. The United States has one national government and fifty state governments, but it has more than 80,000 local governments, which include counties, municipalities, school districts, and special districts, such as water, sewage, and conservation districts.

Local government is the source of most public employment. Compared with the roughly 3 million federal workers and the 3.5 million state employees, 8.5 million people work in local government. They are one of the most heavily unionized groups in the country. Schoolteachers are represented through the American Federation of Teachers (AFT) and the National Education Association (NEA), and other local public employees are represented through such unions as the International Association of Fire Fighters (IAFF) and the American Federation of State, County, and Municipal Employees (AFSCME). These unions have more than 3 million members, and they have been quite successful in obtaining better working conditions and job benefits for their members.

COUNTY GOVERNMENT

The oldest form of local government in the United States is the county, and it remains a top local governing unit in rural areas and in those few states, such as New York, where the county has broad responsibility for providing government services. The county is governed through an elected county commission (which, in some states, is called a county legislature or board of supervisors). In most states, there are also elected county sheriffs and county attorneys, and a few states have elected chief county executives.

In most states, the county functions as an administrative subdivision of the state. The county's responsibility is to carry out programs, such as highway maintenance or welfare services, that are established by the state. Some analysts believe that the county will increase in importance in upcoming years because of the prominence of issues, such as waste disposal, that cannot be addressed adequately at the municipal level but require a regional response.

MUNICIPAL GOVERNMENT

In most parts of the United States, the major unit of local government is the municipality, which can be a city, town,

or village. Municipalities exist partly to carry out activities of the state government, but they also serve their residents directly: most Americans depend on their municipal governments for law enforcement, water, and sanitation services.

The traditional and most common form of municipal government is the mayor–council system, which includes the mayor as the chief executive and the local council as the legislative body. The mayor–council system takes two forms. The more common form is the **strong mayor–council system,** in which the mayor has the veto power and a prescribed responsibility for budgetary and other policy actions. The mayor, rather than the council, is the more powerful policymaker. The alternative is the **weak mayor–council system,** in which the mayor's policymaking powers are less substantial than the council's. The mayor has no power to veto the council's actions and often has no formal role in such activities as budget making.

A different type of municipal government entirely is the **commission system.** This form invests executive and legislative authority in a commission, with each commissioner serving as a member of the local council, but also having a specified executive role, such as police commissioner or public works commissioner. The commission system has lost favor in recent decades. Its major weakness is that it has no chief executive with the power and responsibility to set the local government's overall direction.

A final type of municipal government is the **city-manager system,** which was pioneered in Ohio during the Progressive era as a reaction against inefficiency and partisan corruption in many of the nation's cities. The system entrusts the executive role to a professionally trained manager, who is chosen, and can be fired, by the city council. This arrangement ensures that the manager will be at least somewhat responsive to political and popular pressures.

Most city managers have specialized university training in the operation of municipal government, so they bring expertise to their position. However, the city manager may be an outsider who does not have the political support that is required for major undertakings. Most of the larger cities that installed the city manager system have since reverted to the mayor–council system, but the city-manager form is the most common type of government in smaller cities.

A local chief executive, whether a mayor or city manager, is, above all, an administrator whose main responsibility is to oversee the work of the component units of local government—the police, fire, sanitation, and other departments. Increasingly, local chief executives are also expected to provide economic leadership by fostering a business climate that will keep old firms in the community and attract new ones. In many cities, including Baltimore, San Antonio, and Minneapolis, mayors have played key roles in the revitalization of downtown areas. Of course, not all chief executives accomplish much, or even get the opportunity. In smaller towns and villages particularly, the position of mayor is often more honorary than active; it is a part-time position held by a trusted member of the community.

SCHOOL DISTRICTS

The tradition of local public schools is deeply embedded in the American political experience. Unlike Europe, where private schools and national educational standards have historically been more important, the United States has emphasized public education and local control. This control is exercised through local school boards. In a few places the school board is subordinate to the municipal government, but elsewhere it is an independent body. School policy is established by the local board rather than by the local mayor or council. The chief executive of the local public school system is a specially trained professional, the superintendent of schools.

SPECIAL DISTRICTS

A final form of municipal government, and one of increasing importance, is the special district. As society has become more complex and interdependent, a need has arisen for local governing institutions that are responsive to the resulting policy needs. Special districts that deal with such policy areas as water supply, soil conservation, and waste disposal are an answer. These districts also provide an answer to the problem of coordinating the efforts of independent municipal governments. Issues such as pollution control are not easily addressed within a single community. Special districts bring municipalities together; the typical form of governance of these districts is a board that includes a member from each municipality within the district's boundaries.

LOCAL ELECTIONS

The principle of elective office dominates local government. In addition to an elected mayor, most communities have an elected town or city council. The office of county commissioner is also an elective office throughout the country. Except in a few eastern states, local officials are chosen in nonpartisan elections; no party labels appear on the ballot.

Perhaps no local institution symbolizes the nature of American democracy better than the public schools. School board members are elected and, in many communities, the voters even have the opportunity to approve or reject school budgets and bonding proposals. In contrast, school officials in European countries are typically appointed to their positions, and school budgets are set primarily by national governments.

Voting in local elections is subject to state registration laws. However, as we saw in Chapter 9, many local governments have tried to weaken the link between their level of government and the state and national levels by scheduling local elections for odd-numbered years rather than the even-numbered ones during which all federal and most state elections are held. A predictable effect of this scheduling is that voter turnout is somewhat lower at each level than would be the case if national, state, and local elections were held simultaneously. The average turnout in local elections in most states is very low—30 percent or less. Turnout figures can be deceptive, however. There are countless instances of extraordinary turnout in local elections when a contentious issue is on the ballot. School bonding proposals, for example, often produce a high turnout.

State and Local Policy

Through the Tenth Amendment the states possess what is sometimes called the **police power,** a term that refers to the broad power of government to regulate the health, safety, and morals of the citizenry. Possession of this power has meant that the American states carry out many of the policy responsibilities that in other countries are dealt with at the national level. Law enforcement, public education, public health, and roads are among the policy areas that are defined largely by the state and local governments.

Although the policies enacted by Congress get more attention from the press, the acts of state legislatures have more influence on the day-to-day lives of most Americans. For example, most crimes are defined by state law, most criminal acts are investigated by authorities operating under state law, most trials take place under state law, and most prisoners are held in penitentiaries and jails that operate under laws enacted by state legislatures.

One way to see how the states use their power is to rank policy areas by level of spending. The top spending category for the states is public welfare, followed by public education, health and hospitals, and highways. These four areas are by far the most significant components of state spending. There is a large dropoff in spending between the fourth category, highways, and the fifth one, police.

The policy priorities of local governments are less easily described. Some local units, such as school boards, operate in only one policy area. Municipalities vary in size from the largest cities to the smallest villages, and their policies differ accordingly. Despite such differences, a few patterns to local spending are discernible. Far and away the biggest expense for local governments is public education; it accounts for more than 40 percent of all spending at the local level. Health and hospital spending ranks second at 8 percent. Welfare, roads, and law enforcement follow, in that order.

A brief description of some of the policy activities of state and local governments, and where they get the money to pay for these activities, will provide a broader perspective on the role of states and localities in the American system.

STATE AND LOCAL POLICY PRIORITIES

Education

Public education, including primary schools, secondary schools, and colleges and universities, accounts for the largest share of combined state and local spending, about a third of the total. Education spending by state and local governments dwarfs that of the federal government—roughly 90 percent to 10 percent. Even higher education is mainly a state and local responsibility, which means that the greatest share of the country's investment in the technical research and personnel that underpin the economy is provided by subnational governments. They also make the key substantive policy decisions in the education area, from curriculum to performance standards to length of schooling.

Of the many issues affecting public education in the states, two have stood out in recent years. One is the disparity in spending among school districts, which, in most instances, reflects differences in communities' wealth. Suburban schools, for example, are typically better funded and have better facilities than the inner-city schools in the same metropolitan area. Should such differences be allowed? In a 1976 Texas case, the Supreme Court concluded that a state has no obligation to provide students with an equal education: its obligation is "to provide an 'adequate' education for all children."[9] Nevertheless, state financial contributions to local schools are typically designed to help poorer districts more than wealthier ones. This tendency, however, does not begin to offset the disparity in the quality of schools between a state's poorest communities and its richest ones.

The other conspicuous education issue is the quality of American schools (see Chapter 26). The performance of U.S. students on standardized tests such as the SATs has declined in recent decades, and it is widely conceded that American public schools are not providing the quality of education that is found in Japan and some European countries. The situation has provoked ongoing heated disputes over merit pay for teachers, national tests for all students, and parent-student choice of schools.

Welfare Assistance

The most expensive social-welfare program in the United States is entirely a national one—social security for retirees. However, the states are vitally involved in the provision of most welfare services, particularly public assistance programs for the needy (see Chapter 25). Programs such as AFDC, Medicaid, and food stamps operate within federal guidelines, but the states have discretionary authority over benefit and eligibility levels. These programs are funded jointly by the state and national governments and are administered primarily by the state governments. They have the local offices that are necessary for administering need-based welfare programs, which, as we noted in Chapter 25, require regular contacts between caseworkers and welfare recipients.

Welfare programs account for about 12 percent of all state and local spending. This spending and the American tradition of self-reliance make welfare an ongoing political issue. One response by the states has been "workfare" programs, which require welfare recipients to accept work or education in order to retain their welfare benefits. The states have also devised various ways of holding down spending. In response to the rapid increase in Medicaid costs, for example, the state of Oregon conducted a systematic study of medical procedures in order to identify, and make ineligible for Medicaid reimbursement, those procedures that physicians apply electively.

Health and Hospitals

Nearly 9 percent of state and local expenditures are in the health and hospitals policy area. All states and many localities operate public hospitals, and most of the laws and regulations affecting medical practices are established by state governments. In addition, states and localities have public health programs such as immunization campaigns, mobile X-ray units, and health inspections of motels and restaurants.

Highways

Until the 1950s the roadways of America were built almost entirely with state and local funds. The interstate highway system was begun in the 1950s and was funded largely by the national government. Today, Washington provides about a third of the total spending on highways, and states and localities contribute the rest. State and local governments set most policies governing use of highways, including traffic infractions and shipping methods. Highway spending accounts for 8 percent of state and local expenditures.

Police

Some democracies have a national police force, but the United States does not. It has local and state police forces.

They enforce state laws and local ordinances, which collectively govern most aspects of crime and punishment. The state police include the highway patrol, game wardens, prison guards, and liquor control officers, and they are generally well-trained and highly professional. Local police are less specialized, are more uneven in their training and professionalism, and are required to do most of the "dirty" work of law enforcement—crime control and the maintenance of public order. About 4 percent of state and local spending is for police-related activities.

THE ECONOMICS OF STATE AND LOCAL POLICY

The federal government raises more tax revenues than do all fifty states and the thousands of local governments combined. Although states and localities have a substantial tax base, they are in an inherently competitive situation. People and businesses faced with state or local tax increases can move to another state or locality where taxes are lower. Between the 1960s and 1980s, there was a substantial movement of business firms from the Northeast and Midwest to the South and Southwest. These firms were lured by the cheaper labor and lower energy costs of the Sunbelt, and also by the lower tax rates of southern states.

Local governments are also in a relatively weak tax position. They compete with one another for the jobs and income that business firms represent. Every city of any size in the United States offers tax breaks or other incentives to companies that might relocate there. The predatory nature of the competition makes it difficult for any locality to raise its tax rate substantially and virtually forces them to give tax breaks to firms that could well afford to pay.

The major sources of state revenue are sales taxes, corporate income taxes, personal income taxes, and user fees, such as motor vehicle licenses and hunting and fishing licenses. There are, however, substantial variations in the taxing policies of the states. A few states have no personal income tax. South Dakota is one of these states. It also has no corporate income tax. Not surprisingly, South Dakota has one of the lowest levels of public services in the nation. Its neighboring state of Minnesota, for example, spends about twice as much per capita on public education.

The sales tax is the chief source of revenue for the states, accounting for about half of all taxes they raise. The sales tax is a flat-rate tax on consumer goods and thereby places a relatively heavy burden on lower-income persons, who spend a higher proportion of their income on such goods than do upper-income persons. The regressive nature of the sales tax has been a source of criticism, and some

states exempt food and medicine from the sales tax in order to relieve somewhat the burden it places on lower-income people. Nevertheless, the sales tax is a reliable method of raising large sums of money, and the states have increasingly used it to obtain their revenues.

Local governments rely primarily on the property tax for their revenue. This form of taxation accounts for nearly half of all revenues raised directly by local government, but it has drawbacks. It is paid, for example, in a lump sum, which heightens taxpayers' awareness of its cost and leads them to resist any increase. Accordingly, localities have turned increasingly to sales taxes (shared with the state and collected with the state's permission) and local income taxes (collected with the state's permission). The revenues from these sources increase automatically when the economy expands, thus providing localities with increased revenues without a raise in the tax rate.

States and localities also depend on revenues provided by other governments. About 15 percent of state revenues are provided by federal grant-in-aid programs, while local governments get about 30 percent of their revenues from the state and 5 percent from Washington. The states and localities also benefit from federal spending. The states of the South and West particularly owe many of their jobs to federal programs. In Hawaii, for example, more than 30,000 active U.S. military personnel are stationed on the islands at bases that include Pearl Harbor (Navy), Schofield Barracks (Army), and Hickam Field (Air Force).

Federal grants-in-aid and other federal policies tend to reduce the importance of state-to-state differences in wealth as a factor in state and local policies. Federal assistance is targeted disproportionately for less affluent states and communities. In addition, many federal programs require matching grants and uniform standards of participating states. However, the leveling effect of this federal policy is not very great, and states differ enormously in their economic wealth. The level of public services in all areas—education, welfare, health, and so on—is higher in wealthier states. In comparison with the five poorest states (Mississippi, West Virginia, Utah, Arkansas, and South Carolina), the five wealthiest states (Connecticut, New Jersey, Alaska, Massachusetts, and New York) spend about $400 more per capita on public education and about $50 more per capita on public health each year.[10]

Some analysts have concluded that economics, not politics, is the chief determinant of a state's public policies. Whether or not that observation is literally true, there is no question that the wealth of a state has a great influence on its policies. In the early 1980s, the states were beneficiaries of a sharp upturn in the national economy. As corporate and personal incomes rose, so did the tax revenues flowing into the state treasuries. Policy initiatives flowed from the states, which seemed especially adept at combining programs designed to stimulate economic development with programs designed to tighten fiscal responsibility.

Innovative governors were leaders of the change. Their experimental economic and social programs, from technological development to welfare reform, were widely publicized.[11] An example was the so-called Massachusetts Miracle. In Boston and the surrounding area, dozens of high-technology firms sprang up almost overnight, creating unprecedented prosperity for the state. Its governor, Michael Dukakis, was given much of the credit for the economic boom. He was voted the nation's most effective governor by the other governors, which contributed to the political reputation that helped him gain the Democratic party's 1988 presidential nomination.

By 1990, however, the states were in trouble. More than half had budget deficits and faced the prospect of service cuts and tax increases. Many states faced serious long-term economic problems in the form of declining industries and strong foreign competitors. All the states had no choice but to cut back on either their plans or their programs; they had no money for significant new initiatives.

THE POLITICS OF STATE AND LOCAL POLICY

If general economic conditions and the wealth of a state have a powerful impact on policy, so does the nature of a state's politics. The states vary significantly in their support for one major party or the other. Where the Republicans are stronger, as in the Mountain states, taxes and the quality of public services tend to be lower. Where Democrats are stronger, as in the Northeast, the reverse situation tends to predominate.

The intensity of party competition has a somewhat less obvious, but no less important, relationship to public policy. In states where party competition is weak, politics tends to be somewhat exclusive: a sizable share of the population, usually the poorest groups, will be more or less ignored by government. The dominant party has gained control without the help of these groups, and the minority party could not gain control even with their help. In other words, neither party has a strong incentive to seek their vote. The classic case of a neglected public was the black community in the South in the period before the modern civil rights movement of the 1950s and 1960s. African-Americans were politically powerless. Neither the white Democrats who ran the South nor the white Republicans who offered token opposition had a real interest in bringing black people into their coalition.

Where party competition is more intense, any sizable group in a state is likely to receive the attention of one party or the other and thus to be in a position to influence public policy. In the modern South, which is increasingly competitive between the parties, black voters are a growing force and have tipped the balance in some elections. They are also more likely than at any time in the past to have policy influence.

Interest-group systems can be looked at in a similar way. In those states where interest groups are many in number and somewhat evenly balanced in their political resources, public policy tends to serve a broad range of interests. An example is the state of New York, which has many competing factions, including, for example, business and labor, the upstate and downstate areas, and environmentalists and developers. Almost any legislation that makes it through the New York state legislature requires negotiation among numerous groups.

In states where a particular group or interest is dominant, however, government tends to serve that group or interest above all others. A classic example was the Anaconda Copper Company in Montana, which, during the period that it accounted for nearly all the state's mining and manufacturing, nearly ran the state. A more recent example is the influence of the Church of Latter-Day Saints in Utah. The large share of the state's residents are Mormons, and a policy alternative that is actively opposed by the church has almost no chance of becoming law. Thus, the church for years opposed the sale of hard liquor in Utah, and such sales were prohibited by law. The law was changed recently, but only after Mormon leaders agreed not to oppose the change, which was prompted by the state's desire to improve its ability to attract conventions and perhaps a future Winter Olympics.

Utah with its Mormon population is one of the most distinctive states in the union, but every state has its special characteristics. California is no more like Mississippi than Mississippi is like Rhode Island. Yet, as we have seen, the American states also have many things in common. The differences and similarities among the states are testimony to the enduring nature of the American governing experiment. The states are different enough to provide their residents with a special identity and a special political experience; yet they are alike enough to allow the triumph of the national union that the Framers so keenly envisioned 200 years ago.

Summary

Although developments in the twentieth century have narrowed the differences among the American states, they, and the localities that govern under their authority, remain distinctive and vital systems of government.

All states apply the constitutional principle of separate branches sharing power, but the structure of the state governments differs in some respects from that of the federal government. An example is the more widespread use of elections at the state level. Most states elect by popular vote their judges and a number of executives, including an attorney general and treasurer in addition to a governor. Through the initiative and the referendum, nearly all states also allow their residents to vote directly on issues of policy.

Local governments are chartered by the state. They are not sovereign governments, but most states have chosen to grant local units a considerable level of policymaking discretion. Local governments include counties, municipalities, school districts, and special districts. Of these, the independent school district is the most distinctively American institution, but the municipality is the primary gov-

erning unit. Municipalities are governed by one of four types of systems: the strong mayor–council system, the weak mayor–council system, the commission system, or the city-manager system.

The states and localities have primary responsibility for most of the public policies that directly touch Americans' daily lives. For example, the major share of legislation devoted to public education and about 90 percent of the funding for it are provided by the states and localities. Public welfare, public health, roads, and police are other policy areas dominated by these subnational governments. They do not, however, have the amount of revenue that is available to the federal government; competition between them holds down their taxing capacity. Their policies are also conditioned by the wealth of the state or locality, and by the structure of its party and interest group systems.

Major Concepts

charter	moralistic subculture
city-manager system	police power
commission system	recall
Dillon's rule	referendum
home rule	strong mayor–council system
individualistic subculture	traditionalistic subculture
initiative	weak mayor–council system

[1]Daniel Elazar, *American Federalism: A View from the States,* 2d ed. (New York: Crowell, 1972).

[2]Kim Quaile Hill and Kenneth R. Mladenka, *Democratic Governance in American States and Cities* (Pacific Grove, Calif.: Brooks/Cole Publishing, 1992), 39–44.

[3]John F. Dillon, *Commentaries on the Law of Municipal Corporations* (Boston: Little, Brown, 1881).

[4]Thad L. Beyle, "Governors," in Virginia Gray, Herbert Jacob, and Kenneth N. Vines, eds., *Politics in the American States: A Comparative Analysis,* 4th ed. (Boston: Little, Brown, 1983), 202.

[5]*Baker* v. *Carr,* 369 U.S. 186 (1962); *Gray* v. *Sanders,* 372 U.S. 368 (1963); *Reynolds* v. *Sims* 377 U.S. 533 (1964).

[6]Advisory Commission on Intergovernmental Relations (ACIR), *The Question of State Government Capability* (Washington, D.C.: ACIR, 1985), 123.

[7]V. O. Key, Jr., *Southern Politics* (New York: Knopf, 1949), 495.

[8]Norman R. Luttbeg, "Differential Voting Turnout in the American States, 1960–82," *Social Science Quarterly* 65 (March 1984): 60–73.

[9]*San Antonio Independent School District* v. *Rodriquez,* 411 U.S. 1 (1973).

[10]Advisory Commission on Intergovernmental Relations, *Significant Features of Fiscal Federalism* (Washington, D.C.: U.S. Government Printing Office, 1989): 152, 202.

[11]David Osborne, *Laboratories of Democracy: A New Breed of Governor Creates Models for National Growth* (Cambridge, Mass.: Harvard Business School Press, 1988).

THE DECLARATION OF INDEPENDENCE

In Congress, July 4, 1776,

THE UNANIMOUS DECLARATION
OF THE THIRTEEN UNITED
STATES OF AMERICA

When, in the course of human events, it becomes necessary for one people to dissolve the political bands which have connected them with another, and to assume, among the powers of the earth, the separate and equal station to which the laws of nature and of nature's God entitle them, a decent respect to the opinions of mankind requires that they should declare the causes which impel them to the separation.

We hold these truths to be self-evident, that all men are created equal; that they are endowed by their Creator with certain unalienable rights; that among these, are life, liberty, and the pursuit of happiness. That, to secure these rights, governments are instituted among men, deriving their just powers from the consent of the governed; that, whenever any form of government becomes destructive of these ends, it is the right of the people to alter or to abolish it, and to institute a new government, laying its foundation on such principles, and organizing its powers in such form, as to them shall seem most likely to effect their safety and happiness. Prudence, indeed, will dictate that governments long established, should not be changed for light and transient causes; and, accordingly, all experience hath shown, that mankind are more disposed to suffer, while evils are sufferable, than to right themselves by abolishing the forms to which they are accustomed. But, when a long train of abuses and usurpations, pursuing invariably the same object, evinces a design to reduce them under absolute despotism, it is their right, it is their duty, to throw off such government and to provide new guards for their future security. Such has been the patient sufferance of these colonies, and such is now the necessity which constrains them to alter their former systems of government. The history of the present King of Great Britain is a history of repeated injuries and usurpations, all having, in direct object, the establishment of an absolute tyranny over these States. To prove this, let facts be submitted to a candid world:

He has refused his assent to laws the most wholesome and necessary for the public good.

He has forbidden his governors to pass laws of immediate and pressing importance, unless suspended in their operation till his assent should be obtained; and, when so suspended, he has utterly neglected to attend to them.

He has refused to pass other laws for the accommodation of large districts of people, unless those people would relinquish the right of representation in the legislature; a right inestimable to them, and formidable to tyrants only.

He has called together legislative bodies at places unusual, uncomfortable, and distant from the depository of their public records, for the sole purpose of fatiguing them into compliance with his measures.

He has dissolved representative houses repeatedly for opposing, with manly firmness, his invasions on the rights of the people.

He has refused, for a long time after such dissolutions, to cause others to be elected; whereby the legislative powers, incapable of annihilation, have returned to the people at large for their exercise; the state remaining, in the meantime, exposed to all the danger of invasion from without, and convulsions within.

He has endeavored to prevent the population of these States; for that purpose, obstructing the laws for naturalization of foreigners, refusing to pass others to encourage their migration hither, and raising the conditions of new appropriations of lands.

He has obstructed the administration of justice, by refusing his assent to laws for establishing judiciary powers.

He has made judges dependent on his will alone, for the tenure of their offices, and the amount and payment of their salaries.

He has erected a multitude of new offices, and sent hither swarms of officers to harass our people, and eat out their substance.

He has kept among us, in time of peace, standing armies, without the consent of our legislatures.

He has affected to render the military independent of, and superior to, the civil power.

He has combined, with others, to subject us to a jurisdiction foreign to our Constitution, and unacknowledged by our laws; giving his assent to their acts of pretended legislation:

For quartering large bodies of armed troops among us:

For protecting them by a mock trial, from punishment, for any murders which they should commit on the inhabitants of these States:

For cutting off our trade with all parts of the world:

For imposing taxes on us without our consent:

For depriving us, in many cases, of the benefit of trial by jury:

For transporting us beyond seas to be tried for pretended offences:

For abolishing the free system of English laws in a neighboring province, establishing therein an arbitrary government, and enlarging its boundaries, so as to render it at once an example and fit instrument for introducing the same absolute rule into these colonies:

For taking away our charters, abolishing our most valuable laws, and altering, fundamentally, the powers of our governments:

For suspending our own legislatures, and declaring themselves invested with power to legislate for us in all cases whatsoever.

He has abdicated government here, by declaring us out of his protection, and waging war against us.

He has plundered our seas, ravaged our coasts, burnt our towns, and destroyed the lives of our people.

He is, at this time, transporting large armies of foreign mercenaries to complete the works of death, desolation, and tyranny, already begun, with circumstances of cruelty and perfidy scarcely paralleled in the most barbarous ages, and totally unworthy the head of a civilized nation.

He has constrained our fellow citizens, taken captive on the high seas, to bear arms against their country, to become the executioners of their friends, and brethren, or to fall themselves by their hands.

He has excited domestic insurrections amongst us, and has endeavored to bring on the inhabitants of our frontiers, the merciless Indian savages, whose known rule of warfare is an undistinguished destruction of all ages, sexes, and conditions.

In every stage of these oppressions, we have petitioned for redress, in the most humble terms; our repeated petitions have been answered only by repeated injury. A prince, whose character is thus marked by every act which may define a tyrant, is unfit to be the ruler of a free people.

Nor have we been wanting in attention to our British brethren. We have warned them, from time to time, of attempts made by their legislature to extend an unwarrantable jurisdiction over us. We have reminded them of the circumstances of our emigration and settlement here. We have appealed to their native justice and magnanimity, and we have conjured them, by the ties of our common kindred, to disavow these usurpations, which would inevitably interrupt our connections and correspondence. They, too, have been deaf to the voice of justice and consanguinity. We must, therefore, acquiesce in the necessity which denounces our separation, and hold them as we hold the rest of mankind, enemies in war, in peace, friends.

We, therefore, the representatives of the United States of America, in general Congress assembled, appealing to the Supreme Judge of the world for the rectitude of our intentions, do, in the name, and by the authority of the good people of these colonies, solemnly publish and declare, that these united colonies are, and of right ought to be, free and independent states: that they are absolved from all allegiance to the British Crown, and that all political connection between them and the state of Great Britain is, and ought to be, totally dissolved; and that, as free and independent states, they have full power to levy war, conclude peace, contract alliances, establish commerce, and to do all other acts and things which independent states may of right do. And, for the support of this declaration, with a firm reliance on the protection of Divine Providence, we mutually pledge to each other our lives, our fortunes, and our sacred honor.

The foregoing Declaration was, by order of Congress, engrossed, and signed by the following members:

JOHN HANCOCK

New Hampshire
Josiah Bartlett
William Whipple
Matthew Thornton

Massachusetts Bay
Samuel Adams
John Adams
Robert Treat Paine
Elbridge Gerry

Rhode Island
Stephen Hopkins
William Ellery

Connecticut
Roger Sherman
Samuel Huntington
William Williams
Oliver Wolcott

New York
William Floyd
Philip Livingston
Francis Lewis
Lewis Morris

New Jersey
Richard Stockton
John Witherspoon
Francis Hopkinson
John Hart
Abraham Clark

Pennsylvania
Robert Morris
Benjamin Rush
Benjamin Franklin
John Morton
George Clymer
James Smith
George Taylor
James Wilson
George Ross

Delaware
Caesar Rodney
George Reed
Thomas M'Kean

Maryland
Samuel Chase
William Paca
Thomas Stone
Charles Carroll,
    of Carrollton

Virginia
George Wythe
Richard Henry Lee
Thomas Jefferson
Benjamin Harrison
Thomas Nelson, Jr.
Francis Lightfoot Lee
Carter Braxton

North Carolina
William Hooper
Joseph Hewes
John Penn

South Carolina
Edward Rutledge
Thomas Heyward, Jr.
Thomas Lynch, Jr.
Arthur Middleton

Georgia
Button Gwinnett
Lyman Hall
George Walton

Resolved, That copies of the Declaration be sent to the several assemblies, conventions, and committees, or councils of safety, and to the several commanding officers of the continental troops; that it be proclaimed in each of the United States, at the head of the army.

THE CONSTITUTION OF THE UNITED STATES OF AMERICA[1]

We the People of the United States, in Order to form a more perfect Union, establish Justice, insure domestic Tranquility, provide for the common defence, promote the general Welfare, and secure the Blessings of Liberty to ourselves and our Posterity, do ordain and establish this CONSTITUTION for the United States of America.

Article 1

SECTION 1

All legislative Powers herein granted shall be vested in a Congress of the United States, which shall consist of a Senate and House of Representatives.

SECTION 2

The House of Representatives shall be composed of Members chosen every second Year by the People of the several States, and the Electors in each State shall have the Qualifications requisite for Electors of the most numerous Branch of the State Legislature.

No Person shall be a Representative who shall not have attained to the Age of twenty-five Years, and been seven Years a Citizen of the United States, and who shall not, when elected, be an Inhabitant of that State in which he shall be chosen.

[Representatives and direct Taxes[2] shall be apportioned among the several States which may be included within this Union, according to their respective Numbers, which shall be determined by adding to the whole Number of free Persons, including those bound to Service for a Term of Years, and excluding Indians not taxed, three fifths of all other Persons.][3] The actual Enumeration shall be made within three Years after the first Meeting of the Congress of the United States, and within every subsequent Term of ten Years, in such Manner as they shall by Law direct. The Number of Representatives shall not exceed one for every thirty Thousand, but each State shall have at Least one Representative; and until such enumeration shall be made, the State of New Hampshire shall be entitled to chuse three, Massachusetts eight, Rhode-Island and Providence Plantations one, Connecticut five, New York six, New Jersey four, Pennsylvania eight, Delaware one, Maryland six, Virginia ten, North Carolina five, South Carolina five, and Georgia three.

When vacancies happen in the Representation from any State, the Executive Authority thereof shall issue Writs of Election to fill such Vacancies.

The House of Representatives shall chuse their Speaker and other Officers; and shall have the sole Power of Impeachment.

SECTION 3

The Senate of the United States shall be composed of two Senators from each State, chosen by the Legislature thereof, for six Years; and each Senator shall have one Vote.

Immediately after they shall be assembled in Consequence of the first Election, they shall be divided as equally as may be into three Classes. The Seats of the Senators of the first Class shall be vacated at the Expiration of the second Year, of the second Class at the Expiration of the fourth Year, and of the third Class at the Expiration of the sixth Year, so that one-third may be chosen every second Year; and if Vacancies happen by Resignation, or otherwise, during the Recess of the Legis-

---

[1]This version, which follows the original Constitution in capitalization and spelling, was published by the United States Department of the Interior, Office of Education, in 1935.

[2]Altered by the Sixteenth Amendment.

[3]Negated by the Fourteenth Amendment.

lature of any State, the Executive thereof may make temporary Appointments until the next Meeting of the Legislature, which shall then fill such Vacancies.

No Person shall be a Senator who shall not have attained to the Age of thirty Years, and been nine Years a Citizen of the United States, and who shall not, when elected, be an Inhabitant of that State for which he shall be chosen.

The Vice President of the United States shall be President of the Senate, but shall have no vote, unless they be equally divided.

The Senate shall chuse their other Officers, and also a President pro tempore, in the absence of the Vice President, or when he shall exercise the Office of President of the United States.

The Senate shall have the sole Power to try all Impeachments. When sitting for that purpose they shall be on Oath or Affirmation. When the President of the United States is tried, the Chief Justice shall preside: And no person shall be convicted without the Concurrence of two thirds of the Members present.

Judgment in Cases of Impeachment shall not extend further than to removal from Office, and disqualification to hold and enjoy any Office of honor, Trust, or Profit under the United States: but the Party convicted shall nevertheless be liable and subject to Indictment, Trial, Judgment and Punishment, according to Law.

SECTION 4

The Times, Places and Manner of holding Elections for Senators and Representatives, shall be prescribed in each State by the Legislature thereof; but the Congress may at any time by Law make or alter such Regulations, except as to the Places of Chusing Senators.

The Congress shall assemble at least once in every Year, and such Meeting shall be on the first Monday in December, unless they shall by Law appoint a different Day.

SECTION 5

Each House shall be the Judge of the Elections, Returns and Qualifications of its own Members, and a Majority of each shall constitute a Quorum to do Business; but a smaller number may adjourn from day to day, and may be authorized to compel the Attendance of absent Members, in such Manner, and under such Penalties, as each House may provide.

Each House may determine the Rules of its Proceedings, punish its Members for disorderly Behaviour, and, with the Concurrence of two thirds, expel a Member.

Each House shall keep a Journal of its Proceedings, and from time to time publish the same, excepting such Parts as may in their Judgment require Secrecy; and the Yeas and Nays of the Members of either House on any question shall, at the Desire of one fifth of those Present, be entered on the Journal.

Neither House, during the Session of Congress, shall, without the Consent of the other, adjourn for more than three days, nor to any other Place than that in which the two Houses shall be sitting.

SECTION 6

The Senators and Representatives shall receive a Compensation for their Services, to be ascertained by Law, and paid out of the Treasury of the United States. They shall in all Cases, except Treason, Felony, and Breach of the Peace, be privileged from Arrest during their Attendance at the Session of their respective Houses, and in going to and returning from the same; and for any Speech or Debate in either House, they shall not be questioned in any other Place.

No Senator or Representative shall, during the Time for which he was elected, be appointed to any civil Office under the Authority of the United States, which shall have been created, or the Emoluments whereof shall have been increased, during such time; and no Person holding any Office under the United States shall be a Member of either House during his continuance in Office.

SECTION 7

All Bills for raising Revenue shall originate in the House of Representatives; but the Senate may propose or concur with Amendments as on other bills.

Every Bill which shall have passed the House of Representatives and the Senate, shall, before it becomes a Law, be presented to the President of the United States; If he approve he shall sign it, but if not he shall return it, with his Objections, to that House in which it shall have originated, who shall enter the Objections at large on their Journal, and proceed to reconsider it. If after such Reconsideration two thirds of that House shall agree to pass the bill, it shall be sent, together with the objections, to the other House, by which it shall likewise be reconsidered, and if approved by two thirds of that House, it shall become a Law. But in all such Cases the Votes of both Houses shall be determined by Yeas and Nays, and the Names of the Persons voting for and against the Bill shall be entered on the Journal of each House respectively. If any Bill shall not be returned by the President within ten Days (Sundays excepted) after it shall have been presented to him, the Same shall be a Law, in like Manner as if he had signed it, unless the Congress by their Adjournment prevent its Return, in which Case it shall not be a Law.

Every Order, Resolution, or Vote to which the Concurrence of the Senate and House of Representatives may be necessary (except on a question of Adjournment) shall be presented to the President of the United States; and before the Same shall take Effect, shall be approved by him, or being disapproved by him, shall be repassed by two thirds of the Senate and House of Representatives, according to the Rules and Limitations prescribed in the Case of a Bill.

SECTION 8

The Congress shall have Power To lay and collect Taxes, Duties, Imposts and Excises, to pay the Debts and provide for the common Defence and general Welfare of the United States; but all Duties, Imposts and Excises shall be uniform throughout the United States;

To borrow money on the credit of the United States;

To regulate Commerce with foreign Nations, and among the several States, and with the Indian Tribes;

To establish a uniform rule of Naturalization, and uniform Laws on the subject of Bankruptcies throughout the United States;

To coin Money, regulate the Value thereof, and of foreign Coin, and fix the Standard of Weights and Measures;

To provide for the Punishment of counterfeiting the Securities and current Coin of the United States;

To establish Post Offices and post Roads;

To promote the Progress of Science and useful Arts, by securing for limited Times to Authors and Inventors the exclusive Right to their respective Writings and Discoveries;

To constitute Tribunals inferior to the Supreme Court;

To define and punish Piracies and Felonies committed on the high Seas, and Offenses against the Law of Nations;

To declare War, grant Letters of Marque and Reprisal, and make Rules concerning Captures on Land and Water;

To raise and support Armies, but no Appropriation of Money to that Use shall be for a longer Term than two Years;

To provide and maintain a Navy;

To make Rules for the Government and Regulation of the land and naval forces;

To provide for calling forth the Militia to execute the Laws of the Union, suppress Insurrections and repel Invasions;

To provide for organizing, arming, and disciplining the Militia, and for governing such Part of them as may be employed in the Service of the United States, reserving to the States respectively, the Appointment of the Officers, and the Authority of training the Militia according to the discipline prescribed by Congress;

To exercise exclusive Legislation in all Cases whatsoever, over such District (not exceeding ten Miles square) as may, by Cession of particular States, and the acceptance of Congress, become the Seat of the Government of the United States, and to exercise like Authority over all Places purchased by the Consent of the Legislature of the State in which the Same shall be, for the Erection of Forts, Magazines, Arsenals, Dock-yards, and other needful Buildings;—And

To make all Laws which shall be necessary and proper for carrying into Execution the foregoing Powers, and all other Powers vested by this Constitution in the Government of the United States, or in any Department or Officer thereof.

SECTION 9

The Migration or Importation of such Persons as any of the States now existing shall think proper to admit, shall not be prohibited by the Congress prior to the Year one thousand eight hundred and eight, but a tax or duty may be imposed on such Importation, not exceeding ten dollars for each Person.

The privilege of the Writ of Habeas Corpus shall not be suspended, unless when in Cases of Rebellion or Invasion the public Safety may require it.

No bill of Attainder or ex post facto Law shall be passed.

No capitation, or other direct, Tax shall be laid unless in Proportion to the Census or Enumeration herein before directed to be taken.

No Tax or Duty shall be laid on Articles exported from any State.

No Preference shall be given by any Regulation of Commerce or Revenue to the Ports of one State over those of another: nor shall Vessels bound to, or from, one State, be obliged to enter, clear, or pay Duties in another.

No Money shall be drawn from the Treasury, but in Consequence of Appropriations made by Law; and a regular Statement and Account of the Receipts and Expenditures of all public Money shall be published from time to time.

No Title of Nobility shall be granted by the United States: And no Person holding any Office of Profit or Trust under them, shall, without the Consent of the Congress, accept of any present, Emolument, Office, or Title, of any kind whatever, from any King, Prince, or foreign State.

SECTION 10

No State shall enter into any Treaty, Alliance, or Confederation; grant Letters of Marque and Reprisal; coin Money; emit Bills of Credit; make any Thing but gold and silver Coin a Tender in Payment of Debts; pass any Bill of Attainder, ex post facto Law, or Law impairing the Obligation of Contracts, or grant any Title of Nobility.

No State shall, without the Consent of the Congress, lay any Imposts or Duties on Imports or Exports, except what may be absolutely necessary for executing its inspection Laws; and the net Produce of all Duties and Imposts, laid by any State on Imports or Exports, shall be for the use of the Treasury of the United States; and all such Laws shall be subject to the Revision and Control of the Congress.

No state shall, without the Consent of Congress, lay any duty of Tonnage, keep Troops, or Ships of War in time of Peace, enter into any Agreement or Compact with another State, or with a foreign Power, or engage in War, unless actually invaded, or in such imminent Danger as will not admit of delay.

Article II

SECTION 1

The executive Power shall be vested in a President of the United States of America. He shall hold his Office during the Term of four years, and, together with the Vice President, chosen for the same Term, be elected, as follows:

Each State shall appoint, in such Manner as the Legislature thereof may direct, a Number of Electors, equal to the whole Number of Senators and Representatives to which the State may be entitled in the Congress: but no Senator or Representative, or Person holding an Office of Trust or Profit under the United States, shall be appointed an Elector.

[The Electors shall meet in their respective States, and vote by Ballot for two persons, of whom one at least shall not be an Inhabitant of the same State with themselves. And they shall make a List of all the Persons voted for, and of the Number of Votes for each; which List they shall sign and certify, and transmit sealed to the Seat of the Government of the United States, directed to the President of the Senate. The President of the Senate shall, in the Presence of the Senate and House of Representatives, open all the Certificates, and the Votes shall then be counted. The Person having the greatest Number of Votes shall be the President, if such Number be a Majority of the whole Number of Electors appointed; and if there be more than one who have such Majority, and have an equal Number of Votes, then the House of Representatives shall immediately chuse by Ballot one of them for President; and if no Person have a Majority, then from the five

highest on the List the said House shall in like Manner chuse the President. But in chusing the President, the Votes shall be taken by States, the Representation from each State having one Vote; a quorum for this Purpose shall consist of a Member or Members from two-thirds of the States, and a Majority of all the States shall be necessary to a Choice. In every Case, after the Choice of the President, the Person having the greatest Number of Votes of the Electors shall be the Vice President. But if there should remain two or more who have equal votes, the Senate shall chuse from them by Ballot the Vice President.][4]

The Congress may determine the Time of chusing the Electors, and the Day on which they shall give their Votes; which Day shall be the same throughout the United States.

No person except a natural-born Citizen, or a Citizen of the United States, at the time of the Adoption of this Constitution, shall be eligible to the Office of President; neither shall any Person be eligible to that Office who shall not have attained to the Age of thirty-five years, and been fourteen Years a Resident within the United States.

In Case of the Removal of the President from Office, or of his Death, Resignation, or Inability to discharge the Powers and Duties of the said Office, the same shall devolve on the Vice President, and the Congress may by Law provide for the Case of Removal, Death, Resignation, or Inability, both of the President and Vice President, declaring what Officer shall then act as President, and such Officer shall act accordingly, until the disability be removed, or a President shall be elected.

The President shall, at stated Times, receive for his Services a Compensation, which shall neither be increased nor diminished during the Period for which he shall have been elected, and he shall not receive within that Period any other Emolument from the United States, or any of them.

Before he enter on the execution of his Office, he shall take the following Oath or Affirmation:—"I do solemnly swear (or affirm) that I will faithfully execute the Office of President of the United States, and will, to the best of my Ability, preserve, protect, and defend the Constitution of the United States."

SECTION 2

The President shall be Commander in Chief of the Army and Navy of the United States, and of the Militia of the several States, when called into the actual Service of the

---

[4]Revised by the Twelfth Amendment.

United States; he may require the Opinion, in writing, of the principal Officer in each of the executive Departments, upon any subject relating to the Duties of their respective Offices, and he shall have Power to Grant Reprieves and Pardons for Offenses against the United States, except in Cases of Impeachment.

He shall have Power, by and with the Advice and Consent of the Senate, to make Treaties, provided two-thirds of the Senators present concur; and he shall nominate, and by and with the Advice and Consent of the Senate, shall appoint Ambassadors, other public Ministers and Consuls, Judges of the supreme Court, and all other Officers of the United States, whose Appointments are not herein otherwise provided for, and which shall be established by Law: but the Congress may by Law vest the Appointment of such inferior Officers, as they think proper, in the President alone, in the Courts of Law, or in the Heads of Departments.

The President shall have Power to fill up all Vacancies that may happen during the Recess of the Senate, by granting Commissions which shall expire at the End of their next Session.

SECTION 3

He shall from time to time give to the Congress Information of the State of the Union, and recommend to their Consideration such Measures as he shall judge necessary and expedient; he may, on extraordinary occasions, convene both Houses, or either of them, and in Case of Disagreement between them, with respect to the Time of Adjournment, he may adjourn them to such Time as he shall think proper; he shall receive Ambassadors and other public Ministers; he shall take care that the Laws be faithfully executed, and shall Commission all the Officers of the United States.

SECTION 4

The President, Vice President and all civil Officers of the United States, shall be removed from Office on Impeachment for, and Conviction of, Treason, Bribery, or other high Crimes and Misdemeanors.

Article III

SECTION 1

The judicial Power of the United States, shall be vested in one supreme Court, and in such inferior Courts as the Congress may from time to time ordain and establish. The Judges, both of the supreme and inferior Courts, shall hold their Offices during good Behaviour, and shall, at stated Times, receive for their Services, a Compensation, which shall not be diminished during their Continuance in Office.

SECTION 2

The judicial Power shall extend to all Cases, in Law and Equity, arising under this Constitution, the Laws of the United States, and Treaties made, or which shall be made, under their Authority;—to all Cases affecting ambassadors, other public ministers and consuls;—to all cases of admiralty and maritime Jurisdiction;—to Controversies to which the United States shall be a Party;—to Controversies between two or more States;—between a State and Citizens of another State;[5]—between Citizens of different States—between Citizens of the same State claiming Lands under Grants of different States, and between a State, or the Citizens thereof, and foreign States, Citizens, or Subjects.

In all Cases affecting Ambassadors, other public Ministers and Consuls, and those in which a State shall be Party, the supreme Court shall have original Jurisdiction. In all the other Cases before mentioned, the supreme Court shall have appellate Jurisdiction, both as to Law and Fact, with such Exceptions, and under such Regulations as the Congress shall make.

The trial of all Crimes, except in Cases of Impeachment, shall be by Jury; and such Trial shall be held in the State where the said Crimes shall have been committed; but when not committed within any State, the Trial shall be at such Place or Places as the Congress may by Law have directed.

SECTION 3

Treason against the United States, shall consist only in levying War against them, or in adhering to their Enemies, giving them Aid and Comfort. No Person shall be convicted of Treason unless on the Testimony of two Witnesses to the same overt Act, or on Confession in open Court.

The Congress shall have power to declare the Punishment of Treason, but no Attainder of Treason shall work Corruption of Blood, or Forfeiture except during the Life of the Person attainted.

[5]Qualified by the Eleventh Amendment.

Article IV

SECTION 1

Full Faith and Credit shall be given in each State to the public Acts, Records, and judicial Proceedings of every other State. And the Congress may by general Laws prescribe the Manner in which such Acts, Records and Proceedings shall be proved, and the Effect thereof.

SECTION 2

The Citizens of each State shall be entitled to all Privileges and Immunities of Citizens in the several States.

A Person charged in any State with Treason, Felony, or other Crime, who shall flee from Justice, and be found in another State, shall on demand of the executive Authority of the State from which he fled, be delivered up, to be removed to the State having Jurisdiction of the crime.

No Person held to Service or Labour in one State, under the Laws thereof, escaping into another, shall, in Consequence of any Law or Regulation therein, be discharged from such Service or Labour, but shall be delivered up on Claim of the Party to whom such Service or Labour may be due.

SECTION 3

New States may be admitted by the Congress into this Union; but no new State shall be formed or erected within the Jurisdiction of any other State; nor any State be formed by the Junction of two or more States, or parts of States, without the Consent of the Legislatures of the States concerned as well as of the Congress.

The Congress shall have Power to dispose of and make all needful Rules and Regulations respecting the Territory or other Property belonging to the United States; and nothing in this Constitution shall be so construed as to Prejudice any Claims of the United States, or of any particular State.

SECTION 4

The United States shall guarantee to every State in this Union a Republican Form of Government, and shall protect each of them against Invasion; and on Application of the Legislature, or of the Executive (when the Legislature cannot be convened) against domestic Violence.

Article V

The Congress, whenever two-thirds of both Houses shall deem it necessary, shall propose Amendments to this Constitution, or, on the Application of the Legislatures of two-thirds of the several States, shall call a Convention for proposing Amendments, which, in either Case, shall be valid to all Intents and Purposes, as part of this Constitution, when ratified by the Legislatures of three-fourths of the several States, or by Conventions in three-fourths thereof, as the one or the other Mode of Ratification may be proposed by the Congress; Provided that no Amendment which may be made prior to the Year One thousand eight hundred and eight shall in any Manner affect the first and fourth Clauses in the Ninth Section of the first Article; and that no State, without its Consent, shall be deprived of its equal Suffrage in the Senate.

Article VI

All Debts contracted and Engagements entered into, before the Adoption of this Constitution, shall be as valid against the United States under this Constitution, as under the Confederation.

This Constitution, and the Laws of the United States which shall be made in Pursuance thereof; and all Treaties made, or which shall be made, under the Authority of the United States, shall be the supreme Law of the Land; and the Judges in every State shall be bound thereby, any Thing in the Constitution or Laws of any State to the Contrary notwithstanding.

The Senators and Representatives before mentioned, and the Members of the several State Legislatures, and all executive and judicial Officers, both of the United States and of the several States, shall be bound by Oath or Affirmation to support this Constitution; but no religious Tests shall ever be required as a qualification to any Office or public Trust under the United States.

Article VII

The Ratification of the Conventions of nine States shall be sufficient for the Establishment of this Constitution between the States so ratifying the same.

Done in Convention by the Unanimous Consent of the States present the Seventeenth Day of September in the Year of our Lord one thousand seven hundred and Eighty seven, and of the Independence of the United States of America the Twelfth. In Witness whereof We have hereunto subscribed our Names.[6]

---

[6]These are the full names of the signers, which in some cases are not the signatures on the document.

George Washington
President and deputy from Virginia

New Hampshire
John Langdon
Nicholas Gilman

Massachusetts
Nathaniel Gorham
Rufus King

Connecticut
William Samuel
   Johnson
Roger Sherman

New York
Alexander Hamilton

New Jersey
William Livingston
David Brearley
William Paterson
Jonathan Dayton

Pennsylvania
Benjamin Franklin
Thomas Mifflin
Robert Morris
George Clymer
Thomas FitzSimons
Jared Ingersoll
James Wilson
Gouverneur Morris

Delaware
George Read
Gunning Bedford, Jr.
John Dickinson
Richard Bassett
Jacob Broom

Maryland
James McHenry
Daniel of
   St. Thomas Jenifer
Daniel Carroll

Virginia
John Blair
James Madison, Jr.

North Carolina
William Blount
Richard Dobbs
   Spaight
Hugh Williamson

South Carolina
John Rutledge
Charles Cotesworth
   Pinckney
Charles Pinckney
Pierce Butler

Georgia
William Few
Abraham Baldwin

Articles in Addition to, and Amendment of, the Constitution of the United States of America, Proposed by Congress, and Ratified by the Legislatures of the Several States, Pursuant to the Fifth Article of the Original Constitution[7]

Amendment I

Congress shall make no law respecting an establishment of religion, or prohibiting the free exercise thereof; or abridging the freedom of speech, or of the press; or the right of the people peaceably to assemble, and to petition the Government for a redress of grievances.

Amendment II

A well regulated Militia, being necessary to the security of a free State, the right of the people to keep and bear Arms shall not be infringed.

[7]This heading appears only in the joint resolution submitting the first ten amendments, which are collectively known as the Bill of Rights. They were ratified on December 15, 1791.

Amendment III

No Soldier shall, in time of peace, be quartered in any house, without the consent of the Owner, nor in time of war, but in a manner to be prescribed by law.

Amendment IV

The right of the people to be secure in their persons, houses, papers, and effects, against unreasonable searches and seizures, shall not be violated, and no Warrants shall issue, but upon probable cause, supported by Oath or affirmation, and particularly describing the place to be searched, and the persons or things to be seized.

Amendment V

No person shall be held to answer for a capital or otherwise infamous crime, unless on a presentment or indictment of a Grand Jury, except in cases arising in the land or naval forces, or in the Militia, when in actual service in time of War or public danger; nor shall any person be subject for the same offence to be twice put in jeopardy of life or limb; nor shall be compelled in any criminal case to be a witness against himself, nor be deprived of life, liberty, or property, without due process of law; nor shall private property be taken for public use, without just compensation.

Amendment VI

In all criminal prosecutions, the accused shall enjoy the right to a speedy and public trial, by an impartial jury of the State and district wherein the crime shall have been committed, which district shall have been previously ascertained by law, and to be informed of the nature and cause of the accusation; to be confronted with the witnesses against him; to have compulsory process for obtaining witnesses in his favour, and to have the Assistance of Counsel for his defence.

Amendment VII

In suits at common law, where the value in controversy shall exceed twenty dollars, the right of trial by jury shall be preserved, and no fact tried by a jury, shall be otherwise reexamined in any Court of the United States, than according to the rules of the common law.

Amendment VIII

Excessive bail shall not be required, nor excessive fines imposed, nor cruel and unusual punishments inflicted.

Amendment IX

The enumeration of the Constitution, of certain rights, shall not be construed to deny or disparage others retained by the people.

Amendment X   *reserved*

The powers not delegated to the United States by the Constitution, nor prohibited by it to the States, are reserved to the States respectively, or to the people.

Amendment XI [1798]

The Judicial power of the United States shall not be construed to extend to any suit in law or equity, commenced or prosecuted against one of the United States by Citizens of another State, or by Citizens or Subjects of any Foreign State.

Amendment XII [1804]

The Electors shall meet in their respective States and vote by ballot for President and Vice-President, one of whom, at least, shall not be an inhabitant of the same State with themselves; they shall name in their ballots the person voted for as President, and in distinct ballots the person voted for as Vice-President, and they shall make distinct lists of all persons voted for as President, and of all persons voted for as Vice-President, and of the number of votes for each, which lists they shall sign and certify, and transmit sealed to the seal of the government of the United States, directed to the President of the Senate;—The President of the Senate shall, in the presence of the Senate and House of Representatives, open all the certificates and the votes shall then be counted;—The person having the greatest number of votes for President, shall be the President, if such number be a majority of the whole number of Electors appointed; and if no person have such majority, then from the persons having the highest numbers not exceeding three on the list of those voted for as President, the House of Representatives shall choose immediately, by ballot, the President. But in choosing the President, the votes shall be taken by states, the representation from each state having one vote; a quorum for this purpose shall consist of a member or members from two-thirds of the states, and a majority of all the states shall be necessary to a choice. And if the House of Representatives shall not choose a President whenever the right of choice shall devolve upon them, before the fourth day of March next following, then the Vice-President shall act as President, as in the case of the death or other constitutional disability of the President.—The person having the greatest number of votes as Vice-President, shall be the Vice-President, if such number be a majority of the whole number of Electors appointed, and if no person have a majority, then from the two highest numbers on the list, the Senate shall choose the Vice-President; a quorum for the purpose shall consist of two-thirds of the whole number of Senators, and majority of the whole number shall be necessary to a choice. But no person constitutionally ineligible to the office of President shall be eligible to that of Vice-President of the United States.

Amendment XIII [1865]

SECTION 1

Neither slavery nor involuntary servitude, except as a punishment for crime whereof the party shall have been duly convicted, shall exist within the United States, or any place subject to their jurisdiction.

SECTION 2

Congress shall have power to enforce this article by appropriate legislation.

Amendment XIV [1868]

SECTION 1

All persons born or naturalized in the United States, and subject to the jurisdiction thereof, are citizens of the United States and of the State wherein they reside. No State shall abridge the privileges or immunities of citizens of the United States; nor shall any State deprive any person of life, liberty, or property, without due process of law; nor deny to any person within its jurisdiction the equal protection of the laws.

SECTION 2

Representatives shall be apportioned among the several States according to their respective numbers, counting the whole number of persons in each State, excluding Indians not taxed. But when the right to vote at any election for the choice of electors for President and Vice-President of the United States, Representatives in Congress, the Executive and Judicial officers of a State, or the members of the Legislature thereof, is denied to any of the male inhabitants of such State, being twenty-one years of age, and citizens of the United States, or in any way abridged, except for participation in rebellion, or other crime, the basis of representation therein shall be reduced in the proportion which the number of such male citizens shall bear to the whole number of male citizens twenty-one years of age in such State.

SECTION 3

No person shall be a Senator or Representative in Congress, or elector of President and Vice-President, or hold any office, civil or military, under the United States, or under any State, who, having previously taken an oath, as a member of Congress, or as an officer of the United States, or as a member of any State legislature, or as an executive or judicial officer of any State, to support the Constitution of the United States, shall have engaged in insurrection or rebellion against the same, or given aid or comfort to the enemies thereof. But Congress may by a vote of two-thirds of each House, remove such disability.

SECTION 4

The validity of the public debt of the United States, authorized by law, including debts incurred for payment of pensions and bounties for services in suppressing insurrection or rebellion, shall not be questioned. But neither the United States nor any State shall assume or pay any debts or obligation incurred in aid of insurrection or rebellion against the United States, or any claim for the loss or emancipation of any slave; but all such debts, obligations, and claims shall be held illegal and void.

SECTION 5

The Congress shall have the power to enforce, by appropriate legislation, the provisions of this article.

Amendment XV [1870]

SECTION 1

The right of citizens of the United States to vote shall not be denied or abridged by the United States or by any State on account of race, color, or previous condition of servitude—

SECTION 2

The Congress shall have power to enforce this article by appropriate legislation.

Amendment XVI [1913]

The Congress shall have power to lay and collect taxes on incomes, from whatever source derived, without apportionment among the several States, and without regard to any census or enumeration.

Amendment XVII [1913]

The Senate of the United States shall be composed of two Senators from each State, elected by the people thereof, for six years; and each Senator shall have one vote. The electors in each State shall have the qualifications requisite for electors of the most numerous branch of the State legislatures.

When vacancies happen in the representation of any State in the Senate, the executive authority of such State shall issue writs of election to fill such vacancies: *Provided,* That the legislature of any State may empower the executive thereof to make temporary appointments until the people fill the vacancies by election as the legislature may direct.

This amendment shall not be so constured as to affect the election or term of any Senator chosen before it becomes valid as part of the Constitution.

Amendment XVIII [1919]

SECTION 1

After one year from the ratification of this article the manufacture, sale, or transportation of intoxicating liquors within, the importation thereof into, or the exportation thereof from the United States and all territory subject to the jurisdiction thereof for beverage purposes is hereby prohibited.

SECTION 2

The Congress and the several States shall have concurrent power to enforce this article by appropriate legislation.

SECTION 3

This article shall be inoperative unless it shall have been ratified as an amendment to the Constitution by the legislatures of the several States, as provided in the Constitution, within seven years from the date of the submission hereof to the States by the Congress.

Amendment XIX [1920]

The right of citizens of the United States to vote shall not be denied or abridged by the United States or by any State on account of sex.

Congress shall have power to enforce this article by appropriate legislation.

Amendment XX [1933]

SECTION 1

The terms of the President and Vice-President shall end at noon on the 20th day of January, and the terms of Senators and Representatives at noon on the 3d day of January, of the years in which such terms would have ended if this article had not been ratified; and the terms of their successors shall then begin.

SECTION 2

The Congress shall assemble at least once in every year, and such meeting shall begin at noon on the 3d day of January, unless they shall by law appoint a different day.

SECTION 3

If, at the time fixed for the beginning of the term of the President, the President elect shall have died, the Vice-President elect shall become President. If a President shall not have been chosen before the time fixed for the beginning of his term or if the President elect shall have failed to qualify, then the Vice-President elect shall act as President until a President shall have qualified; and the Congress may by law provide for the case wherein neither a President elect nor a Vice-President elect shall have qualified, declaring who shall then act as President, or the manner in which one who is to act shall be selected, and such person shall act accordingly until a President or Vice-President shall have qualified.

SECTION 4

The Congress may by law provide for the case of the death of any of the persons from whom the House of Representatives may choose a President whenever the right of choice shall have devolved upon them, and for the case of the death of any of the persons from whom the Senate may choose a Vice-President whenever the right of choice shall have devolved upon them.

SECTION 5

Sections 1 and 2 shall take effect on the 15th day of October following the ratification of this article.

SECTION 6

This article shall be inoperative unless it shall have been ratified as an amendment to the Constitution by the legislatures of three-fourths of the several States within seven years from the date of its submission.

Amendment XXI [1933]

SECTION 1

The eighteenth article of amendment to the Constitution of the United States is hereby repealed.

SECTION 2

The transportation or importation into any State, Territory, or possession of the United States for delivery or use therein of intoxicating liquors, in violation of the laws thereof, is hereby prohibited.

SECTION 3

This article shall be inoperative unless it shall have been ratified as an amendment to the Constitution by conventions in the several States, as provided in the Constitution, within seven years from the date of the submission hereof to the States by the Congress.

Amendment XXII [1951]

No person shall be elected to the office of the President more than twice, and no person who has held the office of President, or acted as President, for more than two years of a term to which some other person was elected President shall be elected to the office of the President more than once.

But this Article shall not apply to any person holding the office of President when this Article was proposed by the Congress, and shall not prevent any person who may be holding the office of President, or acting as President, during the term within which this Article becomes operative from holding the office of President or acting as President during the remainder of such term.

This article shall be inoperative unless it shall have been ratified as an amendment to the Constitution by the legislatures of three-fourths of the several states within seven years from the date of its submission to the states by the Congress.

Amendment XXIII [1961]

SECTION 1

The District constituting the seat of Government of the United States shall appoint in such manner as the Congress may direct:

A number of electors of President and Vice-President equal to the whole number of Senators and Representatives in Congress to which the District would be entitled if it were a State, but in no event more than the least populous State; they shall be in addition to those appointed by the States, but they shall be considered, for the purposes of the election of President and Vice-President, to be electors appointed by a State; and they shall meet in the District and perform such duties as provided by the twelfth article of amendment.

SECTION 2

The Congress shall have power to enforce this article by appropriate legislation.

Amendment XXIV [1964]

SECTION 1

The right of citizens of the United States to vote in any primary or other election for President or Vice President, for electors for President or Vice President, or for Senator or Representative in Congress, shall not be denied or abridged by the United States or any state by reason of failure to pay any poll tax or other tax.

SECTION 2

The Congress shall have the power to enforce this article by appropriate legislation.

Amendment XXV [1967]

SECTION 1

In case of the removal of the President from office or of his death or resignation, the Vice President shall become President.

SECTION 2

Whenever there is a vacancy in the office of the Vice President, the President shall nominate a Vice President who shall take office upon confirmation by a majority vote of both Houses of Congress.

SECTION 3

Whenever the President transmits to the President Pro Tempore of the Senate and the Speaker of the House of Representatives his written declaration that he is unable to discharge the powers and duties of his office, and until he transmits to them a written declaration to the contrary, such powers and duties shall be discharged by the Vice President as Acting President.

SECTION 4

Whenever the Vice President and a majority of either the principal officers of the executive departments or of such other body as Congress may by law provide, transmit to the President Pro Tempore of the Senate and the Speaker of the House of Representatives their written declaration that the President is unable to discharge the powers and duties of his office, the Vice President shall immediately assume the powers and duties of the office as Acting President.

Thereafter, when the President transmits to the President Pro Tempore of the Senate and the Speaker of the House of Representatives his written declaration that no inability exists, he shall resume the powers and duties of his office unless the Vice President and a majority of either the principal officers of the executive departments or of such other body as Congress may by law provide, transmit within four days to the President Pro Tempore of the Senate and the Speaker of the House of Representatives their written declaration that the President is unable to discharge the powers and duties of his office. Thereupon Congress shall decide the issue, assembling within forty-eight hours for that purpose if not in session. If the Congress, within twenty-one days after receipt of the latter written declaration, or, if Congress is not in session, within twenty-one days after Congress is required to assemble, determines by two-thirds vote of both Houses that the President is unable to discharge the powers and duties of his office, the Vice President shall continue to discharge the same as Acting President; otherwise, the President shall resume the powers and duties of his office.

Amendment XXVI [1971]

SECTION 1

The right of citizens of the United States, who are eighteen years of age or older, to vote shall not be denied or abridged by the United States or by any State on account of age.

SECTION 2

The Congress shall have power to enforce this article by appropriate legislation.

FEDERALIST NO. 10 (JAMES MADISON)

Among the numerous advantages promised by a well-constructed Union, none deserves to be more accurately developed than its tendency to break and control the violence of faction. The friend of popular governments never finds himself so much alarmed for their character and fate as when he contemplates their propensity to this dangerous vice. He will not fail, therefore, to set a due value on any plan which, without violating the principles to which he is attached, provides a proper cure for it. The instability, injustice, and confusion introduced into the public councils have, in truth, been the mortal diseases under which popular governments have everywhere perished, as they continue to be the favorite and fruitful topics from which the adversaries to liberty derive their most specious declamations. The valuable improvements made by the American constitutions on the popular models, both ancient and modern, cannot certainly be too much admired; but it would be an unwarrantable partiality to contend that they have as effectually obviated the danger on this side, as was wished and expected. Complaints are everywhere heard from our most considerate and virtuous citizens, equally the friends of public and private faith and of public and personal liberty, that our governments are too unstable, that the public good is disregarded in the conflicts of rival parties, and that measures are too often decided, not according to the rules of justice and the rights of the minor party, but by the superior force of an interested and overbearing majority. However anxiously we may wish that these complaints had no foundation, the evidence of known facts will not permit us to deny that they are in some degree true. It will be found, indeed, on a candid review of our situation, that some of the distresses under which we labor have been erroneously charged on the operation of our governments; but it will be found, at the same time, that other causes will not alone account for many of our heaviest misfortunes; and, particularly, for that prevailing and increasing distrust of public engagements and alarm for private rights which are echoed from one end of the continent to the other. These must be chiefly, if not wholly, effects of the unsteadiness and injustice with which a factious spirit has tainted our public administration.

By a faction I understand a number of citizens, whether amounting to a majority or minority of the whole, who are united and actuated by some common impulse of passion, or of interest, adverse to the rights of other citizens, or to the permanent and aggregate interests of the community.

There are two methods of curing the mischiefs of faction: the one, by removing its causes; the other, by controlling its effects.

There are again two methods of removing the causes of faction: the one, by destroying the liberty which is essential to its existence; the other, by giving to every citizen the same opinions, the same passions, and the same interests.

It could never be more truly said than of the first remedy that it was worse than the disease. Liberty is to faction what air is to fire, and aliment without which it instantly expires. But it could not be a less folly to abolish liberty, which is essential to political life, because it nourishes faction than it would be to wish the annihilation of air, which is essential to animal life, because it imparts to fire its destructive agency.

The second expedient is as impracticable as the first would be unwise. As long as the reason of man continues fallible, and he is at liberty to exercise it, different opinions will be formed. As long as the connection subsists between his reason and his self-love, his opinions and his passions will have a reciprocal influence on each other; and the former will be objects to which the latter will attach themselves. The diversity in the faculties of men, from which the rights of property originate, is not less an insuperable obstacle to a uniformity of interest. The protection of these faculties is the first object of government. From the protection of different and unequal faculties of acquiring property, the possession of different degrees and kinds of property immediately results; and from the influence of these on the sentiments and views of the respective proprietors ensues a division of the society into different interests and parties.

The latent causes of faction are thus sown in the nature of man; and we see them everywhere brought into different degrees of activity, acccording to the different circumstances of civil society. A zeal for different opinions concerning religion, concerning government, and many other points, as well of speculation as of practice; an attachment to different leaders ambitiously contending for pre-eminence and power; or to persons of other descriptions whose fortunes have been interesting to the human passions, have, in turn, divided mankind into parties, inflamed them with mutual animosity, and rendered them much more disposed to vex and oppress each other than to co-operate for their common good. So strong is this propensity of mankind to fall into mutual animosities that where no substantial occasion presents itself the most frivolous and fanciful distinctions have been sufficient to kindle their unfriendly passions and excite their most violent conflicts. But the most common and durable source of factions has been the various and unequal distribution of property. Those who hold and those who are without property have ever formed distinct interests in society. Those who are creditors, and those who are debtors, fall under a like discrimination. A landed interest, a manufacturing interest, a mercantile interest, a moneyed interest, with many lesser interests, grow up of necessity in civilized nations, and divide them into different classes, actuated by different sentiments and views. The regulation of these various and interfering interests forms the principal task of modern legislation and involves the spirit of party and faction in the necessary and ordinary operations of government.

No man is allowed to be a judge in his own cause, because his interest would certainly bias his judgment, and, not improbably, corrupt his integrity. With equal, nay with greater reason, a body of men are unfit to be both judges and parties at the same time; yet what are many of the most important acts of legislation but so many judicial determinations, not indeed concerning the rights of single persons, but concerning the rights of large bodies of citizens? And what are the different classes of legislators but advocates and parties to the causes which they determine? Is a law proposed concerning private debts? It is a question to which the creditors are parties on one side and the debtors on the other. Justice ought to hold the balance between them. Yet the parties are, and must be, themselves the judges; and the most numerous party, or in other words, the most powerful faction must be expected to prevail. Shall domestic manufacturers be encouraged, and in what degree, by restrictions on foreign manufacturers? are questions which would be differently decided by the landed and the manufacturing classes, and

probably by neither with a sole regard to justice and the public good. The apportionment of taxes on the various descriptions of property is an act which seems to require the most exact impartiality; yet there is, perhaps, no legislative act in which greater opportunity and temptation are given to a predominant party to trample on the rules of justice. Every shilling with which they overburden the inferior number is a shilling saved to their own pockets.

It is in vain to say that enlightened statesmen will be able to adjust these clashing interests and render them all subservient to the public good. Enlightened statesmen will not always be at the helm. Nor, in many cases, can such an adjustment be made at all without taking into view indirect and remote considerations, which will rarely prevail over the immediate interest which one party may find in disregarding the rights of another or the good of the whole.

The inference to which we are brought is that the *causes* of faction cannot be removed and that relief is only to be sought in the means of controlling its *effects*.

If a faction consists of less than a majority, relief is supplied by the republican principle, which enables the majority to defeat its sinister views by regular vote. It may clog the administration, it may convulse the society; but it will be unable to execute and mask its violence under the forms of the Constitution. When a majority is included in a faction, the form of popular government, on the other hand, enables it to sacrifice to its ruling passion or interest both the public good and the rights of other citizens. To secure the public good and private rights against the danger of such a faction, and at the same time to preserve the spirit and the form of popular government, is then the great object to which our inquiries are directed. Let me add that it is the great desideratum by which alone this form of government can be rescued from the opprobrium under which it has so long labored and be recommended to the esteem and adoption of mankind.

By what means is this object attainable? Evidently by one of two only. Either the existence of the same passion or interest in a majority at the same time must be prevented, or the majority, having such coexistent passion or interest, must be rendered, by their number and local situation, unable to concert and carry into effect schemes of oppression. If the impulse and the opportunity be suffered to coincide, we well know that neither moral nor religious motives can be relied on as an adequate control. They are not found to be such on the injustice and violence of individuals, and lose their efficacy in proportion to the number combined together, that is, in proportion as their efficacy becomes needful.

From this view of the subject it may be concluded that a pure democracy, by which I mean a society consisting of a small number of citizens, who assemble and administer the government in person, can admit of no cure for the mischiefs of faction. A common passion or interest will, in almost every case, be felt by a majority of the whole, a communication and concert results from the form of government itself; and there is nothing to check the inducements to sacrifice the weaker party or an obnoxious individual. Hence it is that such democracies have ever been spectacles of turbulence and contention; have ever been found incompatible with personal security or the rights of property; and have in general been as short in their lives as they have been violent in their deaths. Theoretic politicians, who have patronized this species of government, have erroneously supposed that by reducing mankind to a perfect equality in their political rights, they would at the same time be perfectly equalized and assimilated in their possessions, their opinions, and their passions.

A republic, by which I mean a government in which the scheme of representation takes place, opens a different prospect and promises the cure for which we are seeking. Let us examine the points in which it varies from pure democracy, and we shall comprehend both the nature of the cure and the efficacy which it must derive from the Union.

The two great points of difference between a democracy and a republic are: first, the delegation of the government, in the latter, to a small number of citizens elected by the rest; secondly, the greater number of citizens and greater sphere of country over which the latter may be extended.

The effect of the first difference is, on the one hand, to refine and enlarge the public views by passing them through the medium of a chosen body of citizens, whose wisdom may best discern the true interest of their country and whose patriotism and love of justice will be least likely to sacrifice it to temporary or partial considerations. Under such a regulation it may well happen that the public voice, pronounced by the representatives of the people, will be more consonant to the public good than if pronounced by the people themselves, convened for the purpose. On the other hand, the effect may be inverted. Men of factious tempers, of local prejudices, or of sinister designs, may, by intrigue, by corruption, or by other means, first obtain the suffrages, and then betray the interests of the people. The question resulting is, whether small or extensive republics are most favorable to the election of proper guardians of the public weal; and it is clearly decided in favor of the latter by two obvious considerations.

In the first place it is to be remarked that however small the republic may be the representatives must be raised to a certain number in order to guard against the cabals of a few; and that however large it may be they must be limited to a certain number in order to guard against the confusion of a multitude. Hence, the number of representatives in the two cases not being in proportion to that of the constituents, and being proportionally greatest in the small republic, it follows that if the proportion of fit characters be not less in the large than in the small republic, the former will present a greater option, and consequently a greater probability of a fit choice.

In the next place, as each representative will be chosen by a greater number of citizens in the large than in the small republic, it will be more difficult for unworthy candidates to practice with success the vicious arts by which elections are too often carried; and the suffrages of the people being more free, will be more likely to center on men who possess the most attractive merit and the most diffusive and established characters.

It must be confessed that in this, as in most other cases, there is a mean, on both sides of which inconveniencies will be found to lie. By enlarging too much the number of electors, you render the representative too little acquainted with all their local circumstances and lesser interests; as by reducing it too much, you render him unduly attached to these, and too little fit to comprehend and pursue great and national objects. The federal Constitution forms a happy combination in this respect; the great and aggregate interests being referred to the national, the local and particular to the State legislatures.

The other point of difference is the greater number of citizens and extent of territory which may be brought within the compass of republican than of democratic government; and it is this circumstance principally which renders factious combinations less to be dreaded in the former than in the latter. The smaller the society, the fewer probably will be the distinct parties and interests composing it; the fewer the distinct parties and interests, the more frequently will a majority be found of the same party; and the smaller the number of individuals composing a majority, and the smaller the compass within which they are placed, the more easily will they concert and execute their plans of oppression. Extend the sphere and you take in a greater variety of parties and interests; you make it less probable that a majority of the whole will have a common motive to invade the rights of other citizens; or if such a common motive exists, it will be more difficult for all who feel it to discover their own strength and to act in unison with each other. Besides other impediments, it may be remarked that, where there is a consciousness of unjust or dishonorable purposes, communication is always checked by distrust in proportion to the number whose concurrence is necessary.

Hence, it clearly appears that the same advantage which a republic has over a democracy in controlling the effects of faction is enjoyed by a large over a small republic—is enjoyed by the Union over the States composing it. Does this advantage consist in the substitution of representatives whose enlightened views and virtuous sentiments render them superior to local prejudices and to schemes of injustice? It will not be denied that the representation of the Union will be most likely to possess these requisite endowments. Does it consist in the greater security afforded by a greater variety of parties, against the event of any one party being able to outnumber and oppress the rest? In an equal degree does the increased variety of parties comprised within the Union increase this security. Does it, in fine, consist in the greater obstacles opposed to the concert and accomplishment of the secret wishes of an unjust and interested majority? Here again the extent of the Union gives it the most palpable advantage.

The influence of factious leaders may kindle a flame within their particular States but will be unable to spread a general conflagration through the other States. A religious sect may degenerate into a political faction in a part of the Confederacy; but the variety of sects dispersed over the entire face of it must secure the national councils against any danger from that source. A rage for paper money, for an abolition of debts, for an equal division of property, or for any other improper of wicked project, will be less apt to pervade the whole body of the Union than a particular member of it, in the same proportion as such a malady is more likely to taint a particular county or district than an entire State.

In the extent and proper structure of the Union, therefore, we behold a republican remedy for the diseases most incident to republican government. And according to the degree of pleasure and pride we feel in being republicans ought to be our zeal in cherishing the spirit and supporting the character of federalists.

FEDERALIST NO. 51 (JAMES MADISON)

To what expedient, then, shall we finally resort, for maintaining in practice the necessary partition of power among the several departments as laid down in the Constitution? The only answer that can be given is that as all these exterior provisions are found to be inadequate, the defect must be supplied, by so contriving the interior structure of the government as that its several constituent parts may, by their mutual relations, be the means of keeping each other in their proper places. Without presuming to undertake a full development of this important idea I will hazard few general observations which may perhaps place it in a clearer light, and enable us to form a more correct judgment of the principles and structure of the government planned by the convention.

In order to lay a due foundation for that separate and distinct exercise of the different powers of government, which to a certain extent is admitted on all hands to be essential to the preservation of liberty, it is evident that each department should have a will of its own; and consequently should be so constituted that the members of each should have as little agency as possible in the appointment of the members of the others. Were this principle rigorously adhered to, it would require that all the appointments for the supreme executive, legislative, and judiciary magistracies should be drawn from the same fountain of authority, the people, through channels having no communication whatever with one another. Perhaps such a plan of constructing the several departments would be less difficult in practice than it may in contemplation appear. Some difficulties, however, and some additional expense would attend the execution of it. Some deviations, therefore, from the principle must be admitted. In the constitution of the judiciary department in particular, it might be inexpedient to insist rigorously on the principle: first, because peculiar qualifications being essential in the members, the primary consideration ought to be to select that mode of choice which best secures these qualifications; second, because the permanent tenure by which the appointments are held in that department must soon destroy all sense of dependence on the authority conferring them.

It is equally evident that the members of each department should be as little dependent as possible on those of the others for the emoluments annexed to their offices. Were the executive magistrate, or the judges, not independent of the legislature in this particular, their independence in every other would be merely nominal.

But the great security against a gradual concentration of the several powers in the same department consists in giving to those who administer each department the necessary constitutional means and personal motives to resist encroachments of the others. The provision for defense must in this, as in all other cases, be made commensurate to the danger of attack. Ambition must be made to counteract ambition. The interest of the man must be connected with the constitutional rights of the place. It may be a reflection on human nature that such devices should be necessary to control the abuses of government. But what is government itself but the greatest of all reflections on human nature? If men were angels no government would be necessary. If angels were to govern men, neither external nor internal controls on government would be necessary. In framing a government which is to be administered by men over men, the great difficulty lies in this: you must first enable the government to control the governed; and in the next place oblige it to control itself. A dependence on the people is, no doubt, the primary control on the government; but experience has taught mankind the necessity of auxiliary precautions.

This policy of supplying, by opposite and rival interests, the defect of better motives, might be traced through the whole system of human affairs, private as well as public. We see it particularly displayed in all the subordinate distributions of power, where the constant aim is to divide and arrange the several offices in such a manner as that each may be a check on the other—that the private interest of every individual may be a sentinel over the public rights. These inventions of prudence cannot be less requisite in the distribution of the supreme powers of the State.

But it is not possible to give to each department an equal power of self-defense. In republican government, the legislative authority necessarily predominates. The remedy for this inconveniency is to divide the legislature into different branches; and to render them, by different modes of election and different principles of action, as little connected with each other as the nature of their common functions and their common dependence on the society will admit. It may even be necessary to guard against dangerous encroachments by still further precautions. As the weight of the legislative authority requires that it should be thus divided, the weakness of the executive may require, on the other hand, that it should be fortified. An absolute negative on the legislature appears, at first view, to be the natural defense with which the executive magistrate should be armed. But perhaps it would be neither altogether safe nor alone sufficient. On ordinary occasions it might not be exerted with the requisite firmness, and on extraordinary occasions it might be perfidiously abused. May not this defect of an absolute negative be supplied by some qualified connection between this weaker department and the weaker branch of the stronger department, by which the latter may be led to support the constitutional rights of the former, without being too much detached from the rights of its own department?

If the principles on which these observations are founded be just, as I persuade myself they are, and they be applied as a criterion to the several State constitutions, and to the federal Constitution, it will be found that if the latter does not perfectly correspond with them, the former are infinitely less able to bear such a test.

There are, moreover, two considerations particularly applicable to the federal system of America, which place that system in a very interesting point of view.

First. In a single republic, all the power surrendered by the people is submitted to the administration of a single government; and the usurpations are guarded against by a division of the government into distinct and separate departments. In the compound republic of America, the power surrendered by the people is first divided between two distinct governments, and then the portion allotted to each subdivided among distinct and separate departments. Hence a double security arises to the rights of the people. The different governments will control each other, at the same time that each will be controlled by itself.

Second. It is of great importance in a republic not only to guard the society against the oppression of its rulers, but to guard one part of the society against the injustice of the other part. Different interests necessarily exist in different classes of citizens. If a majority be united by a common interest, the rights of the minority will be insecure. There are but two methods of providing against this evil: the one by creating a will in the community independent of the majority—that is, of the society itself; the other, by comprehending in the society so many separate descriptions of citizens as will render an unjust combination of a majority of the whole very improbable, if not impracticable. The first method prevails in all governments possessing an hereditary or self-appointed authority. This, at best, is but a precarious security; because a power independent of the society may as well espouse the unjust views of the major as the righful interests of the minor party, and may possibly be turned against both parties. The second method will be exemplified in the federal republic of the United States. Whilst all authority in it will be derived from and dependent on the society, the society itself will be broken into so many parts, interests and classes of citizens, that the rights of individuals, or of the minority, will be in little danger from interested combinations of the majority. In a free government the security for civil rights must be the same as that for religious rights. It consists in the one case in the multiplicity of interests, and in the other in the multiplicity of sects. The degree of security in both cases will depend on the number of interests and sects; and this may be presumed to depend on the extent of country and number of people comprehended under the same government. This view of the subject must particularly recommend a proper federal system to all the sincere and considerate friends of republican government, since it shows that in exact proportion as the territory of the Union may be formed into more circumscribed Confederacies, or States, oppressive combinations of a majority will be facilitated; the best security, under the republican forms, for the rights of every class of citizen, will be diminished; and consequently the stability and independence of some member of the government, the only other security, must be proportionally increased. Justice is the end of government. It is the end of civil society. It ever has been and ever will be pursued until it be obtained, or until liberty be lost in the pursuit. In a society under the forms of which the stronger faction can readily unite and oppress the weaker, anarchy may as truly be said to reign as in a state of nature, where the weaker individual is not secured against the violence of the stronger; and as, in the latter state, even the stronger individuals are prompted, by the uncertainty of their condition, to submit to a government which may protect the weak as well as themselves; so, in the former state, will the more powerful factions or parties be gradually induced, by a like motive, to wish for a government which will protect all parties, the weaker as well as the more powerful. It can be little doubted that if the State of Rhode Island was separated from the Confederacy and left to itself, the insecurity of rights under the popular form of government within such narrow limits would be displayed by such reiterated oppressions of factious majorities that some power altogether independent of the people would soon be called for by the voice of the very factions whose misrule had proved the necessity of it. In the extended republic of the United States, and among the great variety of interests, parties, and sects which it embraces, a coalition of a majority of the whole society could seldom take place on any other principles than those of justice and the general good; whilst there being thus less danger to a minor from the will of a major party, there must be less pretext, also, to provide for the security of the former, by introducing into the government a will not dependent on the latter, or, in other words, a will independent of the society itself. It is no less certain than it is important, notwithstanding the contrary opinions which have been entertained, that the larger the society, provided it lie within a practicable sphere, the more duly capable it will be of self-government. And happily for the *republican cause*, the practicable sphere may be carried to a very great extent by a judicious modification and mixture of the federal principle.

GLOSSARY

accountability   The ability of the public to hold government officials responsible for their actions.

affirmative action   A term that refers to programs designed to ensure that women, minorities, and other traditionally disadvantaged groups have full and equal opportunities in employment, education, and other areas of life.

agency point of view   The tendency of bureaucrats to place the interests of their agency ahead of other interests and ahead of the priorities sought by the president or Congress.

alienation   A feeling of personal powerlessness that includes the notion that government does not care about the opinions of people like oneself.

apathy   A feeling of personal noninterest or unconcern with politics.

appellate jurisdiction   The authority of a given court to review cases that have already been tried in lower courts and are appealed to it by the losing party; such a court is called an appeals court or appellate court. (See **original jurisdiction.**)

authority   The recognized right of an official or institution to exercise power. (See **power.**)

bill   A proposed law (legislative act) within Congress or another legislature. (See **law.**)

Bill of Rights   The first ten amendments to the Constitution, which set forth basic protections for individual rights to free expression, fair trial, and property.

block grants   Federal grants-in-aid that permit state and local officials to decide how the money will be spent within a general area, such as education or health. (See **categorical grants.**)

bureaucracy   A system of organization and control based on the principles of hierarchical authority, job specialization, and formalized rules. (See **formalized rules; hierarchical authority; job specialization.**)

cabinet   A group consisting of the heads of the fourteen executive departments, who are appointed by the president, subject to confirmation by the Senate. (See **cabinet departments.**)

cabinet (executive) departments   The fourteen major organizations within the federal executive bureaucracy, each of which has responsibility for a major function of the federal government, such as defense, agriculture, or justice. (See **cabinet.**)

candidate-centered politics   Election campaigns and other political processes in which candidates, not political parties, have most of the initiative and influence. (See **party-centered politics.**)

capitalism   An economic system based on the idea that government should interfere with economic transactions as little as possible. Free enterprise and self-reliance are the collective and individual principles that underpin capitalism.

categorical grants   Federal grants-in-aid to states and localities that can be used only for designated projects. (See **block grants.**)

caucus   An informal group of legislators with a shared interest who meet to exchange information and coordinate a legislative strategy designed to foster that interest.

charter   The chief instrument by which a state governs its local units. No local government can exist without a charter, which is issued by the state and defines the limits, usually quite restrictive, within which a local unit must operate. (See **home rule.**)

checks and balances   The elaborate system of divided spheres of authority provided by the U.S. Constitution as a means of controlling the power of government. The separation of powers among the branches of the national government, federalism, and the different methods of selecting national officers are all part of this system.

city-manager system   A form of municipal government that entrusts the executive role to a professionally trained manager, who is chosen, and can be fired, by the city council.

civic duty   The belief of an individual that civic and political participation is a responsibility of citizenship.

civil liberties   The fundamental individual rights of a free society, such as freedom of speech and the right to a jury trial, which in the United States are protected by the Bill of Rights.

civil (equal) rights   The right of every person to equal protection under the laws and equal access to society's opportunities and public facilities.

civil service system   See **merit system.**

clear-and-present-danger test   A test devised by the Supreme Court in 1919 in order to define the limits of free speech in the context of national security. According to the test, government cannot abridge political expression unless it presents a clear and present danger to the nation's security.

clientele groups Special-interest groups that benefit directly from the activities of a particular bureaucratic agency and are therefore strong advocates of the agency.

cloture A parliamentary maneuver which, if a three-fifths majority votes for it, limits Senate debate to 100 hours and has the effect of defeating a filibuster. (See **filibuster**.)

cold war The period after World War II when the United States and the USSR were not engaged in actual combat (a "hot war") but were nonetheless locked in a state of deep-seated hostility.

collective (public) goods Benefits that are offered by groups (usually noneconomic groups) as an incentive for membership, but that can be obtained by nonmembers as well as members of the particular group. (See **private goods; free-rider problem**.)

comity The legal principle that, when court jurisdictions overlap in a given case, the laws of the relevant governing authority (such as a state) will be respected even though the dispute is being settled by a court of a different authority (such as another state or the national government). (See **jurisdiction**.)

commerce clause A clause of the Constitution (Article I, section 8) that empowers the federal government to regulate commerce among the states and with other nations.

commission system A form of municipal government that invests executive and legislative authority in a commission; each commissioner serves as a member of the local council but also has a specified executive role, such as police commissioner or public works commissioner.

common-carrier role The media's function as an open channel through which political leaders and the public can communicate.

comparable worth The idea that men and women should get equal pay for work that requires similar levels of training and responsibility.

compelling governmental interest The theoretical standard against which claims of constitutional rights are upheld or rejected.

compliance The issue of whether a court's decisions will be respected and obeyed.

concurring opinion A separate opinion written by a Supreme Court justice who votes with the majority in the decision on a case but who disagrees with their reasoning. (See **majority opinion**.)

confederacy A governmental system in which sovereignty is vested entirely in subnational (state) governments. (See **federalism; unitary system**.)

conference committee A temporary committee that is formed to bargain over the differences in the House and Senate versions of a bill. The committee's members are usually appointed from the House and Senate standing committees that originally worked on the bill.

conservatism An ideology that in contemporary U.S. politics includes beliefs in economic individualism, traditional social values, and a strong defense establishment. (See **liberalism**.)

constituency The individuals who live within the geographical area represented by an elected official. More narrowly, the body of citizens eligible to vote for a particular representative.

constitutionalism The idea that there are definable limits on the rightful power of a government over its citizens.

containment A doctrine developed after World War II, based on the assumptions that the Soviet Union was an aggressor nation and that only a determined United States could block Soviet territorial ambitions.

contract clause The clause of the U.S. Constitution (Article I, section 10) that forbids a state to pass laws that impair "the obligation of contracts" or that allow payment of debts by means other than legal tender.

cooperative federalism A federal system in which the national, state, and local levels work together to solve problems.

dealignment A situation in which voters' partisan loyalties have been substantially weakened. (See **party identification; realigning election**.)

decision A vote of the Supreme Court in a particular case that indicates which party the justices side with and by how large a margin.

de facto **discrimination** Discrimination on the basis of race, sex, religion, ethnicity, and the like that results from social, economic, and cultural biases and conditions. (See *de jure* **discrimination**.)

de jure **discrimination** Discrimination on the basis of race, sex, religion, ethnicity, and the like that results from a law. (See *de facto* **discrimination**.)

delegates The idea of elected representatives as obligated to carry out the expressed wishes of the electorate. The delegate model of representation assumes that the people themselves are the best judge of the public interest. (See **trustees**.)

demand-side economics A form of fiscal policy that emphasizes "demand" (consumer spending). Government can use increased spending or tax cuts to place more money in consumers' hands and thereby increase demand. (See **fiscal policy; supply-side economics**.)

democracy A form of government in which the people rule, either directly or through elected representatives.

denials of power A constitutional means of limiting governmental action by listing those powers that government is expressly prohibited from using. For example, the U.S. Constitution prohibits *ex post facto* laws.

deregulation The rescinding of government regulations for the purpose of promoting economic activity.

détente A French word meaning "a relaxing" and used to refer to an era of improved relations between the United States and the Soviet Union that began in the early 1970s.

deterrence The idea that nuclear war can be discouraged if each side in a conflict has the capacity to destroy the other with nuclear weapons.

Dillon's rule The principle that local governments are creatures of their state, which in theory even has the power to abolish them.

dissenting opinion The opinion of a justice in a Supreme Court case that explains the reasons for disagreeing with the majority position. (See **majority opinion**.)

diversity The principle that individual differences should be respected, are a legitimate basis of self-interest, and are a source of strength for the American nation.

divided government The situation in which control of the presidency and one or more chambers of Congress is divided between the major political parties.

economic groups Interest groups that are organized primarily for economic reasons, but which engage in political activity in order to seek favorable policies from government. (See **interest group; noneconomic groups**.)

economy A system of production and consumption of goods and services, which are allocated through exchange among sellers and buyers.

efficiency An economic principle which holds that firms should fulfill as many of society's needs as possible while using as few of its resources as possible.

electoral mastery A strong base of popular support that frees a congressional incumbent from constant worry over reelection.

elite theory The view that the United States is essentially run by a tiny economic elite (composed of wealthy individuals and corporate managers) who control public policy through both direct and indirect means.

entitlement program Any of a number of individual benefit programs, such as social security, that require government to provide a designated benefit to any person who meets the established criteria for eligibility.

enumerated powers The seventeen powers granted to the national government under Article I, section 8 of the Constitution. These powers include taxation and the regulation of commerce as well as the authority to provide for the national defense.

equal rights See **civil rights**.

equality The principle that all individuals have moral worth and are entitled to fair treatment under the law.

equality of opportunity The idea that all individuals should be given an equal chance to succeed on their own.

equality of result The objective of policies intended to reduce or eliminate the effects of discrimination so that members of traditionally disadvantaged groups will have the same benefits of society as do members of advantaged groups.

equal-protection clause A clause of the Fourteenth Amendment that forbids any state to deny equal protection of the laws to any individual within its jurisdiction.

equity (in relation to economic policy) The principle that economic transactions ought to be fair to each party involved. A transaction can be considered equitable if each party enters into it freely and is not unknowingly at a disadvantage.

equity (in relation to court cases) The idea that the courts should resort to general principles of fairness in cases where existing law is inadequate.

establishment clause The First Amendment provision that government may not favor one religion over another, or religion over no religion, and that prohibits Congress from passing laws respecting the establishment of religion.

exclusionary rule The legal principle that government is prohibited from using in trials evidence that was obtained by unconstitutional means (for example, illegal search and seizure).

executive leadership system An approach to managing the bureaucracy that is based on presidential leadership and presidential management tools, such as the president's annual budget proposal. (See **merit system; patronage system**.)

externalities Burdens that society incurs when firms fail to pay the full cost of resources used in production. An example of an externality is the pollution that results when corporations dump industrial wastes into lakes and rivers.

facts (of a court case) The relevant circumstances of a legal dispute or offense as determined by a trial court. The facts of a case are crucial because they help to determine which law or laws are applicable in the case.

federalism (federal system) A governmental system in which authority is divided between two sovereign levels of government: national and regional. (See **confederacy; unitary system**.)

filibuster A procedural tactic in the U.S. Senate whereby a minority of legislators prevent a bill from coming to a vote by holding the floor and talking until the majority gives in and the bill is withdrawn from consideration. (See **cloture**.)

fiscal policy A tool of economic management by which government attempts to maintain a stable economy through its taxing and spending decisions. (See **demand-side economics; monetary policy; supply-side economics.**)

formalized rules A basic principle of bureaucracy that refers to the standardized procedures and established regulations by which a bureaucracy conducts its operations. (See **bureaucracy**.)

freedom of expression A First Amendment right which guarantees individuals freedom of conscience, speech, press, assembly, and petition.

free-exercise clause A First Amendment provision that prohibits the government from interfering with the practice of religion or enacting any law prohibiting the free exercise of religion.

free-rider problem The situation in which the incentives offered by a group to its members are also available to nonmembers. The incentive to join the group and to promote its cause is reduced because nonmembers (free riders) receive the benefits without having to pay any of the group's costs. (See **collective goods.**)

free trade The view that all countries benefit to the degree that trade between them is not impeded by tariffs and other forms of protectionism. (See **protectionism.**)

general revenue sharing Federal grants-in-aid that can be spent as state and local officials see fit.

gerrymandering The deliberate redrawing of an election district's boundaries to give a particular party or candidate an advantage.

government corporations Bodies, such as the U.S. Postal Service and Amtrak, that are similar to private corporations in that they charge for their services, but different in that they receive federal funding to help defray expenses and their directors are appointed by the president with Senate approval.

grants of power The method of limiting the U.S. government by confining its scope of authority to those powers expressly granted in the Constitution.

grass-roots lobbying A form of lobbying designed to persuade officials that a group's policy position has strong public support.

hierarchical authority A basic principle of bureaucracy that refers to the chain of command within an organization, whereby officials and units have control over those below them. (See **bureaucracy**.)

home rule A device for granting local governments more leeway in their policies. It allows a local government to design its own charter, subject to the laws and constitution of the state and also subject to veto by the state. (See **charter**.)

horizontal federalism The constitutional relationship of the states to one another.

ideology A consistent pattern of opinion on political issues that stems from a basic underlying belief or set of beliefs.

implied powers The constitutional principle (Article I, section 8) that Congress shall have the power to enact all laws deemed "necessary and proper" for the carrying out of the powers granted it by the Constitution. (See **necessary and proper clause.**)

in-kind benefits Government benefits that are cash equivalents, such as food stamps or rent vouchers. This form of benefit ensures that recipients will use public assistance in a specified way.

inalienable (natural) rights Those rights which persons theoretically possessed in the state of nature, prior to the formation of governments. These rights, including those of life, liberty, and property, are considered inherent, and as such are inalienable. Since government is established by people, government has the responsibility to preserve these rights.

independent agencies Bureaucratic agencies that are similar to cabinet departments but usually have a narrower area of responsibility. Each such agency is headed by a presidential appointee who is not a cabinet member. An example is the National Aeronautics and Space Administration (NASA). (See **cabinet departments.**)

individual goods See **private goods**.

individualism A philosophical belief that stresses the values of hard work and self-reliance and holds that the individual should be left to succeed or fail on his or her own.

individualistic subculture An orientation toward private life and economic gain, with politics largely an extension of this perspective. This subculture extends across most of the central United States. (See **moralistic subculture; traditonalistic subculture.**)

initiative A device used by some states that allows citizens through signature petitions to place legislative measures on the ballot. If such a measure receives a majority vote, it becomes law, just as if it had been enacted by the state's legislature. (See **referendum.**)

inside lobbying Direct communication between organized interests and policymakers, which is based on the assumed value of close ("inside") contacts with policymakers.

insurgency A type of military conflict in which irregular soldiers rise up against an established regime.

interest group A set of individuals who are organized to promote a shared political interest. (See **economic groups; noneconomic groups.**)

interest-group liberalism The tendency of public officials to support the policy demands of self-interested groups (as opposed to judging policy demands according to whether or not they serve "the public interest").

internationalist(ism) The view that the country should involve itself deeply in world affairs. (See **isolationist.**)

iron triangle A small and informal but relatively stable group of legislators, executives, and lobbyists who are determined to promote policies beneficial to a particular interest. (See **issue network.**)

isolationist(ism) The view that the country should deliberately avoid a large role in world affairs and, instead, concentrate on domestic concerns. (See **internationalist.**)

issue network An informal network of public officials and lobbyists who have a common interest and expertise in a given area and who are brought together by a proposed policy in that area. (See **iron triangle.**)

job specialization A basic principle of bureaucracy which holds that the responsibilities of each job position should be explicitly defined and that a precise division of labor within the organization should be maintained. (See **bureaucracy.**)

judicial activism The doctrine that the courts should develop new legal principles when judges see a compelling need, even if this action places them in conflict with the policy decisions of elected officials. (See **judicial restraint.**)

judicial conference A closed meeting of the justices of the U.S. Supreme Court to discuss the points of the cases before them; the justices are not supposed to discuss conference proceedings with outsiders.

judicial restraint The doctrine that the judiciary should be highly deferential to the judgment of legislatures. The doctrine claims that the job of judges is to work within the confines of laws set down by the lawmaking majorities. (See **judicial activism.**)

judicial review The power of courts to decide whether a governmental institution has acted within its constitutional powers and, if not, to declare its action void.

jurisdiction (of a court) A given court's authority to hear cases of a particular kind. Jurisdiction may be original or appellate. (See **comity.**)

jurisdictions (of congressional committees) The policy areas in which particular congressional committees are authorized to act.

laissez-faire doctrine A classic economic philosophy which holds that owners of business should be allowed to make their own production and distribution decisions without government regulation or control.

law (as enacted by Congress) A legislative proposal, or bill, that is passed by both the House and Senate and is either signed or not vetoed by the president. (See **bill.**)

lawmaking function The responsibility of a legislature to make the laws deemed necessary to meet society's needs. (See **representation function.**)

laws (of a court case) The constitutional provisions, legislative statutes, or judicial precedents that apply to a court case.

legitimacy (in relation to courts) The issue of the proper limits of judicial authority in a political system based on the principle of majority rule.

legitimacy (of election) The idea that the voters must choose the party nominees for public office as well as the final winner if the outcome is truly to reflect the people's will. (See **primary election.**)

liberalism An ideology that in contemporary U.S. politics includes beliefs in social-welfare programs (activist government), tolerance for social change and diversity, and opposition to "excessive" military spending and involvement. (See **conservatism.**)

liberty The principle that the people are the ultimate source of governing authority and that their general welfare is the only legitimate purpose of government.

limited government A government that is subject to strict limits on its lawful uses of powers, and hence on its ability to deprive people of their liberty.

lobbying The process by which interest-group representatives (lobbyists) attempt to influence public policy through contacts with public officials.

logrolling The trading of votes between legislators so that each gets what he or she most wants.

majority opinion A Supreme Court opinion that reflects the agreement of a majority of the justices on the legal basis of their decision. (See **concurring opinion; dissenting opinion; plurality opinion.**)

malapportionment The situation in which election districts have greatly unequal populations, usually as a result of a deliberate attempt to manipulate political power.

means test The criteria for economic need that an applicant for public assistance must meet in order to be eligible for the assistance. (See **public assistance.**)

merit system An approach to managing the bureaucracy whereby people are appointed to government positions on the basis of either competitive examinations or special qualifications, such as professional training. (See **executive leadership system; patronage system.**)

military-industrial complex The three components (the military establishment, the industries that manufacture weapons, and the members of Congress from states and districts that depend heavily on the arms industry) that mutually benefit from a high level of defense spending.

momentum A strong showing by a candidate in early presidential nominating contests, which leads to a buildup of public support for the candidate.

monetary policy A tool of economic management, available to government, based on manipulation of the amount of money in circulation. (See **fiscal policy**.)

moralistic subculture An emphasis on "good government" (the public interest), "clean government" (honesty), and "civic government" (public participation). This subculture typifies many states of the northern tier, such as Minnesota, Maine, and Washington. (See **individualistic subculture; traditionalistic subculture**.)

multilateralism The situation in which nations act together in response to problems and crises.

multinational corporations Firms that have major business operations in more than one country.

multiparty system A system in which three or more political parties have the capacity to gain control of government separately or in coalition.

natural rights See **inalienable rights**.

necessary and proper clause (elastic clause) The authority granted Congress in Article I, section 8 of the Constitution "to make all laws which shall be necessary and proper" for the implementation of its enumerated powers. (See **implied powers**.)

negative government A philosophical belief that government governs best by staying out of people's lives, thus giving individuals as much freedom as possible to determine their own pursuits. (See **positive government**.)

neutral competence The administrative objective of a merit-based bureaucracy. Such a bureaucracy should be "competent" in the sense that its employees are hired and retained on the basis of their expertise and "neutral" in the sense that it operates by objective standards rather than partisan ones.

nomination The designation of a particular individual to run as a political party's candidate (its "nominee") in a given election.

noneconomic groups Organized interests formed by individuals drawn together by opportunities to promote a cause in which they believe but which does not provide them significant individual economic benefits. (See **economic groups; interest group**).

objective journalism A model of news reporting based on the communication of "facts" rather than opinions and which is "fair" in that it presents all sides of partisan debate. (See **partisan press**.)

open party caucuses Meetings at which a party's candidates for nomination are voted upon and which are open to all of the party's rank-and-file voters who want to attend.

open-seat election An election race in which the incumbent is not seeking reelection.

opinion (of a court) A court's written explanation of its decision which serves to inform others of the court's interpretation of laws. (See **concurring opinion; dissenting opinion; majority opinion; plurality opinion**.)

original jurisdiction The authority of a given court to be the first court to hear a case. (See **appellate jurisdiction**.)

outside lobbying A form of lobbying in which an interest group seeks to mobilize public support as a means of influencing officials.

oversight function A supervisory activity of Congress that centers on its constitutional responsibility to see that the executive carries out the laws faithfully and spends appropriations properly.

partisan press Newspapers and other communication media that openly support a political party and whose news in significant part follows the party line. (See **objective journalism**.)

party-centered politics Election campaigns and other political processes in which political parties and political leaders hold most of the initiative and influence. (See **candidate-centered politics**.)

party coalition The groups and interests that support a political party.

party competition A process in which conflict over society's goals is transformed by political parties into electoral competition in which the losers accept the winners' right to make policy decisions.

party identification The personal sense of loyalty that an individual may feel toward a particular political party. (See **dealignment; realigning election**.)

party leaders Members of the House and Senate who are chosen by the Democratic or Republican caucus in each chamber to represent the party's interests in that chamber and who give some central direction to the chamber's deliberations.

party organizations The party organizational units at national, state, and local levels; their influence has decreased over time due to many factors. (See **candidate-centered politics; party-centered politics; primary election**.)

patronage system An approach to managing the bureaucracy whereby people are appointed to important government positions as a reward for political services they have rendered and because of their partisan loyalty. (See **executive leadership system; merit system; spoils system.**)

pluralism A leading theory of American politics which holds that society's interests are substantially represented through the activities of groups. (See **interest group.**)

plurality opinion A court opinion that results when a majority of justices hearing a case agree on a decision in the case but do not agree on the legal basis for the decision. In this instance, the opinion held by most of the justices on the winning side is called a plurality opinion. (See **concurring opinion; majority opinion; opinion.**)

police power The broad power of government to regulate the health, safety, and morals of the citizenry.

policy Generally, any broad course of governmental action; more narrowly, a specific government program or initiative.

policy implementation The primary function of the bureaucracy is policy implementation, which refers to the process of carrying out of the authoritative decisions of Congress, the president, and the courts.

political action committees (PACs) The organizations through which interest groups raise and distribute funds for election purposes. By law, the funds must be raised through voluntary contributions.

political culture The characteristic and deep-seated beliefs of a particular people.

political movements See **social movements.**

political participation A sharing in activities designed to influence public policy and leadership, such as voting, joining political parties and interest groups, writing to elected officials, demonstrating for political causes, and giving money to political candidates.

political party An ongoing coalition of interests joined together to try to get their candidates for public office elected under a common label.

political socialization The learning process by which people acquire their enduring political beliefs and values.

politics The process by which it is determined whose values will prevail in the making of public policy.

population In a public opinion poll, the term *population* refers to the people (for example, the citizens of a nation) whose opinions are being estimated through interviews with a sample of these people.

pork-barrel legislation A law whose tangible benefits are targeted at a particular legislator's constituency.

positive government A philosophical belief that government intervention is necessary in order to enhance personal liberty when individuals are buffeted by economic and social forces beyond their control. (See **negative government.**)

poverty line As defined by the federal government, the poverty line is the annual cost of a thrifty food budget for an urban family of four, multiplied by three to allow also for the cost of housing, clothes, and other expenses.

power The ability of persons or institutions to control policy. (See **authority.**)

precedent A judicial decision in a given case that serves as a rule for settling subsequent cases of a similar nature; courts are generally expected to follow precedent.

preferred position The doctrine that First Amendment rights of free expression, because they are fundamental to a free society, are deserving of utmost protection against infringement by government.

presidential commissions These organizations within the bureaucracy are headed by commissioners appointed by the president. An example of such a commission is the Commission on Civil Rights.

primary election (direct primary) A form of election in which voters choose a party's nominees for public office. Most primaries are closed (only those voters who are registered as members of the party are eligible to participate), with less than a fifth of the states utilizing open primaries (all voters may participate, but they are prohibited from participating in both parties' primaries simultaneously). (See **legitimacy.**)

prior restraint The idea that the government is prohibited from censoring printed materials before publication unless the restriction can be justified by overwhelming national security needs.

private (individual) goods Benefits that a group (most often an economic group) can grant directly and exclusively to the individual members of the group. (See **collective goods.**)

privilege An individual claim that does not have clearly defined legal status and protection. (See **right.**)

probability sample A sample for a poll in which each individual in the population has a known probability of being selected randomly for inclusion in the sample. (See **public opinion poll.**)

procedural due process The constitutional requirement that government must follow proper legal procedures before a person can be legitimately punished for an alleged offense.

progressive tax A tax system in which, as income rises, so does the tax rate on the additional income.

property rights Rights of ownership, use, and contract, which are defined mainly through common law.

proportional representation A form of representation in which seats in the legislature are allocated proportionally according to each political party's share of the popular vote. (See **single-member districts.**)

prospective voting A form of electoral judgment in which voters choose the candidate whose policy stands most closely match their own preferences. (See **retrospective voting.**)

protectionism The view that the immediate interests of domestic producers should have a higher priority (through, for example, protective tariffs) than free trade between nations. (See **free trade.**)

public assistance A term that refers to social-welfare programs funded through general tax revenues and available only to the financially needy. Eligibility for such a program is established by a means test. (See **means test; social insurance.**)

public goods See **collective goods.**

public opinion Those opinions held by ordinary citizens that officials take into account when choosing to act or not to act.

public opinion poll A device for measuring public opinion whereby a relatively small number of individuals (the sample) are interviewed for the purpose of estimating the opinions of a whole community (the population). (See **probability sample.**)

public representative role A role whereby the media act as the public's chosen representatives.

purposive incentives Reasons for joining a noneconomic group. Purposive incentives are opportunities to promote a cause in which an individual believes.

realigning (critical) election An election or set of elections in which the electorate responds strongly to an extraordinarily powerful issue that has disrupted the established political order. A realigning election has a lasting impact on public policy, popular support for the parties, and the composition of the party coalitions. (See **dealignment; party identification.**)

reasonable-basis test A test applied by courts to laws that treat individuals unequally. Such a law may be deemed constitutional if its purpose is held to be "reasonably" related to a legitimate government interest.

recall A procedure that enables citizens to petition for the removal of an elected official before the scheduled completion of his or her term in office.

redistricting The process of rearranging election districts in order to make them as nearly equal in population as possible. Redistricting takes place every ten years, after each population census.

referendum A device that permits a legislature to submit proposals to the voters for approval or rejection. (See **initiative.**)

registration The practice of requiring citizens to put their names on an official list of eligible voters before they can exercise their right to vote.

regulation A term that refers to government restrictions on the economic practices of private firms.

regulatory agencies The bureaucratic executive bodies, such as the Interstate Commerce Commission and the Environmental Protection Agency, that have responsibility for the monitoring and regulation of ongoing economic activities.

representation function The responsibility of a legislature to represent various interests in society. (See **lawmaking function.**)

representative democracy A system in which the people participate in the decision-making process of government not directly but indirectly, through the election of officials to represent their interests. In this way, decisions are reached through the combined workings of deliberative procedures and popular influence.

republic Historically, the form of government in which representative officials met to decide on policy issues. These representatives were expected to serve the public interest but were not subject to the people's immediate control. Today, the term *republic* is used interchangeably with *democracy.*

reserved powers The powers granted to the states under the Tenth Amendment to the Constitution.

retrospective voting A form of electoral judgment in which voters support the incumbent party when its policies are judged to have succeeded and oppose it when its policies are judged to have failed. (See **prospective voting.**)

right An individual claim that has unquestioned legal status and protection. (See **privilege.**)

sample In a public opinion poll, the relatively small number of individuals who are interviewed for the purpose of estimating the opinions of an entire population. (See **public opinion poll.**)

sampling error A measure of the accuracy of a public opinion poll. The sampling error is mainly a function of sample size and is usually expressed in percentage terms. (See **probability sample.**)

select committee A temporary legislative committee that is created to perform specific tasks and is disbanded after it has done so. Unlike a standing committee, a select committee generally does not have authority to draft legislation. (See **standing committee.**)

selective incorporation The absorption of certain provisions of the Bill of Rights (for example, freedom of speech) into the Fourteenth Amendment so that these rights are protected from infringement by the states.

senatorial courtesy The tradition that a U.S. senator from the state in which a federal judicial vacancy has arisen should have a say in the president's nomination of the new judge if the senator is of the same party as the president.

seniority A member of Congress's consecutive years of service on a particular committee.

separated institutions sharing power The principle that, as a way to limit government, its powers should be divided among separate branches, each of which also shares in the power of the others as a means of checking and balancing them. The result is that no one branch can exercise power decisively without the support or acquiescence of the others.

service strategy Use of personal staff by members of Congress to perform services in order to build support among their constituents.

signaler role The perceived responsibility of the media to alert the public to important developments as soon as possible after they happen or are discovered.

single-issue politics The situation in which separate groups are organized around nearly every conceivable policy issue and press their demands and influence to the utmost.

single-member districts A form of representation in which only a single candidate is elected to a particular office by the voters of that district. This system favors major parties because only candidates who can gain a large proportion of votes in an election district have a realistic chance of winning. (See **proportional representation.)**

social insurance Social-welfare programs based on the "insurance" concept, so that individuals must pay into the program in order to be eligible to receive funds from it. An example is social security for retired people. (See **public assistance.)**

social (political) movements Efforts to achieve social and political change by broad groups of people who feel that government has not been properly responsive to their concerns.

sovereignty The ultimate authority to govern within a certain geographical area.

split-ticket voting The pattern of voting in which the individual voter in a given election casts a ballot for one or more candidates of each major party. This pattern is the opposite of straight-ticket voting, in which the voter supports only candidates of one party in a particular election.

spoils system The practice of granting public office to individuals in return for political favors they have rendered. (See **patronage system.)**

standing committee A permanent congressional committee with responsibility for a particular area of public policy. An example is the Senate Foreign Relations Committee. (See **select committee.)**

stewardship theory A theory that argues for a strong, assertive presidential role, with presidential authority limited only at points specifically prohibited by law. (See **Whig theory.)**

strict-scrutiny test A test applied by courts to laws that attempt a racial or ethnic classification. In effect, the strict-scrutiny test eliminates race or ethnicity as a basis for discrimination in law. (See **suspect classifications.)**

strong mayor–council system A form of municipal government in which the mayor has the veto power and prescribed responsibility for budgetary and other policy actions. In this stystem, the mayor, rather than the council, is the more powerful policymaker. (See **weak mayor–council system)**

substantive due process The form of constitutional due process that is based on the questions of whether government has acted reasonably and whether the substance of a law is reasonable.

suffrage The right to vote.

supply-side economics A form of fiscal policy that emphasizes "supply" (production). An example of supply-side economics would be a tax cut for business. (See **demand-side economics; fiscal policy.)**

supremacy clause Article VI of the Constitution, which makes national law supreme over state law when the national government is acting within its constitutional limits.

suspect classifications Legal classifications, such as race and national origin, that have invidious discrimination as their purpose and are therefore unconstitutional. (See **strict-scrutiny test.)**

term limitation A device that deals with the problem of entrenched leadership by restricting elected officials to one or two terms.

traditionalistic subculture A conservative focus with an elitist view of leadership. This subculture reflects the stratified plantation society out of which it grew: the states of the old Confederacy and a few states bordering on it, such as West Virginia. (See **individualistic subculture; moralistic subculture.)**

transfer payments Goverment benefits that are given directly to individuals, as in the case of social security payments to retirees.

trustees The idea of elected representatives as obligated to act in accordance with their own consciences as to what policies are in the best interests of the public. (See **delegates.)**

two-party system A system in which two political parties compete for the chance of acquiring control of the government, thus compelling candidates and voters with diverse opinions to find common ground.

tyranny of the majority The potential of a majority to monopolize power for their own gain and to the detriment of minority rights and interests. In order to avoid this risk, the Framers tempered the power of the majority by dividing power among branches of government and by establishing staggered terms of office and indirect election of the president and U.S. senators.

unitary system   A governmental system in which the national government alone has sovereign (ultimate) authority. (See **confederacy; federalism**)

unity   The principle that Americans are one people who form an indivisible union.

voter turnout   The proportion of persons of voting age who actually vote in a given election.

watchdog role   The accepted responsibility of the media to protect the public from deceitful, careless, incompetent, and corrupt officials by standing ready to expose any official who violates accepted legal, ethical, or performance standards.

weak mayor–council system   A form of municipal government in which the mayor's policymaking powers are less substantial than the council's. In this system, the mayor has no power to veto the council's actions and often has no formal role in such activities as budget making. (See **strong mayor–council system.**)

Whig theory   A theory that prevailed in the nineteenth century and held that the presidency was a limited or restrained office whose occupant was confined to expressly granted constitutional authority. (See **stewardship theory.**)

whistle blowing   An internal check on the bureaucracy whereby individual bureaucrats report instances of mismanagement that they observe.

writ of *certiorari*   Permission granted by a higher court to allow a losing party in a legal case to bring the case before it for a ruling; when such a writ is requested of the U.S. Supreme Court, four of the Court's nine justices must agree to accept the case before it is granted *certiorari*.

CREDITS

Figure 6.1: Adapted from Herbert McClosky and John Zaller, *The American Ethos: Public Attitudes toward Capitalism and Democracy*, Harvard University Press, 1984. Reprinted by permission.

Table 6.1: From 1985 *Los Angeles Times* survey. Copyright © 1985, Los Angeles Times. Reprinted by permission.

How the United States Compares, page 155: From Russell J. Dalton, *Citizen Politics in Western Democracies*. Chatham House Publishers, 1988. Reprinted by permission.

Table 7.2: From *Gallup Reports*, 1982. Reprinted by permission of the Gallup Organization.

Table 8.3: From Benjamin I. Page and Robert Y. Shapiro, "Effects of Public Opinion on Policy," *American Political Science Review*, March 1983. Reprinted by permission of the American Political Science Association.

Figure 9.2: From *Politics in the American States*, 5th edition, by Virginia Gray et al. Copyright © 1990 by Virginia Gray, Herbert Jacob, Robert B. Albritton. Reprinted by permission of HarperCollins Publishers.

Figure 9.3: Adapted from Raymond E. Wolfinger and Steven Rosenstone, *Who Votes?*, Yale University Press, 1980. Reprinted by permission.

Figure 9.4: Adapted from Sidney Verba and Norman Nie, *Participation in America: Political Democracy and Social Equality*, Harper & Row, 1972. Reprinted by permission of the authors.

Table 9.1: From Samuel H. Barnes and Max Kaase (eds.) *Political Action*, Sage Publications, 1979.

How the United States Compares, page 239: From David Glass, Peverill Squire, and Raymond Wolfinger, "Voter Turnout: An International Comparison, " *Public Opinion*, December/January 1984. Reprinted with the permission of the American Enterprise Institute for Public Policy Research, Washington, D.C.

Figure 10.4: From Gerald M. Pomper with Susan S. Lederman, *Elections in America*, Longman, 1980. Reprinted by permission of the author.

Table 10.2: Adapted from Stanley Kelley, Jr., *Interpreting Elections*. Copyright © 1983 by Princeton University Press. Reprinted by permission of Princeton University Press.

Figure 11.2: From *The World Almanac and Book of Facts*, 1991, copyright by Pharos Books, 1990.

Figure 11.3: From *The New York Times*, July 17, 1988. Copyright © 1988 by the New York Times Company. Reprinted by permission.

Figure 11.4: From Adam Clymer, "Poll Finds G.O.P. Growth Erodes Dominant Role of the Democrats," *The New York Times*, July 14, 1991. Copyright © 1991 by The New York Times Company. Reprinted by permission.

Table 11.1: From *The New York Times*, August 14, 1988. Copyright © 1988 by The New York Times Company. Reprinted by permission.

Figure 12.1: From Edie N. Goldenberg and Michael W. Traugott, *Campaigning for Congress*, Congressional Quarterly Press, 1984. Reprinted by permission of Congressional Quarterly, Inc.

Table 12.1: Adapted from James L. Gibson, Cornelius P. Cotter, John F. Bibby, and Robert L. Huckshorn, "Thither the Local Parties?" *American Journal of Political Science. vol. 29:1, February 1985. Reprinted by permission of the University of Texas press and the authors.*

Tables 13.1 and 13.2: From *Encyclopedia of Associations*, 1991, 25th edition, edited by Deborah M. Burek. Copyright © 1990 by Gale Research Inc. Reproduced by permission of the publisher.

Table 13.4: From Sidney Verba and Norman Nie, *Participation in America: Political Democracy and Social Equality*, Harper & Row, 1972. Reprinted by permission.

Figure 16.3: From Roger H. Davidson and Walter J. Oleszek, *Congress and Its Members*, Congressional Quarterly Press, 1981. Reprinted by permission of Congressional Quarterly, Inc.

Table 17.2: Adapted from "Ideological Portrait of Congress," *National Journal*, January 28, 1989. Copyright *National Journal*, 1989. Reprinted with permission.

Figure 19.1: From *Congressional Quarterly Weekly*, December 22, 1990.

Figure 19.2: From William C. Adams, "As New Hampshire Goes . . . ," in Gary R. Orren and Nelson W. Polsby (eds.), *Media and Momentum: The New Hampshire Primary and Nomination Politics*, Chatham House, 1987. Reprinted by permission.

How the United States Compares, page 605: From *The Politics of Bureaucracy*, 3d edition, by B. Guy Peters. Copyright © 1989 by Longman Publishing Group.

Figure 21.1: Adapted from Joel D. Aberbach and Bert A. Rockman, "Clashing Beliefs within the Executive Branch: The Nixon Administration Bureaucracy," *American Political Science Review*, June 1967. Reprinted by permission of the American Political Science Association.

Table 21.1: From Joel D. Aberbach and Bert A. Rockman, "Bureaucrats and Clientele Groups: A view from Capitol Hill," *American Journal of Political Science, vol. 22, November 1978.*

Table 21.2: From Joel D. Aberbach, "The President and the Executive Branch," in Colin Campbell and Bert A. Rockman, *The Bush Presidency: First Appraisals*, Chatham House Publishers, 1991. Reprinted by permission.

Table 22.2 Adapted from Sheldon Goldman, "Reagan's Second-term Judicial Appointments: The Battle at Midway," *Judicature*, vol. 70, April-May 1987. Reprinted by permission of the American Judication Society.

NAME INDEX

SUBJECT INDEX